ITALIAN ENGLISH

ILLUSTRATED DICTIONARY

FREE
AUDIO APP
DK

Author

Thomas Booth worked for 10 years as an English teacher in Poland, Romania, and Russia. He now lives in England, where he works as an editor and English-language materials writer. He has contributed to a number of books in the *English for Everyone* series.

ITALIAN ENGLISH

ILLUSTRATED DICTIONARY

1
2
123

DK

PRODUCED BY
Author / Editor Thomas Booth
Senior Art Editor Sunita Gahir
Art Editors Ali Jayne Scrivens, Samantha Richiardi
Illustrators Edward Byrne, Gus Scott
Project Manager Sunita Gahir / bigmetalfish design

DK UK
Senior Editors Amelia Petersen, Christine Stroyan
Senior Designers Clare Shedden, Vicky Read
Managing Art Editor Anna Hall
Managing Editor Carine Tracanelli
Jacket Editors Stephanie Cheng Hui Tan, Juhi Sheth
Jacket Development Manager Sophia MTT
Production Editors Gillian Reid, Robert Dunn, Jacqueline Street
Production Controller Sian Cheung
Publisher Andrew Macintyre
Art Director Karen Self
Publishing Director Jonathan Metcalf

Translation Andiamo! Language Services Ltd

DK INDIA
Desk Editors Joicy John, Tanya Lohan
DTP Designers Anurag Trivedi, Satish Gaur,
Jaypal Chauhan, Bimlesh Tiwary, Rakesh Kumar
DTP Coordinator Pushpak Tyagi
Jacket Designer Vidushi Chaudhry
Senior Jackets Coordinator Priyanka Sharma Saddi
Managing Editor Saloni Talwar
Creative Head Malavika Talukder

First American Edition, 2023
Published in the United States by DK Publishing,
a division of Penguin Random House LLC
1745 Broadway, 20th Floor, New York, NY 10019

24 25 10 9 8 7 6 5 4 3 2
002–334032–Jul/2023

Published in Great Britain by Dorling Kindersley Limited

A catalog record for this book is available from the Library of Congress.
ISBN 978-0-7440-8076-6

Printed and bound in China

www.dk.com

MIX
Paper | Supporting responsible forestry
FSC
www.fsc.org
FSC™ C018179

This book was made with Forest Stewardship Council™ certified paper – one small step in DK's commitment to a sustainable future.
Learn more at
www.dk.com/uk/information/sustainability

Contents

How to use this book 10

LE PERSONE PEOPLE

01 Le parti del corpo / Parts of the body 12

02 Le mani e i piedi / Hands and feet 14

03 I muscoli e lo scheletro / Muscles and skeleton 16

04 Gli organi interni / Internal organs 18

05 La famiglia / Family 20

06 I sentimenti e gli stati d'animo / Feelings and moods 22

07 Gli eventi della vita / Life events 24

08 La gravidanza e l'infanzia / Pregnancy and childhood 26

09 Le attività quotidiane / Daily routines 28

10 I tratti della personalità / Personality traits 30

11 Le abilità e le azioni / Abilities and actions 32

L'ASPETTO APPEARANCE

12 L'aspetto e i capelli / Appearance and hair 34

13 Gli indumenti / Clothes 36

14 Gli indumenti (continua) / Clothes continued 38

15 Gli indumenti (continua) / Clothes continued 40

16 Gli accessori / Accessories 42

17 Le scarpe / Shoes 44

18 La bellezza / Beauty 46

LA SALUTE HEALTH

19 Le malattie e le lesioni / Illness and injury 48

20 Andare dal medico / Visiting the doctor 50

21 L'ospedale / The hospital 52

22 Il dentista e l'ottico / The dentist and optician 54

23 La dieta e l'alimentazione / Diet and nutrition 56

24 Il corpo sano, la mente sana / Healthy body, healthy mind 58

LA CASA HOME

25 Un luogo in cui vivere / A place to live 60

26 Il salotto e la sala da pranzo / Living room and dining room 62

27 La cucina e le stoviglie / Kitchen and tableware 64

28 Gli utensili da cucina / Kitchenware 66

29 Cucinare / Cooking 68

30 La camera da letto / Bedroom 70

31 Il bagno / Bathroom 72

32 La casa / House and home 74

33 Gli impianti elettrico e idraulico / Electrics and plumbing 76

34 Le faccende domestiche / Household chores 78

35 I lavori di miglioria della casa / Home improvements 80

36 Gli attrezzi / Tools 82

37 La decorazione / Renovating 84

38 Le piante da giardino e le piante da appartamento / Garden plants and houseplants 86

39 Il giardinaggio — Practical gardening 88

40 Gli attrezzi da giardinaggio — Garden tools 90

41 Le caratteristiche del giardino — Garden features 92

LA VITA IN CITTÀ CITY LIFE

42 In città — In town 94

43 In città (continua) — In town continued 96

44 Gli edifici e l'architettura — Buildings and architecture 98

45 La banca e l'ufficio postale — The bank and post office 100

46 Lo shopping — Shopping 102

47 Il centro commerciale — The shopping mall 104

48 Il supermercato — The supermarket 106

49 La farmacia — The pharmacy 108

50 I servizi di pronto intervento — Emergency services 110

51 L'energia e l'alimentazione elettrica — Energy and power supply 112

GLI ALIMENTI FOOD

52 Bere e mangiare — Drinking and Eating 114

53 La carne — Meat 116

54 Il pesce e i frutti di mare — Fish and seafood 118

55 La verdura — Vegetables 120

56 La verdura (continua) — Vegetables continued 122

57 La frutta — Fruit 124

58 La frutta e la frutta a guscio — Fruit and nuts 126

59 Le erbe e le spezie — Herbs and spices 128

60 Nella dispensa — In the pantry 130

61 I prodotti caseari — Dairy produce 132

62 La panetteria — The bakery 134

63 La panetteria (continua) — The bakery continued 136

64 La gastronomia — The delicatessen 138

65 Al bar — At the café 140

66 Al bar (continua) — At the café continued 142

67 I dolciumi — Candy 143

68 Al bar — At the bar 144

69 Al ristorante — At the restaurant 146

70 Il fast food — Fast food 148

71 La colazione — Breakfast 150

72 Il pranzo e la cena — Lunch and dinner 152

LO STUDIO STUDY

73 A scuola — At school 154

74 La matematica — Mathematics 156

75 La fisica — Physics 158

76 La chimica — Chemistry 160

77 La biologia — Biology 162

78 La tavola periodica — The periodic table 164

79 La storia — History 166

80 All'università At college 168

IL LAVORO WORK

81 Al lavoro At work 170
82 In ufficio In the office 172
83 I computer e la tecnologia Computers and technology 174
84 I media Media 176
85 La legge Law 178
86 L'agricoltura Farming 180
87 Le costruzioni Construction 182
88 L'esercito Military 184
89 I lavori Jobs 186
90 I lavori (continua) Jobs continued 188
91 I settori e i reparti Industries and departments 190
92 Fare domanda per un lavoro Applying for a job 192
93 Le competenze sul luogo di lavoro Workplace skills 194
94 Il denaro e la finanza Money and finance 196
95 Le riunioni e le presentazioni Meeting and presenting 198

ANDARE IN GIRO GETTING AROUND

96 Le strade Roads 200
97 Le auto Cars 202
98 Le auto (continua) Cars continued 204
99 Le auto e gli autobus Cars and buses 206
100 I motocicli Motorcycles 208
101 Il ciclismo Cycling 210
102 I treni Trains 212
103 L'aeromobile Aircraft 214
104 In aeroporto At the airport 216
105 Le imbarcazioni Sea vessels 218
106 Il porto The port 220

GLI SPORT SPORTS

107 Il football americano American football 222
108 Il rugby Rugby 224
109 Il calcio Soccer 226
110 L'hockey e il lacrosse Hockey and lacrosse 228
111 Il cricket Cricket 230
112 Il basket e la pallavolo Basketball and volleyball 232
113 Il baseball Baseball 234
114 Il tennis Tennis 236
115 Il golf Golf 238
116 l'atletica Athletics 240
117 Gli sport da combattimento Combat sports 242
118 Il nuoto Swimming 244
119 La vela e gli sport acquatici Sailing and watersports 246
120 L'equitazione Horseback riding 248

121 La pesca — Fishing 250

122 Gli sport invernali — Winter sports 252

123 Gli sport motoristici — Motorsports 254

124 In palestra — At the gym 256

125 Gli altri sport — Other sports 258

IL TEMPO LIBERO LEISURE

126 Sul palco — On stage 260

127 I film — Movies 262

128 La musica — Music 264

129 La musica (continua) — Music continued 266

130 I musei e le gallerie — Museums and galleries 268

131 Il viaggio e l'alloggio — Travel and accommodation 270

132 Fare un giro turistico — Sightseeing 272

133 Le attività all'aperto — Outdoor activities 274

134 In spiaggia — On the beach 276

135 Il campeggio — Camping 278

136 L'home entertainment — Home entertainment 280

137 La televisione — Television 282

138 I libri e la lettura — Books and reading 284

139 Il fantasy e il mito — Fantasy and myth 286

140 I giochi — Games 288

141 Le arti e i mestieri — Arts and crafts 290

142 Le arti e i mestieri (continua) — Arts and crafts continued 292

L'AMBIENTE ENVIRONMENT

143 Lo spazio — Space 294

144 Lo spazio (continua) — Space continued 296

145 Il pianeta Terra — Planet Earth 298

146 La geografia — Geography 300

147 La geografia (continua) — Geography continued 302

148 Le cartine e le direzioni — Maps and directions 304

149 I Paesi — Countries 306

150 I Paesi (continua) — Countries continued 308

151 I Paesi (continua) — Countries continued 310

152 Le nazionalità — Nationalities 312

153 Le nazionalità (continua) — Nationalities continued 314

154 Il tempo atmosferico — Weather 316

155 Il clima e l'ambiente — Climate and the environment 318

156 Le rocce e i minerali — Rocks and minerals 320

IL MONDO NATURALE NATURAL WORLD

157 La storia naturale — Natural history 322

158 I mammiferi — Mammals 324

159 I mammiferi (continua) — Mammals continued 326

160 Gli uccelli — Birds 328

161 Gli uccelli (continua) — Birds continued 330

162 Gli insetti 332
Insects and bugs

163 Gli anfibi e i rettili 334
Amphibians and reptiles

164 Gli animali domestici 336
Pets

165 Gli animali da fattoria 338
Farm animals

166 La vita negli oceani 340
Ocean life

167 Le piante e gli alberi 342
Plants and trees

168 Le piante e gli alberi (continua) 344
Plants and trees continued

169 Le piante e gli alberi (continua) 346
Plants and trees continued

170 I funghi 348
Fungi

IL RIFERIMENTO REFERENCE

171 Il tempo 350
Time

172 Il calendario 352
The calendar

173 I numeri 354
Numbers

174 I pesi e le misure 356
Weights and measures

175 La scrittura 358
Writing

176 Descrivere le cose 360
Describing things

177 Descrivere le cose (continua) 362
Describing things continued

178 I verbi comuni 364
Common phrasal verbs

179 Le espressioni utili 366
Useful expressions

180 Le espressioni utili (continua) 368
Useful expressions continued

WORD LIST (ENGLISH) 370
WORD LIST (ITALIAN) 400
Acknowledgments 432

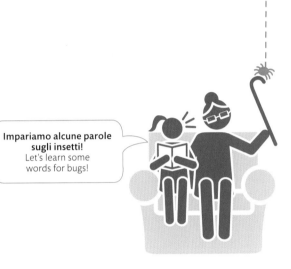

Impariamo alcune parole sugli insetti!
Let's learn some words for bugs!

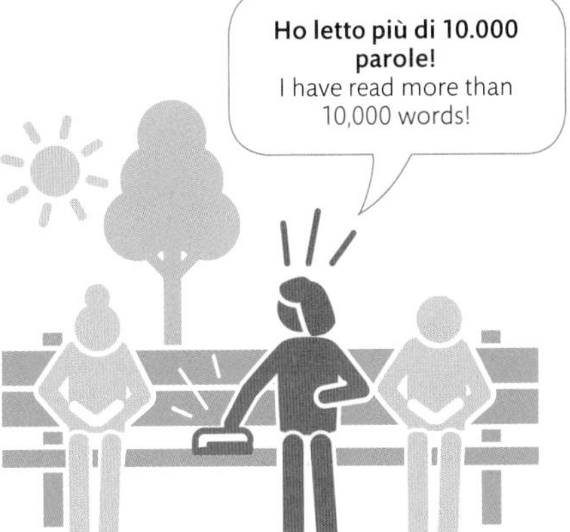

Ho letto più di 10.000 parole!
I have read more than 10,000 words!

How to use this book

This *Italian-English Illustrated Dictionary* will help you understand and remember more than 10,000 of the most useful words and phrases in Italian. Each of the 180 units in the dictionary covers a practical or everyday topic (such as health, food, or the natural world), and words are shown in a visual context to cement them in your memory along with their English equivalents. Using the audio app that accompanies the dictionary will help you learn and remember the new vocabulary.

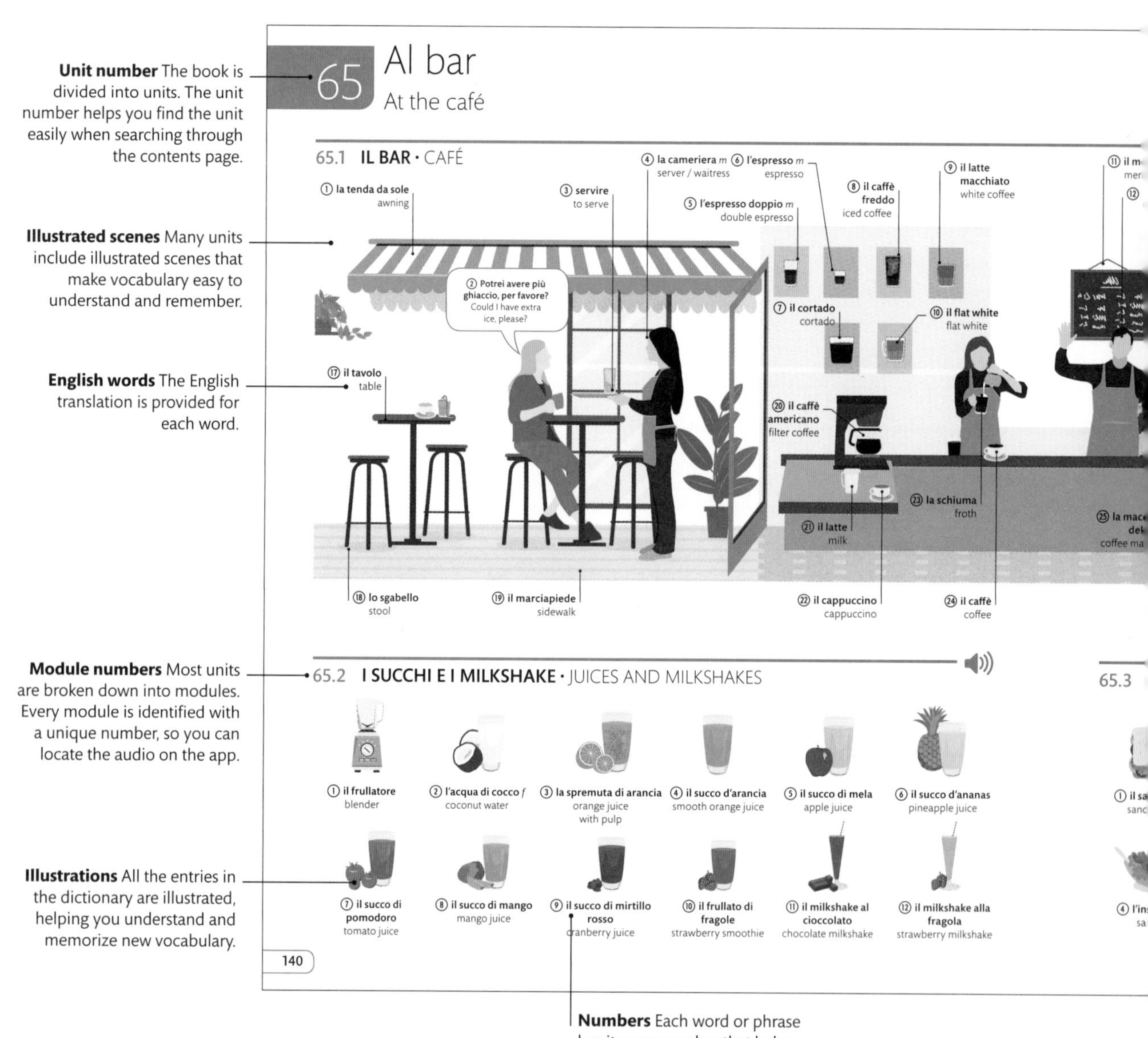

Unit number The book is divided into units. The unit number helps you find the unit easily when searching through the contents page.
Illustrated scenes Many units include illustrated scenes that make vocabulary easy to understand and remember.
English words The English translation is provided for each word.
Module numbers Most units are broken down into modules. Every module is identified with a unique number, so you can locate the audio on the app.
Illustrations All the entries in the dictionary are illustrated, helping you understand and memorize new vocabulary.
Numbers Each word or phrase has its own number that helps you find the audio on the app.
65 Al bar
At the café
65.1 IL BAR · CAFÉ
① la tenda da sole awning
② Potrei avere più ghiaccio, per favore? Could I have extra ice, please?
③ servire to serve
④ la cameriera m server / waitress
⑤ l'espresso doppio m double espresso
⑥ l'espresso m espresso
⑦ il cortado cortado
⑧ il caffè freddo iced coffee
⑨ il latte macchiato white coffee
⑩ il flat white flat white
⑰ il tavolo table
⑱ lo sgabello stool
⑲ il marciapiede sidewalk
⑳ il caffè americano filter coffee
㉑ il latte milk
㉒ il cappuccino cappuccino
㉓ la schiuma froth
㉔ il caffè coffee
65.2 I SUCCHI E I MILKSHAKE · JUICES AND MILKSHAKES
① il frullatore blender
② l'acqua di cocco f coconut water
③ la spremuta di arancia orange juice with pulp
④ il succo d'arancia smooth orange juice
⑤ il succo di mela apple juice
⑥ il succo d'ananas pineapple juice
⑦ il succo di pomodoro tomato juice
⑧ il succo di mango mango juice
⑨ il succo di mirtillo rosso cranberry juice
⑩ il frullato di fragole strawberry smoothie
⑪ il milkshake al cioccolato chocolate milkshake
⑫ il milkshake alla fragola strawberry milkshake
65.3
140

See also Each unit has a "see also" box that directs you to other units with useful or related vocabulary.

See also
27 La cucina e le stoviglie • Kitchen and tableware **52** Bere e mangiare
Drinking and eating **66** Al bar (continua) • At the café continued
70 Il fast food • Fast food **72** Il pranzo e la cena • Lunch and dinner

⑭ **il cacao** cocoa powder
⑮ **l'Irish coffee** *m* Irish coffee
⑯ **l'ombrellone** *m* patio umbrella
il cliente *m* **la cliente** *f* customer
㉗ **il caffè nero** black coffee
㉘ **la terrazza** terrace
㉙ **la ringhiera** railing

LI SNACK • FOOD AND SNACKS

⑩ **Mi dispiace, abbiamo finito i sandwich.** Sorry, we've run out of sandwiches.

② **il pancake** pancake
③ **il waffle** waffle
⑨ **le bevande** beverages
⑧ **gli snack** snacks
⑤ **il cono gelato** ice cream cone
⑥ **la coppa di gelato** ice cream scoop
⑦ **lo snack bar** snack bar

141

Speech bubbles Useful expressions and examples of real-life Italian appear in speech bubbles throughout the book.

Gender and articles

All nouns in the dictionary are preceded by the definite article ("the"). In Italian, nouns are masculine or feminine. The definite articles used for singular masculine nouns are "il" or "lo" and for feminine nouns "la". Plurals are indicated with "i" or "gli" for masculine, "le" for feminine. When nouns start with a vowel so that the articles "lo" and, "la" lose their vowel –"l'"– the gender is indicated with *m* or *f*.

il cotone
cotton

lo zio
uncle

i fusilli
fusilli

gli elastici
rubber bands

la medicina
medicine

le monete
coins

l'ospedale *m*
hospital

Word lists

The Italian and English word lists at the back of the book contain every entry from the dictionary. All the vocabulary is listed in alphabetical order, and each entry is followed by the unit number or numbers in which it is found, enabling you to look up any word in either Italian or English. The Italian words are listed without their articles, so that you can search for words alphabetically. The English word list also provides information about the part of speech (for example noun, verb, or adjective) of each word.

Audio app

The *Italian-English Illustrated Dictionary* is supported by a free audio app containing every Italian word and phrase in the book. Listen to the audio and repeat the words and phrases out loud, until you are confident you understand and can pronounce what has been said. The app can be found by searching for "DK Illustrated Dictionary" in the App Store or Google Play.

FREE
AUDIO APP
DK

01 Le parti del corpo
Parts of the body

1.1 IL CORPO UMANO · THE HUMAN BODY

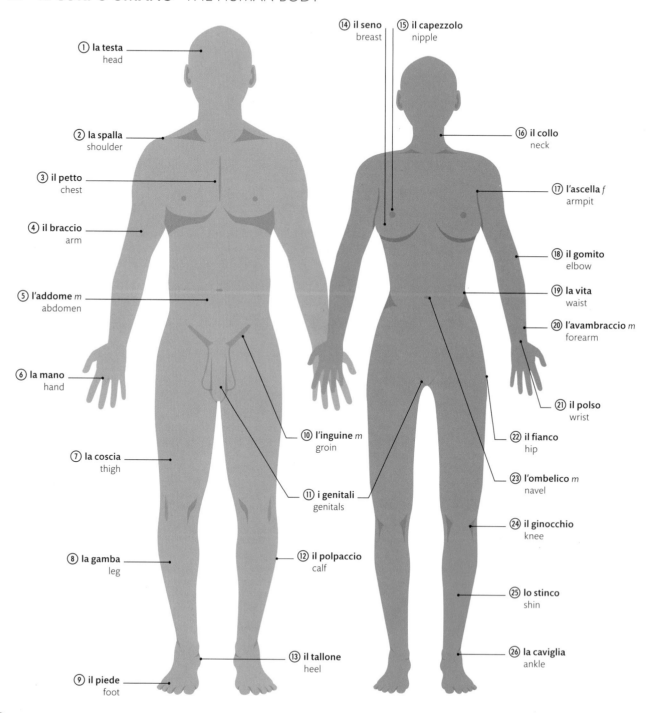

① **la testa** head
② **la spalla** shoulder
③ **il petto** chest
④ **il braccio** arm
⑤ **l'addome** *m* abdomen
⑥ **la mano** hand
⑦ **la coscia** thigh
⑧ **la gamba** leg
⑨ **il piede** foot
⑩ **l'inguine** *m* groin
⑪ **i genitali** genitals
⑫ **il polpaccio** calf
⑬ **il tallone** heel
⑭ **il seno** breast
⑮ **il capezzolo** nipple
⑯ **il collo** neck
⑰ **l'ascella** *f* armpit
⑱ **il gomito** elbow
⑲ **la vita** waist
⑳ **l'avambraccio** *m* forearm
㉑ **il polso** wrist
㉒ **il fianco** hip
㉓ **l'ombelico** *m* navel
㉔ **il ginocchio** knee
㉕ **lo stinco** shin
㉖ **la caviglia** ankle

See also
02 Le mani e i piedi • Hands and feet **03** I muscoli e lo scheletro • Muscles and skeleton
04 Gli organi interni • Internal organs **19** Le malattie e le lesioni • Illness and injury
20 Andare dal medico • Visiting the doctor **22** Il dentista e l'ottico • The dentist and optician

1.2 IL VISO • FACE

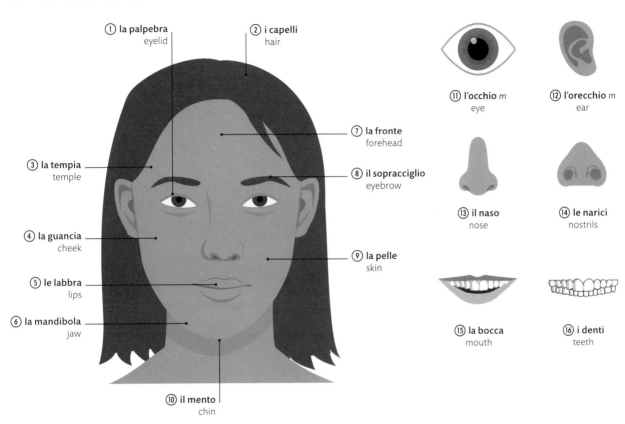

① **la palpebra** eyelid
② **i capelli** hair
③ **la tempia** temple
④ **la guancia** cheek
⑤ **le labbra** lips
⑥ **la mandibola** jaw
⑦ **la fronte** forehead
⑧ **il sopracciglio** eyebrow
⑨ **la pelle** skin
⑩ **il mento** chin
⑪ **l'occhio** *m* eye
⑫ **l'orecchio** *m* ear
⑬ **il naso** nose
⑭ **le narici** nostrils
⑮ **la bocca** mouth
⑯ **i denti** teeth

1.3 GLI OCCHI • EYES

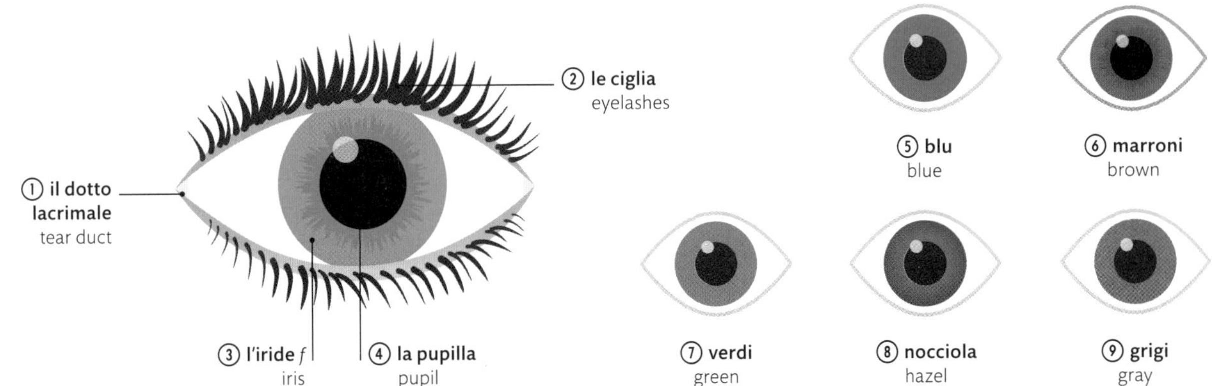
① il dotto lacrimale
tear duct
② le ciglia
eyelashes
③ l'iride f
iris
④ la pupilla
pupil
⑤ blu
blue
⑥ marroni
brown
⑦ verdi
green
⑧ nocciola
hazel
⑨ grigi
gray

02 Le mani e i piedi
Hands and feet

2.1 LE MANI · HANDS

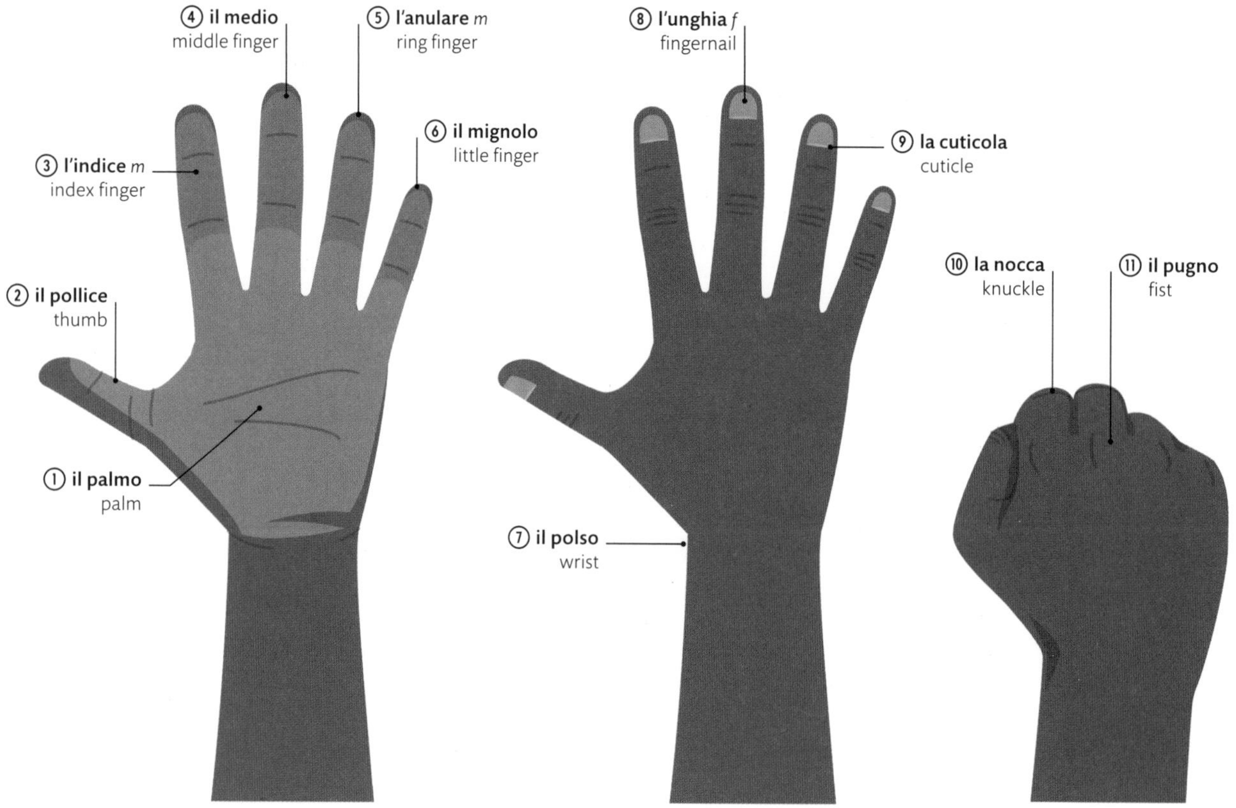

① **il palmo** palm
② **il pollice** thumb
③ **l'indice** *m* index finger
④ **il medio** middle finger
⑤ **l'anulare** *m* ring finger
⑥ **il mignolo** little finger
⑦ **il polso** wrist
⑧ **l'unghia** *f* fingernail
⑨ **la cuticola** cuticle
⑩ **la nocca** knuckle
⑪ **il pugno** fist

2.2 I VERBI DEL CORPO · BODY VERBS

① **sorridere** to smile

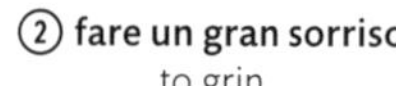
② **fare un gran sorriso** to grin

③ **aggrottare la fronte** to frown

④ **fare l'occhiolino** to wink

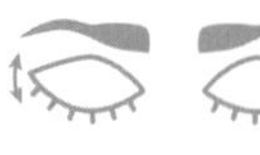
⑤ **sbattere le palpebre** to blink

⑥ **arrossire** to blush

⑦ **sbadigliare** to yawn

⑧ **russare** to snore

⑨ **leccare** to lick

⑩ **succhiare** to suck

⑪ **respirare** to breathe

⑫ **trattenere il respiro** to hold your breath

See also
01 Le parti del corpo • Parts of the body **03** I muscoli e lo scheletro Muscles and skeleton **19** Le malattie e le lesioni • Illness and injury **20** Andare dal medico • Visiting the doctor **21** L'ospedale • The hospital

2.3 I PIEDI • FEET

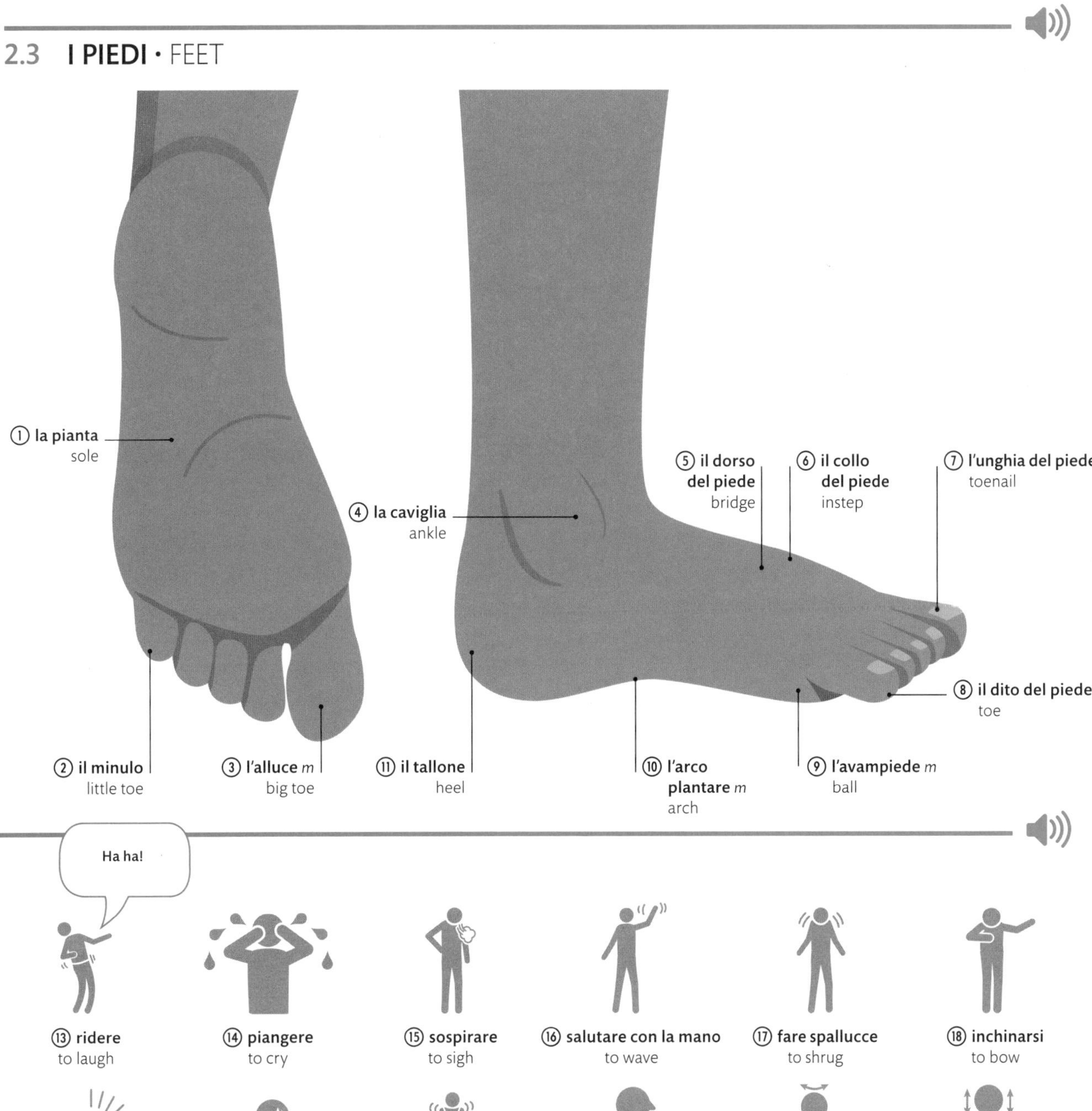
① **la pianta**
sole
② **il minulo**
little toe
③ **l'alluce** *m*
big toe
④ **la caviglia**
ankle
⑤ **il dorso del piede**
bridge
⑥ **il collo del piede**
instep
⑦ **l'unghia del piede** *f*
toenail
⑧ **il dito del piede**
toe
⑨ **l'avampiede** *m*
ball
⑩ **l'arco plantare** *m*
arch
⑪ **il tallone**
heel
Ha ha!
⑬ **ridere**
to laugh
⑭ **piangere**
to cry
⑮ **sospirare**
to sigh
⑯ **salutare con la mano**
to wave
⑰ **fare spallucce**
to shrug
⑱ **inchinarsi**
to bow

⑲ **applaudire**
to clap

⑳ **sudare**
to sweat / to perspire

㉑ **tremare**
to shiver

㉒ **starnutire**
to sneeze

㉓ **scuotere la testa**
to shake your head

㉔ **annuire**
to nod

03 I muscoli e lo scheletro
Muscles and skeleton

3.1 I MUSCOLI
MUSCLES

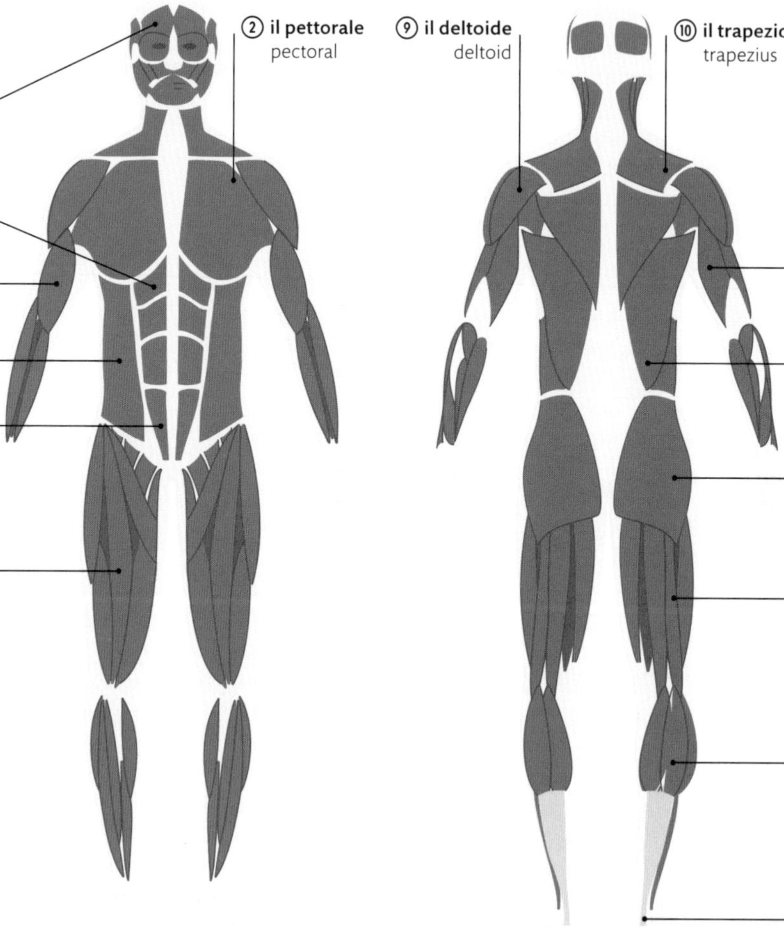

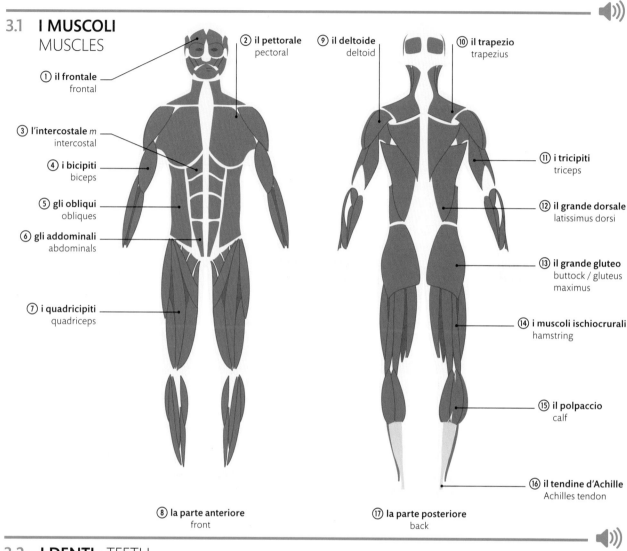

① **il frontale**
frontal

② **il pettorale**
pectoral

③ **l'intercostale** *m*
intercostal

④ **i bicipiti**
biceps

⑤ **gli obliqui**
obliques

⑥ **gli addominali**
abdominals

⑦ **i quadricipiti**
quadriceps

⑧ **la parte anteriore**
front

⑨ **il deltoide**
deltoid

⑩ **il trapezio**
trapezius

⑪ **i tricipiti**
triceps

⑫ **il grande dorsale**
latissimus dorsi

⑬ **il grande gluteo**
buttock / gluteus maximus

⑭ **i muscoli ischiocrurali**
hamstring

⑮ **il polpaccio**
calf

⑯ **il tendine d'Achille**
Achilles tendon

⑰ **la parte posteriore**
back

3.2 I DENTI · TEETH

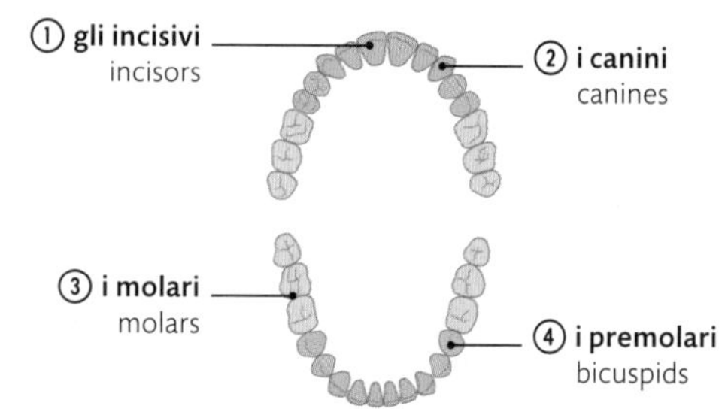
① gli incisivi
incisors
② i canini
canines
③ i molari
molars
④ i premolari
bicuspids

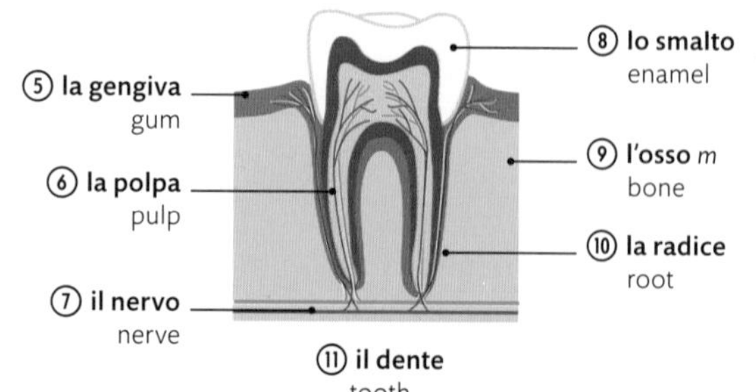
⑤ la gengiva
gum
⑥ la polpa
pulp
⑦ il nervo
nerve
⑧ lo smalto
enamel
⑨ l'osso m
bone
⑩ la radice
root
⑪ il dente
tooth

See also
01 Le parti del corpo • Parts of the body **02** Le mani e i piedi • Hands and feet **04** Gli organi interni • Internal organs **19** Le malattie e le lesioni • Illness and injury **20** Andare dal medico • Visiting the doctor **21** L'ospedale • The hospital

3.3 LO SCHELETRO • SKELETON

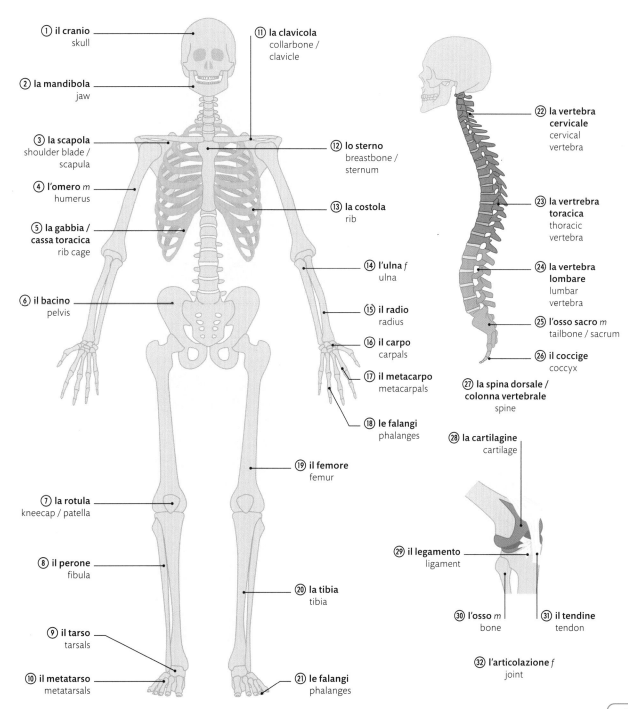

① **il cranio**
skull

② **la mandibola**
jaw

③ **la scapola**
shoulder blade / scapula

④ **l'omero** *m*
humerus

⑤ **la gabbia / cassa toracica**
rib cage

⑥ **il bacino**
pelvis

⑦ **la rotula**
kneecap / patella

⑧ **il perone**
fibula

⑨ **il tarso**
tarsals

⑩ **il metatarso**
metatarsals

⑪ **la clavicola**
collarbone / clavicle

⑫ **lo sterno**
breastbone / sternum

⑬ **la costola**
rib

⑭ **l'ulna** *f*
ulna

⑮ **il radio**
radius

⑯ **il carpo**
carpals

⑰ **il metacarpo**
metacarpals

⑱ **le falangi**
phalanges

⑲ **il femore**
femur

⑳ **la tibia**
tibia

㉑ **le falangi**
phalanges

㉒ **la vertebra cervicale**
cervical vertebra

㉓ **la vertrebra toracica**
thoracic vertebra

㉔ **la vertebra lombare**
lumbar vertebra

㉕ **l'osso sacro** *m*
tailbone / sacrum

㉖ **il coccige**
coccyx

㉗ **la spina dorsale / colonna vertebrale**
spine

㉘ **la cartilagine**
cartilage

㉙ **il legamento**
ligament

㉚ **l'osso** *m*
bone

㉛ **il tendine**
tendon

㉜ **l'articolazione** *f*
joint

04 Gli organi interni
Internal organs

4.1 GLI ORGANI INTERNI • INTERNAL ORGANS

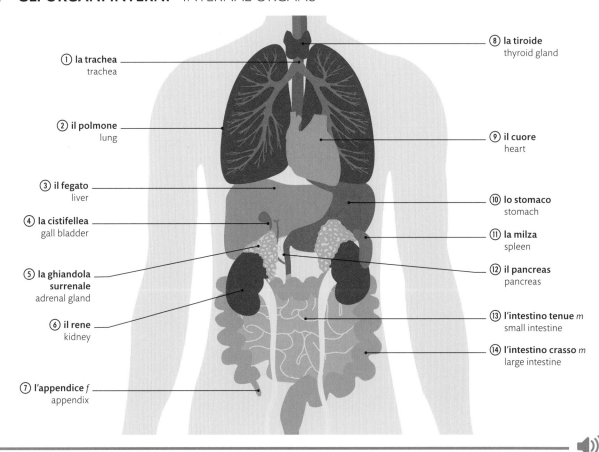

① **la trachea**
trachea

② **il polmone**
lung

③ **il fegato**
liver

④ **la cistifellea**
gall bladder

⑤ **la ghiandola surrenale**
adrenal gland

⑥ **il rene**
kidney

⑦ **l'appendice** *f*
appendix

⑧ **la tiroide**
thyroid gland

⑨ **il cuore**
heart

⑩ **lo stomaco**
stomach

⑪ **la milza**
spleen

⑫ **il pancreas**
pancreas

⑬ **l'intestino tenue** *m*
small intestine

⑭ **l'intestino crasso** *m*
large intestine

4.2 I SISTEMI E GLI APPARATI • BODY SYSTEMS

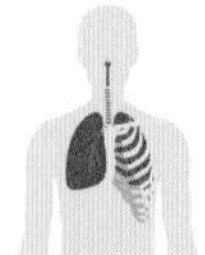

① **l'apparato respiratorio** *m*
respiratory

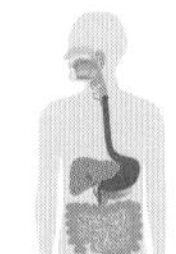

② **l'apparato digerente** *m*
digestive

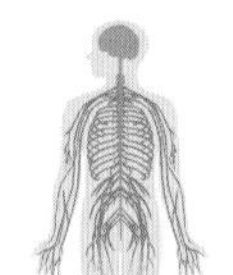

③ **il sistema nervoso**
nervous

④ **l'apparato urinario** *m*
urinary

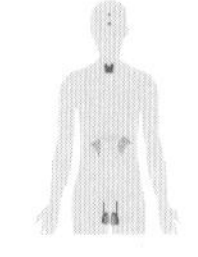

⑤ **il sistema endocrino**
endocrine

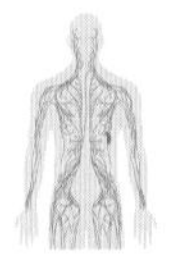

⑥ **il sistema linfatico**
lymphatic

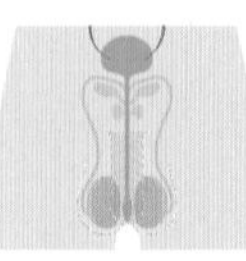

⑦ **l'apparato riproduttivo** *m*
reproductive

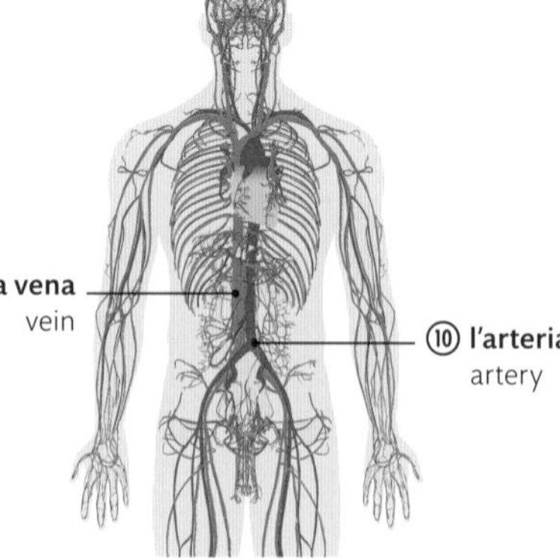
⑨ la vena
vein
⑩ l'arteria f
artery

⑧ **l'apparato cardiocircolatorio** *m*
cardiovascular

See also
01 Le parti del corpo • Parts of the body **03** I muscoli e lo scheletro Muscles and skeleton **19** Le malattie e le lesioni • Illness and injury
20 Andare dal medico • Visiting the doctor **21** L'ospedale • The hospital

4.3 **LA TESTA** • HEAD

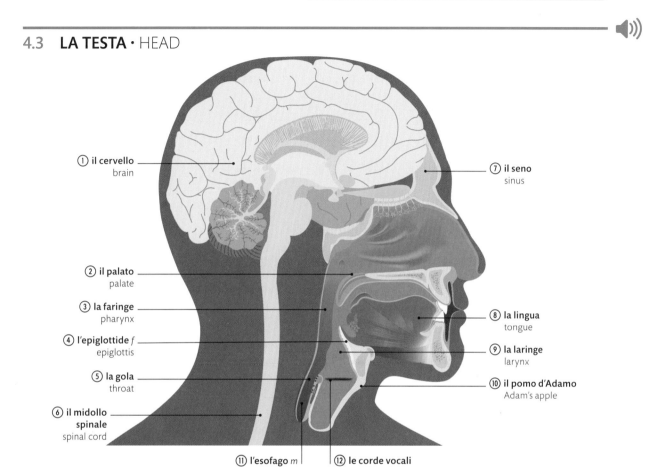

① **il cervello**
brain

② **il palato**
palate

③ **la faringe**
pharynx

④ **l'epiglottide** *f*
epiglottis

⑤ **la gola**
throat

⑥ **il midollo spinale**
spinal cord

⑦ **il seno**
sinus

⑧ **la lingua**
tongue

⑨ **la laringe**
larynx

⑩ **il pomo d'Adamo**
Adam's apple

⑪ **l'esofago** *m*
esophagus

⑫ **le corde vocali**
vocal cords

4.4 **GLI ORGANI RIPRODUTTIVI** • REPRODUCTIVE ORGANS

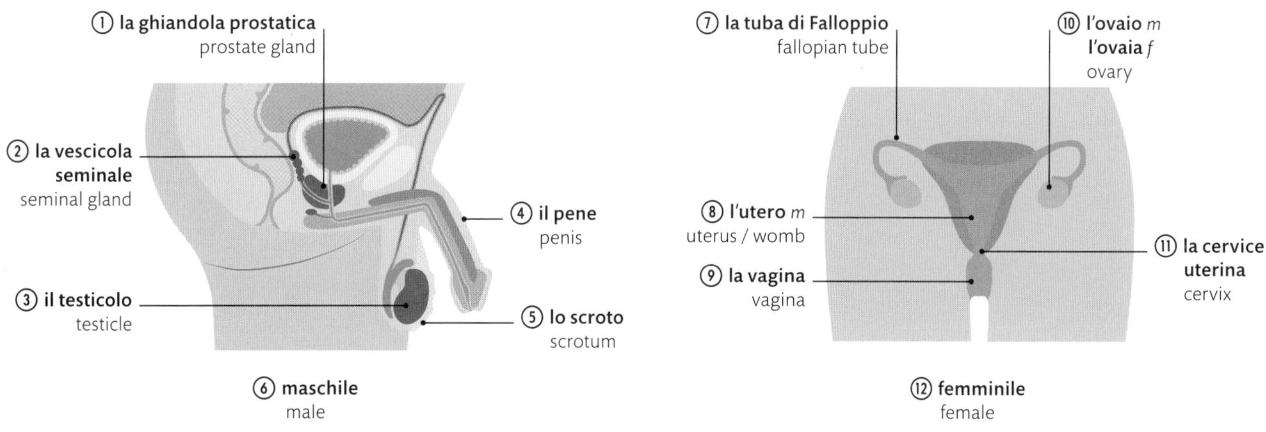
① la ghiandola prostatica
prostate gland
② la vescicola seminale
seminal gland
③ il testicolo
testicle
④ il pene
penis
⑤ lo scroto
scrotum
⑥ maschile
male
⑦ la tuba di Falloppio
fallopian tube
⑧ l'utero m
uterus / womb
⑨ la vagina
vagina
⑩ l'ovaio m
l'ovaia f
ovary
⑪ la cervice uterina
cervix
⑫ femminile
female

05 La famiglia
Family

5.1 LA FAMIGLIA DI CARLO · CARLO'S FAMILY

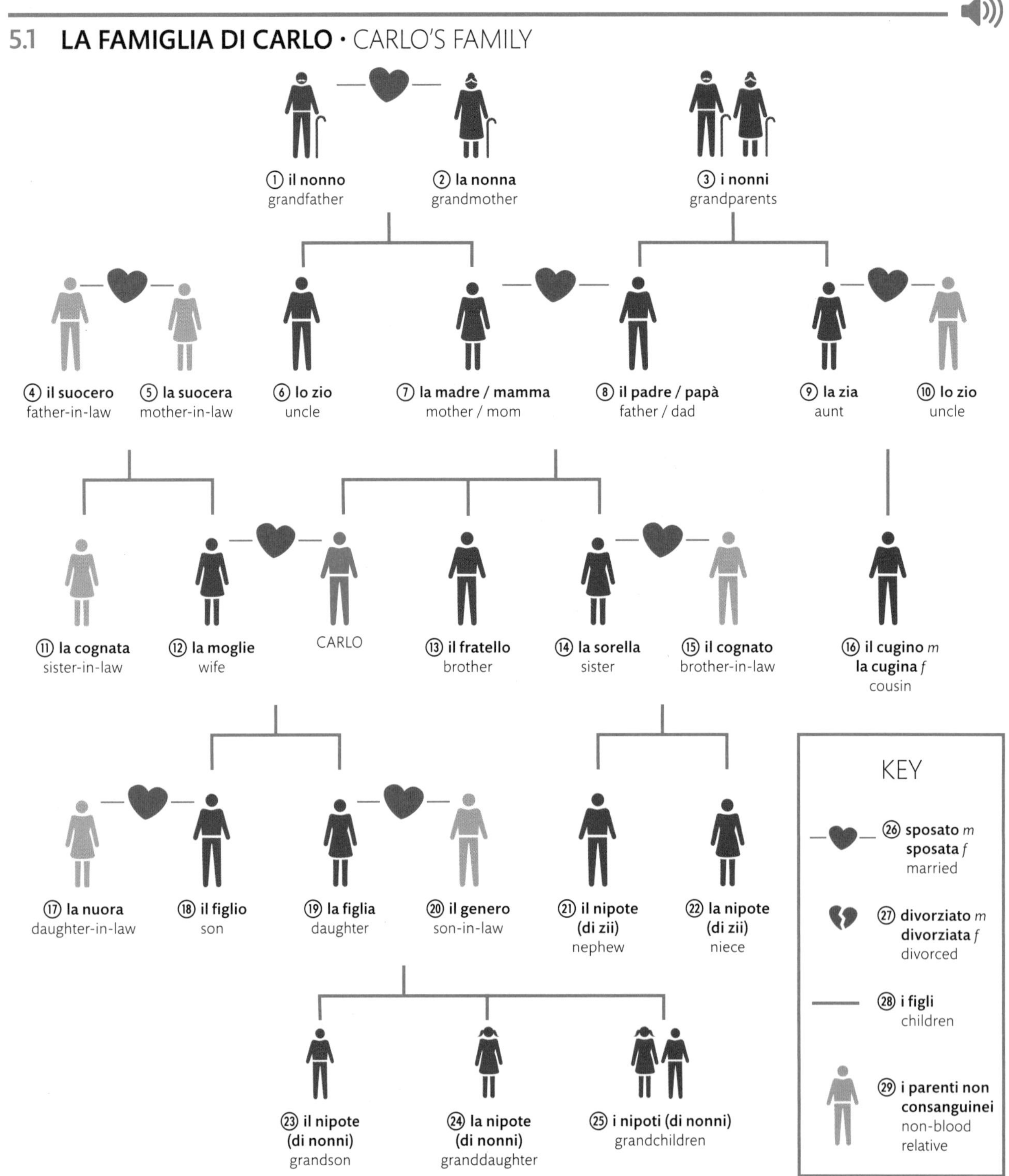

① il nonno
grandfather
② la nonna
grandmother
③ i nonni
grandparents
④ il suocero
father-in-law
⑤ la suocera
mother-in-law
⑥ lo zio
uncle
⑦ la madre / mamma
mother / mom
⑧ il padre / papà
father / dad
⑨ la zia
aunt
⑩ lo zio
uncle
⑪ la cognata
sister-in-law
⑫ la moglie
wife
CARLO
⑬ il fratello
brother
⑭ la sorella
sister
⑮ il cognato
brother-in-law
⑯ il cugino m
la cugina f
cousin
⑰ la nuora
daughter-in-law
⑱ il figlio
son
⑲ la figlia
daughter
⑳ il genero
son-in-law
㉑ il nipote
(di zii)
nephew
㉒ la nipote
(di zii)
niece
㉓ il nipote
(di nonni)
grandson
㉔ la nipote
(di nonni)
granddaughter
㉕ i nipoti (di nonni)
grandchildren
KEY
㉖ sposato m
sposata f
married
㉗ divorziato m
divorziata f
divorced
㉘ i figli
children
㉙ i parenti non consanguinei
non-blood relative

See also
07 Life events • Gli eventi della vita **08** Pregnancy and childhood • La gravidanza e l'infanzia

5.2 LA FAMIGLIA DI SARA
SARA'S FAMILY

① **i nonni**
grandparents

② **la matrigna**
stepmother / stepmom

③ **i genitori**
parents

④ **la sorellastra**
stepsister

⑤ **il fratellastro**
stepbrother

SARA

5.3 LE RELAZIONI • RELATIONSHIPS

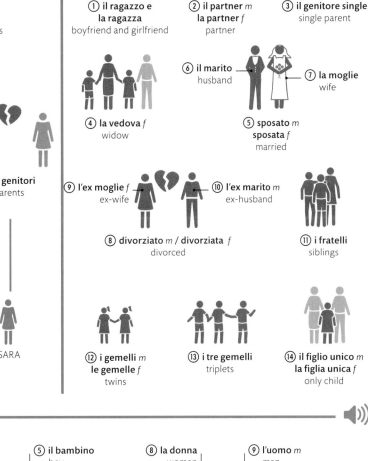

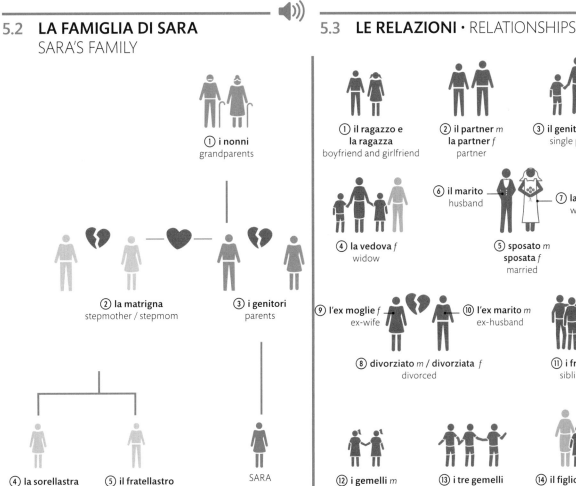

① **il ragazzo e la ragazza**
boyfriend and girlfriend

② **il partner** *m*
la partner *f*
partner

③ **il genitore single**
single parent

④ **la vedova** *f*
widow

⑤ **sposato** *m*
sposata *f*
married

⑥ **il marito**
husband

⑦ **la moglie**
wife

⑧ **divorziato** *m* / **divorziata** *f*
divorced

⑨ **l'ex moglie** *f*
ex-wife

⑩ **l'ex marito** *m*
ex-husband

⑪ **i fratelli**
siblings

⑫ **i gemelli** *m*
le gemelle *f*
twins

⑬ **i tre gemelli**
triplets

⑭ **il figlio unico** *m*
la figlia unica *f*
only child

5.4 CRESCERE • GROWING UP

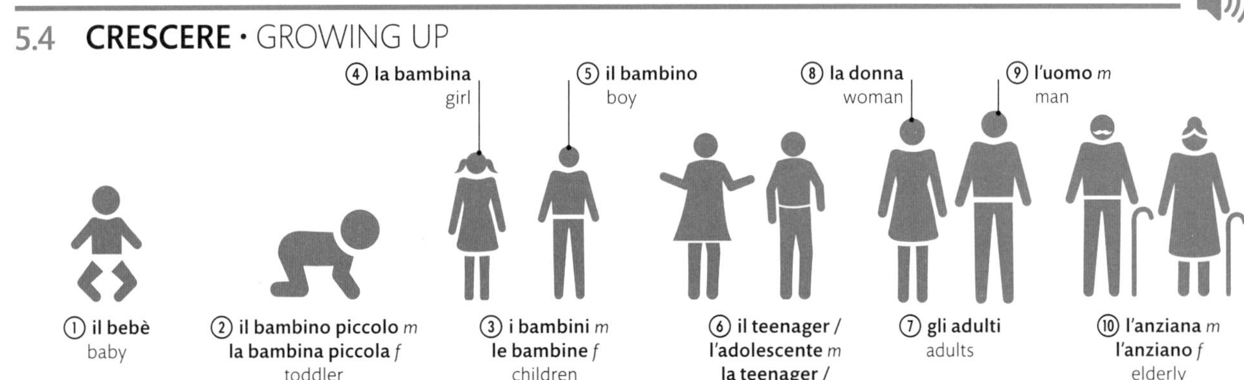
④ la bambina
girl
⑤ il bambino
boy
⑧ la donna
woman
⑨ l'uomo m
man

① **il bebè**
baby

② **il bambino piccolo** *m*
la bambina piccola *f*
toddler

③ **i bambini** *m*
le bambine *f*
children

⑥ **il teenager / l'adolescente** *m*
la teenager / l'adolescente *f*
teenagers

⑦ **gli adulti**
adults

⑩ **l'anziana** *m*
l'anziano *f*
elderly

06 I sentimenti e gli stati d'animo
Feelings and moods

6.1 I SENTIMENTI E GLI STATI D'ANIMO • FEELINGS AND MOODS

① **contento** *m* **contenta** *f* pleased

② **allegro** *m* **allegra** *f* cheerful

③ **felice** happy

④ **felicissimo** *m* **felicissima** *f* delighted

⑤ **al settimo cielo** ecstatic

Ha Ha!
⑥ **divertito** *m* **divertita** *f* amused

⑦ **grato** *m* / **grata** *f* grateful

⑧ **fortunato** *m* **fortunata** *f* lucky

⑨ **interessato** *m* **interessata** *f* interested

⑩ **curioso** *m* **curiosa** *f* curious

⑪ **affascinato** *m* **affascinata** *f* intrigued

⑫ **sbalordito** *m* **sbalordita** *f* amazed

⑬ **sorpreso** *m* **sorpresa** *f* surprised

⑭ **orgoglioso** *m* **orgogliosa** *f* proud

⑮ **entusiasta** excited

⑯ **elettrizzato** *m* **elettrizzata** *f* thrilled

⑰ **calmo** *m* **calma** *f* calm

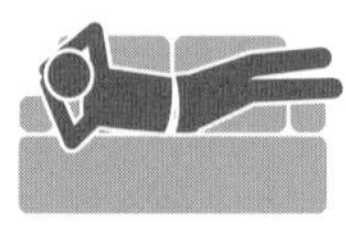
⑱ **rilassato** *m* **rilassata** *f* relaxed

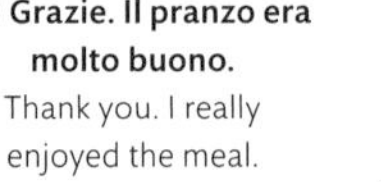
⑳ **Grazie. Il pranzo era molto buono.**
Thank you. I really enjoyed the meal.
⑲ **riconoscente** appreciative

㉑ **sicuro** *m* **sicura** *f* confident

㉒ **fiducioso** *m* **fiduciosa** *f* hopeful

㉓ **comprensivo** *m* **comprensiva** *f* sympathetic

㉔ **infastidito** *m* **infastidita** *f* annoyed

㉕ **geloso** *m* **gelosa** *f* jealous

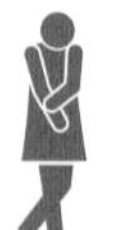
㉖ **imbarazzato** *m* **imbarazzata** *f* embarrassed

See also
10 I tratti della personalità • Personality traits **24** Il corpo sano, la mente sana • Healthy body, healthy mind **93** Le competenze sul luogo di lavoro • Workplace skills

㉘ Non ho passato l'esame nemmeno questa volta. Sono molto deluso.
I failed the exam again. I'm very disappointed.

㉗ **deluso** *m*
delusa *f*
disappointed

㉙ **preoccupato** *m*
preoccupata *f*
worried

㉚ **ansioso** *m*
ansiosa *f*
anxious

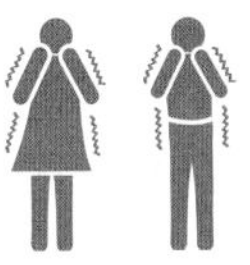

㉛ **nervoso** *m*
nervosa *f*
nervous

㉜ **impaurito** *m*
impaurita *f*
frightened

㉝ **spaventato** *m*
spaventata *f*
scared

㉞ **terrorizzato** *m*
terrorizzata *f*
terrified

㉟ **triste**
sad

㊱ **scontento** *m*
scontenta *f*
unhappy

㊲ **addolorato** *m*
addolorata *f*
tearful

㊳ **infelice**
miserable

㊴ **depresso** *m*
depressa *f*
depressed

㊵ **solo** *m* / **sola** *f*
lonely

㊶ **irritato** *m*
irritata *f*
irritated

㊷ frustrato *m*
frustrata *f*
frustrated

㊸ **arrabbiato** *m*
arrabbiata *f*
angry / mad

㊹ **furioso** *m*
furiosa *f*
furious

㊺ **disgustato** *m*
disgustata *f*
disgusted

㊻ **poco entusiasta**
unenthusiastic

㊼ **stanco** *m*
stanca *f*
tired

㊽ **esausto** *m*
esausta *f*
exhausted

㊾ **confuso** *m*
confusa *f*
confused

㊿ **annoiato** *m*
annoiata *f*
bored

51 **distratto** *m*
distratta *f*
distracted

52 **serio** *m*
seria *f*
serious

53 **indifferente**
indifferent

54 **stressato** *m*
stressata *f*
stressed

55 **colpevole**
guilty

56 **per nulla colpito** *m*
per nulla colpita *f*
unimpressed

57 **turbato** *m*
turbata *f*
upset

58 **scioccato** *m*
scioccata *f*
shocked

07 Gli eventi della vita

Life events

7.1 I RAPPORTI • RELATIONSHIPS

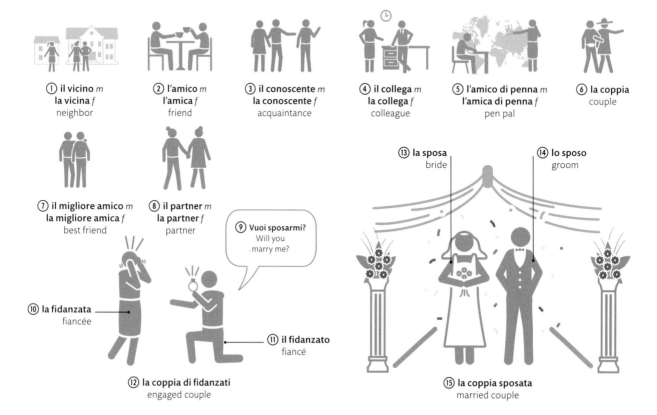

① **il vicino** *m*
la vicina *f*
neighbor

② **l'amico** *m*
l'amica *f*
friend

③ **il conoscente** *m*
la conoscente *f*
acquaintance

④ **il collega** *m*
la collega *f*
colleague

⑤ **l'amico di penna** *m*
l'amica di penna *f*
pen pal

⑥ **la coppia**
couple

⑦ **il migliore amico** *m*
la migliore amica *f*
best friend

⑧ **il partner** *m*
la partner *f*
partner

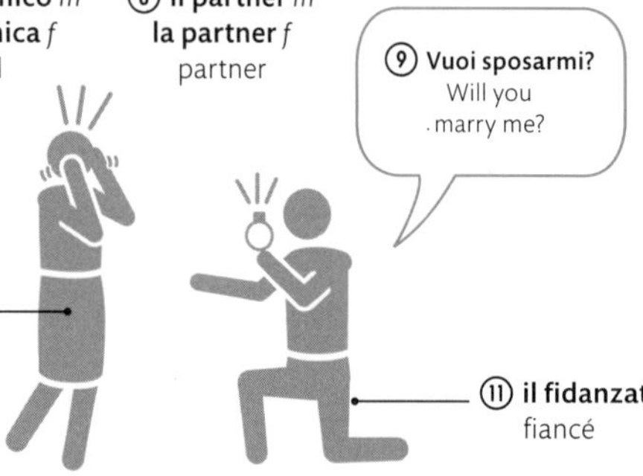

⑨ **Vuoi sposarmi?**
Will you marry me?

⑩ **la fidanzata**
fiancée

⑪ **il fidanzato**
fiancé

⑫ **la coppia di fidanzati**
engaged couple

⑬ **la sposa**
bride

⑭ **lo sposo**
groom

⑮ **la coppia sposata**
married couple

7.2 GLI EVENTI DELLA VITA • LIFE EVENTS

① **nascere**
to be born

② **il certificato di nascita**
birth certificate

③ **andare alla scuola materna**
to go to preschool

④ **iniziare la scuola**
to start school

⑤ **fare amicizia**
to make friends

⑥ **vincere un premio**
to win a prize

⑦ **laurearsi**
to graduate

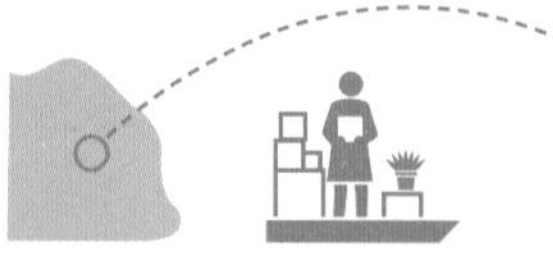

⑧ **emigrare**
to emigrate

⑨ **trovare un lavoro**
to get a job

⑩ **innamorarsi**
to fall in love

⑪ **sposarsi**
to get married

See also
05 La famiglia • Family **08** La gravidanza e l'infanzia • Pregnancy and childhood **19** Le malattie e le lesioni • Illness and injury **73** A scuola • At school **80** All'università • At college **92** Fare domanda per un lavoro • Applying for a job **131** Il viaggio e l'alloggio • Travel and accommodation

7.3 LE FESTE E LE CELEBRAZIONI • FESTIVALS AND CELEBRATIONS

① **il compleanno**
birthday

② **il regalo**
present

③ **il biglietto di buon compleanno**
birthday card

④ **il Natale**
Christmas

⑤ **il Capodanno**
New Year

⑥ **il carnevale**
carnival

⑦ **il Ringraziamento**
Thanksgiving

⑧ **la Pasqua**
Easter

⑨ **Halloween** *m*
Halloween

⑩ **il Kwanzaa**
Kwanzaa

⑪ **la Pasqua ebraica**
Passover

⑫ **il Diwali**
Diwali

⑬ **il giorno dei morti**
Day of the Dead

⑭ **la Eid al-Fitr**
Eid al-Fitr

⑮ **l'Holi** *f*
Holi

⑯ **Hanukkah** *f*
Hanukkah

⑰ **Baisakhi / Vaisakhi** *m*
Baisakhi / Vaisakhi

⑫ **il matrimonio**
wedding

⑬ **la luna di miele**
honeymoon

⑭ **l'anniversario** *m*
anniversary

⑮ **avere un bambino**
to have a baby

⑰ **l'acqua santa** *f*
holy water

⑯ **il battesimo**
christening / baptism

⑱ **il bar mitzvah / bat mitzvah**
bar mitzvah / bat mitzvah

⑲ **andare in pellegrinaggio alla Mecca**
to go on Hajj

⑳ **andare in pensione**
to retire

㉑ **divorziare**
divorce

㉒ **fare testamento**
to write a will

㉓ **morire**
to die

㉔ **il funerale**
funeral

08 La gravidanza e l'infanzia

Pregnancy and childhood

8.1 LA GRAVIDANZA E IL PARTO · PREGNANCY AND CHILDBIRTH

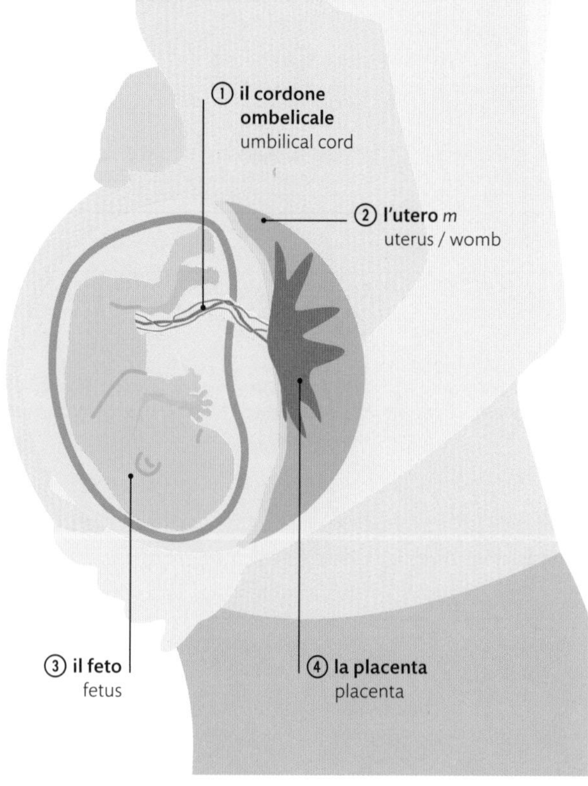

① **il cordone ombelicale**
umbilical cord

② **l'utero** *m*
uterus / womb

③ **il feto**
fetus

④ **la placenta**
placenta

⑤ **il test di gravidanza**
pregnancy test

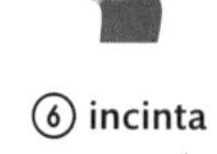

⑥ **incinta**
pregnant

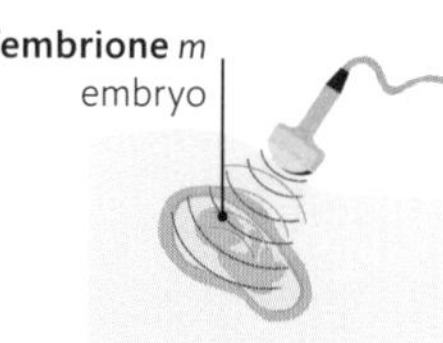

⑧ **l'embrione** *m*
embryo

⑦ **l'ecografia** *f*
ultrasound

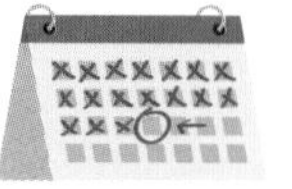

⑨ **la data prevista per il parto**
due date

⑩ **l'ostetrica** *f*
midwife

⑪ **il ginecologo** *m*
la ginecologa *f*
obstetrician

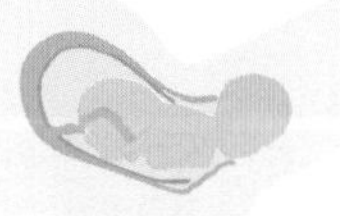

⑫ **la nascita**
birth

⑬ **il neonato** *m*
la neonata *f*
newborn baby

⑭ **la vaccinazione**
vaccination

⑮ **l'incubatrice** *f*
incubator

8.2 I GIOCHI E I GIOCATTOLI · TOYS AND GAMES

① **la bambola**
doll

② **la casa delle bambole**
dollhouse

③ **il peluche**
plsuh toy

④ **il gioco da tavolo**
board game

⑤ **i mattoncini**
building blocks / building bricks

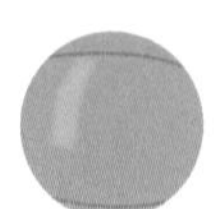

⑥ **la palla**
ball

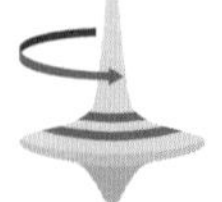

⑦ **la trottola**
top

⑧ **lo yo-yo**
yo-yo

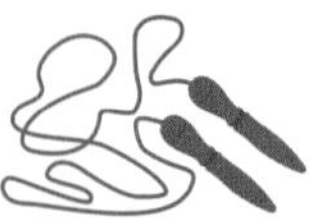

⑨ **la corda per saltare**
jump rope

⑩ **il trampolino**
trampoline

⑪ **il puzzle**
jigsaw puzzle

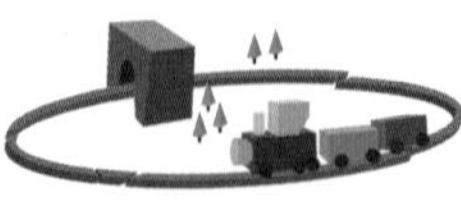

⑫ **il trenino elettrico**
train set

See also
05 La famiglia • Family **13** Gli indumenti • Clothes **20** Andare dal medico • Visiting the doctor
21 L'ospedale • The hospital **30** La camera da letto • Bedroom

8.3 L'INFANZIA • CHILDHOOD

① **il passeggino**
stroller

② **la carrozzina**
baby carriage

③ **il seggiolone**
high chair

④ **il ciuccio**
pacifier

⑤ **il sonaglio**
rattle

⑥ **il baby monitor**
baby monitor

⑦ **il cancelletto di sicurezza**
stair gate

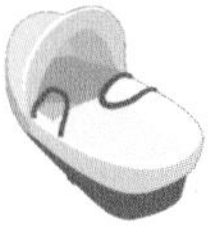

⑧ **la culla di vimini**
Moses basket

⑨ **la vaschetta per il bagnetto**
baby bath

⑩ **il vasino**
potty

⑪ **la salvietta umidificata**
wet wipe

⑫ **il bambino piccolo** *m*
la bambina piccola *f*
toddler

⑬ **la crema per irritazioni da pannolino**
diaper rash cream

⑭ **il pannolino**
diaper

⑮ **la borsa per pannolini**
diaper bag

⑯ **il box**
playpen

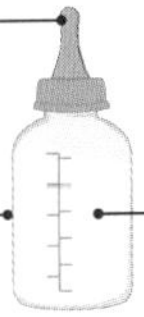

⑱ **la tettarella**
nipple

⑰ **il biberon**
bottle

⑲ **il latte in polvere**
baby formula

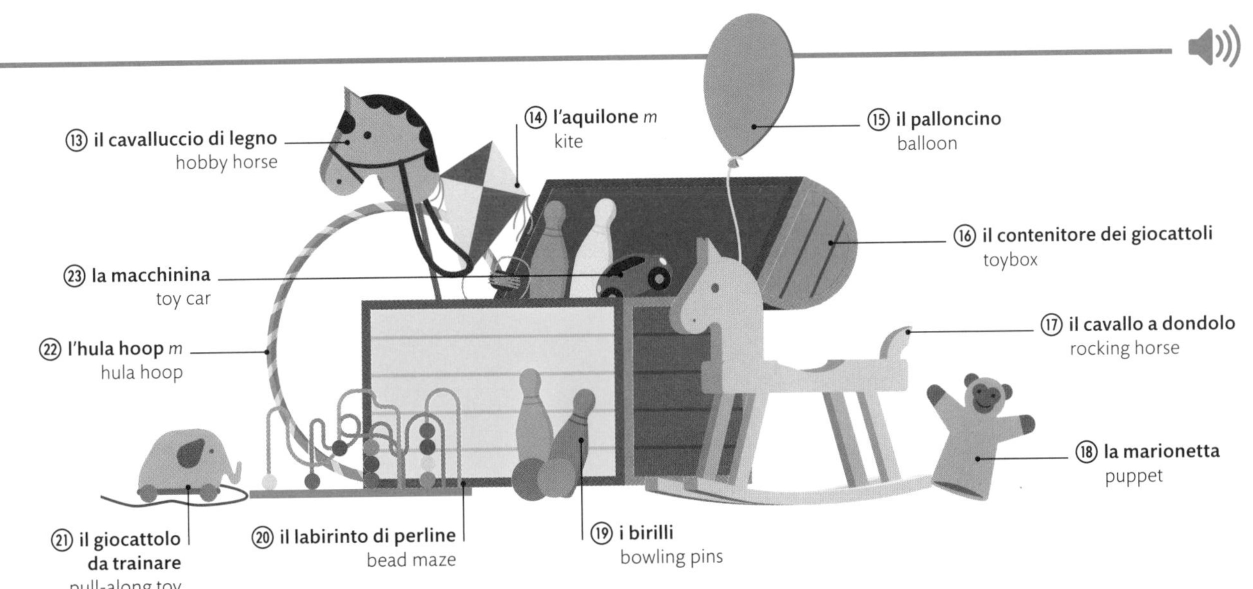

⑬ il cavalluccio di legno
hobby horse
⑭ l'aquilone m
kite
⑮ il palloncino
balloon
⑯ il contenitore dei giocattoli
toybox
㉓ la macchinina
toy car
⑰ il cavallo a dondolo
rocking horse
㉒ l'hula hoop m
hula hoop
⑱ la marionetta
puppet
㉑ il giocattolo da trainare
pull-along toy
⑳ il labirinto di perline
bead maze
⑲ i birilli
bowling pins

09 Le attività quotidiane

Daily routines

9.1 LA MATTINA E IL POMERIGGIO • MORNING AND AFTERNOON

① **suona la sveglia**
alarm goes off

② **svegliarsi**
to wake up

③ **alzarsi**
to get up

④ **fare la doccia**
to take (or have) a shower

⑤ **fare il bagno**
to take (or have) a bath

⑥ **truccarsi**
to put on makeup

⑦ **radersi**
to shave

⑧ **lavarsi i capelli**
to wash your hair

⑨ **asciugarsi i capelli**
to dry your hair

⑩ **stirare una camicia**
to iron a shirt

⑪ **vestirsi**
to get dressed

⑫ **lavarsi i denti**
to brush your teeth

⑬ **lavarsi il viso**
to wash your face

⑭ **pettinarsi**
to brush your hair

⑮ **fare il letto**
to make the bed

⑯ **fare colazione**
to have (or eat) breakfast

⑰ **preparare il pranzo al sacco**
to pack your lunch

⑱ **uscire di casa**
to leave the house

⑲ **andare al lavoro**
to go to work

⑳ **andare a scuola**
to go to school

㉑ **guidare**
to drive

㉒ **prendere l'autobus**
to catch the bus

㉓ **prendere il treno**
to catch the train

㉔ **leggere un giornale**
to read a newspaper

㉕ **arrivare**
to arrive

㉖ **arrivare in anticipo**
to arrive early

㉗ **arrivare in orario**
to arrive on time

㉘ **pranzare**
to have (or eat) lunch

㉙ **controllare le e-mail**
to check your emails

㉚ **fare una pausa**
to take a break

㉜ Mi dispiace di essere di nuovo in ritardo.
I'm sorry I'm late again.

㉛ **arrivare in ritardo / essere in ritardo**
to arrive late / to be late

See also
11 Le abilità e le azioni • Abilities and actions **29** Cucinare • Cooking **81** Al lavoro • At work
82 In ufficio • In the office **171** I sentimenti e gli stati d'animo • Feelings and moods
178 I verbi comuni • Common phrasal verbs

9.2 LA SERA • EVENING

① **finire di lavorare**
to finish work

② **uscire dal lavoro**
to leave work

③ **fare gli straordinari**
to work overtime

④ **Casa dolce casa!**
There's no place like home!

⑤ **arrivare a casa**
to arrive home

⑥ **preparare la cena**
to cook dinner

⑦ **cenare**
to have (or eat) dinner

⑧ **sparecchiare**
to clear the table

⑨ **lavare i piatti**
to do the dishes

⑩ **ascoltare la radio**
to listen to the radio

⑪ **guardare la TV**
to watch TV

⑫ **bere tè o caffè**
to drink tea or coffee

⑬ **portare fuori la spazzatura**
to take out the trash

⑭ **mettere a letto i bambini**
to put the children to bed

⑮ **andare a letto**
to go to bed

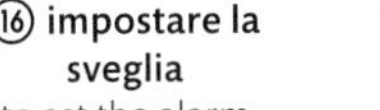

⑯ **impostare la sveglia**
to set the alarm

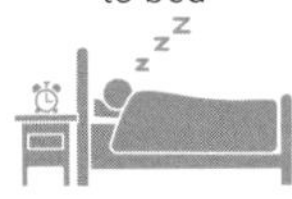

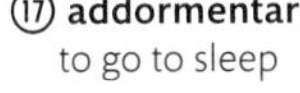

⑰ **addormentarsi**
to go to sleep

9.3 LE ALTRE ATTIVITÀ
OTHER ACTIVITIES

① **fare i compiti**
to do homework

② **portare a spasso il cane**
to walk the dog

③ **dare da mangiare al cane / al gatto**
to feed the dog / cat

④ **fare la spesa**
to buy groceries

⑤ **uscire con gli amici**
to go out with friends

⑥ **andare al bar**
to go to a café

⑦ **chiamare un amico** *m* **/ un'amica** *f* **/ chiamare i familiari**
to call a friend / to call your family

⑧ **tagliare l'erba**
to mow the lawn

⑨ **fare esercizio fisico**
to exercise

⑩ **giocare con i bambini**
to play with your kids

⑪ **pagare le bollette**
to pay the bills

⑫ **fare un riposino**
to take a nap

⑬ **lavare l'auto**
to clean the car

⑭ **suonare uno strumento musicale**
to play a musical instrument

⑮ **chiacchierare con gli amici**
to chat with friends

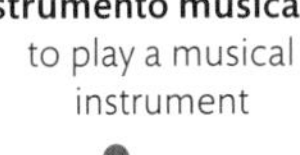

⑯ **chattare online**
to chat online

⑰ **innaffiare le piante**
to water the plants

⑱ **spedire un pacco**
to send a package

10 I tratti della personalità
Personality traits

10.1 DESCRIVERE LE PERSONALITÀ • DESCRIBING PERSONALITIES

① **amichevole**
friendly

② **scortese**
unfriendly

③ **loquace**
talkative

④ **entusiasta**
enthusiastic

⑤ **serio** *m*
seria *f*
serious

⑥ **assertivo** *m*
assertiva *f*
assertive

⑦ **critico** *m*
critica *f*
critical

⑧ **premuroso** *m*
premurosa *f*
caring

⑨ **sensibile**
sensitive

⑩ **insensibile**
insensitive

⑪ **ragionevole**
reasonable

⑫ **irragionevole**
unreasonable

⑬ **gentile**
kind

⑭ **sgarbato** *m*
sgarbata *f*
unkind

⑮ **riservato** *m*
riservata *f*
secretive

⑯ **maturo** *m*
matura *f*
mature

⑰ **immaturo** *m*
immatura *f*
immature

⑱ **cauto** *m* / **cauta** *f*
cautious

⑲ **generoso** *m*
generosa *f*
generous

⑳ **coraggioso** *m*
coraggiosa *f*
brave

Ha Ha!
Ha Ha!
㉑ **divertente**
funny

㉒ **meschino** *m*
meschina *f*
mean

㉓ **paziente**
patient

㉔ **impaziente**
impatient

㉕ **pigro** *m* / **pigra** *f*
lazy

㉖ **ottimista**
optimistic

㉗ **estroverso** *m*
estroversa *f*
outgoing

㉘ **appassionato** *m*
appassionata *f*
passionate

㉙ **educato** *m* / **educata** *f*
polite

㉚ **maleducato** *m*
maleducata *f*
rude

㉛ **timido** *m*
timida *f*
shy

㉜ **intelligente**
intelligent

㉝ **nervoso** *m*
nervosa *f*
nervous

㉞ **sicuro** *m* / **sicura** *f*
confident

㉟ **sciocco** *m*
sciocca *f*
silly

㊱ **egoista**
selfish

See also
05 La famiglia • Family **06** I sentimenti e gli stati d'animo • Feelings and moods **11** Le abilità e le azioni • Abilities and actions **93** Le competenze sul luogo di lavoro • Workplace skills

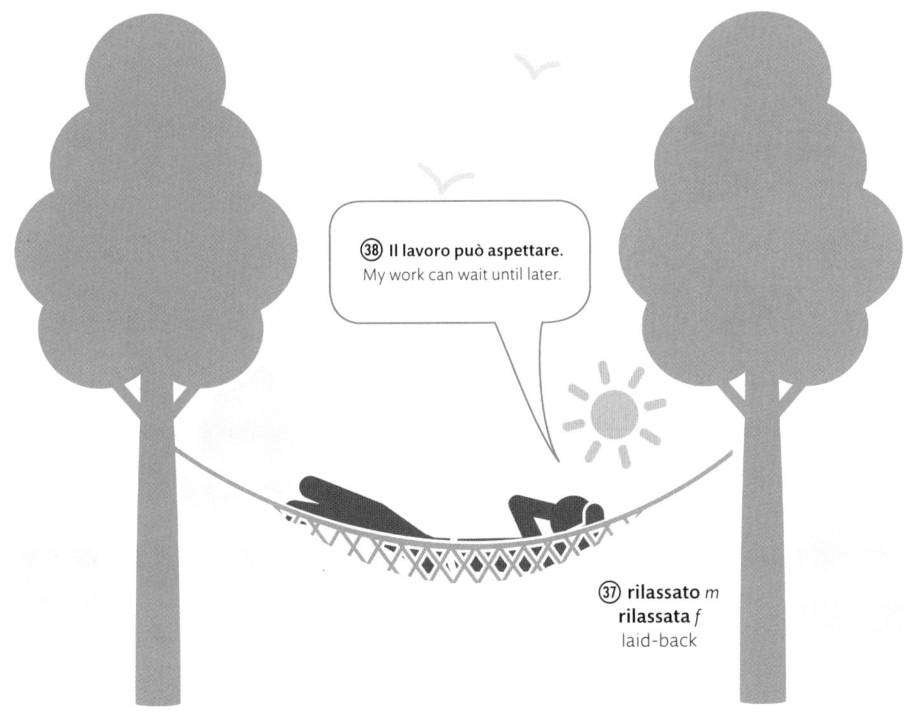
38 **Il lavoro può aspettare.**
My work can wait until later.

37 **rilassato** *m*
rilassata *f*
laid-back

39 **ambizioso** *m*
ambiziosa *f*
ambitious

40 **spontaneo** *m*
spontanea *f*
spontaneous

41 **romantico** *m*
romantica *f*
romantic

42 **calmo** *m* / **calma** *f*
calm

43 **eccentrico** *m*
eccentrica *f*
eccentric

44 **onesto** *m* / **onesta** *f*
honest

?

45 **disonesto** *m*
disonesta *f*
dishonest

46 **di conforto**
supportive

47 **impulsivo** *m*
impulsiva *f*
impulsive

48 **affidabile**
reliable

49 **inaffidabile**
unreliable

50 **talentuoso** *m*
talentuosa *f*
talented

1

51 **arrogante**
arrogant

52 **attento** *m*
attenta *f*
considerate

53 **avventuroso** *m*
avventurosa *f*
adventurous

i

54 **disponibile**
approachable

i

55 **inavvicinabile**
unapproachable

56 **deciso** *m* / **decisa** *f*
decisive

57 **meticoloso** *m*
meticolosa *f*
meticulous

58 **goffo** *m*
goffa *f*
clumsy

59 **irriguardoso** *m*
irriguardosa *f*
thoughtless

11 Le abilità e le azioni

Abilities and actions

11.1 DESCRIVERE LE ABILITÀ E LE AZIONI

DESCRIBING ABILITIES AND ACTIONS

① **vedere**
to see

② **assaggiare**
to taste

③ **annusare**
to smell

④ **andare carponi**
to crawl

⑩ **Amo ballare.**
I love to dance.

⑪ **Anch'io!**
Me too!

⑨ **ballare**
to dance

⑤ **colpire**
to hit

⑥ **giocare**
to play

⑦ **calciare**
to kick

⑧ **lanciare**
to throw

⑫ **afferrare**
to catch

⑬ **correre**
to run

⑭ **saltellare**
to hop

⑮ **saltare**
to jump

⑯ **muoversi furtivamente**
to creep

⑰ **scuotere**
to shake

⑱ **lavorare**
to work

⑲ **soffiare**
to blow

⑳ **fare (un pupazzo di neve)**
to make (a snowman)

㉑ **compitare**
to spell

㉒ **fare (i compiti)**
to do (homework)

㉓ **copiare**
to copy

㉔ **costruire**
to build

㉕ **scavare**
to dig

㉖ **riparare**
to repair

㉗ **aggiustare**
to fix

㉘ **sedersi**
to sit down

㉙ **alzarsi**
to stand up

㉚ **capire**
to understand

㉛ **cadere**
to fall

㉜ **sollevare**
to lift

㉝ **aggiungere**
to add

㉞ **sottrarre**
to subtract

㉟ **contare**
to count

See also
09 Le attività quotidiane • Daily routines **93** Le competenze sul luogo di lavoro • Workplace skills **178** I verbi comuni • Common phrasal verbs

㊱ **ascoltare**
to listen

㊲ **parlare**
to talk

㊳ **parlare**
to speak

㊴ **gridare**
to shout

㊵ **cantare**
to sing

㊶ **recitare**
to act

㊷ **sussurrare**
to whisper

㊸ **pensare**
to think

㊹ **decidere**
to decide

㊺ **ricordare**
to remember

㊻ **dimenticare**
to forget

㊼ **aiutare**
to help

㊽ **indicare**
to point

㊾ **impacchettare**
to pack

㊿ **spacchettare**
to unpack

(51) **volare**
to fly

(52) **andare in**
to ride

(53) **scalare**
to climb

(54) **leccare**
to lick

(55) **prendere**
to take

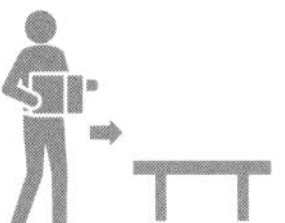
(56) **portare**
to bring

(57) **ritirare**
to pick up

(58) **entrare**
to enter

(59) **uscire**
to exit

(60) **vincere**
to win

(61) **sollevare**
to raise

(62) **portare**
to carry

(63) **fare il giocoliere**
to juggle

(64) **tenere**
to hold

(65) **spostare**
to move

(66) **spingere**
to push

(67) **tirare**
to pull

12 L'aspetto e i capelli
Appearance and hair

12.1 L'ASPETTO GENERALE
GENERAL APPEARANCE

① **di media altezza** medium height

② **alto** *m* **alta** *f* tall

③ **basso** *m* **bassa** *f* short

④ **bella** beautiful

⑤ **bello** handsome

⑥ **giovane** young

⑦ **di mezza età** middle-aged

⑧ **anziano** *m* **anziana** *f* old

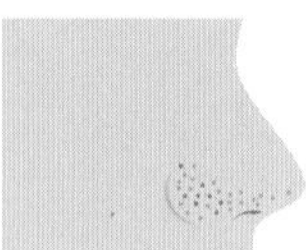

⑨ **i pori** pores

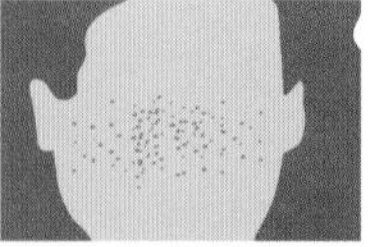

⑩ **le lentiggini** freckles

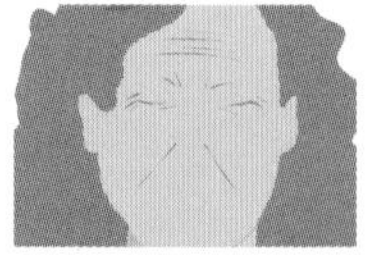

⑪ **le rughe** wrinkles

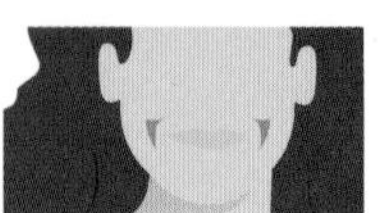

⑫ **le fossette** dimples

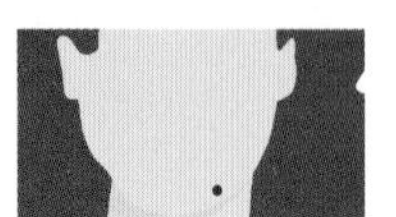

⑬ **il neo** mole

12.2 I CAPELLI · HAIR

① **acconciare i capelli** to style your hair

② **lavarsi i capelli** to wash your hair

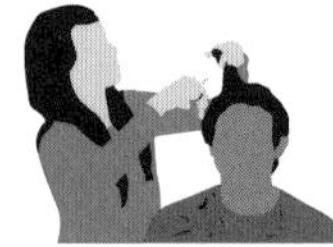

③ **farsi tagliare i capelli** to have (or get) your hair cut

④ **legare i capelli** to tie your hair back

JUNE

⑤ **farsi crescere i capelli** to grow your hair

⑥ **radersi** to shave

⑦ **i capelli lunghi** long hair

⑧ **i capelli corti** short hair

⑨ **i capelli lunghi fino alle spalle** shoulder-length hair

⑩ **la riga laterale** side part

⑪ **la riga centrale** center part

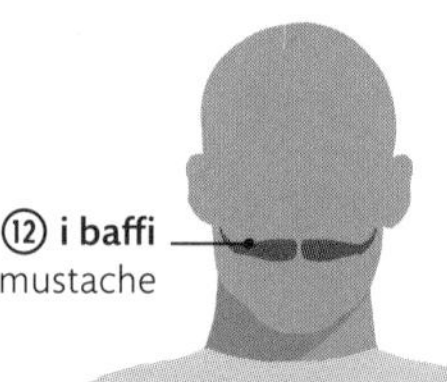

⑫ **i baffi** mustache

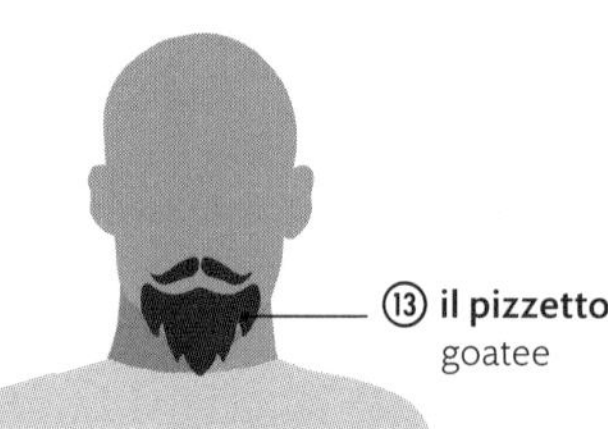

⑬ **il pizzetto** goatee

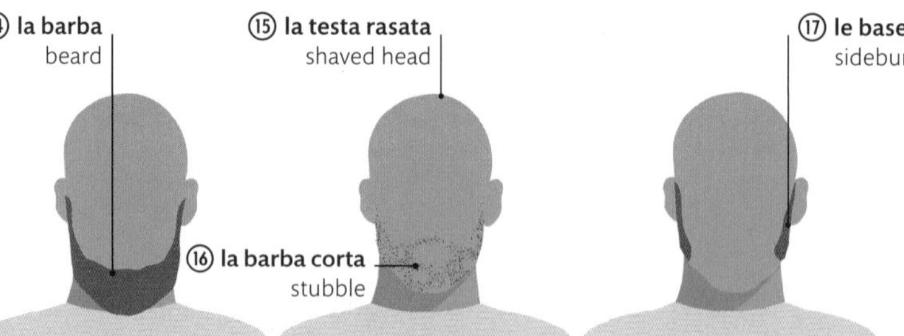

⑭ **la barba** beard

⑮ **la testa rasata** shaved head

⑯ **la barba corta** stubble

⑰ **le basette** sideburns

⑱ **i peli del viso** facial hair

See also
13-15 Gli indumenti • Clothes **16** Gli accessori
Accessories **17** Le scarpe • Shoes **18** La bellezza • Beauty

⑲ **i capelli a spazzola**
crew cut

⑳ **calvo** *m* **/ calva** *f*
bald

㉑ **i capelli lisci**
straight hair

㉒ **i capelli mossi**
wavy hair

㉓ **i capelli ricci**
curly hair

㉔ **i capelli crespi**
frizzy hair

㉕ **la coda di cavallo**
ponytail

㉖ **la treccia**
braid

㉗ **i codini**
pigtails

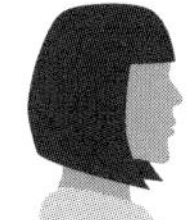
㉘ **il caschetto**
bob

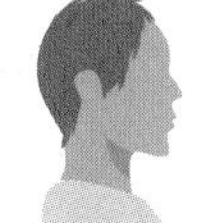
㉙ **il taglio corto**
crop

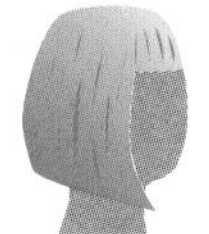
㉚ **la parrucca**
wig

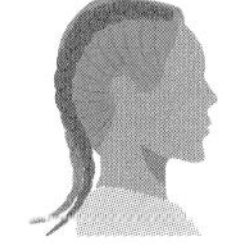
㉛ **la treccia alla francese**
French braid

㉜ **lo chignon**
bun

㉝ **le mèches**
highlights

㉞ **la pettinatura afro**
Afro

㉟ **le treccine**
braids

㊱ **le treccine aderenti alla testa**
cornrows

㊲ **i capelli normali**
normal hair

㊳ **i capelli grassi**
greasy hair

㊴ **i capelli secchi**
dry hair

㊵ **la forfora**
dandruff

㊶ **il gel per capelli**
hair gel

㊷ **lo spray per capelli**
hair spray

㊸ **i capelli neri**
black hair

㊹ **i capelli castani**
brown hair

㊺ **i capelli biondi**
blond / blonde hair

㊻ **i capelli rossi**
red hair

㊼ **i capelli ramati**
auburn hair

㊽ **i capelli grigi**
gray hair

㊾ **la piastra per capelli**
straightening iron

㊿ **il ferro arricciacapelli**
curling iron

(51) **la spazzola**
hairbrush

(52) **il pettine**
comb

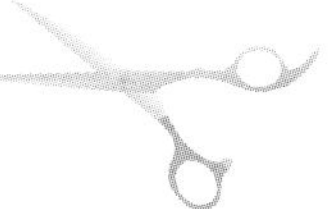
(53) **le forbici per capelli**
hair scissors

(54) **il phon**
hair dryer

13 Gli indumenti

Clothes

13.1 DESCRIVERE GLI INDUMENTI · DESCRIBING CLOTHES

① **la pelle / il cuoio**
leather

② **il cotone**
cotton

③ **di lana**
woolen

④ **la seta**
silk

⑤ **sintetico** *m* **sintetica** *f*
synthetic

⑥ **il denim / jeans**
denim

⑦ **tinta unita**
plain

⑧ **a righe**
striped

⑨ **a quadri / a scacchi**
checkered

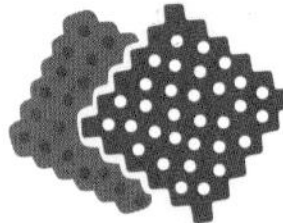
⑩ **a pois**
polka dot

⑪ **con motivo cachemire**
paisley

⑫ **con motivo scozzese**
plaid

⑬ **largo** *m* **/ larga** *f*
loose / baggy

⑭ **aderente**
fitted

⑮ **stretto** *m* **stretta** *f*
tight

⑯ **stropicciato** *m* **stropicciata** *f*
crumpled

⑰ **corto** *m* **/ corta** *f*
cropped

⑱ **vintage**
vintage

13.2 GLI ABITI DA LAVORO E LE UNIFORMI · WORK CLOTHES AND UNIFORMS

① il cappello da cuoco
chef's hat
② la giacca da cuoco
chef's coat

③ **la divisa da cuoco**
chef's uniform

④ **il grembiule**
apron

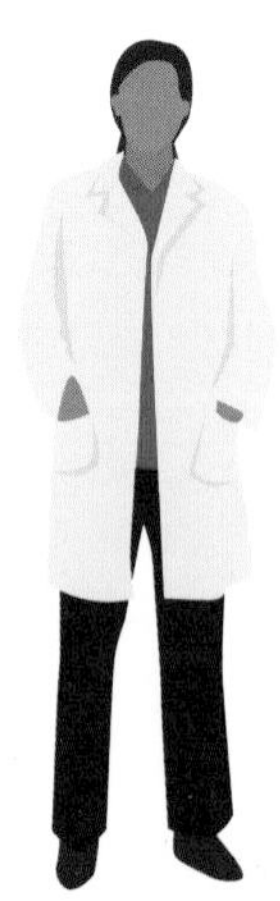
⑤ **il camice da laboratorio**
lab coat

⑥ **l'uniforme da pompiere** *f*
firefighter's uniform

⑦ **la tuta da lavoro**
coveralls

See also
12 L'aspetto e i capelli • Appearance and hair **14-15** Gli indumenti (continua) Clothes continued **16** Gli accessori • Accessories **17** Le scarpe • Shoes

13.3 GLI INDUMENTI DEI BAMBINI • KIDS' AND BABIES' CLOTHES

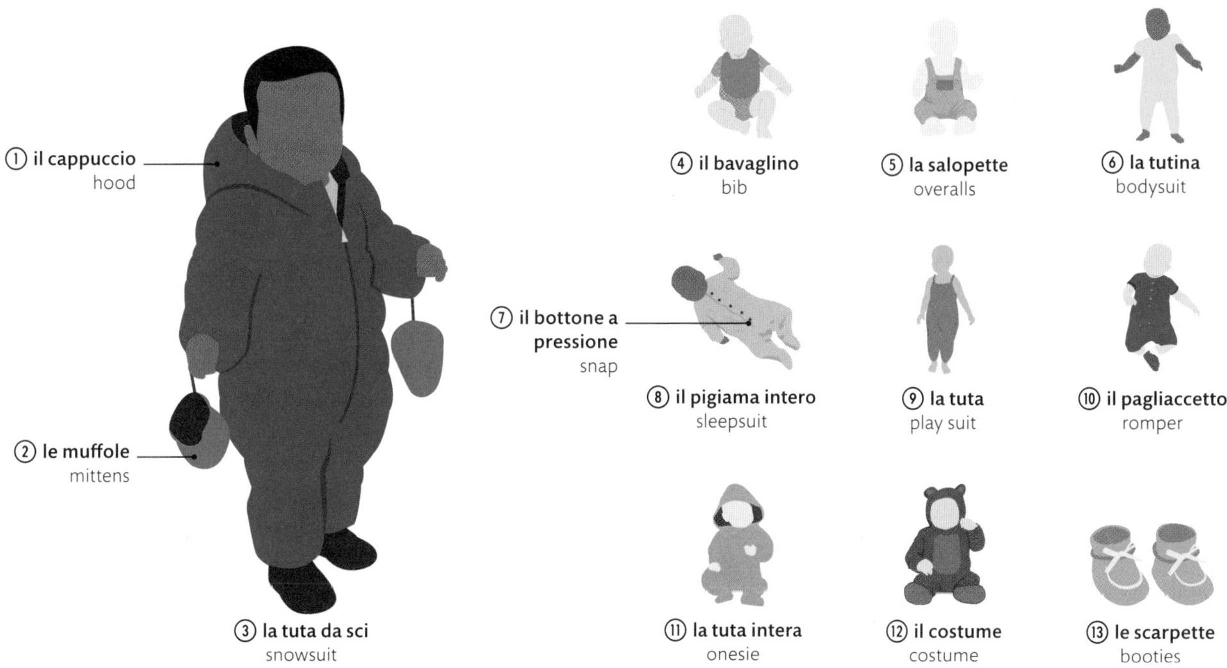
① **il cappuccio** hood
② **le muffole** mittens
③ **la tuta da sci** snowsuit
④ **il bavaglino** bib
⑤ **la salopette** overalls
⑥ **la tutina** bodysuit
⑦ **il bottone a pressione** snap
⑧ **il pigiama intero** sleepsuit
⑨ **la tuta** play suit
⑩ **il pagliaccetto** romper
⑪ **la tuta intera** onesie
⑫ **il costume** costume
⑬ **le scarpette** booties

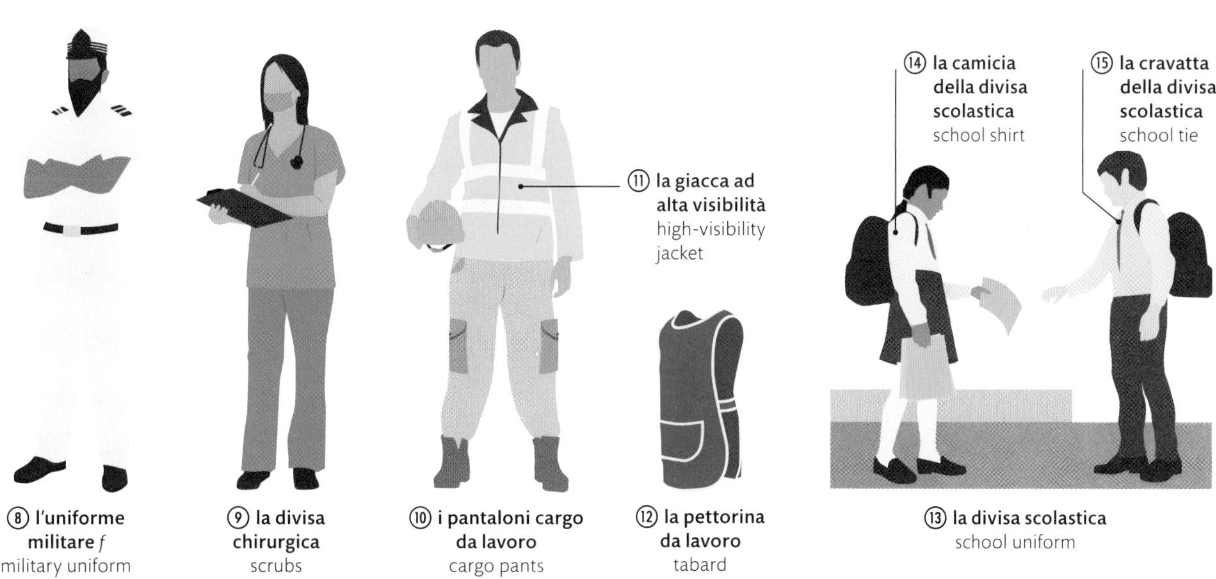
⑧ **l'uniforme militare** *f* military uniform
⑨ **la divisa chirurgica** scrubs
⑩ **i pantaloni cargo da lavoro** cargo pants
⑪ **la giacca ad alta visibilità** high-visibility jacket
⑫ **la pettorina da lavoro** tabard
⑬ **la divisa scolastica** school uniform
⑭ **la camicia della divisa scolastica** school shirt
⑮ **la cravatta della divisa scolastica** school tie

Gli indumenti (continua)

Clothes continued

14.1 L'ABBIGLIAMENTO INFORMALE • CASUAL CLOTHES

① **Preferisco questo abbigliamento informale ai miei abiti da lavoro formali.**
I prefer this casual outfit to my formal work clothes.

⑦ **Dopo il lavoro, mi piace indossare un paio di jeans e una T-shirt.**
After work, I like to change into jeans and a T-shirt.

② **la camicetta / blusa**
blouse

③ **il maglione**
sweater

④ **la gonna**
skirt

⑤ **la piega**
pleat

⑥ **l'orlo** *m*
hem

⑧ **la T-shirt**
T-shirt

⑨ **le righe**
stripes

⑩ **i jeans**
jeans

⑪ **la felpa**
sweatshirt

⑫ **gli shorts**
shorts

⑬ **i bermuda**
bermuda shorts

⑭ **il cardigan**
cardigan

⑮ **la canotta**
tank top

⑯ **il vestito**
dress

⑰ **i leggings**
leggings

⑱ **la camicia a maniche corte**
short-sleeved shirt

⑲ **la polo**
polo shirt

⑳ **il cappello da sole**
sun hat

㉑ **la maglia con scollo a V**
V-neck

㉒ **la maglia girocollo**
round neck

See also
12 L'aspetto e i capelli • Appearance and hair **15** Gli indumenti (continua) • Clothes continued **16** Gli accessori • Accessories **17** Le scarpe • Shoes

14.2 GLI INDUMENTI DA NOTTE
NIGHTWEAR

① **la sottoveste**
camisole

② **le pantofole**
slippers

③ **la mascherina per gli occhi**
eye mask

④ **il pigiama**
pajamas

⑤ **la camicia da notte**
nightgown / nightie

⑥ **la vestaglia**
bathrobe

14.3 LA BIANCHERIA INTIMA • UNDERWEAR

① **le mutandine**
panties

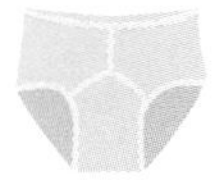
② **le mutande**
briefs

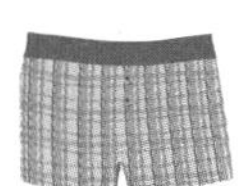
③ **i boxer**
boxer shorts

④ **i calzini**
socks

⑤ **il reggiseno**
bra

⑥ **la sottoveste**
slip

⑦ **la canottiera**
undershirt

⑧ **i collant**
pantyhose

⑨ **le calze**
stockings

⑩ **il corsetto**
corset

⑪ **la giarrettiera**
garter

⑫ **il reggicalze**
garter belt

14.4 I VERBI PER L'ABBIGLIAMENTO • VERBS FOR CLOTHES

① **indossare**
to wear

② **andare bene**
to fit

③ **mettere**
to put on

④ **togliere**
to take off

⑤ **allacciare**
to fasten

⑥ **slacciare**
to unfasten

⑦ **stare bene a (qualcuno)**
to suit (someone)

⑧ **cambiarsi**
to change / to get changed

⑨ **appendere**
to hang up

⑩ **piegare**
to fold

⑪ **fare il risvolto**
to turn up

⑫ **provare qualcosa**
to try something on

15 Gli indumenti (continua)

Clothes continued

15.1 L'ABBIGLIAMENTO FORMALE · FORMAL WEAR

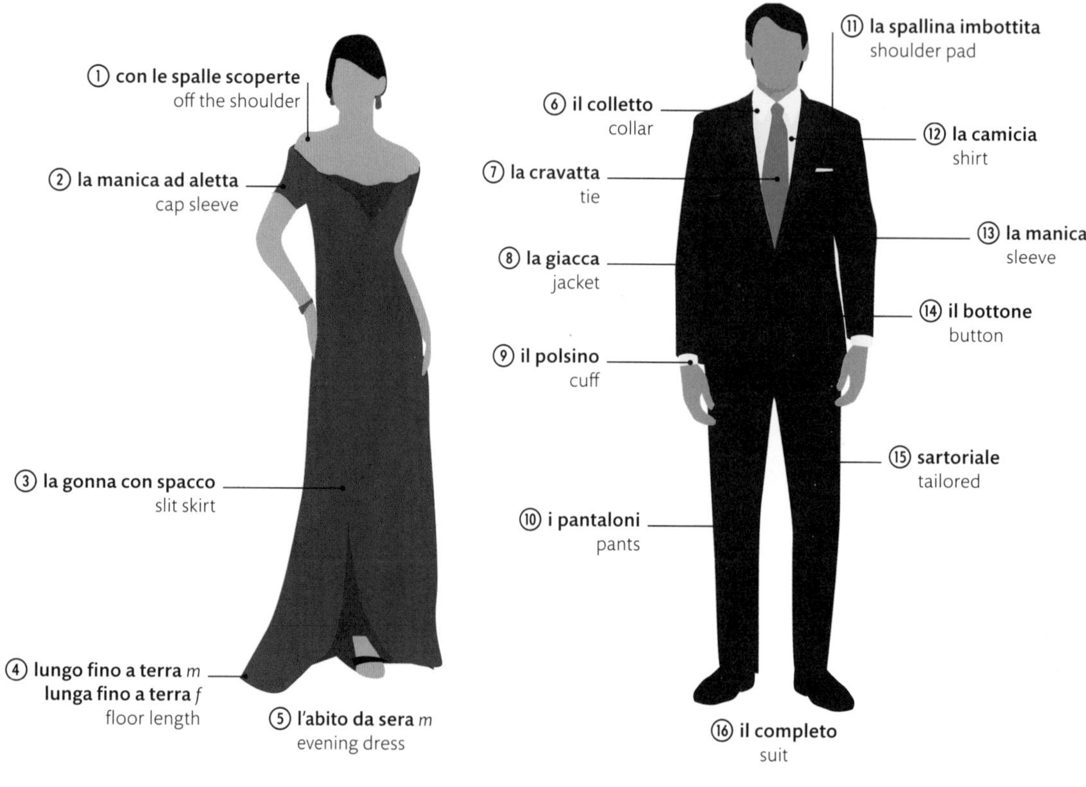

① con le spalle scoperte
off the shoulder
② la manica ad aletta
cap sleeve
③ la gonna con spacco
slit skirt
④ lungo fino a terra *m*
lunga fino a terra *f*
floor length
⑤ l'abito da sera *m*
evening dress
⑥ il colletto
collar
⑦ la cravatta
tie
⑧ la giacca
jacket
⑨ il polsino
cuff
⑩ i pantaloni
pants
⑪ la spallina imbottita
shoulder pad
⑫ la camicia
shirt
⑬ la manica
sleeve
⑭ il bottone
button
⑮ sartoriale
tailored
⑯ il completo
suit

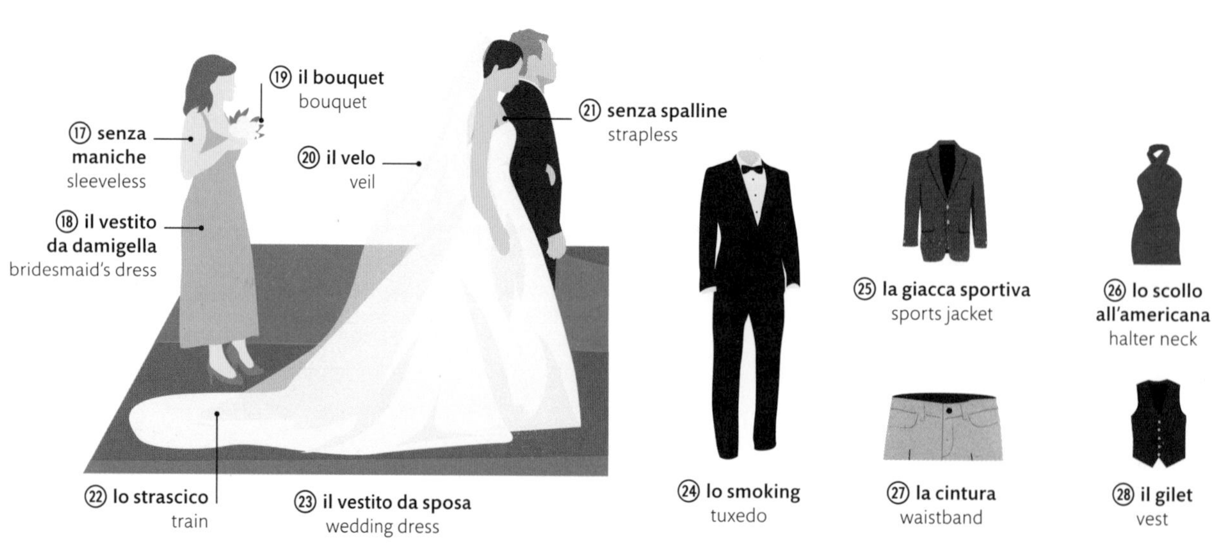

⑰ senza maniche
sleeveless
⑱ il vestito da damigella
bridesmaid's dress
⑲ il bouquet
bouquet
⑳ il velo
veil
㉑ senza spalline
strapless
㉒ lo strascico
train
㉓ il vestito da sposa
wedding dress
㉔ lo smoking
tuxedo
㉕ la giacca sportiva
sports jacket
㉖ lo scollo all'americana
halter neck
㉗ la cintura
waistband
㉘ il gilet
vest

See also
12 L'aspetto e i capelli • Appearance and hair 16 Gli accessori • Accessories
17 Le scarpe • Shoes

15.2 I CAPPOTTI • COATS

② il cappuccio
hood

① l'impermeabile *m*
raincoat

③ la giacca a vento
anorak

④ il montgomery
duffle coat

⑤ il poncho
poncho

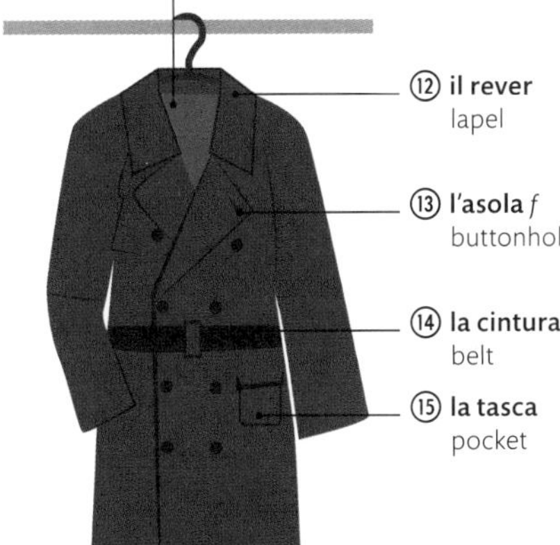

⑪ la fodera
lining

⑫ il rever
lapel

⑬ l'asola *f*
buttonhole

⑭ la cintura
belt

⑮ la tasca
pocket

⑩ il trench
trench coat

⑥ la giacca di jeans
denim jacket

⑦ il giubbotto imbottito
quilted jacket

⑧ il bomber
bomber jacket

⑨ la mantella
cloak

15.3 L'ABBIGLIAMENTO SPORTIVO SPORTSWEAR

① la tuta da ginnastica
tracksuit

② il reggiseno sportivo
sports bra

③ i pantaloni della tuta
sweatpants

④ il body
leotard

⑥ il boccaglio e la maschera
snorkel and mask

⑨ gli occhialini
goggles

⑦ le pinne
fins / flippers

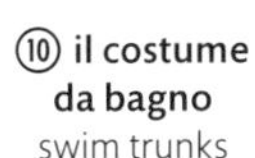

⑤ la maglia da calcio
soccer jersey

⑧ il costume da bagno
swimsuit

⑩ il costume da bagno
swim trunks

15.4 GLI ABITI TRADIZIONALI TRADITIONAL CLOTHES

① l'agbada *m*
agbada

② l'abito da flamenco *m*
flamenco dress

③ i lederhosen
lederhosen

④ il kimono
kimono

⑤ il thawb
thawb

⑥ il sari
sari

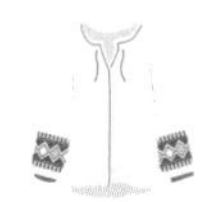

⑦ il kilt
kilt

⑧ il sarong
sarong

⑨ la camicetta folkloristica
folk blouse

16 Gli accessori

Accessories

16.1 GLI ACCESSORI DI MODA · FASHION ACCESSORIES

① **i guanti**
gloves

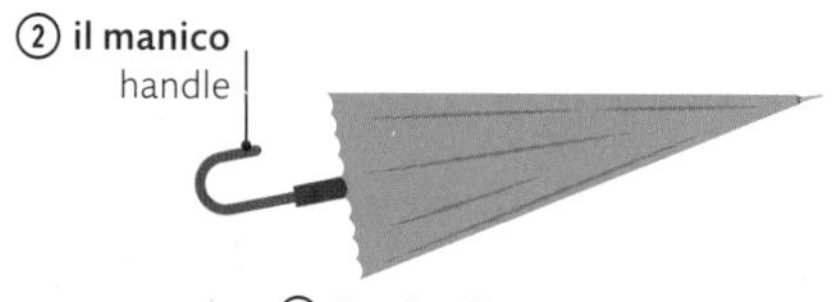
② **il manico**
handle

③ **l'ombrello** *m*
umbrella

④ **il fazzoletto**
handkerchief

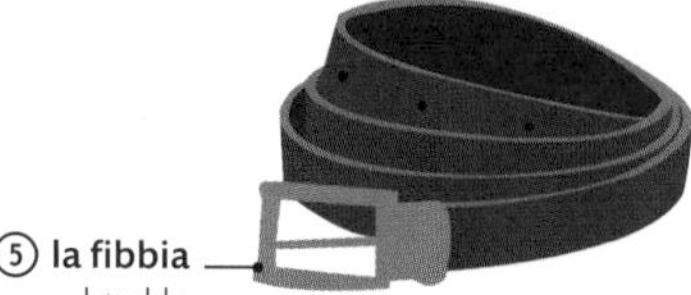
⑤ **la fibbia**
buckle

⑥ **la cintura**
belt

⑦ **la sciarpa**
scarf

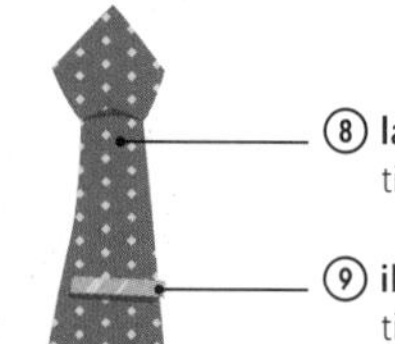
⑧ **la cravatta**
tie

⑨ **il fermacravatta**
tie bar

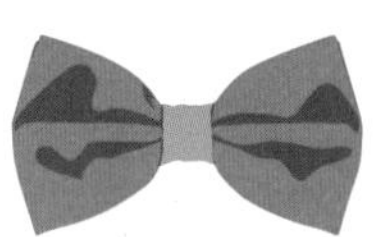
⑩ **il papillon**
bow tie

18
⑪ **la spilla**
pin

⑫ **il cerchietto**
headband

16.2 I GIOIELLI · JEWELRY

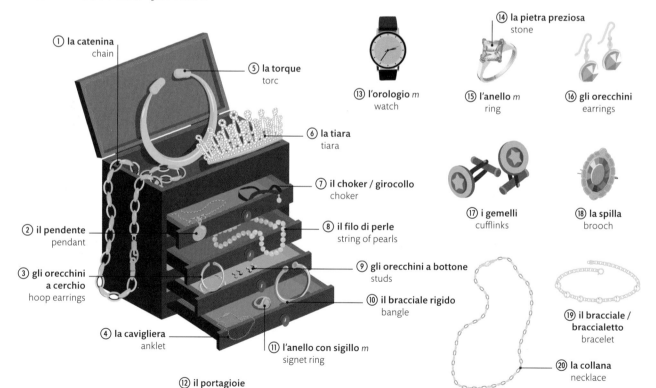

① **la catenina**
chain

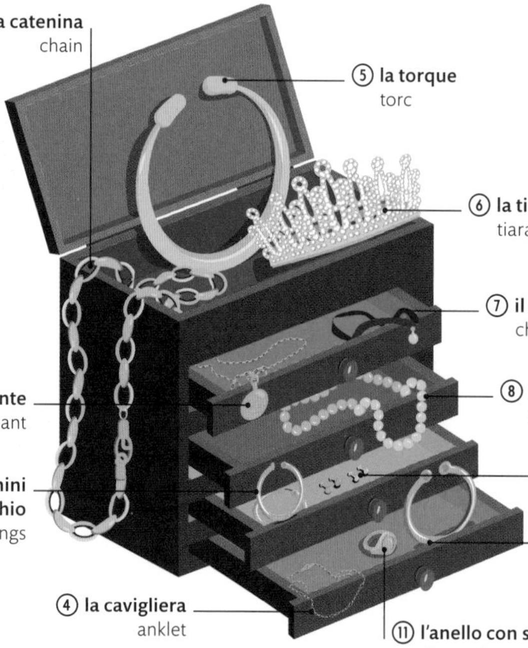

② **il pendente**
pendant

③ **gli orecchini a cerchio**
hoop earrings

④ **la cavigliera**
anklet

⑤ **la torque**
torc

⑥ **la tiara**
tiara

⑦ **il choker / girocollo**
choker

⑧ **il filo di perle**
string of pearls

⑨ **gli orecchini a bottone**
studs

⑩ **il bracciale rigido**
bangle

⑪ **l'anello con sigillo** *m*
signet ring

⑫ **il portagioie**
jewelry box

⑬ **l'orologio** *m*
watch

⑭ **la pietra preziosa**
stone

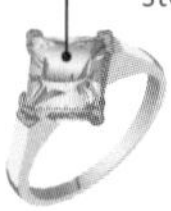

⑮ **l'anello** *m*
ring

⑯ **gli orecchini**
earrings

⑰ **i gemelli**
cufflinks

⑱ **la spilla**
brooch

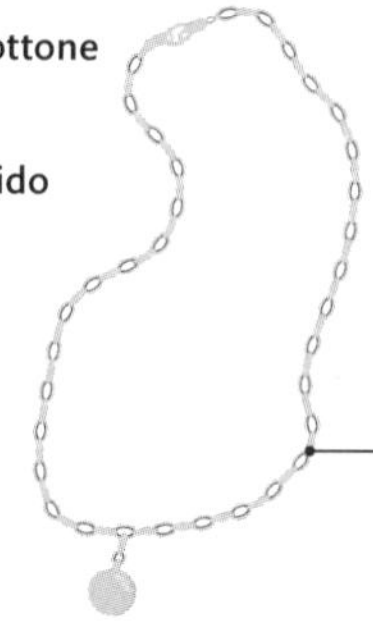

⑲ **il bracciale / braccialetto**
bracelet

⑳ **la collana**
necklace

See also
12 L'aspetto e i capelli • Appearance and hair **13-15** Gli indumenti • Clothes
17 Le scarpe • Shoes

16.3 **I COPRICAPI** • HEADWEAR

1 **il basco**
flat cap

2 **il cappello da baseball**
baseball cap

3 **il berretto con pon pon**
pom pom beanie

4 **l'hijab** *m*
hijab

5 **la kippah**
yarmulke

6 **il turbante**
turban

7 **il berretto**
beret

8 **il fedora**
fedora

9 **il berretto alla Sherlock Holmes**
deerstalker

10 **il fez**
fez

11 **il cappello da cowboy**
cowboy hat

12 **il sombrero**
sombrero

13 **il cappello da sole**
sun hat

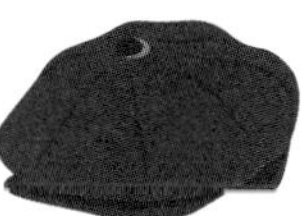

14 **la coppola**
newsboy cap

15 **il panama**
panama

16 **la paglietta**
boater

17 **il berrettino**
beanie

18 **la cloche**
cloche

16.4 **LE BORSE** • BAGS

1 **la valigetta**
briefcase

2 **lo zaino**
backpack

3 **il portafoglio**
wallet

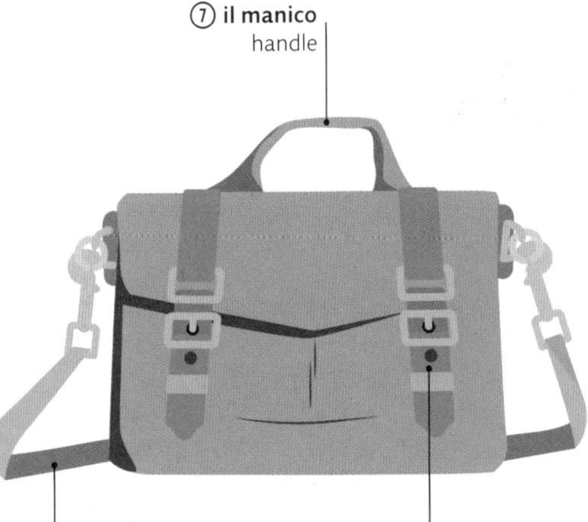

7 **il manico**
handle

8 **la tracolla**
shoulder strap

9 **la chiusura**
fastening

10 **la borsa a tracolla**
shoulder bag

4 **il borsone**
duffel

5 **la borsa**
purse

6 **la valigia**
suitcase

17 Le scarpe

Shoes

17.1 LE SCARPE E GLI ACCESSORI · SHOES AND ACCESSORIES

① **le scarpe col tacco**
high-heeled shoes

② **le scarpe basse**
flats

③ **le infradito**
flip-flops

④ **le espadrillas**
espadrilles

⑤ **le scarpe con tacco a rocchetto**
kitten heels

⑥ **le scarpe con tacco a spillo**
stilettos

⑦ **i sandali**
sandals

⑧ **i sandali in gomma**
jelly sandals

⑨ **i sandali alla schiava**
gladiator sandals

⑩ **i sandali con zeppa**
wedge sandals

⑪ **le scarpe con cinturino a T**
T-strap heels

⑫ **le scarpe con plateau**
platforms

⑬ **le scarpe con tacco e cinturino alla caviglia**
ankle strap heels

⑭ **le scarpe spuntate**
peep toes

⑮ **le scarpe con tacco aperte sul tallone**
slingback heels

⑯ **le ballerine**
ballet flats

⑰ **le sabot**
mules

⑱ **le scarpe Mary Jane**
Mary Janes

17.2 BOOTS · GLI STIVALI

① **gli stivali da lavoro**
work boots

② **gli stivaletti Chelsea**
Chelsea boots

③ **gli scarponcini da trekking**
hiking boots

④ **gli stivaletti**
ankle boots

⑥ la zip
zipper

⑤ **lo stivale alto**
thigh-high boot

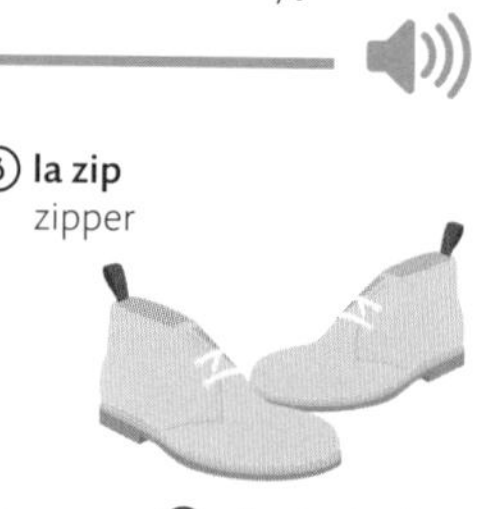
⑦ **gli stivaletti chukka**
chukka boots

⑧ il laccio
lace
⑩ l'occhiello m
eyelet
⑨ la suola
sole
⑪ il tacco
heel

⑫ **gli stivaletti stringati**
lace-up boots

⑬ **gli stivali al ginocchio**
knee-high boots

⑭ **gli stivali di gomma**
rain boots

⑮ **gli stivali da cowboy**
cowboy boots

See also
12 L'aspetto e i capelli • Appearance and hair **13-15** Gli indumenti • Clothes
16 Gli accessori • Accessories **40** Gli attrezzi da giardinaggio • Garden tools

⑲ **le scarpe Oxford**
Oxfords

⑳ **le scarpe Derby**
Derby shoes

㉑ **le scarpe senza lacci**
slip-ons

㉒ **i mocassini**
moccasins

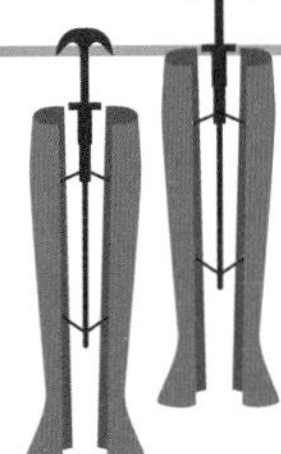
㉓ **la forma per stivali**
boot shapers

㉔ **la forma per scarpe**
shoe trees

㉕ **gli zoccoli**
clogs

㉖ **le scarpe con fibbia**
buckled shoes

㉗ **le ciabatte slider**
slides

㉘ **le pantofole**
slippers

㉙ **i lacci delle scarpe**
shoelaces

㉚ **le solette**
insoles

㉛ **i loafer**
loafers

㉜ **le scarpe da barca**
boat shoes

㉝ **le scarpe per bambini**
kids' shoes

㉞ **le scarpe brogue**
brogues

㉟ **il lucido da scarpe**
shoe polish

㊱ **la spazzola da scarpe**
shoe brush

17.3 **LE SCARPE SPORTIVE** • SPORTS SHOES

① **le scarpe da corsa con tacchetti**
running spikes

② **le scarpe da baseball**
baseball cleats

③ **le scarpe da corsa**
running shoes

④ **le scarpe da ginnastica alte**
high-tops

⑤ **le scarpe da golf**
golf shoes

⑦ **la linguetta**
tongue

⑥ **la scarpa da ginnastica**
sneaker

⑧ **la scarpa da ciclismo**
cycling shoe

⑨ **lo scarpone da sci**
ski boot

⑩ **le scarpe da scoglio**
water shoes

⑪ **gli stivali da equitazione**
riding boots

⑫ **gli stivali Tabi**
tabi boots

⑬ **le scarpe da calcio**
soccer cleats

18 La bellezza

Beauty

18.1 IL TRUCCO · MAKEUP

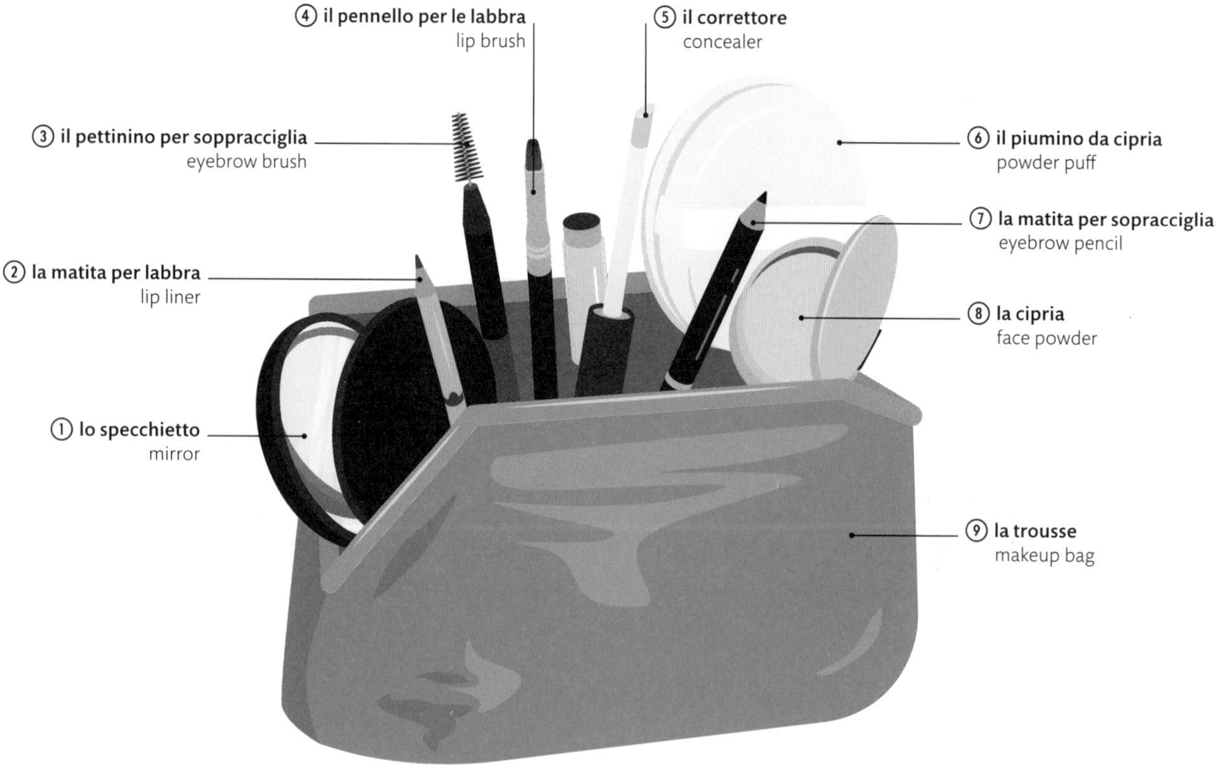

① **lo specchietto** mirror
② **la matita per labbra** lip liner
③ **il pettinino per sopracciglia** eyebrow brush
④ **il pennello per le labbra** lip brush
⑤ **il correttore** concealer
⑥ **il piumino da cipria** powder puff
⑦ **la matita per sopracciglia** eyebrow pencil
⑧ **la cipria** face powder
⑨ **la trousse** makeup bag

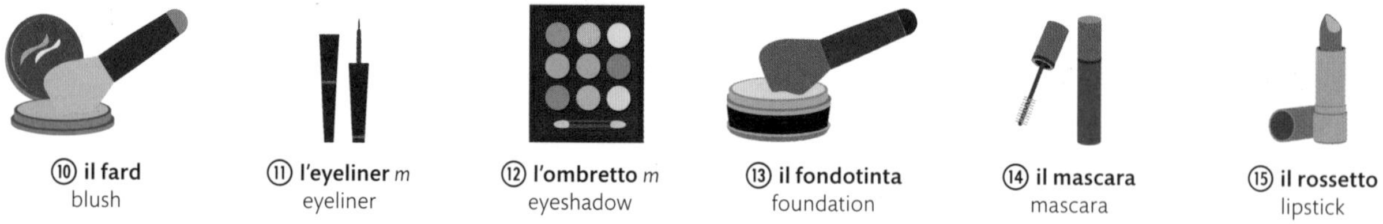

⑩ **il fard**
blush

⑪ **l'eyeliner** *m*
eyeliner

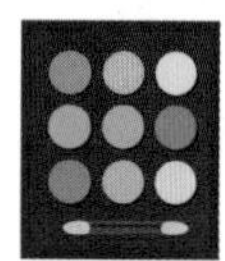

⑫ **l'ombretto** *m*
eyeshadow

⑬ **il fondotinta**
foundation

⑭ **il mascara**
mascara

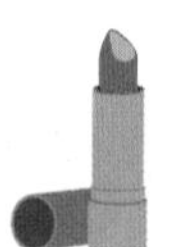

⑮ **il rossetto**
lipstick

18.2 IL TIPO DI PELLE · SKIN TYPE

① **normale**
normal

② **secca**
dry

③ **grassa**
oily

④ **sensibile**
sensitive

⑤ **mista**
combination

See also
12 L'aspetto e i capelli • Appearance and hair **13-15** Gli indumenti • Clothes
16 Gli accessori • Accessories **17** Le scarpe • Shoes **31** Il bagno • Bathroom

18.3 LA MANICURE • MANICURE

① **le forbicine per le unghie**
nail scissors

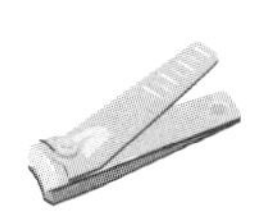

② **il tagliaunghie**
nail clippers

③ **lo smalto per le unghie**
nail polish

④ **il solvente per unghie**
nail polish remover

⑤ **la limetta per unghie**
nail file

⑥ **la crema per le mani**
hand cream

18.4 GLI ARTICOLI DA TOELETTA E I TRATTAMENTI DI BELLEZZA
TOILETRIES AND BEAUTY TREATMENTS

① **la crema idratante**
moisturizer

② **il tonico**
toner

③ **il detergente per il viso**
face wash

④ **il detergente**
cleanser

⑤ **il profumo**
perfume

⑥ **il dopobarba**
aftershave

⑦ **il burrocacao**
lip balm

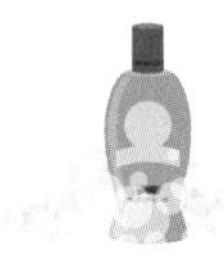

⑧ **il bagnoschiuma**
bubble bath

⑨ **i batuffoli di cotone**
cotton balls

⑩ **la tinta per capelli**
hair dye

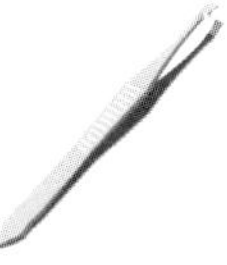

⑪ **le pinzette**
tweezers

⑫ **la ceretta**
wax

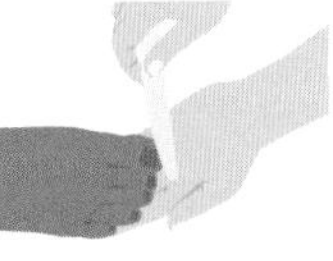

⑬ **la pedicure**
pedicure

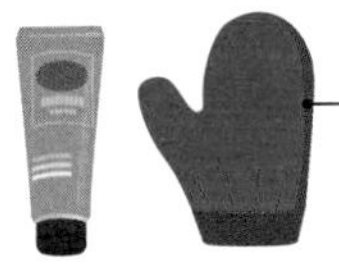

⑭ **l'autoabbronzante** *m*
self tanner

⑮ **il guanto per autoabbronzante**
tanning mitt

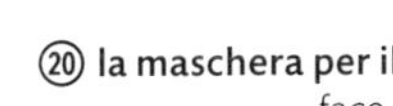

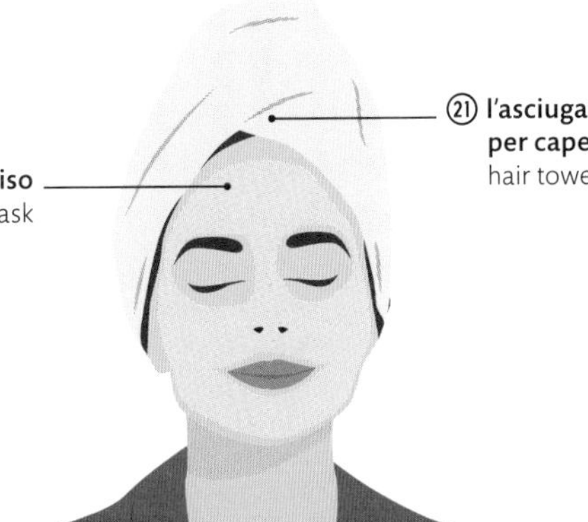

⑳ **la maschera per il viso**
face mask

㉑ **l'asciugamano per capelli** *m*
hair towel wrap

⑲ **facciale**
facial

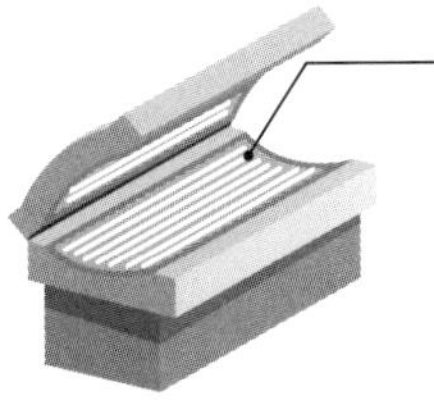

⑰ **i tubi UV**
UV tubes

⑯ **il lettino abbronzante**
tanning bed

⑱ **gli occhiali protettivi per abbronzatura**
tanning goggles

Le malattie e le lesioni

Illness and injury

19.1 **LE MALATTIE** · ILLNESS

① **l'influenza** *f*
flu

② **il raffreddore**
cold

③ **la tosse**
cough

④ **il naso che cola**
runny nose

⑤ **il virus**
virus

⑥ **la febbre**
fever

⑦ **i brividi**
chills

⑧ **il mal di gola**
sore throat

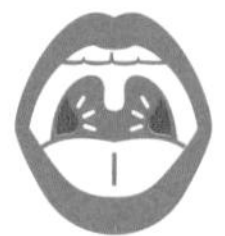
⑨ **la tonsillite**
tonsillitis

⑩ **il mal di testa**
headache

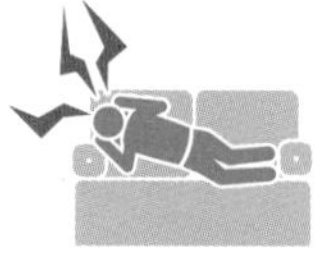
⑪ **l'emicrania** *f*
migraine

⑫ **le vertigini**
dizzy

⑬ **l'intossicazione alimentare** *f*
food poisoning

⑭ **l'avvelenamento** *m*
poisoning

⑮ **l'eruzione cutanea** *f*
rash

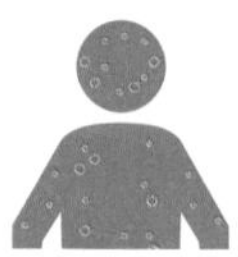
⑯ **la varicella**
chickenpox

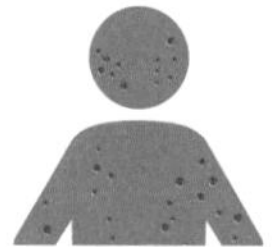
⑰ **il morbillo**
measles

⑱ **la parotite**
mumps

⑲ **l'eczema** *m*
eczema

⑳ **l'asma** *f*
asthma

㉑ **l'allergia** *f*
allergy

㉒ **la febbre da fieno**
hay fever

㉓ **l'infezione** *f*
infection

㉔ **il diabete**
diabetes

㉕ **lo stress**
stress

㉖ **l'epistassi** *f*
nosebleed

㉗ **la nausea**
nausea

㉘ **l'appendicite** *f*
appendicitis

㉙ **l'ipertensione** *f*
high blood pressure

㉚ **i sintomi**
symptoms

㉛ **il crampo**
cramp

㉜ **il mal di schiena**
backache

㉝ **il dolore**
pain

㉞ **il mal di stomaco**
stomachache

㉟ **l'insonnia** *f*
insomnia

㊱ **la diarrea**
diarrhea

See also
01 Le parti del corpo • Parts of the body **03** I muscoli e lo scheletro • Muscles and skeleton **04** Gli organi interni • Internal organs **20** Andare dal medico • Visiting the doctor **21** L'ospedale • The hospital

19.2 LE LESIONI • INJURY

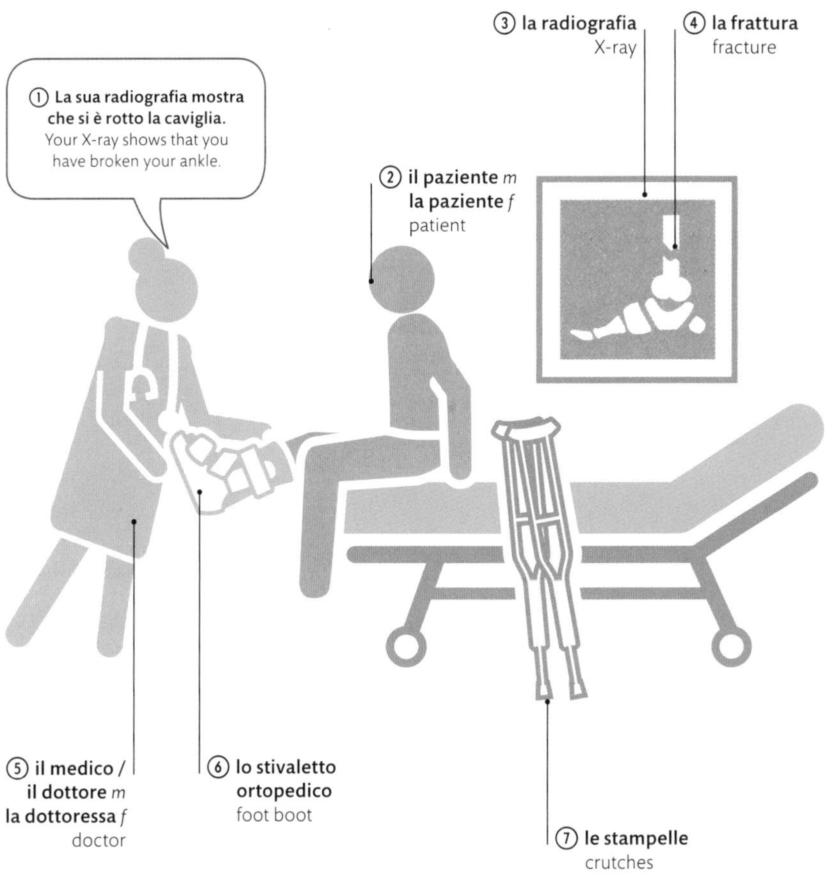
① **La sua radiografia mostra che si è rotto la caviglia.**
Your X-ray shows that you have broken your ankle.
② **il paziente** *m*
la paziente *f*
patient
③ **la radiografia**
X-ray
④ **la frattura**
fracture
⑤ **il medico / il dottore** *m*
la dottoressa *f*
doctor
⑥ **lo stivaletto ortopedico**
foot boot
⑦ **le stampelle**
crutches

⑧ **la slogatura**
sprain

⑨ **l'osso rotto** *m*
broken bone

⑩ **il reggibraccio**
sling

⑪ **il colpo di frusta**
whiplash

⑫ **il collare**
neck brace

⑬ **il taglio**
cut

⑭ **la sbucciatura**
scrape

⑮ **l'ematoma** *m*
bruise

⑯ **la scheggia**
splinter

⑰ **la scottatura**
sunburn

⑱ **la bruciatura**
burn

⑲ **il morso**
bite

⑳ **la puntura**
sting

㉑ **l'incidente** *m*
accident

㉒ **la ferita**
wound

㉓ **l'emorragia** *f*
hemorrhage

㉔ **la vescica**
blister

㉕ **la commozione cerebrale**
concussion

㉖ **la ferita alla testa**
head injury

㉗ **la scossa elettrica**
electric shock

20 Andare dal medico

Visiting the doctor

20.1 LE CURE · TREATMENT

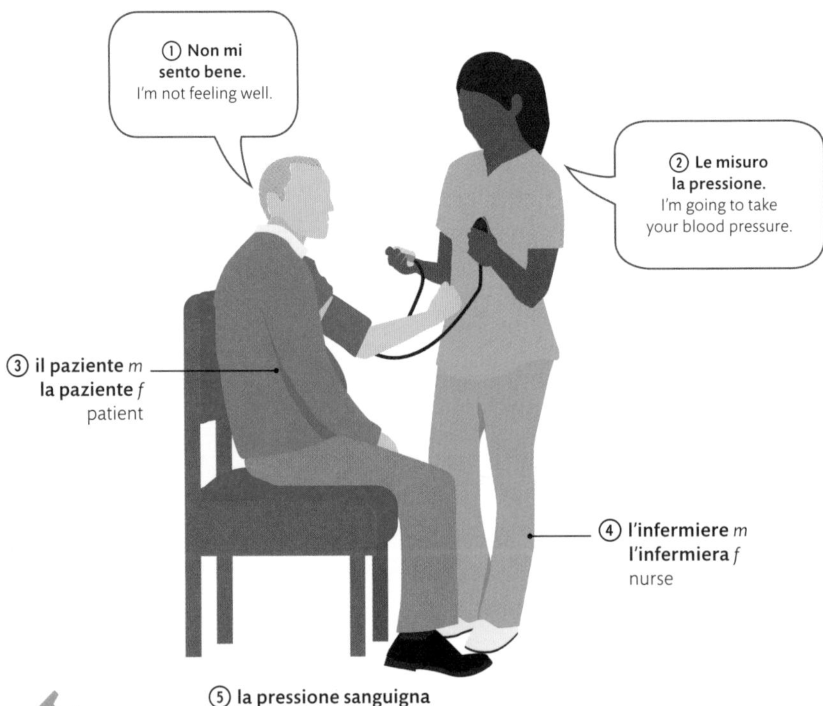

① **Non mi sento bene.** I'm not feeling well.
② **Le misuro la pressione.** I'm going to take your blood pressure.
③ **il paziente** *m* **la paziente** *f* patient
④ **l'infermiere** *m* **l'infermiera** *f* nurse

⑤ **la pressione sanguigna** blood pressure

⑥ **il medico / il dottore** *m* **la dottoressa** *f* doctor

⑦ **lo studio medico** doctor's office

⑧ **la sala d'attesa** waiting room

JUL
17

⑨ **l'appuntamento** *m* appointment

⑩ **la visita medica** medical examination

⑪ **la vaccinazione** inoculation / vaccination

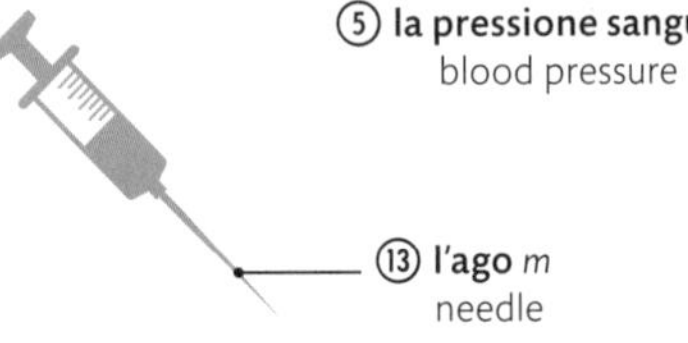

⑬ **l'ago** *m* needle

⑫ **la siringa** syringe

⑭ **l'esame del sangue** *m* blood test

⑮ **i risultati dell'esame** test results

⑯ **la ricetta** prescription

⑰ **il farmaco** medicine / medication

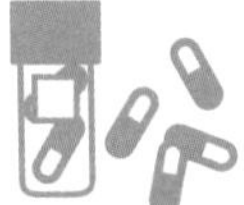

⑱ **le pastiglie / le compresse** pills / tablets

⑲ **la bilancia** scale

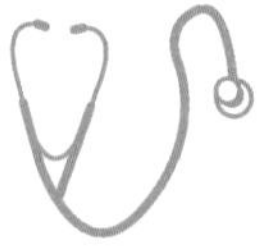

⑳ **lo stetoscopio** stethoscope

㉑ **l'inalatore** *m* inhaler

㉒ **lo spray nasale** nasal spray

㉓ **la mascherina** face mask

㉔ **il reggibraccio** sling

㉕ **la fasciatura** dressing

㉖ **la garza** gauze

㉗ **il nastro medico** tape

㉘ **il termometro** thermometer

㉙ **il termometro auricolare** ear thermometer

See also
01 Le parti del corpo • Parts of the body **02** Le mani e i piedi • Hands and feet
03 I muscoli e lo scheletro • Muscles and skeleton **04** Gli organi interni • Internal organs
19 Le malattie e le lesioni • Illness and injury **21** L'ospedale • The hospital

20.2 IL KIT DI PRONTO SOCCORSO • FIRST-AID KIT

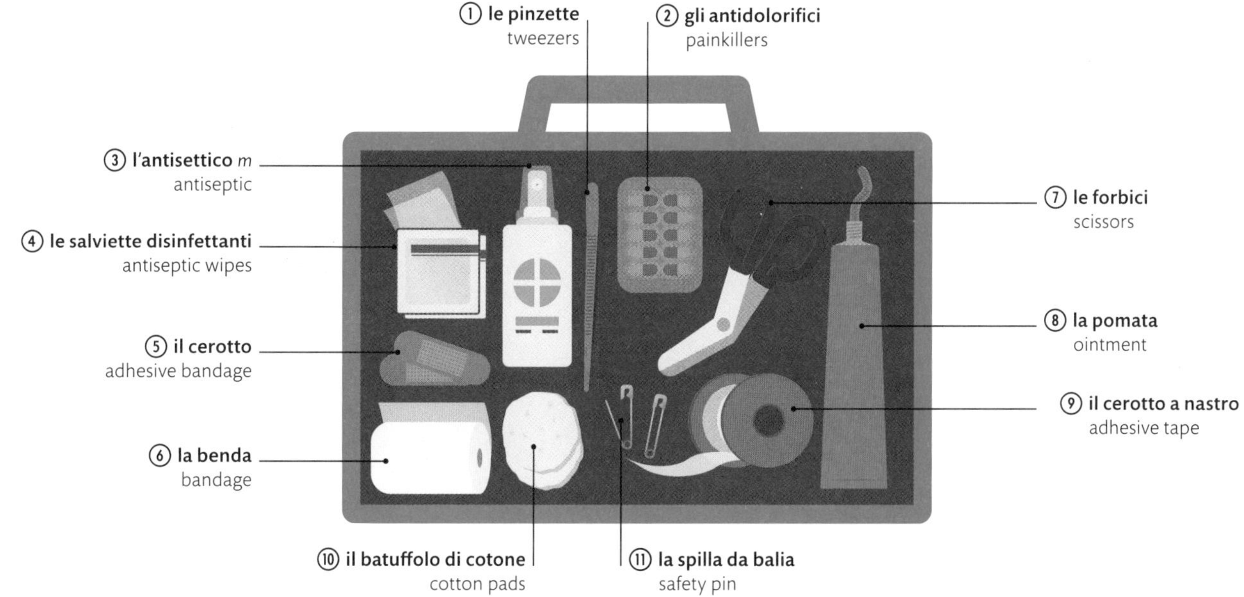
① **le pinzette** tweezers
② **gli antidolorifici** painkillers
③ **l'antisettico** *m* antiseptic
④ **le salviette disinfettanti** antiseptic wipes
⑤ **il cerotto** adhesive bandage
⑥ **la benda** bandage
⑦ **le forbici** scissors
⑧ **la pomata** ointment
⑨ **il cerotto a nastro** adhesive tape
⑩ **il batuffolo di cotone** cotton pads
⑪ **la spilla da balia** safety pin

20.3 I VERBI PER DESCRIVERE LE MALATTIE • VERBS TO DESCRIBE ILLNESS

① **vomitare** to vomit

② **starnutire** to sneeze

③ **tossire** to cough

④ **fare male** to hurt / to ache

⑤ **sanguinare** to bleed

⑥ **svenire** to faint

⑦ **stendersi** to lie down

⑧ **riposare** to rest

⑨ **dimagrire** to lose weight

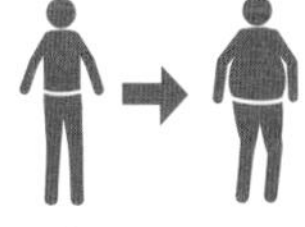
⑩ **ingrassare** to gain weight

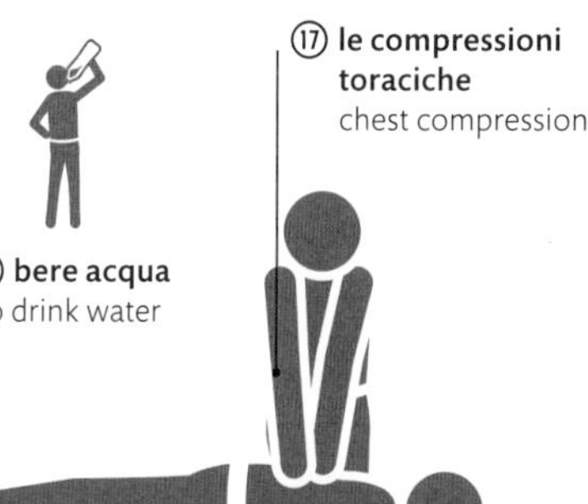
⑪ **bere acqua** to drink water

⑰ **le compressioni toraciche** chest compressions

⑯ **rianimare** to resuscitate

⑫ **fare esercizio fisico** to exercise

⑬ **guarire** to heal

⑭ **riprendersi** to recover

⑮ **sentirsi meglio** to feel better

21 L'ospedale
The hospital

21.1 IN OSPEDALE · AT THE HOSPITAL

① **la maschera di ossigeno**
oxygen mask

② **la flebo**
IV

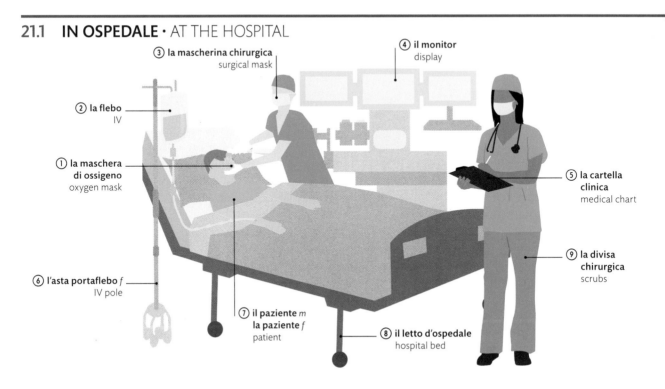

③ **la mascherina chirurgica**
surgical mask

④ **il monitor**
display

⑤ **la cartella clinica**
medical chart

⑥ **l'asta portaflebo** *f*
IV pole

⑦ **il paziente** *m*
la paziente *f*
patient

⑧ **il letto d'ospedale**
hospital bed

⑨ **la divisa chirurgica**
scrubs

⑩ **l'ospedale** *m*
hospital

⑪ **l'ambulanza** *f*
ambulance

⑫ **il paramedico**
paramedic

⑬ **la barella**
stretcher

⑭ **il chirurgo** *m*
la chirurga *f*
surgeon

⑮ **il medico / il dottore** *m*
la dottoressa *f*
doctor

⑯ **l'infermiere** *m*
l'infermiera *f*
nurse

⑰ **il portantino**
orderly

⑱ **la sedia a rotelle**
wheelchair

⑲ **l'ecografia** *f*
scan

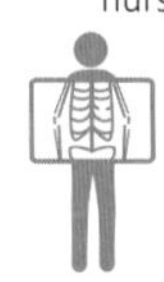

⑳ **la radiografia**
X-ray

㉑ **l'esame del sangue** *m*
blood test

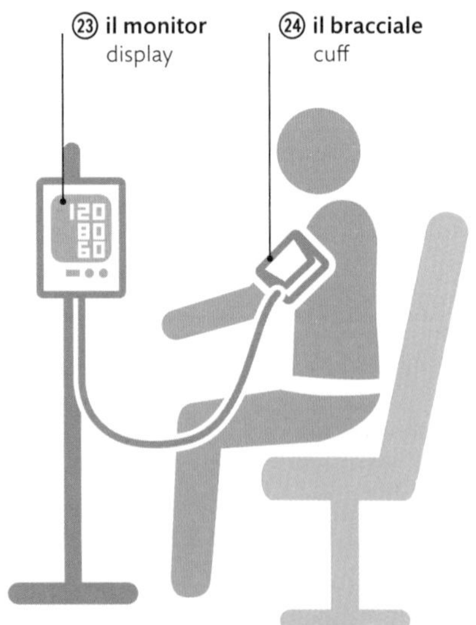
㉓ il monitor
display
㉔ il bracciale
cuff
120
80
60

㉒ **il misuratore di pressione**
blood pressure monitor

See also
01 Le parti del corpo • Parts of the body **03** I muscoli e lo scheletro • Muscles and skeleton
04 Gli organi interni • Internal organs **19** Le malattie e le lesioni • Illness and injury
20 Andare dal medico • Visiting the doctor

㉕ **il bisturi**
scalpel

㉖ **i punti**
stitches

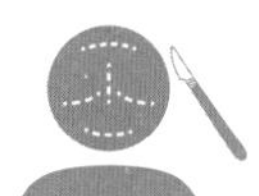

㉗ **la chirurgia plastica**
plastic surgery

㉘ **la terapia**
treatment

㉙ **l'operazione** *f*
operation

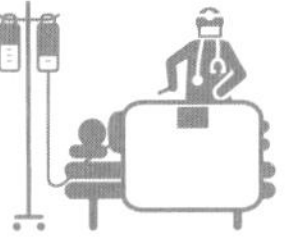

㉚ **il tavolo operatorio**
operating table

㉛ **la sala operatoria**
operating room

㉜ **il pronto soccorso**
emergency room

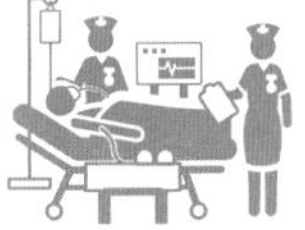

㉝ **il reparto di terapia intensiva**
intensive care unit

㉞ **la sala risveglio**
recovery room

㉟ **la stanza privata**
private room

㊱ **il reparto**
ward

㊲ **il reparto pediatrico**
children's ward

㊳ **il reparto maternità**
maternity ward

㊴ **ricoverare**
to admit

㊵ **dimettere**
to discharge

㊶ **il paziente ambulatoriale**
outpatient

21.2 I REPARTI • DEPARTMENTS

① **l'otorinolaringoiatria** *f*
ENT (ear, nose, and throat)

② **la cardiologia**
cardiology

③ **l'ortopedia** *f*
orthopedics

④ **la neurologia**
neurology

⑤ **la radiologia**
radiology

⑥ **la patologia**
pathology

⑦ **la pediatria**
pediatrics

⑧ **la dermatologia**
dermatology

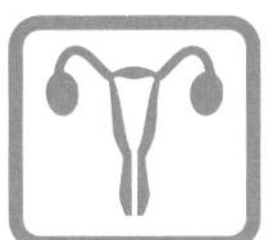

⑨ **la ginecologia**
gynecology

⑩ **la chirurgia**
surgery

⑪ **la fisioterapia**
physical therapy

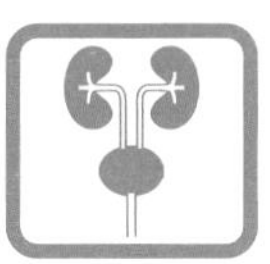

⑫ **l'urologia** *f*
urology

⑬ **la maternità**
maternity

⑭ **la psichiatria**
psychiatry

⑮ **l'oculistica** *f*
ophthalmology

⑯ **l'endocrinologia** *f*
endocrinology

⑰ **l'oncologia** *f*
oncology

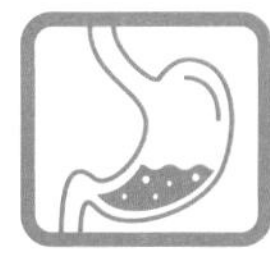

⑱ **la gastroenterologia**
gastroenterology

22 Il dentista e l'ottico

The dentist and optician

22.1 LO STUDIO DENTISTICO · DENTIST'S OFFICE

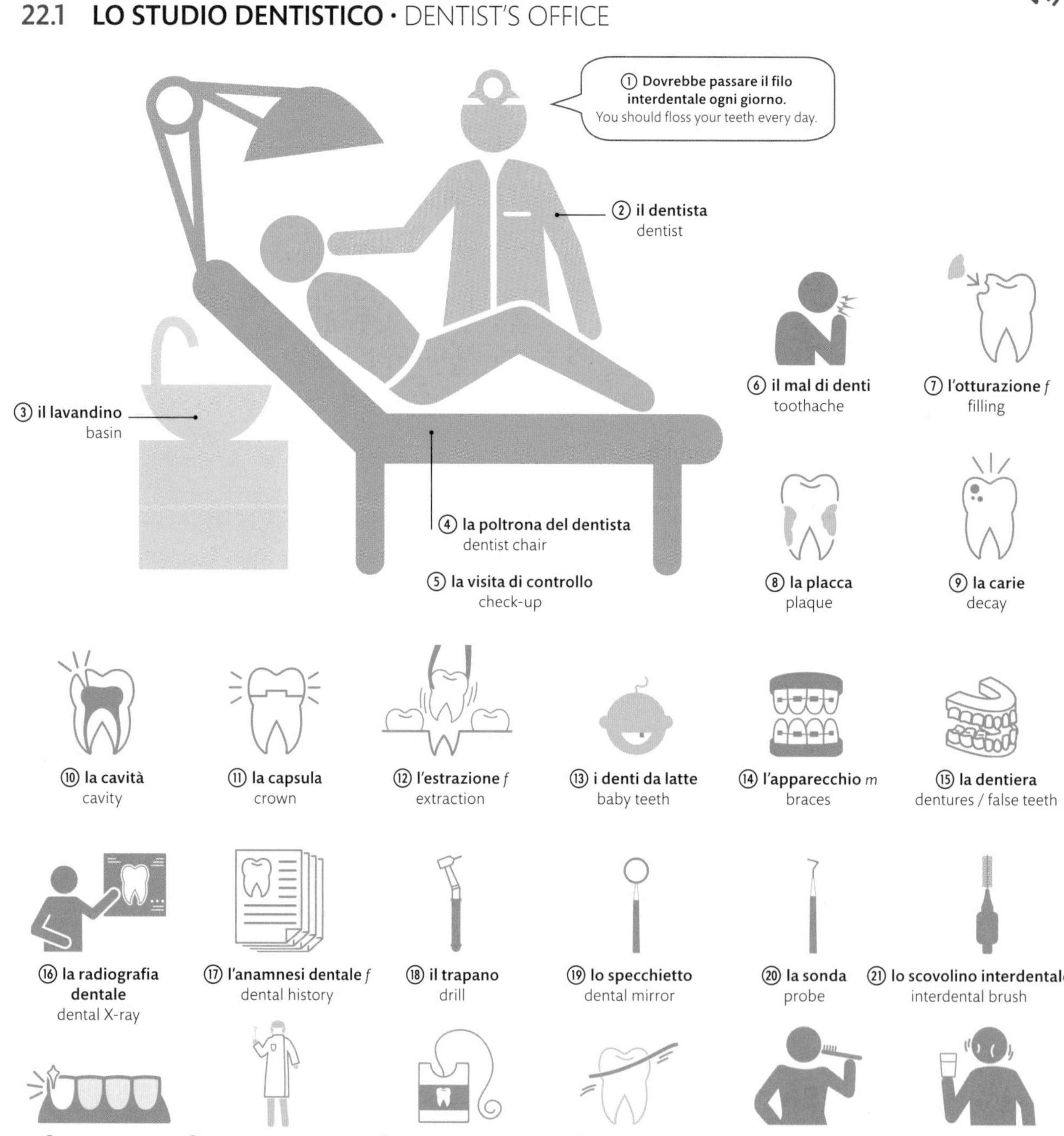

① Dovrebbe passare il filo interdentale ogni giorno.
You should floss your teeth every day.
② il dentista
dentist
③ il lavandino
basin
④ la poltrona del dentista
dentist chair
⑤ la visita di controllo
check-up
⑥ il mal di denti
toothache
⑦ l'otturazione *f*
filling
⑧ la placca
plaque
⑨ la carie
decay
⑩ la cavità
cavity
⑪ la capsula
crown
⑫ l'estrazione *f*
extraction
⑬ i denti da latte
baby teeth
⑭ l'apparecchio *m*
braces
⑮ la dentiera
dentures / false teeth
⑯ la radiografia dentale
dental X-ray
⑰ l'anamnesi dentale *f*
dental history
⑱ il trapano
drill
⑲ lo specchietto
dental mirror
⑳ la sonda
probe
㉑ lo scovolino interdentale
interdental brush
㉒ lo sbiancante
whitening
㉓ l'igienista dentale *m / f*
dental hygienist
㉔ il filo interdentale
dental floss
㉕ passare il filo interdentale
to floss
㉖ spazzolare
to brush
㉗ sciacquare
to rinse

See also
01 Le parti del corpo • Parts of the body **03** I muscoli e lo scheletro • Muscles and skeleton
20 Andare dal medico • Visiting the doctor **21** L'ospedale • The hospital **31** Il bagno • Bathroom

22.2 L'OTTICO • OPTICIAN

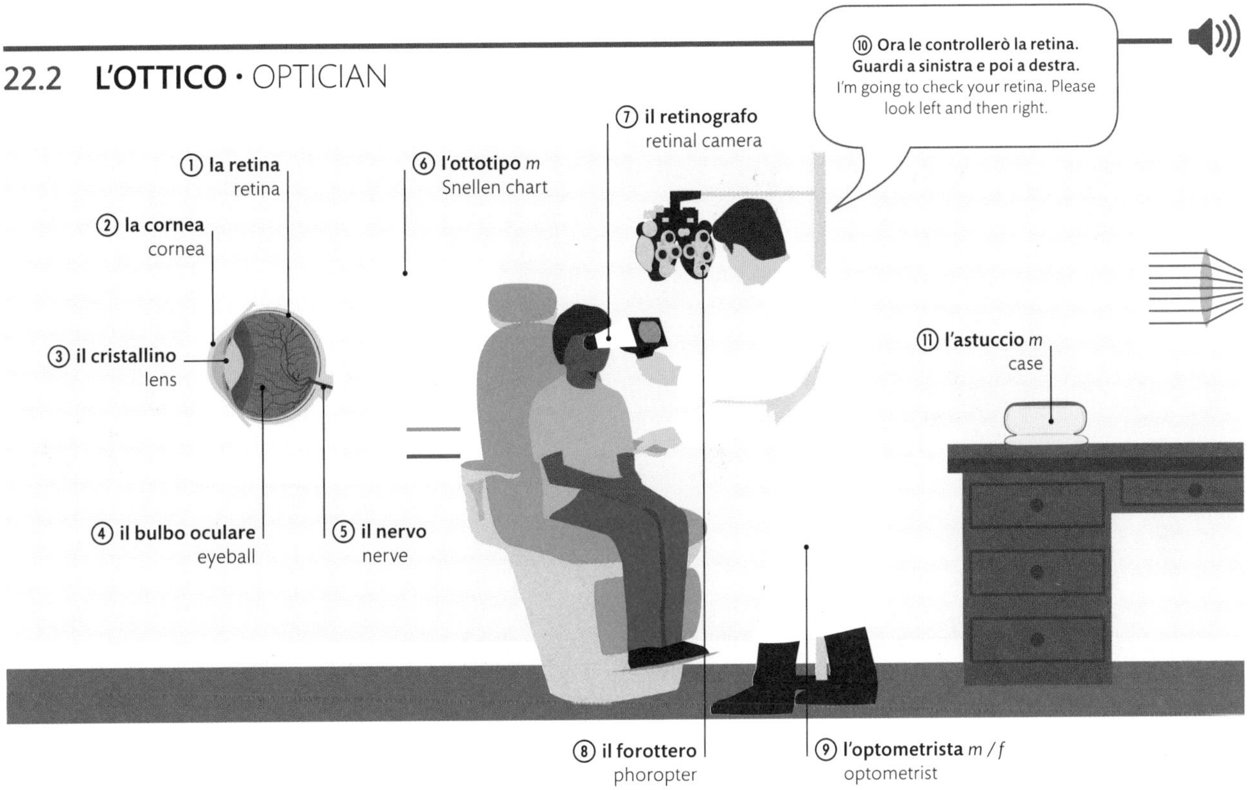

⑩ **Ora le controllerò la retina. Guardi a sinistra e poi a destra.**
I'm going to check your retina. Please look left and then right.

① **la retina**
retina

② **la cornea**
cornea

③ **il cristallino**
lens

④ **il bulbo oculare**
eyeball

⑤ **il nervo**
nerve

⑥ **l'ottotipo** *m*
Snellen chart

⑦ **il retinografo**
retinal camera

⑧ **il forottero**
phoropter

⑨ **l'optometrista** *m / f*
optometrist

⑪ **l'astuccio** *m*
case

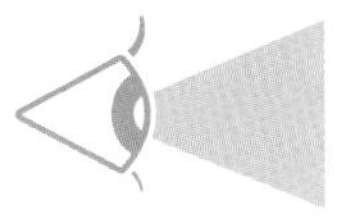

⑫ **la vista**
vision

⑬ **presbite**
farsighted

⑭ **miope**
nearsighted

⑮ **la lacrima**
tear

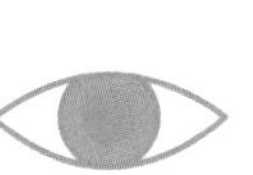

⑯ **la cataratta**
cataract

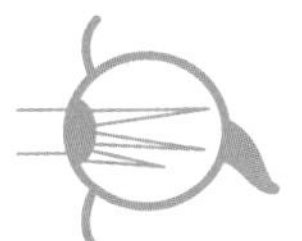

⑰ **l'astigmatismo** *m*
astigmatism

⑱ **gli occhiali da lettura**
reading glasses

⑲ **gli occhiali bifocali**
bifocal

⑳ **il monocolo**
monocle

㉑ **il binocolo**
opera glasses

㉓ **la lente**
lens

㉒ **gli occhiali**
glasses

㉔ **gli occhiali da sole**
sunglasses

㉕ **il panno per la pulizia delle lenti**
lens cleaning cloth

㉖ **le lenti a contatto**
contact lenses

㉗ **la soluzione per lenti a contatto**
contact lens solution

㉘ **il portalenti**
lens case

㉙ **il collirio**
eye drops

23 La dieta e l'alimentazione

Diet and nutrition

23.1 LO STILE DI VITA SANO · HEALTHY LIVING

① **le proteine**
protein

② **i carboidrati**
carbohydrates

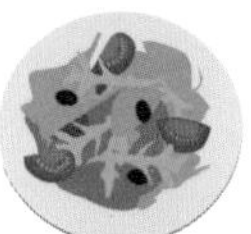
③ **le fibre**
fiber

④ **i latticini**
dairy

⑤ **i legumi**
legumes

⑥ **lo zucchero**
sugar

⑦ **il sale**
salt

⑧ **i grassi saturi**
saturated fat

⑨ **i grassi insaturi**
unsaturated fat

⑩ **le calorie**
calories / energy

A
C
E
D
⑪ **le vitamine**
vitamins

Ca Zn P
Fe Co Mn
⑫ **i minerali**
minerals

⑬ **il calcio**
calcium

⑭ **il ferro**
iron

⑮ **il colesterolo**
cholesterol

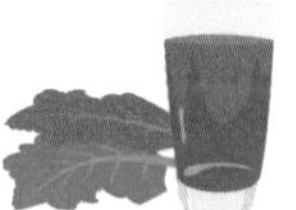
⑯ **la depurazione**
detox

⑰ **la dieta equilibrata**
balanced diet

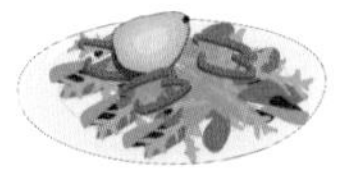
⑱ **la dieta ipocalorica**
calorie-controlled diet

HEALTH FOOD
⑲ **il negozio di cibi biologici**
health food store

⑳ **la sezione di alimenti biologici**
organic food section
㉑ **i prodotti agricoli locali**
local produce
㉒ **Mi piace acquistare frutta e verdura biologiche.**
I like to buy organic fruit and vegetables.
㉓ **il mercato agricolo**
farmers' market

See also
03 I muscoli e lo scheletro • Muscles and skeleton **19** Le malattie e le lesioni • Illness and injury
24 Il corpo sano, la mente sana • Healthy body, healthy mind **29** Cucinare • Cooking
48 Il supermercato • The supermarket **52-72** Gli alimenti • Food

㉔ **gli alimenti lavorati**
processed food

㉕ **i supercibi**
superfoods

㉖ **biologico** *m*
biologica *f*
organic

㉗ **l'integratore** *m*
supplement

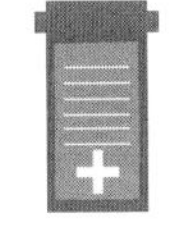
㉘ **gli additivi**
additives

㉙ **senza latticini**
dairy-free

㉚ **vegetariano** *m*
vegetariana *f*
vegetarian

㉛ **vegano** *m*
vegana *f*
vegan

㉜ **pescetariano** *m*
pescetariana *f*
pescatarian

㉝ **senza glutine**
gluten-free

㉞ **perdere peso / dimagrire**
to lose weight

㉟ **i cibi pronti**
convenience food

㊱ **ipercalorico** *m*
ipercalorica *f*
high-calorie

㊲ **ipocalorico** *m*
ipocalorica *f*
low-calorie

㊳ **ridurre**
to cut down on

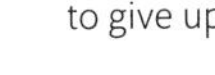
㊴ **rinunciare a**
to give up

㊵ **mettersi a dieta**
to go on a diet

㊶ **mangiare troppo**
to overeat

23.2 LE ALLERGIE ALIMENTARI
FOOD ALLERGIES

① **l'allergia alla frutta a guscio** *f*
nut allergy

② **l'allergia alle arachidi** *f*
peanut allergy

③ **l'allergia ai frutti di mare** *f*
seafood allergy

④ **l'intolleranza al lattosio** *f*
lactose intolerant

⑤ **l'intolleranza al glutine** *f*
gluten intolerant

⑥ **l'intolleranza ai latticini** *f*
dairy allergy

⑦ **l'allergia al grano** *f*
wheat allergy

⑧ **l'allergia alle uova** *f*
egg allergy

⑨ **l'allergia al sesamo** *f*
sesame allergy

⑩ **l'allergia alla soia** *f*
soy allergy

⑪ **l'allergia al sedano** *f*
celery allergy

SO_2
⑫ **l'allergia ai solfiti** *f*
sulfite allergy

⑬ **allergico** *m* **/ allergica** *f*
allergic

⑭ **l'allergia alla senape** *f*
mustard allergy

⑮ **intollerante**
intolerant

24 Il corpo sano, la mente sana

Healthy body, healthy mind

24.1 LO YOGA · YOGA

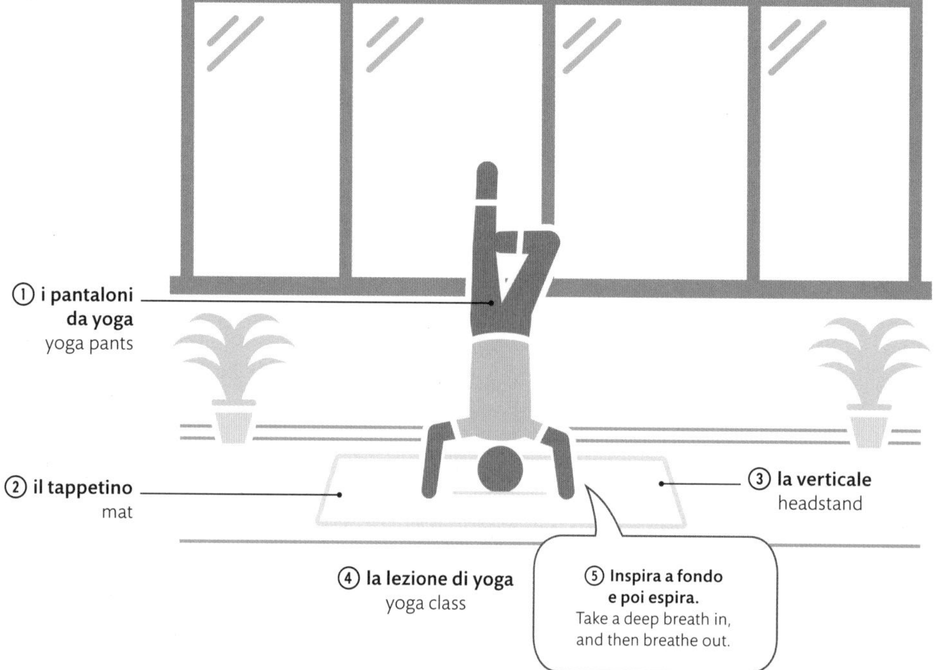

① i pantaloni da yoga
yoga pants
② il tappetino
mat
③ la verticale
headstand
④ la lezione di yoga
yoga class
⑤ Inspira a fondo e poi espira.
Take a deep breath in, and then breathe out.

⑥ **la posizione del bambino**
child's pose

⑦ **la posizione del cobra**
cobra pose

⑧ **la posizione del guerriero**
warrior pose

⑨ **la torsione da seduti**
seated twist

⑩ **la posizione del triangolo**
triangle pose

⑪ **il piegamento in avanti da seduti**
seated forward fold

⑫ **la posizione del cadavere**
corpse pose

⑬ **la posizione del corvo**
crow pose

⑭ **la posizione della sedia**
chair pose

⑮ **la posizione della montagna**
mountain pose

⑯ **la posizione del ponte**
bridge pose

⑰ **la posizione della panca**
plank pose

⑱ **la posizione dell'arco**
bow pose

⑲ **la posizione del piccione**
pigeon pose

⑳ **la posizione dell'albero**
tree pose

㉑ **il cane a testa in giù**
downward dog

㉒ **la posizione dell'angolo legato**
bound ankle pose

㉓ **la posizione del cammello**
camel pose

㉔ **la posizione della ruota**
wheel pose

㉕ **la posizione della mezza luna**
half moon pose

㉖ **la posizione del delfino**
dolphin pose

See also
03 I muscoli e lo scheletro • Muscles and skeleton **04** Gli organi interni • Internal organs **19** Le malattie e le lesioni • Illness and injury **20** Andare dal medico • Visiting the doctor **21** L'ospedale • The hospital **23** La dieta e l'alimentazione • Diet and nutrition **29** Cucinare • Cooking

24.2 I TRATTAMENTI E LE TERAPIE • TREATMENTS AND THERAPY

① **il massaggio**
massage

② **lo shiatsu**
shiatsu

③ **la chiropratica**
chiropractic

④ **l'osteopatia** *f*
osteopathy

⑤ **la riflessologia**
reflexology

⑥ **la meditazione**
meditation

⑦ **il reiki**
reiki

⑧ **l'agopuntura** *f*
acupuncture

⑨ **l'ayurveda** *f*
ayurveda

⑩ **l'ipnoterapia** *f*
hypnotherapy

⑪ **l'idroterapia** *f*
hydrotherapy

⑫ **l'aromaterapia** *f*
aromatherapy

⑬ **l'erbalismo** *m*
herbalism

⑭ **gli oli essenziali**
essential oils

⑮ **l'omeopatia** *f*
homeopathy

⑯ **l'agopressione** *f*
acupressure

⑰ **la cristalloterapia**
crystal healing

⑱ **la naturopatia**
naturopathy

⑲ **il feng shui**
feng shui

⑳ **la poesiaterapia**
poetry therapy

㉑ **l'arteterapia** *f*
art therapy

㉒ **la pet therapy**
pet therapy

㉓ **la naturoterapia**
nature therapy

㉔ **la musicoterapia**
music therapy

㉕ **il rilassamento**
relaxation

㉖ **la mindfulness**
mindfulness

㉗ **l'assistente socio-psicologico** *m* **/ l'assistente socio-psicologica** *f*
counselor

㉘ **la psicoterapia**
psychotherapy

㉚ **Oggi parleremo dello stress sul lavoro.**
Today, we're talking about stress at work.

㉙ **la terapia di gruppo**
group therapy

25 Un luogo in cui vivere
A place to live

25.1 LE CASE • HOUSES

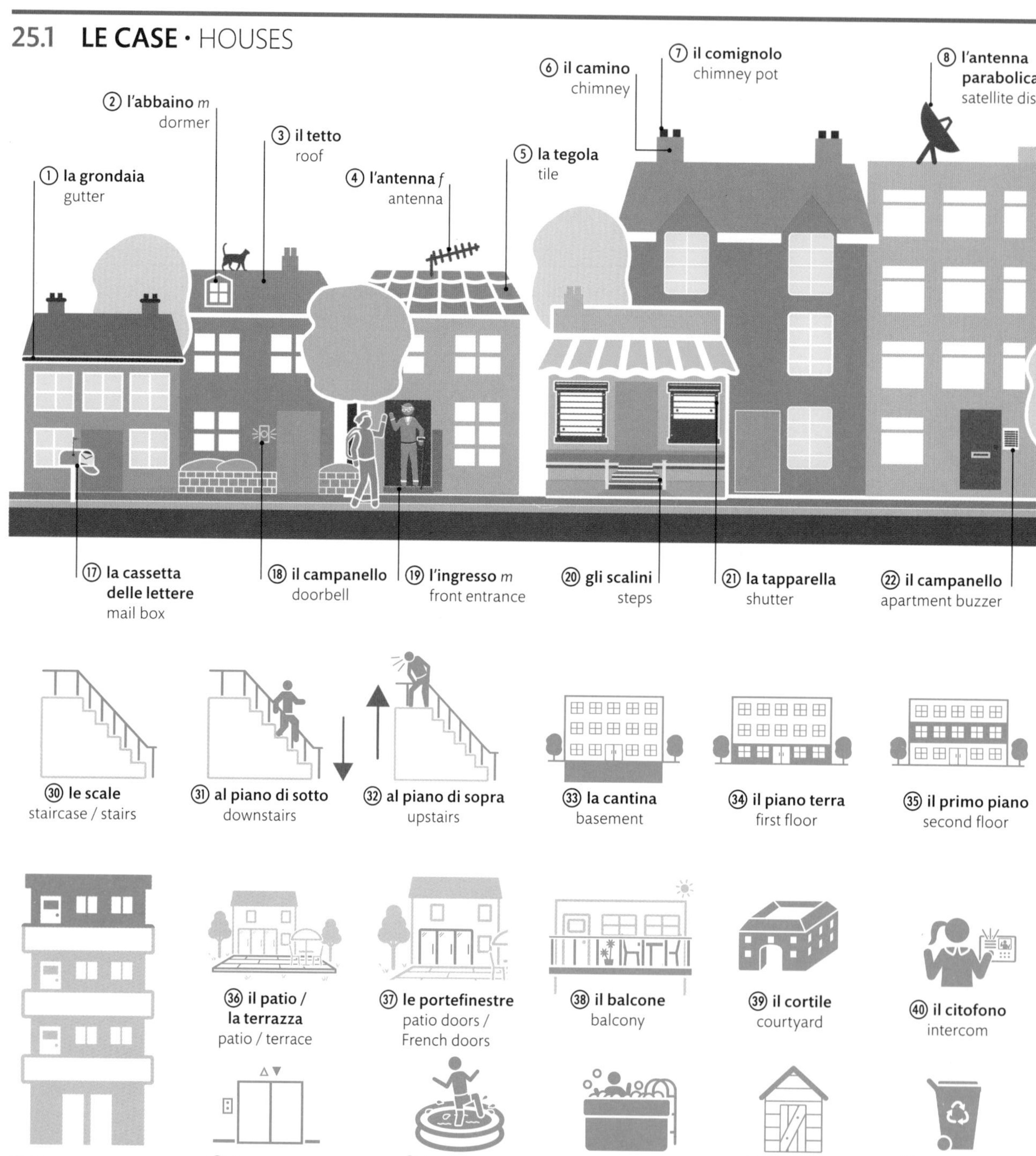

① la grondaia
gutter
② l'abbaino m
dormer
③ il tetto
roof
④ l'antenna f
antenna
⑤ la tegola
tile
⑥ il camino
chimney
⑦ il comignolo
chimney pot
⑧ l'antenna parabolica f
satellite dish
⑰ la cassetta delle lettere
mail box
⑱ il campanello
doorbell
⑲ l'ingresso m
front entrance
⑳ gli scalini
steps
㉑ la tapparella
shutter
㉒ il campanello
apartment buzzer
㉚ le scale
staircase / stairs
㉛ al piano di sotto
downstairs
㉜ al piano di sopra
upstairs
㉝ la cantina
basement
㉞ il piano terra
first floor
㉟ il primo piano
second floor
㊱ il patio / la terrazza
patio / terrace
㊲ le portefinestre
patio doors / French doors
㊳ il balcone
balcony
㊴ il cortile
courtyard
㊵ il citofono
intercom
㊶ l'appartamento m
apartment
㊷ l'ascensore m
elevator
㊸ la piscinetta
wading pool
㊹ la vasca idromassaggio
jacuzzi
㊺ il capanno
shed
㊻ il cassonetto
dumpster

See also
32 La casa • House and home **34** Le faccende domestiche • Household chores **37** La decorazione
Renovating **42-43** In città • In town **44** Gli edifici e l'architettura • Buildings and architecture

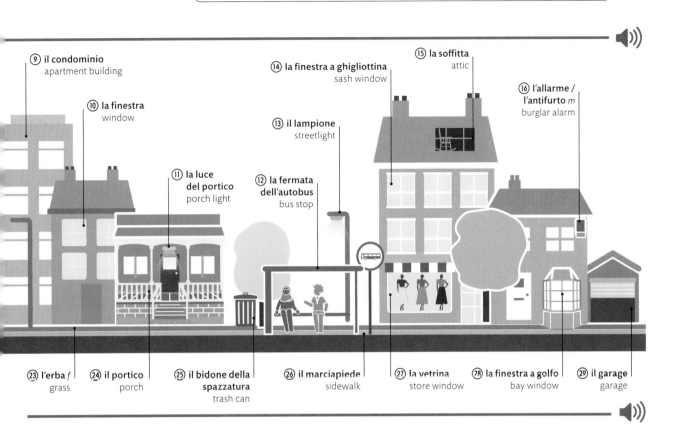

⑨ **il condominio** apartment building

⑩ **la finestra** window

⑪ **la luce del portico** porch light

⑫ **la fermata dell'autobus** bus stop

⑬ **il lampione** streetlight

⑭ **la finestra a ghigliottina** sash window

⑮ **la soffitta** attic

⑯ **l'allarme / l'antifurto** *m* burglar alarm

㉓ **l'erba** *f* grass

㉔ **il portico** porch

㉕ **il bidone della spazzatura** trash can

㉖ **il marciapiede** sidewalk

㉗ **la vetrina** store window

㉘ **la finestra a golfo** bay window

㉙ **il garage** garage

25.2 **L'ATRIO** • HALLWAY

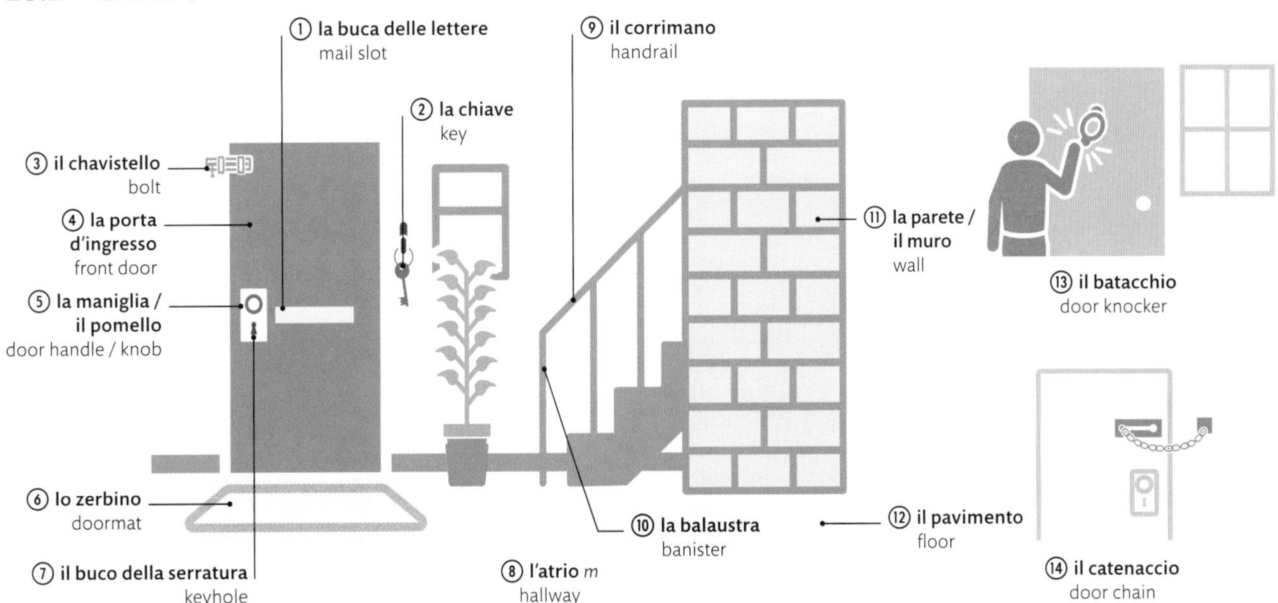
① la buca delle lettere
mail slot
② la chiave
key
③ il chavistello
bolt
④ la porta d'ingresso
front door
⑤ la maniglia / il pomello
door handle / knob
⑥ lo zerbino
doormat
⑦ il buco della serratura
keyhole
⑧ l'atrio m
hallway
⑨ il corrimano
handrail
⑩ la balaustra
banister
⑪ la parete / il muro
wall
⑫ il pavimento
floor
⑬ il batacchio
door knocker
⑭ il catenaccio
door chain

26 Il salotto e la sala da pranzo

Living room and dining room

26.1 IL SALOTTO · LIVING ROOM

① **la lampada** lamp

② **il paralume** lampshade

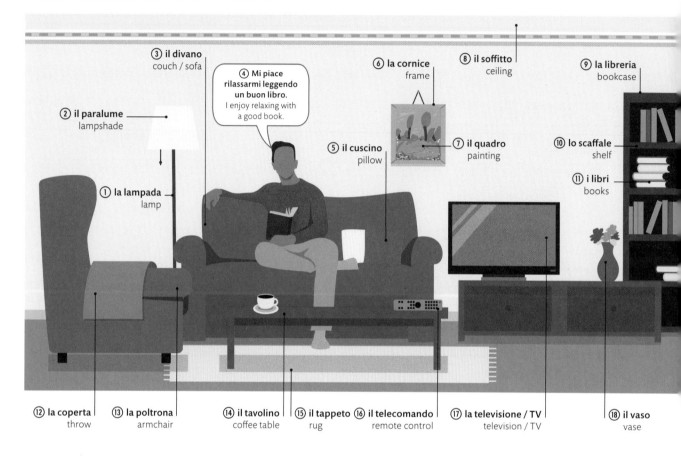

③ **il divano** couch / sofa

④ **Mi piace rilassarmi leggendo un buon libro.** I enjoy relaxing with a good book.

⑤ **il cuscino** pillow

⑥ **la cornice** frame

⑦ **il quadro** painting

⑧ **il soffitto** ceiling

⑨ **la libreria** bookcase

⑩ **lo scaffale** shelf

⑪ **i libri** books

⑫ **la coperta** throw

⑬ **la poltrona** armchair

⑭ **il tavolino** coffee table

⑮ **il tappeto** rug

⑯ **il telecomando** remote control

⑰ **la televisione / TV** television / TV

⑱ **il vaso** vase

⑲ **il caminetto** fireplace

⑳ **la mensola del caminetto** mantlepiece

㉑ **le veneziane** Venetian blinds

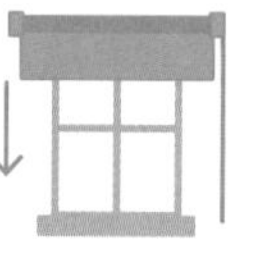

㉒ **le tende avvolgibili** roller shade

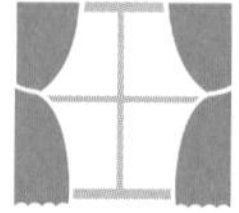

㉓ **le tende** curtains

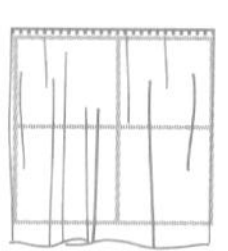

㉔ **le tende di tulle** sheer curtain

㉕ **il divano letto** sofa bed

㉖ **la sedia a dondolo** rocking chair

㉗ **lo sgabello** foot stool

㉘ **l'applique** *f* sconce

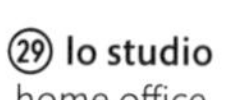

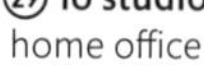

㉙ **lo studio** home office

See also
25 Un luogo in cui vivere • A place to live **27** La cucina e le stoviglie • Kitchen and tableware
34 Le faccende domestiche • Household chores **71** La colazione • Breakfast **72** Il pranzo e la cena • Lunch and dinner **136** L'home entertainment • Home entertainment

26.2 LA SALA DA PRANZO • DINING ROOM

① **lo schienale**
back

② **la sedia**
chair

③ **la gamba**
leg

④ **la candela**
candle

⑤ **il portacandele**
candlestick

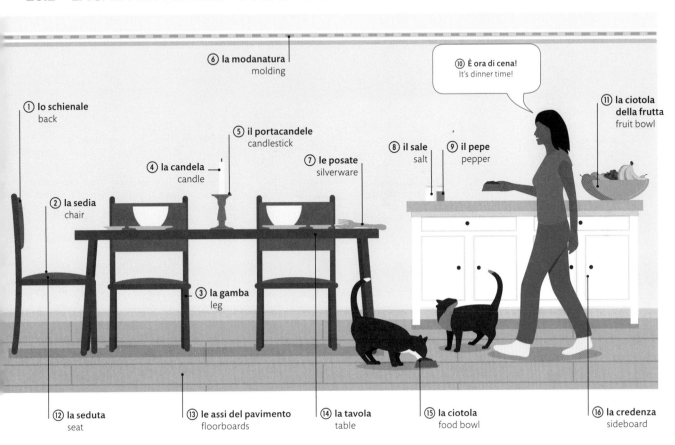

⑥ **la modanatura**
molding

⑦ **le posate**
silverware

⑧ **il sale**
salt

⑨ **il pepe**
pepper

⑩ **È ora di cena!**
It's dinner time!

⑪ **la ciotola della frutta**
fruit bowl

⑫ **la seduta**
seat

⑬ **le assi del pavimento**
floorboards

⑭ **la tavola**
table

⑮ **la ciotola**
food bowl

⑯ **la credenza**
sideboard

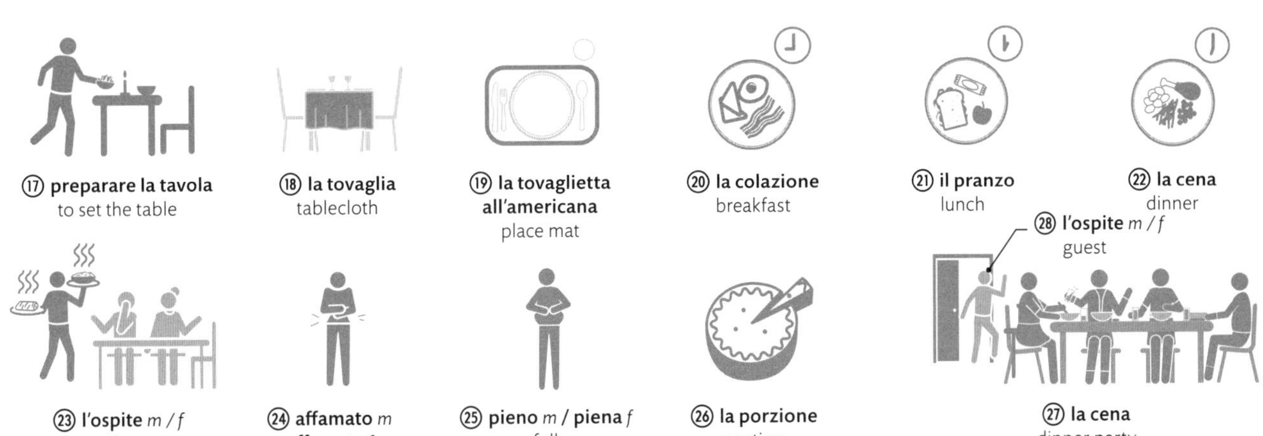

⑰ **preparare la tavola**
to set the table

⑱ **la tovaglia**
tablecloth

⑲ **la tovaglietta all'americana**
place mat

⑳ **la colazione**
breakfast

㉑ **il pranzo**
lunch

㉒ **la cena**
dinner

㉓ **l'ospite** *m / f*
host / hostess

㉔ **affamato** *m*
affamata *f*
hungry

㉕ **pieno** *m* / **piena** *f*
full

㉖ **la porzione**
portion

㉗ **la cena**
dinner party

㉘ **l'ospite** *m / f*
guest

27 La cucina e le stoviglie

Kitchen and tableware

27.1 GLI ELETTRODOMESTICI DA CUCINA

KITCHEN APPLIANCES

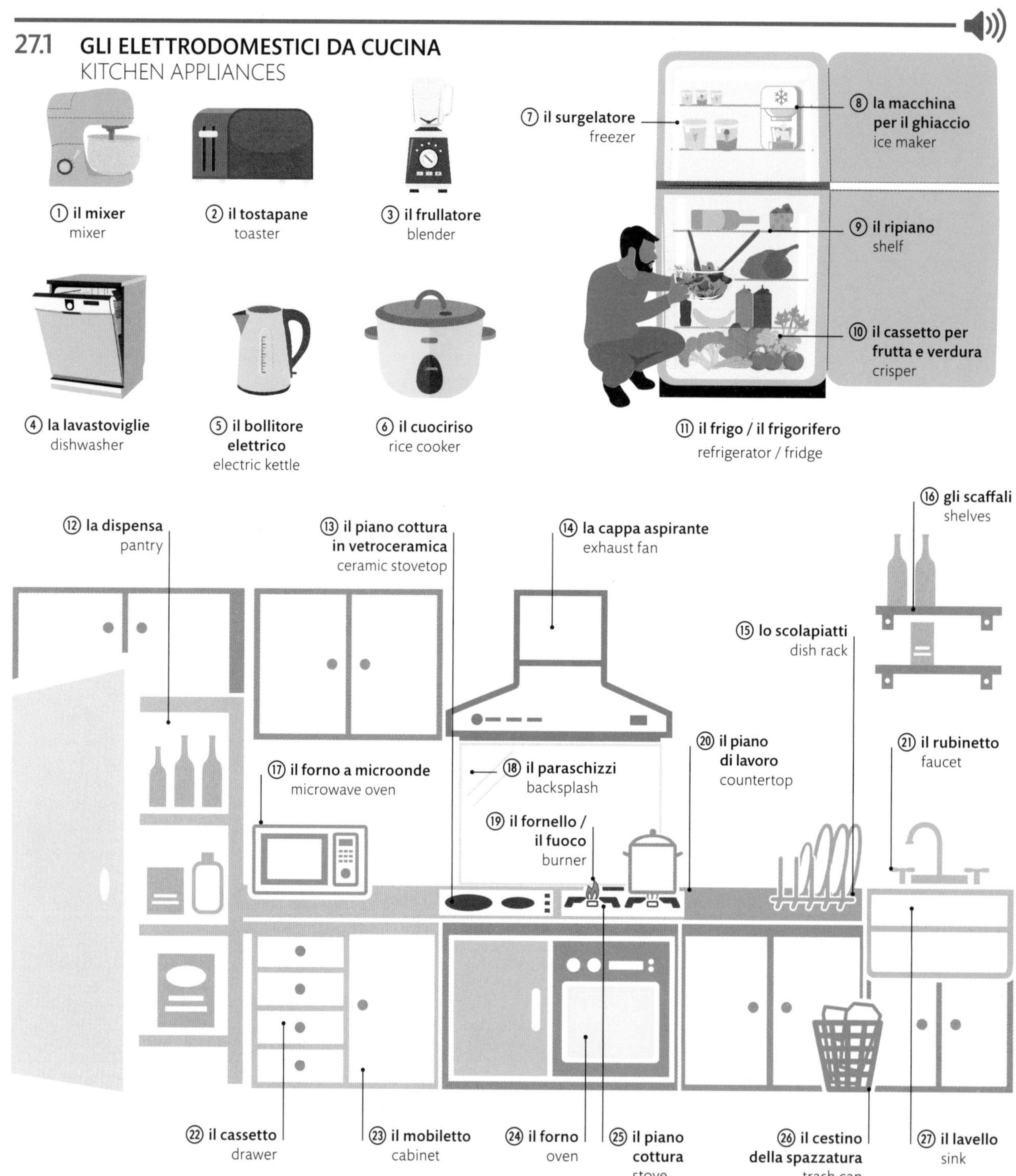

① il mixer
mixer
② il tostapane
toaster
③ il frullatore
blender
④ la lavastoviglie
dishwasher
⑤ il bollitore elettrico
electric kettle
⑥ il cuociriso
rice cooker
⑦ il surgelatore
freezer
⑧ la macchina per il ghiaccio
ice maker
⑨ il ripiano
shelf
⑩ il cassetto per frutta e verdura
crisper
⑪ il frigo / il frigorifero
refrigerator / fridge
⑫ la dispensa
pantry
⑬ il piano cottura in vetroceramica
ceramic stovetop
⑭ la cappa aspirante
exhaust fan
⑮ lo scolapiatti
dish rack
⑯ gli scaffali
shelves
⑰ il forno a microonde
microwave oven
⑱ il paraschizzi
backsplash
⑲ il fornello / il fuoco
burner
⑳ il piano di lavoro
countertop
㉑ il rubinetto
faucet
㉒ il cassetto
drawer
㉓ il mobiletto
cabinet
㉔ il forno
oven
㉕ il piano cottura
stove
㉖ il cestino della spazzatura
trash can
㉗ il lavello
sink

See also
28 Gli utensili da cucina • Kitchenware **29** Cucinare • Cooking
59 Le erbe e le spezie • Herbs and spices **60** Nella dispensa • In the pantry
71 La colazione • Breakfast **72** Il pranzo e la cena • Lunch and dinner

27.2 LE STOVIGLIE • TABLEWARE

① **la forchetta**
fork

② **il coltello**
knife

③ **il cucchiaio**
tablespoon

④ **il cucchiaino**
teaspoon

⑤ **il cucchiaio da minestra**
soup spoon

⑥ **il cucchiaio da portata**
serving spoon

⑦ **le posate**
silverware

⑧ **il coltello da burro**
butter knife

⑨ **le bacchette**
chopsticks

⑩ **il mestolo**
ladle

⑪ **il piatto piano**
dinner plate

⑫ **il piattino**
side plate

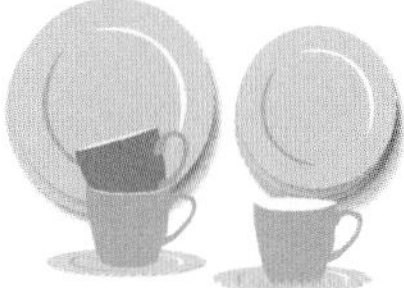
⑬ **le stoviglie**
dinnerware

⑭ **la tazzina da caffè**
coffee cup

⑮ **la tazza da tè**
teacup

⑯ **la tazza**
mug

⑰ **la caffettiera**
espresso maker

⑱ **la teiera**
teapot

⑲ **il posto a tavola**
place setting

⑳ **il tovagliolo**
napkin

㉑ **il portatovagliolo**
napkin ring

㉒ **la ciotola**
bowl

㉓ **il piatto fondo**
la scodella
soup bowl

㉔ **la ciotola del riso**
rice bowl

㉕ **il portauovo**
egg cup

㉖ **il set da sushi**
sushi set

㉗ **la caraffa graduata**
measuring cup

㉘ **il tumbler**
tumbler

㉙ **il bicchiere da vino**
wineglass

㉚ **il bicchiere da birra**
pint glass

㉛ **i calici**
stemware

㉜ **i bicchieri**
glasses / glassware

㉝ **il barattolo**
jar

㉞ **il bicchiere**
sippy cup

㉟ **il bicchiere da sakè**
sake cup

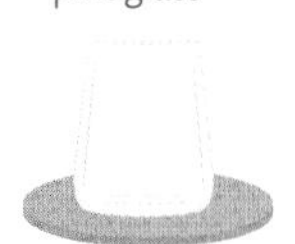
㊱ **il sottobicchiere**
coaster

28 Gli utensili da cucina
Kitchenware

28.1 GLI UTENSILI DA CUCINA · KITCHEN EQUIPMENT

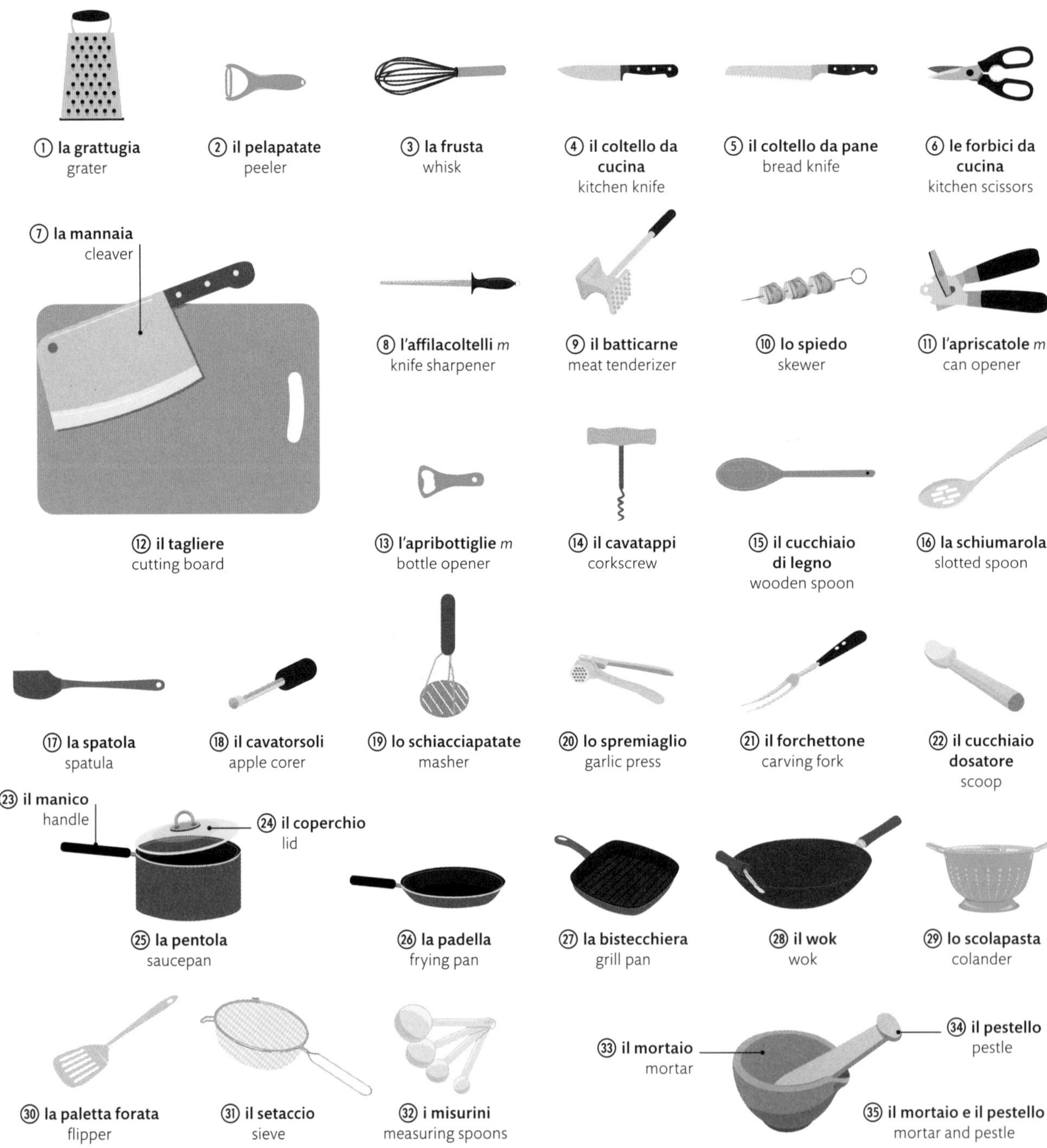

① la grattugia
grater
② il pelapatate
peeler
③ la frusta
whisk
④ il coltello da cucina
kitchen knife
⑤ il coltello da pane
bread knife
⑥ le forbici da cucina
kitchen scissors
⑦ la mannaia
cleaver
⑧ l'affilacoltelli m
knife sharpener
⑨ il batticarne
meat tenderizer
⑩ lo spiedo
skewer
⑪ l'apriscatole m
can opener
⑫ il tagliere
cutting board
⑬ l'apribottiglie m
bottle opener
⑭ il cavatappi
corkscrew
⑮ il cucchiaio di legno
wooden spoon
⑯ la schiumarola
slotted spoon
⑰ la spatola
spatula
⑱ il cavatorsoli
apple corer
⑲ lo schiacciapatate
masher
⑳ lo spremiaglio
garlic press
㉑ il forchettone
carving fork
㉒ il cucchiaio dosatore
scoop
㉓ il manico
handle
㉔ il coperchio
lid
㉕ la pentola
saucepan
㉖ la padella
frying pan
㉗ la bistecchiera
grill pan
㉘ il wok
wok
㉙ lo scolapasta
colander
㉚ la paletta forata
flipper
㉛ il setaccio
sieve
㉜ i misurini
measuring spoons
㉝ il mortaio
mortar
㉞ il pestello
pestle
㉟ il mortaio e il pestello
mortar and pestle

See also
27 La cucina e le stoviglie • Kitchen and tableware **29** Cucinare • Cooking
59 Le erbe e le spezie • Herbs and spices **60** Nella dispensa • In the pantry
71 La colazione • Breakfast **72** Il pranzo e la cena • Lunch and dinner

㊱ **il tajine**
tagine

㊲ **la terrina**
mixing bowl

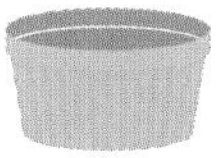

㊳ **lo stampo per soufflé**
soufflé dish

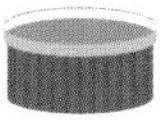

㊴ **il pirottino**
ramekin

㊵ **la casseruola**
casserole dish

㊶ **il cestello per friggere**
frying basket

㊷ **la burriera**
butter dish

㊸ **il contaminuti**
timer

㊹ **il timer da cucina**
egg timer

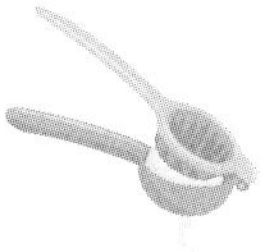

㊺ **lo spremiagrumi**
lemon squeezer

㊻ **la caffettiera a stantuffo**
coffee press / cafetière

㊼ **il termometro da carne**
meat thermometer

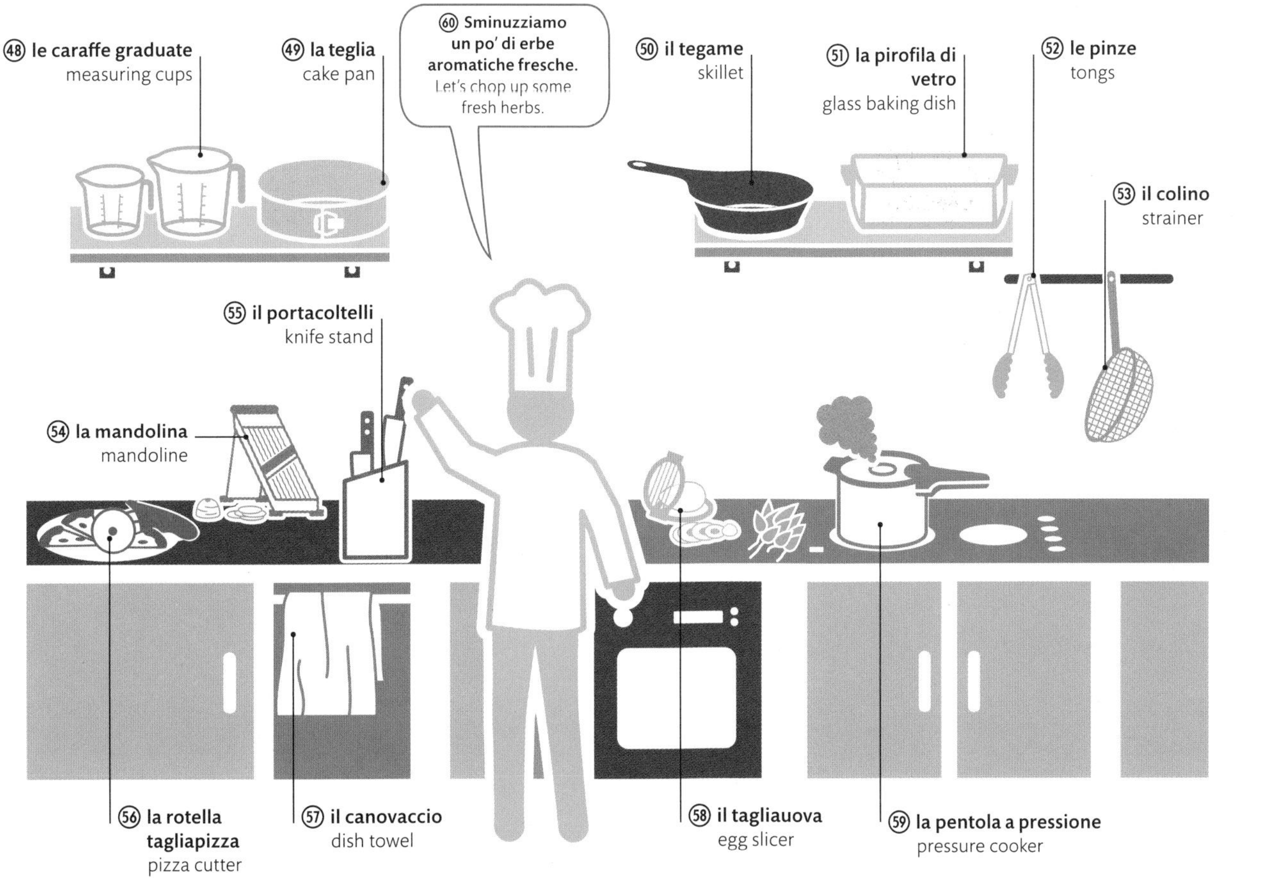

㊽ **le caraffe graduate**
measuring cups

㊾ **la teglia**
cake pan

⑥⓪ **Sminuzziamo un po' di erbe aromatiche fresche.**
Let's chop up some fresh herbs.

㊿ **il tegame**
skillet

51 **la pirofila di vetro**
glass baking dish

52 **le pinze**
tongs

53 **il colino**
strainer

55 **il portacoltelli**
knife stand

54 **la mandolina**
mandoline

56 **la rotella tagliapizza**
pizza cutter

57 **il canovaccio**
dish towel

58 **il tagliauova**
egg slicer

59 **la pentola a pressione**
pressure cooker

29 Cucinare
Cooking

29.1 I VERBI DELLA CUCINA • COOKING VERBS

① cospargere
to sprinkle
② cuocere in forno
to bake
③ guarnire
to garnish
④ ungere
to grease
⑤ stendere
to roll
⑥ assaggiare
to taste
⑬ Lo guarnirò con un po' di erbe fresche.
I'll garnish this with some fresh herbs.
⑭ tagliare a pezzetti
to chop
⑫ saltare in padella
to stir-fry

⑳ **grigliare**
to broil

㉑ **arrostire**
to roast

㉒ **friggere**
to fry

㉓ **far bollire / fare in camicia (le uova)**
to poach

㉔ **cuocere a fuoco lento**
to simmer

㉕ **bollire**
to boil

㉖ **congelare**
to freeze

㉗ **aggiungere**
to add

㉘ **mescolare**
to mix

㉙ **mescolare**
to stir

㉚ **sbattere con la frusta**
to whisk

㉛ **schiacciare**
to mash

㉜ **tagliare a fette**
to slice

㉝ **un pizzico**
a pinch

㉞ **un goccio**
a dash

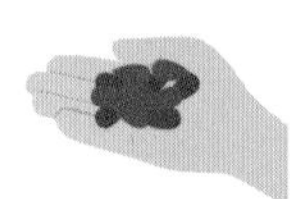
㉟ **una manciata**
a handful

㊱ **macinare**
to mince

㊲ **sbucciare**
to peel

㊳ **tagliare**
to cut

㊴ **grattugiare**
to grate

㊵ **versare**
to pour

See also
27 La cucina e le stoviglie • Kitchen and tableware **28** Gli utensili da cucina • Kitchenware
59 Le erbe e le spezie • Herbs and spices **60** Nella dispensa • In the pantry **62-63** La panetteria
The bakery **71** La colazione • Breakfast **72** Il pranzo e la cena • Lunch and dinner

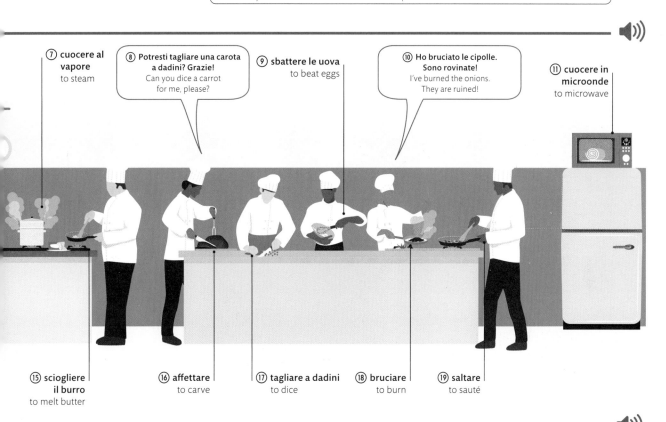

⑦ **cuocere al vapore**
to steam

⑧ **Potresti tagliare una carota a dadini? Grazie!**
Can you dice a carrot for me, please?

⑨ **sbattere le uova**
to beat eggs

⑩ **Ho bruciato le cipolle. Sono rovinate!**
I've burned the onions. They are ruined!

⑪ **cuocere in microonde**
to microwave

⑮ **sciogliere il burro**
to melt butter

⑯ **affettare**
to carve

⑰ **tagliare a dadini**
to dice

⑱ **bruciare**
to burn

⑲ **saltare**
to sauté

29.2 CUOCERE IN FORNO • BAKING

① **il grembiule**
apron

② **il guanto da forno**
oven mitt

③ **la teglia**
cake pan

④ **la teglia da flan**
flan pan

⑤ **il tegame da forno**
pie pan

⑥ **il pennello per dolci**
pastry brush

⑦ **il mattarello**
rolling pin

⑧ **la placca da forno**
baking pan

⑨ **la teglia da muffin**
muffin tin

⑩ **la gratella**
cooling rack

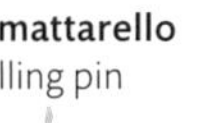

⑪ **la glassa**
icing

⑫ **la sac-a-poche**
piping bag

⑬ **la bilancia**
scale

⑭ **la caraffa graduata**
measuring cup

⑮ **decorare**
to decorate

30 La camera da letto
Bedroom

30.1 LA CAMERA DA LETTO · BEDROOM

① **la gruccia appendiabiti**
coat hanger

② **la biancheria da letto**
bed linen

③ **la sveglia**
alarm clock

④ **la testiera**
headboard

⑤ **la federa**
pillowcase

⑭ **l'armadio** *m*
wardrobe

⑮ **la moquette**
carpeting

⑯ **il cassetto**
drawer

⑰ **la radiosveglia**
clock radio

⑱ **il comodino**
nightstand

⑲ **il piumone**
duvet

⑳ **la pediera**
foot board

㉑ **il cuscino**
pillow

㉒ **il letto**
bed

㉗ **il letto singolo**
twin bed

㉘ **il letto matrimoniale**
double bed

㉙ **la rete**
box spring

㉚ **l'ottomana** *f*
Ottoman

㉛ **la cassapanca**
linen chest

㉜ **il copriletto**
throw

㉝ **la trapunta**
quilt

㉞ **la coperta**
blanket

㉟ **la coperta elettrica**
electric blanket

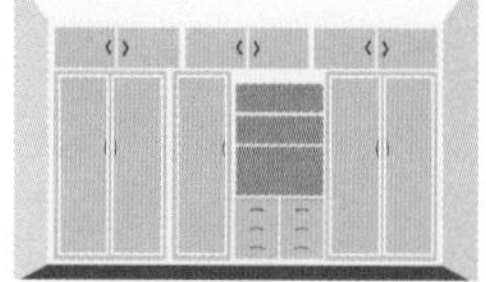

㊱ **l'armadio a muro** *m*
closet

㊲ **la borsa dell'acqua calda**
hot-water bottle

See also
08 La gravidanza e l'infanzia • Pregnancy and childhood **13-15** Gli indumenti
Clothes **25** Un luogo in cui vivere • A place to live **32** La casa • House and home

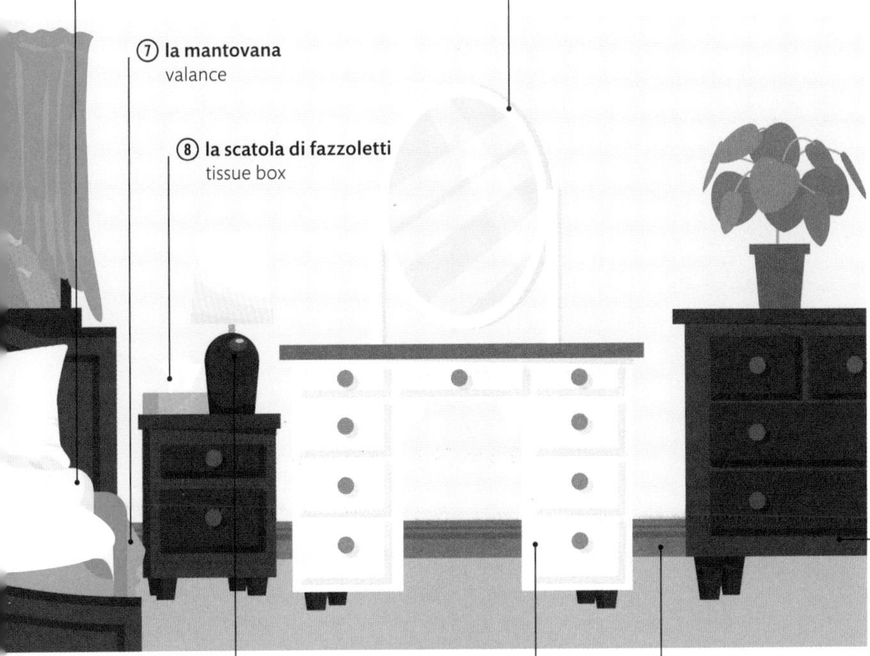

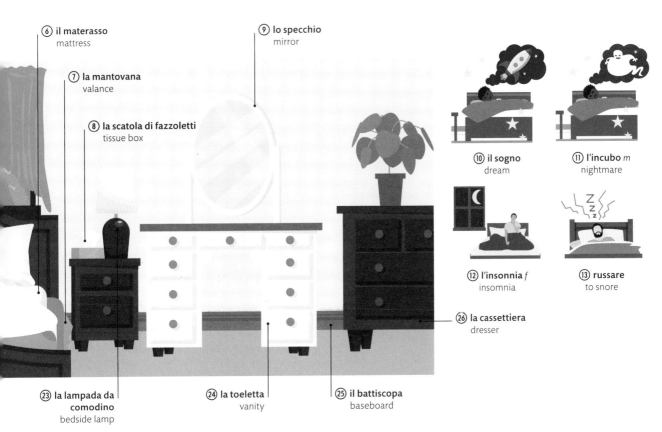

⑥ **il materasso**
mattress

⑦ **la mantovana**
valance

⑧ **la scatola di fazzoletti**
tissue box

⑨ **lo specchio**
mirror

⑩ **il sogno**
dream

⑪ **l'incubo** *m*
nightmare

⑫ **l'insonnia** *f*
insomnia

⑬ **russare**
to snore

㉖ **la cassettiera**
dresser

㉓ **la lampada da comodino**
bedside lamp

㉔ **la toeletta**
vanity

㉕ **il battiscopa**
baseboard

30.2 LA STANZA DEL BEBÈ • NURSERY

① **il baby monitor**
baby monitor
② **il lettino**
crib
③ **le sbarre**
bars
④ **il lenzuolo**
sheet
⑤ **la culla di vimini**
Moses basket
⑥ **la luce notturna**
night-light
⑦ **la giostrina**
mobile
⑧ **il materassino del fasciatoio**
changing mat
⑨ **il fasciatoio**
changing table
⑩ **l'orsacchiotto** *m*
teddy bear
⑪ **il pavimento**
floor

31 Il bagno
Bathroom

31.1 IN BAGNO · IN THE BATHROOM

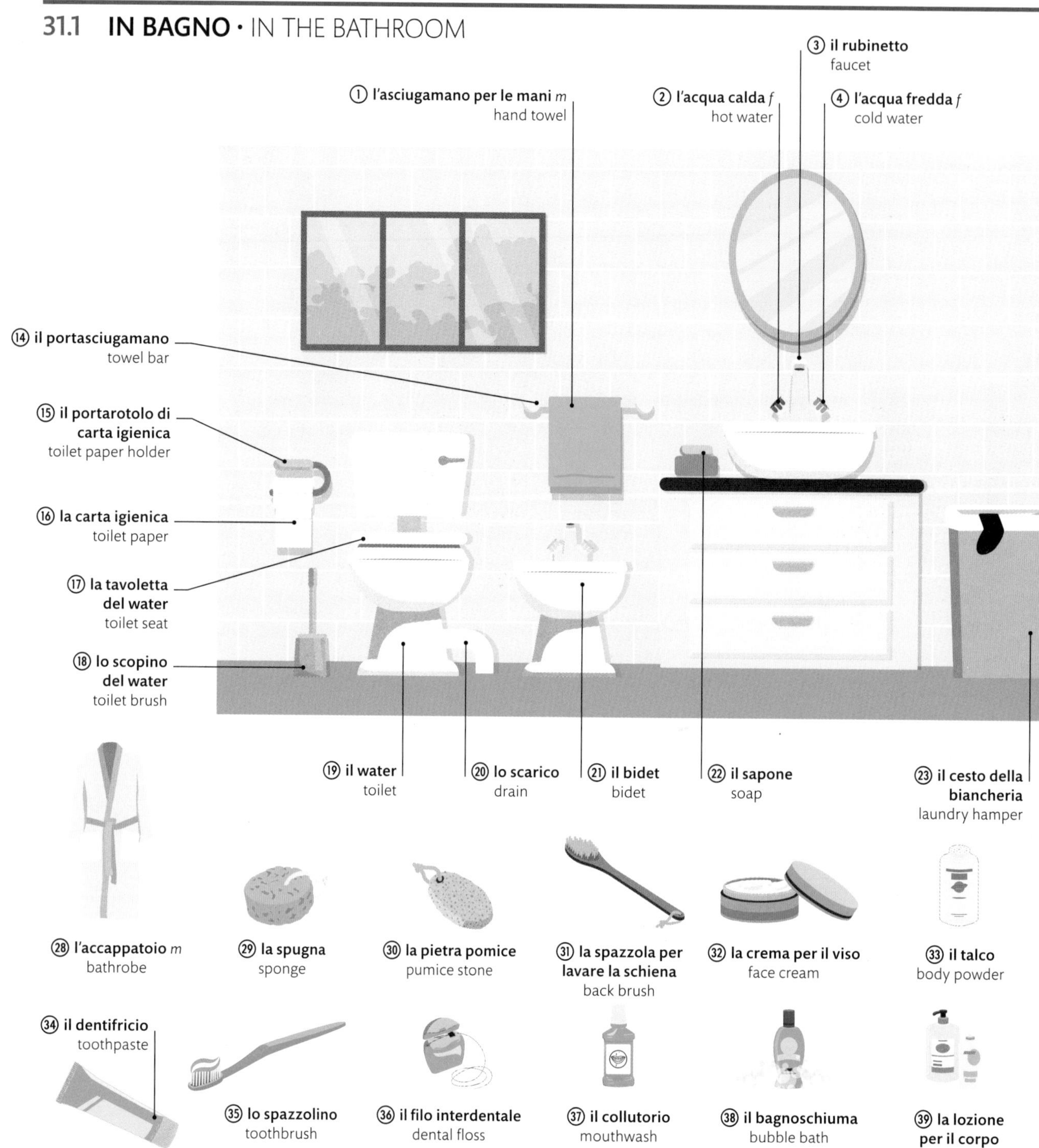

③ il rubinetto
faucet
① l'asciugamano per le mani *m*
hand towel
② l'acqua calda *f*
hot water
④ l'acqua fredda *f*
cold water
⑭ il portasciugamano
towel bar
⑮ il portarotolo di carta igienica
toilet paper holder
⑯ la carta igienica
toilet paper
⑰ la tavoletta del water
toilet seat
⑱ lo scopino del water
toilet brush
⑲ il water
toilet
⑳ lo scarico
drain
㉑ il bidet
bidet
㉒ il sapone
soap
㉓ il cesto della biancheria
laundry hamper
㉘ l'accappatoio *m*
bathrobe
㉙ la spugna
sponge
㉚ la pietra pomice
pumice stone
㉛ la spazzola per lavare la schiena
back brush
㉜ la crema per il viso
face cream
㉝ il talco
body powder
㉞ il dentifricio
toothpaste
㉟ lo spazzolino
toothbrush
㊱ il filo interdentale
dental floss
㊲ il collutorio
mouthwash
㊳ il bagnoschiuma
bubble bath
㊴ la lozione per il corpo
body lotion

See also
18 La bellezza • Beauty **25** Un luogo in cui vivere • A place to live **32** La casa House and home **33** Gli impianti elettrico e idraulico • Electrics and plumbing

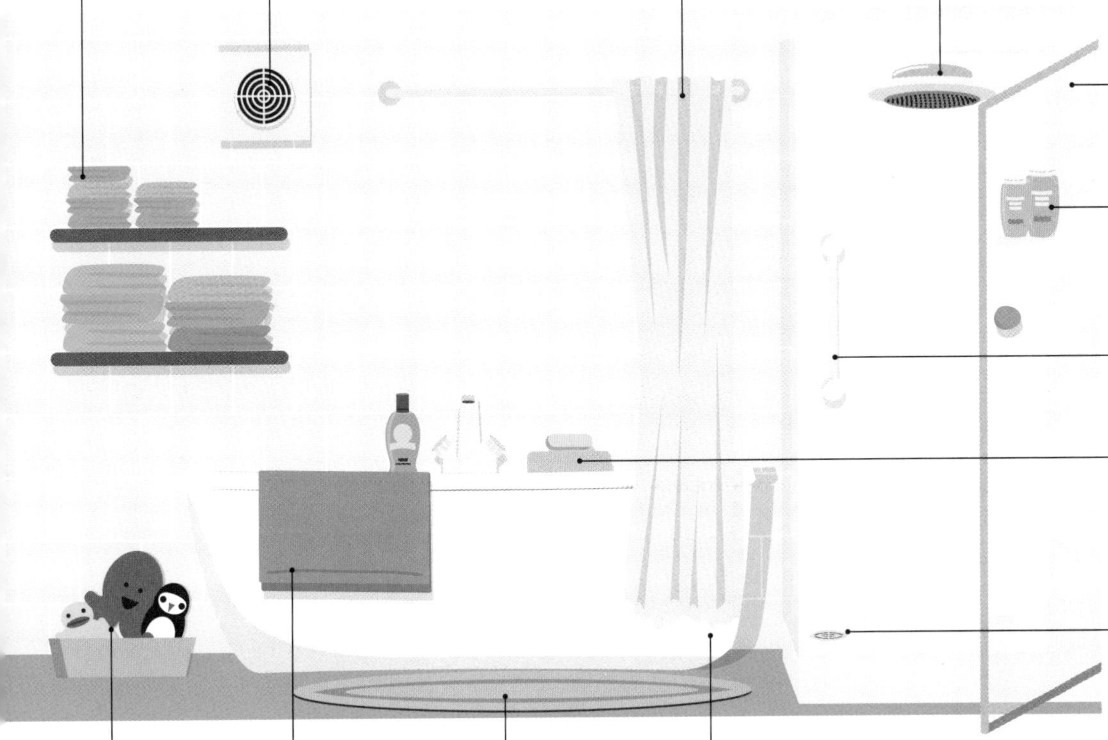

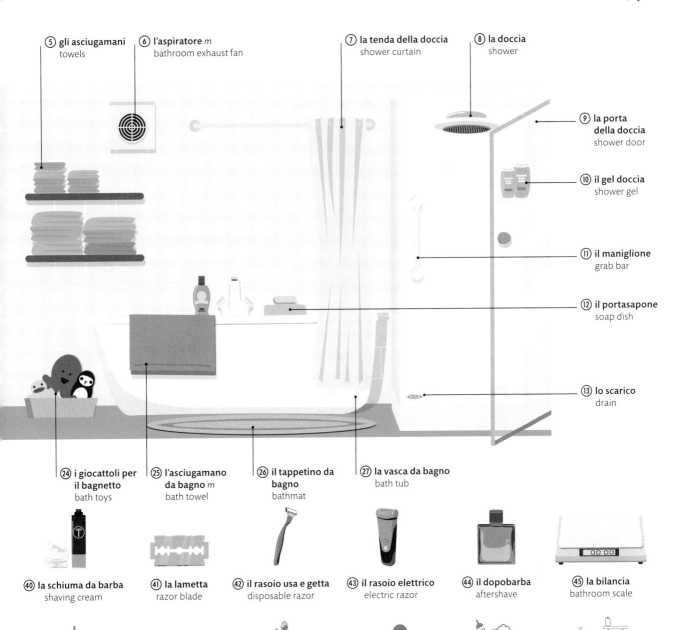

⑤ **gli asciugamani**
towels

⑥ **l'aspiratore** *m*
bathroom exhaust fan

⑦ **la tenda della doccia**
shower curtain

⑧ **la doccia**
shower

⑨ **la porta della doccia**
shower door

⑩ **il gel doccia**
shower gel

⑪ **il maniglione**
grab bar

⑫ **il portasapone**
soap dish

⑬ **lo scarico**
drain

㉔ **i giocattoli per il bagnetto**
bath toys

㉕ **l'asciugamano da bagno** *m*
bath towel

㉖ **il tappetino da bagno**
bathmat

㉗ **la vasca da bagno**
bath tub

㊵ **la schiuma da barba**
shaving cream

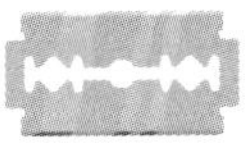

㊶ **la lametta**
razor blade

㊷ **il rasoio usa e getta**
disposable razor

㊸ **il rasoio elettrico**
electric razor

㊹ **il dopobarba**
aftershave

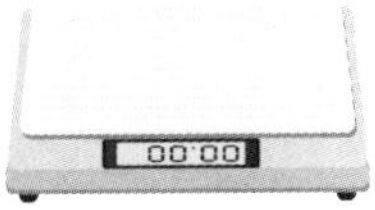

㊺ **la bilancia**
bathroom scale

㊻ **lo sturalavandini**
plunger

㊼ **il tappo**
plug

㊽ **asciugarsi**
to dry yourself

㊾ **radersi**
to shave

㊿ **fare la doccia**
to take (or have) a shower

51 **fare il bagno**
to take (or have) a bath

32 La casa
House and home

32.1 I TIPI DI CASE · TYPES OF HOUSE

① **la casa indipendente**
detached house

② **la casa bifamiliare**
duplex

③ **la casa a schiera**
row house

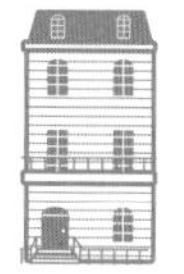
④ **la casa di città**
town house

⑤ **il cottage**
cottage

⑥ **la villa**
villa

⑦ **il bungalow**
ranch house

⑧ **la villa**
mansion

⑨ **la roulotte**
mobile home

⑩ **la baita**
cabin

⑪ **la casa sull'albero**
tree house

⑫ **lo chalet**
chalet

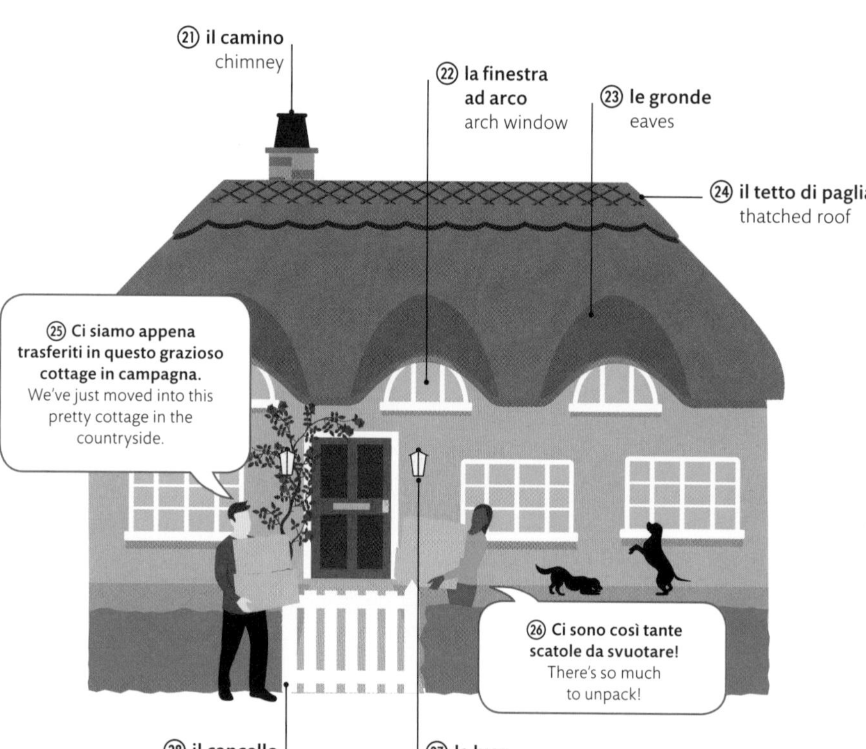

㉑ il camino
chimney
㉒ la finestra ad arco
arch window
㉓ le gronde
eaves
㉔ il tetto di paglia
thatched roof
㉕ Ci siamo appena trasferiti in questo grazioso cottage in campagna.
We've just moved into this pretty cottage in the countryside.
㉖ Ci sono così tante scatole da svuotare!
There's so much to unpack!
㉗ la luce
light
㉘ il cancello
gate

㉙ **il cottage con il tetto di paglia**
thatched cottage

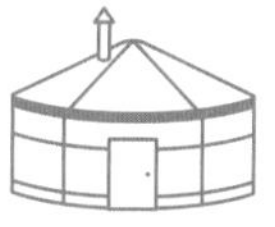
⑬ **la iurta**
yurt

⑭ **la capanna**
hut

⑮ **il wigwam**
wigwam

⑯ **l'igloo** *m*
igloo

⑰ **il tepee**
teepee

⑱ **la casa galleggiante**
houseboat

⑲ **la casa prefabbricata**
prefab house

⑳ **la palafitta**
stilt house

See also
25 Un luogo in cui vivere • A place to live **33** Gli impianti elettrico e idraulico • Electrics and plumbing **35** I lavori di miglioria della casa • Home improvements **37** La decorazione Renovating **42-43** In città • In town **44** Gli edifici e l'architettura • Buildings and architecture

32.2 L'ACQUISTO E L'AFFITTO DI UNA CASA • BUYING AND RENTING A HOUSE

$$$

① **l'agente immobiliare** *m / f*
realtor

② **l'immobile** *m*
real estate

$$

③ **vedere una casa**
to view a house

④ **arredato** *m* **arredata** *f*
furnished

⑤ **non arredato** *m* **non arredata** *f*
unfurnished

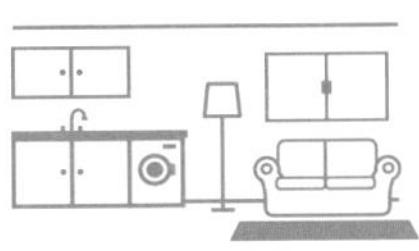

⑥ **open space**
open-plan

P

⑦ **il parcheggio**
parking space

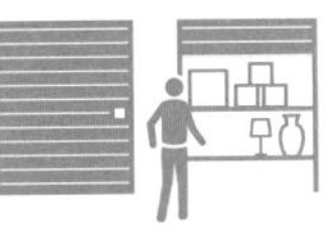

⑧ **il magazzino**
storage

⑨ **risparmiare**
to save up

$$$

⑩ **acquistare**
to buy

⑪ **possedere**
to own

⑫ **le scatole**
boxes

⑬ **il nastro adesivo**
tape

⑭ **le chiavi**
keys

⑮ **imballare**
to pack

⑯ **il camion dei traslochi**
moving truck

⑰ **traslocare**
to move out

⑱ **trasferirsi**
to move in

⑲ **spacchettare**
to unpack

⑳ **dare in affitto**
to rent out

MAY

㉑ **prendere in affitto**
to rent

㉒ **il contratto d'affitto**
lease

㉓ **l'affittuario** *m* **l'affittuaria** *f*
tenant

㉔ **il padrone di casa** *m* **la padrona di casa** *f*
landlord

㉕ **la cauzione**
deposit

㉖ **dare il preavviso**
to give notice

㉗ **l'ipoteca** *f*
mortgage

㉘ **le bollette**
bills

㉙ **l'inquilino** *m* **l'inquilina** *f*
roomer

㉚ **il coinquilino** *m* **la coinquilina** *f*
roommate

㉛ **l'area residenziale** *f*
residential area

33 Gli impianti elettrico e idraulico
Electrics and plumbing

33.1 L'ELETTRICITÀ · ELECTRICITY

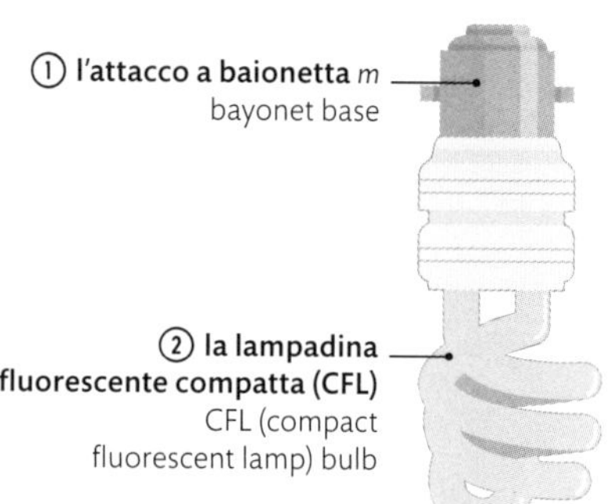

① **l'attacco a baionetta** *m*
bayonet base

② **la lampadina fluorescente compatta (CFL)**
CFL (compact fluorescent lamp) bulb

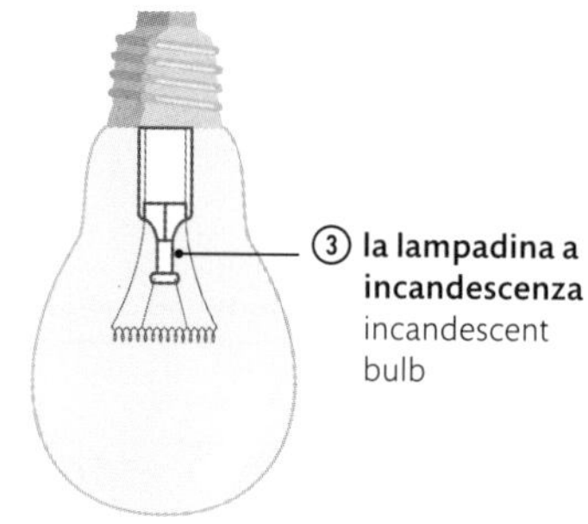

③ **la lampadina a incandescenza**
incandescent bulb

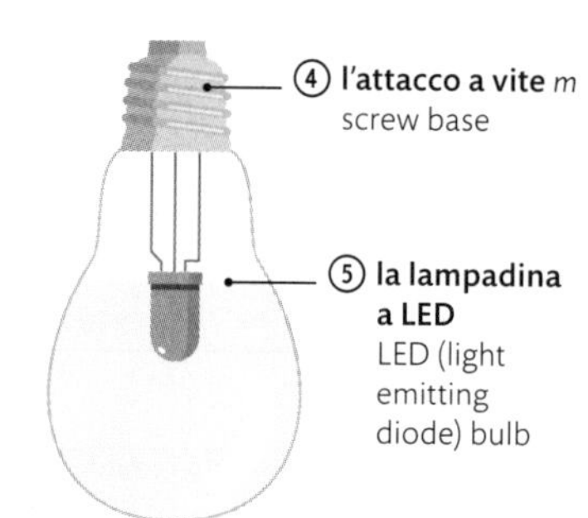

④ **l'attacco a vite** *m*
screw base

⑤ **la lampadina a LED**
LED (light emitting diode) bulb

⑥ **le lampadine**
light bulbs

⑦ **la presa elettrica**
socket

⑧ **l'interruttore** *m*
light switch

⑨ **la corrente continua**
direct current

⑩ **la corrente alternata**
alternating current

⑪ **il generatore**
generator

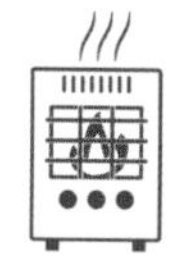

⑫ **la stufetta a gas**
gas space heater

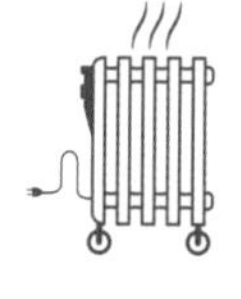

⑬ **il radiatore a olio**
oil-filled radiator

⑭ **la stufetta**
fan space heater

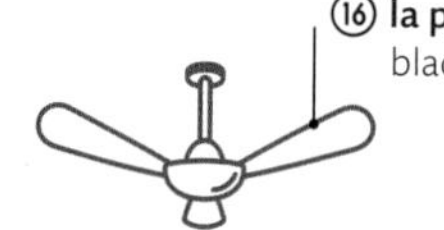

⑮ **il ventilatore da soffitto**
ceiling fan

⑯ **la pala**
blade

⑰ **il ventilatore**
fan

⑱ **l'aria condizionata** *f*
air conditioning

⑲ **la corrente elettrica**
power

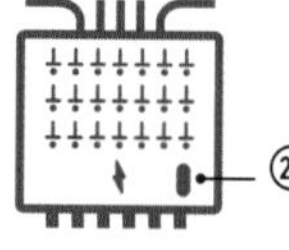

⑳ **il quadro elettrico**
fuse box

㉑ **il salvavita**
breaker

㉒ **l'ampere** *m*
amp

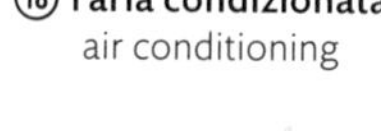

㉓ **sotto tensione**
live

㉔ **neutro**
neutral

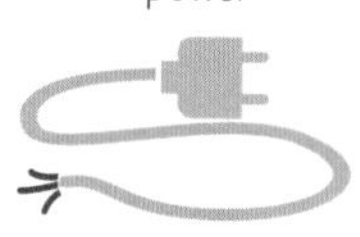

㉕ **i cavi**
wires

㉖ **la messa a terra**
ground

㉗ **il voltaggio**
voltage

㉘ **la spina**
plug

㉙ **lo spinotto**
pin

㉟ **Stacca la corrente prima di toccare un cavo sotto tensione.**
Switch off the power before touching a live wire.

㉚ **il contatore elettrico**
electricity meter

㉛ **il trasformatore**
transformer

㉜ **l'interruzione di corrente** *f*
power outage

㉝ **la rete elettrica**
utility power

㉞ **il cablaggio**
wiring

See also
31 Il bagno • Bathroom **35** I lavori di miglioria della casa • Home improvements
36 Gli attrezzi • Tools **37** La decorazione • Renovating **87** Le costruzioni • Construction

33.2 **L'IMPIANTO IDRAULICO** • PLUMBING

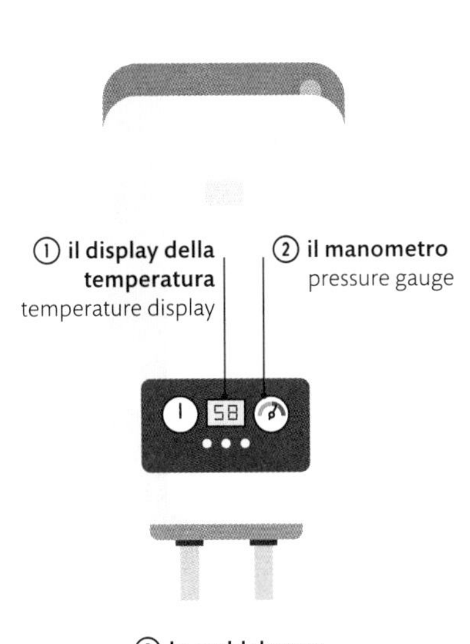
① **il display della temperatura**
temperature display
② **il manometro**
pressure gauge
58

③ **lo scaldabagno**
on-demand boiler

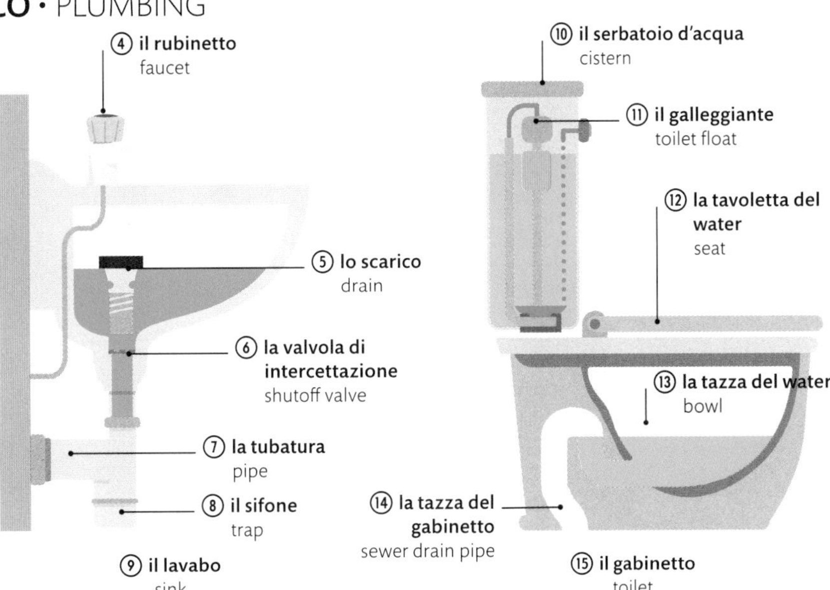
④ **il rubinetto**
faucet
⑤ **lo scarico**
drain
⑥ **la valvola di intercettazione**
shutoff valve
⑦ **la tubatura**
pipe
⑧ **il sifone**
trap
⑩ **il serbatoio d'acqua**
cistern
⑪ **il galleggiante**
toilet float
⑫ **la tavoletta del water**
seat
⑬ **la tazza del water**
bowl
⑭ **la tazza del gabinetto**
sewer drain pipe

⑨ **il lavabo**
sink

⑮ **il gabinetto**
toilet

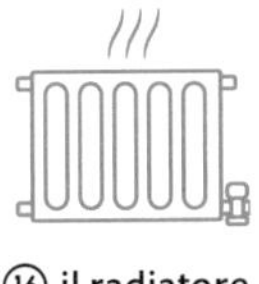

⑯ **il radiatore**
radiator

⑰ **il rubinetto**
faucet

⑱ **avere una perdita**
to spring a leak

⑲ **chiamare un idraulico**
to call a plumber

⑳ **riparare**
to repair

㉑ **installare**
to install

33.3 **I RIFIUTI** • WASTE

① **il cestino della spazzatura**
trash can

② **il cestino per la raccolta differenziata**
recycling bin

③ **l'unità per la raccolta differenziata** *f*
sorting unit

④ **il contenitore per il compost**
food compost bin

⑤ **il sacco dell'immondizia**
trash bag

⑥ **i rifiuti biodegradabili**
biodegradable waste

⑦ **i rifiuti pericolosi**
hazardous waste

⑧ **i rifiuti elettrici**
electrical waste

⑨ **i rifiuti edili**
construction waste

34 Le faccende domestiche

Household chores

34.1 I LAVORI DI CASA · HOUSEHOLD TASKS

① **cambiare le lenzuola**
to change the sheets

② **fare il letto**
to make the bed

③ **dare da mangiare agli animali**
to feed the pets

④ **annaffiare le piante**
to water the plants

⑤ **lavare l'auto**
to wash the car

⑥ **spazzare il pavimento**
to sweep the floor

⑦ **lavare il pavimento**
to scrub the floor

⑧ **pulire il forno**
to clean the oven

⑨ **pulire le finestre**
to clean the windows

⑩ **sbrinare il frigo**
to defrost the freezer

⑪ **passare l'aspirapolvere sul tappeto** *m*
to vacuum the carpet

⑫ **spolverare**
to dust

⑬ **pulire il bagno**
to clean the bathroom

⑭ **riordinare**
to clean up

⑮ **fare la spesa**
to buy groceries

⑯ **fare il bucato**
to do the laundry

⑰ **stendere il bucato**
to hang clothes

⑱ **stirare**
to do the ironing

⑳ **Solitamente faccio i lavori di casa alla sera.**
I usually do the housework in the evening.

⑲ **passare il mocio**
to mop the floor

㉑ **piegare i vestiti**
to fold clothes

㉒ **preparare la tavola / apparecchiare**
to set the table

㉓ **sparecchiare**
to clear the table

㉔ **riempire la lavastoviglie**
to load the dishwasher

㉕ **svuotare la lavastoviglie**
to unload the dishwasher

㉖ **pulire le superfici**
to wipe the surfaces

㉗ **lavare i piatti**
to do the dishes

㉘ **asciugare i piatti**
to dry the dishes

㉙ **portare fuori la spazzatura**
to take out the trash

See also
09 Le attività quotidiane • Daily routines **25** Un luogo in cui vivere • A place to live **33** Gli impianti elettrico e idraulico • Electrics and plumbing **35** I lavori di miglioria della casa • Home improvements **37** La decorazione • Renovating **39** Il giardinaggio • Practical gardening

34.2 IL BUCATO E LE PULIZIE • LAUNDRY AND CLEANING

① **la spugnetta abrasiva**
scouring pad

② **la spugna**
sponge

③ **il panno**
cloth

④ **il panno per spolverare**
duster

⑤ **il piumino per la polvere**
feather duster

⑥ **il lavavetri**
squeegee

⑦ **il secchio**
bucket

⑧ **il mocio**
mop

⑨ **lo spazzolone**
scrubbing brush

⑩ **la paletta**
dustpan

⑪ **la scopetta**
brush

⑫ **la scopa**
broom

⑬ **il cestino per la raccolta differenziata**
recycling bin

⑭ **il sacco dell'immondizia**
trash bag

⑮ **il lucidante**
polish

⑯ **il detergente per superfici**
surface cleaner

⑰ **il detergente per bagno**
toilet cleaner

⑱ **la tavoletta attiva**
automatic toilet cleaner

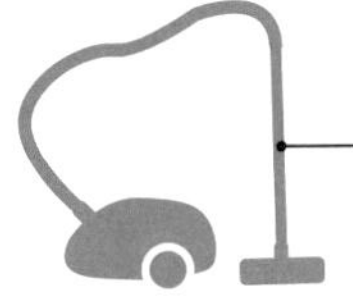
⑳ **il tubo di aspirazione**
suction hose

⑲ **l'aspirapolvere** *m*
vacuum cleaner

㉑ **i guanti di gomma**
rubber gloves

㉒ **l'aceto bianco** *m*
white vinegar

㉓ **i panni sporchi**
dirty clothes

㉔ **il cesto della biancheria**
laundry hamper

㉕ **la lavatrice**
washing machine

㉖ **l'asciugatrice** *f*
tumble dryer

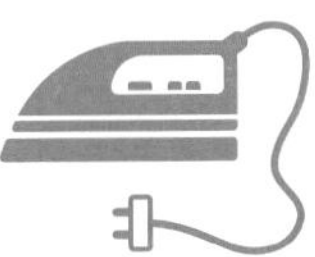
㉗ **il ferro da stiro**
iron

㉘ **l'asse da stiro** *m*
ironing board

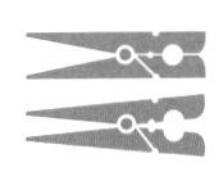
㉙ **la molletta**
clothes pin

㉚ **il filo stendibiancheria**
clothesline

㉛ **il detersivo per il bucato**
laundry detergent

㉜ **l'ammorbidente** *m*
fabric softener

㉝ **la lavastoviglie**
dishwasher

㉞ **le pastiglie per lavastoviglie**
dishwasher tablets

㉟ **il detersivo per piatti**
dishwashing liquid

㊱ **la candeggina**
bleach

35 I lavori di miglioria della casa

Home improvements

35.1 GLI ATTREZZI E GLI UTENSILI PER IL BRICOLAGE · TOOLS AND DIY EQUIPMENT

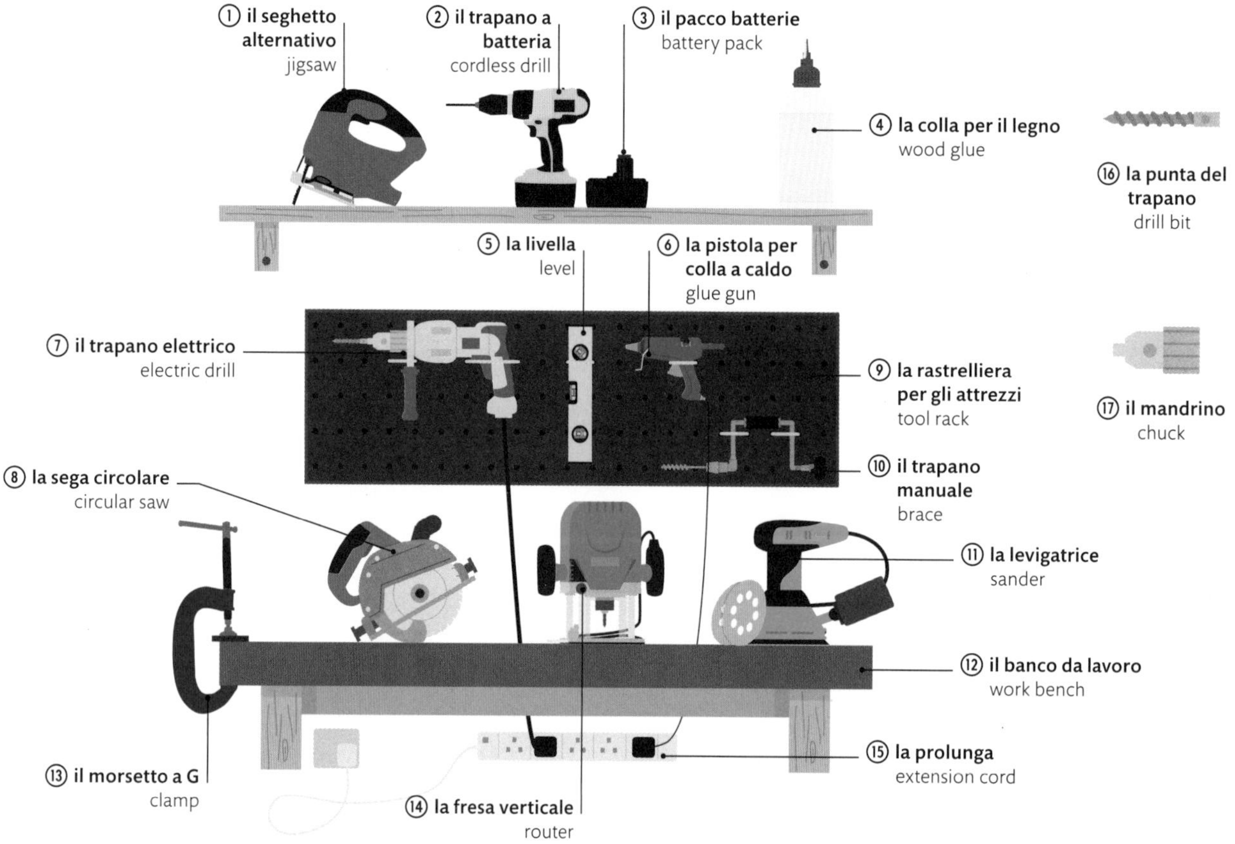

1. **il seghetto alternativo** jigsaw
2. **il trapano a batteria** cordless drill
3. **il pacco batterie** battery pack
4. **la colla per il legno** wood glue
5. **la livella** level
6. **la pistola per colla a caldo** glue gun
7. **il trapano elettrico** electric drill
8. **la sega circolare** circular saw
9. **la rastrelliera per gli attrezzi** tool rack
10. **il trapano manuale** brace
11. **la levigatrice** sander
12. **il banco da lavoro** work bench
13. **il morsetto a G** clamp
14. **la fresa verticale** router
15. **la prolunga** extension cord
16. **la punta del trapano** drill bit
17. **il mandrino** chuck

35.2 I VERBI DEL BRICOLAGE · DIY VERBS

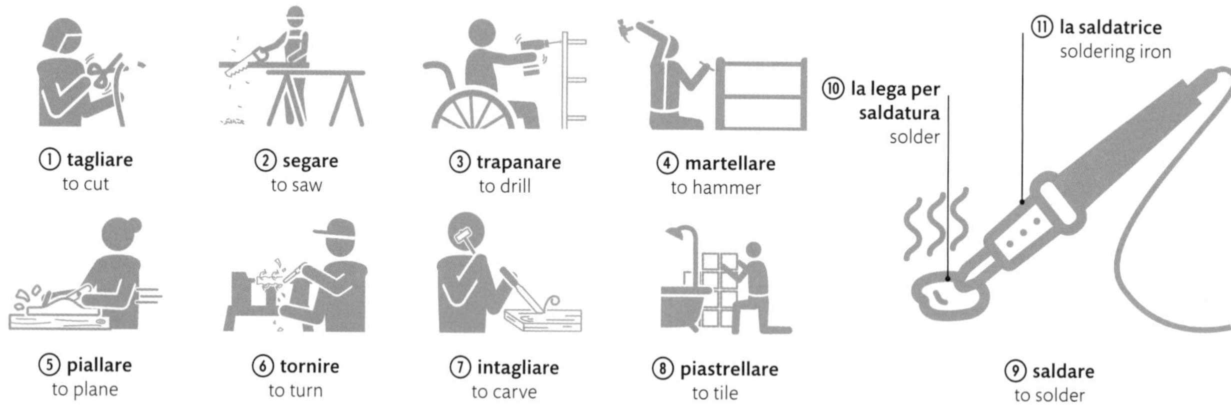
① tagliare
to cut
② segare
to saw
③ trapanare
to drill
④ martellare
to hammer
⑤ piallare
to plane
⑥ tornire
to turn
⑦ intagliare
to carve
⑧ piastrellare
to tile
⑨ saldare
to solder
⑩ la lega per saldatura
solder
⑪ la saldatrice
soldering iron

See also
33 Gli impianti elettrico e idraulico • Electrics and plumbing **36** Gli attrezzi • Tools **37** La decorazione • Renovating **87** Le costruzioni • Construction

35.3 I MATERIALI • MATERIALS

① **il legno**
wood

② **il legno massiccio**
hardwood

③ **il legno tenero**
softwood

④ **la faesite**
hardboard

⑤ **il truciolato**
particle board

⑥ **il compensato**
plywood

⑦ **l'MDF** *m*
MDF

⑧ **le piastrelle**
tiles

⑨ **il cemento**
concrete

⑩ **il metallo**
metal

⑪ **il fil di ferro**
wire

⑫ **il lastricato**
flagstone

⑬ **l'isolamento** *m*
insulation

⑭ **la sabbia**
sand

⑮ **la ghiaia**
gravel

⑰ **Sto costruendo un nuovo ampliamento.**
I'm building a new extension.

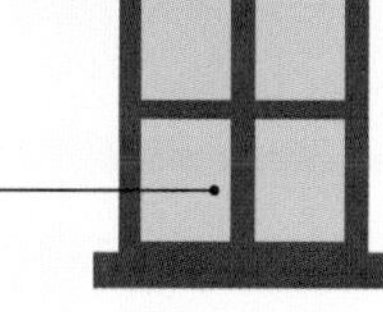
⑱ **il vetro**
glass

⑲ **la malta**
mortar

⑯ **i mattoni**
bricks

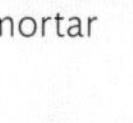

⑫ **posare la moquette**
to install a carpet

⑬ **sturare il lavandino**
to unclog the sink

⑭ **rifare l'impianto elettrico della casa**
to rewire the house

⑮ **posare i mattoni**
to lay bricks

⑯ **convertire il loft**
to convert the attic

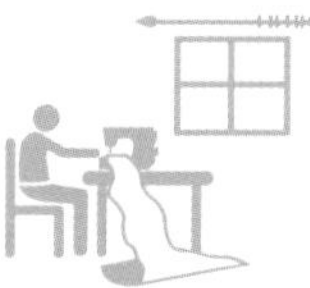
⑰ **realizzare le tende**
to make curtains

⑱ **appendere gli scaffali**
to put up shelves

⑲ **cambiare una lampadina**
to change a light bulb

⑳ **sturare il water**
to unclog the toilet

㉑ **abbattere un muro**
to knock down a wall

㉒ **dipingere un muro**
to paint a wall

㉓ **riparare una recinzione**
to fix a fence

36 Gli attrezzi
Tools

36.1 LA CASSETTA DEGLI ATTREZZI · TOOLBOX

① **la chiave a rullino**
monkey wrench

② **la chiave a bussola**
socket wrench

③ **le pinze a becchi lunghi**
needle-nose pliers

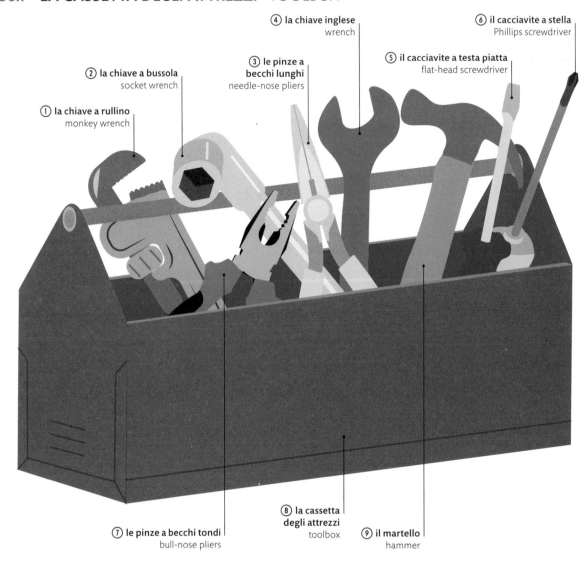

④ **la chiave inglese**
wrench

⑤ **il cacciavite a testa piatta**
flat-head screwdriver

⑥ **il cacciavite a stella**
Phillips screwdriver

⑦ **le pinze a becchi tondi**
bull-nose pliers

⑧ **la cassetta degli attrezzi**
toolbox

⑨ **il martello**
hammer

36.2 LE PUNTE DEL TRAPANO · DRILL BITS

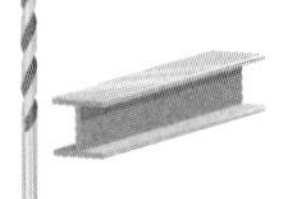

① **la punta da metallo**
metal bit

② **la punta da muro**
masonry bit

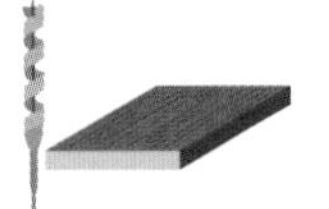

③ **la punta da legno**
carpentry bit

④ **la punta piatta da legno**
flat wood bit

⑤ **la punta di sicurezza**
security bit

⑥ **l'alesatore** *m*
reamer

See also
33 Gli impianti elettrico e idraulico • Electrics and plumbing
35 I lavori di miglioria della casa • Home improvements
37 La decorazione • Renovating **87** Le costruzioni • Construction

36.3 GLI ATTREZZI • TOOLS

① **la cintura porta attrezzi**
tool belt

② **il chiodo**
nail

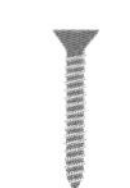
③ **la vite**
screw

④ **il bullone**
bolt

⑤ **la guarnizione**
washer

⑥ **il dado**
nut

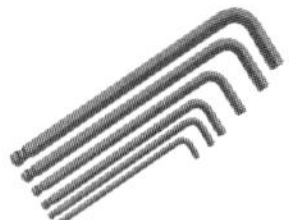
⑦ **le brugole**
Allen wrenches

⑧ **il metro a nastro**
tape measure

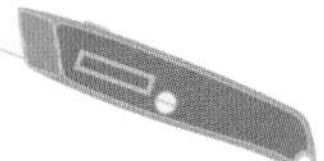
⑨ **il taglierino**
utility knife

⑩ **il seghetto**
hacksaw

⑪ **la sega per tenoni**
tenon saw

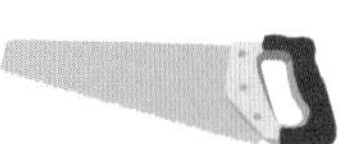
⑫ **la sega**
handsaw

⑬ **la pialla**
plane

⑭ **il trapano manuale**
hand drill

⑮ **la chiave inglese**
wrench

⑯ **lo scalpello**
chisel

⑰ **la lima**
file

⑱ **la pietra per affilare**
sharpening stone

⑳ **il piolo**
rung

⑲ **la scala**
ladder

㉑ **le pinze spelafili**
wire strippers

㉒ **il tronchese**
wire cutters

㉓ **il nastro isolante**
insulating tape

㉔ **il tagliatubi**
pipe cutter

㉕ **lo sturalavandini**
plunger

㉖ **il mazzuolo**
mallet

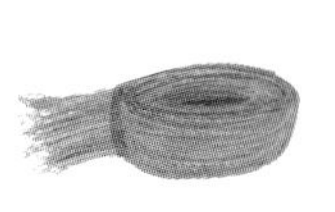
㉗ **l'ascia** *f*
ax

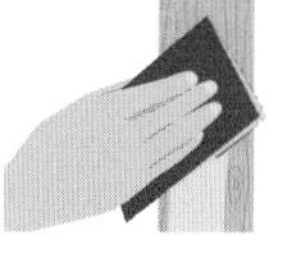
㉘ **la lana d'acciaio**
steel wool

㉙ **la carta vetrata**
sandpaper

㉚ **gli occhiali protettivi**
safety goggles

㉛ **la saldatrice**
soldering iron

㉜ **la lega per saldatura**
solder

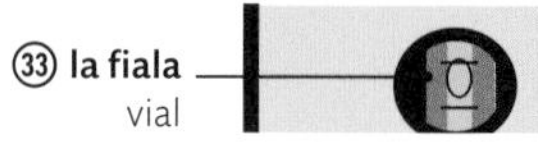

㉝ **la fiala**
vial

㉞ **la livella**
level

37 La decorazione
Renovating

37.1 LA RISTRUTTURAZIONE DELLA CASA · HOUSEHOLD RENOVATION

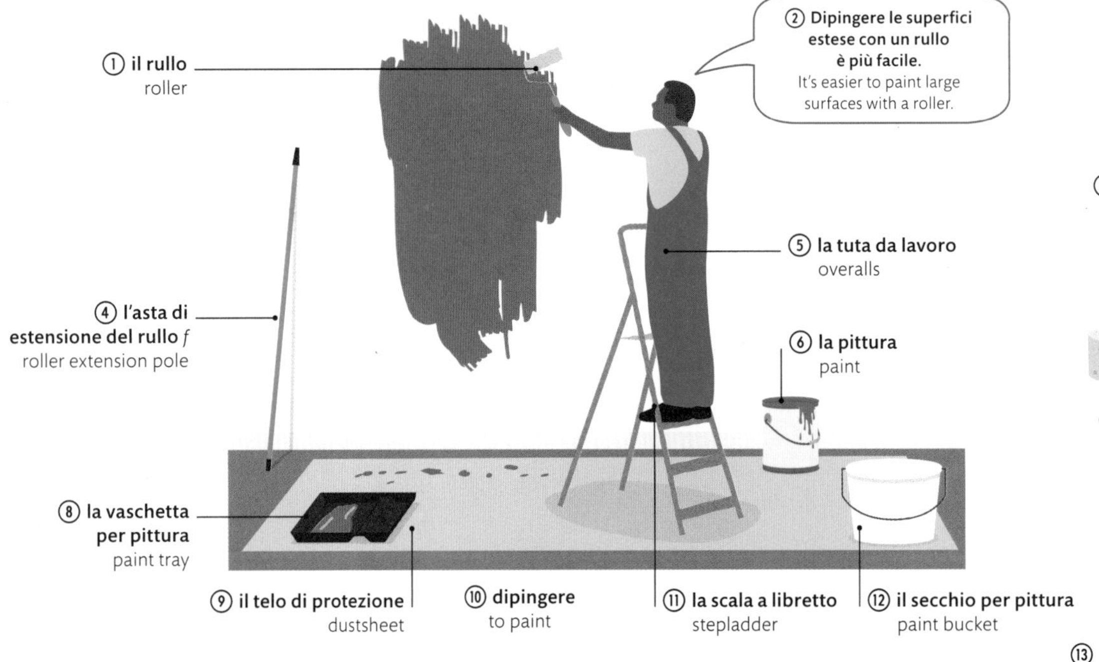

① il rullo
roller
② Dipingere le superfici estese con un rullo è più facile.
It's easier to paint large surfaces with a roller.
④ l'asta di estensione del rullo *f*
roller extension pole
⑤ la tuta da lavoro
overalls
⑥ la pittura
paint
⑧ la vaschetta per pittura
paint tray
⑨ il telo di protezione
dustsheet
⑩ dipingere
to paint
⑪ la scala a libretto
stepladder
⑫ il secchio per pittura
paint bucket

③ **il pennello**
paintbrush

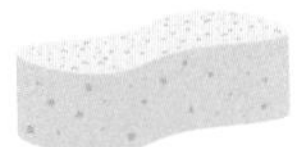

⑦ **la spugna**
sponge

⑬ **il nastro adesivo di carta**
masking tape

⑭ **il taglierino**
utility knife

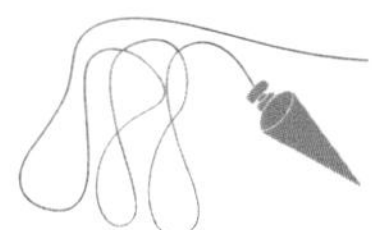

⑮ **il filo a piombo**
plumb line

⑯ **la carta vetrata**
sandpaper

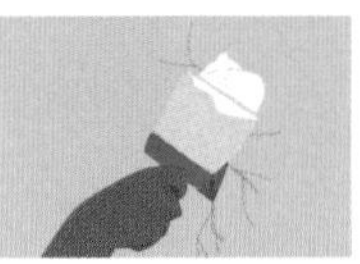

⑰ **lo stucco**
spackle

⑱ **l'acqua ragia** *f*
mineral spirits

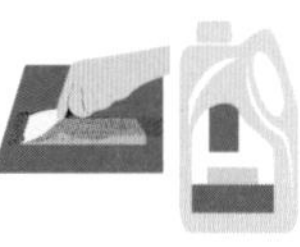

⑲ **lo sverniciatore**
paint stripper

⑳ **l'intonaco** *m*
plaster

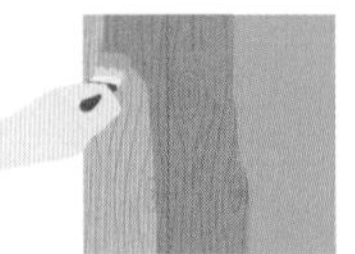

㉑ **la vernice di base**
sealer

㉒ **la mano di fondo**
primer

㉓ **l'emulsione** *f*
paint

㉔ **opaco** *m* **/ opaca** *f*
matte

㉕ **lucido** *m* **lucida** *f*
gloss

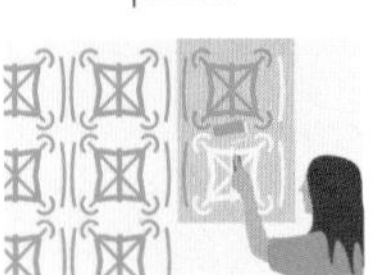

㉖ **lo stencil**
stencil

㉗ **il solvente**
solvent

㉘ **il sigillante per bagno**
sealant / caulk

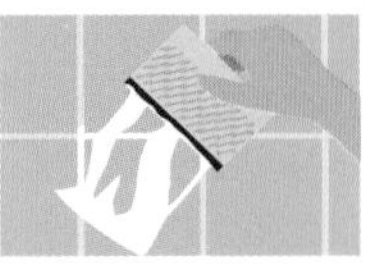

㉙ **la malta**
grout

㉚ **l'impregnante** *m*
wood preserver

㉛ **la vernice**
varnish

See also
32 La casa • House and home **33** Gli impianti elettrico e idraulico • Electrics and plumbing **34** Le faccende domestiche • Household chores **35** I lavori di miglioria della casa • Home improvements

(32) **le forbici**
scissors

(33) **la carta di fondo**
lining paper

(34) **la macchina per rimuovere la carta da parati**
wallpaper stripper

(35) **il raschietto**
scraper

(36) **il rotolo di carta da parati**
wallpaper roll

(37) **il bordo della carta da parati**
wallpaper border

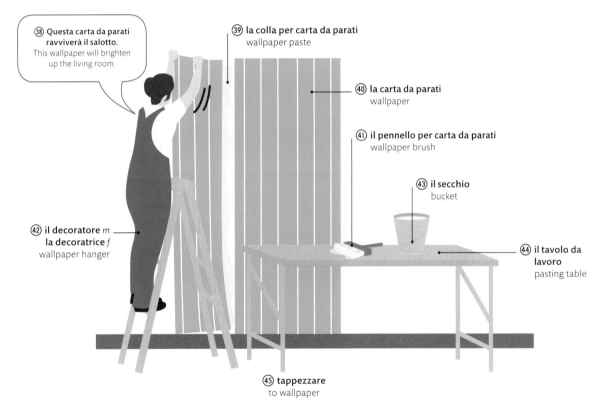

(38) **Questa carta da parati ravviverà il salotto.**
This wallpaper will brighten up the living room.

(39) **la colla per carta da parati**
wallpaper paste

(40) **la carta da parati**
wallpaper

(41) **il pennello per carta da parati**
wallpaper brush

(42) **il decoratore** *m*
la decoratrice *f*
wallpaper hanger

(43) **il secchio**
bucket

(44) **il tavolo da lavoro**
pasting table

(45) **tappezzare**
to wallpaper

37.2 I VERBI DELLA DECORAZIONE • VERBS FOR RENOVATION

(1) **staccare**
to strip

(2) **stuccare**
to spackle

(3) **scartavetrare**
to sand

(4) **intonacare**
to plaster

(5) **appendere**
to hang

(6) **piastrellare**
to tile

38 Le piante da giardino e le piante da appartamento • Garden plants and houseplants

38.1 LE PIANTE DA GIARDINO E I FIORI • GARDEN PLANTS AND FLOWERS

1 **il dente di leone**
dandelion

2 **l'enagra** *f*
evening primrose

3 **il cardo**
thistle

4 **il tulipano**
tulip

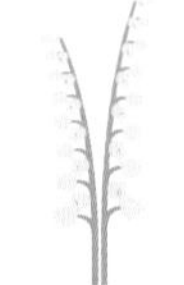
5 **il mughetto**
lily of the valley

6 **il garofano**
carnation

8 **la margherita**
daisy

9 **il ranuncolo**
buttercup

10 **il papavero**
poppy

11 **la viola del pensiero**
pansy

12 **il geranio**
geranium

13 **la digitale**
foxglove

15 **il lupino**
lupin

16 **la rosa**
rose

17 **il girasole**
sunflower

18 **l'orchidea** *f*
orchid

19 **la begonia**
begonia

20 **il giglio**
lily

22 **la viola**
violet

23 **il croco**
crocus

24 **la giunchiglia**
daffodil

25 **il lillà**
lilac

26 **la gardenia**
gardenia

27 **la lavanda**
lavender

29 **la calendula**
marigold

30 **l'azalea** *f*
azalea

31 **il crisantemo**
chrysanthemum

32 **il rododendro**
rhododendron

33 **l'ibisco** *m*
rose of Sharon / hibiscus

35 **il caprifoglio**
honeysuckle

36 **l'iris** *f*
iris

37 **il loto**
lotus

38 **il glicine**
wisteria

39 **la margherita africana**
African daisy

40 **l'ortensia** *f*
hydrangea

See also
39 Il giardinaggio • Practical gardening 40 Gli attrezzi da giardinaggio • Garden tools
41 Le caratteristiche del giardino • Garden features 167-169 Le piante e gli alberi • Plants and trees

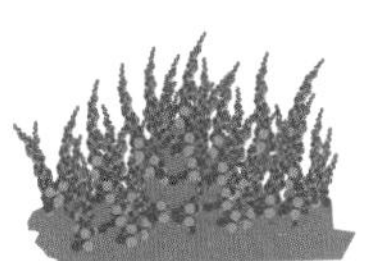
⑦ **l'erica** *f*
heather

⑭ **la camelia**
camellia

㉑ **il ginerio**
pampas grass

㉘ **la protea**
protea

㉞ **il rosmarino**
rosemary

㊶ **l'alloro** *m*
bay tree

38.2 LE PIANTE DA APPARTAMENTO • HOUSEPLANTS

① **lo spatifillo**
peace lily

② **la sansevieria**
snake plant

③ **la pianta ragno**
spider plant

④ **la yucca**
yucca

⑤ **la dracena**
dragon tree

⑥ **il bonsai**
bonsai tree

⑦ **l'aracea americana** *f*
Swiss cheese plant

⑧ **le piante grasse**
succulents

⑨ **la pianta delle monete cinesi**
Chinese money plant

⑩ **il fico del caucciù**
rubber plant

⑪ **il falso papiro**
umbrella plant

⑫ **l'hypoestes phyllostachya** *f*
polka dot plant

⑬ **il pothos regina di marmo**
marble queen

⑭ **il pothos Jade**
jade pothos

38.3 L'ANATOMIA DEL FIORE
FLOWER ANATOMY

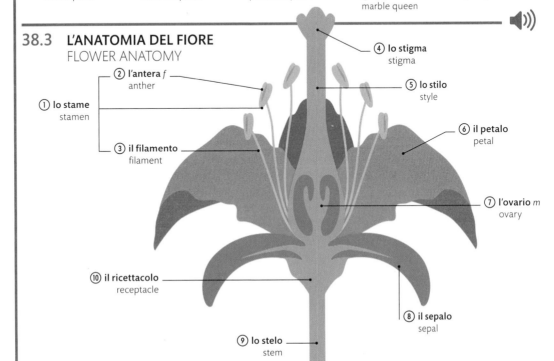

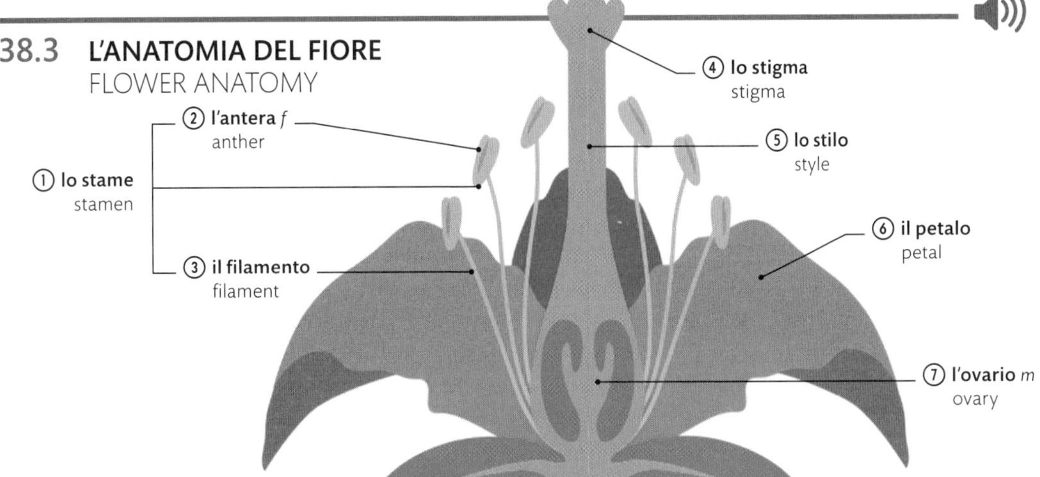
① lo stame
stamen
② l'antera f
anther
③ il filamento
filament
④ lo stigma
stigma
⑤ lo stilo
style
⑥ il petalo
petal
⑦ l'ovario m
ovary
⑧ il sepalo
sepal
⑨ lo stelo
stem
⑩ il ricettacolo
receptacle

39 Il giardinaggio

Practical gardening

39.1 I VERBI DEL GIARDINAGGIO · GARDENING VERBS

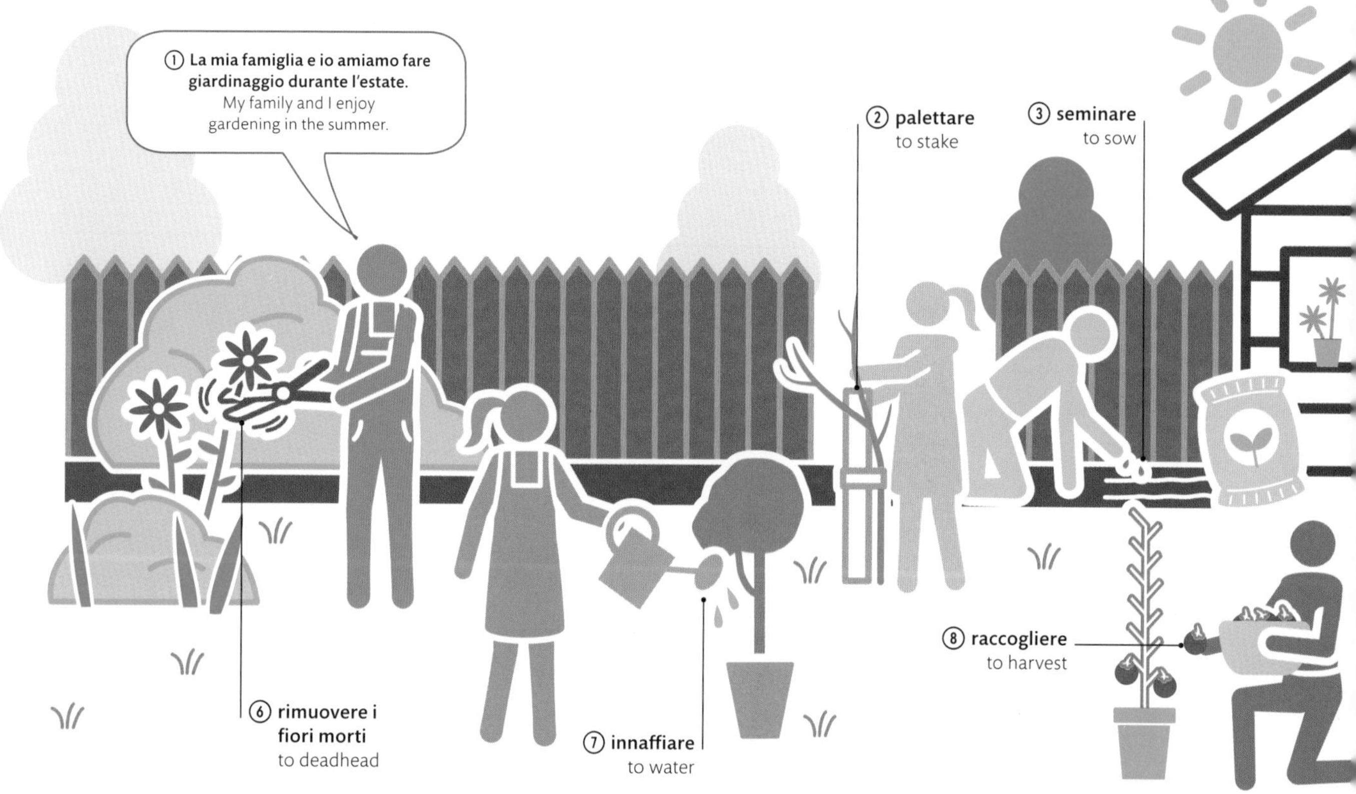

① **La mia famiglia e io amiamo fare giardinaggio durante l'estate.**
My family and I enjoy gardening in the summer.

② **palettare**
to stake

③ **seminare**
to sow

⑥ **rimuovere i fiori morti**
to deadhead

⑦ **innaffiare**
to water

⑧ **raccogliere**
to harvest

⑮ **tagliare l'erba**
to mow the lawn

⑯ **coprire con zolle erbose**
to lay sod

⑰ **spianare (il terreno)**
to rake (soil)

⑱ **rastrellare (le foglie)**
to rake (leaves)

⑲ **aerare**
to aerate

⑳ **la miniserra**
cold frame

㉔ **innestare**
to graft

㉕ **far crescere**
to propagate

㉖ **piantare**
to plant

㉗ **pacciamare**
to mulch

㉘ **togliere le erbacce**
to do the weeding

㉙ **trapiantare**
to transplant

㉞ **coltivare**
to cultivate

㉟ **potare**
to trim

㊱ **sfrondare**
to prune

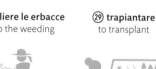

㊲ **tagliare**
to chop

㊳ **setacciare**
to sieve

㊴ **progettare l'architettura paesaggistica**
to landscape

See also
38 Le piante da giardino e le piante da appartamento • Garden plants and houseplants **40** Gli attrezzi da giardinaggio • Garden tools **41** Le caratteristiche del giardino • Garden features **167-169** Le piante e gli alberi • Plants and trees

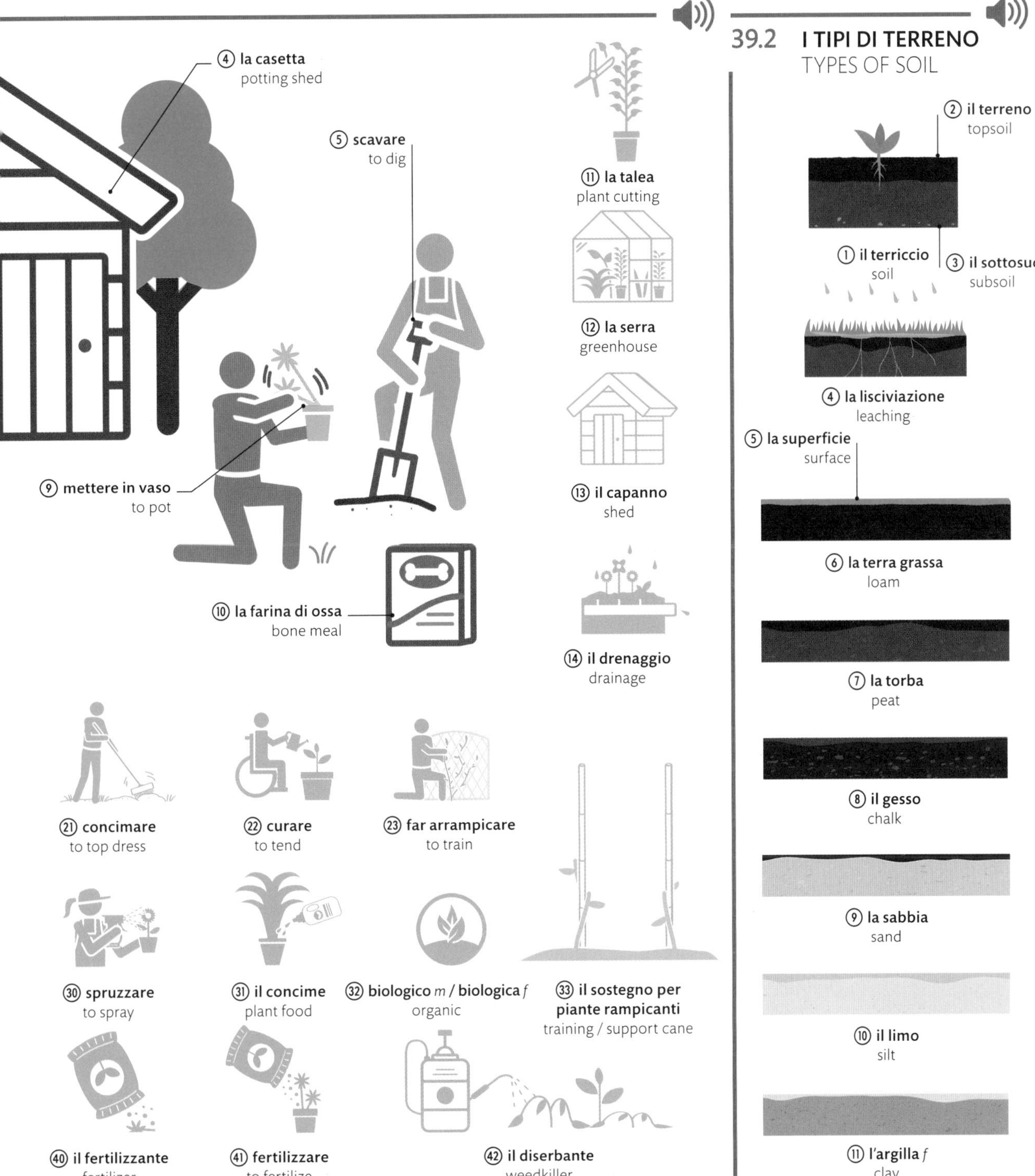
④ la casetta
potting shed
⑤ scavare
to dig
⑪ la talea
plant cutting
⑫ la serra
greenhouse
⑬ il capanno
shed
⑨ mettere in vaso
to pot
⑩ la farina di ossa
bone meal
⑭ il drenaggio
drainage
㉑ concimare
to top dress
㉒ curare
to tend
㉓ far arrampicare
to train
㉚ spruzzare
to spray
㉛ il concime
plant food
㉜ biologico m / biologica f
organic
㉝ il sostegno per piante rampicanti
training / support cane
㊵ il fertilizzante
fertilizer
㊶ fertilizzare
to fertilize
㊷ il diserbante
weedkiller

39.2 I TIPI DI TERRENO
TYPES OF SOIL

② **il terreno** topsoil

① **il terriccio** soil

③ **il sottosuolo** subsoil

④ **la lisciviazione** leaching

⑤ **la superficie** surface

⑥ **la terra grassa** loam

⑦ **la torba** peat

⑧ **il gesso** chalk

⑨ **la sabbia** sand

⑩ **il limo** silt

⑪ **l'argilla** *f* clay

40 Gli attrezzi da giardinaggio
Garden tools

40.1 L'ATTREZZATURA PER IL GIARDINAGGIO • GARDENING EQUIPMENT

② il raccoglierba
grass collector
③ la forca
fork
④ il dissodatore
soil tiller
⑤ il forcone
potato fork
⑥ le cesoie tagliabordi
long-handled shears
① il tagliaerba
lawnmower
⑦ la zappa
hoe
⑧ la vanga
spade
⑨ il badile
shovel
⑩ il tagliabordi
trimmer
⑬ la compostiera
compost
⑪ la protezione
shield
⑫ il compost
composter
⑭ il bidone di compostaggio
compost bin
⑮ i semi
seeds
⑯ il cesto da giardinaggio
gardening basket
⑰ la ghiaia
gravel
⑲ il manico
handle
㉑ l'aspirafoglie m
leaf blower
㉒ il rastrello aeratore
lawn rake
㉓ il rastrello
rake
⑳ l'appoggio m
stand
⑱ la carriola
wheelbarrow
㉔ la paletta
trowel
㉕ il troncarami
loppers
㉖ il potatore
tree pruner
㉗ i bastoni
canes
㉘ la vaschetta per i semi
seed tray
㉙ l'inginocchiatoio m
kneeler
㉚ lo spago
twine
㉛ le etichette
labels
㉜ i legacci
twist ties

See also
38 Le piante da giardino e le piante da appartamento • Garden plants and houseplants **39** Il giardinaggio • Practical gardening **41** Le caratteristiche del giardino • Garden features **167-169** Le piante e gli alberi • Plants and trees

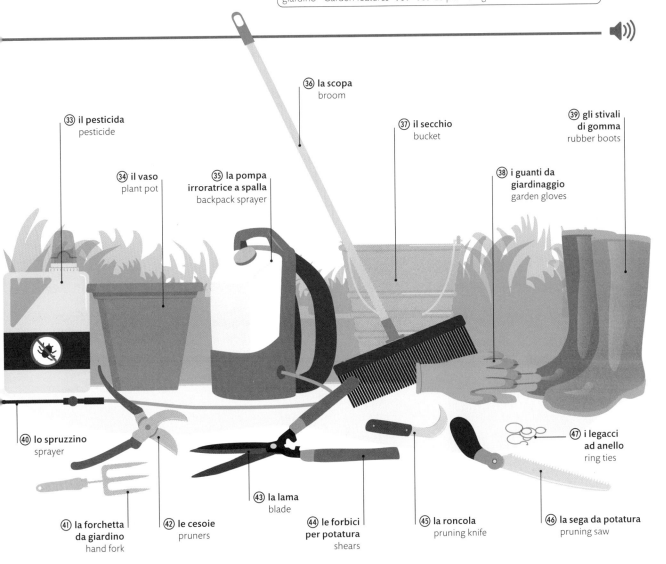

㉝ **il pesticida**
pesticide

㉞ **il vaso**
plant pot

㉟ **la pompa irroratrice a spalla**
backpack sprayer

㊱ **la scopa**
broom

㊲ **il secchio**
bucket

㊳ **i guanti da giardinaggio**
garden gloves

㊴ **gli stivali di gomma**
rubber boots

㊵ **lo spruzzino**
sprayer

㊶ **la forchetta da giardino**
hand fork

㊷ **le cesoie**
pruners

㊸ **la lama**
blade

㊹ **le forbici per potatura**
shears

㊺ **la roncola**
pruning knife

㊻ **la sega da potatura**
pruning saw

㊼ **i legacci ad anello**
ring ties

40.2 L'ANNAFFIATURA • WATERING

① **l'annaffiatoio** *m*
watering can

② **l'ugello spruzzatore** *m*
spray nozzle

③ **l'irrigatore a pioggia** *m*
sprinkler

④ **l'avvolgitubo** *m*
hose reel

⑤ **l'ugello** *m*
nozzle

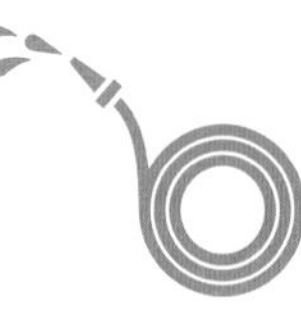

⑥ **la canna da giardino** *m*
garden hose

41 Le caratteristiche del giardino

Garden features

41.1 I TIPI DI GIARDINO E GLI ORNAMENTI · GARDEN TYPES AND FEATURES

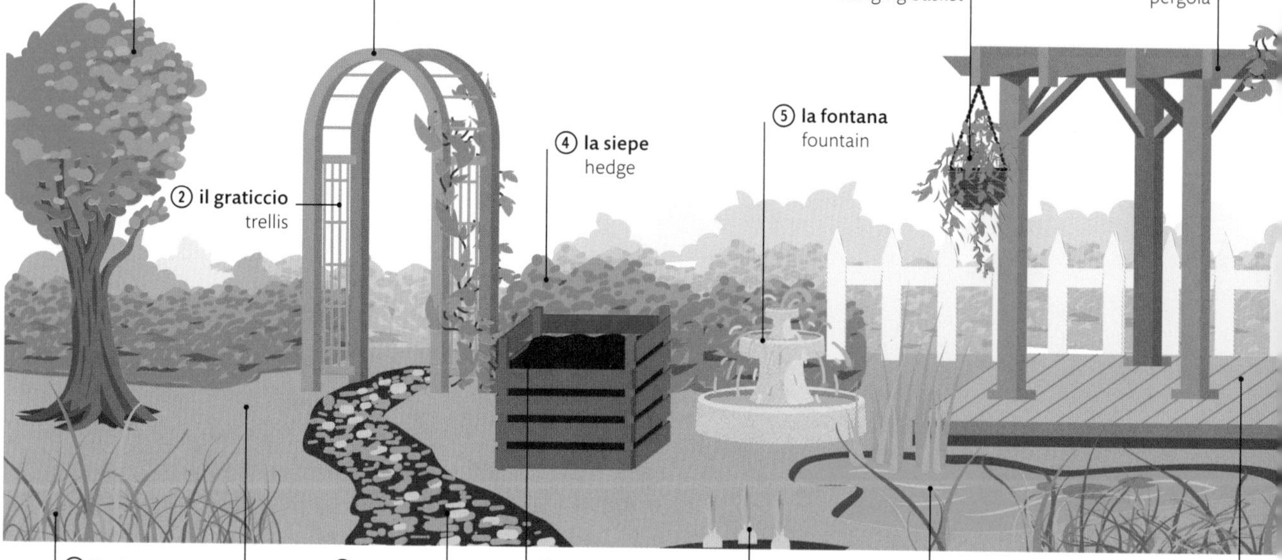

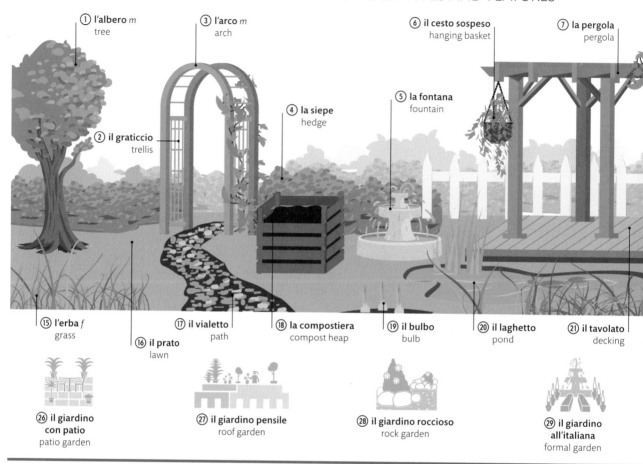

① **l'albero** *m*
tree

③ **l'arco** *m*
arch

⑥ **il cesto sospeso**
hanging basket

⑦ **la pergola**
pergola

⑤ **la fontana**
fountain

④ **la siepe**
hedge

② **il graticcio**
trellis

⑮ **l'erba** *f*
grass

⑯ **il prato**
lawn

⑰ **il vialetto**
path

⑱ **la compostiera**
compost heap

⑲ **il bulbo**
bulb

⑳ **il laghetto**
pond

㉑ **il tavolato**
decking

㉖ **il giardino con patio**
patio garden

㉗ **il giardino pensile**
roof garden

㉘ **il giardino roccioso**
rock garden

㉙ **il giardino all'italiana**
formal garden

41.2 I TIPI DI PIANTE · TYPES OF PLANTS

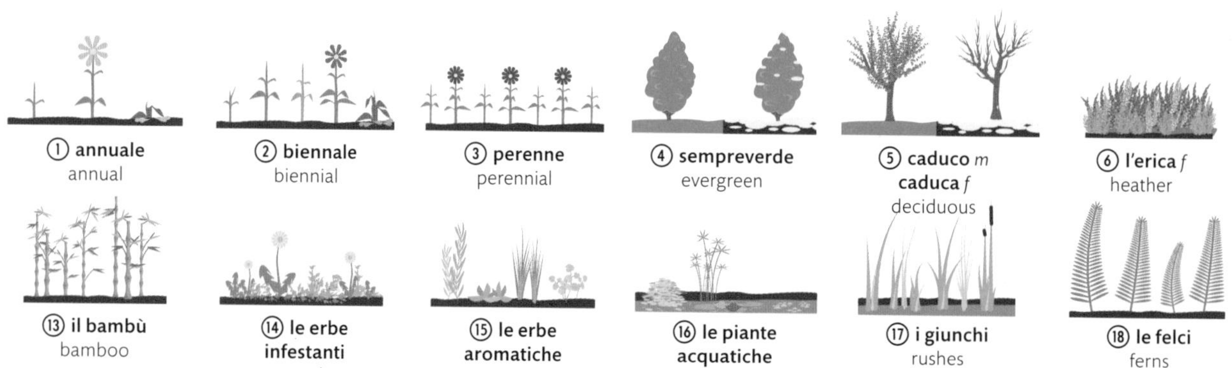
① annuale
annual
② biennale
biennial
③ perenne
perennial
④ sempreverde
evergreen
⑤ caduco m
caduca f
deciduous
⑥ l'erica f
heather
⑬ il bambù
bamboo
⑭ le erbe infestanti
weeds
⑮ le erbe aromatiche
herbs
⑯ le piante acquatiche
water plants
⑰ i giunchi
rushes
⑱ le felci
ferns

See also
38 Le piante da giardino e le piante da appartamento • Garden plants and houseplants **39** Il giardinaggio • Practical gardening **40** Gli attrezzi da giardinaggio • Garden tools **167-169** Le piante e gli alberi • Plants and trees

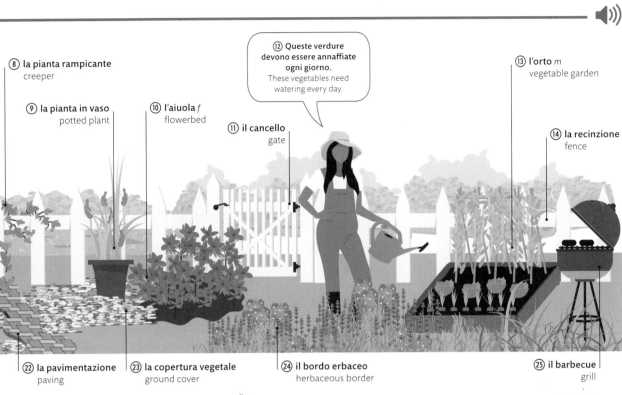

⑧ **la pianta rampicante**
creeper

⑨ **la pianta in vaso**
potted plant

⑩ **l'aiuola** *f*
flowerbed

⑪ **il cancello**
gate

⑫ **Queste verdure devono essere annaffiate ogni giorno.**
These vegetables need watering every day.

⑬ **l'orto** *m*
vegetable garden

⑭ **la recinzione**
fence

㉒ **la pavimentazione**
paving

㉓ **la copertura vegetale**
ground cover

㉔ **il bordo erbaceo**
herbaceous border

㉕ **il barbecue**
grill

㉚ **il giardino di erbe aromatiche**
herb garden

㉛ **il giardino d'acqua**
water garden

㉜ **il giardino all'inglese**
cottage garden

㉝ **il cortile**
courtyard

⑦ **le palme**
palms

⑧ **le conifere**
conifers

⑨ **l'arte topiaria** *f*
topiary

⑩ **la pianta rampicante**
climber

⑪ **le piante ornamentali**
ornamental plants

⑫ **le piante ombreggianti**
shade plants

⑲ **le piante alpine**
alpine plants

⑳ **le piante grasse**
succulents

㉑ **i cactus**
cacti

㉒ **gli arbusti**
shrubs

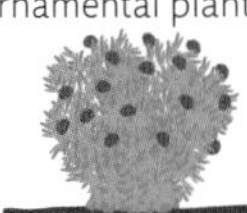
㉓ **gli arbusti da fiore**
flowering shrub

㉔ **le piante erbacee**
grasses

42 In città
In town

42.1 GLI EDIFICI E LE ALTRE CARATTERISTICHE
BUILDINGS AND OTHER FEATURES

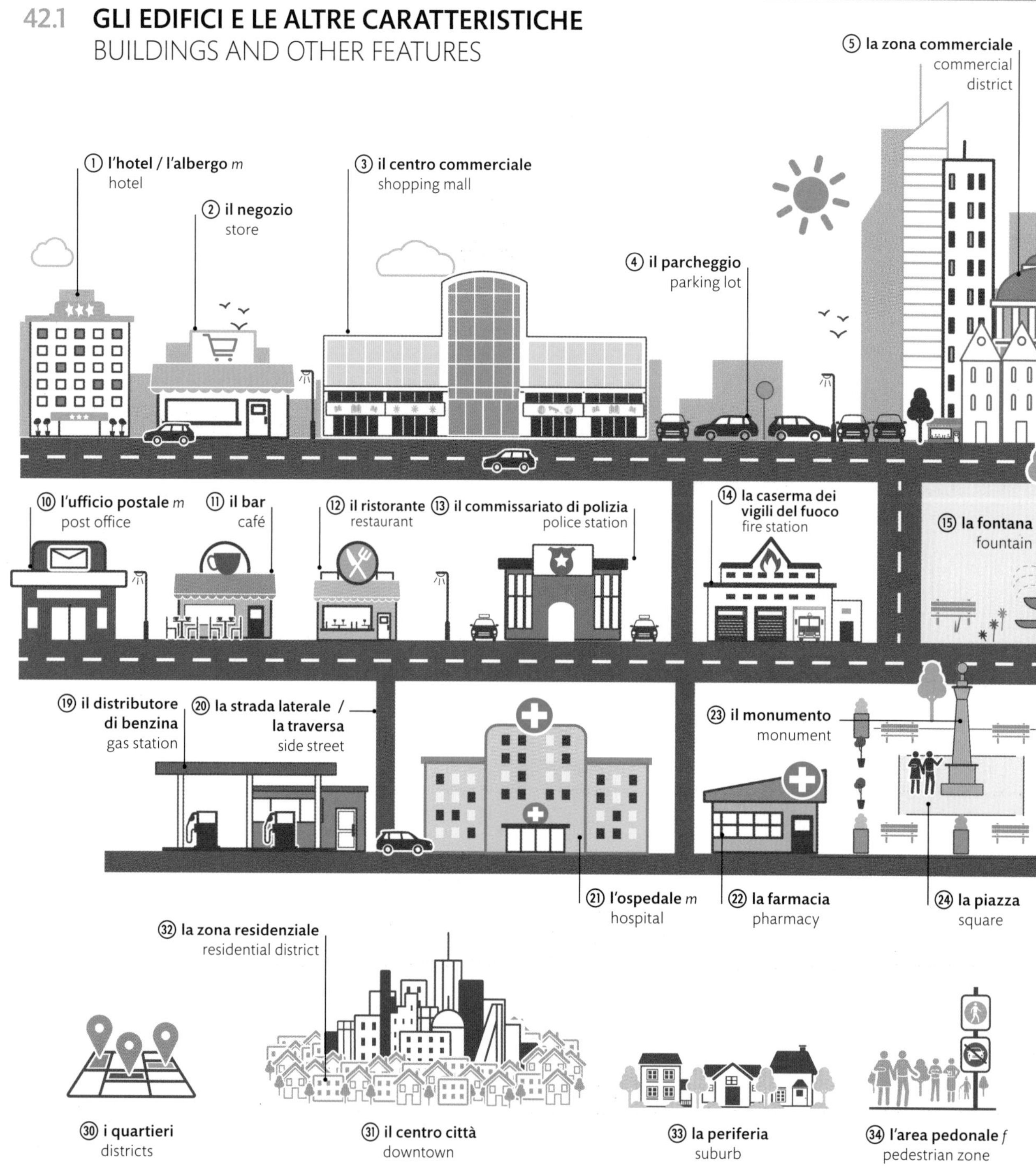

① l'hotel / l'albergo *m*
hotel
② il negozio
store
③ il centro commerciale
shopping mall
④ il parcheggio
parking lot
⑤ la zona commerciale
commercial district
⑩ l'ufficio postale *m*
post office
⑪ il bar
café
⑫ il ristorante
restaurant
⑬ il commissariato di polizia
police station
⑭ la caserma dei vigili del fuoco
fire station
⑮ la fontana
fountain
⑲ il distributore di benzina
gas station
⑳ la strada laterale / la traversa
side street
㉑ l'ospedale *m*
hospital
㉒ la farmacia
pharmacy
㉓ il monumento
monument
㉔ la piazza
square
㉜ la zona residenziale
residential district
㉚ i quartieri
districts
㉛ il centro città
downtown
㉝ la periferia
suburb
㉞ l'area pedonale *f*
pedestrian zone

See also
25 Un luogo in cui vivere • A place to live 43 In città (continua) • In town continued 44 Gli edifici e l'architettura • Buildings and architecture 46 Lo shopping • Shopping 47 Il centro commerciale The shopping mall 102 I treni • Trains 104 In aeroporto • At the airport 106 Il porto • The port

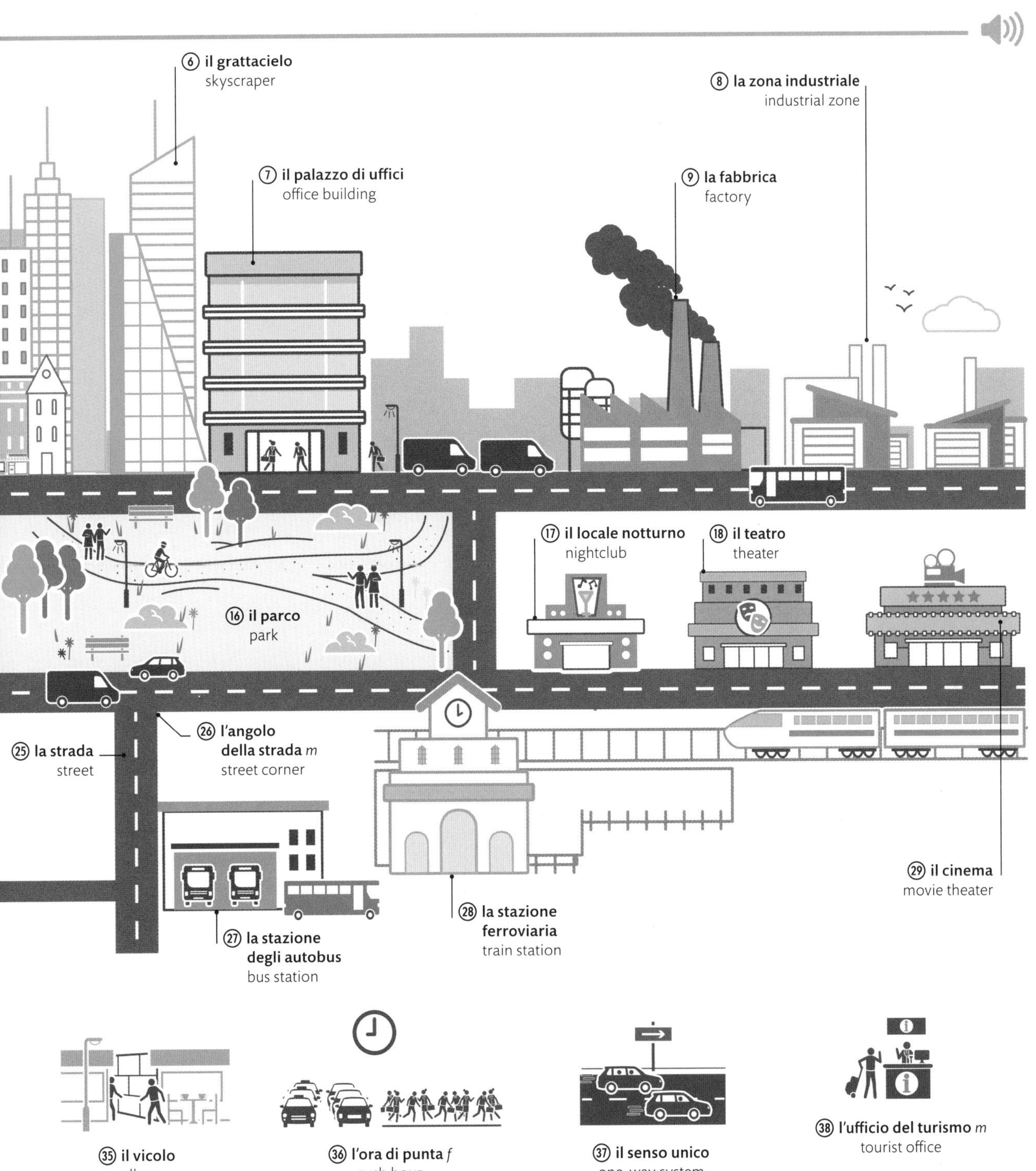
⑥ il grattacielo
skyscraper
⑦ il palazzo di uffici
office building
⑧ la zona industriale
industrial zone
⑨ la fabbrica
factory
⑯ il parco
park
⑰ il locale notturno
nightclub
⑱ il teatro
theater
㉕ la strada
street
㉖ l'angolo della strada m
street corner
㉗ la stazione degli autobus
bus station
㉘ la stazione ferroviaria
train station
㉙ il cinema
movie theater

㉟ il vicolo
alley

㊱ l'ora di punta *f*
rush hour

㊲ il senso unico
one-way system

㊳ l'ufficio del turismo *m*
tourist office

43 In città (continua)

In town continued

43.1 GLI EDIFICI E LE ALTRE CARATTERISTICHE · BUILDINGS AND OTHER FEATURES

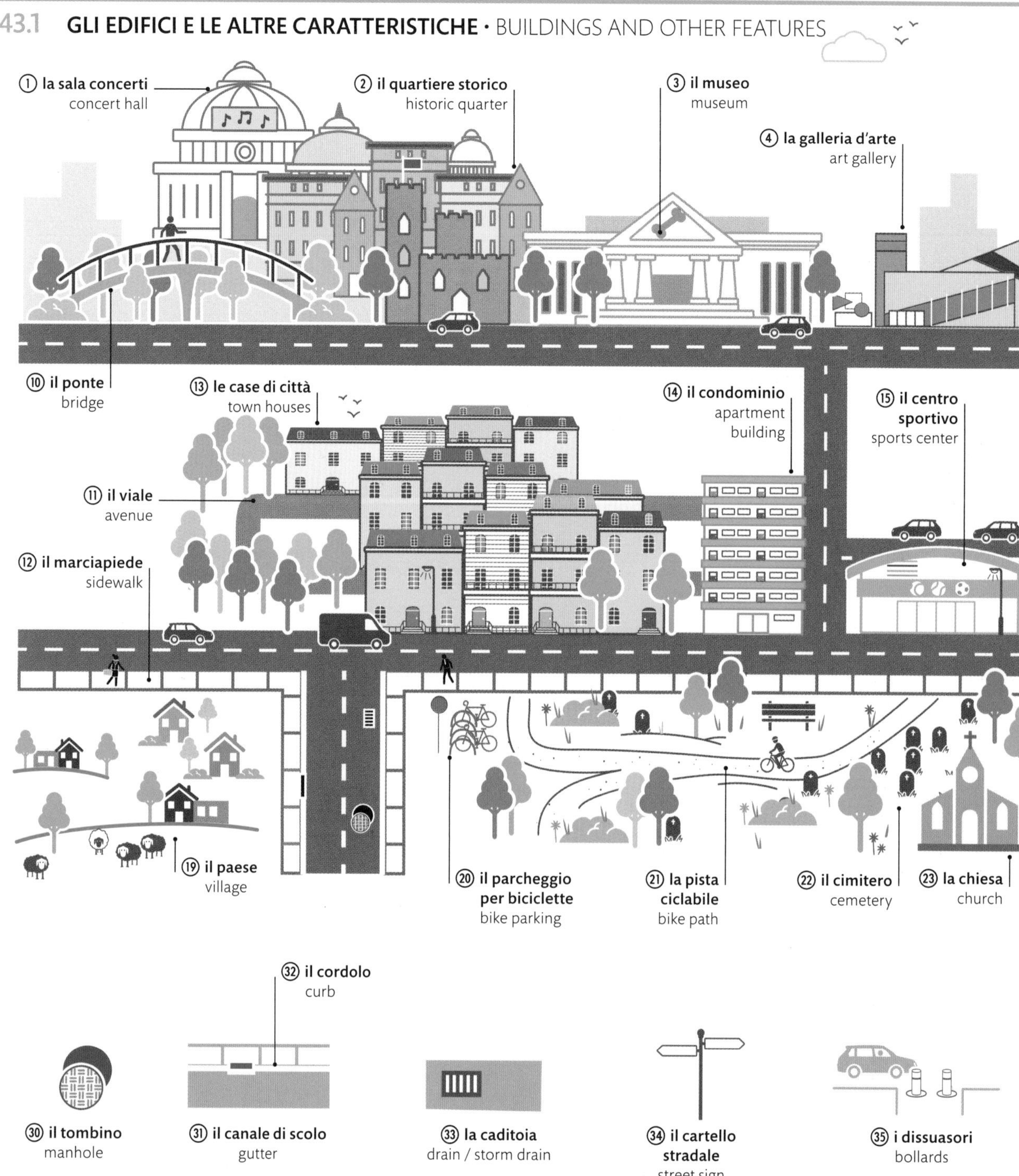

① la sala concerti
concert hall
② il quartiere storico
historic quarter
③ il museo
museum
④ la galleria d'arte
art gallery
⑩ il ponte
bridge
⑬ le case di città
town houses
⑭ il condominio
apartment building
⑮ il centro sportivo
sports center
⑪ il viale
avenue
⑫ il marciapiede
sidewalk
⑲ il paese
village
⑳ il parcheggio per biciclette
bike parking
㉑ la pista ciclabile
bike path
㉒ il cimitero
cemetery
㉓ la chiesa
church
㉜ il cordolo
curb
㉚ il tombino
manhole
㉛ il canale di scolo
gutter
㉝ la caditoia
drain / storm drain
㉞ il cartello stradale
street sign
㉟ i dissuasori
bollards

See also
25 Un luogo in cui vivere • A place to live **44** Gli edifici e l'architettura • Buildings and architecture **46** Lo shopping • Shopping **47** Il centro commerciale • The shopping mall **102** I treni • Trains **104** In aeroporto • At the airport **106** Il porto • The port

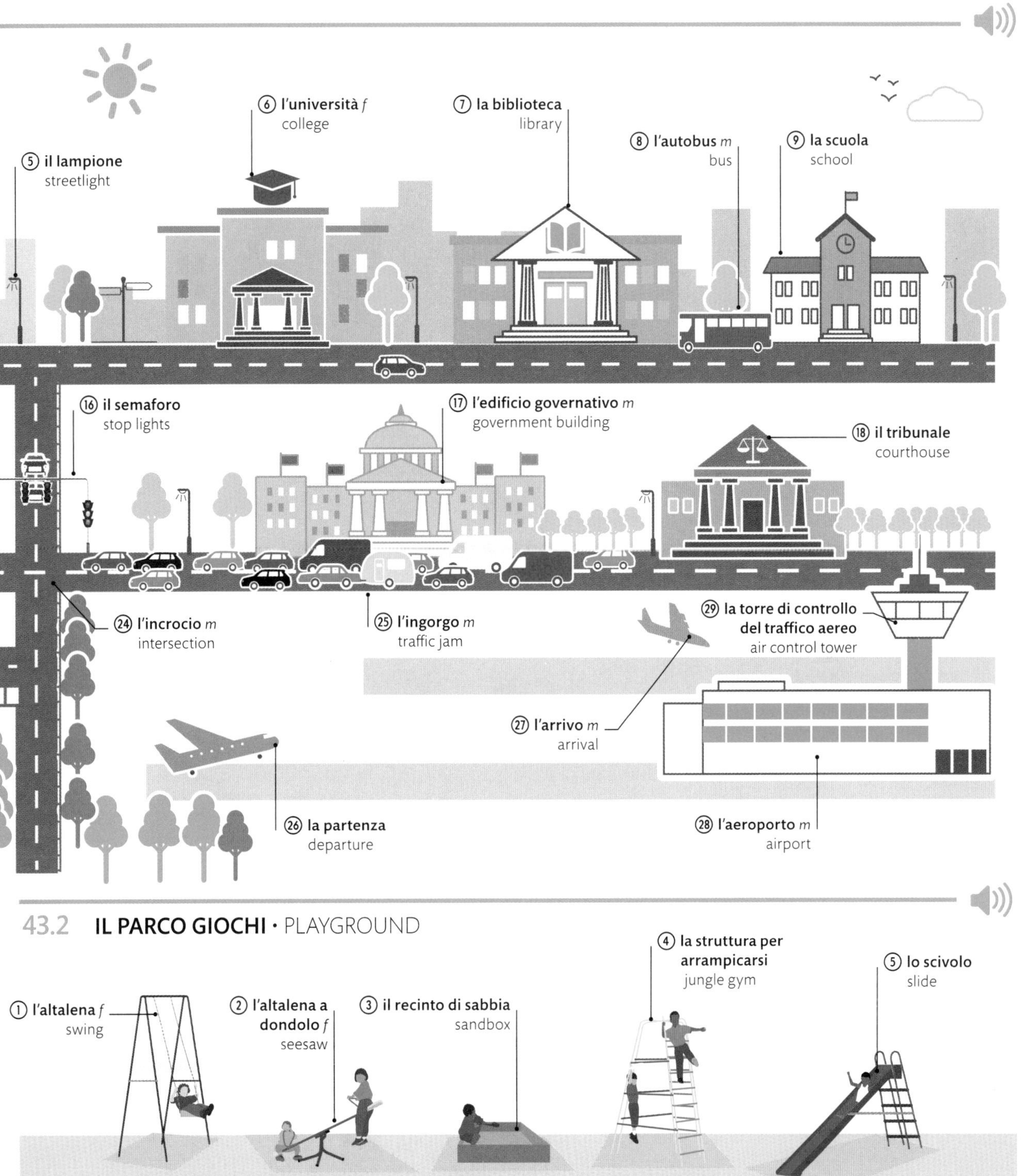
⑤ il lampione
streetlight
⑥ l'università f
college
⑦ la biblioteca
library
⑧ l'autobus m
bus
⑨ la scuola
school
⑯ il semaforo
stop lights
⑰ l'edificio governativo m
government building
⑱ il tribunale
courthouse
㉔ l'incrocio m
intersection
㉕ l'ingorgo m
traffic jam
㉙ la torre di controllo del traffico aereo
air control tower
㉗ l'arrivo m
arrival
㉖ la partenza
departure
㉘ l'aeroporto m
airport

43.2 IL PARCO GIOCHI • PLAYGROUND

① l'altalena f
swing
② l'altalena a dondolo f
seesaw
③ il recinto di sabbia
sandbox
④ la struttura per arrampicarsi
jungle gym
⑤ lo scivolo
slide

44 Gli edifici e l'architettura
Buildings and architecture

44.1 I TIPI DI EDIFICI · TYPES OF BUILDINGS

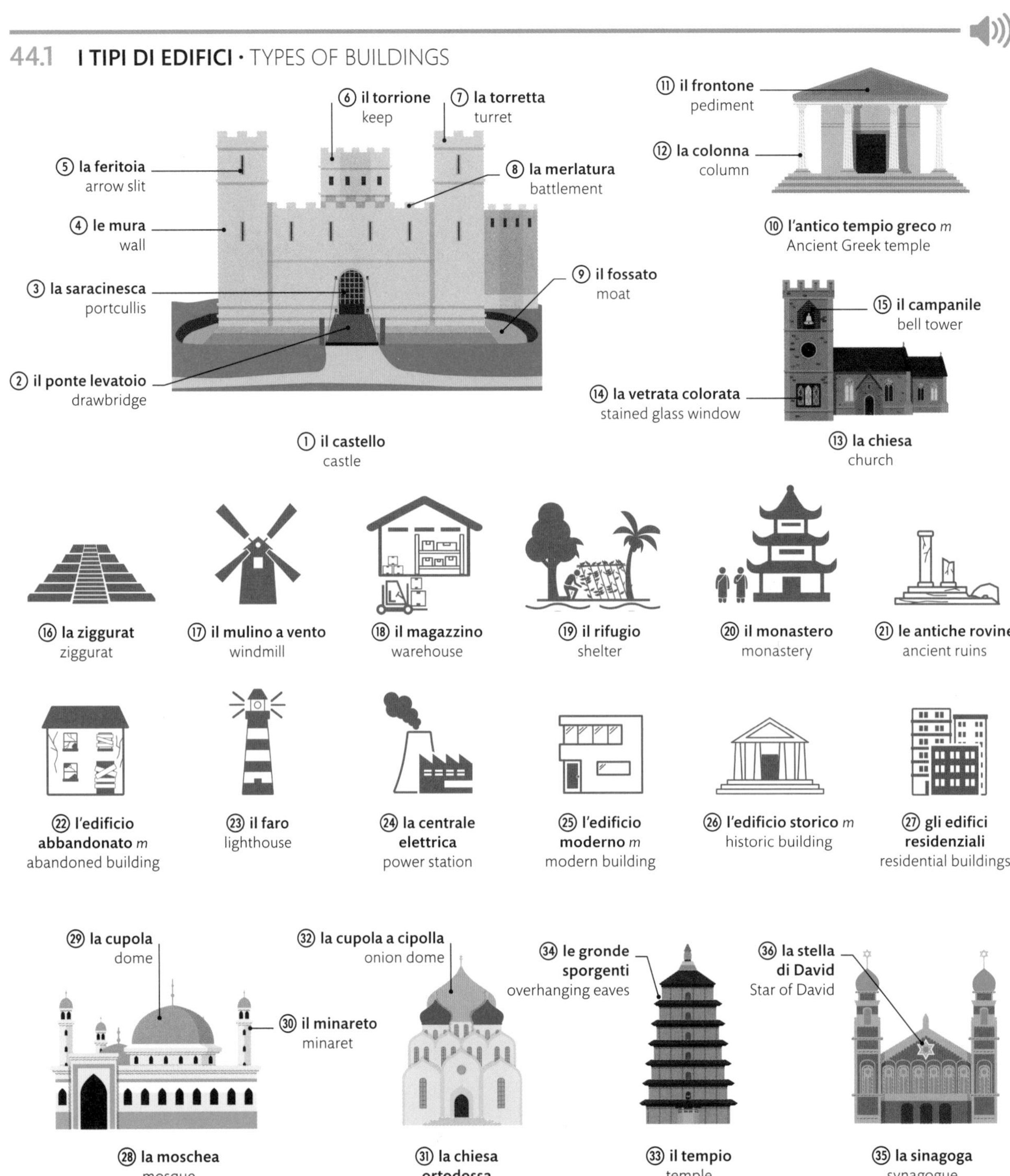

⑥ il torrione
keep
⑦ la torretta
turret
⑤ la feritoia
arrow slit
⑧ la merlatura
battlement
④ le mura
wall
③ la saracinesca
portcullis
⑨ il fossato
moat
② il ponte levatoio
drawbridge
① il castello
castle
⑪ il frontone
pediment
⑫ la colonna
column
⑩ l'antico tempio greco m
Ancient Greek temple
⑮ il campanile
bell tower
⑭ la vetrata colorata
stained glass window
⑬ la chiesa
church
⑯ la ziggurat
ziggurat
⑰ il mulino a vento
windmill
⑱ il magazzino
warehouse
⑲ il rifugio
shelter
⑳ il monastero
monastery
㉑ le antiche rovine
ancient ruins
㉒ l'edificio abbandonato m
abandoned building
㉓ il faro
lighthouse
㉔ la centrale elettrica
power station
㉕ l'edificio moderno m
modern building
㉖ l'edificio storico m
historic building
㉗ gli edifici residenziali
residential buildings
㉙ la cupola
dome
㉚ il minareto
minaret
㉘ la moschea
mosque
㉜ la cupola a cipolla
onion dome
㉛ la chiesa ortodossa
Orthodox church
㉞ le gronde sporgenti
overhanging eaves
㉝ il tempio
temple
㊱ la stella di David
Star of David
㉟ la sinagoga
synagogue

See also
25 Un luogo in cui vivere • A place to live **32** La casa • House and home **42-43** In città • In town **132** Fare un giro turistico • Sightseeing

44.2 I MONUMENTI E GLI EDIFICI FAMOSI • FAMOUS BUILDINGS AND MONUMENTS

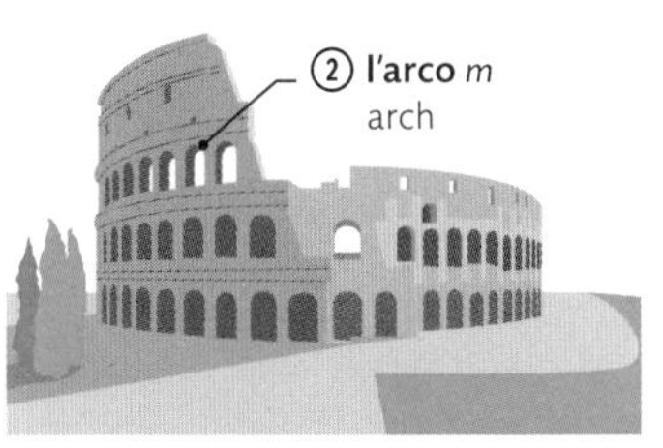
② **l'arco** *m*
arch

① **il Colosseo**
the Colosseum

③ **le piramidi di Giza**
the pyramids of Giza

⑤ **il muro della qibla**
qibla prayer wall
⑥ **la torre**
tower

④ **la Grande Moschea di Djenné**
the Great Mosque of Djenné

⑦ **la Casa Bianca**
the White House

⑧ **il Taj Mahal**
the Taj Mahal

⑨ **la Città Proibita**
the Forbidden City

⑩ **la cattedrale di San Basilio**
St. Basil's cathedral

⑪ **il Teatro dell'Opera di Sydney**
Sydney Opera House

⑭ **l'orologio** *m*
clock

⑰ **la piattaforma di osservazione**
viewing platform

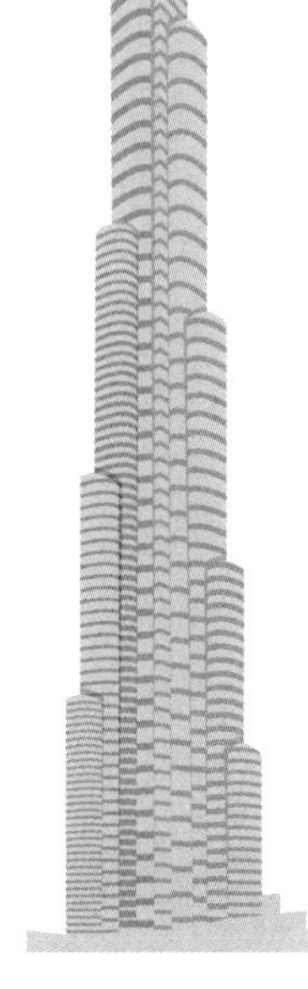

⑫ **il castello di Himeji**
Himeji Castle

⑬ **il Big Ben**
Big Ben

⑮ **la torre pendente di Pisa**
the Leaning Tower of Pisa

⑯ **la Torre Eiffel**
the Eiffel Tower

⑱ **l'Empire State Building** *m*
the Empire State Building

⑲ **il Burj Khalifa**
Burj Khalifa

45 La banca e l'ufficio postale

The bank and post office

45.1 LA BANCA · BANK

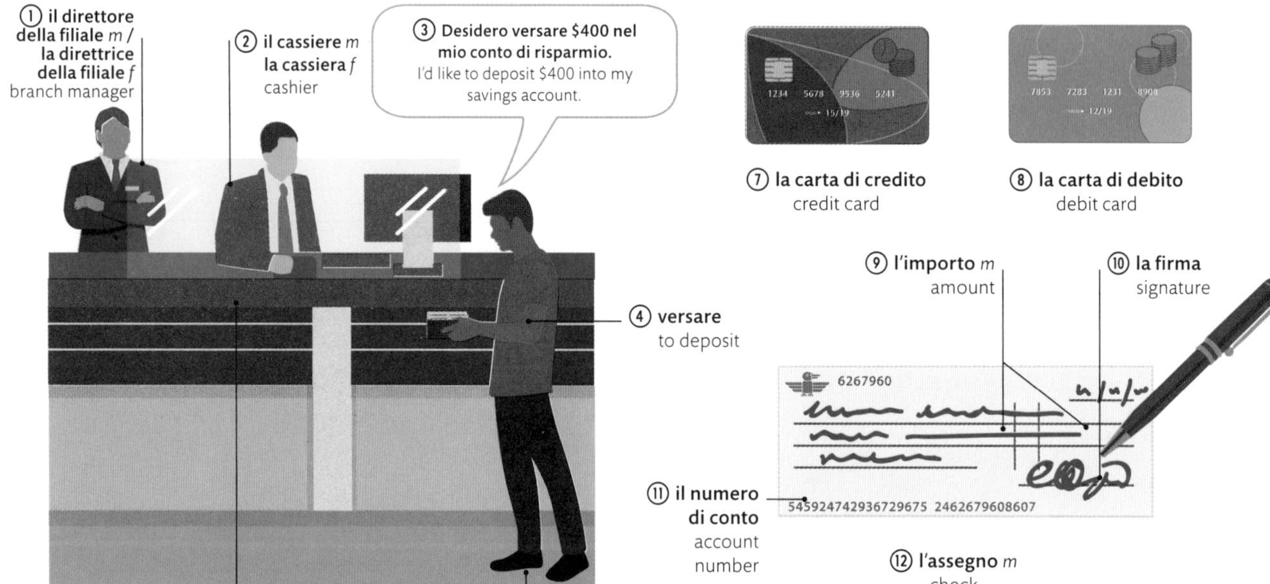

6267960
545924742936729675 2462679608607

① **il direttore della filiale** *m* / **la direttrice della filiale** *f*
branch manager

② **il cassiere** *m* **la cassiera** *f*
cashier

③ **Desidero versare $400 nel mio conto di risparmio.**
I'd like to deposit $400 into my savings account.

④ **versare**
to deposit

⑤ **lo sportello**
counter

⑥ **il cliente** *m* **la cliente** *f*
customer

⑦ **la carta di credito**
credit card

⑧ **la carta di debito**
debit card

⑨ **l'importo** *m*
amount

⑩ **la firma**
signature

⑪ **il numero di conto**
account number

⑫ **l'assegno** *m*
check

⑬ **il conto di risparmio**
savings account

⑭ **i risparmi**
savings

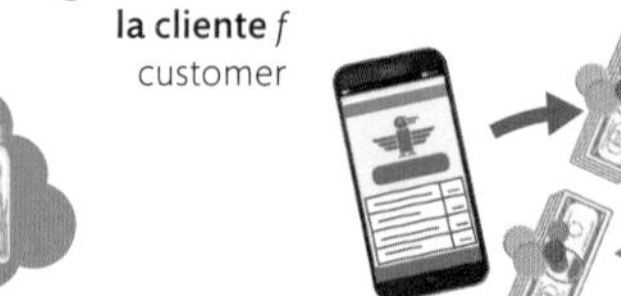

⑮ **il conto corrente**
checking account

⑯ **l'addebito diretto** *m*
direct debit

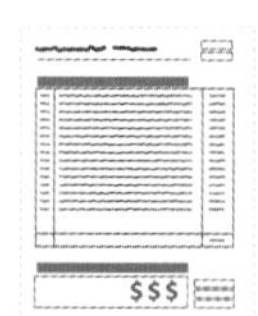

$$$

⑰ **l'estratto conto** *m*
bank statement

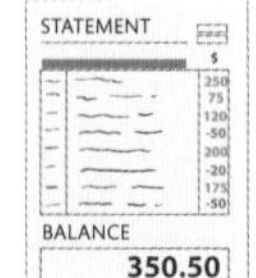

STATEMENT
BALANCE
350.50

⑱ **in attivo**
in the black / in credit

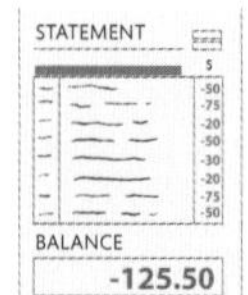

STATEMENT
BALANCE
-125.50

⑲ **in passivo / in rosso**
in the red / in debt

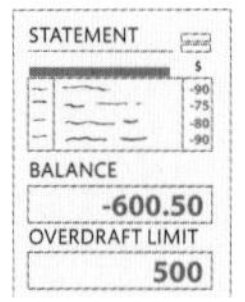

STATEMENT
BALANCE
-600.50
OVERDRAFT LIMIT
500

⑳ **lo scoperto**
overdraft

㉑ **i servizi bancari online**
online banking

㉒ **il tasso d'interesse**
interest rate

㉓ **il mutuo**
bank loan

㉔ **l'ipoteca** *f*
mortgage

㉕ **prelevare denaro**
to withdraw money

㉖ **trasferire denaro**
to transfer money

See also
94 Il denaro e la finanza • Money and finance
131 Il viaggio e l'alloggio • Travel and accommodation

45.2 IL DENARO • MONEY

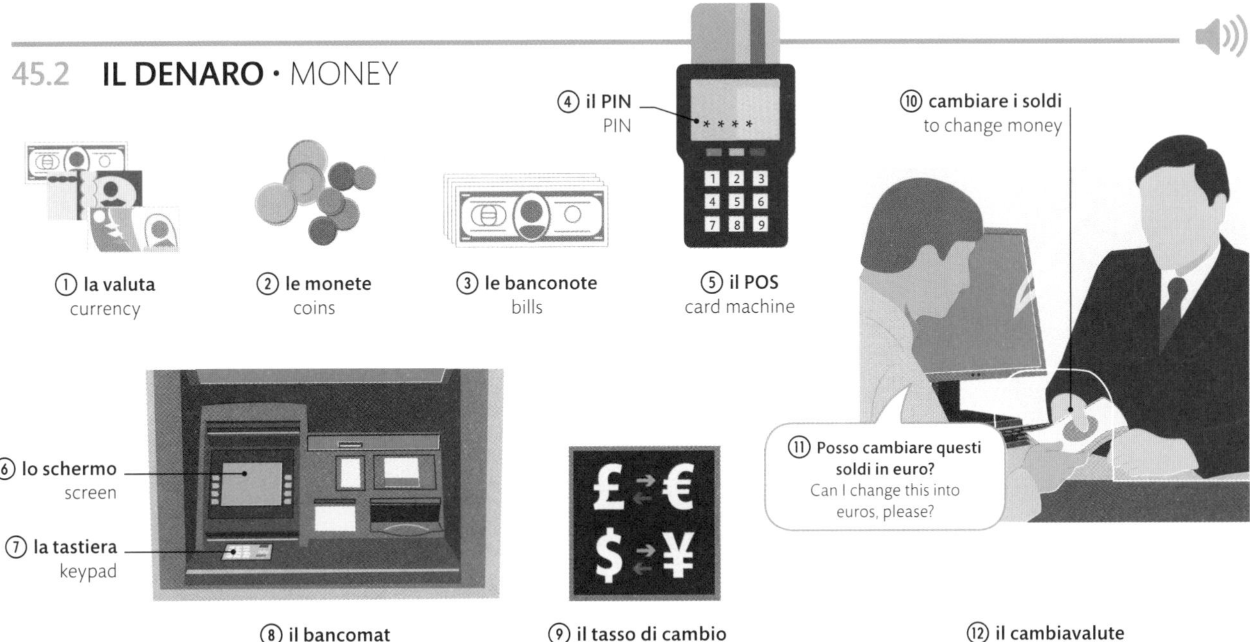

① **la valuta**
currency

② **le monete**
coins

③ **le banconote**
bills

④ **il PIN**
PIN

⑤ **il POS**
card machine

⑥ **lo schermo**
screen

⑦ **la tastiera**
keypad

⑧ **il bancomat**
cash machine / ATM

⑨ **il tasso di cambio**
exchange rate

⑩ **cambiare i soldi**
to change money

⑪ **Posso cambiare questi soldi in euro?**
Can I change this into euros, please?

⑫ **il cambiavalute**
currency exchange

45.3 L'UFFICIO POSTALE • POST OFFICE

① **l'impiegato delle poste** *m*
l'impiegata delle poste *f*
postal worker

② **la bilancia**
scale

③ **la lettera**
letter

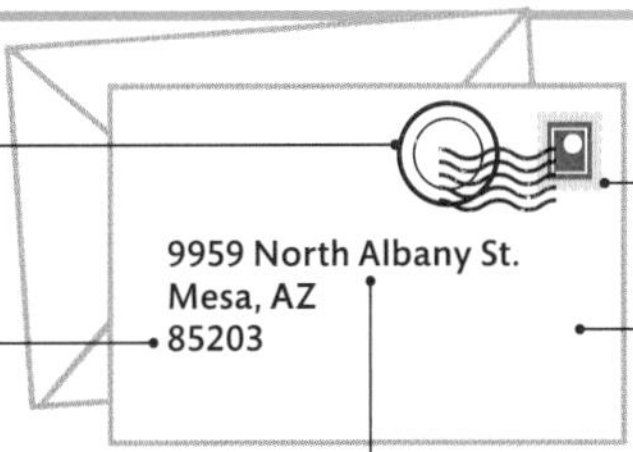

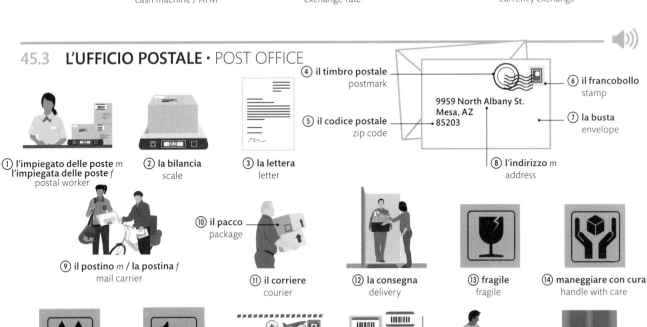

④ **il timbro postale**
postmark

⑤ **il codice postale**
zip code

9959 North Albany St.
Mesa, AZ
85203

⑥ **il francobollo**
stamp

⑦ **la busta**
envelope

⑧ **l'indirizzo** *m*
address

⑨ **il postino** *m* / **la postina** *f*
mail carrier

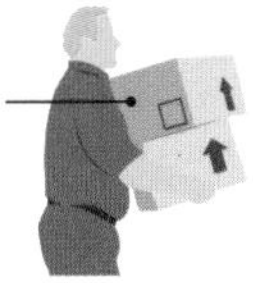

⑩ **il pacco**
package

⑪ **il corriere**
courier

⑫ **la consegna**
delivery

⑬ **fragile**
fragile

⑭ **maneggiare con cura**
handle with care

⑮ **alto**
this way up

⑯ **non piegare**
do not bend

⑰ **la posta aerea**
airmail

⑱ **la raccomandata**
registered mail

⑲ **la cassetta delle lettere**
mailbox

⑳ **la buca delle lettere**
mail slot

46 Lo shopping
Shopping

46.1 NELLA VIA PRINCIPALE · ON THE HIGH STREET

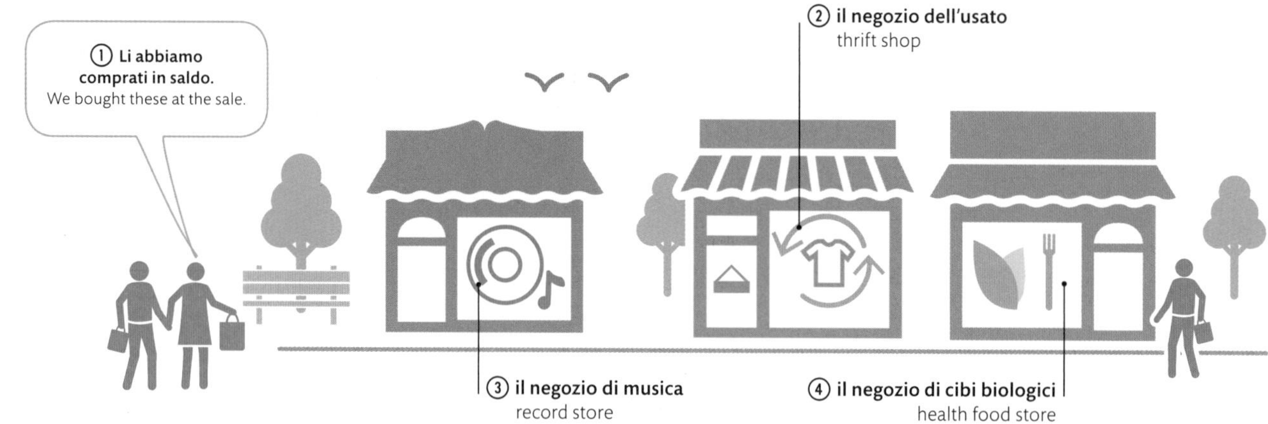

① **Li abbiamo comprati in saldo.**
We bought these at the sale.
② **il negozio dell'usato**
thrift shop
③ **il negozio di musica**
record store
④ **il negozio di cibi biologici**
health food store

⑤ **il negozio di articoli da regalo**
gift shop

⑥ **la boutique**
boutique

⑦ **la gioielleria**
jeweler

⑧ **il negozio d'arte**
art store

⑨ **il negozio di antiquariato**
antiques store

⑩ **il negozio di giocattoli**
toy store

⑪ **l'ottico** *m*
optician

⑫ **la ferramenta**
hardware store

⑬ **il negozio specializzato in chiavi**
key cutting shop

⑭ **il negozio di elettronica**
electronics store

⑮ **il negozio di animali**
pet store

⑯ **l'agenzia di viaggi** *f*
travel agent

⑰ **il mercato**
street market

⑱ **la pescheria**
fishmonger

⑲ **il macellaio**
butcher

⑳ **il panificio**
bakery

㉑ **il fruttivendolo**
grocery store

㉒ **la gastronomia**
delicatessen

㉓ **la pasticceria**
bakery

㉔ **il bar**
café / coffee shop

㉕ **il negozio di alcolici**
liquor store

㉖ **l'edicola** *f*
il chiosco
newsstand / kiosk

㉗ **la libreria**
bookstore

㉘ **il negozio di scarpe**
shoe store

See also
42-43 In città • In town **47** Il centro commerciale
The shopping mall **48** Il supermercato • The supermarket

㉙ **il vivaio**
garden center

㉚ **il fiorista** *m*
la fiorista *f*
florist

㉛ **il sarto**
la sarta
tailor

㉜ **la cabina per fototessere**
photo booth

㉝ **la lavanderia self-service**
Laundromat

㉞ **la lavanderia a secco**
dry cleaner's

㉟ **le spese folli**
shopping spree

㊱ **guardare le vetrine**
window shopping

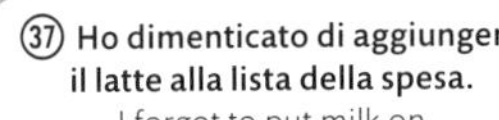

㊲ **Ho dimenticato di aggiungere il latte alla lista della spesa.**
I forgot to put milk on my shopping list.

㊳ **la lista della spesa**
shopping list

46.2 I VERBI DELLO SHOPPING • SHOPPING VERBS

① **scegliere**
to choose

② **vendere**
to sell

③ **comprare**
to buy

④ **volere**
to want

⑤ **andare bene**
to fit

⑥ **pagare**
to pay

⑦ **provare**
to try on

⑧ **contrattare**
to haggle

⑨ **reclamare**
to complain

⑩ **sostituire**
to exchange

⑪ **rimborsare**
to refund

⑫ **restituire**
to return

46.3 ORDINARE ONLINE • ORDERING ONLINE

① **aggiungere al carrello**
to add to the cart

② **aggiungere alla lista dei desideri**
to add to wishlist

③ **procedere al pagamento**
to proceed to checkout

④ **ordinare**
to order

⑤ **tracciare l'ordine**
to track your order

47 Il centro commerciale
The shopping mall

47.1 IL CENTRO COMMERCIALE · SHOPPING MALL

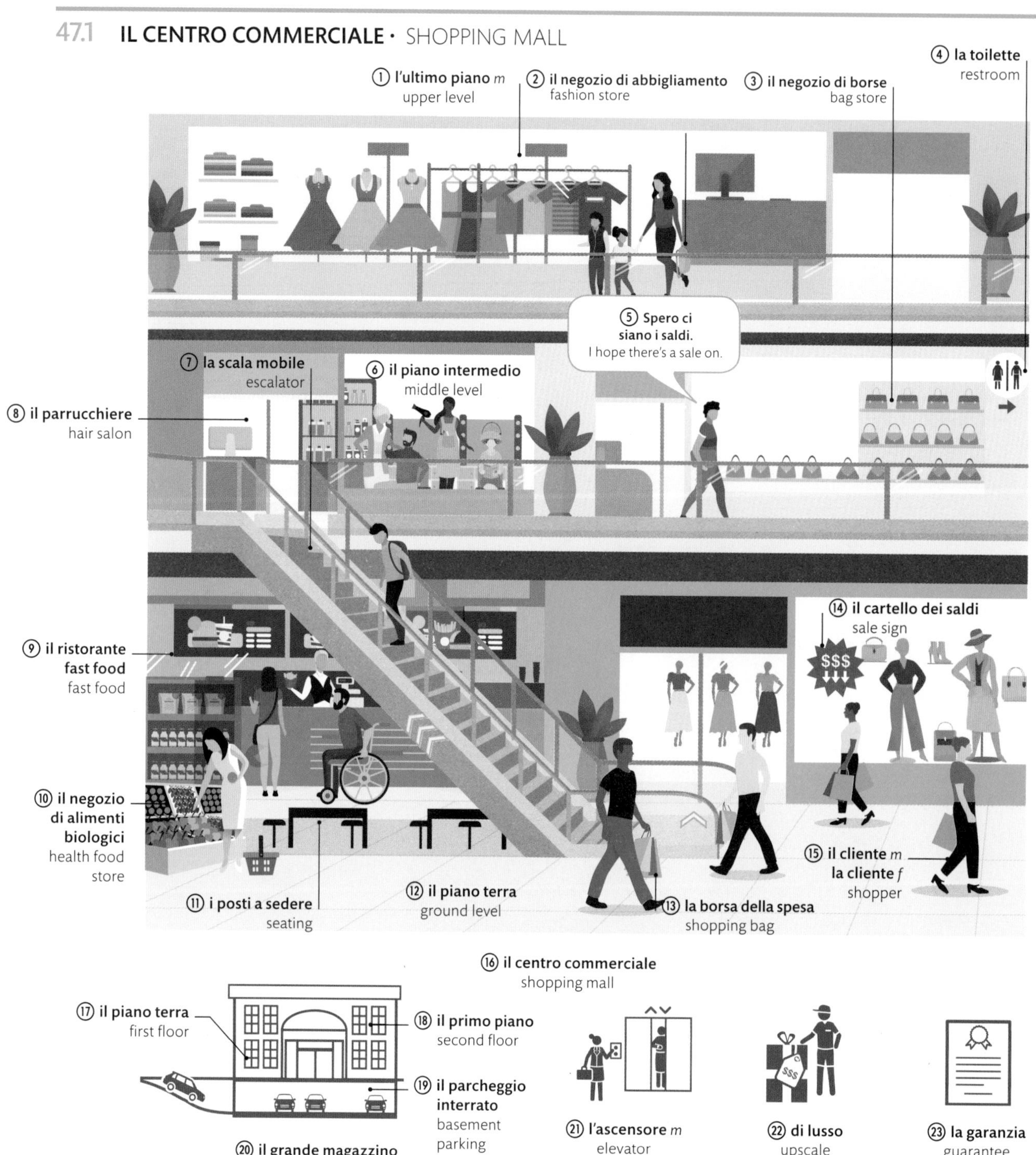

① l'ultimo piano *m*
upper level
② il negozio di abbigliamento
fashion store
③ il negozio di borse
bag store
④ la toilette
restroom
⑤ Spero ci siano i saldi.
I hope there's a sale on.
⑥ il piano intermedio
middle level
⑦ la scala mobile
escalator
⑧ il parrucchiere
hair salon
⑨ il ristorante fast food
fast food
⑩ il negozio di alimenti biologici
health food store
⑪ i posti a sedere
seating
⑫ il piano terra
ground level
⑬ la borsa della spesa
shopping bag
⑭ il cartello dei saldi
sale sign
$$$
⑮ il cliente *m*
la cliente *f*
shopper
⑯ il centro commerciale
shopping mall
⑰ il piano terra
first floor
⑱ il primo piano
second floor
⑲ il parcheggio interrato
basement parking
⑳ il grande magazzino
department store
㉑ l'ascensore *m*
elevator
$$$
㉒ di lusso
upscale
㉓ la garanzia
guarantee

See also
13-15 Gli indumenti • Clothes **16** Gli accessori • Accessories **17** Le scarpe • Shoes
18 La bellezza • Beauty **42-43** In città • In town **46** Lo shopping • Shopping mall

24 i camerini
changing rooms

25 l'abbigliamento da donna *m*
womenswear

26 l'abbigliamento da uomo *m*
menswear

27 i fasciatoi
baby changing facilities

28 il reparto bambini
children's department

29 le firme
designer labels

30 i saldi
sale

31 la lingerie
lingerie

32 l'arredamento *m*
home furnishings

33 il cartellino del prezzo
price tag

34 l'illuminazione *m*
lighting

35 gli elettrodomestici
electrical appliances

36 la carta fedeltà
loyalty card

37 il fai da te
DIY (do it yourself)

38 la bellezza
beauty

39 il servizio clienti
customer service

40 la profumeria
cosmetics

41 l'area ristorazione *f*
food court

47.2 IL CHIOSCO DEI FIORI • FLOWER STALL

1 il chiosco
stall / kiosk

2 il fiorista *m*
la fiorista *f*
florist

3 la ghirlanda
garland

4 il mazzo
bunch

5 il gladiolo
gladiolus

6 la pianta in vaso
pot plant

7 il fogliame
foliage

8 la gerbera
gerbera

9 la peonia
peony

10 la gipsofila
gypsophila

11 il bouquet
bouquet

12 l'acacia *f*
acacia

13 l'orchidea *f*
orchid

14 la violacciocca
stocks

15 la fresia
freesia

48 Il supermercato
The supermarket

48.1 IL SUPERMERCATO · SUPERMARKET

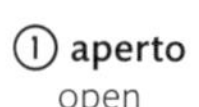

① **aperto**
open

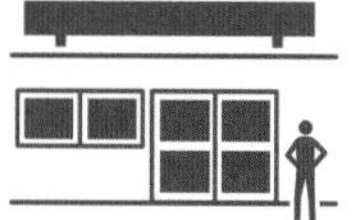

② **chiuso**
closed

③ **il cliente** *m*
la cliente *f*
customer

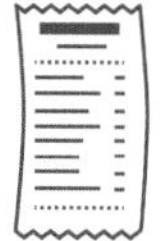

④ **lo scontrino**
receipt

⑤ **l'offerta speciale** *f*
special offer

$$
$$$

⑥ **l'affare** *m*
bargain

⑦ **la grande varietà**
wide range

⑧ **la fila**
line

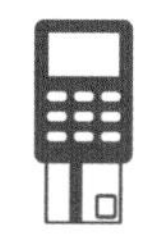

⑨ **il POS**
card machine

⑩ **lo shopping online**
online shopping

⑪ **il fattorino**
delivery man

⑫ **la consegna a domicilio**
home delivery

48.2 LA CASSA · CHECKOUT

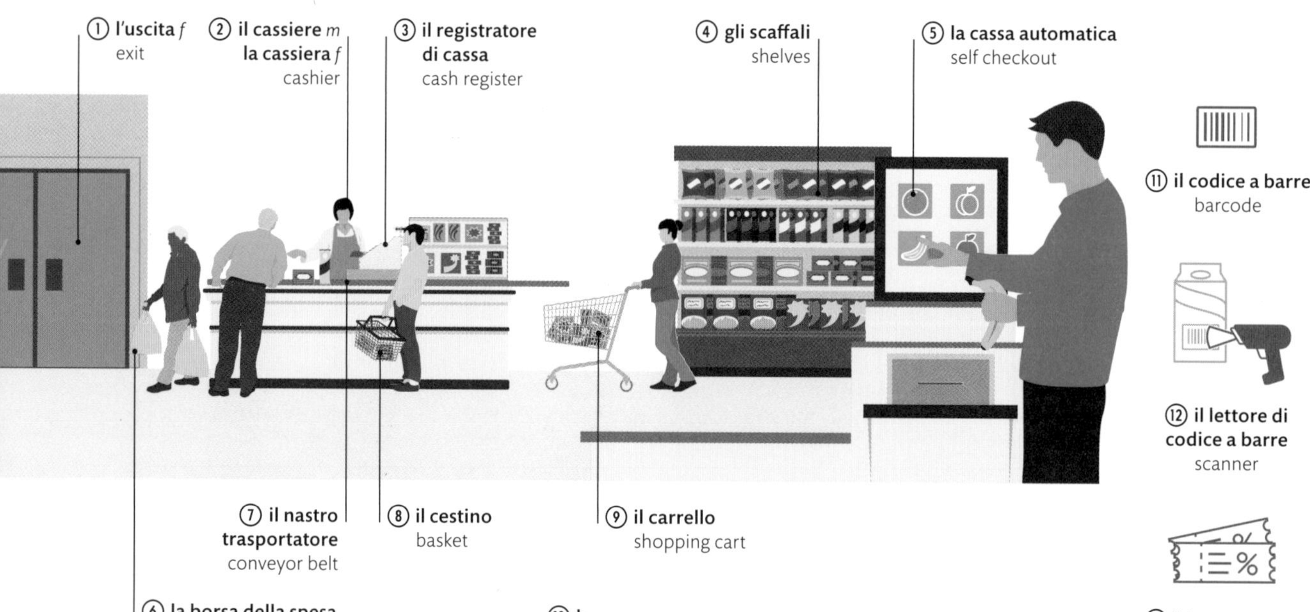

① **l'uscita** *f*
exit

② **il cassiere** *m*
la cassiera *f*
cashier

③ **il registratore di cassa**
cash register

④ **gli scaffali**
shelves

⑤ **la cassa automatica**
self checkout

⑥ **la borsa della spesa**
shopping bag

⑦ **il nastro trasportatore**
conveyor belt

⑧ **il cestino**
basket

⑨ **il carrello**
shopping cart

⑩ **la cassa**
checkout

⑪ **il codice a barre**
barcode

⑫ **il lettore di codice a barre**
scanner

⑬ **il buono sconto**
coupon

See also
46 Lo shopping • Shopping **53** La carne • Meat **54** Il pesce e i frutti di mare • Fish and seafood **55-56** La verdura Vegetables **57** La frutta • Fruit **58** La frutta e la frutta a guscio • Fruit and nuts **59** Le erbe e le spezie • Herbs and spices **60** Nella dispensa • In the pantry **61** I prodotti caseari • Dairy produce **62-63** La panetteria • The bakery

48.3 LE CORSIE / I REPARTI • AISLES / SECTIONS

① **la panetteria**
bakery

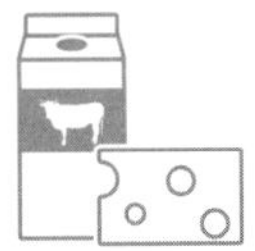
② **i latticini**
dairy

③ **i cereali per la colazione**
breakfast cereals

④ **il cibo in scatola**
canned food

⑤ **i dolciumi**
candy

⑥ **la verdura**
vegetables

⑦ **la frutta**
fruit

⑧ **la carne e il pollame**
meat and poultry

⑨ **il pesce**
fish

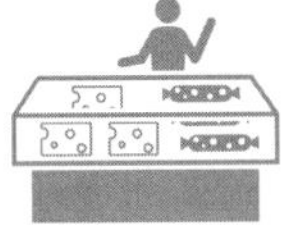
⑩ **la gastronomia**
deli

⑪ **i surgelati**
frozen food

⑫ **i cibi pronti**
convenience food

⑬ **le bevande**
drinks

⑭ **i prodotti per la casa**
household products

⑮ **gli articoli da toeletta**
toiletries

⑯ **i prodotti per bambini**
baby products

⑰ **l'elettronica** *f*
electrical goods

⑱ **il cibo per animali**
pet food

48.4 L'EDICOLA / IL CHIOSCO • NEWSSTAND / KIOSK

① **il quotidiano**
newspaper

② **la rivista**
magazine

③ **il fumetto**
comic

④ **la cartolina**
postcard

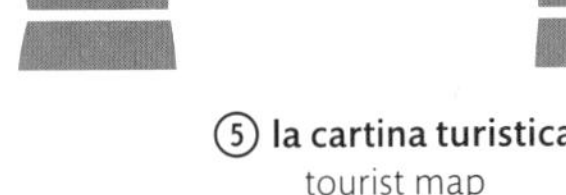
⑤ **la cartina turistica**
tourist map

1
2
⑥ **i francobolli**
stamps

⑦ **la tessera per i trasporti**
travel card

⑧ **la carta SIM**
sim card

⑨ **la barretta**
snack bar

⑩ **le patatine**
chips

⑪ **l'acqua** *f*
water

49 La farmacia

The pharmacy

49.1 LA FARMACIA · PHARMACY

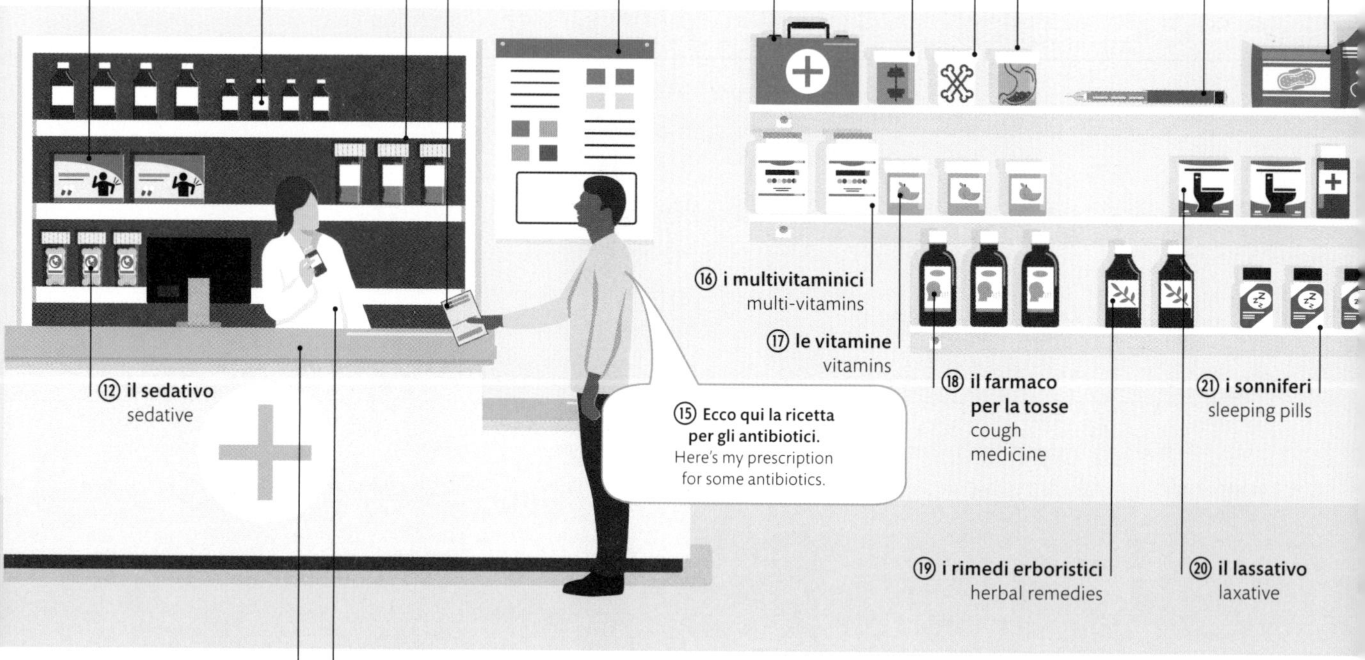

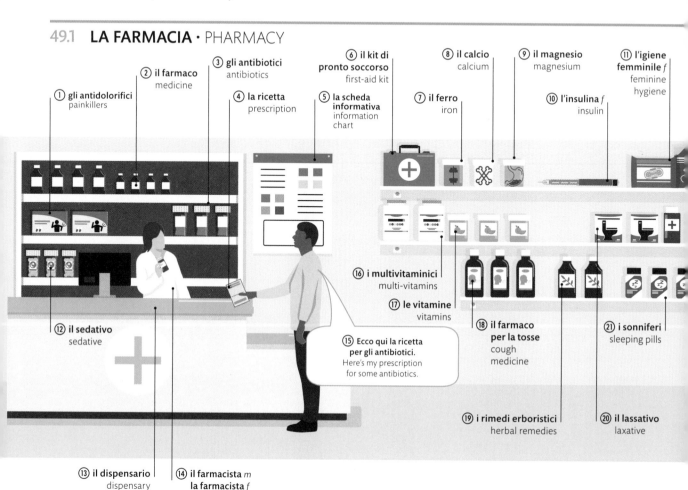

① **gli antidolorifici** painkillers

② **il farmaco** medicine

③ **gli antibiotici** antibiotics

④ **la ricetta** prescription

⑤ **la scheda informativa** information chart

⑥ **il kit di pronto soccorso** first-aid kit

⑦ **il ferro** iron

⑧ **il calcio** calcium

⑨ **il magnesio** magnesium

⑩ **l'insulina** *f* insulin

⑪ **l'igiene femminile** *f* feminine hygiene

⑫ **il sedativo** sedative

⑮ **Ecco qui la ricetta per gli antibiotici.** Here's my prescription for some antibiotics.

⑯ **i multivitaminici** multi-vitamins

⑰ **le vitamine** vitamins

⑱ **il farmaco per la tosse** cough medicine

⑲ **i rimedi erboristici** herbal remedies

⑳ **il lassativo** laxative

㉑ **i sonniferi** sleeping pills

⑬ **il dispensario** dispensary

⑭ **il farmacista** *m* **la farmacista** *f* pharmacist

㉒ **gli effetti collaterali** side effects

㉓ **il medicinale** medication

㉖ **il dosaggio** dosage

㉔ **le capsule** capsules

㉗ **l'antinfiammatorio** *m* anti-inflammatory

㉕ **le pastiglie le compresse** pills / tablets

㉘ **i farmaci da banco** over-the-counter drugs

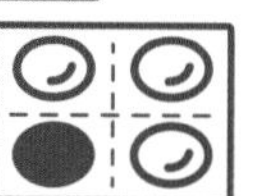

㉙ **la pastiglia per la gola** throat lozenge

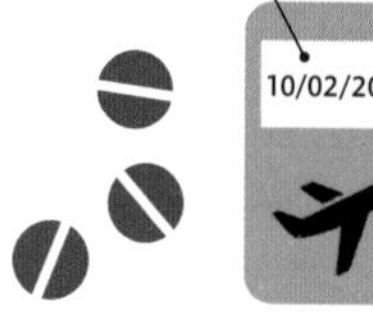
10/02/2028

㉛ **la data di scadenza** expiration date

㉚ **le pillole per il mal di viaggio** motion-sickness medication

See also
19 Le malattie e le lesioni • Illness and injury **20** Andare dal medico • Visiting the doctor **21** L'ospedale • The hospital **46** Lo shopping • Shopping

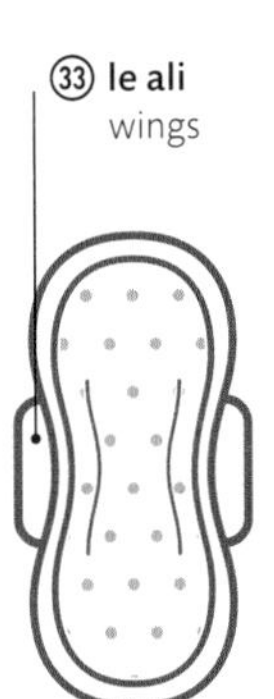

㉝ **le ali**
wings

㉜ **l'assorbente** *m*
sanitary pad

㉞ **l'assorbente interno** *m*
tampon

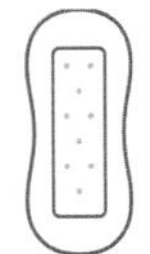

㉟ **il salvaslip**
panty liner

㊱ **i pannoloni per l'incontinenza**
incontinence pads

㊲ **la supposta**
suppository

㊳ **il deodorante**
deodorant

㊴ **i prodotti per la pelle**
skin care

㊵ **la crema solare**
sunscreen

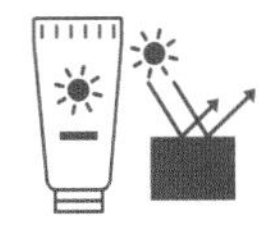

㊶ **la crema solare ad alta protezione**
sunblock

㊷ **la fasciatura**
bandage

㊸ **il cerotto**
adhesive bandage

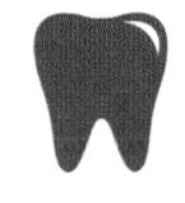

㊹ **i prodotti per l'igiene orale**
dental care

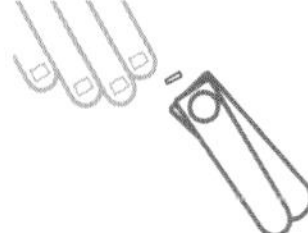

㊺ **il tagliaunghie**
nail clippers

㊻ **le salviette umidificate**
wet wipes

㊼ **il fazzoletto**
tissue

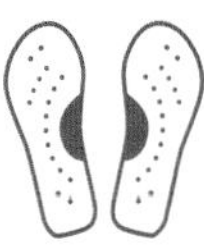

㊽ **le solette**
insoles

㊾ **gli occhiali da lettura**
reading glasses

㊿ **il repellente per gli insetti**
insect repellent

(51) **le lenti a contatto**
contact lens

(52) **la soluzione per lenti a contatto**
lens solution

(53) **la siringa**
syringe

(54) **l'inalatore** *m*
inhaler

(55) **le gocce**
drops

(56) **l'integratore** *m*
supplement

(57) **solubile**
soluble

(58) **la pomata**
ointment

(64) **il misurino**
measuring spoon

(63) **lo sciroppo**
syrup

(59) **la polvere**
powder

(60) **lo spray**
spray

(61) **il gel**
gel

(62) **la crema**
cream

50 I servizi di pronto intervento
Emergency services

50.1 IL PRONTO SOCCORSO · ACCIDENT AND EMERGENCY

① **il paramedico**
paramedic

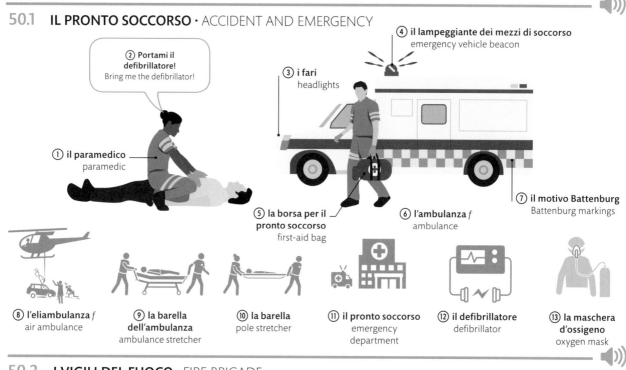

② **Portami il defibrillatore!**
Bring me the defibrillator!

③ **i fari**
headlights

④ **il lampeggiante dei mezzi di soccorso**
emergency vehicle beacon

⑤ **la borsa per il pronto soccorso**
first-aid bag

⑥ **l'ambulanza** *f*
ambulance

⑦ **il motivo Battenburg**
Battenburg markings

⑧ **l'eliambulanza** *f*
air ambulance

⑨ **la barella dell'ambulanza**
ambulance stretcher

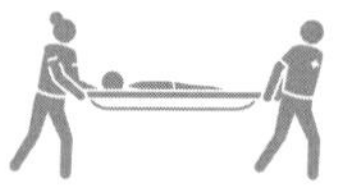

⑩ **la barella**
pole stretcher

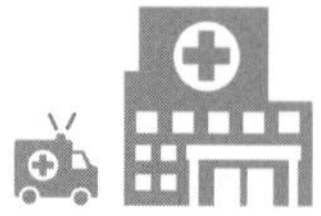

⑪ **il pronto soccorso**
emergency department

⑫ **il defibrillatore**
defibrillator

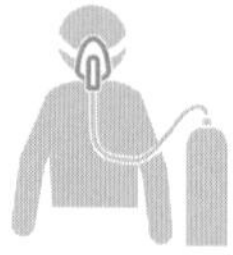

⑬ **la maschera d'ossigeno**
oxygen mask

50.2 I VIGILI DEL FUOCO · FIRE BRIGADE

① **il rilevatore di fumo**
smoke alarm

② **l'allarme antincendio** *m*
fire alarm

③ **la scala antincendio**
fire escape

④ **la caserma dei vigili del fuoco**
fire station

⑤ **la bombola d'aria compressa**
compressed-air cylinder

⑥ **l'estintore** *m*
fire extinguisher

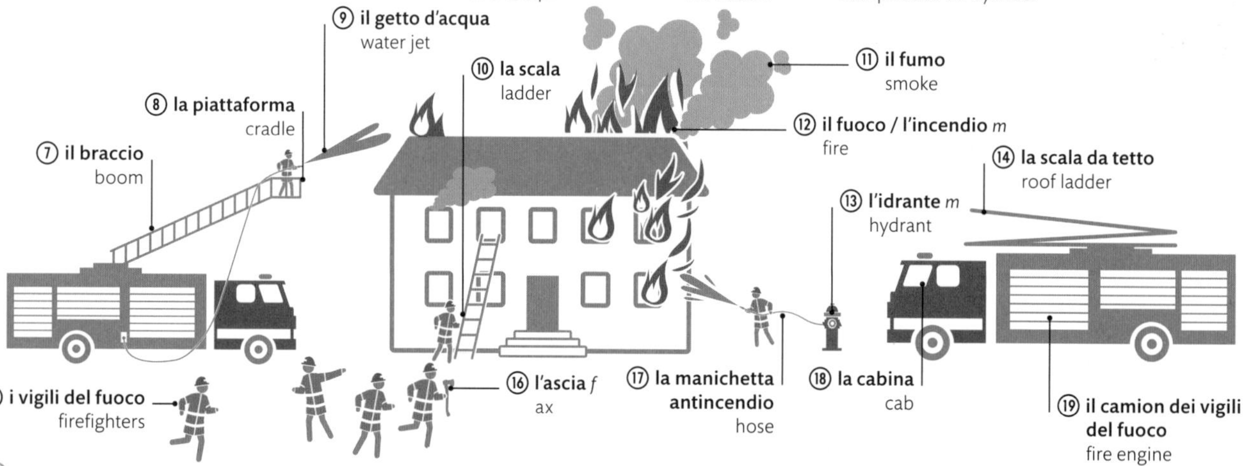

⑦ **il braccio**
boom

⑧ **la piattaforma**
cradle

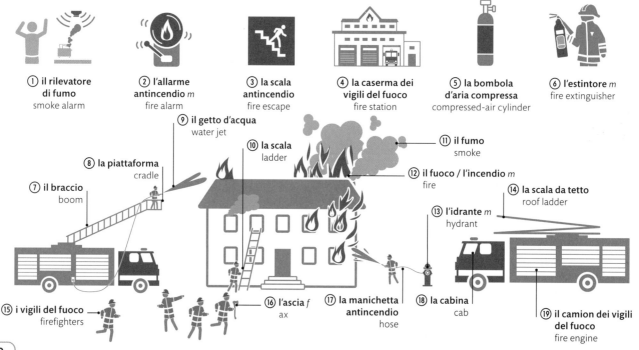

⑨ **il getto d'acqua**
water jet

⑩ **la scala**
ladder

⑪ **il fumo**
smoke

⑫ **il fuoco / l'incendio** *m*
fire

⑬ **l'idrante** *m*
hydrant

⑭ **la scala da tetto**
roof ladder

⑮ **i vigili del fuoco**
firefighters

⑯ **l'ascia** *f*
ax

⑰ **la manichetta antincendio**
hose

⑱ **la cabina**
cab

⑲ **il camion dei vigili del fuoco**
fire engine

See also
19 Le malattie e le lesioni • Illness and injury
21 L'ospedale • The hospital **85** La legge • Law

50.3 LA POLIZIA • POLICE

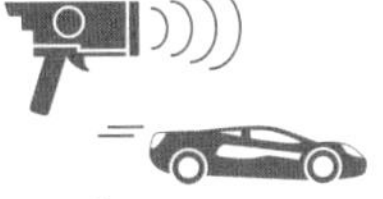

① **il rilevatore di velocità**
radar speed gun

② **l'etilometro** *m*
breathalyzer

③ **la ricetrasmittente**
walkie-talkie

④ **il cane della polizia**
police dog

⑤ **la denuncia**
complaint

⑥ **il commissariato di polizia**
police station

⑦ **la cella**
police cell

⑧ **la sala interrogatori**
interrogation room

⑨ **l'investigatore** *m*
l'investigatrice *f*
detective

⑩ **l'ispettore** *m*
l'ispettrice *f*
inspector

⑪ **l'impronta digitale** *f*
fingerprint

⑫ **l'accusa** *f*
charge

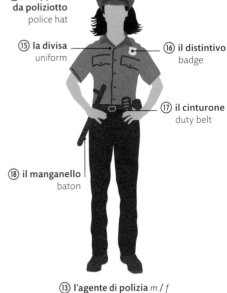

⑭ **il cappello da poliziotto**
police hat

⑮ **la divisa**
uniform

⑯ **il distintivo**
badge

⑰ **il cinturone**
duty belt

⑱ **il manganello**
baton

⑬ **l'agente di polizia** *m / f*
police officer

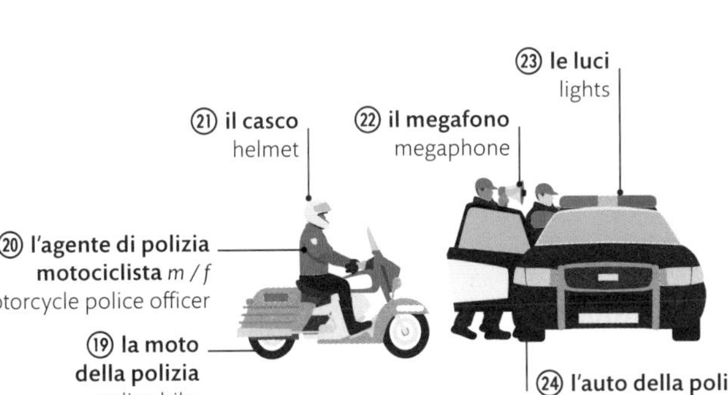

㉓ **le luci**
lights

㉑ **il casco**
helmet

㉒ **il megafono**
megaphone

⑳ **l'agente di polizia motociclista** *m / f*
otorcycle police officer

⑲ **la moto della polizia**
police bike

㉔ **l'auto della polizia** *f*
police car

BANK

㉖ **l'allarme** *m*
alarm

㉗ **l'irruzione** *f*
break in

㉘ **i rapinatori**
robbers

㉕ **la rapina**
robbery

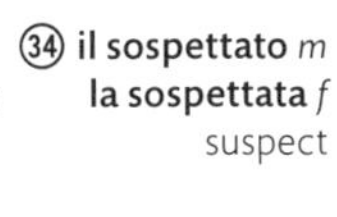

㉛ **la prova**
evidence

㉜ **la radio**
radio

㉚ **l'indagine** *f*
investigation

㉙ **la scena del crimine**
crime scene

㉞ **il sospettato** *m*
la sospettata *f*
suspect

㉝ **l'arresto** *m*
arrest

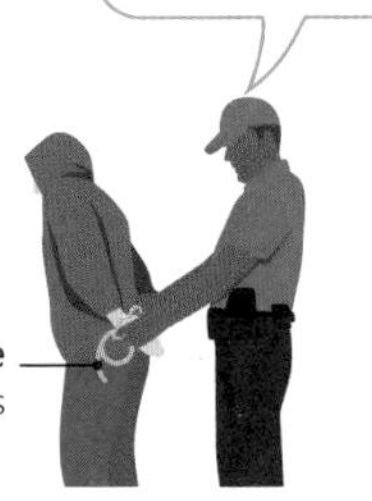

㊱ **Sei in arresto!**
You're under arrest!

㉟ **le manette**
handcuffs

51 L'energia e l'alimentazione elettrica
Energy and power supply

51.1 L'ENERGIA NUCLEARE E I COMBUSTIBILI FOSSILI
NUCLEAR ENERGY AND FOSSIL FUELS

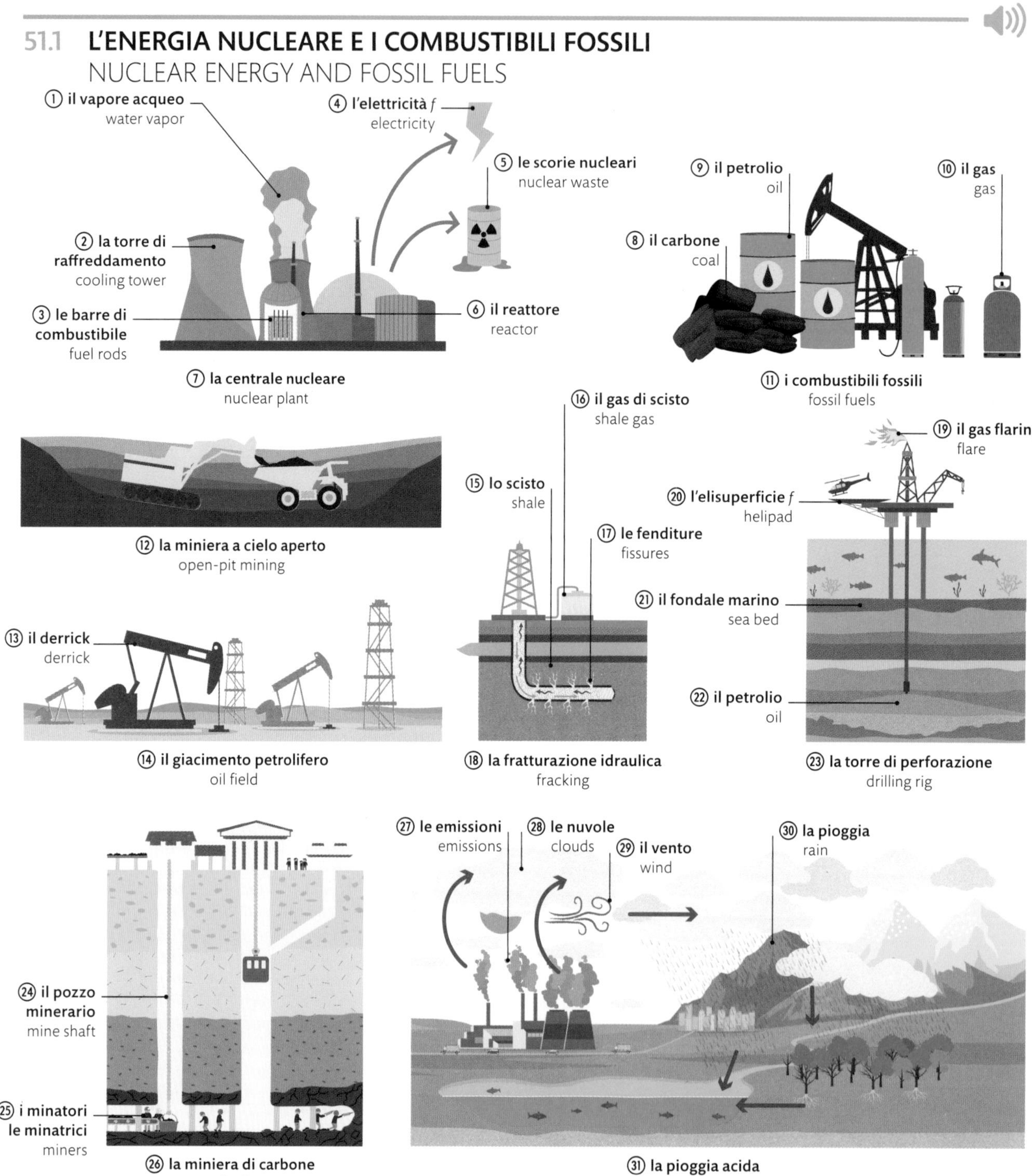

① il vapore acqueo
water vapor
④ l'elettricità *f*
electricity
⑤ le scorie nucleari
nuclear waste
② la torre di raffreddamento
cooling tower
③ le barre di combustibile
fuel rods
⑥ il reattore
reactor
⑦ la centrale nucleare
nuclear plant
⑨ il petrolio
oil
⑩ il gas
gas
⑧ il carbone
coal
⑪ i combustibili fossili
fossil fuels
⑯ il gas di scisto
shale gas
⑲ il gas flaring
flare
⑮ lo scisto
shale
⑳ l'elisuperficie *f*
helipad
⑰ le fenditure
fissures
⑫ la miniera a cielo aperto
open-pit mining
㉑ il fondale marino
sea bed
⑬ il derrick
derrick
㉒ il petrolio
oil
⑭ il giacimento petrolifero
oil field
⑱ la fratturazione idraulica
fracking
㉓ la torre di perforazione
drilling rig
㉗ le emissioni
emissions
㉘ le nuvole
clouds
㉙ il vento
wind
㉚ la pioggia
rain
㉔ il pozzo minerario
mine shaft
㉕ i minatori
le minatrici
miners
㉖ la miniera di carbone
coal mine
㉛ la pioggia acida
acid rain

See also
33 Gli impianti elettrico e idraulico • Electrics and plumbing **42-43** In città • In town
145 Il pianeta Terra • Planet Earth **155** Il clima e l'ambiente • Climate and the environment

51.2 L'ENERGIA RINNOVABILE • RENEWABLE ENERGY

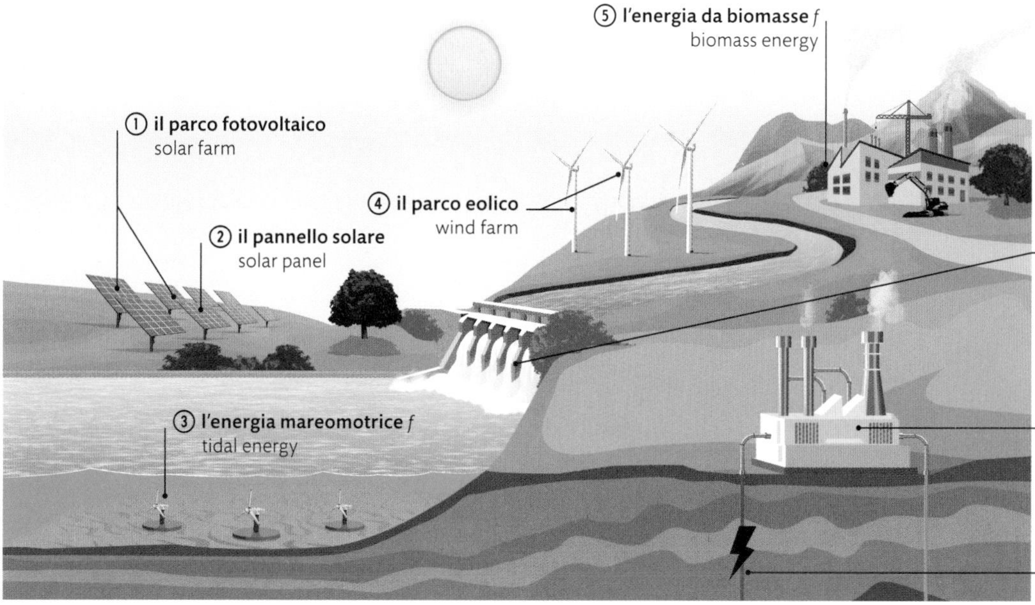

① **il parco fotovoltaico**
solar farm

② **il pannello solare**
solar panel

③ **l'energia mareomotrice** *f*
tidal energy

④ **il parco eolico**
wind farm

⑤ **l'energia da biomasse** *f*
biomass energy

⑥ **l'energia idroelettrica** *f*
hydroelectric energy

⑦ **la centrale geotermica**
geothermal plant

⑧ **l'energia geotermica** *f*
geothermal energy

⑨ **l'energia pulita** *f*
green energy

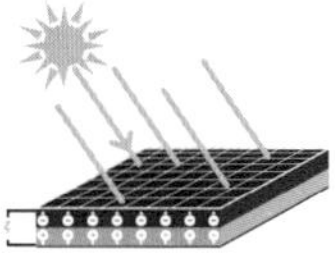

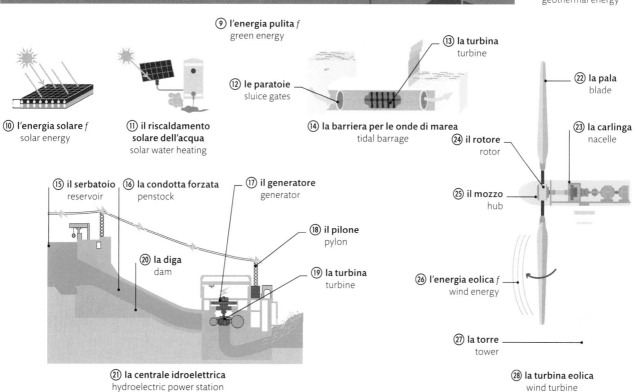

⑩ **l'energia solare** *f*
solar energy

⑪ **il riscaldamento solare dell'acqua**
solar water heating

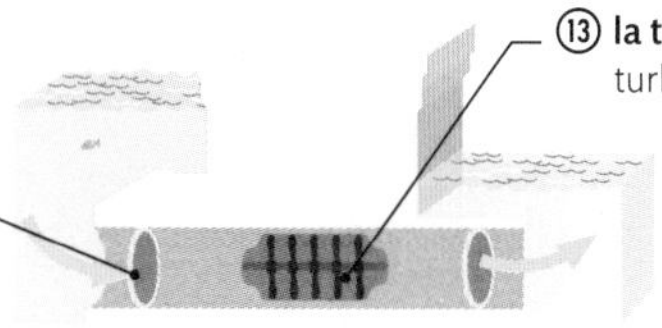

⑫ **le paratoie**
sluice gates

⑬ **la turbina**
turbine

⑭ **la barriera per le onde di marea**
tidal barrage

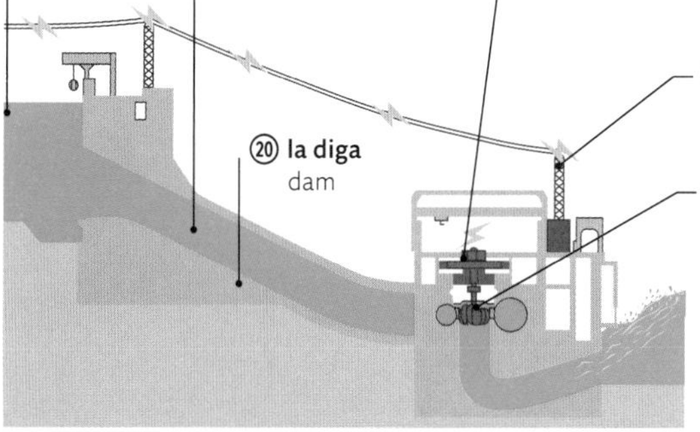

⑮ **il serbatoio**
reservoir

⑯ **la condotta forzata**
penstock

⑰ **il generatore**
generator

⑱ **il pilone**
pylon

⑲ **la turbina**
turbine

⑳ **la diga**
dam

㉑ **la centrale idroelettrica**
hydroelectric power station

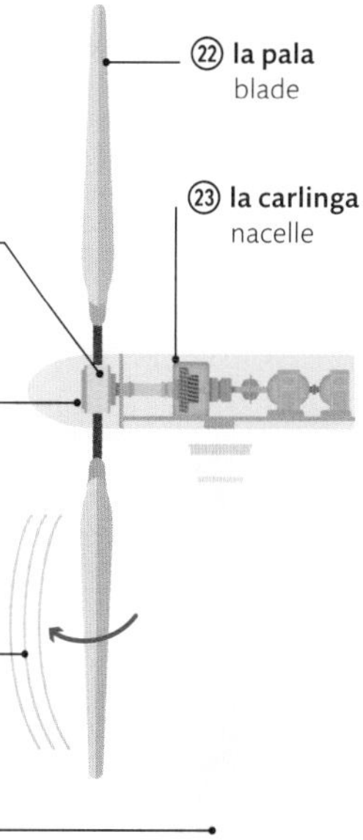

㉒ **la pala**
blade

㉓ **la carlinga**
nacelle

㉔ **il rotore**
rotor

㉕ **il mozzo**
hub

㉖ **l'energia eolica** *f*
wind energy

㉗ **la torre**
tower

㉘ **la turbina eolica**
wind turbine

52 Bere e mangiare

Drinking and eating

52.1 LE BEVANDE · DRINKS

① **il caffè**
coffee

② **il tè**
tea

③ **la cioccolata calda**
hot chocolate

④ **la tisana**
herbal tea

⑤ **il tè freddo**
iced tea

⑥ **la limonata**
lemonade

⑦ **il succo**
juice

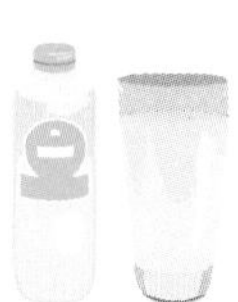

⑧ **l'acqua minerale** *f*
mineral water

⑨ **l'acqua del rubinetto** *f*
tap water

⑩ **il frullato**
smoothie

⑪ **l'aranciata** *f*
orangeade

⑫ **la coca cola**
cola

⑬ **il frappè**
milkshake

⑭ **la bevanda energetica**
sports drink / energy drink

⑮ **il vino rosso**
red wine

⑯ **il vino bianco**
white wine

⑰ **il vino rosé**
rosé wine

⑱ **la birra**
beer

52.2 I CONTENITORI · CONTAINERS

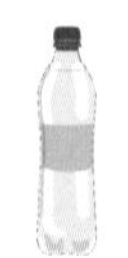

① **la bottiglia**
bottle

② **il bicchiere**
glass

③ **il cartone**
carton

④ **il barattolo**
jar

⑤ **il sacchetto**
bag

⑥ **il pacchetto**
package

⑦ **la scatola**
box

⑧ **la lattina**
can

⑨ **il thermos**
thermal flask

⑩ **la ciotola**
bowl

⑪ **il contenitore ermetico**
airtight container

⑫ **il barattolo in vetro**
Mason jar

See also
27 La cucina e le stoviglie • Kitchen and tableware **28** Gli utensili da cucina • Kitchenware **29** Cucinare • Cooking **52-72** Gli alimenti • Food

52.3 GLI AGGETTIVI • ADJECTIVES

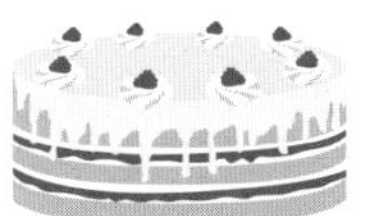

① **dolce**
sweet

② **saporito** *m* / **saporita** *f*
savory

③ **acido**
sour

④ **salato** *m* / **salata** *f*
salty

⑤ **amaro** *m* / **amara** *f*
bitter

⑥ **piccante**
spicy / hot

⑦ **fresco** *m* / **fresca** *f*
fresh

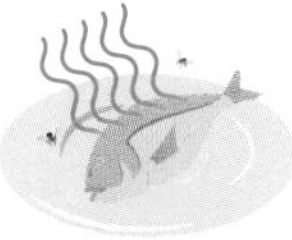

⑧ **andato a male**
andata a male
bad

⑨ **forte**
strong

⑩ **con ghiaccio / freddo** *m*
con ghiaccio / fredda *f*
iced / chilled

⑪ **frizzante**
carbonated / sparkling

⑫ **naturale / non frizzante**
non-carbonated / still

⑬ **gustoso** *m*
gustosa *f*
rich

⑭ **succoso** *m*
succosa *f*
juicy

⑮ **croccante**
crunchy

⑯ **delizioso** *m*
deliziosa *f*
delicious

⑰ **disgustoso** *m*
disgustosa *f*
disgusting

⑱ **saporito** *m*
saporita *f*
tasty

52.4 I VERBI PER MANGIARE E BERE
DRINKING AND EATING VERBS

① **mangiare**
to eat

② **masticare**
to chew

③ **assaggiare**
to taste

④ **Alla salute!**
Cheers!

⑤ **cenare**
to dine

⑥ **piluccare**
to nibble

⑦ **addentare**
to bite

⑧ **inghiottire**
to swallow

⑨ **sorseggiare**
to sip

⑩ **bere**
to drink

⑪ **deglutire**
to gulp

53 La carne
Meat

53.1 IL MACELLAIO · THE BUTCHER

① **biologico / bilogica**
organic

② **allevato a terra allevata a terra**
free-range

③ **la carne bianca**
white meat

④ **la carne rossa**
red meat

⑤ **la carne magra**
lean meat

⑥ **la carne macinata**
ground meat

⑦ **il salame**
salami

⑧ **il chorizo**
chorizo

⑨ **il prosciutto**
ham

⑩ **il fegato**
liver

⑪ **la cotoletta**
chop

⑫ **il gancio da macellaio**
meat hook

⑬ **lo scamone**
rump roast

⑭ **il macellaio** *m*
la macellaia *f*
butcher

⑮ **il coniglio**
rabbit

⑯ **le salsicce**
sausages

⑰ **la selvaggina**
game

⑱ **la pancetta**
bacon

⑲ **la lonza**
Canadian bacon

⑳ **il controfiletto**
sirloin steak

See also
29 Cucinare • Cooking **52** Bere e mangiare • Drinking and eating **54** Il pesce e i frutti di mare • Fish and seafood **69** Al ristorante • At the restaurant **72** Il pranzo e la cena • Lunch and dinner **165** Gli animali da fattoria • Farm animals

53.2 **I TIPI DI CARNE** • TYPES OF MEAT

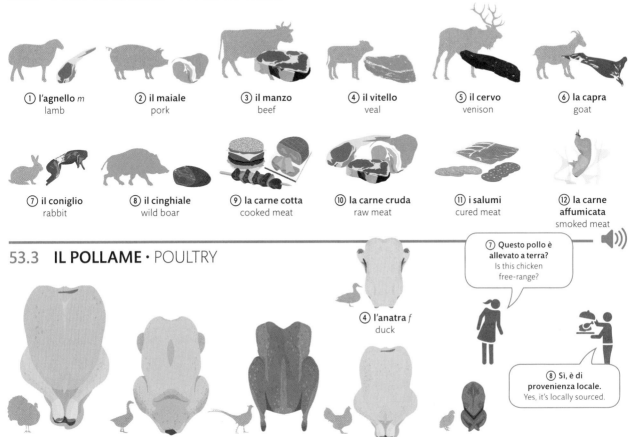

① **l'agnello** *m*
lamb

② **il maiale**
pork

③ **il manzo**
beef

④ **il vitello**
veal

⑤ **il cervo**
venison

⑥ **la capra**
goat

⑦ **il coniglio**
rabbit

⑧ **il cinghiale**
wild boar

⑨ **la carne cotta**
cooked meat

⑩ **la carne cruda**
raw meat

⑪ **i salumi**
cured meat

⑫ **la carne affumicata**
smoked meat

53.3 **IL POLLAME** • POULTRY

① **il tacchino**
turkey

② **l'oca** *f*
goose

③ **il fagiano**
pheasant

④ **l'anatra** *f*
duck

⑤ **il pollo**
chicken

⑥ **la quaglia**
quail

⑦ **Questo pollo è allevato a terra?**
Is this chicken free-range?

⑧ **Sì, è di provenienza locale.**
Yes, it's locally sourced.

53.4 **I TAGLI DI CARNE** • CUTS OF MEAT

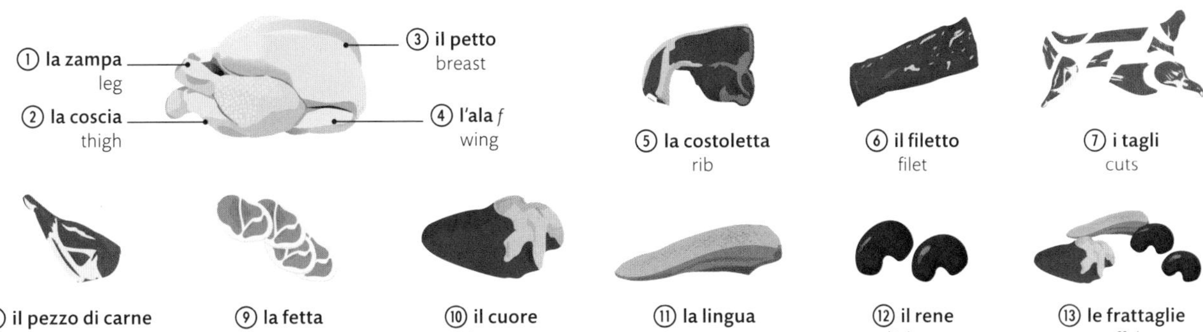

① **la zampa**
leg

② **la coscia**
thigh

③ **il petto**
breast

④ **l'ala** *f*
wing

⑤ **la costoletta**
rib

⑥ **il filetto**
filet

⑦ **i tagli**
cuts

⑧ **il pezzo di carne**
cut

⑨ **la fetta**
slice

⑩ **il cuore**
heart

⑪ **la lingua**
tongue

⑫ **il rene**
kidney

⑬ **le frattaglie**
offal

54 Il pesce e i frutti di mare
Fish and seafood

54.1 IL PESCE · FISH

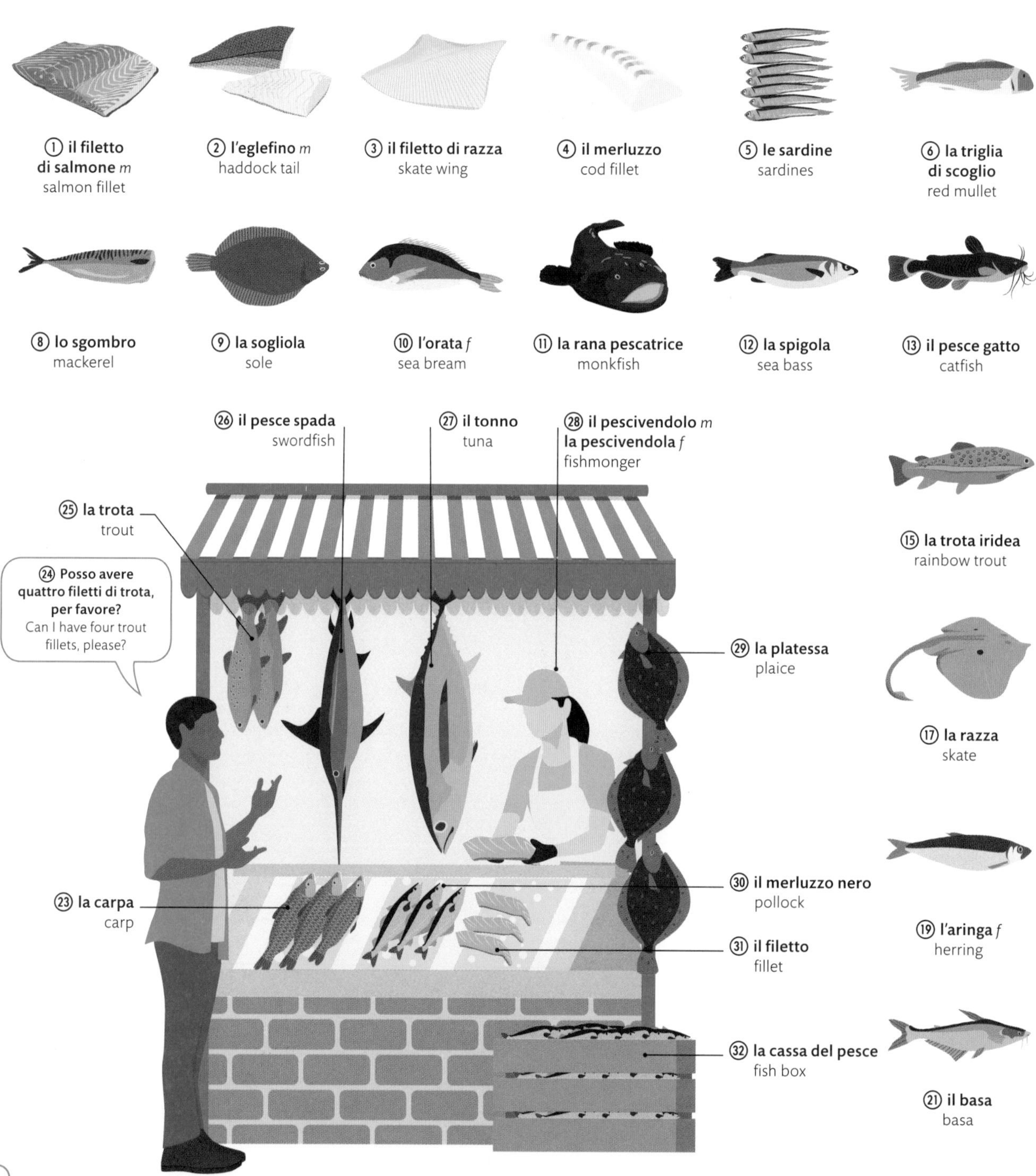

① il filetto di salmone *m*
salmon fillet
② l'eglefino *m*
haddock tail
③ il filetto di razza
skate wing
④ il merluzzo
cod fillet
⑤ le sardine
sardines
⑥ la triglia di scoglio
red mullet
⑧ lo sgombro
mackerel
⑨ la sogliola
sole
⑩ l'orata *f*
sea bream
⑪ la rana pescatrice
monkfish
⑫ la spigola
sea bass
⑬ il pesce gatto
catfish
㉖ il pesce spada
swordfish
㉗ il tonno
tuna
㉘ il pescivendolo *m*
la pescivendola *f*
fishmonger
㉕ la trota
trout
㉔ Posso avere quattro filetti di trota, per favore?
Can I have four trout fillets, please?
⑮ la trota iridea
rainbow trout
㉙ la platessa
plaice
⑰ la razza
skate
㉓ la carpa
carp
㉚ il merluzzo nero
pollock
⑲ l'aringa *f*
herring
㉛ il filetto
fillet
㉜ la cassa del pesce
fish box
㉑ il basa
basa

See also
29 Cucinare • Cooking **52** Bere e mangiare • Drinking and eating
55-56 La verdura • Vegetables **69** Al ristorante • At the restaurant
72 Il pranzo e la cena • Lunch and dinner **166** La vita negli oceani • Ocean life

⑦ **il merlano**
whiting

⑭ **l'halibut** *m*
halibut

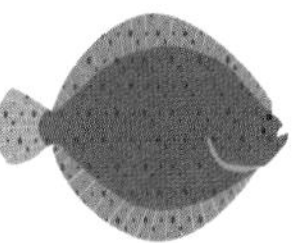

⑯ **il rombo**
turbot

⑱ **l'anguilla** *f*
eel

⑳ **il pesce persico**
perch

㉒ **il lucioperca**
pike perch

54.2 I FRUTTI DI MARE • SEAFOOD

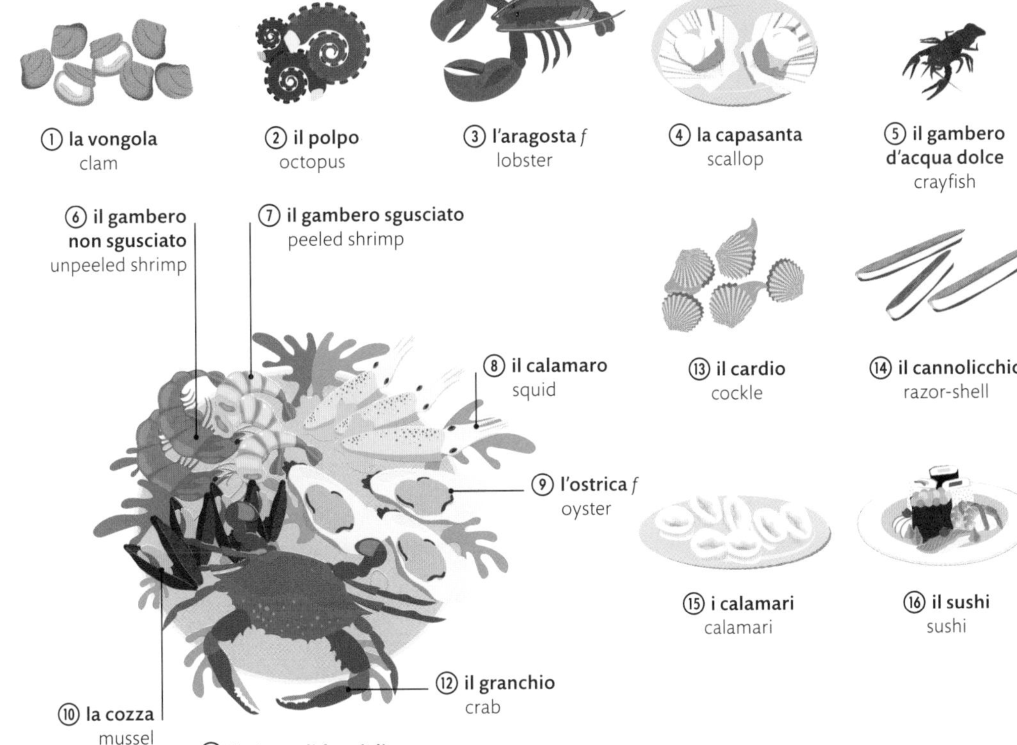
① la vongola
clam
② il polpo
octopus
③ l'aragosta f
lobster
④ la capasanta
scallop
⑤ il gambero d'acqua dolce
crayfish
⑥ il gambero non sgusciato
unpeeled shrimp
⑦ il gambero sgusciato
peeled shrimp
⑧ il calamaro
squid
⑨ l'ostrica f
oyster
⑩ la cozza
mussel
⑪ il piatto di frutti di mare
seafood platter
⑫ il granchio
crab
⑬ il cardio
cockle
⑭ il cannolicchio
razor-shell
⑮ i calamari
calamari
⑯ il sushi
sushi

54.3 LA PREPARAZIONE • PREPARATION

① la squama
scale
③ la coda
tail

② **fresco** *m* / **fresca** *f*
fresh

④ **surgelato** *m*
surgelata *f*
frozen

⑤ **affumicato** *m*
affumicata *f*
smoked

⑥ **salato** *m* / **salata** *f*
salted

⑦ **squamato** *m*
squamata *f*
descaled

⑧ **pulito** *m* / **pulita** *f*
cleaned

⑨ **spinato** *m*
spinata *f*
boned

⑩ **il filetto**
loin

55 La verdura
Vegetables

55.1 LA VERDURA · VEGETABLES

① **le fave**
fava beans

② **i fagiolini**
runner beans

③ **i fagiolini**
green beans

④ **i fagioli secchi**
dried beans

⑤ **il sedano**
celery

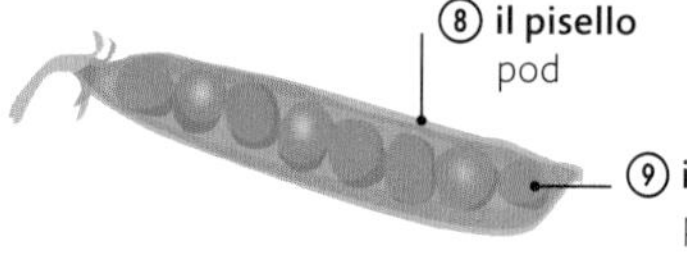
⑧ il pisello
pod
⑨ il baccello
pea

⑦ **i piselli**
garden peas

⑩ **la taccola**
snow peas

⑪ **l'okra** *f*
okra

⑫ **il bambù**
bamboo

⑬ **i germogli di soia**
bean sprouts

⑮ **la cicoria**
chicory

⑯ **il finocchio**
fennel

⑰ **i cuori di palma**
palm hearts

⑱ **le mini pannocchie di mais**
baby corn

⑲ i chicchi
kernel

⑳ **il mais**
corn

㉓ **l'indivia** *f*
endive

㉔ **il dente di leone**
dandelion

㉕ **la bietola**
Swiss chard

㉖ **il cavolo riccio**
kale

㉗ **l'acetosella** *f*
sorrel

㉘ **gli spinaci**
spinach

㉛ **il cavolo cinese**
bok choi

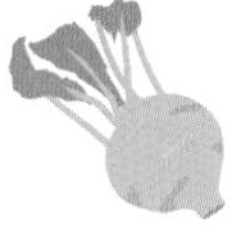

㉜ **il cavolo rapa**
kohlrabi

㉝ **i cavolini di Bruxelles**
Brussels sprouts

㉞ **le verdure primaverili**
spring greens

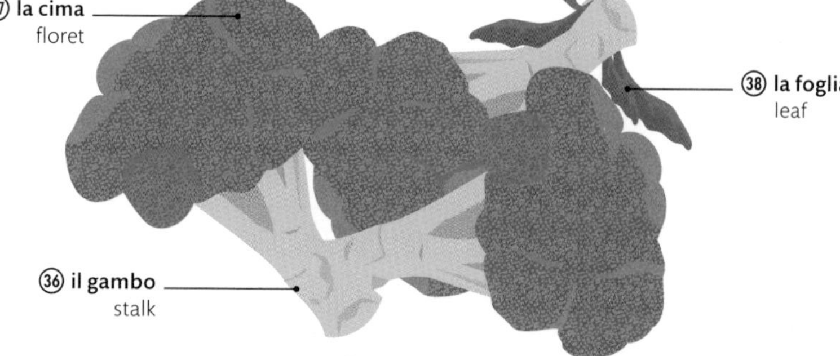
㊲ la cima
floret
㊳ la foglia
leaf
㊱ il gambo
stalk

㉟ **i broccoli**
broccoli

See also
29 Cucinare • Cooking **52** Bere e mangiare • Drinking and eating **56** La verdura (continua) • Vegetables continued **57** La frutta • Fruit **58** La frutta e la frutta a guscio • Fruit and nuts **59** Le erbe e le spezie Herbs and spices **69** Al ristorante • At the restaurant **72** Il pranzo e la cena • Lunch and dinner

⑥ **il cavolo**
collards

⑭ **la verza**
savoy cabbage

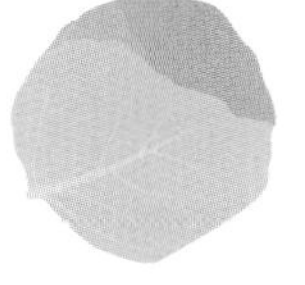

㉑ **il cavolo**
cabbage

㉒ **il cavolo rosso**
red cabbage

㉙ **il cavolo nero**
cavolo nero

㉚ **le foglie di barbabietola**
beet greens

㊵ **i pesticidi**
pesticides

㊴ **le verdure biologiche**
organic vegetables

55.2 LE VERDURE DA INSALATA • SALAD VEGETABLES

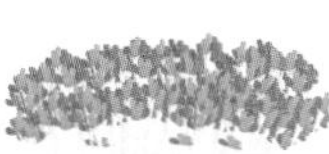

① **il crescione**
cress

② **la rucola**
arugula

③ **l'insalata iceberg** *f*
iceberg lettuce

④ **la lattuga romana**
romaine lettuce

⑤ **la lattuga Little Gem**
little gem

⑥ **il cipollotto**
spring onions

⑦ **i pomodori ciliegini**
cherry tomatoes

⑧ **il cetriolo**
cucumber

⑨ **l'indivia riccia** *f*
frisée

⑩ **il crescione d'acqua**
watercress

⑪ **il radicchio**
radicchio

⑫ **la lattuga**
lettuce

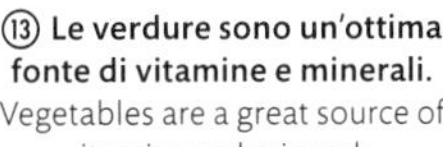

⑬ **Le verdure sono un'ottima fonte di vitamine e minerali.**
Vegetables are a great source of vitamins and minerals.

⑭ **l'insalata** *f*
salad

56 La verdura (continua)

Vegetables continued

56.1 DAL FRUTTIVENDOLO · AT THE GROCERY STORE

① **la rapa**
turnip

② **il ravanello**
radish

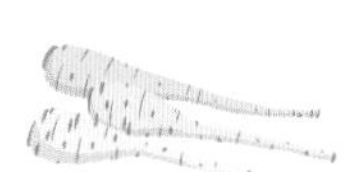

③ **la pastinaca**
parsnip

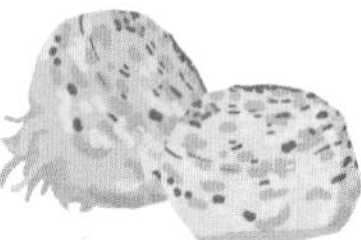

④ **il sedano rapa**
celeriac

⑤ **la manioca**
cassava

⑥ **la patata**
potato

⑦ **la castagna d'acqua**
water chestnut

⑧ **l'igname** *m*
yam

⑨ **la barbabietola**
beets

⑩ **la rapa svedese**
rutabagas

⑪ **il topinambur**
Jerusalem artichoke

⑫ **il taro**
taro root

⑬ **il rafano**
horseradish

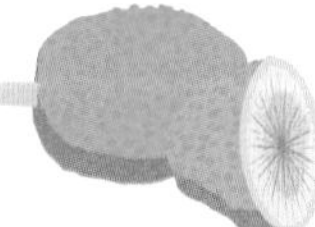

⑭ **il frutto dell'albero del pane**
breadfruit

⑮ **lo scalogno**
shallot

⑯ **il peperoncino**
chili

⑰ **il pomodoro San Marzano**
plum tomato

⑱ **la punta di asparago**
asparagus tip

⑲ **il cuore di carciofo**
artichoke heart

⑳ **il fungo pleurotus**
oyster mushroom

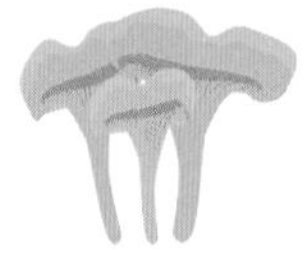

㉑ **il finferlo**
chanterelle

㉒ **il fungo shiitake**
shiitake mushroom

㉓ **il tartufo**
truffle

㉔ **il fungo enoki**
enoki mushroom

㉕ **lo zucchino**
marrow

㉖ **la zucca violina**
butternut squash

㉗ **la zucca acorn**
acorn squash

㉘ **la zucca**
pumpkin

㉙ **la zucca invernale**
buttercup squash

㉚ **la zucca bianca**
patty pan

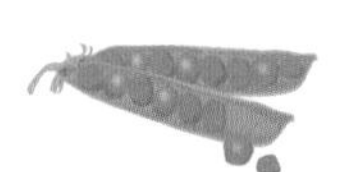

㉛ **fresco** *m* **/ fresca** *f*
fresh

㉜ **surgelato** *m* **surgelata** *f*
frozen

㉝ **in scatola**
canned

㉞ **crudo** *m* **/ cruda** *f*
raw

㉟ **cotto** *m* **/ cotta** *f*
cooked

㊱ **piccante**
hot / spicy

See also
29 Cucinare • Cooking **52** Bere e mangiare • Drinking and eating
57 La frutta • Fruit **58** La frutta e la frutta a guscio • Fruit and nuts
69 Al ristorante • At the restaurant **72** Il pranzo e la cena • Lunch and dinner

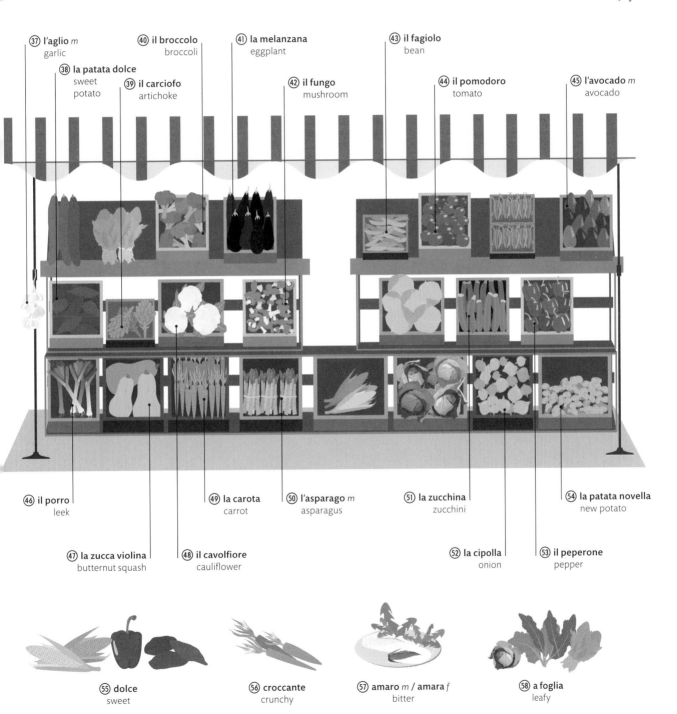

(37) **l'aglio** *m*
garlic

(38) **la patata dolce**
sweet potato

(39) **il carciofo**
artichoke

(40) **il broccolo**
broccoli

(41) **la melanzana**
eggplant

(42) **il fungo**
mushroom

(43) **il fagiolo**
bean

(44) **il pomodoro**
tomato

(45) **l'avocado** *m*
avocado

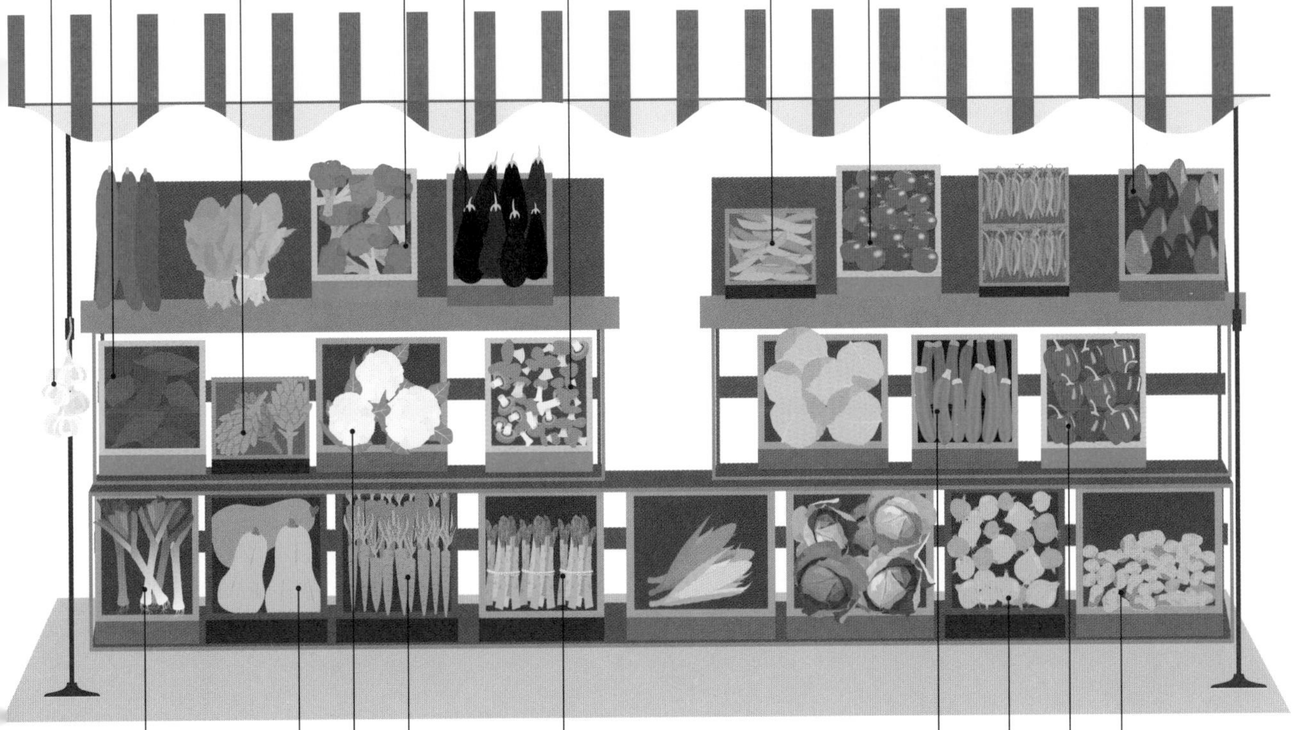

(46) **il porro**
leek

(47) **la zucca violina**
butternut squash

(48) **il cavolfiore**
cauliflower

(49) **la carota**
carrot

(50) **l'asparago** *m*
asparagus

(51) **la zucchina**
zucchini

(52) **la cipolla**
onion

(53) **il peperone**
pepper

(54) **la patata novella**
new potato

(55) **dolce**
sweet

(56) **croccante**
crunchy

(57) **amaro** *m* / **amara** *f*
bitter

(58) **a foglia**
leafy

57 La frutta
Fruit

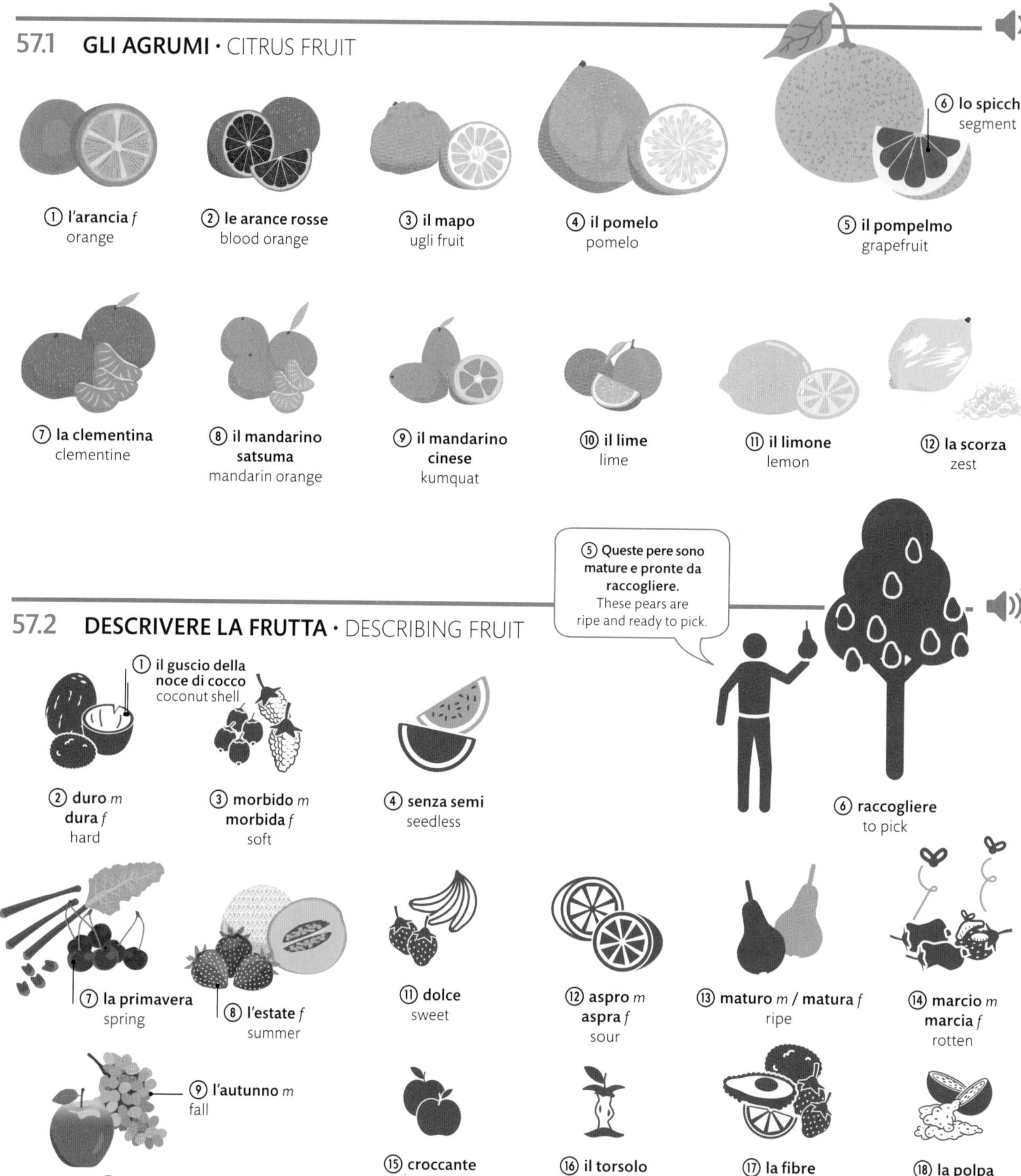
57.1 GLI AGRUMI · CITRUS FRUIT
① l'arancia f
orange
② le arance rosse
blood orange
③ il mapo
ugli fruit
④ il pomelo
pomelo
⑤ il pompelmo
grapefruit
⑥ lo spicchio
segment
⑦ la clementina
clementine
⑧ il mandarino satsuma
mandarin orange
⑨ il mandarino cinese
kumquat
⑩ il lime
lime
⑪ il limone
lemon
⑫ la scorza
zest
57.2 DESCRIVERE LA FRUTTA · DESCRIBING FRUIT
① il guscio della noce di cocco
coconut shell
② duro m
dura f
hard
③ morbido m
morbida f
soft
④ senza semi
seedless
⑤ Queste pere sono mature e pronte da raccogliere.
These pears are ripe and ready to pick.
⑥ raccogliere
to pick
⑦ la primavera
spring
⑧ l'estate f
summer
⑨ l'autunno m
fall
⑩ la frutta stagionale
seasonal fruit
⑪ dolce
sweet
⑫ aspro m
aspra f
sour
⑬ maturo m / matura f
ripe
⑭ marcio m
marcia f
rotten
⑮ croccante
crisp
⑯ il torsolo
core
⑰ la fibre
fiber
⑱ la polpa
pulp

See also
29 Cucinare • Cooking **52** Bere e mangiare • Drinking and eating **55-56** La verdura • Vegetables **58** La frutta e la frutta a guscio • Fruit and nuts **65-66** Al bar • At the café **69** Al ristorante At the restaurant **71** La colazione • Breakfast **72** Il pranzo e la cena • Lunch and dinner

57.3 LE BACCHE E LA FRUTTA CON IL NOCCIOLO • BERRIES AND STONE FRUIT

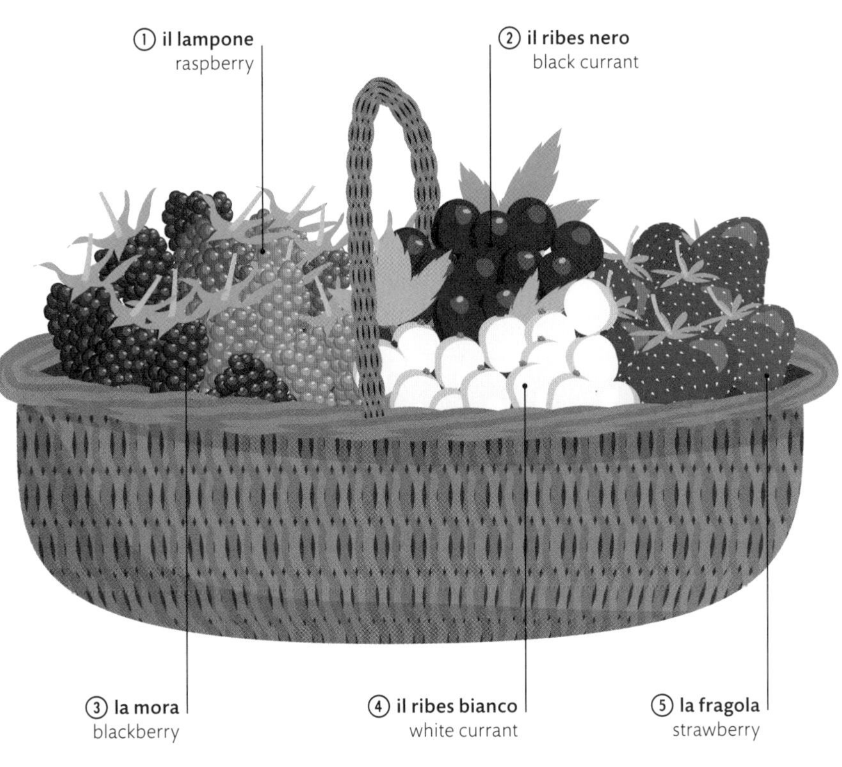

① **il lampone**
raspberry

② **il ribes nero**
black currant

③ **la mora**
blackberry

④ **il ribes bianco**
white currant

⑤ **la fragola**
strawberry

⑥ **il cesto di frutta** *f*
basket of fruit

⑦ **il mirtillo rosso**
cranberry

⑧ **il mirtillo**
blueberry

⑨ **il loganberry**
loganberry

⑩ **l'alchechengi** *f*
cape gooseberry

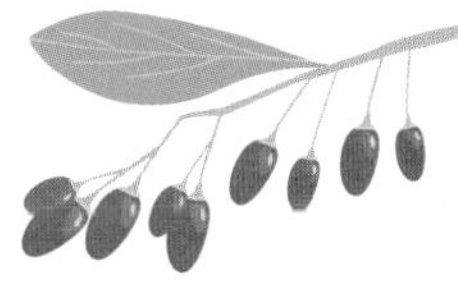

⑪ **la bacca di goji**
goji berry

⑫ **l'uva spina** *f*
gooseberry

⑬ **il ribes rosso**
red currant

⑭ **il mirtillo**
bilberry

⑮ **la bacca di sambuco**
elderberry

⑯ **l'uva** *f*
grapes

⑰ **la mora di gelso**
mulberry

⑱ **la pesca**
peach

⑲ **la pesca nettarina**
nectarine

⑳ **l'albicocca** *f*
apricot

㉑ **il mango**
mango

㉒ **la prugna**
plum

㉓ **la ciliegia**
cherry

㉔ **il dattero**
date

㉕ **il litchi**
lychee

58 La frutta e la frutta a guscio

Fruit and nuts

58.1 I MELONI · MELONS

① **l'anguria** *f*
watermelon

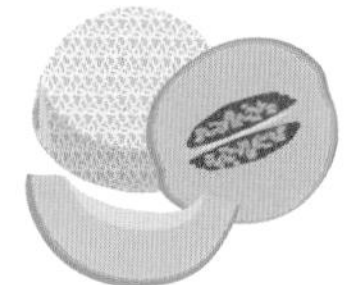

② **il cantalupo**
cantaloupe

③ **il melone verde**
honeydew melon

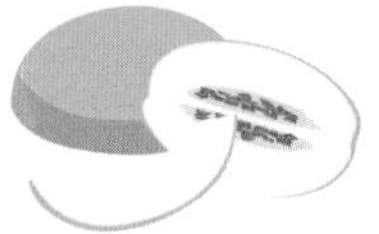

④ **il melone d'inverno**
Canary melon

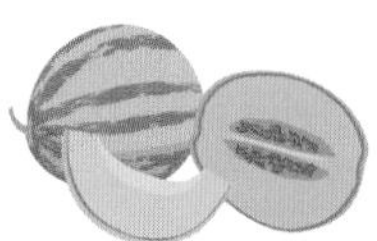

⑤ **il melone charentais**
charentais

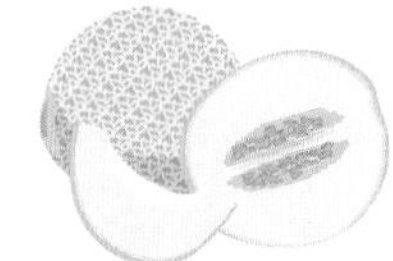

⑥ **il melone galia**
galia

58.2 GLI ALTRI FRUTTI · OTHER FRUIT

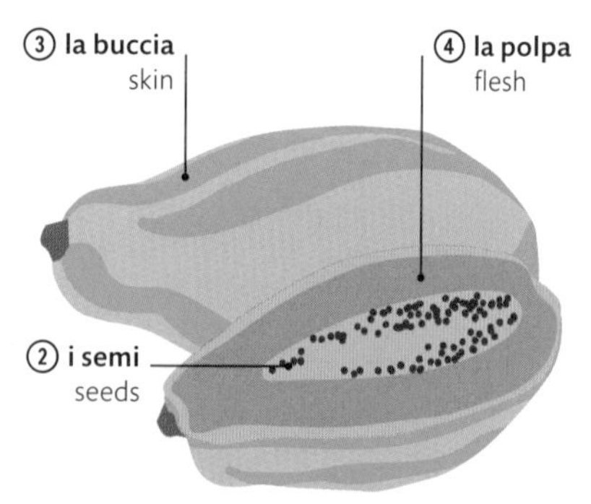
③ la buccia
skin
④ la polpa
flesh
② i semi
seeds

① **la papaia**
papaya

⑤ **la mela cotogna**
quince

⑥ **il frutto della passione**
passion fruit

⑦ **la guava**
guava

⑧ **la carambola**
starfruit

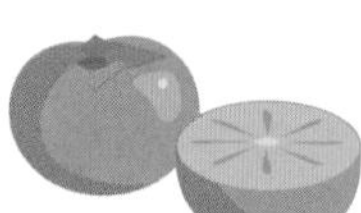

⑨ **il caco**
persimmon

⑩ **la feijoa**
feijoa

⑪ **l'ananas** *m*
pineapple

⑫ **il fico d'India**
prickly pear

⑬ **il tamarillo**
tamarillo

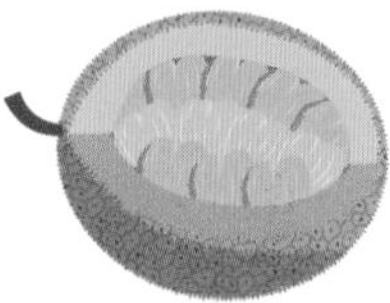

⑭ **il giaca**
jackfruit

⑮ **il mangostano**
mangosteen

⑯ **il melograno**
pomegranate

⑰ **la banana**
banana

⑱ **il kiwi**
kiwi

⑲ **la mela**
apple

⑳ **le mele selvatiche**
crab apples

㉑ **la pera**
pear

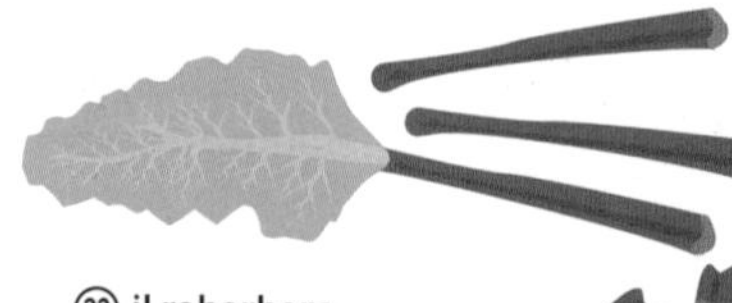

㉒ **il rabarbaro**
rhubarb

See also
29 Cucinare • Cooking **52** Bere e mangiare • Drinking and eating **55-56** La verdura Vegetables **57** La frutta • Fruit **65-66** Al bar • At the café **69** Al ristorante • At the restaurant **71** La colazione • Breakfast **72** Il pranzo e la cena • Lunch and dinner

58.3 **LA FRUTTA A GUSCIO E LA FRUTTA SECCA** • NUTS AND DRIED FRUIT

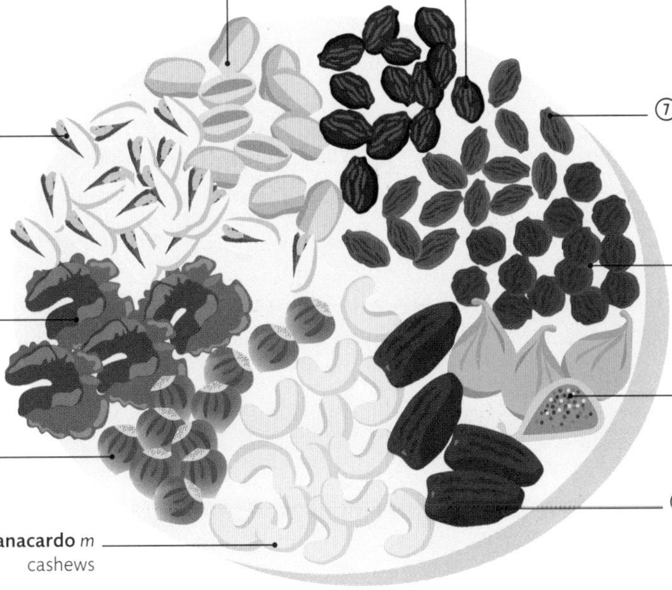

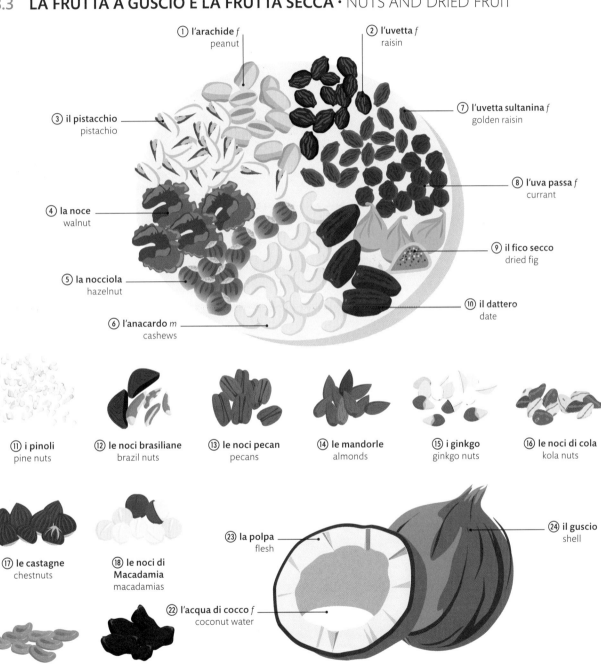

① **l'arachide** *f*
peanut

② **l'uvetta** *f*
raisin

③ **il pistacchio**
pistachio

④ **la noce**
walnut

⑤ **la nocciola**
hazelnut

⑥ **l'anacardo** *m*
cashews

⑦ **l'uvetta sultanina** *f*
golden raisin

⑧ **l'uva passa** *f*
currant

⑨ **il fico secco**
dried fig

⑩ **il dattero**
date

⑪ **i pinoli**
pine nuts

⑫ **le noci brasiliane**
brazil nuts

⑬ **le noci pecan**
pecans

⑭ **le mandorle**
almonds

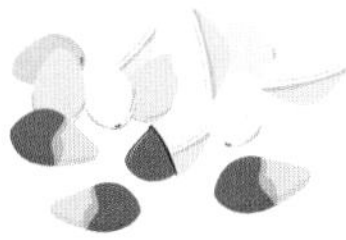

⑮ **i ginkgo**
ginkgo nuts

⑯ **le noci di cola**
kola nuts

⑰ **le castagne**
chestnuts

⑱ **le noci di Macadamia**
macadamias

⑲ **le albicocche secche**
dried apricots

⑳ **le prugne secche**
prunes

㉑ **la noce di cocco**
coconut

㉒ **l'acqua di cocco** *f*
coconut water

㉓ **la polpa**
flesh

㉔ **il guscio**
shell

59 Le erbe e le spezie

Herbs and spices

59.1 LE SPEZIE · SPICES

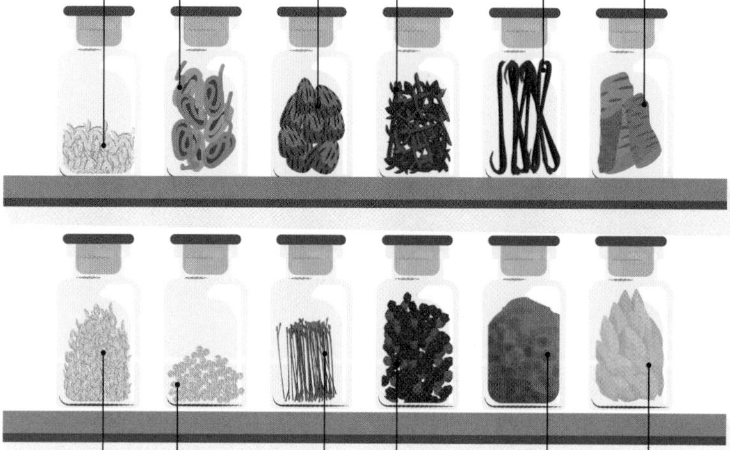

① **l'anice** *m*
anise

② **il macis**
mace

③ **la noce moscata**
nutmeg

④ **i chiodi di garofano**
cloves

⑤ **la vaniglia**
vanilla

⑥ **la curcuma**
turmeric

⑦ **il cumino**
cumin

⑧ **i semi di coriandolo**
coriander seeds

⑨ **lo zafferano**
saffron

⑩ **i grani di pepe**
peppercorns

⑪ **la paprika**
paprika

⑫ **il cardamomo**
cardamom

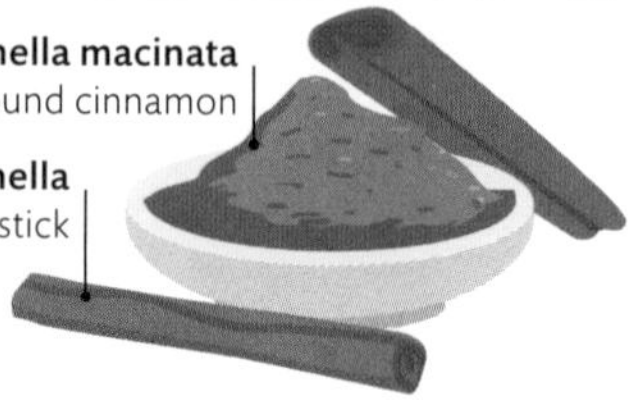

⑬ **la cannella**
cinnamon

⑭ **la stecca di cannella**
cinnamon stick

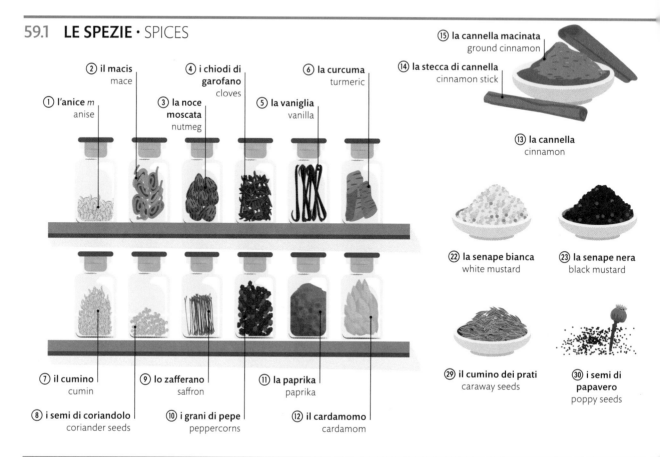

⑮ **la cannella macinata**
ground cinnamon

㉒ **la senape bianca**
white mustard

㉓ **la senape nera**
black mustard

㉙ **il cumino dei prati**
caraway seeds

㉚ **i semi di papavero**
poppy seeds

59.2 LE ERBE · HERBS

① **il finocchio**
fennel

② **la foglia d'alloro**
bay leaf

③ **il prezzemolo**
parsley

④ **l'erba cipollina** *f*
chives

⑤ **la menta**
mint

⑥ **il coriandolo**
cilantro

⑬ **il timo**
thyme

⑭ **la salvia**
sage

⑮ **il dragoncello**
tarragon

⑯ **la maggiorana**
marjoram

⑰ **il basilico**
basil

⑱ **l'origano** *m*
oregano

See also
29 Cucinare • Cooking **52** Bere e mangiare • Drinking and eating **53** La carne • Meat **55-56** La verdura • Vegetables **60** Nella dispensa • In the pantry

⑯ **l'anice stellato** *m*
star anise

⑰ **lo scotano**
sumac

⑱ **le cinque spezie**
five spice

⑲ **il ras el hanout**
ras el hanout

⑳ **il pimento**
allspice

㉑ **il curry**
curry powder

㉔ **lo zenzero**
ginger

㉕ **il peperoncino di Cayenna**
cayenne pepper

㉖ **il jalapeño**
jalapeños

㉗ **il peperoncino Thai**
bird's eye chili

㉘ **il peperoncino in polvere**
ground chili

㉛ **i semi di finocchio**
fennel seeds

㉜ **i semi di Nigella**
nigella seeds

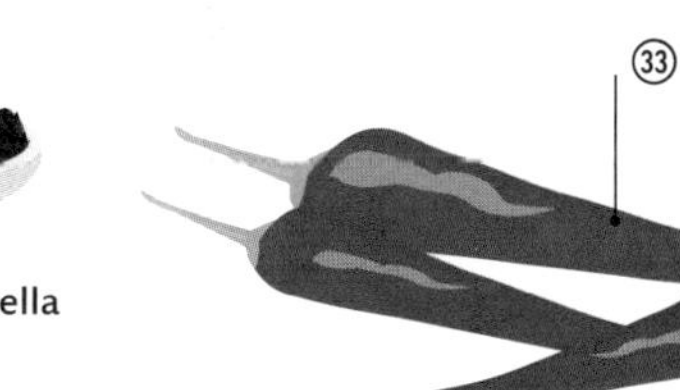

㉝ **i peperoncini freschi**
fresh chili

㉞ **il peperoncino a scaglie**
chili flakes

⑦ **l'issopo** *m*
hyssop

⑧ **l'aneto** *m*
dill

⑨ **il rosmarino**
rosemary

⑩ **il cerfoglio**
chervil

⑪ **il levistico**
lovage

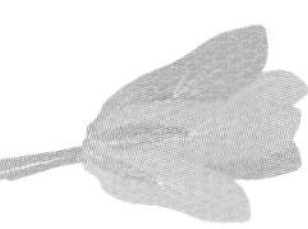
⑫ **l'acetosella** *f*
sorrel

⑲ **la citronella**
lemongrass

⑳ **la melissa**
lemon balm

㉑ **la borragine**
borage

㉒ **le foglie di fieno greco**
fenugreek leaves

㉓ **il mazzetto aromatico**
bouquet garni

60 Nella dispensa

In the pantry

60.1 GLI OLI IN BOTTIGLIA • BOTTLED OILS

① l'olio *m*
oil

② l'olio di palma *m*
palm oil

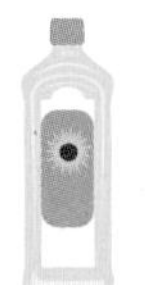

③ l'olio di girasole *m*
sunflower oil

④ l'olio di colza *m*
canola / rapeseed oil

⑤ l'olio di mais *m*
corn oil

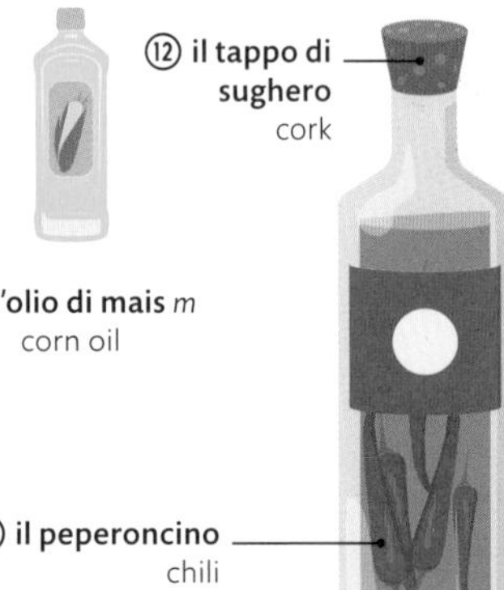

⑫ il tappo di sughero
cork

⑪ il peperoncino
chili

⑥ l'olio di soia *m*
soybean oil

⑦ l'olio di arachide *m*
peanut oil

⑧ l'olio di nocciola *m*
hazelnut oil

⑨ l'olio di cocco *m*
coconut oil

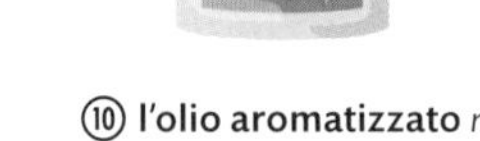

⑩ l'olio aromatizzato *m*
flavored oil

⑬ l'olio di sesamo *m*
sesame oil

⑭ l'olio di mandorle *m*
almond oil

⑮ l'olio di noci *m*
walnut oil

⑯ l'olio di vinaccioli *m*
grapeseed oil

⑱ extra vergine
extra virgin

⑰ l'olio di oliva *m*
olive oil

60.2 LE CREME SPALMABILI DOLCI • SWEET SPREADS

① la crema al limone
lemon curd

② la confettura di lamponi
raspberry jam

④ il vasetto
jar

③ la confettura di fragole
strawberry jam

⑤ il miele cristallizzato
crystalized honey

⑦ il favo
honeycomb

⑧ lo spargimiele
honey dipper

⑥ il miele
honey

⑨ la marmellata di arance
marmalade

⑩ lo sciroppo d'acero
maple syrup

⑪ il burro di arachidi
peanut butter

⑫ la crema spalmabile al cioccolato
chocolate spread

⑭ la frutta conservata
preserved fruit

⑬ il barattolo
preserving jar

See also
27 La cucina e le stoviglie • Kitchen and tableware **29** Cucinare • Cooking
52 Bere e mangiare • Drinking and eating **53** La carne • Meat **55-56** La verdura
Vegetables **65-66** Al bar • At the café **69** Al ristorante • At the restaurant

60.3 **LE SALSE E I CONDIMENTI** • SAUCES AND CONDIMENTS

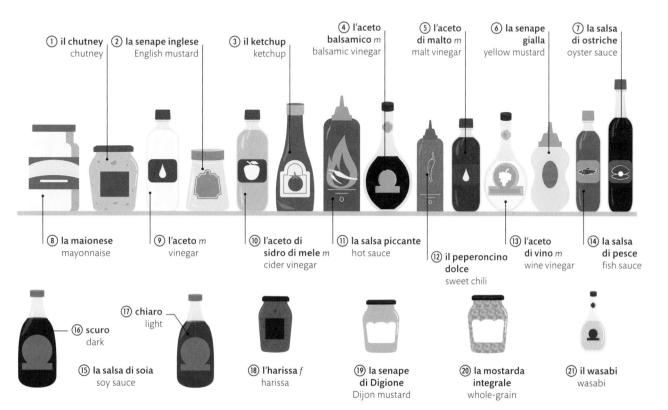

① **il chutney**
chutney

② **la senape inglese**
English mustard

③ **il ketchup**
ketchup

④ **l'aceto balsamico** *m*
balsamic vinegar

⑤ **l'aceto di malto** *m*
malt vinegar

⑥ **la senape gialla**
yellow mustard

⑦ **la salsa di ostriche**
oyster sauce

⑧ **la maionese**
mayonnaise

⑨ **l'aceto** *m*
vinegar

⑩ **l'aceto di sidro di mele** *m*
cider vinegar

⑪ **la salsa piccante**
hot sauce

⑫ **il peperoncino dolce**
sweet chili

⑬ **l'aceto di vino** *m*
wine vinegar

⑭ **la salsa di pesce**
fish sauce

⑯ **scuro**
dark

⑰ **chiaro**
light

⑮ **la salsa di soia**
soy sauce

⑱ **l'harissa** *f*
harissa

⑲ **la senape di Digione**
Dijon mustard

⑳ **la mostarda integrale**
whole-grain

㉑ **il wasabi**
wasabi

60.4 **I SOTTACETI** • PICKLES

① **l'aneto** *m*
dill
② **il cetriolino**
gherkin
③ **i semi di senape**
mustard seeds
④ **i crauti**
sauerkraut
⑤ **il kimchi**
kimchi
⑥ **il lime sott'aceto** *m*
lime pickle
⑦ **le cipolline sott'aceto** *m*
pickled onions
⑧ **le barbabietole sott'aceto** *m*
pickled beets
⑨ **il sottaceto per sandwich**
sandwich pickle
⑩ **la giardiniera**
piccalilli
⑪ **i cetriolini sott'aceto** *m*
cornichons

61 I prodotti caseari
Dairy produce

61.1 IL FORMAGGIO · CHEESE

① il formaggio a pasta dura
hard cheese

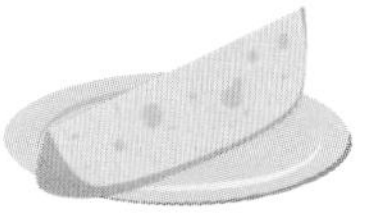
② il formaggio a pasta semidura
semi-hard cheese

③ il formaggio a pasta semimolle
semi-soft cheese

④ il formaggio a pasta molle
soft cheese

⑤ il pecorino
sheep's milk cheese

⑥ il formaggio di capra
goat's cheese

⑦ il formaggio erborinato
blue cheese

⑧ la crosta
rind

⑨ il formaggio grattugiato
grated cheese

⑩ il formaggio fresco
fresh cheese

⑪ i fiocchi di latte
cottage cheese

⑫ il formaggio spalmabile
cream cheese

61.2 LE UOVA · EGGS

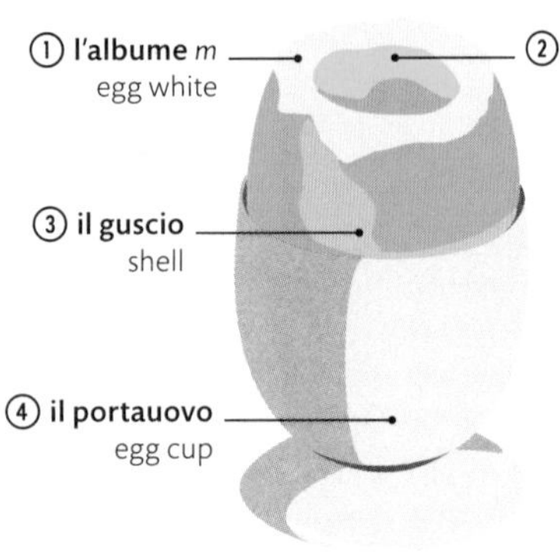
① l'albume *m*
egg white
② il tuorlo
yolk
③ il guscio
shell
④ il portauovo
egg cup
⑤ l'uovo sodo *m*
boiled egg

⑥ l'uovo al tegamino *m*
fried egg

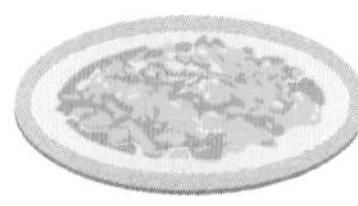
⑦ le uova strapazzate
scrambled eggs

⑧ l'uovo in camicia *m*
poached egg

⑨ l'omelette *f*
omelet

⑩ l'uovo d'oca *m*
goose egg

⑪ l'uovo d'anatra *m*
duck egg

⑫ l'uovo di gallina *m*
chicken egg

⑬ l'uovo di quaglia *m*
quail egg

61.3 IL LATTE · MILK

① pastorizzato
pasteurized

② non pastorizzato
unpasteurized

③ senza lattosio
lactose free

④ omogeneizzato
homogenized

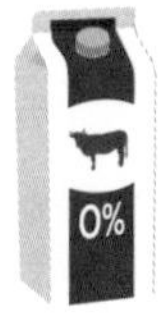
0%
⑤ senza grassi
fat free

⑥ il latte in polvere
powdered milk

See also
29 Cucinare • Cooking **52** Bere e mangiare • Drinking and eating **65-66** Al bar • At the café **69** Al ristorante • At the restaurant **71** La colazione • Breakfast

61.4 I DERIVATI DEL LATTE • MILK PRODUCTS

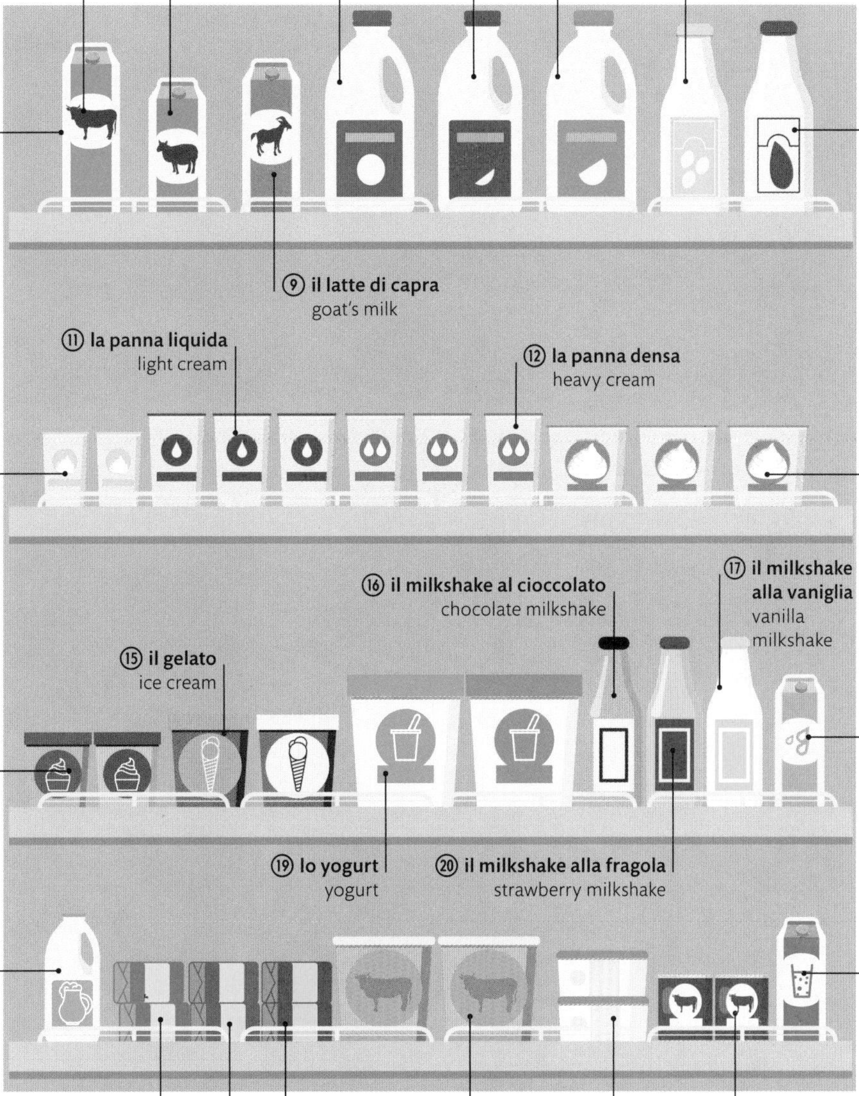

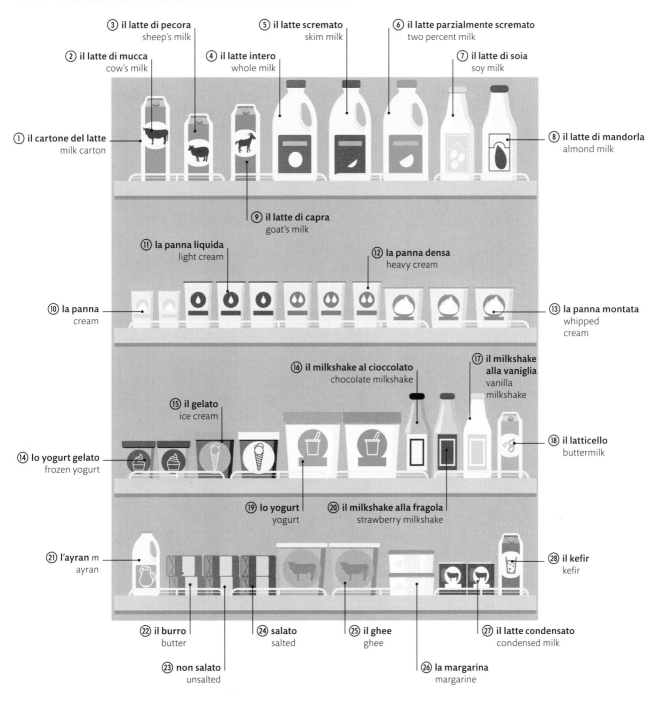

① il cartone del latte
milk carton
② il latte di mucca
cow's milk
③ il latte di pecora
sheep's milk
④ il latte intero
whole milk
⑤ il latte scremato
skim milk
⑥ il latte parzialmente scremato
two percent milk
⑦ il latte di soia
soy milk
⑧ il latte di mandorla
almond milk
⑨ il latte di capra
goat's milk
⑩ la panna
cream
⑪ la panna liquida
light cream
⑫ la panna densa
heavy cream
⑬ la panna montata
whipped cream
⑭ lo yogurt gelato
frozen yogurt
⑮ il gelato
ice cream
⑯ il milkshake al cioccolato
chocolate milkshake
⑰ il milkshake alla vaniglia
vanilla milkshake
⑱ il latticello
buttermilk
⑲ lo yogurt
yogurt
⑳ il milkshake alla fragola
strawberry milkshake
㉑ l'ayran *m*
ayran
㉒ il burro
butter
㉓ non salato
unsalted
㉔ salato
salted
㉕ il ghee
ghee
㉖ la margarina
margarine
㉗ il latte condensato
condensed milk
㉘ il kefir
kefir

62 La panetteria
The bakery

62.1 I TIPI DI PANE E DI FARINA · BREADS AND FLOURS

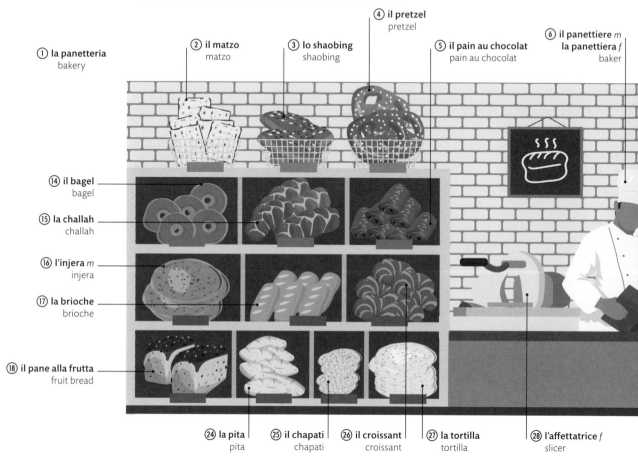

① **la panetteria**
bakery

② **il matzo**
matzo

③ **lo shaobing**
shaobing

④ **il pretzel**
pretzel

⑤ **il pain au chocolat**
pain au chocolat

⑥ **il panettiere** *m*
la panettiera *f*
baker

⑭ **il bagel**
bagel

⑮ **la challah**
challah

⑯ **l'injera** *m*
injera

⑰ **la brioche**
brioche

⑱ **il pane alla frutta**
fruit bread

㉔ **la pita**
pita

㉕ **il chapati**
chapati

㉖ **il croissant**
croissant

㉗ **la tortilla**
tortilla

㉘ **l'affettatrice** *f*
slicer

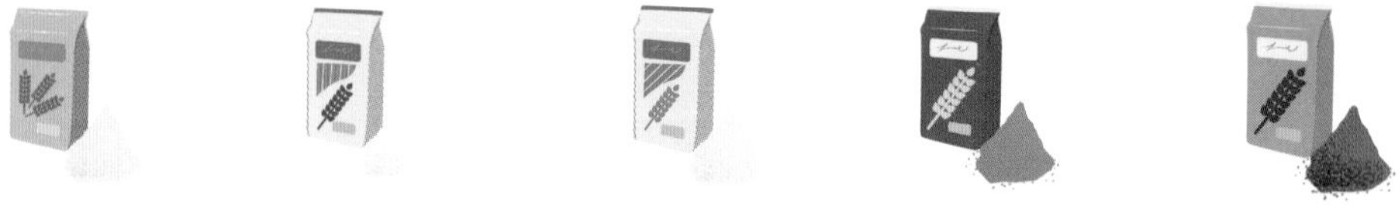

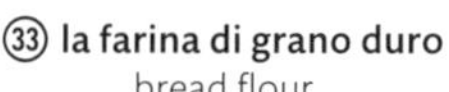

㉝ **la farina di grano duro**
bread flour

㉞ **la farina**
plain flour

㉟ **la farina autolievitante**
self-rising flour

㊱ **la farina marrone**
brown flour

㊲ **la farina integrale**
whole-wheat flour

㊹ **le bolle di CO_2**
CO_2 bubbles

㊳ **la farina bianca**
white flour

㊴ **la farina senza glutine**
gluten-free flour

㊵ **la farina di grano saraceno**
buckwheat flour

㊶ **il lievito disidratato**
dried yeast

㊷ **il lievito fresco**
fresh yeast

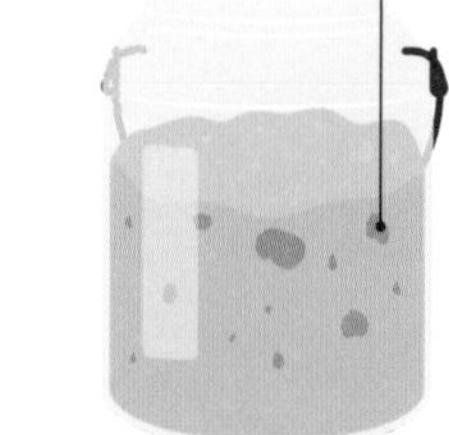

㊸ **il lievito madre**
sourdough starter

See also
29 Cucinare • Cooking **52** Bere e mangiare • Drinking and eating **63** La panetteria (continua) • The bakery continued **65-66** Al bar • At the café **69** Al ristorante • At the restaurant **71** La colazione • Breakfast

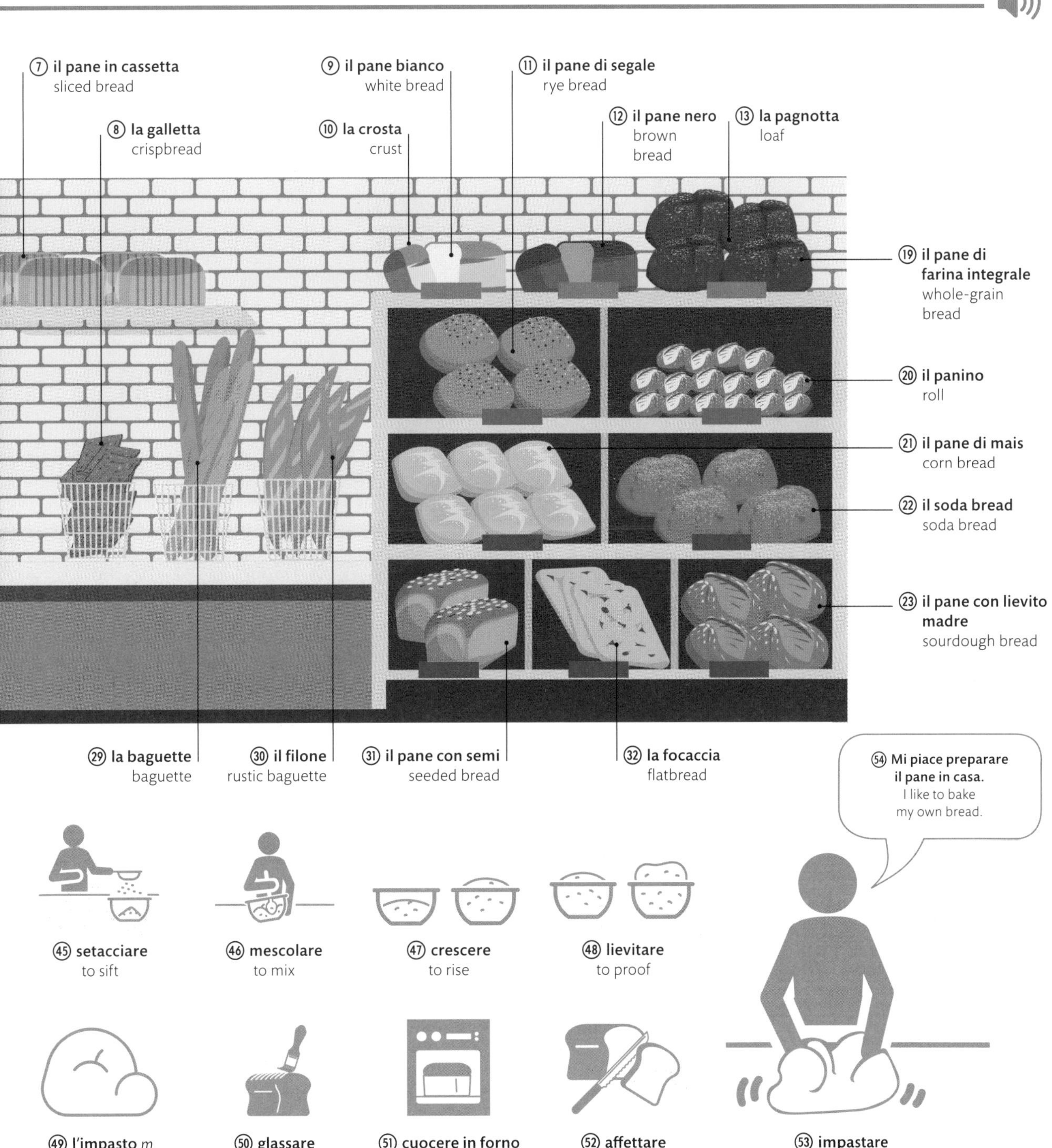
⑦ **il pane in cassetta**
sliced bread
⑧ **la galletta**
crispbread
⑨ **il pane bianco**
white bread
⑩ **la crosta**
crust
⑪ **il pane di segale**
rye bread
⑫ **il pane nero**
brown bread
⑬ **la pagnotta**
loaf
⑲ **il pane di farina integrale**
whole-grain bread
⑳ **il panino**
roll
㉑ **il pane di mais**
corn bread
㉒ **il soda bread**
soda bread
㉓ **il pane con lievito madre**
sourdough bread
㉙ **la baguette**
baguette
㉚ **il filone**
rustic baguette
㉛ **il pane con semi**
seeded bread
㉜ **la focaccia**
flatbread
㊹ **Mi piace preparare il pane in casa.**
I like to bake my own bread.
㊺ **setacciare**
to sift
㊻ **mescolare**
to mix
㊼ **crescere**
to rise
㊽ **lievitare**
to proof
㊾ **l'impasto** *m*
dough
㊿ **glassare**
to glaze
51 **cuocere in forno**
to bake
52 **affettare**
to slice
53 **impastare**
to knead

63 La panetteria (continua)

The bakery continued

63.1 LE TORTE E I DESSERT · CAKES AND DESSERTS

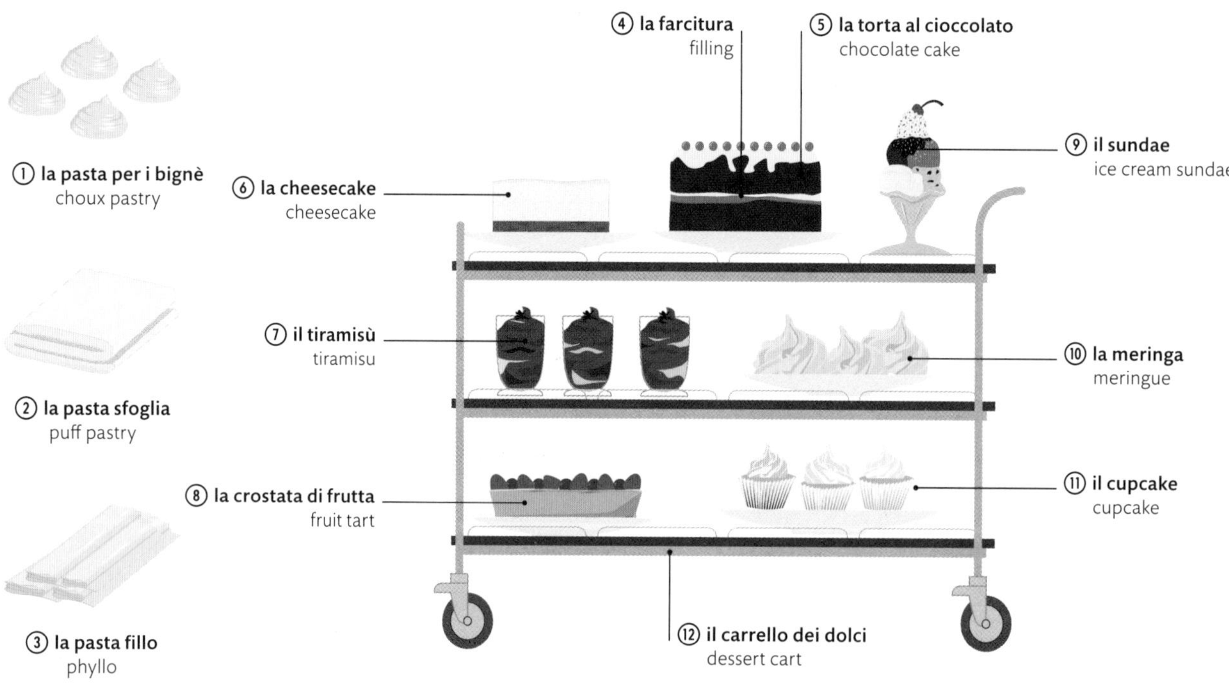

① la pasta per i bignè
choux pastry
② la pasta sfoglia
puff pastry
③ la pasta fillo
phyllo
④ la farcitura
filling
⑤ la torta al cioccolato
chocolate cake
⑥ la cheesecake
cheesecake
⑦ il tiramisù
tiramisu
⑧ la crostata di frutta
fruit tart
⑨ il sundae
ice cream sundae
⑩ la meringa
meringue
⑪ il cupcake
cupcake
⑫ il carrello dei dolci
dessert cart

⑬ **la crema pasticcera**
crème pâtissière

⑭ **il mochi**
mochi

⑮ **la ciambella**
donut

⑯ **la ciambella alla marmellata**
jelly donut

⑰ **la ciambella al cioccolato**
chocolate donut

⑱ **il muffin**
muffin

⑲ **il baklava**
baklava

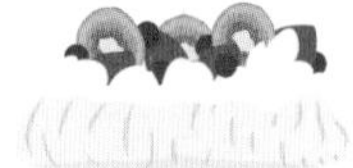
⑳ **la pavlova**
pavlova

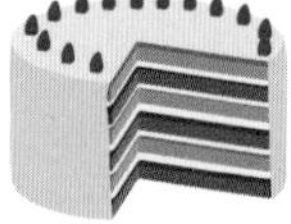
㉑ **la torta a strati**
layer cake

㉒ **il pan di Spagna**
sponge cake

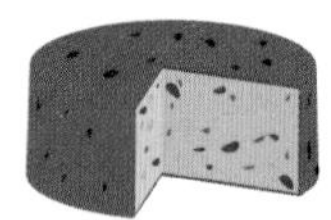
㉓ **la torta alla frutta**
fruitcake

㉔ **la torta**
gateau

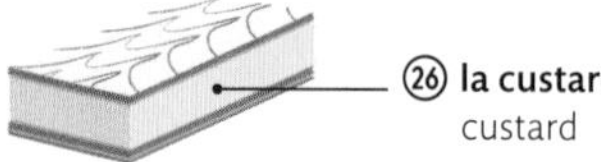
㉖ **la custard**
custard

㉕ **la fetta di custard**
Napoleon

㉗ **l'éclair** *m*
éclair

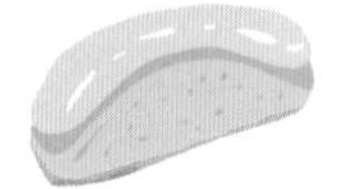
㉘ **il panino glassato**
iced bun

㉙ **la pasta dolce**
pastry

㉚ **il budino di riso**
rice pudding

See also
29 Cucinare • Cooking **52** Bere e mangiare • Drinking and eating
67 I dolciumi • Candy **71** La colazione • Breakfast

63.2 I DOLCETTI E I BISCOTTI • COOKIES AND BISCUITS

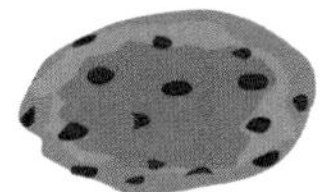
① **il biscotto con gocce di cioccolato**
chocolate chip cookie

② **il biscotto fiorentino**
Florentine

③ **il frollino**
shortbread

④ **il macaron**
macaron

⑤ **l'omino di pan di zenzero** *m*
gingerbread man

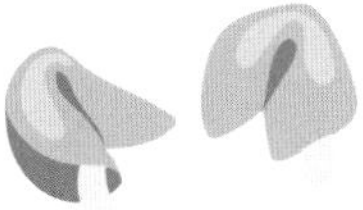
⑥ **i biscotti della fortuna**
fortune cookies

63.3 LE TORTE PER LE RICORRENZE • CELEBRATION CAKES

① **Vuoi un pezzo di torta?**
Would you like a piece of cake?
② **Sì, sembra davvero deliziosa.**
Yes, it looks absolutely delicious.
③ **lo strato superiore**
top tier
④ **la decorazione**
decoration
⑤ **la glassa**
icing
⑥ **il centrotorta**
cake topper
⑦ **il marzapane**
marzipan
⑧ **il nastro**
ribbon

⑨ **la torta nuziale**
wedding cake

⑩ **glassare**
to glaze

⑪ **cuocere in forno**
to bake

⑫ **decorare**
to decorate

⑬ **la torta di compleanno**
birthday cake
⑭ **le candeline**
birthday candles
⑮ **spegnere**
to blow out

64 La gastronomia
The delicatessen

64.1 LA GASTRONOMIA · DELICATESSEN

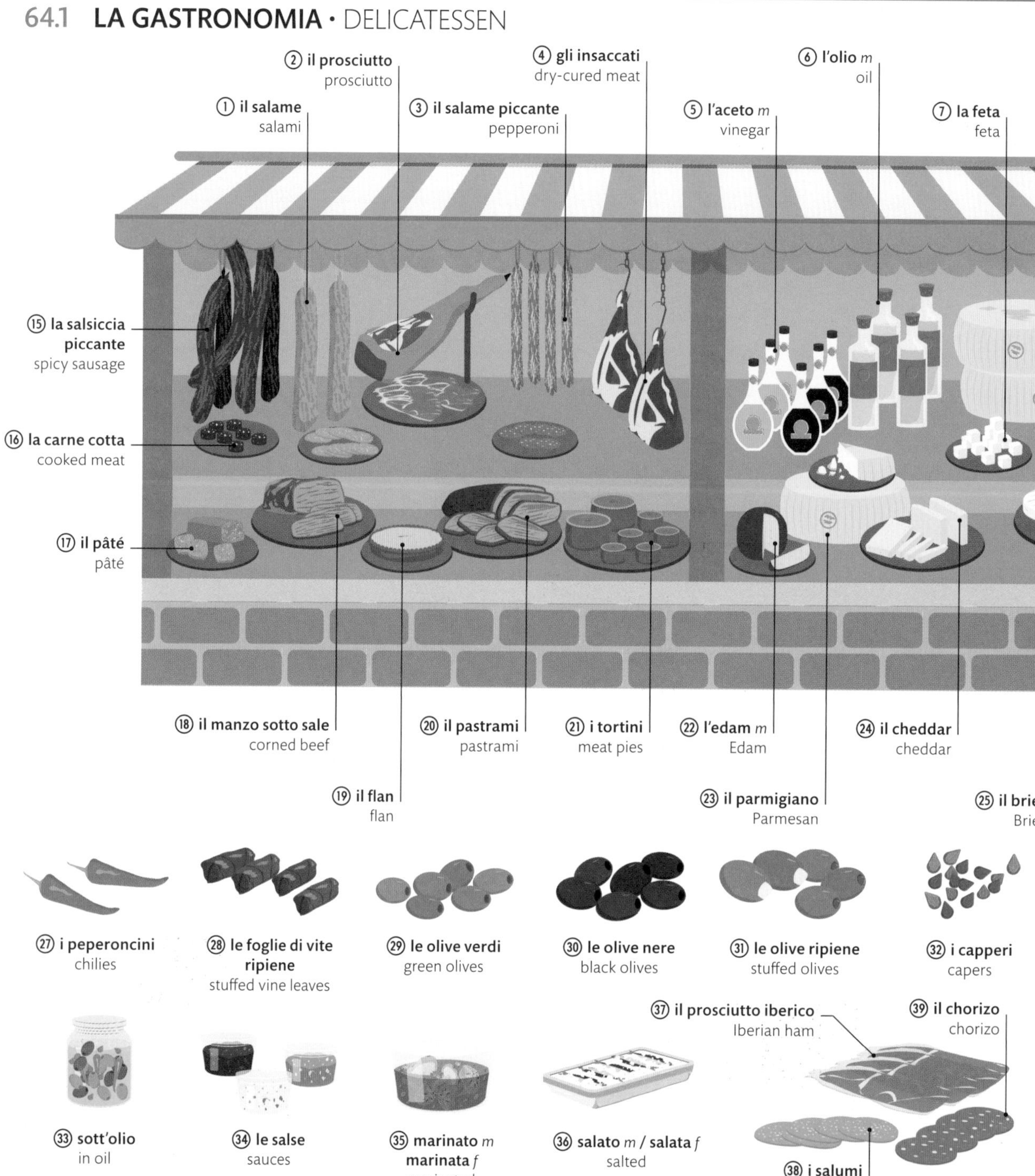

① il salame
salami
② il prosciutto
prosciutto
③ il salame piccante
pepperoni
④ gli insaccati
dry-cured meat
⑤ l'aceto *m*
vinegar
⑥ l'olio *m*
oil
⑦ la feta
feta
⑮ la salsiccia piccante
spicy sausage
⑯ la carne cotta
cooked meat
⑰ il pâté
pâté
⑱ il manzo sotto sale
corned beef
⑲ il flan
flan
⑳ il pastrami
pastrami
㉑ i tortini
meat pies
㉒ l'edam *m*
Edam
㉓ il parmigiano
Parmesan
㉔ il cheddar
cheddar
㉕ il brie
Brie
㉗ i peperoncini
chilies
㉘ le foglie di vite ripiene
stuffed vine leaves
㉙ le olive verdi
green olives
㉚ le olive nere
black olives
㉛ le olive ripiene
stuffed olives
㉜ i capperi
capers
㉝ sott'olio
in oil
㉞ le salse
sauces
㉟ marinato *m* marinata *f*
marinated
㊱ salato *m* / salata *f*
salted
㊲ il prosciutto iberico
Iberian ham
㊳ i salumi
cured meat
㊴ il chorizo
chorizo

See also
29 Cucinare • Cooking **52** Bere e mangiare • Drinking and eating **53** La carne • Meat **60** Nella dispensa • In the pantry **61** I prodotti caseari • Dairy produce **65-66** Al bar • At the café **69** Al ristorante • At the restaurant **71** La colazione • Breakfast **72** Il pranzo e la cena • Lunch and dinner

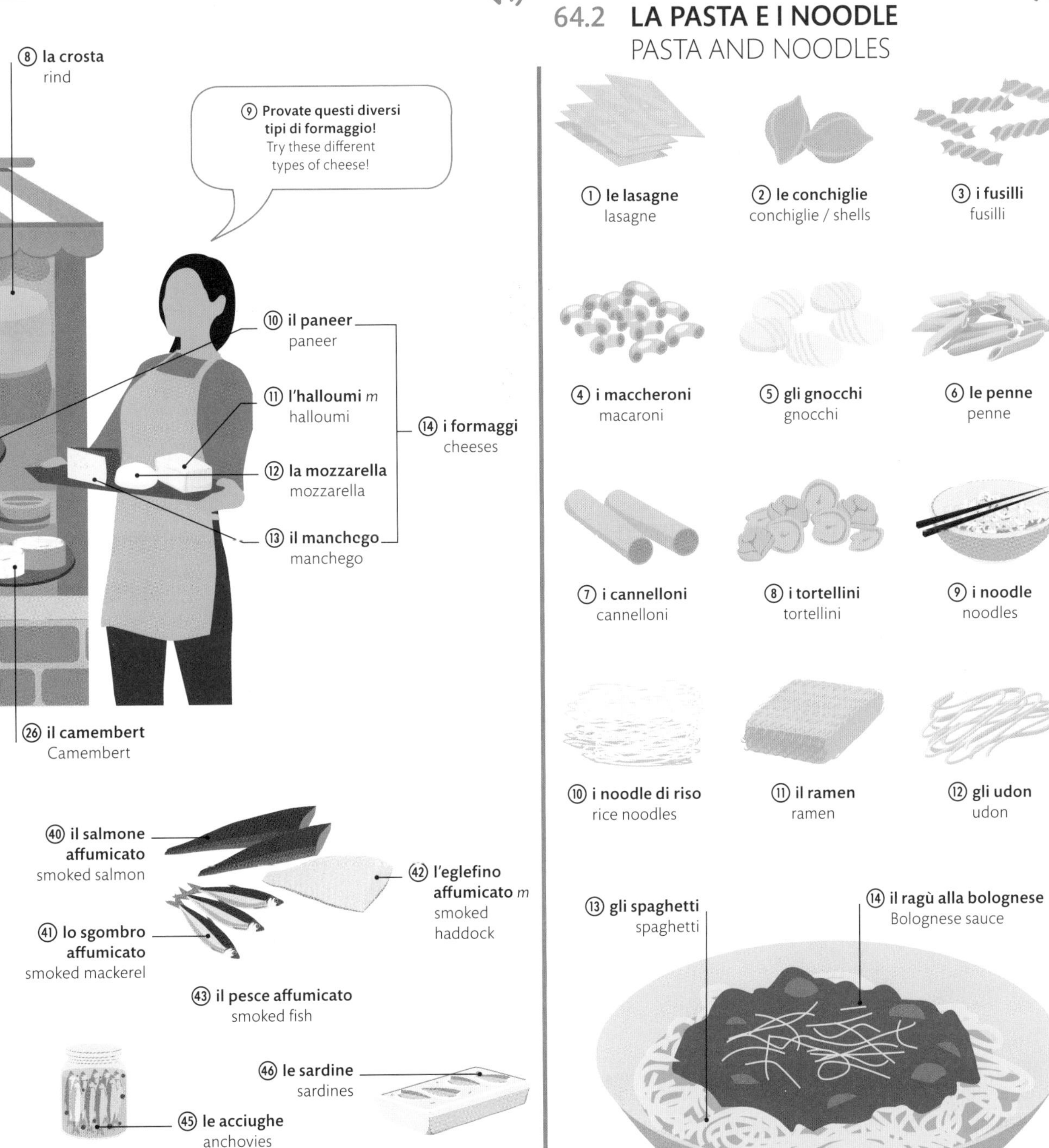
(8) la crosta
rind
(9) Provate questi diversi tipi di formaggio!
Try these different types of cheese!
(10) il paneer
paneer
(11) l'halloumi m
halloumi
(12) la mozzarella
mozzarella
(13) il manchego
manchego
(14) i formaggi
cheeses
(26) il camembert
Camembert
(40) il salmone affumicato
smoked salmon
(41) lo sgombro affumicato
smoked mackerel
(42) l'eglefino affumicato m
smoked haddock
(43) il pesce affumicato
smoked fish
(44) in salamoia
in brine
(45) le acciughe
anchovies
(46) le sardine
sardines
(47) il pesce marinato
marinated fish

64.2 LA PASTA E I NOODLE
PASTA AND NOODLES

(1) **le lasagne**
lasagne

(2) **le conchiglie**
conchiglie / shells

(3) **i fusilli**
fusilli

(4) **i maccheroni**
macaroni

(5) **gli gnocchi**
gnocchi

(6) **le penne**
penne

(7) **i cannelloni**
cannelloni

(8) **i tortellini**
tortellini

(9) **i noodle**
noodles

(10) **i noodle di riso**
rice noodles

(11) **il ramen**
ramen

(12) **gli udon**
udon

(13) **gli spaghetti**
spaghetti

(14) **il ragù alla bolognese**
Bolognese sauce

65 Al bar
At the café

65.1 IL BAR · CAFÉ

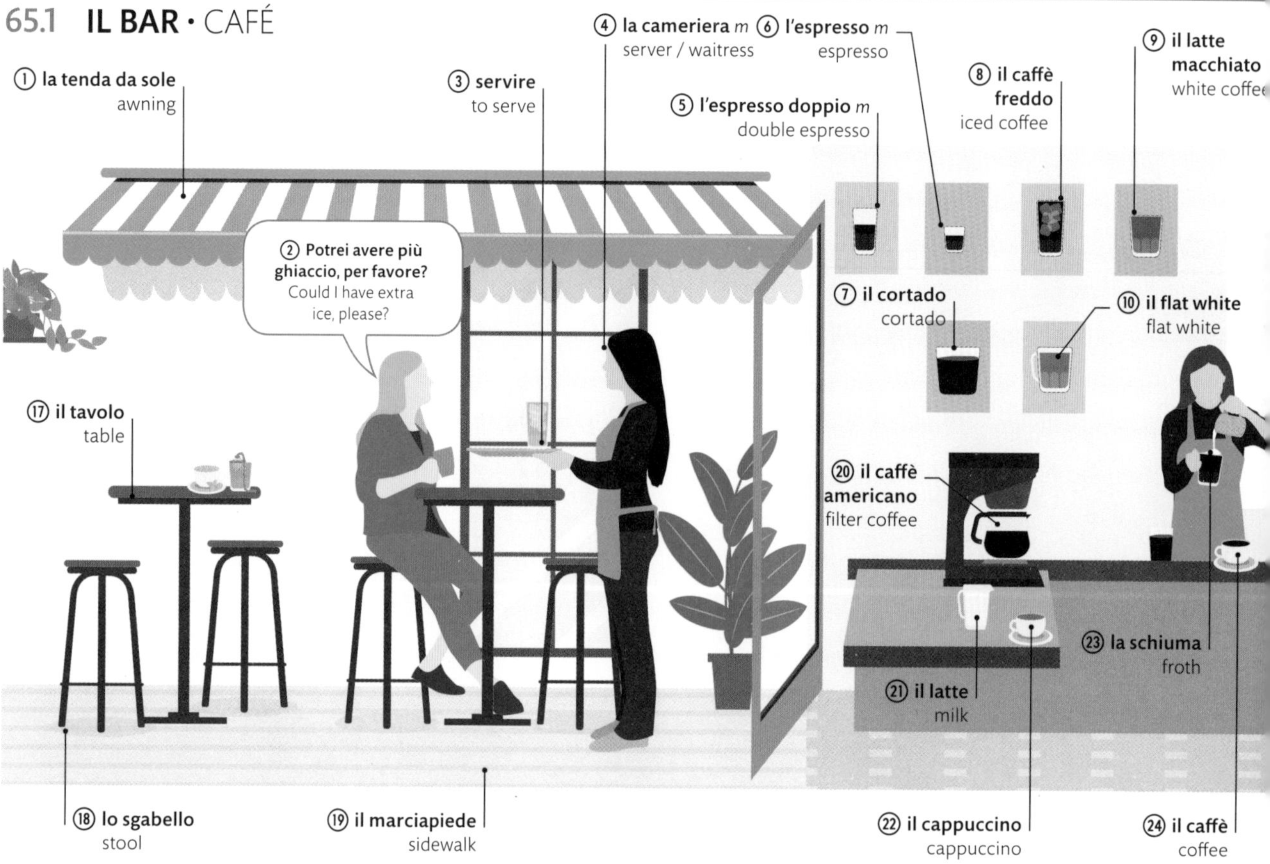

① la tenda da sole
awning

② Potrei avere più ghiaccio, per favore?
Could I have extra ice, please?

③ servire
to serve

④ la cameriera *m*
server / waitress

⑤ l'espresso doppio *m*
double espresso

⑥ l'espresso *m*
espresso

⑦ il cortado
cortado

⑧ il caffè freddo
iced coffee

⑨ il latte macchiato
white coffee

⑩ il flat white
flat white

⑰ il tavolo
table

⑱ lo sgabello
stool

⑲ il marciapiede
sidewalk

⑳ il caffè americano
filter coffee

㉑ il latte
milk

㉒ il cappuccino
cappuccino

㉓ la schiuma
froth

㉔ il caffè
coffee

65.2 I SUCCHI E I MILKSHAKE · JUICES AND MILKSHAKES

① il frullatore
blender

② l'acqua di cocco *f*
coconut water

③ la spremuta di arancia
orange juice
with pulp

④ il succo d'arancia
smooth orange juice

⑤ il succo di mela
apple juice

⑥ il succo d'ananas
pineapple juice

⑦ il succo di pomodoro
tomato juice

⑧ il succo di mango
mango juice

⑨ il succo di mirtillo rosso
cranberry juice

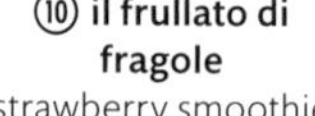
⑩ il frullato di fragole
strawberry smoothie

⑪ il milkshake al cioccolato
chocolate milkshake

⑫ il milkshake alla fragola
strawberry milkshake

See also
27 La cucina e le stoviglie • Kitchen and tableware **52** Bere e mangiare
Drinking and eating **66** Al bar (continua) • At the café continued
70 Il fast food • Fast food **72** Il pranzo e la cena • Lunch and dinner

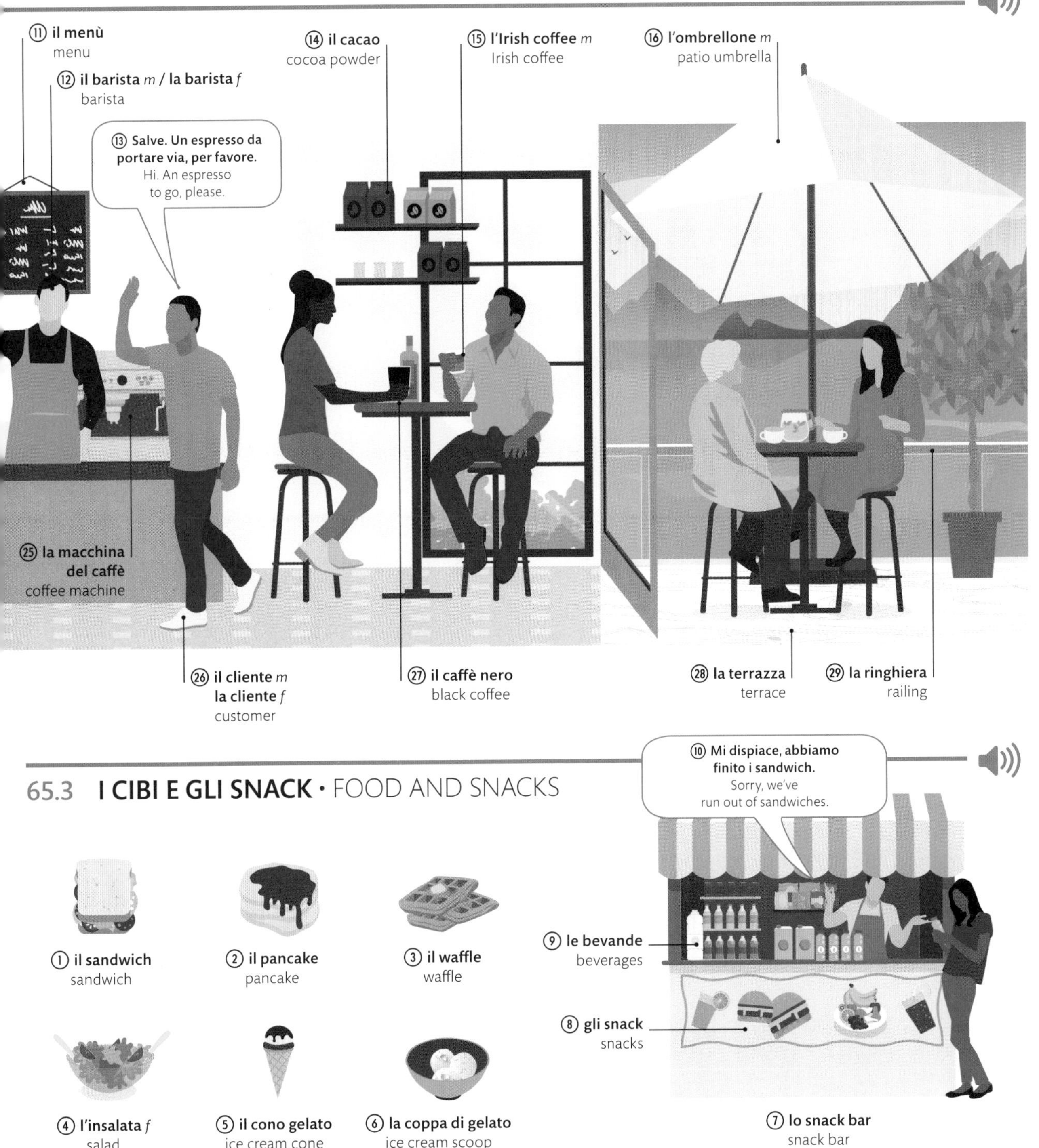
⑪ **il menù** menu
⑫ **il barista** *m* / **la barista** *f* barista
⑬ **Salve. Un espresso da portare via, per favore.** Hi. An espresso to go, please.
⑭ **il cacao** cocoa powder
⑮ **l'Irish coffee** *m* Irish coffee
⑯ **l'ombrellone** *m* patio umbrella
㉕ **la macchina del caffè** coffee machine
㉖ **il cliente** *m* **la cliente** *f* customer
㉗ **il caffè nero** black coffee
㉘ **la terrazza** terrace
㉙ **la ringhiera** railing

65.3 I CIBI E GLI SNACK • FOOD AND SNACKS

⑩ **Mi dispiace, abbiamo finito i sandwich.** Sorry, we've run out of sandwiches.
① **il sandwich** sandwich
② **il pancake** pancake
③ **il waffle** waffle
④ **l'insalata** *f* salad
⑤ **il cono gelato** ice cream cone
⑥ **la coppa di gelato** ice cream scoop
⑦ **lo snack bar** snack bar
⑧ **gli snack** snacks
⑨ **le bevande** beverages

66 Al bar (continua)
At the café continued

See also
27 La cucina e le stoviglie • Kitchen and tableware
52 Bere e mangiare • Drinking and eating
72 Il pranzo e la cena • Lunch and dinner

66.1 IL TÈ • TEA

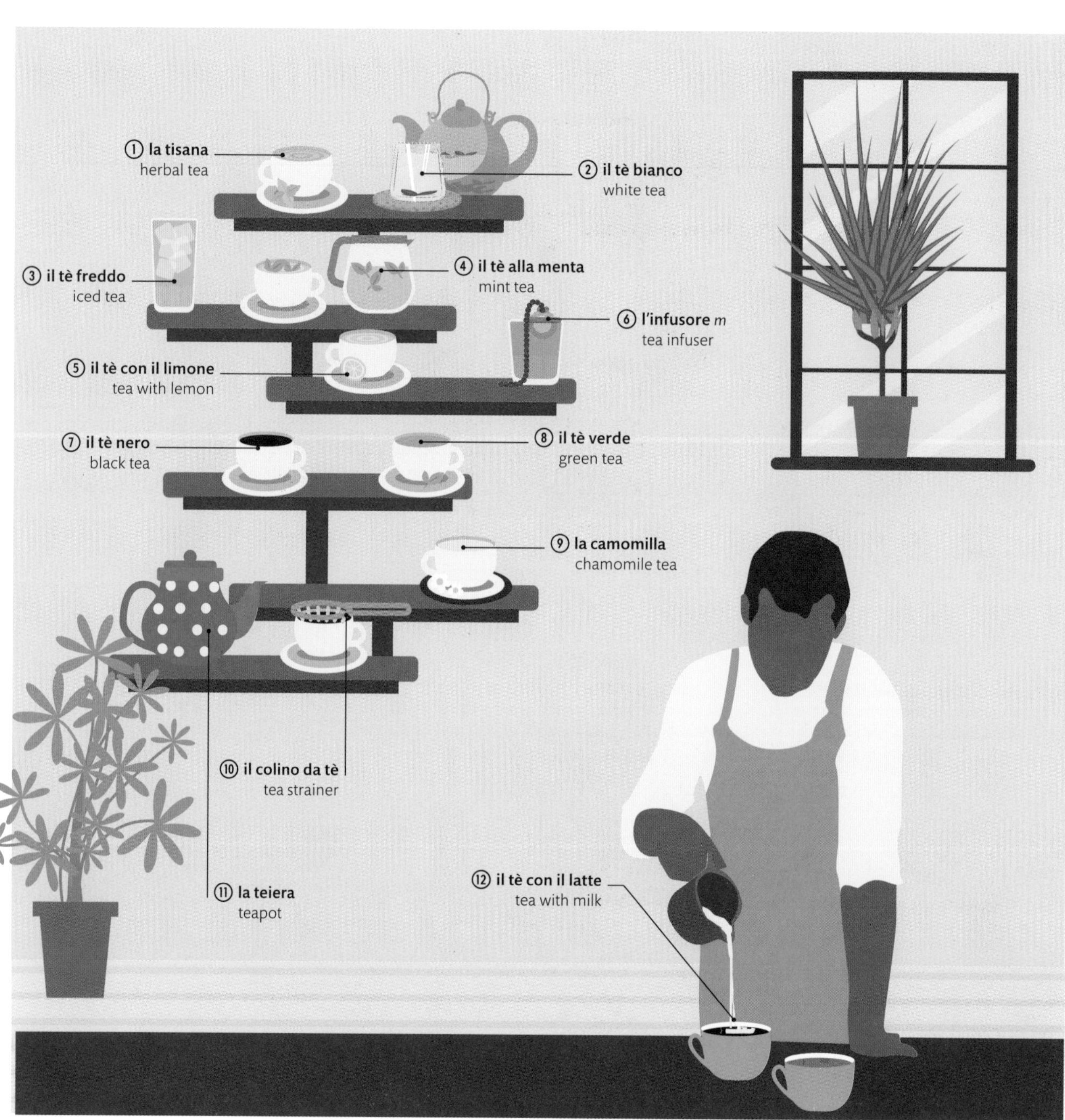
① la tisana
herbal tea
② il tè bianco
white tea
③ il tè freddo
iced tea
④ il tè alla menta
mint tea
⑤ il tè con il limone
tea with lemon
⑥ l'infusore *m*
tea infuser
⑦ il tè nero
black tea
⑧ il tè verde
green tea
⑨ la camomilla
chamomile tea
⑩ il colino da tè
tea strainer
⑪ la teiera
teapot
⑫ il tè con il latte
tea with milk

I dolciumi
Candy

See also
48 Il supermercato • The supermarket
62-63 La panetteria • The bakery

67.1 IL NEGOZIO DI DOLCIUMI • CANDY STORE

① **la caramella gommosa alla frutta**
fruit gummies
② **l'halva** *m*
halva
③ **la mentina**
mint
④ **il toffee**
toffee
⑤ **le caramelle morbide**
soft candy
⑥ **la liquirizia**
licorice
⑦ **il bastoncino di zucchero**
candy cane
⑧ **la caramella gommosa**
jelly beans
⑨ **la barretta di cioccolato**
chocolate bar
⑩ **il cioccolato fondente**
dark chocolate
⑪ **le caramelle**
hard candy
⑫ **il lokum**
Turkish delight
⑬ **il lecca lecca**
lollipop
⑭ **il torrone**
nougat
⑮ **il cioccolato al latte**
milk chocolate
⑯ **il cioccolato bianco**
white chocolate
⑰ **lo zucchero filato**
cotton candy
⑱ **le caramelle assortite**
penny candy
⑲ **il marshmallow**
marshmallow
⑳ **la gomma da masticare**
chewing gum

68 Al bar
At the bar

68.1 IL BAR • BAR

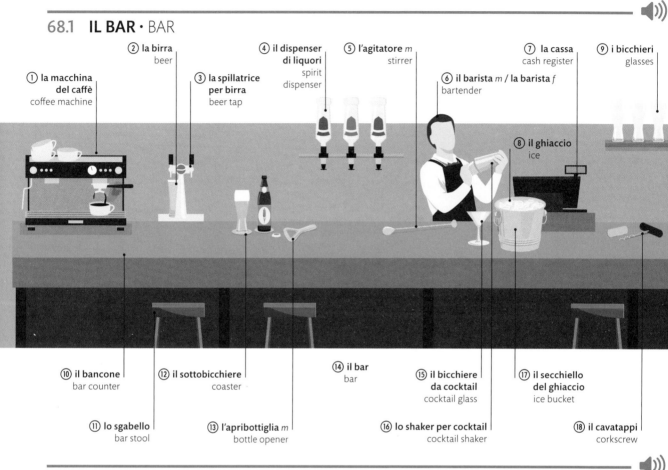

1. **la macchina del caffè** coffee machine
2. **la birra** beer
3. **la spillatrice per birra** beer tap
4. **il dispenser di liquori** spirit dispenser
5. **l'agitatore** *m* stirrer
6. **il barista** *m* / **la barista** *f* bartender
7. **la cassa** cash register
8. **il ghiaccio** ice
9. **i bicchieri** glasses
10. **il bancone** bar counter
11. **lo sgabello** bar stool
12. **il sottobicchiere** coaster
13. **l'apribottiglia** *m* bottle opener
14. **il bar** bar
15. **il bicchiere da cocktail** cocktail glass
16. **lo shaker per cocktail** cocktail shaker
17. **il secchiello del ghiaccio** ice bucket
18. **il cavatappi** corkscrew

68.2 LA BIRRA E IL VINO • BEER AND WINE

1. **la birra lager** lager

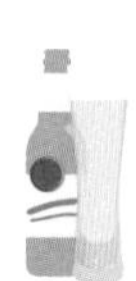

2. **la Pilsner** Pilsner

3. **la birra di frumento** wheat beer

4. **l'India Pale Ale (IPA)** *f* Indian pale ale (IPA)

5. **la birra ale** ale

6. **la birra stout** stout

0%

7. **la birra analcolica** alcohol-free beer

8. **il vino rosso** red wine

9. **il vino bianco** white wine

10. **il rosé** rosé

11. **lo spumante** sparkling wine

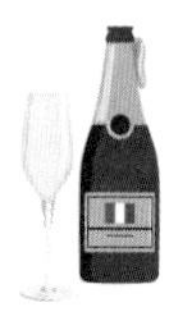

12. **lo champagne** Champagne

See also
52 Bere e mangiare • Drinking and eating **69** Al ristorante
At the restaurant **72** Il pranzo e la cena • Lunch and dinner

68.3 I DRINK • DRINKS

① **l'acqua minerale** *f*
mineral water

② **il sidro**
cider

③ **il rum**
rum

④ **il rum e cola**
rum and cola

⑤ **la vodka**
vodka

⑥ **la vodka con succo d'arancia**
vodka and orange

⑦ **il gin tonic**
gin and tonic

⑧ **il Martini**
Martini

⑨ **il cocktail**
cocktail

⑩ **il cocktail analcolico**
mocktail

⑪ **lo sherry**
sherry

⑫ **il porto**
port

⑬ **il whisky**
whiskey

⑭ **lo scotch con acqua**
Scotch and water

⑮ **il brandy**
brandy

⑯ **il liquore**
liqueur

⑰ **con ghiaccio**
with ice

⑱ **senza ghiaccio**
without ice

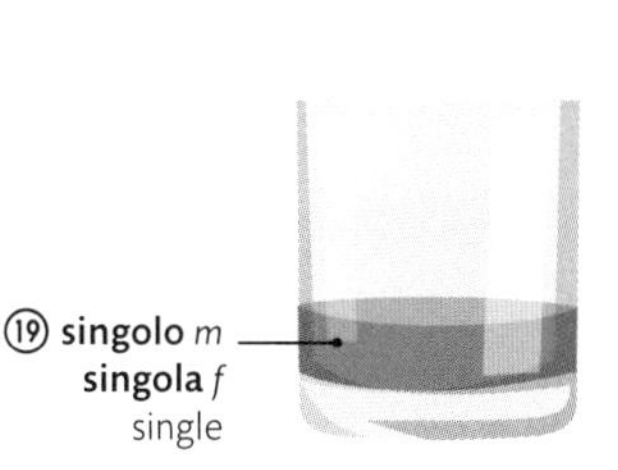
⑲ **singolo** *m* **singola** *f*
single

⑳ **doppio** *m* / **doppia** *f*
double

㉑ **lo shottino**
shot

㉒ **la quantità**
measure

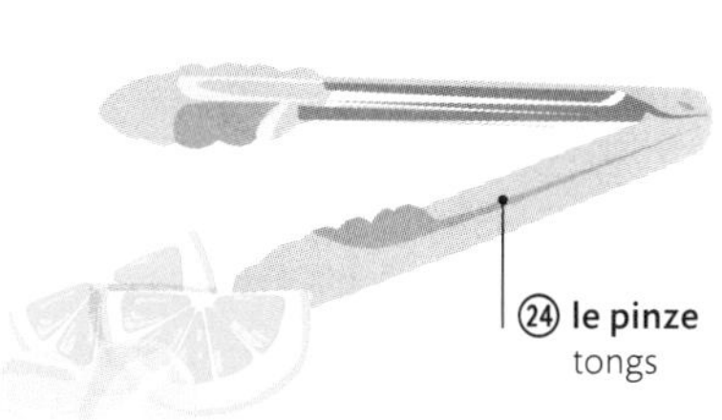
㉔ **le pinze**
tongs

㉓ **il ghiaccio e il limone**
ice and lemon

68.4 GLI SNACK • BAR SNACKS

① **le patatine**
chips

② **le noci**
nuts

③ **le mandorle**
almonds

④ **gli anacardi**
cashews

⑤ **le arachidi**
peanuts

⑥ **le olive**
olives

69 Al ristorante
At the restaurant

69.1 IL RISTORANTE • RESTAURANT

① Quali sono le specialità del giorno?
What are today's specials?
② la carta dei vini
wine list
③ il barista *m* / la barista *f*
bartender
④ i clienti
customers
⑫ il direttore di sala *m*
la direttrice di sala *f*
restaurant manager
⑭ Possiamo avere un tavolo per due?
May we have a table for two, please?

⑪ la cameriera
server / waitress

⑬ il coperto
table setting

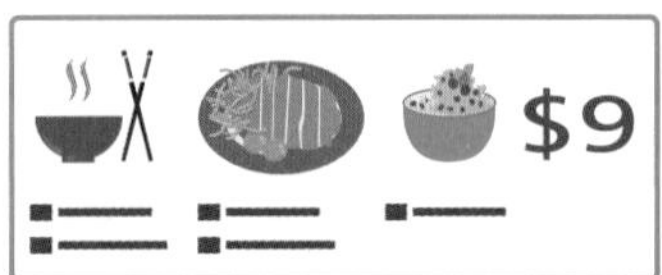

$9

⑱ il menù fisso
fixed menu

⑲ il brunch
brunch

⑳ il menù del pranzo
lunch menu

㉑ il menù alla carta
à la carte menu

㉒ le specialità
specials

㉓ il menù per bambini
kids meal

㉔ il buffet
buffet

㉕ il pasto di tre portate
three-course meal

㉖ la zuppa
soup

㉗ l'antipasto *m*
appetizer

㉘ il primo piatto
entrée

㉙ il contorno
side / side order

㉚ il tagliere di formaggi
cheese platter

㉛ il dessert
dessert

㉜ la bevanda
beverage

㉝ il caffè
coffee

㉞ il digestivo
digestif

See also
27 La cucina e le stoviglie • Kitchen and tableware **52** Bere e mangiare • Drinking and eating **53** La carne • Meat **54** Il pesce e i frutti di mare • Fish and seafood **55-56** La verdura • Vegetables **72** Il pranzo e la cena • Lunch and dinner

⑤ **il prezzo**
price

⑥ **il vassoio**
tray

⑦ **Buon appetito!**
Enjoy your meal!

⑧ **la cucina**
kitchen

⑨ **lo chef** *m*
la chef *f*
chef

⑩ **l'aiuto cuoco** *m / f*
commis chef

⑮ **il menù della cena**
dinner menu

⑯ **il cameriere**
server / waiter

⑰ **il carrello dei dolci**
dessert cart

㉟ **il sommelier**
la sommelier
sommelier

㊱ **mangiare fuori**
to eat out

㊲ **prenotare**
to make a reservation

㊳ **cancellare**
to cancel

㊴ **ordinare**
to order

㊵ **il contorno**
il conto
check

㊶ **pagare separatamente**
to pay separately

㊷ **dividere il conto**
to split the check

㊸ **il prezzo del servizio**
service charge

㊹ **servizio incluso**
service included

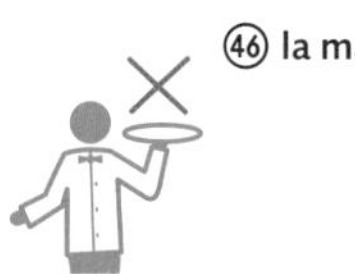

㊺ **servizio non incluso**
service not included

㊻ **la mancia**
tip

㊼ **lo scontrino**
receipt

㊽ **il bistrot**
bistro

70 Il fast food

Fast food

70.1 IN UN FAST FOOD

IN A FAST-FOOD RESTAURANT

① il listino prezzi
price list
② la cannuccia
straw
③ la bibita
soft drink
④ le patatine fritte
fries
⑤ È da mangiare qui?
Is this to eat in?
⑥ l'hamburger *m*
hamburger
⑦ il tovagliolo di carta
paper napkin
⑧ il vassoio
tray
⑨ il fast food
burger bar
⑩ mangiare sul posto
to eat in
⑪ il cibo da asporto
carry out
⑫ la consegna a domicilio
home delivery
⑬ la bancarella
street stall
⑭ il menù
menu
⑮ il milkshake
milkshake
⑯ la bibita in lattina
canned drink
⑰ la bibita gassata
soda
⑱ l'offerta del giorno *f*
meal deal
⑲ la tazza riutilizzabile
reusable cup
⑳ la salsa
condiment
㉑ il food truck
food truck
㉒ il waffle
waffle
㉓ il gelato
ice cream
㉔ il muffin
muffin
㉕ la ciambella
donut
㉖ il fattorino di cibo a domicilio
food delivery driver
㉗ Il tuo ordine sta arrivando.
Your order is on its way.

See also
52 Bere e mangiare • Drinking and eating **60** Nella dispensa • In the pantry **65-66** Al bar • At the café **67** I dolciumi • Candy

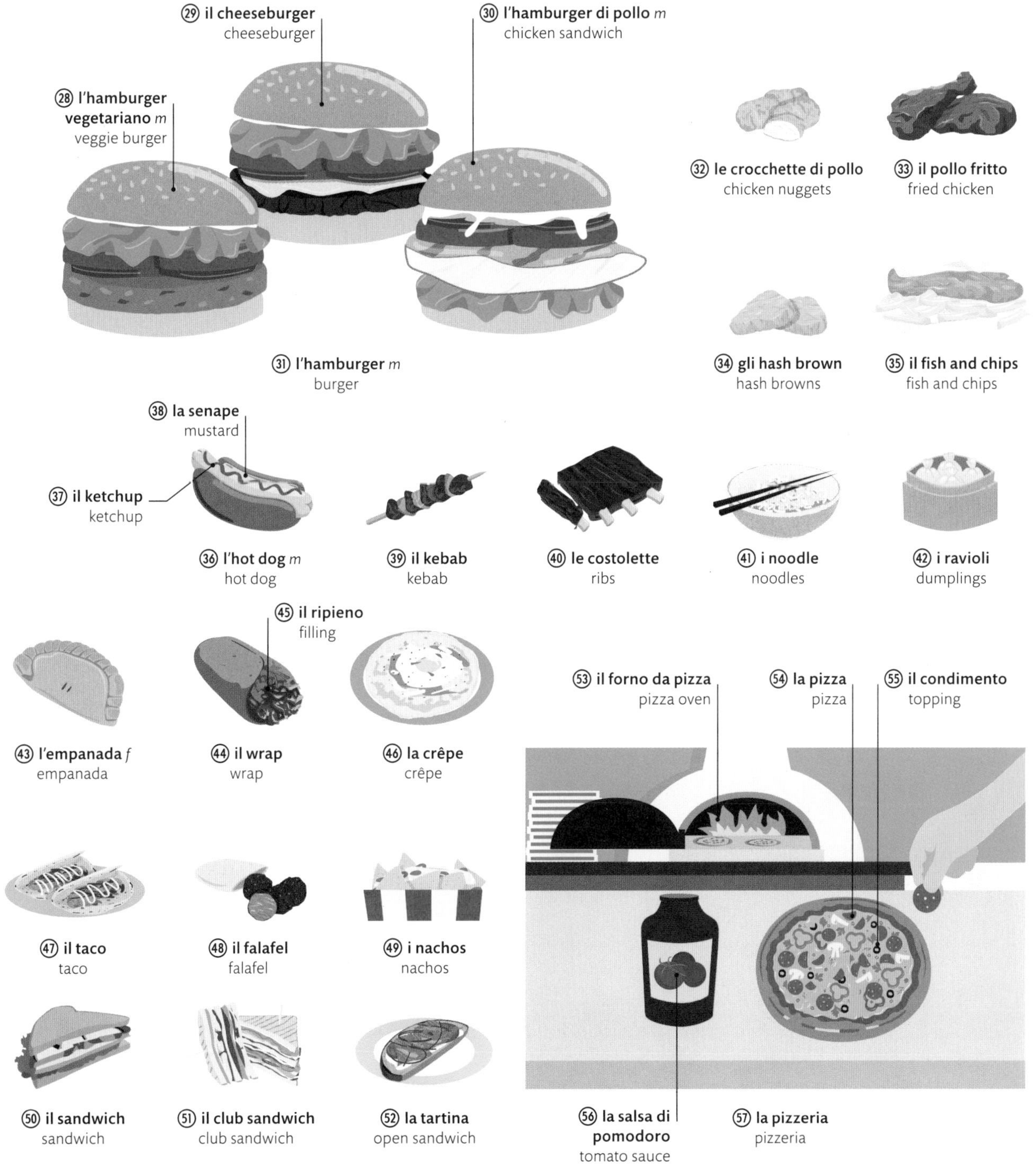

㉙ **il cheeseburger**
cheeseburger
㉚ **l'hamburger di pollo** *m*
chicken sandwich
㉘ **l'hamburger vegetariano** *m*
veggie burger
㉛ **l'hamburger** *m*
burger
㊳ **la senape**
mustard
㊲ **il ketchup**
ketchup
㊺ **il ripieno**
filling
㊸ **il forno da pizza**
pizza oven
㊹ **la pizza**
pizza
㊺ **il condimento**
topping
㊻ **la salsa di pomodoro**
tomato sauce

㉜ **le crocchette di pollo**
chicken nuggets

㉝ **il pollo fritto**
fried chicken

㉞ **gli hash brown**
hash browns

㉟ **il fish and chips**
fish and chips

㊱ **l'hot dog** *m*
hot dog

㊴ **il kebab**
kebab

㊵ **le costolette**
ribs

㊶ **i noodle**
noodles

㊷ **i ravioli**
dumplings

㊸ **l'empanada** *f*
empanada

㊹ **il wrap**
wrap

㊻ **la crêpe**
crêpe

㊼ **il taco**
taco

㊽ **il falafel**
falafel

㊾ **i nachos**
nachos

㊿ **il sandwich**
sandwich

51 **il club sandwich**
club sandwich

52 **la tartina**
open sandwich

57 **la pizzeria**
pizzeria

71 La colazione
Breakfast

71.1 LA COLAZIONE A BUFFET · BREAKFAST BUFFET

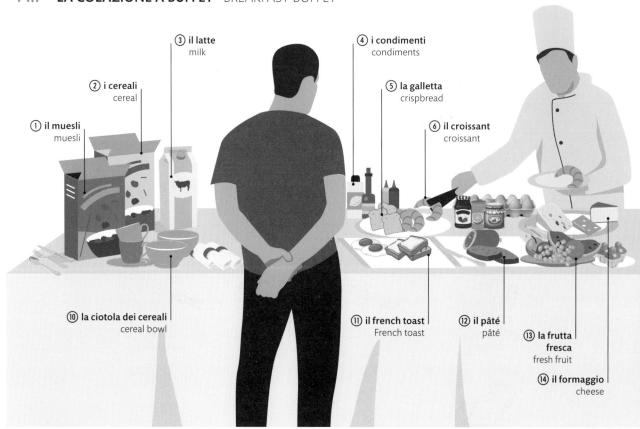

① **il muesli**
muesli

② **i cereali**
cereal

③ **il latte**
milk

④ **i condimenti**
condiments

⑤ **la galletta**
crispbread

⑥ **il croissant**
croissant

⑩ **la ciotola dei cereali**
cereal bowl

⑪ **il french toast**
French toast

⑫ **il pâté**
pâté

⑬ **la frutta fresca**
fresh fruit

⑭ **il formaggio**
cheese

⑰ **il prosciutto**
ham

⑱ **il toast**
toasted sandwich

⑲ **l'omelette** *f*
omelet

⑳ **l'avocado toast** *m*
avocado toast

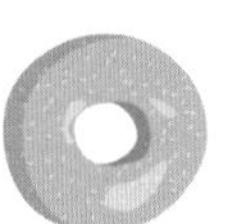
㉑ **il bagel**
bagel

㉒ **il rotolo alla cannella**
cinnamon rolls

㉕ **la confettura**
jam

㉖ **la marmellata di arance**
marmalade

㉗ **il miele**
honey

㉘ **il tè**
tea

㉙ **il caffè**
coffee

㉚ **il succo di frutta**
fruit juice

See also
29 Cucinare • Cooking **52** Bere e mangiare • Drinking and eating **53** La carne • Meat
57 La frutta • Fruit **58** La frutta e la frutta a guscio • Fruit and nuts **61** I prodotti caseari
Dairy produce **64** La gastronomia • The delicatessen **65-66** Al bar • At the café

⑨ **il cestino del pane**
bread basket

⑦ **gli affettati**
cold meats

⑧ **la brioche**
brioche

⑯ **il pane**
bread

⑮ **il burro**
butter

㉓ **i waffle**
waffles

㉔ **la panna**
cream

㉛ **la frutta secca**
dried fruit

㉜ **lo yogurt alla frutta**
fruit yogurt

71.2 LA COLAZIONE ALL'INGLESE • COOKED BREAKFAST

① **la salsiccia**
sausage

② **le polpette di salsiccia**
sausage patties

③ **la pancetta**
bacon

④ **le aringhe affumicate**
kippers

⑤ **il salmone affumicato**
smoked salmon

⑥ **lo sgombro affumicato**
smoked mackerel

⑦ **il sanguinaccio**
black pudding

⑧ **i reni**
kidneys

⑨ **le uova strapazzate**
scrambled eggs

⑩ **l'uovo in camicia** *m*
poached egg

⑫ **l'albume** *m*
egg white

⑪ **l'uovo sodo** *m*
boiled egg

⑬ **il tuorlo**
yolk

⑭ **l'uovo al tegamino** *m*
fried egg

⑮ **il pane tostato**
toast

⑯ **i funghi fritti**
fried mushrooms

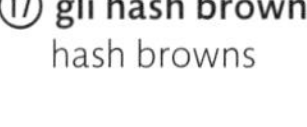

⑰ **gli hash brown**
hash browns

⑱ **il pomodoro grigliato**
grilled tomato

⑲ **il pomodoro in scatola**
canned tomato

⑳ **i fagioli stufati**
baked beans

㉑ **il breakfast roll**
breakfast roll

㉒ **il burrito**
breakfast burrito

㉓ **le frittelle di patate**
potato cakes

㉔ **i pancake**
pancakes

㉕ **il porridge**
oatmeal

72 Il pranzo e la cena
Lunch and dinner

72.1 I CIBI E I PIATTI · MEALS AND DISHES

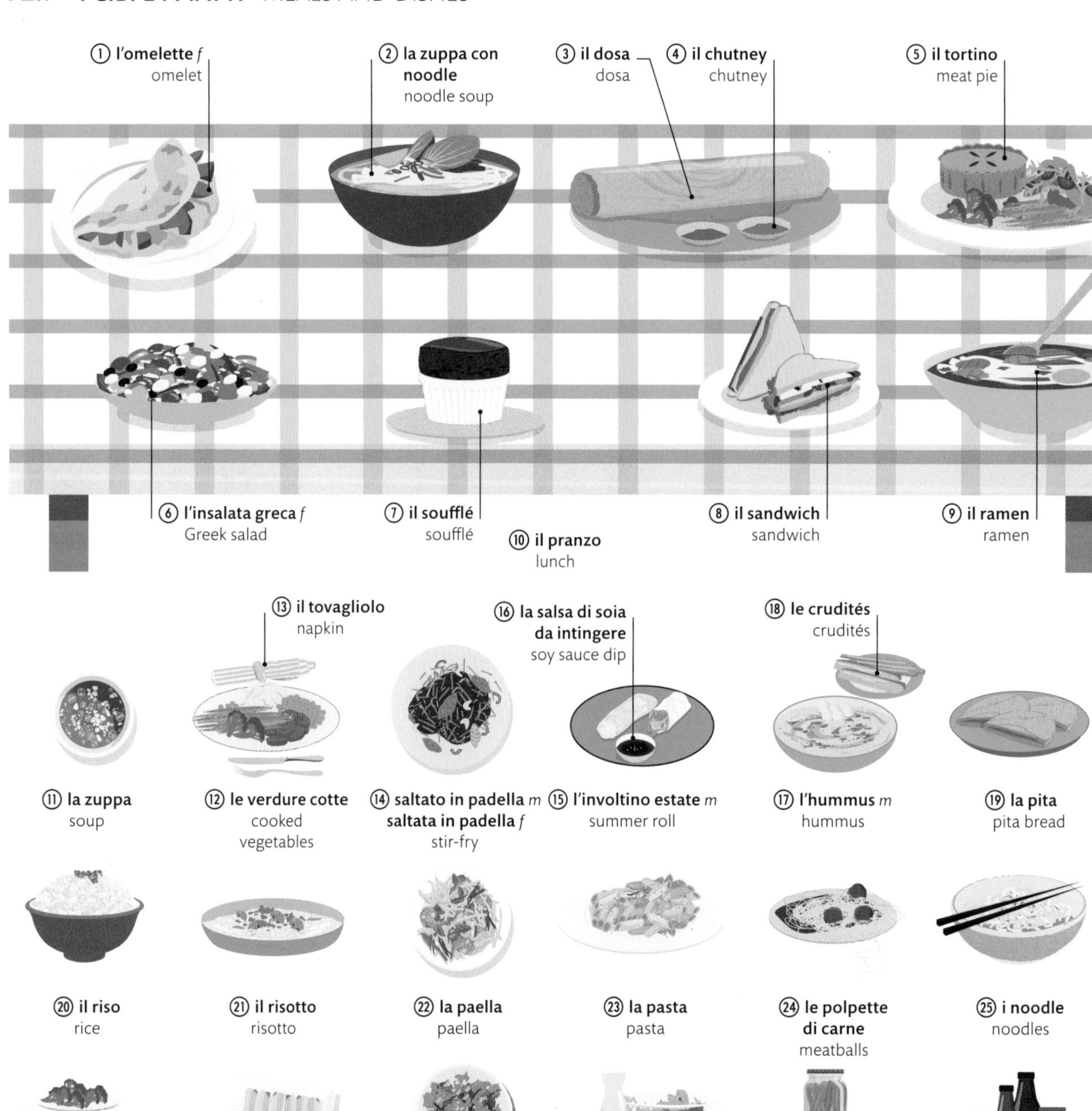

① **l'omelette** *f*
omelet
② **la zuppa con noodle**
noodle soup
③ **il dosa**
dosa
④ **il chutney**
chutney
⑤ **il tortino**
meat pie
⑥ **l'insalata greca** *f*
Greek salad
⑦ **il soufflé**
soufflé
⑧ **il sandwich**
sandwich
⑨ **il ramen**
ramen
⑩ **il pranzo**
lunch
⑪ **la zuppa**
soup
⑫ **le verdure cotte**
cooked vegetables
⑬ **il tovagliolo**
napkin
⑭ **saltato in padella** *m* **saltata in padella** *f*
stir-fry
⑮ **l'involtino estate** *m*
summer roll
⑯ **la salsa di soia da intingere**
soy sauce dip
⑰ **l'hummus** *m*
hummus
⑱ **le crudités**
crudités
⑲ **la pita**
pita bread
⑳ **il riso**
rice
㉑ **il risotto**
risotto
㉒ **la paella**
paella
㉓ **la pasta**
pasta
㉔ **le polpette di carne**
meatballs
㉕ **i noodle**
noodles

㉖ **i contorni**
side dishes

㉗ **l'involtino primavera** *m*
spring roll

㉘ **l'insalata tritata** *f*
chopped salad

㉙ **il condimento**
dressing

㉚ **i sottaceti**
pickles

㉛ **i condimenti**
condiments

See also
27 La cucina e le stoviglie • Kitchen and tableware **29** Cucinare • Cooking
52 Bere e mangiare • Drinking and eating **53** La carne • Meat **55-56** La verdura
Vegetables **65-66** Al bar • At the café **69** Al ristorante • At the restaurant

㉜ **l'insalata mista** *f*
mixed salad
㉝ **il kebab**
kebab
㉞ **il brodo**
broth
㉟ **i ravioli**
dumplings
㊱ **l'hot pot cinese** *m*
Chinese hotpot
㊲ **il pollo arrosto**
roast chicken
㊳ **il curry**
curry
㊴ **le lasagne**
lasagna
㊵ **gli spaghetti**
spaghetti
㊶ **lo stufato**
stew
㊷ **la cena**
dinner

72.2 LA PREPARAZIONE DEL CIBO · FOOD PREPARATION

① **farcito** *m* **farcita** *f*
stuffed

② **grigliato** *m* **grigliata** *f*
grilled

③ **marinato** *m* **marinata** *f*
marinated

④ **in salsa**
in sauce

⑤ **in camicia**
poached

⑥ **bollito** *m* **bollita** *f*
boiled

⑦ **cotto al forno** *m* **cotta al forno** *f*
baked

⑧ **saltato in padella** *m* **saltata in padella** *f*
stir-fried

⑨ **al tegame**
fried

⑩ **fritto** *m* / **fritta** *f*
deep-fried

⑪ **affumicato** *m* **affumicata** *f*
smoked

⑫ **al vapore**
steamed

⑬ **schiacciato** *m* **schiacciata** *f*
mashed

⑭ **condito** *m* **condita** *f*
dressed

⑮ **stagionato** *m* **stagionata** *f*
cured

⑯ **sott'aceto**
pickled

⑰ **il kosher**
kosher

⑱ **l'halal** *m*
halal

73 A scuola
At school

73.1 LA SCUOLA E LO STUDIO · SCHOOL AND STUDY

① **la scuola**
school

② **l'aula** *f*
classroom

③ **la classe**
class

④ **l'insegnante** *m / f*
teacher

⑤ **la lavagna**
whiteboard

⑥ **l'alunno** *m*
l'alunna *f*
pupil

⑦ **il banco**
desk

⑧ **gli studenti** *m*
le studentesse *f*
school students

⑨ **lo zaino**
school bag

⑩ **la letteratura**
literature

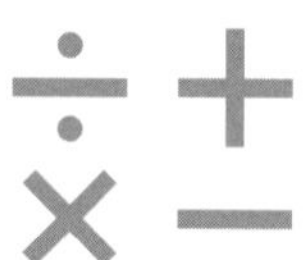
⑪ **la matematica**
math

⑫ **la geografia**
geography

⑬ **la storia**
history

⑭ **le scienze**
science

⑮ **la chimica**
chemistry

⑯ **la fisica**
physics

⑰ **la biologia**
biology

HELLO
⑱ **l'inglese** *m*
English

Bonjour!
Hallo!
¡Hola!
⑲ **le lingue**
languages

⑳ **il disegno tecnico e la tecnologia**
design and technology

@
㉑ **l'informatica** *f*
information technology

㉒ **l'arte** *f*
art

㉓ **la musica**
music

㉔ **il teatro**
drama

㉕ **l'educazione fisica** *f*
physical education

㉖ **il preside** *m*
la preside *f*
principal

㉗ **i compiti per casa**
homework

㉘ **la lezione**
lesson

㉙ **il compito in classe**
exam

㉚ **il tema**
essay

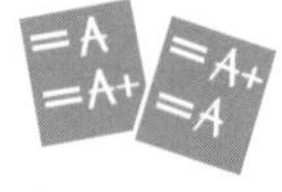
=A
=A+
=A+
=A
㉛ **il voto**
grade

㉜ **l'enciclopedia** *f*
encyclopedia

A
Z
㉝ **il dizionario**
dictionary

㉞ **l'atlante** *m*
atlas

㉟ **la verifica**
test

See also
74 La matematica • Mathematics **75** La fisica • Physics **76** La chimica • Chemistry
77 La biologia • Biology **79** La storia • History **80** All'università • At college
83 I computer e la tecnologia • Computers and technology

73.2 I VERBI DELLA SCUOLA • SCHOOL VERBS

① **leggere**
to read

② **scrivere**
to write

③ **domandare**
to question

④ **fare una verifica**
to take a test

⑤ **imparare**
to learn

⑥ **disegnare**
to draw

⑦ **rispondere**
to answer

CAT

⑧ **computare**
to spell

⑨ **ripassare**
to review

⑩ **recuperare il compito**
to retake

⑪ **prendere appunti**
to take notes

⑫ **discutere**
to discuss

⑬ **andare male**
to fail

⑭ **andare bene**
to pass

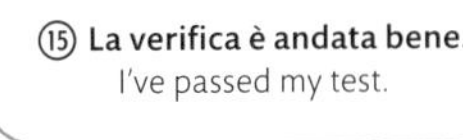

⑮ **La verifica è andata bene.**
I've passed my test.

10
10

73.3 I MATERIALI • EQUIPMENT

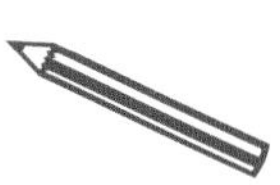

① **la matita**
pencil

② **il temperino**
pencil sharpener

③ **la penna**
pen

④ **il pennino**
nib

⑤ **la gomma da cancellare**
eraser

⑥ **le matite colorate**
colored pencils

⑦ **l'astuccio** *m*
pencil case

⑧ **il righello**
ruler

⑨ **la squadra**
triangle

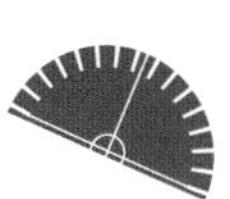

⑩ **il goniometro**
protractor

⑪ **la calcolatrice**
calculator

⑫ **il compasso**
compass

⑬ **il libro di testo**
textbook

⑭ **il quaderno**
notebook / exercise book

⑮ **il videoproiettore**
digital projector

⑯ **l'evidenziatore** *m*
highlighter

⑰ **la graffetta**
paper clip

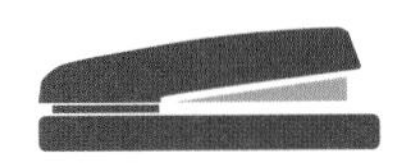

⑱ **la cucitrice**
stapler

74 La matematica
Mathematics

74.1 LE FORME · SHAPES

74.2 I SOLIDI · SOLIDS

74.3 LE LINEE · LINES

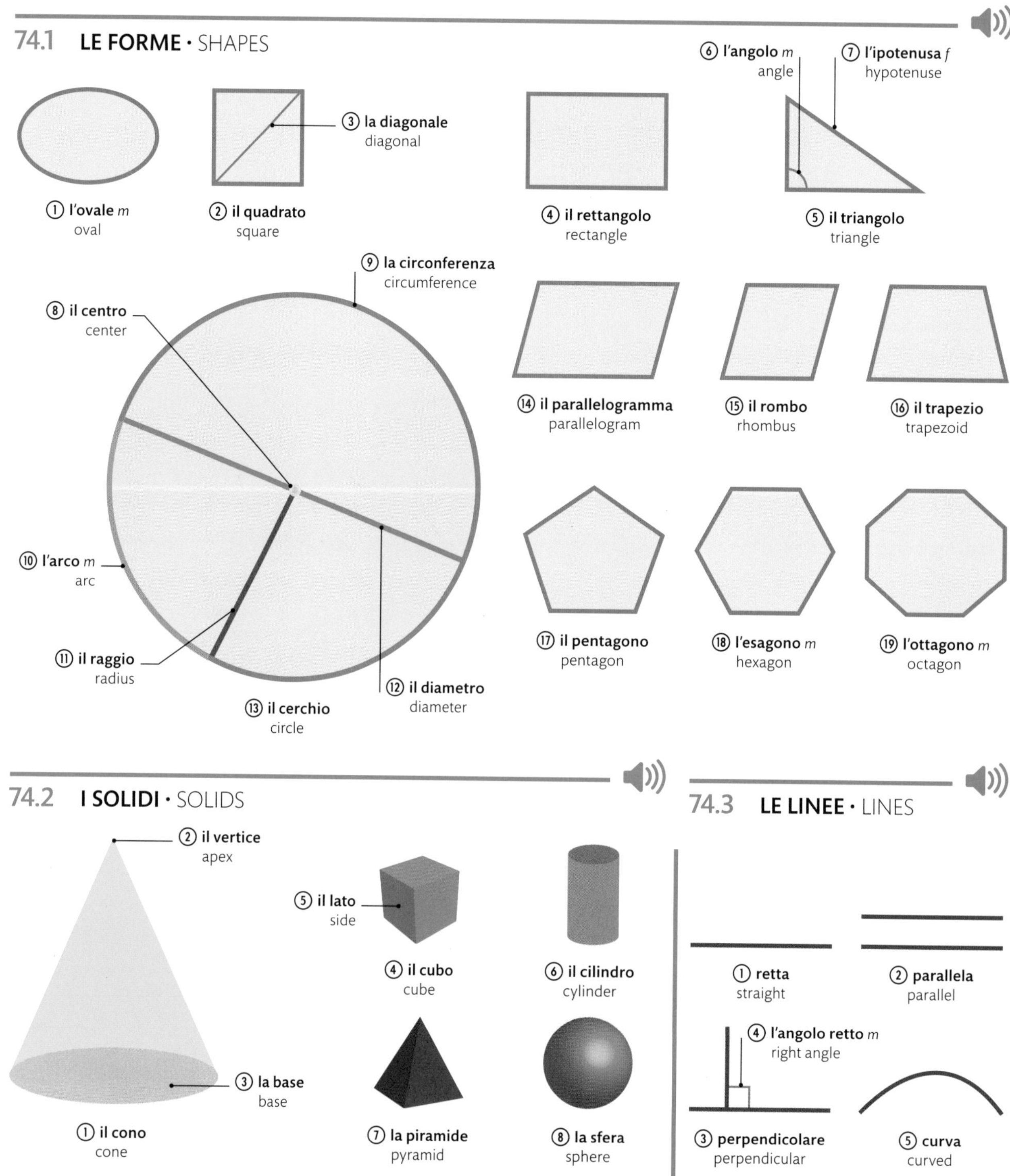

① l'ovale m
oval
② il quadrato
square
③ la diagonale
diagonal
④ il rettangolo
rectangle
⑤ il triangolo
triangle
⑥ l'angolo m
angle
⑦ l'ipotenusa f
hypotenuse
⑧ il centro
center
⑨ la circonferenza
circumference
⑩ l'arco m
arc
⑪ il raggio
radius
⑫ il diametro
diameter
⑬ il cerchio
circle
⑭ il parallelogramma
parallelogram
⑮ il rombo
rhombus
⑯ il trapezio
trapezoid
⑰ il pentagono
pentagon
⑱ l'esagono m
hexagon
⑲ l'ottagono m
octagon
① il cono
cone
② il vertice
apex
③ la base
base
④ il cubo
cube
⑤ il lato
side
⑥ il cilindro
cylinder
⑦ la piramide
pyramid
⑧ la sfera
sphere
① retta
straight
② parallela
parallel
③ perpendicolare
perpendicular
④ l'angolo retto m
right angle
⑤ curva
curved

See also
73 A scuola • At school **94** Il denaro e la finanza • Money and finance
173 I numeri • Numbers **174** I pesi e le misure • Weights and measures

74.4 LE MISURE • MEASUREMENTS

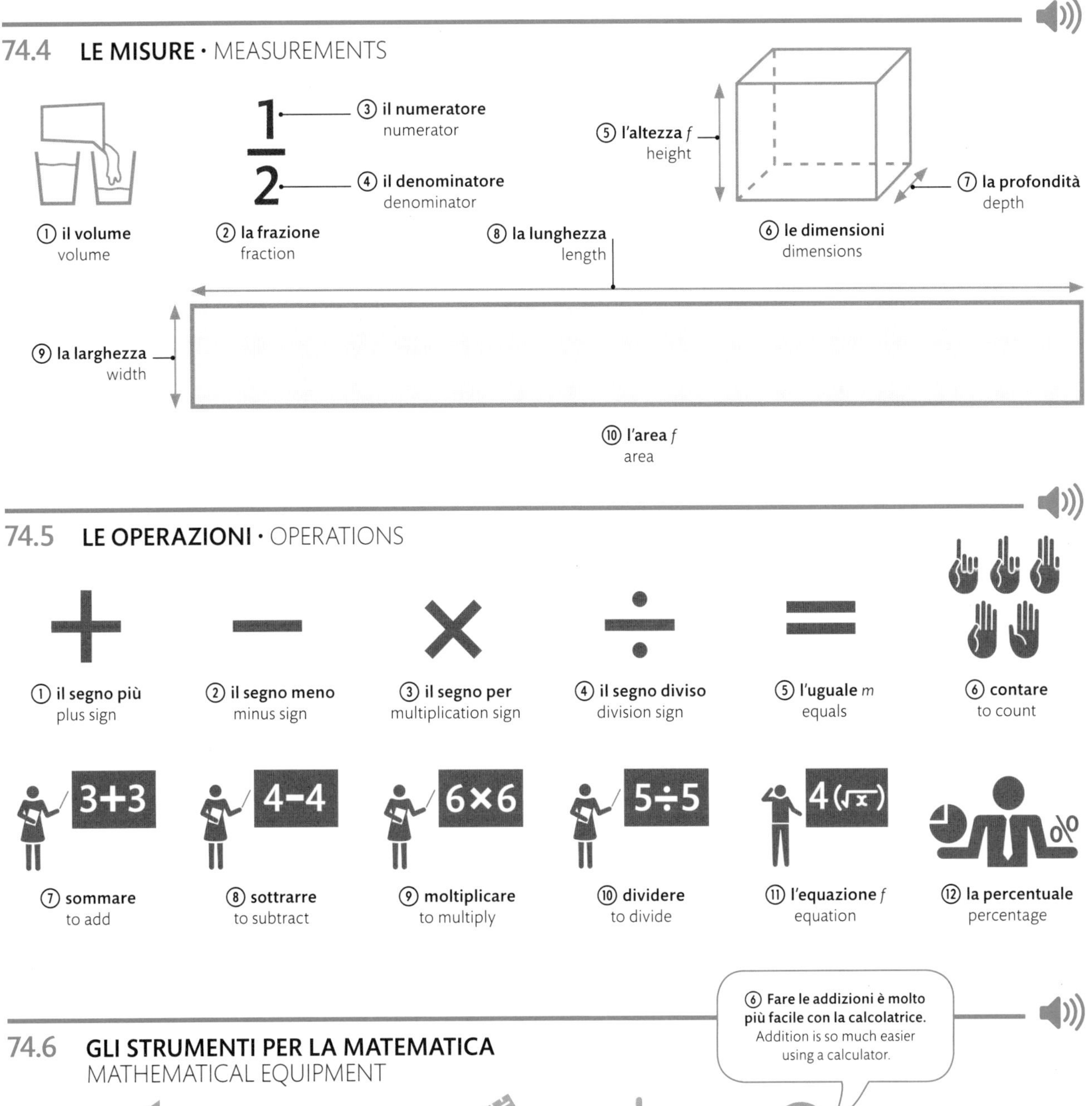
1
2
① **il volume**
volume
② **la frazione**
fraction
③ **il numeratore**
numerator
④ **il denominatore**
denominator
⑤ **l'altezza** *f*
height
⑥ **le dimensioni**
dimensions
⑦ **la profondità**
depth
⑧ **la lunghezza**
length
⑨ **la larghezza**
width
⑩ **l'area** *f*
area

74.5 LE OPERAZIONI • OPERATIONS

3+3
4−4
6×6
5÷5
4(√x)
%

① **il segno più**
plus sign

② **il segno meno**
minus sign

③ **il segno per**
multiplication sign

④ **il segno diviso**
division sign

⑤ **l'uguale** *m*
equals

⑥ **contare**
to count

⑦ **sommare**
to add

⑧ **sottrarre**
to subtract

⑨ **moltiplicare**
to multiply

⑩ **dividere**
to divide

⑪ **l'equazione** *f*
equation

⑫ **la percentuale**
percentage

74.6 GLI STRUMENTI PER LA MATEMATICA
MATHEMATICAL EQUIPMENT

⑥ **Fare le addizioni è molto più facile con la calcolatrice.**
Addition is so much easier using a calculator.

① **la squadra**
triangle

② **il goniometro**
protractor

③ **il righello**
ruler

④ **il compasso**
compass

⑤ **la calcolatrice**
calculator

75 La fisica
Physics

75.1 LA FISICA · PHYSICS

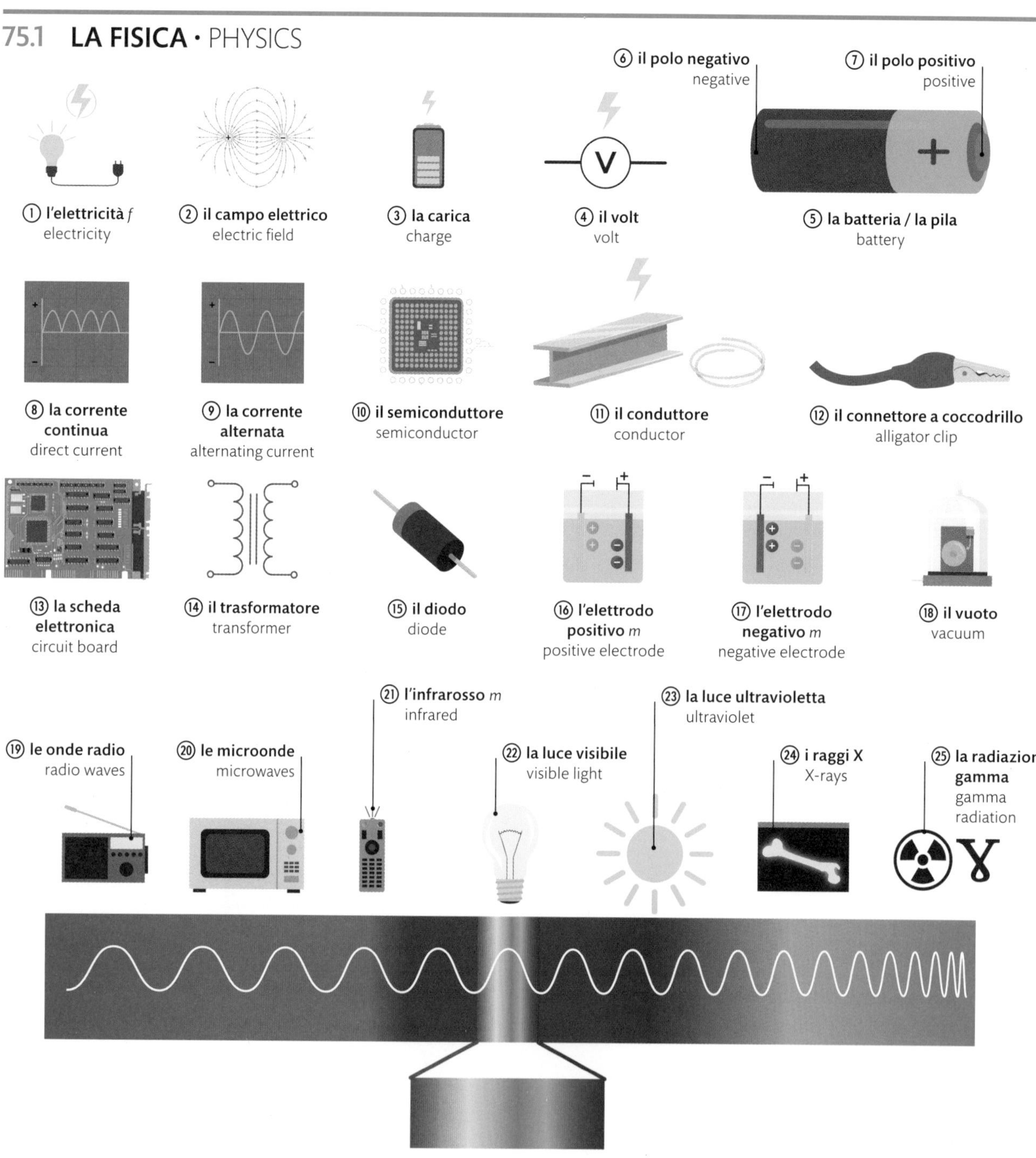

① l'elettricità *f*
electricity
② il campo elettrico
electric field
③ la carica
charge
④ il volt
volt
V
⑤ la batteria / la pila
battery
⑥ il polo negativo
negative
⑦ il polo positivo
positive
⑧ la corrente continua
direct current
⑨ la corrente alternata
alternating current
⑩ il semiconduttore
semiconductor
⑪ il conduttore
conductor
⑫ il connettore a coccodrillo
alligator clip
⑬ la scheda elettronica
circuit board
⑭ il trasformatore
transformer
⑮ il diodo
diode
⑯ l'elettrodo positivo *m*
positive electrode
⑰ l'elettrodo negativo *m*
negative electrode
⑱ il vuoto
vacuum
⑲ le onde radio
radio waves
⑳ le microonde
microwaves
㉑ l'infrarosso *m*
infrared
㉒ la luce visibile
visible light
㉓ la luce ultravioletta
ultraviolet
㉔ i raggi X
X-rays
㉕ la radiazione gamma
gamma radiation
㉖ lo spettro elettromagnetico
electromagnetic spectrum

See also
73 A scuola • At school **74** La matematica • Mathematics **76** La chimica • Chemistry
77 La biologia • Biology **78** La tavola periodica • The periodic table

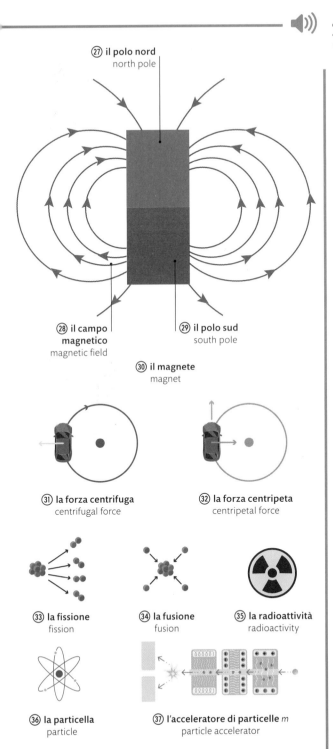

(27) **il polo nord**
north pole

(28) **il campo magnetico**
magnetic field

(29) **il polo sud**
south pole

(30) **il magnete**
magnet

(31) **la forza centrifuga**
centrifugal force

(32) **la forza centripeta**
centripetal force

(33) **la fissione**
fission

(34) **la fusione**
fusion

(35) **la radioattività**
radioactivity

(36) **la particella**
particle

(37) **l'acceleratore di particelle** *m*
particle accelerator

75.2 L'OTTICA • OPTICS

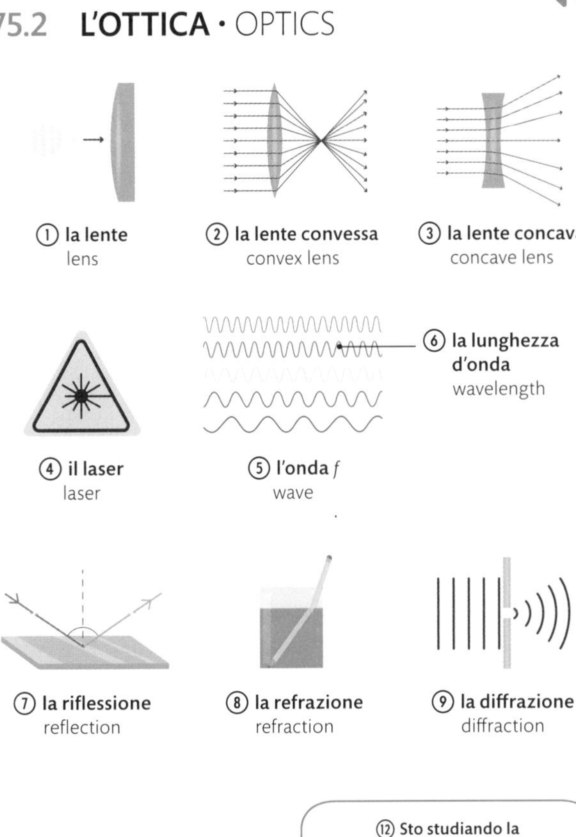
(6) **la lunghezza d'onda**
wavelength

(1) **la lente**
lens

(2) **la lente convessa**
convex lens

(3) **la lente concava**
concave lens

(4) **il laser**
laser

(5) **l'onda** *f*
wave

(7) **la riflessione**
reflection

(8) **la refrazione**
refraction

(9) **la diffrazione**
diffraction

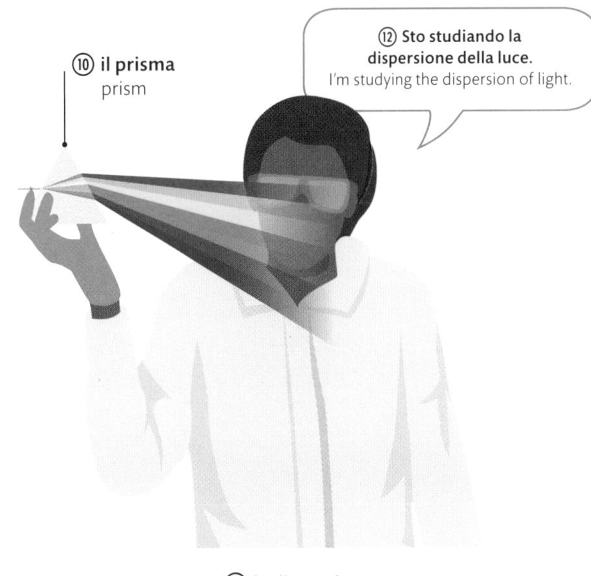
(10) **il prisma**
prism
(12) **Sto studiando la dispersione della luce.**
I'm studying the dispersion of light.

(11) **la dispersione**
dispersion

76 La chimica
Chemistry

76.1 IN LABORATORIO · IN THE LABORATORY

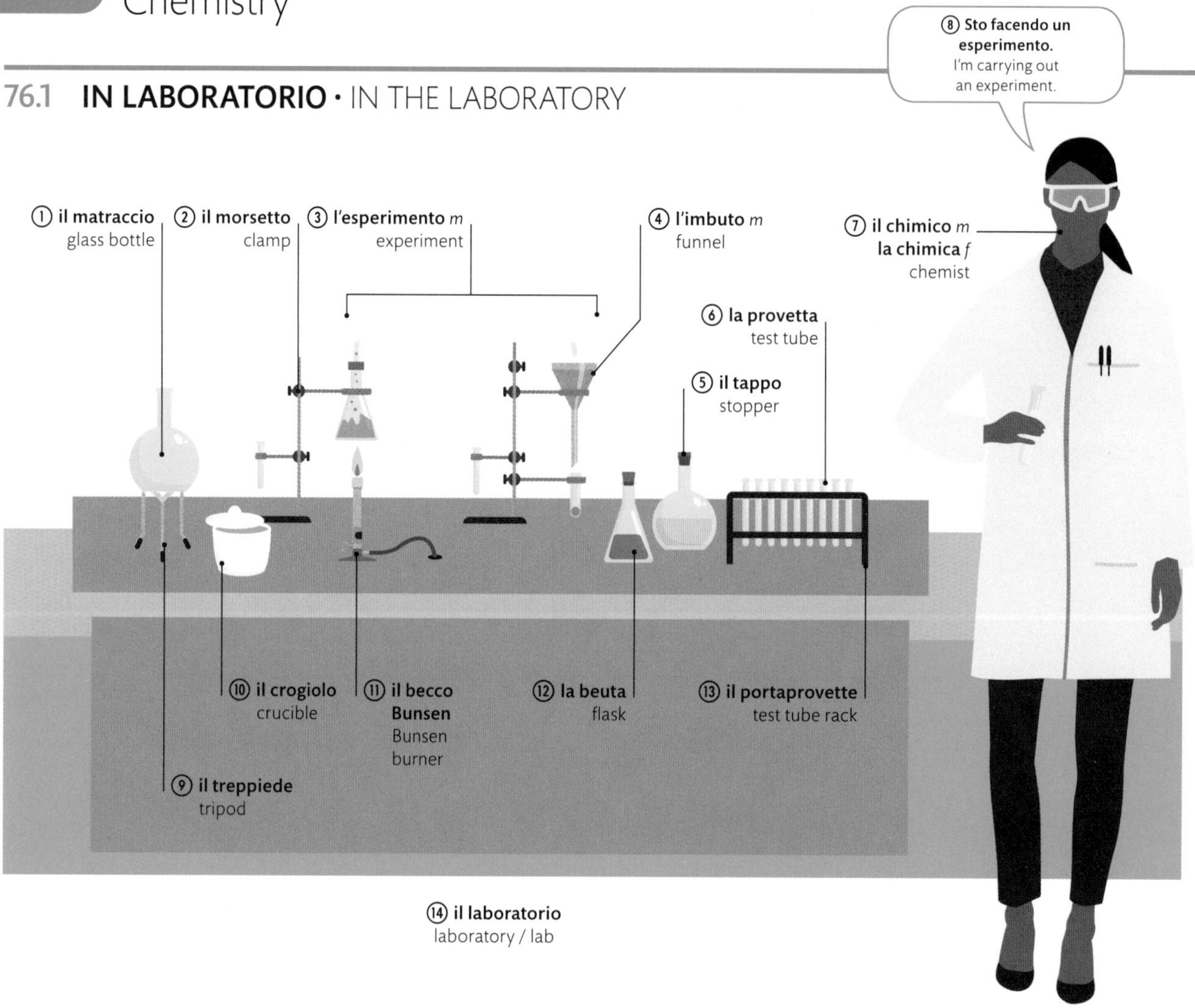

① **il matraccio** glass bottle
② **il morsetto** clamp
③ **l'esperimento** *m* experiment
④ **l'imbuto** *m* funnel
⑤ **il tappo** stopper
⑥ **la provetta** test tube
⑦ **il chimico** *m* **la chimica** *f* chemist
⑧ **Sto facendo un esperimento.** I'm carrying out an experiment.
⑨ **il treppiede** tripod
⑩ **il crogiolo** crucible
⑪ **il becco Bunsen** Bunsen burner
⑫ **la beuta** flask
⑬ **il portaprovette** test tube rack
⑭ **il laboratorio** laboratory / lab

⑮ **la bilancia** scale

⑯ **il timer** timer

⑰ **il termometro** thermometer

⑱ **le pinze** tongs

⑲ **la spatola** spatula

⑳ **il pestello** pestle
㉑ **il mortaio** mortar

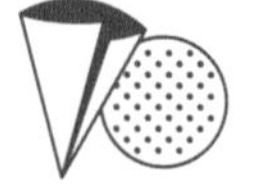
㉒ **la carta da filtro** filter paper

㉓ **il contagocce** dropper

㉔ **la pipetta** pipette

㉕ **il becher** beaker

㉖ **la bacchetta di vetro** glass rod

㉗ **gli occhiali protettivi** safety goggles

See also
73 A scuola • At school **74** La matematica • Mathematics **75** La fisica
Physics **77** La biologia • Biology **78** La tavola periodica • The periodic table

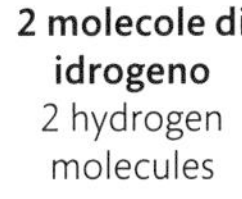

2 molecole di idrogeno
2 hydrogen molecules

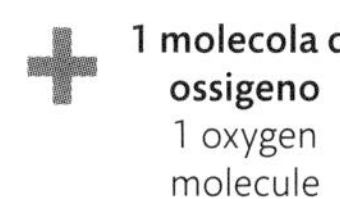

1 molecola di ossigeno
1 oxygen molecule

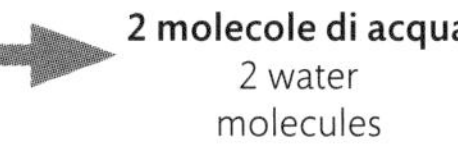

2 molecole di acqua
2 water molecules

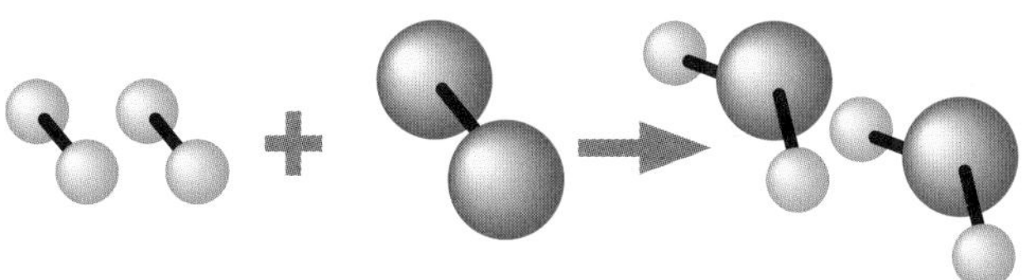

$$2H_2 + O_2 \rightarrow 2H_2O$$

㉙ **il simbolo chimico**
chemical symbol

㉚ **il pedice**
subscript

㉘ **l'equazione chimica** *f*
chemical equation

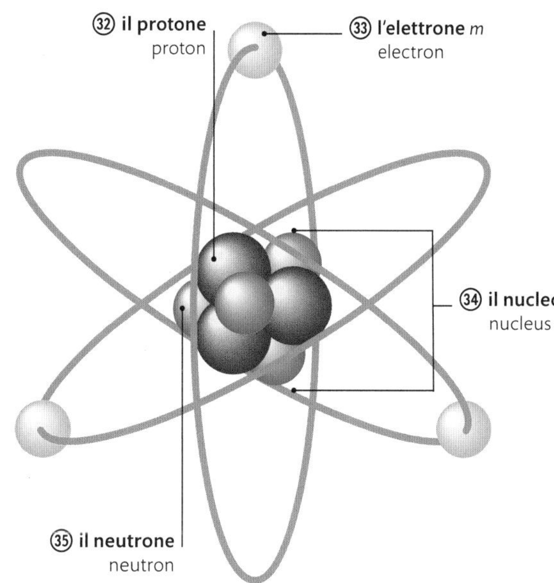

㉜ **il protone**
proton

㉝ **l'elettrone** *m*
electron

㉞ **il nucleo**
nucleus

㉟ **il neutrone**
neutron

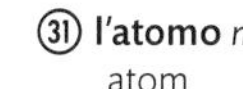

㉛ **l'atomo** *m*
atom

H_2O

㊱ **la formula chimica**
chemical formula

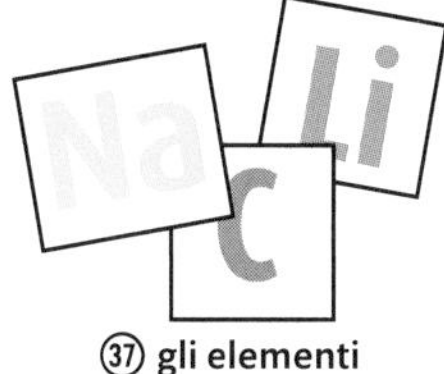
Na
Li
C

㊲ **gli elementi**
elements

㊳ **la molecola**
molecule

1 2 3 5 6 7 8 9 10 11 13 14

㊵ **l'acido** *m*
acid

㊶ **l'alcale** *m*
alkali

㊴ **il valore di pH**
pH level

㊷ **la reazione**
reaction

Q<K

㊸ **la direzione di una reazione**
reaction direction

Q⇌K

㊹ **la direzione inversa**
reversible direction

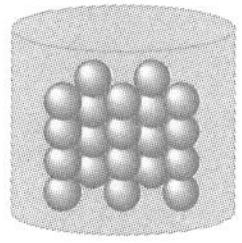

㊺ **il solido**
solid

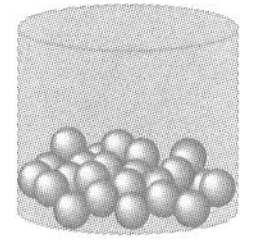

㊻ **il liquido**
liquid

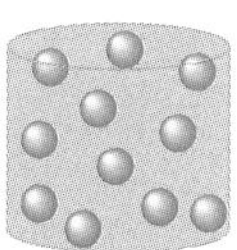

㊼ **il gas**
gas

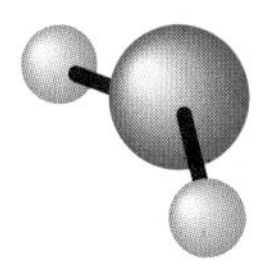

㊽ **il composto**
compound

㊾ **la base**
base

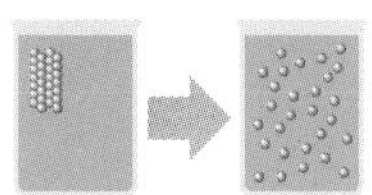

㊿ **la diffusione**
diffusion

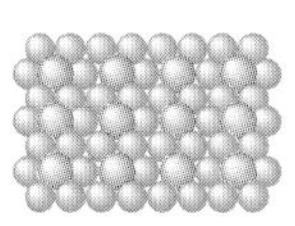

51 **la lega**
alloy

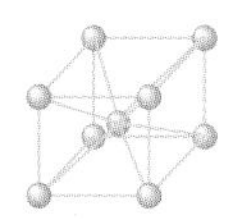

52 **il cristallo**
crystal

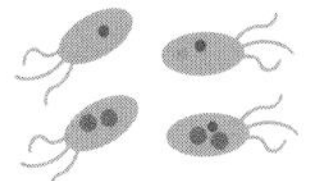

53 **la biochimica**
biochemistry

77 La biologia
Biology

77.1 LA BIOLOGIA · BIOLOGY

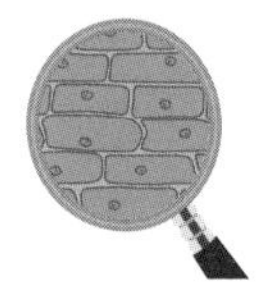

① **il biologo** *m* **la biologa** *f*
biologist

② **la microbiologia**
microbiology

③ **il microbiologo** *m* **la microbiologa** *f*
microbiologist

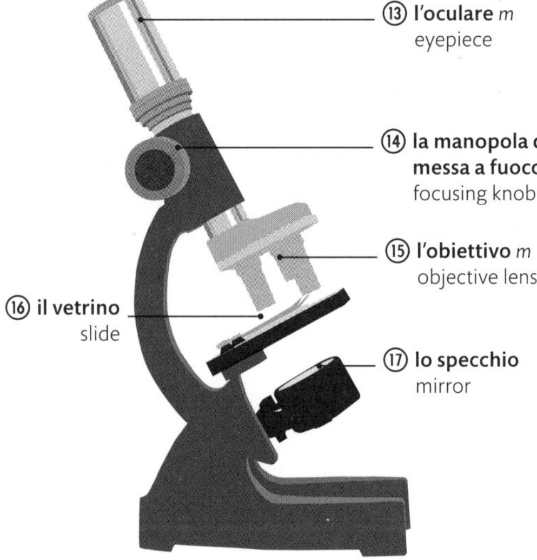

⑬ **l'oculare** *m*
eyepiece

⑭ **la manopola di messa a fuoco**
focusing knob

⑮ **l'obiettivo** *m*
objective lens

⑯ **il vetrino**
slide

⑰ **lo specchio**
mirror

⑱ **il microscopio**
microscope

④ **il nucleo**
nucleus

⑤ **il mitocondrio**
mitochondria

⑥ **la membrana cellulare**
cell membrane

⑦ **il citoplasma**
cytoplasm

⑧ **la cellula animale**
animal cell

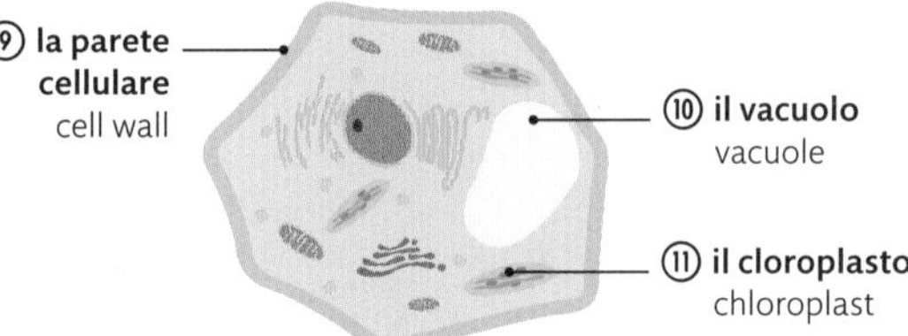

⑨ **la parete cellulare**
cell wall

⑩ **il vacuolo**
vacuole

⑪ **il cloroplasto**
chloroplast

⑫ **la cellula vegetale**
plant cell

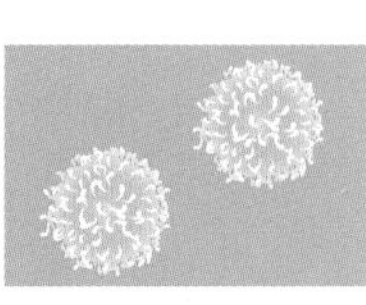
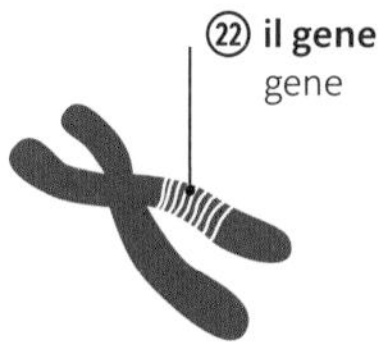

⑲ **il globulo rosso**
red blood cell

⑳ **il globulo bianco**
white blood cell

㉑ **il cromosoma**
chromosome

㉒ **il gene**
gene

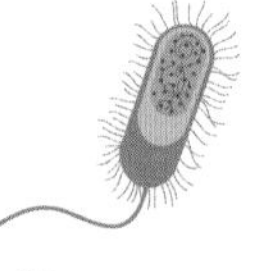

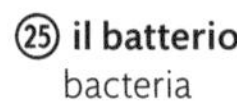

㉓ **il DNA**
DNA

㉔ **il virus**
virus

㉕ **il batterio**
bacteria

㉖ **la capsula Petri**
petri dish

㉗ **le pinzette**
tweezers

㉘ **il bisturi**
scalpel

㉙ **la siringa**
syringe

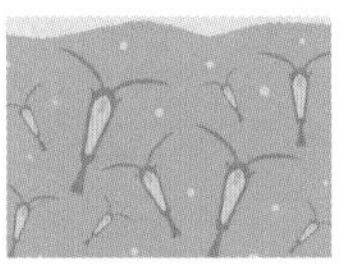

㉚ **la zoologia**
zoology

㉛ **lo zoologo** *m* **la zoologa** *f*
zoologist

㉜ **il plancton**
plankton

㉝ **invertebrato** *m* **invertebrata** *f*
invertebrate

㉞ **vertebrato** *m* **vertebrata** *f*
vertebrate

㉟ **la specie**
species

See also
157 La storia naturale • Natural history **158-159** I mammiferi • Mammals **160-161** Gli uccelli Birds **162** Gli insetti • Insects and bugs **163** Gli anfibi e i rettili • Amphibians and reptiles **166** La vita negli oceani • Ocean life **167-169** Le piante e gli alberi • Plants and trees **170** I funghi • Fungi

(36) **l'ecosistema** *m*
ecosystem

(37) **l'esoscheletro** *m*
exoskeleton

(38) **l'endoscheletro** *m*
endoskeleton

(39) **la riproduzione**
reproduction

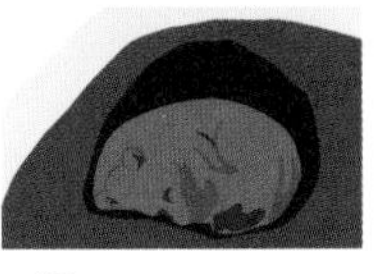

(40) **l'ibernazione** *f*
hibernation

(41) **la botanica**
botany

(42) **il botanico** *m*
la botanica *f*
botanist

(43) **la pianta**
plant

(44) **i funghi**
fungi

(45) **la fotosintesi**
photosynthesis

(46) **il paleontologo** *m*
la paleontologa *f*
paleontologist

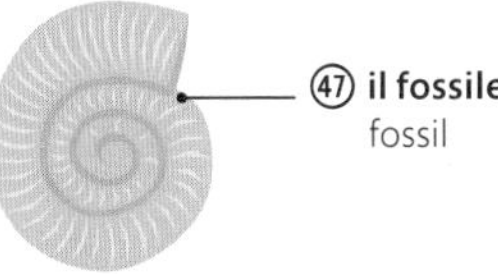

(47) **il fossile**
fossil

(48) **l'evoluzione** *f*
evolution

77.2 LA METAMORFOSI • METAMORPHOSIS

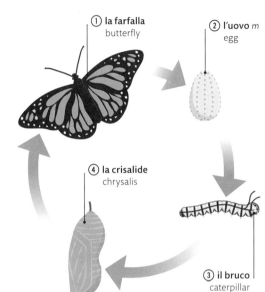

(1) **la farfalla**
butterfly

(2) **l'uovo** *m*
egg

(3) **il bruco**
caterpillar

(4) **la crisalide**
chrysalis

(5) **il ciclo di vita di una farfalla**
life cycle of a butterfly

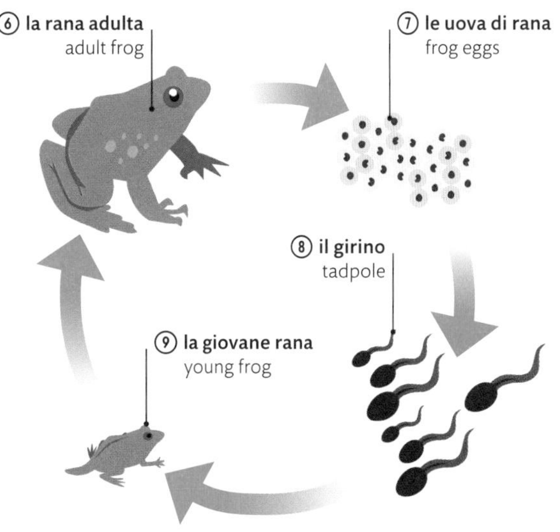

(6) **la rana adulta**
adult frog

(7) **le uova di rana**
frog eggs

(8) **il girino**
tadpole

(9) **la giovane rana**
young frog

(10) **il ciclo di vita di una rana**
life cycle of a frog

78 La tavola periodica
The periodic table

78.1 LA TAVOLA PERIODICA · THE PERIODIC TABLE

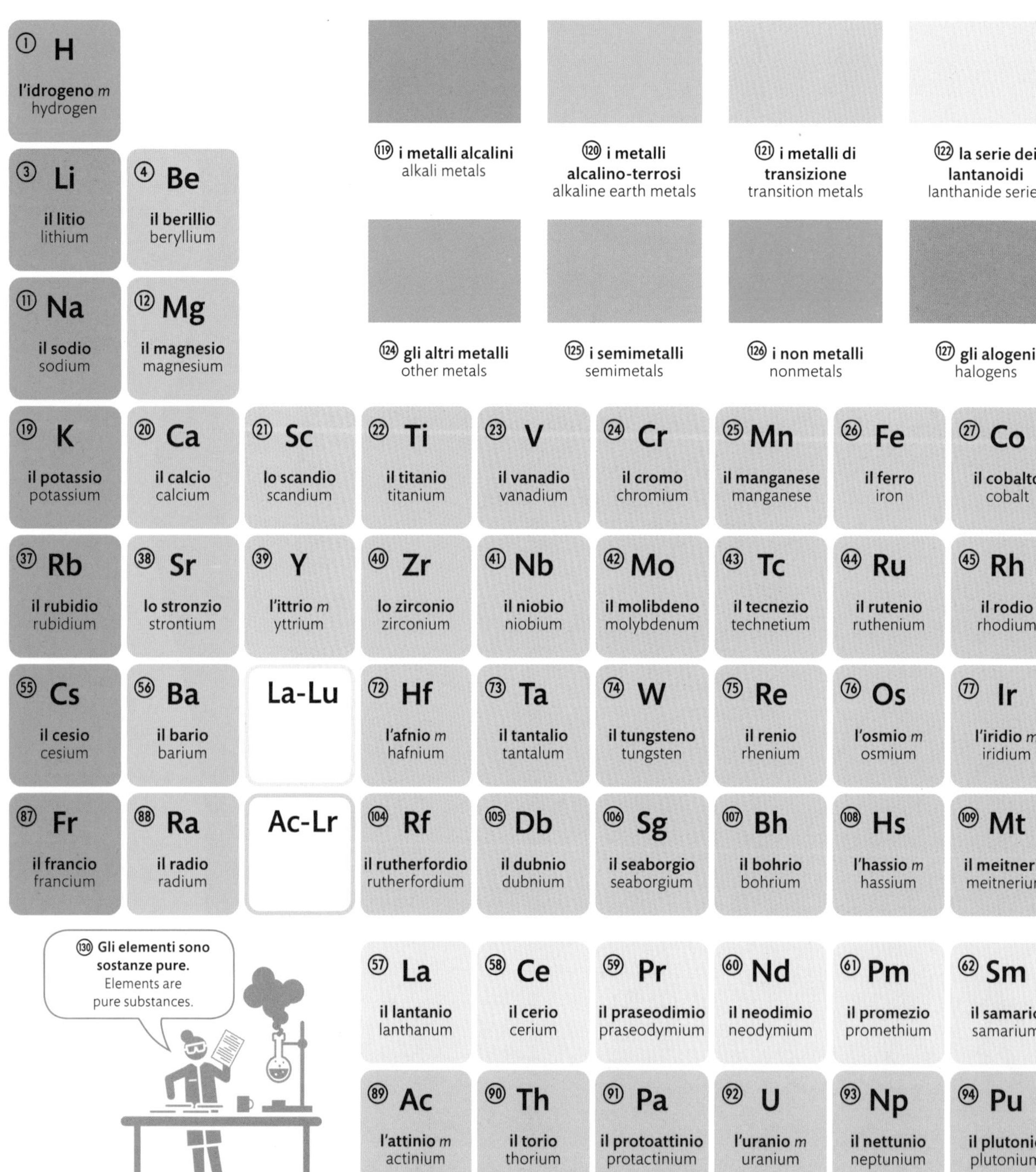

① H l'idrogeno *m* hydrogen
③ Li il litio lithium
④ Be il berillio beryllium
⑪ Na il sodio sodium
⑫ Mg il magnesio magnesium
⑲ K il potassio potassium
⑳ Ca il calcio calcium
㉑ Sc lo scandio scandium
㉒ Ti il titanio titanium
㉓ V il vanadio vanadium
㉔ Cr il cromo chromium
㉕ Mn il manganese manganese
㉖ Fe il ferro iron
㉗ Co il cobalto cobalt
㊲ Rb il rubidio rubidium
㊳ Sr lo stronzio strontium
㊴ Y l'ittrio *m* yttrium
㊵ Zr lo zirconio zirconium
㊶ Nb il niobio niobium
㊷ Mo il molibdeno molybdenum
㊸ Tc il tecnezio technetium
㊹ Ru il rutenio ruthenium
㊺ Rh il rodio rhodium
55 Cs il cesio cesium
56 Ba il bario barium
La-Lu
72 Hf l'afnio *m* hafnium
73 Ta il tantalio tantalum
74 W il tungsteno tungsten
75 Re il renio rhenium
76 Os l'osmio *m* osmium
77 Ir l'iridio *m* iridium
87 Fr il francio francium
88 Ra il radio radium
Ac-Lr
104 Rf il rutherfordio rutherfordium
105 Db il dubnio dubnium
106 Sg il seaborgio seaborgium
107 Bh il bohrio bohrium
108 Hs l'hassio *m* hassium
109 Mt il meitnerio meitnerium
57 La il lantanio lanthanum
58 Ce il cerio cerium
59 Pr il praseodimio praseodymium
60 Nd il neodimio neodymium
61 Pm il promezio promethium
62 Sm il samario samarium
89 Ac l'attinio *m* actinium
90 Th il torio thorium
91 Pa il protoattinio protactinium
92 U l'uranio *m* uranium
93 Np il nettunio neptunium
94 Pu il plutonio plutonium
119 **i metalli alcalini** alkali metals
120 **i metalli alcalino-terrosi** alkaline earth metals
121 **i metalli di transizione** transition metals
122 **la serie dei lantanoidi** lanthanide series
124 **gli altri metalli** other metals
125 **i semimetalli** semimetals
126 **i non metalli** nonmetals
127 **gli alogeni** halogens
130 **Gli elementi sono sostanze pure.** Elements are pure substances.

See also
73 A scuola • At school **75** La fisica • Physics **76** La chimica • Chemistry
156 Le rocce e i minerali • Rocks and minerals

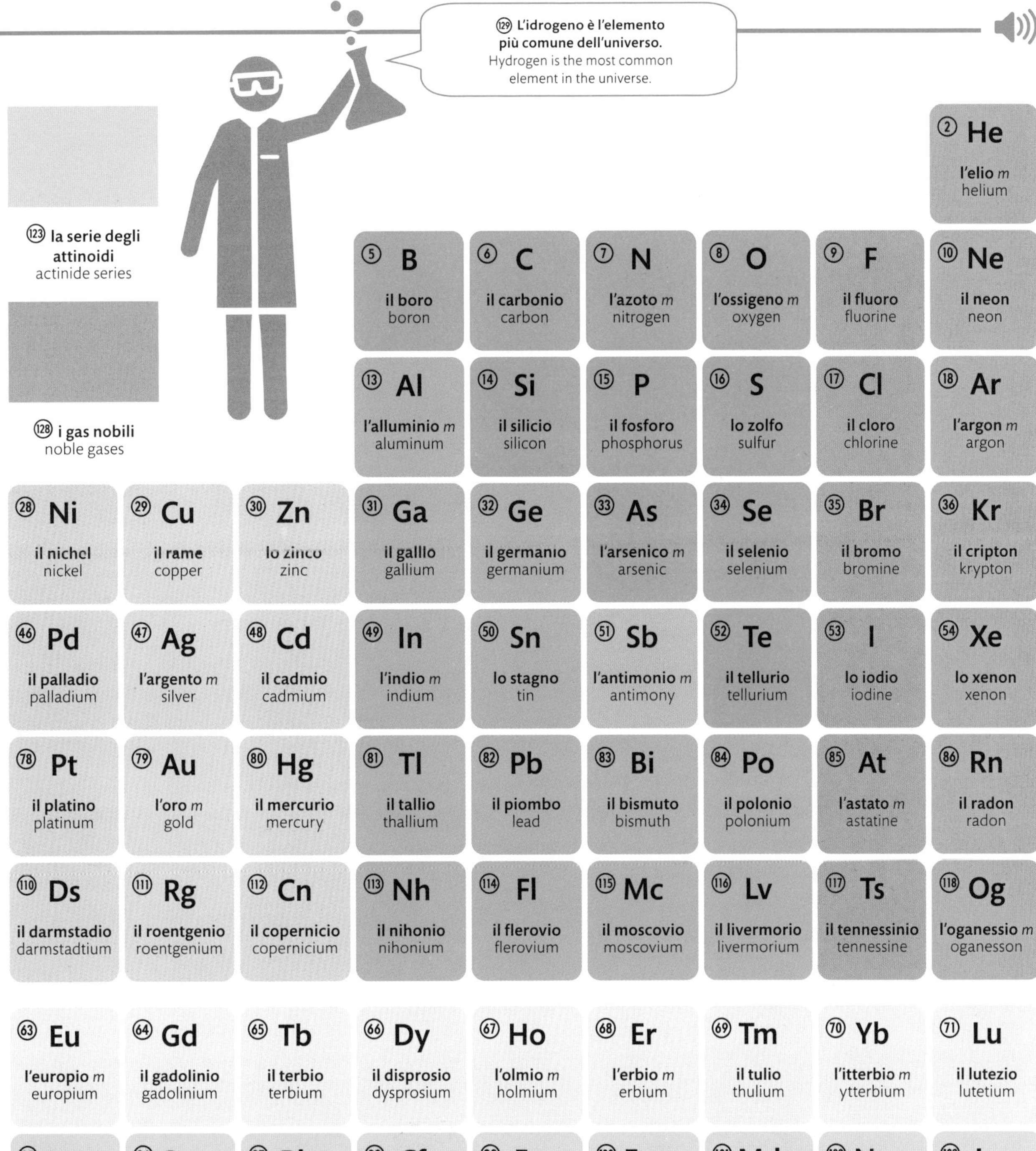
129 L'idrogeno è l'elemento più comune dell'universo.
Hydrogen is the most common element in the universe.
123 la serie degli attinoidi
actinide series
128 i gas nobili
noble gases
2 He **l'elio** *m* helium
5 B **il boro** boron
6 C **il carbonio** carbon
7 N **l'azoto** *m* nitrogen
8 O **l'ossigeno** *m* oxygen
9 F **il fluoro** fluorine
10 Ne **il neon** neon
13 Al **l'alluminio** *m* aluminum
14 Si **il silicio** silicon
15 P **il fosforo** phosphorus
16 S **lo zolfo** sulfur
17 Cl **il cloro** chlorine
18 Ar **l'argon** *m* argon
28 Ni **il nichel** nickel
29 Cu **il rame** copper
30 Zn **lo zinco** zinc
31 Ga **il gallio** gallium
32 Ge **il germanio** germanium
33 As **l'arsenico** *m* arsenic
34 Se **il selenio** selenium
35 Br **il bromo** bromine
36 Kr **il cripton** krypton
46 Pd **il palladio** palladium
47 Ag **l'argento** *m* silver
48 Cd **il cadmio** cadmium
49 In **l'indio** *m* indium
50 Sn **lo stagno** tin
51 Sb **l'antimonio** *m* antimony
52 Te **il tellurio** tellurium
53 I **lo iodio** iodine
54 Xe **lo xenon** xenon
78 Pt **il platino** platinum
79 Au **l'oro** *m* gold
80 Hg **il mercurio** mercury
81 Tl **il tallio** thallium
82 Pb **il piombo** lead
83 Bi **il bismuto** bismuth
84 Po **il polonio** polonium
85 At **l'astato** *m* astatine
86 Rn **il radon** radon
110 Ds **il darmstadio** darmstadtium
111 Rg **il roentgenio** roentgenium
112 Cn **il copernicio** copernicium
113 Nh **il nihonio** nihonium
114 Fl **il flerovio** flerovium
115 Mc **il moscovio** moscovium
116 Lv **il livermorio** livermorium
117 Ts **il tennessinio** tennessine
118 Og **l'oganessio** *m* oganesson
63 Eu **l'europio** *m* europium
64 Gd **il gadolinio** gadolinium
65 Tb **il terbio** terbium
66 Dy **il disprosio** dysprosium
67 Ho **l'olmio** *m* holmium
68 Er **l'erbio** *m* erbium
69 Tm **il tulio** thulium
70 Yb **l'itterbio** *m* ytterbium
71 Lu **il lutezio** lutetium
95 Am **l'americio** *m* americium
96 Cm **il curio** curium
97 Bk **il berkelio** berkelium
98 Cf **il californio** californium
99 Es **l'einsteinio** *m* einsteinium
100 Fm **il fermio** fermium
101 Md **il mendelevio** mendelevium
102 No **il nobelio** nobelium
103 Lr **il laurenzio** lawrencium

79 La storia
History

79.1 LA GUERRA E LE ARMI · WAR AND WEAPONS

① **la biga**
chariot

② **l'arco** *m*
bow

③ **la freccia**
arrow

⑤ **la mazza ferrata**
mace

⑥ **la scimitarra**
scimitar

⑦ **la guerra**
warfare

⑧ **l'ascia** *f*
ax

⑨ **lo scudo**
shield

⑩ **la spada**
sword

79.2 LE PERSONE NELLA STORIA · PEOPLE THROUGH TIME

② **gli utensili di selce**
flint tools

① **l'età della pietra** *f*
the Stone Age

③ **l'età del bronzo** *f*
the Bronze Age

④ **l'età del ferro** *f*
the Iron Age

⑤ **il contadino** *m* / **la contadina** *f*
farmer

⑥ **il mercante**
merchant

⑦ **l'artigiano** *f*
artisan

⑫ **l'imperatore** *m*
emperor

⑬ **l'imperatrice** *f*
empress

⑭ **il re**
king

⑮ **la regina**
queen

⑯ **il principe / la principessa**
prince / princess

⑰ **i nobili**
nobles

㉒ **l'epoca d'oro islamica** *f*
the Islamic Golden Age

㉓ **il filosofo**
philosopher

㉔ **l'illuminismo** *m*
the Enlightenment

㉕ **la rivoluzione industriale**
the Industrial Revolution

See also
44 Gli edifici e l'architettura • Buildings and architecture **73** A scuola • At school
80 All'università • At college **88** L'esercito • Military

④ **la lancia**
spear

⑪ **il cavallo da battaglia**
warhorse

⑫ **l'elefante da battaglia** *m*
war elephant

⑬ **la battaglia**
battle

⑭ **il cannone**
cannon

⑮ **la catapulta**
catapult

⑯ **l'ariete** *m*
battering ram

⑰ **il cavaliere**
knight

⑱ **l'armatura** *f*
armor

⑲ **il guerriero**
warrior

⑧ **il fabbro**
blacksmith

⑨ **i popolani**
peasants

⑩ **il regno**
kingdom

⑪ **l'impero** *m*
empire

⑱ **il lord** *m*
la lady *f*
lord / lady

⑲ **il menestrello**
minstrel

⑳ **il giullare**
jester

㉑ **lo scrivano**
scribe

㉖ **la rivoluzione tecnologica** *f*
the Technological Revolution

㉗ **l'era dell'informazione** *f*
the Information Age

79.3 LO STUDIO DEL PASSATO
STUDYING THE PAST

① **lo storico** *m* / **la storica** *f*
historian

② **l'archivio** *m*
archive

③ **le fonti**
sources

④ **la pergamena**
scroll

⑤ **il documento**
document

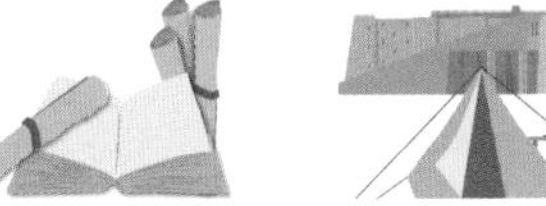

⑥ **l'archeologia** *f*
archeology

⑦ **l'archeologo** *m*
l'archeologa *f*
archeologist

⑧ **lo scavo**
dig / excavation

⑩ **la torbiera**
peat bog

⑨ **i resti**
remains

⑪ **le scoperte**
finds

⑫ **la tomba**
tomb

⑬ **il sito storico**
historical site

80 All'università
At college

80.1 L'UNIVERSITÀ · COLLEGE

① **il campus universitario**
campus

② **l'auditorium** *m*
auditorium

③ **il professore** *m*
la professoressa *f*
lecturer

④ **il campo sportivo**
sports field

⑤ **la mensa**
dining hall

⑥ **il dormitorio**
dorms

⑦ **la borsa di studio**
scholarship

⑧ **le ammissioni**
admissions

⑨ **lo studente della laurea triennale** *m* / **la studentessa della laurea triennale** *f*
undergraduate

⑩ **il diploma di laurea**
diploma

⑪ **la tesi**
dissertation

⑫ **la laurea**
degree

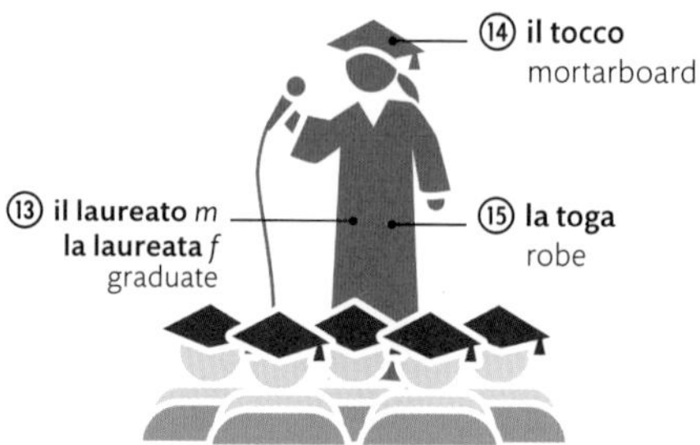
⑬ **il laureato** *m*
la laureata *f*
graduate

⑭ **il tocco**
mortarboard

⑮ **la toga**
robe

⑯ **la cerimonia di laurea**
graduation ceremony

⑰ **lo studente della laurea magistrale** *m*
la studentessa della laurea magistrale *f*
postgraduate

⑱ **la tesi**
thesis

⑲ **la laurea magistrale**
master's degree

⑳ **il dottorato**
doctorate

80.2 I DIPARTIMENTI E LE FACOLTÀ · DEPARTMENTS AND SCHOOLS

① **gli studi umanistici**
humanities

② **le scienze politiche**
politics

③ **la letteratura**
literature

④ **le lingue**
languages

⑤ **l'economia** *f*
economics

%

⑥ **la filosofia**
philosophy

⑦ **la storia**
history

⑧ **le scienze sociali**
social sciences

⑨ **la sociologia**
sociology

⑩ **la legge**
law

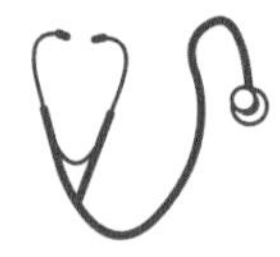
⑪ **la medicina**
medicine

⑫ **l'infermieristica** *f*
nursing

See also
73 A scuola • At school **74** La matematica • Mathematics **75** La fisica • Physics
76 La chimica • Chemistry **77** La biologia • Biology **79** La storia • History
85 La legge • Law **138** I libri e la lettura • Books and reading

80.3 LA BIBLIOTECA • LIBRARY

① **la sala di lettura**
reading room

② **la lista dei libri da leggere**
reading list

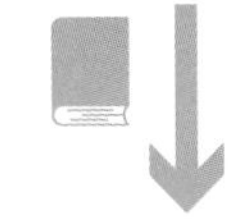
③ **prendere in prestito**
to borrow

④ **rinnovare**
to renew

⑤ **restituire**
to return

⑥ **prenotare**
to reserve

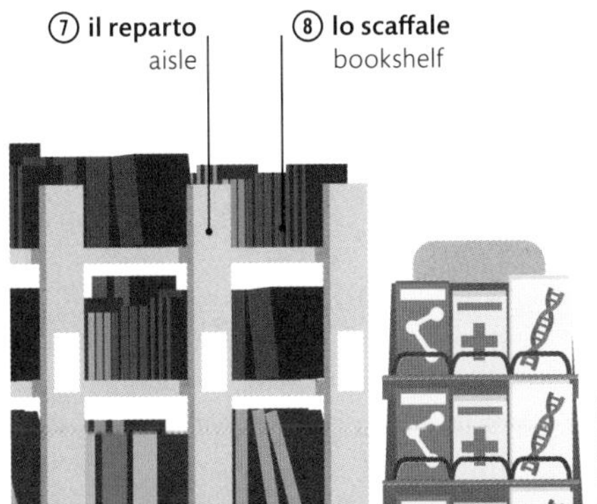

⑦ **il reparto**
aisle

⑧ **lo scaffale**
bookshelf

⑨ **il bibliotecario** *m*
la bibliotecaria *f*
librarian

⑩ **la tessera della biblioteca**
library card

⑪ **la rivista**
periodical / journal

⑫ **il libro**
book

⑬ **la biblioteca**
library

⑭ **lo sportello prestiti**
circulation desk

⑭ **Ho ricevuto una borsa di studio per condurre una ricerca scientifica.**
I received a grant to do scientific research.

⑬ **le scienze**
sciences

⑮ **la chimica**
chemistry

⑯ **la fisica**
physics

⑰ **la biologia**
biology

⑱ **l'ingegneria** *f*
engineering

⑲ **la zoologia**
zoology

⑳ **la scuola di musica**
music school

㉑ **la scuola di danza**
dance school

㉒ **l'istituto d'arte** *m*
art college / school

81 Al lavoro
At work

81.1 IL LAVORO D'UFFICIO • OFFICE WORK

① **l'azienda** *f*
company

② **la filiale**
branch

③ **l'impiego** *m*
employment

④ **guadagnare**
to earn

⑤ **il lavoro fisso**
permanent

⑥ **il lavoro temporaneo**
temporary

⑩ **il lavoro di otto ore regolari**
nine-to-five job

⑪ **lavorare part-time**
to work part-time

⑫ **fare i turni**
to work shifts

⑬ **le ferie annuali**
vacation

⑭ **avere un giorno libero**
to have a day off

⑮ **andare in maternità**
to go on maternity leave

⑲ **prendersi un giorno di malattia**
to call in sick

⑳ **presentare le dimissioni**
to hand in your notice

㉑ **essere licenziato** *m* **essere licenziata** *f*
to get fired

㉒ **essere licenziato** *m* **essere licenziata** *f*
to be laid off

㉓ **essere disoccupato** *m* / **essere disoccupata** *f*
to be unemployed

㉔ **il sussidio di disoccupazione**
unemployment benefit

㉞ **l'uomo d'affari** *m*
businessman

㊴ **il manager** *m* **la manager** *f*
manager

㉙ **la sede principale**
headquarters

㉚ **l'addetto alla reception** *m* / **l'addetta alla reception** *f*
receptionist

㉝ **l'AD (amministratore delegato)** *m*
CEO (chief executive officer)

㊳ **il tirocinante** *m* **la tirocinante** *f*
apprentice

㊵ **l'assistente personale** *m* / *f*
PA (personal assistant)

㊶ **il responsabile** *m* **la responsabile** *f*
leader

㉛ **la sala d'attesa**
waiting area

㉟ **l'accordo commerciale** *m*
business deal

㊱ **la donna d'affari**
businesswoman

㊷ **i clienti**
clients

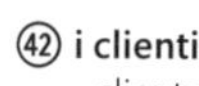

㉘ **la reception dell'ufficio**
office reception

㉜ **l'ufficio dell'amministratore delegato** *m*
CEO's office

㊲ **la riunione**
meeting

See also
82 In ufficio • In the office **89-90** I lavori • Jobs **91** I settori e i reparti • Industries and departments **92** Fare domanda per un lavoro • Applying for a job **93** Le competenze sul luogo di lavoro • Workplace skills **95** Riunirsi e presentare • Meeting and presenting

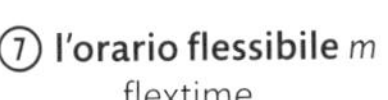

⑦ **l'orario flessibile** *m*
flextime

⑧ **lavorare da casa**
to work from home

⑨ **lavorare a tempo pieno**
to work full-time

⑯ **essere promosso** *m* **essere promossa** *f*
to be promoted

⑰ **dimettersi**
to resign

⑱ **andare in pensione**
to retire

㉕ **il viaggio di lavoro**
business trip

㉖ **l'appuntamento** *m*
appointment

㉗ **il pranzo di lavoro**
business lunch

81.2 LA PAGA • PAY

① **la tariffa oraria**
hourly rate

② **gli straordinari**
overtime

③ **il salario**
salary

④ **lo stipendio**
wages

⑤ **la busta paga**
pay slip

⑥ **l'incentivo** *m*
bonus

⑦ **i benefit**
benefits

25%

⑧ **l'aumento** *m*
raise

25%

⑨ **la riduzione dello stipendio**
pay cut

㊹ **il responsabile del colloquio** *m* **la responsabile del colloquio** *f*
interviewer

㊺ **il candidato** *m* **la candidata** *f*
applicant

㊻ **il datore di lavoro** *m* / **la datrice di lavoro** *f*
employer

㊸ **il colloquio**
interview

㊽ **il lavoratore** *m* **la lavoratrice** *f*
worker

㊾ **il collega** *m* / **la collega** *f*
co-worker / colleague

㊿ **il dipendente** *m* **la dipendente** *f*
employee

51 **il supervisore**
supervisor

52 **lo stagista** *m* **la stagista** *f*
intern

53 **il capoufficio** *m* **la capoufficio** *f*
office manager

㊼ **lo staff**
staff

82 In ufficio
In the office

82.1 L'UFFICIO · OFFICE

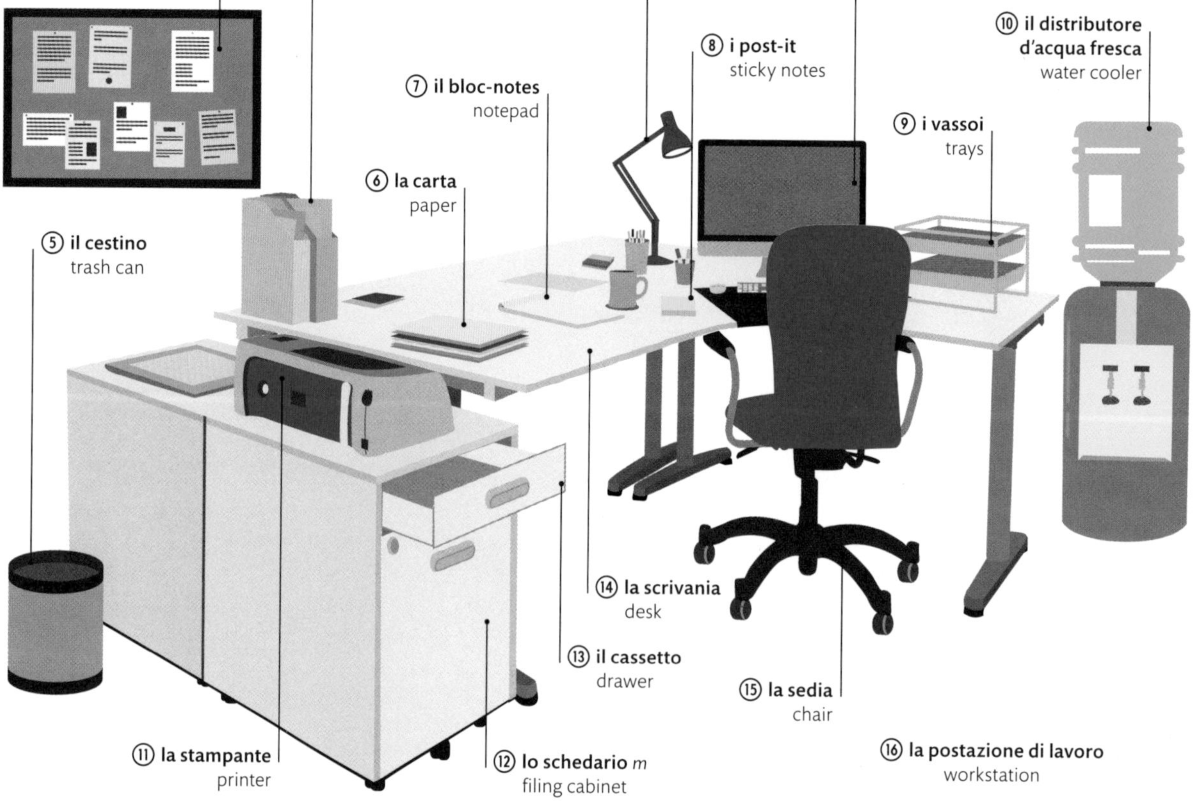

① **la bacheca** bulletin board
② **i raccoglitori** files / folders
③ **la lampada** lamp
④ **il computer** computer
⑤ **il cestino** trash can
⑥ **la carta** paper
⑦ **il bloc-notes** notepad
⑧ **i post-it** sticky notes
⑨ **i vassoi** trays
⑩ **il distributore d'acqua fresca** water cooler
⑪ **la stampante** printer
⑫ **lo schedario** *m* filing cabinet
⑬ **il cassetto** drawer
⑭ **la scrivania** desk
⑮ **la sedia** chair
⑯ **la postazione di lavoro** workstation

82.2 L'ATTREZZATURA PER LE SALE RIUNIONI · MEETING-ROOM EQUIPMENT

① la presentazione
presentation
② la proposta
proposal
③ la relazione
report
④ il proiettore
digital projector
⑤ la riunione
meeting
⑥ la lavagna fogli mobi
flip chart
⑦ il cavallett
easel

See also
81 Al lavoro • At work **83** I computer e la tecnologia • Computers and technology **91** I settori e i reparti Industries and departments **92** Fare domanda per un lavoro • Applying for a job **93** Le competenze sul luogo di lavoro • Workplace skills **95** Riunirsi e presentare • Meeting and presenting

82.3 **L'ATTREZZATURA DELL'UFFICIO** • OFFICE EQUIPMENT

① **la fotocopiatrice**
photocopier

② **lo scanner**
scanner

③ **il telefono**
telephone / phone

④ **il computer portatile**
laptop

⑤ **il proiettore**
projector

⑥ **le cuffie**
headset

⑦ **il tritadocumenti**
shredder

⑧ **il cellulare**
cell phone

⑨ **il poggiapiedi**
footrest

⑩ **la sedia con appoggio per ginocchia**
kneeling chair

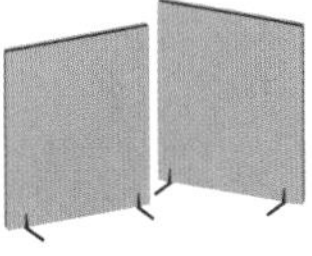
⑪ **il pannello mobile**
movable panel

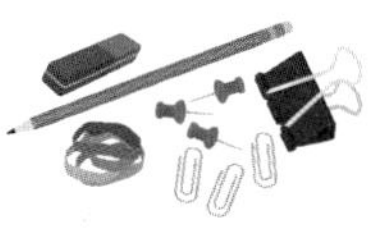
⑫ **la cancelleria**
stationery

⑬ **la lettera**
letter

⑭ **la busta**
envelope

JUNE
⑮ **il calendario**
calendar

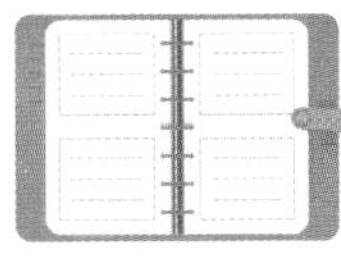
⑯ **l'agenda** *f*
planner

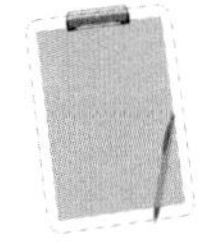
⑰ **il fermablocco**
clipboard

⑱ **la pinzatrice**
hole punch

⑲ **gli elastici**
rubber bands

⑳ **la pinza fermacarte**
binder clip

㉑ **le forbici**
scissors

㉒ **il temperino**
pencil sharpener

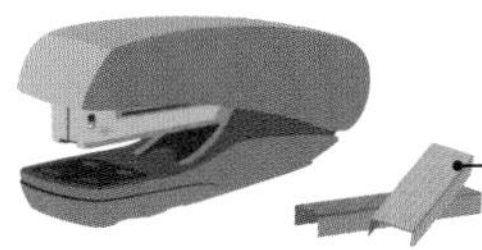
㉓ **la cucitrice**
stapler

㉔ **le graffette**
staples

㉕ **il bianchetto**
correction fluid

MINUTES
㉖ **il verbale**
minutes

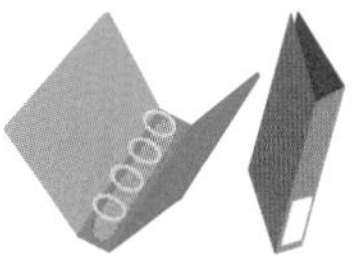
㉗ **il raccoglitore ad anelli**
ring binder

㉘ **l'evidenziatore** *m*
highlighter

㉙ **la colla**
glue

㉚ **lo scotch**
tape

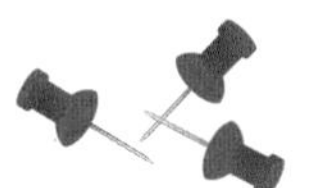
㉛ **la puntina da disegno**
thumbtack

㉜ **la matita**
pencil

㉝ **la penna**
pen

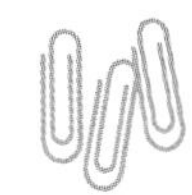
㉞ **le graffette**
paper clips

㉟ **la gomma da cancellare**
eraser

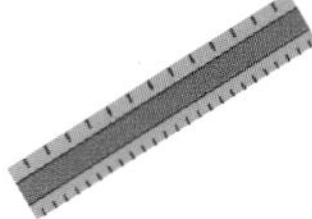
㊱ **il righello**
ruler

83 I computer e la tecnologia

Computers and technology

83.1 GLI APPARECCHI E LA TECNOLOGIA · GADGETS AND TECHNOLOGY

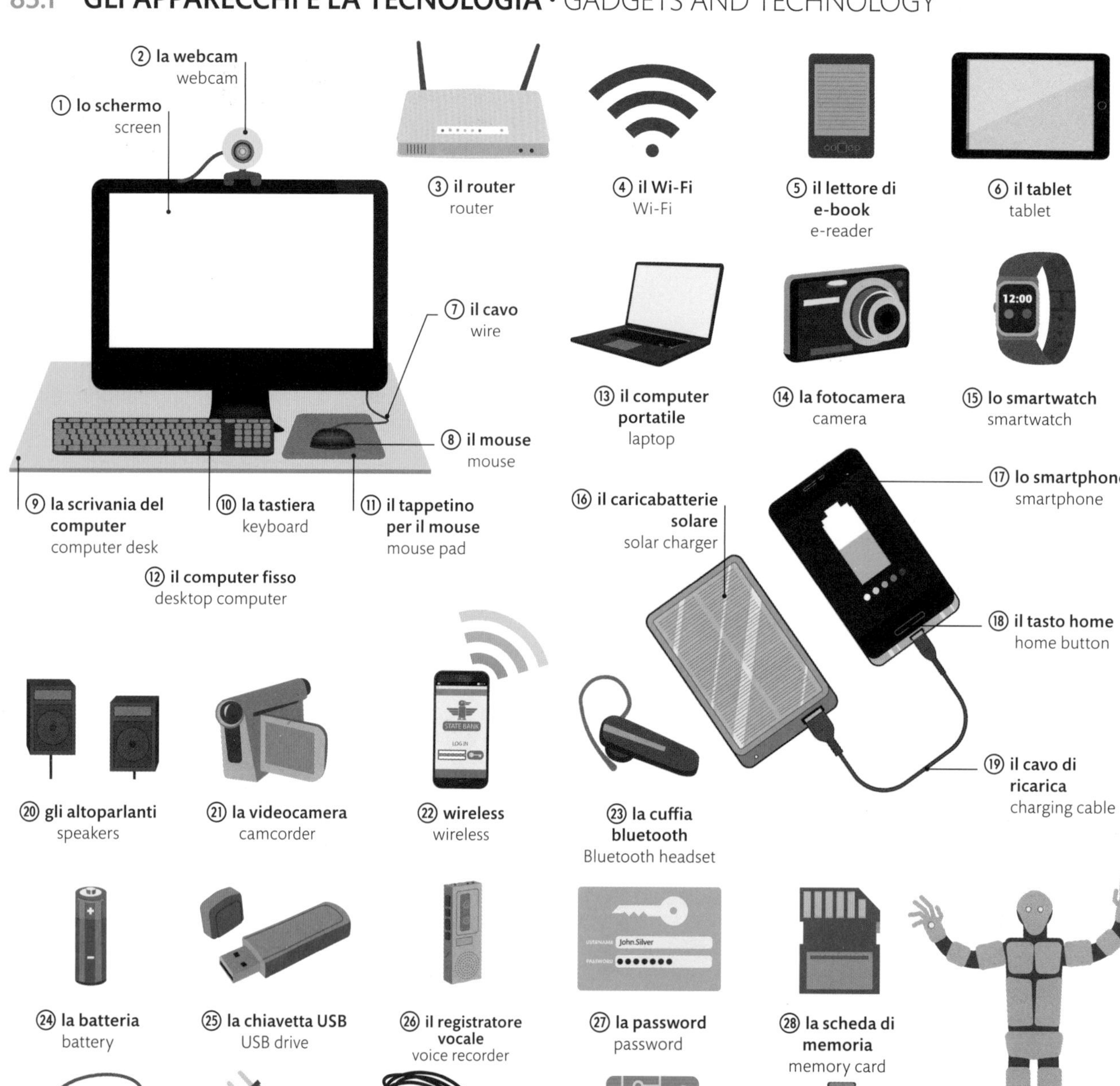

① lo schermo
screen
② la webcam
webcam
③ il router
router
④ il Wi-Fi
Wi-Fi
⑤ il lettore di e-book
e-reader
⑥ il tablet
tablet
⑦ il cavo
wire
⑧ il mouse
mouse
⑨ la scrivania del computer
computer desk
⑩ la tastiera
keyboard
⑪ il tappetino per il mouse
mouse pad
⑫ il computer fisso
desktop computer
⑬ il computer portatile
laptop
⑭ la fotocamera
camera
12:00
⑮ lo smartwatch
smartwatch
⑯ il caricabatterie solare
solar charger
⑰ lo smartphone
smartphone
⑱ il tasto home
home button
⑲ il cavo di ricarica
charging cable
STATE BANK
LOG IN
⑳ gli altoparlanti
speakers
㉑ la videocamera
camcorder
㉒ wireless
wireless
㉓ la cuffia bluetooth
Bluetooth headset
John Silver
㉔ la batteria
battery
㉕ la chiavetta USB
USB drive
㉖ il registratore vocale
voice recorder
㉗ la password
password
㉘ la scheda di memoria
memory card
㉙ il disco fisso
hard drive
㉚ la presa elettrica
plug
㉛ il cavo di alimentazione
power cord
㉜ il circuito
circuit
㉝ il telecomando
remote control
㉞ l'intelligenza artificiale *f*
artificial intelligence

See also
73 A scuola • At school **80** All'università • At college **81** Al lavoro • At work **82** In ufficio • In the office **95** Riunirsi e presentare • Meeting and presenting **140** I giochi • Games

83.2 **LA COMUNICAZIONE ONLINE** • ONLINE COMMUNICATION

① **accendere**
to turn on

② **spegnere**
to turn off

③ **accedere**
to log in

④ **uscire**
to log out

⑤ **scaricare**
to download

⑥ **caricare**
to upload

⑦ **fare il back up**
to back up

⑧ **cliccare**
to click

⑨ **collegare**
to plug in

⑩ **eliminare**
to delete

⑪ **stampare**
to print

⑫ **il contatto**
contact

⑬ **l'e-mail** *f*
email

⑭ **rispondere**
to reply

⑮ **rispondere a tutti**
to reply to all

⑯ **inviare**
to send

⑰ **inoltrare**
to forward

⑱ **la bozza**
draft

⑲ **la posta in arrivo**
inbox

⑳ **la posta in uscita**
outbox

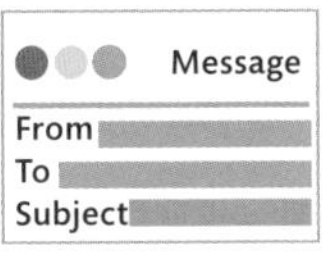
Message
From
To
Subject

㉑ **l'oggetto** *m*
subject

㉒ **lo spam**
junk mail / spam

㉓ **il cestino**
trash

㉔ **l'allegato** *m*
attachment

㉕ **la chat**
chat

㉖ **la videochiamata**
video chat

㉗ **la firma**
signature

㉘ **l'hashtag** *m*
hashtag

㉙ **la chiocciola**
at sign /
at symbol

㉚ **Liz, devi accendere il microfono.**
You need to turn on your microphone, Liz.

㉛ **la videoconferenza**
video conference

84 I media
Media

84.1 LO STUDIO TELEVISIVO · TELEVISION STUDIO

① **la luce**
light

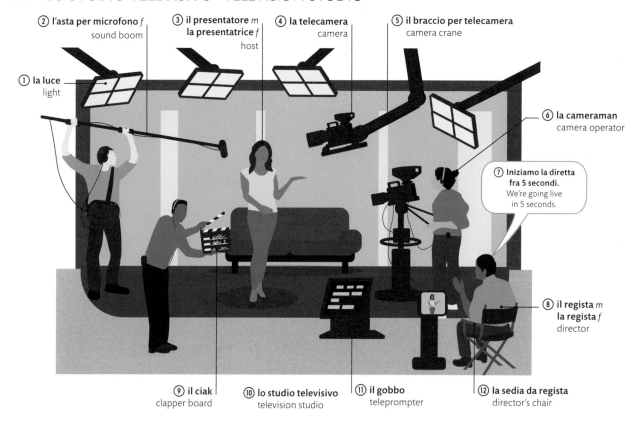

② **l'asta per microfono** *f*
sound boom

③ **il presentatore** *m*
la presentatrice *f*
host

④ **la telecamera**
camera

⑤ **il braccio per telecamera**
camera crane

⑥ **la cameraman**
camera operator

⑦ **Iniziamo la diretta fra 5 secondi.**
We're going live in 5 seconds.

⑧ **il regista** *m*
la regista *f*
director

⑨ **il ciak**
clapper board

⑩ **lo studio televisivo**
television studio

⑪ **il gobbo**
teleprompter

⑫ **la sedia da regista**
director's chair

84.2 LA RADIO · RADIO

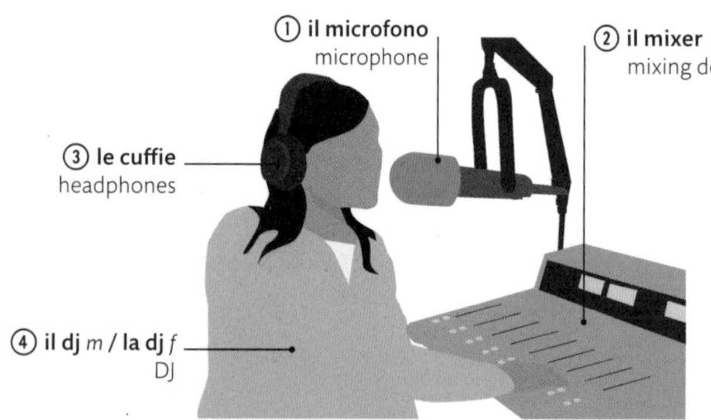

① **il microfono**
microphone

② **il mixer**
mixing desk

③ **le cuffie**
headphones

④ **il dj** *m* / **la dj** *f*
DJ

⑤ **la sala di registrazione**
recording studio

⑥ **il tecnico del suono**
sound technician

⑦ **la stazione radio**
radio station

⑧ **trasmettere**
to broadcast

⑨ **digitale**
digital

⑩ **FM**
FM

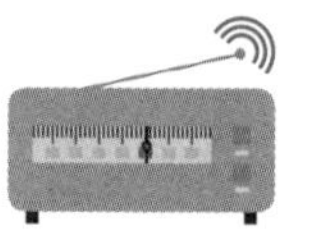

⑪ **la frequenza**
frequency

See also
83 I computer e la tecnologia • Computers and technology **128-129** La musica • Music
136 L'home entertainment • Home entertainment **137** La televisione • Television

84.3 I SOCIAL MEDIA E I MEDIA ONLINE
SOCIAL AND ONLINE MEDIA

① **seguire**
to follow

② **mettere mi piace**
to like

③ **diventare virale**
to go viral

④ **essere di tendenza**
to trend

⑨ Il mio blog ha oltre 500 follower.
My blog has over 500 followers.

⑤ **l'avatar** *m*
avatar

⑥ **il vlog**
vlog

⑦ **il vlogger** *m*
la vlogger *f*
vlogger

⑧ **il blog**
blog

⑩ **il blogger** *m*
la blogger *f*
blogger

⑪ **condividere**
to share

⑫ **bloccare**
to block

⑬ **postare**
to post

⑭ **inviare un messaggio diretto**
to DM someone

⑮ **l'influencer** *m / f*
influencer

⑯ **il follower**
follower

⑰ **il podcast**
podcast

⑱ **l'emoji** *f*
emoji

⑲ **l'hashtag** *m*
hashtag

⑳ **il thread**
thread

㉑ **la sezione notizie**
newsfeed

㉒ **l'aggiornamento dello stato** *m*
status update

㉓ **il sistema di gestione dei contenuti**
CMS (content management system)

㉔ **la piattaforma**
platform

㉕ **il cookie**
cookie

㉖ **la finestra pop-up**
pop-up

㉗ **il sito web di notizie**
news website

㉘ **il sito web di una rivista**
magazine website

㉙ **il sito web della community**
community website

㉚ **il trolling**
trolling

85 La legge
Law

85.1 IL SISTEMA LEGALE • THE LEGAL SYSTEM

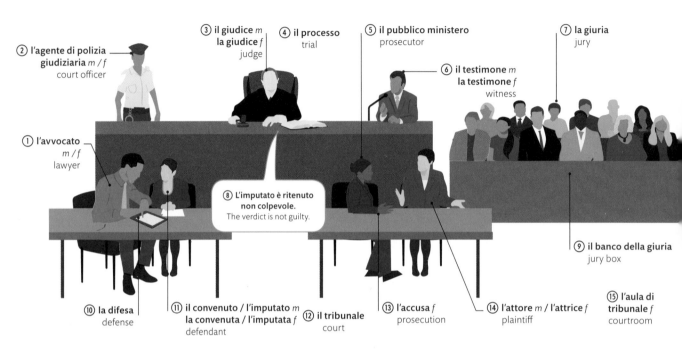

1. **l'avvocato** *m / f* — lawyer
2. **l'agente di polizia giudiziaria** *m / f* — court officer
3. **il giudice** *m* / **la giudice** *f* — judge
4. **il processo** — trial
5. **il pubblico ministero** — prosecutor
6. **il testimone** *m* / **la testimone** *f* — witness
7. **la giuria** — jury
8. **L'imputato è ritenuto non colpevole.** — The verdict is not guilty.
9. **il banco della giuria** — jury box
10. **la difesa** — defense
11. **il convenuto / l'imputato** *m* / **la convenuta / l'imputata** *f* — defendant
12. **il tribunale** — court
13. **l'accusa** *f* — prosecution
14. **l'attore** *m* / **l'attrice** *f* — plaintiff
15. **l'aula di tribunale** *f* — courtroom

16. **lo stenografo** *m* / **la stenografa** *f* — court reporter

17. **l'ufficiale giudiziario** *m* / **l'ufficiale giudiziaria** *f* — court official

18. **l'ufficio dell'avvocato** *m* — lawyer's office

19. **la citazione** — summons

20. **il cliente** *m* / **la cliente** *f* — client

21. **il mandato** — warrant

22. **l'ordinanza** *f* — writ

23. **l'accusa** *f* — charge

24. **la consulenza legale** — legal advice

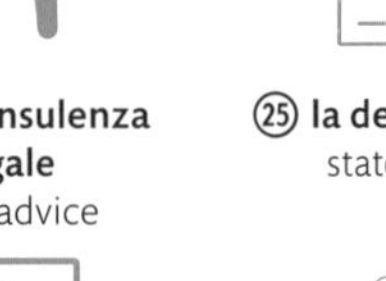

25. **la deposizione** — statement

26. **l'udienza** *f* — court date

27. **il processo** — court case

28. **la sentenza** — verdict

29. **condannare** — to sentence

30. **la delibera della giuria** — jury deliberation
31. **il presidente della giuria** *m* / **la presidentessa della giuria** *f* — foreperson
32. **il voto** — vote

See also
50 | servizi di pronto intervento • Emergency services
91 | settori e i reparti • Industries and departments

㉝ **l'identikit** *m*
composite

㉞ **la prova**
evidence

㉟ **il sospettato** *m*
la sospettata *f*
suspect

㊱ **i precedenti penali**
criminal record

㊲ **il criminale** *m*
la criminale *f*
criminal

㊳ **l'imputato** *m*
l'imputata *f*
accused

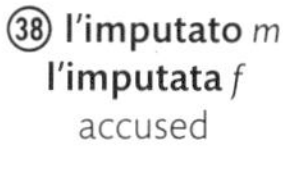
㊴ **perorare / dichiararsi**
to plead

㊵ **innocente** *m / f*
innocent

㊶ **colpevole** *m / f*
guilty

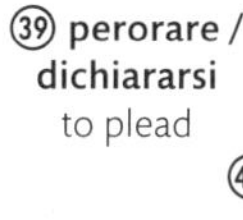
㊷ **ricorrere in appello**
to appeal

㊸ **i carcerati** *m*
le carcerate *f*
prisoners

㊹ **le guardie carcerarie**
prison guards

㊺ **il carcere**
prison

㊻ **la cella**
cell

㊼ **la cauzione**
bail

㊽ **la libertà condizionale**
parole

㊾ **la multa**
fine

㊿ **essere assolto** *m*
essere assolta *f*
to be acquitted

85.2 I CRIMINI • CRIME

① **la rapina**
robbery / burglary

② **lo scippo**
mugging

③ **il furto d'auto**
car theft

④ **la violenza dei tifosi**
hooliganism

⑤ **il vandalismo**
vandalism

⑥ **il contrabbando**
smuggling

⑦ **la frode**
fraud

⑧ **l'hackeraggio** *m*
hacking

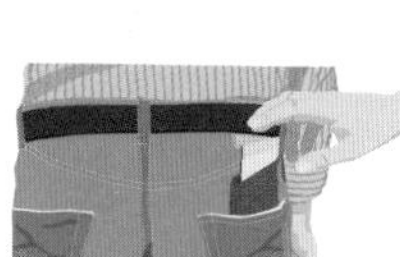
⑨ **il borseggio**
pickpocketing

⑩ **la corruzione**
bribery

⑪ **l'eccesso di velocità** *m*
speeding

⑫ **lo spaccio di droga**
drug dealing

⑬ **i graffiti**
graffiti

⑭ **il taccheggio**
shoplifting

86 L'agricoltura
Farming

86.1 NELLA FATTORIA • ON THE FARM

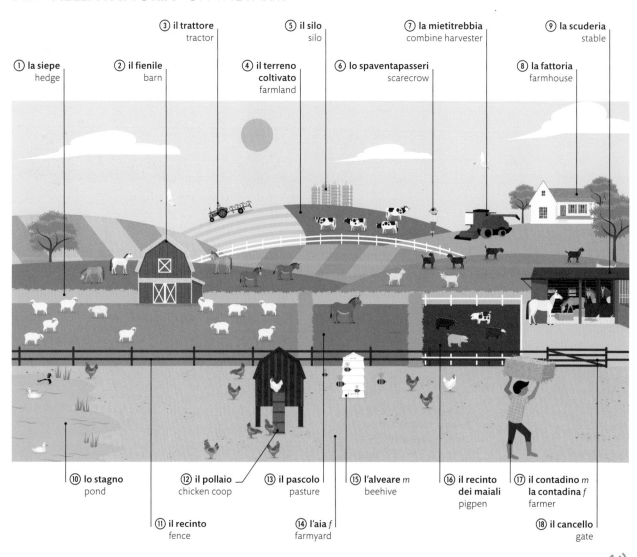

① **la siepe** hedge
② **il fienile** barn
③ **il trattore** tractor
④ **il terreno coltivato** farmland
⑤ **il silo** silo
⑥ **lo spaventapasseri** scarecrow
⑦ **la mietitrebbia** combine harvester
⑧ **la fattoria** farmhouse
⑨ **la scuderia** stable
⑩ **lo stagno** pond
⑪ **il recinto** fence
⑫ **il pollaio** chicken coop
⑬ **il pascolo** pasture
⑭ **l'aia** *f* farmyard
⑮ **l'alveare** *m* beehive
⑯ **il recinto dei maiali** pigpen
⑰ **il contadino** *m* **la contadina** *f* farmer
⑱ **il cancello** gate

86.2 I VERBI DELL'AGRICOLTURA • FARMING VERBS

① **arare** to plow

② **seminare** to sow

③ **mungere** to milk

④ **nutrire** to feed

⑤ **piantare** to plant

⑥ **raccogliere** to harvest

See also
53 La carne • Meat **55-56** La verdura • Vegetables **57** La frutta • Fruit **58** La frutta e la frutta a guscio Fruit and nuts **61** I prodotti caseari • Dairy produce **165** Gli animali da fattoria • Farm animals

86.3 I TERMINI DELL'AGRICOLTURA • FARMING TERMS

① **l'azienda agricola** *f*
crop farm

② **l'azienda casearia** *f*
dairy farm

③ **l'azienda di ovinicoltura** *f*
sheep farm

④ **l'azienda avicola** *f*
poultry farm

⑤ **l'azienda suinicola** *f*
pig farm

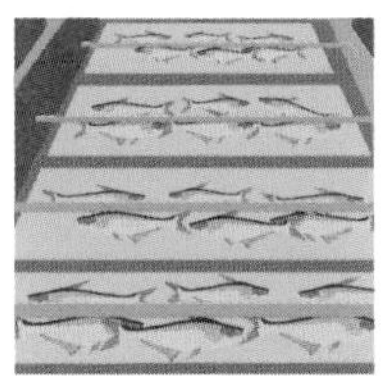
⑥ **l'allevamento ittico** *m*
fish farm

⑦ **la mandria**
herd

⑧ **l'azienda ortofrutticola** *f*
fruit farm

⑨ **il vigneto**
vineyard

⑩ **l'orto** *m*
vegetable garden

⑪ **l'erbicida** *m*
herbicide

⑫ **il pesticida**
pesticide

86.4 LE COLTURE • CROPS

① **il grano**
wheat

② **il mais**
corn

③ **l'orzo** *m*
barley

④ **i semi di colza**
rapeseed

⑤ **i girasoli**
sunflowers

⑥ **il fieno**
hay

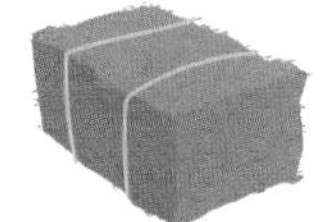
⑦ **l'erba medica** *f*
alfalfa

⑧ **il tabacco**
tobacco

⑨ **il riso**
rice

⑩ **il tè**
tea

⑪ **il caffè**
coffee

⑫ **la canna da zucchero**
sugar cane

⑬ **il lino**
flax

⑭ **il cotone**
cotton

⑮ **le patate**
potatoes

⑯ **gli ignami** *m*
yams

⑰ **il miglio**
millet

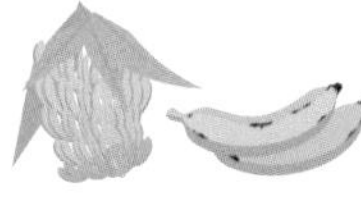
⑱ **le banane platano**
plantains

87 Le costruzioni
Construction

87.1 IL CANTIERE • BUILDING SITE

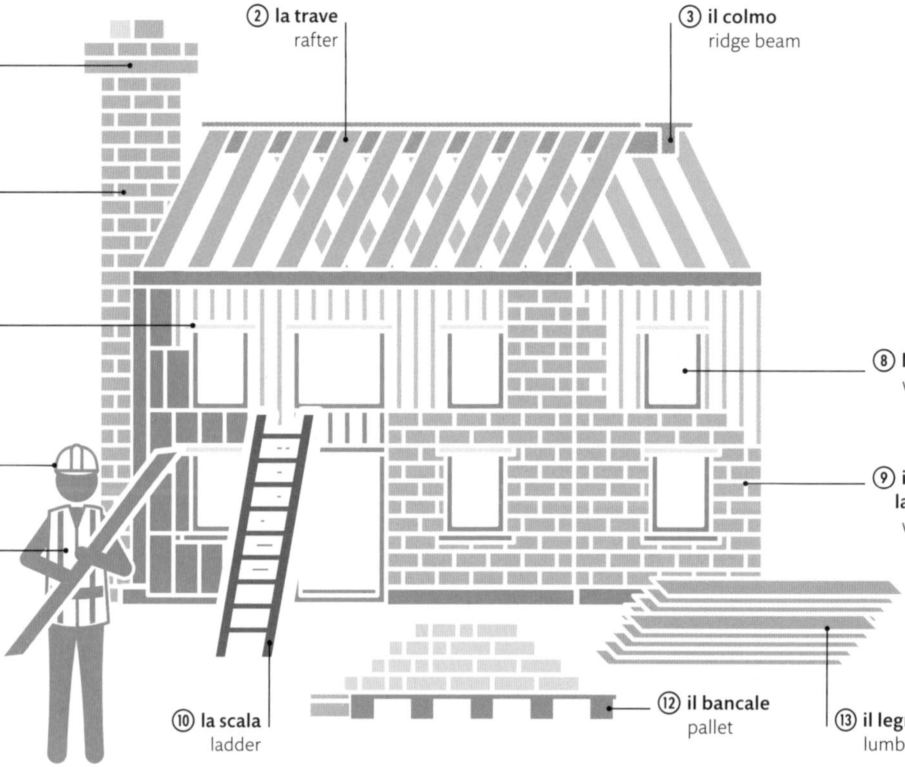

① **il camino** chimney

② **la trave** rafter

③ **il colmo** ridge beam

④ **il mattone** brick

⑤ **l'architrave** *m* lintel

⑥ **il casco di protezione** hard hat

⑦ **l'operaio edile** *m* **l'operaia edile** *f* construction worker

⑧ **la finestra** window

⑨ **il muro / la parete** wall

⑩ **la scala** ladder

⑫ **il bancale** pallet

⑬ **il legname** lumber

⑪ **il cantiere** construction site

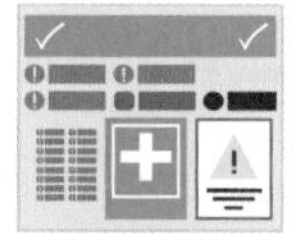

⑭ **la bacheca degli avvisi di sicurezza** safety notice board

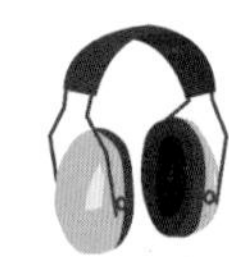

⑮ **il paraorecchie** ear protectors

⑯ **il gilet ad alta visibilità** high-visibility vest

⑰ **i guanti protettivi** safety gloves

⑱ **gli occhiali protettivi** safety glasses

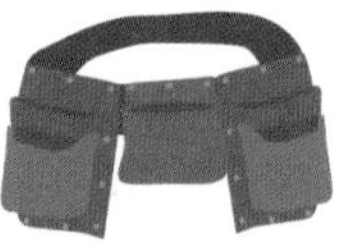

⑲ **la cintura degli attrezzi** tool belt

⑳ **la trave metallica** girder

㉑ **la tubatura** pipe

㉒ **la malta** cement / mortar

㉓ **il blocco di calcestruzzo** cinder block

㉔ **le tegole** shingles

㉕ **costruire** to build

See also
25 Un luogo in cui vivere • A place to live **32** La casa • House and home **33** Gli impianti elettrico e idraulico • Electrics and plumbing **35** I lavori di miglioria della casa • Home improvements **36** Gli attrezzi • Tools **37** La decorazione • Renovating

87.2 I MACCHINARI • MACHINERY

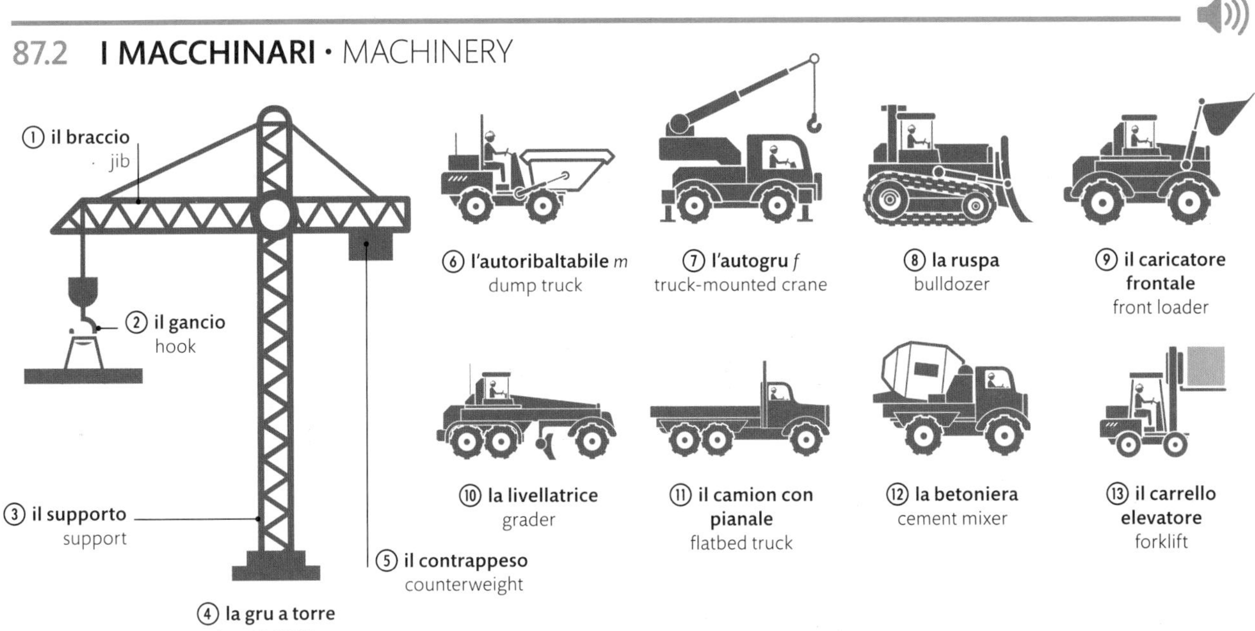
① il braccio
jib
② il gancio
hook
③ il supporto
support
④ la gru a torre
tower crane
⑤ il contrappeso
counterweight
⑥ l'autoribaltabile m
dump truck
⑦ l'autogru f
truck-mounted crane
⑧ la ruspa
bulldozer
⑨ il caricatore frontale
front loader
⑩ la livellatrice
grader
⑪ il camion con pianale
flatbed truck
⑫ la betoniera
cement mixer
⑬ il carrello elevatore
forklift

87.3 GLI ATTREZZI E I CANTIERI STRADALI
TOOLS AND ROADWORKS

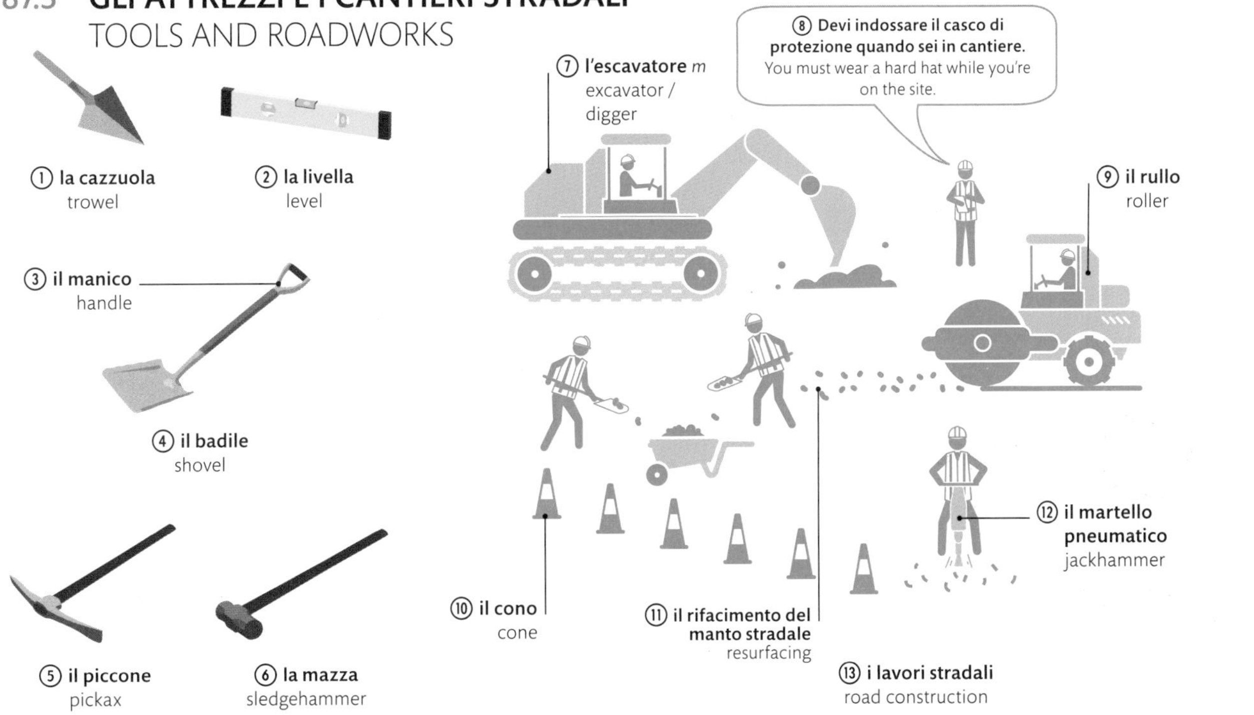

① **la cazzuola**
trowel

② **la livella**
level

③ **il manico**
handle

④ **il badile**
shovel

⑤ **il piccone**
pickax

⑥ **la mazza**
sledgehammer

⑦ **l'escavatore** *m*
excavator / digger

⑧ **Devi indossare il casco di protezione quando sei in cantiere.**
You must wear a hard hat while you're on the site.

⑨ **il rullo**
roller

⑩ **il cono**
cone

⑪ **il rifacimento del manto stradale**
resurfacing

⑫ **il martello pneumatico**
jackhammer

⑬ **i lavori stradali**
road construction

88 L'esercito
Military

88.1 LE FORZE ARMATE
ARMED FORCES

① **l'esercito** *m*
army

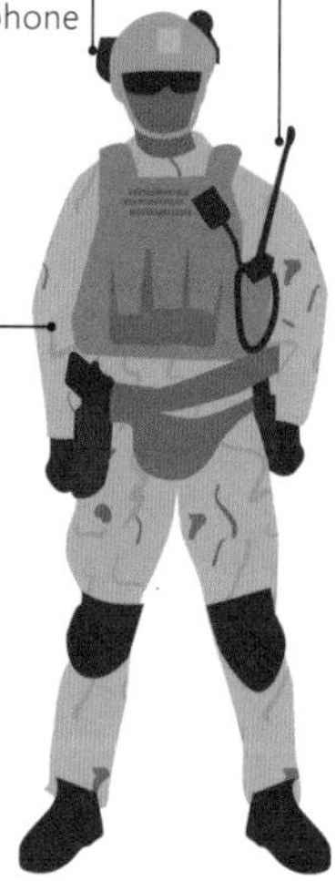

② **il marinaio**
marine

③ **la marina militare**
navy

④ **il soldato** *m*
la soldatessa *f*
soldier

⑤ **la radiotrasmittente**
radio

⑥ **l'auricolare** *m*
ear phone

⑦ **la tuta mimetica**
camouflage

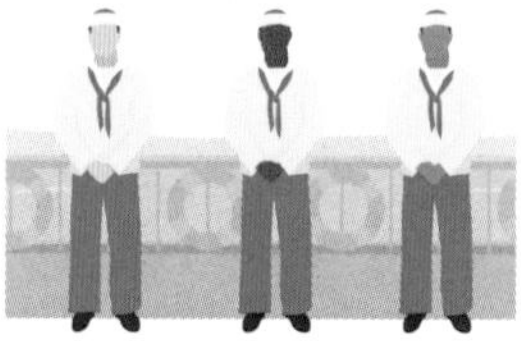

⑧ **i marinai**
sailors

⑨ **il generale**
general

⑩ **l'ammiraglio** *m*
admiral

⑪ **l'aeronautica militare** *f*
airforce

⑫ **l'aviatore** *m*
airman

⑬ **la divisa**
uniform

⑭ **il veterano di guerra**
veteran

⑮ **la medaglia**
medal

88.2 I VEICOLI MILITARI
MILITARY VEHICLES

① **il cannone**
gun

② **il veicolo corazzato**
armored vehicle

③ **il carro armato**
tank

④ **il camion militare**
military truck

⑤ **il veicolo anfibio**
amphibious vehicle

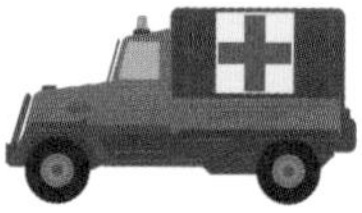

⑥ **l'ambulanza militare** *f*
military ambulance

⑦ **il veicolo da ricognizione**
reconnaissance vehicle

88.3 LE NAVI DELLA MARINA MILITARE
NAVY VESSELS

① **la portaerei**
aircraft carrier

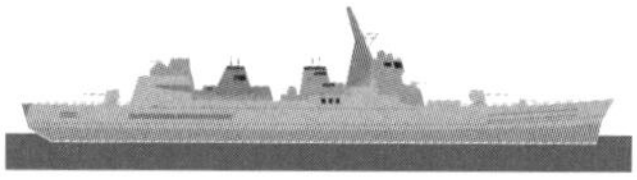

② **l'isola** *f*
island

③ **il cacciatorpediniere**
destroyer

④ **l'incrociatore** *m*
cruiser

⑤ **la fregata**
frigate

⑥ **il sottomarino**
submarine

See also
79 La storia • History **148** Le cartine e le direzioni Maps and directions **149-151** I Paesi • Countries

88.4 IL VELIVOLO DA COMBATTIMENTO • COMBAT AIRCRAFT

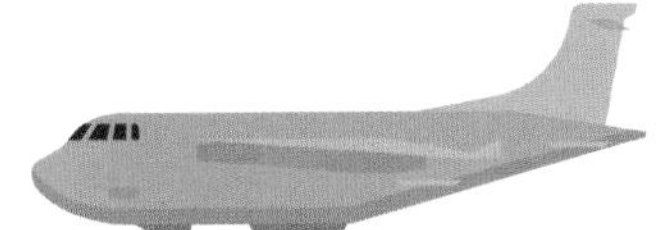

① **l'aereo da trasporto militare** *m*
military transport aircraft

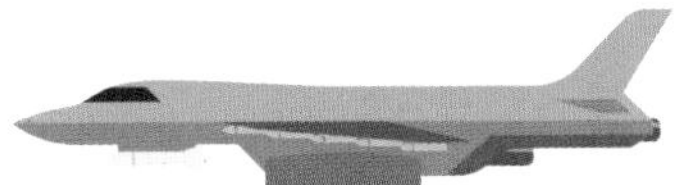

② **il bombardiere**
bomber

③ **l'elicottero d'attacco** *m*
attack helicopter

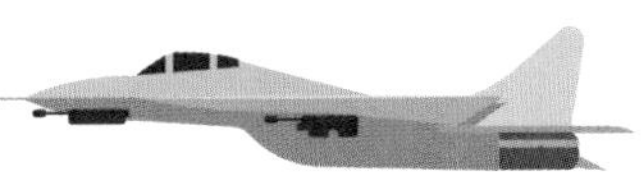

④ **il caccia**
fighter

⑤ **l'aereo da ricognizione** *m*
reconnaissance aircraft

⑥ **l'elicottero da trasporto** *m*
transport helicopter

88.5 LA GUERRA E LE ARMI • WAR AND WEAPONS

① **la battaglia**
battle

② **il fronte**
front

③ **gli spari**
gunfire

④ **il ferito**
casualty

⑤ **l'ospedale da campo** *m*
field hospital

⑥ **la mensa militare**
mess

⑦ **le armi**
guns

⑧ **il mitra**
machine gun

⑨ **la pistola**
pistol

⑩ **il fucile a canna liscia**
shotgun

⑪ **il fucile**
rifle

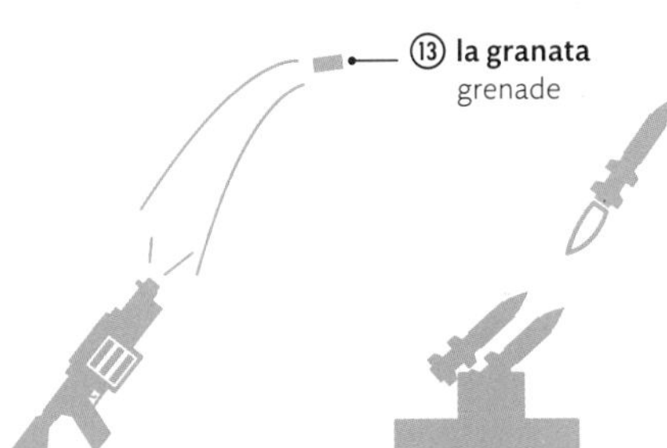

⑫ **il lanciagranate**
grenade launcher

⑬ **la granata**
grenade

⑭ **il missile terra-aria**
surface-to-air missile

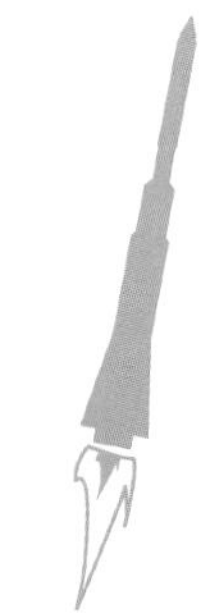

⑮ **il missile balistico**
ballistic missile

⑯ **il missile spalleggiabile**
shoulder-launched missile

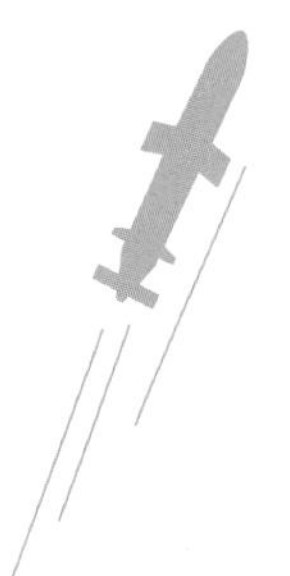

⑰ **il missile da crociera**
cruise missile

⑱ **il drone armato**
armed drone

89 I lavori
Jobs

89.1 LE OCCUPAZIONI · OCCUPATIONS

① **l'attore** *m*
l'attrice *f*
actor

② **il sociologo** *m*
la sociologa *f*
sociologist

③ **il barbiere**
barber

④ **l'editore** *m*
l'editrice *f*
editor

⑩ Questo tubo ha una perdita.
This pipe has sprung a leak.

⑤ **il barista** *m*
la barista *f*
bartender

⑥ **il pescatore** *m*
la pescatrice *f*
fisherman

⑦ **il fisioterapista** *m*
la fisioterapista *f*
physical therapist

⑧ **l'ottico** *m* / **l'ottica** *f*
optician

⑨ **l'idraulico** *m* / **l'idraulica** *f*
plumber

⑪ **il falegname** *m*
la falegname *f*
carpenter

⑫ **il capitano della nave** *m / f*
ship's captain

⑬ **il docente** *m*
la docente *f*
lecturer

⑭ **il comico** *m*
la comica *f*
comedian

⑮ **il ballerino** *m*
la ballerina *f*
dancer

⑯ **il clown** *m*
la clown *f*
clown

⑰ **l'addetto alle pulizie** *m* / **l'addetta alle pulizie** *f*
cleaner

⑱ **il dottore** *m*
la dottoressa *f*
doctor

⑲ **l'istruttore di guida** *m*
l'istruttrice di guida *f*
driving instructor

⑳ **l'imbianchino** *m*
l'imbianchina *f*
painter

㉑ **l'elettricista** *m / f*
electrician

㉒ **il designer** *m*
la designer *f*
designer

㉓ **il barista** *m*
la barista *f*
barista

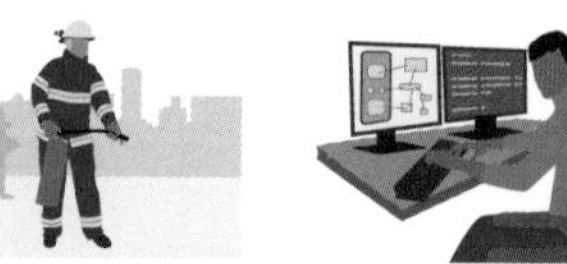
㉔ **il vigile del fuoco** *m*
la vigilessa del fuoco *f*
firefighter

㉕ **lo sviluppatore di app** *m*
la sviluppatrice di app *f*
app developer

㉖ **la spia** *m / f*
spy

㉗ **il fiorista** *m*
la fiorista *f*
florist

㉘ **la manutenzione delle aree verdi**
ground maintenance

㉙ **il giardiniere** *m*
la giardiniera *f*
gardener

㉚ **il fruttivendolo** *m*
la fruttivendola *f*
grocer

㉛ **il minatore** *m*
la minatrice *f*
miner

㉜ **il responsabile IT** *m*
la responsabile IT *f*
IT manager

㉝ **il gioielliere** *m*
la gioielliera *f*
jeweler

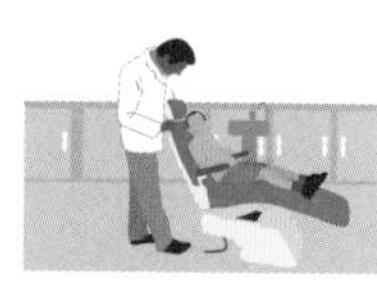
㉞ **il dentista** *m*
la dentista *f*
dentist

See also
81 Al lavoro • At work **82** In ufficio • In the office **90** I lavori (continua) • Jobs continued **91** I settori e i reparti • Industries and departments **92** Fare domanda per un lavoro • Applying for a job **93** Le competenze sul luogo di lavoro • Workplace skills **95** Riunirsi e presentare • Meeting and presenting

(35) **il domestico** *m*
la domestica *f*
maid / housekeeper

(36) **il parrucchiere** *m*
la parrucchiera *f*
hairdresser / stylist

(37) **il meccanico** *m*
la meccanica *f*
mechanic

(38) **l'interprete** *m / f*
interpreter

(39) **il curatore del museo** *m* / **la curatrice del museo** *f*
museum curator

(40) **l'investigatore privato** *m*
l'investigatrice privata *f*
private investigator

(41) **il capo cantiere** *m*
la capo cantiere *f*
site manager

(42) **l'odontoiatra** *m / f*
orthodontist

(43) **il conduttore** *m*
la conduttrice *f*
broadcaster

(44) **il farmacista** *m*
la farmacista *f*
pharmacist

(45) **il macellaio** *m*
la macellaia *f*
butcher

(46) **il fotografo** *m*
la fotografa *f*
photographer

(47) **il poliziotto** *m*
la poliziotta *f*
police officer

(48) **l'infermiere** *m*
l'infermiera *f*
nurse

(49) **il marinaio** *m*
la marinaia *f*
sailor

(50) **il commesso** *m*
la commessa *f*
sales assistant

(51) **la cameriera**
server / waitress

(52) **il cameriere**
server / waiter

(53) **lo scultore** *m*
la scultrice *f*
sculptor

(54) **la guardia di sicurezza**
security guard

(55) **il sarto** *m*
la sarta *f*
tailor

(56) **il maestro di sci** *m*
la maestra di sci *f*
ski instructor

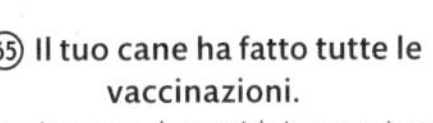

(65) **Il tuo cane ha fatto tutte le vaccinazioni.**

Your dog is up to date with its vaccinations.

(57) **il soldato** *m*
la soldatessa *f*
soldier

(58) **il contadino** *m*
la contadina *f*
farmer

(59) **l'atleta** *m / f*
athlete / sportsperson

(60) **il pescivendolo** *m*
la pescivendola *f*
fishmonger

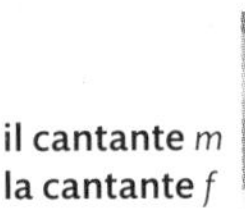

(61) **il cantante** *m*
la cantante *f*
singer

(62) **l'agente immobiliare** *m / f*
real estate agent

(63) **il ricercatore di mercato** *m* / **la ricercatrice di mercato** *f*
market researcher

(64) **il veterinario** *m* / **la veterinaria** *f*
vet

90 I lavori (continua)
Jobs continued

90.1 LE OCCUPAZIONI · OCCUPATIONS

① **la guardia di sicurezza** *m / f*
security guard

② **il lavavetri** *m*
la lavavetri *f*
window cleaner

③ **l'artista** *m / f*
artist

④ **la guardia del corpo** *m / f*
bodyguard

⑤ **lo psicologo** *m*
la psicologa *f*
psychologist

⑥ **l'uomo d'affari** *m*
businessman

⑦ **la donna d'affari**
businesswoman

⑧ **il commercialista** *m*
la commercialista *f*
accountant

⑨ **lo chef** *m*
la chef *f*
chef

⑩ **l'operaio edile** *m*
l'operaia edile *f*
construction worker

⑪ **il dj radiofonico** *m*
la dj radiofonica *f*
radio DJ

⑫ **l'ingegnere** *m*
l'ingegnera *f*
engineer

⑬ **lo stilista** *m*
la stilista *f*
fashion designer

⑭ **la rock star** *m / f*
rock star

⑮ **l'istruttore di volo** *m*
l'istruttrice di volo *f*
flight instructor

⑯ **l'inserviente** *m / f*
janitor

⑰ **la guida turistica** *m / f*
tour guide

⑱ **il postino** *m*
la postina *f*
mail carrier

⑲ **l'assistente personale** *m / f*
personal assistant (PA)

⑳ **il bibliotecario** *m*
la bibliotecaria *f*
librarian

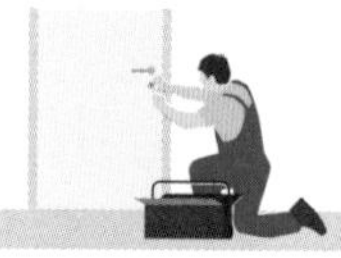

㉑ **il fabbro** *m / f*
locksmith

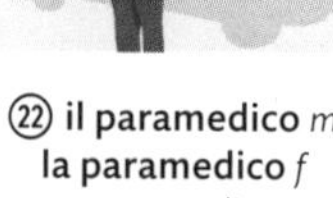
㉒ **il paramedico** *m*
la paramedico *f*
paramedic

㉓ **l'insegnante di musica** *m / f*
music teacher

㉔ **l'assistente all'infanzia** *m / f*
childcare provider

㉕ **l'installatore di cucine** *m*
l'installatrice di cucine *f*
kitchen installer

㉖ **il tassista** *m*
la tassista *f*
taxi driver

㉗ **il custode dello zoo** *m*
la custode dello zoo *f*
zookeeper

㉙ **Devi fare molta esperienza in aula prima di diventare giudice.**
You should have a lot of courtroom experience before you become a judge.

㉘ **il giudice** *m* / **la giudice** *f*
judge

See also
81 Al lavoro • At work **82** In ufficio • In the office **91** I settori e i reparti • Industries and departments **92** Fare domanda per un lavoro • Applying for a job **93** Le competenze sul luogo di lavoro • Workplace skills **95** Riunirsi e presentare • Meeting and presenting

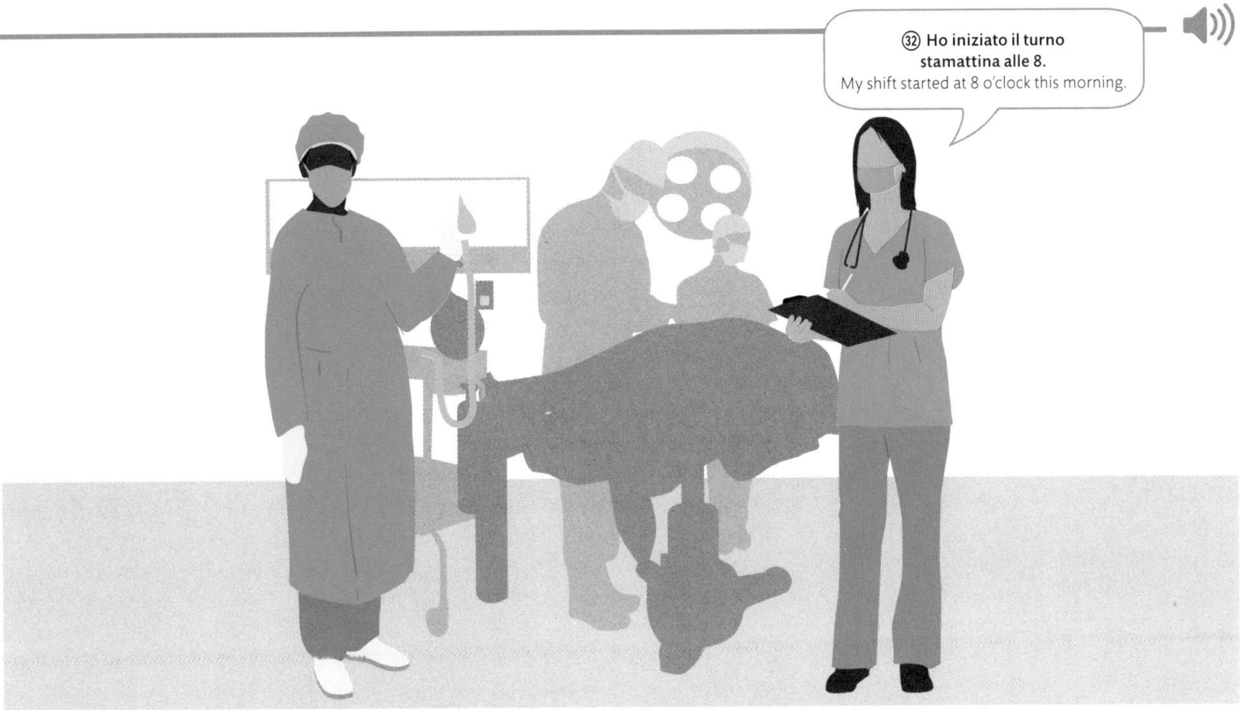

㉜ **Ho iniziato il turno stamattina alle 8.**
My shift started at 8 o'clock this morning.

㉚ **l'anestesista** *m / f*
anesthesiologist

㉛ **il chirurgo** *m* / **la chirurga** *f*
surgeon

㉝ **l'autista** *m / f*
driver

㉞ **il segretario** *m*
la segretaria *f*
secretary

㉟ **l'addetto alla reception** *m*
l'addetta alla reception *f*
receptionist

㊱ **lo steward** *m*
l'hostess *f*
flight attendant

㊲ **lo scienziato** *m*
la scienziata *f*
scientist

㊳ **l'autista di autobus** *m / f*
bus driver

㊴ **il musicista** *m*
la musicista *f*
musician

㊵ **il perito** *m / f*
surveyor

㊶ **l'avvocato** *m / f*
lawyer

㊷ **l'insegnante** *m / f*
teacher

㊸ **il giornalista** *m*
la giornalista *f*
journalist

㊹ **il macchinista ferroviario** *m*
la macchinista ferroviaria *f*
train driver

㊺ **l'agente di viaggio** *m / f*
travel agent

㊻ **il camionista** *m*
la camionista *f*
truck driver

㊼ **l'architetto** *m / f*
architect

㊽ **lo scrittore** *m*
la scrittrice *f*
writer

㊾ **l'insegnante di yoga** *m / f*
yoga teacher

㊿ **il pilota** *m*
la pilota *f*
pilot

91 I settori e i reparti
Industries and departments

91.1 I SETTORI · INDUSTRIES

(1) **la pubblicità**
advertising

(2) **i servizi alla persona**
personal services

(3) **l'agricoltura** *f*
agriculture / farming

(4) **l'esercito** *m*
military

(5) **il settore immobiliare**
real estate

(6) **il settore automobilistico**
automotive industry

(10) **il settore bancario**
banking

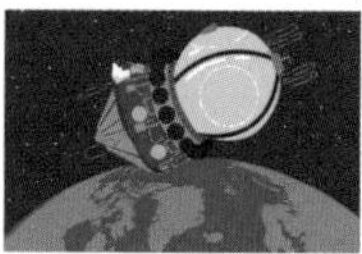
(11) **l'industria aerospaziale** *f*
aerospace

(12) **l'ingegneria del petrolio** *f*
petroleum engineering

(13) **l'industria chimica** *f*
chemical industry

(14) **le arti**
arts

(15) **l'istruzione** *f*
education

(19) **i videogiochi**
gaming

(20) **l'energia** *f*
energy

(21) **la ricerca**
research

(22) **la moda**
fashion

(23) **il riciclo**
recycling

(24) **l'intrattenimento** *m*
entertainment

(28) **le spedizioni**
shipping

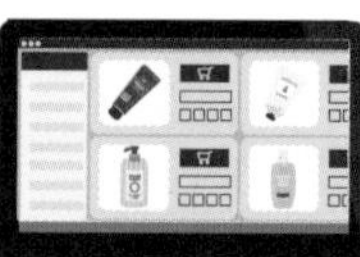
(29) **la vendita al dettaglio online**
online retail

(30) **il giornalismo**
journalism

(31) **il settore tessile**
textiles

(32) **i media**
media

(33) **il settore hospitality**
hospitality

(37) **la consegna online**
online delivery

(38) **l'acqua** *f*
water

(39) **le arti dello spettacolo**
performing arts

(40) **le biotecnologie**
biotechnology

(42) **Le nostre azioni sono precipitate.**
Our stocks have fallen dramatically.
(41) **la finanza**
finance

See also
81 Al lavoro • At work **82** In ufficio • In the office **89-90** I lavori • Jobs **92** Fare domanda per un lavoro • Applying for a job **93** Le competenze sul luogo di lavoro • Workplace skills

⑧ **Questo è uno dei nostri edifici più famosi.**
This is one of our most famous buildings.

⑦ **il turismo**
tourism

⑨ **i servizi per animali domestici**
pet services

⑯ **la ristorazione**
catering / food

⑰ **l'industria farmaceutica** *f*
pharmaceuticals

⑱ **il settore edile**
construction

㉕ **la pesca**
fishing

㉖ **l'elettronica** *f*
electronics

㉗ **la vendita al dettaglio**
retail

㉞ **la sanità**
healthcare

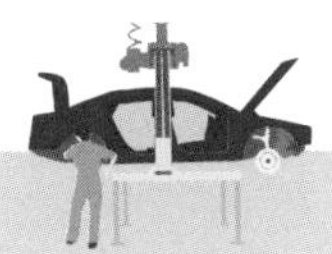

㉟ **l'industria manifatturiera** *f*
manufacturing

㊱ **l'attività mineraria** *f*
mining

㊸ **il trasporto**
transportation

91.2 I REPARTI • DEPARTMENTS

① **il reparto contabile**
accounts / finance

② **la produzione**
production

CONTRACT

③ **l'ufficio legale** *m*
legal

④ **il marketing**
marketing

⑤ **l'informatica** *f*
information technology (IT)

⑥ **i servizi per l'ufficio**
facilities / office services

⑦ **le vendite**
sales

⑧ **l'amministrazione** *f*
administration

⑨ **le relazioni pubbliche**
public relations (PR)

⑩ **gli acquisti**
purchasing

⑪ **le risorse umane**
human resources (HR)

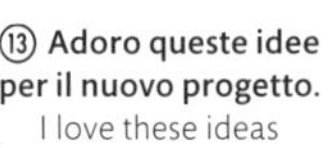

⑬ **Adoro queste idee per il nuovo progetto.**
I love these ideas for the new project.

⑫ **il reparto ricerca e sviluppo**
research and development (R&D)

92 Fare domanda per un lavoro
Applying for a job

92.1 LE CANDIDATURE · JOB APPLICATIONS

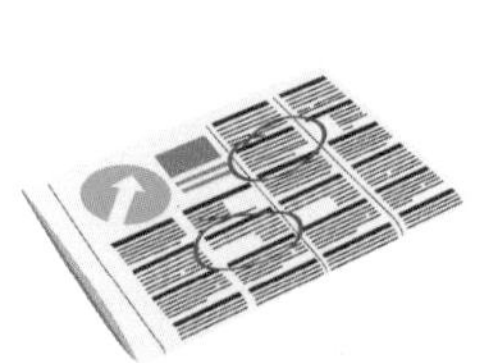

① **le offerte di lavoro**
job ads

② **il modulo di candidatura**
application form

③ **la lettera di accompagnamento**
cover letter

⑧ **Che tipo di lavoro sta cercando?**
What kind of work are you looking for?

⑦ **compilare un modulo**
to fill out a form

④ **il portfolio**
portfolio

⑤ **il curriculum**
résumé

⑥ **il centro per l'impiego**
recruiter

92.2 FARE DOMANDA PER UN LAVORO
APPLYING FOR A JOB

② **i posti vacanti**
vacancies
④ **Che cosa la rende la candidata perfetta per questo lavoro?**
What makes you the perfect candidate for this job?
⑤ **Sono una gran lavoratrice e ho un forte spirito di squadra.**
I'm hardworking and I'm a team player.

① **fare domanda per un lavoro**
to apply for a job

③ **sostenere un colloquio**
to have an interview

See also
81 Al lavoro • At work **89-90** I lavori • Jobs **91** I settori e i reparti • Industries and departments **93** Le competenze sul luogo di lavoro • Workplace skills **95** Riunirsi e presentare • Meeting and presenting

92.3 IL LAVORO DI SQUADRA
TEAMWORK

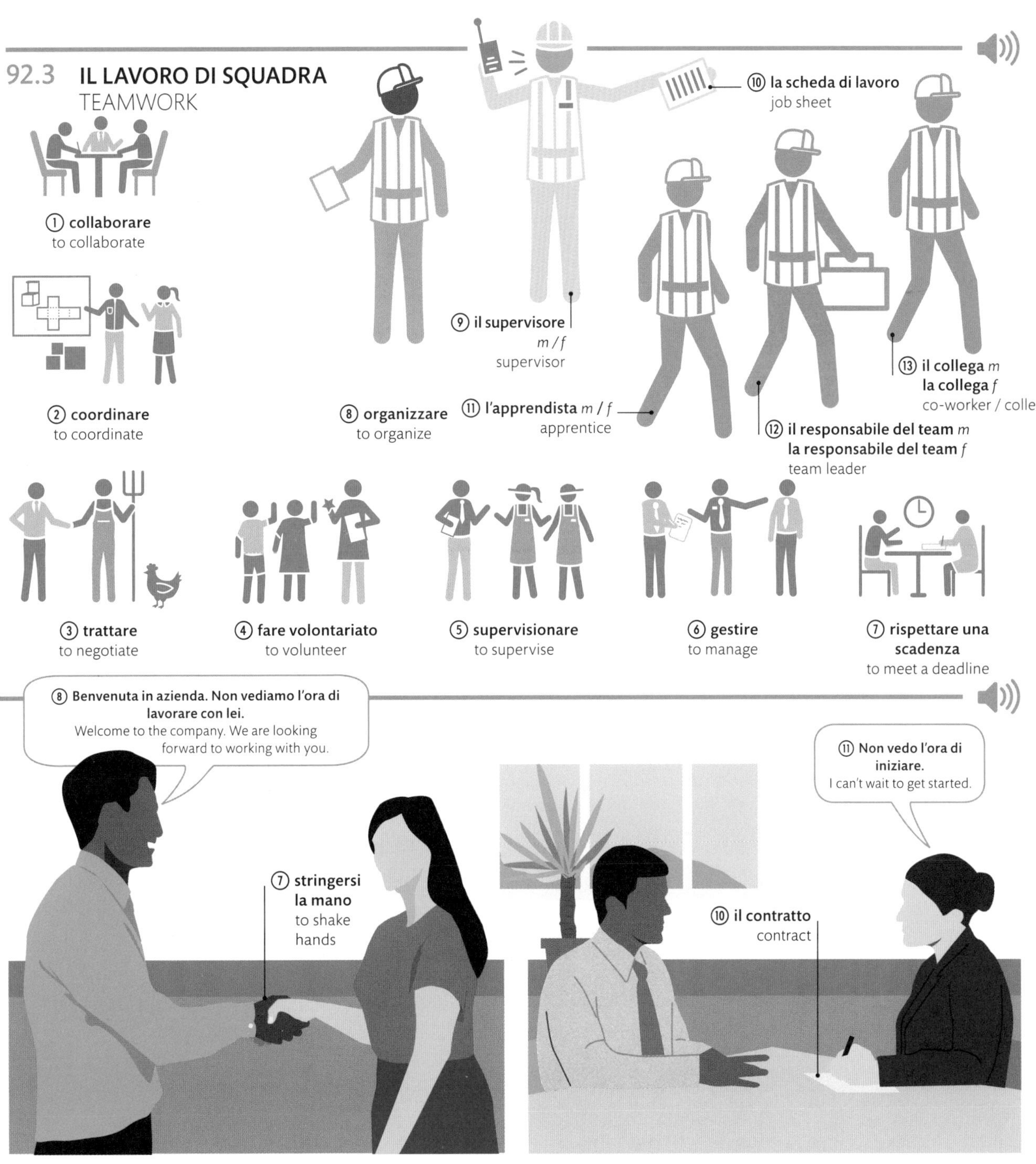
① **collaborare**
to collaborate
② **coordinare**
to coordinate
③ **trattare**
to negotiate
④ **fare volontariato**
to volunteer
⑤ **supervisionare**
to supervise
⑥ **gestire**
to manage
⑦ **rispettare una scadenza**
to meet a deadline
⑧ **organizzare**
to organize
⑨ **il supervisore** *m / f*
supervisor
⑩ **la scheda di lavoro**
job sheet
⑪ **l'apprendista** *m / f*
apprentice
⑫ **il responsabile del team** *m*
la responsabile del team *f*
team leader
⑬ **il collega** *m*
la collega *f*
co-worker / colleague
⑧ **Benvenuta in azienda. Non vediamo l'ora di lavorare con lei.**
Welcome to the company. We are looking forward to working with you.
⑦ **stringersi la mano**
to shake hands
⑪ **Non vedo l'ora di iniziare.**
I can't wait to get started.
⑩ **il contratto**
contract

⑥ **ottenere il lavoro**
to get the job

⑨ **firmare un contratto**
to sign a contract

93 Le competenze sul luogo di lavoro
Workplace skills

93.1 LE QUALITÀ PROFESSIONALI • PROFESSIONAL ATTRIBUTES

① **organizzato** *m* **organizzata** *f* organized

② **paziente** patient

③ **creativo** *m* **creativa** *f* creative

④ **onesto** *m* / **onesta** *f* honest

⑤ **pratico** *m* **pratica** *f* practical

⑥ **professionale** professional

⑦ **capace di adattarsi** adaptable

⑧ **ambizioso** *m* **ambiziosa** *f* ambitious

⑨ **calmo** *m* / **calma** *f* calm

⑩ **sicuro** *m* / **sicura** *f* confident

⑪ **puntuale** punctual

⑫ **affidabile** reliable

⑬ **orientato al cliente** *m* **orientata al cliente** *f* customer-focused

⑭ **indipendente** independent

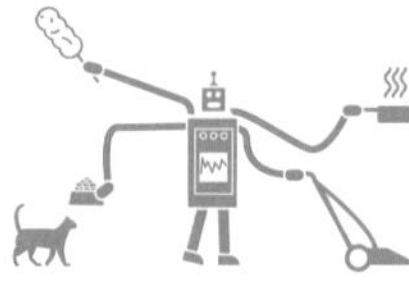
⑮ **efficiente** efficient

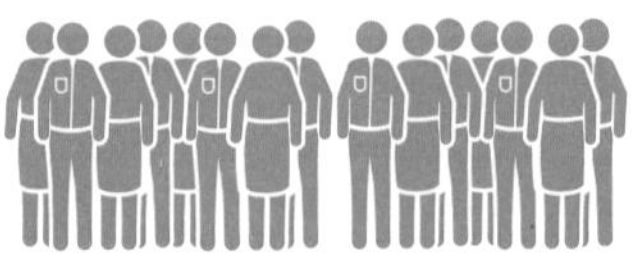
⑯ **capace di lavorare in gruppo** team player

⑰ **responsabile** responsible

⑱ **inventivo** *m* **inventiva** *f* innovative

⑲ **motivato** *m* **motivata** *f* motivated

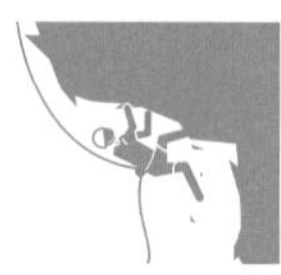

⑳ **determinato** *m* **determinata** *f* determined

㉑ **energico** *m* **energica** *f* energetic

㉓ **Tra tutti quelli che conosco, Carlo è lo chef che lavora più duramente.** Carlo is the hardest-working chef I've ever met.

㉒ **gran lavoratore** *m* **gran lavoratrice** *f* hard-working

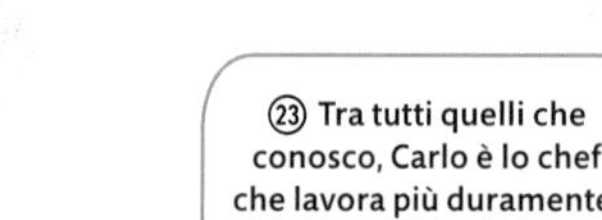
㉔ **competitivo** *m* **competitiva** *f* competitive

㉕ **assertivo** *m* **assertiva** *f* assertive

㉖ **ingegnoso** *m* **ingegnosa** *f* imaginative

㉗ **curioso** *m* / **curiosa** *f* curious

㉘ **originale** original

㉙ **preciso** *m* **precisa** *f* accurate

㉚ **buon ascoltatore** *m* **buona ascoltatrice** *f* good listener

㉛ **flessibile** flexible

See also
10 I tratti della personalità • Personality traits **11** Le abilità e le azioni Abilities and actions **81** Al lavoro • At work **82** In ufficio • In the office

93.2 LE COMPETENZE PROFESSIONALI • PROFESSIONAL EXPERTISE

① **l'organizzazione** *f*
organization

② **le competenze informatiche**
computer literacy

③ **l'utilizzo del computer** *m*
computing

④ **la risoluzione dei problemi**
problem-solving

⑤ **l'analisi** *f*
analytics

A
B

⑥ **la capacità decisionale**
decision-making

⑦ **il lavoro di squadra**
teamwork

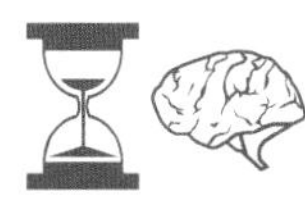

⑧ **imparare in fretta**
being a fast learner

⑨ **prestare attenzione ai dettagli**
paying attention to detail

⑩ **il servizio clienti**
customer service

⑪ **la leadership**
leadership

⑫ **la ricerca**
research

⑬ **fluente nelle lingue** *m / f*
fluent in languages

⑭ **le competenze tecnologiche**
technology literate

⑮ **le capacità oratorie**
public speaking

⑯ **la negoziazione**
negotiating

⑰ **la comunicazione scritta**
written communication

⑱ **l'iniziativa** *f*
initiative

⑲ **il galateo telefonico**
telephone manner

⑳ **lavorare bene sotto pressione**
working well under pressure

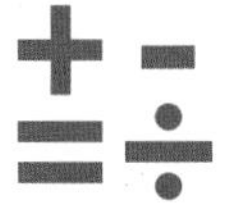

㉑ **le abilità di calcolo**
numeracy

㉒ **la capacità di guidare**
ability to drive

㉓ **ampiamente qualificato** *m* **ampiamente qualificata** *f*
well-qualified

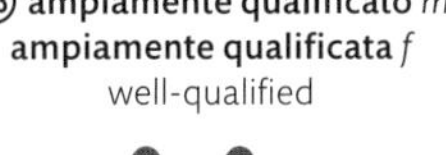

㉔ **l'autogestione** *f*
self management

㉕ **orientato al servizio** *m* **/ orientata al servizio** *f*
service focused

㉖ **capace di influenzare le persone**
influencer

㉗ **l'atteggiamento pragmatico** *m*
businesslike attitude

㉘ **le capacità relazionali**
interpersonal skills

㉙ **la gestione dei progetti**
project management

㉚ **l'amministrazione** *f*
administration

㉜ **Devi imparare a gestire meglio il tempo! Questa relazione è in ritardo.**
You must improve your time management! This report is late.

㉛ **la gestione del tempo**
time management

94 Il denaro e la finanza
Money and finance

94.1 IL DENARO · MONEY

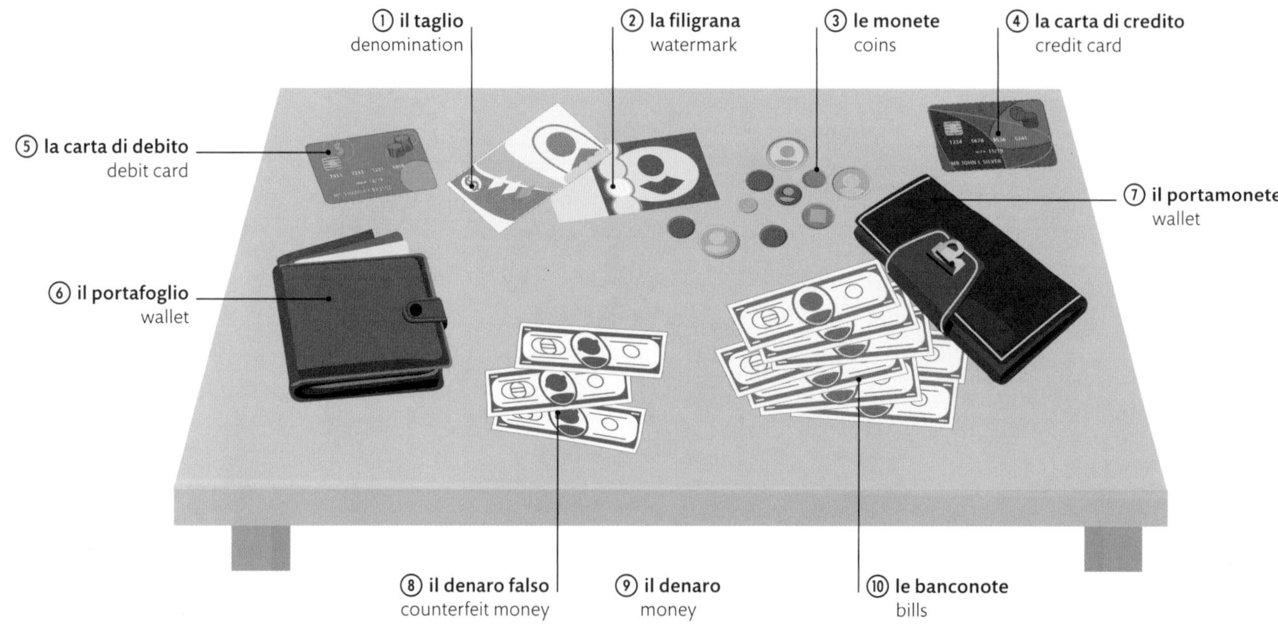

① il taglio
denomination
② la filigrana
watermark
③ le monete
coins
④ la carta di credito
credit card
⑤ la carta di debito
debit card
⑥ il portafoglio
wallet
⑦ il portamonete
wallet
⑧ il denaro falso
counterfeit money
⑨ il denaro
money
⑩ le banconote
bills

⑪ **il portafoglio digitale**
digital wallet

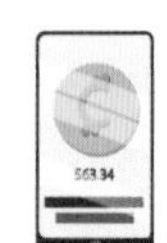

⑫ **la valuta digitale**
digital currency

⑬ **la banca**
bank

⑭ **i servizi bancari online**
online banking

⑮ **il mobile banking**
mobile banking

⑯ **i servizi bancari telefonici**
telephone banking

⑰ **la ricevuta**
receipt

⑱ **la valuta**
currency

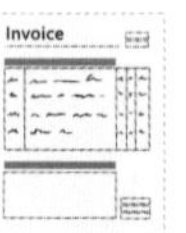

⑲ **la fattura**
invoice

㉔ Accettate i contanti qui?
Do you accept cash here?

⑳ **l'assegno** *m*
check

㉑ **la cassa**
cash register

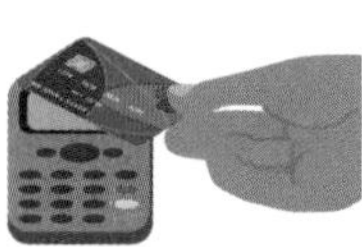

㉒ **pagare con carta**
to pay by card

㉓ **pagare in contanti**
to pay with cash

See also
45 La banca e l'ufficio postale • The bank and post office
91 I settori e i reparti • Industries and departments

94.2 **LA FINANZA** • FINANCE

① **l'agente di borsa** *m / f*
stockbroker

② **la Borsa**
stock exchange

③ **le azioni**
shares

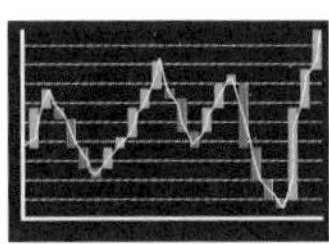

④ **il prezzo delle azioni**
share price

⑤ **i dividendi**
dividends

5%

⑥ **la commissione**
commission

VIDEO STORE

⑦ **il capitale netto**
equity

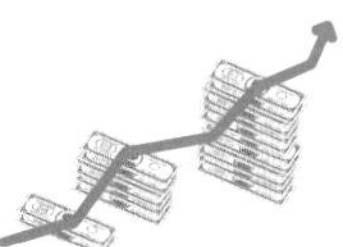

⑧ **l'investimento** *m*
investment

⑨ **il portfolio**
portfolio

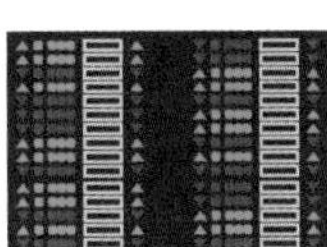

⑩ **le quote azionarie**
stocks

£ € $ ¥

⑪ **il tasso di cambio**
exchange rate

⑫ **il reddito**
income

$
Q1 Q2 Q3 Q4

⑬ **il budget**
budget

⑭ **indebitarsi**
to get into debt

⑮ **guadagnare**
to make a profit

⑯ **perdere**
to take a loss

⑰ **essere in pareggio**
to break even

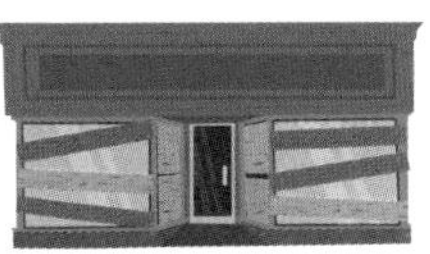

⑱ **fallire**
to go out of business

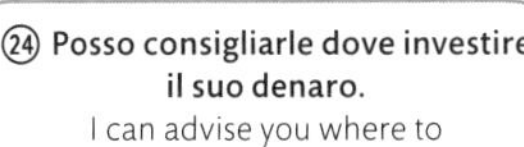

㉔ **Posso consigliarle dove investire il suo denaro.**
I can advise you where to invest your money.

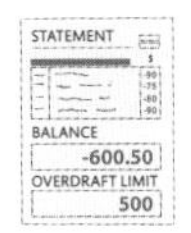
STATEMENT
BALANCE
-600.50
OVERDRAFT LIMIT
500

⑲ **lo scoperto**
overdraft

⑳ **le spese**
expenditure / outlay

㉑ **la recessione economica**
economic downturn

㉒ **il commercialista** *m*
la commercialista *f*
accountant

㉓ **il consulente finanziario** *m*
la consulente finanziaria *f*
financial advisor

95 Riunirsi e presentare
Meeting and presenting

95.1 RIUNIRSI · MEETING

② **Maria, qual è l'ordine del giorno di oggi?**
What's on the agenda today, Maria?

③ **Discuteremo le presentazioni per la prossima settimana.**
We're discussing the presentations for next week.

① **partecipare a una riunione**
to attend a meeting

④ **tenere una teleconferenza**
to have a conference call

⑤ **redigere il verbale**
to take minutes

⑥ **rispondere alle domande**
to take questions

⑦ **essere assente**
to be absent

⑧ **interrompere**
to interrupt

⑨ **raggiungere un consenso**
to reach a consensus

⑩ **il voto unanime**
unanimous vote

⑪ **i punti di azione**
action points

⑫ **l'alzata di mano** *f*
show of hands

⑬ **varie ed eventuali**
any other business

⑭ **la sala riunioni del consiglio di amministrazione**
boardroom

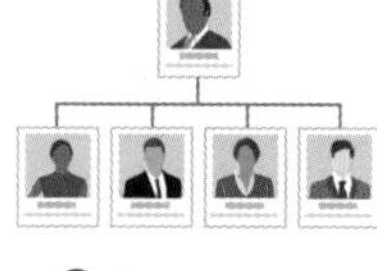

⑮ **il consiglio di amministrazione**
board of directors

⑯ **raggiungere un accordo**
to reach an agreement

⑰ **l'assemblea generale annuale** *f*
annual general meeting (AGM)

⑱ **concludere una riunione**
to wrap up the meeting

⑲ **la lavagna**
whiteboard

⑳ **il bloc-notes**
notebook

AGENDA

㉑ **l'ordine del giorno** *m*
agenda

See also
81 Al lavoro • At work **82** In ufficio • In the office **83** I computer e la tecnologia • Computers and technology **84** I media • Media

95.2 **PRESENTARE** • PRESENTING

① **avviare**
to commence

② **riassumere**
to sum up

③ **esaurire il tempo a disposizione**
to run out of time

④ **la diapositiva**
slide

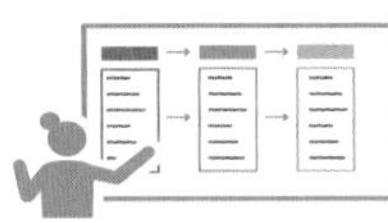

⑤ **il piano d'azione**
roadmap

⑥ **fare una presentazione**
to give a presentation

⑦ **il proiettore**
projector

⑧ **il timer**
timer

⑨ **il cavo HDMI**
HDMI cable

⑩ **le casse portatili**
portable speakers

⑪ **i documenti della presentazione**
handouts

⑫ **gli appunti**
notes

⑬ **la smartpen**
smartpen

⑭ **il microfono**
microphone

⑮ **le cuffie**
headphones

⑯ **la lavagna a fogli mobili**
flip chart

⑰ **condividere lo schermo**
to share your screen

⑱ **il telecomando per presentazioni**
presenter remote

⑲ **la conferenza**
conference

⑳ **il relatore ospite** *m* / **la relatrice ospite** *f*
guest speaker

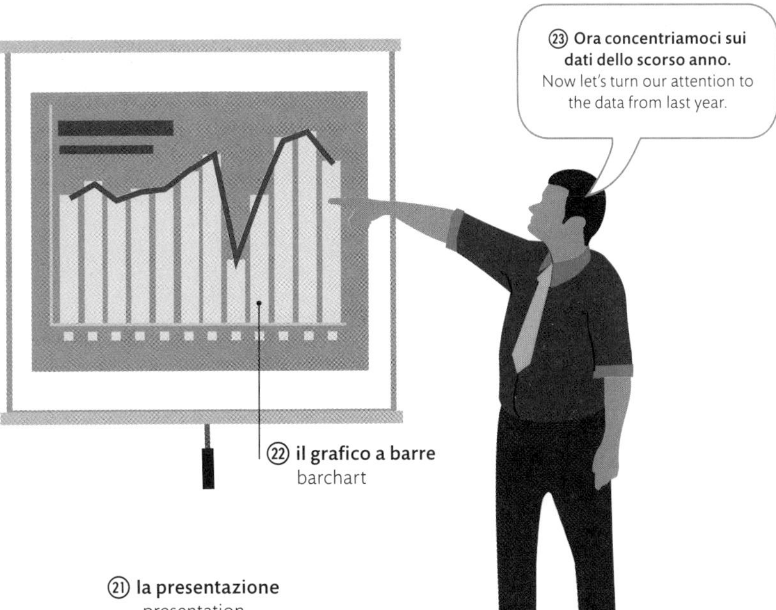
㉓ **Ora concentriamoci sui dati dello scorso anno.**
Now let's turn our attention to the data from last year.
㉒ **il grafico a barre**
barchart

㉑ **la presentazione**
presentation

96 Le strade
Roads

96.1 PER LA STRADA · ON THE ROAD

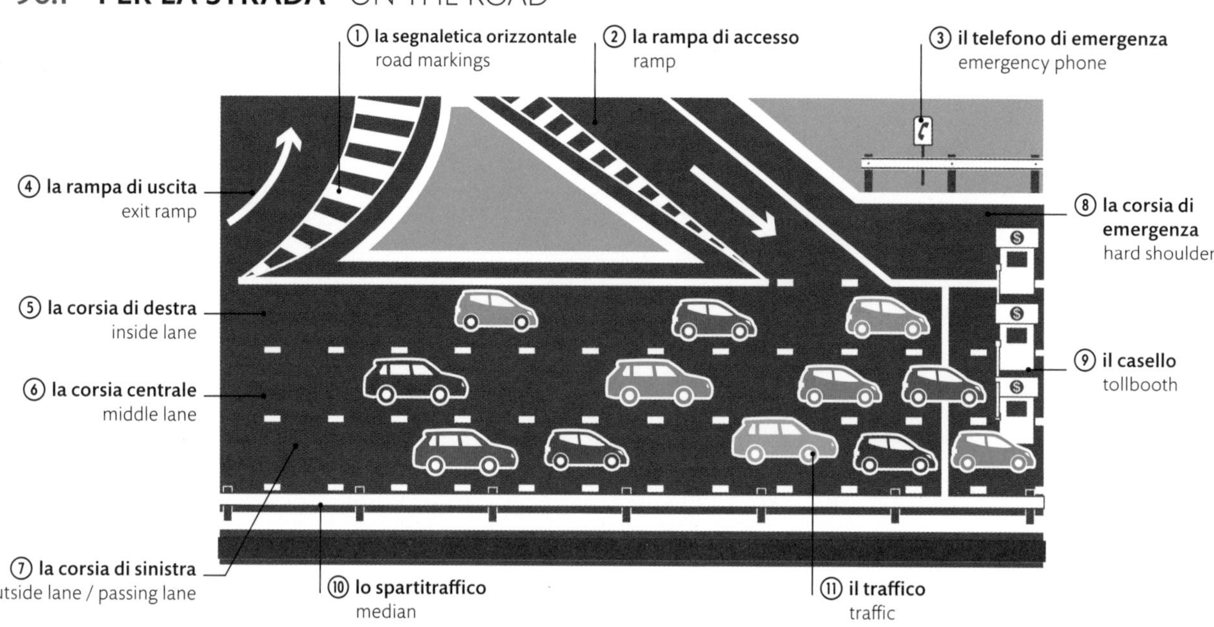

① **la segnaletica orizzontale**
road markings

② **la rampa di accesso**
ramp

③ **il telefono di emergenza**
emergency phone

④ **la rampa di uscita**
exit ramp

⑤ **la corsia di destra**
inside lane

⑥ **la corsia centrale**
middle lane

⑦ **la corsia di sinistra**
outside lane / passing lane

⑧ **la corsia di emergenza**
hard shoulder

⑨ **il casello**
tollbooth

⑩ **lo spartitraffico**
median

⑪ **il traffico**
traffic

⑫ **l'autostrada** *f*
highway

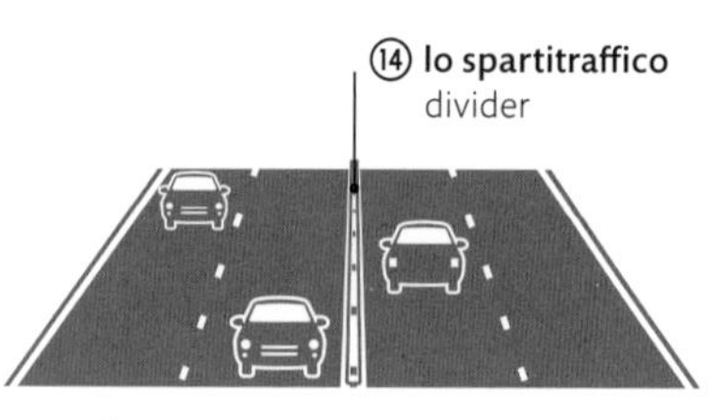

⑭ **lo spartitraffico**
divider

⑬ **la strada a doppia carreggiata**
divided highway

⑮ **lo svincolo**
junction

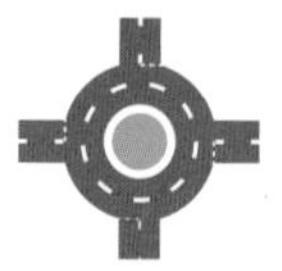

⑯ **la rotonda**
roundabout

⑰ **il cavalcavia**
flyover

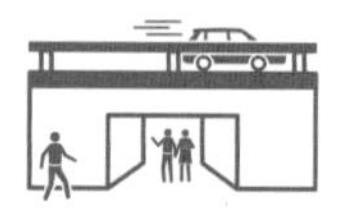

⑱ **il sottopassaggio**
underpass

⑲ **la barriera di sicurezza**
traffic barrier

⑳ **la deviazione**
detour

30

㉑ **l'autovelox** *m*
speed camera

㉒ **il semaforo**
stop light

㉓ **l'ingorgo** *m*
traffic jam

㉔ **la strada a senso unico**
one-way street

㉕ **le strisce pedonali**
pedestrian crossing

㉖ **i lavori stradali**
road construction

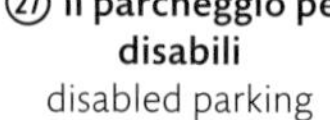

㉗ **il parcheggio per disabili**
disabled parking

P

㉘ **il posteggiatore** *m*
la posteggiatrice *f*
parking attendant

P

㉙ **il parchimetro**
parking meter

See also
42-43 In città • In town **97-98** Le auto • Cars **99** Le auto e gli autobus • Cars and buses **100** I motocicli • Motorcycles **101** Il ciclismo • Cycling **123** Gli sport motoristici • Motorsports **148** Le cartine e le direzioni • Maps and directions

96.2 I CARTELLI STRADALI • ROAD SIGNS

① **il divieto di accesso**
no entry

30
② **il limite di velocità**
speed limit

③ **il pericolo**
hazard

④ **il divieto di svolta a destra**
no right turn

⑤ **il divieto di inversione a U**
no U-turn

⑥ **la curva a destra**
right bend

⑦ **il dare la precedenza**
yield

⑧ **il senso unico alternato**
right of way

⑨ **il divieto di sorpasso**
no passing

⑩ **l'attraversamento di bambini** *m*
school zone

⑪ **la strada deformata**
bumps

⑫ **l'attraversamento di animali selvatici** *m*
deer crossing

⑬ **la direzione obbligatoria**
direction to follow

⑭ **i lavori in corso**
construction ahead

⑮ **il preavviso di semaforo**
stop light ahead

⑯ **il divieto di transito ai velocipedi**
closed to bicycles

⑰ **il divieto di transito ai pedoni**
closed to pedestrians

96.3 I VERBI DELLA GUIDA • VERBS FOR DRIVING

① **guidare**
to drive

② **fare retromarcia**
to reverse

③ **fermarsi**
to stop

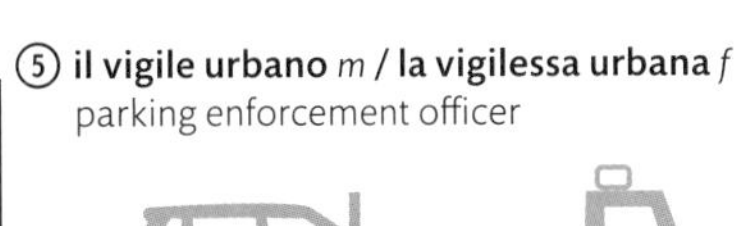
⑤ **il vigile urbano** *m* **/ la vigilessa urbana** *f*
parking enforcement officer

④ **rimuovere**
to tow away

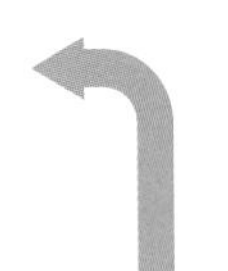
⑥ **girare a sinistra**
to turn left

⑦ **girare a destra**
to turn right

⑧ **andare dritto**
to go straight ahead

⑨ **prendere la prima a sinistra**
to take the first left

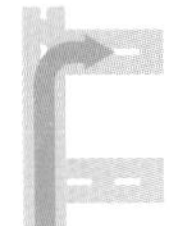
⑩ **prendere la seconda a destra**
to take the second right

97 Le auto
Cars

97.1 L'ESTERNO DELL'AUTO · CAR EXTERIOR

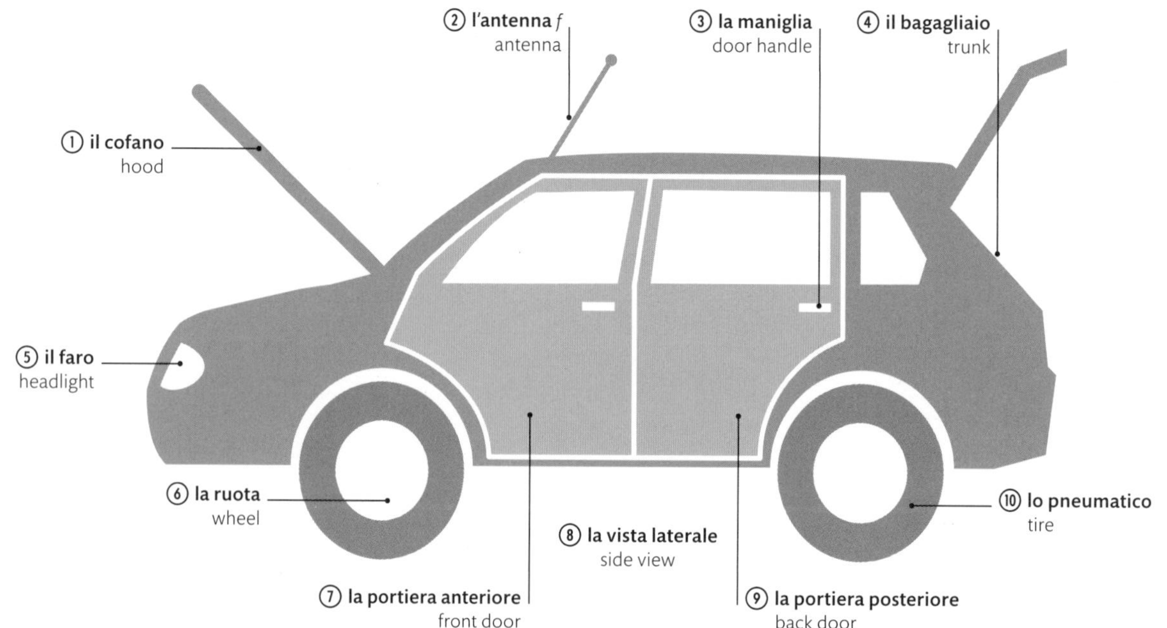

① il cofano
hood
② l'antenna *f*
antenna
③ la maniglia
door handle
④ il bagagliaio
trunk
⑤ il faro
headlight
⑥ la ruota
wheel
⑦ la portiera anteriore
front door
⑧ la vista laterale
side view
⑨ la portiera posteriore
back door
⑩ lo pneumatico
tire

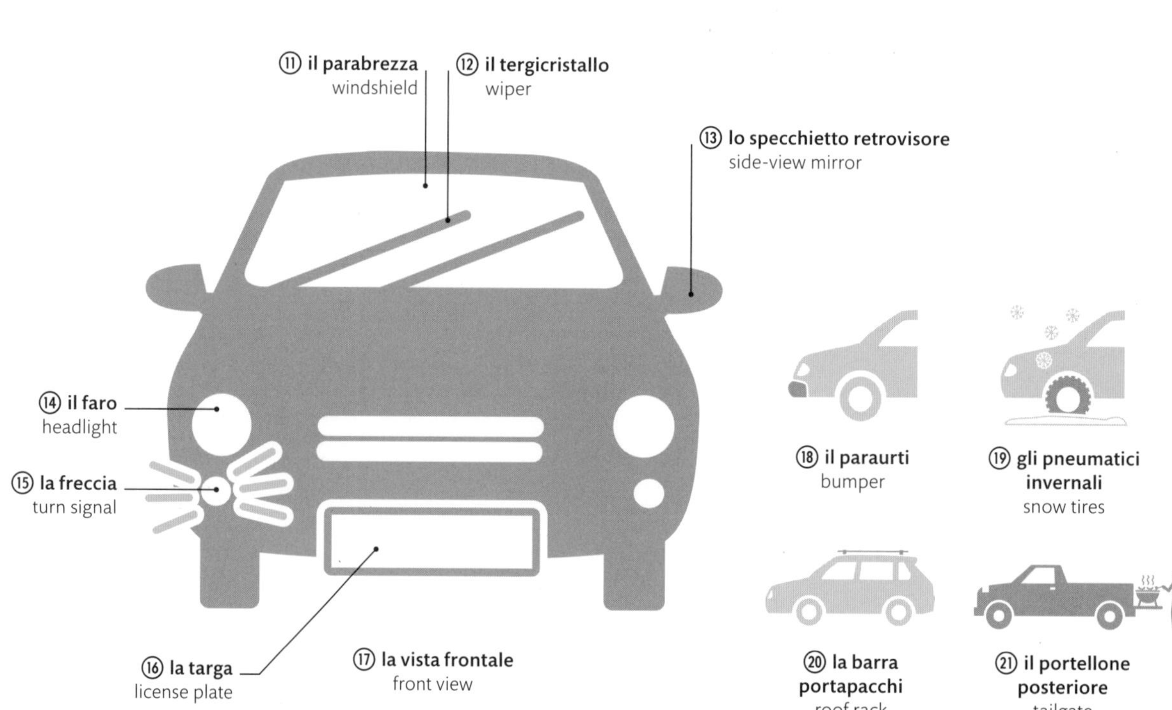

⑪ il parabrezza
windshield
⑫ il tergicristallo
wiper
⑬ lo specchietto retrovisore
side-view mirror
⑭ il faro
headlight
⑮ la freccia
turn signal
⑯ la targa
license plate
⑰ la vista frontale
front view
⑱ il paraurti
bumper
⑲ gli pneumatici invernali
snow tires
⑳ la barra portapacchi
roof rack
㉑ il portellone posteriore
tailgate

See also
42-43 In città • In town **96** Le strade • Roads **98** Le auto (continua) • Cars continued **99** Le auto e gli autobus • Cars and buses **100** I motocicli • Motorcycles **123** Gli sport motoristici • Motorsports

97.2 I TIPI DI AUTO • TYPES OF CARS

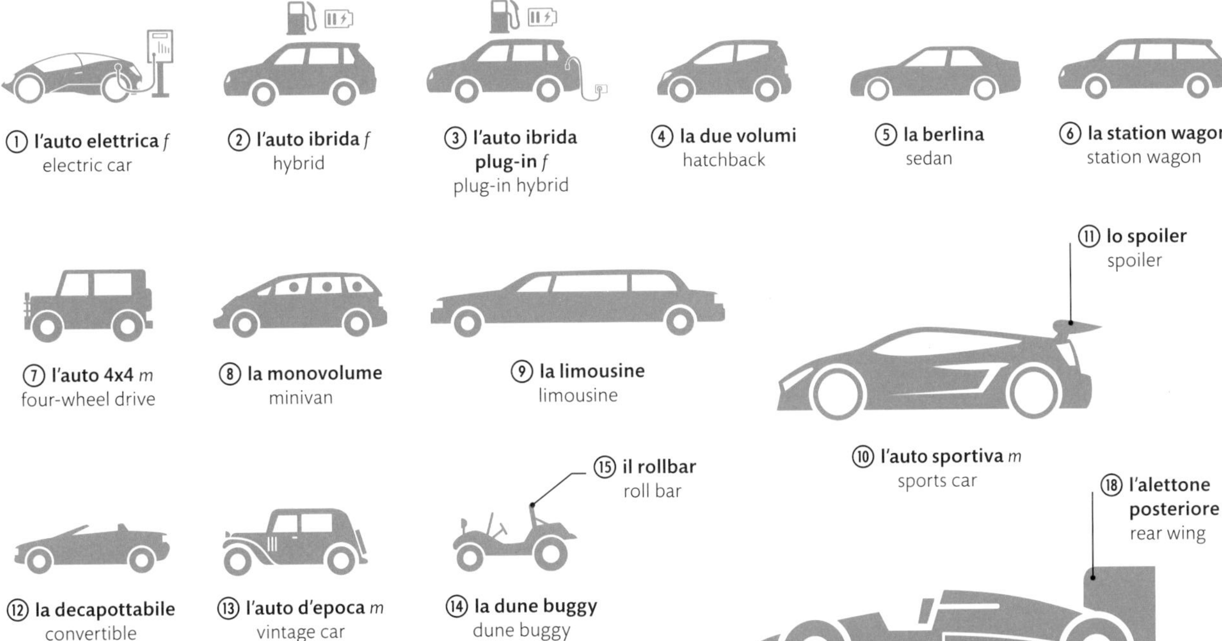
① **l'auto elettrica** *f*
electric car
② **l'auto ibrida** *f*
hybrid
③ **l'auto ibrida plug-in** *f*
plug-in hybrid
④ **la due volumi**
hatchback
⑤ **la berlina**
sedan
⑥ **la station wagon**
station wagon
⑦ **l'auto 4x4** *m*
four-wheel drive
⑧ **la monovolume**
minivan
⑨ **la limousine**
limousine
⑩ **l'auto sportiva** *m*
sports car
⑪ **lo spoiler**
spoiler
⑫ **la decapottabile**
convertible
⑬ **l'auto d'epoca** *m*
vintage car
⑭ **la dune buggy**
dune buggy
⑮ **il rollbar**
roll bar
⑯ **l'auto da corsa** *m*
race car
⑰ **l'alettone anteriore** *m*
front wing
⑱ **l'alettone posteriore** *m*
rear wing

97.3 IL DISTRIBUTORE DI BENZINA • GAS STATION

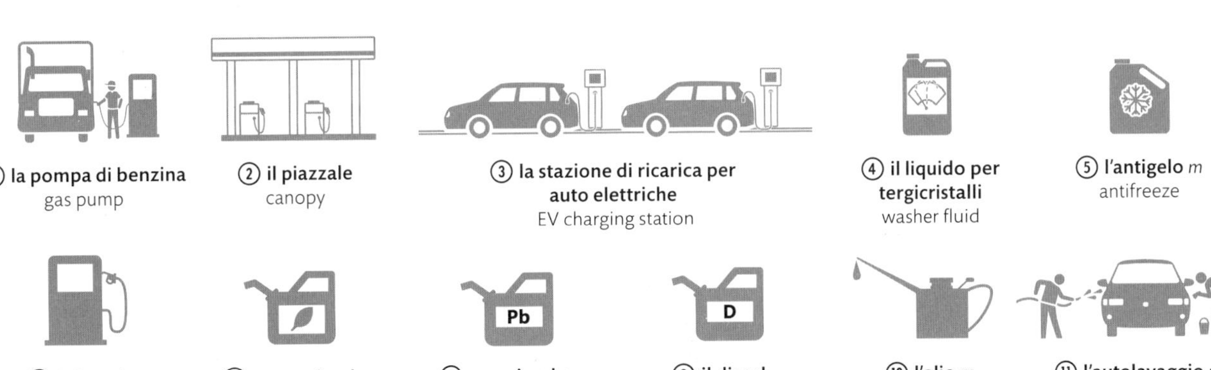
① **la pompa di benzina**
gas pump
② **il piazzale**
canopy
③ **la stazione di ricarica per auto elettriche**
EV charging station
④ **il liquido per tergicristalli**
washer fluid
⑤ **l'antigelo** *m*
antifreeze
⑥ **la benzina**
gasoline
⑦ **senza piombo**
unleaded
⑧ **con piombo**
leaded
Pb
⑨ **il diesel**
diesel
D
⑩ **l'olio** *m*
oil
⑪ **l'autolavaggio** *m*
car wash

98 Le auto (continua)
Cars continued

98.1 IL SOCCORSO STRADALE · BREAKDOWN ASSISTANCE

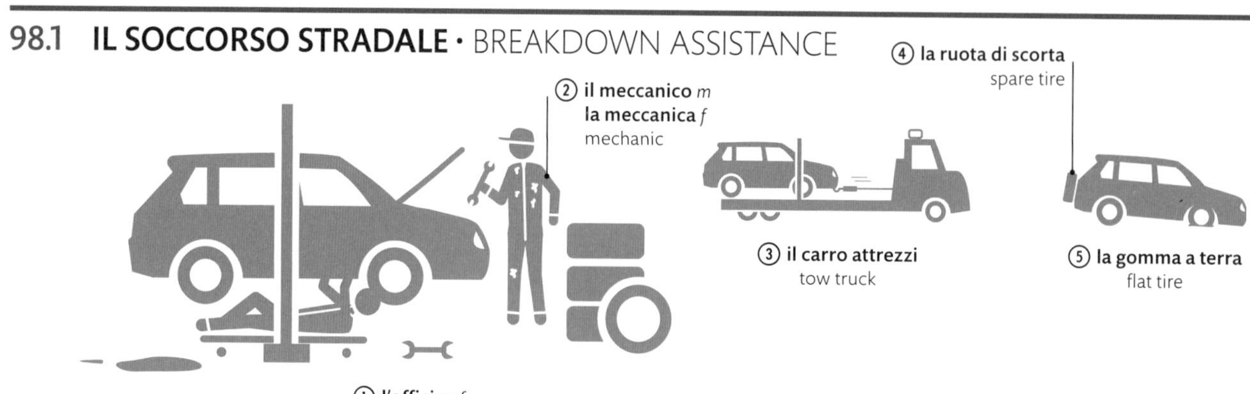

① l'officina *f*
auto repair shop
② il meccanico *m*
la meccanica *f*
mechanic
③ il carro attrezzi
tow truck
④ la ruota di scorta
spare tire
⑤ la gomma a terra
flat tire

98.2 LA MECCANICA · MECHANICS

① **la cinghia della ventola**
fan belt

② **il filtro dell'aria**
air filter

③ **il radiatore**
radiator

④ **la candela**
spark plug

⑤ **la scatola dei fusibili**
fuse box

⑥ **la distribuzione**
distributor

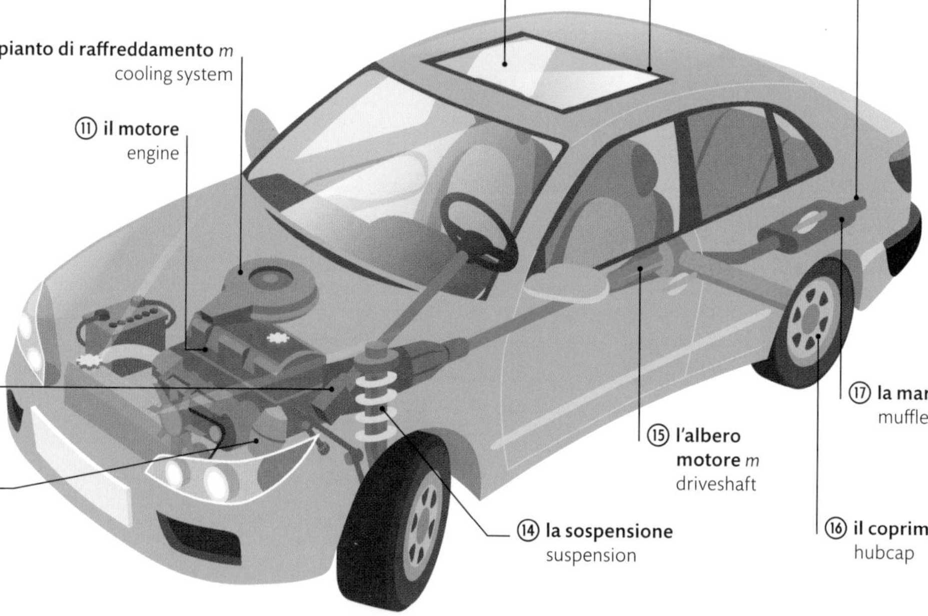

⑦ **il tettuccio apribile**
sunroof

⑧ **il tetto**
roof

⑨ **il tubo di scarico**
exhaust pipe

⑩ **l'impianto di raffreddamento** *m*
cooling system

⑪ **il motore**
engine

⑫ **la scatola del cambio**
gearbox

⑬ **la trasmissione**
transmission

⑭ **la sospensione**
suspension

⑮ **l'albero motore** *m*
driveshaft

⑯ **il coprimozzo**
hubcap

⑰ **la marmitta**
muffler

See also
42-43 In città • In town **96** Le strade • Roads **99** Le auto e gli autobus • Cars and buses **100** I motocicli • Motorcycles **123** Gli sport motoristici • Motorsports

⑥ **la chiave inglese**
wrench

⑦ **i bulloni delle ruote**
lug nuts

⑧ **il cric**
jack

⑱ **il serbatoio del liquido per tergicristalli**
washer fluid reservoir

⑲ **il cofano**
hood

⑳ **il serbatoio del liquido freni**
brake fluid reservoir

㉑ **l'astina di livello** *f*
dipstick

㉒ **il tubo di scarico**
pipe

㉓ **il serbatoio del liquido di raffreddamento**
coolant reservoir

㉔ **la batteria**
battery

㉕ **la carrozzeria**
bodywork

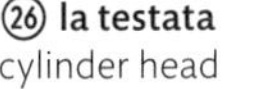

㉖ **la testata**
cylinder head

98.3 I VERBI DELLA GUIDA
VERBS FOR DRIVING

① **rifornire**
to fill up

② **controllare l'olio**
to check the oil

③ **controllare gli pneumatici**
to check the tires

④ **revisionare l'auto**
to service the car

⑤ **parcheggiare**
to park

⑥ **partire**
to take off

⑦ **mettere la freccia**
to signal

⑧ **frenare**
to brake

40
30

⑨ **rallentare**
to slow down

⑩ **accelerare**
to speed up

⑪ **andare a prendere qualcuno**
to pick someone up

⑫ **accompagnare qualcuno**
to drop someone off

⑬ **avere un incidente**
to have a car accident

⑭ **rompersi**
to break down

⑮ **sorpassare**
to pass

99 Le auto e gli autobus

Cars and buses

99.1 L'INTERNO DELL'AUTO · CAR INTERIOR

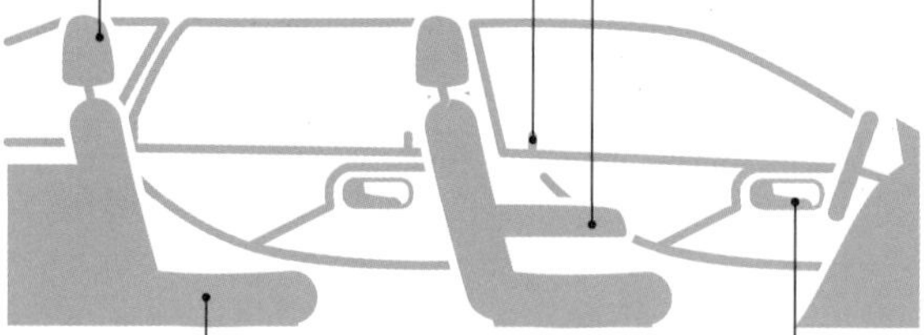

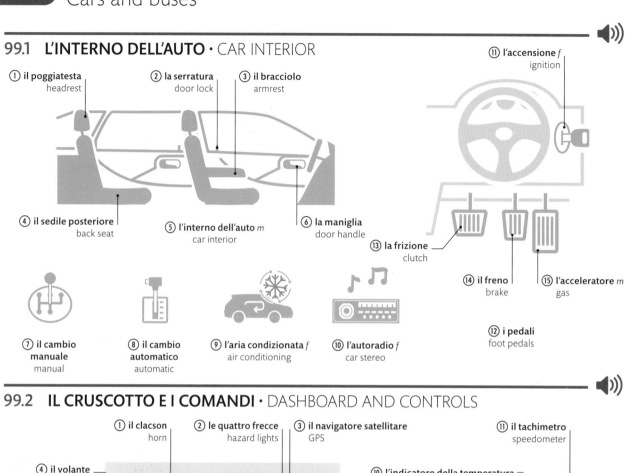

① **il poggiatesta** headrest

② **la serratura** door lock

③ **il bracciolo** armrest

④ **il sedile posteriore** back seat

⑤ **l'interno dell'auto** *m* car interior

⑥ **la maniglia** door handle

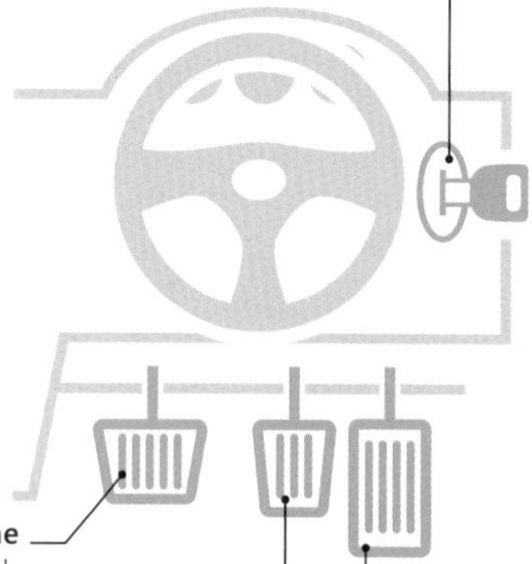

⑦ **il cambio manuale** manual

⑧ **il cambio automatico** automatic

⑨ **l'aria condizionata** *f* air conditioning

⑩ **l'autoradio** *f* car stereo

⑪ **l'accensione** *f* ignition

⑫ **i pedali** foot pedals

⑬ **la frizione** clutch

⑭ **il freno** brake

⑮ **l'acceleratore** *m* gas

99.2 IL CRUSCOTTO E I COMANDI · DASHBOARD AND CONTROLS

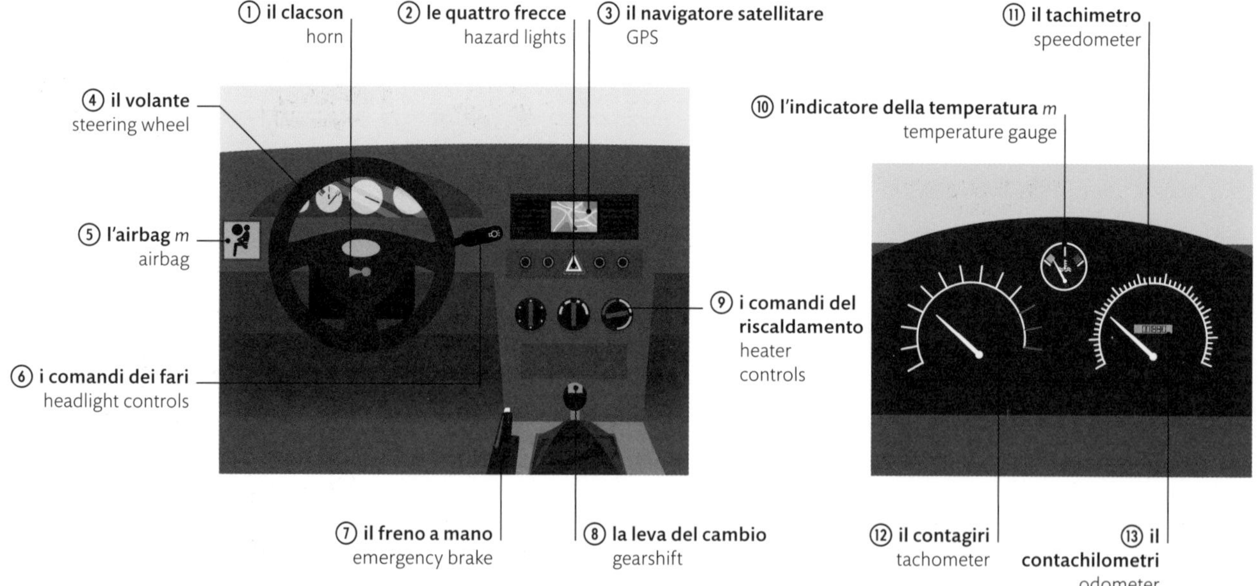
① il clacson
horn
② le quattro frecce
hazard lights
③ il navigatore satellitare
GPS
④ il volante
steering wheel
⑤ l'airbag m
airbag
⑥ i comandi dei fari
headlight controls
⑦ il freno a mano
emergency brake
⑧ la leva del cambio
gearshift
⑨ i comandi del riscaldamento
heater controls
⑩ l'indicatore della temperatura m
temperature gauge
⑪ il tachimetro
speedometer
⑫ il contagiri
tachometer
⑬ il contachilometri
odometer

See also
42-43 In città • In town **96** Le strade • Roads **97-98** Le auto • Cars
100 I motocicli • Motorcycles **123** Gli sport motoristici • Motorsports

99.3 L'AUTOBUS • BUS

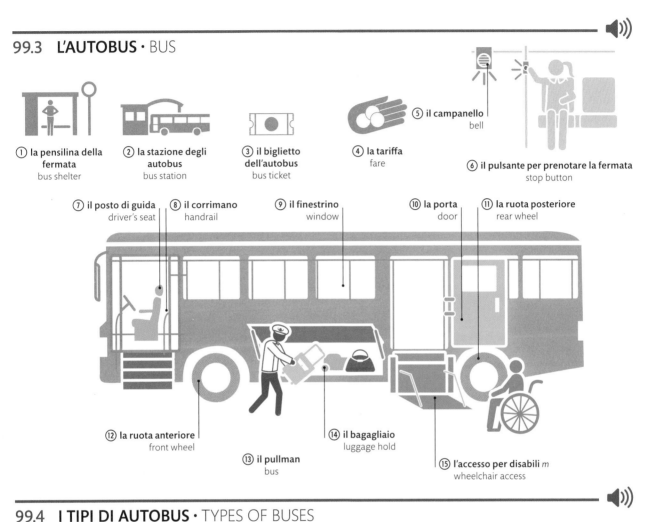

① **la pensilina della fermata**
bus shelter

② **la stazione degli autobus**
bus station

③ **il biglietto dell'autobus**
bus ticket

④ **la tariffa**
fare

⑤ **il campanello**
bell

⑥ **il pulsante per prenotare la fermata**
stop button

⑦ **il posto di guida**
driver's seat

⑧ **il corrimano**
handrail

⑨ **il finestrino**
window

⑩ **la porta**
door

⑪ **la ruota posteriore**
rear wheel

⑫ **la ruota anteriore**
front wheel

⑬ **il pullman**
bus

⑭ **il bagagliaio**
luggage hold

⑮ **l'accesso per disabili** *m*
wheelchair access

99.4 I TIPI DI AUTOBUS • TYPES OF BUSES

24

① **l'autobus a due piani** *m*
double-decker bus

② **il piano superiore**
upper deck

③ **il piano inferiore**
lower deck

④ **l'autista** *m / f*
driver

⑤ **l'autobus turistico** *m*
tourist bus

⑥ **fare un giro turistico** *m*
sightseeing

⑦ **il numero della linea**
route number

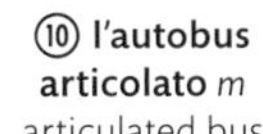

⑧ **lo scuolabus**
school bus

⑨ **il pulmino**
minibus

⑩ **l'autobus articolato** *m*
articulated bus

⑪ **la navetta**
shuttle bus

⑫ **il filobus**
trolley bus

⑬ **il tram**
tram

I motocicli
Motorcycles

100.1 LA MOTO · MOTORCYCLE

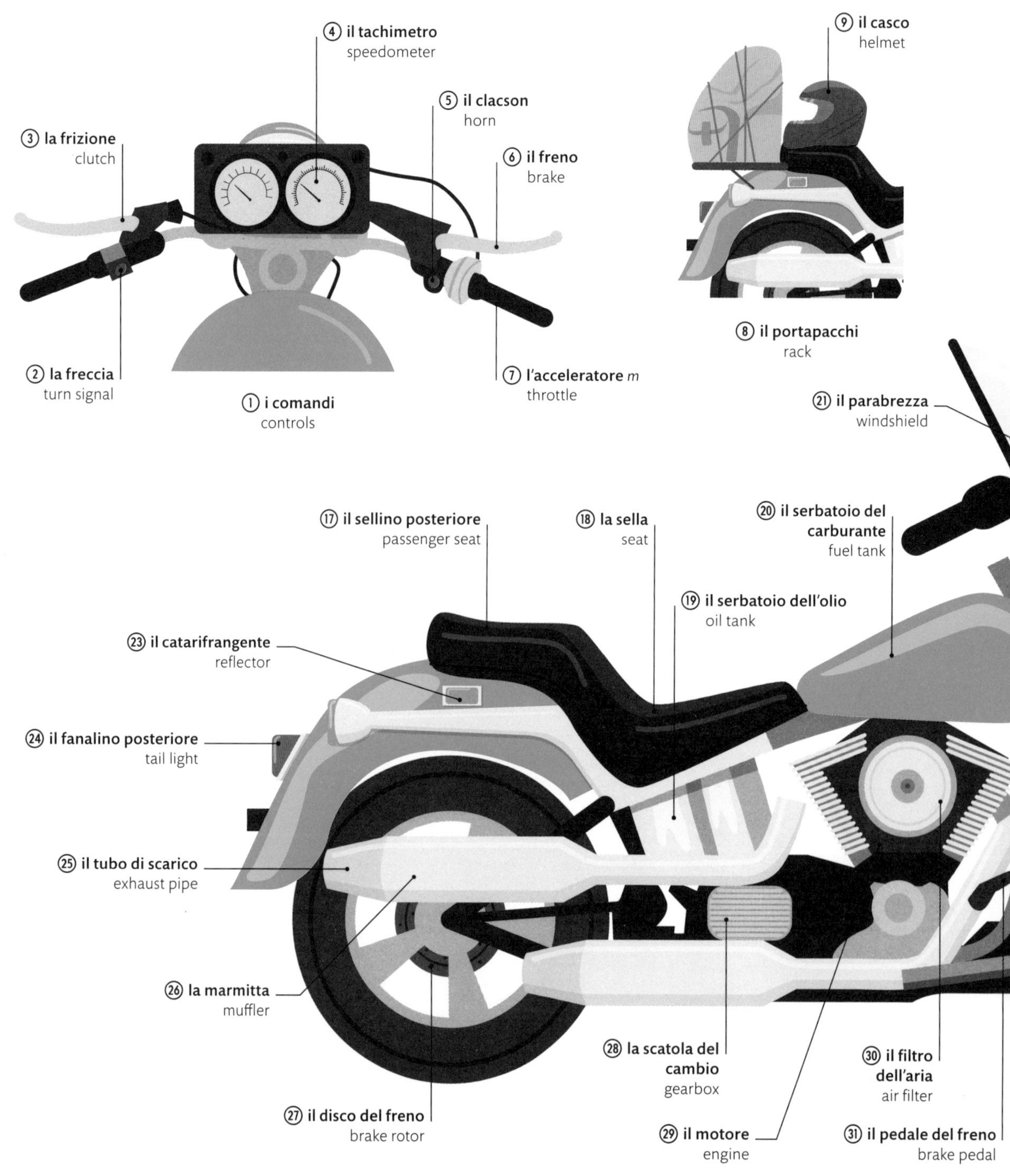

④ il tachimetro
speedometer
⑨ il casco
helmet
⑤ il clacson
horn
③ la frizione
clutch
⑥ il freno
brake
⑧ il portapacchi
rack
② la freccia
turn signal
⑦ l'acceleratore m
throttle
① i comandi
controls
㉑ il parabrezza
windshield
⑰ il sellino posteriore
passenger seat
⑱ la sella
seat
⑳ il serbatoio del carburante
fuel tank
⑲ il serbatoio dell'olio
oil tank
㉓ il catarifrangente
reflector
㉔ il fanalino posteriore
tail light
㉕ il tubo di scarico
exhaust pipe
㉖ la marmitta
muffler
㉘ la scatola del cambio
gearbox
㉚ il filtro dell'aria
air filter
㉗ il disco del freno
brake rotor
㉙ il motore
engine
㉛ il pedale del freno
brake pedal

See also
42-43 In città • In town **96** Le strade • Roads **97-98** Le auto
Cars **123** Gli sport motoristici • Motorsports

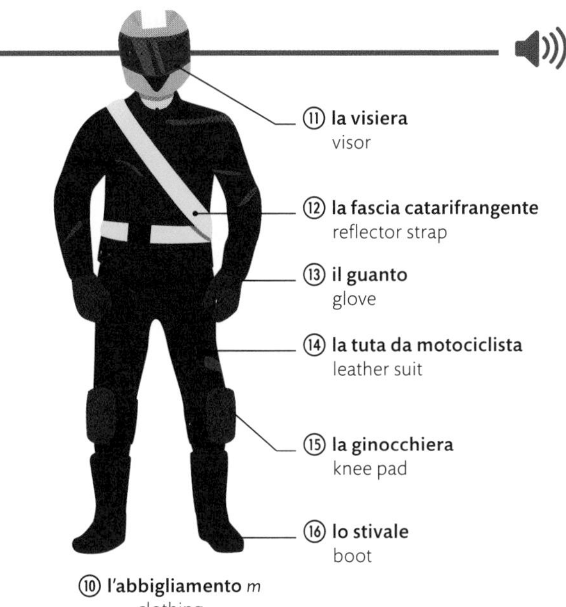
⑪ **la visiera**
visor
⑫ **la fascia catarifrangente**
reflector strap
⑬ **il guanto**
glove
⑭ **la tuta da motociclista**
leather suit
⑮ **la ginocchiera**
knee pad
⑯ **lo stivale**
boot

⑩ **l'abbigliamento** *m*
clothing

㉒ **il faro**
headlight

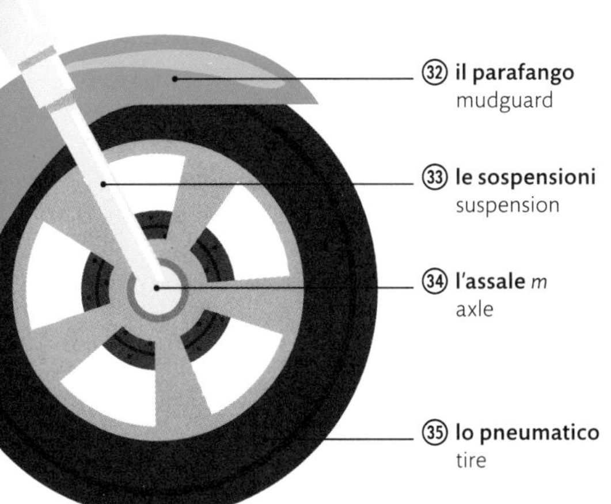
㉜ **il parafango**
mudguard
㉝ **le sospensioni**
suspension
㉞ **l'assale** *m*
axle
㉟ **lo pneumatico**
tire

100.2 I TIPI DI MOTOCICLI
TYPES OF MOTORCYCLES

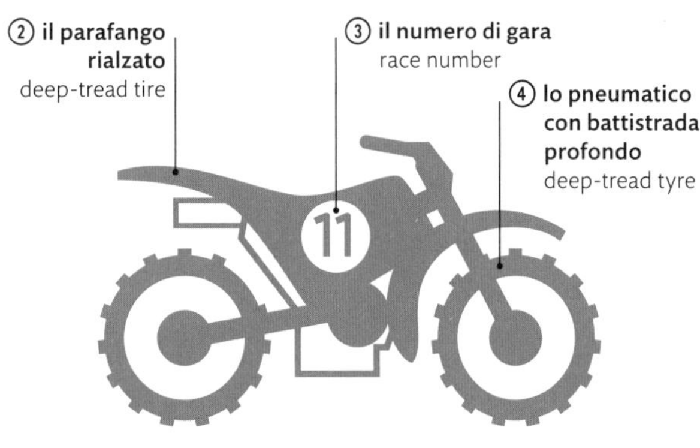
② **il parafango rialzato**
deep-tread tire
③ **il numero di gara**
race number
④ **lo pneumatico con battistrada profondo**
deep-tread tyre
11

① **la moto fuoristrada**
off-road motorcycle

⑤ **la moto da corsa**
racing bike

⑥ **la moto da turismo**
tourer

⑦ **il quad**
all-terrain vehicle / quad bike

⑧ **il sidecar**
side car

⑨ **la moto elettrica**
electric motorcycle

⑩ **il monopattino elettrico**
electric scooter

⑪ **la moto a tre ruote**
three-wheeler

⑫ **lo scooter**
motor scooter

⑬ **il motociclista** *m*
la motociclista *f*
rider

⑭ **viaggiare dietro**
to ride passenger

⑮ **salire**
to get on / mount

⑯ **scendere**
to get off / dismount

101 Il ciclismo
Cycling

101.1 LA BICICLETTA · BICYCLE

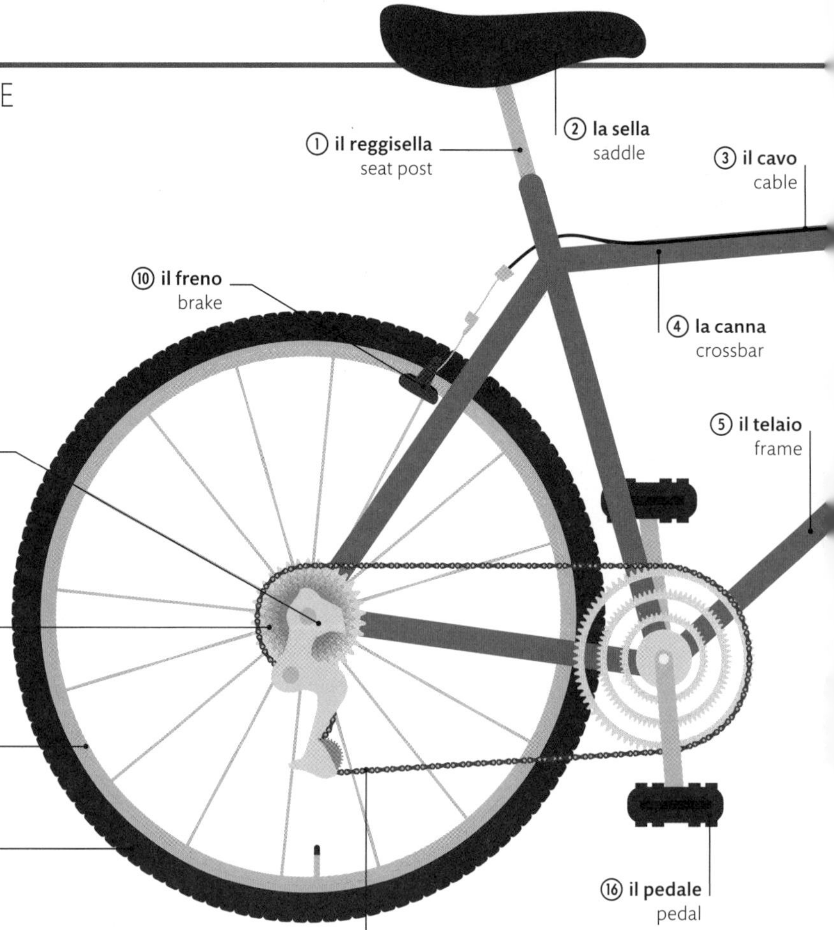

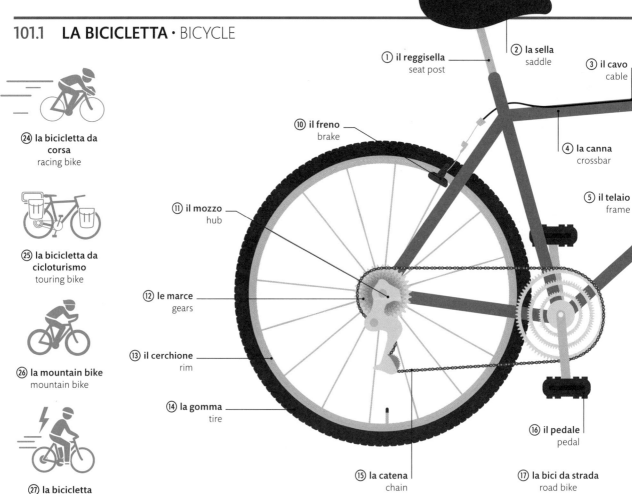

① **il reggisella**
seat post

② **la sella**
saddle

③ **il cavo**
cable

④ **la canna**
crossbar

⑤ **il telaio**
frame

⑩ **il freno**
brake

⑪ **il mozzo**
hub

⑫ **le marce**
gears

⑬ **il cerchione**
rim

⑭ **la gomma**
tire

⑮ **la catena**
chain

⑯ **il pedale**
pedal

⑰ **la bici da strada**
road bike

㉔ **la bicicletta da corsa**
racing bike

㉕ **la bicicletta da cicloturismo**
touring bike

㉖ **la mountain bike**
mountain bike

㉗ **la bicicletta elettrica**
electric bike

㉘ **il tandem**
tandem

㉙ **il cestino**
basket

㉚ **il seggiolino per bambini**
child seat

㉛ **il cavalletto**
kickstand

㉜ **la pastiglia dei freni**
brake pad

㉝ **le rotelle**
training wheels

㉞ **il monociclo**
unicycle

㉟ **il fermapiede**
toe clip

㊱ **il cinturino per pedali**
toe strap

㊲ **la lampadina**
lamp

㊳ **la luce posteriore**
rear light

㊴ **la camera d'aria**
inner tube

See also
42-43 In città • In town **96** Le strade • Roads **100** I motocicli Motorcycles **133** Le attività all'aperto • Outdoor activities

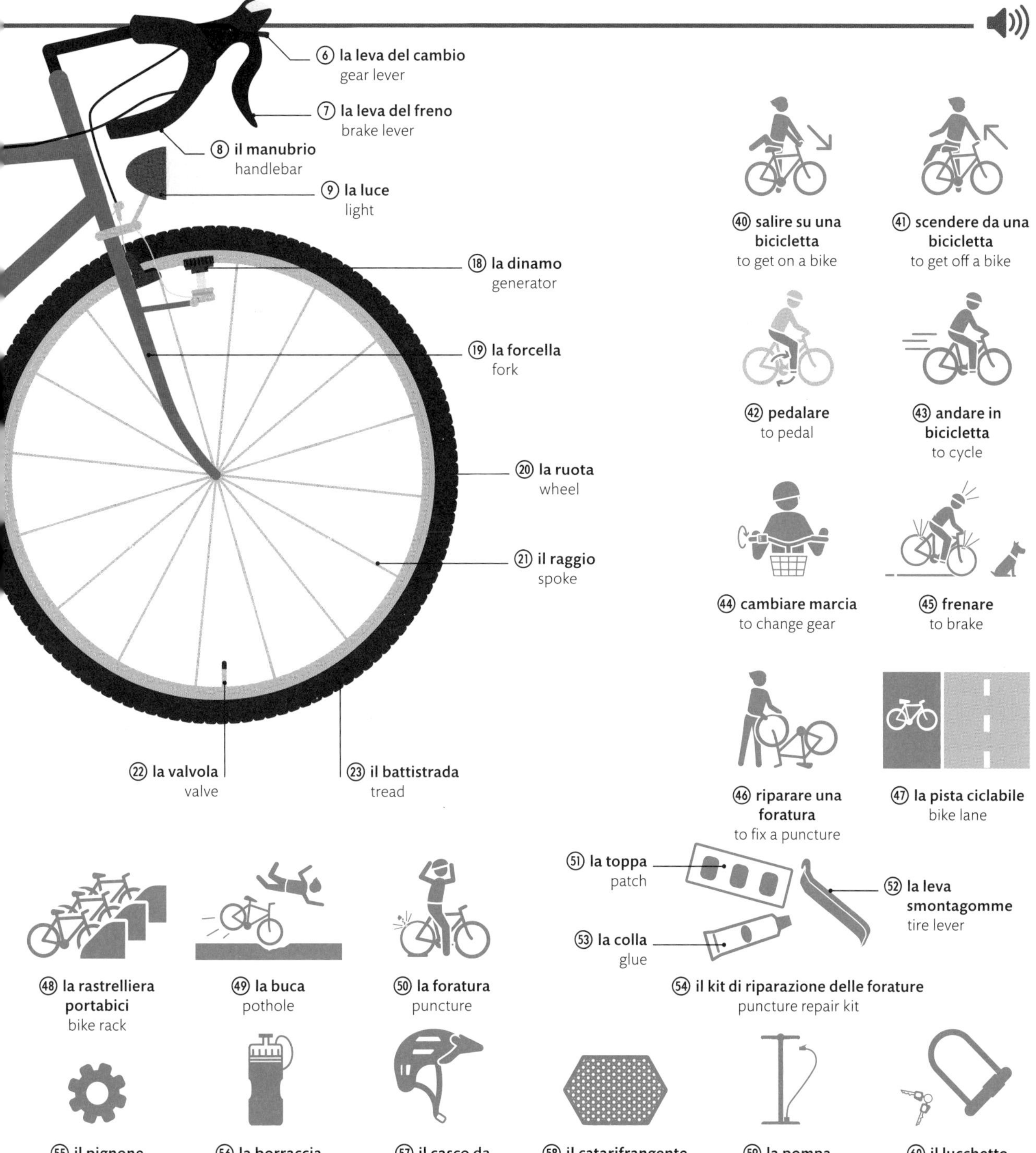
⑥ la leva del cambio
gear lever
⑦ la leva del freno
brake lever
⑧ il manubrio
handlebar
⑨ la luce
light
⑱ la dinamo
generator
⑲ la forcella
fork
⑳ la ruota
wheel
㉑ il raggio
spoke
㉒ la valvola
valve
㉓ il battistrada
tread
㊵ salire su una bicicletta
to get on a bike
㊶ scendere da una bicicletta
to get off a bike
㊷ pedalare
to pedal
㊸ andare in bicicletta
to cycle
㊹ cambiare marcia
to change gear
㊺ frenare
to brake
㊻ riparare una foratura
to fix a puncture
㊼ la pista ciclabile
bike lane
㊽ la rastrelliera portabici
bike rack
㊾ la buca
pothole
㊿ la foratura
puncture
51 la toppa
patch
52 la leva smontagomme
tire lever
53 la colla
glue
54 il kit di riparazione delle forature
puncture repair kit
55 il pignone
sprocket
56 la borraccia
water bottle
57 il casco da bicicletta
bike helmet
58 il catarifrangente
reflector
59 la pompa
pump
60 il lucchetto
lock

102 I treni

Trains

102.1 LA STAZIONE FERROVIARIA · TRAIN STATION

① **il treno**
train

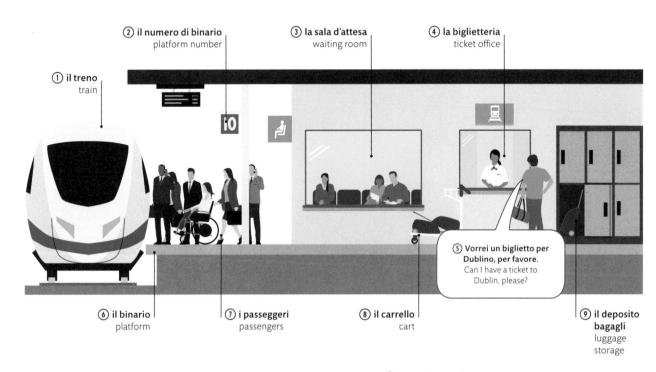

② **il numero di binario**
platform number

③ **la sala d'attesa**
waiting room

④ **la biglietteria**
ticket office

⑤ **Vorrei un biglietto per Dublino, per favore.**
Can I have a ticket to Dublin, please?

⑥ **il binario**
platform

⑦ **i passeggeri**
passengers

⑧ **il carrello**
cart

⑨ **il deposito bagagli**
luggage storage

⑩ **l'ufficio oggetti smarriti** *m*
lost property office

⑪ **il biglietto**
ticket

⑫ **la tariffa**
fare

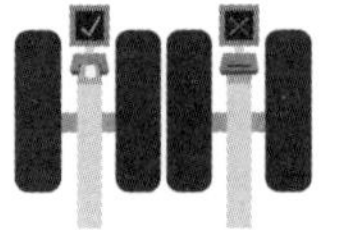

⑬ **il tornello**
ticket barrier

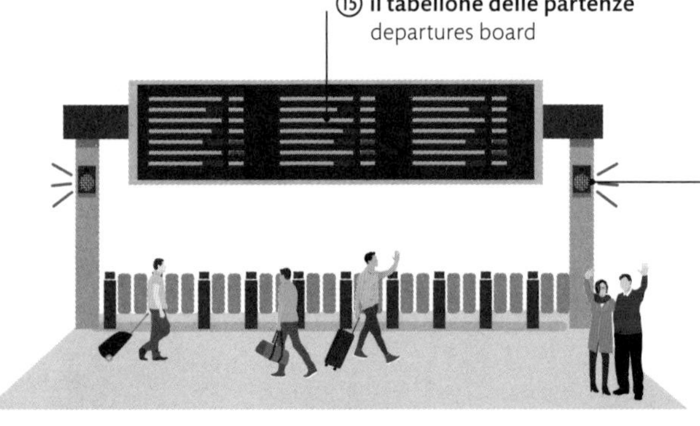

⑮ **il tabellone delle partenze**
departures board

⑯ **l'altoparlante** *m*
public address system

⑭ **l'atrio** *m*
concourse

⑰ **la rete ferroviaria**
rail network

⑱ **la cartina della metropolitana**
subway map

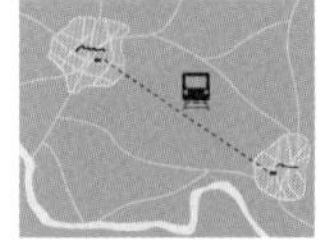

⑲ **l'intercity** *m*
intercity train

⑳ **il ritardo**
delay

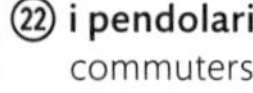

㉒ **i pendolari**
commuters

㉑ **l'orario di punta** *m*
rush hour

㉓ **prendere un treno**
to catch a train

See also
42-43 In città • In town **131** Il viaggio e l'alloggio • Travel and accommodation

(27) la rotaia sotto tensione
live rail

(24) perdere un treno
to miss a train

(25) cambiare
to change trains

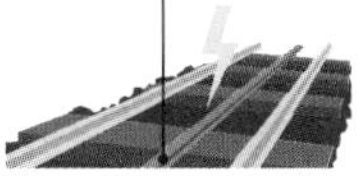

(26) la rotaia
track

(28) le linee elettriche
electric lines

(29) il sottopassaggio
underpass

(30) il passaggio sopraelevato
overpass

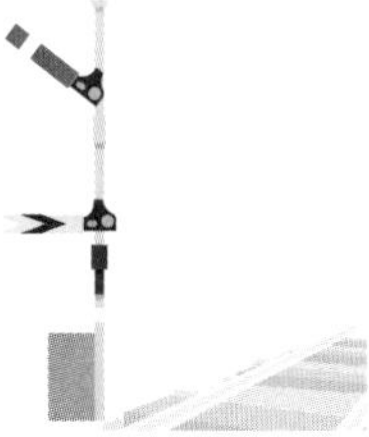

(34) il finestrino
window

(35) la porta
door

(33) la rastrelliera
luggage rack

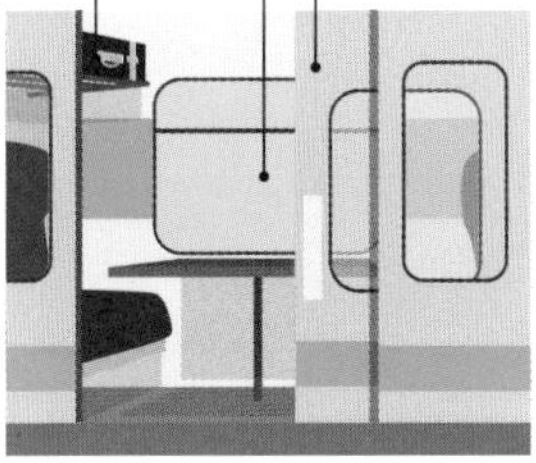

(31) il segnale
signal

(32) lo scompartimento
compartment

(36) il vagone
car / carriage

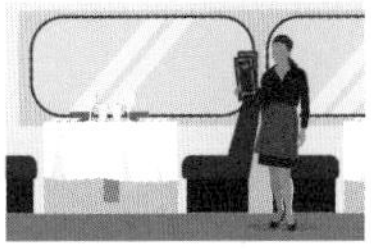

(37) il vagone ristorante
dining car

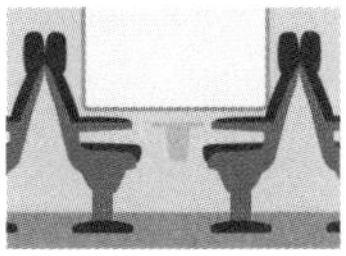

(38) il sedile
seat

(39) il vagone letto
sleeping compartment

(40) il controllore
conductor

(41) la leva d'emergenza
emergency signal

102.2 I TIPI DI TRENI
TYPES OF TRAINS

(1) il duomo
steam dome

(2) il respingente
buffer

(3) la biella di accoppiamento
coupling rod

(4) il treno a vapore
steam train

(5) il cacciapietre
cowcatcher

(6) il pantografo
pantograph

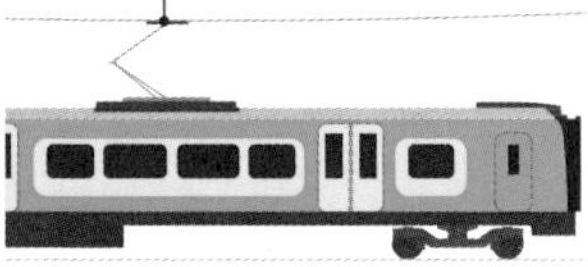

(8) la cabina di guida
driver's cab

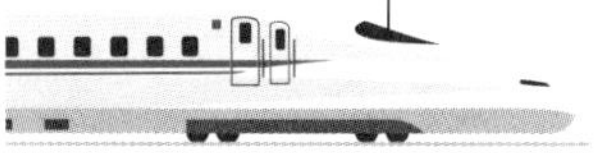

(7) il treno elettrico
electric train

(9) il treno proitelle
bullet train

(10) il treno ad alta velocità
high-speed train

(11) il treno diesel
diesel train

(12) il carico
cargo

(13) il treno merci
freight train

(14) il treno a levitazione magnetica
maglev

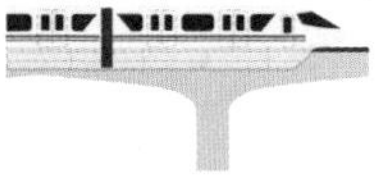

(15) il monorotaia
monorail

(16) la metropolitana
subway train

(17) il tram
tram

103 L'aeromobile
Aircraft

103.1 L'AEREO PASSEGGERI · PASSENGER AIRPLANE

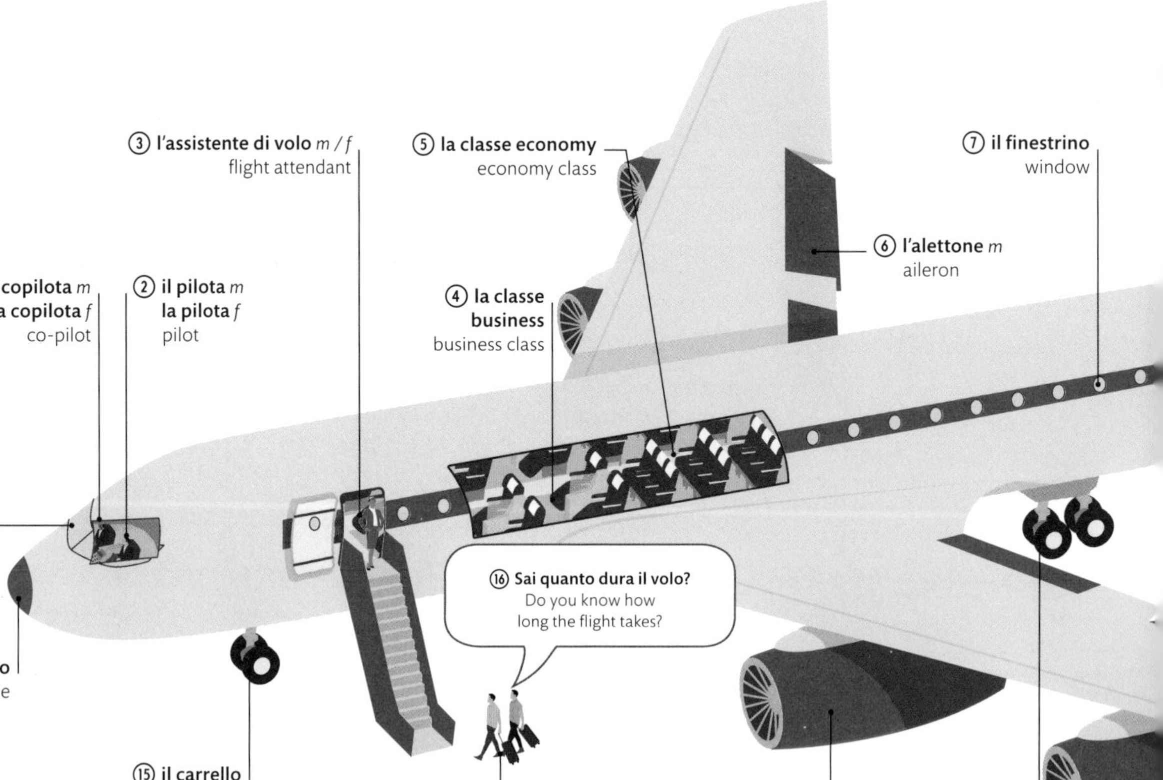

① **il copilota** *m*
la copilota *f*
co-pilot

② **il pilota** *m*
la pilota *f*
pilot

③ **l'assistente di volo** *m / f*
flight attendant

④ **la classe business**
business class

⑤ **la classe economy**
economy class

⑥ **l'alettone** *m*
aileron

⑦ **il finestrino**
window

⑬ **la cabina di pilotaggio** *f*
cockpit

⑭ **il muso**
nose

⑮ **il carrello anteriore**
nosewheel

⑯ **Sai quanto dura il volo?**
Do you know how long the flight takes?

⑰ **il bagaglio a mano**
carry-on

⑱ **il jumbo jet**
jumbo jet

⑲ **il motore**
engine

⑳ **il carrello di atterraggio**
landing gear

103.3 I TIPI DI AEROMOBILE · TYPES OF AIRCRAFT

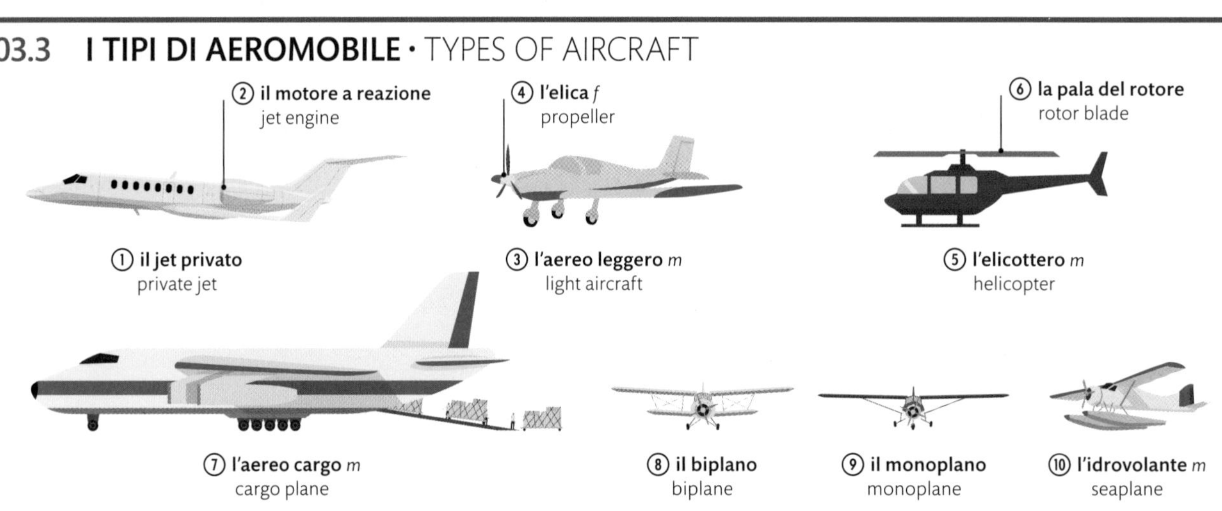
② il motore a reazione
jet engine
④ l'elica f
propeller
⑥ la pala del rotore
rotor blade
① il jet privato
private jet
③ l'aereo leggero m
light aircraft
⑤ l'elicottero m
helicopter
⑦ l'aereo cargo m
cargo plane
⑧ il biplano
biplane
⑨ il monoplano
monoplane
⑩ l'idrovolante m
seaplane

See also
42-43 In città · In town 104 In aeroporto · At the airport
131 Il viaggio e l'alloggio · Travel and accommodation

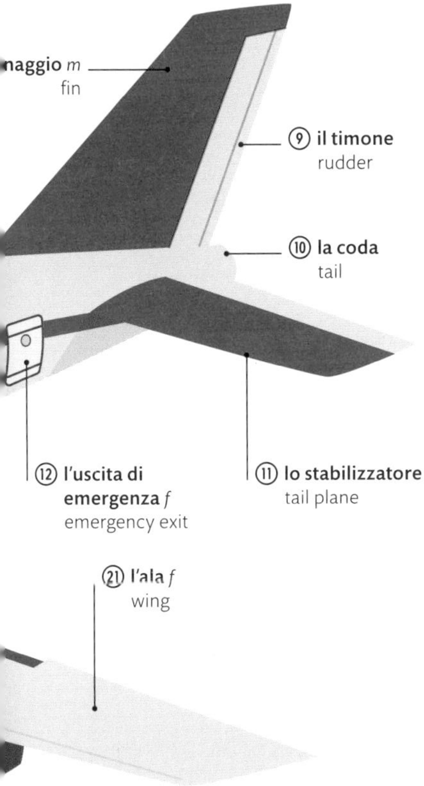

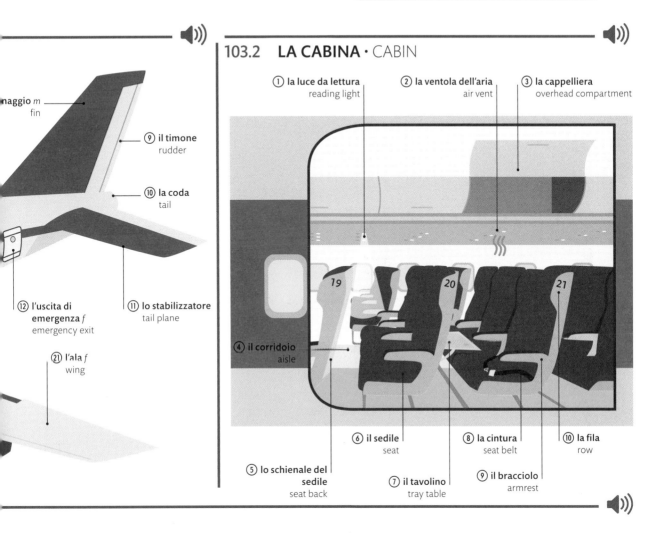

naggio *m*
fin

⑨ **il timone**
rudder

⑩ **la coda**
tail

⑫ **l'uscita di emergenza** *f*
emergency exit

⑪ **lo stabilizzatore**
tail plane

㉑ **l'ala** *f*
wing

103.2 LA CABINA · CABIN

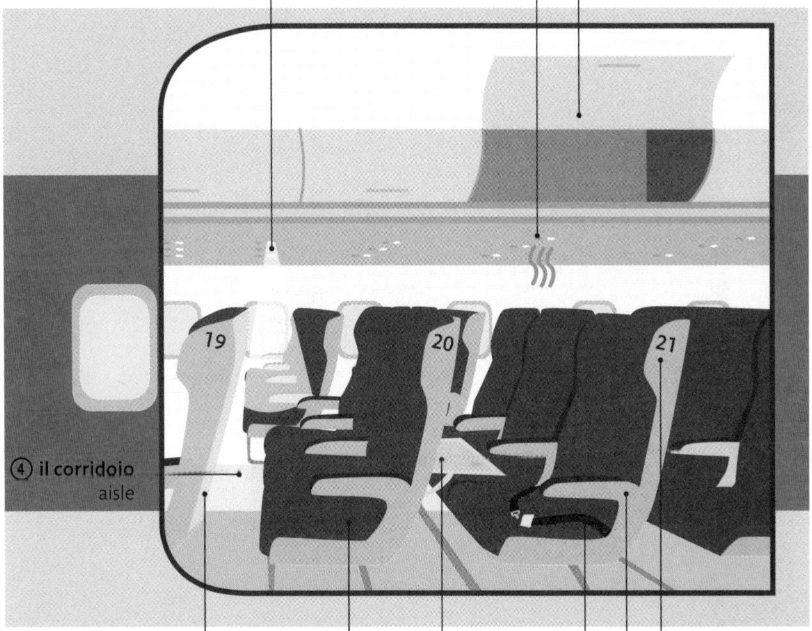

① **la luce da lettura**
reading light

② **la ventola dell'aria**
air vent

③ **la cappelliera**
overhead compartment

④ **il corridoio**
aisle

⑤ **lo schienale del sedile**
seat back

⑥ **il sedile**
seat

⑦ **il tavolino**
tray table

⑧ **la cintura**
seat belt

⑨ **il bracciolo**
armrest

⑩ **la fila**
row

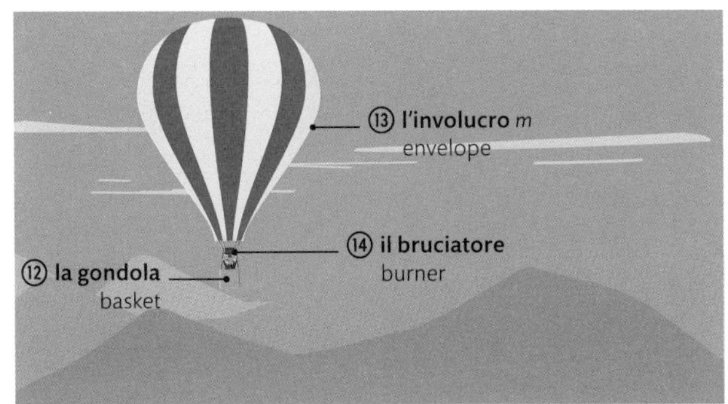
⑬ l'involucro m
envelope
⑭ il bruciatore
burner
⑫ la gondola
basket

⑪ **la mongolfiera**
hot-air balloon

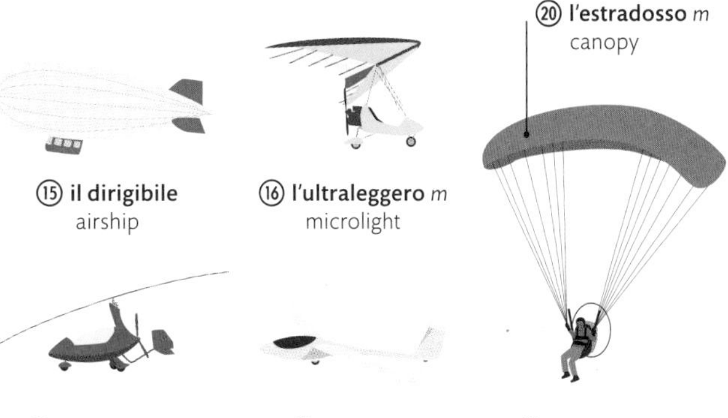
⑳ l'estradosso m
canopy

⑮ **il dirigibile**
airship

⑯ **l'ultraleggero** *m*
microlight

⑰ **il girocottero**
gyrocopter

⑱ **l'aliante** *m*
glider

⑲ **il paramotore**
paramotor

104 In aeroporto
At the airport

104.1 AL TERMINAL • AT THE TERMINAL

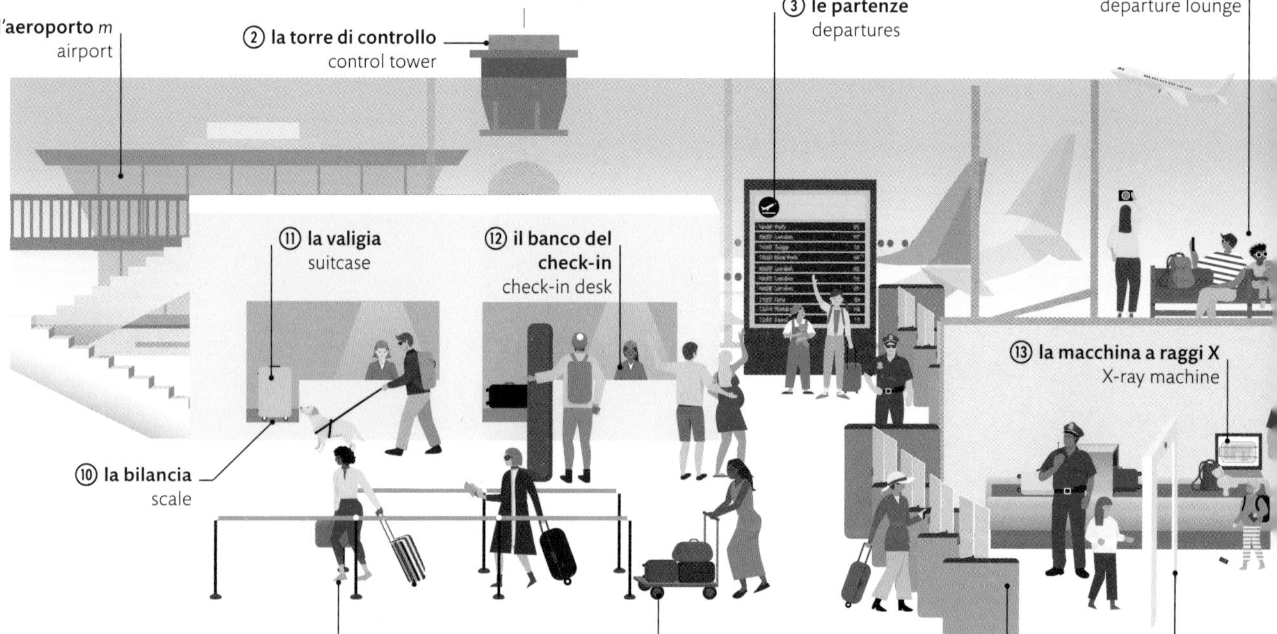

(1) **l'aeroporto** *m*
airport

(2) **la torre di controllo**
control tower

(3) **le partenze**
departures

(4) **la sala d'imbarco**
departure lounge

(11) **la valigia**
suitcase

(12) **il banco del check-in**
check-in desk

(13) **la macchina a raggi X**
X-ray machine

(10) **la bilancia**
scale

(17) **fare la coda**
to wait in line

(18) **il terminal**
terminal

(19) **il carrello**
cart

(20) **la sicurezza**
security

(21) **lo scanner**
scanner

(28) **il passaporto**
passport

(29) **il passaporto biometrico**
biometric passport

(30) **il visto**
visa

(31) **il biglietto**
ticket

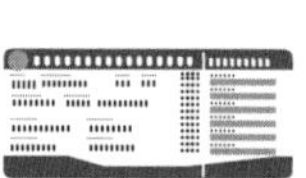
(32) **la carta d'imbarco**
boarding pass

(33) **il check-in online**
online check-in

(40) **la vacanza**
vacation

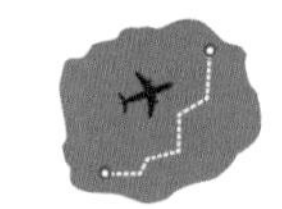
(41) **il volo interno**
domestic flight

(42) **il volo internazionale**
international flight

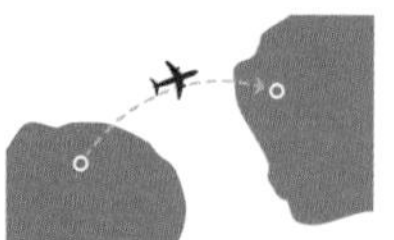
(43) **andare all'estero** *m*
to go abroad

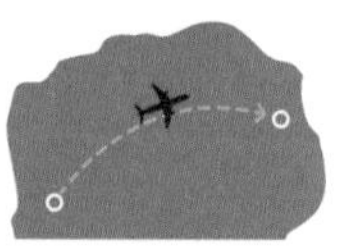
(44) **il volo diretto**
direct flight

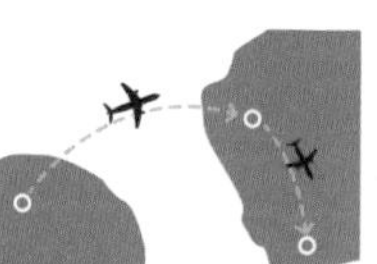
(45) **la coincidenza**
connection

(51) **i bagagli in eccedenza**
excess baggage

(52) **il controllo passaporti**
passport control

(53) **il cambio**
currency exchange

(54) **il negozio duty-free**
duty-free shop

(55) **l'ufficio bagagli smarriti** *m*
lost and found

(56) **essere in ritardo**
to be delayed

See also
103 L'aeromobile • Aircraft **131** Il viaggio e l'alloggio
Travel and accommodation **149-151** I Paesi • Countries

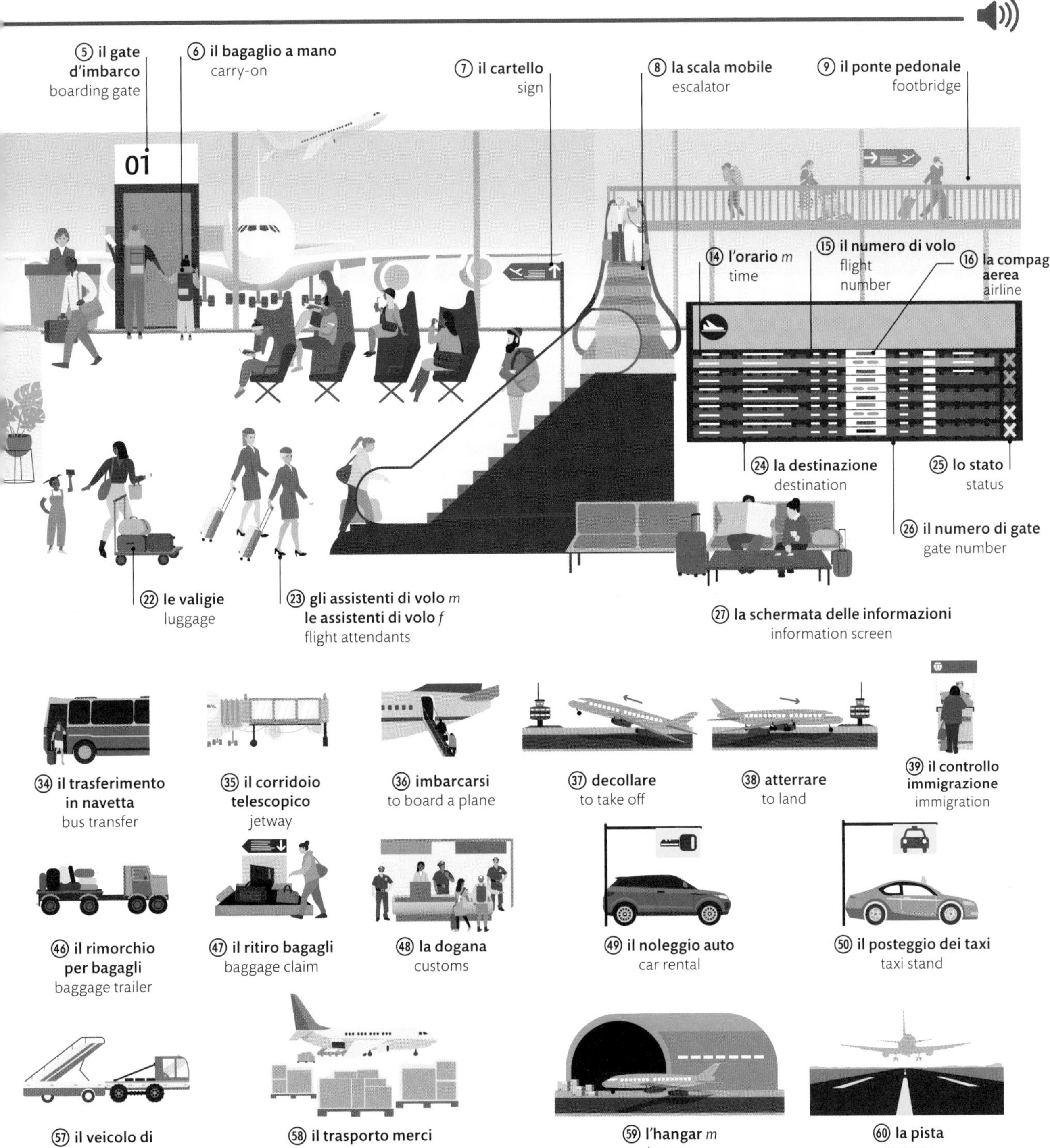

⑤ il gate d'imbarco
boarding gate
01
⑥ il bagaglio a mano
carry-on
⑦ il cartello
sign
⑧ la scala mobile
escalator
⑨ il ponte pedonale
footbridge
⑭ l'orario m
time
⑮ il numero di volo
flight number
⑯ la compagnia aerea
airline
㉔ la destinazione
destination
㉕ lo stato
status
㉖ il numero di gate
gate number
㉒ le valigie
luggage
㉓ gli assistenti di volo m
le assistenti di volo f
flight attendants
㉗ la schermata delle informazioni
information screen
㉞ il trasferimento in navetta
bus transfer
㉟ il corridoio telescopico
jetway
㊱ imbarcarsi
to board a plane
㊲ decollare
to take off
㊳ atterrare
to land
㊴ il controllo immigrazione
immigration
㊻ il rimorchio per bagagli
baggage trailer
㊼ il ritiro bagagli
baggage claim
㊽ la dogana
customs
㊾ il noleggio auto
car rental
㊿ il posteggio dei taxi
taxi stand
57 il veicolo di servizio
service vehicle
58 il trasporto merci per via aerea
air cargo
59 l'hangar m
hangar
60 la pista
runway

105 Le imbarcazioni
Sea vessels

105.1 LA NAVE · SHIP

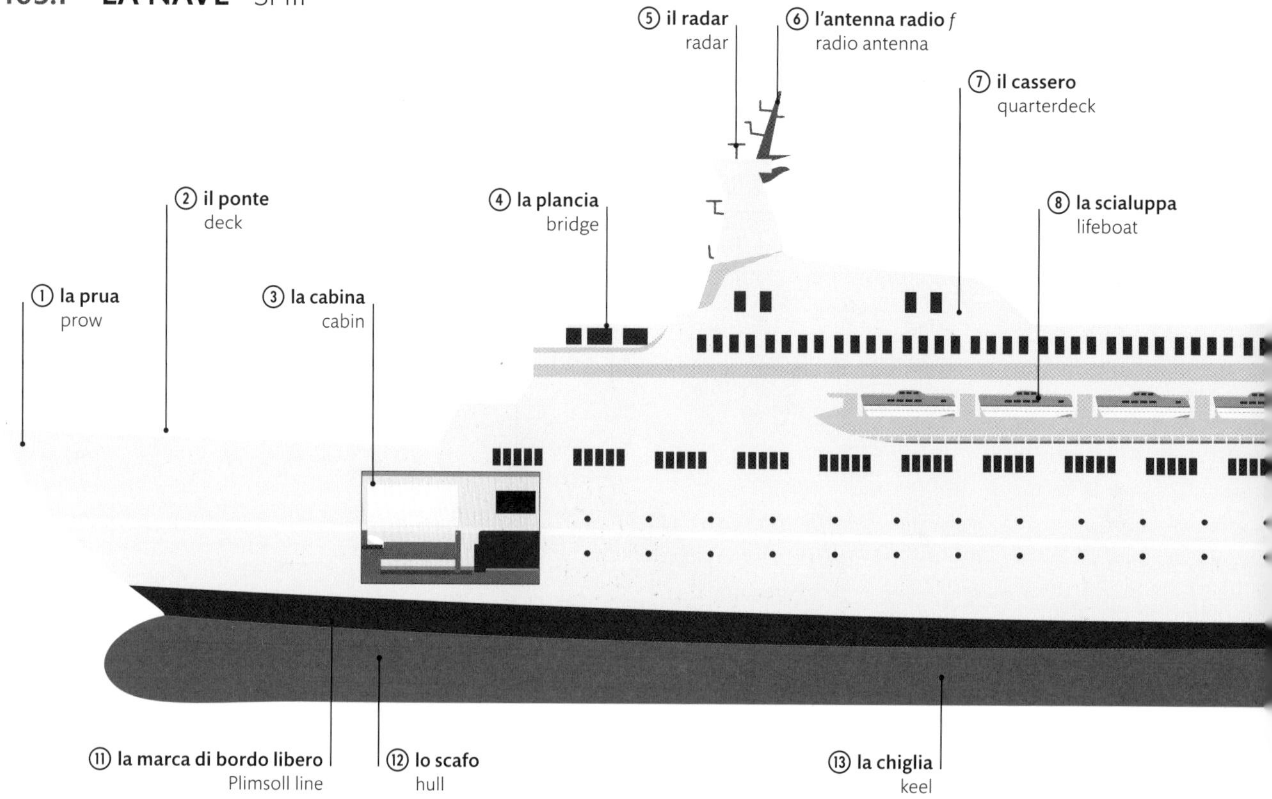

① **la prua** prow

② **il ponte** deck

③ **la cabina** cabin

④ **la plancia** bridge

⑤ **il radar** radar

⑥ **l'antenna radio** *f* radio antenna

⑦ **il cassero** quarterdeck

⑧ **la scialuppa** lifeboat

⑪ **la marca di bordo libero** Plimsoll line

⑫ **lo scafo** hull

⑬ **la chiglia** keel

105.2 LE ALTRE BARCHE E NAVI · OTHER BOATS AND SHIPS

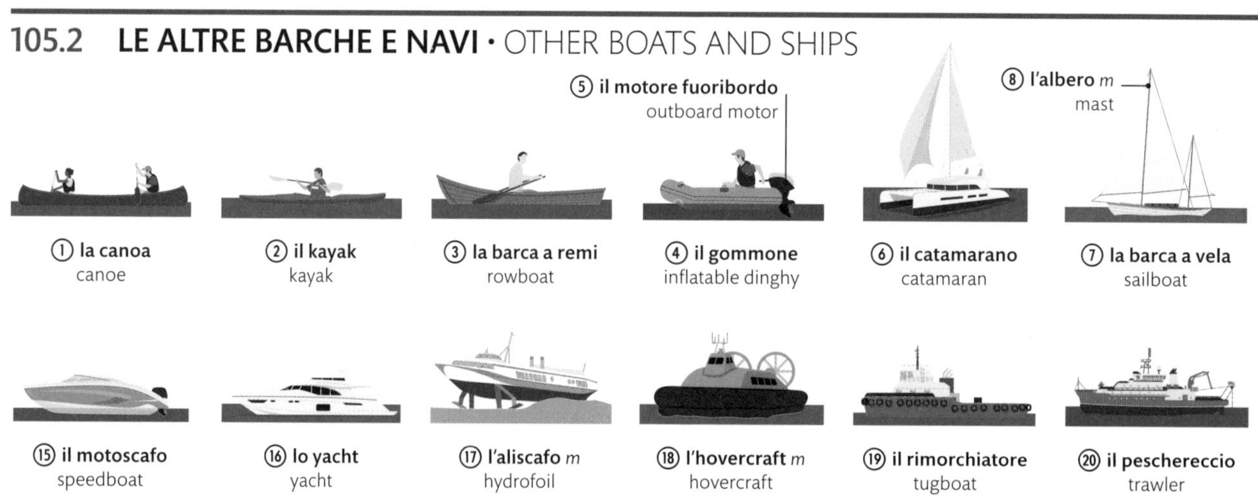
⑤ il motore fuoribordo
outboard motor
⑧ l'albero m
mast
① la canoa
canoe
② il kayak
kayak
③ la barca a remi
rowboat
④ il gommone
inflatable dinghy
⑥ il catamarano
catamaran
⑦ la barca a vela
sailboat
⑮ il motoscafo
speedboat
⑯ lo yacht
yacht
⑰ l'aliscafo m
hydrofoil
⑱ l'hovercraft m
hovercraft
⑲ il rimorchiatore
tugboat
⑳ il peschereccio
trawler

See also
106 Il porto • The port **119** La vela e gli sport acquatici • Sailing and watersports **131** Il viaggio e l'alloggio • Travel and accommodation

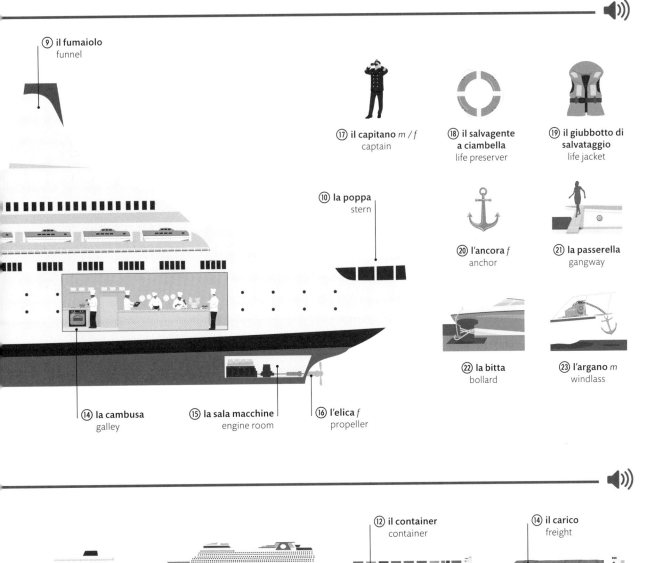

⑨ **il fumaiolo**
funnel

⑩ **la poppa**
stern

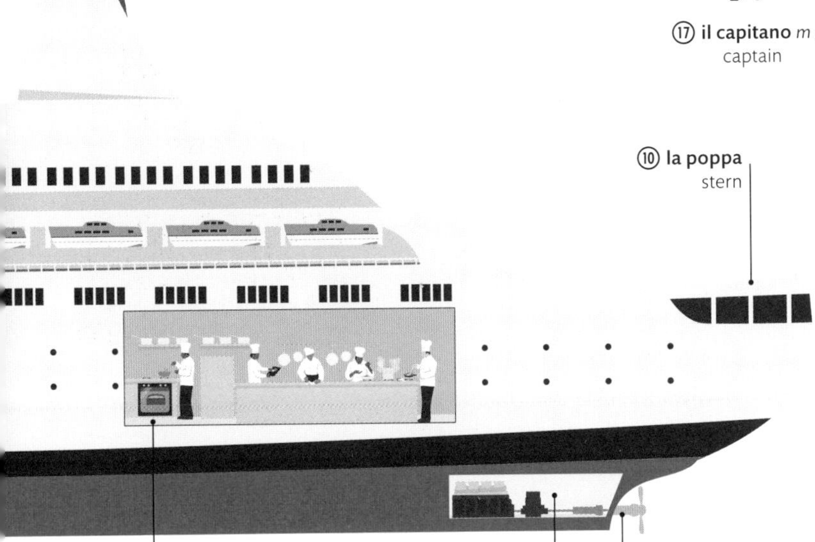

⑭ **la cambusa**
galley

⑮ **la sala macchine**
engine room

⑯ **l'elica** *f*
propeller

⑰ **il capitano** *m / f*
captain

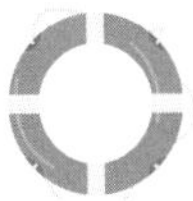

⑱ **il salvagente a ciambella**
life preserver

⑲ **il giubbotto di salvataggio**
life jacket

⑳ **l'ancora** *f*
anchor

㉑ **la passerella**
gangway

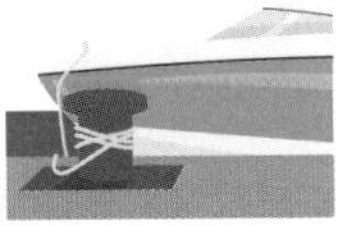

㉒ **la bitta**
bollard

㉓ **l'argano** *m*
windlass

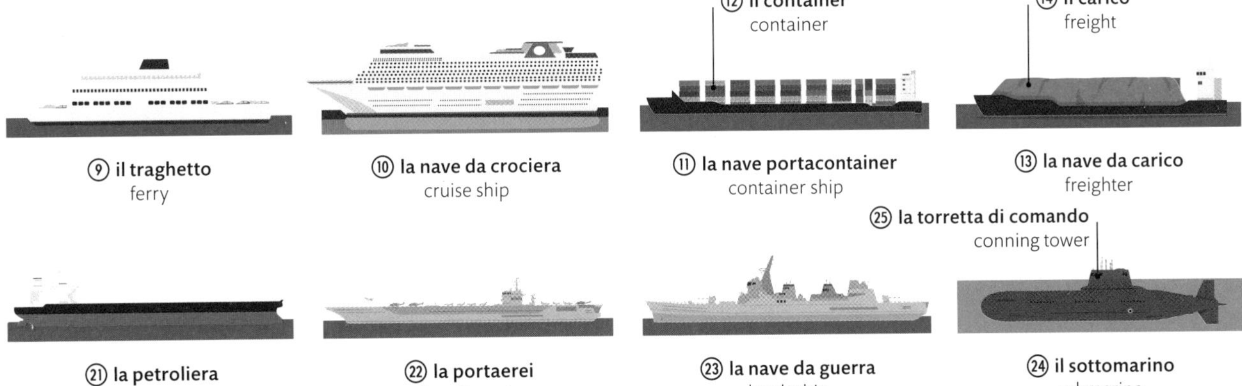
⑫ il container
container
⑭ il carico
freight
⑨ il traghetto
ferry
⑩ la nave da crociera
cruise ship
⑪ la nave portacontainer
container ship
⑬ la nave da carico
freighter
㉕ la torretta di comando
conning tower
㉑ la petroliera
oil tanker
㉒ la portaerei
aircraft carrier
㉓ la nave da guerra
battleship
㉔ il sottomarino
submarine

106 Il porto
The port

106.1 AL MOLO · AT THE DOCKS

① **la nave portacontainer**
container ship

② **la gru**
crane

③ **il container**
shipping container

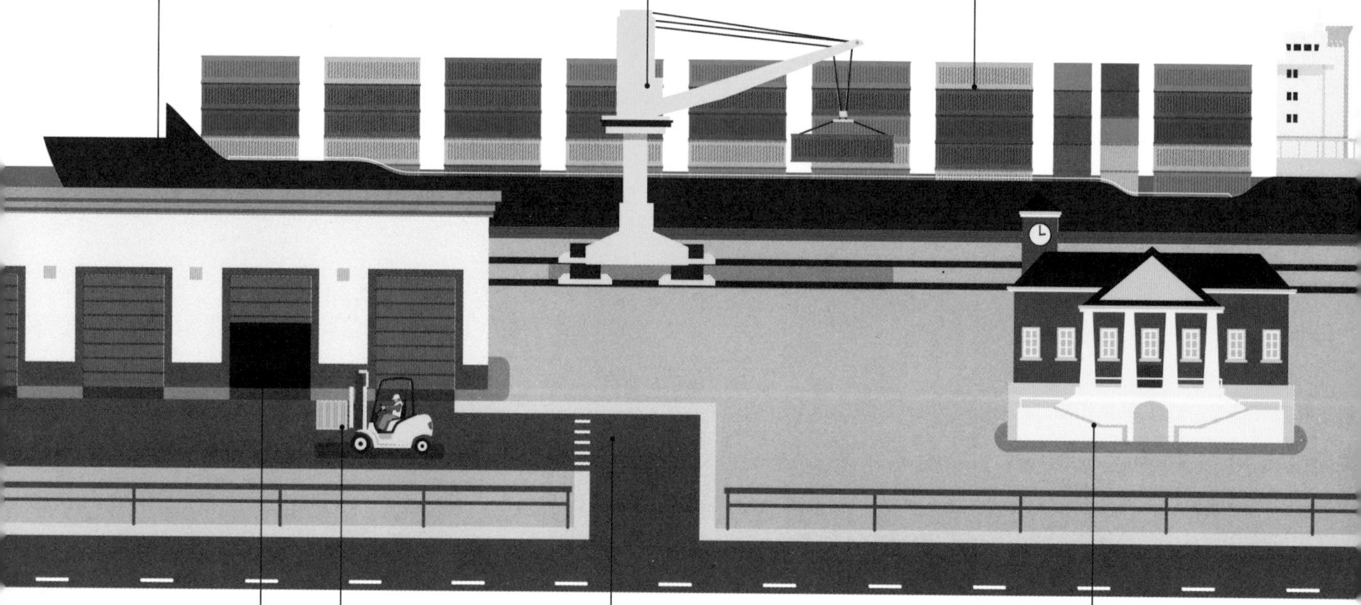

④ **il magazzino**
warehouse

⑤ **il carrello elevatore**
forklift

⑥ **la strada d'accesso**
access road

⑦ **il molo**
dock

⑧ **la dogana**
customhouse

⑱ **il traghetto**
ferry

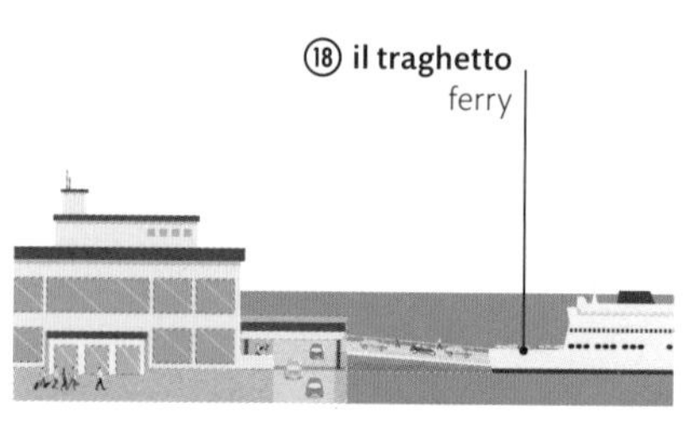

⑰ **il terminal traghetti**
ferry terminal

⑳ **i passeggeri**
passengers

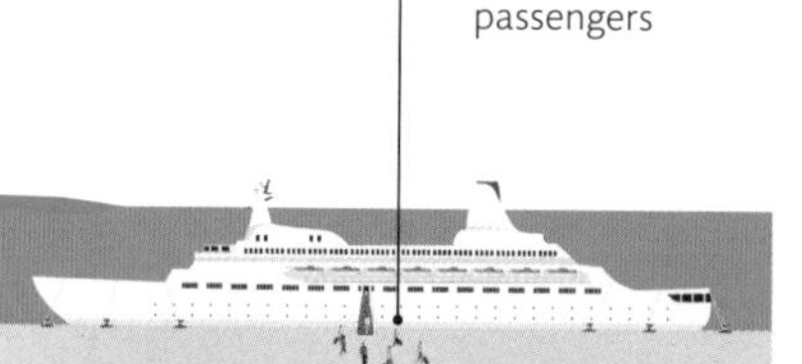

⑲ **il porto passeggeri**
passenger port

㉑ **il porto di pesca**
fishing port

㉒ **la biglietteria**
ticket office

㉗ **l'ormeggio** *m*
mooring

㉘ **il porto**
harbor

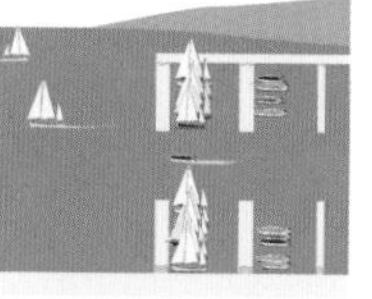

㉙ **la marina**
marina

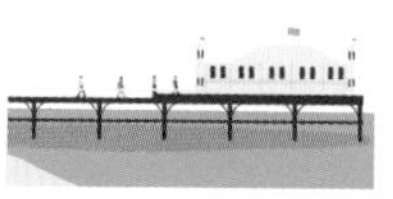

㉚ **il pontile**
pier

㉛ **l'imbarcadero** *m*
jetty

㉜ **il cantiere navale**
shipyard

See also
96 Le strade • Roads **102** I treni • Trains
105 Le imbarcazioni • Sea vessels

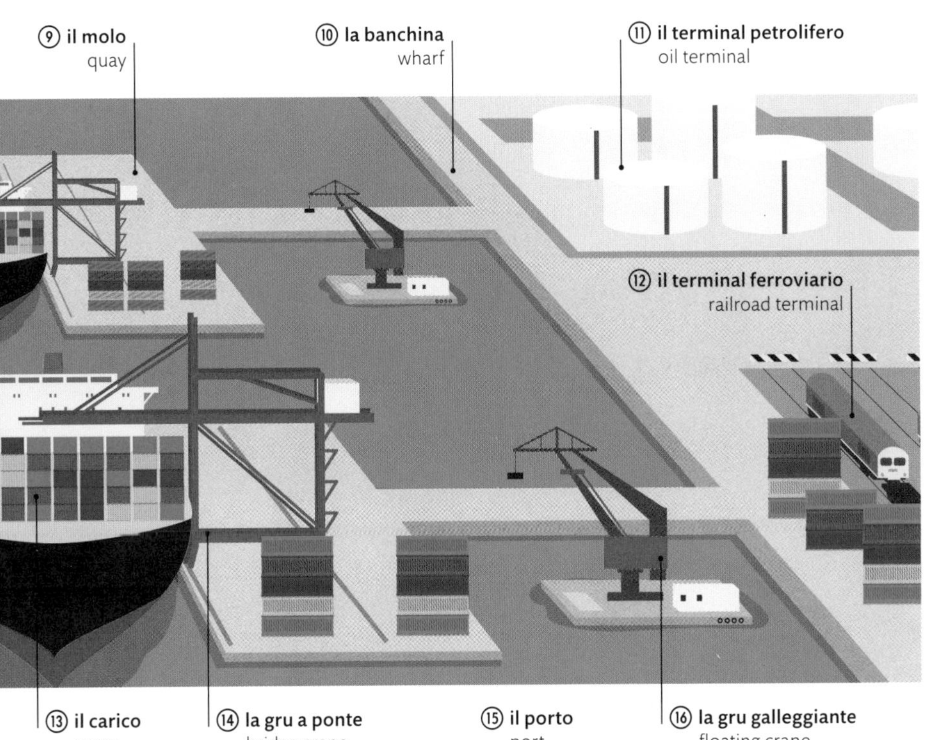

⑨ **il molo**
quay

⑩ **la banchina**
wharf

⑪ **il terminal petrolifero**
oil terminal

⑫ **il terminal ferroviario**
railroad terminal

⑬ **il carico**
cargo

⑭ **la gru a ponte**
bridge crane

⑮ **il porto**
port

⑯ **la gru galleggiante**
floating crane

㉓ **il bacino di carenaggio**
dry dock

㉔ **la boa**
buoy

㉖ **la lampada**
lamp

㉕ **il faro**
lighthouse

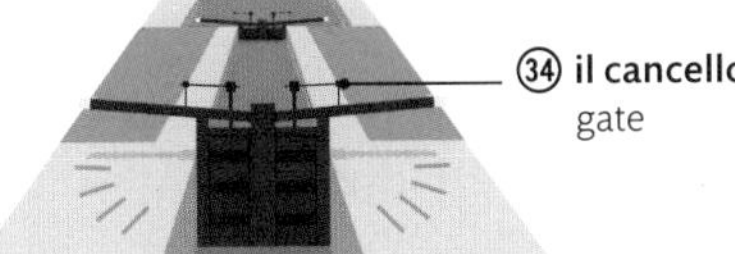

㉞ **il cancello**
gate

㉝ **la chiusa**
lock

㉟ **la guardia costiera** *m / f*
coastguard

㊱ **il capitano di porto** *m / f*
harbor master

106.2 I VERBI
VERBS

① **imbarcarsi**
to board

② **ormeggiare**
to moor

③ **sbarcare**
to disembark

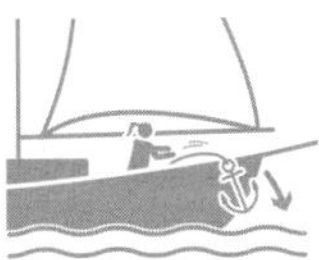

④ **calare l'ancora**
to drop anchor

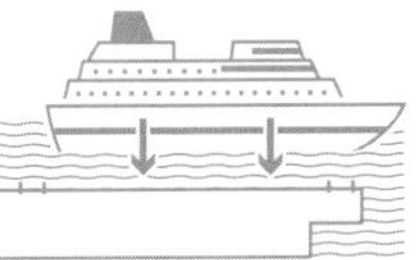

⑤ **attraccare**
to dock

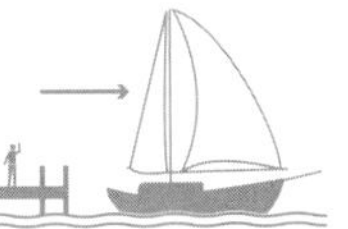

⑥ **salpare**
to set sail

107 Il football americano
American football

107.1 IL FOOTBALL AMERICANO • AMERICAN FOOTBALL

① **il cornerback sinistro** *m / f*
left cornerback

② **il linebacker esterno** *m / f*
outside linebacker

③ **il defensive end sinistro** *m / f*
left defensive end

④ **il safety sinistro** *m / f*
left safety

⑤ **il defensive tackle sinistro** *m / f*
left defensive tackle

⑥ **il linebacker centrale** *m / f*
middle linebacker

⑦ **il defensive tackle destro** *m / f*
right defensive tackle

⑧ **il safety destro** *m / f*
right safety

⑨ **il defensive end destro** *m / f*
right defensive end

⑩ **il linebacker esterno** *m / f*
outside linebacker

⑪ **il cornerback destro** *m / f*
right cornerback

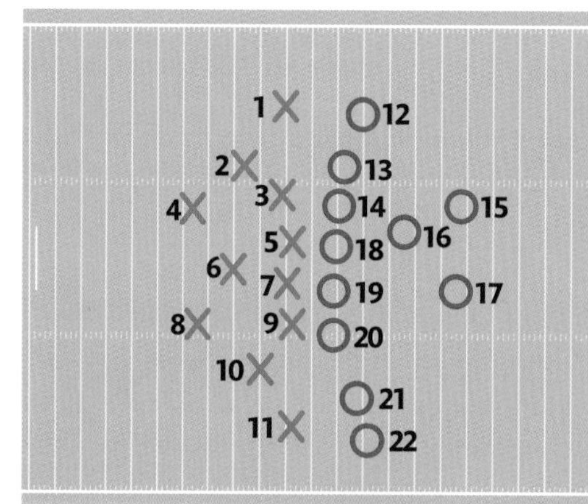

1
2
3
4
5
6
7
8
9
10
11
12
13
14
15
16
17
18
19
20
21
22

㉔ **la difesa** *m / f*
defense

㉓ **le posizioni del football americano**
American football positions

㉕ **l'attacco** *m / f*
offense

⑫ **il ricevitore** *m* **la ricevitrice** *f*
wide receiver

⑬ **l'offensive tackle destro** *m / f*
right tackle

⑭ **la guardia destra** *m / f*
right guard

⑮ **il running back / l'halfback** *m / f*
running back / halfback

⑯ **il fullback** *m / f*
fullback

⑰ **il quarterback** *m / f*
quarterback

⑱ **il centro** *m / f*
center

⑲ **la guardia sinistra** *m / f*
left guard

⑳ **l'offensive tackle sinistro** *m / f*
left tackle

㉑ ㉒ **il ricevitore** *m* **la ricevitrice** *f*
wide receiver

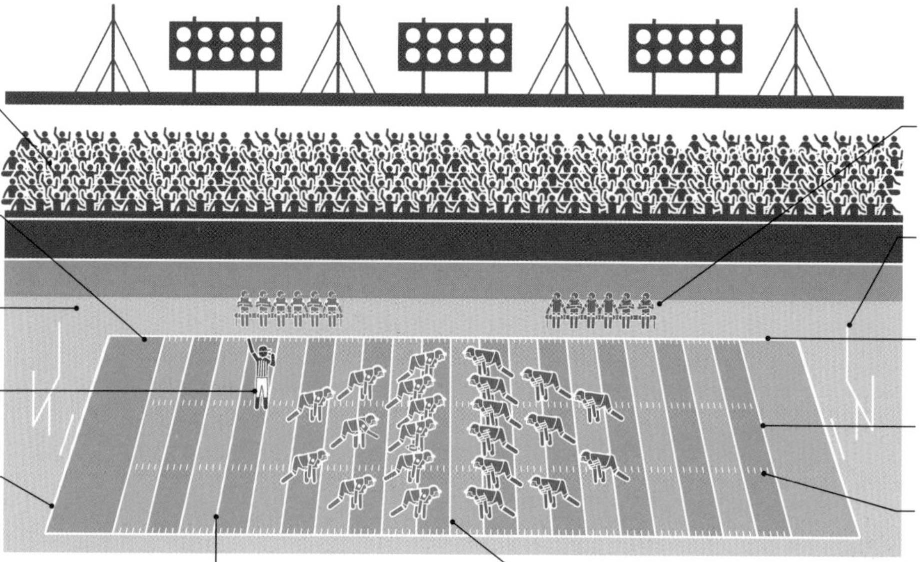

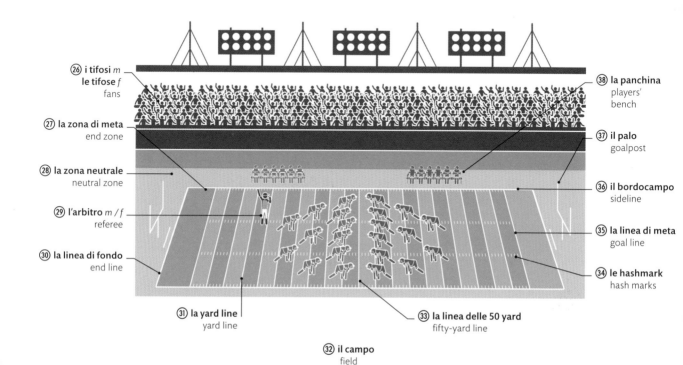

㉖ **i tifosi** *m* **le tifose** *f*
fans

㉗ **la zona di meta**
end zone

㉘ **la zona neutrale**
neutral zone

㉙ **l'arbitro** *m / f*
referee

㉚ **la linea di fondo**
end line

㉛ **la yard line**
yard line

㉜ **il campo**
field

㉝ **la linea delle 50 yard**
fifty-yard line

㉞ **le hashmark**
hash marks

㉟ **la linea di meta**
goal line

㊱ **il bordocampo**
sideline

㊲ **il palo**
goalpost

㊳ **la panchina**
players' bench

See also
108 Il rugby • Rugby 109 Il calcio • Soccer
110 L'hockey e il lacrosse • Hockey and lacrosse

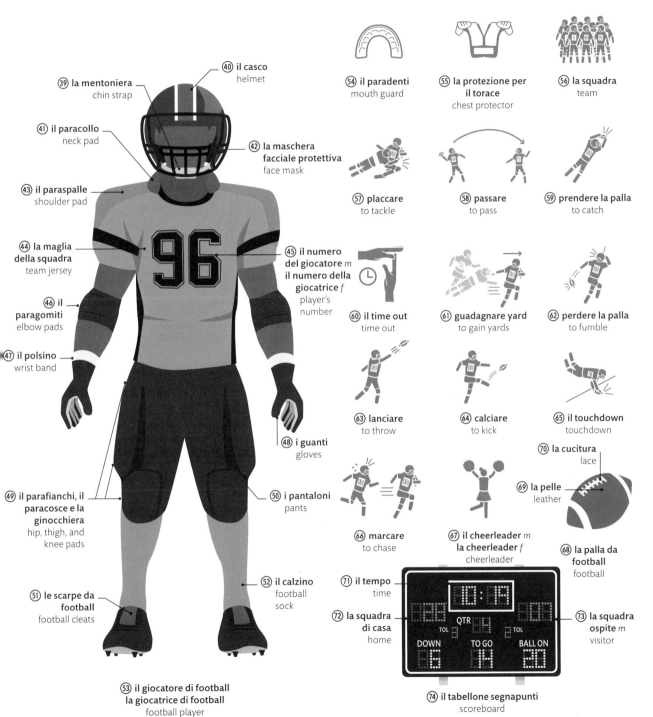

39 **la mentoniera** chin strap
40 **il casco** helmet
41 **il paracollo** neck pad
42 **la maschera facciale protettiva** face mask
43 **il paraspalle** shoulder pad
44 **la maglia della squadra** team jersey
45 **il numero del giocatore** *m* **il numero della giocatrice** *f* player's number
46 **il paragomiti** elbow pads
47 **il polsino** wrist band
48 **i guanti** gloves
49 **il parafianchi, il paracosce e la ginocchiera** hip, thigh, and knee pads
50 **i pantaloni** pants
51 **le scarpe da football** football cleats
52 **il calzino** football sock
53 **il giocatore di football la giocatrice di football** football player

54 **il paradenti** mouth guard
55 **la protezione per il torace** chest protector 
56 **la squadra** team 
57 **placcare** to tackle 
58 **passare** to pass 
59 **prendere la palla** to catch 
60 **il time out** time out 
61 **guadagnare yard** to gain yards 
62 **perdere la palla** to fumble 
63 **lanciare** to throw 
64 **calciare** to kick 
65 **il touchdown** touchdown 
66 **marcare** to chase 
67 **il cheerleader** *m* **la cheerleader** *f* cheerleader 
68 **la palla da football** football 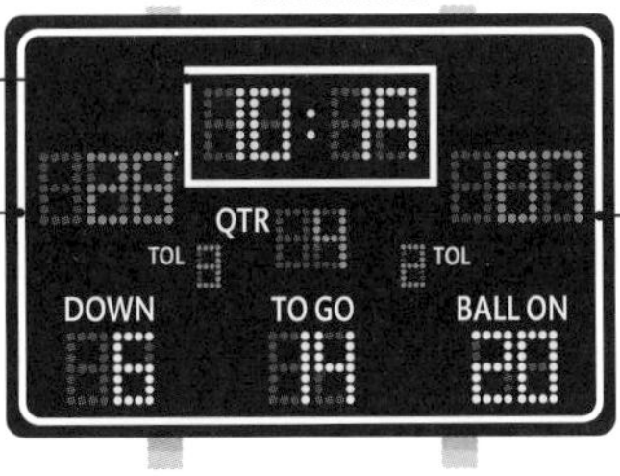
69 **la pelle** leather
70 **la cucitura** lace
71 **il tempo** time
72 **la squadra di casa** home
73 **la squadra ospite** *m* visitor
74 **il tabellone segnapunti** scoreboard

QTR
TOL
TOL
DOWN
TO GO
BALL ON

108.1 **IL RUGBY** · RUGBY

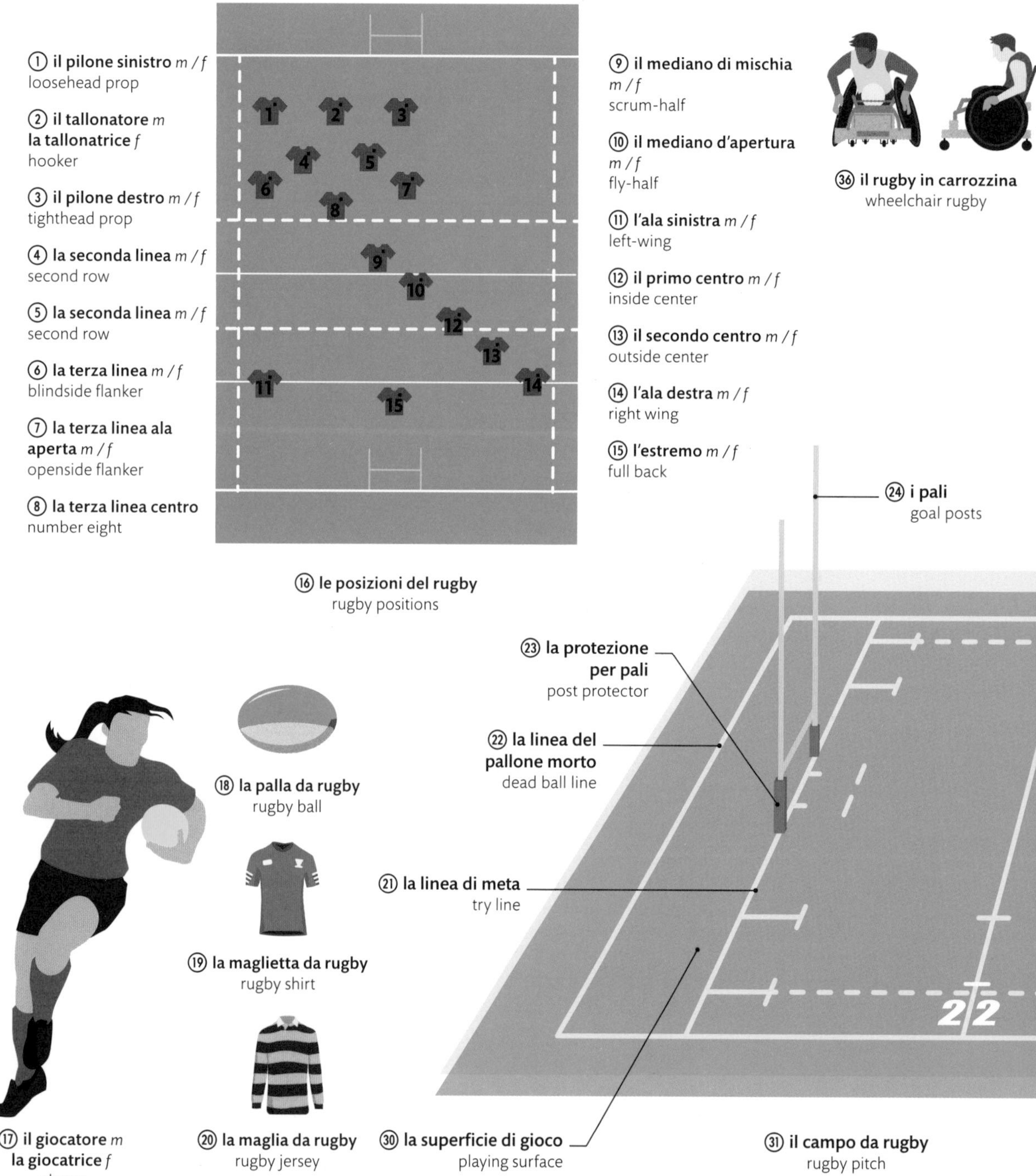
1
2
3
4
5
6
7
8
9
10
11
12
13
14
15
22

① **il pilone sinistro** *m / f*
loosehead prop

② **il tallonatore** *m*
la tallonatrice *f*
hooker

③ **il pilone destro** *m / f*
tighthead prop

④ **la seconda linea** *m / f*
second row

⑤ **la seconda linea** *m / f*
second row

⑥ **la terza linea** *m / f*
blindside flanker

⑦ **la terza linea ala aperta** *m / f*
openside flanker

⑧ **la terza linea centro**
number eight

⑨ **il mediano di mischia** *m / f*
scrum-half

⑩ **il mediano d'apertura** *m / f*
fly-half

⑪ **l'ala sinistra** *m / f*
left-wing

⑫ **il primo centro** *m / f*
inside center

⑬ **il secondo centro** *m / f*
outside center

⑭ **l'ala destra** *m / f*
right wing

⑮ **l'estremo** *m / f*
full back

⑯ **le posizioni del rugby**
rugby positions

㊱ **il rugby in carrozzina**
wheelchair rugby

㉔ **i pali**
goal posts

㉓ **la protezione per pali**
post protector

㉒ **la linea del pallone morto**
dead ball line

㉑ **la linea di meta**
try line

⑱ **la palla da rugby**
rugby ball

⑲ **la maglietta da rugby**
rugby shirt

⑰ **il giocatore** *m*
la giocatrice *f*
player

⑳ **la maglia da rugby**
rugby jersey

㉚ **la superficie di gioco**
playing surface

㉛ **il campo da rugby**
rugby pitch

See also
107 Il football americano • American football **109** Il calcio • Soccer **110** L'hockey e il lacrosse • Hockey and lacrosse **112** Il basket e la pallavolo • Basketball and volleyball

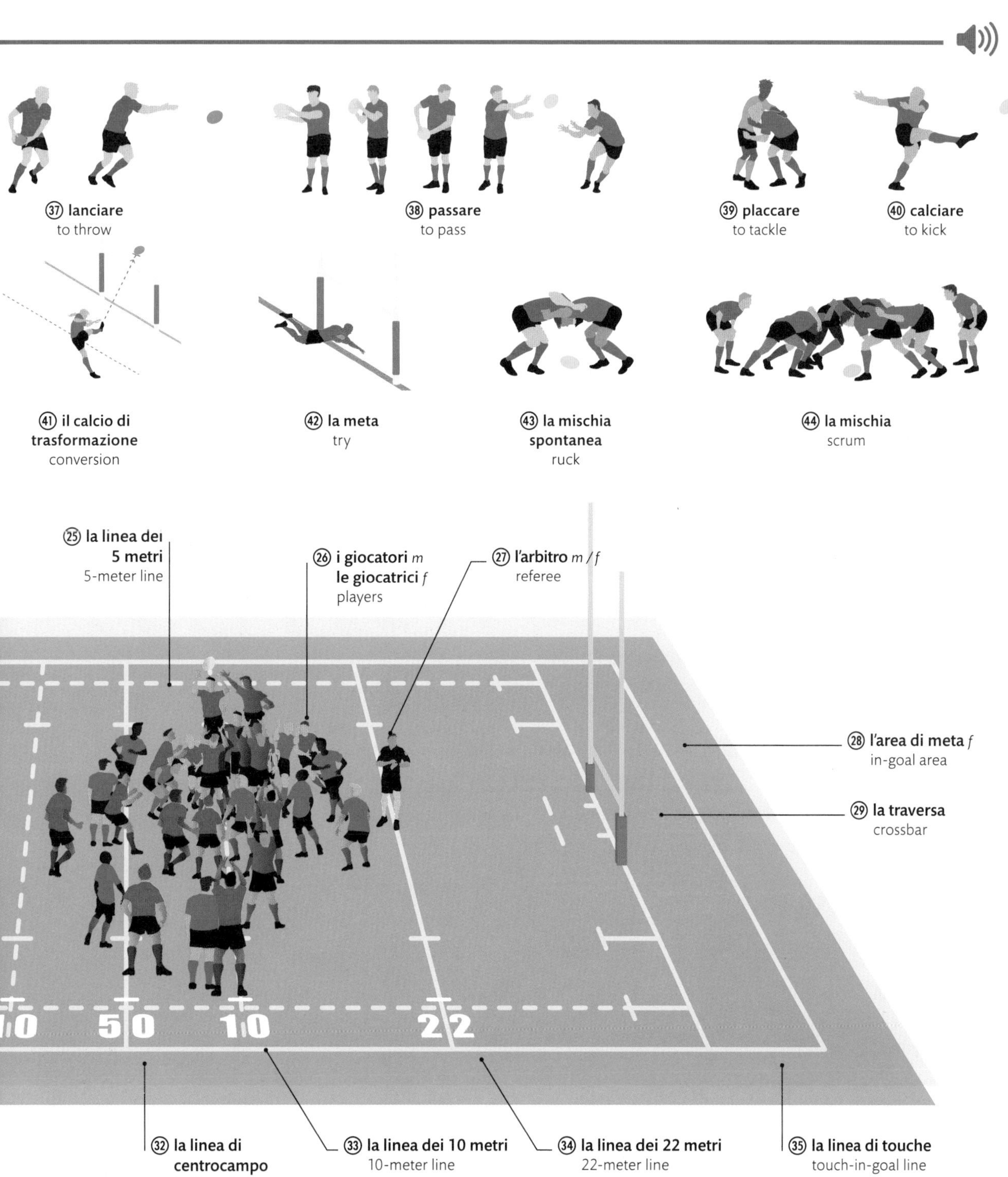

㊲ **lanciare**
to throw
㊳ **passare**
to pass
㊴ **placcare**
to tackle
㊵ **calciare**
to kick
㊶ **il calcio di trasformazione**
conversion
㊷ **la meta**
try
㊸ **la mischia spontanea**
ruck
㊹ **la mischia**
scrum
㉕ **la linea dei 5 metri**
5-meter line
㉖ **i giocatori** *m* **le giocatrici** *f*
players
㉗ **l'arbitro** *m / f*
referee
㉘ **l'area di meta** *f*
in-goal area
㉙ **la traversa**
crossbar
10
50
10
22
㉜ **la linea di centrocampo**
halfway line
㉝ **la linea dei 10 metri**
10-meter line
㉞ **la linea dei 22 metri**
22-meter line
㉟ **la linea di touche**
touch-in-goal line

109 Il calcio
Soccer

109.1 LA PARTITA DI CALCIO · SOCCER GAME

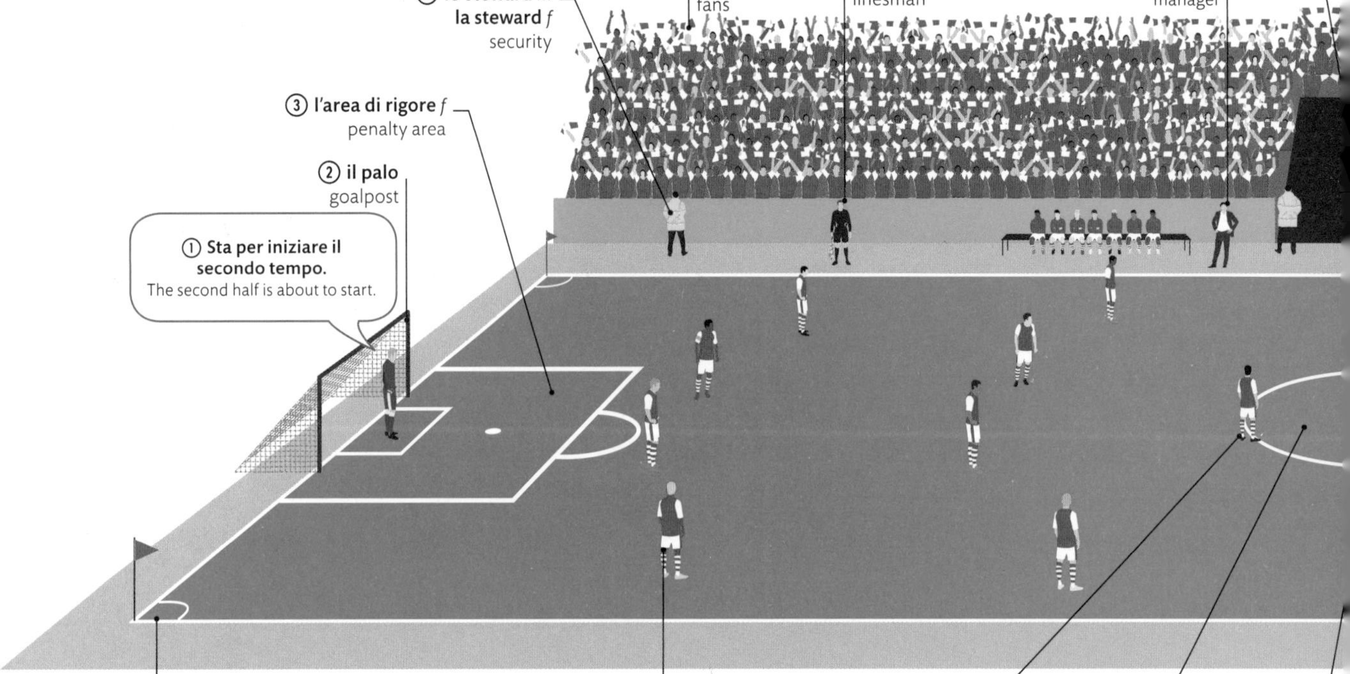

① **Sta per iniziare il secondo tempo.**
The second half is about to start.

② **il palo**
goalpost

③ **l'area di rigore** *f*
penalty area

④ **lo steward** *m*
la steward *f*
security

⑤ **i tifosi** *m*
le tifose *f*
fans

⑥ **il guardalinee** *m*
la guardalinee *f*
linesman

⑦ **l'allenatore** *m*
l'allenatrice *f*
manager

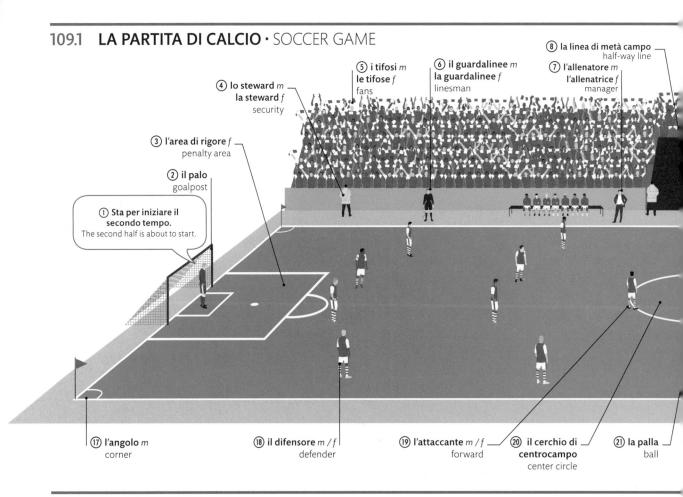

⑧ **la linea di metà campo**
half-way line

⑰ **l'angolo** *m*
corner

⑱ **il difensore** *m / f*
defender

⑲ **l'attaccante** *m / f*
forward

⑳ **il cerchio di centrocampo**
center circle

㉑ **la palla**
ball

109.2 I TEMPI E LE REGOLE · TIMING AND RULES

00:00
① **il calcio d'inizio**
kickoff

45:00
② **l'intervallo** *m*
half time

90:00
③ **la fine della partita**
full time

④ **la rimessa**
throw-in

⑤ **il fischio finale**
final whistle

⑥ **il recupero**
stoppage time

⑨ **il calcio d'angolo**
corner kick

⑩ **il cartellino giallo**
yellow card

⑪ **il cartellino rosso**
red card

⑫ **essere espulso**
to be sent off

00
00
⑬ **pareggiare**
to tie

00
05
⑭ **perdere**
to lose

See also
107 Il football americano • American football **108** Il rugby • Rugby **110** L'hockey e il lacrosse • Hockey and lacrosse **112** Il basket e la pallavolo • Basketball and volleyball

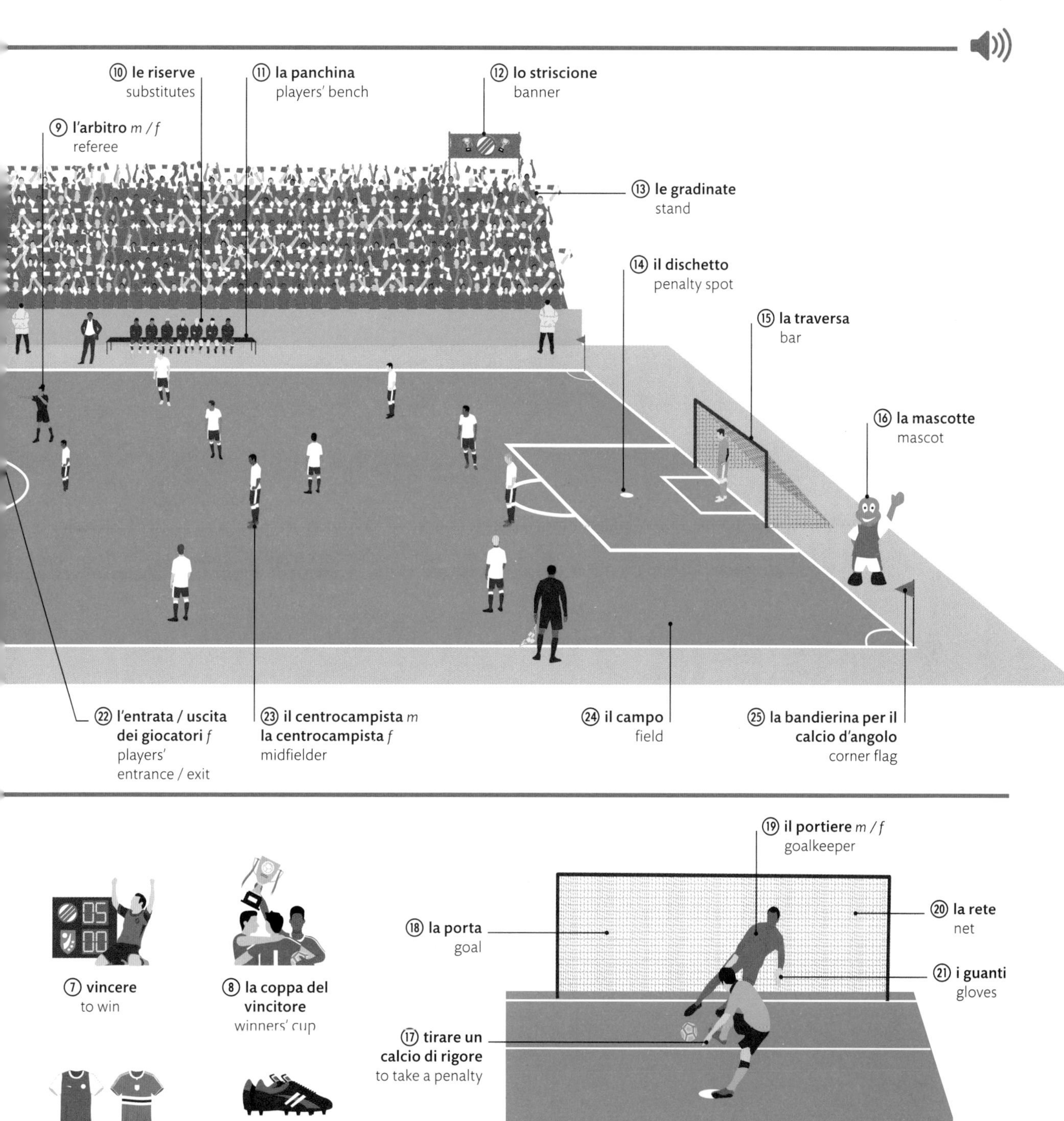
⑨ **l'arbitro** *m / f*
referee
⑩ **le riserve**
substitutes
⑪ **la panchina**
players' bench
⑫ **lo striscione**
banner
⑬ **le gradinate**
stand
⑭ **il dischetto**
penalty spot
⑮ **la traversa**
bar
⑯ **la mascotte**
mascot
㉒ **l'entrata / uscita dei giocatori** *f*
players' entrance / exit
㉓ **il centrocampista** *m*
la centrocampista *f*
midfielder
㉔ **il campo**
field
㉕ **la bandierina per il calcio d'angolo**
corner flag
⑦ **vincere**
to win
⑧ **la coppa del vincitore**
winners' cup
⑮ **la maglia da calcio**
soccer jersey
⑯ **le scarpe da calcio**
soccer cleats
⑲ **il portiere** *m / f*
goalkeeper
⑱ **la porta**
goal
⑳ **la rete**
net
㉑ **i guanti**
gloves
⑰ **tirare un calcio di rigore**
to take a penalty
㉒ **il calcio di rigore**
penalty kick

110 L'hockey e il lacrosse
Hockey and lacrosse

110.1 L'HOCKEY SU GHIACCIO · ICE HOCKEY

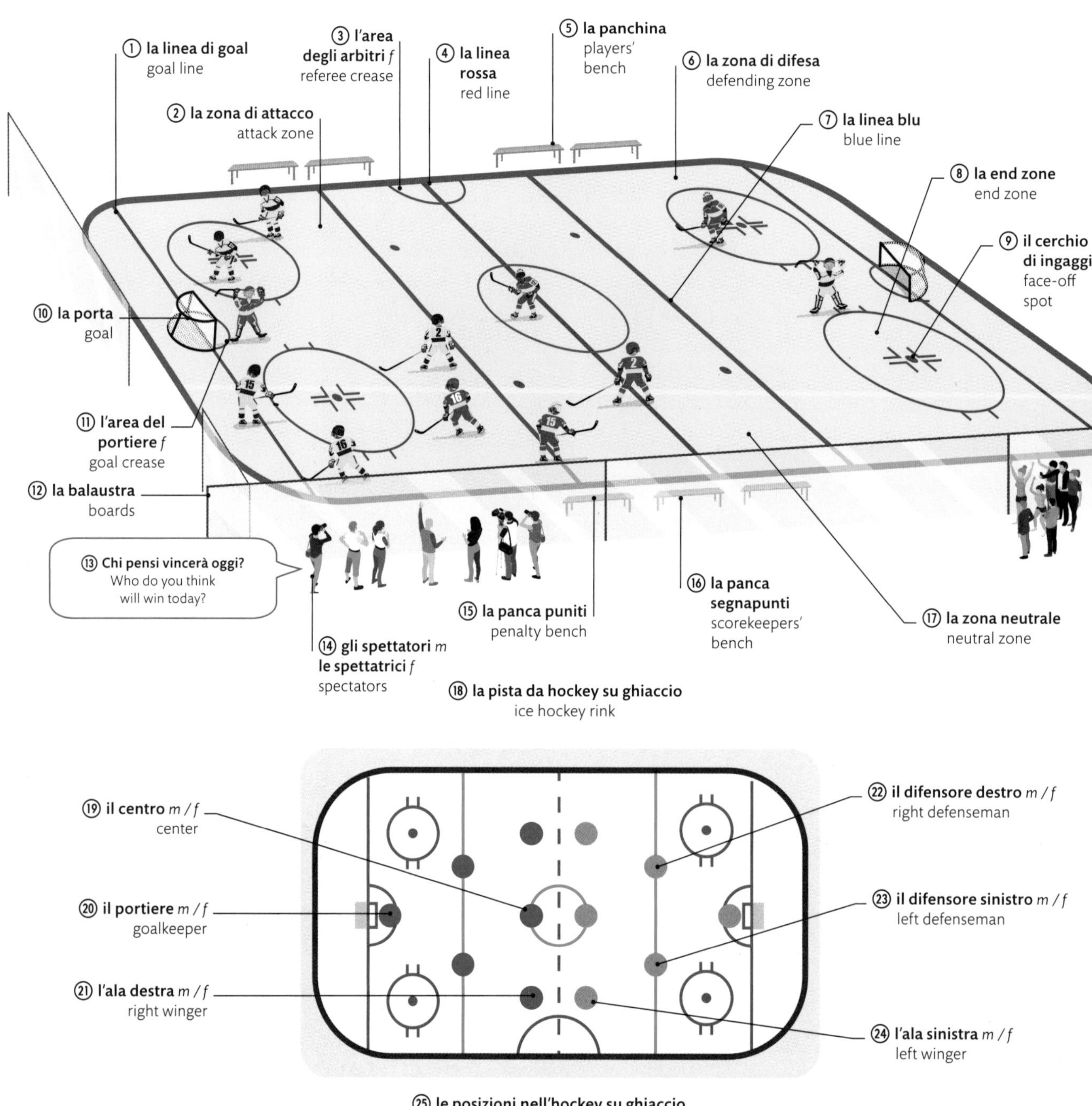

① la linea di goal
goal line
② la zona di attacco
attack zone
③ l'area degli arbitri *f*
referee crease
④ la linea rossa
red line
⑤ la panchina
players' bench
⑥ la zona di difesa
defending zone
⑦ la linea blu
blue line
⑧ la end zone
end zone
⑨ il cerchio di ingaggio
face-off spot
⑩ la porta
goal
⑪ l'area del portiere *f*
goal crease
⑫ la balaustra
boards
⑬ Chi pensi vincerà oggi?
Who do you think will win today?
⑭ gli spettatori *m* le spettatrici *f*
spectators
⑮ la panca puniti
penalty bench
⑯ la panca segnapunti
scorekeepers' bench
⑰ la zona neutrale
neutral zone
⑱ la pista da hockey su ghiaccio
ice hockey rink
⑲ il centro *m / f*
center
⑳ il portiere *m / f*
goalkeeper
㉑ l'ala destra *m / f*
right winger
㉒ il difensore destro *m / f*
right defenseman
㉓ il difensore sinistro *m / f*
left defenseman
㉔ l'ala sinistra *m / f*
left winger

㉕ **le posizioni nell'hockey su ghiaccio**
ice hockey positions

See also
107 Il football americano • American football **111** Il cricket • Cricket **112** Il basket e la pallavolo • Basketball and volleyball **113** Il baseball • Baseball **114** Il tennis • Tennis

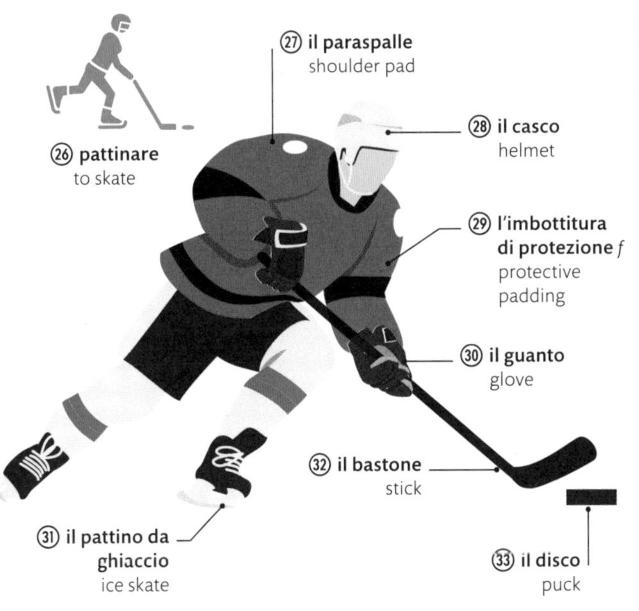
26 pattinare
to skate
27 il paraspalle
shoulder pad
28 il casco
helmet
29 l'imbottitura di protezione f
protective padding
30 il guanto
glove
31 il pattino da ghiaccio
ice skate
32 il bastone
stick
33 il disco
puck

34 **il giocatore di hockey su ghiaccio** *m*
la giocatrice di hockey su ghiaccio *f*
ice hockey player

35 lo scudo
blocking glove
36 la maschera facciale protettiva
face mask
37 il guanto da presa
catcher glove
38 il paragambe
leg guard
39 il bastone da portiere
goalie stick

40 **il portiere** *m / f*
goalkeeper

110.2 L'HOCKEY SU PRATO • FIELD HOCKEY

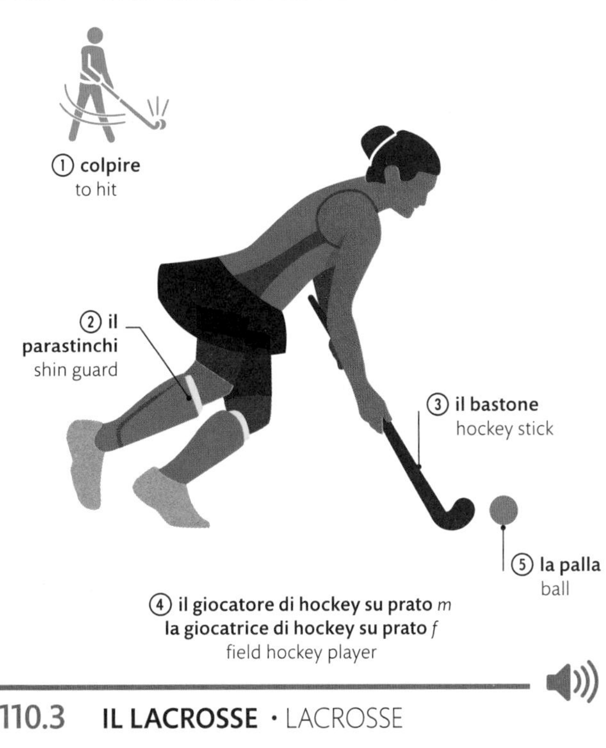
1 colpire
to hit
2 il parastinchi
shin guard
3 il bastone
hockey stick
5 la palla
ball

4 **il giocatore di hockey su prato** *m*
la giocatrice di hockey su prato *f*
field hockey player

110.3 IL LACROSSE • LACROSSE

1 il cesto
head pocket
2 la mazza
crosse
3 il parabraccia
arm protection
4 il manico
handle

5 **il giocatore di lacrosse** *m*
la giocatrice di lacrosse *f*
lacrosse player

6 **passare**
to pass

7 **raccogliere**
to scoop

8 **l'ingaggio** *m*
face-off

111 Il cricket
Cricket

111.1 IL CAMPO DA CRICKET E LE POSIZIONI
CRICKET PITCH AND POSITIONS

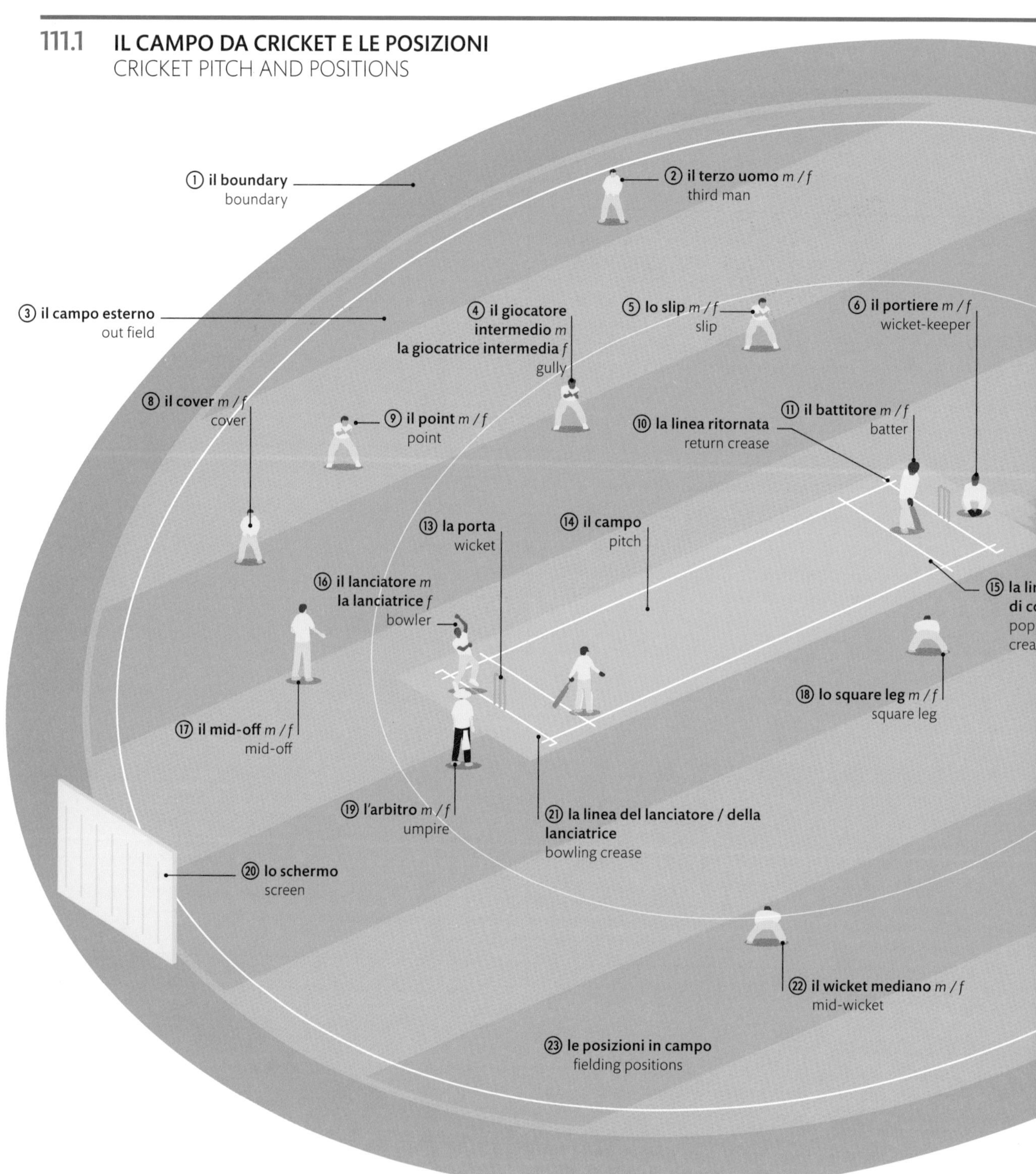

① il boundary
boundary
② il terzo uomo m / f
third man
③ il campo esterno
out field
④ il giocatore intermedio m
la giocatrice intermedia f
gully
⑤ lo slip m / f
slip
⑥ il portiere m / f
wicket-keeper
⑧ il cover m / f
cover
⑨ il point m / f
point
⑩ la linea ritornata
return crease
⑪ il battitore m / f
batter
⑬ la porta
wicket
⑭ il campo
pitch
⑮ la lin
di co
popp
creas
⑯ il lanciatore m
la lanciatrice f
bowler
⑰ il mid-off m / f
mid-off
⑱ lo square leg m / f
square leg
⑲ l'arbitro m / f
umpire
⑳ lo schermo
screen
㉑ la linea del lanciatore / della lanciatrice
bowling crease
㉒ il wicket mediano m / f
mid-wicket
㉓ le posizioni in campo
fielding positions

See also
109 Il calcio • Soccer **110** L'hockey e il lacrosse • Hockey and lacrosse **113** Il baseball • Baseball **115** Il golf • Golf

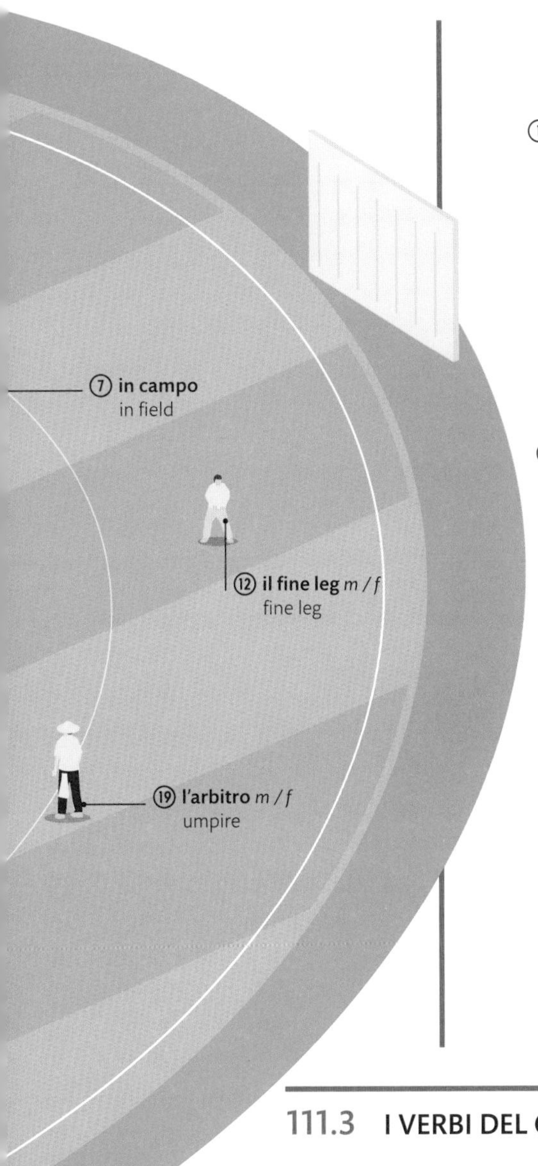

⑦ **in campo**
in field

⑫ **il fine leg** *m / f*
fine leg

⑲ **l'arbitro** *m / f*
umpire

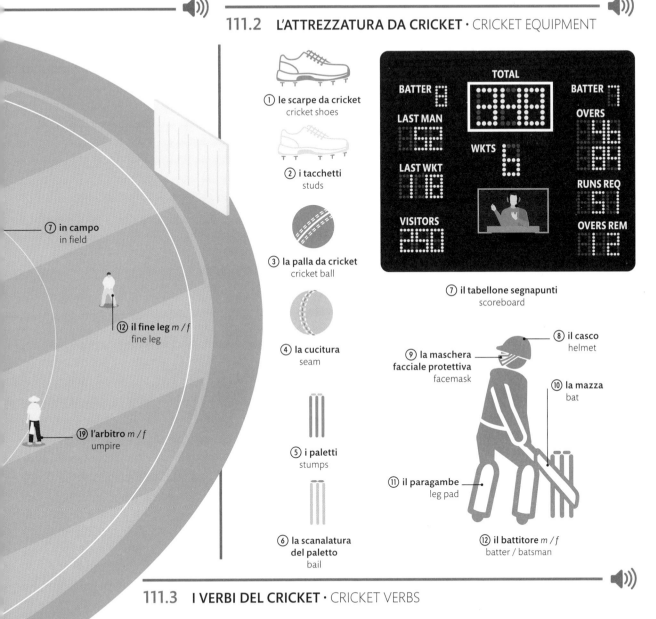

111.2 L'ATTREZZATURA DA CRICKET • CRICKET EQUIPMENT

① **le scarpe da cricket**
cricket shoes

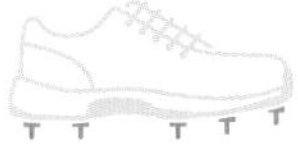

② **i tacchetti**
studs

③ **la palla da cricket**
cricket ball

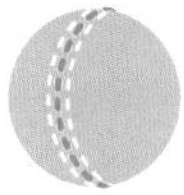

④ **la cucitura**
seam

⑤ **i paletti**
stumps

⑥ **la scanalatura del paletto**
bail

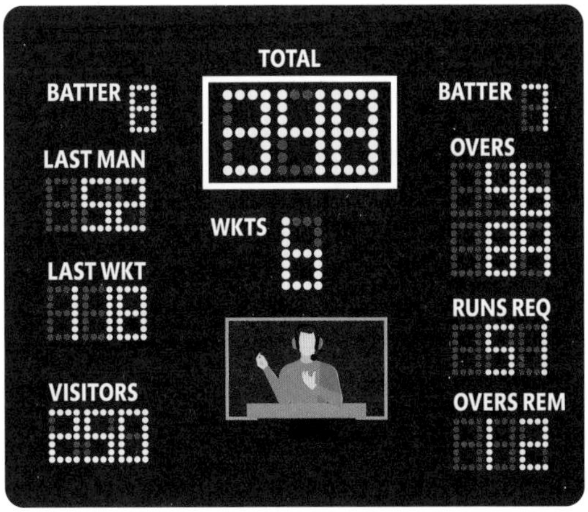

TOTAL
BATTER
LAST MAN
LAST WKT
VISITORS
WKTS
BATTER
OVERS
RUNS REQ
OVERS REM

⑦ **il tabellone segnapunti**
scoreboard

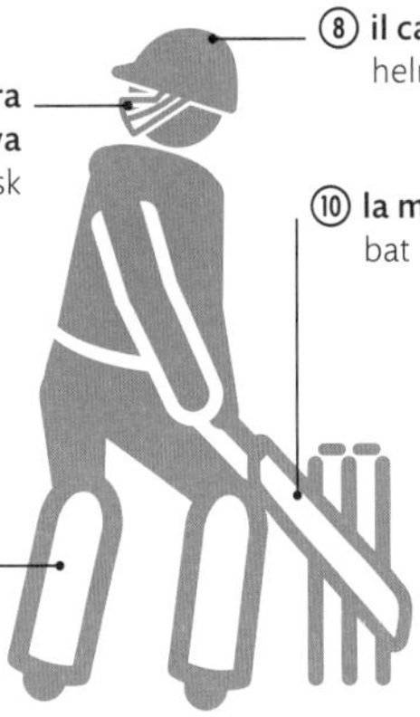

⑧ **il casco**
helmet

⑨ **la maschera facciale protettiva**
facemask

⑩ **la mazza**
bat

⑪ **il paragambe**
leg pad

⑫ **il battitore** *m / f*
batter / batsman

111.3 I VERBI DEL CRICKET • CRICKET VERBS

① **correre**
to run

② **lanciare**
to bowl

③ **battere**
to bat

④ **prendere la palla**
to field

⑤ **essere eliminato** *m*
essere eliminata *f*
to strike out

⑥ **eliminare colpendo il wicket**
to stump

112 Il basket e la pallavolo

Basketball and volleyball

112.1 IL BASKET • BASKETBALL

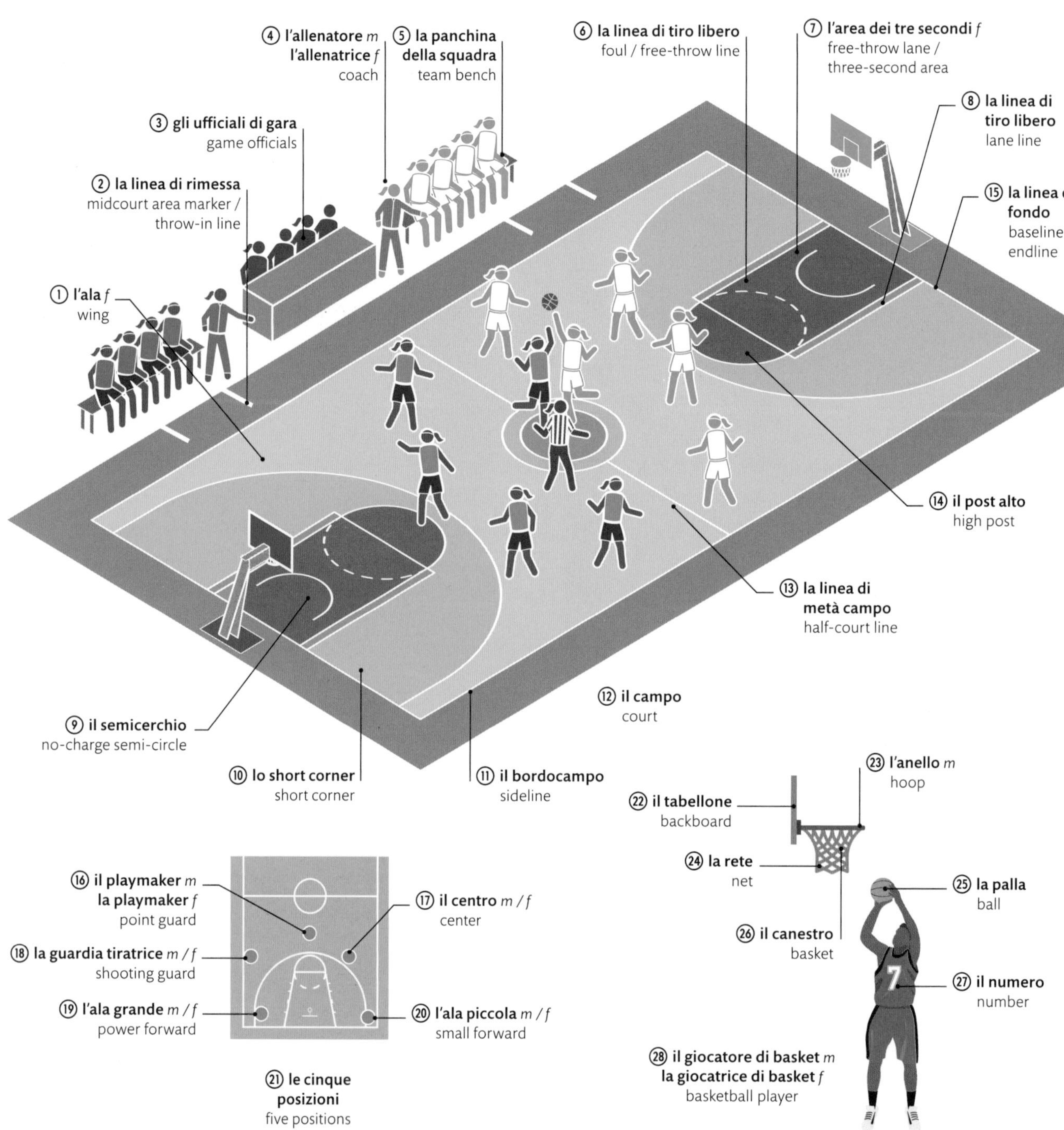

① l'ala f
wing
② la linea di rimessa
midcourt area marker / throw-in line
③ gli ufficiali di gara
game officials
④ l'allenatore m
l'allenatrice f
coach
⑤ la panchina della squadra
team bench
⑥ la linea di tiro libero
foul / free-throw line
⑦ l'area dei tre secondi f
free-throw lane / three-second area
⑧ la linea di tiro libero
lane line
⑨ il semicerchio
no-charge semi-circle
⑩ lo short corner
short corner
⑪ il bordocampo
sideline
⑫ il campo
court
⑬ la linea di metà campo
half-court line
⑭ il post alto
high post
⑮ la linea di fondo
baseline / endline
⑯ il playmaker m
la playmaker f
point guard
⑰ il centro m / f
center
⑱ la guardia tiratrice m / f
shooting guard
⑲ l'ala grande m / f
power forward
⑳ l'ala piccola m / f
small forward
㉑ le cinque posizioni
five positions
㉒ il tabellone
backboard
㉓ l'anello m
hoop
㉔ la rete
net
㉕ la palla
ball
㉖ il canestro
basket
㉗ il numero
number
㉘ il giocatore di basket m
la giocatrice di basket f
basketball player
7

See also
107 Il football americano • American football **108** Il rugby • Rugby **109** Il calcio • Soccer **124** In palestra • At the gym **125** Gli altri sport • Other sports

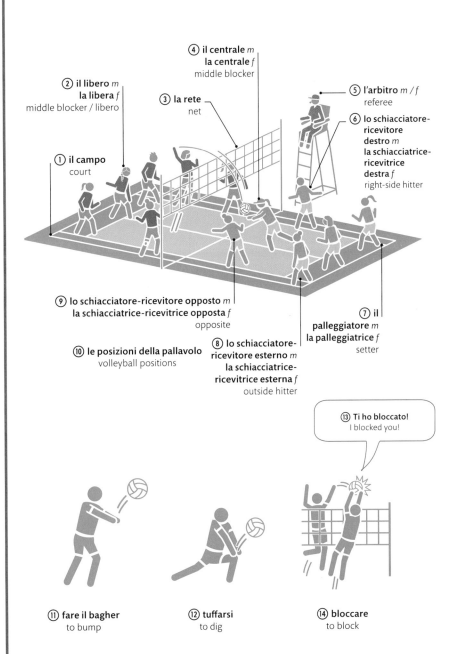

㉙ **passare**
pass

㉚ **il fuori campo**
out of bounds

㉛ **la rimessa**
throw-in

㉜ **il rimbalzo**
rebound

㉝ **l'airball** *m*
airball

㉞ **il salto a due**
jump ball

㉟ **il fallo**
foul

㊱ **marcare**
to mark

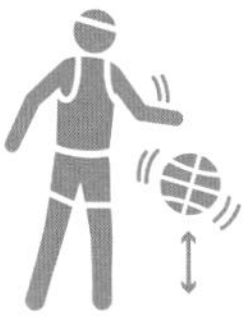

㊲ **palleggiare**
to bounce

㊳ **schiacciare**
to dunk

㊴ **tirare**
to shoot

㊵ **bloccare**
to block

112.2 LA PALLAVOLO • VOLLEYBALL

① **il campo**
court

② **il libero** *m*
la libera *f*
middle blocker / libero

③ **la rete**
net

④ **il centrale** *m*
la centrale *f*
middle blocker

⑤ **l'arbitro** *m / f*
referee

⑥ **lo schiacciatore-ricevitore destro** *m*
la schiacciatrice-ricevitrice destra *f*
right-side hitter

⑦ **il palleggiatore** *m*
la palleggiatrice *f*
setter

⑧ **lo schiacciatore-ricevitore esterno** *m*
la schiacciatrice-ricevitrice esterna *f*
outside hitter

⑨ **lo schiacciatore-ricevitore opposto** *m*
la schiacciatrice-ricevitrice opposta *f*
opposite

⑩ **le posizioni della pallavolo**
volleyball positions

⑪ **fare il bagher**
to bump

⑫ **tuffarsi**
to dig

⑬ **Ti ho bloccato!**
I blocked you!

⑭ **bloccare**
to block

113 Il baseball
Baseball

113.1 LA PARTITA DI BASEBALL · BASEBALL GAME

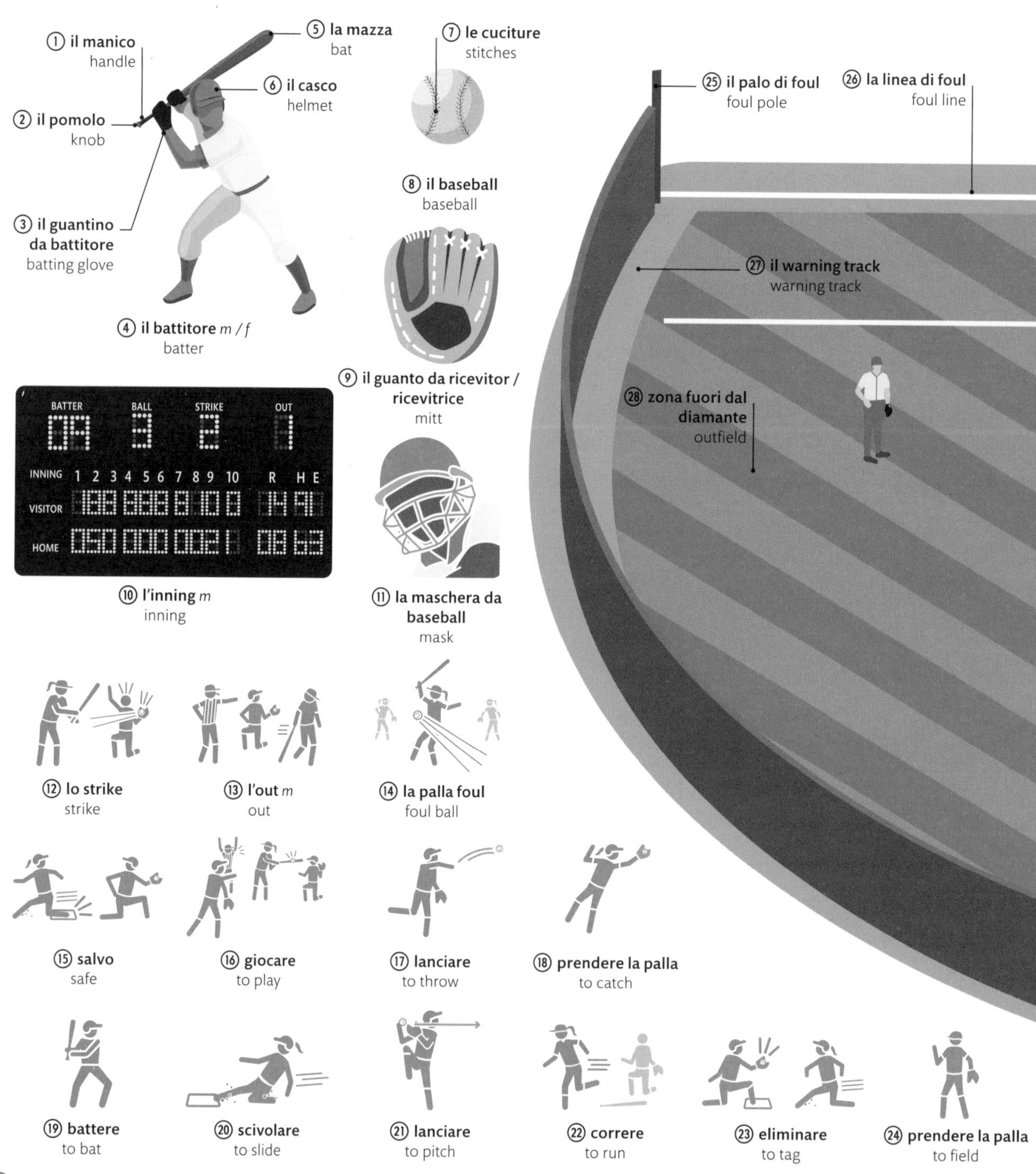

① il manico
handle
② il pomolo
knob
③ il guantino da battitore
batting glove
④ il battitore m / f
batter
⑤ la mazza
bat
⑥ il casco
helmet
⑦ le cuciture
stitches
⑧ il baseball
baseball
⑨ il guanto da ricevitor / ricevitrice
mitt
BATTER
BALL
STRIKE
OUT
INNING 1 2 3 4 5 6 7 8 9 10 R H E
VISITOR
HOME
⑩ l'inning m
inning
⑪ la maschera da baseball
mask
⑫ lo strike
strike
⑬ l'out m
out
⑭ la palla foul
foul ball
⑮ salvo
safe
⑯ giocare
to play
⑰ lanciare
to throw
⑱ prendere la palla
to catch
⑲ battere
to bat
⑳ scivolare
to slide
㉑ lanciare
to pitch
㉒ correre
to run
㉓ eliminare
to tag
㉔ prendere la palla
to field
㉕ il palo di foul
foul pole
㉖ la linea di foul
foul line
㉗ il warning track
warning track
㉘ zona fuori dal diamante
outfield

See also
107 Il football americano • American football **110** L'hockey e il lacrosse • Hockey and lacrosse **111** Il cricket • Cricket **112** Il basket e la pallavolo • Basketball and volleyball

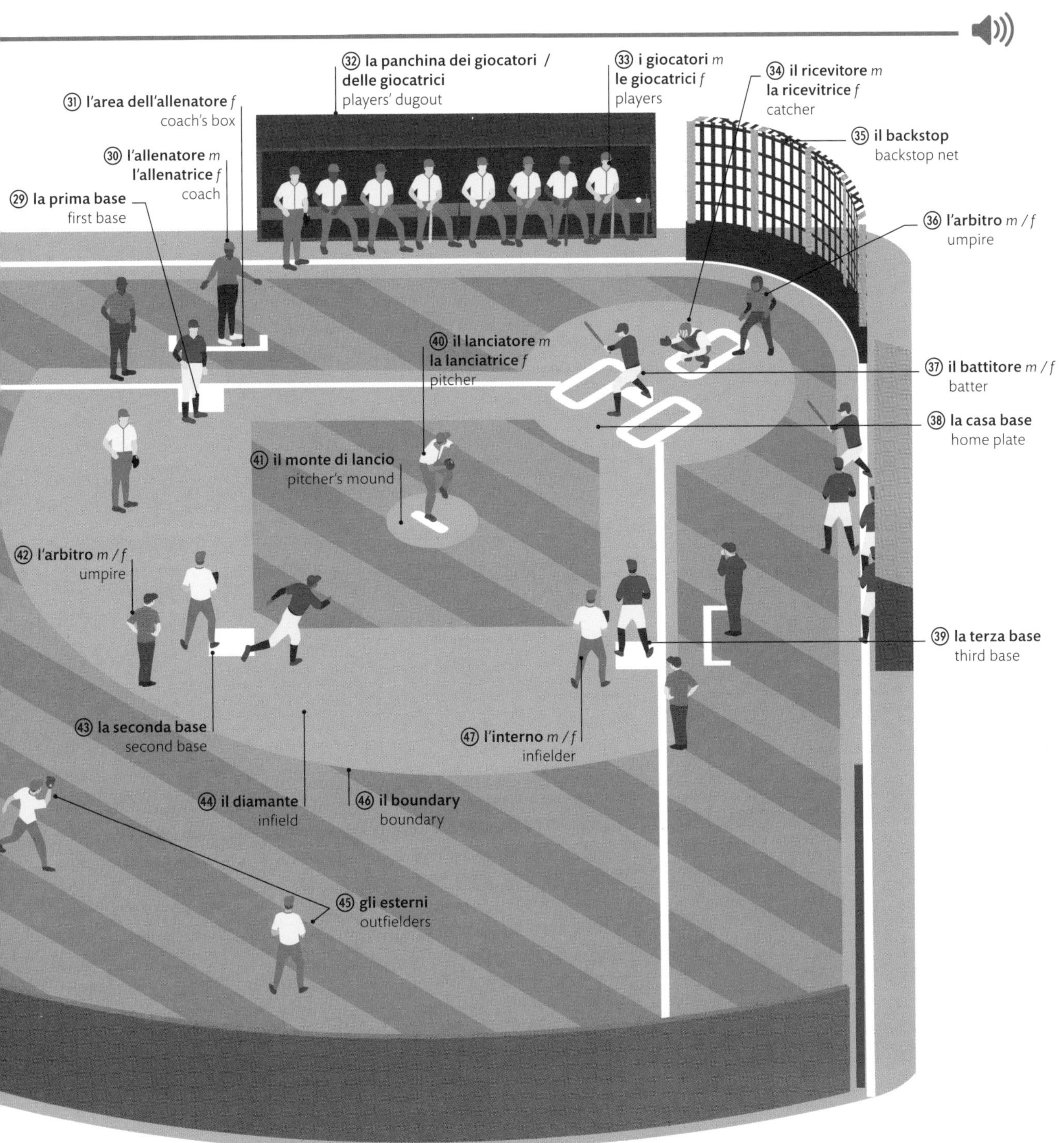
29 la prima base
first base
30 l'allenatore m
l'allenatrice f
coach
31 l'area dell'allenatore f
coach's box
32 la panchina dei giocatori / delle giocatrici
players' dugout
33 i giocatori m
le giocatrici f
players
34 il ricevitore m
la ricevitrice f
catcher
35 il backstop
backstop net
36 l'arbitro m / f
umpire
37 il battitore m / f
batter
38 la casa base
home plate
39 la terza base
third base
40 il lanciatore m
la lanciatrice f
pitcher
41 il monte di lancio
pitcher's mound
42 l'arbitro m / f
umpire
43 la seconda base
second base
44 il diamante
infield
45 gli esterni
outfielders
46 il boundary
boundary
47 l'interno m / f
infielder

48 il campo da baseball
baseball field

114 Il tennis
Tennis

114.1 L'INCONTRO DI TENNIS • TENNIS MATCH

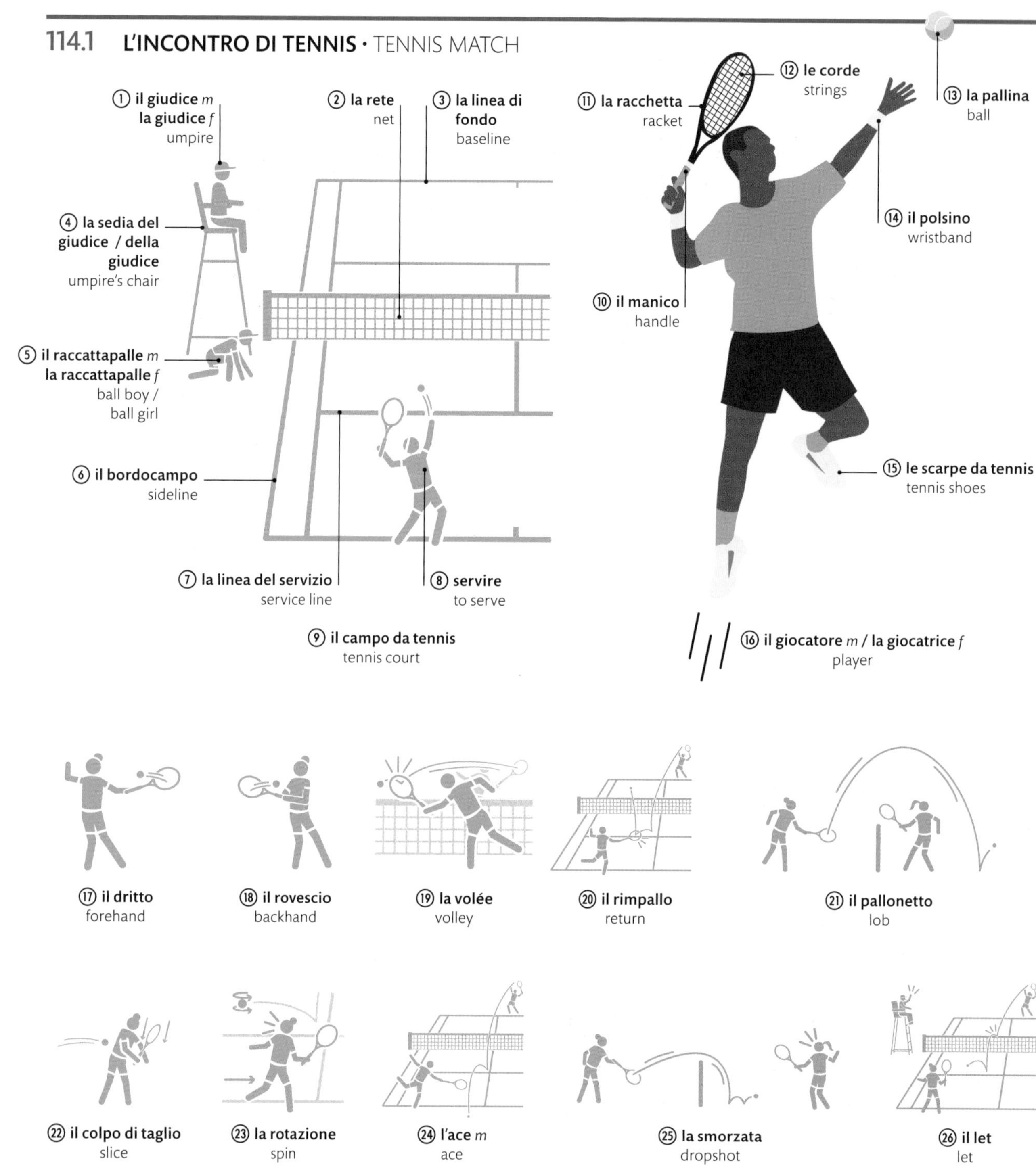

① il giudice *m*
la giudice *f*
umpire
② la rete
net
③ la linea di fondo
baseline
④ la sedia del giudice / della giudice
umpire's chair
⑤ il raccattapalle *m*
la raccattapalle *f*
ball boy / ball girl
⑥ il bordocampo
sideline
⑦ la linea del servizio
service line
⑧ servire
to serve
⑨ il campo da tennis
tennis court
⑩ il manico
handle
⑪ la racchetta
racket
⑫ le corde
strings
⑬ la pallina
ball
⑭ il polsino
wristband
⑮ le scarpe da tennis
tennis shoes
⑯ il giocatore *m* / la giocatrice *f*
player
⑰ il dritto
forehand
⑱ il rovescio
backhand
⑲ la volée
volley
⑳ il rimpallo
return
㉑ il pallonetto
lob
㉒ il colpo di taglio
slice
㉓ la rotazione
spin
㉔ l'ace *m*
ace
㉕ la smorzata
dropshot
㉖ il let
let

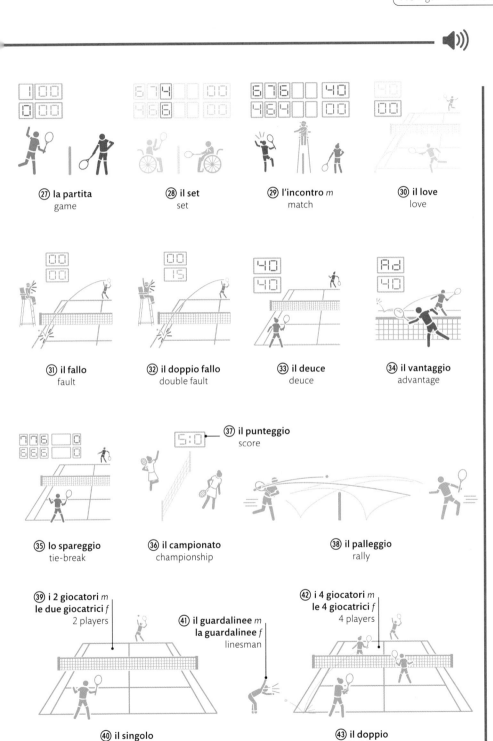

See also
111 Il cricket • Cricket **113** Il baseball • Baseball
115 Il golf • Golf **116** L'atletica • Athletics

(27) **la partita**
game

(28) **il set**
set

(29) **l'incontro** *m*
match

(30) **il love**
love

(31) **il fallo**
fault

(32) **il doppio fallo**
double fault

(33) **il deuce**
deuce

(34) **il vantaggio**
advantage

(35) **lo spareggio**
tie-break

(36) **il campionato**
championship

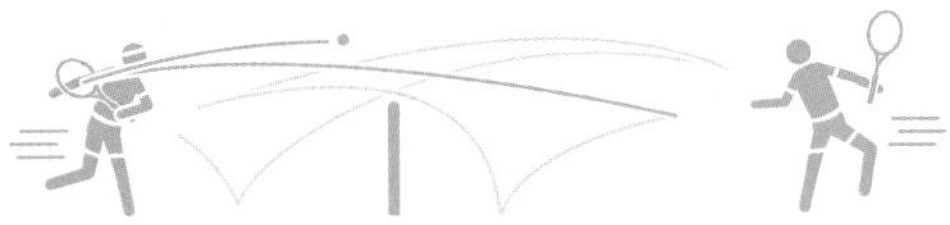

(37) **il punteggio**
score

(38) **il palleggio**
rally

(39) **i 2 giocatori** *m*
le due giocatrici *f*
2 players

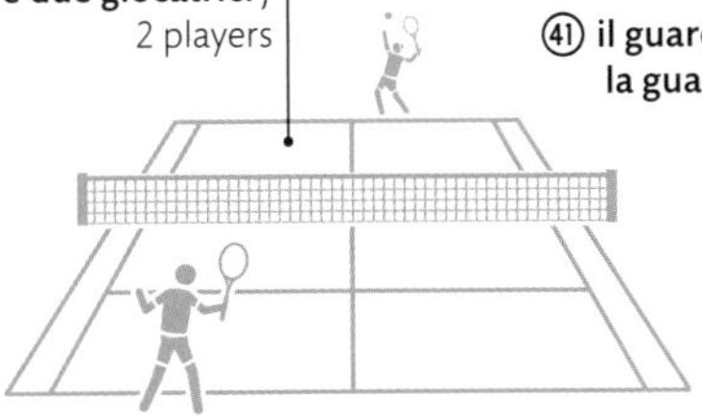

(40) **il singolo**
singles

(41) **il guardalinee** *m*
la guardalinee *f*
linesman

(42) **i 4 giocatori** *m*
le 4 giocatrici *f*
4 players

(43) **il doppio**
doubles

114.2 I GIOCHI CON LE RACCHETTE
RACKET GAMES

(1) **lo squash**
squash

(2) **il racquetball**
racquetball

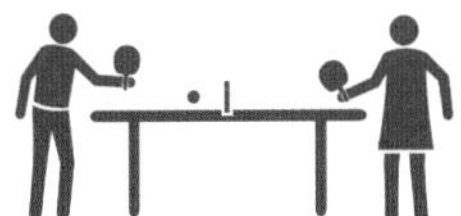

(3) **il ping pong**
ping pong /
table tennis

(4) **il paddle**
paddle

(5) **il badminton**
badminton

(6) **il volano**
shuttlecock

115 Il golf
Golf

115.1 SUL CAMPO DA GOLF · ON THE GOLF COURSE

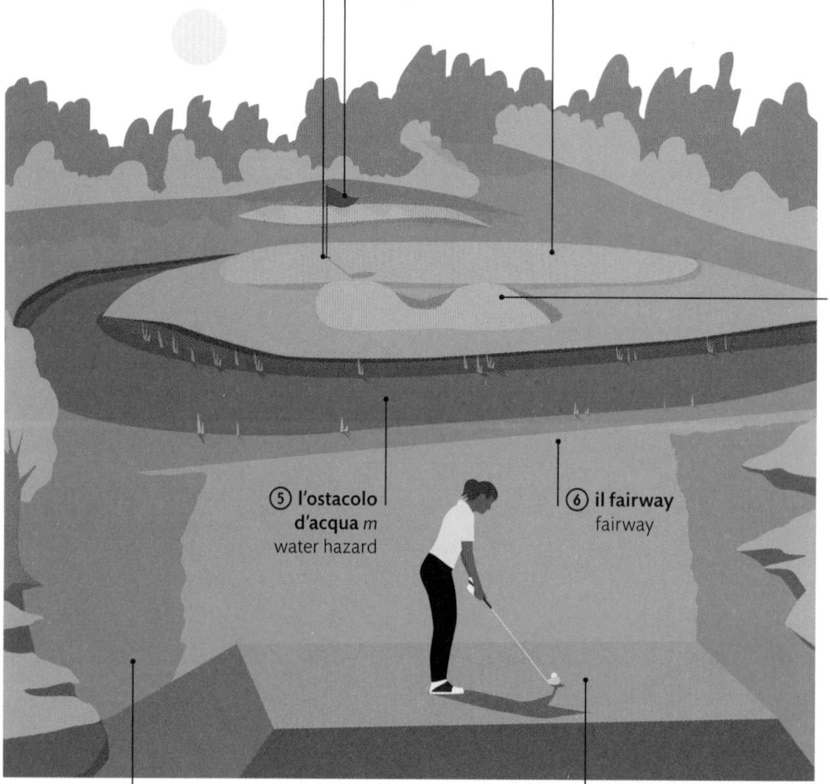

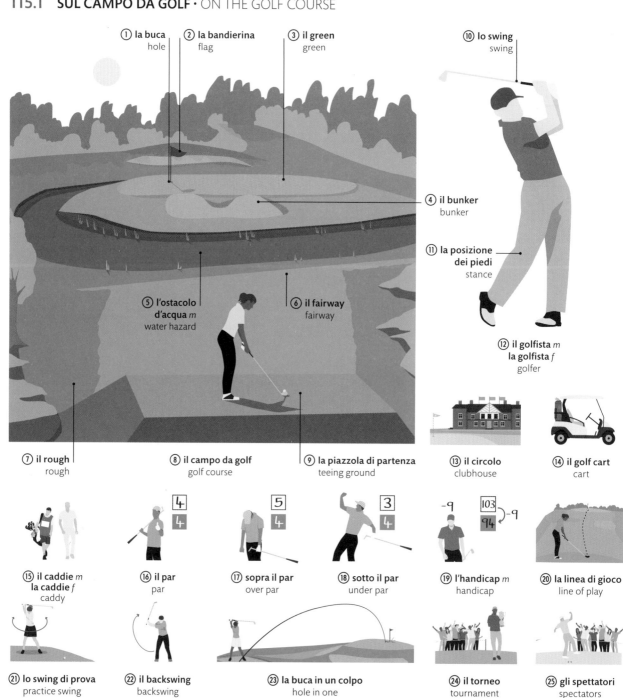

1. **la buca** hole
2. **la bandierina** flag
3. **il green** green
4. **il bunker** bunker
5. **l'ostacolo d'acqua** *m* water hazard
6. **il fairway** fairway
7. **il rough** rough
8. **il campo da golf** golf course
9. **la piazzola di partenza** teeing ground
10. **lo swing** swing 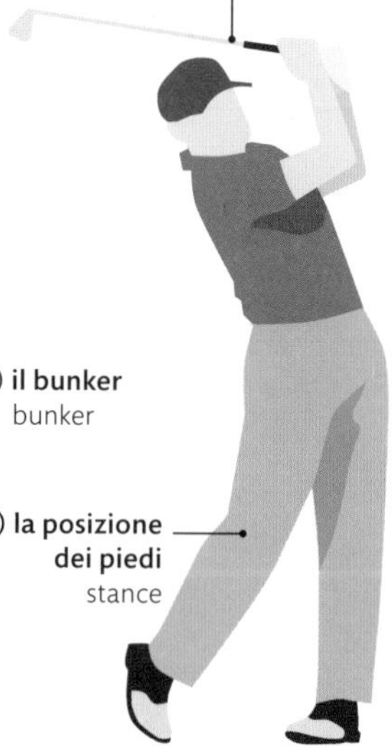
11. **la posizione dei piedi** stance
12. **il golfista** *m* **la golfista** *f* golfer
13. **il circolo** clubhouse 
14. **il golf cart** cart 
15. **il caddie** *m* **la caddie** *f* caddy 
16. **il par** par 
17. **sopra il par** over par 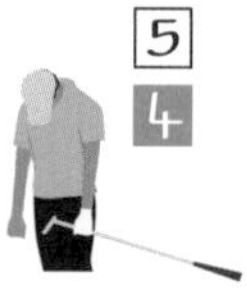
18. **sotto il par** under par 
19. **l'handicap** *m* handicap 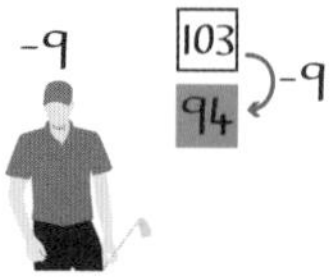
20. **la linea di gioco** line of play 
21. **lo swing di prova** practice swing 
22. **il backswing** backswing 
23. **la buca in un colpo** hole in one 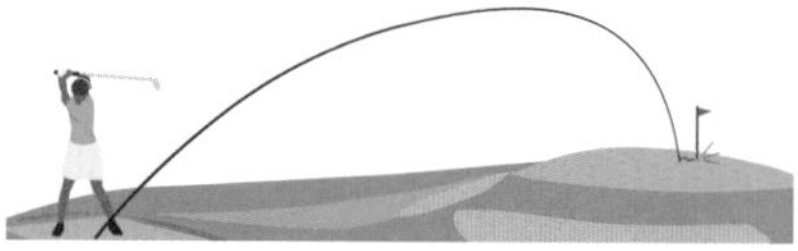
24. **il torneo** tournament 
25. **gli spettatori** spectators

See also
111 Il cricket • Cricket **113** Il baseball
Baseball **114** Il tennis • Tennis

115.2 L'ATTREZZATURA DA GOLF
GOLF EQUIPMENT

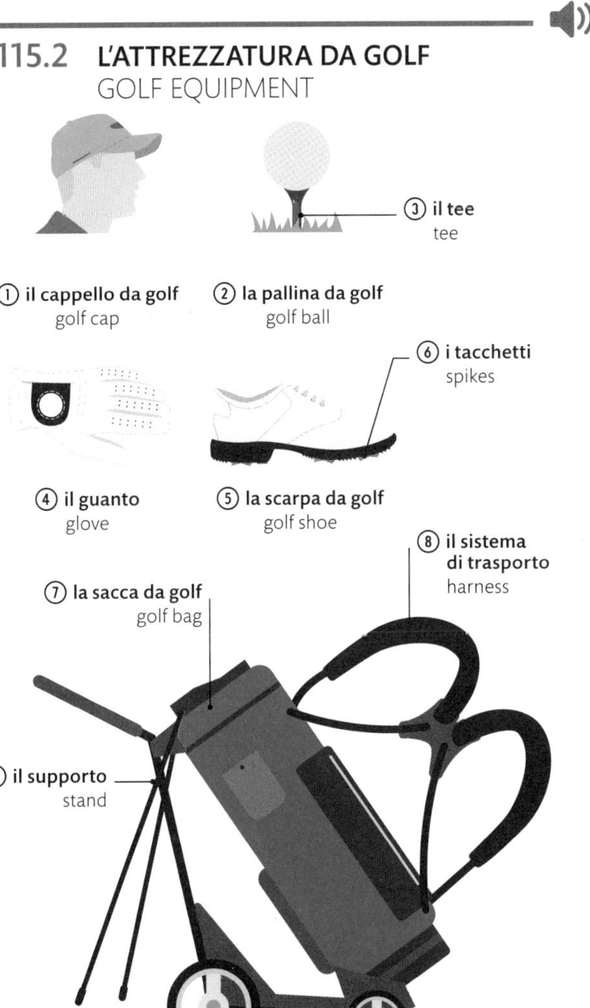
③ il tee
tee
① il cappello da golf
golf cap
② la pallina da golf
golf ball
⑥ i tacchetti
spikes
④ il guanto
glove
⑤ la scarpa da golf
golf shoe
⑧ il sistema di trasporto
harness
⑦ la sacca da golf
golf bag
⑨ il supporto
stand
⑩ il carrello per sacca da golf
golf push cart

115.3 LE MAZZE DA GOLF • GOLF CLUBS

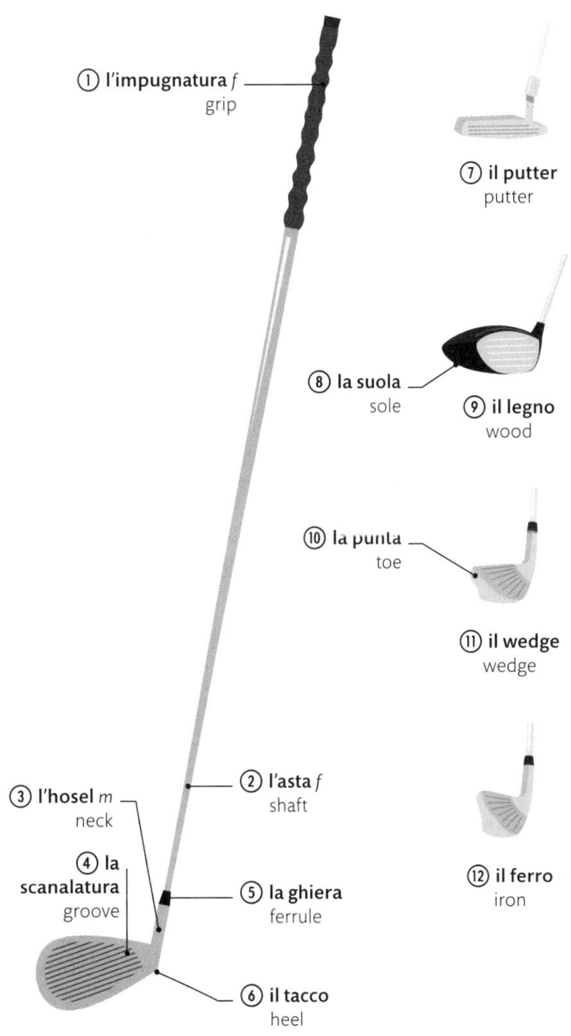
① l'impugnatura *f*
grip
⑦ il putter
putter
⑧ la suola
sole
⑨ il legno
wood
⑩ la punta
toe
⑪ il wedge
wedge
③ l'hosel *m*
neck
② l'asta *f*
shaft
④ la scanalatura
groove
⑤ la ghiera
ferrule
⑫ il ferro
iron
⑥ il tacco
heel

115.4 I VERBI DEL GOLF • GOLF VERBS

① **iniziare una partita**
to tee off

② **tirare il drive**
to drive

③ **fare uno swing**
to swing

④ **puttare**
to putt

⑤ **tirare un chip**
to chip

⑥ **vincere**
to win

116 L'atletica
Athletics

116.1 LA PISTA DI ATLETICA · ATHLETICS TRACK

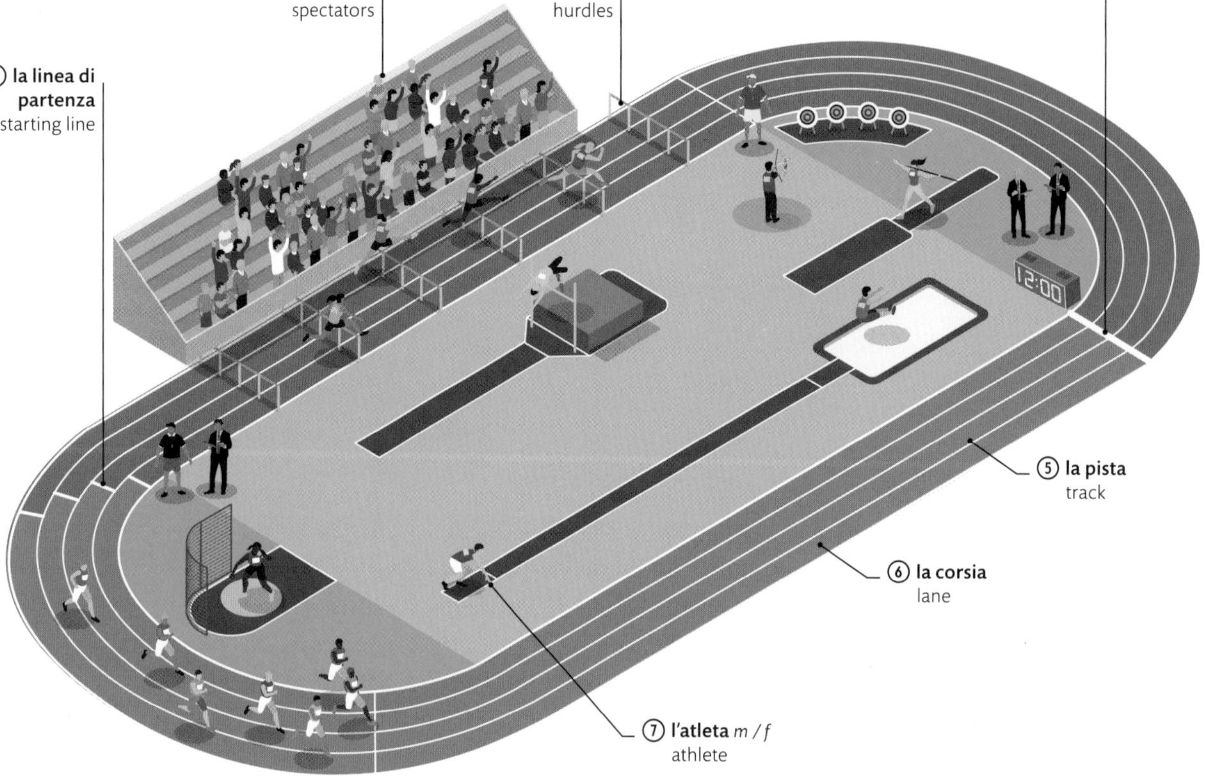

① **la linea di partenza**
starting line

② **gli spettatori**
spectators

③ **gli ostacoli**
hurdles

④ **il traguardo**
finish line

⑤ **la pista**
track

⑥ **la corsia**
lane

⑦ **l'atleta** *m / f*
athlete

116.2 LE GARE DI CORSA · RACING EVENTS

① **la gara**
race

② **il blocco di partenza**
starting block

③ **il velocista** *m*
la velocista *f*
sprinter

④ **la corsa T11 (per atleti non vedenti)**
T11 (visual impairment) race

⑤ **la corsa in carrozzina**
wheelchair race

⑥ **la staffetta**
relay race

⑦ **il testimone**
baton

⑧ **la maratona**
marathon

⑨ **il fotofinish**
photo finish

See also
117 Gli sport da combattimento • Combat sports **118** Il nuoto • Swimming **119** La vela e gli sport acquatici • Sailing and watersports **120** L'equitazione • Horseback riding **122** Gli sport invernali • Winter sports **124** In palestra • At the gym **125** Gli altri sport • Other sports

116.3 L'ATLETICA LEGGERA • FIELD EVENTS

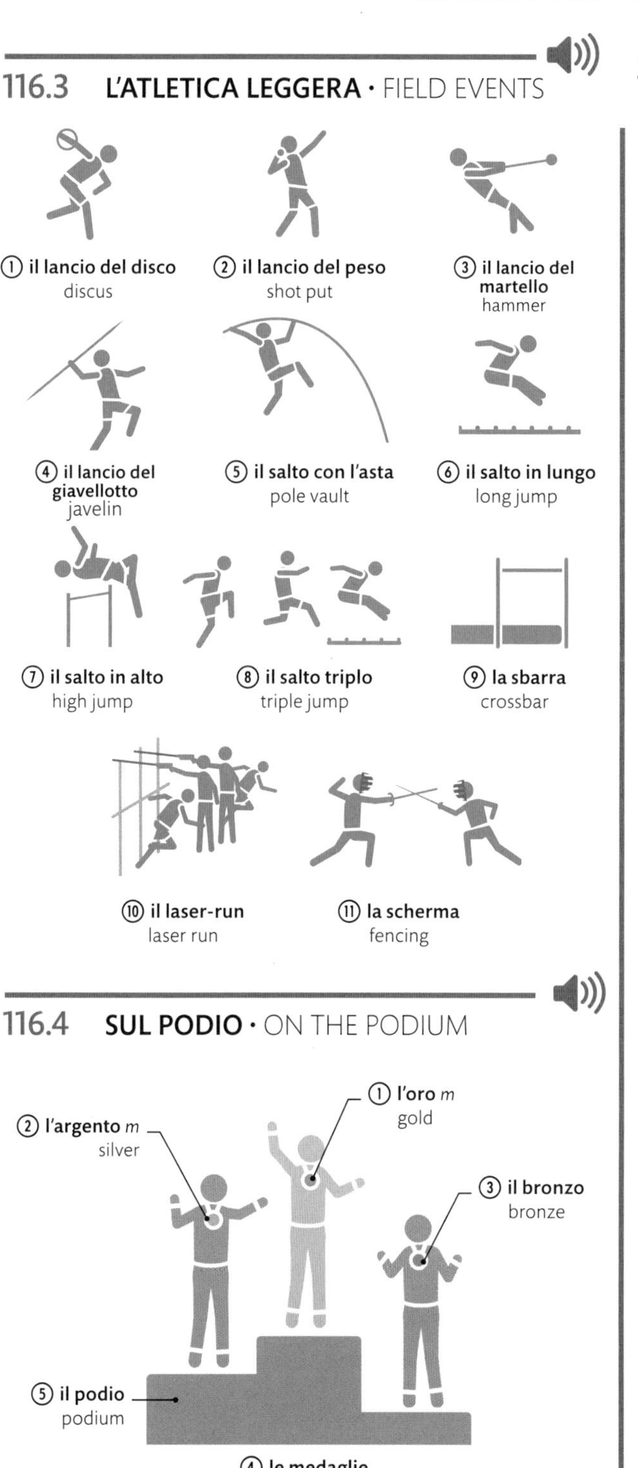

① **il lancio del disco**
discus

② **il lancio del peso**
shot put

③ **il lancio del martello**
hammer

④ **il lancio del giavellotto**
javelin

⑤ **il salto con l'asta**
pole vault

⑥ **il salto in lungo**
long jump

⑦ **il salto in alto**
high jump

⑧ **il salto triplo**
triple jump

⑨ **la sbarra**
crossbar

⑩ **il laser-run**
laser run

⑪ **la scherma**
fencing

116.4 SUL PODIO • ON THE PODIUM

① **l'oro** *m*
gold

② **l'argento** *m*
silver

③ **il bronzo**
bronze

④ **le medaglie**
medals

⑤ **il podio**
podium

116.5 LE PROVE MULTIPLE
COMBINED EVENTS

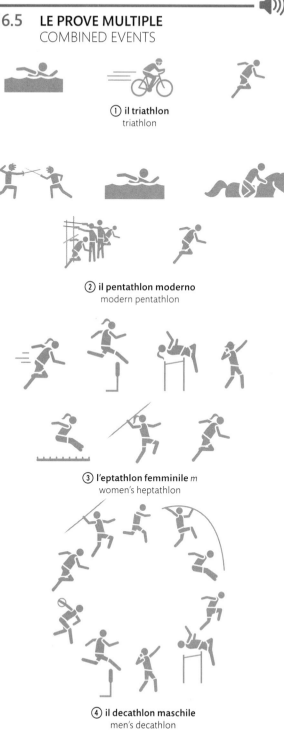

① **il triathlon**
triathlon

② **il pentathlon moderno**
modern pentathlon

③ **l'eptathlon femminile** *m*
women's heptathlon

④ **il decathlon maschile**
men's decathlon

117 Gli sport da combattimento
Combat sports

117.1 LE ARTI MARZIALI • MARTIAL ARTS

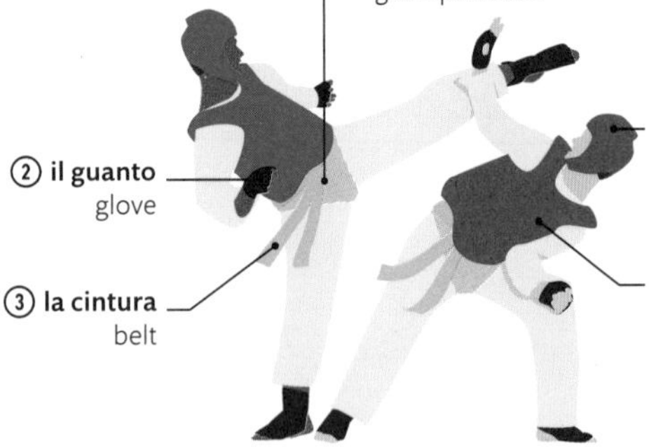

① **la protezione inguinale** groin protector
② **il guanto** glove
③ **la cintura** belt
④ **il casco** head guard
⑤ **la protezione per il torace** chest protection
⑥ **il taekwondo** taekwondo
⑦ **la cintura nera** black belt 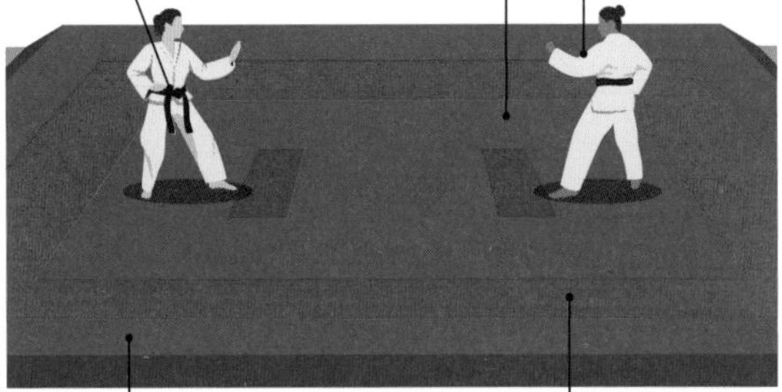
⑧ **il tatami** karate mat
⑨ **l'avversario** *m* **l'avversaria** *f* opponent
⑩ **la zona di sicurezza** safety area
⑪ **il karate** karate
⑫ **la zona di pericolo** danger area
⑬ **il judo** judo 
⑭ **l'aikido** *m* aikido 
⑮ **l'hakama** *m* hakama
⑯ **il kung fu** kung fu 
⑰ **il jujitsu** jujitsu 
⑱ **la capoeira** capoeira 
⑲ **il kickboxing** kickboxing 
⑳ **il tai chi** tai chi 
㉑ **il wrestling** wrestling 
㉒ **il sumo** sumo wrestling 
㉓ **la maschera protettiva** mask 
㉔ **la spada** sword
㉕ **il kendo** kendo

117.2 LE AZIONI • ACTIONS

① **cadere** to fall

② **tenere** to hold

③ **lanciare** to throw

④ **bloccare** to pin

⑤ **il calcio frontale** front kick

⑥ **il calcio volante** flying kick

See also
116 L'atletica • Athletics **124** In palestra At the gym **125** Gli altri sport • Other sports

117.3 LA BOXE • BOXING

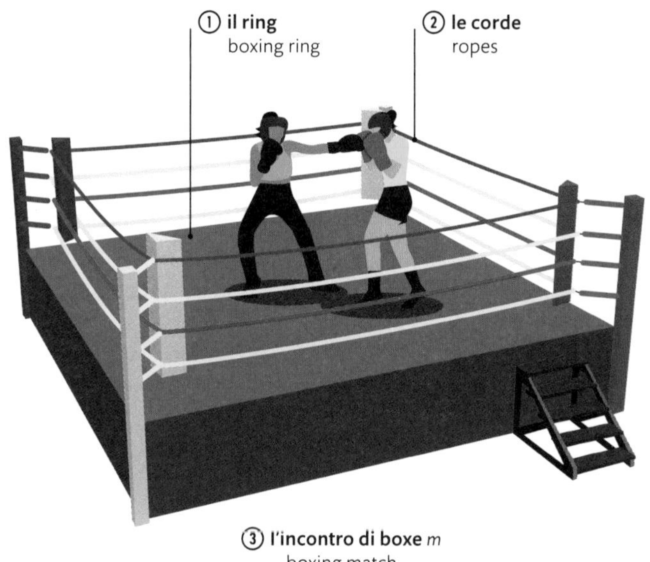

① **il ring**
boxing ring

② **le corde**
ropes

③ **l'incontro di boxe** *m*
boxing match

1

④ **il round**
round

⑤ **il K.O.**
knock out

⑥ **i guanti da boxe**
boxing gloves

⑦ **il paradenti**
mouth guard

⑧ **il sacco da boxe**
punching bag

117.4 LA SCHERMA • FENCING

① **affondare**
to lunge

② **parare**
to parry

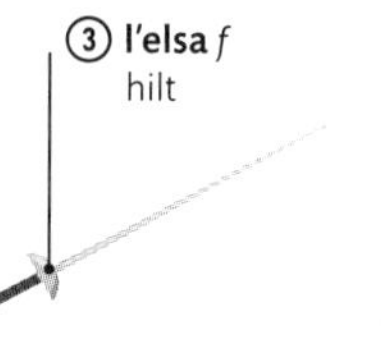

③ **l'elsa** *f*
hilt

④ **il fioretto**
foil

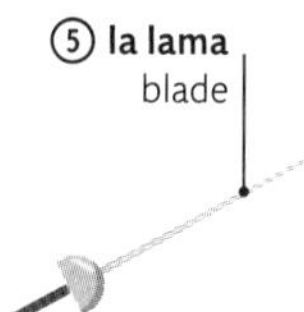

⑤ **la lama**
blade

⑥ **la spada**
épée

⑦ **la sciabola**
saber

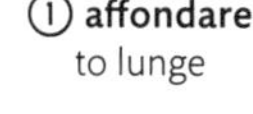

⑦ **colpire con un pugno**
to punch

⑧ **colpire**
to strike

⑨ **bloccare**
to block

⑩ **saltare**
to jump

⑪ **spaccare**
to chop

118 Il nuoto
Swimming

118.1 IL NUOTO • SWIMMING

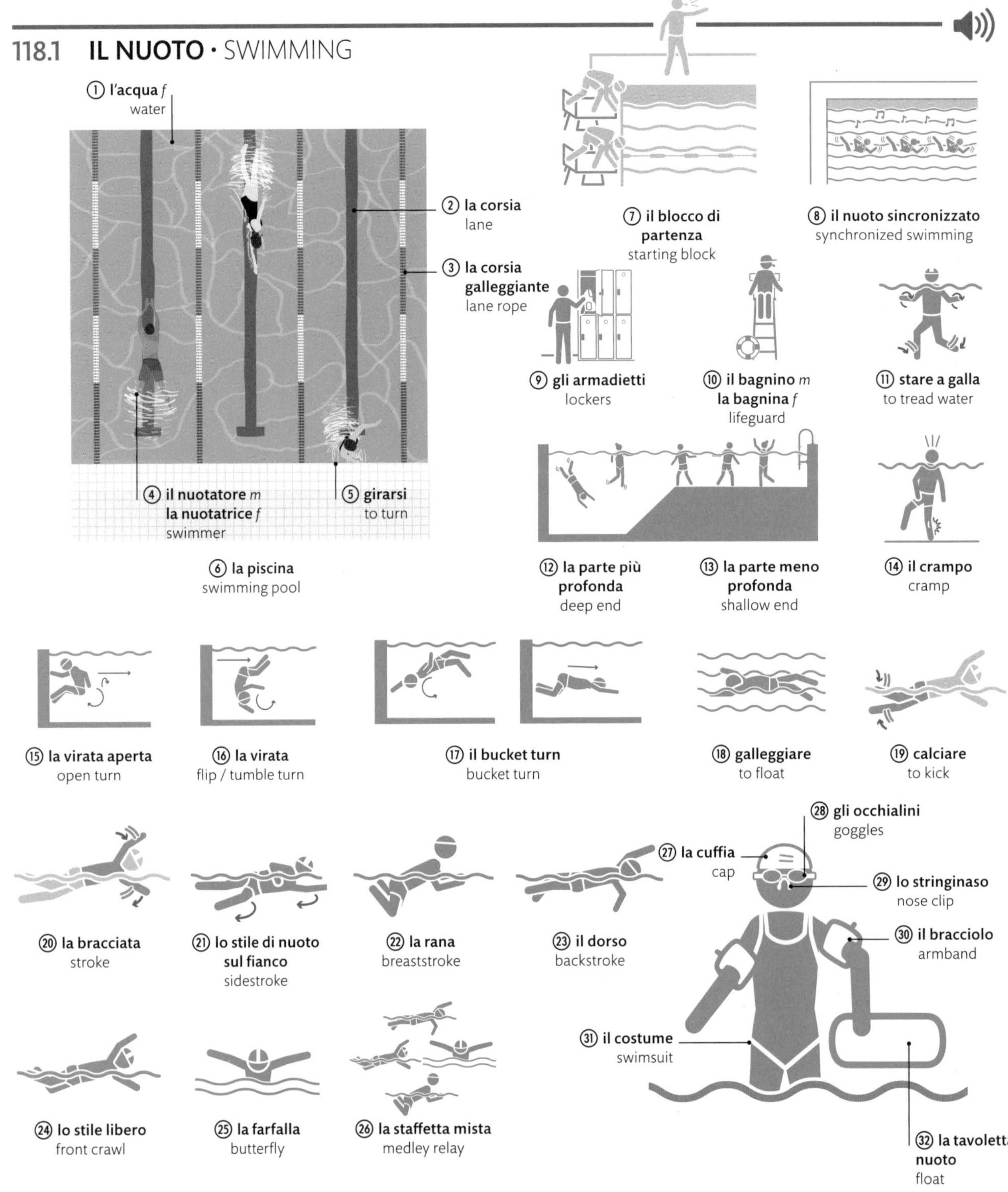

① l'acqua *f*
water
② la corsia
lane
③ la corsia galleggiante
lane rope
④ il nuotatore *m*
la nuotatrice *f*
swimmer
⑤ girarsi
to turn
⑥ la piscina
swimming pool
⑦ il blocco di partenza
starting block
⑧ il nuoto sincronizzato
synchronized swimming
⑨ gli armadietti
lockers
⑩ il bagnino *m*
la bagnina *f*
lifeguard
⑪ stare a galla
to tread water
⑫ la parte più profonda
deep end
⑬ la parte meno profonda
shallow end
⑭ il crampo
cramp
⑮ la virata aperta
open turn
⑯ la virata
flip / tumble turn
⑰ il bucket turn
bucket turn
⑱ galleggiare
to float
⑲ calciare
to kick
⑳ la bracciata
stroke
㉑ lo stile di nuoto sul fianco
sidestroke
㉒ la rana
breaststroke
㉓ il dorso
backstroke
㉔ lo stile libero
front crawl
㉕ la farfalla
butterfly
㉖ la staffetta mista
medley relay
㉗ la cuffia
cap
㉘ gli occhialini
goggles
㉙ lo stringinaso
nose clip
㉚ il bracciolo
armband
㉛ il costume
swimsuit
㉜ la tavoletta nuoto
float

See also
119 La vela e gli sport acquatici • Sailing and watersports
134 In spiaggia • On the beach **166** La vita negli oceani • Ocean life

118.2 I TUFFI
DIVING

il trampolino
diving board

② **tuffarsi**
to dive

③ **la gara di tuffi**
racing dive

④ **la piattaforma**
platform

⑤ **il trampolino**
diving tower

⑥ **il tuffo da grandi altezze**
high dive

⑦ **il tuffatore** *m*
la tuffatrice *f*
diver

⑧ **la capovolta in avanti**
front-flip

⑨ **la capriola all'indietro**
back-flip

⑩ **il tuffo di testa**
head-first

⑪ **il tuffo di piedi**
feet-first

⑫ **il trampolino**
springboard

118.3 LE IMMERSIONI • UNDERWATER DIVING

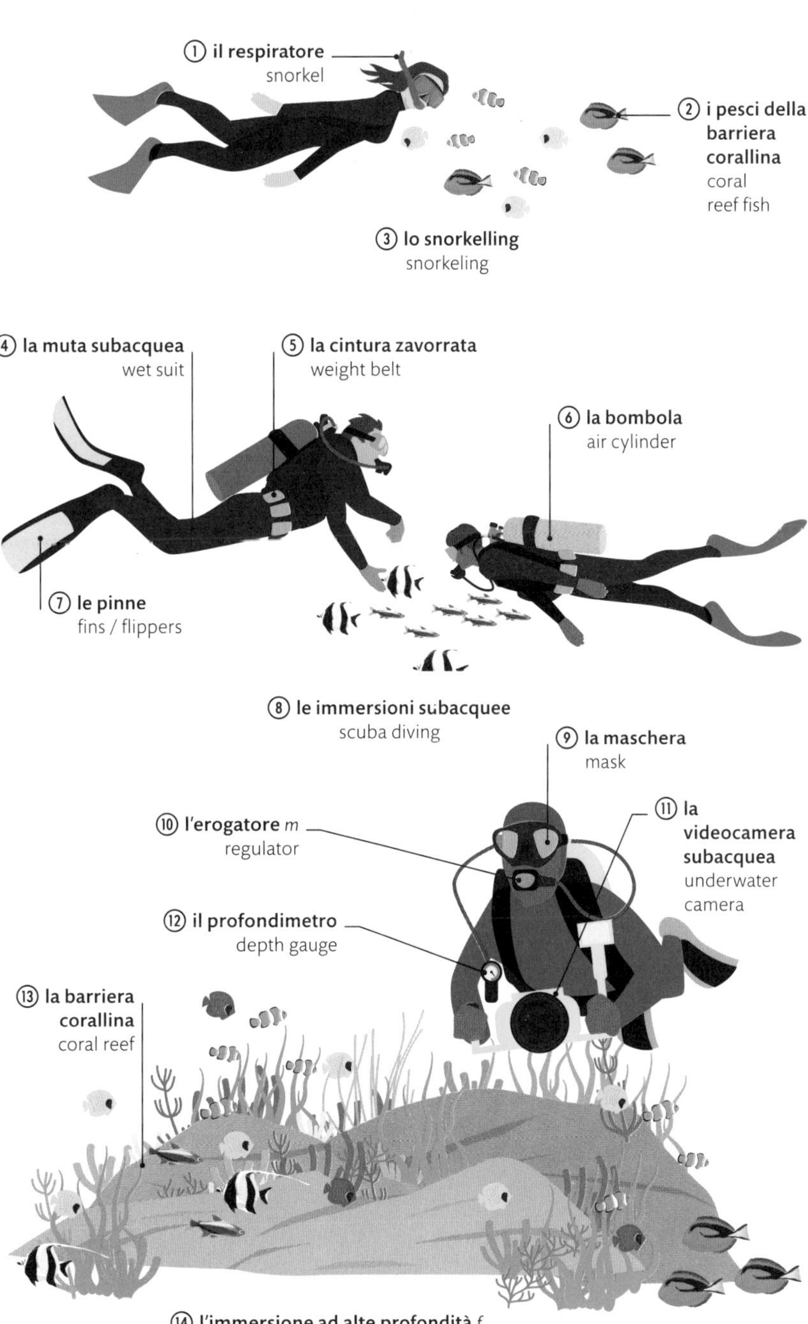
① il respiratore
snorkel
② i pesci della barriera corallina
coral reef fish
③ lo snorkelling
snorkeling
④ la muta subacquea
wet suit
⑤ la cintura zavorrata
weight belt
⑥ la bombola
air cylinder
⑦ le pinne
fins / flippers
⑧ le immersioni subacquee
scuba diving
⑨ la maschera
mask
⑩ l'erogatore m
regulator
⑪ la videocamera subacquea
underwater camera
⑫ il profondimetro
depth gauge
⑬ la barriera corallina
coral reef
⑭ l'immersione ad alte profondità f
deep diving

119 La vela e gli sport acquatici
Sailing and watertsports

119.1 LA VELA · SAILING

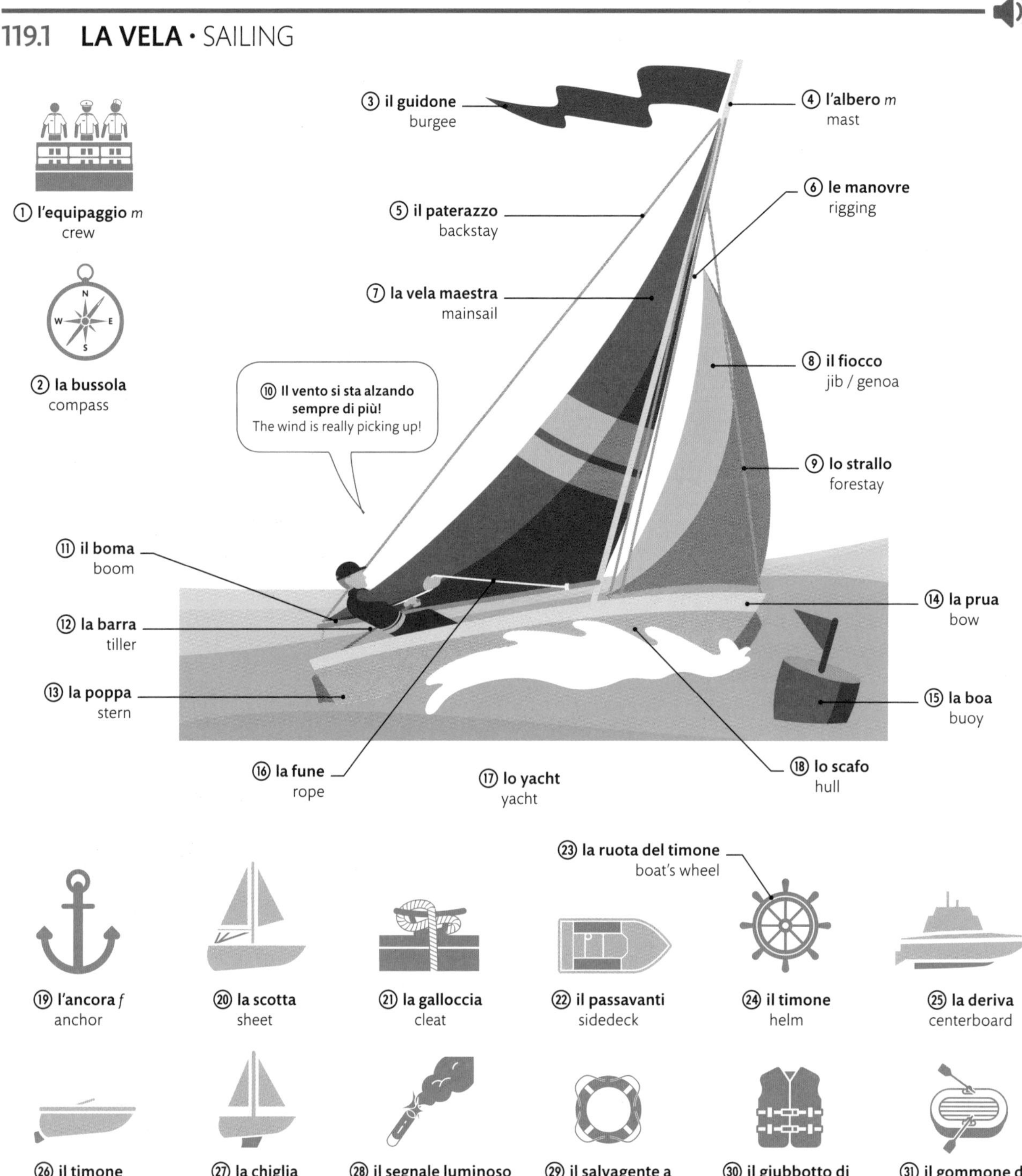

① l'equipaggio m
crew
② la bussola
compass
③ il guidone
burgee
④ l'albero m
mast
⑤ il paterazzo
backstay
⑥ le manovre
rigging
⑦ la vela maestra
mainsail
⑧ il fiocco
jib / genoa
⑨ lo strallo
forestay
⑩ Il vento si sta alzando sempre di più!
The wind is really picking up!
⑪ il boma
boom
⑫ la barra
tiller
⑬ la poppa
stern
⑭ la prua
bow
⑮ la boa
buoy
⑯ la fune
rope
⑰ lo yacht
yacht
⑱ lo scafo
hull
⑲ l'ancora f
anchor
⑳ la scotta
sheet
㉑ la galloccia
cleat
㉒ il passavanti
sidedeck
㉓ la ruota del timone
boat's wheel
㉔ il timone
helm
㉕ la deriva
centerboard
㉖ il timone
rudder
㉗ la chiglia
keel
㉘ il segnale luminoso
flare
㉙ il salvagente a ciambella
life preserver
㉚ il giubbotto di salvataggio
life jacket
㉛ il gommone di salvataggio
life raft

See also
105 Le imbarcazioni • Sea vessels **106** Il porto • The port **118** Il nuoto Swimming **121** La pesca • Fishing **134** In spiaggia • On the beach

119.2 GLI SPORT D'ACQUA • WATERSPORTS

il canottiere
rower
③ il remo
oar
② il canottaggio
rowing
④ il kayak
kayak
⑥ la pagaia
paddle
⑤ andare in kayak
kayaking
⑨ il surf
surfboard
⑦ il surfista m
la surfista f
surfer
⑧ la tavola da surf
surfing
⑩ il
oogie-board
boogie board
⑪ il bodyboarding
bodyboarding
⑫ il paddle-boarding
paddleboarding
⑬ il parasailing
parasailing
⑭ il kitesurf
kite surfing
⑳ lo sci
ski
㉑ lo sciatore d'acqua m
la sciatrice d'acqua f
water skier
⑮ andare in motoscafo
speed boating
⑯ il rafting
rafting
⑰ andare in moto d'acqua
jet skiing
⑱ la pallanuoto
water polo
⑲ lo sci d'acqua
water skiing
㉒ ribaltarsi
to capsize
㉓ navigare
to navigate
㉔ virare
to tack
㉚ il surfista m
la surfista f
windsurfer
㉛ la vela
sail
㉙ la tavola
board
㉝ il boma
boom
㉜ la cinghia fermapiedi
foot strap
㉘ il windsurf
windsurfing
㉗ la schiuma
surf
㉖ le rapide
rapids
㉕ l'onda f
wave

120 L'equitazione
Horseback riding

120.1 L'EQUITAZIONE · HORSEBACK RIDING

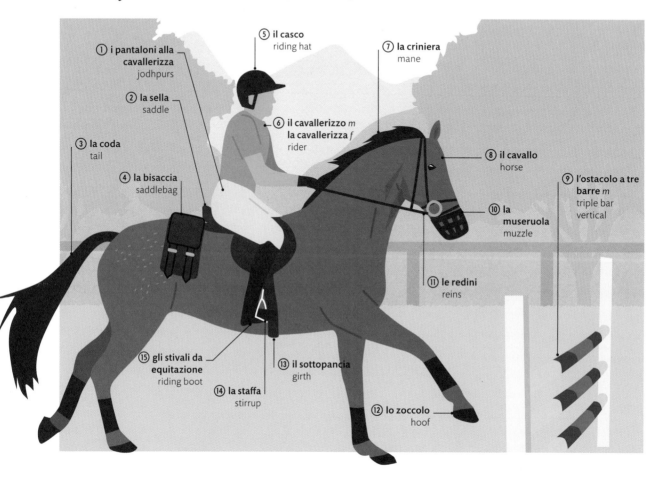

1. **i pantaloni alla cavallerizza** jodhpurs
2. **la sella** saddle
3. **la coda** tail
4. **la bisaccia** saddlebag
5. **il casco** riding hat
6. **il cavallerizzo** *m* **la cavallerizza** *f* rider
7. **la criniera** mane
8. **il cavallo** horse
9. **l'ostacolo a tre barre** *m* triple bar vertical
10. **la museruola** muzzle
11. **le redini** reins
12. **lo zoccolo** hoof
13. **il sottopancia** girth
14. **la staffa** stirrup
15. **gli stivali da equitazione** riding boot

16. **il ferro di cavallo** horseshoe

17. **la cavezza** halter

18. **la museruola** noseband

19. **il morso** bit

20. **il frontalino** browband

21. **le briglie** bridle

22. **il pomolo** pommel

23. **la sella** seat

24. **il frustino** riding crop

5

25. **il fantino** jockey

5

26. **il cavallo da corsa** racehorse

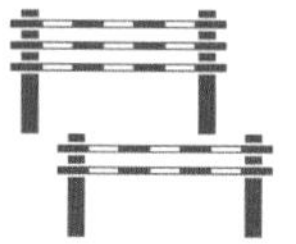

27. **gli ostacoli** verticals

See also
116 L'atletica · Athletics 125 Gli altri sport · Other sports 133 Le attività all'aperto · Outdoor activities

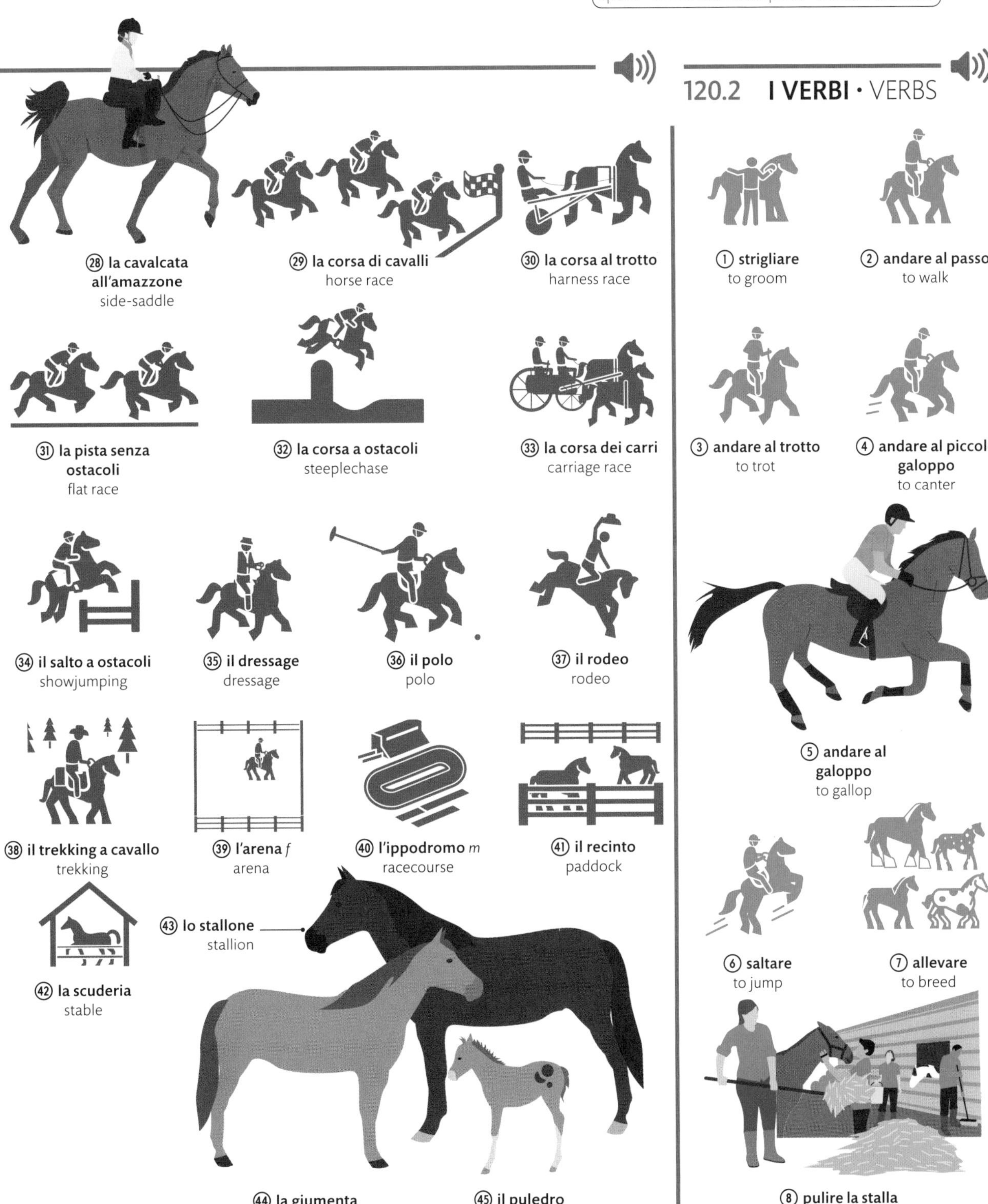
㉘ la cavalcata all'amazzone
side-saddle
㉙ la corsa di cavalli
horse race
㉚ la corsa al trotto
harness race
㉛ la pista senza ostacoli
flat race
㉜ la corsa a ostacoli
steeplechase
㉝ la corsa dei carri
carriage race
㉞ il salto a ostacoli
showjumping
㉟ il dressage
dressage
㊱ il polo
polo
㊲ il rodeo
rodeo
㊳ il trekking a cavallo
trekking
㊴ l'arena *f*
arena
㊵ l'ippodromo *m*
racecourse
㊶ il recinto
paddock
㊷ la scuderia
stable
㊸ lo stallone
stallion
㊹ la giumenta
mare
㊺ il puledro
foal

120.2 I VERBI · VERBS

① strigliare
to groom
② andare al passo
to walk
③ andare al trotto
to trot
④ andare al piccolo galoppo
to canter
⑤ andare al galoppo
to gallop
⑥ saltare
to jump
⑦ allevare
to breed
⑧ pulire la stalla
to muck out

121 La pesca
Fishing

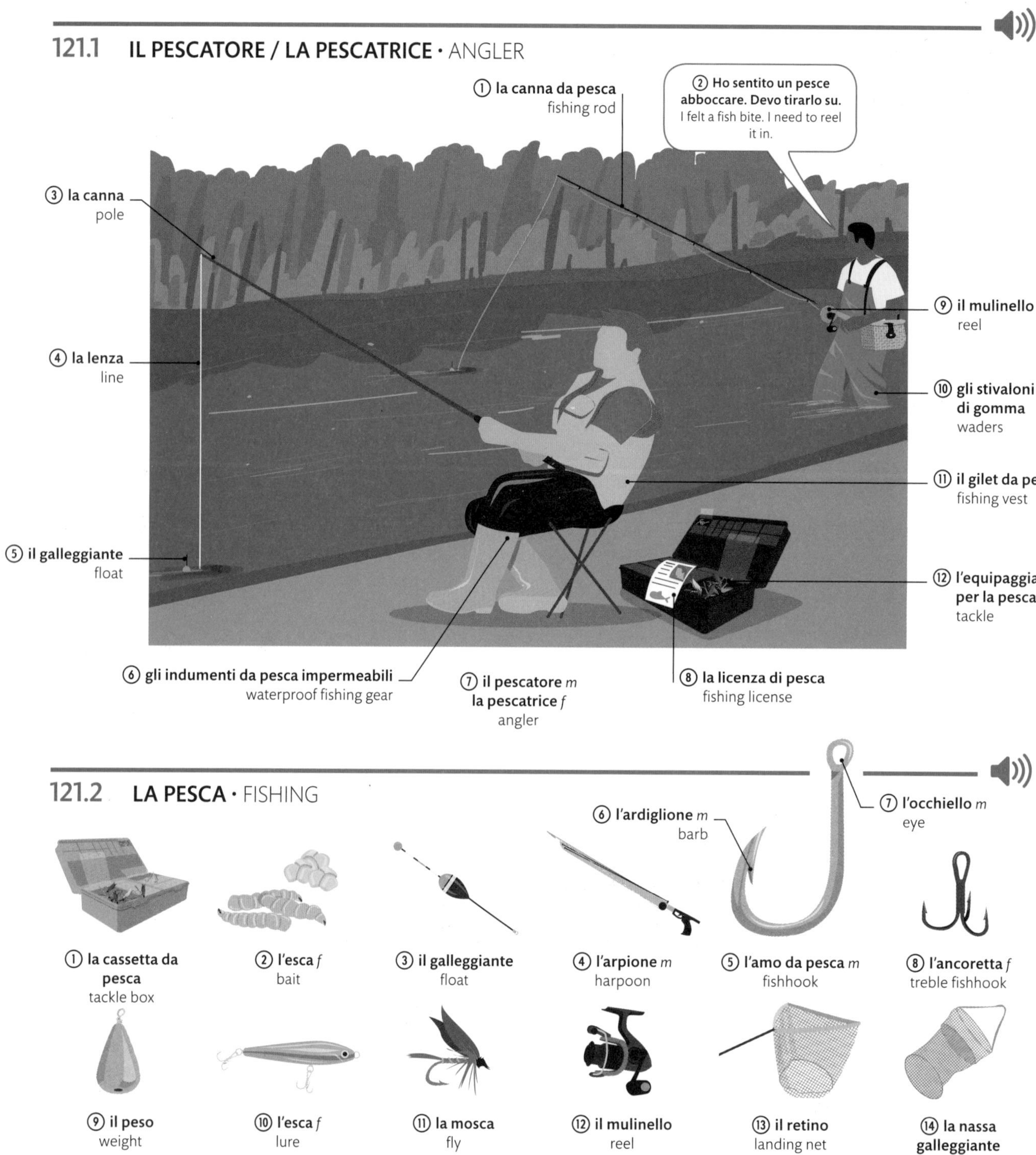
121.1 IL PESCATORE / LA PESCATRICE · ANGLER
① la canna da pesca
fishing rod
② Ho sentito un pesce abboccare. Devo tirarlo su.
I felt a fish bite. I need to reel it in.
③ la canna
pole
④ la lenza
line
⑤ il galleggiante
float
⑥ gli indumenti da pesca impermeabili
waterproof fishing gear
⑦ il pescatore m
la pescatrice f
angler
⑧ la licenza di pesca
fishing license
⑨ il mulinello
reel
⑩ gli stivaloni di gomma
waders
⑪ il gilet da pesc
fishing vest
⑫ l'equipaggiam
per la pesca m
tackle
121.2 LA PESCA · FISHING
① la cassetta da pesca
tackle box
② l'esca f
bait
③ il galleggiante
float
④ l'arpione m
harpoon
⑤ l'amo da pesca m
fishhook
⑥ l'ardiglione m
barb
⑦ l'occhiello m
eye
⑧ l'ancoretta f
treble fishhook
⑨ il peso
weight
⑩ l'esca f
lure
⑪ la mosca
fly
⑫ il mulinello
reel
⑬ il retino
landing net
⑭ la nassa galleggiante
keep net

See also
54 Il pesce e i frutti di mare • Fish and seafood
119 La vela e gli sport acquatici • Sailing and watersports **166** La vita negli oceani • Ocean life

121.3 I TIPI DI PESCA • TYPES OF FISHING

① **la pesca a mosca**
fly fishing

② **la pesca in acqua dolce**
freshwater fishing

③ **la pesca marittima**
marine fishing

④ **la pesca d'altura**
deep sea fishing

⑤ **la pesca sportiva**
sport fishing

⑥ **la pesca subacquea**
spearfishing

⑦ **la pesca su ghiaccio**
ice fishing

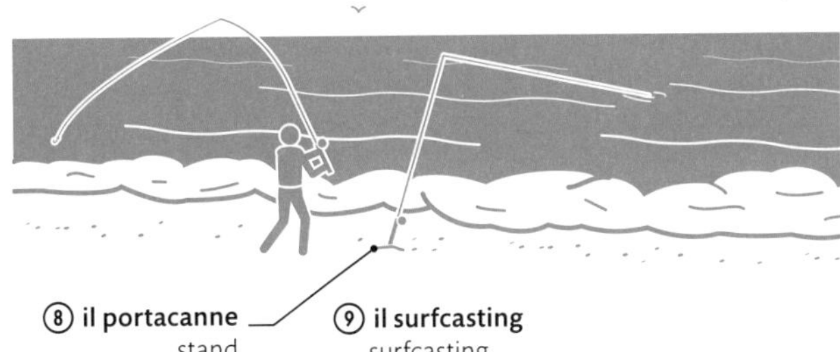

⑧ **il portacanne**
stand

⑨ **il surfcasting**
surfcasting

121.4 I VERBI DELLA PESCA • FISHING VERBS

① **mettere l'esca**
to bait

② **lanciare la lenza**
to cast

③ **abboccare**
to bite

④ **catturare**
to catch

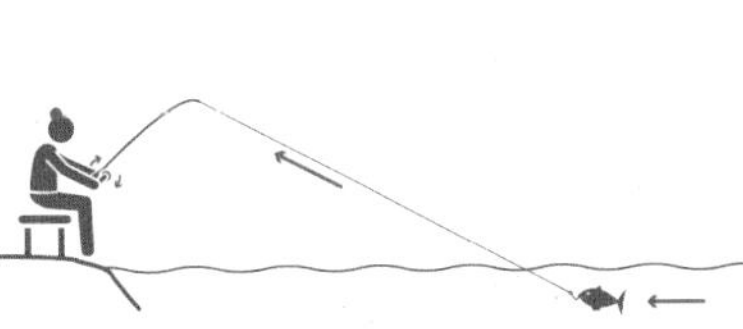

⑤ **tirare su**
to reel in

⑥ **catturare con la rete**
to net

⑦ **liberare**
to release

121.5 I NODI • KNOTS

① **il nodo clinch**
clinch knot

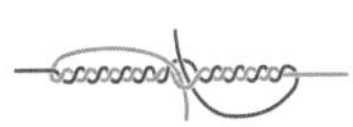

② **il nodo di sangue**
blood knot

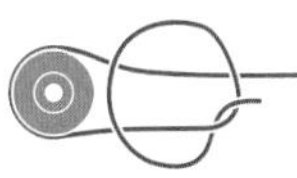

③ **il nodo Arbor**
arbor knot

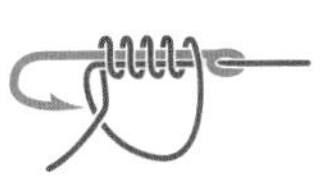

④ **il nodo Snell**
snell knot

⑤ **il nodo Turle**
turle knot

⑥ **il nodo Palomar**
palomar knot

122 Gli sport invernali
Winter sports

122.1 LO SCI • SKIING

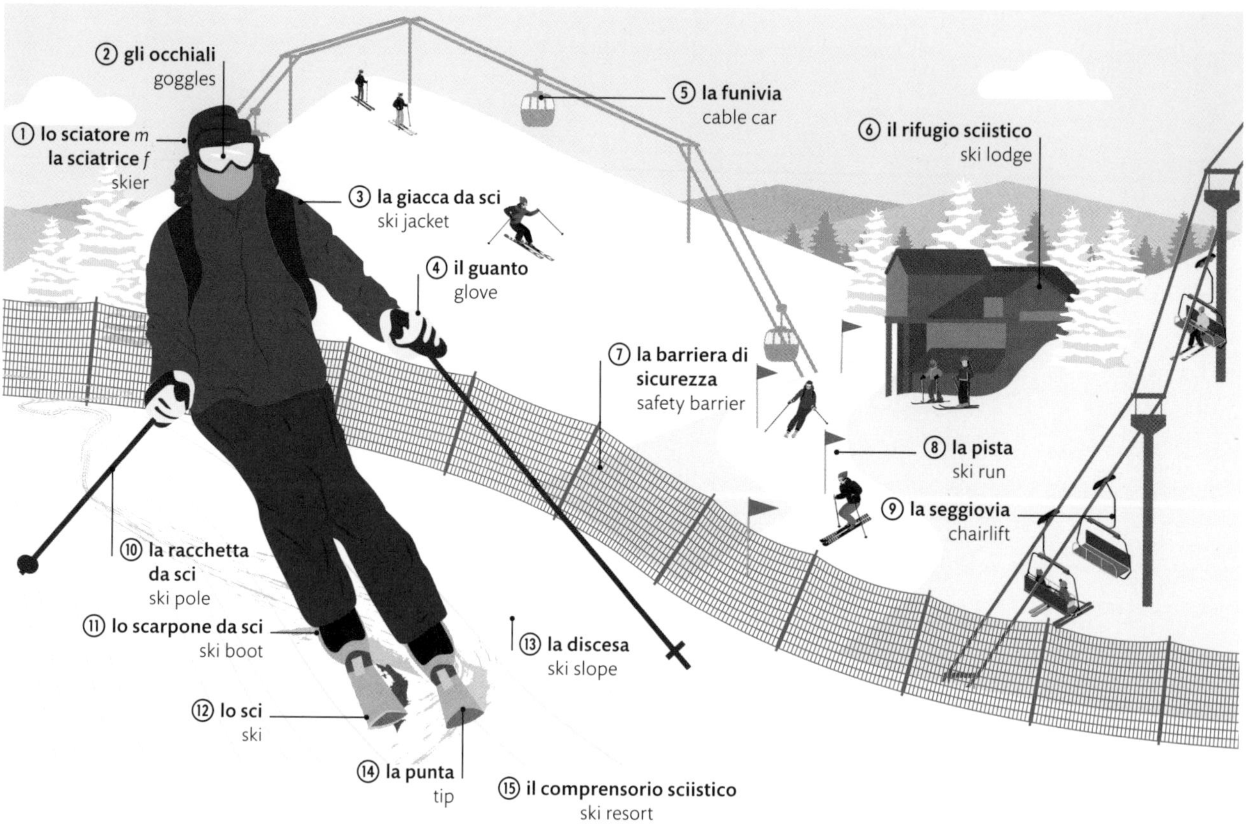

① **lo sciatore** *m* **la sciatrice** *f*
skier

② **gli occhiali**
goggles

③ **la giacca da sci**
ski jacket

④ **il guanto**
glove

⑤ **la funivia**
cable car

⑥ **il rifugio sciistico**
ski lodge

⑦ **la barriera di sicurezza**
safety barrier

⑧ **la pista**
ski run

⑨ **la seggiovia**
chairlift

⑩ **la racchetta da sci**
ski pole

⑪ **lo scarpone da sci**
ski boot

⑫ **lo sci**
ski

⑬ **la discesa**
ski slope

⑭ **la punta**
tip

⑮ **il comprensorio sciistico**
ski resort

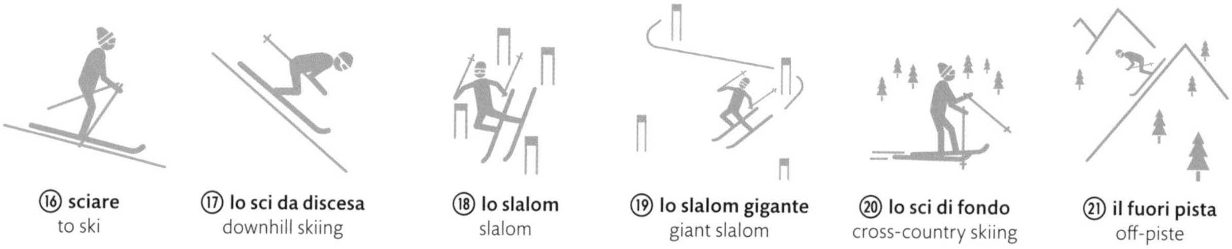

⑯ **sciare**
to ski

⑰ **lo sci da discesa**
downhill skiing

⑱ **lo slalom**
slalom

⑲ **lo slalom gigante**
giant slalom

⑳ **lo sci di fondo**
cross-country skiing

㉑ **il fuori pista**
off-piste

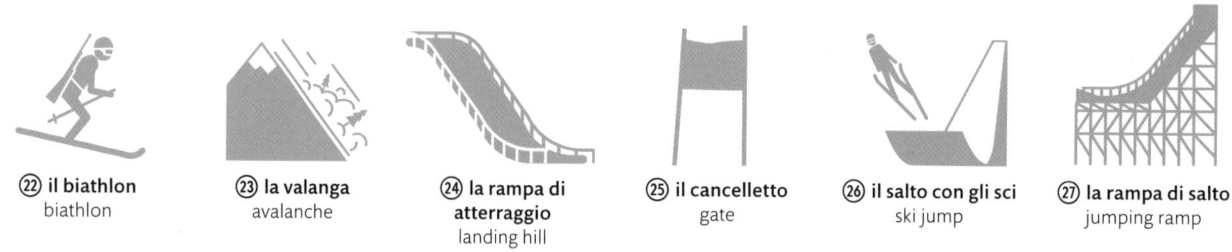

㉒ **il biathlon**
biathlon

㉓ **la valanga**
avalanche

㉔ **la rampa di atterraggio**
landing hill

㉕ **il cancelletto**
gate

㉖ **il salto con gli sci**
ski jump

㉗ **la rampa di salto**
jumping ramp

See also
116 L'atletica • Athletics **124** In palestra
At the gym **125** Gli altri sport • Other sports

122.2 GLI ALTRI SPORT INVERNALI • OTHER WINTER SPORTS

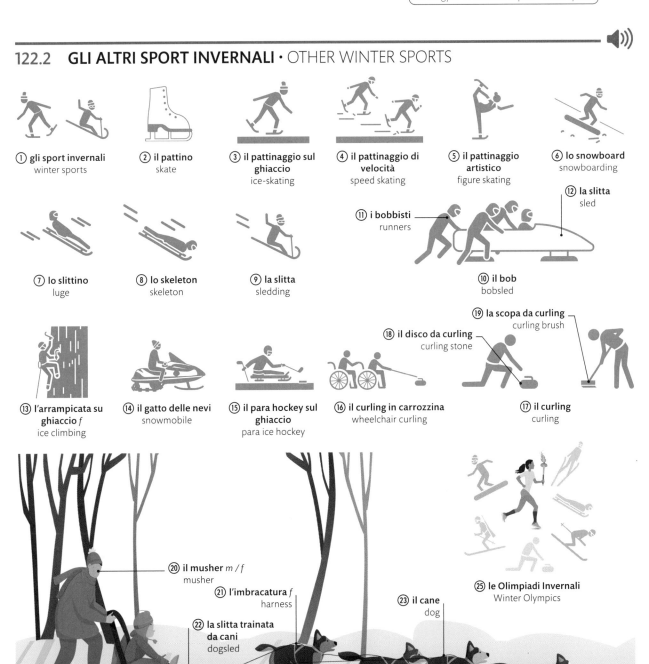

① **gli sport invernali**
winter sports

② **il pattino**
skate

③ **il pattinaggio sul ghiaccio**
ice-skating

④ **il pattinaggio di velocità**
speed skating

⑤ **il pattinaggio artistico**
figure skating

⑥ **lo snowboard**
snowboarding

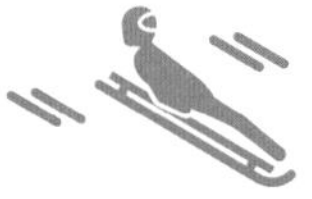

⑦ **lo slittino**
luge

⑧ **lo skeleton**
skeleton

⑨ **la slitta**
sledding

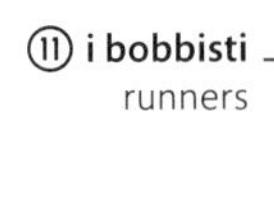

⑪ i bobbisti
runners
⑫ la slitta
sled

⑩ **il bob**
bobsled

⑬ **l'arrampicata su ghiaccio** *f*
ice climbing

⑭ **il gatto delle nevi**
snowmobile

⑮ **il para hockey sul ghiaccio**
para ice hockey

⑯ **il curling in carrozzina**
wheelchair curling

⑲ la scopa da curling
curling brush
⑱ il disco da curling
curling stone

⑰ **il curling**
curling

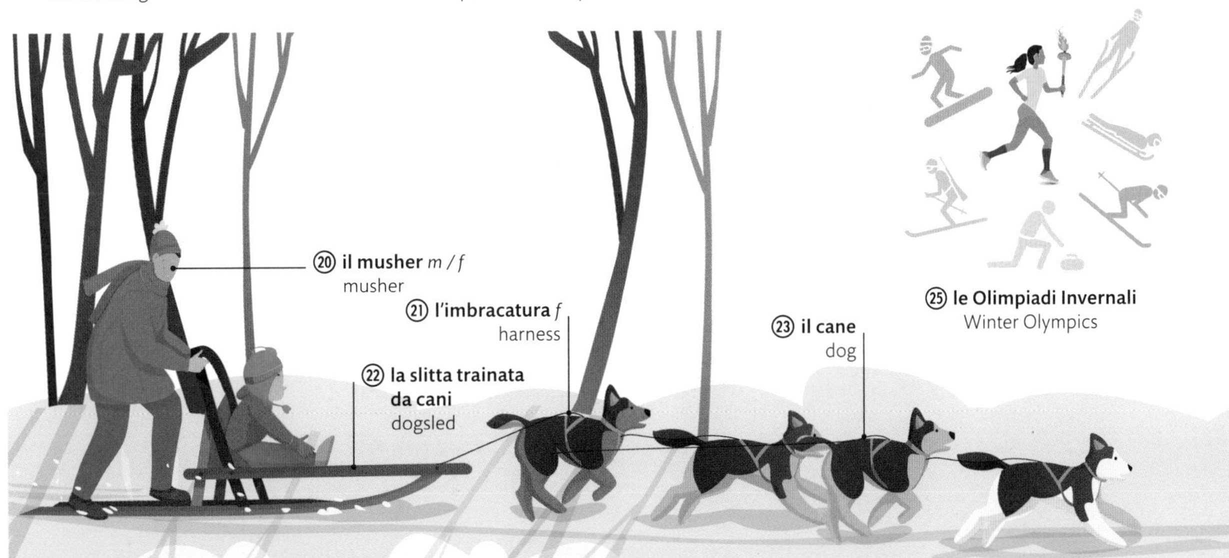
⑳ il musher m / f
musher
㉑ l'imbracatura f
harness
㉒ la slitta trainata da cani
dogsled
㉓ il cane
dog
㉕ le Olimpiadi Invernali
Winter Olympics

㉔ **andare sulla slitta**
dog sledding

123 Gli sport motoristici
Motorsports

123.1 L'AUTO DA CORSA • RACE CAR

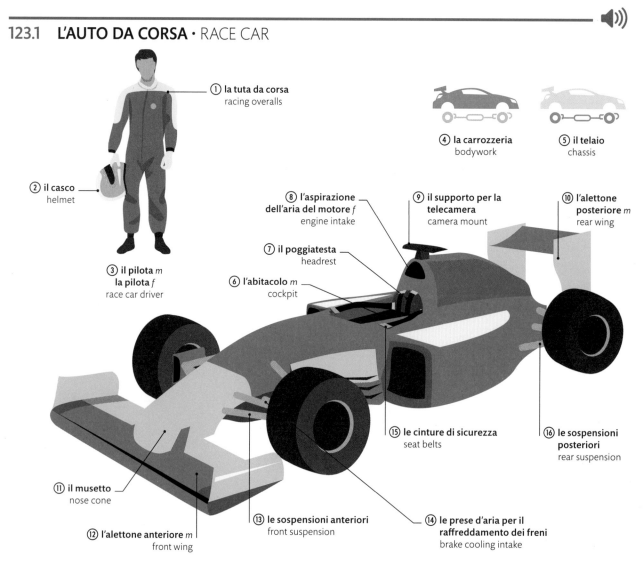

① **la tuta da corsa**
racing overalls

② **il casco**
helmet

③ **il pilota** *m*
la pilota *f*
race car driver

④ **la carrozzeria**
bodywork

⑤ **il telaio**
chassis

⑥ **l'abitacolo** *m*
cockpit

⑦ **il poggiatesta**
headrest

⑧ **l'aspirazione dell'aria del motore** *f*
engine intake

⑨ **il supporto per la telecamera**
camera mount

⑩ **l'alettone posteriore** *m*
rear wing

⑪ **il musetto**
nose cone

⑫ **l'alettone anteriore** *m*
front wing

⑬ **le sospensioni anteriori**
front suspension

⑭ **le prese d'aria per il raffreddamento dei freni**
brake cooling intake

⑮ **le cinture di sicurezza**
seat belts

⑯ **le sospensioni posteriori**
rear suspension

123.2 I TIPI DI SPORT MOTORISTICI • TYPES OF MOTORSPORTS

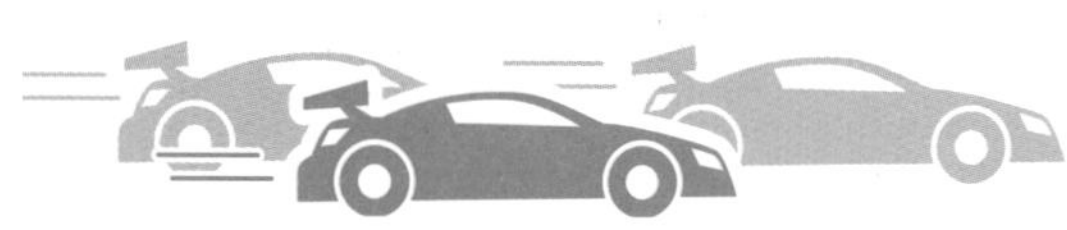

① **la gara automobilistica**
auto racing

② **il rally**
rally driving

③ **la gara di accelerazione**
drag racing

See also
96 Le strade • Roads **97-98** Le auto • Cars **99** Le auto e gli autobus • Cars and buses **100** I motocicli • Motorcycles

123.3 **IL CIRCUITO** • RACE TRACK

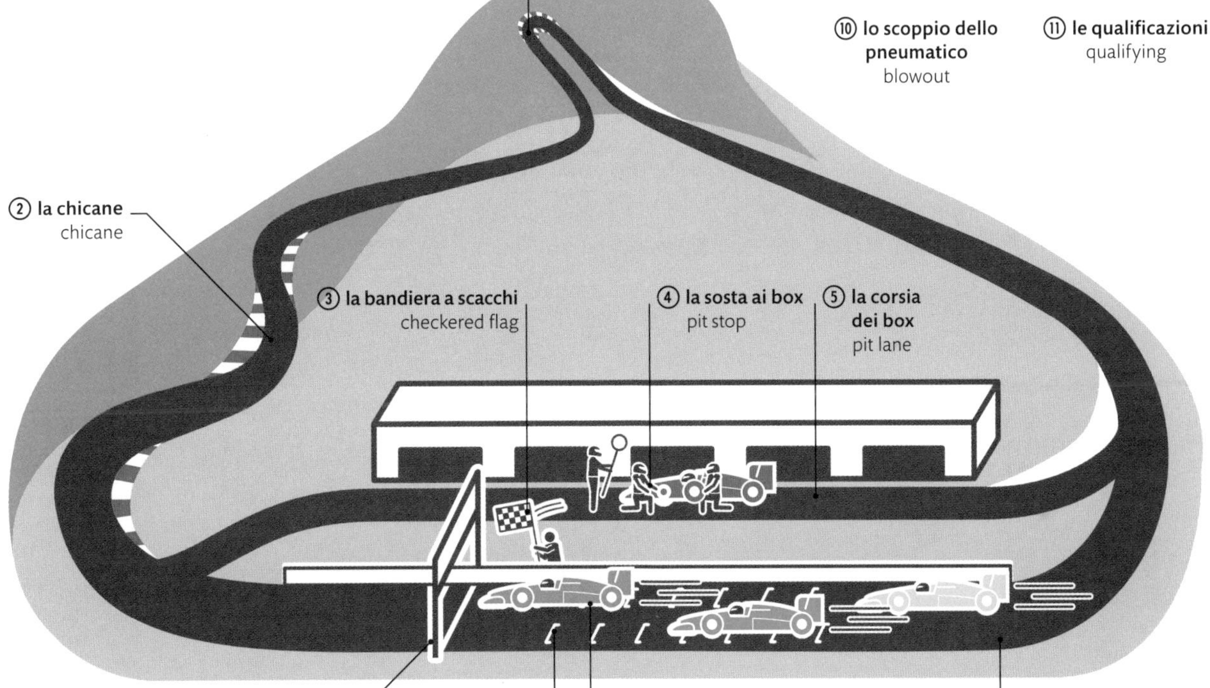

① **il tornante**
hairpin turn

② **la chicane**
chicane

③ **la bandiera a scacchi**
checkered flag

④ **la sosta ai box**
pit stop

⑤ **la corsia dei box**
pit lane

⑥ **il traguardo**
finish line

⑦ **la griglia di partenza**
starting grid

⑧ **la prima posizione**
pole position

⑨ **il rettilineo d'arrivo**
homestretch

⑩ **lo scoppio dello pneumatico**
blowout

⑪ **le qualificazioni**
qualifying

④ **il motociclismo**
motorcycle racing

⑤ **la corsa motociclistica su pista**
speedway

⑥ **il motocross**
motocross

⑦ **la gara di Monster Truck**
monster truck

⑧ **il go cart**
go-cart

124 In palestra
At the gym

124.1 L'ALLENAMENTO · WORKING OUT

① Quanto spesso ti alleni?
How often do you work out?
② Faccio esercizio tre volte alla settimana.
I exercise three times a week.
③ l'ellittica *f*
elliptical
④ l'allenamento *m*
working out
⑤ il vogatore
rowing machine
⑥ la cyclette
exercise bike
⑫ i macchinari da palestra
gym machines

⑭ **gli armadietti**
lockers

⑬ **lo spogliatoio**
locker room

⑮ **la lezione di ginnastica**
exercise class

⑯ **il Pilates**
Pilates

⑰ **lo stretching**
stretch

⑲ **gli esercizi**
exercises

⑱ **l'allenamento a circuito** *m*
circuit training

⑳ **l'aerobica** *f*
aerobics

㉑ **i jumping jack**
jumping jacks

㉒ **le circonduzioni delle braccia**
arm circles

㉓ **i salti laterali**
side shuffles

㉔ **la corsa**
running

㉕ **l'affondo** *m*
lunge

㉖ **il curl dei bicipiti**
bicep curl

㉗ **lo squat**
squat

㉘ **gli addominali**
sit-up

㉙ **la fit boxe**
boxercise

㉚ **saltare la corda**
to skip

㉛ **contrarre i muscoli**
to flex

㉜ **fare corsa sul posto**
to jog in place

㉝ **allenarsi**
to train

㉞ **fare trazioni alla sbarra**
to pull up

㉟ **allungare**
to extend

㊱ **riscaldarsi**
to warm up

㊲ **raffreddarsi**
to cool down

See also
116 L' atletica • Athletics **117** Gli sport da combattimento • Combat sports **118** Il nuoto • Swimming **122** Gli sport invernali • Winter sports **125** Gli altri sport • Other sports

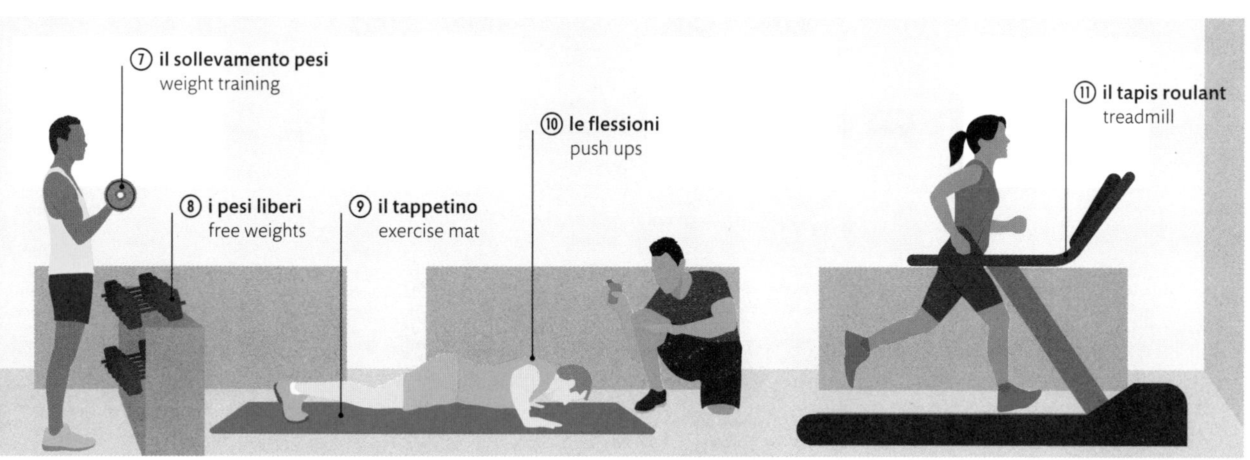
⑦ **il sollevamento pesi**
weight training
⑧ **i pesi liberi**
free weights
⑨ **il tappetino**
exercise mat
⑩ **le flessioni**
push ups
⑪ **il tapis roulant**
treadmill

㊳ **l'iscrizione** *f*
membership

㊴ **l'attrezzatura da palestra** *f*
gym equipment

㊵ **lo step**
aerobics step

㊶ **il manubrio**
dumbbell

㊷ **le manopole**
hand grips

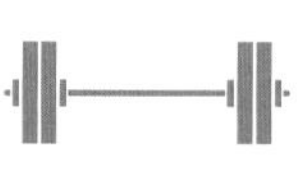

㊸ **la barra dei pesi**
barbell

㊹ **la sbarra**
bar

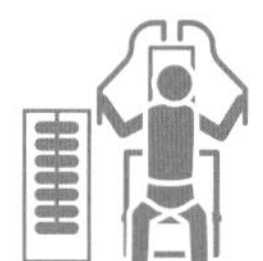

㊺ **la chest press**
chest press

㊻ **la corda da saltare**
jump rope

㊼ **la palla fitness**
exercise ball

㊽ **il bastone per torsioni**
twist bar

㊾ **la cavigliera / la polsiera**
ankle weights / wrist weights

㊿ **la leg press**
leg press

(51) **l'estensore per torace** *m*
chest expander

(52) **la ruota per addominali** *m*
ab wheel

(53) **il tapis roulant**
running machine

(54) **la panca**
bench

(55) **il battito cardiaco**
heart rate

(56) **la sauna**
sauna

(57) **la vasca idromassaggio**
hot tub

(58) **il personal trainer** *m*
la personal trainer *f*
personal trainer

125 Gli altri sport
Other sports

125.1 LA GINNASTICA · GYMNASTICS

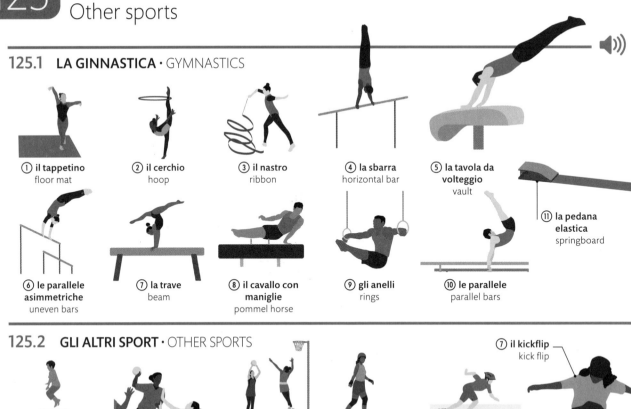

1. **il tappetino** floor mat
2. **il cerchio** hoop
3. **il nastro** ribbon
4. **la sbarra** horizontal bar
5. **la tavola da volteggio** vault
6. **le parallele asimmetriche** uneven bars
7. **la trave** beam
8. **il cavallo con maniglie** pommel horse
9. **gli anelli** rings
10. **le parallele** parallel bars
11. **la pedana elastica** springboard

125.2 GLI ALTRI SPORT · OTHER SPORTS

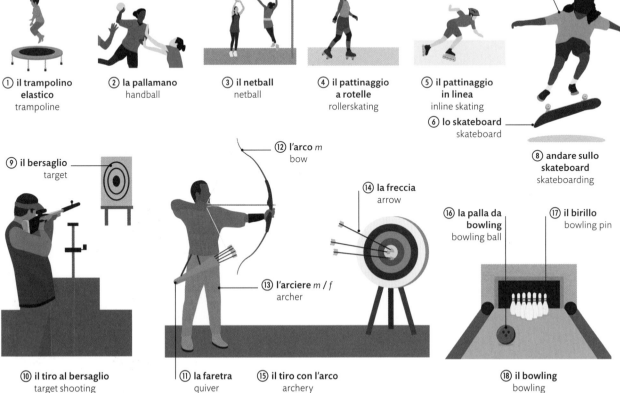

1. **il trampolino elastico** trampoline
2. **la pallamano** handball
3. **il netball** netball
4. **il pattinaggio a rotelle** rollerskating
5. **il pattinaggio in linea** inline skating
6. **lo skateboard** skateboard
7. **il kickflip** kick flip
8. **andare sullo skateboard** skateboarding

9. **il bersaglio** target

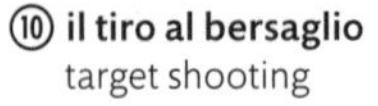

10. **il tiro al bersaglio** target shooting

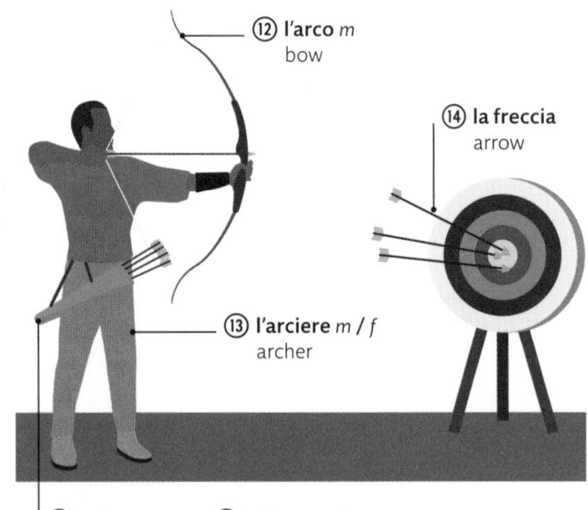

11. **la faretra** quiver
12. **l'arco** *m* bow
13. **l'arciere** *m / f* archer
14. **la freccia** arrow
15. **il tiro con l'arco** archery
16. **la palla da bowling** bowling ball
17. **il birillo** bowling pin
18. **il bowling** bowling

See also
116 L'atletica • Athletics 117 Gli sport da combattimento • Combat sports 118 Il nuoto • Swimming
120 L'equitazione • Horseback riding 122 Gli sport invernali • Winter sports 124 In palestra • At the gym

125.3 I PARASPORT • PARASPORTS

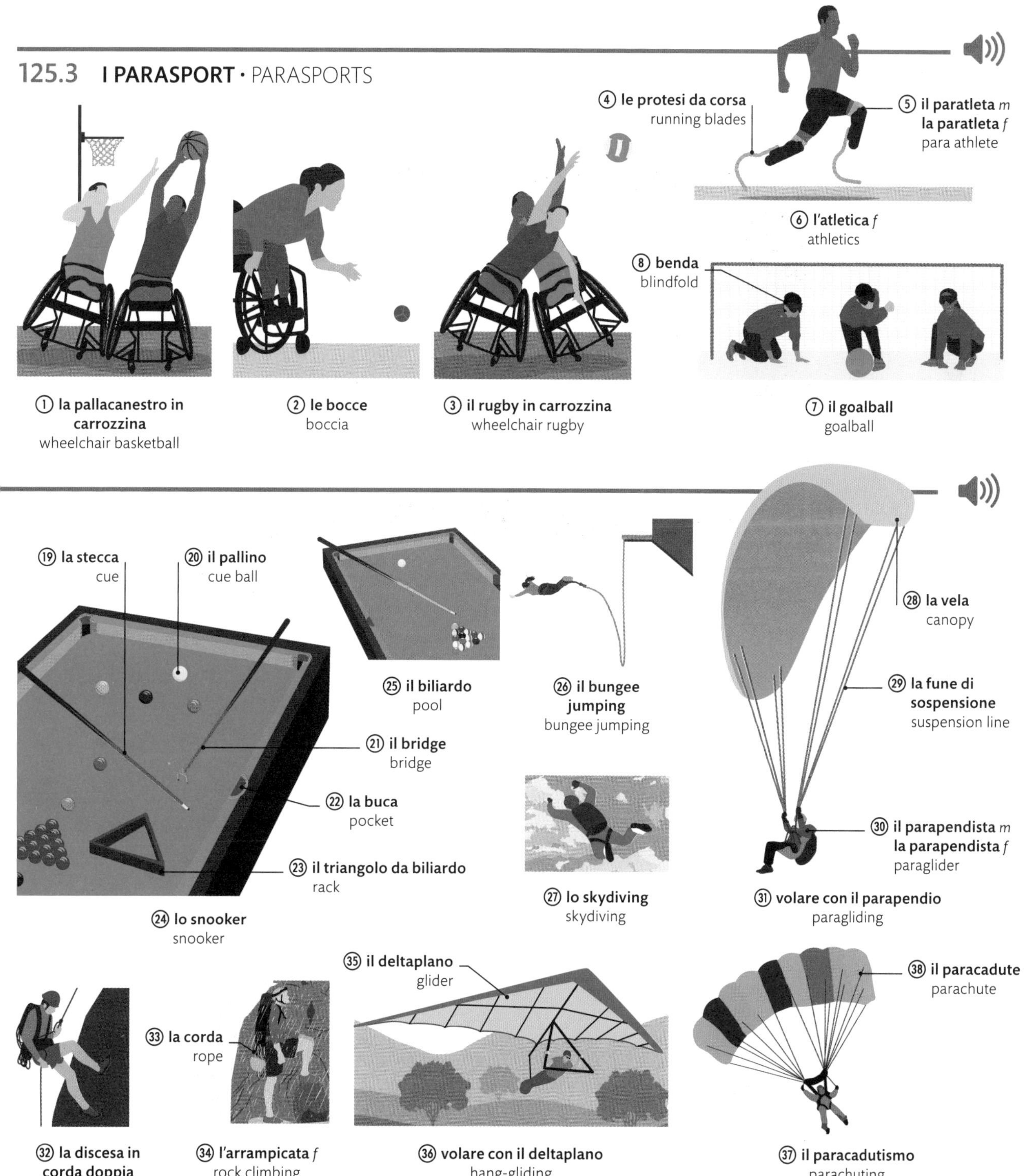
④ le protesi da corsa
running blades
⑤ il paratleta m
la paratleta f
para athlete
⑥ l'atletica f
athletics
⑧ benda
blindfold
① la pallacanestro in carrozzina
wheelchair basketball
② le bocce
boccia
③ il rugby in carrozzina
wheelchair rugby
⑦ il goalball
goalball
⑲ la stecca
cue
⑳ il pallino
cue ball
㉑ il bridge
bridge
㉒ la buca
pocket
㉓ il triangolo da biliardo
rack
㉔ lo snooker
snooker
㉕ il biliardo
pool
㉖ il bungee jumping
bungee jumping
㉗ lo skydiving
skydiving
㉘ la vela
canopy
㉙ la fune di sospensione
suspension line
㉚ il parapendista m
la parapendista f
paraglider
㉛ volare con il parapendio
paragliding
㉜ la discesa in corda doppia
abseiling
㉝ la corda
rope
㉞ l'arrampicata f
rock climbing
㉟ il deltaplano
glider
㊱ volare con il deltaplano
hang-gliding
㊲ il paracadutismo
parachuting
㊳ il paracadute
parachute

126 Sul palco
On stage

126.1 IL TEATRO · THEATER

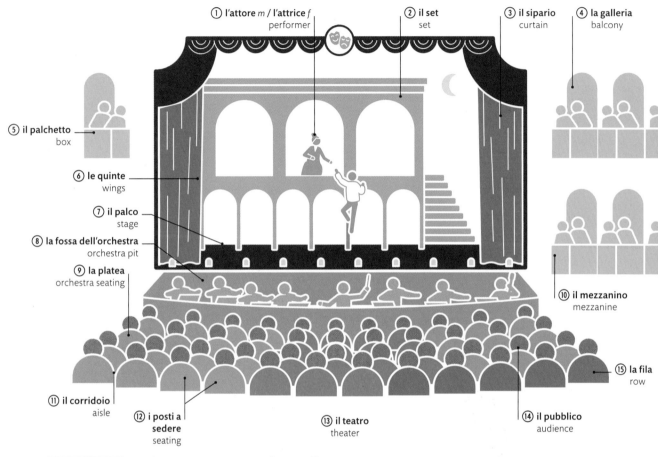

① **l'attore** *m* / **l'attrice** *f*
performer

② **il set**
set

③ **il sipario**
curtain

④ **la galleria**
balcony

⑤ **il palchetto**
box

⑥ **le quinte**
wings

⑦ **il palco**
stage

⑧ **la fossa dell'orchestra**
orchestra pit

⑨ **la platea**
orchestra seating

⑩ **il mezzanino**
mezzanine

⑪ **il corridoio**
aisle

⑫ **i posti a sedere**
seating

⑬ **il teatro**
theater

⑭ **il pubblico**
audience

⑮ **la fila**
row

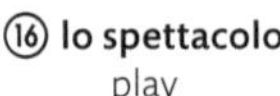

⑯ **lo spettacolo**
play

⑰ **i costumi**
costumes

⑱ **il materiale di scena**
props

⑲ **le scenografie**
sets

⑳ **lo sfondo**
backdrop

㉑ **il copione**
script

㉒ **il produttore** *m*
la produttrice *f*
producer

㉓ **il regista** *m*
la regista *f*
director

㉔ **l'attore** *m*
l'attrice *f*
actor

㉕ **il cast**
cast

㉖ **la prima**
opening night

㉗ **l'intervallo** *m*
intermission

See also
127 I film • Movies **128-129** La musica • Music
139 Il fantasy e il mito • Fantasy and myth

126.2 IL BALLETTO • BALLET

㉘ **il programma**
program

㉙ **l'usciere** *m*
l'usciera *f*
usher

㉚ **la tragedia**
tragedy

㉛ **la commedia**
comedy

㉜ **il musical**
musical

㉝ **la standing ovation**
standing ovation

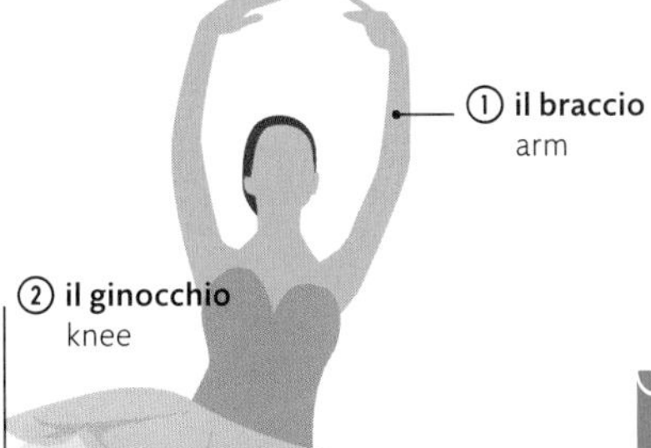
① **il braccio**
arm

② **il ginocchio**
knee

③ **la punta**
toe box

④ **fare la pirouette**
to pirouette / to turn

⑤ **fare il plié**
to plié / to bend

⑥ **il ballerino**
male ballet dancer

⑦ **la ballerina**
ballerina

⑧ **il tutù**
tutu

⑨ **il body**
ballet leotard

⑩ **le scarpette**
ballet slippers

⑪ **l'esibizione** *f*
performance

⑫ **il bis**
encore

⑬ **l'applauso** *m*
applause

126.3 L'OPERA • OPERA

① **il basso**
bass

② **il baritono**
baritone

③ **il tenore**
tenor

④ **il teatro dell'opera**
opera house

⑤ **il contralto**
alto

⑥ **il mezzo soprano**
mezzo-soprano

⑦ **il soprano**
soprano

⑧ **la primadonna**
prima donna

⑨ **il libretto**
libretto

127 I film
Movies

127.1 AL CINEMA · AT THE MOVIES

① **il film drammatico**
drama

② **il musical**
musical

③ **il film di fantascienza**
science fiction

④ **il thriller**
thriller

⑤ **la commedia**
comedy

⑥ **il film d'azione**
action movie

⑦ **l'horror** *m*
horror

⑧ **il cartone animato**
animation

⑨ **la commedia romantica**
romantic comedy

⑩ **il poliziesco**
crime drama

⑪ **il film western**
western

⑫ **il film storico**
historical drama

⑬ **il fantasy**
fantasy

⑭ **il film di arti marziali**
martial arts

⑮ **gli effetti speciali**
special effects

⑯ **il botteghino**
box office

⑰ **il cinema multisala**
multiplex

⑱ **i popcorn**
popcorn

⑲ **la star del cinema**
movie star

⑳ **lo schermo**
screen

㉑ **il pubblico**
audience

㉒ **il cinema**
movie theater

㉓ **il protagonista** *m*
la protagonista *f*
main character

㉔ **l'eroe** *m* / **l'eroina** *f*
hero

㉕ **il cattivo** *m*
la cattiva *f*
villain

See also
126 Sul palco • On stage **136** L'home entertainment
Home entertainment **137** La televisione • Television

127.2 LO STUDIO CINEMATOGRAFICO • FILM STUDIO

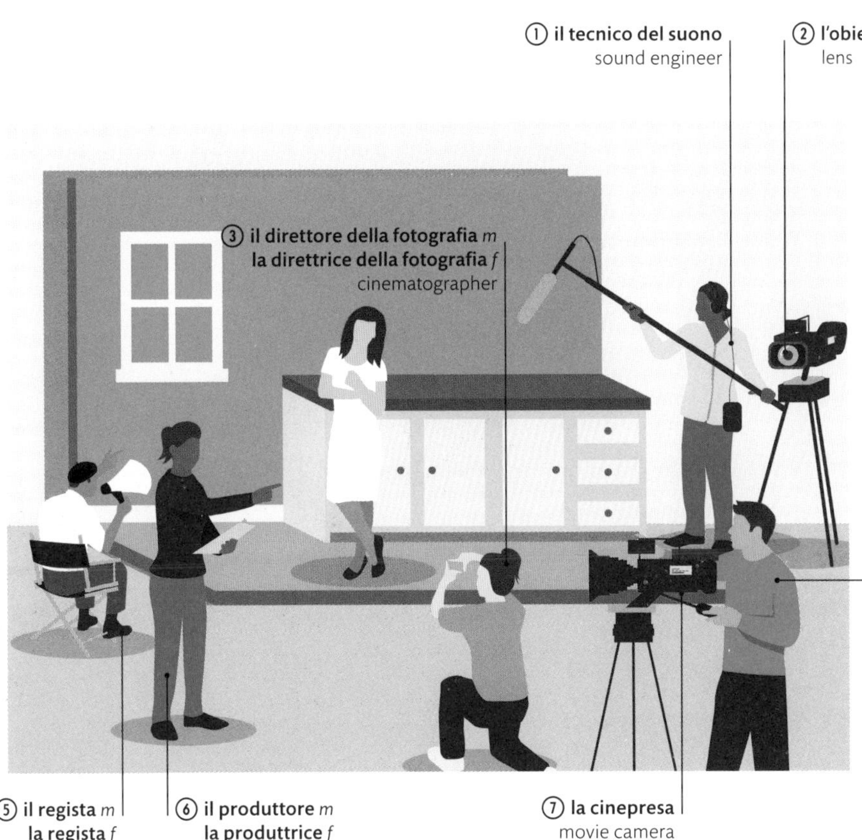

① **il tecnico del suono**
sound engineer

② **l'obiettivo** *m*
lens

③ **il direttore della fotografia** *m*
la direttrice della fotografia *f*
cinematographer

④ **il cameraman** *m*
la cameraman *f*
camera operator

⑤ **il regista** *m*
la regista *f*
director

⑥ **il produttore** *m*
la produttrice *f*
producer

⑦ **la cinepresa**
movie camera

⑧ **il set cinematografico**
film set

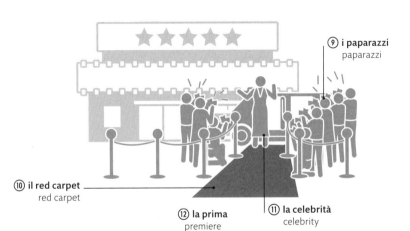

⑨ **i paparazzi**
paparazzi

⑩ **il red carpet**
red carpet

⑪ **la celebrità**
celebrity

⑫ **la prima**
premiere

⑬ **l'audizione** *f*
audition

⑭ **il cast**
cast

⑮ **le comparse**
extras

⑯ **la controfigura**
stunt

⑰ **il materiale di scena**
props

⑱ **la sceneggiatura**
screenplay

⑲ **i costumi**
costumes

⑳ **la colonna sonora**
soundtrack

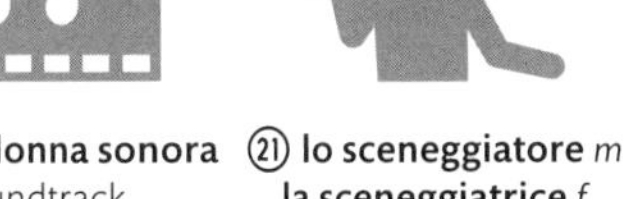

㉑ **lo sceneggiatore** *m*
la sceneggiatrice *f*
screenwriter

La musica
Music

128.1 GLI STRUMENTI DELL'ORCHESTRA · ORCHESTRAL INSTRUMENTS

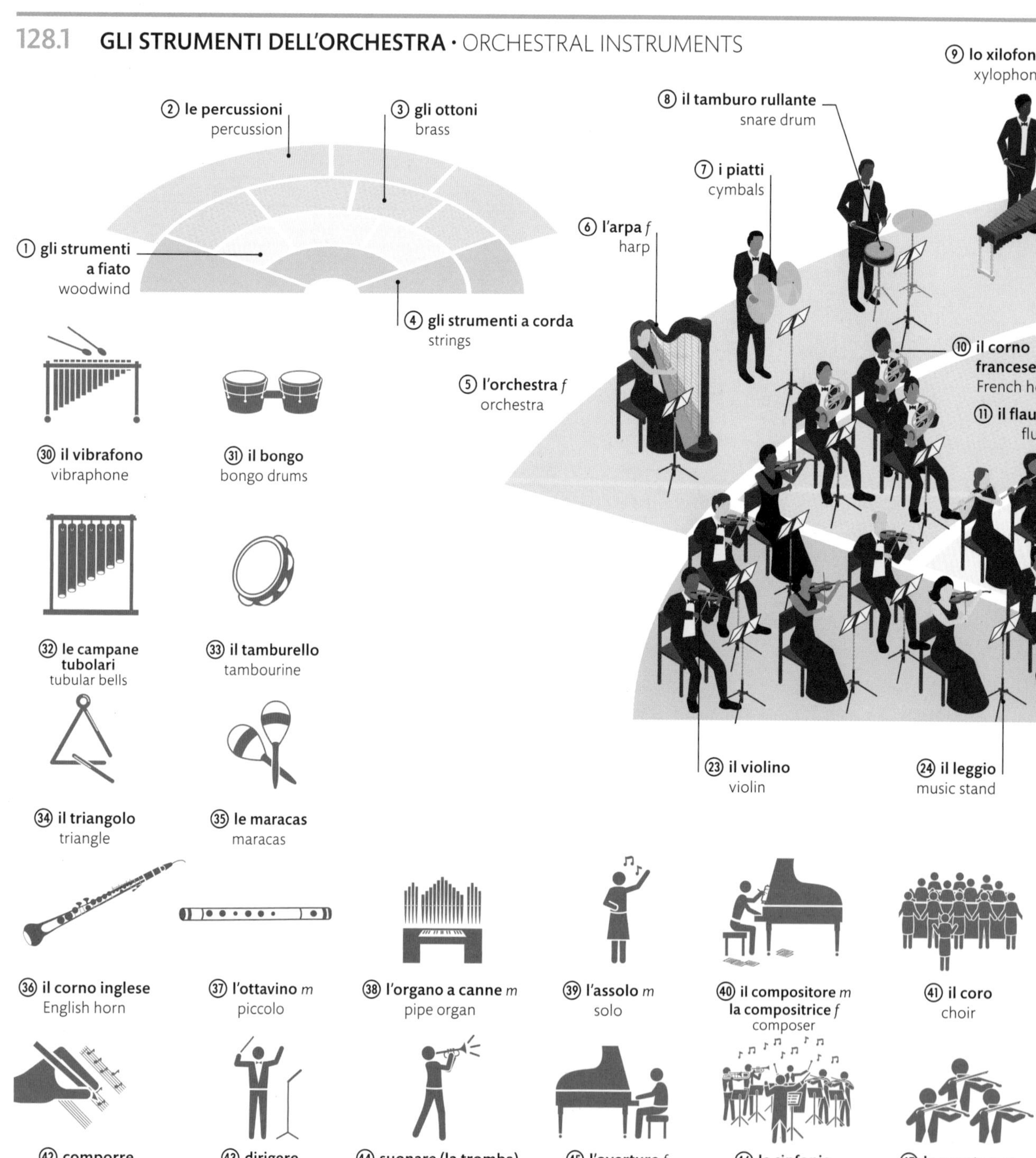

① gli strumenti a fiato
woodwind
② le percussioni
percussion
③ gli ottoni
brass
④ gli strumenti a corda
strings
⑤ l'orchestra *f*
orchestra
⑥ l'arpa *f*
harp
⑦ i piatti
cymbals
⑧ il tamburo rullante
snare drum
⑨ lo xilofono
xylophone
⑩ il corno francese
French horn
⑪ il flauto
flute
㉓ il violino
violin
㉔ il leggio
music stand
㉚ il vibrafono
vibraphone
㉛ il bongo
bongo drums
㉜ le campane tubolari
tubular bells
㉝ il tamburello
tambourine
㉞ il triangolo
triangle
㉟ le maracas
maracas
㊱ il corno inglese
English horn
㊲ l'ottavino *m*
piccolo
㊳ l'organo a canne *m*
pipe organ
㊴ l'assolo *m*
solo
㊵ il compositore *m* la compositrice *f*
composer
㊶ il coro
choir
㊷ comporre
to compose
㊸ dirigere
to conduct
㊹ suonare (la tromba)
to play (the trumpet)
㊺ l'overture *f*
piano overture
㊻ la sinfonia
symphony
㊼ la sonata per violino
violin sonata

See also
126 Sul palco • On stage **127** I film • Movies **129** La musica (continua) Music continued **136** L'home entertainment • Home entertainment

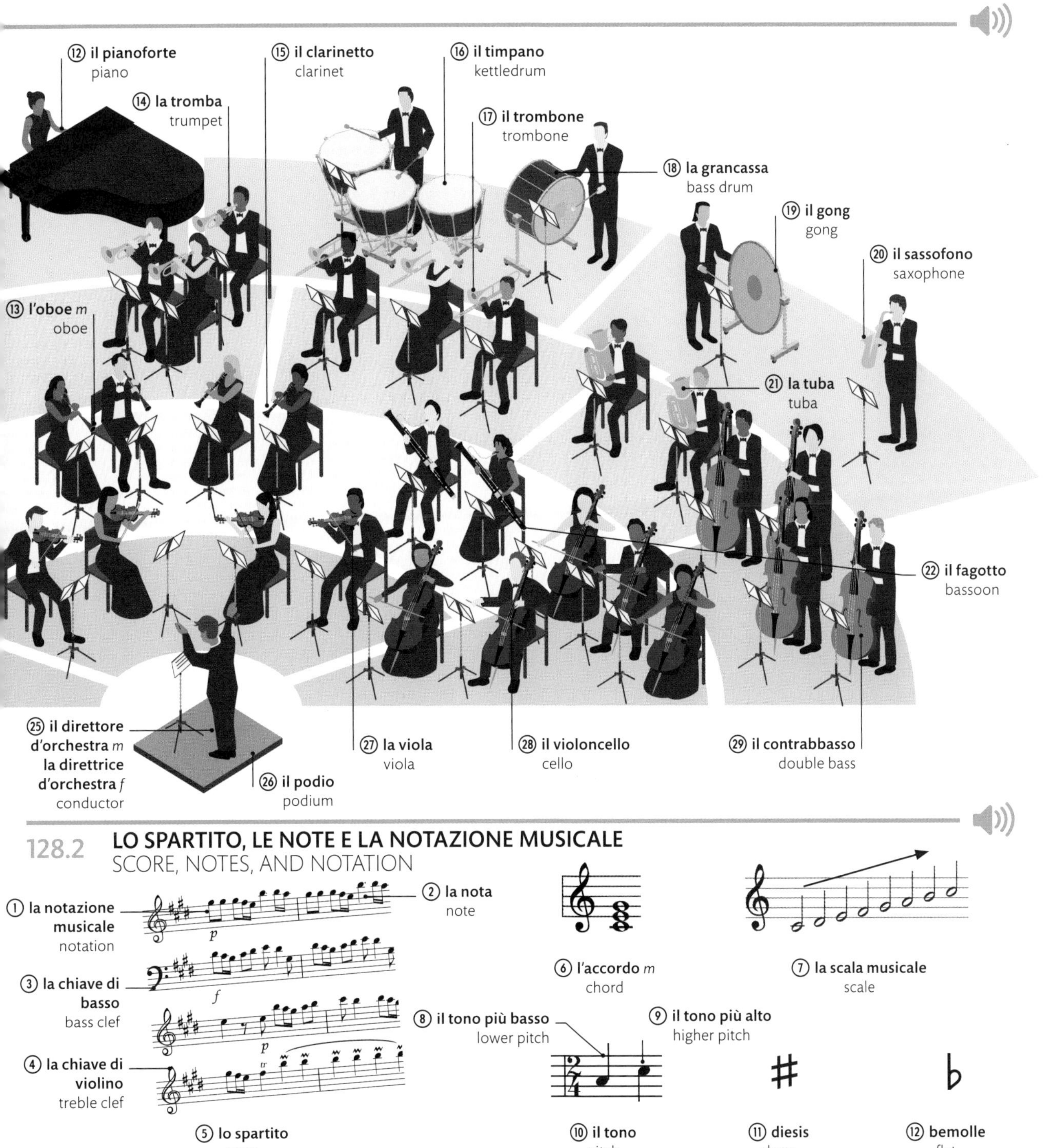
⑫ **il pianoforte**
piano
⑭ **la tromba**
trumpet
⑮ **il clarinetto**
clarinet
⑯ **il timpano**
kettledrum
⑰ **il trombone**
trombone
⑱ **la grancassa**
bass drum
⑲ **il gong**
gong
⑳ **il sassofono**
saxophone
⑬ **l'oboe** *m*
oboe
㉑ **la tuba**
tuba
㉒ **il fagotto**
bassoon
㉕ **il direttore d'orchestra** *m*
la direttrice d'orchestra *f*
conductor
㉖ **il podio**
podium
㉗ **la viola**
viola
㉘ **il violoncello**
cello
㉙ **il contrabbasso**
double bass

128.2 LO SPARTITO, LE NOTE E LA NOTAZIONE MUSICALE
SCORE, NOTES, AND NOTATION

① **la notazione musicale**
notation
② **la nota**
note
③ **la chiave di basso**
bass clef
④ **la chiave di violino**
treble clef
⑤ **lo spartito**
score
⑥ **l'accordo** *m*
chord
⑦ **la scala musicale**
scale
⑧ **il tono più basso**
lower pitch
⑨ **il tono più alto**
higher pitch
⑩ **il tono**
pitch
⑪ **diesis**
sharp
⑫ **bemolle**
flat

La musica (continua)

Music continued

129.1 LA MUSICA POP • POPULAR MUSIC

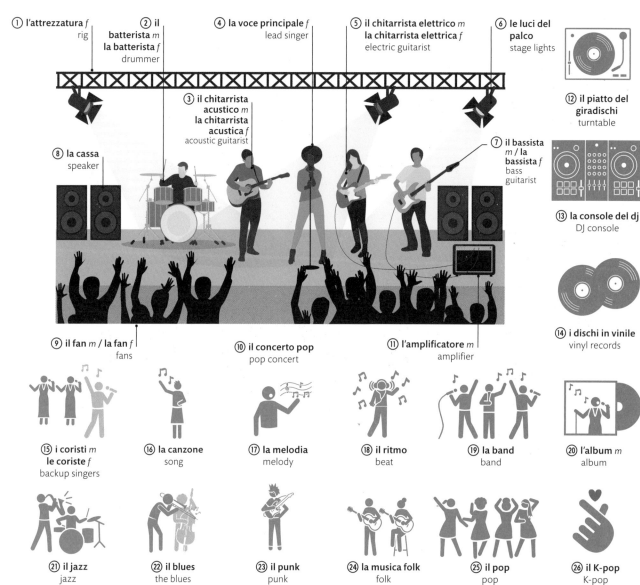

① l'attrezzatura *f*
rig

② il batterista *m* la batterista *f*
drummer

③ il chitarrista acustico *m* la chitarrista acustica *f*
acoustic guitarist

④ la voce principale *f*
lead singer

⑤ il chitarrista elettrico *m* la chitarrista elettrica *f*
electric guitarist

⑥ le luci del palco
stage lights

⑦ il bassista *m* / la bassista *f*
bass guitarist

⑧ la cassa
speaker

⑨ il fan *m* / la fan *f*
fans

⑩ il concerto pop
pop concert

⑪ l'amplificatore *m*
amplifier

⑫ il piatto del giradischi
turntable

⑬ la console del dj
DJ console

⑭ i dischi in vinile
vinyl records

⑮ i coristi *m* le coriste *f*
backup singers

⑯ la canzone
song

⑰ la melodia
melody

⑱ il ritmo
beat

⑲ la band
band

⑳ l'album *m*
album

㉑ il jazz
jazz

㉒ il blues
the blues

㉓ il punk
punk

㉔ la musica folk
folk

㉕ il pop
pop

㉖ il K-pop
K-pop

㉗ l'heavy metal *m*
heavy metal

㉘ l'hip hop *m*
hip-hop

㉙ la musica country
country

㉚ il rock
rock

㉛ il soul
soul

㉜ la musica latina
Latin

See also
126 Sul palco • On stage **127** I film • Movies
136 L'home entertainment • Home entertainment

129.2 GLI ALTRI STRUMENTI • MORE INSTRUMENTS

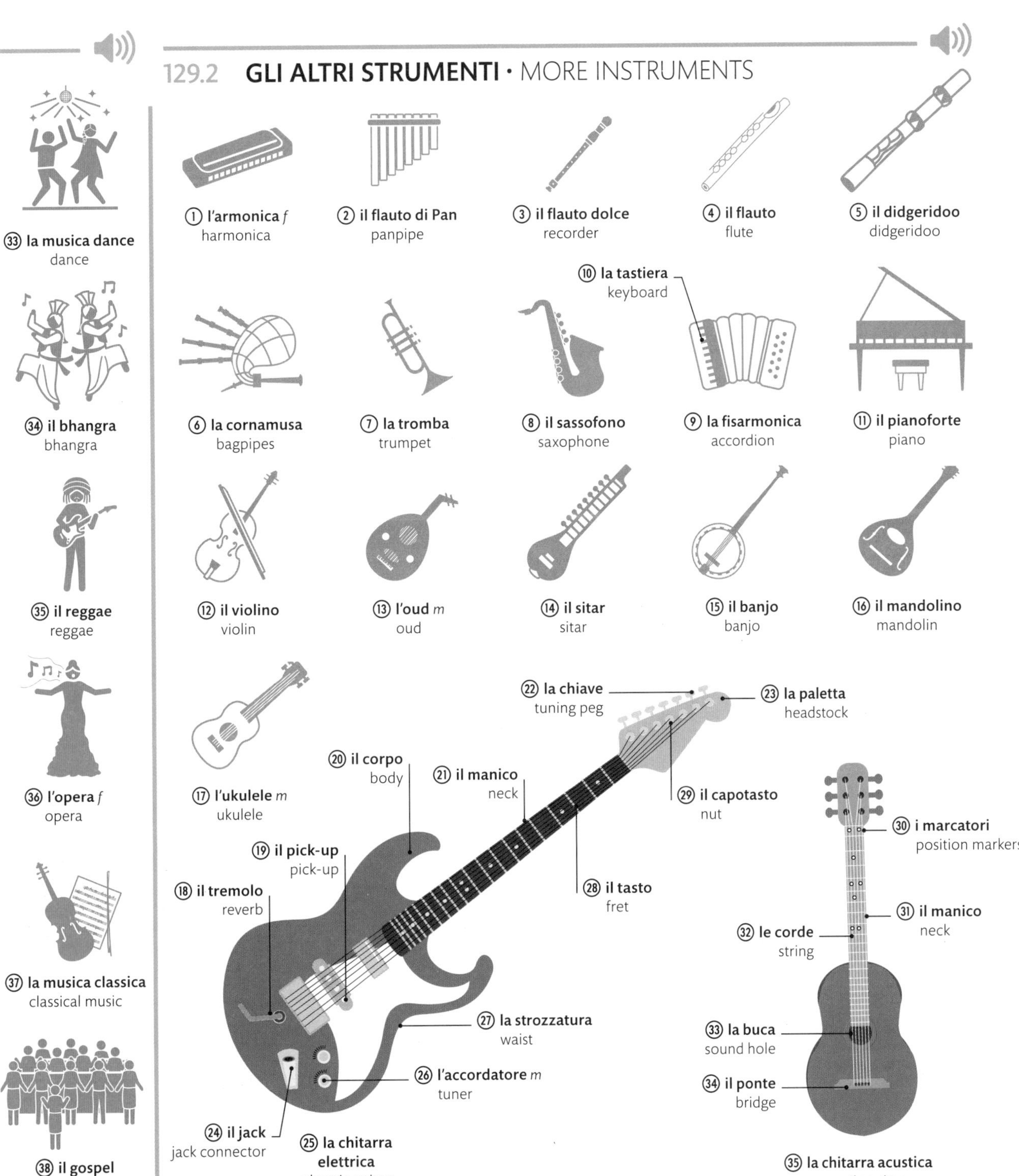

(33) la musica dance
dance
(34) il bhangra
bhangra
(35) il reggae
reggae
(36) l'opera *f*
opera
(37) la musica classica
classical music
(38) il gospel
gospel
(1) l'armonica *f*
harmonica
(2) il flauto di Pan
panpipe
(3) il flauto dolce
recorder
(4) il flauto
flute
(5) il didgeridoo
didgeridoo
(6) la cornamusa
bagpipes
(7) la tromba
trumpet
(8) il sassofono
saxophone
(9) la fisarmonica
accordion
(10) la tastiera
keyboard
(11) il pianoforte
piano
(12) il violino
violin
(13) l'oud *m*
oud
(14) il sitar
sitar
(15) il banjo
banjo
(16) il mandolino
mandolin
(17) l'ukulele *m*
ukulele
(18) il tremolo
reverb
(19) il pick-up
pick-up
(20) il corpo
body
(21) il manico
neck
(22) la chiave
tuning peg
(23) la paletta
headstock
(24) il jack
jack connector
(25) la chitarra elettrica
electric guitar
(26) l'accordatore *m*
tuner
(27) la strozzatura
waist
(28) il tasto
fret
(29) il capotasto
nut
(30) i marcatori
position markers
(31) il manico
neck
(32) le corde
string
(33) la buca
sound hole
(34) il ponte
bridge
(35) la chitarra acustica
acoustic guitar

130 I musei e le gallerie

Museums and galleries

130.1 AL MUSEO E ALLA GALLERIA D'ARTE · AT THE MUSEUM AND ART GALLERY

① **la galleria**
gallery

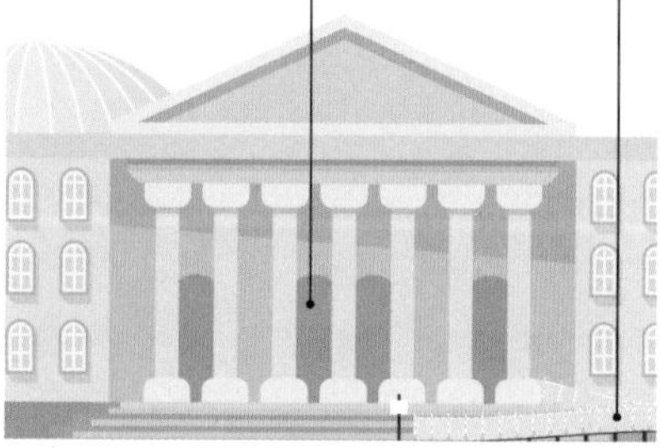

② **l'ingresso** *m*
entrance

③ **la rampa per sedie a rotelle**
wheelchair ramp

④ **il museo**
museum

⑤ **la toilette**
restrooms

⑥ **il guardaroba**
cloakroom

⑦ **la tariffa d'ingresso**
admission fee

⑧ **il biglietto**
ticket

⑨ **la biglietteria**
ticket office

⑩ **la donazione**
donation

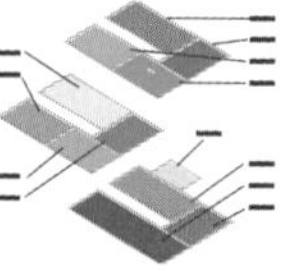

⑪ **la piantina**
floor plan

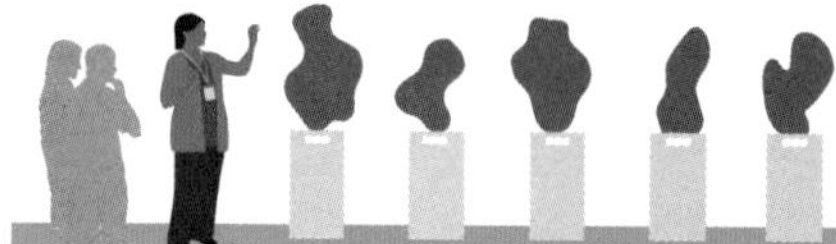

⑫ **il curatore** *m* / **la curatrice** *f*
curator

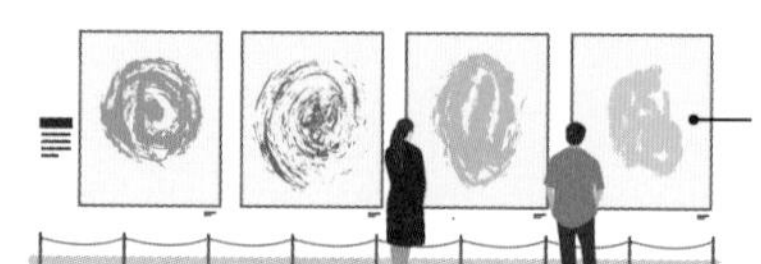

⑬ **la mostra**
exhibition

⑭ **l'opera esposta** *f*
exhibit

⑮ **la mostra permanente**
permanent exhibition

UNTIL
MAY 14

⑰ **l'installazione** *f*
installation

⑯ **la mostra temporanea**
temporary exhibition

⑱ **la collezione**
collection

⑲ **il restauro**
conservation

⑳ **la guida turistica**
tour guide

㉑ **l'audioguida** *f*
audio guide

㉒ **il divieto di fotografare**
no photography

㉓ **il negozio di souvenir**
gift shop

See also
42-43 In città • In town **132** Fare un giro turistico • Sightseeing
141-142 Le arti e i mestieri • Arts and crafts

㉙ Questo capolavoro è di valore inestimabile!
This masterpiece is priceless!

㉔ **la scultura**
sculpture

㉕ **la telecamera di sorveglianza**
surveillance camera

㉖ **il cartellino**
label

㉗ **il capolavoro**
masterpiece

㉘ **l'addetto alla sicurezza** *m*
l'addetta alla sicurezza *f*
security guard

㉚ **la cornice**
frame

㉛ **il dipinto**
painting

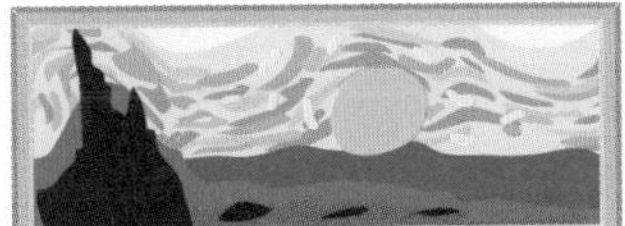

㉜ **il dipinto a olio**
oil painting

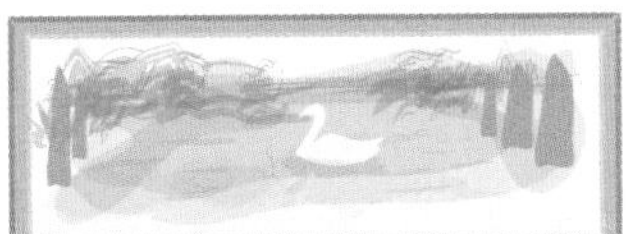

㉝ **l'acquerello** *m*
watercolor

㉞ **il Classicismo**
Classicism

㉟ **l'Impressionismo** *m*
Impressionism

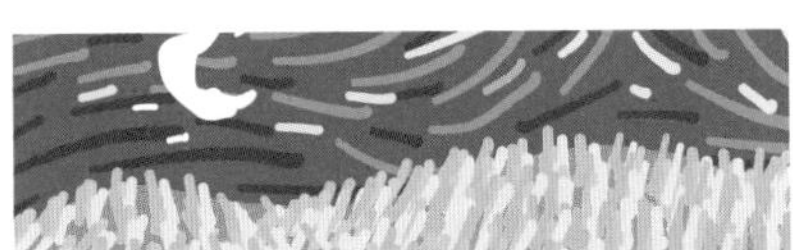

㊱ **il Post-impressionismo**
Post-Impressionism

㊶ **l'Art déco** *f*
Art Deco

㊷ **lo stile Liberty**
Art Nouveau

㊲ **il Cubismo**
Cubism

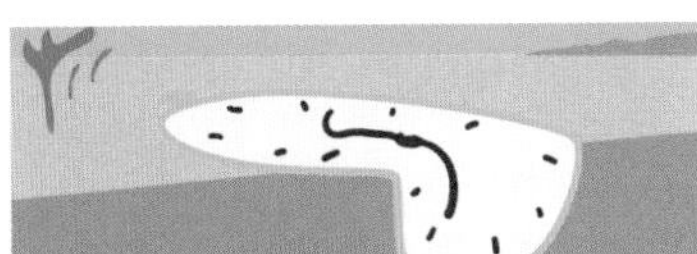

㊳ **il Surrealismo**
Surrealism

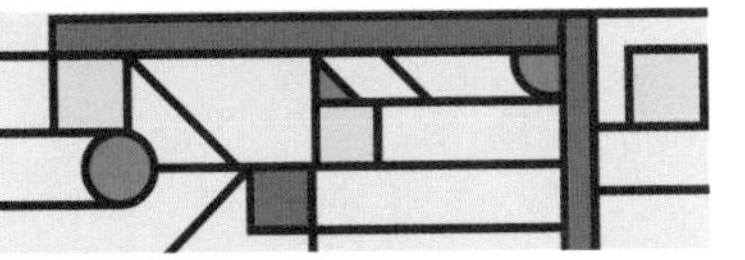

㊴ **il Bauhaus**
Bauhaus

㊵ **la Pop art**
Pop Art

㊸ **l'arte concettuale** *f*
conceptual art

131 Il viaggio e l'alloggio
Travel and accommodation

131.1 IL VIAGGIO · TRAVEL

① **la guida**
guidebook

② **il frasario**
phrasebook

③ **il biglietto di sola andata**
one-way ticket

④ **il biglietto di andata e ritorno**
round-trip

⑤ **prenotare una vacanza**
to book a vacation

⑥ **fare i bagagli**
to pack your bags

⑦ **andare in vacanza**
to go on a vacation

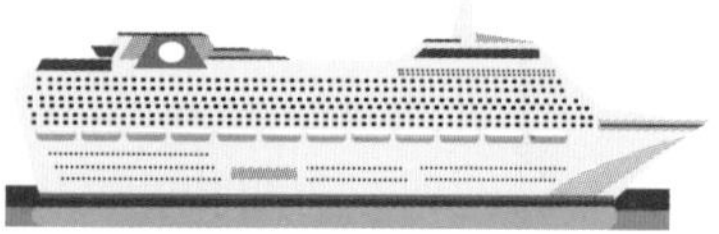
⑧ **andare in crociera**
to go on a cruise

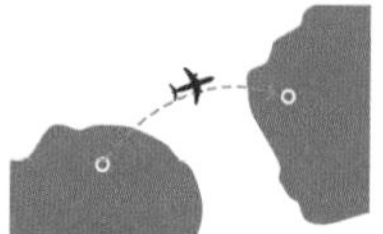
⑨ **andare all'estero**
to go abroad

⑩ **fare una prenotazione**
to make a reservation

⑪ **affittare un cottage**
to rent a cottage

⑫ **viaggiare con lo zaino in spalla**
to go backpacking

⑬ **fare il check-in**
to check in

⑭ **fare il check-out**
to check out

⑮ **alloggiare in albergo**
to stay in a hotel

131.2 L'ALLOGGIO · ACCOMMODATION

① **l'albergo** *m*
hotel

② **l'appartamento** *m*
apartment

③ **l'ostello** *m*
hostel

B&B
⑨ **la pensione**
guest house

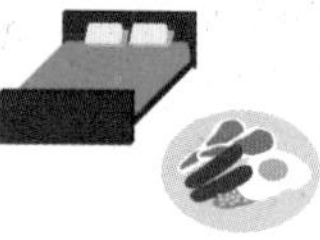
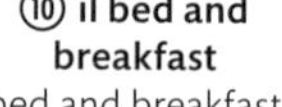
⑩ **il bed and breakfast**
bed and breakfast

⑪ **la casa vacanze**
villa

⑱ **l'ascensore** *m*
elevator

⑲ **gli ospiti**
guests

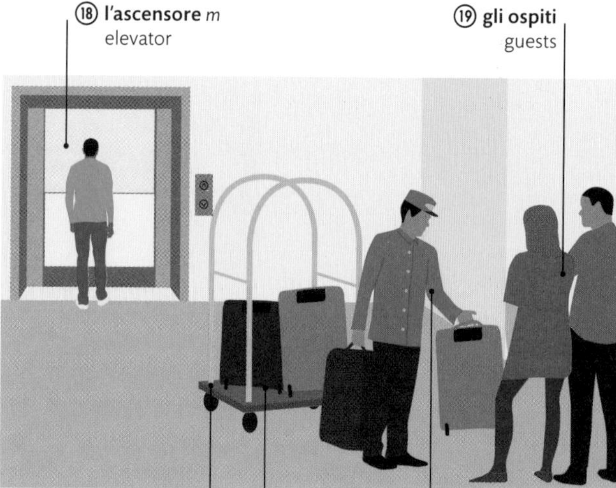

㉔ **il carrello**
trolley

㉕ **le valigie**
luggage

㉖ **il facchino** *m*
la facchina *f*
porter

131.3 I SERVIZI · SERVICES

① **il ristorante**
restaurant

② **la palestra**
gym

③ **la piscina**
swimming pool

See also
104 In aeroporto • At the airport **132** Fare un giro turistico • Sightseeing
133 Le attività all'aperto • Outdoor activities **134** In spiaggia • On the beach

④ **lo chalet**
chalet

⑤ **la baita**
cabin

⑥ **l'ecoturismo** *m*
ecotourism

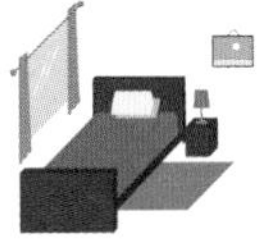

⑦ **la camera singola**
single room

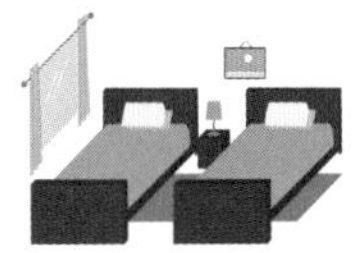

⑧ **la camera doppia con letti singoli**
twin room

⑫ **la camera doppia**
double room

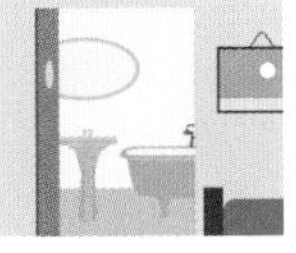

⑬ **il bagno in camera**
private bathroom

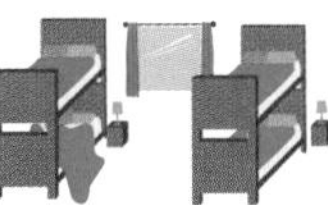

⑭ **il dormitorio**
dorm

⑮ **la camera con vista**
room with a view

1 2 3
4 5 6
7 8 9

⑯ **con camere libere**
vacancies

1 2 3
4 5 6
7 8 9

⑰ **al completo**
no vacancies

⑳ **il receptionist** *m*
la receptionist *f*
receptionist

㉑ **la reception**
front desk

㉒ **la toilette**
restrooms

㉓ **l'uscita di emergenza** *f*
emergency exit

㉗ **il bancone**
counter

㉘ **la hall dell'albergo**
hotel lobby

⑤ **il vassoio della colazione**
breakfast tray

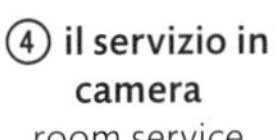

④ **il servizio in camera**
room service

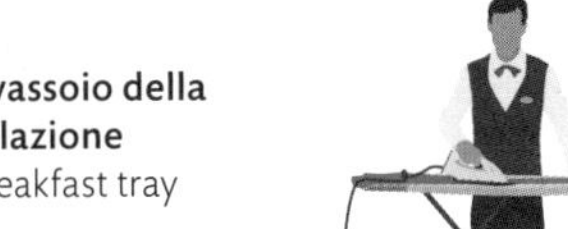

⑥ **il servizio di lavanderia**
laundry service

⑦ **il servizio di pulizie**
maid service

⑧ **il minibar**
minibar

⑨ **la cassaforte**
safe

Fare un giro turistico
Sightseeing

132.1 L'ATTRAZIONE TURISTICA · TOURIST ATTRACTION

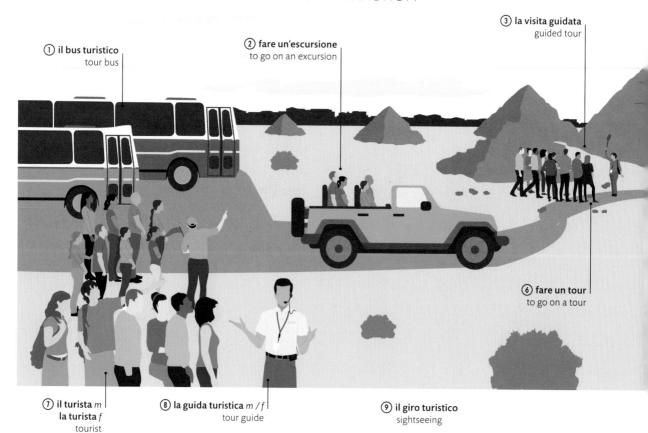

① **il bus turistico**
tour bus

② **fare un'escursione**
to go on an excursion

③ **la visita guidata**
guided tour

⑥ **fare un tour**
to go on a tour

⑦ **il turista** *m*
la turista *f*
tourist

⑧ **la guida turistica** *m / f*
tour guide

⑨ **il giro turistico**
sightseeing

132.2 LE ATTRAZIONI · ATTRACTIONS

① **la galleria d'arte**
art gallery

② **il museo**
museum

③ **il monumento**
monument

④ **il palazzo**
palace

⑤ **l'edificio storico** *m*
historic building

⑥ **il giardino botanico**
botanical gardens

⑧ il paesaggio
landscape
⑨ panoramico m
panoramica f
scenic

⑦ **il parco nazionale**
national park

See also
99 Le auto e gli autobus • Cars and buses **130** I musei e le gallerie • Museums and galleries
131 Il viaggio e l'alloggio • Travel and accommodation **149-151** I Paesi • Countries

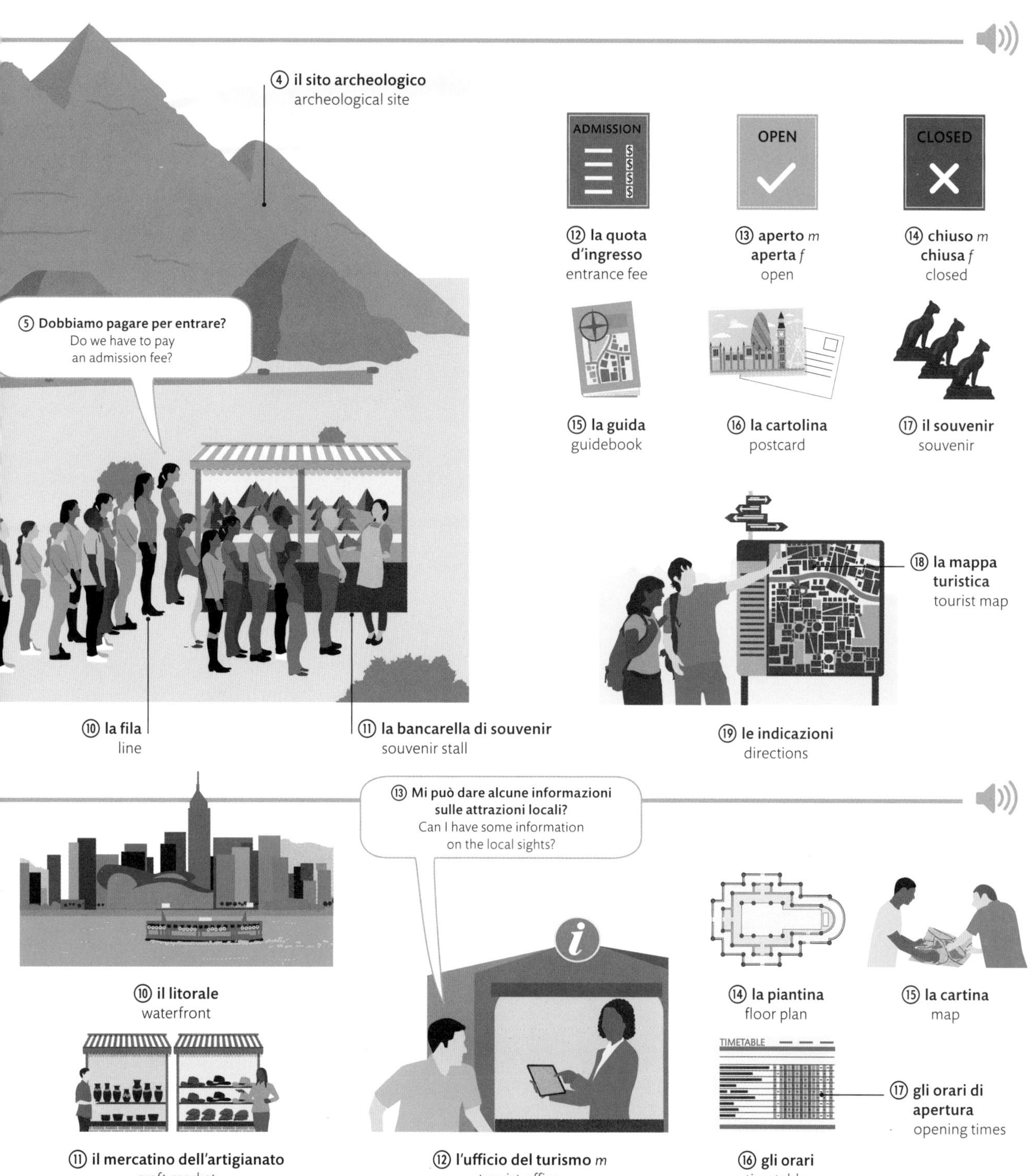
ADMISSION
$ $ $ $
OPEN
CLOSED
TIMETABLE

④ **il sito archeologico**
archeological site

⑤ **Dobbiamo pagare per entrare?**
Do we have to pay an admission fee?

⑩ **la fila**
line

⑪ **la bancarella di souvenir**
souvenir stall

⑫ **la quota d'ingresso**
entrance fee

⑬ **aperto** *m* **aperta** *f*
open

⑭ **chiuso** *m* **chiusa** *f*
closed

⑮ **la guida**
guidebook

⑯ **la cartolina**
postcard

⑰ **il souvenir**
souvenir

⑱ **la mappa turistica**
tourist map

⑲ **le indicazioni**
directions

⑩ **il litorale**
waterfront

⑪ **il mercatino dell'artigianato**
craft market

⑬ **Mi può dare alcune informazioni sulle attrazioni locali?**
Can I have some information on the local sights?

⑫ **l'ufficio del turismo** *m*
tourist office

⑭ **la piantina**
floor plan

⑮ **la cartina**
map

⑯ **gli orari**
timetable

⑰ **gli orari di apertura**
opening times

Le attività all'aperto
Outdoor activities

133.1 LE ATTIVITÀ ALL'APERTO • OPEN-AIR ACTIVITIES

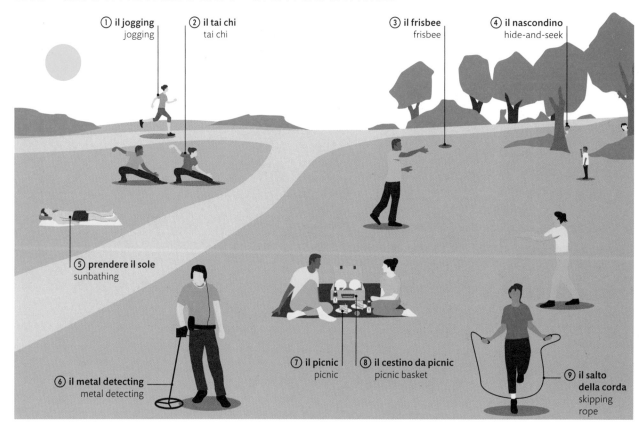

① **il jogging**
jogging

② **il tai chi**
tai chi

③ **il frisbee**
frisbee

④ **il nascondino**
hide-and-seek

⑤ **prendere il sole**
sunbathing

⑥ **il metal detecting**
metal detecting

⑦ **il picnic**
picnic

⑧ **il cestino da picnic**
picnic basket

⑨ **il salto della corda**
skipping rope

⑩ **il parco**
park

㉓ **la casa sull'albero**
tree house

㉔ **l'altalena** *f*
swing

㉒ **l'arrampicata sugli alberi** *f*
tree climbing

㉕ **il giardinaggio**
gardening

㉖ **il croquet**
croquet

㉗ **il bird watching**
bird-watching

㉘ **il paintball**
paintballing

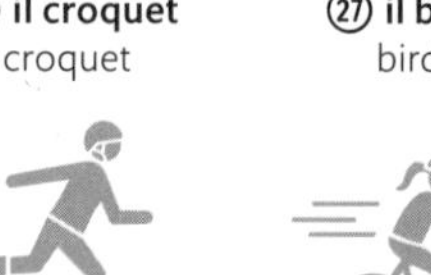

㉛ **la piscina per bambini**
wading pool

㉜ **lo skateboard**
skateboarding

㉝ **il monopattino**
scootering

㉞ **il pattinaggio in linea**
rollerblading

㉟ **andare in bicicletta**
bicycling

㊱ **il parkour**
parkour

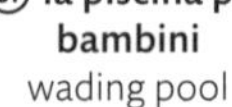
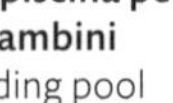
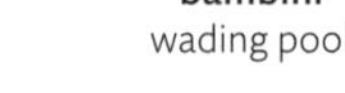

See also
11 Le abilità e le azioni • Abilities and actions **134** In spiaggia • On the beach
135 Il campeggio • Camping **148** Le cartine e le direzioni • Maps and directions

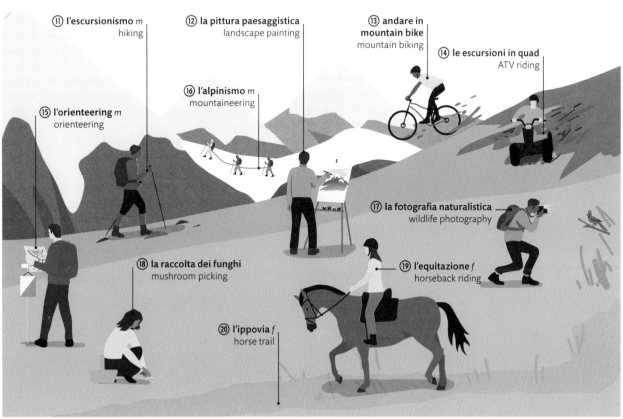

⑪ **l'escursionismo** *m*
hiking

⑫ **la pittura paesaggistica**
landscape painting

⑬ **andare in mountain bike**
mountain biking

⑭ **le escursioni in quad**
ATV riding

⑮ **l'orienteering** *m*
orienteering

⑯ **l'alpinismo** *m*
mountaineering

⑰ **la fotografia naturalistica**
wildlife photography

⑱ **la raccolta dei funghi**
mushroom picking

⑲ **l'equitazione** *f*
horseback riding

⑳ **l'ippovia** *f*
horse trail

㉑ **il parco nazionale**
national park

㉙ **lo zoosafari**
safari park

㉚ **la riserva naturale**
nature reserve

㊲ **lo zoo**
zoo

㊳ **l'area giochi per bambini** *f*
adventure playground

㊵ **la giostra dei cavalli**
carousel

㊶ **la ruota panoramica**
Ferris wheel

㊷ **le montagne russe**
roller-coaster

㊴ **il parco divertimenti**
theme park

134 In spiaggia
On the beach

134.1 LA SPIAGGIA · THE BEACH

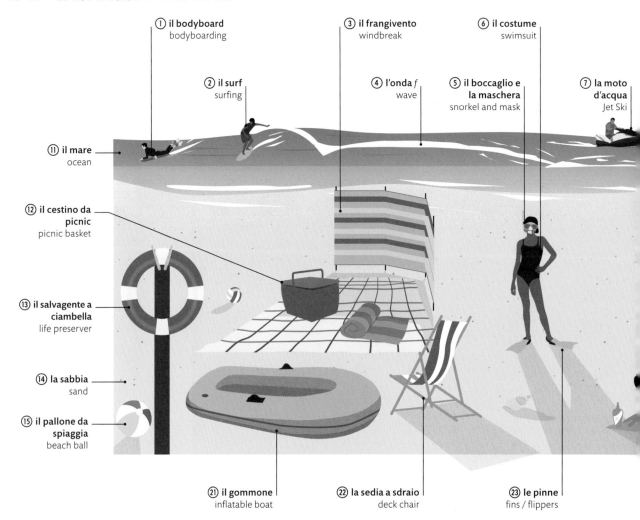

① **il bodyboard**
bodyboarding

② **il surf**
surfing

③ **il frangivento**
windbreak

④ **l'onda** *f*
wave

⑤ **il boccaglio e la maschera**
snorkel and mask

⑥ **il costume**
swimsuit

⑦ **la moto d'acqua**
Jet Ski

⑪ **il mare**
ocean

⑫ **il cestino da picnic**
picnic basket

⑬ **il salvagente a ciambella**
life preserver

⑭ **la sabbia**
sand

⑮ **il pallone da spiaggia**
beach ball

㉑ **il gommone**
inflatable boat

㉒ **la sedia a sdraio**
deck chair

㉓ **le pinne**
fins / flippers

㉕ **la vela**
sail

㉖ **lo yacht**
yacht

㉗ **il pontile**
boardwalk

㉘ **il lungomare**
promenade

㉙ **la cabina**
beach hut

See also
105 Le imbarcazioni • Sea vessels **118** Il nuoto • Swimming **119** La vela e gli sport acquatici • Sailing and watersports **121** La pesca • Fishing **133** Le attività all'aperto • Outdoor activities **166** La vita negli oceani • Ocean life

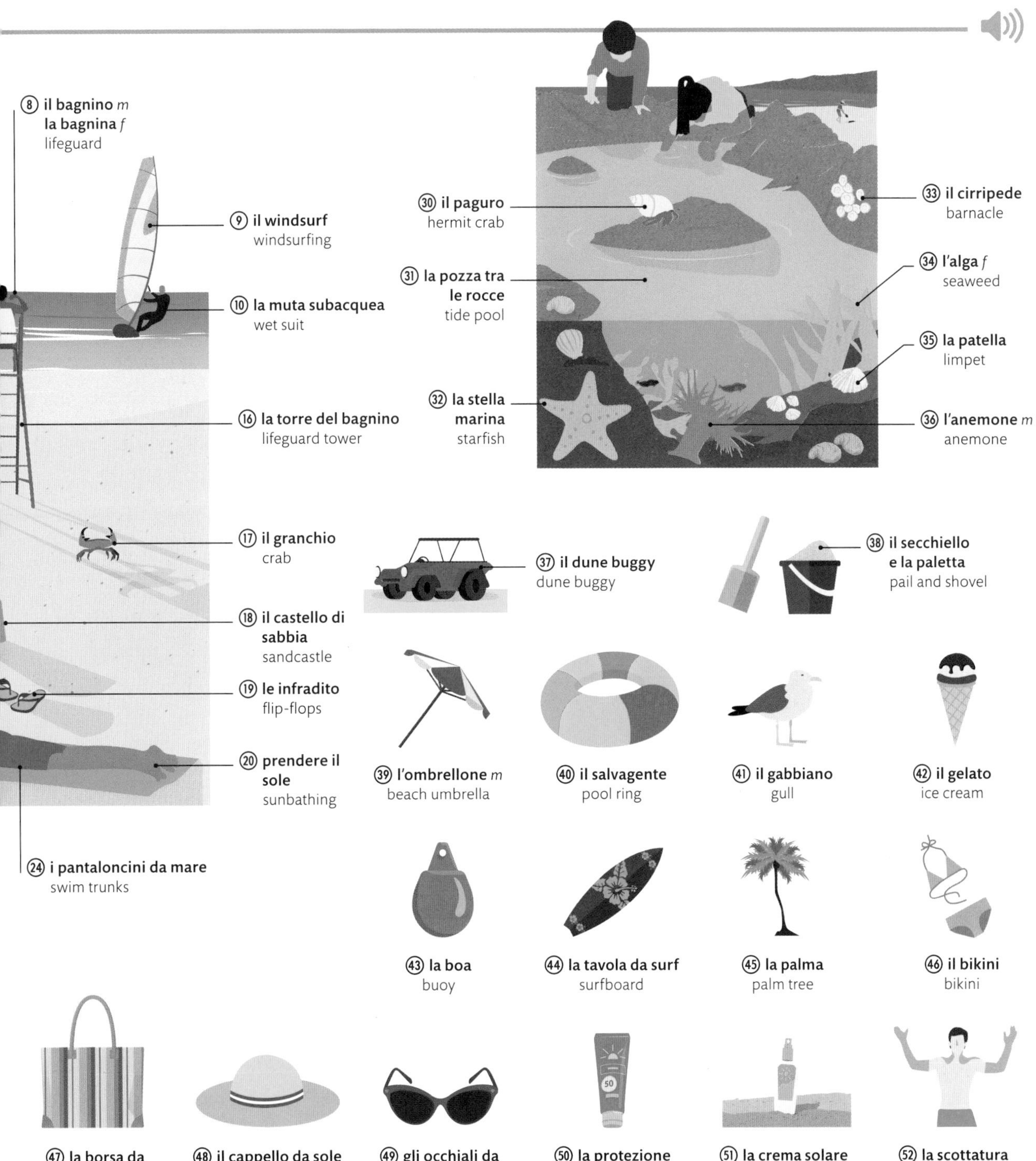
⑧ **il bagnino** *m*
la bagnina *f*
lifeguard
⑨ **il windsurf**
windsurfing
⑩ **la muta subacquea**
wet suit
⑯ **la torre del bagnino**
lifeguard tower
⑰ **il granchio**
crab
⑱ **il castello di sabbia**
sandcastle
⑲ **le infradito**
flip-flops
⑳ **prendere il sole**
sunbathing
㉔ **i pantaloncini da mare**
swim trunks
㉚ **il paguro**
hermit crab
㉛ **la pozza tra le rocce**
tide pool
㉜ **la stella marina**
starfish
㉝ **il cirripede**
barnacle
㉞ **l'alga** *f*
seaweed
㉟ **la patella**
limpet
㊱ **l'anemone** *m*
anemone
㊲ **il dune buggy**
dune buggy
㊳ **il secchiello e la paletta**
pail and shovel
㊴ **l'ombrellone** *m*
beach umbrella
㊵ **il salvagente**
pool ring
㊶ **il gabbiano**
gull
㊷ **il gelato**
ice cream
㊸ **la boa**
buoy
㊹ **la tavola da surf**
surfboard
㊺ **la palma**
palm tree
㊻ **il bikini**
bikini
㊼ **la borsa da spiaggia**
beach bag
㊽ **il cappello da sole**
sun hat
㊾ **gli occhiali da sole**
sunglasses
㊿ **la protezione solare**
sunblock
51 **la crema solare**
sunscreen
52 **la scottatura**
sunburn

Il campeggio
Camping

135.1 LE ATTREZZATURE E LE STRUTTURE PER IL CAMPEGGIO · CAMPING EQUIPMENT AND FACILITIES

① **fare campeggio**
to camp

② **montare la tenda**
to pitch a tent

③ **la tenda per due persone**
two-person tent

5
④ **l'area di campeggio** *f*
site

⑤ **le aree disponibili**
sites available

⑥ **pieno**
full

⑧ **l'allaccio della luce** *m*
electric hook-up

⑨ **la roulotte**
trailer

⑩ **il camper**
motor home

⑪ **l'amaca** *f*
hammock

⑫ **il falò**
campfire

⑬ **accendere il fuoco**
to light a fire

⑮ **la carbonella**
charcoal

⑯ **il barbecue**
barbecue

⑰ **il fornello da campeggio**
single-burner camping stove

⑱ **il fornello da campeggio a due fuochi**
double-burner camping stove

⑲ **la griglia pieghevole**
folding grill

⑳ **la panca da picnic**
picnic bench

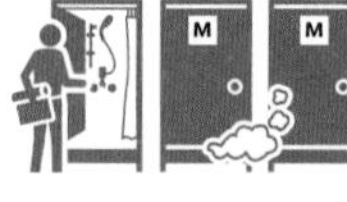
M
M
㉒ **l'area docce** *f*
shower block

W
W
㉓ **l'area bagni** *f*
toilet block

㉔ **lo smaltimento dei rifiuti**
waste disposal

㉕ **l'ufficio del responsabile dello stabilimento** *m*
l'ufficio della responsabile dello stabilimento *f*
site manager's office

㉖ **lo zaino**
backpack

㉗ **la torcia**
flashlight

N
W
E
S
㉙ **la bussola**
compass

㉚ **l'abbigliamento termico** *m*
thermals

㉛ **le scarpe da trekking**
walking boots

㉜ **gli indumenti impermeabili**
rain gear

㉝ **il coltellino svizzero**
multi-purpose knife

㉞ **il repellente per insetti**
insect repellent

㊱ **il sacco a pelo**
sleeping bag

㊲ **il materassino**
sleeping mat

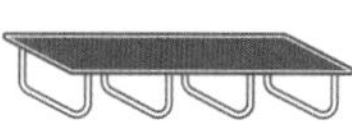
㊳ **la branda**
camp bed

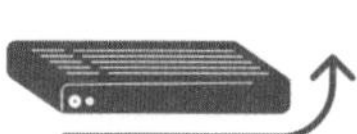
㊴ **il materassino autogonfiante**
self-inflating mattress

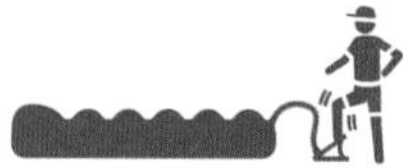
㊵ **il materasso ad aria**
air bed / air mattress

㊶ **la pompa ad aria**
air pump

See also
131 Il viaggio e l'alloggio • Travel and accommodation **133** Le attività all'aperto • Outdoor activities **146-147** La geografia • Geography

135.2 IL CAMPEGGIO • CAMPGROUND

⑦ **il caravan**
camper

⑭ **l'accendifuoco** *m*
firestarter

㉑ **le bottiglie d'acqua**
water bottles

㉘ **la torcia frontale**
headlamp

㉟ **la zanzariera**
mosquito net

㊷ **la pompa elettrica**
electric pump

① **la tenda familiare**
family tent

② **la struttura**
frame

③ **il piolo**
tent pole

④ **il tirante**
guy line

⑤ **la tenda automatica**
pop-up tent

⑥ **il frigo portatile**
cooler

⑦ **il thermos**
thermal flask

⑧ **il picchetto**
tent peg

⑨ **il pozzo del fuoco**
firepit

⑩ **il recipiente per l'acqua**
water carrier

⑪ **il sovratelo**
rainfly

⑫ **la lanterna**
lamp / lantern

⑬ **il telo impermeabile**
groundsheet

L'home entertainment

Home entertainment

136.1 LA TELEVISIONE E I SISTEMI AUDIO · TELEVISION AND AUDIO

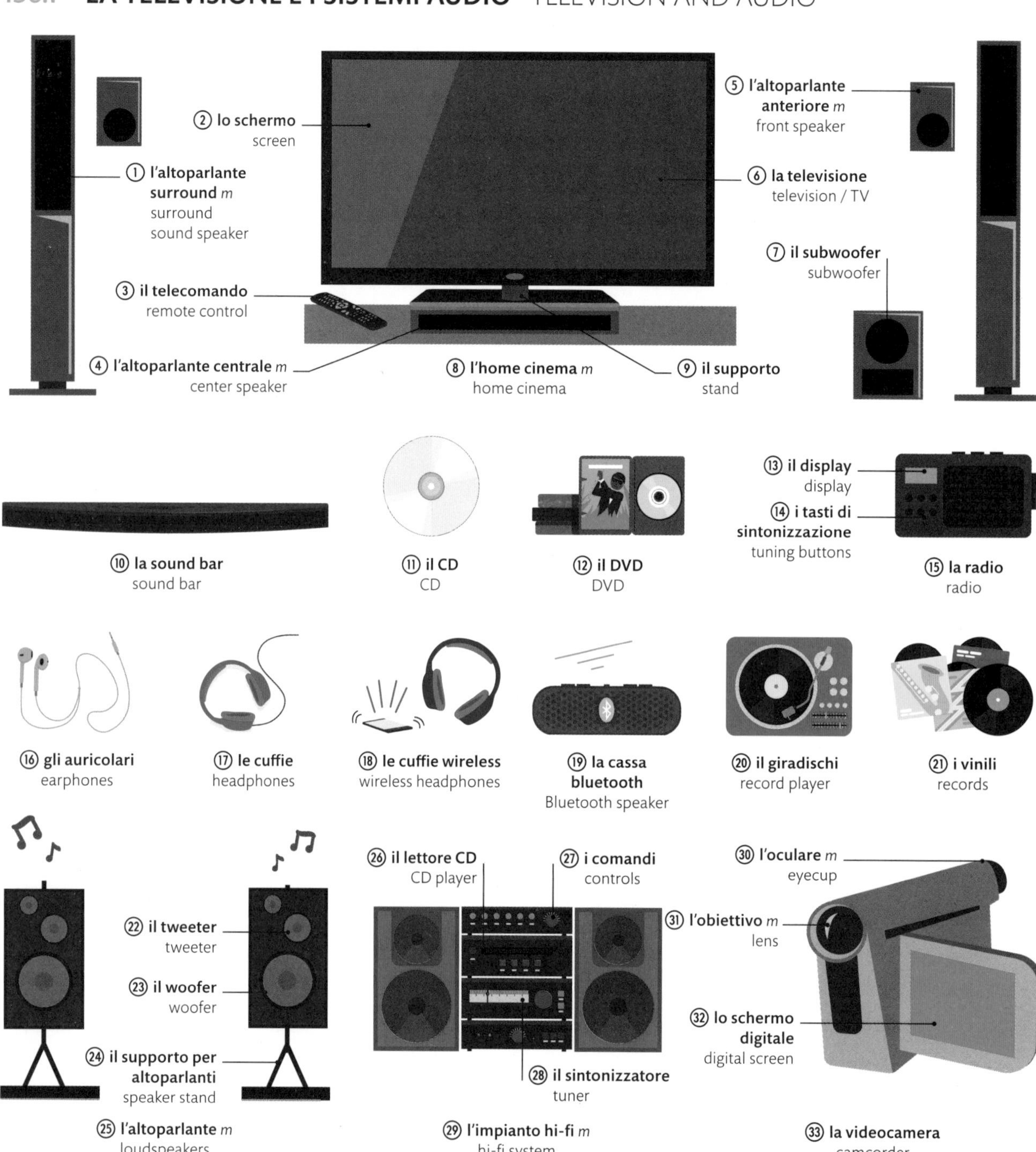

① l'altoparlante surround *m*
surround sound speaker
② lo schermo
screen
③ il telecomando
remote control
④ l'altoparlante centrale *m*
center speaker
⑤ l'altoparlante anteriore *m*
front speaker
⑥ la televisione
television / TV
⑦ il subwoofer
subwoofer
⑧ l'home cinema *m*
home cinema
⑨ il supporto
stand
⑩ la sound bar
sound bar
⑪ il CD
CD
⑫ il DVD
DVD
⑬ il display
display
⑭ i tasti di sintonizzazione
tuning buttons
⑮ la radio
radio
⑯ gli auricolari
earphones
⑰ le cuffie
headphones
⑱ le cuffie wireless
wireless headphones
⑲ la cassa bluetooth
Bluetooth speaker
⑳ il giradischi
record player
㉑ i vinili
records
㉒ il tweeter
tweeter
㉓ il woofer
woofer
㉔ il supporto per altoparlanti
speaker stand
㉕ l'altoparlante *m*
loudspeakers
㉖ il lettore CD
CD player
㉗ i comandi
controls
㉘ il sintonizzatore
tuner
㉙ l'impianto hi-fi *m*
hi-fi system
㉚ l'oculare *m*
eyecup
㉛ l'obiettivo *m*
lens
㉜ lo schermo digitale
digital screen
㉝ la videocamera
camcorder

See also
127 I film • Movies **128-129** La musica • Music
137 La televisione • Television **140** I giochi • Games

㉞ **lo stereo**
stereo

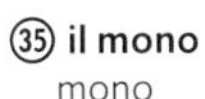
㉟ **il mono**
mono

㊱ **sintonizzarsi**
to tune in

㊲ **il volume**
volume

㊳ **alzare il volume**
to turn up

㊴ **abbassare il volume**
to turn down

㊵ **l'antenna parabolica** *f*
satellite dish

㊶ **il decoder digitale**
digital box

㊷ **il microfono**
microphone

㊸ **il karaoke**
karaoke

136.2 I VIDEOGIOCHI • VIDEO GAMES

① **la console**
console

② **il controller**
controller

③ **il gioco di strategia**
strategy game

④ **il gioco a quiz**
trivia game

⑤ **il gioco a piattaforme**
platform game

⑥ **il gioco d'avventura**
adventure game

⑦ **il gioco di ruolo**
role-playing game

⑧ **il gioco d'azione**
action game

⑨ **il gioco multigiocatore**
multiplayer game

⑩ **il gioco di simulazione**
simulation game

⑪ **il gioco di sport**
sports game

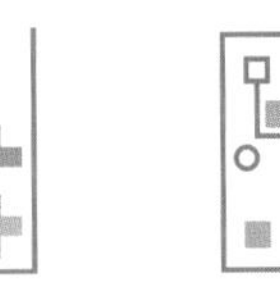
⑫ **il puzzle**
puzzle game

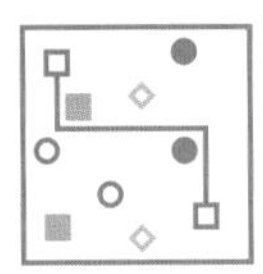
⑬ **il gioco di logica**
logic game

137 La televisione
Television

137.1 GUARDARE LA TELEVISIONE • WATCHING TELEVISION

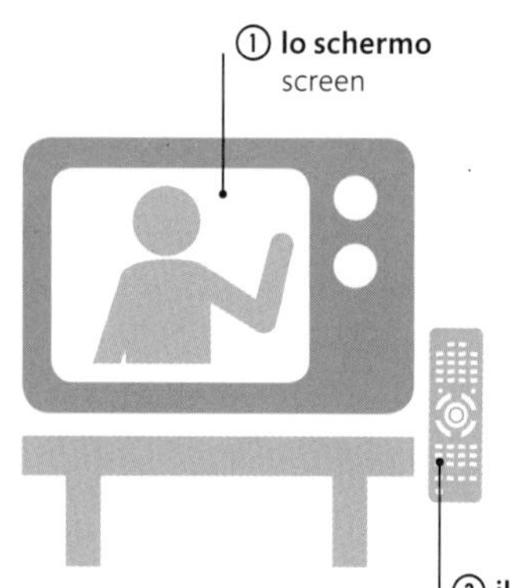

(1) **lo schermo**
screen

(2) **il televisore**
TV set

(3) **il telecomando**
remote control

(4) **l'alta definizione** *f*
high-definition

(5) **la tv via cavo**
cable TV

(6) **la tv satellitare**
satellite TV

(7) **il video on demand**
video on demand

(8) **il canale**
channel

(9) **il canale pay per view**
pay-per-view channel

(10) **l'episodio** *m*
episode

(11) **la stagione**
season

(12) **il programma**
show

(13) **i sottotitoli**
subtitles

(14) **l'intervista** *f*
interview

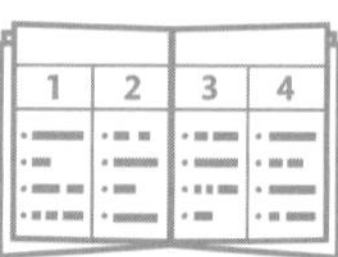
1
2
3
4

(15) **la guida tv**
TV guide / schedule

(16) **l'anticipazione** *f*
preview

(17) **il reporter** *m* **la reporter** *f*
reporter

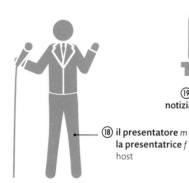

(18) **il presentatore** *m* **la presentatrice** *f*
host

(19) **il conduttore del notiziario** *m* / **la conduttrice del notiziario** *f*
news anchor

(20) **la pubblicità**
commercial break

(21) **le previsioni del tempo**
weather forecaster

(22) **il pantofolaio** *m* **la pantofolaia** *f*
couch potato

137.2 I VERBI DELLA TELEVISIONE • TELEVISION VERBS

(1) **accendere**
to turn on

(2) **spegnere**
to turn off

(3) **alzare il volume**
to turn up the volume

(4) **abbassare il volume**
to turn down the volume

(5) **cambiare canale**
to change the channel

(6) **trasmettere in streaming**
to stream

See also
26 Il salotto e la sala da pranzo • Living room and dining room **84** I media • Media
127 I film • Movies **136** L'home entertainment • Home entertainment

137.3 I PROGRAMMI E I CANALI TELEVISIVI • TV SHOWS AND CHANNELS

① **il programma di cucina**
cooking show

② **il talk show**
talk show

③ **il programma sportivo**
sports

④ **il documentario**
documentary

⑤ **il documentario sulla natura**
nature documentary

⑥ **il dramma in costume**
period drama / costume drama

⑦ **la sitcom**
sitcom

⑧ **il quiz televisivo**
quiz show

⑨ **il programma di attualità**
current affairs

⑩ **il notiziario**
news

⑪ **il meteo**
weather

⑫ **la telenovela**
soap opera

⑬ **il gioco a premi**
game show

⑭ **la commedia**
comedy

⑮ **il cartone animato**
cartoon

⑯ **il poliziesco**
crime

⑰ **il thriller**
thriller

⑱ **la satira**
satire

⑲ **la tv per bambini**
children's show

⑳ **il programma del mattino**
morning show

㉑ **il reality**
reality TV

㉒ **la catch-up tv**
catch-up TV

㉓ **il canale di televendite**
shopping channel

㉔ **il canale musicale**
music channel

⑦ **riprodurre**
to play

⑧ **fermare**
to stop

⑨ **mettere in pausa**
to pause

⑩ **tornare indietro**
to rewind

⑪ **mandare avanti**
to fast forward

•REC
⑫ **registrare**
to record

138 I libri e la lettura

Books and reading

138.1 I LIBRI • BOOKS

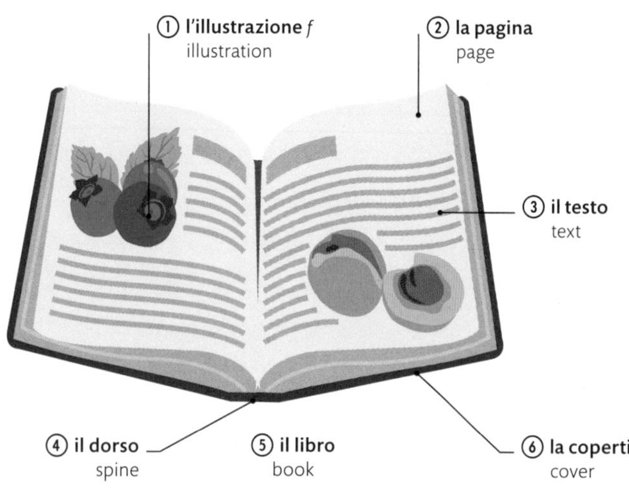

① l'illustrazione *f*
illustration

② la pagina
page

③ il testo
text

④ il dorso
spine

⑤ il libro
book

⑥ la copertina
cover

⑦ l'autore *m*
l'autrice *f*
author

⑧ il libro tascabile
paperback

⑨ il libro con copertina rigida
hardback

⑬ la recensione
review

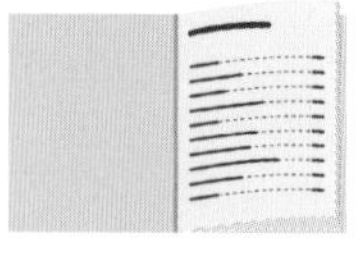

⑭ l'indice *m*
contents

2

⑮ il capitolo
chapter

138.2 LA LETTURA E I GENERI • READING AND GENRES

① la saggistica
nonfiction

B

② il dizionario
dictionary

1 2 3 4 5

③ l'enciclopedia *f*
encyclopedia

④ il libro di giardinaggio
gardening book

⑤ la guida tv
TV guide

⑥ il manuale di auto-aiuto
self-help

⑦ l'autobiografia *f*
autobiography

⑧ la biografia
biography

⑨ il libro di cucina
cookbook

⑩ la guida turistica
guidebook

⑪ il libro sulla natura
nature writing

⑫ il libro di testo
textbook / course book

⑬ la narrativa
fiction

Great Adventure Stories

⑭ il romanzo
novel

⑮ il libro di fantascienza
science fiction

⑯ il libro fantasy
fantasy

⑰ il fumetto
comic

⑱ la letteratura di viaggio
travel writing

See also
127 I film • Movies **136** L'home entertainment • Home entertainment
139 Il fantasy e il mito • Fantasy and myth **175** La scrittura • Writing

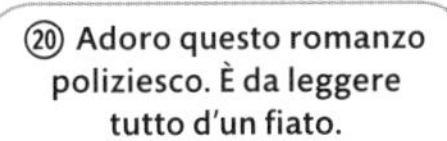
⑳ **Adoro questo romanzo poliziesco. È da leggere tutto d'un fiato.**
I love this crime novel. It's a real page-turner.

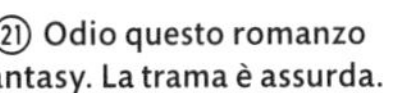
㉑ **Odio questo romanzo fantasy. La trama è assurda.**
I hate this fantasy novel. The plot is ridiculous.

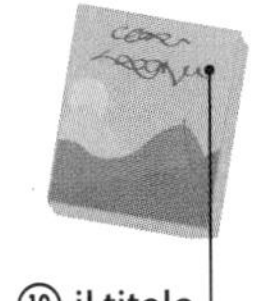

⑩ **il titolo**
title

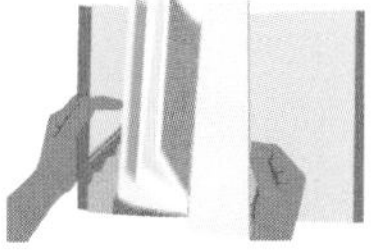

⑪ **sfogliare**
to flip through

⑫ **il lettore di e-book**
e-reader

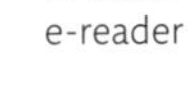
Bibliography

⑯ **la bibliografia**
bibliography

Glossary

⑰ **il glossario**
glossary

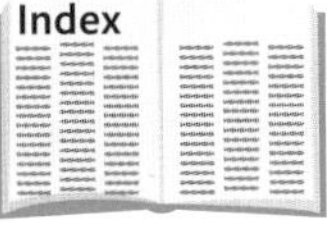
Index

⑱ **l'indice** *m*
index

⑲ **la lettura**
reading

Jane Austen
Charles Dickens
Chinua Achebe
SHAKESPEARE
Virginia Woolf
MARY SHELLEY
Gabriel Garcia Marquez
G. FLAUBERT

⑲ **la narrativa letteraria**
literary fiction

㉑ **il personaggio**
character

⑳ **il libro per bambini**
children's book

㉒ **il libro da colorare**
coloring book

㉓ **la favola**
fairy tale

㉔ **la storia d'amore**
romance

㉕ **il romanzo poliziesco**
crime fiction

㉖ **il libro umoristico**
humor

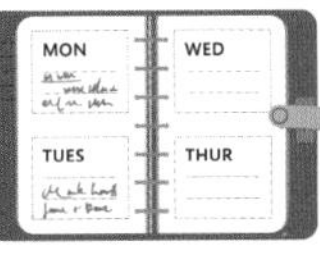
MON
WED
TUES
THUR

㉗ **l'agenda** *f*
planner

#1

㉘ **il bestseller**
bestseller

㉙ **l'oroscopo** *m*
horoscope

㉚ **la rivista di gossip**
gossip magazine

㉛ **l'enigmistica** *f*
puzzles

㉝ **il titolo**
headline

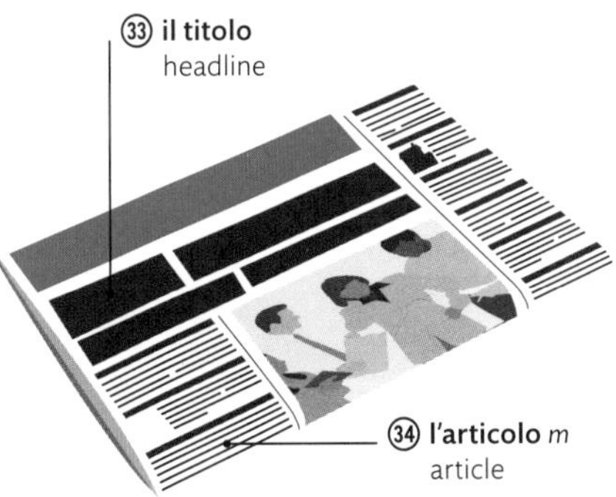

㉞ **l'articolo** *m*
article

㉜ **il giornale**
newspaper

139 Il fantasy e il mito
Fantasy and myth

139.1 I MITI, LE STORIE E LE CREATURE FANTASTICHE · MYTHS, STORIES, AND FANTASTIC CREATURES

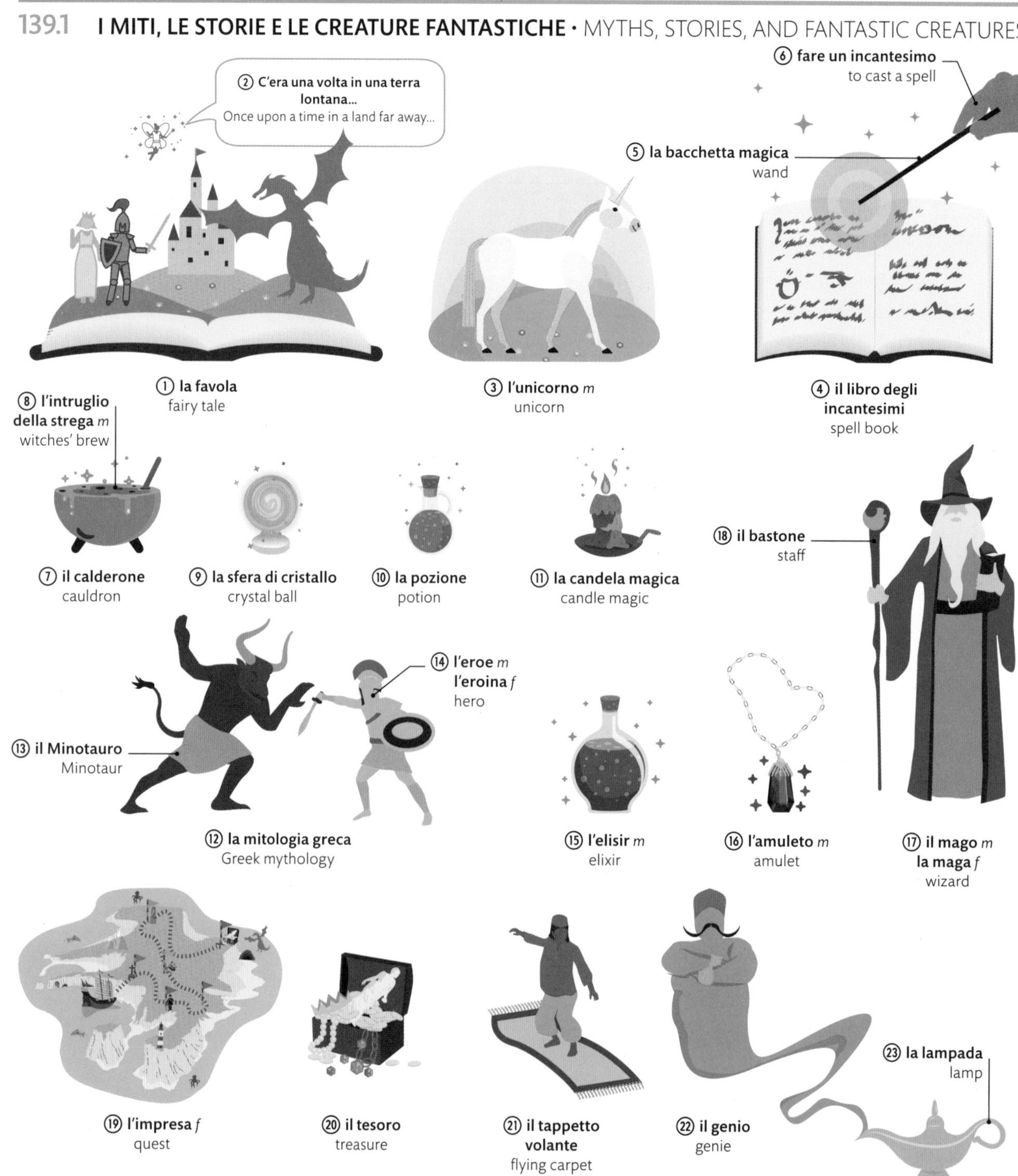

② C'era una volta in una terra lontana...
Once upon a time in a land far away...
⑥ fare un incantesimo
to cast a spell
⑤ la bacchetta magica
wand
① la favola
fairy tale
③ l'unicorno m
unicorn
④ il libro degli incantesimi
spell book
⑧ l'intruglio della strega m
witches' brew
⑦ il calderone
cauldron
⑨ la sfera di cristallo
crystal ball
⑩ la pozione
potion
⑪ la candela magica
candle magic
⑱ il bastone
staff
⑭ l'eroe m
l'eroina f
hero
⑬ il Minotauro
Minotaur
⑫ la mitologia greca
Greek mythology
⑮ l'elisir m
elixir
⑯ l'amuleto m
amulet
⑰ il mago m
la maga f
wizard
⑲ l'impresa f
quest
⑳ il tesoro
treasure
㉑ il tappetto volante
flying carpet
㉒ il genio
genie
㉓ la lampada
lamp

See also
127 I film • Movies **137** La televisione • Television
138 I libri e la lettura • Books and reading

㉔ **il serpente marino**
sea serpent

㉕ **Hugin e Munin**
Hugin and Munin

㉖ **le Disir**
the Disir

㉗ **il mostro**
monster

㉘ **lo zombie**
zombie

㉙ **il licantropo**
werewolf

㉚ **il vampiro**
vampire

㉛ **il fantasma**
ghost

㉜ **la zucca di Halloween**
jack-o'-lantern

㉝ **il drago**
dragon

㉞ **il cavaliere**
knight

㊱ **la scopa**
broomstick

㉟ **la strega**
witch

㊲ **la fata**
fairy

㊳ **il folletto**
pixie

㊴ **il fauno**
faun

㊵ **lo gnomo**
gnome

㊶ **il leprecauno**
leprechaun

㊷ **il gremlin**
gremlin

㊸ **il goblin**
goblin

㊹ **il troll**
troll

㊺ **l'ogre** *m*
ogre

㊻ **l'orco** *m*
orc

㊼ **il gigante** *m*
la gigantessa *f*
giant

㊽ **l'elfo** *m*
elf

㊾ **il nano**
dwarf

㊿ **la sirena**
mermaid

51 **il tritone**
merman

52 **la fenice**
phoenix

53 **il grifone**
griffin

54 **l'idra** *f*
hydra

55 **il centauro**
centaur

56 **la sfinge**
sphinx

57 **Cerbero**
Cerberus

58 **il robot cattivo**
bad robot

59 **l'alieno** *m*
l'aliena *f*
alien

140 I giochi
Games

140.1 GLI SCACCHI · CHESS

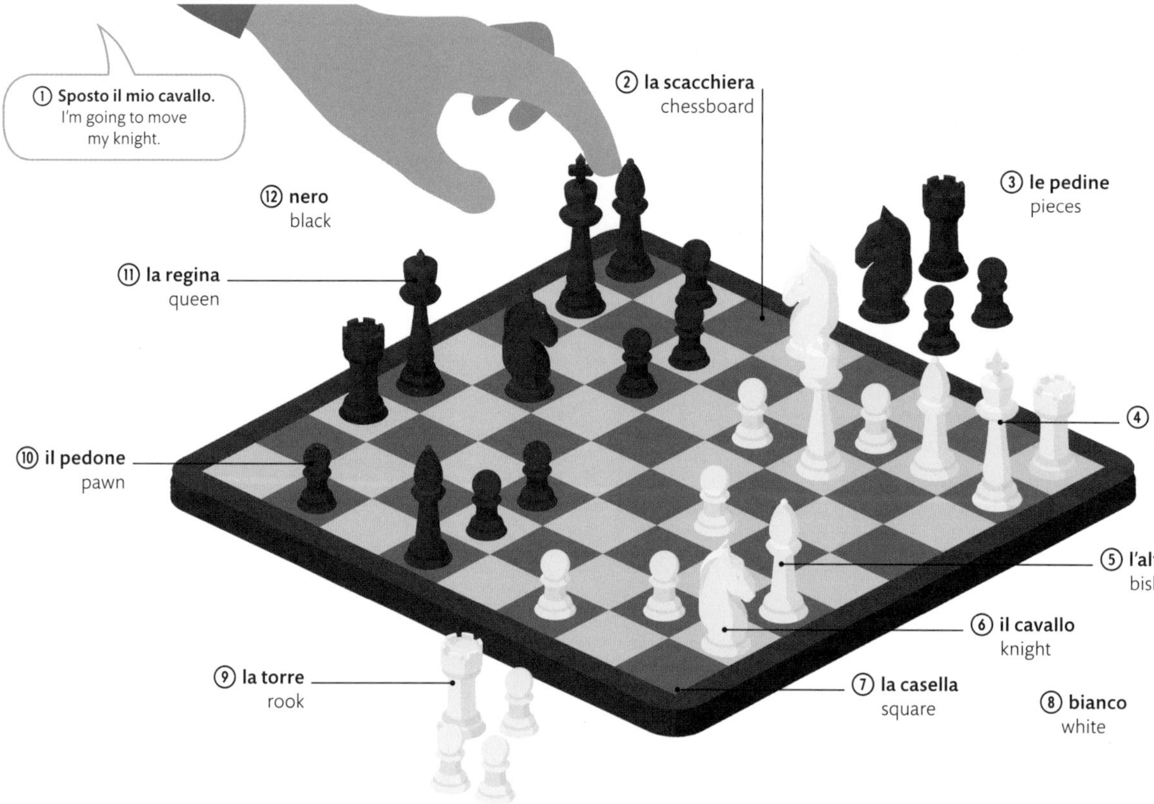

① **Sposto il mio cavallo.**
I'm going to move my knight.

② **la scacchiera**
chessboard

③ **le pedine**
pieces

④ **il re**
king

⑤ **l'alfiere** *m*
bishop

⑥ **il cavallo**
knight

⑦ **la casella**
square

⑧ **bianco**
white

⑨ **la torre**
rook

⑩ **il pedone**
pawn

⑪ **la regina**
queen

⑫ **nero**
black

140.3 I GIOCHI · GAMES

① **i giochi da tavolo**
board games

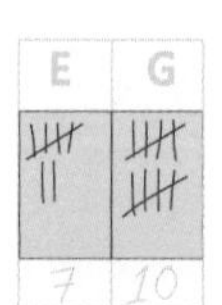
E
G
7
10
② **i punti**
points

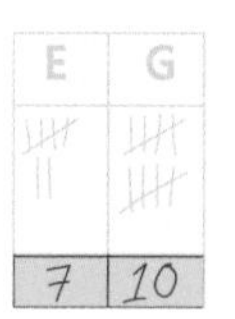
E
G
7
10
③ **il punteggio**
score

④ **il tris**
tic-tac-toe

⑤ **i dadi**
dice

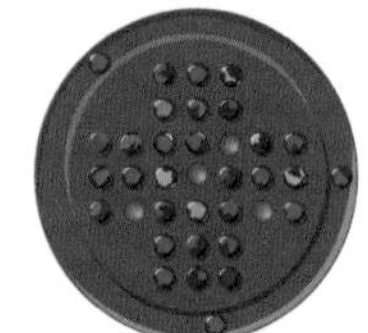
⑥ **il solitario**
solitaire

⑦ **le pedine**
pieces

⑧ **il puzzle**
jigsaw puzzle

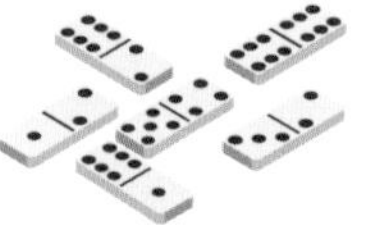
⑨ **il domino**
dominoes

⑩ **le freccette**
darts

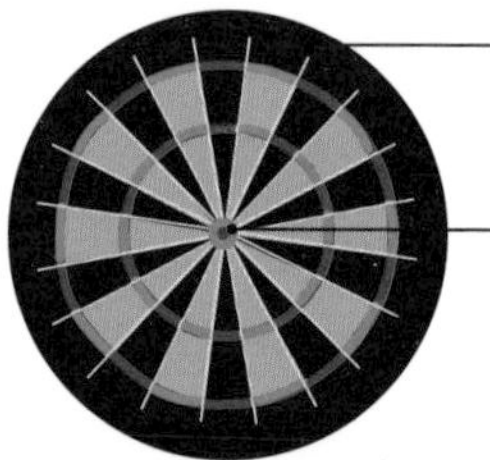
⑪ **il bersaglio**
dartboard

⑫ **il centro del bersaglio**
bull's-eye

See also
136 L'home entertainment • Home entertainment **138** I libri e la lettura
Books and reading **141-142** Le arti e i mestieri • Arts and crafts

140.2 GIOCARE A CARTE • PLAYING CARDS

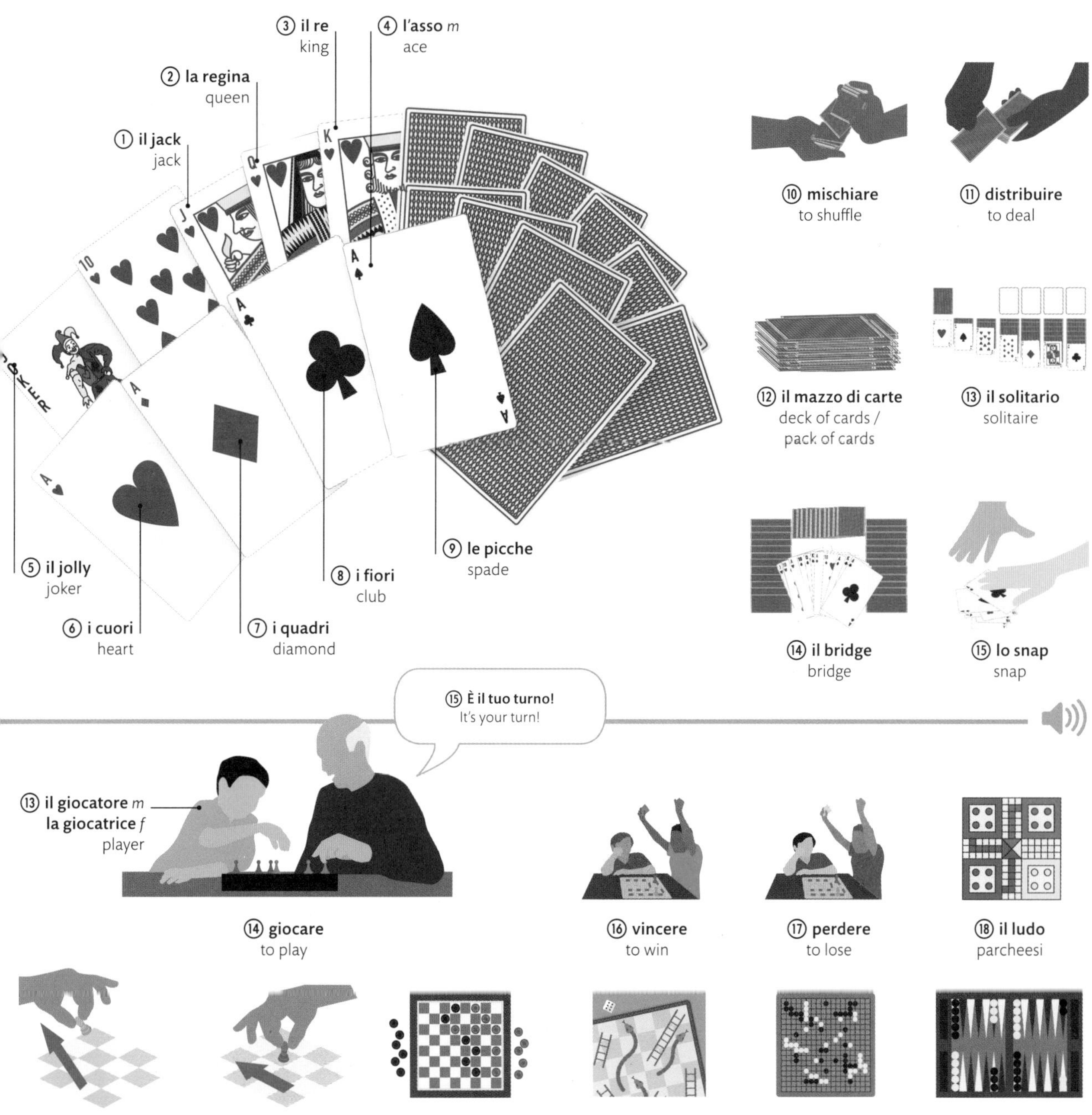
① **il jack**
jack
② **la regina**
queen
③ **il re**
king
④ **l'asso** *m*
ace
⑤ **il jolly**
joker
⑥ **i cuori**
heart
⑦ **i quadri**
diamond
⑧ **i fiori**
club
⑨ **le picche**
spade
⑩ **mischiare**
to shuffle
⑪ **distribuire**
to deal
⑫ **il mazzo di carte**
deck of cards / pack of cards
⑬ **il solitario**
solitaire
⑭ **il bridge**
bridge
⑮ **lo snap**
snap
⑮ **È il tuo turno!**
It's your turn!
⑬ **il giocatore** *m*
la giocatrice *f*
player
⑭ **giocare**
to play
⑯ **vincere**
to win
⑰ **perdere**
to lose
⑱ **il ludo**
parcheesi
⑲ **catturare**
to take
⑳ **muovere**
to move
㉑ **la dama**
checkers
㉒ **scale e serpenti**
chutes and ladders
㉓ **il go**
go
㉔ **il backgammon**
backgammon

141 Le arti e i mestieri
Arts and crafts

141.1 LA PITTURA • PAINTING

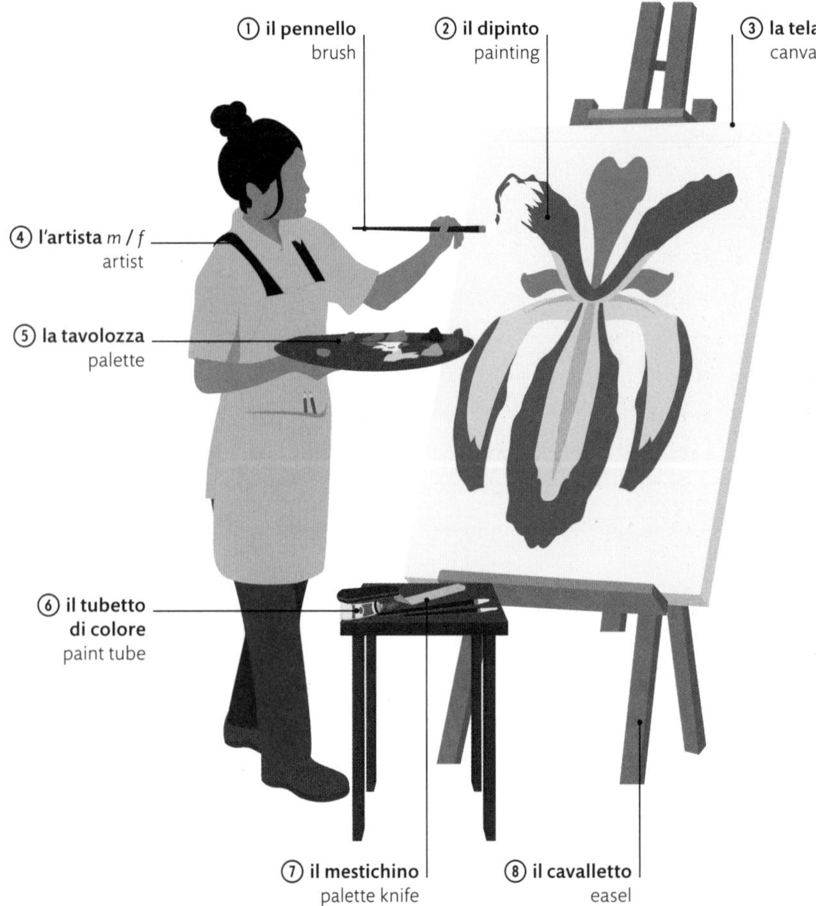

① il pennello
brush
② il dipinto
painting
③ la tela
canvas
④ l'artista *m / f*
artist
⑤ la tavolozza
palette
⑥ il tubetto di colore
paint tube
⑦ il mestichino
palette knife
⑧ il cavalletto
easel

⑨ **il rosso**
red

⑩ **lo scarlatto**
scarlet

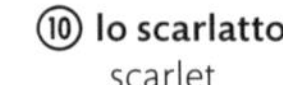

⑪ **il blu**
blue

⑫ **il turchese**
turquoise

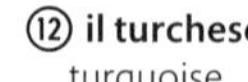

⑬ **il blu marino**
navy blue

⑭ **il giallo**
yellow

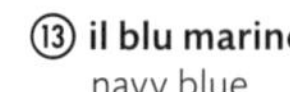

⑮ **il verde**
green

⑯ **l'arancione** *m*
orange

⑰ **il viola**
purple

⑱ **l'indaco** *m*
indigo

⑲ **il rosa**
pink

⑳ **il marrone**
brown

㉑ **il grigio**
gray

㉒ **il nero**
black

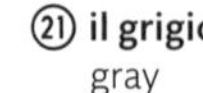

㉓ **il bianco**
white

㉔ **i colori a olio**
oil paints

㉕ **gli acquerelli**
watercolors

㉖ **i pastelli**
pastels

㉗ **i colori acrilici**
acrylic paints

㉘ **la tempera**
poster paint

See also
37 La decorazione • Renovating **130** I musei e le gallerie • Museums and galleries **142** Le arti e i mestieri (continua) • Arts and crafts continued

141.2 LE ALTRE ARTI E I MESTIERI • OTHER ARTS AND CRAFTS

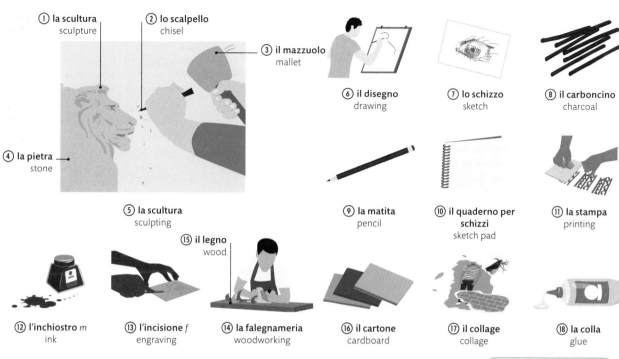

① **la scultura**
sculpture

② **lo scalpello**
chisel

③ **il mazzuolo**
mallet

④ **la pietra**
stone

⑤ **la scultura**
sculpting

⑥ **il disegno**
drawing

⑦ **lo schizzo**
sketch

⑧ **il carboncino**
charcoal

⑨ **la matita**
pencil

⑩ **il quaderno per schizzi**
sketch pad

⑪ **la stampa**
printing

⑮ **il legno**
wood

⑫ **l'inchiostro** *m*
ink

⑬ **l'incisione** *f*
engraving

⑭ **la falegnameria**
woodworking

⑯ **il cartone**
cardboard

⑰ **il collage**
collage

⑱ **la colla**
glue

⑲ **l'origami** *m*
origami

⑳ **la modellistica**
model making

㉑ **la cartapesta**
papier-mâché

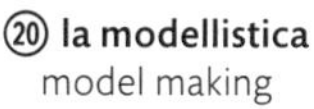

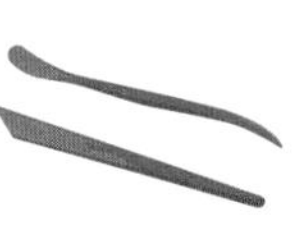

㉒ **l'utensile di modellazione** *m*
modeling tool

㉓ **la gioielleria**
making jewelry

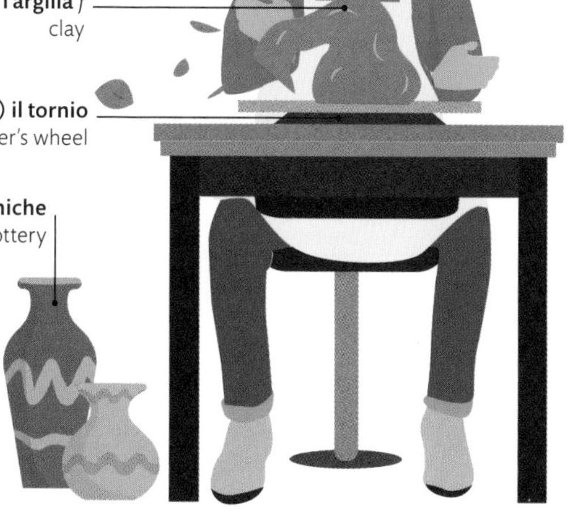

㉘ **Nel tempo libero creo vasi.**
I make pots in my spare time.

㉔ **il vasaio** *m*
la vasaia *f*
potter

㉕ **l'argilla** *f*
clay

㉖ **il tornio**
potter's wheel

㉗ **le ceramiche**
pottery

142 Le arti e i mestieri (continua)
Arts and crafts continued

142.1 IL CUCITO · SEWING

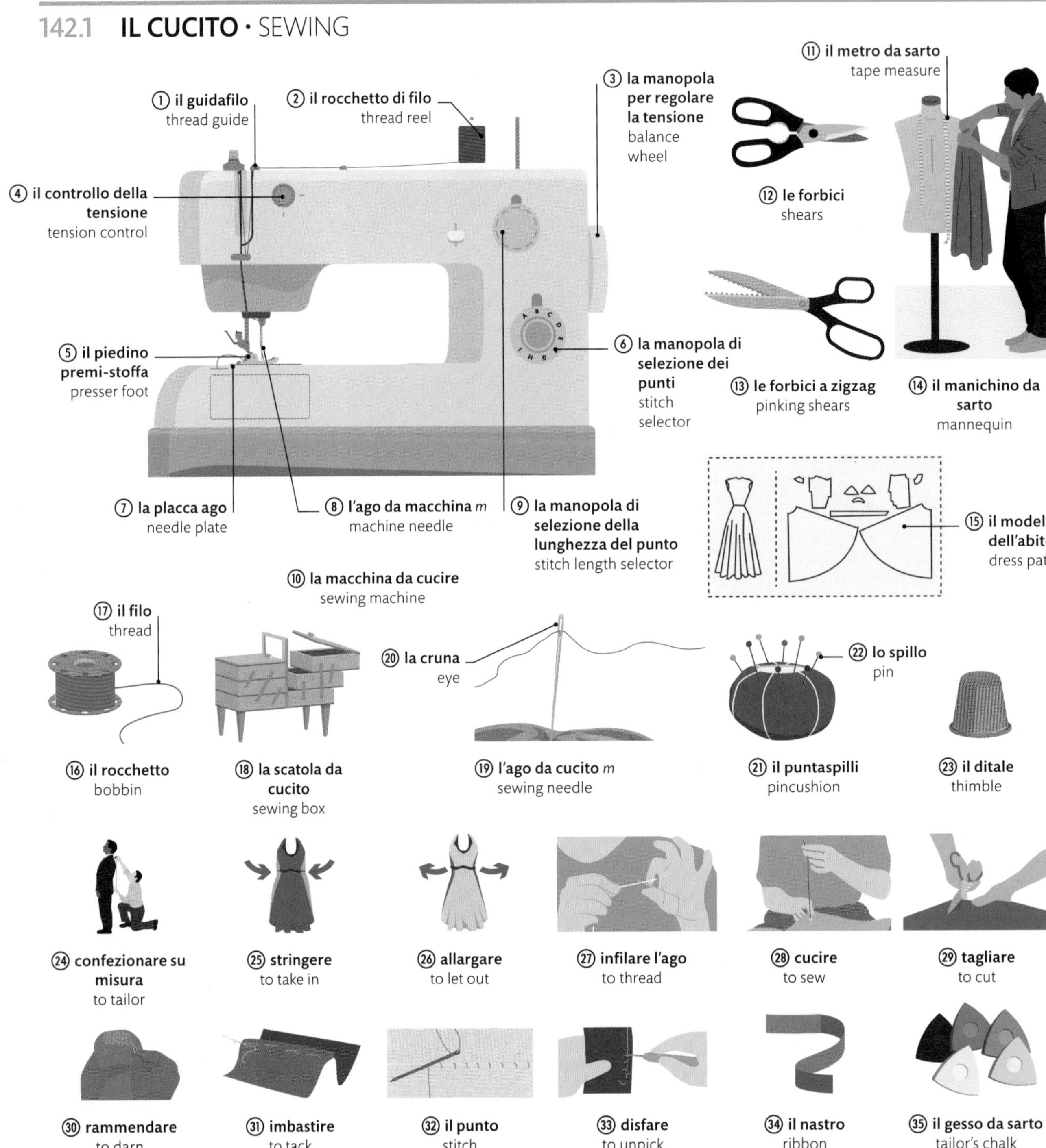

① il guidafilo
thread guide
② il rocchetto di filo
thread reel
③ la manopola per regolare la tensione
balance wheel
④ il controllo della tensione
tension control
⑤ il piedino premi-stoffa
presser foot
⑥ la manopola di selezione dei punti
stitch selector
⑦ la placca ago
needle plate
⑧ l'ago da macchina *m*
machine needle
⑨ la manopola di selezione della lunghezza del punto
stitch length selector
⑩ la macchina da cucire
sewing machine
⑪ il metro da sarto
tape measure
⑫ le forbici
shears
⑬ le forbici a zigzag
pinking shears
⑭ il manichino da sarto
mannequin
⑮ il modello dell'abito
dress pattern
⑯ il rocchetto
bobbin
⑰ il filo
thread
⑱ la scatola da cucito
sewing box
⑲ l'ago da cucito *m*
sewing needle
⑳ la cruna
eye
㉑ il puntaspilli
pincushion
㉒ lo spillo
pin
㉓ il ditale
thimble
㉔ confezionare su misura
to tailor
㉕ stringere
to take in
㉖ allargare
to let out
㉗ infilare l'ago
to thread
㉘ cucire
to sew
㉙ tagliare
to cut
㉚ rammendare
to darn
㉛ imbastire
to tack
㉜ il punto
stitch
㉝ disfare
to unpick
㉞ il nastro
ribbon
㉟ il gesso da sarto
tailor's chalk

See also
11 Le abilità e le azioni • Abilities and actions **13-15** Gli indumenti • Clothes
37 La decorazione • Renovating **39** Il giardinaggio • Practical gardening

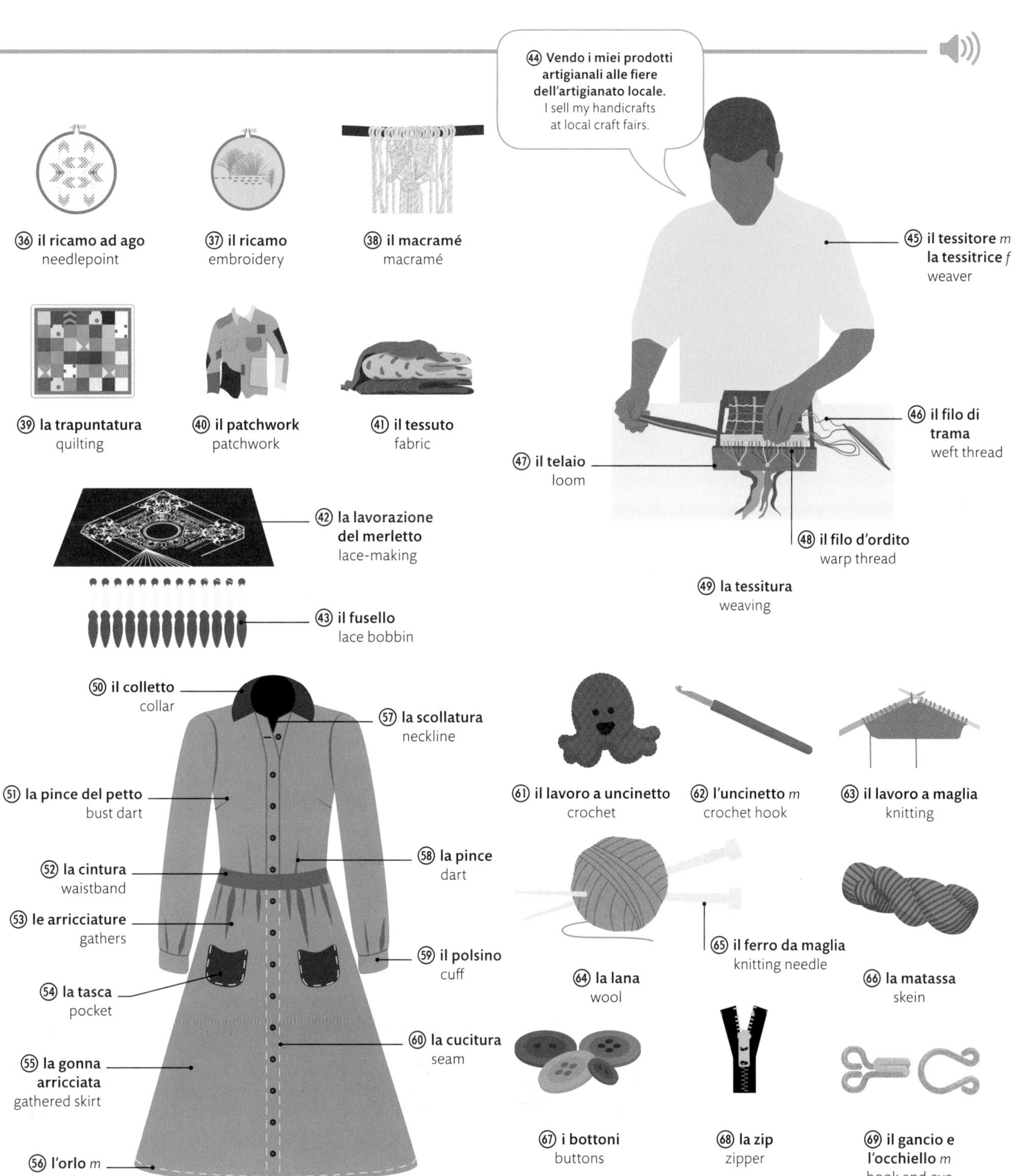
44 Vendo i miei prodotti artigianali alle fiere dell'artigianato locale.
I sell my handicrafts at local craft fairs.
36 il ricamo ad ago
needlepoint
37 il ricamo
embroidery
38 il macramé
macramé
45 il tessitore m
la tessitrice f
weaver
39 la trapuntatura
quilting
40 il patchwork
patchwork
41 il tessuto
fabric
46 il filo di trama
weft thread
47 il telaio
loom
42 la lavorazione del merletto
lace-making
48 il filo d'ordito
warp thread
49 la tessitura
weaving
43 il fusello
lace bobbin
50 il colletto
collar
57 la scollatura
neckline
51 la pince del petto
bust dart
61 il lavoro a uncinetto
crochet
62 l'uncinetto m
crochet hook
63 il lavoro a maglia
knitting
52 la cintura
waistband
58 la pince
dart
53 le arricciature
gathers
59 il polsino
cuff
65 il ferro da maglia
knitting needle
54 la tasca
pocket
64 la lana
wool
66 la matassa
skein
60 la cucitura
seam
55 la gonna arricciata
gathered skirt
67 i bottoni
buttons
68 la zip
zipper
69 il gancio e l'occhiello m
hook and eye
56 l'orlo m
hem

143 Lo spazio
Space

143.1 IL SISTEMA SOLARE · THE SOLAR SYSTEM

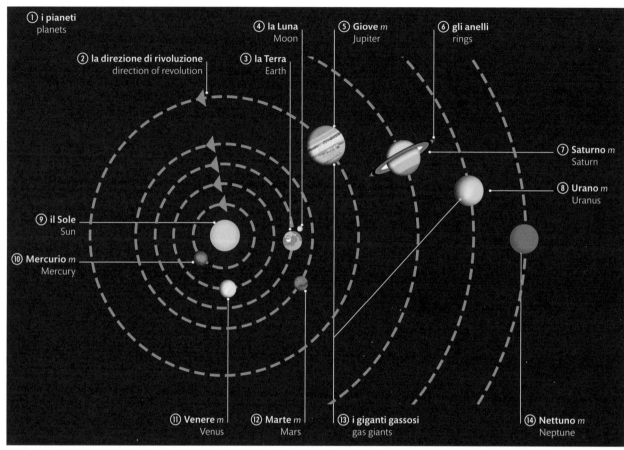

1. **i pianeti** planets
2. **la direzione di rivoluzione** direction of revolution
3. **la Terra** Earth
4. **la Luna** Moon
5. **Giove** *m* Jupiter
6. **gli anelli** rings
7. **Saturno** *m* Saturn
8. **Urano** *m* Uranus
9. **il Sole** Sun
10. **Mercurio** *m* Mercury
11. **Venere** *m* Venus
12. **Marte** *m* Mars
13. **i giganti gassosi** gas giants
14. **Nettuno** *m* Neptune

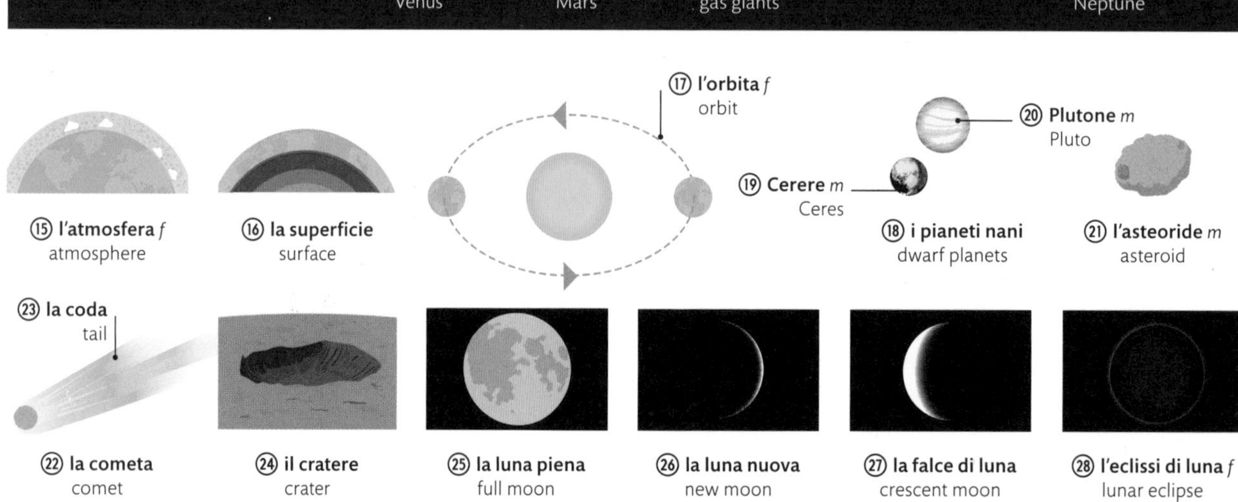

⑰ l'orbita f
orbit
⑳ Plutone m
Pluto
⑲ Cerere m
Ceres
⑮ l'atmosfera f
atmosphere
⑯ la superficie
surface
⑱ i pianeti nani
dwarf planets
㉑ l'asteroide m
asteroid
㉓ la coda
tail
㉒ la cometa
comet
㉔ il cratere
crater
㉕ la luna piena
full moon
㉖ la luna nuova
new moon
㉗ la falce di luna
crescent moon
㉘ l'eclissi di luna f
lunar eclipse

See also
74 La matematica • Mathematics **75** La fisica • Physics **83** I computer e la tecnologia • Computers and technology **144** Lo spazio (continua) • Space continued **145** Il pianeta Terra • Planet Earth **156** Le rocce e i minerali • Rocks and minerals

143.2 L'ESPLORAZIONE DELLO SPAZIO • SPACE EXPLORATION

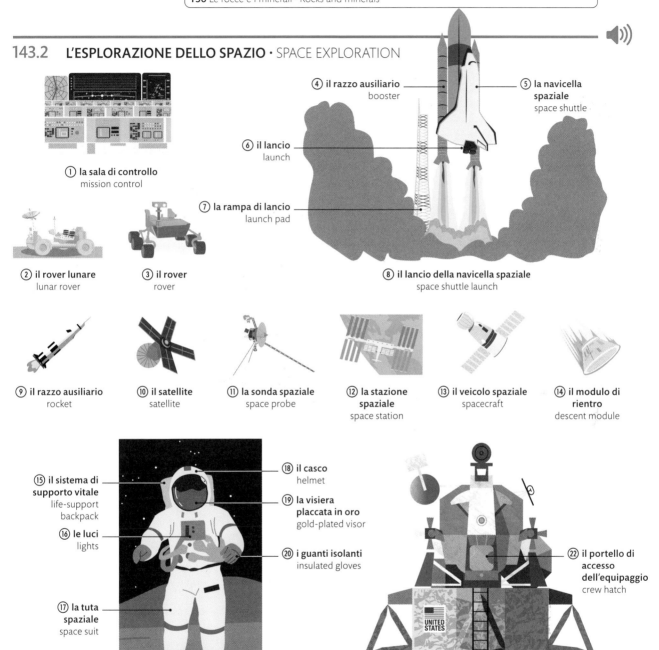

① **la sala di controllo**
mission control

② **il rover lunare**
lunar rover

③ **il rover**
rover

④ **il razzo ausiliario**
booster

⑤ **la navicella spaziale**
space shuttle

⑥ **il lancio**
launch

⑦ **la rampa di lancio**
launch pad

⑧ **il lancio della navicella spaziale**
space shuttle launch

⑨ **il razzo ausiliario**
rocket

⑩ **il satellite**
satellite

⑪ **la sonda spaziale**
space probe

⑫ **la stazione spaziale**
space station

⑬ **il veicolo spaziale**
spacecraft

⑭ **il modulo di rientro**
descent module

⑮ **il sistema di supporto vitale**
life-support backpack

⑯ **le luci**
lights

⑰ **la tuta spaziale**
space suit

⑱ **il casco**
helmet

⑲ **la visiera placcata in oro**
gold-plated visor

⑳ **i guanti isolanti**
insulated gloves

㉑ **l'astronauta** *m / f*
astronaut

㉒ **il portello di accesso dell'equipaggio**
crew hatch

㉓ **il propulsore**
thruster

㉔ **il modulo lunare**
lunar module

UNITED STATES

144 Lo spazio (continua)

Space continued

144.1 L'ASTRONOMIA · ASTRONOMY

① **il binocolo**
binoculars

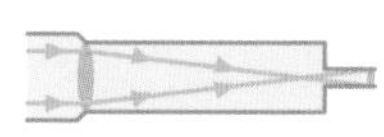

② **il telescopio rifrattore**
refractor telescope

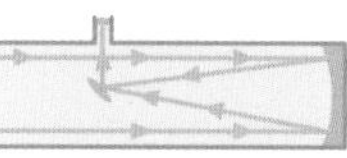

③ **il telescopio riflettore**
reflector telescope

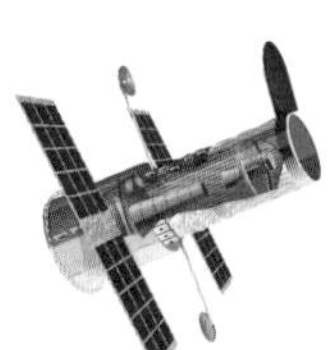

④ **il radiotelescopio**
radio telescope

⑤ **l'osservatorio** *m*
observatory

⑥ **il telescopio spaziale**
space telescope

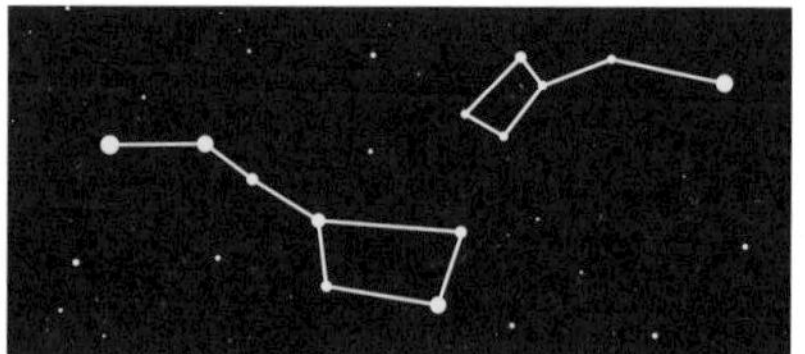

⑦ **la costellazione**
constellation

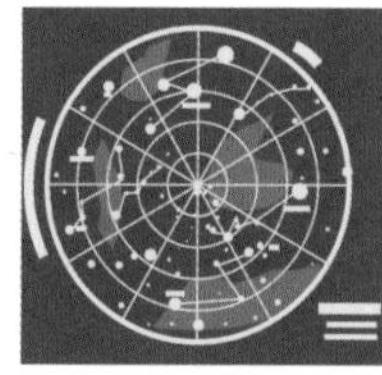

⑧ **la carta celeste**
star chart

⑨ **Ho avvistato una cometa.**
I've just spotted a comet.

⑩ **l'oculare** *m*
eyepiece

⑪ **il cercatore**
finderscope

⑫ **la cometa**
comet

⑬ **il treppiede**
tripod

⑭ **la manopola di messa a fuoco**
focusing knob

⑮ **il telescopio**
telescope

144.2 LE STELLE E LE COSTELLAZIONI · STARS AND CONSTELLATIONS

① **la gravità**
gravity

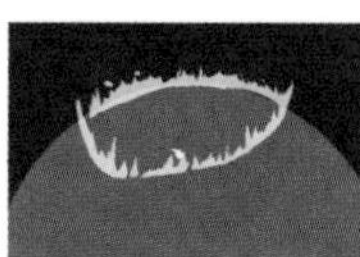

② **l'aurora** *f*
aurora

③ **la stella**
star

④ **il bagliore**
flare

⑤ **la stella binaria**
double star

⑥ **la stella di neutroni**
neutron star

⑬ **la Stella Polare**
the Pole Star / Polaris

⑭ **l'Orsa Maggiore** *f*
the Big Dipper

⑮ **la Croce del Sud**
the Southern Cross

⑯ **Orione** *m*
Orion

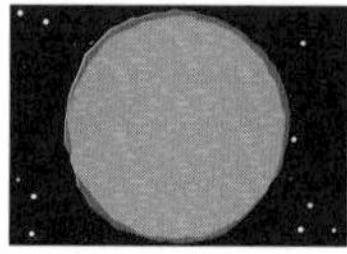

⑰ **la gigante rossa**
red giant

⑱ **la nana bianca**
white dwarf

See also
74 La matematica • Mathematics **75** La fisica • Physics **83** I computer e la tecnologia • Computers and technology **145** Il pianeta Terra • Planet Earth **156** Le rocce e i minerali • Rocks and minerals

144.3 LO ZODIACO • THE ZODIAC

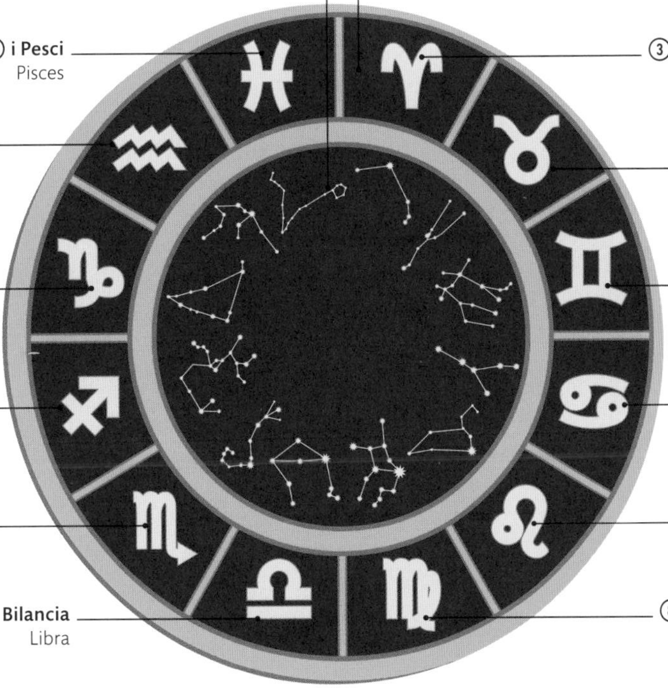

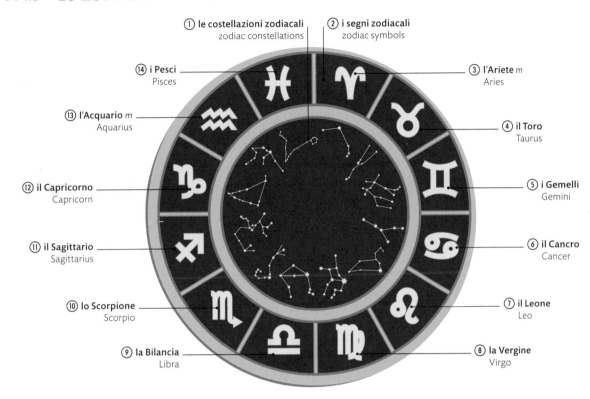

① **le costellazioni zodiacali**
zodiac constellations

② **i segni zodiacali**
zodiac symbols

③ **l'Ariete** *m*
Aries

④ **il Toro**
Taurus

⑤ **i Gemelli**
Gemini

⑥ **il Cancro**
Cancer

⑦ **il Leone**
Leo

⑧ **la Vergine**
Virgo

⑨ **la Bilancia**
Libra

⑩ **lo Scorpione**
Scorpio

⑪ **il Sagittario**
Sagittarius

⑫ **il Capricorno**
Capricorn

⑬ **l'Acquario** *m*
Aquarius

⑭ **i Pesci**
Pisces

⑰ **la supernova**
supernova

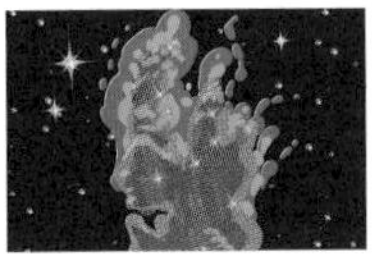

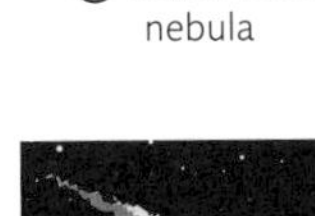
⑱ **la nebulosa**
nebula

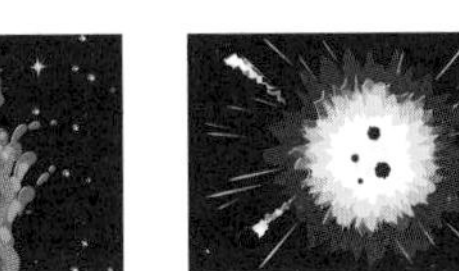
⑲ **il Big Bang**
the Big Bang

⑩ **l'ammasso stellare** *m*
star cluster

⑪ **la galassia ellittica**
elliptical galaxy

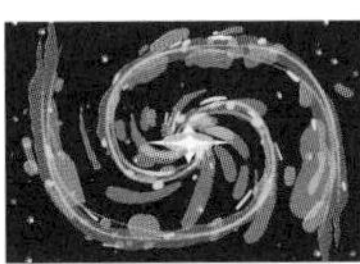
⑫ **la galassia a spirale**
spiral galaxy

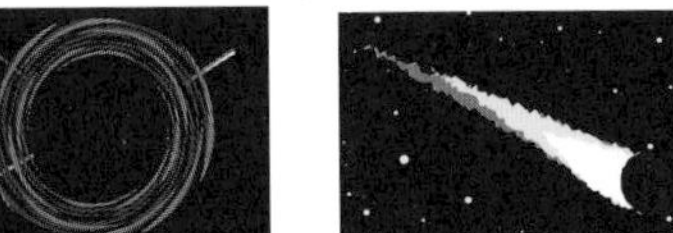
⑲ **il buco nero**
black hole

⑳ **la meteora**
meteor

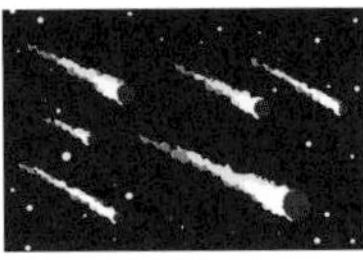
㉑ **lo sciame meteorico**
meteor shower

㉒ **la Via Lattea**
the Milky Way

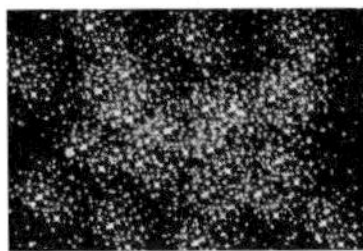
㉓ **l'universo** *m*
the universe

145 Il pianeta Terra
Planet Earth

145.1 LA TERRA · THE EARTH

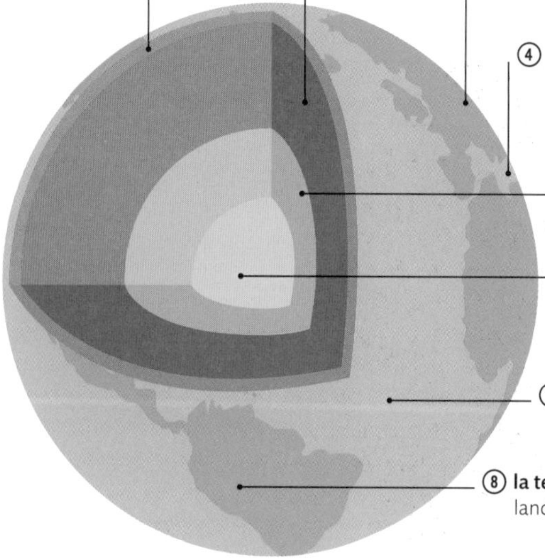

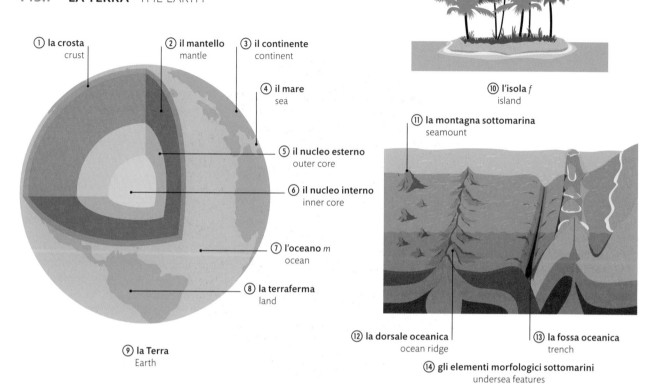

① **la crosta**
crust

② **il mantello**
mantle

③ **il continente**
continent

④ **il mare**
sea

⑤ **il nucleo esterno**
outer core

⑥ **il nucleo interno**
inner core

⑦ **l'oceano** *m*
ocean

⑧ **la terraferma**
land

⑨ **la Terra**
Earth

⑩ **l'isola** *f*
island

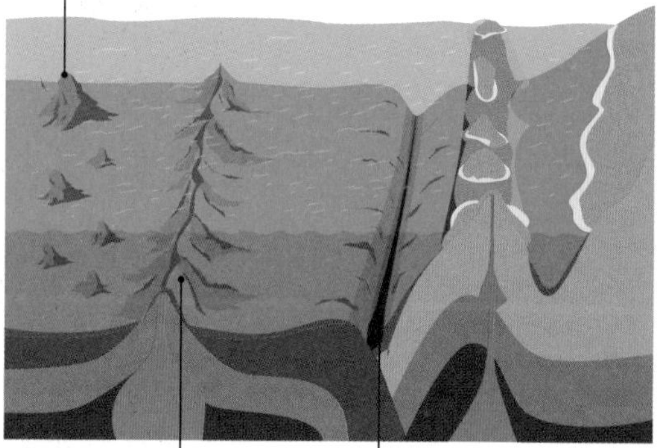

⑪ **la montagna sottomarina**
seamount

⑫ **la dorsale oceanica**
ocean ridge

⑬ **la fossa oceanica**
trench

⑭ **gli elementi morfologici sottomarini**
undersea features

145.2 LA TETTONICA DELLE PLACCHE · PLATE TECTONICS

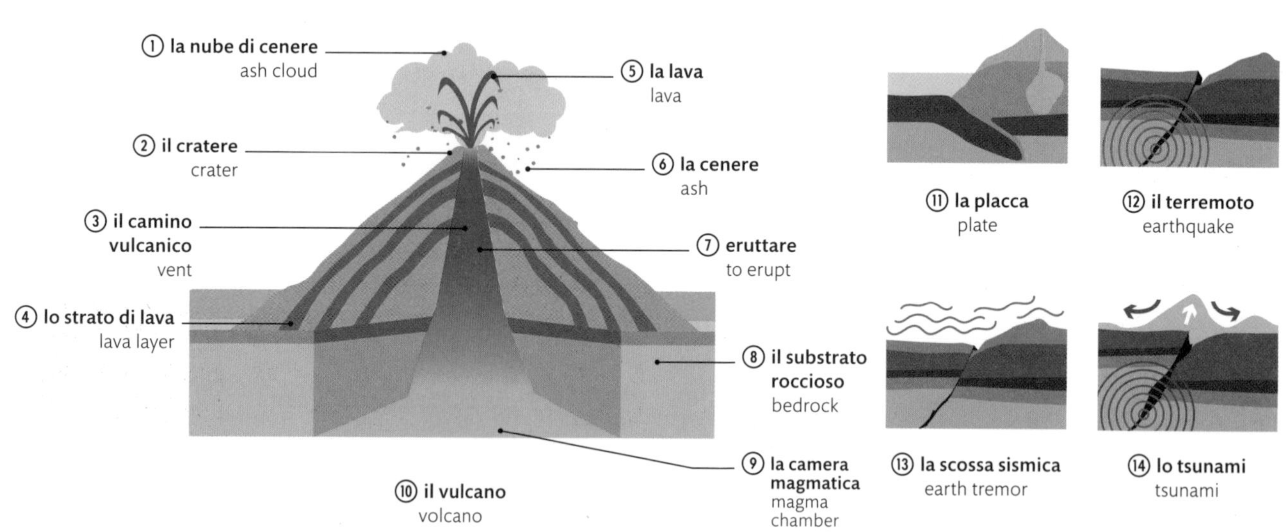

① la nube di cenere
ash cloud
② il cratere
crater
③ il camino vulcanico
vent
④ lo strato di lava
lava layer
⑤ la lava
lava
⑥ la cenere
ash
⑦ eruttare
to erupt
⑧ il substrato roccioso
bedrock
⑨ la camera magmatica
magma chamber
⑩ il vulcano
volcano
⑪ la placca
plate
⑫ il terremoto
earthquake
⑬ la scossa sismica
earth tremor
⑭ lo tsunami
tsunami

See also
143-144 Lo spazio • Space **146-147** La geografia • Geography
148 Le cartine e le direzioni • Maps and directions **149-151** I Paesi • Countries

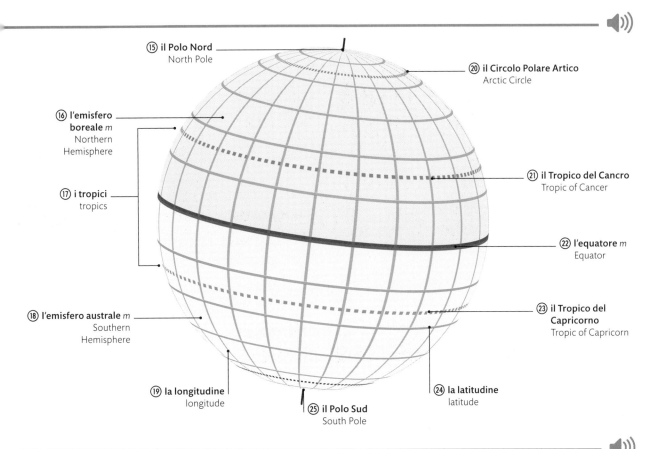

⑮ **il Polo Nord**
North Pole

⑯ **l'emisfero boreale** *m*
Northern Hemisphere

⑰ **i tropici**
tropics

⑱ **l'emisfero australe** *m*
Southern Hemisphere

⑲ **la longitudine**
longitude

⑳ **il Circolo Polare Artico**
Arctic Circle

㉑ **il Tropico del Cancro**
Tropic of Cancer

㉒ **l'equatore** *m*
Equator

㉓ **il Tropico del Capricorno**
Tropic of Capricorn

㉔ **la latitudine**
latitude

㉕ **il Polo Sud**
South Pole

145.3 LE FORMAZIONI E I FENOMENI ACQUATICI • WATER FEATURES AND PHENOMENA

① **le Cascate Vittoria**
Victoria Falls

② **la Hang Son Doong**
Hang Son Doong

③ **il Rio delle Amazzoni**
the Amazon

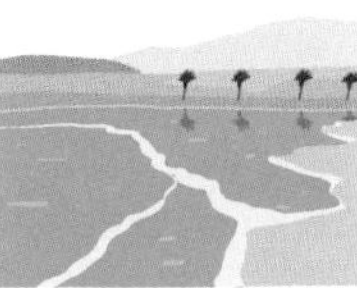
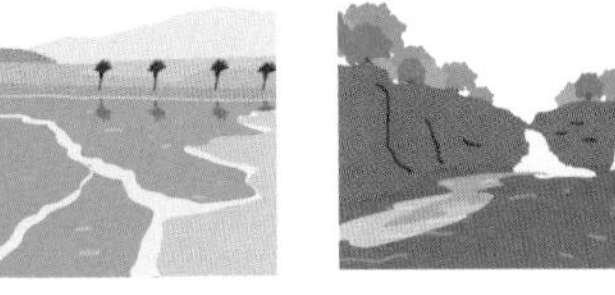
④ **il Mar Morto**
the Dead Sea

⑤ **il Caño Cristales**
Caño Cristales

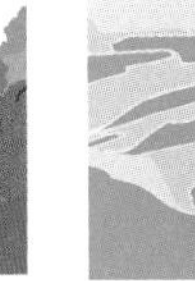
⑥ **Pamukkale**
Pamukkale

⑦ **la barriera corallina**
the Barrier Reef

⑧ **il Gange**
the Ganges

⑨ **il Salto Ángel**
Angel Falls

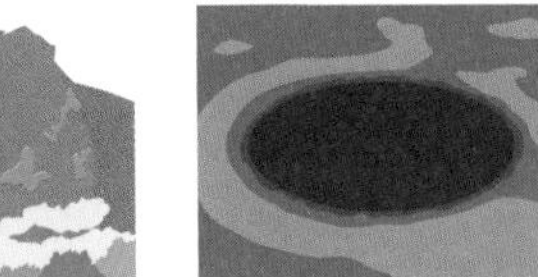
⑩ **il Great Blue Hole**
the Great Blue Hole

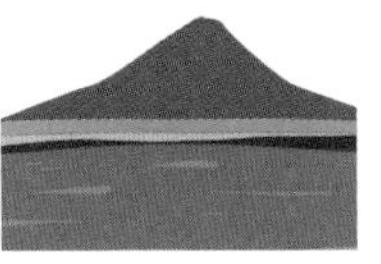
⑪ **il lago Natron**
Lake Natron

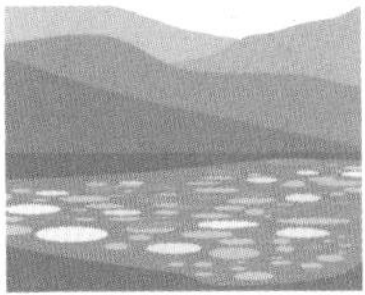
⑫ **lo Spotted Lake**
Spotted Lake

146 La geografia
Geography

146.1 LE CARATTERISTICHE GEOGRAFICHE E IL PAESAGGIO
GEOGRAPHICAL FEATURES AND LANDSCAPE

① **il bosco**
woods

② **la foresta pluviale**
rain forest

③ **la foresta di conifere**
coniferous forest

④ **la foresta decidua**
deciduous forest

⑤ **le rapide**
rapids

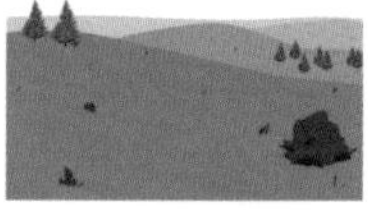

⑥ **la campagna**
countryside

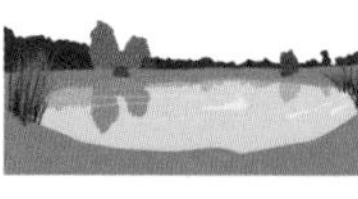

⑦ **il lago**
lake

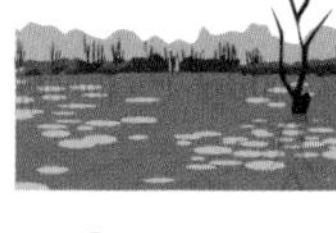

⑧ **la palude**
swamp

⑨ **la cascata**
waterfall

⑩ **il campo**
field

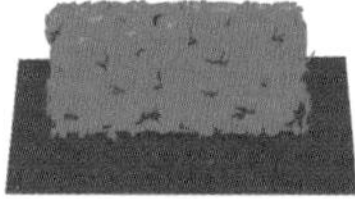

⑪ **la siepe**
hedge

⑫ **la valle**
valley

⑬ **il terreno coltivato**
farmland

⑭ **le zone umide**
wetlands

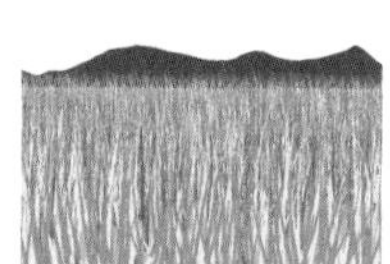

⑮ **il terreno erboso**
grassland

⑯ **la prateria**
prairie

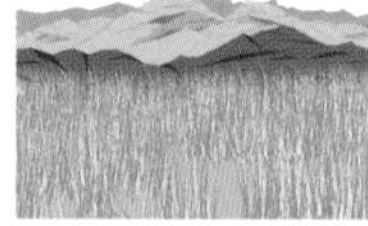

⑰ **la steppa**
steppe

⑱ **la mesa**
mesa

⑲ **l'altura** *f*
highland

⑳ **il crinale**
ridge

㉑ **il massiccio montuoso**
mountain range

㉒ **la savana**
savannah

㉓ **la catena montuosa**
mountain chain

㉔ **il geyser**
geyser

㉕ **la pianura**
plain

㉖ **l'oasi** *f*
oasis

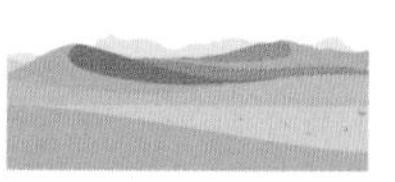

㉗ **il deserto**
desert

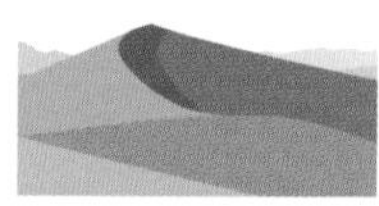

㉘ **la duna**
sand dune

See also
133 Le attività all'aperto • Outdoor activites **145** Il pianeta Terra • Planet Earth **147** La geografia (continua) Geography continued **148** Le cartine e le direzioni • Maps and directions **149-151** I Paesi • Countries

㉙ **il canyon**
canyon

㉚ **l'iceberg** *m*
iceberg

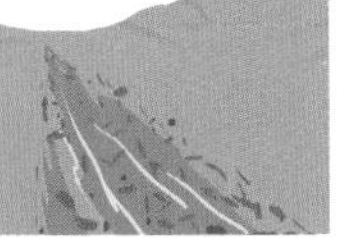

㉛ **la colata di fango**
mudslide

㉜ **la frana**
landslide

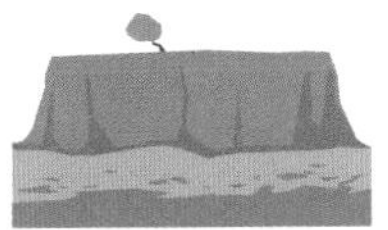

㉝ **l'altopiano** *m*
plateau

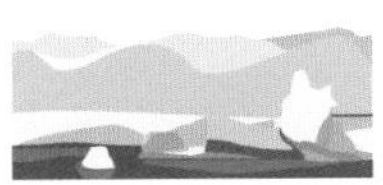

㉞ **la regione polare**
polar region

㉟ **la tundra**
tundra

㊱ **il ghiacciaio**
glacier

146.2 LE GROTTE E LA SPELEOLOGIA • CAVES AND CAVING

① il ghiacciolo
icicle
② la torcia frontale
headlamp
③ la colonna
column
④ il corso d'acqua sotterraneo
subterranean stream
⑤ Un casco e una torcia frontale sono fondamentali quando si esplorano le grotte.
A helmet and headlamp are essential when caving.
⑥ la stalattite
stalactite
⑦ il casco
helmet
⑧ lo speleologo m
la speleologa f
caver
⑨ la stalagmite
stalagmite

147 La geografia (continua)

Geography continued

147.1 LE CARATTERISTICHE COSTIERE · COASTAL FEATURES

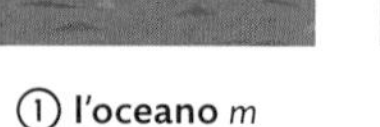

① **l'oceano** *m*
ocean

② **l'onda** *f*
wave

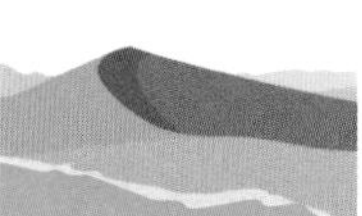

③ **la duna**
dune

④ **l'isola** *f*
island

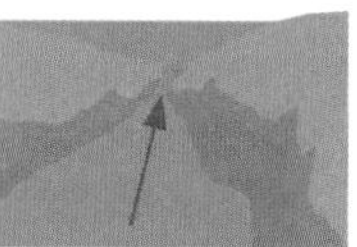

⑤ **lo stretto**
strait

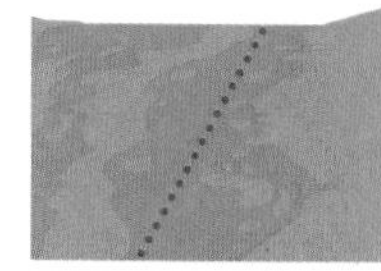

⑥ **il canale**
channel

⑦ **l'alta marea** *f*
high tide

⑧ **la bassa marea**
low tide

⑨ **il banco di scogli**
reef

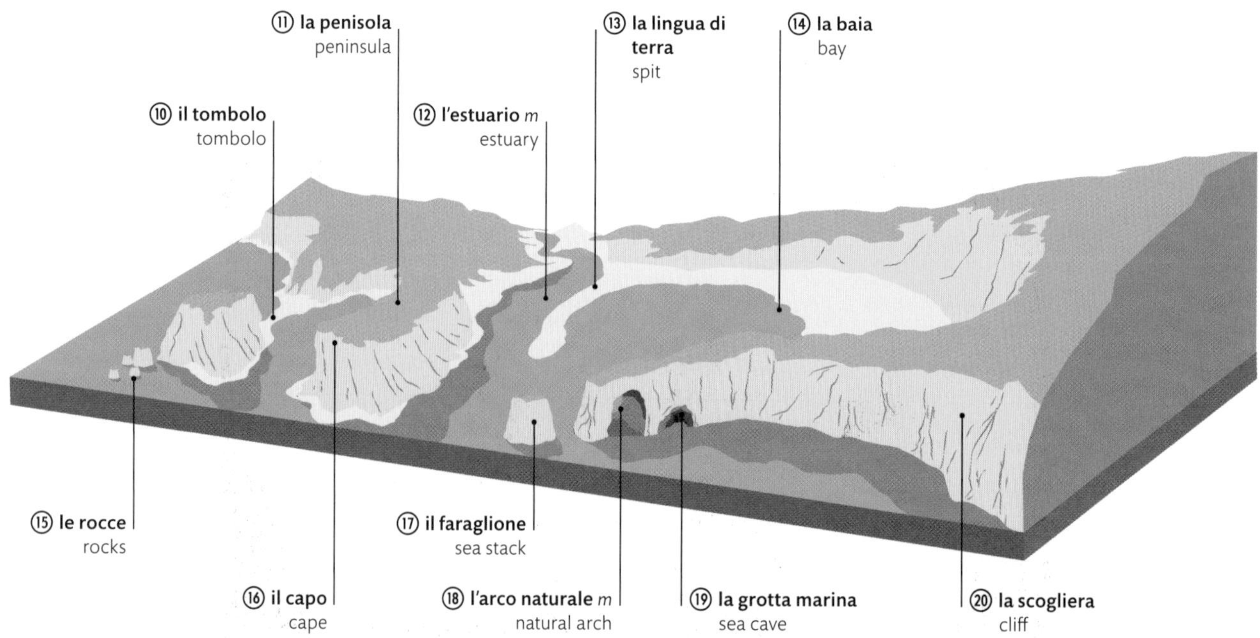
⑩ il tombolo
tombolo
⑪ la penisola
peninsula
⑫ l'estuario m
estuary
⑬ la lingua di terra
spit
⑭ la baia
bay
⑮ le rocce
rocks
⑯ il capo
cape
⑰ il faraglione
sea stack
⑱ l'arco naturale m
natural arch
⑲ la grotta marina
sea cave
⑳ la scogliera
cliff

See also
133 Le attività all'aperto • Outdoor activities **145** Il pianeta Terra • Planet Earth
148 Le cartine e le direzioni • Maps and directions **149-151** I Paesi • Countries

㉑ **la palude**
marsh

㉒ **il delta**
delta

㉓ **il golfo**
gulf

㉔ **il fiordo**
fjord

㉕ **l'arcipelago** *m*
archipelago

㉖ **l'istmo** *m*
isthmus

㉗ **l'atollo** *m*
atoll

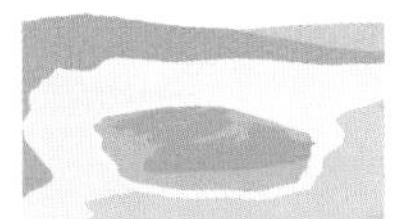

㉘ **la laguna**
lagoon

147.2 LE CARATTERISTICHE FLUVIALI • RIVER FEATURES

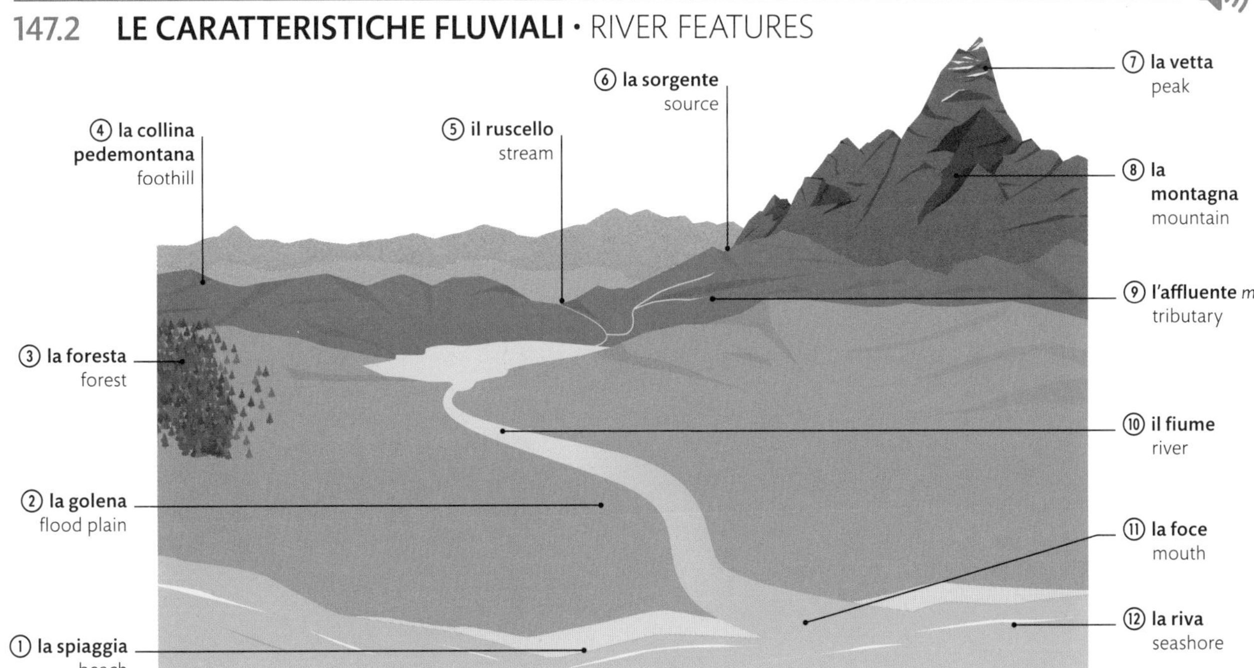
① la spiaggia
beach
② la golena
flood plain
③ la foresta
forest
④ la collina pedemontana
foothill
⑤ il ruscello
stream
⑥ la sorgente
source
⑦ la vetta
peak
⑧ la montagna
mountain
⑨ l'affluente m
tributary
⑩ il fiume
river
⑪ la foce
mouth
⑫ la riva
seashore

Le cartine e le direzioni

Maps and directions

148.1 LEGGERE UNA CARTINA · READING A MAP

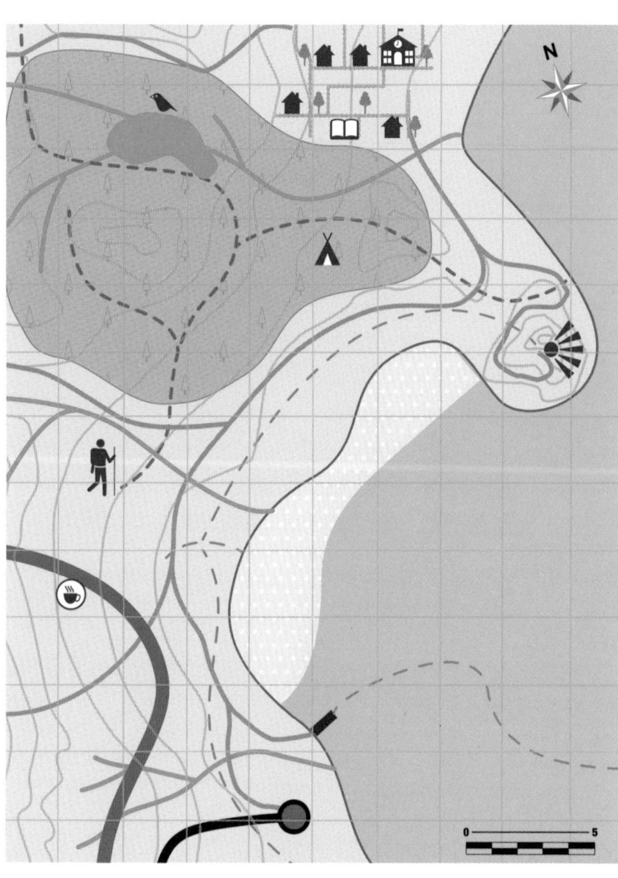
N
0
5

① **la cartina**
map

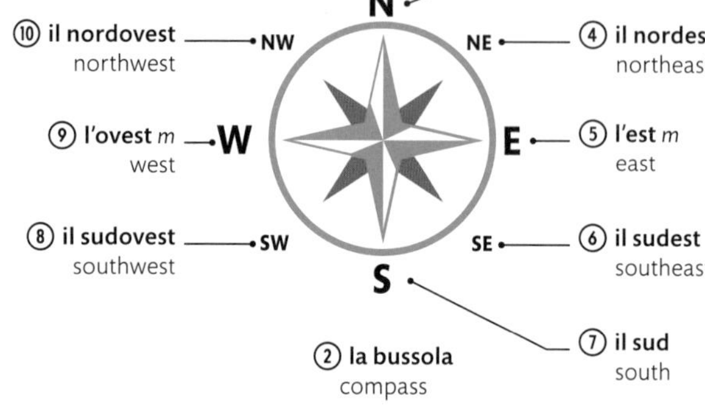
N
NE
E
SE
S
SW
W
NW

③ **il nord**
north

⑩ **il nordovest**
northwest

④ **il nordest**
northeast

⑨ **l'ovest** *m*
west

⑤ **l'est** *m*
east

⑧ **il sudovest**
southwest

⑥ **il sudest**
southeast

② **la bussola**
compass

⑦ **il sud**
south

⑪ **la strada principale**
main road

⑫ **la strada secondaria**
secondary road

⑬ **il sentiero pubblico**
public footpath

⑭ **la linea ferroviaria**
railroad

⑮ **la stazione ferroviaria**
train station

⑯ **l'area campeggio** *f*
campground

⑰ **l'area di sosta** *f*
rest stop

⑱ **le linee della griglia**
grid lines

⑲ **la riserva naturale**
nature reserve

⑳ **il punto panoramico**
viewpoint

㉑ **il percorso a piedi**
walking trail

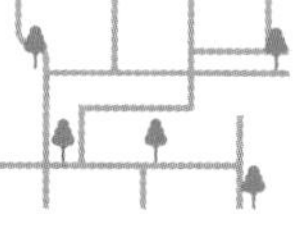

㉒ **la città**
town

㉓ **la casa / l'edificio** *m*
house / building

㉔ **la scuola**
school

㉕ **la biblioteca**
library

㉖ **il percorso del traghetto**
ferry route

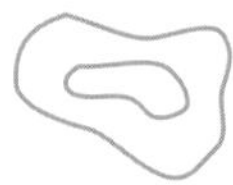

㉗ **i contorni**
contours

㉘ **il fiume**
river

㉙ **il lago**
lake

㉚ **la foresta**
forest

㉛ **la spiaggia**
beach

See also
96 Le strade • Roads **133** Le attività all'aperto • Outdoor activities **145** Il pianeta Terra • Planet Earth **146-147** La geografia • Geography **149-151** I Paesi • Countries

㉜ **in senso orario**
clockwise

㉝ **in senso antiorario**
counterclockwise

㉞ **le coordinate**
coordinates

㉟ **l'orienteering** *m*
orienteering

㊱ **la latitudine**
latitude

㊲ **la longitudine**
longitude

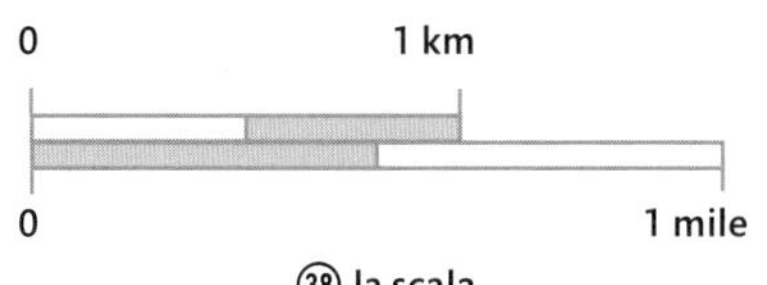
0
1 km
0
1 mile

㊳ **la scala**
scale

㊴ **il cartografo** *m*
la cartografa *f*
cartographer

㊵ **la cartina online**
online map

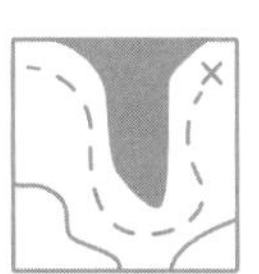

㊶ **la cartina escursionistica**
trail map

㊷ **la carta stradale**
roadmap

148.2 LE PREPOSIZIONI DI LUOGO PREPOSITIONS OF PLACE

① **accanto**
next to / beside

② **di fronte**
across from

③ **tra**
between

④ **all'angolo** *m*
on the corner

⑤ **davanti a**
in front of

⑥ **dietro**
behind

⑦ **a sinistra**
on the left

⑧ **a destra**
on the right

148.3 I VERBI DI DIREZIONE • DIRECTION VERBS

① **girare a sinistra**
to go left /
to turn left

② **girare a destra**
to go right /
to turn right

③ **andare dritto**
to go straight ahead

④ **tornare indietro**
to go back

⑤ **oltrepassare**
to go past
(the restaurant)

⑥ **prendere la prima a sinistra**
to take the first left

⑦ **prendere la seconda a destra**
to take the
second right

⑧ **fermarsi a**
to stop at
(the hotel)

⑨ **pianificare il percorso**
to plan your route

⑩ **perdersi**
to lose
your way

⑪ **leggere una cartina**
to read a map

⑫ **chiedere indicazioni**
to ask directions

149 I Paesi
Countries

149.1 L'AFRICA • AFRICA

① **il Marocco**
Morocco

② **la Mauritania**
Mauritania

③ **Capo Verde**
Cape Verde

④ **il Senegal**
Senegal

⑤ **il Gambia**
Gambia

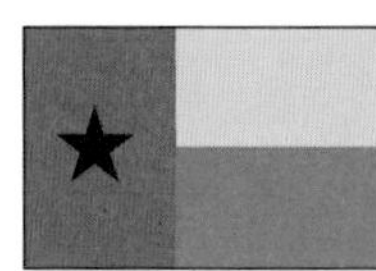
⑥ **la Guinea-Bissau**
Guinea-Bissau

⑦ **la Guinea**
Guinea

⑧ **la Sierra Leone**
Sierra Leone

⑨ **la Liberia**
Liberia

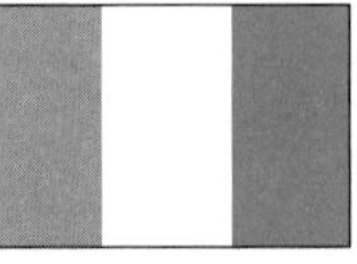
⑩ **la Costa d'Avorio**
Ivory Coast

⑪ **il Burkina Faso**
Burkina Faso

⑫ **il Mali**
Mali

⑬ **l'Algeria** *f*
Algeria

⑭ **la Tunisia**
Tunisia

⑮ **la Libia**
Libya

⑯ **il Niger**
Niger

⑰ **il Ghana**
Ghana

⑱ **il Togo**
Togo

⑲ **il Benin**
Benin

⑳ **la Nigeria**
Nigeria

㉑ **São Tomé e Príncipe**
São Tomé and Príncipe

㉒ **la Guinea Equatoriale**
Equatorial Guinea

㉓ **il Gabon**
Gabon

㉔ **il Camerun**
Cameroon

㉕ **il Ciad**
Chad

㉖ **il Ruanda**
Rwanda

㉗ **il Burundi**
Burundi

㉘ **la Tanzania**
Tanzania

㉙ **il Mozambico**
Mozambique

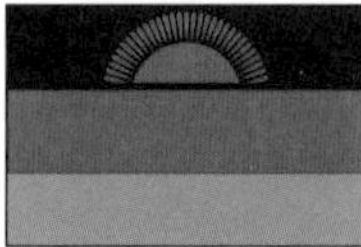
㉚ **il Malawi**
Malawi

㉛ **la Repubblica del Congo**
Republic of the Congo

㉜ **la Repubblica Democratica del Congo**
Democratic Republic of the Congo

㉝ **lo Zambia**
Zambia

㉞ **l'Angola** *f*
Angola

㉟ **la Namibia**
Namibia

㊱ **il Botswana**
Botswana

See also
145 Il pianeta Terra • Planet Earth **146-147** La geografia • Geography **148** Le cartine e le direzioni • Maps and directions **150-151** I Paesi (continua) • Countries continued **152-153** Le nazionalità • Nationalities

㊲ **lo Zimbabwe**
Zimbabwe

㊳ **il Sudafrica**
South Africa

㊴ **il Lesotho**
Lesotho

㊵ **le Comore**
Comoros

㊶ **il Madagascar**
Madagascar

㊷ **l'Egitto** *m*
Egypt

㊸ **il Sudan**
Sudan

㊹ **il Sudan del Sud**
South Sudan

㊺ **l'Etiopia** *f*
Ethiopia

㊻ **l'Eritrea** *f*
Eritrea

㊼ **la Somalia**
Somalia

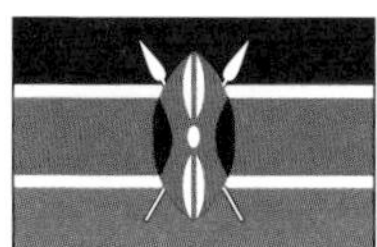

㊽ **il Kenya**
Kenya

㊾ **l'Uganda** *f*
Uganda

㊿ **il Gibuti**
Djibouti

(51) **le Seychelles**
Seychelles

(52) **le Mauritius**
Mauritius

(53) **la Repubblica Centrafricana**
Central African Republic

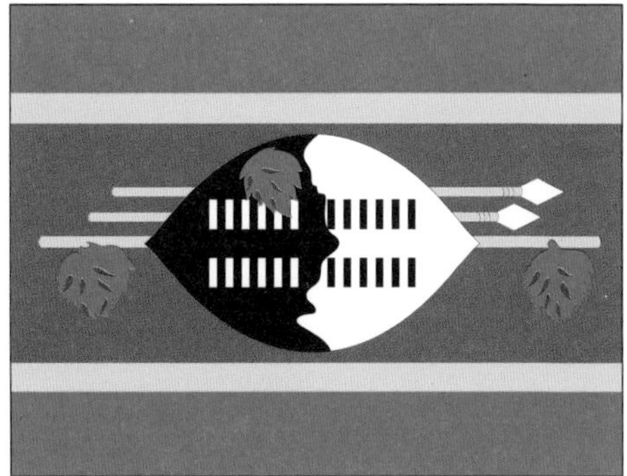

(54) **l'Eswatini** *m*
Eswatini

149.2 IL SUD AMERICA
SOUTH AMERICA

① **il Venezuela**
Venezuela

② **la Colombia**
Colombia

③ **il Brasile**
Brazil

④ **la Bolivia**
Bolivia

⑤ **l'Ecuador** *m*
Ecuador

⑥ **il Perù**
Peru

⑦ **il Cile**
Chile

⑧ **l'Argentina** *f*
Argentina

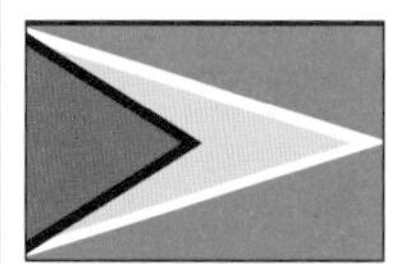

⑨ **la Guyana**
Guyana

⑩ **il Suriname**
Suriname

⑪ **il Paraguay**
Paraguay

⑫ **l'Uruguay** *m*
Uruguay

150 I Paesi (continua)
Countries continued

150.1 IL NORD AMERICA, L'AMERICA CENTRALE E I CARAIBI
NORTH AND CENTRAL AMERICA AND THE CARIBBEAN

① **il Canada**
Canada

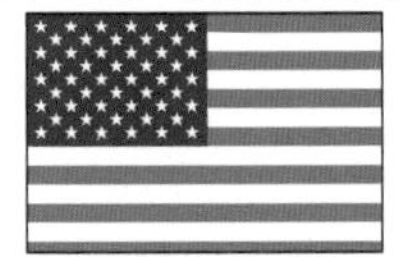
② **gli Stati Uniti d'America**
United States of America

③ **il Messico**
Mexico

④ **il Guatemala**
Guatemala

⑤ **il Belize**
Belize

⑥ **El Salvador**
El Salvador

⑧ **l'Honduras** *m*
Honduras

⑨ **il Nicaragua**
Nicaragua

⑩ **il Costa Rica**
Costa Rica

⑪ **Panama**
Panama

⑫ **Cuba**
Cuba

⑬ **le Bahamas**
Bahamas

⑮ **la Giamaica**
Jamaica

⑯ **Haiti**
Haiti

⑰ **la Repubblica Dominicana**
Dominican Republic

⑱ **le Barbados**
Barbados

⑲ **Trinidad e Tobago**
Trinidad and Tobago

⑳ **Saint Kitts e Nevis**
St. Kitts and Nevis

㉒ **Dominica**
Dominica

㉓ **Antigua e Barbuda**
Antigua and Barbuda

150.2 L'OCEANIA · OCEANIA

① **la Papua Nuova Guinea**
Papua New Guinea

② **l'Australia** *f*
Australia

③ **la Nuova Zelanda**
New Zealand

④ **le Isole Marshall**
Marshall Islands

⑤ **Palau**
Palau

⑥ **la Micronesia**
Micronesia

⑧ **Nauru**
Nauru

⑨ **le Kiribati**
Kiribati

⑩ **le Tuvalu**
Tuvalu

⑪ **le Samoa**
Samoa

⑫ **Tonga**
Tonga

⑬ **le Vanuatu**
Vanuatu

See also
145 Il pianeta Terra • Planet Earth **146-147** La geografia • Geography **148** Le cartine e le direzioni • Maps and directions **151** I Paesi (continua) • Countries continued **152-153** Le nazionalità • Nationalities

⑦ **Grenada**
Grenada

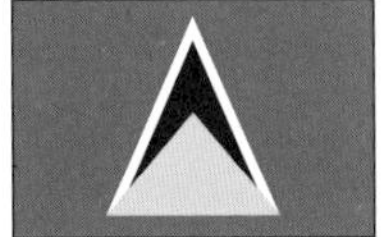

⑭ **Saint Lucia**
St. Lucia

㉑ **Saint Vincent e Grenadine**
St. Vincent and The Grenadines

⑦ **le Isole Salomone**
Solomon Islands

⑭ **le Figi**
Fiji

150.3 **L'ASIA** • ASIA

① **la Turchia**
Türkiye

② **la Federazione Russa**
Russian Federation

③ **la Georgia**
Georgia

④ **l'Armenia** *f*
Armenia

⑤ **l'Azerbaigian** *m*
Azerbaijan

⑥ **l'Iraq** *m*
Iraq

⑦ **la Siria**
Syria

⑧ **il Libano**
Lebanon

⑨ **Israele**
Israel

⑩ **la Giordania**
Jordan

⑪ **il Pakistan**
Pakistan

⑫ **l'India** *f*
India

⑬ **le Maldive**
Maldives

⑭ **lo Sri Lanka**
Sri Lanka

⑮ **la Cina**
China

⑯ **la Mongolia**
Mongolia

⑰ **la Corea del Nord**
North Korea

⑱ **la Corea del Sud**
South Korea

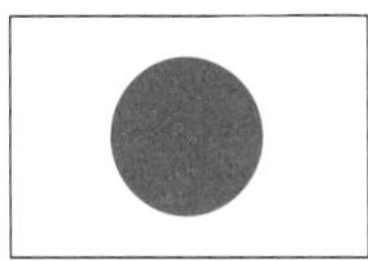

⑲ **il Giappone**
Japan

⑳ **il Bangladesh**
Bangladesh

㉑ **il Bhutan**
Bhutan

㉒ **il Myanmar**
Myanmar (Burma)

㉓ **la Tailandia**
Thailand

㉔ **il Laos**
Laos

㉕ **il Vietnam**
Vietnam

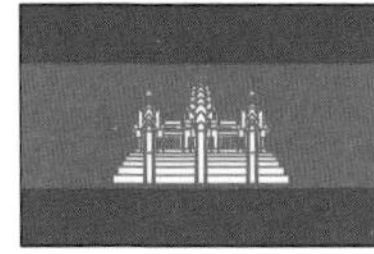

㉖ **la Cambogia**
Cambodia

㉗ **il Nepal**
Nepal

151 I Paesi (continua)

Countries continued

151.1 L'ASIA (CONTINUA) · ASIA CONTINUED

① **Singapore**
Singapore

② **l'Indonesia** *f*
Indonesia

③ **il Brunei**
Brunei

④ **le Filippine**
Philippines

⑤ **Timor Est**
East Timor

⑥ **la Malesia**
Malaysia

⑦ **gli Emirati Arabi Uniti**
United Arab Emirates

⑧ **l'Oman** *m*
Oman

⑨ **il Bahrein**
Bahrain

⑩ **il Qatar**
Qatar

⑪ **il Kuwait**
Kuwait

⑫ **l'Iran** *m*
Iran

⑬ **lo Yemen**
Yemen

⑭ **l'Arabia Saudita** *f*
Saudi Arabia

⑮ **l'Uzbekistan** *m*
Uzbekistan

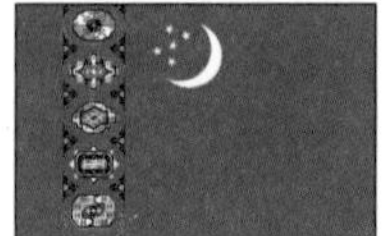

⑯ **il Turkmenistan**
Turkmenistan

⑰ **l'Afghanistan** *m*
Afghanistan

⑱ **il Tagikistan**
Tajikistan

⑲ **il Kirghizistan**
Kyrgyzstan

⑳ **il Kazakistan**
Kazakhstan

151.2 L'EUROPA · EUROPE

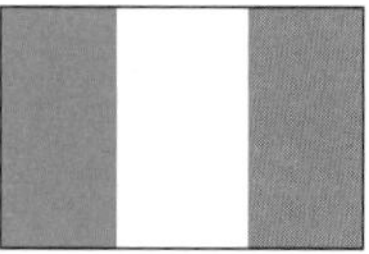

① **l'Irlanda** *f*
Ireland

② **il Regno Unito**
United Kingdom

⑨ **il Belgio**
Belgium

⑩ **i Paesi Bassi**
Netherlands

⑰ **il Portogallo**
Portugal

⑱ **la Spagna**
Spain

㉕ **il Lussemburgo**
Luxembourg

㉖ **la Germania**
Germany

㉝ **Andorra**
Andorra

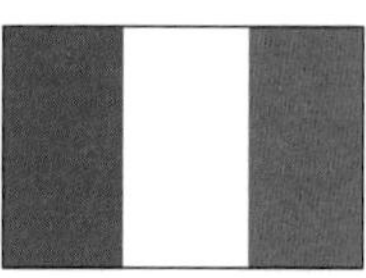

㉞ **la Francia**
France

㊶ **la Danimarca**
Denmark

㊷ **la Norvegia**
Norway

See also
145 Il pianeta Terra • Planet Earth **146-147** La geografia • Geography **148** Le cartine e le direzioni • Maps and directions **152-153** Le nazionalità • Nationalities

③ **la Svezia**
Sweden

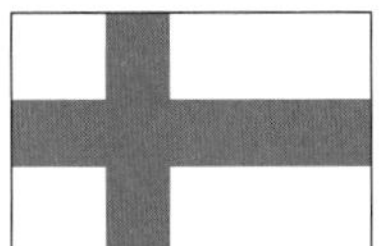
④ **la Finlandia**
Finland

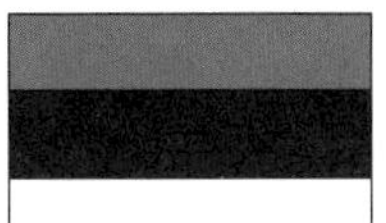
⑤ **l'Estonia** *f*
Estonia

⑥ **la Lettonia**
Latvia

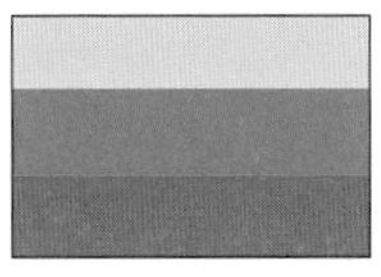
⑦ **la Lituania**
Lithuania

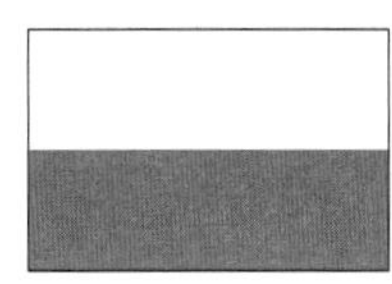
⑧ **la Polonia**
Poland

⑪ **la Repubblica Ceca**
Czech Republic

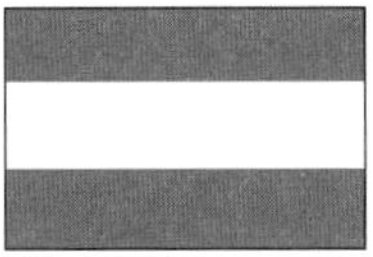
⑫ **l'Austria** *f*
Austria

⑬ **il Liechtenstein**
Liechtenstein

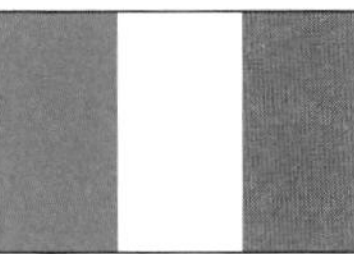
⑭ **l'Italia** *f*
Italy

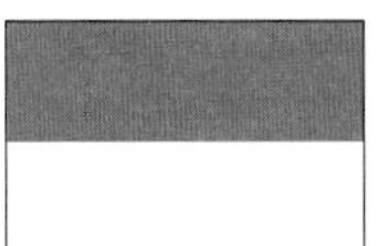
⑮ **il Principato di Monaco**
Monaco

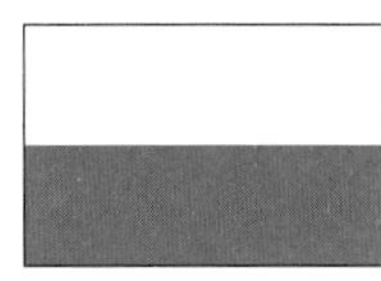
⑯ **San Marino**
San Marino

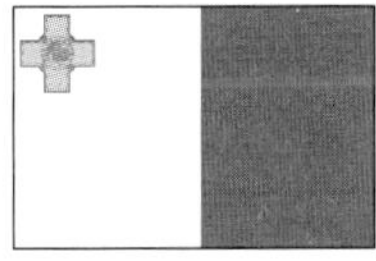
⑲ **Malta**
Malta

⑳ **la Slovenia**
Slovenia

㉑ **la Croazia**
Croatia

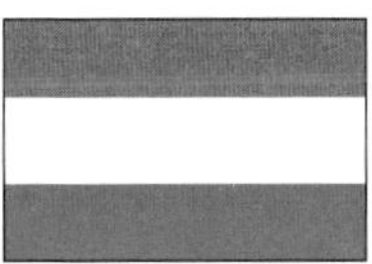
㉒ **l'Ungheria** *f*
Hungary

㉓ **la Slovacchia**
Slovakia

㉔ **l'Ucraina** *f*
Ukraine

㉗ **la Bielorussia**
Belarus

㉘ **la Moldavia**
Moldova

㉙ **la Romania**
Romania

㉚ **la Serbia**
Serbia

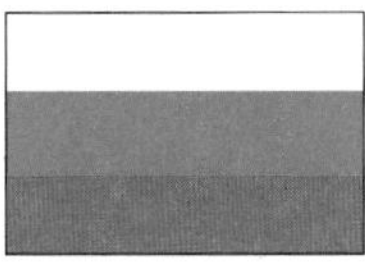
㉛ **la Bulgaria**
Bulgaria

㉜ **l'Albania** *f*
Albania

㉟ **la Grecia**
Greece

㊱ **l'Islanda** *f*
Iceland

㊲ **Cipro**
Cyprus

㊳ **il Montenegro**
Montenegro

㊴ **Città del Vaticano**
Vatican City

㊵ **la Turchia**
Türkiye

㊸ **la Bosnia-Erzegovina**
Bosnia and Herzegovina

㊹ **la Macedonia del Nord**
North Macedonia

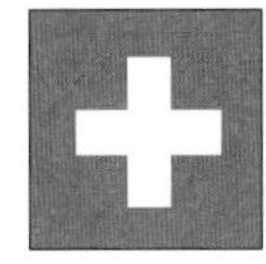
㊺ **la Svizzera**
Switzerland

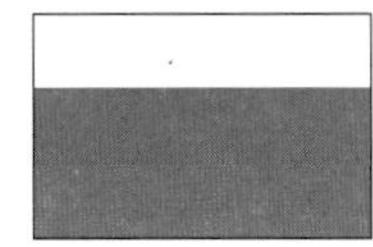
㊻ **la Federazione Russa**
Russian Federation

152 Le nazionalità

Nationalities

152.1 L'AFRICA • AFRICA

Country	Adjective	English Adjective
① **l'Africa** Africa	**africano** *m* / **africana** *f*	African
② **il Marocco** Morocco	**marocchino** *m* **marocchina** *f*	Moroccan
③ **la Mauritania** Mauritania	**mauritano** *m* / **mauritana** *f*	Mauritanian
④ **Capo Verde** Cape Verde	**capoverdiano** *m* **capoverdiana** *f*	Cape Verdean
⑤ **il Senegal** Senegal	**senegalese** *m / f*	Senegalese
⑥ **il Gambia** Gambia	**gambiano** *m* **gambiana** *f*	Gambian
⑦ **la Guinea-Bissau** Guinea-Bissau	**guineense** *m / f*	Bissau-Guinean
⑧ **la Guinea** Guinea	**guineano** *m* / **guineana** *f*	Guinean
⑨ **la Sierra Leone** Sierra Leone	**sierraleonese** *m / f*	Sierra Leonean
⑩ **la Liberia** Liberia	**liberiano** *m* / **liberiana** *f*	Liberian
⑪ **la Costa d'Avorio** Ivory Coast	**ivoriano** *m* / **ivoriana** *f*	Ivorian
⑫ **il Burkina Faso** Burkina Faso	**burkinabé** *m / f*	Burkinabe
⑬ **il Mali** Mali	**maliano** *m* / **maliana** *f*	Malian
⑭ **l'Algeria** Algeria	**algerino** *m* / **algerina** *f*	Algerian
⑮ **la Tunisia** Tunisia	**tunisino** *m* / **tunisina** *f*	Tunisian
⑯ **la Libia** Libya	**libico** *m* / **libica** *f*	Libyan
⑰ **il Niger** Niger	**nigerino** *m* / **nigerina** *f*	Nigerien
⑱ **il Ghana** Ghana	**ghanese** *m* / **ghanese** *f*	Ghanaian
⑲ **il Togo** Togo	**togolese** *m* / **togolese** *f*	Togolese
⑳ **il Benin** Benin	**beninese** *m* / **beninese** *f*	Beninese
㉑ **la Nigeria** Nigeria	**nigeriano** *m* / **nigeriana** *f*	Nigerian
㉒ **São Tomé e Príncipe** São Tomé and Príncipe	**saotomense** *m / f*	São Toméan
㉓ **la Guinea Equatoriale** Equatorial Guinea	**equatoguineano** *m* **equatoguineana** *f*	Equatorial Guinean
㉔ **il Camerun** Cameroon	**camerunense** *m / f*	Cameroonian
㉕ **il Ciad** Chad	**ciadiano** *m* / **ciadiana** *f*	Chadian
㉖ **l'Egitto** Egypt	**egiziano** *m* / **egiziana** *f*	Egyptian
㉗ **il Sudan** Sudan	**sudanese** *m / f*	Sudanese
㉘ **il Sudan del Sud** South Sudan	**sudsudanese** *m / f*	South Sudanese
㉙ **l'Eritrea** Eritrea	**eritreo** *m* / **eritrea** *f*	Eritrean
㉚ **il Gibuti** Djibouti	**gibutiano** *m* / **gibutiana** *f*	Djiboutian
㉛ **l'Etiopia** Ethiopia	**etiope** *m / f*	Ethiopian
㉜ **la Somalia** Somalia	**somalo** *m* / **somala** *f*	Somalian
㉝ **il Kenya** Kenya	**keniano** *m* / **keniana** *f*	Kenyan
㉞ **l'Uganda** Uganda	**ugandese** *m / f*	Ugandan
㉟ **la Repubblica Centrafricana** Central African Republic	**centrafricano** *m* **centrafricana** *f*	Central African
㊱ **il Gabon** Gabon	**gabonese** *m / f*	Gabonese
㊲ **la Repubblica del Congo** Republic of the Congo	**congolese** *m / f*	Congolese
㊳ **la Repubblica Democratica del Congo** Democratic Republic of the Congo	**congolese** *m / f*	Congolese
㊴ **il Ruanda** Rwanda	**ruandese** *m / f*	Rwandan
㊵ **il Burundi** Burundi	**burundese** *m / f*	Burundian
㊶ **la Tanzania** Tanzania	**tanzaniano** *m* **tanzaniana** *f*	Tanzanian
㊷ **il Mozambico** Mozambique	**mozambicano** *m* **mozambicana** *f*	Mozambican
㊸ **il Malawi** Malawi	**malawiano** *m* **malawiana** *f*	Malawian
㊹ **lo Zambia** Zambia	**zambiano** *m* **zambiana** *f*	Zambian
㊺ **l'Angola** Angola	**angolano** *m* **angolana** *f*	Angolan
㊻ **la Namibia** Namibia	**namibiano** *m* **namibiana** *f*	Namibian
㊼ **il Botswana** Botswana	**botswaniano** *m* **botswaniana** *f*	Botswanan
㊽ **lo Zimbabwe** Zimbabwe	**zimbabweano** *m* **zimbabweana** *f*	Zimbabwean
㊾ **il Sudafrica** South Africa	**sudafricano** *m* **sudafricana** *f*	South African
㊿ **il Lesotho** Lesotho	**lesothiano** *m* **lesothiana** *f*	Basotho
(51) **l'Eswatini** *m* Eswatini	**swazi** *m / f*	Swazi
(52) **le Comore** Comoros	**comoriano** *m* **comoriana** *f*	Comoran
(53) **il Madagascar** Madagascar	**malgascio** *m* **malgascia** *f*	Madagascan
(54) **le Seychelles** Seychelles	**seychellese** *m / f*	Seychelloi
(55) **le Mauritius** Mauritius	**mauriziano** *m* **mauriziana** *f*	Mauritian

See also
145 Il pianeta Terra • Planet Earth **146-147** La geografia • Geography
148 Le cartine e le direzioni • Maps and directions **149-151** I Paesi
Countries **153** Le nazionalità (continua) • Nationalities continued

152.2 IL SUD AMERICA • SOUTH AMERICA

Country	Adjective	English Adjective
① **Il Sud America** South America	**sudamericano** *m* **sudamericana** *f*	South American
② **il Venezuela** Venezuela	**venezuelano** *m* **venezuelana** *f*	Venezuelan
③ **la Colombia** Colombia	**colombiano** *m* **colombiana** *f*	Colombian
④ **l'Ecuador** *m* Ecuador	**ecuadoregno** *m* **ecuadoregna** *f*	Ecuadorian
⑤ **il Perù** Peru	**peruviano** *m* **peruviana** *f*	Peruvian
⑥ **la Guyana** Guyana	**guianese** *m / f*	Guyanese
⑦ **il Suriname** Suriname	**surinamese** *m / f*	Surinamese
⑧ **il Brasile** Brazil	**brasiliano** *m* **brasiliana** *f*	Brazilian
⑨ **la Bolivia** Bolivia	**boliviano** *m* **boliviana** *f*	Bolivian
⑩ **il Cile** Chile	**cileno** *m* / **cilena** *f*	Chilean
⑪ **l'Argentina** Argentina	**argentino** *m* **argentina** *f*	Argentinian
⑫ **il Paraguay** Paraguay	**paraguaiano** *m* **paraguaiana** *f*	Paraguayan
⑬ **l'Uruguay** Uruguay	**uruguaiano** *m* **uruguaiana** *f*	Uruguayan

152.3 L'AMERICA DEL NORD, L'AMERICA CENTRALE E I CARAIBI
NORTH AND CENTRAL AMERICA AND THE CARIBBEAN

Country	Adjective	English Adjective
① **l'America del Nord, l'America centrale e i Caraibi** North and Central America and the Caribbean	**nordamericano, centroamericano e caraibico** *m*, **nordamericana centroamericana e caraibica** *f*	North American, Central American, and Caribbean
② **il Canada** Canada	**canadese** *m / f*	Canadian
③ **gli Stati Uniti d'America** United States of America	**statunitense** *m / f*	American
④ **il Messico** Mexico	**messicano** *m* **messicana** *f*	Mexican
⑤ **il Guatemala** Guatemala	**guatemalteco** *m* **guatemalteca** *f*	Guatemalan
⑥ **il Belize** Belize	**beliziano** *m* / **beliziana** *f*	Belizean
⑦ **El Salvador** El Salvador	**salvadoregno** *m* **salvadoregna** *f*	Salvadoran
⑧ **Honduras** Honduras	**honduregno** *m* **honduregna** *f*	Honduran
⑨ **il Nicaragua** Nicaragua	**nicaraguense** *m / f*	Nicaraguan
⑩ **il Costa Rica** Costa Rica	**costaricano** *m* **costaricana** *f*	Costa Rican
⑪ **Panama** Panama	**panamense** *m / f*	Panamanian
⑫ **Cuba** Cuba	**cubano** *m* / **cubana** *f*	Cuban
⑬ **le Bahamas** Bahamas	**bahamense** *m / f*	Bahamian
⑭ **la Giamaica** Jamaica	**giamaicano** *m* **giamaicana** *f*	Jamaican
⑮ **Haiti** Haiti	**haitiano** *m* **haitiana** *f*	Haitian
⑯ **la Repubblica Dominicana** Dominican Republic	**dominicano** *m* **dominicana** *f*	Dominican
⑰ **le Barbados** Barbados	**barbadiano** *m* **barbadiana** *f*	Barbadian
⑱ **Trinidad e Tobago** Trinidad and Tobago	**trinidadiano o tobagoniano** *m* **trinidadiana o tobagoniana** *f*	Trinidadian or Tobagonian
⑲ **Saint Kitts e Nevis** St. Kitts and Nevis	**kittitiano o nevisiano** *m* **kittitiana o nevisiana** *f*	Kittitian or Nevisian
⑳ **Antigua e Barbuda** Antigua and Barbuda	**antiguo-barbudano** *m* **antiguo-barbudana** *f*	Antiguan or Barbudan
㉑ **Dominica** Dominica	**dominicense** *m / f*	Dominican
㉒ **Santa Lucia** St. Lucia	**santaluciano** *m* **santaluciana** *f*	St. Lucian
㉓ **Saint Vincent e Grenadine** St. Vincent and The Grenadines	**sanvicentino** *m* **sanvincentina** *f*	Vincentian
㉔ **Grenada** Grenada	**grenadino** *m* **grenadina** *f*	Grenadian

153 Le nazionalità (continua)

Nationalities continued

153.1 L'OCEANIA · OCEANIA

Country	Adjective	English Adjective
① l'Oceania Oceania	**oceaniano** *m* / **oceaniana** *f*	Oceanian
② **la Papua Nuova Guinea** Papua New Guinea	**papuano** *m* **papuana** *f*	Papua New Guinean
③ **l'Australia** Australia	**australiano** *m* **australiana** *f*	Australian
④ **la Nuova Zelanda** New Zealand	**neozelandese** *m* / *f*	New Zealand
⑤ **le Isole Marshall** Marshall Islands	**marshallese** *m* / *f*	Marshallese
⑥ **Palau** Palau	**palauano** *m* / **palauana** *f*	Palauan
⑦ **la Micronesia** Micronesia	**micronesiano** *m* **micronesiana** *f*	Micronesian
⑧ **Nauru** Nauru	**nauruano** *m* / **nauruana** *f*	Nauruan
⑨ **le Kiribati** Kiribati	**gilbertese** *m* / *f*	Kiribati
⑩ **le Tuvalu** Tuvalu	**tuvaluano** *m* / **tuvaluana** *f*	Tuvaluan
⑪ **le Samoa** Samoa	**samoano** *m* / **samoana** *f*	Samoan
⑫ **Tonga** Tonga	**tongano** *m* / **tongana** *f*	Tongan
⑬ **Vanuatu** Vanuatu	**vanuatiano** *m* **vanuatiana** *f*	Vanuatuan
⑭ **le Isole Salomone** Solomon Islands	**salomonese** *m* / *f*	Solomon Island
⑮ **le Figi** Fiji	**figiano** *m* / **figiana** *f*	Fijian

153.2 L'ASIA · ASIA

Country	Adjective	English Adjective
① **l'Asia** • Asia	**asiatico** *m* / **asiaticia** *f*	Asian
② **la Turchia** Türkiye	**turco** *m* / **turca** *f*	Turkish
③ **la Federazione Russa** Russian Federation	**russo** *m* / **russa** *f*	Russian
④ **la Georgia** Georgia	**georgiano** *m* / **georgiana** *f*	Georgian
⑤ **l'Armenia** Armenia	**armeno** *m* / **armena** *f*	Armenian
⑥ **l'Arzebaigian** Azerbaijan	**azerbaigiano** *m* **azerbaigiana** *f*	Azerbaijani
⑦ **l'Iran** Iran	**iraniano** *m* / **iraniana** *f*	Iranian
⑧ **l'Iraq** Iraq	**iracheno** *m* / **irachena** *f*	Iraqi
⑨ **la Siria** Syria	**siriano** *m* / **siriana** *f*	Syrian
⑩ **il Libano** Lebanon	**libanese** *m* / *f*	Lebanese
⑪ **Israele** Israel	**israeliano** *m* **istraeliana** *f*	Israeli
⑫ **la Giordania** Jordan	**giordano** *m* / **giordana** *f*	Jordanian
⑬ **l'Arabia Saudita** Saudi Arabia	**saudita** *m* / *f*	Saudi
⑭ **il Kuwait** Kuwait	**kuwaitiano** *m* **kuwaitiana** *f*	Kuwaiti
⑮ **il Bahrein** Bahrain	**bahreinita** *m* / *f*	Bahraini
⑯ **il Qatar** Qatar	**qatariota** *m* / *f*	Qatari
⑰ **gli Emirati Arabi Uniti** United Arab Emirates	**emiratino** *m* **emiratina** *f*	Emirati
⑱ **l'Oman** Oman	**omanita** *m* / *f*	Omani
⑲ **lo Yemen** Yemen	**yemenita** *m* / *f*	Yemeni
⑳ **il Kazakistan** Kazakhstan	**kazako** *m* / **kazaka** *f*	Kazakh
㉑ **l'Uzbekistan** Uzbekistan	**uzbeko** *m* / **uzbeka** *f*	Uzbek
㉒ **il Turkmenistan** Turkmenistan	**turkmeno** *m* **turkmena** *f*	Turkmen
㉓ **l'Afghanistan** Afghanistan	**afgano** *m* / **afgana** *f*	Afghan
㉔ **il Tagikistan** Tajikistan	**tagico** *m* / **tagica** *f*	Tajikistani
㉕ **il Kirghizistan** Kyrgyzstan	**kirghiso** *m* / **kirghisa** *f*	Kyrgyz
㉖ **il Pakistan** Pakistan	**pakistano** *m* / **pakistana** *f*	Pakistani
㉗ **l'India** India	**indiano** *m* / **indiana** *f*	Indian
㉘ **le Maldive** Maldives	**maldiviano** *m* **maldiviana** *f*	Maldivian
㉙ **lo Sri Lanka** Sri Lanka	**srilankese** *m* / *f*	Sri Lankan
㉚ **la Cina** China	**cinese** *m* / *f*	Chinese
㉛ **la Mongolia** Mongolia	**mongolo** *m* / **mongola** *f*	Mongolian
㉜ **la Corea del Nord** North Korea	**nordcoreano** *m* **nordcoreana** *f*	North Korean
㉝ **la Corea del Sud** South Korea	**sudcoreano** *m* **sudcoreana** *f*	South Korean
㉞ **il Giappone** Japan	**giapponese** *m* / *f*	Japanese
㉟ **il Nepal** Nepal	**nepalese** *m* / *f*	Nepalese
㊱ **il Bhutan** Bhutan	**butanese** *m* / *f*	Bhutanese
㊲ **il Bangladesh** Bangladesh	**bangladese** *m* / *f*	Bangladeshi
㊳ **il Myanmar** Myanmar (Burma)	**birmano** *m* / **birmana** *f*	Burmese
㊴ **la Tailandia** Thailand	**tailandese** *m* / *f*	Thai

See also
145 Il pianeta Terra • Planet Earth **146-147** La geografia • Geography
148 Le cartine e le direzioni • Maps and directions **149-151** I Paesi • Countries

153.2 L'ASIA (CONTINUA) • ASIA CONTINUED

Country	Adjective	English Adjective
㊵ **il Laos** Laos	**laotiano** *m* / **laotiana** *f*	Laotian
㊶ **il Vietnam** Vietnam	**vietnamita** *m / f*	Vietnamese
㊷ **la Cambogia** Cambodia	**cambogiano** *m* **cambogiana** *f*	Cambodian
㊸ **la Malesia** Malaysia	**malese** *m / f*	Malaysian
㊹ **Singapore** Singapore	**singaporiano** *m* **singaporiana** *f*	Singaporean
㊺ **l'Indonesia** *f* Indonesia	**indonesiano** *m* **indonesiana** *f*	Indonesian
㊻ **il Brunei** Brunei	**bruneiano** *m* **bruneiana** *f*	Bruneian
㊼ **le Filippine** Philippines	**filippino** *m* / **filippina** *f*	Filipino
㊽ **il Timor Est** East Timor	**est-timorese** *m / f*	Timorese

153.3 L'EUROPA • EUROPE

Country	Adjective	English Adjective
① **l'Europa** • Europe	**europeo** *m* / **europea** *f*	European
② **l'Irlanda** Ireland	**irlandese** *m / f*	Irish
③ **il Regno Unito** United Kingdom	**britannico** *m* / **britannica** *f*	British
④ **il Portogallo** Portugal	**portoghese** *m / f*	Portuguese
⑤ **la Spagna** Spain	**spagnolo** *m* / **spagnola** *f*	Spanish
⑥ **Andorra** Andorra	**andorrano** *m* **andorrana** *f*	Andorran
⑦ **la Francia** France	**francese** *m / f*	French
⑧ **il Belgio** Belgium	**belga** *m / f*	Belgian
⑨ **i Paesi Bassi** Netherlands	**olandese** *m / f*	Dutch
⑩ **il Lussemburgo** Luxembourg	**lussemburghese** *m / f*	Luxembourg
⑪ **la Germania** Germany	**tedesco** *m* / **tedesca** *f*	German
⑫ **la Danimarca** Denmark	**danese** *m / f*	Danish
⑬ **la Norvegia** Norway	**norvegese** *m / f*	Norwegian
⑭ **la Svezia** Sweden	**svedese** *m / f*	Swedish
⑮ **la Finlandia** Finland	**finlandese** *m / f*	Finnish
⑯ **l'Estonia** Estonia	**estone** *m / f*	Estonian
⑰ **la Lettonia** Latvia	**lettone** *m / f*	Latvian
⑱ **la Lituania** Lithuania	**lituano** *m* / **lituana** *f*	Lithuanian
⑲ **la Polonia** Poland	**polacco** *m* / **polacca** *f*	Polish
⑳ **la Repubblica Ceca** Czech Republic	**ceco** *m* / **ceca** *f*	Czech
㉑ **l'Austria** *f* Austria	**austriaco** *m* / **austriaca** *f*	Austrian
㉒ **il Liechtenstein** Liechtenstein	**liechtensteinese** *m / f*	Liechtensteiner
㉓ **la Svizzera** Switzerland	**svizzero** *m* **svizzera** *f*	Swiss
㉔ **l'Italia** Italy	**italiano** *m* / **italiana** *f*	Italian
㉕ **il Principato di Monaco** Monaco	**monegasco** *m* **monegasca** *f*	Monacan
㉖ **San Marino** San Marino	**sammarinese** *m / f*	Sammarinese
㉗ **Malta** Malta	**maltese** *m / f*	Maltese
㉘ **la Slovenia** Slovenia	**sloveno** *m* / **slovena** *f*	Slovenian
㉙ **Croazia** Croatia	**croato** *m* / **croata** *f*	Croatian
㉚ **l'Ungheria** Hungary	**ungherese** *m / f*	Hungarian
㉛ **la Slovacchia** Slovakia	**slovacco** *m* **slovacca** *f*	Slovakian
㉜ **l'Ucraina** Ukraine	**ucraino** *m* / **ucraina** *f*	Ukrainian
㉝ **la Bielorussia** Belarus	**bielorusso** *m* / **bielorussa** *f*	Belarusian
㉞ **la Moldavia** Moldova	**moldavo** *m* / **moldava** *f*	Moldovan
㉟ **la Romania** Romania	**rumeno** *m* / **rumena** *f*	Romanian
㊱ **la Serbia** Serbia	**serbo** *m* / **serba** *f*	Serbian
㊲ **la Bosnia -Erzegovina** Bosnia and Herzegovina	**bosniaco o erzegovino** *m* **bosniaca o erzegovina** *f*	Bosnian or Herzegovinian
㊳ **l'Albania** Albania	**albanese** *m / f*	Albanian
㊴ **la Macedonia del Nord** North Macedonia	**macedone** *m / f*	North Macedonian
㊵ **la Bulgaria** Bulgaria	**bulgaro** *m* / **bulgara** *f*	Bulgarian
㊶ **la Grecia** Greece	**greco** *m* / **greca** *f*	Greek
㊷ **il Montenegro** Montenegro	**montenegrino** *m* **montenegrina** *f*	Montenegrin
㊸ **l'Islanda** Iceland	**islandese** *m / f*	Icelandic
㊹ **Cipro** Cyprus	**cipriota** *m / f*	Cypriot
㊺ **la Turchia** Türkiye	**turco** *m* / **turca** *f*	Turkish
㊻ **la Federazione Russa** Russian Federation	**russo** *m* / **russa** *f*	Russian

154 Il tempo atmosferico
Weather

154.1 IL TEMPO ATMOSFERICO · WEATHER

① **l'umidità** *f*
humidity

② **l'ondata di caldo** *f*
heat wave

③ **la siccità**
drought

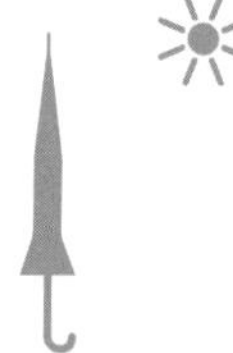
④ **secco**
dry

⑤ **umido**
wet

⑥ **coperto**
overcast

⑦ **lo smog**
smog

⑧ **la goccia di pioggia**
raindrop

⑨ **il leggero piovasco**
light shower

⑩ **la pioggerella**
drizzle

⑪ **l'acquazzone** *m*
downpour

⑫ **l'alluvione** *f*
flood

⑬ **la tempesta di sabbia**
sandstorm

⑭ **la burrasca**
gale

⑮ **il temporale**
storm

⑯ **il tuono**
thunder

⑰ **il fulmine**
lightning

⑱ **l'arcobaleno** *m*
rainbow

⑲ **il nevischio**
sleet

⑳ **il fiocco di neve**
snowflake

㉑ **il cumulo di neve**
snowdrift

㉒ **la tormenta**
blizzard

㉓ **la tempesta di neve**
snowstorm

㉔ **il chicco di grandine**
hailstone

㉕ **l'uragano** *m*
hurricane

㉖ **il tornado**
tornado

㉘ **Oggi piove a dirotto.**
It's raining cats
and dogs today.
㉗ **la pozzanghera**
puddle

See also
145 Il pianeta Terra • Planet Earth **146-147** La geografia • Geography
155 Il clima e l'ambiente • Climate and the environment

154.2 LA TEMPERATURA • TEMPERATURE

① **gelido** *m* / **gelida** *f*
freezing

② **freddo** *m* / **fredda** *f*
cold

③ **freddo** *m* / **fredda** *f*
chilly

④ **caldo** *m* / **calda** *f*
warm

⑤ **caldissimo** *m* **caldissima** *f*
hot

⑥ **soffocante**
stifling

⑦ **il punto di congelamento**
freezing point

⑧ **il punto di ebollizione**
boiling point

⑨ **meno 10**
minus 10

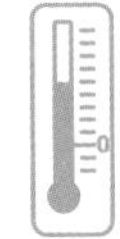

⑩ **25 gradi**
25 degrees

⑪ **Celsius**
Celsius

⑫ **Fahrenheit**
Fahrenheit

⑬ **fresco** *m* / **fresca** *f*
cool

⑭ **mite**
mild

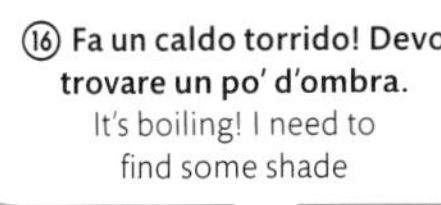

⑯ **Fa un caldo torrido! Devo trovare un po' d'ombra.**
It's boiling! I need to find some shade

⑮ **torrido** *m* / **torrida** *f*
boiling

154.3 GLI AGGETTIVI DEL TEMPO • WEATHER ADJECTIVES

① **il sole → soleggiato** *m* **soleggiata** *f*
sun → sunny

② **la nuvola → nuvoloso** *m* / **nuvolosa** *f*
cloud → cloudy

③ **la nebbia → nebbioso** *m* **nebbiosa** *f*
fog → foggy

④ **la pioggia → piovoso** *m* / **piovosa** *f*
rain → rainy

⑤ **la neve → nevoso** *m* / **nevosa** *f*
snow → snowy

⑥ **il ghiaccio → ghiacciato** *m* **ghiacciata** *f*
ice → icy

⑦ **la gelata → gelido** *m* **gelida** *f*
frost → frosty

⑧ **il vento → ventoso** *m* / **ventosa** *f*
wind → windy

⑨ **il temporale → temporalesco** *m* **temporalesca** *f*
storm → stormy

⑩ **il tuono → tempestoso** *m* **tempestosa** *f*
thunder → thundery

⑪ **la nebbiolina → nebbioso** *m* **nebbiosa** *f*
mist → misty

⑫ **la brezza → ventilato** *m* **ventilata** *f*
breeze → breezy

155 Il clima e l'ambiente
Climate and the environment

155.1 L'ATMOSFERA · ATMOSPHERE

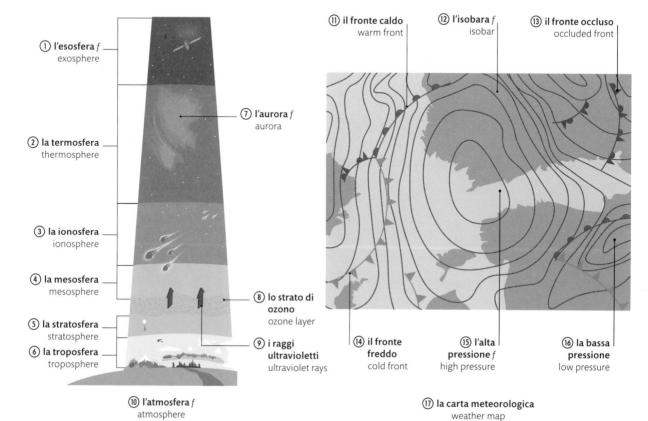

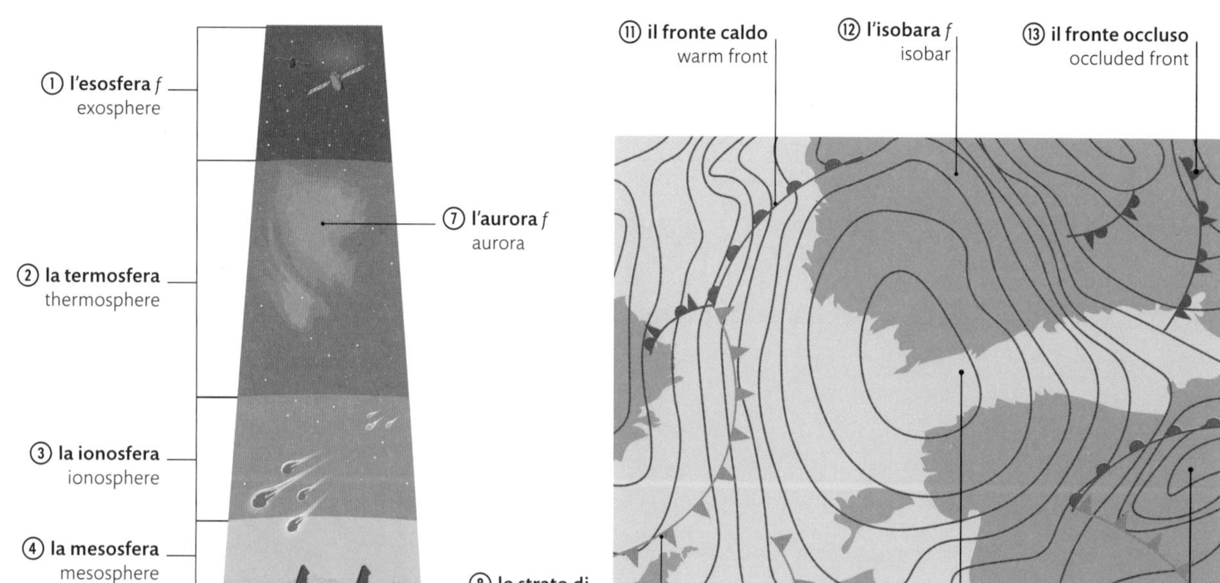
① l'esosfera f
exosphere
② la termosfera
thermosphere
③ la ionosfera
ionosphere
④ la mesosfera
mesosphere
⑤ la stratosfera
stratosphere
⑥ la troposfera
troposphere
⑦ l'aurora f
aurora
⑧ lo strato di ozono
ozone layer
⑨ i raggi ultravioletti
ultraviolet rays
⑪ il fronte caldo
warm front
⑫ l'isobara f
isobar
⑬ il fronte occluso
occluded front
⑭ il fronte freddo
cold front
⑮ l'alta pressione f
high pressure
⑯ la bassa pressione
low pressure

⑩ **l'atmosfera** *f*
atmosphere

⑰ **la carta meteorologica**
weather map

155.2 I PROBLEMI AMBIENTALI · ENVIRONMENTAL ISSUES

① **la deforestazione**
deforestation

② **la perdita di habitat**
habitat loss

③ **le specie a rischio**
endangered species

④ **i rifiuti plastici**
plastic waste

⑤ **la sovrapesca**
overfishing

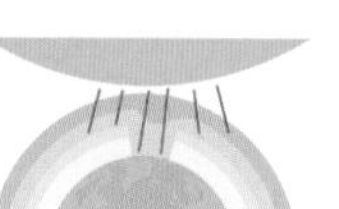

⑥ **il buco dell'ozono**
ozone depletion

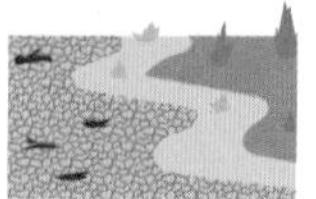

⑦ **la desertificazione**
desertification

⑧ **la chiazza di petrolio**
oil slick

⑨ **la pioggia acida**
acid rain

See also
145 Il pianeta Terra • Planet Earth **146-147** La geografia • Geography **154** Il tempo atmosferico • Weather

155.3 IL CAMBIAMENTO CLIMATICO • CLIMATE CHANGE

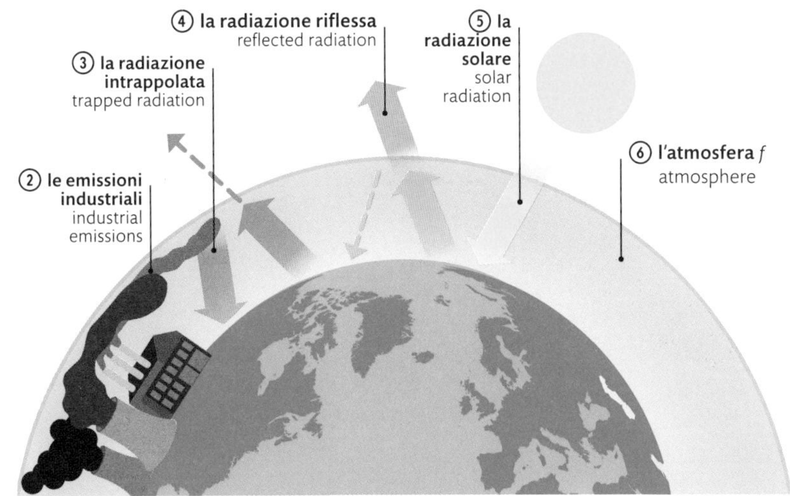
② le emissioni industriali
industrial emissions
③ la radiazione intrappolata
trapped radiation
④ la radiazione riflessa
reflected radiation
⑤ la radiazione solare
solar radiation
⑥ l'atmosfera *f*
atmosphere

① **l'effetto serra** *m*
greenhouse effect

⑧ l'anidride carbonica *f*
carbon dioxide
⑨ il metano
methane
CH4
CO2

⑦ **i gas serra**
greenhouse gases

⑩ **i combustibili fossili**
fossil fuels

⑪ **le emissioni**
emissions

⑫ **l'inquinamento** *m*
pollution

⑬ **l'ecosistema** *m*
ecosystem

CO2

⑭ **emissioni zero**
zero carbon

⑮ **il restringimento dei ghiacciai**
shrinking glaciers

⑯ **lo scioglimento delle calotte polari**
melting ice caps

155.4 I RIFIUTI E IL RICICLAGGIO • WASTE AND RECYCLING

② **Cerco di riciclare il più possibile la plastica e la carta.**
I try to recycle plastic and paper as much as possible.

① **differenziare i rifiuti**
to sort your trash

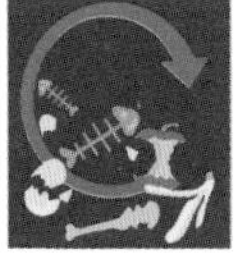

③ **i rifiuti alimentari**
food waste

④ **la carta**
paper

⑤ **la plastica**
plastic

⑥ **il vetro**
glass

⑦ **il metallo**
metal

⑧ **il sacchetto compostabile**
compostable bags

⑨ **la discarica**
landfill

Le rocce e i minerali

Rocks and minerals

156.1 **LE ROCCE** · ROCKS

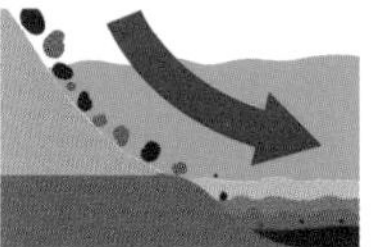

① **la roccia sedimentaria**
sedimentary

② **l'arenaria** *f*
sandstone

③ **il calcare**
limestone

④ **il gesso**
chalk

⑤ **la selce**
flint

⑥ **il conglomerato**
conglomerate

⑦ **la pietra metamorfica**
metamorphic

⑧ **l'ardesia** *f*
slate

⑨ **lo scisto**
schist

⑩ **lo gneis**
gneiss

⑪ **il marmo**
marble

⑫ **la quarzite**
quartzite

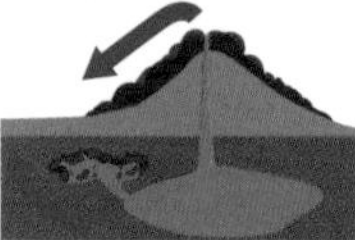

⑬ **la roccia ignea**
igneous

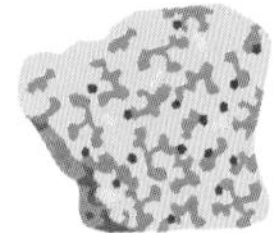

⑭ **il granito**
granite

⑮ **l'ossidiana** *f*
obsidian

⑯ **il basalto**
basalt

⑰ **il tufo vulcanico**
tuff

⑱ **la pietra pomice**
pumice

156.2 **I MINERALI** · MINERALS

① **il quarzo**
quartz

② **la mica**
mica

③ **l'agata** *f*
agate

④ **l'ematite** *f*
hematite

⑤ **la calcite**
calcite

⑥ **la malachite**
malachite

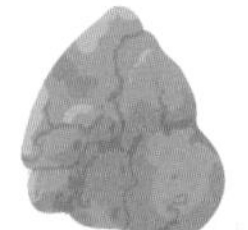

⑦ **il turchese**
turquoise

⑧ **l'onice** *f*
onyx

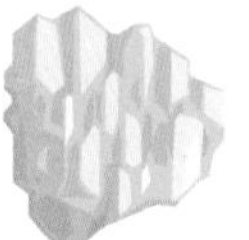

⑨ **lo zolfo**
sulfur

⑩ **la grafite**
graphite

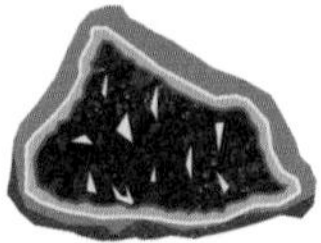

⑪ **il geode**
geode

⑫ **la rosa del deserto**
sand rose

See also
76 La chimica · Chemistry 78 La tavola periodica · The periodic table
145 Il pianeta Terra · Planet Earth 146-147 La geografia · Geography

156.3 LE GEMME · GEMS

① **il diamante**
diamond

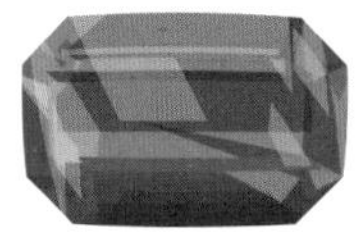
② **lo zaffiro**
sapphire

③ **lo smeraldo**
emerald

④ **il rubino**
ruby

⑤ **l'ametista** *f*
amethyst

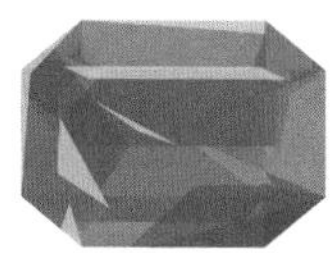
⑥ **il topazio**
topaz

⑦ **l'acquamarina** *f*
aquamarine

⑧ **la pietra di luna**
moonstone

⑨ **l'opale** *m*
opal

⑩ **la tormalina**
tourmaline

⑪ **il granato**
garnet

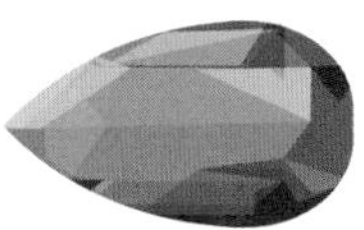
⑫ **il citrino**
citrine

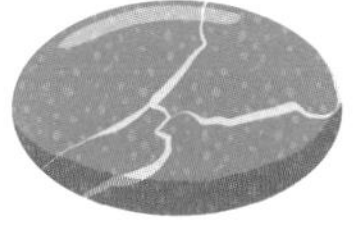
⑬ **la giada**
jade

⑭ **il giaietto**
jet

⑮ **il lapislazzulo**
lapis lazuli

⑯ **il diaspro**
jasper

⑰ **l'occhio di tigre** *m*
tiger's eye

⑱ **la corniola**
carnelian

156.4 I METALLI · METALS

① **l'oro** *m*
gold

② **l'argento** *m*
silver

③ **il platino**
platinum

④ **il magnesio**
magnesium

⑤ **il ferro**
iron

⑥ **il rame**
copper

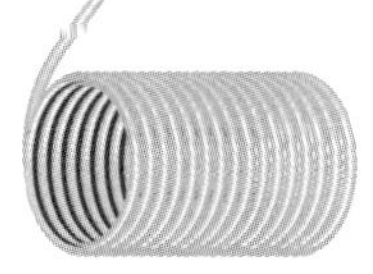
⑦ **lo stagno**
tin

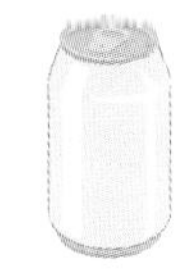
⑧ **l'alluminio** *m*
aluminum

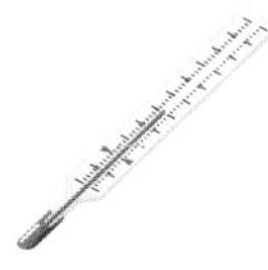
⑨ **il mercurio**
mercury

⑩ **il nichel**
nickel

⑪ **lo zinco**
zinc

⑫ **il cromo**
chromium

157 La storia naturale
Natural history

157.1 I PERIODI GEOLOGICI • GEOLOGICAL PERIODS

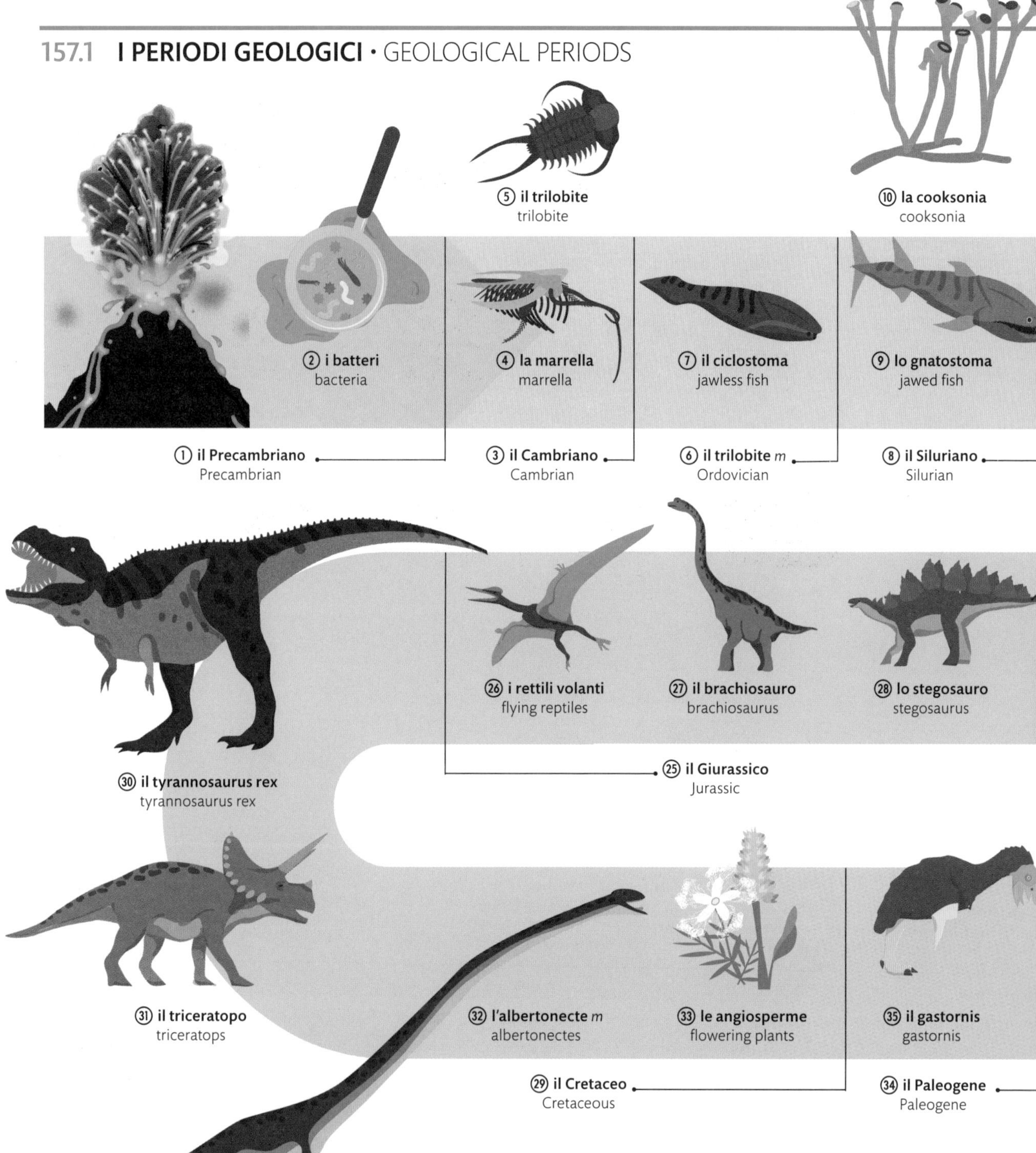

⑤ il trilobite
trilobite
⑩ la cooksonia
cooksonia
② i batteri
bacteria
④ la marrella
marrella
⑦ il ciclostoma
jawless fish
⑨ lo gnatostoma
jawed fish
① il Precambriano
Precambrian
③ il Cambriano
Cambrian
⑥ il trilobite m
Ordovician
⑧ il Siluriano
Silurian
㉖ i rettili volanti
flying reptiles
㉗ il brachiosauro
brachiosaurus
㉘ lo stegosauro
stegosaurus
㉚ il tyrannosaurus rex
tyrannosaurus rex
㉕ il Giurassico
Jurassic
㉛ il triceratopo
triceratops
㉜ l'albertonecte m
albertonectes
㉝ le angiosperme
flowering plants
㉟ il gastornis
gastornis
㉙ il Cretaceo
Cretaceous
㉞ il Paleogene
Paleogene

See also
145 Il pianeta Terra • Planet Earth **158-159** I mammiferi • Mammals **160-161** Gli uccelli • Birds **162** Gli insetti • Insects and bugs **163** Gli anfibi e i rettili • Amphibians and reptiles **166** La vita negli oceani • Ocean life **167-169** Le piante e gli alberi • Plants and trees

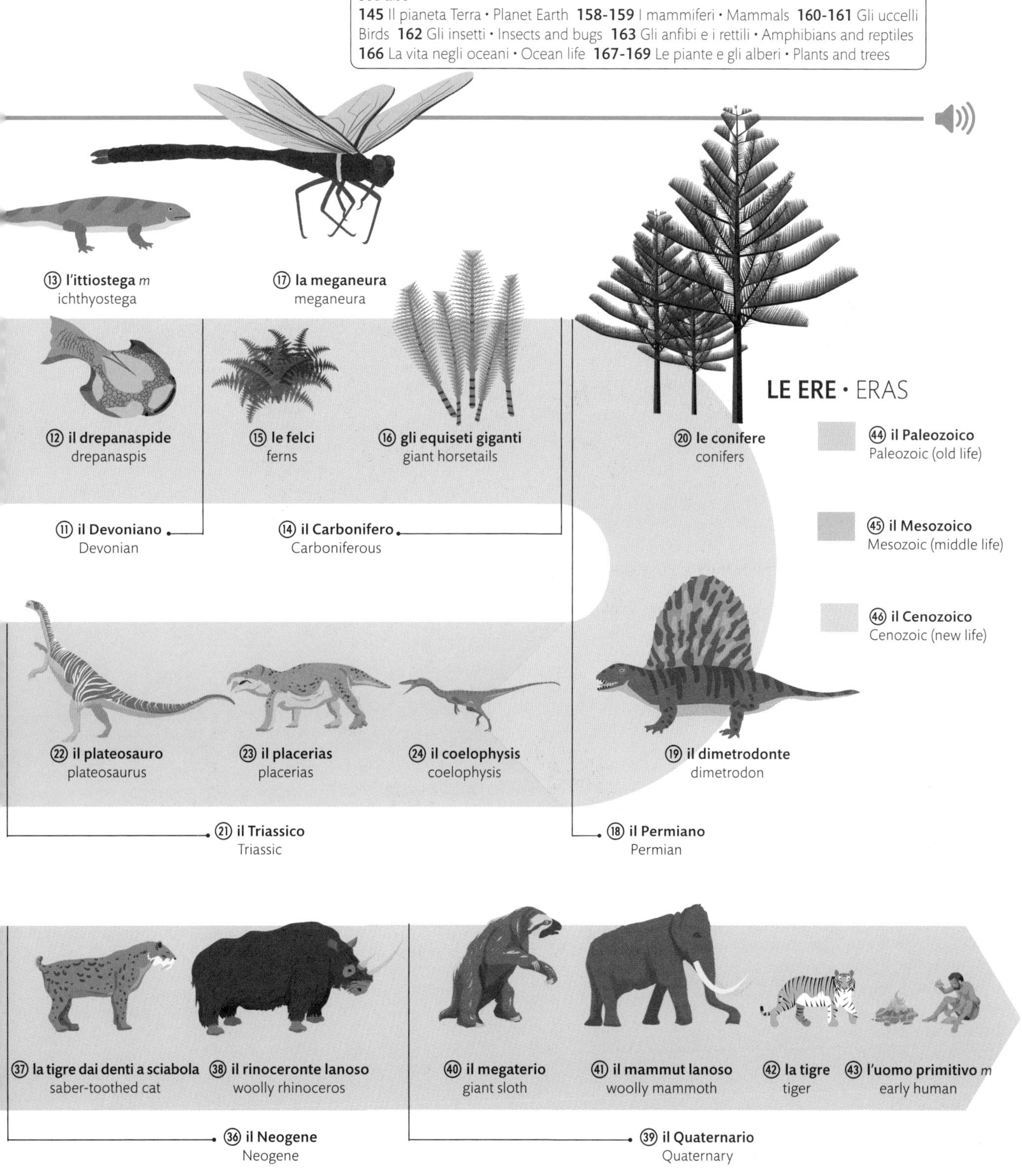
⑬ l'ittiostega *m*
ichthyostega
⑰ la meganeura
meganeura
⑫ il drepanaspide
drepanaspis
⑮ le felci
ferns
⑯ gli equiseti giganti
giant horsetails
⑳ le conifere
conifers
⑪ il Devoniano
Devonian
⑭ il Carbonifero
Carboniferous
㉒ il plateosauro
plateosaurus
㉓ il placerias
placerias
㉔ il coelophysis
coelophysis
⑲ il dimetrodonte
dimetrodon
㉑ il Triassico
Triassic
⑱ il Permiano
Permian
㊲ la tigre dai denti a sciabola
saber-toothed cat
㊳ il rinoceronte lanoso
woolly rhinoceros
㊵ il megaterio
giant sloth
㊶ il mammut lanoso
woolly mammoth
㊷ la tigre
tiger
㊸ l'uomo primitivo *m*
early human
㊱ il Neogene
Neogene
㊴ il Quaternario
Quaternary

LE ERE • ERAS

㊹ **il Paleozoico**
Paleozoic (old life)

㊺ **il Mesozoico**
Mesozoic (middle life)

㊻ **il Cenozoico**
Cenozoic (new life)

158 I mammiferi
Mammals

158.1 LE SPECIE DI MAMMIFERI • SPECIES OF MAMMALS

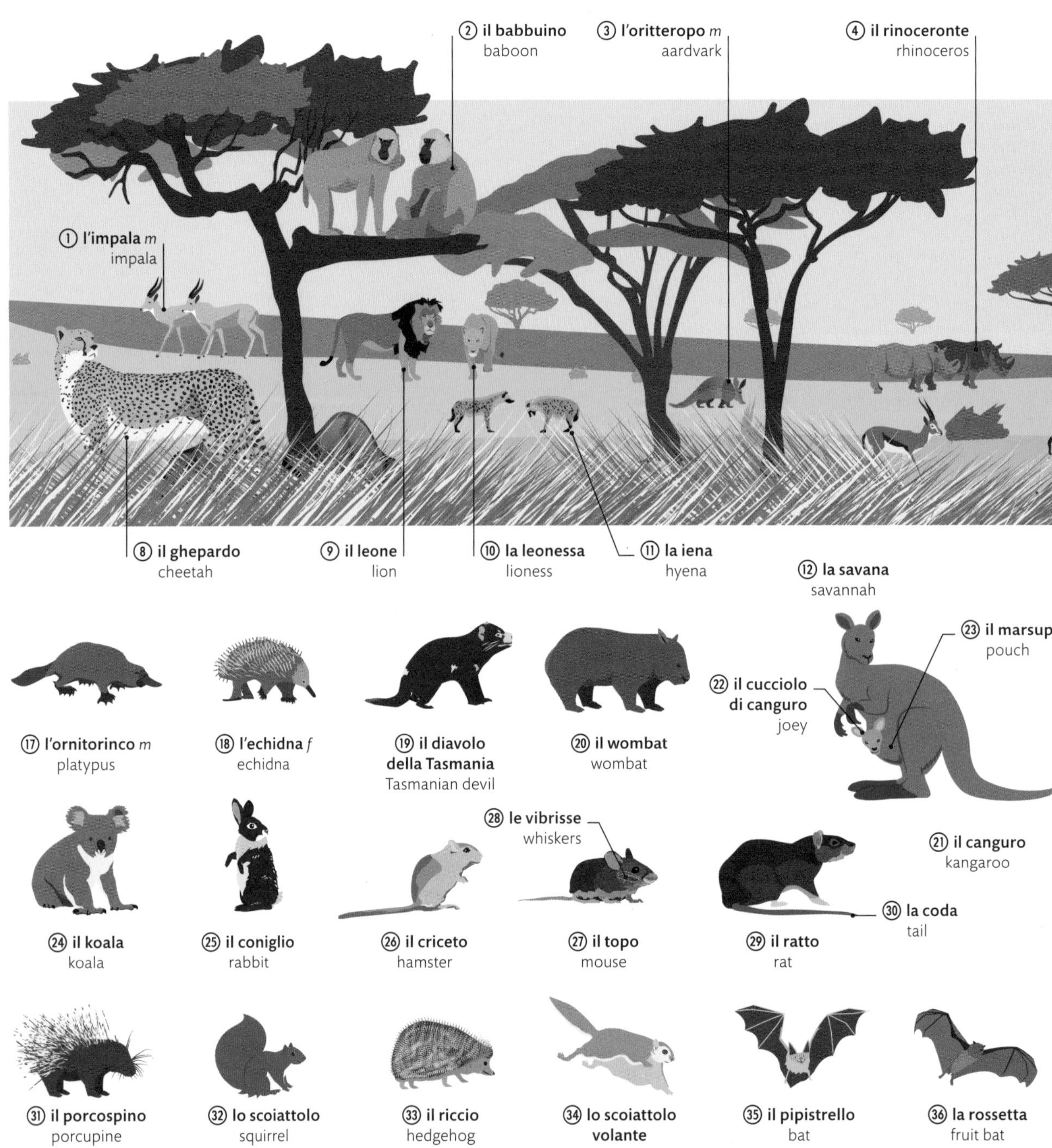

② il babbuino
baboon
③ l'oritteropo m
aardvark
④ il rinoceronte
rhinoceros
① l'impala m
impala
⑧ il ghepardo
cheetah
⑨ il leone
lion
⑩ la leonessa
lioness
⑪ la iena
hyena
⑫ la savana
savannah
㉓ il marsupio
pouch
㉒ il cucciolo di canguro
joey
⑰ l'ornitorinco m
platypus
⑱ l'echidna f
echidna
⑲ il diavolo della Tasmania
Tasmanian devil
⑳ il wombat
wombat
㉘ le vibrisse
whiskers
㉑ il canguro
kangaroo
㉚ la coda
tail
㉔ il koala
koala
㉕ il coniglio
rabbit
㉖ il criceto
hamster
㉗ il topo
mouse
㉙ il ratto
rat

㉛ **il porcospino**
porcupine

㉜ **lo scoiattolo**
squirrel

㉝ **il riccio**
hedgehog

㉞ **lo scoiattolo volante**
flying squirrel

㉟ **il pipistrello**
bat

㊱ **la rossetta**
fruit bat

See also
157 La storia naturale • Natural history 159 I mammiferi (continua) • Mammals continued 164 Gli animali domestici • Pets 165 Gli animali da fattoria • Farm animals 166 La vita negli oceani • Ocean life

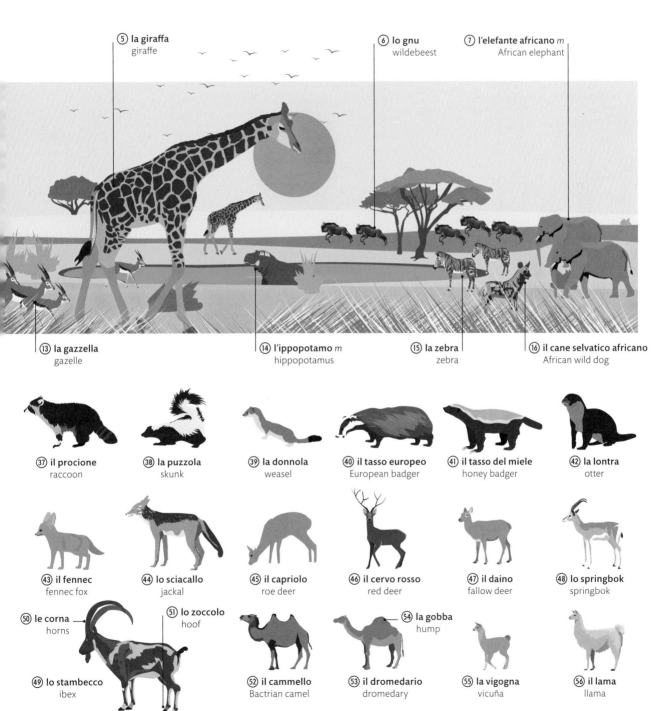

⑤ **la giraffa**
giraffe

⑥ **lo gnu**
wildebeest

⑦ **l'elefante africano** *m*
African elephant

⑬ **la gazzella**
gazelle

⑭ **l'ippopotamo** *m*
hippopotamus

⑮ **la zebra**
zebra

⑯ **il cane selvatico africano**
African wild dog

㊲ **il procione**
raccoon

㊳ **la puzzola**
skunk

㊴ **la donnola**
weasel

㊵ **il tasso europeo**
European badger

㊶ **il tasso del miele**
honey badger

㊷ **la lontra**
otter

㊸ **il fennec**
fennec fox

㊹ **lo sciacallo**
jackal

㊺ **il capriolo**
roe deer

㊻ **il cervo rosso**
red deer

㊼ **il daino**
fallow deer

㊽ **lo springbok**
springbok

㊿ **le corna**
horns

51 **lo zoccolo**
hoof

49 **lo stambecco**
ibex

52 **il cammello**
Bactrian camel

54 **la gobba**
hump

53 **il dromedario**
dromedary

55 **la vigogna**
vicuña

56 **il lama**
llama

159 I mammiferi (continua)

Mammals continued

159.1 LE SPECIE DI MAMMIFERI • SPECIES OF MAMMALS

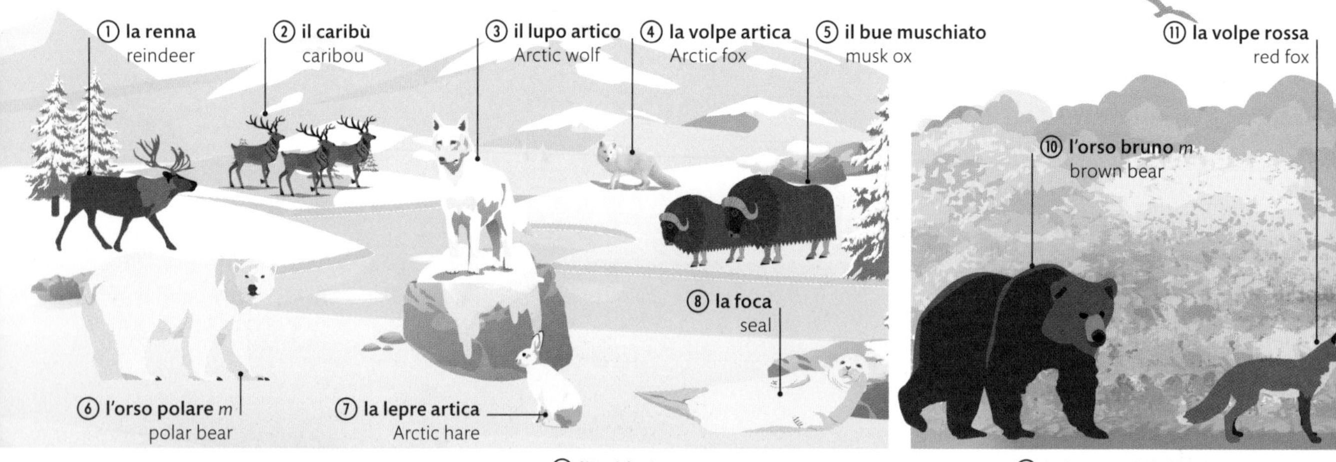

① la renna
reindeer
② il caribù
caribou
③ il lupo artico
Arctic wolf
④ la volpe artica
Arctic fox
⑤ il bue muschiato
musk ox
⑪ la volpe rossa
red fox
⑩ l'orso bruno *m*
brown bear
⑧ la foca
seal
⑥ l'orso polare *m*
polar bear
⑦ la lepre artica
Arctic hare

⑨ **l'Artide** *f*
Arctic

⑮ **la foresta di latifoglie**
broadleaf forest

㉔ **la proboscide**
trunk

㉓ **l'elefante asiatico** *m*
Asian elephant

㉕ **il formichiere**
anteater

㉗ **il cucciolo** *m* **/ la cucciola** *f*
cub

㉖ **la tigre**
tiger

㉘ **il leopardo**
leopard

㉙ **il gatto selvatico**
wildcat

㉚ **la lince rossa**
bobcat

㉛ **il leopardo delle nevi**
snow leopard

㉜ **il lemure dalla coda ad anelli**
ring-tailed lemur

㉝ **la scimmia cappuccina**
capuchin monkey

㉟ **la coda**
tail

㉞ **la scimmia ragno**
spider monkey

㊲ **il naso pendulo**
pendulous nose

㊱ **la nasica**
proboscis monkey

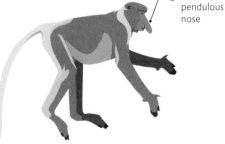

㊳ **il macaco**
macaque

㊴ **il mandrillo**
mandrill

㊵ **la marmosetta**
marmoset

㊶ **l'orangotango** *m*
orangutan

㊷ **lo scimpanzé**
chimpanzee

㊸ **il gibbone**
gibbon

㊹ **il gorilla**
gorilla

㊺ **il panda**
panda

See also
157 La storia naturale • Natural history 164 Gli animali domestici • Pets
165 Gli animali da fattoria • Farm animals 166 La vita negli oceani • Ocean life

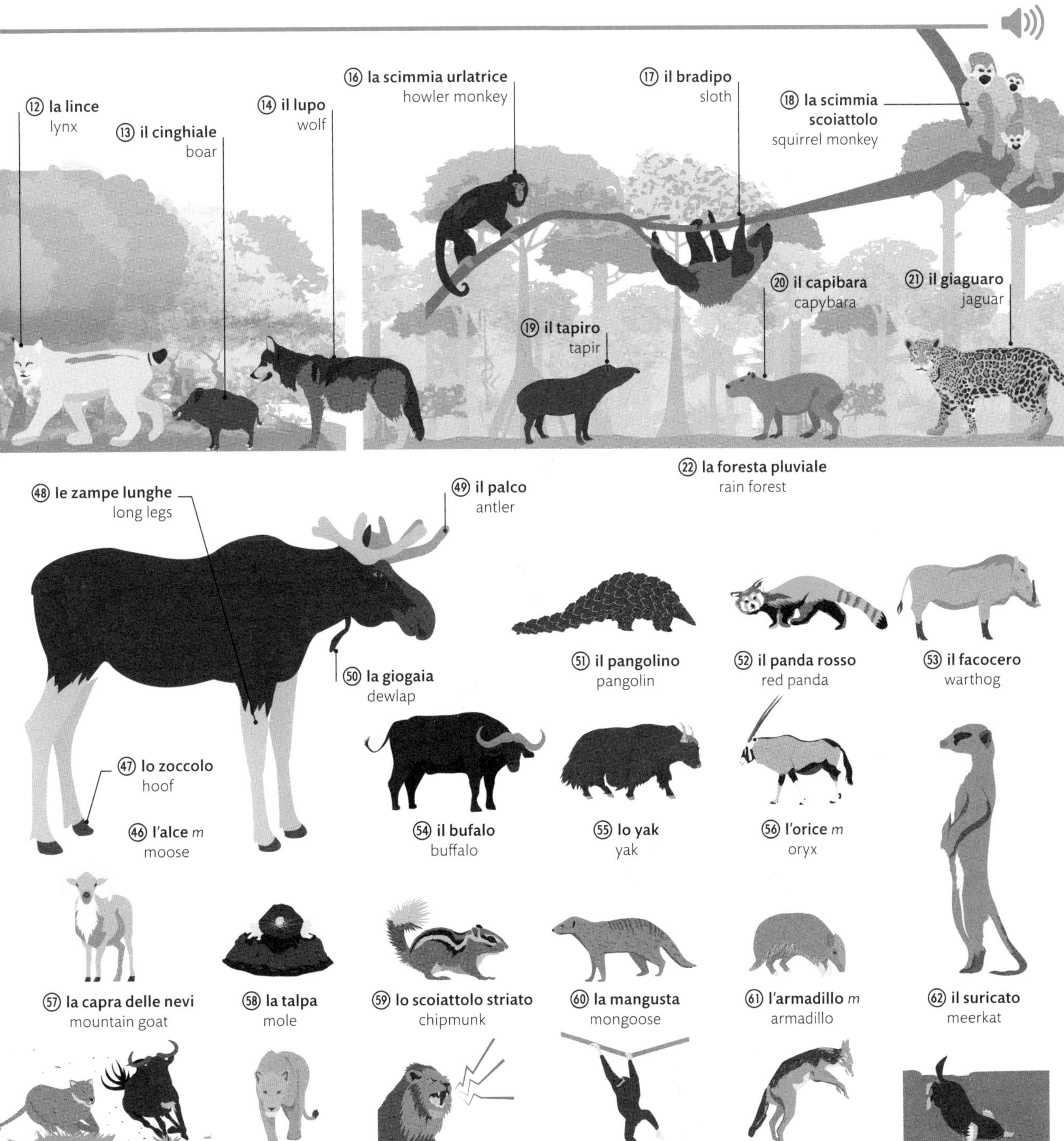
⑫ la lince
lynx
⑬ il cinghiale
boar
⑭ il lupo
wolf
⑯ la scimmia urlatrice
howler monkey
⑰ il bradipo
sloth
⑱ la scimmia scoiattolo
squirrel monkey
⑲ il tapiro
tapir
⑳ il capibara
capybara
㉑ il giaguaro
jaguar
㉒ la foresta pluviale
rain forest
㊽ le zampe lunghe
long legs
㊾ il palco
antler
㊿ la giogaia
dewlap
㊼ lo zoccolo
hoof
㊻ l'alce m
moose
(51) il pangolino
pangolin
(52) il panda rosso
red panda
(53) il facocero
warthog
(54) il bufalo
buffalo
(55) lo yak
yak
(56) l'orice m
oryx
(57) la capra delle nevi
mountain goat
(58) la talpa
mole
(59) lo scoiattolo striato
chipmunk
(60) la mangusta
mongoose
(61) l'armadillo m
armadillo
(62) il suricato
meerkat
(63) cacciare
to hunt
(64) aggirarsi furtivamente
to prowl
(65) ruggire
to roar
(66) oscillare
to swing
(67) balzare
to pounce
(68) scavare una galleria
to burrow

160 Gli uccelli
Birds

160.1 LE SPECIE DI UCCELLI · SPECIES OF BIRDS

① il picchio verde
green woodpecker
② il picchio nero
black woodpecker
③ il colibrì
hummingbird
④ il balestruccio
house martin
⑤ il gabbiano
seagull
⑥ il rondone
swift
⑦ la rondine riparia
sand martin
⑧ la sterna artica
Arctic tern
⑨ il picchio pileato
pileated woodpecker
⑩ il picchio rosso maggiore
greater spotted woodpecker
⑪ la coda
tail
⑫ la rondine
swallow
⑬ il canarino
canary
⑭ il parrocchetto ondulato
budgerigar
⑮ lo storno
starling
⑯ l'usignolo m
nightingale
⑰ il tessitore
weaverbird
⑱ l'acchiappamosche vermiglio m
vermilion flycatcher
⑲ l'albatro m
albatross
⑳ la fregata
frigate
㉑ l'aquila reale f
golden eagle
㉒ l'aquila calva f
bald eagle
㉓ il falco pescatore
osprey
㉔ il cormorano
cormorant
㉕ la sula
gannet
㉖ il condor delle Ande
Andean condor
㉗ il falco pellegrino
peregrine falcon
㉘ l'avvoltoio m
vulture
㉙ l'aquila arpia f
harpy eagle
㉚ l'uria f
guillemot
㉛ la pulcinella di mare
Atlantic puffin

See also
157 La storia naturale • Natural history **161** Gli uccelli (continua) Birds continued **165** Gli animali da fattoria • Farm animals

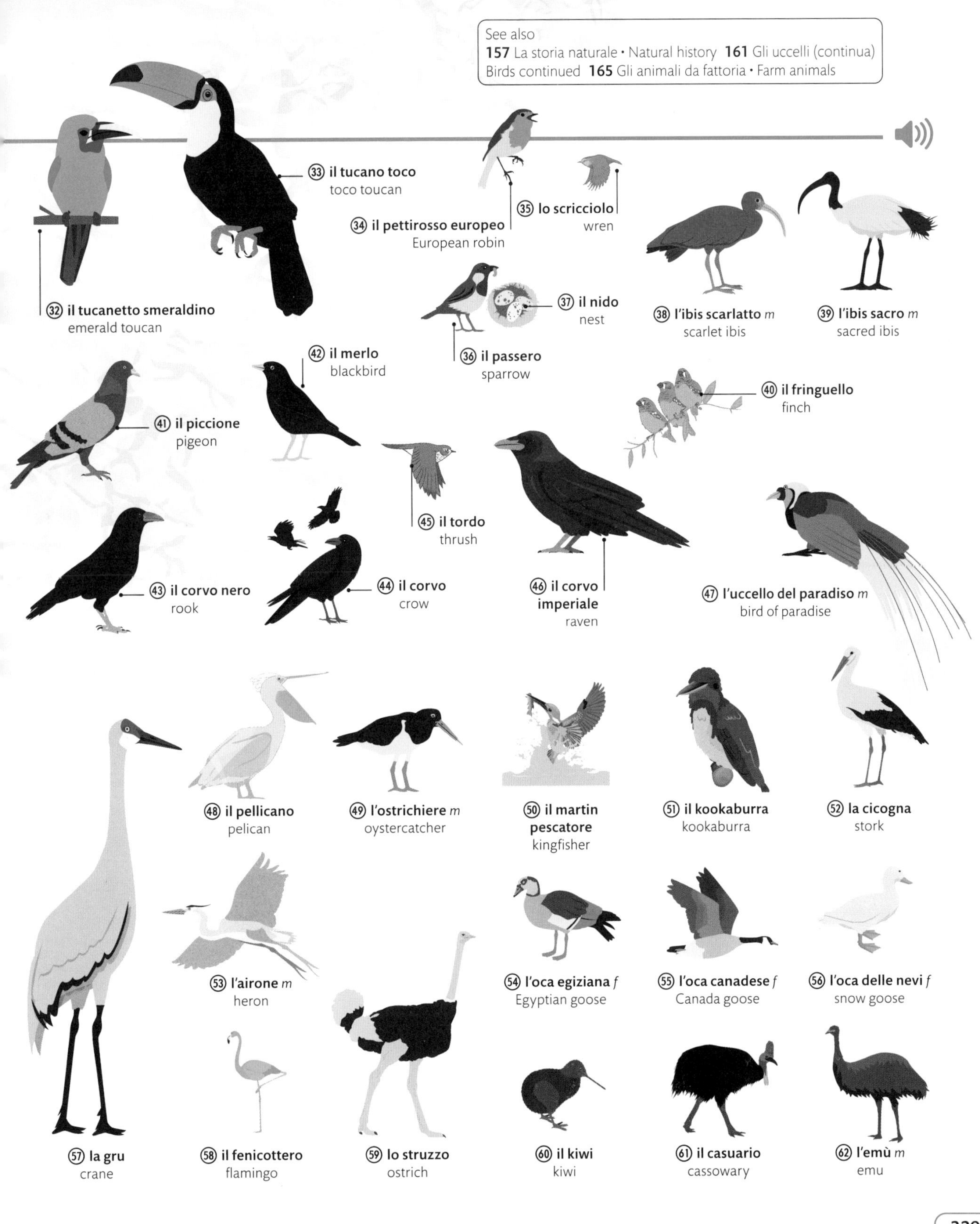
(32) il tucanetto smeraldino
emerald toucan
(33) il tucano toco
toco toucan
(34) il pettirosso europeo
European robin
(35) lo scricciolo
wren
(36) il passero
sparrow
(37) il nido
nest
(38) l'ibis scarlatto m
scarlet ibis
(39) l'ibis sacro m
sacred ibis
(40) il fringuello
finch
(41) il piccione
pigeon
(42) il merlo
blackbird
(43) il corvo nero
rook
(44) il corvo
crow
(45) il tordo
thrush
(46) il corvo imperiale
raven
(47) l'uccello del paradiso m
bird of paradise
(48) il pellicano
pelican
(49) l'ostrichiere m
oystercatcher
(50) il martin pescatore
kingfisher
(51) il kookaburra
kookaburra
(52) la cicogna
stork
(53) l'airone m
heron
(54) l'oca egiziana f
Egyptian goose
(55) l'oca canadese f
Canada goose
(56) l'oca delle nevi f
snow goose
(57) la gru
crane
(58) il fenicottero
flamingo
(59) lo struzzo
ostrich
(60) il kiwi
kiwi
(61) il casuario
cassowary
(62) l'emù m
emu

161 Gli uccelli (continua)

Birds continued

161.1 LE SPECIE DI UCCELLI · SPECIES OF BIRDS

① il cacatua rosa
galah
② il pappagallo ecletto
eclectus parrot
③ il parrocchetto dal collare
rose-ringed parakeet
④ l'ara scarlatta *f*
scarlet macaw
⑤ il lorichetto
lorikeet
⑩ la civetta delle nevi
snowy owl
⑪ il gufo reale
eagle owl
⑫ il grande gufo grigio
great gray owl
⑬ il gufo crestato
crested owl
⑭ il barbagianni
barn owl
⑮ bubolare
to hoot
㉒ il cigno reale
mute swan
㉓ il cigno nero
black swan
㉔ il cigno selvatico
whooper swan
㉕ la folaga
coot
㉖ il germano reale
mallard
㉗ l'anatra mandarina *f*
mandarin duck
㉘ lo svasso
grebe
㉙ l'anatra sposa *f*
wood duck
㉚ il porciglione europeo
water rail
㉛ il chiurlo
curlew
㉜ il fagiano
pheasant
㉝ il tacchino
turkey
㉟ la ruota
feathers displayed
㊱ il collo
neck
㉞ il pavone
peacock

See also
157 La storia naturale • Natural history
165 Gli animali da fattoria • Farm animals

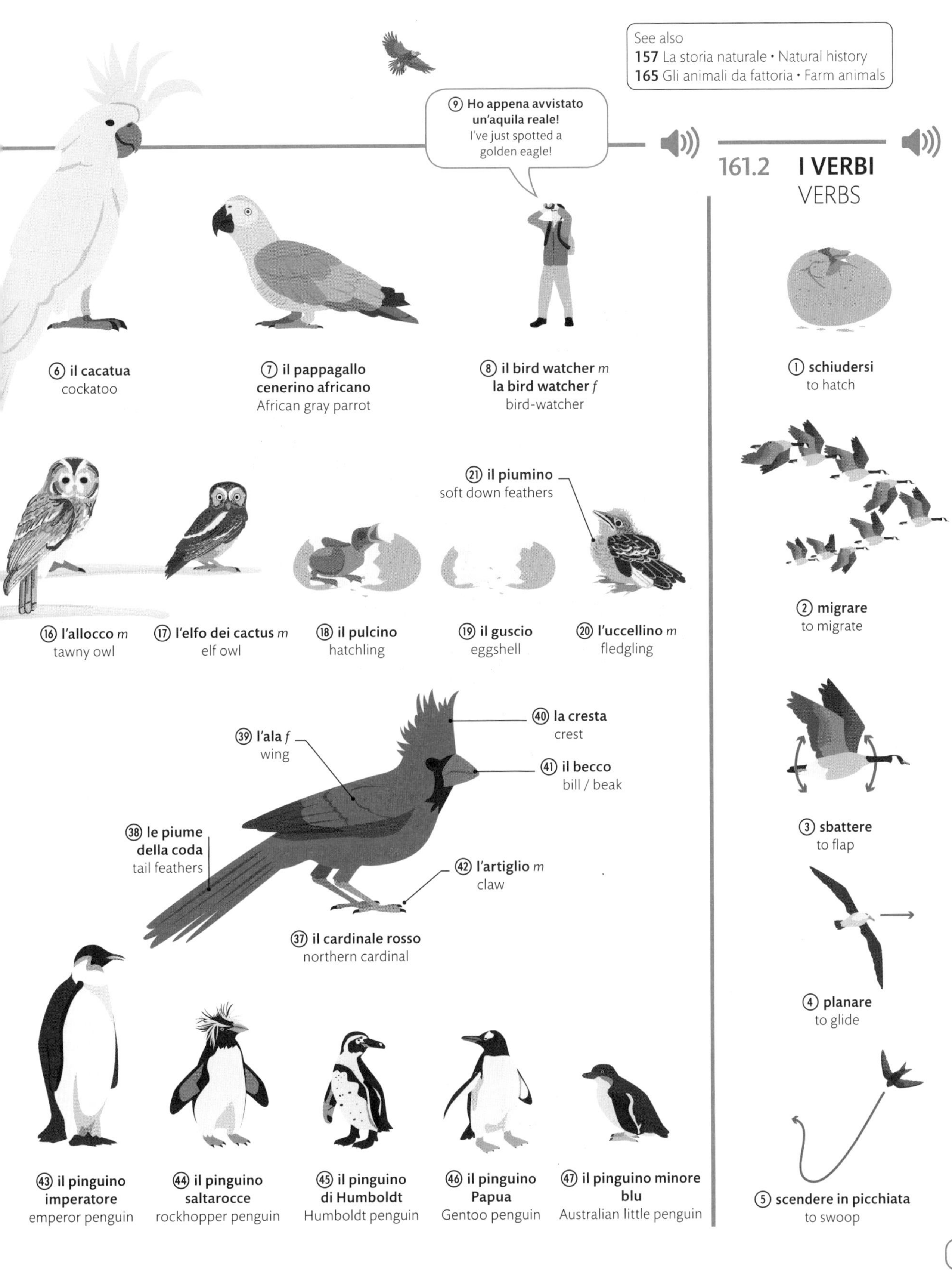
⑨ Ho appena avvistato un'aquila reale!
I've just spotted a golden eagle!
⑥ il cacatua
cockatoo
⑦ il pappagallo cenerino africano
African gray parrot
⑧ il bird watcher m
la bird watcher f
bird-watcher
⑯ l'allocco m
tawny owl
⑰ l'elfo dei cactus m
elf owl
⑱ il pulcino
hatchling
⑲ il guscio
eggshell
㉑ il piumino
soft down feathers
⑳ l'uccellino m
fledgling
㊴ l'ala f
wing
㊵ la cresta
crest
㊶ il becco
bill / beak
㊳ le piume della coda
tail feathers
㊷ l'artiglio m
claw
㊲ il cardinale rosso
northern cardinal
㊸ il pinguino imperatore
emperor penguin
㊹ il pinguino saltarocce
rockhopper penguin
㊺ il pinguino di Humboldt
Humboldt penguin
㊻ il pinguino Papua
Gentoo penguin
㊼ il pinguino minore blu
Australian little penguin

161.2 I VERBI
VERBS

① schiudersi
to hatch
② migrare
to migrate
③ sbattere
to flap
④ planare
to glide
⑤ scendere in picchiata
to swoop

Gli insetti

Insects and bugs

162.1 LE FARFALLE E LE FALENE • BUTTERFLIES AND MOTHS

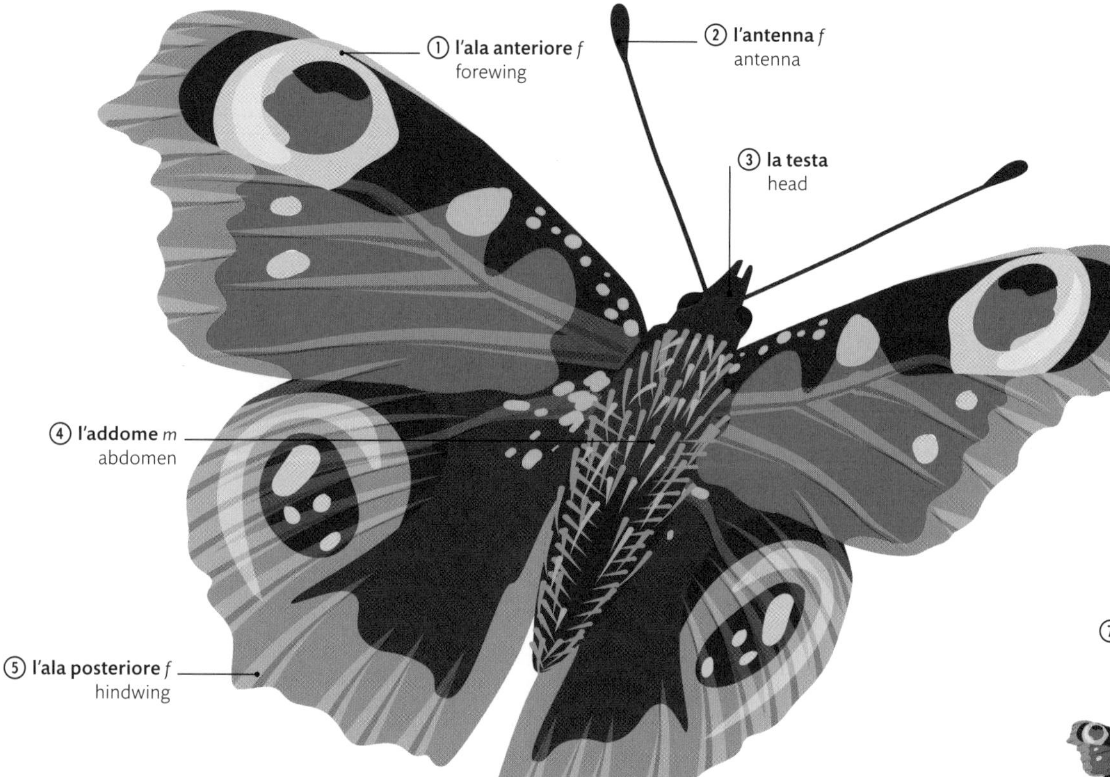

① **l'ala anteriore** *f*
forewing

② **l'antenna** *f*
antenna

③ **la testa**
head

④ **l'addome** *m*
abdomen

⑤ **l'ala posteriore** *f*
hindwing

⑥ **la farfalla**
butterfly

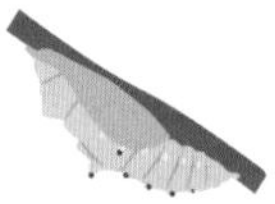

⑦ **il bozzolo**
cocoon

⑧ **il bruco**
caterpillar

⑨ **la vanessa io**
peacock butterfly

⑩ **la farfalla monarca**
monarch butterfly

⑪ **la vanessa del cardo**
painted lady butterfly

⑫ **la farfalla papilionide**
swallowtail butterfly

⑬ **la farfalla dalle ali di vetro**
glasswing butterfly

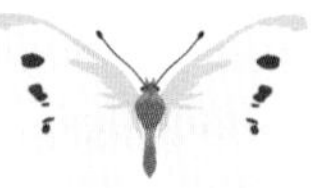

⑭ **la farfalla cavolaia**
cabbage white butterfly

⑮ **la farfalla punteggiata delle betulle**
peppered moth

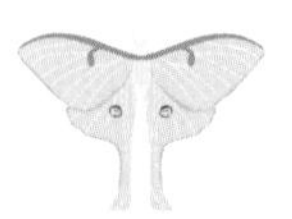

⑯ **la falena di luna**
luna moth

⑰ **la sfinge del galio**
hummingbird hawksmoth

⑱ **la falena imperatrice**
emperor moth

⑲ **la farfalla cobra**
atlas moth

⑳ **la falena dei vestiti**
clothes moth

㉑ **lo sfingide**
hawk moth

See also
157 La storia naturale • Natural history **158-159** I mammiferi • Mammals
160-161 Gli uccelli • Birds **163** Gli anfibi e i rettili • Amphibians and reptiles

162.2 GLI ALTRI INSETTI E GLI INVERTEBRATI • OTHER BUGS AND INVERTEBRATES

① **il dinastino**
rhinoceros beetle

② **il cervo volante**
stag beetle

③ **il tonchio**
weevil

④ **lo scarafaggio**
cockroach

⑤ **la coccinella**
ladybug

⑥ **la mosca**
fly

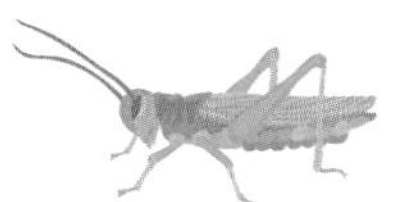
⑦ **la cavalletta**
grasshopper

⑧ **la locusta**
locust

⑨ **il fillio**
leaf insect

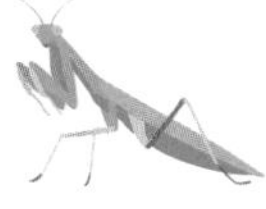
⑩ **la mantide religiosa**
praying mantis

⑫ **il pungiglione**
sting

⑪ **lo scorpione**
scorpion

⑬ **il grillo**
cricket

⑭ **il centopiedi**
centipede

⑮ **il millepiedi**
millipede

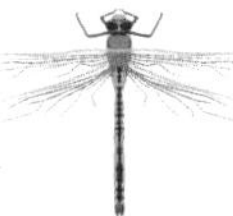
⑯ **la libellula**
dragonfly

⑰ **la zanzara**
mosquito

⑱ **il verme**
worm

⑲ **la tarantola**
tarantula

⑳ **la vedova nera**
black widow spider

㉑ **il ragno saltatore**
jumping spider

㉒ **il ragno tessitore**
orb weaver

㉓ **la lumaca**
slug

㉔ **la chiocciola**
snail

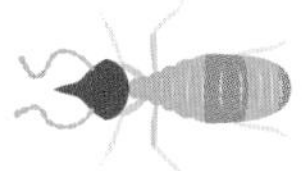
㉕ **la termite**
termite

㉖ **la formica**
ant

㉗ **il bombo**
bumble bee

㉘ **la vespa**
wasp

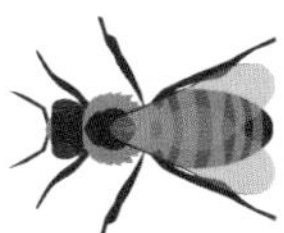
㉙ **l'ape** *f*
honey bee

㉚ **pungere**
to sting

㉛ **volare**
to fly

㉜ **ronzare**
to buzz

㉝ **il nido di vespe**
wasp nest

㉞ **l'alveare** *m*
beehive

㉟ **lo sciame**
swarm

163 Gli anfibi e i rettili

Amphibians and reptiles

163.1 GLI ANFIBI • AMPHIBIANS

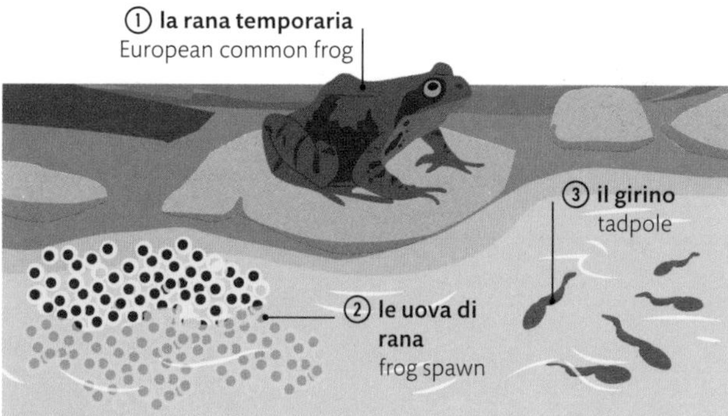
① la rana temporaria
European common frog
② le uova di rana
frog spawn
③ il girino
tadpole

④ **la rana volante di Wallace**
Wallace's flying frog

⑤ **la rana freccia**
poison dart frog

⑥ **la rana di Darwin**
Darwin's frog

⑦ **la raganella dagli occhi rossi**
red-eyed tree frog

⑧ **il rospo comune**
common toad

⑨ **la rana toro africana**
African bullfrog

⑩ **l'ululone dal ventre di fuoco** *m*
Oriental fire-bellied toad

⑪ **il rospo delle grandi pianure**
Great Plains toad

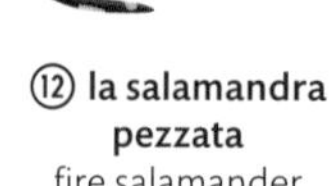

⑫ **la salamandra pezzata**
fire salamander

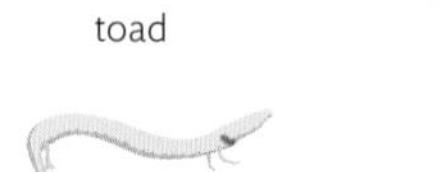

⑬ **il proteo**
olm

⑭ **l'axolotl** *m*
Mexican axolotl

⑮ **il tritone crestato**
great crested newt

⑯ **la salamandra rossa**
red salamander

163.2 I RETTILI • REPTILES

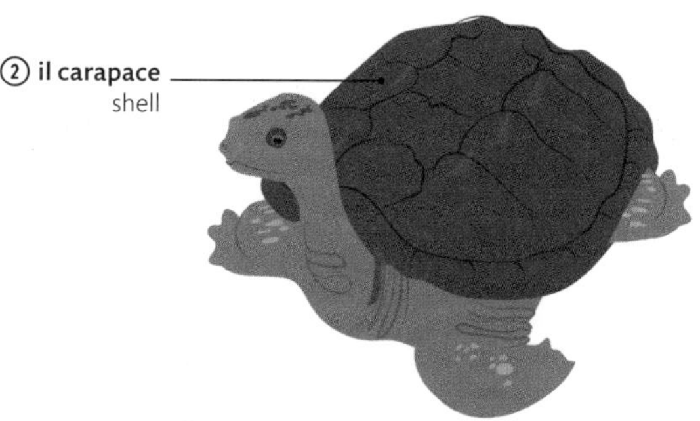
② il carapace
shell

① **la tartaruga delle Galápagos**
Galápagos turtle

③ **la testuggine raggiata**
radiated tortoise

④ **la mata mata**
matamata

⑤ **la tartaruga dal dorso di diamante**
diamond back terrapin

⑥ **la tartaruga dal collo di serpente**
common snake-necked turtle

⑦ **la tartaruga verde**
green sea turtle

⑧ **la tartaruga liuto**
leatherback sea turtle

⑨ **il camaleonte di Parson**
parson's chameleon

⑩ **il camaleonte del Madagascar**
panther chameleon

⑪ **il camaleonte di Jackson**
Jackson's chameleon

⑫ **il varano di Komodo**
Komodo dragon

See also
77 La biologia • Biology **157** La storia naturale • Natural history **158-159** I mammiferi Mammals **160-161** Gli uccelli • Birds **162** Gli insetti • Bugs and insects

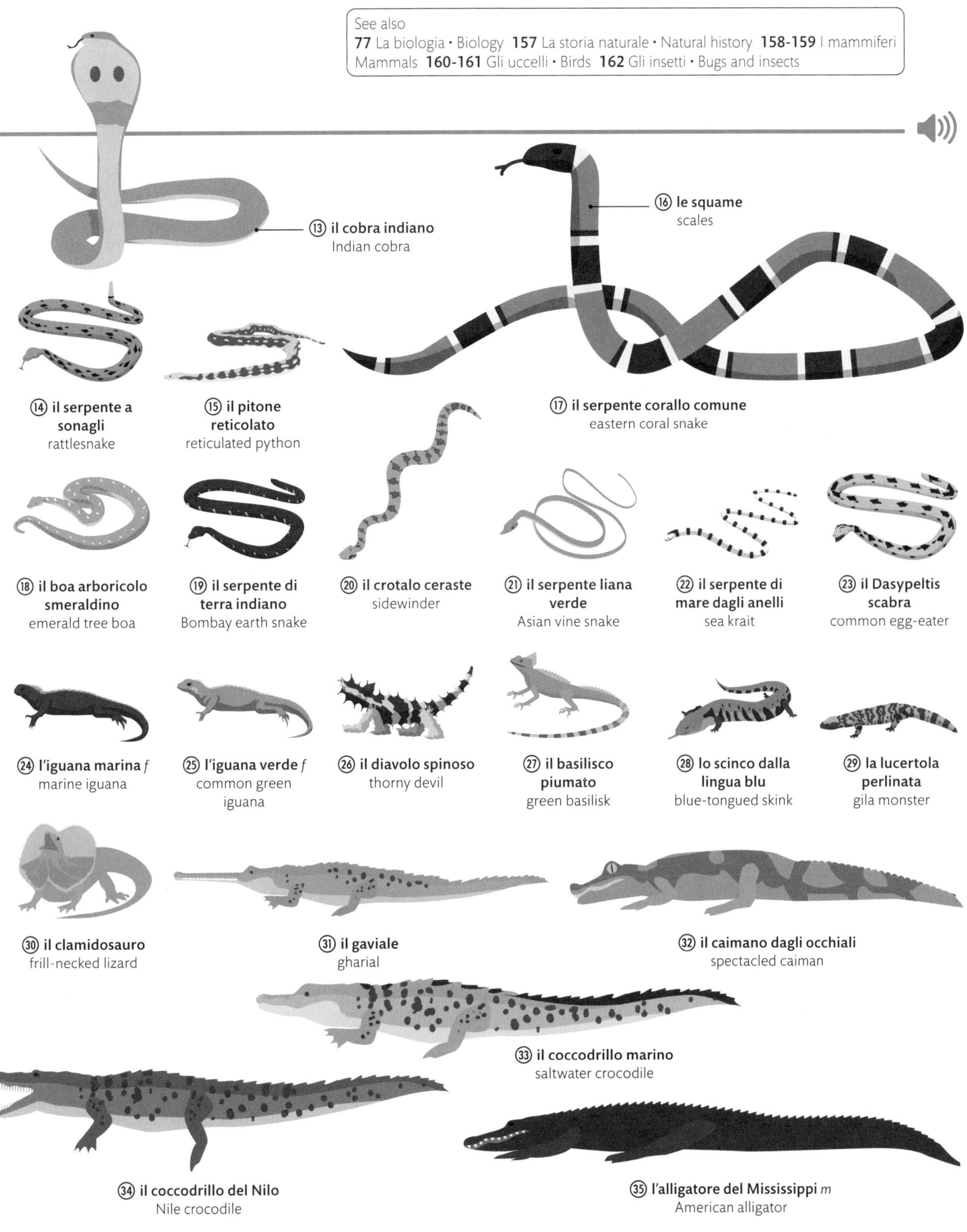
⑬ **il cobra indiano**
Indian cobra
⑯ **le squame**
scales
⑭ **il serpente a sonagli**
rattlesnake
⑮ **il pitone reticolato**
reticulated python
⑰ **il serpente corallo comune**
eastern coral snake
⑱ **il boa arboricolo smeraldino**
emerald tree boa
⑲ **il serpente di terra indiano**
Bombay earth snake
⑳ **il crotalo ceraste**
sidewinder
㉑ **il serpente liana verde**
Asian vine snake
㉒ **il serpente di mare dagli anelli**
sea krait
㉓ **il Dasypeltis scabra**
common egg-eater
㉔ **l'iguana marina** *f*
marine iguana
㉕ **l'iguana verde** *f*
common green iguana
㉖ **il diavolo spinoso**
thorny devil
㉗ **il basilisco piumato**
green basilisk
㉘ **lo scinco dalla lingua blu**
blue-tongued skink
㉙ **la lucertola perlinata**
gila monster
㉚ **il clamidosauro**
frill-necked lizard
㉛ **il gaviale**
gharial
㉜ **il caimano dagli occhiali**
spectacled caiman
㉝ **il coccodrillo marino**
saltwater crocodile
㉞ **il coccodrillo del Nilo**
Nile crocodile
㉟ **l'alligatore del Mississippi** *m*
American alligator

164 Gli animali domestici

Pets

164.1 LE RAZZE DI GATTI · CAT BREEDS

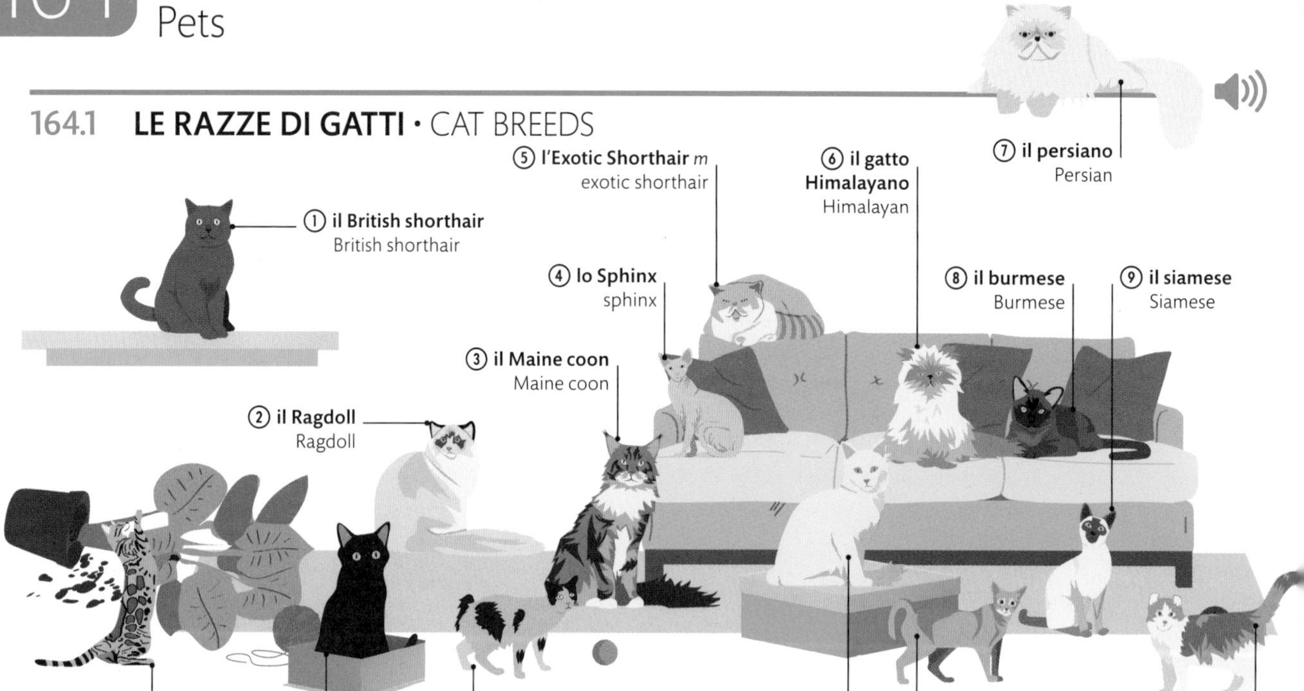

① **il British shorthair**
British shorthair

② **il Ragdoll**
Ragdoll

③ **il Maine coon**
Maine coon

④ **lo Sphinx**
sphinx

⑤ **l'Exotic Shorthair** *m*
exotic shorthair

⑥ **il gatto Himalayano**
Himalayan

⑦ **il persiano**
Persian

⑧ **il burmese**
Burmese

⑨ **il siamese**
Siamese

⑩ **il gatto del Bengala**
Bengal

⑪ **il gatto Bombay**
Bombay

⑫ **il bobtail giapponese**
Japanese bobtail

⑬ **il gatto d'Angora**
Angora

⑭ **l'abissino** *m*
Abyssinian

⑮ **l'American curl** *m*
American curl

⑯ **miagolare**
to meow

⑰ **fare le fusa**
to purr

⑱ **nascondersi**
to hide

⑲ **fare la muta**
to molt

⑳ **il gattino** *m*
la gattina *f*
kitten

164.3 GLI ALTRI ANIMALI DOMESTICI · OTHER PETS

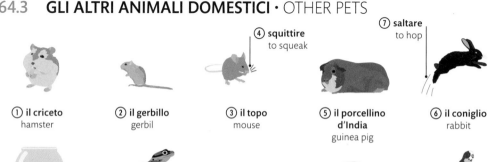

① **il criceto**
hamster

② **il gerbillo**
gerbil

③ **il topo**
mouse

④ **squittire**
to squeak

⑤ **il porcellino d'India**
guinea pig

⑥ **il coniglio**
rabbit

⑦ **saltare**
to hop

⑧ **il furetto**
ferret

⑨ **il pesce**
fish

⑩ **la lucertola**
lizard

⑪ **l'insetto stecco** *m*
stick insect

⑫ **la tartaruga**
tortoise

⑬ **il pappagallino**
budgerigar / budgie

⑭ **il cacatua**
cockatiel

See also
158-159 I mammiferi • Mammals **160-161** Gli uccelli • Birds **162** Gli insetti
Insects and bugs **163** Gli anfibi e i rettili • Amphibians and reptiles

164.2 LE RAZZE DI CANI • DOG BREEDS

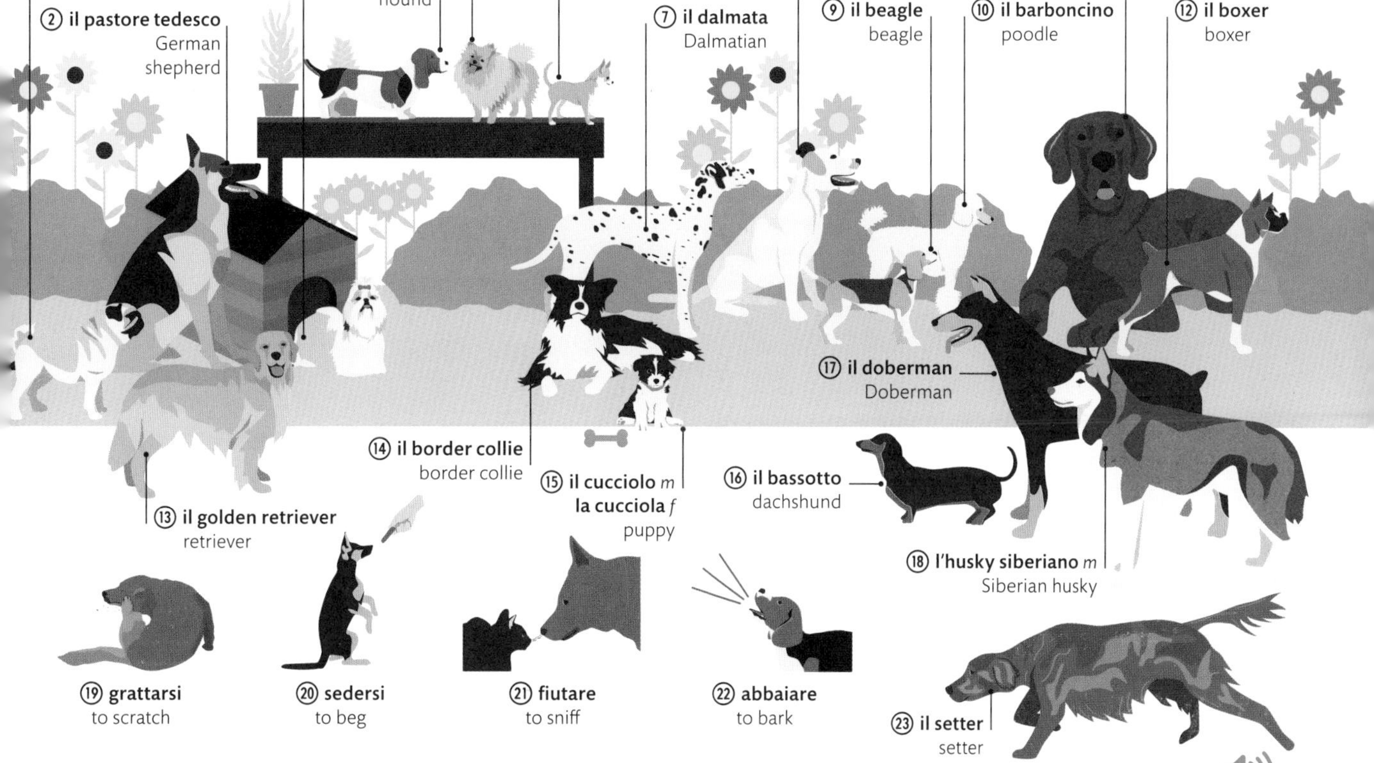

① **il carlino**
pug

② **il pastore tedesco**
German shepherd

③ **lo shih-tzu**
shih tzu

④ **il basset hound**
basset hound

⑤ **il volpino della Pomerania**
Pomeranian

⑥ **il chihuahua**
chihuahua

⑦ **il dalmata**
Dalmatian

⑧ **il labrador**
labrador

⑨ **il beagle**
beagle

⑩ **il barboncino**
poodle

⑪ **l'alano** *m*
Great Dane

⑫ **il boxer**
boxer

⑬ **il golden retriever**
retriever

⑭ **il border collie**
border collie

⑮ **il cucciolo** *m*
la cucciola *f*
puppy

⑯ **il bassotto**
dachshund

⑰ **il doberman**
Doberman

⑱ **l'husky siberiano** *m*
Siberian husky

⑲ **grattarsi**
to scratch

⑳ **sedersi**
to beg

㉑ **fiutare**
to sniff

㉒ **abbaiare**
to bark

㉓ **il setter**
setter

164.4 I PRODOTTI PER ANIMALI DOMESTIC • PET SUPPLIES

① **l'acquario** *m*
fish tank / aquarium

② **la cesta**
basket

③ **la cuccia**
doghouse

④ **la gabbia**
cage

⑤ **la conigliera**
rabbit hutch

⑥ **la lettiera**
litterbox

⑦ **il guinzaglio**
leash

⑧ **il terrario**
vivarium

⑨ **il becchime**
birdseed

⑩ **i premi**
treats

⑪ **i giocattoli**
toys

Gli animali da fattoria
Farm animals

165.1 NELLA FATTORIA · ON THE FARM

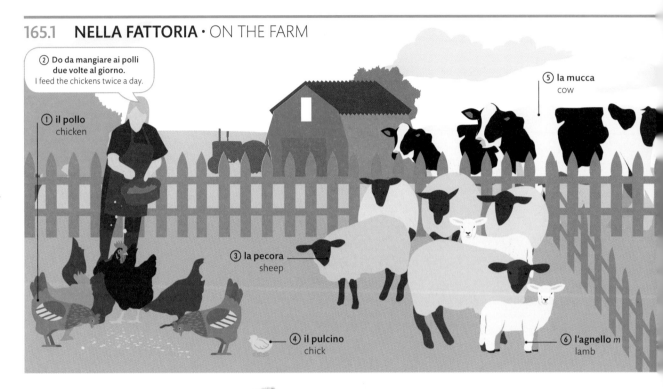

② **Do da mangiare ai polli due volte al giorno.**
I feed the chickens twice a day.

① **il pollo**
chicken

⑤ **la mucca**
cow

③ **la pecora**
sheep

④ **il pulcino**
chick

⑥ **l'agnello** *m*
lamb

⑭ **il gallo**
rooster

⑮ **la gallina**
hen

⑯ **il tacchino**
turkey

⑰ **il pollame**
poultry

㉑ **l'ape** *f*
bee

⑳ **l'arnia** *f*
hive

㉒ **il gregge di pecore**
flock of sheep

㉓ **la mandria di mucche**
herd of cows

⑱ **il montone**
ram

⑲ **la pecora**
ewe

㉔ **il toro**
bull

㉕ **il vitello** *m*
la vitella *f*
calf

㉖ **il bestiame**
cattle

㉗ **l'asino** *m*
donkey

See also
53 La carne • Meat **86** L'agricoltura • Farming
158-159 I mammiferi • Mammals **164** Gli animali domestici • Pets

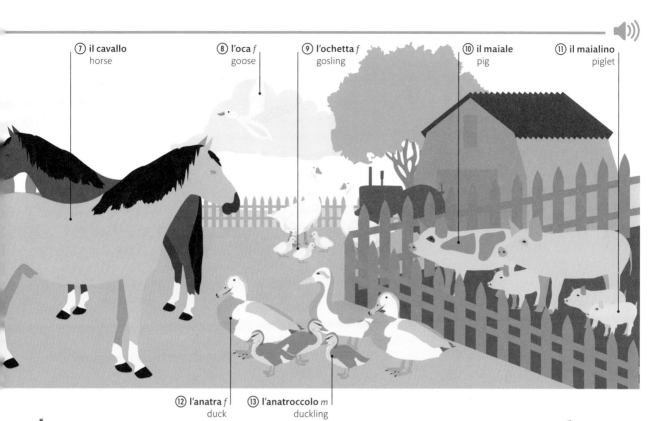

⑦ **il cavallo**
horse

⑧ **l'oca** *f*
goose

⑨ **l'ochetta** *f*
gosling

⑩ **il maiale**
pig

⑪ **il maialino**
piglet

⑫ **l'anatra** *f*
duck

⑬ **l'anatroccolo** *m*
duckling

㉘ **lo stallone**
stallion

㉙ **la giumenta**
mare

㉚ **il puledro** *m*
la puledra *f*
foal

㉛ **la capra**
goat

㉜ **il capretto** *m*
la capretta *f*
kid

㉝ **lo struzzo**
ostrich

㉞ **il lama**
llama

㉟ **l'alpaca** *m*
alpaca

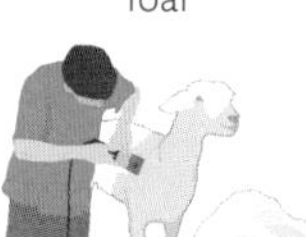

㊱ **tosare**
to shear

㊲ **trottare**
to trot

㊳ **galoppare**
to gallop

㊴ **caricare**
to charge

㊵ **cantare**
to crow

㊶ **belare**
to bleat

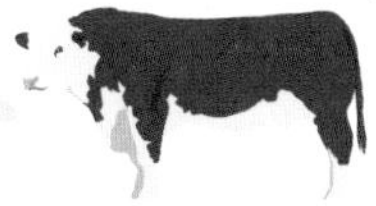

㊷ **sbuffare**
to snort

㊸ **grugnire**
to grunt

㊹ **ragliare**
to bray

㊺ **fare qua qua**
to quack

La vita negli oceani
Ocean life

166.1 LE SPECIE MARINE • MARINE SPECIES

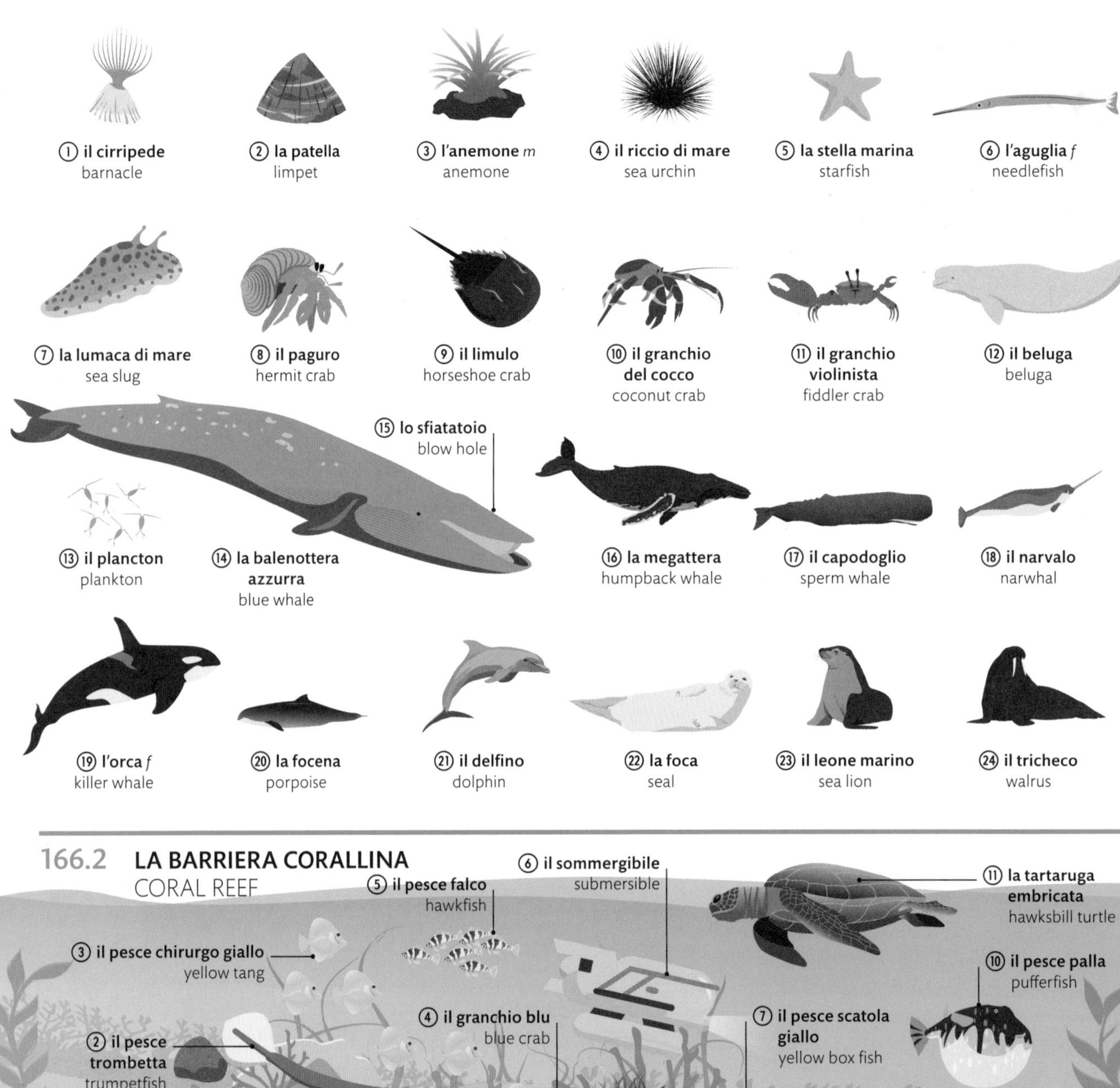

① il cirripede
barnacle
② la patella
limpet
③ l'anemone *m*
anemone
④ il riccio di mare
sea urchin
⑤ la stella marina
starfish
⑥ l'aguglia *f*
needlefish
⑦ la lumaca di mare
sea slug
⑧ il paguro
hermit crab
⑨ il limulo
horseshoe crab
⑩ il granchio del cocco
coconut crab
⑪ il granchio violinista
fiddler crab
⑫ il beluga
beluga
⑬ il plancton
plankton
⑭ la balenottera azzurra
blue whale
⑮ lo sfiatatoio
blow hole
⑯ la megattera
humpback whale
⑰ il capodoglio
sperm whale
⑱ il narvalo
narwhal
⑲ l'orca *f*
killer whale
⑳ la focena
porpoise
㉑ il delfino
dolphin
㉒ la foca
seal
㉓ il leone marino
sea lion
㉔ il tricheco
walrus

166.2 LA BARRIERA CORALLINA
CORAL REEF

① la trota corallina
coral trout
② il pesce trombetta
trumpetfish
③ il pesce chirurgo giallo
yellow tang
④ il granchio blu
blue crab
⑤ il pesce falco
hawkfish
⑥ il sommergibile
submersible
⑦ il pesce scatola giallo
yellow box fish
⑧ la cicala di mare
mantis shrimp
⑨ il pesce chirurgo blu
blue tang
⑩ il pesce palla
pufferfish
⑪ la tartaruga embricata
hawksbill turtle

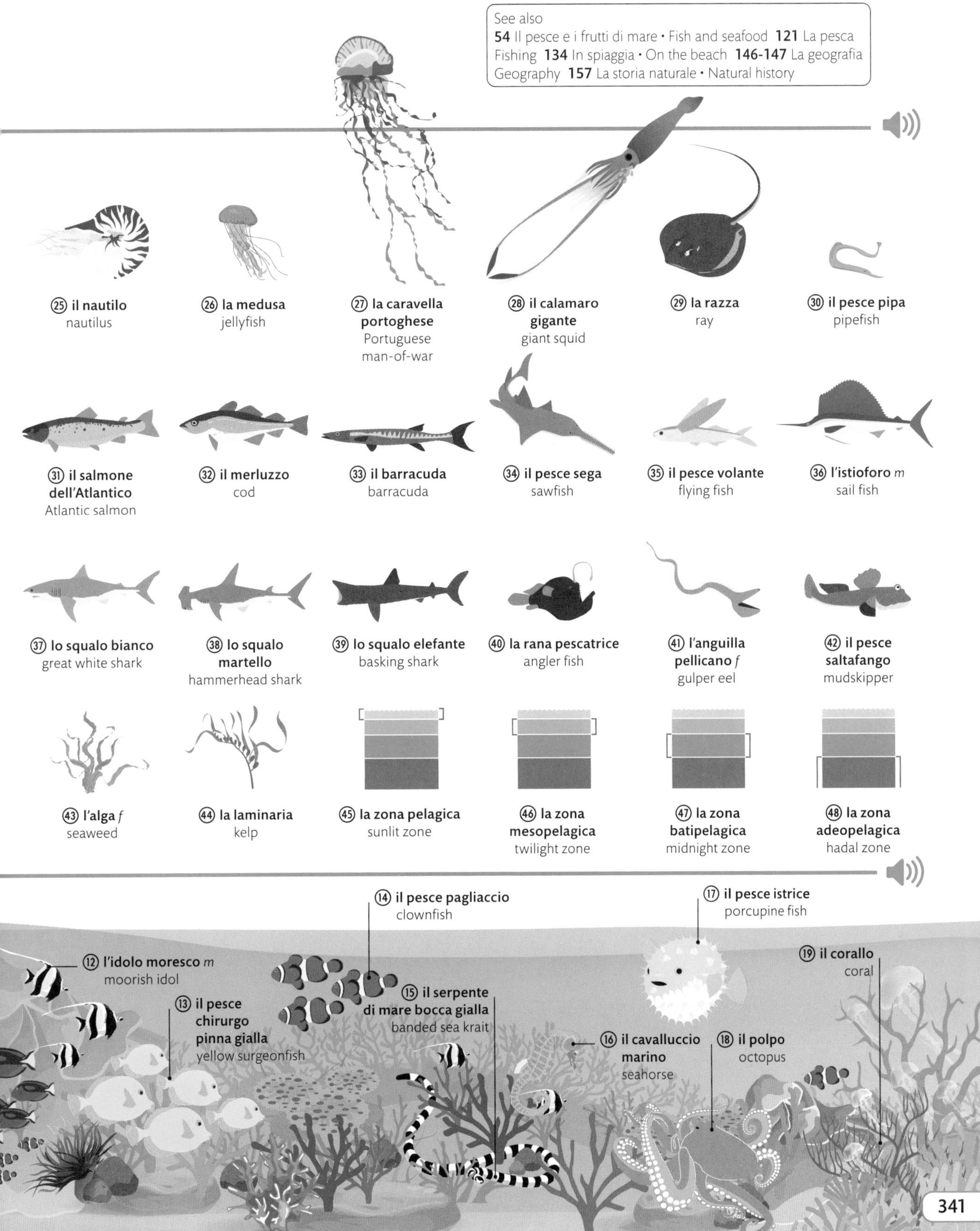
See also
54 Il pesce e i frutti di mare • Fish and seafood 121 La pesca Fishing 134 In spiaggia • On the beach 146-147 La geografia Geography 157 La storia naturale • Natural history
25 il nautilo
nautilus
26 la medusa
jellyfish
27 la caravella portoghese
Portuguese man-of-war
28 il calamaro gigante
giant squid
29 la razza
ray
30 il pesce pipa
pipefish
31 il salmone dell'Atlantico
Atlantic salmon
32 il merluzzo
cod
33 il barracuda
barracuda
34 il pesce sega
sawfish
35 il pesce volante
flying fish
36 l'istioforo m
sail fish
37 lo squalo bianco
great white shark
38 lo squalo martello
hammerhead shark
39 lo squalo elefante
basking shark
40 la rana pescatrice
angler fish
41 l'anguilla pellicano f
gulper eel
42 il pesce saltafango
mudskipper
43 l'alga f
seaweed
44 la laminaria
kelp
45 la zona pelagica
sunlit zone
46 la zona mesopelagica
twilight zone
47 la zona batipelagica
midnight zone
48 la zona adeopelagica
hadal zone
14 il pesce pagliaccio
clownfish
17 il pesce istrice
porcupine fish
12 l'idolo moresco m
moorish idol
19 il corallo
coral
13 il pesce chirurgo pinna gialla
yellow surgeonfish
15 il serpente di mare bocca gialla
banded sea krait
16 il cavalluccio marino
seahorse
18 il polpo
octopus

167 Le piante e gli alberi
Plants and trees

167.1 LE PIANTE E GLI ALBERI • PLANTS AND TREES

① **l'epatica** *f*
liverwort

② **il muschio**
moss

③ **l'equiseto** *m*
horsetail

④ **la felce**
fern

⑤ **la cycas**
cycad

⑥ **il gingko**
ginkgo

⑦ **il peccio**
spruce

⑧ **l'abete** *m*
fir

⑨ **l'araucaria** *f*
monkey puzzle

⑩ **il tasso**
yew

⑪ **le conifere**
conifers

⑫ **il larice**
larch

⑬ **il cedro del Libano**
cedar of Lebanon

⑭ **il pino domestico**
umbrella pine

⑮ **la ninfea**
water lily

⑯ **la magnolia**
magnolia

⑰ **l'albero di avocado** *m*
avocado tree

⑱ **l'alloro** *m*
laurel

⑲ **la calla**
arum lily

⑳ **la sequoia gigante**
giant sequoia

㉑ **l'albero di Giosuè** *m*
Joshua tree

㉒ **l'amarillide** *f*
amaryllis

㉓ **l'aspidistra** *f*
cast-iron plant

㉔ **la dracena**
dragon tree

㉕ **la campanula**
English bluebell

㉖ **il bucaneve**
snowdrop

㉗ **il croco**
crocus

See also
38 Le piante da giardino e le piante da appartamento • Garden plants and houseplants **57** La frutta • Fruit **58** La frutta e la frutta a guscio • Fruit and nuts **157** La storia naturale • Natural history **168-169** Le piante e gli alberi (continua) • Plants and trees continued **170** I funghi • Fungi

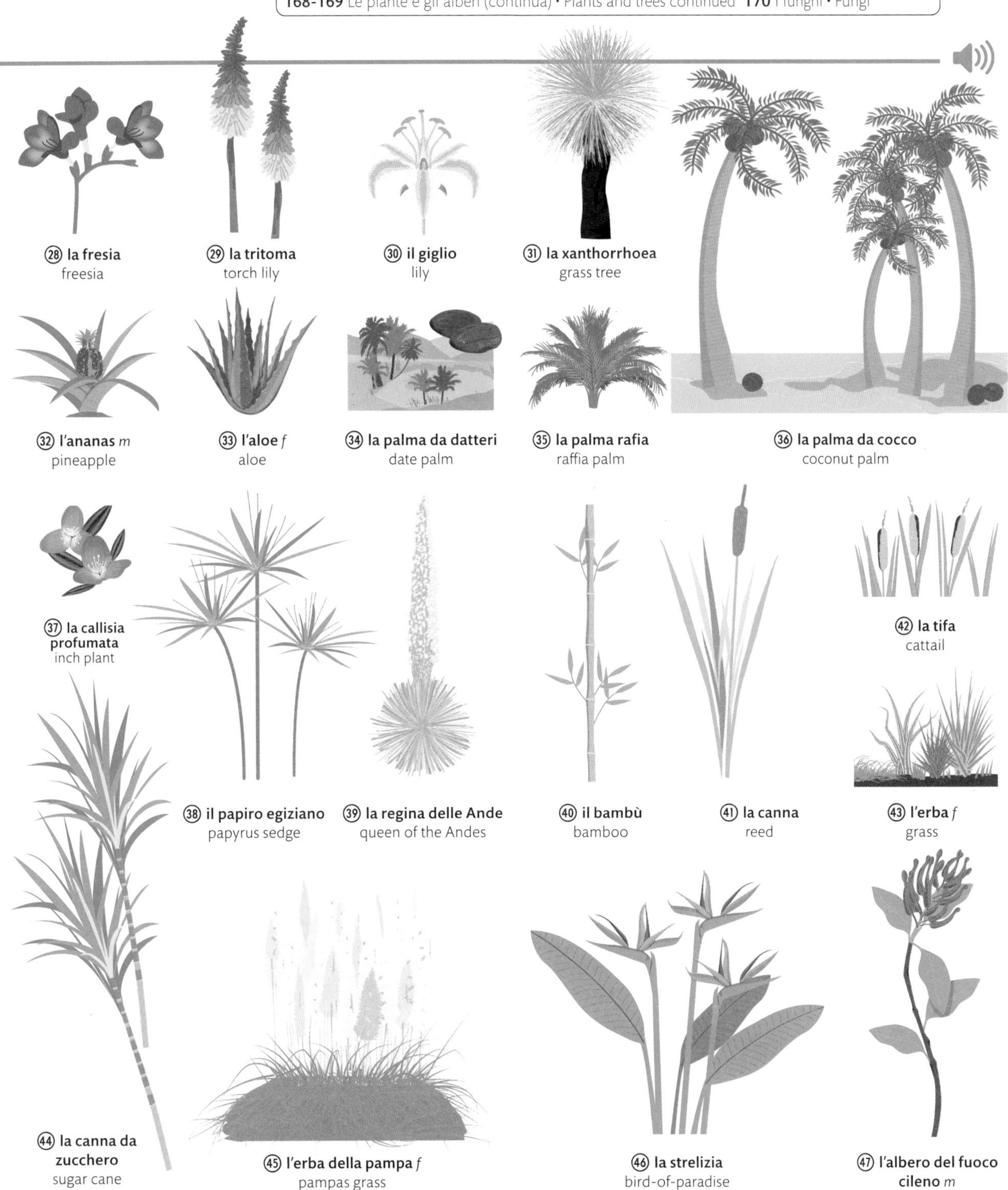

㉘ **la fresia**
freesia

㉙ **la tritoma**
torch lily

㉚ **il giglio**
lily

㉛ **la xanthorrhoea**
grass tree

㉜ **l'ananas** *m*
pineapple

㉝ **l'aloe** *f*
aloe

㉞ **la palma da datteri**
date palm

㉟ **la palma rafia**
raffia palm

㊱ **la palma da cocco**
coconut palm

㊲ **la callisia profumata**
inch plant

㊳ **il papiro egiziano**
papyrus sedge

㊴ **la regina delle Ande**
queen of the Andes

㊵ **il bambù**
bamboo

㊶ **la canna**
reed

㊷ **la tifa**
cattail

㊸ **l'erba** *f*
grass

㊹ **la canna da zucchero**
sugar cane

㊺ **l'erba della pampa** *f*
pampas grass

㊻ **la strelizia**
bird-of-paradise

㊼ **l'albero del fuoco cileno** *m*
Chilean fire bush

Le piante e gli alberi (continua)

Plants and trees continued

168.1 LE PIANTE E GLI ALBERI • PLANTS AND TREES

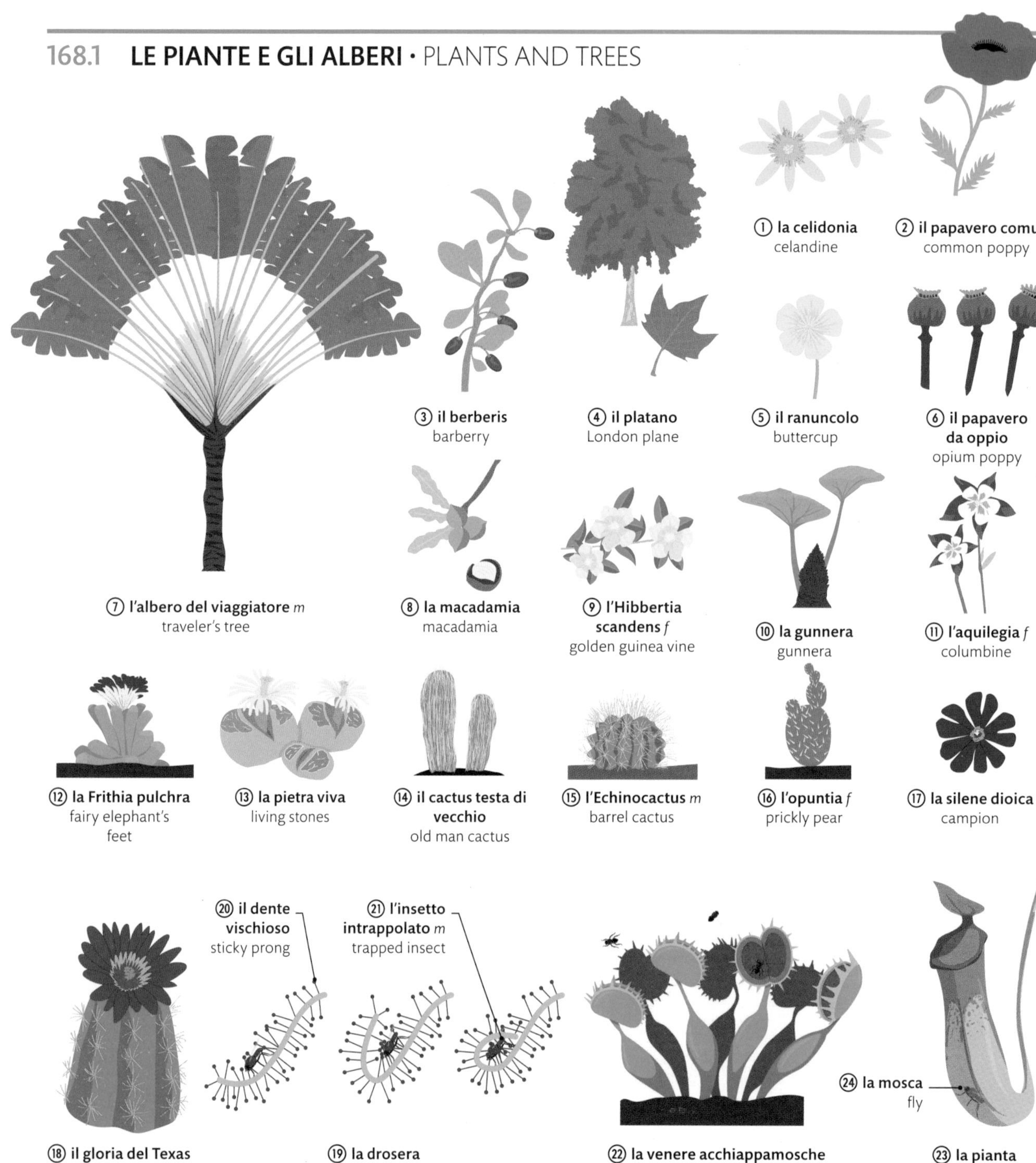

① la celidonia
celandine
② il papavero comune
common poppy
③ il berberis
barberry
④ il platano
London plane
⑤ il ranuncolo
buttercup
⑥ il papavero da oppio
opium poppy
⑦ l'albero del viaggiatore *m*
traveler's tree
⑧ la macadamia
macadamia
⑨ l'Hibbertia scandens *f*
golden guinea vine
⑩ la gunnera
gunnera
⑪ l'aquilegia *f*
columbine
⑫ la Frithia pulchra
fairy elephant's feet
⑬ la pietra viva
living stones
⑭ il cactus testa di vecchio
old man cactus
⑮ l'Echinocactus *m*
barrel cactus
⑯ l'opuntia *f*
prickly pear
⑰ la silene dioica
campion
⑳ il dente vischioso
sticky prong
㉑ l'insetto intrappolato *m*
trapped insect
⑱ il gloria del Texas
glory of Texas
⑲ la drosera
sundew
㉒ la venere acchiappamosche
Venus fly-trap
㉔ la mosca
fly
㉓ la pianta carnivora
pitcher plant

See also
38 Le piante da giardino e le piante da appartamento • Garden plants and houseplants **57** La frutta • Fruit **58** La frutta e la frutta a guscio • Fruit and nuts **157** La storia naturale • Natural history **169** Le piante e gli alberi (continua) • Plants and trees continued **170** I funghi • Fungi

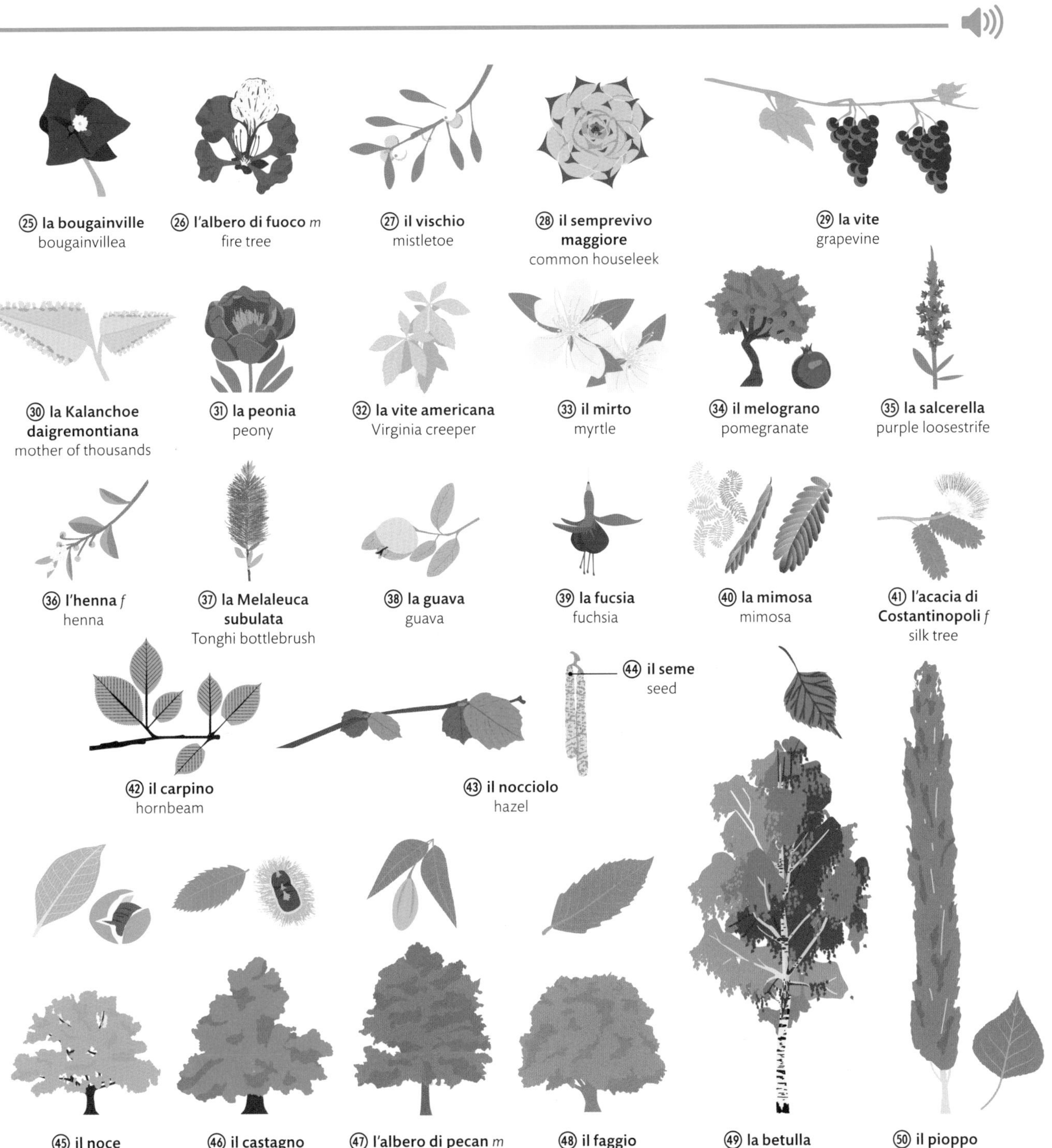
(25) **la bougainville**
bougainvillea
(26) **l'albero di fuoco** *m*
fire tree
(27) **il vischio**
mistletoe
(28) **il semprevivo maggiore**
common houseleek
(29) **la vite**
grapevine
(30) **la Kalanchoe daigremontiana**
mother of thousands
(31) **la peonia**
peony
(32) **la vite americana**
Virginia creeper
(33) **il mirto**
myrtle
(34) **il melograno**
pomegranate
(35) **la salcerella**
purple loosestrife
(36) **l'henna** *f*
henna
(37) **la Melaleuca subulata**
Tonghi bottlebrush
(38) **la guava**
guava
(39) **la fucsia**
fuchsia
(40) **la mimosa**
mimosa
(41) **l'acacia di Costantinopoli** *f*
silk tree
(42) **il carpino**
hornbeam
(43) **il nocciolo**
hazel
(44) **il seme**
seed
(45) **il noce**
walnut
(46) **il castagno**
Spanish chestnut
(47) **l'albero di pecan** *m*
pecan
(48) **il faggio**
beech
(49) **la betulla**
birch
(50) **il pioppo**
poplar

Le piante e gli alberi (continua)

Plants and trees continued

169.1 LE PIANTE E GLI ALBERI • PLANTS AND TREES

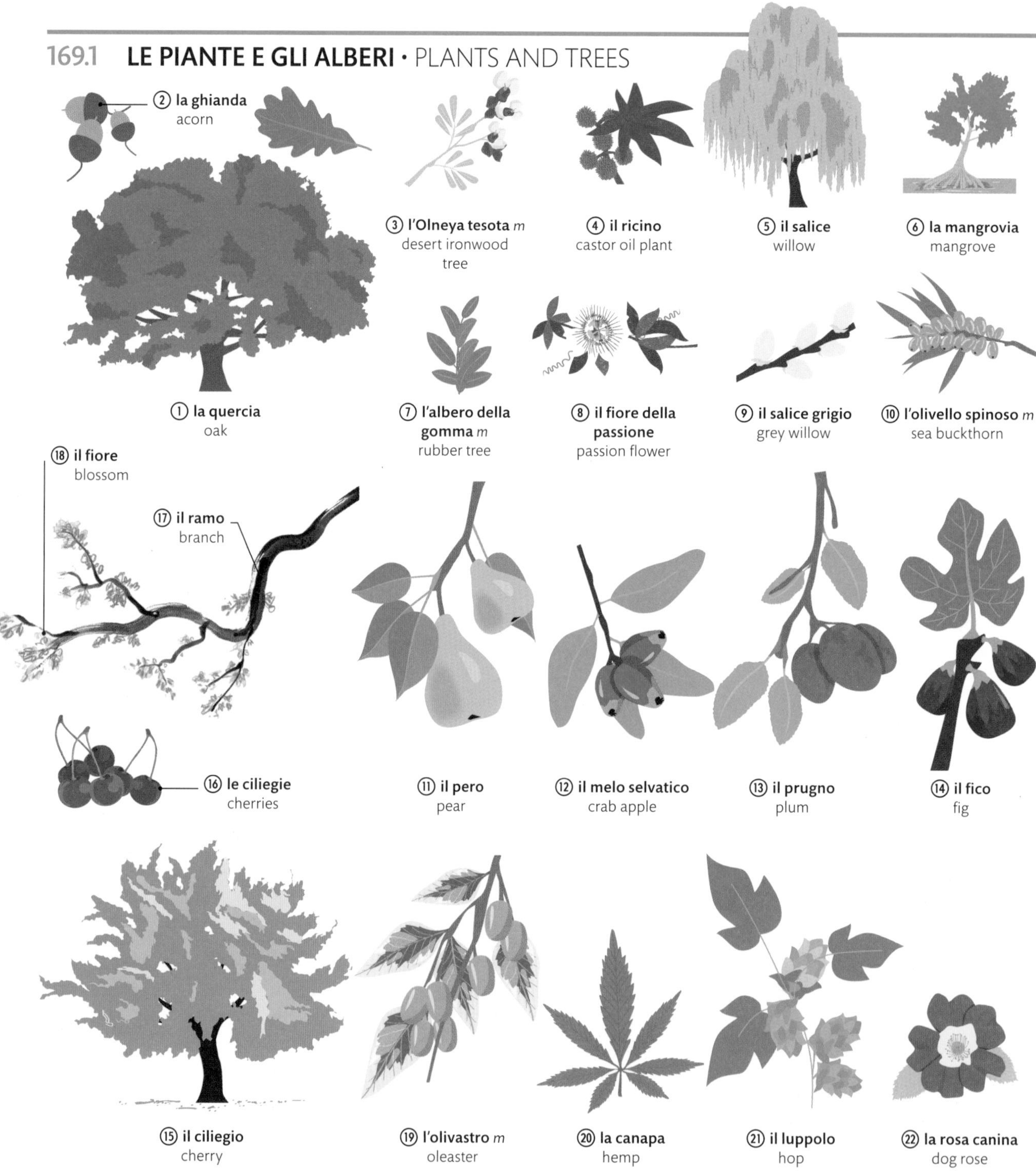
② la ghianda
acorn
① la quercia
oak
③ l'Olneya tesota m
desert ironwood tree
④ il ricino
castor oil plant
⑤ il salice
willow
⑥ la mangrovia
mangrove
⑦ l'albero della gomma m
rubber tree
⑧ il fiore della passione
passion flower
⑨ il salice grigio
grey willow
⑩ l'olivello spinoso m
sea buckthorn
⑱ il fiore
blossom
⑰ il ramo
branch
⑯ le ciliegie
cherries
⑪ il pero
pear
⑫ il melo selvatico
crab apple
⑬ il prugno
plum
⑭ il fico
fig
⑮ il ciliegio
cherry
⑲ l'olivastro m
oleaster
⑳ la canapa
hemp
㉑ il luppolo
hop
㉒ la rosa canina
dog rose

See also
38 Le piante da giardino e le piante da appartamento • Garden plants and houseplants **57** La frutta • Fruit **58** La frutta e la frutta a guscio • Fruit and nuts **157** La storia naturale • Natural history **170** I funghi • Fungi

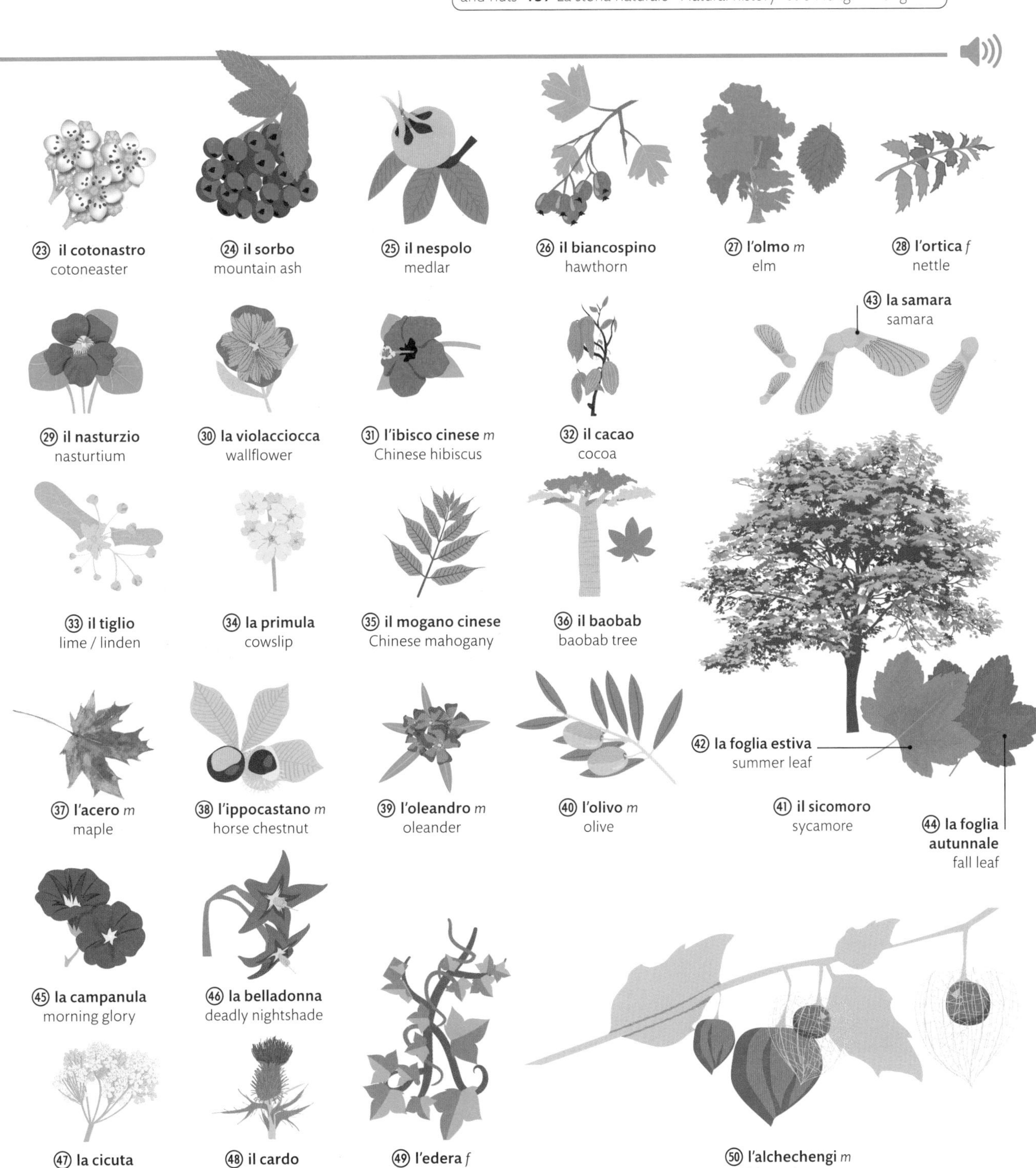

㉓ **il cotonastro**
cotoneaster
㉔ **il sorbo**
mountain ash
㉕ **il nespolo**
medlar
㉖ **il biancospino**
hawthorn
㉗ **l'olmo** *m*
elm
㉘ **l'ortica** *f*
nettle
㉙ **il nasturzio**
nasturtium
㉚ **la violacciocca**
wallflower
㉛ **l'ibisco cinese** *m*
Chinese hibiscus
㉜ **il cacao**
cocoa
㊸ **la samara**
samara
㉝ **il tiglio**
lime / linden
㉞ **la primula**
cowslip
㉟ **il mogano cinese**
Chinese mahogany
㊱ **il baobab**
baobab tree
㊲ **l'acero** *m*
maple
㊳ **l'ippocastano** *m*
horse chestnut
㊴ **l'oleandro** *m*
oleander
㊵ **l'olivo** *m*
olive
㊷ **la foglia estiva**
summer leaf
㊶ **il sicomoro**
sycamore
㊹ **la foglia autunnale**
fall leaf
㊺ **la campanula**
morning glory
㊻ **la belladonna**
deadly nightshade
㊼ **la cicuta**
hemlock
㊽ **il cardo**
thistle
㊾ **l'edera** *f*
ivy
㊿ **l'alchechengi** *m*
Chinese lantern

I funghi
Fungi

170.1 LE SPECIE DI FUNGHI · SPECIES OF FUNGI

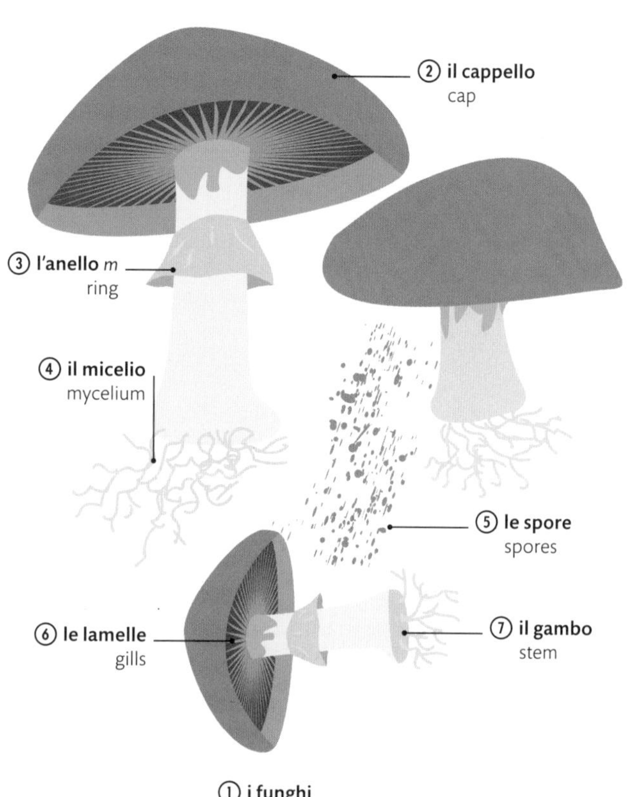
② il cappello
cap
③ l'anello *m*
ring
④ il micelio
mycelium
⑤ le spore
spores
⑥ le lamelle
gills
⑦ il gambo
stem
① i funghi
mushrooms

⑧ **l'Inonotus hispidus** *m*
shaggy bracket fungus

⑨ **andare a funghi**
to forage / to pick mushrooms

⑭ **Alcuni funghi sono velenosi. Controllo sempre prima di raccoglierli.**
Some fungi are poisonous. I always check before picking.

⑬ **la vescia**
common puffball

㉑ **i funghi coltivati**
cultivated mushrooms

㉒ **i funghi velenosi**
toadstools

㉓ **il cerchio delle streghe**
fairy ring

㉔ **il Pleurotus ostreatus**
oyster mushroom

㉕ **il boletus dal cappello arancione**
orange-cap boletus

㉖ **il fungo Laetiporus**
chicken of the woods

㉗ **l'Hydnum repandum** *m*
hedgehog mushroom

㉘ **l'Hericium** *m*
bear's head tooth

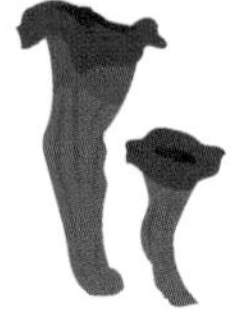
㉙ **la trombetta dei morti**
black trumpet

㉚ **il fungo dell'inchiostro**
shaggy mane mushroom

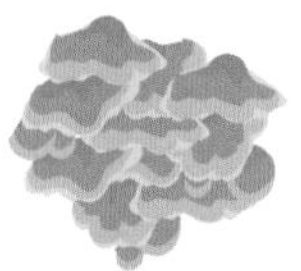
㉛ **la grifola frondosa**
hen of the wood

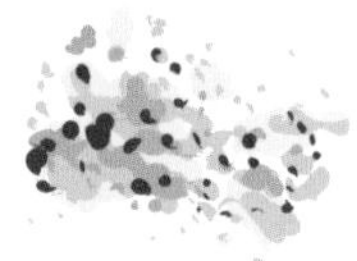
㉜ **la muffa**
mold

See also
55-56 La verdura • Vegetables **133** Le attività all'aperto • Outdoor activities
167-169 Le piante e gli alberi • Plants and trees

⑩ **il fungo enoki**
enoki mushroom

⑪ **il fungo shiitake**
shiitake mushroom

⑫ **il cappello di cera**
waxcap

⑮ **la morchella**
morel

⑯ **la vescia gigante**
giant puffball

⑰ **il prataiolo**
field mushroom

⑱ **il tartufo**
truffle

⑲ **il porcino**
porcini

⑳ **il finferlo**
chanterelle

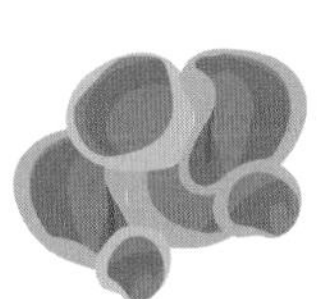

㉟ **l'Aleuria aurantia** *f*
orange peel fungus

㊱ **il satirione**
stinkhorn

㊲ **l'orecchio di lepre** *m*
hare's ear

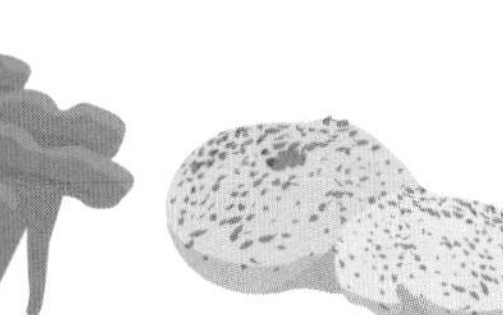

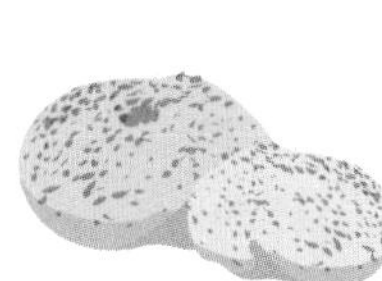

㉝ **l'amanita falloide** *f*
death cap

㉞ **l'amanita virosa** *f*
death angel

㊳ **il fungo dell'olivo**
jack-o'-lantern

㊴ **lo Scleroderma citrinum**
common earthball

㊵ **il Conocybe apala**
milky conecap

㊶ **l'ovolo malefico** *m*
fly agaric

171 Il tempo

Time

171.1 DIRE L'ORA • TELLING THE TIME

① **Che ore sono?**
What time is it?

② **Sono le tre.**
It's three o'clock.

③ **l'una** *f*
one o'clock

④ **l'una e cinque** *f*
five past one

⑤ **l'una e dieci** *f*
ten past one

⑥ **l'una e un quarto** *f*
quarter past one

⑦ **l'una e venti** *f*
twenty past one

⑧ **l'una e venticinque** *f*
twenty-five past one

⑨ **l'una e mezza** *f*
one thirty / half past one

⑩ **l'una e trentacinque** *f*
twenty-five to two

⑪ **le due meno venti**
twenty to two

⑫ **le due meno un quarto**
quarter to two

⑬ **le due meno dieci**
ten to two

⑭ **le due meno cinque**
five to two

⑮ **le due**
two o'clock

⑯ **il secondo**
second

⑰ **il minuto**
minute

⑱ **il quarto d'ora**
quarter of an hour

171.2 LE PARTI DEL GIORNO • PARTS OF THE DAY

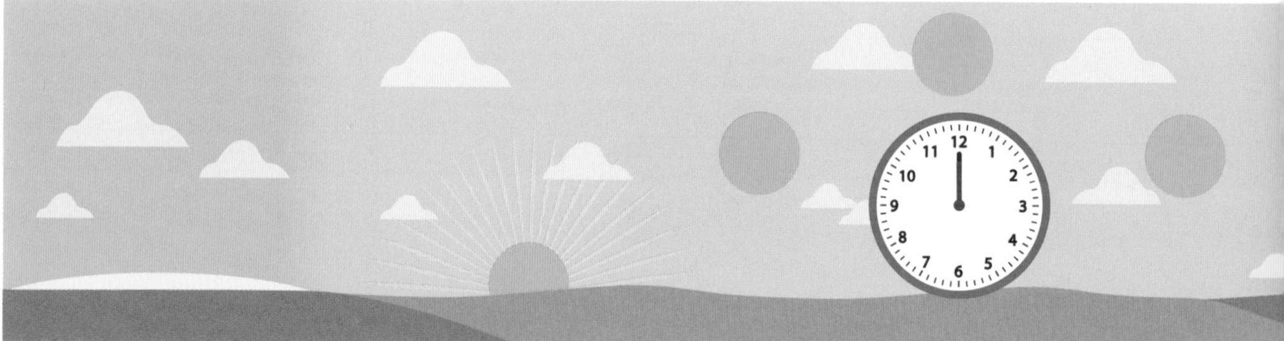

① **l'alba** *f*
dawn

② **il sorgere del sole**
sunrise

③ **la mattina**
morning

④ **il mezzogiorno**
midday

⑤ **il pomeriggio**
afternoon

See also
172 Il calendario • The calendar **173** I numeri • Numbers
174 I pesi e le misure • Weights and measures

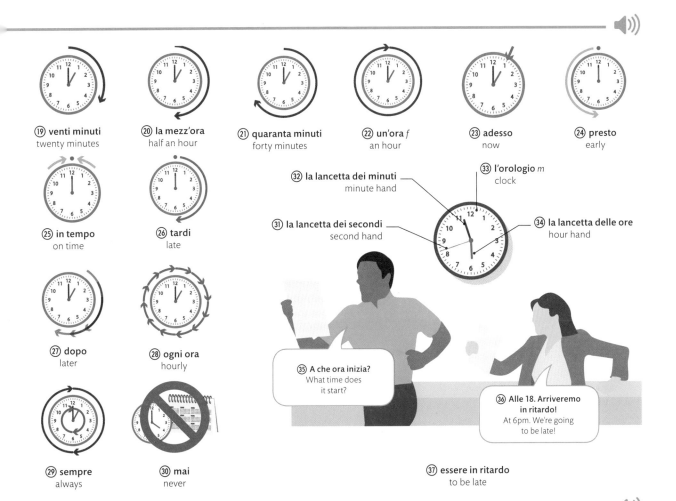

⑲ **venti minuti**
twenty minutes

⑳ **la mezz'ora**
half an hour

㉑ **quaranta minuti**
forty minutes

㉒ **un'ora** *f*
an hour

㉓ **adesso**
now

㉔ **presto**
early

㉕ **in tempo**
on time

㉖ **tardi**
late

㉗ **dopo**
later

㉘ **ogni ora**
hourly

㉙ **sempre**
always

㉚ **mai**
never

㉛ **la lancetta dei secondi**
second hand

㉜ **la lancetta dei minuti**
minute hand

㉝ **l'orologio** *m*
clock

㉞ **la lancetta delle ore**
hour hand

㉟ **A che ora inizia?**
What time does it start?

㊱ **Alle 18. Arriveremo in ritardo!**
At 6pm. We're going to be late!

㊲ **essere in ritardo**
to be late

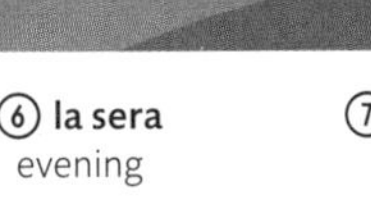

⑥ **la sera**
evening

⑦ **il tramonto**
sunset

⑧ **il crepuscolo**
dusk

⑨ **la mezzanotte**
midnight

⑩ **la notte**
night

⑪ **il giorno**
day

172 Il calendario
The calendar

172.1 IL CALENDARIO E LE STAGIONI • CALENDAR AND SEASONS

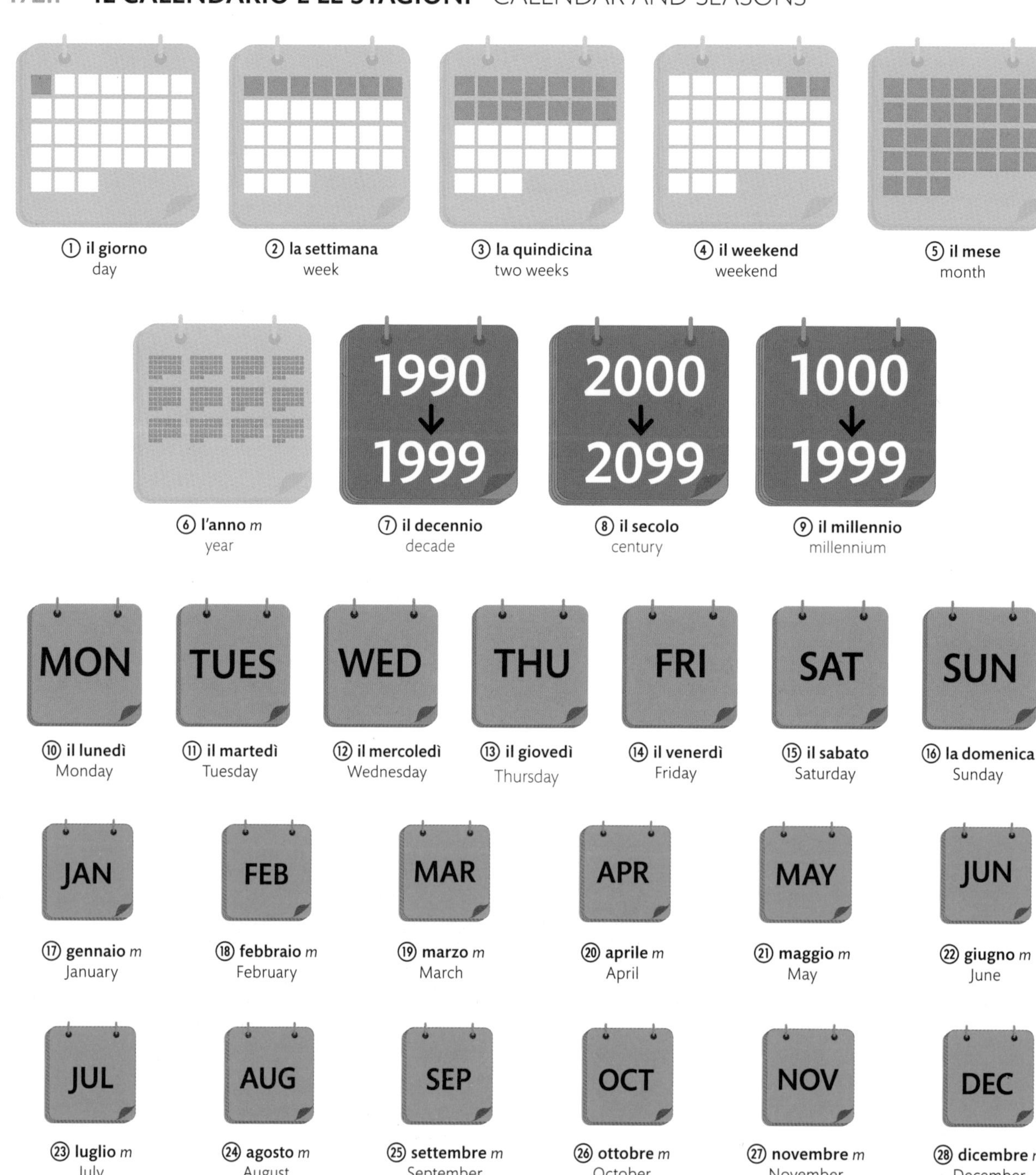

1990
1999
2000
2099
1000
1999
MON
TUES
WED
THU
FRI
SAT
SUN
JAN
FEB
MAR
APR
MAY
JUN
JUL
AUG
SEP
OCT
NOV
DEC

① **il giorno** day
② **la settimana** week
③ **la quindicina** two weeks
④ **il weekend** weekend
⑤ **il mese** month
⑥ **l'anno** *m* year
⑦ **il decennio** decade
⑧ **il secolo** century
⑨ **il millennio** millennium
⑩ **il lunedì** Monday
⑪ **il martedì** Tuesday
⑫ **il mercoledì** Wednesday
⑬ **il giovedì** Thursday
⑭ **il venerdì** Friday
⑮ **il sabato** Saturday
⑯ **la domenica** Sunday
⑰ **gennaio** *m* January
⑱ **febbraio** *m* February
⑲ **marzo** *m* March
⑳ **aprile** *m* April
㉑ **maggio** *m* May
㉒ **giugno** *m* June
㉓ **luglio** *m* July
㉔ **agosto** *m* August
㉕ **settembre** *m* September
㉖ **ottobre** *m* October
㉗ **novembre** *m* November
㉘ **dicembre** *m* December

See also
171 Il tempo • Time
173 I numeri • Numbers

1900
㉙ **millenovecento**
nineteen hundred

1901
㉚ **millenovecentouno**
nineteen-oh-one

1910
㉛ **millenovecentodieci**
nineteen ten

2000
㉜ **duemila**
two thousand

2001
㉝ **duemilauno**
two thousand and one

2033
㉞ **duemilatrentatré**
twenty thirty-three

㉟ **una volta alla settimana**
once a week

㊱ **due volte alla settimana**
twice a week

㊲ **tre volte alla settimana**
three times a week

㊳ **ogni giorno**
every day

㊴ **ogni due giorni**
every other day

㊵ **soltanto il weekend**
only weekends

9AM
10AM
11AM
12PM
1PM
2PM
3PM
4PM
㊶ **ogni ora**
hourly

MON
TUES
WED
THU
FRI
SAT
SUN
㊷ **ogni giorno**
daily

JAN 1
JAN 8
JAN 15
JAN 22
JAN 29
FEB 05
FEB 12
FEB 19
㊸ **ogni settimana**
weekly

JAN
FEB
MAR
APR
MAY
JUNE
JULY
AUG
㊹ **ogni mese**
monthly

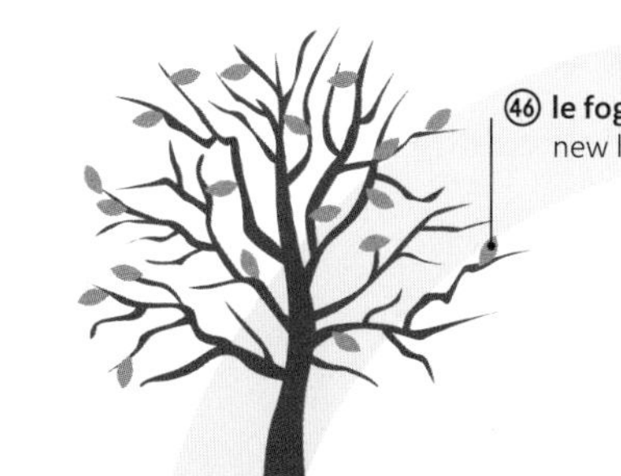
㊻ **le foglie nuove**
new leaves

㊺ **la primavera**
spring

㊽ **il fogliame verde**
green foliage

㊼ **l'estate** *f*
summer

㊾ **le stagioni**
seasons

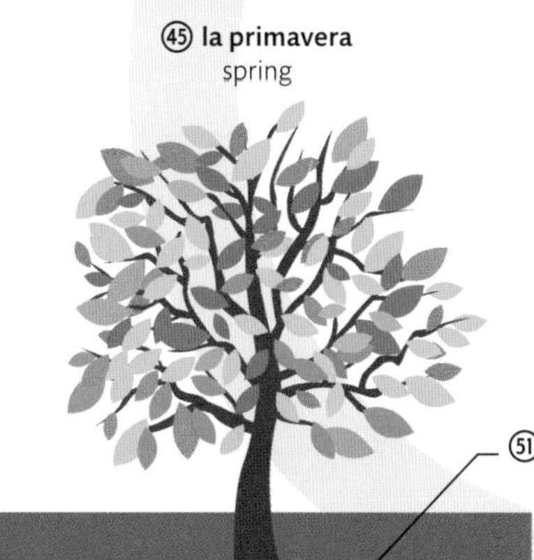
㊿ **l'autunno** *m*
fall

(51) **la caduta delle foglie**
leaf fall

(53) **i rami spogli**
bare branches

(52) **l'inverno** *m*
winter

173 I numeri

Numbers

173.1 I NUMERI CARDINALI · CARDINAL NUMBERS

1	2	3	4	5	6
① **uno** one	② **due** two	③ **tre** three	④ **quattro** four	⑤ **cinque** five	⑥ **sei** six
7	**8**	**9**	**10**	**11**	**12**
⑦ **sette** seven	⑧ **otto** eight	⑨ **nove** nine	⑩ **dieci** ten	⑪ **undici** eleven	⑫ **dodici** twelve
13	**14**	**15**	**16**	**17**	**18**
⑬ **tredici** thirteen	⑭ **quattordici** fourteen	⑮ **quindici** fifteen	⑯ **sedici** sixteen	⑰ **diciassette** seventeen	⑱ **diciotto** eighteen
19	**20**	**21**	**22**	**30**	**40**
⑲ **diciannove** nineteen	⑳ **venti** twenty	㉑ **ventuno** twenty-one	㉒ **ventidue** twenty-two	㉓ **trenta** thirty	㉔ **quaranta** forty

50	60	70	80	90	100	0
㉕ **cinquanta** fifty	㉖ **sessanta** sixty	㉗ **settanta** seventy	㉘ **ottanta** eighty	㉙ **novanta** ninety	㉚ **cento** one hundred	㉛ **zero** zero

173.2 I NUMERI ORDINALI · ORDINAL NUMBERS

1st	2nd	3rd	4th	5th	6th
① **primo** *m* / **prima** *f* first	② **secondo** *m* **seconda** *f* second	③ **terzo** *m* / **terza** *f* third	④ **quarto** *m* **quarta** *f* fourth	⑤ **quinto** *m* **quinta** *f* fifth	⑥ **sesto** *m* / **sesta** *f* sixth
7th	**8th**	**9th**	**10th**	**20th**	**21st**
⑦ **settimo** *m* **settima** *f* seventh	⑧ **ottavo** *m* **ottava** *f* eighth	⑨ **nono** *m* / **nona** *f* ninth	⑩ **decimo** *m* **decima** *f* tenth	⑪ **ventesimo** *m* **ventesima** *f* twentieth	⑫ **ventunesimo** *m* **ventunesima** *f* twenty-first

See also
74 La matematica • Mathematics **171** Il tempo • Time **172** Il calendario
The calendar **174** I pesi e le misure • Weights and measures

173.3 I GRANDI NUMERI • LARGE NUMBERS

200
① **duecento**
two hundred

250
② **duecentocinquanta**
two hundred and fifty

500
③ **cinquecento**
five hundred

750
④ **settecentocinquanta**
seven hundred and fifty

1,000
⑤ **mille**
one thousand

1,200
⑥ **milleduecento**
one thousand two hundred

10,000
⑦ **diecimila**
ten thousand

100,000
⑧ **centomila**
one hundred thousand

1,000,000
⑨ **un milione**
one million

5,000,000
⑩ **cinque milioni**
five million

500,000,000
⑪ **cinquecento milioni / mezzo miliardo**
five hundred million / half a billion

1,000,000,000
⑫ **un miliardo**
one billion

3,846
⑬ **tremilaottocentoquarantasei**
three thousand, eight hundred and forty-six

82,043
⑭ **ottantaduemilaquarantatrè**
eighty-two thousand and forty-three

⑮ Ho perso il conto!
I've lost count!

234,407
⑯ **duecentotrentaquattromila quattrocentosette**
two hundred and thirty-four thousand, four hundred and seven

3,089,342
⑰ **tre milioni ottantanovemila trecentoquarantadue**
three million, eighty-nine thousand, three hundred and forty-two

173.4 LE FRAZIONI, I DECIMALI E LE PERCENTUALI
FRACTIONS, DECIMALS, AND PERCENTAGES

⅛
① **un ottavo**
an eighth

¼
② **un quarto**
a quarter

⅓
③ **un terzo**
a third

½
④ **la metà**
a half

⅗
⑤ **i tre quinti**
three-fifths

⅞
⑥ **i sette ottavi**
seven-eighths

0.5
⑦ **zero virgola cinque**
zero point five

1.7
⑧ **uno virgola sette**
one point seven

3.97
⑨ **tre virgola novantasette**
three point nine seven

1%
⑩ **uno percento**
one percent

99%
⑪ **novantanove percento**
ninety-nine percent

100%
⑫ **cento percento**
one hundred percent

174 I pesi e le misure
Weights and measures

174.1 IL PESO · WEIGHT

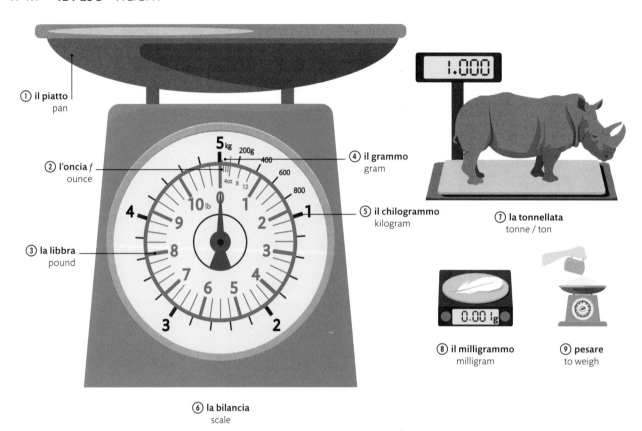

① **il piatto**
pan

② **l'oncia** *f*
ounce

③ **la libbra**
pound

④ **il grammo**
gram

⑤ **il chilogrammo**
kilogram

⑥ **la bilancia**
scale

⑦ **la tonnellata**
tonne / ton

⑧ **il milligrammo**
milligram

⑨ **pesare**
to weigh

174.2 LA DISTANZA, L'AREA E LA LUNGHEZZA · DISTANCE, AREA, AND LENGTH

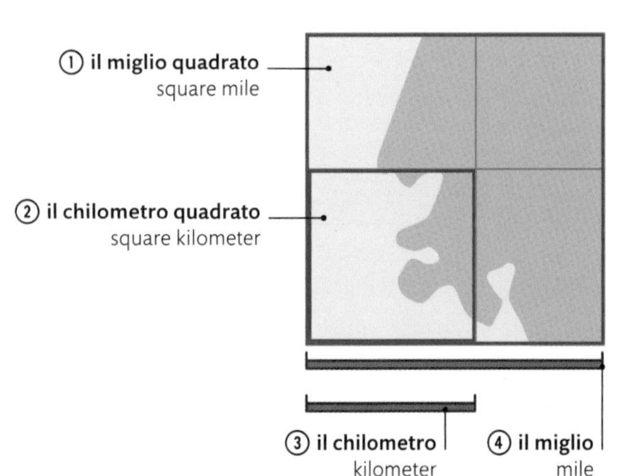
① il miglio quadrato
square mile
② il chilometro quadrato
square kilometer
③ il chilometro
kilometer
④ il miglio
mile

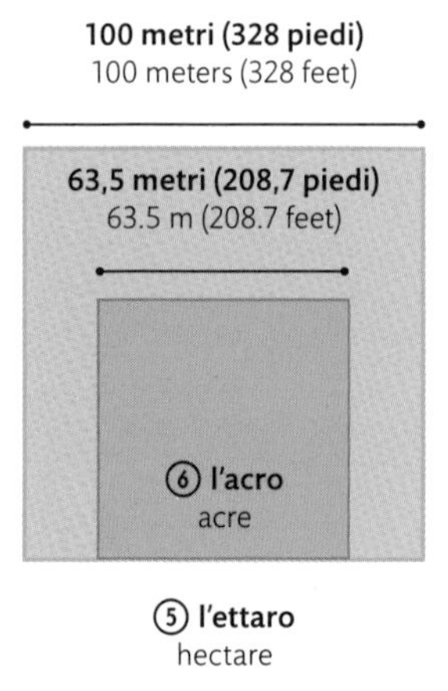
100 metri (328 piedi)
100 meters (328 feet)
63,5 metri (208,7 piedi)
63.5 m (208.7 feet)
⑥ l'acro
acre
⑤ l'ettaro
hectare

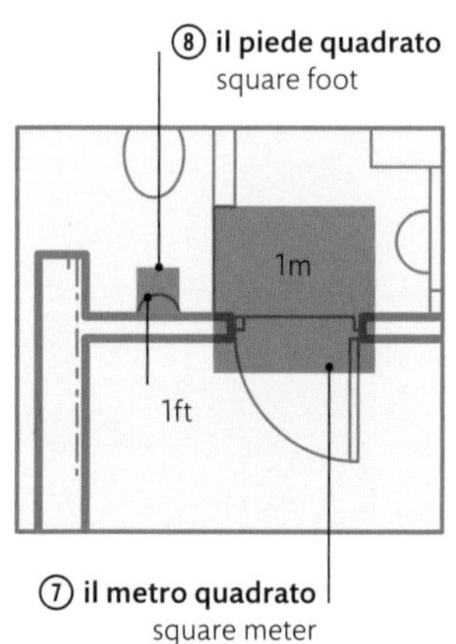
⑧ il piede quadrato
square foot
1m
1ft
⑦ il metro quadrato
square meter

See also
29 Cucinare • Cooking **35** I lavori di miglioria della casa • Home improvements **74** La matematica • Mathematics **173** I numeri • Numbers

174.3 LE MISURE / IL VOLUME DEI LIQUIDI • LIQUID MEASUREMENTS / VOLUME

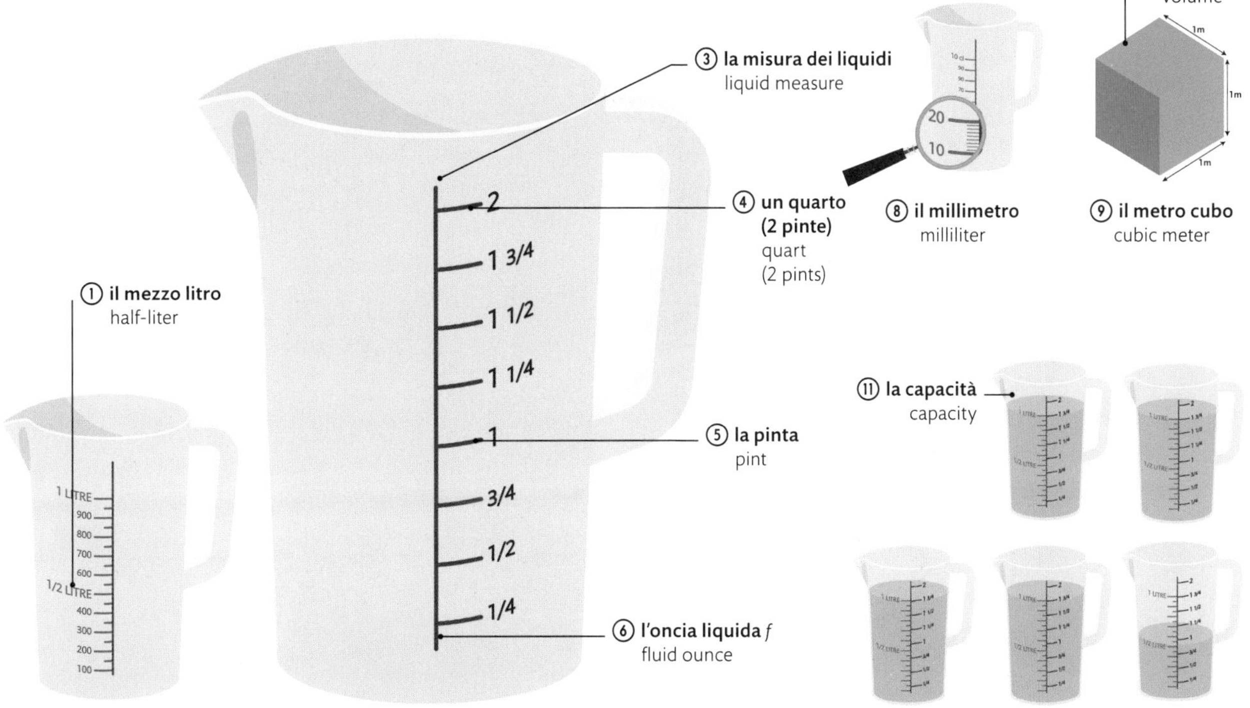

① **il mezzo litro**
half-liter

② **il litro**
liter

1 LITRE
900
800
700
600
1/2 LITRE
400
300
200
100

③ **la misura dei liquidi**
liquid measure

④ **un quarto (2 pinte)**
quart (2 pints)

⑤ **la pinta**
pint

⑥ **l'oncia liquida** *f*
fluid ounce

2
1 3/4
1 1/2
1 1/4
1
3/4
1/2
1/4

⑦ **la caraffa graduata**
measuring cup

⑧ **il millimetro**
milliliter

20
10

⑨ **il metro cubo**
cubic meter

⑩ **il volume**
volume

1m
1m
1m

⑪ **la capacità**
capacity

⑫ **il gallone - 4,6 litri**
gallon = 4.6 liters

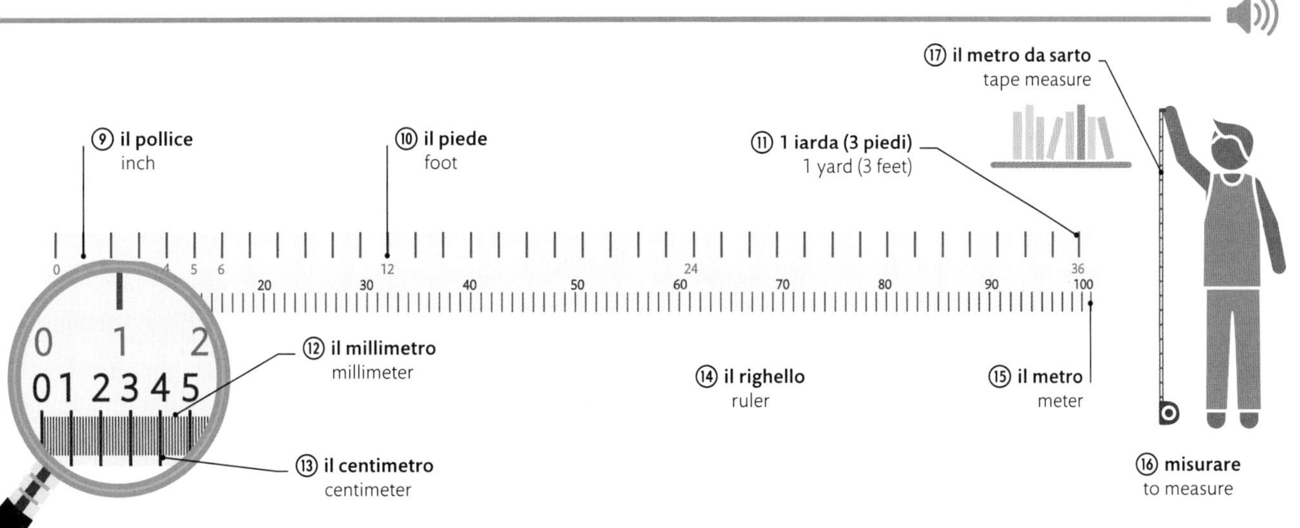
⑨ il pollice
inch
⑩ il piede
foot
⑪ 1 iarda (3 piedi)
1 yard (3 feet)
⑰ il metro da sarto
tape measure
0 4 5 6 12 24 36
20 30 40 50 60 70 80 90 100
0 1 2
0 1 2 3 4 5
⑫ il millimetro
millimeter
⑬ il centimetro
centimeter
⑭ il righello
ruler
⑮ il metro
meter
⑯ misurare
to measure

175 La scrittura
Writing

175.1 LA SCRITTURA E IL MATERIALE PER SCRIVERE · WRITING AND WRITING EQUIPMENT

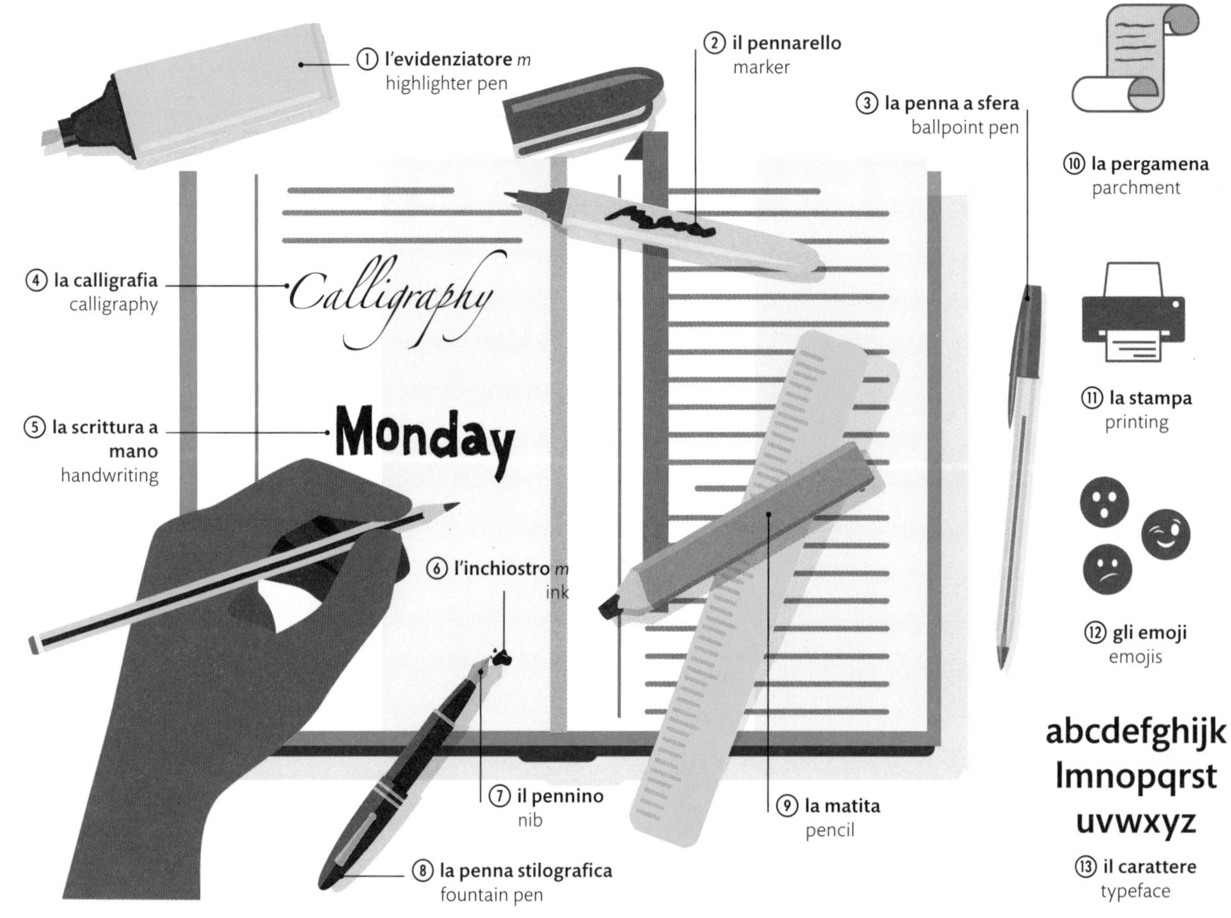

① l'evidenziatore *m*
highlighter pen
② il pennarello
marker
③ la penna a sfera
ballpoint pen
④ la calligrafia
calligraphy
Calligraphy
⑤ la scrittura a mano
handwriting
Monday
⑥ l'inchiostro *m*
ink
⑦ il pennino
nib
⑧ la penna stilografica
fountain pen
⑨ la matita
pencil
⑩ la pergamena
parchment
⑪ la stampa
printing
⑫ gli emoji
emojis
abcdefghijk
lmnopqrst
uvwxyz
⑬ il carattere
typeface

Aa	ABC	abc	**abc**	*abc*	123
⑭ **le lettere** letters	⑮ **le lettere maiuscole** uppercase / capital letters	⑯ **le lettere minuscole** lowercase	⑰ **il grassetto** bold	⑱ **il corsivo** italic	⑲ **le cifre** numerals

ft	.	-	—	_	,
⑳ **la legatura** ligature	㉑ **il punto** period	㉒ **il trattino** hyphen	㉓ **la lineetta** dash	㉔ **il trattino basso** underscore	㉕ **la virgola** comma

See also
73 A scuola • At school
138 I libri e la lettura • Books and reading

㉖ **il punto e virgola**
semicolon

㉗ **i due punti**
colon

㉘ **i puntini di sospensione**
ellipsis

㉙ **il punto esclamativo**
exclamation mark

㉚ **il punto interrogativo**
question mark

㉛ **l'apostrofo** *m*
apostrophe

㉜ **la virgoletta singola**
single quotation mark

㉝ **la virgoletta doppia**
double quotation mark

㉞ **l'asterisco** *m*
asterisk

㉟ **la chiocciola**
at sign / at symbol

㊱ **la e commerciale**
ampersand

㊲ **la tilde**
tilde

㊳ **l'accento acuto** *m*
acute accent

㊴ **l'accento grave** *m*
grave accent

㊵ **la dieresi**
umlaut

㊶ **l'accento circonflesso** *m*
circumflex

㊷ **la cediglia**
cedilla

㊸ **il copyright**
copyright

cat

Γάτα кошка

㊹ **il marchio registrato**
registered trademark

㊺ **le parentesi**
brackets

㊻ **l'hashtag** *m*
hashtag

㊼ **l'alfabeto latino** *m*
Latin alphabet

㊽ **l'alfabeto greco** *m*
Greek alphabet

㊾ **l'alfabeto cirillico** *m*
Cyrillic alphabet

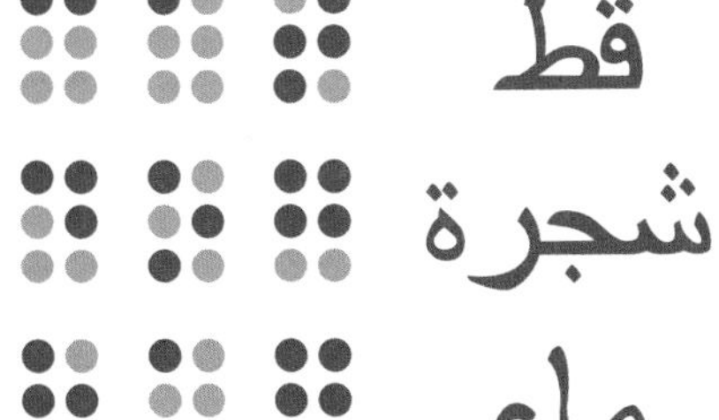

قط
شجرة
ماء

市
車両
道

桃
橘子
柠檬

खेत
घोड़ा
नदी

㊿ **il Braille**
Braille

(51) **i caratteri arabi**
Arabic script

(52) **i caratteri giapponesi**
Japanese characters

(53) **i caratteri cinesi**
Chinese characters

(54) **l'alfabeto devanagari** *m*
Devanagari script

(55) **i geroglifici dell'Antico Egitto**
Ancient Egyptian hieroglyphs

176 Descrivere le cose
Describing things

176.1 I MATERIALI · MATERIALS

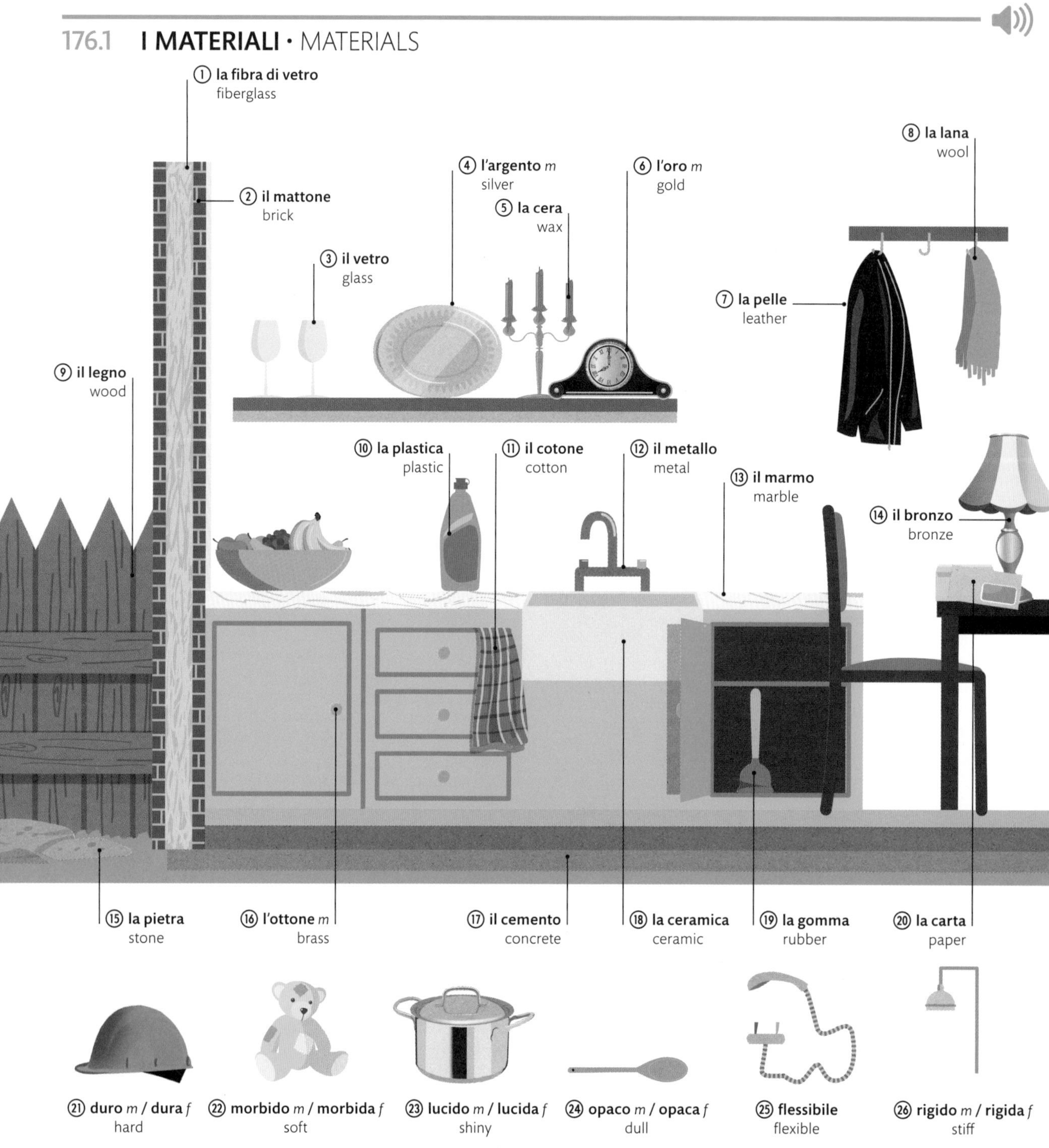

① la fibra di vetro
fiberglass
② il mattone
brick
③ il vetro
glass
④ l'argento m
silver
⑤ la cera
wax
⑥ l'oro m
gold
⑦ la pelle
leather
⑧ la lana
wool
⑨ il legno
wood
⑩ la plastica
plastic
⑪ il cotone
cotton
⑫ il metallo
metal
⑬ il marmo
marble
⑭ il bronzo
bronze
⑮ la pietra
stone
⑯ l'ottone m
brass
⑰ il cemento
concrete
⑱ la ceramica
ceramic
⑲ la gomma
rubber
⑳ la carta
paper
㉑ duro m / dura f
hard
㉒ morbido m / morbida f
soft
㉓ lucido m / lucida f
shiny
㉔ opaco m / opaca f
dull
㉕ flessibile
flexible
㉖ rigido m / rigida f
stiff

See also
32 La casa • House and home **35** I lavori di miglioria della casa • Home improvements **37** La decorazione • Renovating **87** Le costruzioni • Construction **177** Descrivere le cose (continua) • Describing things continued

176.2 GLI AGGETTIVI • ADJECTIVES

① **grande**
big / large

② **piccolo** *m*
piccola *f*
small / little

③ **largo** *m* / **larga** *f*
wide

④ **stretto** *m* / **stretta** *f*
narrow

⑤ **profondo** *m*
profonda *f*
deep

⑥ **poco profondo** *m*
poco profonda *f*
shallow

⑦ **alto** *m* / **alta** *f*
high

⑧ **basso** *m* / **bassa** *f*
low

⑨ **pesante**
heavy

⑩ **leggero** *m* / **leggera** *f*
light

⑪ **pulito** *m* / **pulita** *f*
clean

⑫ **sporco** *m* / **sporca** *f*
dirty

⑬ **caldo** *m* / **calda** *f*
hot

⑭ **freddo** *m* / **fredda** *f*
cold

⑮ **lungo** *m* / **lunga** *f*
long

⑯ **corto** *m* / **corta** *f*
short

⑰ **allentato** *m*
allentata *f*
loose

⑱ **stretto** *m* / **stretta** *f*
tight

⑲ **sottile**
thin

⑳ **spesso** *m* / **spessa** *f*
thick

㉑ **vicino** *m* / **vicina** *f*
near

㉒ **lontano** *m* / **lontana** *f*
far

㉓ **lento** *m* / **lenta** *f*
slow

㉔ **veloce**
fast

㉕ **nuovo** *m* / **nuova** *f*
new

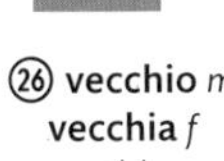

㉖ **vecchio** *m*
vecchia *f*
old

㉗ **vuoto** *m* / **vuota** *f*
empty

㉘ **pieno** *m* / **piena** *f*
full

㉙ **rumoroso** *m*
rumorosa *f*
noisy

㉚ **silenzioso** *m*
silenziosa *f*
quiet

㉛ **giusto** *m* / **giusta** *f*
correct

㉜ **sbagliato** *m*
sbagliata *f*
incorrect

㉝ **luminoso** *m*
luminosa *f*
light

㉞ **scuro** *m* / **scura** *f*
dark

177 Descrivere le cose (continua)

Describing things continued

177.1 LE OPINIONI · OPINIONS

② **La vista da qui è davvero mozzafiato.**
The view here is absolutely breathtaking.

① **mozzafiato**
breathtaking

③ **entusiasmante**
exciting

④ **stupendo** *m*
stupenda *f*
beautiful

⑤ **elettrizzante**
thrilling

⑥ **divertente**
fun

⑦ **romantico** *m*
romantica *f*
romantic

⑧ **sbalorditivo** *m*
sbalorditiva *f*
stunning

⑨ **favoloso** *m*
favolosa *f*
great

10
10
10

⑩ **incredibile**
incredible

⑪ **importante**
important

⑫ **adorabile**
cute

⑬ **rispettoso** *m*
rispettosa *f*
respectful

⑭ **speciale**
special

⑮ **aggraziato** *m*
aggraziata *f*
graceful

⑯ **notevole**
remarkable

⑰ **eccezionale**
outstanding

⑱ **esilarante**
hilarious

⑲ **spassoso** *m*
spassosa *f*
funny

⑳ **straordinario** *m*
straordinaria *f*
extraordinary

㉑ **meraviglioso** *m*
meravigliosa *f*
wonderful

㉒ **innocuo** *m*
innocua *f*
harmless

㉓ **all'antica**
old-fashioned

See also
06 I sentimenti e gli stati d'animo • Feelings and moods **10** I tratti della personalità • Personality traits
11 Le abilità e le azioni • Abilities and actions **93** Le competenze sul luogo di lavoro • Workplace skills

㉔ **bravo** *m* / **brava** *f*
good

㉕ **incapace**
bad

㉖ **fantastico** *m*
fantastica *f*
fantastic

㉗ **terribile**
terrible

㉘ **gradevole**
pleasant

㉙ **sgradevole**
unpleasant

㉚ **brillante**
brilliant

㉛ **tremendo** *m*
tremenda *f*
dreadful

㉜ **utile**
useful

㉝ **inutile**
useless

㉞ **delizioso** *m*
deliziosa *f*
delicious

㉟ **disgustoso** *m*
disgustosa *f*
disgusting

㊱ **bello** *m* / **bella** *f*
pretty

㊲ **brutto** *m* / **brutta** *f*
ugly

㊳ **interessante**
interesting

㊴ **noioso** *m* / **noiosa** *f*
boring

㊵ **rilassante**
relaxing

㊶ **estenuante**
exhausting

㊷ **eccellente**
superb

㊸ **pessimo** *m*
pessima *f*
awful

㊹ **gentile**
nice

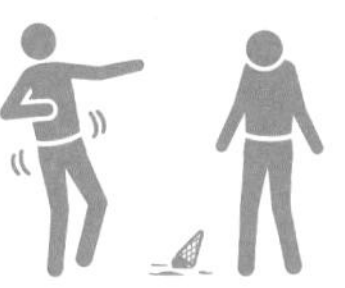
㊺ **sgarbato** *m*
sgarbata *f*
nasty

㊻ **formidabile**
amazing

5
5
4
㊼ **mediocre**
mediocre

㊽ **spaventoso** *m*
spaventosa *f*
frightening

㊾ **terrificante**
terrifying

㊿ **strano** *m* / **strana** *f*
strange / odd

(51) **scioccante**
shocking

(52) **fastidioso** *m*
fastidiosa *f*
annoying

(53) **orribile**
horrible

(54) **disastroso** *m*
disastrosa *f*
disastrous

(55) **poco chiaro** *m*
poco chiara *f*
confusing

(56) **stancante**
tiring

(57) **irritante**
irritating

(58) **disastroso** *m*
disastrosa *f*
dire

(59) **deludente**
disappointing

I verbi comuni

Common phrasal verbs

178.1 I VERBI DELLA VITA QUOTIDIANA • VERBS FOR DAILY LIFE

1 **calmarsi**
to calm down

2 **rilassarsi**
to chill out

3 **cercare**
to look for

4 **crescere**
to grow up

5 **telefonare a**
to call up

6 **indossare**
to put on

7 **vestirsi elegante**
to dress up

8 **vantarsi**
to show off

9 **ammucchiare**
to pile up

10 **restituire**
to give back

11 **appisolarsi**
to doze off

12 **dormire fino a tardi**
to sleep in

13 **alzarsi**
to get up

14 **salire**
to go up

15 **scendere**
to go down

16 **raggiungere**
to catch up

17 **svagarsi**
to mess around

18 **appendere**
to hang up

19 **far entrare**
to let in

20 **strappare**
to rip out

21 **rimanere senza**
to run out (of)

22 **far scattare**
to set off

23 **inciampare**
to trip over

24 **dosare**
to measure

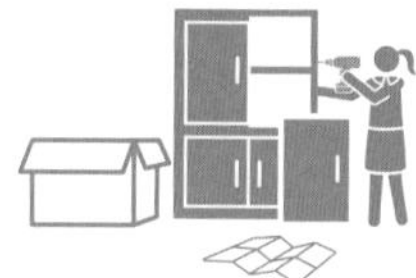

25 **montare**
to put together

26 **ristrutturare**
to fix up

27 **mettere via**
to put away

29 **Vi ho aspettati alzato tutta la notte!**
I've been waiting up all night!

28 **aspettare alzato** *m* / **aspettare alzata** *f*
to wait up

30 **compilare**
to fill out

31 **effettuare l'accesso**
to log in

32 **uscire**
to log out

See also
09 Le attività quotidiane • Daily routines 11 Le abilità e le azioni
Abilities and actions 179-180 Le espressioni utili • Useful expressions

33 **svegliarsi**
to wake up

34 **pesare**
to weigh

35 **accendere**
to turn on

36 **spegnere**
to turn off

37 **alzare**
to turn up

38 **abbassare**
to turn down

39 **rompersi**
to break down

40 **fare il pieno**
to fill up

41 **fare il check-in**
to check in

42 **fare il check-out**
to check out

43 **mangiare fuori**
to eat out

44 **servire**
to wait on

45 **salire**
to get on

46 **scendere**
to get off

47 **diluviare**
to pour down

48 **andare via / partire**
to go away / to get away

49 **indicare**
to point out

50 **accudire**
to care for

51 **osservare**
to look at

52 **regalare**
to give away

53 **distribuire**
to give out

54 **rinunciare**
to give up

60 **Ciao! Sono davvero felice che siate potuti venire!**
Hi! So glad you could join us!

55 **lasciarsi**
to break up

56 **annullare**
to call off

57 **fare pace**
to make up

58 **vedersi**
to meet up

59 **incontrarsi**
to get together

61 **distribuire**
to hand out

62 **fare le pulizie**
to clean up

63 **raccogliere**
to pick up

64 **buttare via**
to throw away

65 **scappare**
to run away

66 **decollare**
to take off

179 Le espressioni utili

Useful expressions

179.1 I SALUTI • GREETINGS

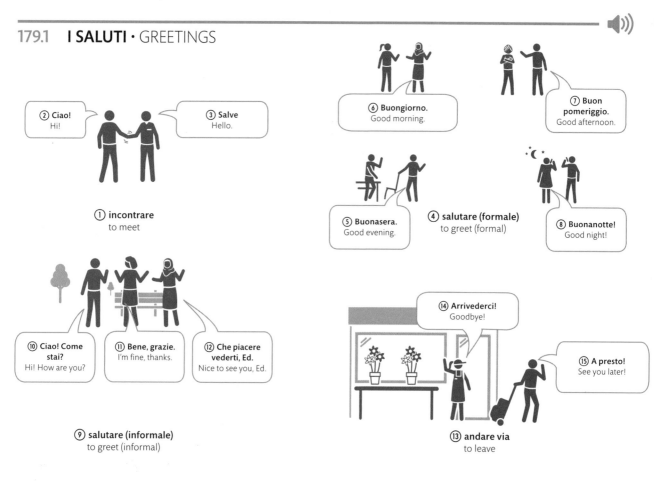

① **incontrare**
to meet

② **Ciao!**
Hi!

③ **Salve**
Hello.

④ **salutare (formale)**
to greet (formal)

⑤ **Buonasera.**
Good evening.

⑥ **Buongiorno.**
Good morning.

⑦ **Buon pomeriggio.**
Good afternoon.

⑧ **Buonanotte!**
Good night!

⑨ **salutare (informale)**
to greet (informal)

⑩ **Ciao! Come stai?**
Hi! How are you?

⑪ **Bene, grazie.**
I'm fine, thanks.

⑫ **Che piacere vederti, Ed.**
Nice to see you, Ed.

⑬ **andare via**
to leave

⑭ **Arrivederci!**
Goodbye!

⑮ **A presto!**
See you later!

179.2 CONOSCERE QUALCUNO • GETTING TO KNOW SOMEONE

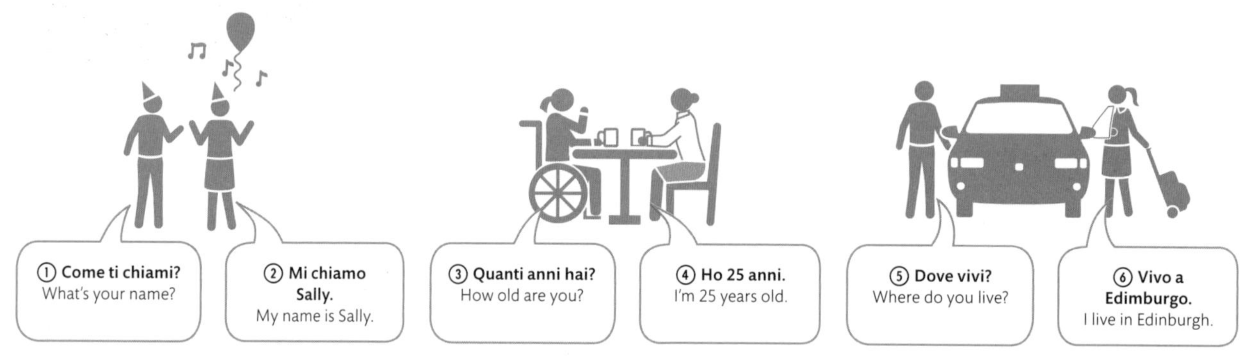

① Come ti chiami?
What's your name?
② Mi chiamo Sally.
My name is Sally.
③ Quanti anni hai?
How old are you?
④ Ho 25 anni.
I'm 25 years old.
⑤ Dove vivi?
Where do you live?
⑥ Vivo a Edimburgo.
I live in Edinburgh.

See also
09 Le attività quotidiane • Daily routines **07** Gli eventi della vita Life events **46** Lo shopping • Shopping **180** Espressioni utili (continua) • Useful expressions continued

179.3 LO SHOPPING • SHOPPING

① **Quanto costa?**
How much is this?

② **Costa 15 dollari.**
It's 15 dollars

③ **Posso pagare qui?**
Can I pay here?

④ **Potrebbe prendermi la tazza rossa, per favore?**
Could you get the red cup for me, please?

⑤ **Posso aiutarla?**
Can I help you?

⑥ **Sto solo dando un'occhiata, grazie.**
I'm just browsing, thanks.

⑦ **Vendete ombrelli?**
Do you sell umbrellas?

⑧ **Avete una taglia più piccola di questo modello?**
Do you have this in a smaller size?

⑨ **Controllo subito.**
Let me check for you.

⑪ **Parla inglese?**
Do you speak English?

⑦ **Da dove vieni?**
Where are you from?

⑧ **Vengo dall'Italia.**
I'm from Italy.

⑨ **Che lavoro fa?**
What do you do?

⑩ **Sono una diplomatica in pensione.**
I'm a retired diplomat.

⑫ **Poco. Potrebbe parlare più lentamente, per favore?**
Only a little. Could you speak more slowly, please?

180 Le espressioni utili (continua)

Useful expressions continued

180.1 LE DIREZIONI · DIRECTIONS

① Mi può aiutare, per favore?
Can you help me, please?
② Sì, certo.
Yes, of course.
③ Dove si trova la stazione ferroviaria?
Where is the train station?
④ Dista 15 minuti a piedi. Giri a sinistra al supermercato.
It's a 15-minute walk. Turn left at the supermarket.

⑤ Quanto dista l'hotel?
How far is it to the hotel?

⑥ Ci siamo persi!
We've lost our way!
⑦ Dovremmo chiedere aiuto.
We should ask for help.

⑧ Può mostrarci come si arriva al lago?
Can you show us the way to the lake?

⑨ Come si arriva alla spiaggia?
How do we get to the beach?
⑩ Sempre dritti!
It's straight ahead!

⑪ Dove posso trovare un buon posto dove mangiare?
Where can I find a good place to eat?
⑫ Provi al bar accanto alle poste.
Try the café next to the post office.

See also
42-43 In città • In town **148** Le cartine e le direzioni • Maps and directions

180.2 LE PREPOSIZIONI • PREPOSITIONS

① **dentro**
in

② **fuori**
out

③ **all'interno**
inside

④ **all'esterno**
outside

⑤ **tra**
between

⑥ **sotto**
under

⑦ **sopra**
on

⑧ **accanto a**
next to / beside

⑨ **davanti a**
in front of

⑩ **dietro a**
behind

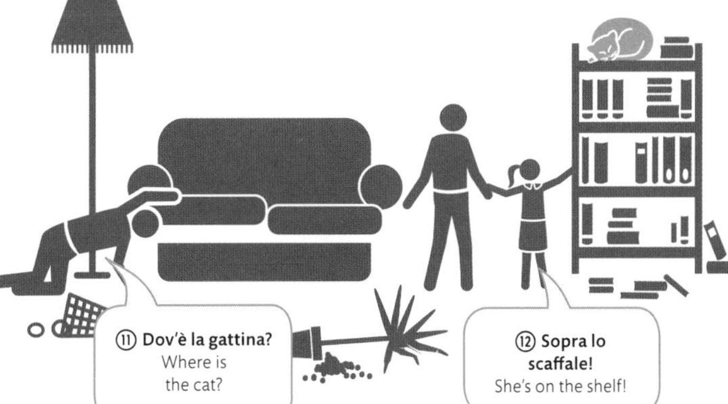

⑪ **Dov'è la gattina?**
Where is the cat?

⑫ **Sopra lo scaffale!**
She's on the shelf!

English word list

The numbers after each word or phrase refer to the units in which they can be found.

KEY
adj - adjective
adv - adverb
n - noun
num - number
phr - phrase
prep - preposition
v - verb

A

à la carte menu *n* **69**
aardvark *n* **158**
ab wheel *n* **124**
abandoned building *n* **44**
abdomen *n* **01, 162**
abdominals *n* **03**
abilities *n* **11**
ability to drive *n* **93**
abseiling *n* **125**
Abyssinian *n* **164**
acacia *n* **47**
access road *n* **106**
accessories *n* **16**
accident *n* **19**
accident and emergency *n* **50**
accommodation *n* **131**
accordion *n* **129**
account number *n* **45**
accountant *n* **90, 94**
accounts *n* **91**
accurate *adj* **93**
ace *n* **114, 140**
ache *v* **20**
Achilles tendon *n* **03**
acid *n* **76**
acid rain *n* **51, 155**
acorn *n* **169**
acorn squash *n* **56**
acoustic guitar *n* **129**
acoustic guitarist *n* **129**
acquaintance *n* **07**
acquitted *adj* **85**
acre *n* **174**
across from *prep* **148**
acrylic paint *n* **141**
act *v* **11**
actinide series *n* **78**
actinium *n* **78**
action game *n* **136**
action movie *n* **127**
action points *n* **95**
actions *n* **11**
actor *n* **89, 126**
acupressure *n* **24**
acupuncture *n* **24**
acute accent *n* **175**
Adam's apple *n* **04**
adaptable *adj* **93**
add *v* **11, 29, 74**
add to cart *v* **46**
add to wishlist *v* **46**
additives *n* **23**
address *n* **45**
adhesive bandage *n* **20**
adhesive tape *n* **20**
administration *n* **91, 93**
admiral *n* **88**
admission fee *n* **130**
admissions *n* **80**
admit *v* **21**
adrenal gland *n* **04**
adult frog *n* **77**
adult teeth *n* **03**
adults *n* **05**
advantage *n* **114**
adventure game *n* **136**
adventure playground *n* **133**
adventurous *adj* **10**
advertising *n* **91**
aerate *v* **39**
aerobics *n* **124**
aerobics step *n* **124**
aerospace *n* **91**
Afghan *adj* **153**
Afghanistan *n* **151, 153**
Africa *n* **149, 152**
African *adj* **152**
African bullfrog *n* **163**
African daisy *n* **38**
African elephant *n* **158**
African gray parrot *n* **161**
African wild dog *n* **158**
Afro *n* **12**
afternoon *n* **09, 171**
aftershave *n* **18, 31**
agate *n* **156**
agbada *n* **15**
agenda *n* **95**
agriculture *n* **91**
aikido *n* **117**
aileron *n* **103**
air ambulance *n* **50**
air bed *n* **135**
air cargo *n* **104**
air conditioning *n* **33, 99**
air control tower *n* **43**
air cylinder *n* **118**
air filter *n* **98, 100**
air mattress *n* **135**
air pump *n* **135**
air vent *n* **103**
airbag *n* **99**
airball *n* **112**
aircraft carrier *n* **88, 105**
aircraft *n* **103**
airforce *n* **88**
airline *n* **104**
airmail *n* **45**
airman *n* **88**
airport *n* **43, 104**
airship *n* **103**
airtight container *n* **52**
aisle, aisles *n* **48, 80, 103, 126**
alarm *n* **50**
alarm clock *n* **30**
alarm goes off *phr* **09**
Albania *n* **151, 153**
Albanian *adj* **153**
albatross *n* **160**
albertonectes *n* **157**
album *n* **129**
alcohol-free beer *n* **68**
ale *n* **68**
alfalfa *n* **86**
Algeria *n* **149, 152**
Algerian *adj* **152**
alien *n* **139**
alkali *n* **76**
alkali metals *n* **78**
alkaline earth metals *n* **78**
all-terrain vehicle *n* **100**
allergic *adj* **23**
allergy *n* **19**
alley *n* **42**
alligator clip *n* **75**
alloy *n* **76**
allspice *n* **59**
almond milk *n* **61**
almond oil *n* **60**
almonds *n* **58, 68**
aloe *n* **167**
alpaca *n* **165**
alpine plants *n* **41**
alternating current *n* **33, 75**
alto *n* **126**
aluminum *n* **78, 156**
always *adj* **171**
amaryllis *n* **167**
amazed *adj* **06**
amazing *adj* **177**
Amazon *n* **145**
ambitious *adj* **10, 93**
ambulance *n* **21, 50**
ambulance stretcher *n* **50**
American *adj* **152**
American alligator *n* **163**
American curl *n* **164**
American football field *n* **107**
American football *n* **107**
American football positions *n* **107**
americium *n* **78**
amethyst *n* **156**
amount *n* **45**
amp *n* **33**
ampersand *n* **175**
amphibians *n* **163**
amphibious vehicle *n* **88**
amplifier *n* **129**
amulet *n* **139**
amused *adj* **06**
analytics *n* **93**
anchor *n* **105, 119**
anchovies *n* **64**
Ancient Egyptian hieroglyphs *n* **175**
Ancient Greek temple *n* **44**
ancient ruins *n* **44**
Andean condor *n* **160**
Andorra *n* **151, 153**
Andorran *adj* **153**
anemone *n* **134, 166**
anesthesiologist *n* **90**
Angel Falls *n* **145**
angle *n* **74**
angler *n* **121**
angler fish *n* **166**
Angola *n* **149, 152**
Angolan *adj* **152**
Angora *n* **164**
angry *adj* **06**
animal cell *n* **77**
animation *n* **127**
anise *n* **59**
ankle *n* **01-02**
ankle boots *n* **17**
ankle strap heels *n* **17**
ankle weights *n* **124**
anklet *n* **16**
anniversary *n* **07**
annoyed *adj* **06**
annoying *adj* **177**
annual *n* **41**
annual general meeting (AGM) *n* **95**
anorak *n* **15**
answer *v* **73**
ant *n* **162**
anteater *n* **159**
antenna *n* **25, 97**
antenna *n* **162**
anther *n* **38**
anti-inflammatory *n* **49**
antibiotics *n* **49**
antifreeze *n* **97**
Antigua and Barbuda *n* **150, 152**
Antiguan *adj* **152**
antimony *n* **78**
antiques store *n* **46**
antiseptic *n* **20**
antiseptic wipes *n* **20**
antler *n* **159**
anxious *adj* **06**
any other business *phr* **95**
apartment *n* **25**
apartment *n* **131**
apartment building *n* **25, 43**
apartment buzzer *n* **25**
apex *n* **74**
apostrophe *n* **175**
app developer *n* **89**
appeal *n* **85**
appearance *n* **12**
appendicitis *n* **19**
appendix *n* **04**
appetizer *n* **69**
applause *n* **126**
apple *n* **58**
apple corer *n* **28**
apple juice *n* **65**
applicant *n* **81**
application form *n* **92**
apply for a job *v* **92**
applying for a job *n* **92**
appointment *n* **20, 81**
appreciative *adj* **06**
apprentice *n* **81, 92**
approachable *adj* **10**
apricot *n* **57**
April *n* **172**
apron *n* **13, 29**
aquamarine *n* **156**
aquarium *n* **164**
Aquarius *n* **144**
Arabic script *n* **175**
arbor knot *n* **121**
arc *n* **74, 112**
arch *n* **02, 41, 44**
arch window *n* **32**
archeological site *n* **132**
archeologist *n* **79**
archeology *n* **79**
archer *n* **125**
archery *n* **125**
archipelago *n* **147**

architect *n* **90**
architecture *n* **44**
archive *n* **79**
Arctic *n* **159**
Arctic Circle *n* **145**
Arctic fox *n* **159**
Arctic hare *n* **159**
Arctic tern *n* **160**
Arctic wolf *n* **159**
area *n* **74, 174**
arena *n* **120**
Argentina *n* **149, 152**
Argentinian *adj* **152**
argon *n* **78**
Aries *n* **144**
arm, arms *n* **01, 126**
arm circles *n* **124**
arm protection *n* **110**
armadillo *n* **159**
armband *n* **118**
armchair *n* **26**
armed drone *n* **88**
armed forces *n* **88**
Armenia *n* **150, 153**
Armenian *adj* **153**
armor *n* **79**
armored vehicle *n* **88**
armpit *n* **01**
armrest *n* **99, 103**
army *n* **88**
aromatherapy *n* **24**
arrest *n* **50**
arrival *n* **43**
arrive *v* **09**
arrive early *v* **09**
arrive home *v* **09**
arrive late *v* **09**
arrive on time *v* **09**
arrogant *adj* **10**
arrow *n* **79, 125**
arrow slit *n* **44**
arsenic *n* **78**
art, arts *n* **73, 91, 141-142**
art college *n* **80**
Art Deco *n* **130**
art gallery *n* **43, 130, 132**
Art Nouveau *n* **130**
art school *n* **80**
art store *n* **46**
art therapy *n* **24**
artery *n* **04**
artichoke heart *n* **56**
artichoke *n* **56**
article *n* **138**
articulated bus *n* **99**
artificial intelligence *n* **83**
artisan *n* **79**
artist *n* **90, 141**
arugula *n* **55**
arum lily *n* **167**
ash *n* **145**
ash cloud *n* **145**
Asia *n* **150, 153**
Asian *adj* **153**
Asian elephant *n* **159**
Asian vine snake *n* **163**
ask directions *v* **148**
asparagus *n* **56**
asparagus tip *n* **56**
assertive *adj* **10, 93**
astatine *n* **78**
asterisk *n* **175**
asteroid *n* **143**
asthma *n* **19**
astigmatism *n* **22**
astronaut *n* **143**
astronomy *n* **144**
at sign *n* **83, 175**
at symbol *n* **83, 175**
athlete *n* **89, 116**
athletics *n* **116, 125**
athletics track *n* **116**
Atlantic puffin *n* **160**
Atlantic salmon *n* **166**
atlas moth *n* **162**
atlas *n* **73**
ATM *n* **45**
ATV riding *n* **133**
atmosphere *n* **143, 155**
atoll *n* **147**
atom *n* **76**
attachment *n* **83**
attack helicopter *n* **88**
attack zone *n* **110**
attend a meeting *v* **95**
attic *n* **25**
attractions *n* **132**
aubergines *n* **56**
auburn hair *n* **12**
audience *n* **126, 127**
audio *n* **136**
audio guide *n* **130**
audition *n* **127**
auditorium *n* **80**
August *n* **172**
aunt *n* **05**
aurora *n* **144, 155**
Australia *n* **150, 153**
Australian *adj* **153**
Australian little penguin *n* **161**
Austria *n* **151, 153**
Austrian *adj* **153**
author *n* **138**
auto racing *n* **123**
auto repair shop *n* **98**
autobiography *n* **138**
autocue *n* **84**
automatic *n* **99**
automatic toilet cleaner *n* **34**
automotive industry *n* **91**
autumn leaf *n* **169**
avalanche *n* **122**
avatar *n* **84**
avenue *n* **43**
avocado *n* **56**
avocado toast *n* **71**
avocado tree *n* **167**
awful *adj* **177**
awning *n* **65**
ax *n* **36, 50, 79**
axle *n* **100**
ayran *n* **61**
ayurveda *n* **24**
azalea *n* **38**
Azerbaijan *n* **150, 153**
Azerbaijani *adj* **153**

B

babies' clothes *n* **13**
baboon *n* **158**
baby *n* **05**
baby bath *n* **08**
baby carriage *n* **08**
baby changing facilities *n* **47**
baby corn *n* **55**
baby formula *n* **08**
baby monitor *n* **08, 30**
baby products *n* **48**
baby teeth *n* **22**
back *adj* **03**
back *n* **26**
back bacon *n* **53**
back brush *n* **31**
back door *n* **97**
back seat *n* **99**
back up *v* **83**
back-flip *n* **118**
backache *n* **19**
backboard *n* **112**
backdrop *n* **126**
backgammon *n* **140**
backhand *n* **114**
backing singers *n* **129**
backpack *n* **16, 135**
backpack sprayer *n* **40**
backsplash *n* **27**
backstay *n* **119**
backstop net *n* **113**
backstroke *n* **118**
backswing *n* **115**
bacon *n* **53, 71**
bacteria *n* **77, 157**
Bactrian camel *n* **158**
bad *adj* **52, 177**
bad robot *n* **139**
badge *n* **50**
badminton *n* **114**
bag, bags *n* **16, 52**
bag store *n* **47**
bagel *n* **62, 71**
baggage claim *n* **104**
baggage trailer *n* **104**
bagpipes *n* **129**
baguette *n* **62**
baggy *adj* **13, 176**
Bahamas *n* **150, 162**
Bahamian *adj* **152**
Bahrain *n* **151, 153**
Bahraini *adj* **153**
bail *n* **85, 111**
Baisakhi *n* **07**
bait *n* **121**
bait *v* **121**
bake *v* **29, 62-63**
baked *adj* **72**
baked beans *n* **71**
baker *n* **62**
bakery *n* **46, 48, 62-63**
baking *n* **29**
baking pan *n* **29**
baklava *n* **63**
balance wheel *n* **142**
balanced diet *n* **23**
balcony *n* **126**
balcony *n* **25**
bald *adj* **12**
bald eagle *n* **160**
ball *n* **02, 08, 109-110, 112, 114**
ball boy *n* **114**
ball girl *n* **114**
ballerina *n* **126**
ballet *n* **126**
ballet flats *n* **17**
ballet leotard *n* **126**
ballet slippers *n* **126**
ballistic missile *n* **88**
balloon *n* **08**
ballpoint pen *n* **175**
balsamic vinegar *n* **60**
bamboo *n* **41, 55, 167**
banana *n* **58**
band *n* **129**
bandage *n* **20, 49**
banded sea krait *n* **166**
Bangladesh *n* **150, 153**
Bangladeshi *adj* **153**
bangle *n* **16**
banister *n* **25-26**
banjo *n* **129**
bank *n* **45, 94**
bank loan *n* **45**
bank statement *n* **45**
banking *n* **91**
banner *n* **109**
baobab tree *n* **169**
baptism *n* **07**
bar, bars *n* **30, 68, 109, 124**
bar chart *n* **95**
bar counter *n* **68**
bar mitzvah *n* **07**
bar snacks *n* **68**
bar stool *n* **68**
bar tender *n* **69**
barb *n* **121**
Barbadian *adj* **152**
Barbados *n* **150, 152**
barbecue *n* **135**
barbell *n* **124**
barber *n* **89**
barberry *n* **168**
Barbudan *adj* **152**
barcode *n* **48**
bare branches *n* **172**
bargain *n* **48**
barista *n* **65, 89**
baritone *n* **126**
barium *n* **78**
bark *v* **164**
barley *n* **86**
barn *n* **86**
barn owl *n* **161**
barnacle *n* **134, 166**
barracuda *n* **166**
barrel cactus *n* **168**
Barrier Reef *n* **145**
bartender *n* **68, 89**
basa *n* **54**
basalt *n* **156**
base *n* **74, 76**
baseball *n* **113**
baseball cap *n* **16**
baseball cleats *n* **17**
baseball game *n* **113**
baseboard *n* **30**
baseline *n* **114**
basement *n* **25, 47**
basil *n* **59**
basin *n* **22, 33**
basket *n* **48, 101, 103, 112, 164**
basket of fruit *n* **57**
basketball *n* **112**
basketball player *n* **112**
basking shark *n* **166**
Basotho *adj* **152**
bass *n* **126**
bass clef *n* **128**
bass drum *n* **128**
bass guitarist *n* **129**
basset hound *n* **164**
bassoon *n* **128**
bat *n* **111, 113-114, 158**
bat *v* **111, 113**
bat mitzvah *n* **07**
bath towel *n* **31**
bath toys *n* **31**
bath tub *n* **31**
bathmat *n* **31**
bathrobe *n* **14, 31**
bathroom *n* **31**

bathroom exhaust fan *n* **31**
bathroom scale *n* **31**
baton *n* **50**
baton *n* **116**
batsman *n* **111**
Battenberg markings *n* **50**
batter *n* **111, 113**
battering ram *n* **79**
battery *n* **75, 83, 98**
battery pack *n* **35**
batting glove *n* **113**
battle *n* **79, 88**
battlement *n* **44**
battleship *n* **105**
Bauhaus *n* **130**
bay *n* **147**
bay leaf *n* **59**
bay tree *n* **38**
bay window *n* **25**
bayonet base *n* **33**
be absent *v* **95**
be born *v* **07**
be delayed *v* **104**
be laid off *v* **81**
be late *v* **09, 171**
be promoted *v* **81**
be sent off *v* **109**
be unemployed *v* **81**
beach *n* **134, 147–148**
beach bag *n* **134**
beach ball *n* **134**
beach hut *n* **134**
beach umbrella *n* **134**
bead maze *n* **08**
beagle *n* **164**
beak *n* **161**
beaker *n* **76**
beam *n* **125**
bean sprouts *n* **55**
beanie *n* **16**
bean *n* **56**
bear's head tooth *n* **170**
beard *n* **12**
beat *n* **129**
beat eggs *v* **29**
beautiful *adj* **12, 177**
beauty *n* **18, 47**
beauty treatments *n* **18**
bed *n* **30**
bed and breakfast *n* **131**
bed linen *n* **30**
bedrock *n* **145**
bedroom *n* **30**
bedside lamp *n* **30**
bee *n* **165**
beech *n* **168**
beef *n* **53**
beehive *n* **86, 162**
beer *n* **52, 68**
beer tap *n* **68**
beet greens *n* **55**
beet *n* **56**
beg *v* **164**
begonia *n* **38**
behind *prep* **148, 180**
being a fast learner *n* **93**
Belarus *n* **151, 153**
Belarusian *adj* **153**
Belgian *adj* **153**
Belgium *n* **151, 153**
Belize *n* **150, 152**
Belizean *adj* **152**
bell *n* **99**
bell tower *n* **44**
belt *n* **15–16, 117**
beluga *n* **166**
bench *n* **124**
bend *v* **126**
benefits *n* **81**
Bengal *n* **164**
Benin *n* **149, 152**
Beninese *adj* **152**
beret *n* **16**
berkelium *n* **78**
Bermuda shorts *n* **14**
berries *n* **57**
beryllium *n* **78**
beside *prep* **180**
best friend *n* **07**
bestseller *n* **138**
between *prep* **148, 180**
beverage, beverages *n* **65, 69**
bhangra *n* **129**
Bhutan *n* **150, 153**
Bhutanese *adj* **153**
biathlon *n* **122**
bib *n* **13**
bibliography *n* **138**
bicep curl *n* **124**
biceps *n* **03**
bicuspids *n* **03**
bicycle *n* **101**
bicycling *n* **133**
bidet *n* **31**
biennial *n* **41**
bifocal *n* **22**
big *adj* **176**
Big Bang *n* **144**
Big Ben *n* **44**
Big Dipper *n* **144**
big toe *n* **02**
bike helmet *n* **101**
bike lane *n* **101**
bike parking *n* **43**
bike path *n* **43**
bike rack *n* **101**
bikini *n* **134**
bilberry *n* **57**
bill *n* **161, 32**
bill *n* **45, 94**
binder clip *n* **82**
binoculars *n* **144**
biochemistry *n* **76**
biodegradable waste *n* **33**
biography *n* **138**
biologist *n* **77**
biology *n* **73, 77, 80**
biomass energy *n* **51**
biometric passport *n* **104**
biotechnology *n* **91**
biplane *n* **103**
birch *n* **168**
bird of paradise *n* **160**
bird-of-paradise *n* **167**
bird seed *n* **164**
bird-watching *n* **133**
bird's eye chiles *n* **59**
birds *n* **160, 161**
birdwatcher *n* **161**
birth *n* **08**
birth certificate *n* **07**
birthday *n* **07**
birthday cake *n* **63**
birthday candles *n* **63**
birthday card *n* **07**
biscuits *n* **63**
bishop *n* **140**
bismuth *n* **78**
Bissau-Guinean *adj* **152**
bistro *n* **69**
bit *n* **120**
bite *n* **19**
bite *v* **52, 121**
bitter *adj* **52, 56**
black *adj* **140–141**
black *n* **140–141**
black belt *n* **117**
black coffee *n* **65**
black currant *n* **57**
black hair *n* **12**
black hole *n* **144**
black mustard *n* **59**
black olives *n* **64**
black pudding *n* **70**
black swan *n* **161**
black tea *n* **66**
black trumpet *n* **170**
black widow spider *n* **162**
black woodpecker *n* **160**
blackberry *n* **57**
blackbird *n* **160**
blacksmith *n* **79**
blade *n* **33, 40, 51, 117**
blanket *n* **30**
bleach *n* **34**
bleat *v* **165**
bleed *v* **20**
blender *n* **27, 65**
blindfold *n* **125**
blindside flanker *n* **108**
blink *v* **02**
blister *n* **19**
blizzard *n* **154**
block *v* **84, 112, 117**
blocker *n* **112**
blocking glove *n* **110**
blog *n* **84**
blogger *n* **84**
blond hair *n* **12**
blonde hair *n* **12**
blood knot *n* **121**
blood orange *n* **57**
blood pressure *n* **20**
blood pressure monitor *n* **21**
blood sausage *n* **71**
blood test *n* **20–21**
blossom *n* **169**
blouse *n* **14**
blow *v* **11**
blow hole *n* **166**
blow out *v* **63**
blowout *n* **123**
blue *adj* **01, 141**
blue *n* **01, 141**
blue cheese *n* **61**
blue crab *n* **166**
blue line *n* **110**
blue tang *n* **166**
blue whale *n* **166**
blue-tongued skink *n* **163**
blueberry *n* **57**
blues *n* **129**
Bluetooth headset *n* **83**
Bluetooth speaker *n* **136**
blush *v* **02**
blush *n* **18**
boar *n* **53, 159**
board *n* **119**
board *v* **106**
board a plane *v* **104**
board game *n* **08**
board games *n* **140**
board of directors *n* **95**
boarding gate *n* **104**
boarding pass *n* **104**
boardroom *n* **95**
boards *n* **110**
boardwalk *n* **134**
boat shoes *n* **17**
boat's wheel *n* **119**
boater *n* **16**
boats *n* **105**
bob *n* **12**
bobbin *n* **142**
bobcat *n* **159**
bobsled *n* **122**
boccia *n* **125**
body *n* **129**
body lotion *n* **31**
body powder *n* **31**
body systems *n* **04**
bodyboarding *n* **119, 134**
bodyguard *n* **90**
bodysuit *n* **13**
bodywork *n* **98, 123**
bohrium *n* **78**
boil *v* **29**
boiled *adj* **72**
boiled egg *n* **61, 71**
boiling *adj* **154**
boiling point *n* **154**
bok choi *n* **55**
bold *adj* **175**
bold *n* **175**
Bolivia *n* **149, 152**
Bolivian *adj* **152**
bollard, bollards *n* **43, 105**
Bolognese sauce *n* **64**
bolt *n* **25, 36**
Bombay *n* **164**
Bombay earth snake *n* **163**
bomber *n* **88**
bomber jacket *n* **15**
bone *n* **03**
bone meal *n* **39**
boned *adj* **54**
bongo drums *n* **128**
bonsai tree *n* **38**
bonus *n* **81**
boogie board *n* **119**
book, books *n* **26, 80, 138**
book a vacation *v* **131**
bookcase *n* **26**
bookshelf *n* **80**
bookstore *n* **46**
boom *n* **50, 119**
booster *n* **143**
boot, boots *n* **17, 100**
boot shapers *n* **17**
booties *n* **13**
borage *n* **59**
border collie *n* **164**
bored *adj* **06**
boring *adj* **177**
boron *n* **78**
borrow *v* **80**
Bosnia and Herzegovina *n* **151, 153**
Bosnian *adj* **153**
boss *n* **81**
botanical gardens *n* **132**
botanist *n* **77**
botany *n* **77**
Botswana *n* **149, 152**
Botswanan *adj* **152**
bottle *n* **08, 52**
bottle opener *n* **28, 68**
bottled oils *n* **60**
bougainvillea *n* **168**
bounce *v* **112**
bound ankle pose *n* **24**
boundary *n* **111, 113**
bouquet *n* **15, 47**
bouquet garni *n* **59**
boutique *n* **46**
bow *n* **79, 119, 125**
bow *v* **02**
bow pose *n* **24**
bow tie *n* **16**
bowl *n* **27, 33, 52**
bowl *v* **111**
bowler *n* **111**

bowling *n* **125**
bowling ball *n* **125**
bowling crease *n* **111**
bowling pin *n* **125, 08**
box, boxes *n* **32, 52, 126**
box office *n* **127**
box spring *n* **30**
boxer *n* **164**
boxer shorts *n* **14**
boxercise *n* **124**
boxing *n* **117**
boxing gloves *n* **117**
boxing match *n* **117**
boxing ring *n* **117**
boy *n* **05**
boyfriend *n* **05**
bra *n* **14**
brace *n* **35**
bracelet *n* **16**
braces *n* **22**
brachiosaurus *n* **157**
brackets *n* **175**
braids *n* **12**
Braille *n* **175**
brain *n* **04**
brake *n* **99-101**
brake cooling intake *n* **123**
brake fluid reservoir *n* **98**
brake lever *n* **101**
brake pad *n* **101**
brake pedal *n* **100**
brake rotor *n* **100**
brake *v* **98, 101**
branch *n* **81, 169**
branch manager *n* **45**
brandy *n* **68**
brass *adj* **176**
brass *n* **128, 176**
brave *adj* **10**
bray *v* **165**
Brazil *n* **149, 152**
brazil nuts *n* **58**
Brazilian *adj* **152**
bread, breads *n* **62, 71**
bread basket *n* **71**
bread flour *n* **62**
bread knife *n* **28**
breadfruit *n* **56**
break down *v* **98, 178**
break even *v* **94**
break in *n* **50**
break up *v* **178**
breakdown assistance *n* **98**
breaker *n* **33**
breakfast *n* **26, 71**
breakfast buffet *n* **71**
breakfast burrito *n* **71**
breakfast cereals *n* **48**
breakfast roll *n* **71**
breakfast tray *n* **131**
breast *n* **01, 53**
breastbone *n* **03**
breaststroke *n* **118**
Breathalyzer *n* **50**
breathe *v* **02**
breathtaking *adj* **177**
breed *v* **120**
breeze *n* **154**
breezy *adj* **154**
bribery *n* **85**
brick *adj* **176**
brick, bricks *n* **35, 87, 176**
bride *n* **07**
bridesmaid's dress *n* **15**
bridge crane *n* **106**
bridge *n* **02, 43, 105, 125, 129, 140**
bridge pose *n* **24**
bridle *n* **120**
Brie *n* **64**
briefs *n* **14**
briefcase *n* **16**
brilliant *adj* **177**
bring *v* **11**
brioche *n* **62, 71**
British *adj* **153**
British shorthair *n* **164**
broadcast *v* **84**
broadcaster *n* **89**
broadleaf forest *n* **159**
broccoli *n* **55-56**
brogues *n* **17**
broil *v* **29**
broken bone *n* **19**
bromine *n* **78**
bronze *adj* **176**
bronze *n* **116, 176**
Bronze age *n* **79**
brooch *n* **16**
broom *n* **34, 40**
broomstick *n* **139**
broth *n* **72**
brother *n* **05**
brother-in-law *n* **05**
browband *n* **120**
brown *adj* **01**
brown *n* **01, 141**
brown bear *n* **159**
brown bread *n* **62**
brown flour *n* **62**
brown hair *n* **12**
bruise *n* **19**
brunch *n* **69**
Brunei *n* **151, 153**
Bruneian *adj* **153**
brush *n* **34, 141**
brush *v* **22**
brush your hair *v* **09**
brush your teeth *v* **09**
Brussels sprouts *n* **55**
bubble bath *n* **18, 31**
bucket *n* **34, 37, 40**
bucket turn *n* **118**
buckle *n* **16**
buckled shoes *n* **17**
buckwheat flour *n* **62**
budgerigar *n* **160, 164**
budget *n* **94**
budgie *n* **160, 164**
buffalo *n* **159**
buffer *n* **102**
buffet *n* **69**
bugs *n* **162**
build *v* **11, 87**
building, buildings *n* **42-44, 148**
building blocks/ bricks *n* **08**
Bulgaria *n* **151, 153**
Bulgarian *adj* **153**
bull *n* **165**
bull-nose pliers *n* **36**
bull's-eye *n* **140**
bulldozer *n* **87**
bullet train *n* **102**
bulletin board *n* **82**
bumble bee *n* **162**
bump *v* **112**
bumper *n* **97**
bumps *n* **96**
bun *n* **12**
bunch *n* **47**
bungee jumping *n* **125**
bunker *n* **115**
Bunsen burner *n* **76**
buoy *n* **106, 119, 134**
burgee *n* **119**
burger *n* **70**
burger bar *n* **70**
burglar alarm *n* **25**
burglary *n* **85**
Burj Khalifa *n* **44**
Burkina Faso *n* **149, 152**
Burkinabe *adj* **152**
Burma (Myanmar) *n* **150, 153**
Burmese *adj* **153**
burn *n* **19, 29**
burner *n* **27, 103**
burrow *v* **159**
Burundi *n* **149, 152**
Burundian *adj* **152**
bus, buses *n* **43, 99**
bus driver *n* **90**
bus shelter *n* **99**
bus station *n* **42, 99**
bus stop *n* **25**
bus ticket *n* **99**
bus transfer *n* **104**
business class *n* **103**
business deal *n* **81**
business lunch *n* **81**
business man *n* **81**
business trip *n* **81**
businesslike attitude *n* **93**
businessman *n* **90**
businesswoman *n* **81, 90**
bust dart *n* **142**
butcher *n* **46, 53, 89**
butter *n* **61, 71**
butter dish *n* **28**
butter knife *n* **27**
buttercup *n* **38, 168**
buttercup squash *n* **56**
butterfly, butterflies *n* **77, 118, 162**
buttermilk *n* **61**
butternut squash *n* **56**
buttock *n* **03**
button, buttons *n* **15, 142**
button hole *n* **15**
buy *v* **32, 46**
buy groceries *v* **09, 34**
buying a house *n* **32**
buzz *v* **162**

C

cab *n* **50**
cabbage *n* **55**
cabbage white butterfly *n* **162**
cabin *n* **32, 103, 105, 131**
cabinet *n* **27**
cable *n* **101**
cable car *n* **122**
cable TV *n* **137**
cacti *n* **41**
caddy *n* **115**
caddy bin *n* **155**
cadmium *n* **78**
café *n* **42, 46, 65-66**
cafetière *n* **28**
cage *n* **164**
cake, cakes *n* **63**
cake pan *n* **28-29**
cake topper *n* **63**
calamari *n* **54**
calcite *n* **156**
calcium *n* **23, 49, 78**
calculator *n* **73-74**
calendar *n* **82, 172**
calf *n* **01, 03, 165**
californium *n* **78**
call a friend *v* **09**
call a plumber *v* **33**
call in sick *v* **81**
call off *v* **178**
call up *v* **178**
call your family *v* **09**
calligraphy *n* **175**
calm *adj* **06, 10, 93**
calm down *v* **178**
calorie-controlled diet *n* **23**
calories *n* **23**
Cambodia *n* **150, 153**
Cambodian *adj* **153**
Cambrian *adj* **157**
Cambrian *n* **157**
camel pose *n* **24**
camellia *n* **38**
Camembert *n* **64**
camera *n* **83-84**
camera crane *n* **84**
camera mount *n* **123**
camera operator *n* **84, 127**
Cameroon *n* **149, 152**
Cameroonian *adj* **152**
camisole *n* **14**
camouflage *n* **88**
camp *v* **135**
camp bed *n* **135**
campfire *n* **135**
campground *n* **135, 148**
camping *n* **135**
camping equipment *n* **135**
camping facilities *n* **135**
campion *n* **168**
campus *n* **80**
can *n* **52**
can opener *n* **28**
Canada *n* **150, 152**
Canada goose *n* **160**
Canadian *adj* **152**
canary *n* **160**
Canary melon *n* **58**
cancel *v* **69**
Cancer *n* **144**
candle *n* **26, 30**
candle magic *n* **139**
candlestick *n* **26**
candy *n* **67**
candy cane *n* **67**
candy store *n* **67**
canes *n* **40**
canines *n* **03**
canned *adj* **56**
canned drink *n* **70**
canned food *n* **48**
canned tomato *n* **71**
cannelloni *n* **64**
cannon *n* **79**
Caño Cristales *n* **145**
canoe *n* **105**
canola oil *n* **60**
canopy *n* **103, 125**
canopy *n* **97**
cantaloupe *n* **58**
canter *v* **120**
canvas *n* **141**
canyon *n* **146**
cap *n* **118, 170**
cap sleeve *n* **15**
capacity *n* **174**
cape *n* **147**

cape gooseberry *n* **57**
Cape Verde *n* **149, 152**
Cape Verdean *adj* **152**
capers *n* **64**
capital letters *n* **175**
capoeira *n* **117**
cappuccino *n* **65**
Capricorn *n* **144**
capsize *v* **119**
capsules *n* **49**
captain *n* **105**
capuchin monkey *n* **159**
capybara *n* **159**
car, cars *n* **97-99, 102**
car exterior *n* **97**
car interior *n* **99**
car rental *n* **104**
car stereo *n* **99**
car theft *n* **85**
car wash *n* **97**
caravan *n* **135**
caraway seeds *n* **59**
carbohydrates *n* **23**
carbon *n* **78**
carbon dioxide *n* **155**
carbonated *adj* **52**
Carboniferous *adj* **157**
card machine *n* **45, 48**
cardamom *n* **59**
cardboard *n* **141**
cardigan *n* **14**
cardinal numbers *n* **173**
cardiology *n* **21**
cardiovascular *n* **04**
care for *v* **178**
cargo *n* **102, 106**
cargo pants *n* **12**
cargo plane *n* **103**
Caribbean *n* **152**
Caribbean *adj* **152**
caribou *n* **159**
caring *adj* **10**
carnation *n* **38**
carnelian *n* **156**
carnival *n* **07**
carousel *n* **133**
carp *n* **54**
carpenter *n* **89**
carpentry bit *n* **36**
carpeting *n* **30**
carriage *n* **102**
carriage race *n* **120**
carrot *n* **56**
carry *v* **11**
carry-on *n* **103-104**
carryout *n* **70**
cart *n* **102, 104, 115**
cartilage *n* **03**
cartographer *n* **148**
carton *n* **52**
cartoon *n* **137**
carve *v* **29, 35**
carving fork *n* **28**
case *n* **22**
cash machine *n* **45**
cash register *n* **48, 68, 94**
cashew, cashews *n* **58, 68**
cashier *n* **45, 48**
cassava *n* **56**
casserole dish *n* **28**
cassowary *n* **160**
cast *n* **126-127**
cast *v* **121**
cast a spell *v* **139**
cast-iron plant *n* **167**
castle *n* **44**
castor oil plant *n* **169**
casual clothes *n* **14**
casualty *n* **88**
cat breeds *n* **164**
catamaran *n* **105**
catapult *n* **79**
cataract *n* **22**
catch *v* **11, 107, 113, 121**
catch a train *v* **102**
catch the bus *v* **09**
catch the train *v* **09**
catch up *v* **178**
catch-up TV *n* **137**
catcher *n* **113**
catcher glove *n* **110**
catering *n* **91**
caterpillar *n* **77, 162**
catfish *n* **54**
cattail *n* **167**
cattle *n* **165**
cauldron *n* **139**
cauliflower *n* **56**
caulk *n* **37**
cautious *adj* **10**
caver *n* **146**
caves *n* **146**
caving *n* **146**
cavity *n* **22**
cavolo nero *n* **55**
cayenne pepper *n* **59**
CD *n* **136**
CD player *n* **136**
cedar of Lebanon *n* **167**
cedilla *n* **175**
ceiling *n* **26**
ceiling fan *n* **33**
celandine *n* **168**
celebration cakes *n* **63**
celebrations *n* **07**
celebrity *n* **127**
celeriac *n* **56**
celery *n* **55**
celery allergy *n* **23**
cell *n* **85**
cell membrane *n* **77**
cell phone *n* **82**
cell wall *n* **77**
cello *n* **128**
Celsius *n* **154**
cement *n* **87**
cement mixer *n* **87**
cemetery *n* **43**
Cenozoic (new life) *adj* **157**
Cenozoic (new life) *n* **157**
centaur *n* **139**
center *n* **74, 107, 110, 112**
center part *n* **12**
center speaker *n* **136**
centerboard *n* **119**
centimeter *n* **174**
centipede *n* **162**
Central African *adj* **152**
Central African Republic *n* **149, 152**
Central America *n* **150, 152**
Central American *adj* **152**
centre circle *n* **109**
centrifugal force *n* **75**
centripetal force *n* **75**
century *n* **172**
CEO (chief executive officer) *n* **81**
ceramic *adj* **176**
ceramic *n* **176**
Cerberus *n* **139**
cereal *n* **71**
cereal bowl *n* **71**
Ceres *n* **143**
cerium *n* **78**
cervical vertebrae *n* **03**
cervix *n* **04**
cesium *n* **78**
CFL (compact fluorescent lamp) bulb *n* **33**
Chad *n* **149, 152**
Chadian *adj* **152**
chain *n* **16, 101**
chair *n* **26, 82**
chair pose *n* **24**
chairlift *n* **122**
chalet *n* **32, 131**
chalk *n* **39, 156**
challah *n* **62**
chamomile tea *n* **66**
Champagne *n* **68**
championship *n* **114**
change *v* **14**
change a light bulb *v* **35**
change gear *v* **101**
change money *v* **45**
change the channel *v* **137**
change the sheets *v* **34**
change trains *v* **102**
changing mat *n* **30**
changing rooms *n* **47**
changing table *n* **30**
channel *n* **137, 147**
chanterelle *n* **56, 170**
chapati *n* **62**
chapter *n* **138**
character *n* **138**
charcoal *n* **135, 141**
charentais *n* **58**
charge *n* **50, 75, 85**
charge *v* **165**
charging cable *n* **83**
chariot *n* **79**
chase *v* **107**
chassis *n* **123**
chat *n* **83**
chat online *v* **09**
chat with friends *v* **09**
check *n* **45, 69, 94**
check in *v* **131, 178**
check out *v* **131, 178**
check the oil *v* **98**
check the tires *v* **98**
check your emails *v* **09**
check-in desk *n* **104**
check-up *n* **22**
checkered *adj* **12**
checkers *n* **140**
checking account *n* **45**
checkout *n* **48**
cheddar *n* **64**
cheek *n* **01**
cheerful *adj* **06**
cheerleader *n* **107**
cheese, cheeses *n* **61, 64, 71**
cheese platter *n* **69**
cheeseburger *n* **70**
cheesecake *n* **63**
cheetah *n* **158**
chef *n* **69, 90**
chef's coat *n* **13**
chef's hat *n* **13**
chef's uniform *n* **13**
Chelsea boots *n* **17**
chemical equation *n* **76**
chemical formula *n* **76**
chemical industry *n* **91**
chemical symbol *n* **76**
chemist *n* **76**
chemistry *n* **73, 76, 80**
chequered flag *n* **123**
cherry, cherries *n* **57, 169**
cherry tomatoes *n* **55**
chervil *n* **59**
chess *n* **140**
chessboard *n* **140**
chest *n* **01**
chest compressions *n* **20**
chest expander *n* **124**
chest press *n* **124**
chest protection *n* **117**
chest protector *n* **107**
chestnuts *n* **58**
chew *v* **52**
chewing gum *n* **67**
chicane *n* **123**
chick *n* **165**
chicken *n* **53, 165**
chicken coop *n* **86**
chicken egg *n* **61**
chicken nuggets *n* **70**
chicken of the woods *n* **170**
chicken sandwich *n* **70**
chickenpox *n* **19**
chicory *n* **55**
chihuahua *n* **164**
child *n* **05**
child seat *n* **101**
childcare provider *n* **90**
child's pose *n* **24**
childbirth *n* **08**
childhood *n* **08**
children's book *n* **138**
children's department *n* **47**
children's show *n* **137**
children's ward *n* **21**
Chile *n* **149, 152**
chile, chiles *n* **56, 60, 64**
chile flakes *n* **59**
Chilean *adj* **152**
Chilean fire bush *n* **167**
chill out *v* **178**
chilled *adj* **52**
chills *n* **19**
chily *n* **56**
chimney *n* **25, 32, 87**
chimney pot *n* **25**
chimpanzee *n* **159**
chin *n* **01**
chin strap *n* **107**
China *n* **150, 153**
Chinese *adj* **153**
Chinese characters *n* **175**
Chinese hibiscus *n* **169**
Chinese hotpot *n* **72**
Chinese lantern *n* **169**
Chinese mahogany *n* **169**
Chinese money plant *n* **38**
chip *v* **115**
chipmunk *n* **159**
chips *n* **48, 68**
chiropractic *n* **24**
chisel *n* **36, 141**
chives *n* **59**
chlorine *n* **78**
chloroplast *n* **77**
chocolate bar *n* **67**
chocolate cake *n* **63**
chocolate chip cookie *n* **63**
chocolate milkshake *n* **61, 65**
chocolate spread *n* **60**
choir *n* **128**
choker *n* **16**
cholesterol *n* **23**
choose *v* **46**
chop *n* **53**
chop *v* **29, 39, 117**
chopped salad *n* **72**

chopsticks *n* **27**
chord *n* **128**
chorizo *n* **53, 64**
choux pastry *n* **63**
christening *n* **07**
Christmas *n* **07**
chromium *n* **78, 156**
chromosome *n* **77**
chrysalis *n* **77**
chrysanthemum *n* **38**
chuck *n* **35**
chukka boots *n* **17**
church *n* **43-44**
chutes and ladders *n* **140**
chutney *n* **60, 72**
cider *n* **68**
cider vinegar *n* **60**
cilantro *n* **59**
cinder block *n* **87**
cinematographer *n* **127**
cinnamon *n* **59**
cinnamon rolls *n* **71**
cinnamon stick *n* **59**
circle *n* **74**
circuit *n* **83**
circuit board *n* **75**
circuit training *n* **124**
circular saw *n* **35**
circulation desk *n* **80**
circumference *n* **74**
circumflex *n* **175**
cistern *n* **33**
citrine *n* **156**
citrus fruit *n* **57**
clam *n* **54**
clamp *n* **35, 76**
clap *v* **02**
clapper board *n* **84**
clarinet *n* **128**
class *n* **73**
classical *adj* **129**
Classicism *n* **130**
classroom *n* **73**
clavicle *n* **03**
claw *n* **161**
clay *n* **39, 141**
clean *adj* **176**
clean the bathroom *v* **34**
clean the car *v* **09**
clean the oven *v* **34**
clean the windows *v* **34**
clean up *v* **34, 178**
cleaned *adj* **54**
cleaner *n* **89**
cleaning *n* **34**
cleanser *n* **18**
clear the table *v* **09, 34**
cleat *n* **119**
cleaver *n* **28**
clementine *n* **57**
click *n* **83**
client, clients *n* **81, 85**
cliff *n* **147**
climate *n* **155**
climate change *n* **155**
climb *v* **11**
climber *n* **41**
clinch knot *n* **121**
clipboard *n* **82**
cloak *n* **15**
cloakroom *n* **130**
cloche *n* **16**
clock *n* **44, 171**
clock radio *n* **30**
clockwise *adv* **148**
clogs *n* **17**
closed *adj* **48, 132**
closed to bicycles *adj* **96**
closed to pedestrians *adj* **96**
closet *n* **30**
cloth *n* **34**
clothes *n* **13-15**
clothes moth *n* **162**
clothes pin *n* **34**
clothesline *n* **34**
clothing *n* **100**
cloud, clouds *n* **51, 154**
cloudy *adj* **154**
cloves *n* **59**
clown *n* **89**
clownfish *n* **166**
club *n* **140**
club sandwich *n* **70**
clubhouse *n* **115**
clumsy *adj* **10**
clutch *n* **99-100**
CMS (content management system) *n* **84**
co-pilot *n* **103**
co-worker *n* **81**
CO_2 bubbles *n* **62**
coach *n* **112-113**
coach's box *n* **113**
coal *n* **51**
coal mine *n* **51**
coastal features *n* **147**
coaster *n* **27, 68**
coastguard *n* **106**
coat hanger *n* **30**
coats *n* **15**
cobalt *n* **78**
cobra pose *n* **24**
coccyx *n* **03**
cockatiel *n* **164**
cockatoo *n* **161**
cockle *n* **54**
cockpit *n* **103, 123**
cockroach *n* **162**
cocktail *n* **68**
cocktail glass *n* **68**
cocktail shaker *n* **68**
cocoa *n* **169**
cocoa powder *n* **65**
coconut *n* **58**
coconut crab *n* **166**
coconut oil *n* **60**
coconut palm *n* **167**
coconut shell *n* **57**
coconut water *n* **58, 65**
cocoon *n* **162**
cod *n* **166**
cod fillet *n* **54**
coelophysis *n* **157**
coffee *n* **52, 65, 69, 71, 86**
coffee cup *n* **27**
coffee machine *n* **65, 68**
coffee press *n* **28**
coffee shop *n* **46**
coffee table *n* **26**
coins *n* **45, 94**
cola *n* **52**
colander *n* **28**
cold *adj* **154, 176**
cold *n* **19**
cold frame *v* **39**
cold front *n* **155**
cold meats *n* **71**
cold water *n* **31**
collaborate *v* **92**
collage *n* **141**
collar *n* **15, 142**
collarbone *n* **03**
collards *n* **55**
colleague *n* **07, 81, 92**
collection *n* **130**
college *n* **43, 80**
college departments *n* **80**
college schools *n* **80**
Colombia *n* **149, 152**
Colombian *adj* **152**
colon *n* **175**
colored pencils *n* **73**
coloring book *n* **138**
Colosseum *n* **44**
columbine *n* **168**
column *n* **44, 146**
comb *n* **12**
combat aircraft *n* **88**
combat sports *n* **117**
combination *adj* **18**
combine harvester *n* **86**
combined events *n* **116**
comedian *n* **89**
comedy *n* **126-127, 137**
comet *n* **143-144**
comic *n* **48, 138**
comma *n* **175**
commence *v* **95**
commercial break *n* **137**
commercial district *n* **42**
commis chef *n* **69**
commission *n* **94**
common earthball *n* **170**
common egg-eater *n* **163**
common green iguana *n* **163**
common houseleek *n* **168**
common poppy *n* **168**
common puffball *n* **170**
common snake-necked turtle *n* **163**
common toad *n* **163**
community website *n* **84**
commuters *n* **102**
Comoran *adj* **152**
Comoros *n* **149, 152**
company *n* **81**
compartment *n* **102**
compass *n* **73-74, 119, 135, 148**
competitive *adj* **93**
complain *v* **46**
complaint *n* **50**
compose *v* **128**
composer *n* **128**
composite *n* **85**
compost *n* **40**
compost bin *n* **40**
compost heap *n* **41**
compostable bags *n* **155**
composter *n* **40**
compound *n* **76**
compressed-air cylinder *n* **50**
computer, computers *n* **82-83**
computer desk *n* **83**
computer literacy *n* **93**
computing *n* **93**
concave lens *n* **75**
concealer *n* **18**
conceptual art *n* **130**
concert hall *n* **43**
conchiglie *n* **64**
concourse *n* **102**
concrete *adj* **176**
concrete *n* **35, 176**
concussion *n* **19**
condensed milk *n* **61**
condiment, condiments *n* **60, 70, 71-72**
conduct *v* **128**
conductor *n* **75, 102, 128**
cone *n* **74, 87**
conference *n* **95**
confident *adj* **06, 10, 93**
confused *adj* **06**
confusing *adj* **177**
conglomerate *n* **156**
Congolese *adj* **152**
coniferous forest *n* **146**
conifers *n* **41, 157, 167**
connection *n* **104**
conning tower *n* **105**
conservation *n* **130**
considerate *adj* **10**
console *n* **136**
constellation, constellations *n* **144**
construction *n* **87, 91**
construction ahead *n* **96**
construction site *n* **87**
construction waste *n* **33**
construction worker *n* **87, 90**
contact *n* **83**
contact lens, contact lenses *n* **22, 49**
contact lens solution *n* **22**
container *n* **105**
container port *n* **106**
container ship *n* **105-106**
containers *n* **52**
contents *n* **138**
continent *n* **145**
contours *n* **148**
contract *n* **92**
control tower *n* **104**
controller *n* **136**
controls *n* **100, 136**
convenience food *n* **23, 48**
conversion *n* **108**
convert the attic *v* **35**
convertible *n* **97**
convex lens *n* **75**
conveyor belt *n* **48**
cook dinner *v* **09**
cookbook *n* **138**
cooked *adj* **56**
cooked breakfast *n* **71**
cooked meat *n* **53, 64**
cooked vegetables *n* **72**
cookie *n* **63, 84**
cooking *n* **29**
cooking show *n* **137**
cooksonia *n* **157**
cool *adj* **154**
cool down *v* **124**
coolant reservoir *n* **98**
cooler *n* **135**
cooling rack *n* **29**
cooling system *n* **98**
cooling tower *n* **51**
coordinate *v* **92**
coordinates *n* **148**
coot *n* **161**
copernicium *n* **78**
copper *n* **78, 156**
copy *v* **11**
copyright *n* **175**
coral *n* **166**
coral reef *n* **118, 166**
coral reef fish *n* **118**
coral trout *n* **166**
cordless drill *n* **35**
core *n* **57**
coriander seeds *n* **59**
cork *n* **60**

corkscrew *n* **28, 68**
cormorant *n* **160**
corn *n* **55, 86**
corn bread *n* **62**
corn oil *n* **60**
cornea *n* **22**
corned beef *n* **64**
corner *n* **109**
corner flag *n* **109**
corner kick *n* **109**
cornerback *n* **107**
cornichons *n* **60**
cornrows *n* **12**
corpse pose *n* **24**
correct *adj* **176**
correction fluid *n* **82**
corset *n* **14**
cortado *n* **65**
cosmetics *n* **47**
Costa Rica *n* **150, 152**
Costa Rican *adj* **152**
costume, costumes *n* **13, 126-127**
cotoneaster *n* **169**
cottage *n* **32**
cottage cheese *n* **61**
cottage garden *n* **41**
cotton *adj* **176**
cotton *n* **13, 86, 176**
cotton balls *n* **18**
cotton candy *n* **67**
cotton pads *n* **20**
couch *n* **26**
couch potato *n* **137**
cough *n* **19**
cough *v* **20**
cough medicine *n* **49**
counselor *n* **24**
count *v* **11, 74**
counter *n* **45, 131**
counterfeit money *n* **94**
countertop *n* **27**
counterweight *n* **87**
country, countries *n* **129, 149-150**
countryside *n* **146**
couple *n* **07**
coupling rod *n* **102**
coupon *n* **48**
courier *n* **45**
course book *n* **138**
court *n* **85, 112**
court case *n* **85**
court date *n* **85**
court officer *n* **85**
court official *n* **85**
court reporter *n* **85**
courthouse *n* **43**
courtroom *n* **85**
courtyard *n* **25, 41**
cousin *n* **05**
cover *n* **111, 138**
coveralls *n* **13**
cover letter *n* **92**
cow *n* **165**
cowcatcher *n* **102**
co-worker *n* **92**
cow's milk *n* **61**
cowboy boots *n* **17**
cowboy hat *n* **16**
cowslip *n* **169**
crab *n* **54, 134**
crab apple *n* **58, 169**
cradle *n* **50**
craft market *n* **132**
crafts *n* **141-142**
cramp, cramps *n* **19, 118**
cranberry *n* **57**
cranberry juice *n* **65**
crane *n* **106, 160**
crater *n* **143, 145**
crawl *v* **11**
crayfish *n* **54**
cream *n* **49, 61, 71**
cream cheese *n* **61**
creative *adj* **93**
credit card *n* **45, 94**
creep *v* **11**
creeper *n* **41**
crème pâtissière *n* **63**
crêpe *n* **70**
crescent moon *n* **143**
cress *n* **55**
crest *n* **161**
crested owl *n* **161**
Cretaceous *adj* **157**
Cretaceous *n* **157**
crew *n* **119**
crew cut *n* **12**
crew hatch *n* **143**
crib *n* **30**
cricket *n* **111, 162**
cricket ball *n* **111**
cricket equipment *n* **111**
cricket pitch *n* **111**
cricket positions *n* **111**
cricket shoes *n* **111**
crime *n* **85, 137**
crime drama *n* **127**
crime fiction *n* **138**
crime scene *n* **50**
criminal *n* **85**
criminal record *n* **85**
crisp *adj* **57**
crispbread *n* **62, 71**
crisper *n* **27**
critical *adj* **10**
Croatia *n* **151, 153**
Croatian *adj* **153**
crochet *n* **142**
crochet hook *n* **142**
crockery *n* **27**
crocus *n* **38, 167**
croissant *n* **62, 71**
crop *n* **12**
crop farm *n* **86**
cropped *adj* **13**
crops *n* **86**
croquet *n* **133**
cross-country skiing *n* **122**
cross-section of tooth *n* **03**
crossbar *n* **101, 108, 116**
crosse *n* **110**
crow *n* **160**
crow *v* **165**
crow pose *n* **24**
crown *n* **22**
crucible *n* **76**
crudités *n* **72**
cruise missile *n* **88**
cruise ship *n* **105**
cruiser *n* **88**
crumpled *adj* **13**
crunchy *adj* **52, 56**
crust *n* **62, 145**
crutches *n* **19**
cry *v* **02**
crystal *n* **76**
crystal ball *n* **139**
crystal healing *n* **24**
crystalized honey *n* **60**
cub *n* **159**
Cuba *n* **150, 152**
Cuban *adj* **152**
cube *n* **74**
cubic meter *n* **174**
Cubism *n* **130**
cucumber *n* **55**
cue *n* **125**
cue ball *n* **125**
cuff *n* **15, 21, 142**
cufflinks *n* **16**
cultivate *v* **39**
cultivated mushrooms *n* **170**
cumin *n* **59**
cupcake *n* **63**
curator *n* **130**
curb *n* **43**
cured *adj* **72**
cured meat *n* **53, 64**
curious *adj* **06, 93**
curium *n* **78**
curlew *n* **161**
curling *n* **122**
curling brush *n* **122**
curling iron *n* **12**
curling stone *n* **122**
curly hair *n* **12**
currant *n* **58**
currency *n* **45, 94**
currency exchange *n* **45, 104**
current affairs *n* **137**
curry *n* **72**
curry powder *n* **59**
curtain, curtains *n* **26, 126**
curved *adj* **74**
custard *n* **63**
customer, customers *n* **45, 48, 65, 69**
customer service *n* **47, 93**
customer-focused *adj* **93**
customs *n* **104**
customhouse *n* **106**
cut *n* **19**
cut *n* **53**
cut *v* **29, 35, 142**
cut down on *v* **23**
cute *adj* **177**
cuticle *n* **02**
cuts *n* **53**
cuts of meat *n* **53**
cutting board *n* **28**
cycad *n* **167**
cycle *v* **101**
cycle lane *n* **101**
cycling *n* **101**
cycling shoe *n* **17**
cylinder *n* **74**
cylinder head *n* **98**
cymbals *n* **128**
Cypriot *adj* **153**
Cyprus *n* **151, 153**
Cyrillic alphabet *n* **175**
cytoplasm *n* **77**
Czech *adj* **153**
Czech Republic *n* **151, 153**

D

dachshund *n* **164**
dad *n* **05**
daffodil *n* **38**
daily *adj* **172**
daily *adv* **172**
daily life *n* **178**
daily routines *n* **09**
dairy *n* **23, 48**
dairy allergy *n* **23**
dairy farm *n* **86**
dairy produce *n* **61**
dairy-free *adj* **23**
daisy *n* **38**
Dalmatian *n* **164**
dam *n* **51**
dance *n* **129**
dance *v* **11**
dance school *n* **80**
dancer *n* **89**
dandelion *n* **38, 55**
dandruff *n* **12**
danger area *n* **117**
Danish *adj* **153**
dark *adj* **60, 176**
dark chocolate *n* **67**
darmstadtium *n* **78**
darn *v* **142**
dart, darts *n* **140, 142**
dartboard *n* **140**
Darwin's frog *n* **163**
dash *n* **29, 175**
dashboard and controls *n* **99**
date *n* **57-58**
date palm *n* **167**
daughter *n* **05**
daughter-in-law *n* **05**
dawn *n* **171**
day *n* **171-172**
Day of the Dead *n* **07**
dead ball line *n* **108**
Dead sea *n* **145**
deadhead *v* **39**
deadly nightshade *n* **169**
deal *v* **140**
death angel *n* **170**
death cap *n* **170**
debit card *n* **45, 94**
decade *n* **172**
decay *n* **22**
December *n* **172**
decide *v* **11**
deciduous *n* **41**
decimals *n* **173**
decision-making *n* **93**
decisive *adj* **10**
deck *n* **105**
deck chair *n* **134**
deck of cards *n* **140**
decking *n* **41**
decorate *v* **29, 63**
decoration *n* **63**
deep *adj* **176**
deep diving *n* **118**
deep end *n* **118**
deep sea fishing *n* **121**
deep-fried *adj* **72**
deep-tread tire *n* **100**
deer crossing *n* **96**
deerstalker *n* **16**
defendant *n* **85**
defender *n* **109**
defending zone *n* **110**
defense *n* **85, 107**
defensive specialist *n* **112**
defibrillator *n* **50**
deforestation *n* **155**
defrost the freezer *v* **34**
degree *n* **80**
degrees *n* **154**
delay *n* **102**
delete *v* **83**
deli *n* **48**
delicatessen *n* **46, 64**
delicious *adj* **52, 177**

delighted *adj* **06**
delivery *n* **45**
delivery man *n* **48**
delta *n* **147**
deltoid *n* **03**
Democratic Republic of the Congo *n* **149, 152**
den *n* **26**
denim *n* **13**
denim jacket *n* **15**
Denmark *n* **151, 153**
denomination *n* **74, 94**
dental care *n* **49**
dental floss *n* **22**
dental floss *n* **31**
dental history *n* **22**
dental hygienist *n* **22**
dental mirror *n* **22**
dental X-ray *n* **22**
dentist *n* **22, 89**
dentist chair *n* **22**
dentist's office *n* **22**
dentures *n* **22**
deodorant *n* **49**
department store *n* **47**
departments *n* **21, 91**
departure, departures *n* **43, 104**
departure board *n* **102**
departure lounge *n* **104**
deposit *n* **32**
deposit *v* **45**
depressed *adj* **06**
depth *n* **74**
depth gauge *n* **118**
Derby shoes *n* **17**
dermatology *n* **21**
derrick *n* **51**
descaled *adj* **54**
descent module *n* **143**
describing abilities *n* **11**
describing actions *n* **11**
describing clothes *n* **13**
describing fruit *n* **57**
describing personalities *n* **10**
describing things *n* **176-177**
desert *n* **146**
desert boots *n* **17**
desert ironwood tree *n* **169**
desertification *n* **155**
design and technology *n* **73**
designer *n* **89**
designer labels *n* **47**
desk *n* **73, 82**
desktop computer *n* **83**
dessert, desserts *n* **63, 69**
dessert cart *n* **69**
destination *n* **104**
destroyer *n* **88**
detached house *n* **32**
detective *n* **50**
determined *adj* **93**
detour *n* **96**
detox *n* **23**
deuce *n* **114**
Devanagari script *n* **175**
Devonian *adj* **157**
Devonian *n* **157**
dewlap *n* **159**
diabetes *n* **19**
diagonal *adj* **74**
diameter *n* **74**
diamond *n* **140, 156**
diamond back terrapin *n* **163**
diaper *n* **08**
diaper bag *n* **08**
diaper rash cream *n* **08**
diarrhea
dice *n* **140**
dice *v* **29**
dictionary *n* **73, 138**
didgeridoo *n* **129**
die *v* **07**
diesel *n* **97**
diesel train *n* **102**
diffraction *n* **75**
diffusion *n* **76**
dig *n* **79**
dig *v* **11, 39, 112**
digestif *n* **69**
digestive *n* **04**
digger *n* **87**
digital *adj* **84**
digital box *n* **136**
digital currency *n* **94**
digital projector *n* **73, 82**
digital screen *n* **136**
digital wallet *n* **94**
Dijon mustard *n* **60**
dill *n* **59-60**
dimensions *n* **74**
dimetrodon *n* **157**
dimples *n* **12**
dine *v* **52**
dining car *n* **102**
dining hall *n* **80**
dining room *n* **26**
dinner *n* **26, 72**
dinner menu *n* **69**
dinner party *n* **26**
dinner plate *n* **27**
dinnerware *n* **27**
diode *n* **75**
diploma *n* **80**
dipstick *n* **98**
dire *adj* **177**
direct current *n* **33, 75**
direct debit *n* **45**
direct flight *n* **104**
direction of revolution *n* **143**
direction to follow *n* **96**
directions *n* **132, 148, 180**
director *n* **84, 126-127**
director's chair *n* **84**
dirty *adj* **176**
dirty clothes *n* **34**
disabled parking *n* **96**
disappointed *adj* **06, 177**
disastrous *adj* **177**
discharge *v* **21**
discus *n* **116**
discuss *v* **73**
disembark *v* **106**
disgusted *adj* **06**
disgusting *adj* **52, 177**
dish rack *n* **27**
dish towel *n* **28**
dishes *n* **72**
dishonest *adj* **10**
dishwasher *n* **27, 34**
dishwasher tablets *n* **34**
dishwashing liquid *n* **34**
Disir *n* **139**
dismount *v* **100**
dispensary *n* **49**
dispersion *n* **75**
display *n* **21, 136**
disposable razor *n* **31**
dissertation *n* **80**
distance *n* **174**
distracted *adj* **06**
distributor *n* **98**
districts *n* **42**
dive *v* **118**
diver *n* **118**
divide *v* **74**
divided highway *n* **96**
dividends *n* **94**
divider *n* **96**
diving *n* **118**
diving board *n* **118**
diving tower *n* **118**
division sign *n* **74**
divorce *n* **07**
divorced *adj* **05**
Diwali *n* **07**
DIY (do it yourself) *n* **47**
DIY equipment *n* **35**
dizzy *adj* **19**
DJ *n* **84**
DJ console *n* **129**
Djibouti *n* **149, 152**
Djiboutian *adj* **152**
DM someone *v* **84**
DNA *n* **77**
do homework *v* **09, 11**
do not bend *phr* **45**
do the dishes *v* **09, 34**
do the ironing *v* **34**
do the laundry *v* **34**
do the weeding *v* **39**
Doberman *n* **164**
dock *v* **106**
docks *n* **106**
doctor *n* **19-21, 89**
doctor's office *n* **20**
doctorate *n* **80**
document *n* **79**
documentary *n* **137**
dog *n* **122**
dog breeds *n* **164**
dog rose *n* **169**
dog sledding *n* **122**
doghouse *n* **164**
dogsled *n* **122**
doll *n* **08**
dollhouse **08**
dolphin *n* **166**
dolphin pose *n* **24**
dome *n* **44**
domestic flight *n* **104**
Dominica *n* **150, 152**
Dominican *adj* **152**
Dominican Republic *n* **150, 152**
dominoes *n* **140**
donation *n* **130**
donkey *n* **165**
donut *n* **63, 70**
door *n* **99, 102**
door chain *n* **25-26**
door handle *n* **25-26, 97, 99**
door knocker *n* **25**
door lock *n* **99**
doorbell *n* **25**
doormat *n* **25-26**
dorm *n* **131**
dormer *n* **25**
dorms *n* **80**
dosa *n* **72**
dosage *n* **49**
double *adj* **68**
double bass *n* **128**
double bed *n* **30**
double burner camping stove *n* **135**
double espresso *n* **65**
double fault *n* **114**
double quotation mark *n* **175**
double room *n* **131**
double star *n* **144**
double-decker bus *n* **99**
doubles *n* **114**
dough *n* **62**
downhill skiing *n* **122**
download *v* **83**
downpour *n* **154**
downstairs *adv, n* **25**
downtown *n* **42**
downward dog *n* **24**
doze off *v* **178**
draft *n* **83**
drag racing *n* **123**
dragon *n* **139**
dragon tree *n* **38, 167**
dragonfly *n* **162**
drain *n* **31, 33, 43**
drainage *n* **39**
drama *n* **73, 127**
draw *v* **73**
drawbridge *n* **44**
drawer *n* **27, 30, 82**
drawing *n* **141**
dreadful *adj* **177**
dream *n* **30**
drepanaspis *n* **157**
dress *n* **14**
dress pattern *n* **142**
dress up *v* **178**
dressage *n* **120**
dressed *adj* **72**
dresser *n* **30**
dressing *n* **20, 72**
dried apricots *n* **58**
dried beans *n* **55**
dried fig *n* **58**
dried fruit *n* **58, 71**
dried yeast *n* **62**
drill *n* **22**
drill *v* **35**
drill bit, drill bits *n* **35-36**
drilling rig *n* **51**
drink *v* **52**
drink tea or coffee *v* **09**
drink water *v* **20**
drinking *n* **52**
drinks *n* **48, 52, 68**
drive *v* **09, 95, 115**
driver *n* **90, 99**
driver's cab *n* **102**
driver's seat *n* **99**
driveshaft *n* **98**
driving instructor *n* **89**
drizzle *n* **154**
dromedary *n* **158**
drop anchor *v* **106**
drop someone off *v* **98**
dropper *n* **76**
drops *n* **49**
dropshot *n* **114**
drought *n* **154**
drug dealing *n* **85**
drummer *n* **129**
dry *adj* **18, 154**
dry hair *n* **12**
dry-cleaner's *n* **46**
dry dock *n* **106**
dry the dishes *v* **34**
dry your hair *v* **09**
dry yourself *v* **31**
dry-cured meat *n* **64**
dubnium *n* **78**
duck *n* **53, 165**
duck egg *n* **61**
duckling *n* **165**
due date *n* **08**
duffel *n* **16**
duffle coat *n* **15**

dull *adj* **176**
dumbbell *n* **124**
dump truck *n* **87**
dumplings *n* **70, 72**
dumpster *n* **25**
dune *n* **147**
dune buggy *n* **97, 134**
dunk *v* **112**
duplex *n* **32**
dusk *n* **171**
dust *v* **34**
dustbin *n* **25**
duster *n* **34**
dustpan *n* **34**
dustsheet *n* **37**
Dutch *adj* **153**
duty belt *n* **50**
duty-free shop *n* **104**
duvet *n* **30**
DVD *n* **136**
dwarf *n* **139**
dwarf planets *n* **143**
dysprosium *n* **78**

E

e-reader *n* **83, 138**
eagle owl *n* **161**
ear *n* **01**
ear phone *n* **88**
ear protectors *n* **87**
ear thermometer *n* **20**
early *adj* **171**
early *adv* **171**
early human *n* **157**
earn *v* **81**
earphones *n* **136**
earrings *n* **16**
Earth *n* **143, 145**
earth tremor *n* **145**
earthquake *n* **145**
easel *n* **82, 141**
east *n* **148**
East Timor *n* **151, 153**
Easter *n* **07**
eastern coral snake *n* **163**
eat *v* **52**
eat breakfast *v* **09**
eat dinner *v* **09**
eat in *v* **70**
eat lunch *v* **09**
eat out *v* **69, 178**
eating *n* **52**
eccentric *adj* **10**
echidna *n* **158**
éclair *n* **63**
eclectus parrot *n* **161**
economic downturn *n* **94**
economics *n* **80**
economy class *n* **103**
ecosystem *n* **77, 155**
ecotourism *n* **131**
ecstatic *adj* **06**
Ecuador *n* **149, 152**
Ecuadorian *adj* **152**
eczema *n* **19**
Edam *n* **64**
editor *n* **89**
education *n* **91**
eel *n* **54**
efficient *adj* **93**
egg, eggs *n* **61, 77**
egg allergy *n* **23**
egg cup *n* **27, 61**
egg slicer *n* **28**
egg timer *n* **28**
egg white *n* **61, 71**
eggplant *n* **56**
eggshell *n* **161**
Egypt *n* **149, 152**
Egyptian *adj* **152**
Egyptian goose *n* **160**
Eid al-Fitr *n* **07**
Eiffel Tower *n* **44**
eight *num* **173**
eighteen *num* **173**
eighth *num* **173**
eighty *num* **173**
einsteinium *n* **78**
El Salvador *n* **150, 152**
elbow *n* **01**
elbow pads *n* **107**
elderberry *n* **57**
elderly *adj* **05**
electric bike *n* **101**
electric blanket *n* **30**
electric car *n* **97**
electric drill *n* **35**
electric field *n* **75**
electric guitar *n* **129**
electric guitarist *n* **129**
electric hook-up *n* **135**
electric kettle *n* **27**
electric lines *n* **102**
electric motorcycle *n* **100**
electric pump *n* **135**
electric razor *n* **31**
electric scooter *n* **100**
electric shock *n* **19**
electric train *n* **102**
electrical appliances *n* **47**
electrical goods *n* **48**
electrical waste *n* **33**
electrician *n* **89**
electricity *n* **33, 51, 75**
electricity meter *n* **33**
electrics *n* **33**
electromagnetic spectrum *n* **75**
electron *n* **76**
electronics *n* **91**
electronics store *n* **46**
elements *n* **76**
elevator *n* **25, 47, 131**
eleven *num* **173**
elf *n* **139**
elf owl *n* **161**
elixir *n* **139**
ellipsis *n* **175**
elliptical *n* **124**
elliptical galaxy *n* **144**
elm *n* **169**
email *n* **83**
embarrassed *adj* **06**
embroidery *n* **142**
embryo *n* **08**
emerald *n* **156**
emerald toucan *n* **160**
emerald tree boa *n* **163**
emergency brake *n* **99**
emergency department *n* **50**
emergency exit *n* **103, 131**
emergency phone *n* **96**
emergency room *n* **21**
emergency services *n* **50**
emergency signal *n* **102**
emergency vehicle beacon *n* **50**
emigrate *v* **07**
Emirati *adj* **153**
emissions *n* **51, 155**
emoji, emojis *n* **84, 175**
empanada *n* **70**
emperor *n* **79**
emperor moth *n* **162**
emperor penguin *n* **161**
empire *n* **79**
Empire State Building *n* **44**
employee *n* **81**
employer *n* **81**
employment *adj* **81**
empress *n* **79**
empty *adj* **176**
emu *n* **160**
enamel *n* **03**
encore *n* **126**
encyclopedia *n* **73, 138**
end line *n* **107**
end zone *n* **107, 110**
endangered species *n* **155**
endive *n* **55**
endocrine *n* **04**
endocrinology *n* **21**
endoskeleton *n* **77**
energetic *adj* **93**
energy *n* **23, 51, 91**
energy drink *n* **52**
engaged couple *n* **07**
engine *n* **98, 100, 103**
engine intake *n* **123**
engine room *n* **105**
engineer *n* **90**
engineering *n* **80**
English *n* **73**
English bluebell *n* **167**
English horn *n* **128**
English mustard *n* **60**
engraving *n* **141**
Enlightenment *n* **79**
enoki mushroom *n* **56, 170**
ENT *n* **21**
enter *v* **11**
entertainment *n* **91**
enthusiastic *adj* **10**
entrance *n* **130**
entrance fee *n* **132**
entrée *n* **69**
envelope *n* **45, 82, 103**
environment *n* **155**
environmental issues *n* **155**
épée *n* **117**
epiglottis *n* **04**
episode *n* **137**
equals *n* **74**
equation *n* **74**
Equator *n* **145**
Equatorial Guinea *n* **149, 152**
Equatorial Guinean *adj* **152**
equity *n* **94**
eraser *n* **73, 82**
erbium *n* **78**
Eritrea *n* **149, 152**
Eritrean *adj* **152**
erupt *v* **145**
escalator *n* **47, 104**
esophagus *n* **04**
espadrilles *n* **17**
espresso *n* **65**
espresso maker *n* **27**
essay *n* **73**
essential oils *n* **24**
Estonia *n* **151, 153**
Estonian *adj* **153**
estuary *n* **147**
Eswatini *n* **149, 152**
Ethiopia *n* **149, 152**
Ethiopian *adj* **152**
Europe *n* **151, 153**
European *adj* **153**
European badger *n* **158**
European common frog *n* **163**
European robin *n* **160**
europium *n* **78**
EV charging station *n* **97**
eave *n* **32, 44**
evening *n* **09, 171**
evening dress *n* **15**
evening primrose *n* **38**
evergreen *n* **41**
every day *adv* **172**
every other day *adv* **172**
evidence *n* **50, 85**
evolution *n* **77**
ewe *n* **165**
ex-husband *n* **05**
ex-wife *n* **05**
exam *n* **73**
excavation *n* **79, 87**
excess baggage *n* **104**
exchange *v* **46**
exchange rate *n* **45, 94**
excited *adj* **06**
exciting *adj* **177**
exclamation mark *n* **175**
exercise *v* **09, 20**
exercise ball *n* **124**
exercise bike *n* **124**
exercise book *n* **73**
exercise class *n* **124**
exercise mat *n* **124**
exercises *n* **124**
exhaust fan *n* **27**
exhaust pipe *n* **98, 100**
exhausted *adj* **06**
exhausting *adj* **177**
exhibit *n* **130**
exhibition *n* **130**
exit *n* **48**
exit *v* **11**
exit ramp *n* **96**
exoskeleton *n* **77**
exosphere *n* **155**
exotic shorthair *n* **164**
expenditure *n* **94**
experiment *n* **76**
expiration date *n* **49**
extend *v* **124**
extension cord *n* **35**
extra virgin *adj* **60**
extraction *n* **22**
extraordinary *adj* **177**
extras *n* **127**
eye, eyes *n* **01, 121, 142**
eye drops *n* **22**
eye mask *n* **14**
eyeball *n* **22**
eyebrow *n* **01**
eyebrow brush *n* **18**
eyebrow pencil *n* **18**
eyecup *n* **136**
eyelashes *n* **01**
eyelet *n* **17**
eyelid *n* **01**
eyeliner *n* **18**
eyepiece *n* **77, 144**
eyeshadow *n* **18**

F

fabric n 142
fabric softener n 34
face n 01
face cream n 31
face mask n 18
face mask n 20, 107, 110
face powder n 18
face wash n 18
face-off n 110
face-off spot n 110
facemask n 111
facial n 18
facial hair n 12
facilities n 91
factory n 42
Fahrenheit n 154
fail v 73
faint v 20
fairway n 115
fairy n 139
fairy elephant's feet n 168
fairy ring n 170
fairy tale n 138-139
falafel n 70
fall n 57, 172
fall v 11, 117
fall in love v 07
fall leaf n 169
fallopian tube n 04
fallow deer n 158
false teeth n 22
family n 05
family tent n 135
famous buildings n 44
fan n 33
fan belt n 98
fan space heater n 33
fans n 107, 109, 129
fantastic adj 177
fantastic creatures n 139
fantasy n 127, 138-139
far adj 176
fare n 99, 102
farm n 86, 165
farm animals n 165
farmer n 79, 86, 89
farmers' market n 23
farmhouse n 86
farming n 86, 91
farming terms n 86
farmland n 86, 146
farmyard n 86
farsighted adj 22
fashion n 91
fashion accessories n 16
fashion designer n 90
fashion store n 47
fast adj 176
fast food n 47, 70
fast forward v 137
fast-food restaurant n 70
fasten v 14
fastening n 16
fat free adj 61
father n 05
father-in-law n 05
faucet n 27, 31, 33
fault n 114
faun n 139
fava beans n 55
feather duster n 34
feather n 161
feathers displayed n 161
February n 172
fedora n 16
feed v 86
feed the cat v 09
feed the dog v 09
feed the pets v 34
feel better v 20
feelings n 06
feet n 02
feet-first adj 118
feijoa n 58
female n 04
feminine hygiene n 49
femur n 03
fence n 41, 86
fencing n 116-117
feng shui n 24
fennec fox n 158
fennel n 55, 59
fennel seeds n 59
fenugreek leaves n 59
fermium n 78
fern, ferns n 41, 156, 167
ferret n 164
ferris wheel n 133
ferrule n 115
ferry n 105-106
ferry route n 148
ferry terminal n 106
fertilize v 39
fertilizer n 39
festivals n 07
feta n 64
fetus n 08
fever n 19
fez n 16
fiancé n 07
fiancée n 07
fiber n 23, 57
fiberglass adj 176
fiberglass n 176
fibula n 03
fiction n 138
fiddler crab n 166
field n 107, 113, 146
field n 109
field v 111, 113
field events n 116
field hockey n 110
field hockey player n 110
field hospital n 88
field mushroom n 170
fielding positions n 111
fifteen num 173
fifth num 173
fifty num 173
fifty-yard line n 107
fig n 169
fighter n 88
figure skating n 122
Fiji n 150, 153
Fijian adj 153
filament n 38
file, files n 36, 82
filet n 53
filing cabinet n 82
Filipino adj 153
fill v 37
fill out v 178
fill out a form v 92
fill up v 98, 178
fillet n 54
filling n 22, 63, 70
film set n 127
film studio n 127
filter coffee n 65
filter paper n 76
fin n 103
final whistle n 109
finance n 91, 94
financial advisor n 94
finch n 160
finderscope n 144
finds n 79
fine n 85
fine leg n 111
fingernail n 02
fingerprint n 50
finish line n 116, 123
finish work v 09
Finland n 151, 153
Finnish adj 153
fins n 118, 134
fir n 167
fire n 50
fire alarm n 50
fire department n 50
fire engine n 50
fire escape n 50
fire extinguisher n 50
fire salamander n 163
fire station n 42, 50
fire tree n 168
firefighter, firefighters n 50, 89
firefighter's uniform n 13
firepit n 135
fireplace n 26
firestarter n 135
first num 173
first aid bag n 50
first base n 113
first floor n 25, 47
first-aid kit n 20, 49
fish n 48, 54, 164
fish and chips n 70
fish box n 54
fish farm n 86
fish sauce n 60
fish tank n 164
fisherman n 89
fishhook n 121
fishing n 91, 121
fishing license n 121
fishing port n 106
fishing rod n 121
fishing vest n 121
fishmonger n 18, 54, 89
fission n 75
fissures n 51
fist n 02
fit v 14, 46
fitted adj 13
five num 173
five hundred num 173
five past one n 171
five positions n 112
five spice n 59
five to two n 171
fix v 11
fix a fence v 35
fix a puncture v 101
fix up v 178
fixed menu n 69
fjord n 147
flag n 115
flagstone n 35
flamenco dress n 15
flamingo n 160
flan n 64
flan pan n 29
flap v 161
flare n 51, 119, 144
flashlight n 135
flask n 76
flat adj 128
flat cap n 16
flat head screwdriver n 36
flat race n 120
flat tire n 98
flat white n 65
flat wood bit n 36
flatbed truck n 87
flatbread n 62
flats n 17
flavored oil n 60
flax n 86
fledgling n 161
flerovium n 78
flesh n 58
flex v 124
flexible adj 93, 176
flextime n 81
flight attendant, flight attendants n 90, 103-104
flight instructor n 90
flight number n 104
flint n 156
flint tools n 79
flip n 118
flip chart n 82, 95
flip through v 138
flip-flops n 17, 134
flipper, flippers n 15, 118, 134
flipper n 28
float n 118, 121
float v 118
floating crane n 106
flock of sheep n 165
flood n 154
flood plain n 147
floor n 25-26, 30
floor length adj 15
floor mat n 125
floor plan n 130, 132
floorboards n 26
Florentine n 63
floret n 55
florist n 46-47, 89
floss v 22
flours n 62
flower anatomy n 38
flower stall n 47
flowerbed n 41
flowering plants n 157
flowering shrub n 41
flu n 19
fluent in languages adj 93
fluid ounce n 174
fluorine n 78
flute n 128-129
fly n 121, 162, 168
fly v 11, 162
fly agaric n 170
fly fishing n 121
fly-half n 108
flying carpet n 139
flying fish n 166
flying kick n 117
flying reptiles n 157
flying squirrel n 158
flyover n 96
FM adj 84
foal n 120, 165
focusing knob n 77, 144
fog n 154
foggy adj 154
foil n 117
fold v 14
fold clothes v 34
folders n 82
folding grill n 135
foliage n 47
folk blouse n 15

folk music *n* **129**
follow *v* **84**
follower *n* **84**
food *n* **65, 91**
food allergies *n* **23**
food bowl *n* **26**
food compost bin *n* **33**
food court *n* **47**
food poisoning *n* **19**
food preparation *n* **72**
food truck *n* **70**
food waste *n* **155**
foot *n* **01, 174**
foot board *n* **30**
foot boot *n* **19**
foot pedals *n* **99**
foot stool *n* **26**
foot strap *n* **119**
football *n* **107**
football cleats *n* **107**
football player *n* **107**
football rules *n* **109**
football timing *n* **109**
footbridge *n* **104**
foothill *n* **147**
footrest *n* **82**
forage mushrooms *v* **170**
Forbidden City *n* **44**
forearm *n* **01**
forehand *n* **114**
forehead *n* **01**
foreperson *n* **85**
forest *n* **147-148**
forestay *n* **119**
forewing *n* **162**
forget *v* **11**
fork *n* **27, 40, 101**
forklift *n* **87, 106**
formal garden *n* **41**
formal wear *n* **15**
fortune cookies *n* **63**
forty *num* **173**
forty minutes *n* **171**
forward *n* **109**
forward *v* **83**
fossil *n* **77**
fossil fuels *n* **51, 155**
foul *n* **112**
foul ball *n* **113**
foul line *n* **112-113**
foul pole *n* **113**
foundation *n* **18**
fountain *n* **41-42**
fountain pen *n* **175**
four *num* **173**
four-wheel drive *n* **97**
fourteen *num* **173**
fourth *num* **173**
foxglove *n* **38**
fracking *n* **51**
fraction, fractions *n* **74, 173**
fracture *n* **19**
fragile *adj* **45**
frame *n* **26, 101, 130, 135**
France *n* **151, 153**
francium *n* **78**
fraud *n* **85**
freckles *n* **12**
free weights *n* **124**
free-range *adj* **53**
free-throw lane *n* **112**
free-throw line *n* **112**
freesia *n* **47, 167**
freeze *v* **29**
freezer *n* **27**
freezing *adj* **154**
freezing point *n* **154**
freight *n* **105**
freight train *n* **102**
freighter *n* **105**
French braid *n* **12**
French doors *n* **25**
French horn *n* **128**
French toast *n* **71**
frequency *n* **84**
fresh *adj* **52, 54, 56**
fresh cheese *n* **61**
fresh chili *n* **59**
fresh fruit *n* **71**
fresh yeast *n* **62**
freshwater fishing *n* **121**
fret *n* **129**
Friday *n* **172**
fried *adj* **72**
fried chicken *n* **70**
fried egg *n* **61, 71**
fried mushrooms *n* **71**
friend *n* **07**
friendly *adj* **10**
fries *n* **70**
frigate *n* **88, 160**
frightened *adj* **06**
frightening *adj* **177**
frill-necked lizard *n* **163**
frisbee *n* **133**
frisée *n* **55**
frizzy hair *n* **12**
frog eggs *n* **77, 163**
front *adj* **03**
front *n* **88**
front crawl *n* **118**
front desk *n* **131**
front door *n* **25, 97**
front entrance *n* **25**
front kick *n* **117**
front loader *n* **87**
front speaker *n* **136**
front suspension *n* **123**
front view *n* **97**
front wheel *n* **99**
front wing *n* **97, 123**
front-flip *n* **118**
frontal *n* **03**
frost *n* **154**
frosty *adj* **154**
froth *n* **65**
frown *v* **02**
frozen *adj* **54, 56**
frozen food *n* **48**
frozen yoghurt *n* **61**
fruit *n* **48, 57-58**
fruit bat *n* **158**
fruit bowl *n* **26**
fruit bread *n* **62**
fruit farm *n* **86**
fruit gummies *n* **67**
fruit juice *n* **71**
fruit tart *n* **63**
fruit yogurt *n* **71**
fruitcake *n* **63**
frustrated *adj* **06**
fry *v* **29**
frying basket *n* **28**
frying pan *n* **28**
fuchsia *n* **168**
fuel rods *n* **51**
fuel tank *n* **100**
full *adj* **26, 135, 176**
full back *n* **108**
full moon *n* **143**
full time *n* **109**
fullback *n* **107**
fumble *v* **107**
fun *adj* **177**
funeral *n* **07**
fungi *n* **77, 170**
funnel *n* **76, 105**
funny *adj* **10, 177**
furious *adj* **06**
furnished *n* **32**
fuse box *n* **33, 98**
fusilli *n* **64**
fusion *n* **75**

G

Gabon *n* **149, 152**
Gabonese *adj* **152**
gadgets *n* **83**
gadolinium *n* **78**
gain weight *v* **20**
gain yards *v* **107**
galah *n* **161**
Galápagos turtle *n* **163**
gale *n* **154**
galia *n* **58**
gall bladder *n* **04**
gallery *n* **105, 130**
gallium *n* **78**
gallon *n* **174**
gallop *v* **120, 165**
Gambia *n* **149, 152**
Gambian *adj* **152**
game, games *n* **08, 53, 114, 140**
game officials *n* **112**
game show *n* **137**
gaming *n* **91**
gamma radiation *n* **75**
Ganges *n* **145**
gangway *n* **105**
gannet *n* **160**
garage *n* **25**
garden center *n* **46**
garden features *n* **41**
garden flowers *n* **38**
garden gloves *n* **40**
garden hose *n* **40**
garden peas *n* **55**
garden plants *n* **38**
garden salad *n* **72**
garden tools *n* **40**
garden types *n* **41**
gardener *n* **89**
gardenia *n* **38**
gardening *n* **39, 133**
gardening basket *n* **40**
gardening book *n* **138**
gardening features *n* **41**
garland *n* **47**
garlic *n* **56**
garlic press *n* **28**
garnet *n* **156**
garnish *v* **29**
garter *n* **14**
garter belt *n* **14**
gas *n* **51, 76**
gas *n* **99**
gas giants *n* **143**
gas pump *n* **97**
gas space heater *n* **33**
gas station *n* **42, 97**
gasoline *n* **97**
gastornis *n* **157**
gastroenterology *n* **21**
gate *n* **32, 41, 86, 106, 122**
gate number *n* **104**
gateau *n* **63**
gathered skirt *n* **142**
gathers *n* **142**
gauze *n* **20**
gazelle *n* **158**
gear lever *n* **101**
gearbox *n* **98, 100**
gears *n* **101**
gearshift *n* **99**
gel *n* **49**
Gemini *n* **144**
gems *n* **156**
gene *n* **77**
general *n* **88**
general appearance *n* **12**
generator *n* **33, 51, 101**
generous *adj* **10**
genie *n* **139**
genitals *n* **01**
genoa *n* **119**
genres *n* **138**
Gentoo penguin *n* **161**
geode *n* **156**
geographical features *n* **146**
geography *n* **73, 146-147**
geological periods *n* **157**
geometry *n* **74**
Georgia *n* **150, 153**
Georgian *adj* **153**
geothermal energy *n* **51**
geothermal power plant *n* **51**
geranium *n* **38**
gerbera *n* **47**
gerbil *n* **164**
German *adj* **153**
German shepherd *n* **164**
germanium *n* **78**
Germany *n* **151, 153**
get a job *v* **07**
get away *v* **178**
get changed *v* **14**
get dressed *v* **09**
get fired *v* **81**
get into debt *v* **94**
get married *v* **07**
get off *v* **100, 178**
get off a bike *v* **101**
get on *v* **100, 178**
get on a bike *v* **101**
get the job *v* **92**
get together *v* **178**
get up *v* **09, 178**
get your hair cut *v* **12**
getting to know someone *n* **179**
geyser *n* **146**
Ghana *n* **149, 152**
Ghanaian *adj* **152**
gharial *n* **163**
ghee *n* **61**
gherkin *n* **60**
ghost *n* **139**
giant *n* **139**
giant horsetails *n* **157**
giant puffball *n* **170**
giant sequoia *n* **167**
giant slalom *n* **122**
giant sloth *n* **157**
giant squid *n* **166**
gibbon *n* **159**
gift shop *n* **46, 130**
gila monster *n* **163**
gills *n* **170**
gin and tonic *n* **68**
ginger *n* **59**

gingerbread man *n* **63**
ginkgo *n* **167**
ginkgo nuts *n* **58**
giraffe *n* **158**
girder *n* **87**
girl *n* **05**
girlfriend *n* **05**
girth *n* **120**
give a presentation *v* **95**
give away *v* **178**
give back *v* **178**
give notice *v* **32**
give out *v* **178**
give up *v* **23, 178**
glacier *n* **146**
gladiator sandals *n* **17**
gladiolus *n* **47**
glass *adj* **176**
glass, glasses *n* **27, 52, 68, 155, 176**
glass baking dish *n* **28**
glass bottle *n* **76**
glass rod *n* **76**
glasses *n* **22**
glassware *n* **27**
glasswing butterfly *n* **162**
glaze *v* **62-63**
glide *v* **161**
glider *n* **103, 125**
glory of Texas *n* **168**
gloss *n* **37**
glossary *n* **138**
glove, gloves *n* **16, 100, 110, 115, 117, 122, 107, 109**
glue *n* **82, 101, 141**
glue gun *n* **35**
gluten intolerant *adj* **23**
gluten-free *adj* **23**
gluten-free flour *n* **62**
gluteus maximus *n* **03**
gneiss *n* **156**
gnocchi *n* **64**
gnome *n* **139**
go *n* **140**
go abroad *v* **104, 141**
go away *v* **178**
go back *v* **148**
go backpacking *v* **131**
go down *v* **178**
go on a cruise *v* **131**
go on a diet *v* **23**
go on a vacation *v* **131**
go on an excursion *v* **132**
go on a tour *v* **132**
go on Hajj *v* **07**
go on maternity leave *v* **81**
go out of business *v* **94**
go out with friends *v* **09**
go past (the restaurant) *v* **148**
go straight ahead *v* **96, 148**
go to a café *v* **09**
go to bed *v* **09**
go to preschool *v* **07**
go to school *v* **09**
go to sleep *v* **09**
go to work *v* **09**
go up *v* **178**
go viral *v* **84**
go-cart *n* **123**
goal *n* **108-110**
goal crease *n* **110**
goal line *n* **107, 110**
goal posts *n* **108**
goalball *n* **125**
goalie stick *n* **110**
goalkeeper *n* **109-110**
goalpost *n* **107-09**
goat *n* **53, 165**
goat's cheese *n* **61**
goat's milk *n* **61**
goatee *n* **12**
goblin *n* **139**
goggles *n* **15, 118, 122**
goji berry *n* **57**
gold *adj* **176**
gold *n* **78, 116, 156, 176**
gold-plated visor *n* **143**
golden eagle *n* **160**
golden guinea vine *n* **168**
golden raisin *n* **58**
golf *n* **115**
golf bag *n* **115**
golf ball *n* **115**
golf cap *n* **115**
golf clubs *n* **115**
golf course *n* **115**
golf equipment *n* **115**
golf push cart *n* **115**
golf shoe, golf shoes *n* **17, 115**
golfer *n* **115**
gong *n* **128**
good *adj* **177**
good afternoon *phr* **179**
good evening *phr* **179**
good listener *n* **93**
good morning *phr* **179**
good night *phr* **179**
goodbye *phr* **179**
goose *n* **53, 165**
goose egg *n* **61**
gooseberry *n* **57**
gorilla *n* **159**
gosling *n* **165**
gospel *n* **129**
gossip magazine *n* **138**
government building *n* **43**
GPS *n* **99**
grab bar *n* **31**
graceful *adj* **177**
grade *n* **73**
grader *n* **87**
graduate *n* **80**
graduate *v* **07**
graduation ceremony *n* **80**
graffiti *n* **85**
graft *v* **39**
gram *n* **174**
granddaughter *n* **05**
grandfather *n* **05**
grandmother *n* **05**
grandparents *n* **05**
grandson *n* **05**
granite *n* **156**
grapefruit *n* **57**
grapes *n* **57**
grapeseed oil *n* **60**
grapevine *n* **168**
graphite *n* **156**
grass, grasses *n* **25, 41, 167**
grass collector *n* **40**
grass tree *n* **167**
grasshopper *n* **162**
grassland *n* **146**
grate *v* **29**
grated cheese *n* **61**
grateful *adj* **06**
grater *n* **28**
grave accent *n* **175**
gravel *n* **35, 40**
gravity *n* **144**
gray *adj* **01, 141**
gray *n* **01, 141**
gray hair *n* **12**
grease *v* **29**
greasy hair *n* **12**
great *adj* **177**
Great Blue Hole *n* **145**
great crested newt *n* **163**
Great Dane *n* **164**
great gray owl *n* **161**
Great Mosque of Djenné *n* **44**
Great Plains toad *n* **163**
great white shark *n* **166**
greater spotted woodpecker *n* **160**
grebe *n* **161**
Greece *n* **151, 153**
Greek *adj* **153**
Greek alphabet *n* **175**
Greek mythology *n* **139**
Greek salad *n* **72**
green *adj* **01, 141**
green *n* **115, 141**
green basilisk *n* **163**
green beans *n* **55**
green energy *n* **51**
green foliage *n* **172**
green olives *n* **64**
green sea turtle *n* **163**
green tea *n* **66**
green woodpecker *n* **160**
greenhouse *n* **39**
greenhouse effect *n* **155**
greenhouse gases *n* **155**
greet *v* **179**
greetings *n* **179**
gremlin *n* **139**
Grenada *n* **150, 152**
grenade *n* **88**
grenade launcher *n* **88**
Grenadian *adj* **152**
gray willow *n* **169**
grid lines *n* **148**
griffin *n* **139**
grill *n* **41**
grill pan *n* **28**
grilled *adj* **72**
grilled tomato *n* **71**
grin *v* **02**
grip *n* **115**
grocer *n* **89**
grocery store *n* **46, 56**
groin *n* **01**
groin protector *n* **117**
groom *n* **07**
groom *v* **120**
groove *n* **115**
ground *n* **33**
ground chili *n* **59**
ground cinnamon *n* **59**
ground cover *n* **41**
ground level *n* **47**
ground maintenance *n* **89**
ground meat *n* **53**
ground sheet *n* **135**
group therapy *n* **24**
grout *n* **37**
grow up *v* **178**
grow your hair *v* **12**
growing up *n* **05**
grunt *v* **165**
guarantee *n* **47**
Guatemala *n* **150, 152**
Guatemalan *adj* **152**
guava *n* **58, 168**
guest *n* **26**
guest house *n* **131**
guest speaker *n* **95**
guests *n* **131**
guidebook *n* **131-132, 138**
guided tour *n* **132**
guillemot *n* **160**
guilty *adj* **06, 85**
Guinea *n* **149, 152**
guinea pig *n* **164**
Guinea-Bissau *n* **149, 152**
Guinean *adj* **152**
gulf *n* **147**
gull *n* **134**
gully *n* **111**
gulp *v* **52**
gulper eel *n* **166**
gum *n* **03**
gun, guns *n* **88**
gunfire *n* **88**
gunnera *n* **168**
gutter *n* **25, 43**
guy line *n* **135**
Guyana *n* **149, 152**
Guyanese *adj* **152**
gym *n* **124, 131**
gym equipment *n* **124**
gym machines *n* **124**
gymnastics *n* **125**
gynecology *n* **21**
gypsophila *n* **47**
gyrocopter *n* **103**

habitat loss *n* **155**
hacking *n* **85**
hacksaw *n* **36**
hadal zone *n* **166**
haddock tail *n* **54**
hafnium *n* **78**
haggle *v* **46**
hailstone *n* **154**
hair *n* **01, 12**
hair dryer *n* **12**
hair dye *n* **18**
hair gel *n* **12**
hair salon *n* **47**
hair scissors *n* **12**
hair spray *n* **12**
hair towel wrap *n* **18**
hairbrush *n* **12**
hairdresser *n* **89**
hairpin turn *n* **123**
Haiti *n* **150, 152**
Haitian *adj* **152**
hakama *n* **117**
halal *adj* **72**
half *num* **173**
half an hour *n* **171**
half moon pose *n* **24**
half time *n* **109**
half-court line *n* **112**
half-liter *n* **174**
half-way line *n* **109**
halfback *n* **107**
halfway line *n* **108**
halibut *n* **54**
halloumi *n* **64**
Halloween *n* **07**
hallway *n* **25-26**
halogens *n* **78**
halter *n* **120**
halter neck *n* **15**
halva *n* **67**
ham *n* **53, 71**
hamburger *n* **70**

hammer *n* **36, 116**
hammer *v* **35**
hammerhead shark *n* **166**
hammock *n* **135**
hamster *n* **158, 164**
hamstrings *n* **03**
hand, hands *n* **01-02**
hand cream *n* **18**
hand drill *n* **36**
hand fork *n* **40**
hand grips *n* **124**
hand in your notice *v* **81**
hand out *v* **178**
hand towel *n* **31**
handball *n* **125**
handcuffs *n* **50**
handful *n* **29**
handicap *n* **115**
handkerchief *n* **16**
handle *n* **16, 28, 40, 87, 110, 113-114**
handle with care *phr* **45**
handlebar *n* **101**
handouts *n* **95**
handrail *n* **25, 99**
handsaw *n* **36**
handsome *adj* **12**
handwriting *n* **175**
hang *v* **37**
hang clothes *v* **34**
hang glider *n* **125**
Hang Son Doong *n* **145**
hang up *v* **14, 178**
hang-gliding *n* **125**
hangar *n* **104**
hanging basket *n* **41**
hangman *n* **140**
Hanukkah *n* **07**
happy *adj* **06**
harbor *n* **106**
harbor master *n* **106**
hard *adj* **57, 176**
hard candy *n* **67**
hard cheese *n* **61**
hard drive *n* **83**
hard hat *n* **87**
hard shoulder *n* **96**
hard-working *adj* **93**
hardback *n* **138**
hardboard *n* **35**
hardware store *n* **46**
hardwood *n* **35**
hare's ear *n* **170**
harissa *n* **60**
harmless *adj* **177**
harmonica *n* **129**
harness *n* **115, 122**
harness race *n* **120**
harp *n* **128**
harpoon *n* **121**
harpy eagle *n* **160**
harvest *v* **39, 86**
hash browns *n* **70-71**
hash marks *n* **107**
hashtag *n* **83-84, 175**
hassium *n* **78**
hatch *v* **161**
hatchback *n* **97**
hatchling *n* **161**
have a baby *v* **07, 09**
have a car accident *v* **98**
have a conference call *v* **95**
have a day off *v* **81**
have a shower *v* **09**
have an interview *v* **92**
have breakfast *v* **09**
have dinner *v* **09**
have lunch *v* **09**
have tea or coffee *v* **09**
have your hair cut *v* **12**
hawk moth *n* **162**
hawkfish *n* **166**
hawksbill turtle *n* **166**
hawthorn *n* **169**
hay *n* **86**
hay fever *n* **19**
hazard *n* **96**
hazard lights *n* **99**
hazardous waste *n* **33**
hazel *adj* **01**
hazel *n* **01, 168**
hazelnut *n* **58**
hazelnut oil *n* **60**
HDMI cable *n* **95**
head *n* **01, 04, 162**
headband *n* **16**
head guard *n* **117**
head injury *n* **19**
head pocket *n* **110**
head-first *adj* **118**
headache *n* **19**
headboard *n* **30**
headlamp *n* **135, 146**
headlight, headlights *n* **50, 97, 100**
headlight controls *n* **99**
headline *n* **138**
headphones *n* **84, 95, 136**
headquarters *n* **81**
headrest *n* **99, 123**
headset *n* **82**
headstand *n* **24**
headstock *n* **129**
headwear *n* **16**
heal *v* **20**
health food store *n* **23, 46-47**
healthcare *n* **91**
healthy body *n* **24**
healthy living *n* **23**
healthy mind *n* **24**
heart *n* **04, 53, 140**
heart rate *n* **124**
heat wave *n* **154**
heater controls *n* **99**
heather *n* **38, 41**
heavy *adj* **176**
heavy cream *n* **61**
heavy metal *n* **129**
hectare *n* **174**
hedge *n* **41, 86, 146**
hedgehog *n* **158**
hedgehog mushroom *n* **170**
heel *n* **01-02, 17, 115**
height *n* **74**
helicopter *n* **103**
helipad *n* **51**
helium *n* **78**
hello *phr* **179**
helm *n* **119**
helmet *n* **50, 100, 107, 111, 113, 123, 143, 146**
help *v* **11**
hem *n* **14, 142**
hematite *n* **156**
hemlock *n* **169**
hemorrhage *n* **19**
hemp *n* **169**
hen *n* **165**
hen of the wood *n* **170**
henna *n* **168**
herb garden *n* **41**
herbaceous border *n* **41**
herbal remedies *n* **49**
herbal tea *n* **52, 66**
herbalism *n* **24**
herbicide *n* **86**
herbs *n* **41, 59**
herd *n* **86**
herd of cows *n* **165**
hermit crab *n* **134, 166**
hero *n* **127, 139**
heron *n* **160**
herring *n* **54**
Herzegovinian *adj* **153**
hex keys *n* **36**
hexagon *n* **74**
hi *phr* **179**
hi-fi system *n* **136**
hibernation *n* **77**
hibiscus *n* **38**
hide *v* **164**
hide-and-seek *n* **133**
high *adj* **176**
high blood pressure *n* **19**
high calorie *adj* **23**
high chair *n* **08**
high dive *n* **118**
high jump *n* **116**
high pressure *n* **155**
high tide *n* **147**
high-definition *adj* **137**
high-heeled shoes *n* **17**
high-speed train *n* **102**
high-tops *n* **17**
high-visibility jacket *n* **13**
high-visibility vest *n* **87**
higher pitch *n* **128**
highland *n* **146**
highlighter *n* **73, 82**
highlighter pen *n* **175**
highlights *n* **12**
highway *n* **96**
hijab *n* **16**
hiking *n* **133**
hiking boots *n* **17**
hilarious *adj* **177**
hilt *n* **117**
Himalayan *n* **164**
Himeji Castle *n* **44**
hindwing *n* **162**
hip *n* **01**
hip-hop *n* **129**
hip pads *n* **107**
hippopotamus *n* **158**
historian *n* **79**
historic building *n* **44, 132**
historic quarter *n* **43**
historical drama *n* **127**
historical site *n* **79**
history *n* **73, 79-80**
hit *v* **11, 110**
hive *n* **165**
hobby horse *n* **08**
hockey *n* **110**
hockey stick *n* **110**
hoe *n* **40**
hold *v* **11, 117**
hold your breath *v* **02**
hole *n* **115**
hole in one *n* **115**
hole punch *n* **82**
Holi *n* **07**
holmium *n* **78**
holy water *n* **07**
home *n* **32, 107**
home button *n* **83**
home cinema *n* **136**
home delivery *n* **48, 70**
home entertainment *n* **136**
home furnishings *n* **47**
home improvements *n* **35**
home office *n* **26**
home plate *n* **113**
homeopathy *n* **24**
homestretch *n* **123**
homework *n* **73**
homogenized *adj* **61**
Honduran *adj* **152**
Honduras *n* **150, 152**
honest *adj* **10, 93**
honey *n* **60, 71**
honey badger *n* **158**
honey bee *n* **162**
honey dipper *n* **60**
honeycomb *n* **60**
honeydew melon *n* **58**
honeymoon *n* **07**
honeysuckle *n* **38**
hood *n* **13, 15**
hood *n* **97**
hoof *n* **120, 158-159**
hook *n* **87**
hook and eye *n* **142**
hooker *n* **108**
hooliganism *n* **85**
hoop *n* **16, 112, 125**
hoot *v* **161**
hop *n* **169**
hop *v* **11, 164**
hopeful *adj* **06**
horizontal bar *n* **125**
horn, horns *n* **99, 100, 158**
hornbeam *n* **168**
horoscope *n* **138**
horrible *adj* **177**
horror *n* **127**
horse *n* **120, 165**
horse chestnut *n* **169**
horse race *n* **120**
horse riding *n* **120**
horse trail *n* **133**
horseback riding *n* **120, 133**
horseradish *n* **56**
horseshoe *n* **120**
horseshoe crab *n* **166**
horsetail *n* **167**
hose *n* **50**
hose reel *n* **40**
hospital *n* **21, 42**
hospital bed *n* **21**
hospital porter *n* **21**
hospitality *n* **91**
host *n* **84, 137**
host *n* **26**
hostel *n* **131**
hostess *n* **26**
hot *adj* **52, 56, 154, 176**
hot chocolate *n* **52**
hot dog *n* **70**
hot sauce *n* **60**
hot tub *n* **124**
hot water *n* **31**
hot-air balloon *n* **103**
hot-water bottle *n* **30**
hotel *n* **42, 131**
hotel lobby *n* **131**
hour *n* **171**
hour hand *n* **171**
hourly *adj, adv* **171-172**
hourly rate *n* **81**
house, houses *n* **25, 32, 148**
house martin *n* **160**
houseboat *n* **32**
household chores *n* **34**
household products *n* **48**
household renovation *n* **37**
household tasks *n* **34**

housekeeper n 89
houseplants n 38
hovercraft n 105
howler monkey n 159
hub n 51, 101
hubcap n 98
Hugin and Munin n 139
hula hoop n 08
hull n 105, 119
human body n 01
human resources (HR) n 91
humanities n 80
Humboldt penguin n 161
humerus n 03
humidity n 154
hummingbird n 160
hummingbird hawksmoth n 162
hummus n 72
humor n 138
hump n 158
humpback whale n 166
Hungarian adj 153
Hungary n 151, 153
hungry adj 26
hunt v 159
hurdles n 116
hurricane n 154
hurt v 20
husband n 05
hut n 32
hybrid n 97
Hydra n 139
hydrangea n 38
hydrant n 50
hydroelectric energy n 51
hydroelectric power station n 51
hydrofoil n 105
hydrogen n 78
hydrotherapy n 24
hyena n 158
hyphen n 175
hypnotherapy n 24
hypotenuse n 74
hyssop n 59

I

Iberian ham n 64
ibex n 158
ice n 68, 154
ice and lemon n 68
ice bucket n 68
ice climbing n 122
ice cream n 61, 70, 134
ice cream cone n 65
ice cream scoop n 65
ice cream sundae n 63
ice fishing n 121
ice hockey n 110
ice hockey player n 110
ice hockey rink n 110
ice maker n 27
ice skate n 110
ice-skating n 122
iceberg lettuce n 55
iceberg n 146
iced adj 52
iced bun n 63
iced coffee n 65
iced tea n 52, 66
Iceland n 151, 153
Icelandic adj 153
ichthyostega n 157
icicle n 146
icing n 29, 63
icy adj 154
igloo n 32
igneous adj 156
ignition n 99
illness n 19
illustration n 138
imaginative adj 93
immature adj 10
immigration n 104
impala n 158
impatient adj 10
important adj 177
Impressionism n 130
impulsive adj 10
in brine phr 64
in credit phr 45
in debt phr 45
in field n 111
in front of prep 148, 180
in oil phr 64
in prep 180
in sauce phr 72
in the black phr 45
in the red phr 45
in town n 42
in-goal area n 108
inbox n 83
incandescent bulb n 33
inch n 174
inch plant n 167
incisors n 03
income n 94
incontinence pads n 49
incorrect adj 176
incredible adj 177
incubator n 08
independent adj 93
index n 138
index finger n 02
India n 150, 153
Indian adj 153
Indian cobra n 163
Indian pale ale (IPA) n 68
indifferent adj 06
indigo n 141
indium n 78
Indonesia n 151, 153
Indonesian adj 153
industrial emissions n 155
industrial revolution n 79
industrial zone n 42
industries n 91
infection n 19
infield n 113
infielders n 113
inflatable boat n 134
inflatable dinghy n 105
influencer n 84, 93
information age n 79
information chart n 49
information screen n 104
information technology (IT) n 73, 91
infrared n 75
inhaler n 20, 49
initiative n 93
injera n 62
injury n 19
ink n 141, 175
inline skating n 125
inner core n 145
inner tube n 101
inning n 113
innocent adj 85
innovative adj 93
inoculation n 20
insect repellent n 49, 135
insects n 162
insensitive adj 10
inside prep 180
inside center n 108
inside lane n 96
insoles n 17, 49
insomnia n 19, 30
inspector n 50
install v 33
install a carpet v 35
installation n 130
instep n 02
instruments n 129
insulated gloves n 143
insulating tape n 36
insulation n 35
insulin n 49
intelligent adj 10
intensive care unit n 21
intercity train n 102
intercom n 25
intercostal n 03
interdental brush n 22
interest rate n 45
interested adj 06
interesting adj 177
intermission n 126
intern n 81
internal organs n 04
international flight n 104
interpersonal skills n 93
interrogation room n 50
interrupt v 95
intersection n 43
interview n 81, 137
interviewer n 81
intolerant adj 23
intrigued adj 06
invertebrate n 77
investigation n 50
investment n 94
invoice n 94
iodine n 78
ionosphere n 155
Iran n 151, 153
Iranian adj 153
Iraq n 150, 153
Iraqi adj 153
Ireland n 151, 153
iridium n 78
iris n 01, 38
Irish adj 153
Irish coffee n 65
iron n 23, 34, 49, 78, 115, 156
iron a shirt v 09
Iron age n 79
ironing board n 34
irritated adj 06
irritating adj 177
Islamic Golden Age n 79
island n 88, 145, 147
isobar n 155
Israel n 150, 153
Israeli adj 153
isthmus n 147
IT manager n 89
Italian adj 153
italic adj 175
italic n 175
Italy n 151, 153
IV n 21
IV pole n 21
Ivorian adj 152
Ivory Coast n 149, 152
ivy n 169

J

jack n 98, 140
jack connector n 129
jack-o'-lantern n 139, 170
jackal n 158
jacket n 15
jackfruit n 58
jackhammer n 87
Jackson's chameleon n 163
jacuzzi n 25
jade n 156
jade pothos n 38
jaguar n 159
jalapeños n 59
jam n 71
Jamaica n 150, 152
Jamaican adj 152
janitor n 90
January n 172
Japan n 150, 153
Japanese adj 153
Japanese bobtail n 164
Japanese characters n 175
jar n 27, 52, 60
jasper n 156
javelin n 116
jaw n 01, 03
jawed fish n 157
jawless fish n 157
jazz n 129
jealous adj 06
jeans n 14
jelly beans n 67
jelly donut n 63
jelly sandals n 17
jellyfish n 166
Jerusalem artichoke n 56
jester n 79
jet n 156
jet engine n 103
Jet Ski n 134
jet skiing n 119
jetty n 106
jetway n 104
jeweler n 46, 89
jewelry n 16
jewelry box n 16
jewelry making n 141
jib n 87, 119
jigsaw n 35
jigsaw puzzle n 08, 140
job ads n 92
job applications n 92
job sheet n 92
job skills n 92
jobs n 89–90
jockey n 120
jodhpurs n 120
joey n 158
jog in place v 124
jogging n 133
joker n 140
Jordan n 150, 153
Jordanian adj 153
Joshua tree n 167
journal n 80

journalism *n* **91**
journalist *n* **90**
judge *n* **85, 90**
judo *n* **117**
juggle *v* **11**
juice, juices *n* **52, 65**
juicy *adj* **52**
jujitsu *n* **117**
July *n* **172**
jumbo jet *n* **103**
jump *v* **11, 117, 120**
jump ball *n* **112**
jump rope *n* **08, 124**
jumping jacks *n* **124**
jumping ramp *n* **122**
jumping spider *n* **162**
junction *n* **96**
June *n* **172**
jungle gym *n* **43**
junk mail *n* **83**
Jupiter *n* **143**
Jurassic *adj* **157**
Jurassic *n* **157**
jury *n* **85**
jury box *n* **85**
jury deliberation *n* **85**

K

K-pop *n* **129**
kale *n* **55**
kangaroo *n* **158**
karaoke *n* **136**
karate *n* **117**
karate mat *n* **117**
kayak *n* **105, 119**
kayaking *n* **119**
Kazakhstan *n* **151, 153**
Kazakh *adj* **153**
kebab *n* **70, 72**
keel *n* **105, 119**
keep *n* **44**
keep net *n* **121**
kefir *n* **61**
kelp *n* **166**
kendo *n* **117**
Kenya *n* **149, 152**
Kenyan *adj* **152**
kernel *n* **55**
ketchup *n* **60, 70**
kettledrum *n* **128**
key, keys *n* **25, 32**
key cutting shop *n* **46**
keyboard *n* **83, 129**
keyhole *n* **25-26**
keypad *n* **45**
kick *n* **108, 118**
kick *v* **11, 107**
kick flip *n* **125**
kickboxing *n* **117**
kickoff *n* **109**
kickstand *n* **101**
kid *n* **165**
kidney,
kidneys *n* **04, 53, 71**
kids meal *n* **69**
kids' clothes *n* **13**
kids' shoes *n* **17**
killer whale *n* **166**
kilogram *n* **174**
kilometer *n* **174**
kilt *n* **15**
kimchi *n* **60**
kimono *n* **15**
kind *adj* **10**
king *n* **79, 140**
kingdom *n* **79**
kingfisher *n* **160**
kiosk *n* **46-48**
kippers *n* **71**
Kiribati *adj* **153**
Kiribati *n* **150, 153**
kitchen *n* **27, 69**
kitchen appliances *n* **27**
kitchen equipment *n* **28**
kitchen installer *n* **90**
kitchen knife *n* **28**
kitchen scissors *n* **28**
kitchenware *n* **28**
kite *n* **08**
kite surfing *n* **119**
kitten *n* **164**
kitten heels *n* **17**
Kittitian *adj* **152**
kiwi *n* **160**
knead *v* **62**
knee *n* **01, 126**
knee joint *n* **03**
knee pad *n* **107, 100**
knee-high boots *n*
kneecap *n* **03**
kneeler *n* **40**
kneeling chair *n* **82**
knife *n* **27**
knife sharpener *n* **28**
knife stand *n* **28**
knight *n* **79, 139-140**
knitting *n* **142**
knitting needle *n* **142**
knob *n* **25-26, 113**
knock down
a wall *v* **35**
knock out *n* **117**
knots *n* **121**
knuckle *n* **02**
koala *n* **158**
kohlrabi *n* **55**
kola nuts *n* **58**
Komodo dragon *n* **163**
kookaburra *n* **160**
kosher *adj* **72**
krypton *n* **78**
kumquat *n* **57**
kung fu *n* **117**
Kuwait *n* **151, 153**
Kuwaiti *adj* **153**
Kwanzaa *n* **07**
Kyrgyz *adj* **153**
Kyrgyzstan *n* **151, 153**

L

lab *n* **76**
lab coat *n* **13**
label, labels *n* **40, 130**
laboratory *n* **76**
labrador *n* **164**
lace *n* **17, 107**
lace bobbin *n* **142**
lace-making *n* **142**
lace-up boots *n* **17**
lacrosse *n* **110**
lacrosse player *n* **110**
lactose free *adj* **61**
lactose intolerant *adj* **23**
ladder *n* **36, 50, 87**
ladle *n* **27**
lady *n* **79**
ladybug *n* **162**
lager *n* **68**
lagoon *n* **147**
laid-back *adj* **10**
lake *n* **146, 148**
Lake Natron *n* **145**
lamb *n* **53, 165**
lamp *n* **26, 82, 101, 106, 135, 139**
lampshade *n* **26**
land *n* **145**
land *v* **104**
landfill *n* **155**
landing gear *n* **103**
landing hill *n* **122**
landing net *n* **121**
landlord *n* **32**
landscape *n* **132**
landscape *v* **39**
landscape painting *n* **133**
landslide *n* **146**
lane *n* **116, 118**
lane line *n* **112**
lane rope *n* **118**
languages *n* **73, 80**
lantern *n* **135**
lanthanum *n* **78**
lanthanide series *n* **78**
Laos *n* **150, 153**
Laotian *adj* **153**
lapel *n* **15**
lapis lazuli *n* **156**
laptop *n* **82-83**
larch *n* **167**
large *adj* **176**
large intestine *n* **04**
larynx *n* **04**
lasagna *n* **64, 72**
laser *n* **75**
laser run *n* **116**
late *adj* **171**
later *adj* **171**
later *adv* **171**
Latin *n* **129**
Latin alphabet *n* **175**
latissimus dorsi *n* **03**
latitude *n* **145, 148**
Latvia *n* **151, 153**
Latvian *adj* **153**
laugh *v* **02**
launch *n* **143**
launch pad *n* **143**
Laundromat *n* **46**
laundry *n* **34**
laundry detergent *n* **34**
laundry
hamper *n* **31, 34**
laundry service *n* **131**
laurel *n* **167**
lava *n* **145**
lava layer *n* **145**
lavender *n* **38**
law *n* **80, 85**
lawn *n* **41**
lawn rake *n* **40**
lawnmower *n* **40**
lawrencium *n* **78**
lawyer *n* **85, 90**
lawyer's office *n* **85**
laxative *n* **49**
lay bricks *v* **35**
lay sod *v* **39**
layer cake *n* **63**
lazy *adj* **10**
leaching *n* **39**
lead *n* **78**
lead singer *n* **129**
leaded *n* **97**
leader *n* **81**
leadership *n* **93**
leaf *n* **55**
leaf blower *n* **40**
leaf fall *n* **172**
leafy *adj* **56**
lean meat *n* **53**
Leaning Tower
of Pisa *n* **44**
learn *v* **73**
lease *n* **32**
leash *n* **164**
leather *adj* **176**
leather *n* **13, 107, 176**
leather suit *n* **100**
leatherback
sea turtle *n* **163**
leave *v* **179**
leave the house *v* **09**
leave work *v* **09**
Lebanese *adj* **153**
Lebanon *n* **150, 153**
lecture theatre *n* **80**
lecturer *n* **80, 89**
LED (light emitting diode)
bulb *n* **33**
lederhosen *n* **15**
leek *n* **56**
left defenseman *n* **110**
left defensive end *n* **107**
left defensive tackle *n* **107**
left guard *n* **107**
left safety *n* **107**
left tackle *n* **107**
left winger *n* **110**
left-wing *n* **108**
leg *n* **01, 26, 53**
leg guard *n* **110**
leg pad *n* **111**
leg press *n* **124**
legal *n* **91**
legal advice *n* **85**
legal system *n* **85**
leggings *n* **14**
legumes *n* **23**
lemon *n* **57**
lemon balm *n* **59**
lemon curd *n* **60**
lemon squeezer *n* **28**
lemonade *n* **52**
lemongrass *n* **59**
length *n* **74, 174**
lens *n* **22, 75, 127, 136**
lens case *n* **22**
lens cleaning cloth *n* **22**
lens solution *n* **49**
Leo *n* **144**
leopard *n* **159**
leotard *n* **15**
leprechaun *n* **139**
Lesotho *n* **149, 152**
lesson *n* **73**
let *n* **114**
let in *v* **178**
let out *v* **142**
letter *n* **45, 82**
letters *n* **175**
lettuce *n* **55**
level *n* **35-36, 87**
Liberia *n* **149, 152**
Liberian *adj* **152**
libero *n* **112**
Libra *n* **144**

librarian *n* **80, 90**
library *n* **43, 80, 148**
library card *n* **80**
libretto *n* **126**
Libya *n* **149, 152**
Libyan *adj* **152**
license plate *n* **97**
lick *v* **02, 11**
licorice *n* **67**
lid *n* **28**
lie down *v* **20**
Liechtenstein *n* **151, 153**
Liechtensteiner *adj* **153**
life cycle *n* **77**
life events *n* **07**
life jacket *n* **105, 119**
life preserver *n* **105, 119, 134**
life raft *n* **119**
life-support backpack *n* **143**
lifeboat *n* **105**
lifeguard *n* **118, 134**
lifeguard tower *n* **134**
lift *v* **11**
ligament *n* **03**
ligature *n* **175**
light *adj* **60, 176**
light, lights *n* **32, 50, 84, 101, 143**
light a fire *v* **135**
light aircraft *n* **103**
light bulbs *n* **33**
light cream *n* **61**
light shower *n* **154**
light switch *n* **33**
lighthouse *n* **44, 106**
lighting *n* **47**
lightning *n* **154**
like *v* **84**
lilac *n* **38**
lily *n* **38, 167**
lily of the valley *n* **38**
lime *n* **57, 169**
lime pickle *n* **60**
limestone *n* **156**
limousine *n* **97**
limpet *n* **134, 166**
linden *n* **169**
line, lines *n* **74, 121**
line *n* **48, 132**
line of play *n* **115**
linen chest *n* **30**
linesman *n* **109, 114**
lingerie *n* **47**
lining *n* **15**
lining paper *n* **37**
lintel *n* **87**
lion *n* **158**
lioness *n* **158**
lip balm *n* **18**
lip brush *n* **18**
lip liner *n* **18**
lips *n* **01**
lipstick *n* **18**
liqueur *n* **68**
liquid *n* **76**
liquid measure *n* **174**
liquid measurements *n* **174**
liquor store *n* **46**
listen *v* **11**
listen to the radio *v* **09**
liter *n* **174**
literary fiction *n* **138**
literature *n* **73, 80**
lithium *n* **78**
Lithuania *n* **151, 153**
Lithuanian *adj* **153**
little finger *n* **02**
little gem *n* **55**
little toe *n* **02**
litterbox *n* **164**
live *n* **33**
live rail *n* **102**
liver *n* **04, 53**
livermorium *n* **78**
liverwort *n* **167**
living room *n* **26**
living stones *n* **168**
lizard *n* **164**
llama *n* **158, 165**
load the dishwasher *v* **34**
loaf *n* **62**
loafers *n* **17**
loam *n* **39**
lob *n* **114**
lobster *n* **54**
local produce *n* **23**
lock *n* **101, 106**
locker room *n* **124**
lockers *n* **118, 124**
locksmith *n* **90**
locust *n* **162**
log in *v* **83, 178**
log out *v* **83, 178**
loganberry *n* **57**
logic game *n* **136**
loin *n* **54**
lollipop *n* **67**
London plane *n* **168**
lonely *adj* **06**
long *adj* **176**
long hair *n* **12**
long jump *n* **116**
long legs *n* **159**
long-handled shears *n* **40**
longitude *n* **145, 148**
look at *v* **178**
look for *v* **178**
loom *n* **142**
loose *adj* **13, 176**
loosehead prop *n* **108**
loppers *n* **40**
lord *n* **79**
lorikeet *n* **161**
lose *v* **109, 140**
lose weight *v* **20, 23**
lose your way *v* **148**
lost and found *n* **104**
lost property office *n* **102**
lotus *n* **38**
loudspeakers *n* **136**
lovage *n* **59**
love *n* **114**
low *adj* **176**
low calorie *adj* **23**
low pressure *n* **155**
low tide *n* **147**
lower deck *n* **99**
lower pitch *n* **128**
lowercase *n* **175**
loyalty card *n* **47**
lucky *adj* **06**
ludo *n* **140**
lug nuts *n* **98**
luge *n* **122**
luggage *n* **104, 131**
luggage hold *n* **99**
luggage rack *n* **102**
luggage storage *n* **102**
lumbar vertebrae *n* **03**
lumber *n* **87**
luna moth *n* **162**
lunar eclipse *n* **143**
lunar module *n* **143**
lunar rover *n* **143**
lunch *n* **26, 72**
lunch menu *n* **69**
lung *n* **04**
lunge *n* **117, 124**
lupin *n* **38**
lure *n* **121**
lutetium *n* **78**
Luxembourg *adj* **153**
Luxembourg *n* **151, 153**
lychee *n* **57**
lymphatic *n* **04**
lynx *n* **159**

M

macadamia, macadamias *n* **58, 168**
macaque *n* **159**
macaron *n* **63**
macaroni *n* **64**
mace *n* **59, 79**
machine gun *n* **88**
machine needle *n* **142**
machinery *n* **87**
mackerel *n* **54**
macramé *n* **142**
mad *adj* **06**
Madagascan *adj* **152**
Madagascar *n* **149, 152**
magazine website *n* **84**
maglev *n* **102**
magma chamber *n* **145**
magnesium *n* **49, 78, 156**
magnet *n* **75**
magnetic field *n* **75**
magnolia *n* **167**
maid *n* **89**
maid service *n* **131**
mail carrier *n* **45, 90**
mail slot *n* **25, 45**
mailbox *n* **25, 45**
main character *n* **127**
main road *n* **148**
main street *n* **46**
Maine coon *n* **164**
mainsail *n* **119**
make *v* **11**
make a loss *v* **94**
make a profit *v* **94**
make a reservation *v* **69, 131**
make curtains *v* **35**
make friends *v* **07**
make the bed *v* **09, 34**
make up *v* **178**
makeup *n* **18**
makeup bag *n* **18**
malachite *n* **156**
Malawi *n* **149, 152**
Malawian *adj* **152**
Malaysia *n* **151, 153**
Malaysian *adj* **153**
Maldives *n* **150, 153**
Maldivian *adj* **153**
male *n* **04**
Mali *n* **149, 152**
Malian *adj* **152**
mallard *n* **161**
mallet *n* **36, 141**
malt vinegar *n* **60**
Malta *n* **151, 153**
Maltese *adj* **153**
mammals *n* **158, 159**
man *n* **05**
manage *v* **92**
manager *n* **81, 109**
managing director *n* **81**
manchego *n* **64**
mandarin duck *n* **161**
mandarin orange *n* **57**
mandolin *n* **129**
mandoline *n* **28**
mandrill *n* **159**
mane *n* **120**
manganese *n* **78**
mango *n* **57**
mango juice *n* **65**
mangosteen *n* **58**
mangrove *n* **169**
manhole *n* **43**
manicure *n* **18**
mannequin *n* **142**
mansion *n* **32**
mantis shrimp *n* **166**
mantle *n* **145**
mantlepiece *n* **26**
manual *n* **99**
manufacturing *n* **91**
map *n* **132**
maple *n* **169**
maple syrup *n* **60**
maps *n* **148**
maracas *n* **128**
marathon *n* **116**
marble *adj* **176**
marble *n* **156, 176**
marble queen *n* **38**
March *n* **172**
mare *n* **120, 165**
margarine *n* **61**
marigold *n* **38**
marina *n* **106**
marinated *adj* **64, 72**
marinated fish *n* **64**
marine *n* **88**
marine fishing *n* **121**
marine iguana *n* **163**
marine species *n* **166**
marjoram *n* **59**
mark *v* **112**
marker *n* **175**
market researcher *n* **89**
marketing *n* **91**
marmalade *n* **60, 71**
marmoset *n* **159**
marrella *n* **157**
married *n* **05**
married couple *n* **07**
marrow *n* **56**
Mars *n* **143**
marsh *n* **147**
Marshall Islands *n* **150, 153**
Marshallese *adj* **153**
marshmallow *n* **67**
martial arts *n* **117, 127**
Martini *n* **68**
Mary Janes *n* **17**
marzipan *n* **63**
mascara *n* **18**
mascot *n* **109**
mash *v* **29**
mashed *adj* **72**
masher *n* **28**
mask *n* **113, 117–118**
masking tape *n* **37**
Mason jar *n* **52**
masonry bit *n* **36**
massage *n* **24**

mast *n* **105, 119**
master's degree *n* **80**
masterpiece *n* **130**
mat *n* **24**
matamata *n* **163**
match *n* **114**
materials *n* **35, 176**
maternity *n* **21**
maternity ward *n* **21**
math *n* **73**
mathematical equipment *n* **74**
mathematics *n* **74**
matte *n* **37**
mattress *n* **30**
mature *adj* **10**
matzo *n* **62**
Mauritania *n* **149, 152**
Mauritanian *adj* **152**
Mauritian *adj* **152**
Mauritius *n* **149, 152**
May *n* **172**
mayonnaise *n* **60**
MDF *n* **35**
meal deal *n* **70**
meals *n* **72**
mean *adj* **10**
measles *n* **19**
measure *n* **68**
measure *v* **174, 178**
measurements *n* **74**
measures *n* **174**
measuring cup *n* **27–29, 174**
measuring spoon *n* **28, 49**
meat *n* **48, 53**
meat hook *n* **53**
meat pie *n* **72**
meat pies *n* **64**
meat tenderizer *n* **28**
meat thermometer *n* **28**
meatballs *n* **72**
mechanic *n* **89, 98**
mechanics *n* **98**
medal *n* **88, 116**
media *n* **84, 91**
median *n* **96**
medical chart *n* **21**
medical examination *n* **20**
medication *n* **20, 49**
medicine *n* **20, 49, 80**
mediocre *adj* **177**
meditation *n* **24**
medium height *adj* **12**
medlar *n* **169**
medley relay *n* **118**
meerkat *n* **159**
meet *v* **179**
meet a deadline *v* **92**
meet up *v* **178**
meeting *n* **81, 82, 95**
meeting-room equipment *n* **82**
meganeura *n* **157**
megaphone *n* **50**
meitnerium *n* **78**
melody *n* **129**
melons *n* **58**
melt butter *v* **29**
melting ice caps *n* **155**
membership *n* **124**
memory card *n* **83**
mendelevium *n* **78**
men's decathlon *n* **116**
menswear *n* **47**
menu *n* **65, 70**
meow *v* **164**
merchant *n* **79**
Mercury *n* **143**
mercury *n* **78, 156**
meringue *n* **63**
mermaid *n* **139**
merman *n* **139**
mesa *n* **146**
mesosphere *n* **155**
Mesozoic (middle life) *adj* **157**
Mesozoic (middle life) *n* **157**
mess *n* **88**
mess around *v* **178**
metacarpals *n* **03**
metal *adj* **176**
metal, metals *n* **35, 155, 156, 176**
metal bit *n* **36**
metal detecting *n* **133**
metamorphic *adj* **156**
metamorphosis *n* **77**
metatarsals *n* **03**
meteor *n* **144**
meteor shower *n* **144**
meter *n* **174**
meter line *n* **108**
methane *n* **155**
meticulous *adj* **10**
Mexican *adj* **152**
Mexican axolotl *n* **163**
Mexico *n* **150, 152**
mezzanine *n* **126**
mezzo-soprano *n* **126**
mica *n* **156**
microbiologist *n* **77**
microbiology *n* **77**
microlight *n* **103**
Micronesia *n* **150, 153**
Micronesian *adj* **153**
microphone *n* **84, 95, 136**
microscope *n* **77**
microwave *v* **29**
microwave oven *n* **27**
microwaves *n* **75**
mid-off *n* **111**
mid-wicket *n* **111**
midcourt area marker *n* **112**
midday *n* **171**
middle blocker *n* **112**
middle finger *n* **02**
middle lane *n* **96**
middle level *n* **47**
middle linebacker *n* **107**
middle-aged *adj* **12**
midfielder *n* **109**
midnight *n* **171**
midnight zone *n* **166**
midwife *n* **08**
migraine *n* **19**
migrate *v* **161**
mild *adj* **154**
mile *n* **174**
military *n* **88, 91**
military ambulance *n* **88**
military transport aircraft *n* **88**
military truck *n* **88**
military uniform *n* **13**
military vehicles *n* **88**
milk *n* **61, 65, 71**
milk *v* **86**
milk carton *n* **61**
milk chocolate *n* **67**
milk products *n* **61**
milkshake *n* **52, 65, 70**
milky conecap *n* **170**
Milky Way *n* **144**
millennium *n* **172**
millet *n* **86**
milligram *n* **174**
milliliter *n* **174**
millimeter *n* **174**
millipede *n* **162**
mimosa *n* **168**
minaret *n* **44**
mince *v* **29**
mindfulness *n* **24**
mine shaft *n* **51**
miner, miners *n* **51, 89**
mineral spirits *n* **37**
mineral water *n* **52, 68**
minerals *n* **23, 156**
minibar *n* **131**
minibus *n* **99**
mining *n* **91**
minivan *n* **97**
Minotaur *n* **139**
minstrel *n* **79**
mint *n* **59, 67**
mint tea *n* **66**
minus sign *n* **74**
minute *n* **82, 171**
minute hand *n* **171**
mirror *n* **18, 30, 77**
miserable *adj* **06**
miss a train *v* **102**
mission control *n* **143**
mist *n* **154**
mistletoe *n* **168**
misty *adj* **154**
mitochondria *n* **77**
mitt *n* **113**
mittens *n* **13**
mix *v* **29, 62**
mixing bowl *n* **28**
mixing desk *n* **84**
moat *n* **44**
mobile *n* **30**
mobile banking *n* **94**
mobile home *n* **32**
moccasins *n* **17**
mochi *n* **63**
mocktail *n* **68**
model making *n* **141**
modeling tool *n* **141**
modern building *n* **44**
modern pentathlon *n* **116**
moisturizer *n* **18**
molars *n* **03**
mold *n* **170**
molding *n* **26**
Moldova *n* **151, 153**
Moldovan *adj* **153**
mole *n* **12, 159**
molecule *n* **76**
molt *v* **164**
molybdenum *n* **78**
mom *n* **05**
Monacan *adj* **153**
Monaco *n* **151, 153**
monarch butterfly *n* **162**
monastery *n* **44**
Monday *n* **172**
money *n* **45, 94**
Mongolia *n* **150, 153**
Mongolian *adj* **153**
mongoose *n* **159**
monkey puzzle *n* **167**
monkey wrench *n* **36**
monkfish *n* **54**
mono *adj* **136**
monocle *n* **22**
monoplane *n* **103**
monorail *n* **102**
monster *n* **139**
monster truck *n* **123**
Montenegrin *adj* **153**
Montenegro *n* **151, 153**
month *n* **172**
monthly *adj* **172**
monthly *adv* **172**
monument *n* **42, 44, 132**
moods *n* **06**
Moon *n* **143**
moonstone *n* **156**
moor *v* **106**
mooring *n* **106**
moorish idol *n* **166**
moose *n* **159**
mop *n* **34**
mop the floor *v* **34**
morel *n* **170**
morning *n* **09, 171**
morning glory *n* **169**
morning show *n* **137**
Moroccan *adj* **152**
Morocco *n* **149, 152**
mortar *n* **28, 35, 76, 87**
mortar and pestle *n* **28**
mortarboard *n* **80**
mortgage *n* **32, 45**
moscovium *n* **78**
Moses basket *n* **08, 30**
mosque *n* **44**
mosquito *n* **162**
mosquito net *n* **135**
moss *n* **167**
mother *n* **05**
mother-in-law *n* **05**
mother of thousands *n* **168**
moths *n* **162**
motion-sickness medication *n* **49**
motivated *adj* **93**
motor home *n* **135**
motor scooter *n* **100**
motocross *n* **123**
motorcycle *n* **100**
motorcycle officer *n* **50**
motorcycle racing *n* **123**
motorsports *n* **123**
mount *v* **100**
mountain *n* **147**
mountain ash *n* **169**
mountain bike *n* **101**
mountain biking *n* **133**
mountain chain *n* **146**
mountain goat *n* **159**
mountain pose *n* **24**
mountain range *n* **146**
mountaineering *n* **133**
mouse *n* **83, 158, 164**
mouse pad *n* **83**
mouth *n* **01, 147**
mouth guard *n* **107, 117**
mouthwash *n* **31**
movable panel *n* **82**
move *v* **11, 140**
move in *v* **32**
move out *v* **32**
movie camera *n* **127**
movie star *n* **127**
movie theater *n* **42, 127**
movies *n* **127**
moving truck *n* **32**
mow the lawn *v* **09, 39**
Mozambican *adj* **152**
Mozambique *n* **149, 152**
mozzarella *n* **64**
muck out *v* **120**
mudguard *n* **100**

mudskipper n 166
mudslide n 146
muesli n 71
muffin n 63, 70
muffin tin n 29
muffler n 98, 100
mug n 27
mugging n 85
mulberry n 57
mulch v 39
mules n 17
multi-purpose knife n 135
multi-vitamins n 49
multiplayer game n 136
multiplex n 127
multiplication sign n 74
multiply v 74
mumps n 19
muscles n 03
museum n 43, 130, 132
museum curator n 89
musher n 122
mushroom picking n 133
mushroom, mushrooms n 56, 170
music n 73, 128, 129
music channel n 137
music school n 80
music stand n 128
music teacher n 90
music therapy n 24
musical n 126, 127
musician n 90
musk ox n 159
mussel n 54
mustache n 12
mustard n 70
mustard allergy n 23
mustard seeds n 60
mute swan n 161
muzzle n 120
Myanmar (Burma) n 150, 153
mycelium n 170
myrtle n 168
myths n 139

N

nacelle n 51
nachos n 70
nail n 36
nail clippers n 18, 49
nail file n 18
nail polish n 18
nail polish remover n 18
nail scissors n 18
Namibia n 149, 152
Namibian adj 152
napkin n 27, 72
napkin ring n 27
Napoleon n 63
narrow adj 176
narwhal n 166
nasal spray n 20
nasturtium n 169
nasty adj 177
national park n 132, 133
nationalities n 152, 153
natural arch n 147
natural history n 157
nature documentary n 137
nature reserve n 133, 148
nature therapy n 24
nature writing n 138
naturopathy n 24
Nauru n 150, 153
Nauruan adj 153
nausea n 19
nautilus n 166
navel n 01
navigate v 119
navy n 88
navy blue n 141
navy vessels n 88
near adj 176
nearsighted adj 22
nebula n 144
neck n 01, 115, 129, 161
neck brace n 19
neck pad n 107
necklace n 16
neckline n 142
nectarine n 57
needle n 20
needlefish n 166
needle-nose pliers n 36
needle plate n 142
needlepoint n 142
negative adj 75
negative electrode n 75
negotiate v 92
negotiating n 93
neighbor n 07
neodymium n 78
Neogene adj 157
Neogene n 157
neon n 78
Nepal n 150, 153
Nepalese adj 153
nephew n 05
Neptune n 143
neptunium n 78
nerve n 03, 22
nervous adj 04, 06, 10
nest n 160
net n 109, 112, 114
net v 121
netball n 125
Netherlands n 151, 153
nettle n 169
neurology n 21
neutral n 33
neutral zone n 107, 110
neutron n 76
neutron star n 144
never adv 171, 172
Nevisian adj 152
new adj 176
new leaves n 172
new moon n 143
new potato n 56
New Year n 07
New Zealand adj 153
New Zealand n 150, 153
newborn baby n 08
news anchor n 137
news n 137
news website n 84
newsboy cap n 16
newsfeed n 84
newspaper n 48, 138
newsstand n 46, 48
next to prep 148, 180
nib n 73, 175
nibble v 52
Nicaragua n 150, 152
Nicaraguan adj 152
nice adj 177
nickel n 78, 156
niece n 05
nigella seeds n 59
Niger n 149, 152
Nigeria n 149, 152
Nigerian adj 152
Nigerien adj 152
night n 171
night-light n 30
nightclub n 42
nightgown n 14
nightie n 14
nightingale n 160
nightmare n 30
nightstand n 30
nightwear n 14
nihonium n 78
Nile crocodile n 163
nine num 173
nine-to-five job n 81
nineteen num 173
ninety num 173
ninth num 173
niobium n 78
nipple n 01, 08
nitrogen n 78
no entry n 96
no passing phr 96
no photography phr 130
no right turn phr 96
no U-turn phr 96
no vacancies phr 131
no-charge semi-circle n 112
nobelium n 78
noble gases n 78
nobles n 79
nod v 02
noisy adj 176
non-blood relative n 05
non-carbonated adj 52
nonfiction n 138
nonmetals n 78
noodle soup n 72
noodles n 64, 70, 72
normal adj 18
normal hair n 12
north n 148
North America n 150, 152
North American adj 152
North Korea n 150, 153
North Korean adj 153
North Macedonia n 151, 153
North Macedonian adj 153
North Pole n 75, 145
northeast n 148
northern cardinal n 161
Northern Hemisphere n 145
northwest n 148
Norway n 151, 153
Norwegian adj 153
nose n 01, 103
nose clip n 118
nose cone n 123
noseband n 120
nosebleed n 19
nosewheel n 103
nostrils n 01
notation n 128
notebook n 73, 95
notepad n 82
notes n 95, 128
nougat n 67
novel n 138
November n 172
now adv 171
nozzle n 40
nuclear energy n 51
nuclear power plant n 51
nuclear waste n 51
nucleus n 76, 77
number n 112
number eight n 108
numbers n 173
numeracy n 93
numerals n 175
numerator n 74
nurse n 20, 21, 89
nursery n 30
nursing n 80
nut allergy n 23
nut, nuts n 36, 58, 68, 129
nutmeg n 59
nutrition n 23

oak n 169
oar n 119
oasis n 146
oatmeal n 70
objective lens n 77
obliques n 03
oboe n 128
observatory n 144
obsidian n 156
obstetrician n 08
occupations n 89-90
occluded front n 155
ocean n 134, 145, 147
ocean life n 166
ocean ridge n 145
Oceania n 150, 153
Oceanian adj 153
octagon n 74
October n 172
octopus n 54, 166
odd adj 177
odometer n 99
off the shoulder adj 15
off-piste n 122
off-road motorcycle n 100
offal n 53
offense n 107
office n 82
office building n 42
office equipment n 82
office manager n 81
office reception n 81
office services n 91
office work n 81
often adv 172
oganesson n 78
ogre n 139
oil n 51, 60, 64, 97
oil field n 51
oil painting n 130
oil paints n 141
oil slick n 155
oil tank n 100
oil tanker n 105
oil terminal n 106
oil-filled radiator n 33
oily adj 18
ointment n 20, 49
okra n 55

old *adj* **12, 176**
old man cactus *n* **168**
old-fashioned *adj* **177**
oleander *n* **169**
oleaster *n* **169**
olive *n* **68, 169**
olive oil *n* **60**
olm *n* **163**
Oman *n* **151, 153**
Omani *adj* **153**
omelet *n* **61, 71, 72**
on-demand boiler *n* **33**
on *prep* **180**
on stage *adj* **126**
on the corner *phr* **148**
on the left *phr* **148**
on the right *phr* **148**
on time *adj* **171**
once a week *adv* **172**
oncology *n* **21**
one *num* **173**
one billion *num* **173**
one hundred *num* **173**
one million *num* **173**
one o'clock *n* **171**
one thirty *n* **171**
one thousand *num* **173**
one-way street *n* **96**
one-way system *n* **42**
one-way ticket *n* **131**
onesie *n* **13**
onion dome *n* **44**
onion *n* **56**
online banking *n* **45, 94**
online check-in *n* **104**
online communication *n* **83**
online delivery *n* **91**
online map *n* **148**
online media *n* **84**
online retail *n* **91**
online shopping *n* **48**
only child *n* **05**
only weekends *adv* **172**
onyx *n* **156**
opal *n* **156**
open *adj* **48, 132**
open sandwich *n* **70**
open turn *n* **118**
open-air activities *n* **133**
open-air hobbies *n* **133**
open-pit mining *n* **51**
open-plan *n* **32**
opening night *n* **126**
opening times *n* **132**
openside flanker *n* **108**
opera *n* **126, 129**
opera glasses *n* **22**
opera house *n* **126**
operating room *n* **21**
operating table *n* **21**
operation *n* **21**
ophthalmology *n* **21**
opinions *n* **177**
opium poppy *n* **168**
opponent *n* **117**
opposite *prep* **112, 148**
optician *n* **22, 46, 89**
optics *n* **75**
optimistic *adj* **10**
optometrist *n* **22**
orange *n* **57, 141**
orange juice with pulp *n* **65**
orange peel fungus *n* **170**
orange-cap boletus *n* **170**
orangeade *n* **52**
orangutan *n* **159**
orb weaver *n* **162**
orbit *n* **143**
orc *n* **139**
orchestra *n* **128**
orchestra pit *n* **126**
orchestra seating *n* **126**
orchestral instruments *n* **128**
orchid *n* **38, 47**
order *v* **46, 69**
ordering online *n* **46**
ordinal numbers *n* **173**
Ordovician *adj* **157**
Ordovician *n* **157**
oregano *n* **59**
organic *adj* **23, 39, 53**
organic food section *n* **23**
organic vegetables *n* **55**
organization *n* **93**
organize *v* **92**
organized *adj* **93**
oriental fire-bellied toad *n* **163**
orienteering *n* **133, 148**
origami *n* **141**
original *adj* **93**
Orion *n* **144**
ornamental plants *n* **41**
orthodontist *n* **89**
Orthodox church *n* **44**
orthopedics *n* **21**
oryx *n* **159**
osmium *n* **78**
osprey *n* **160**
osteopathy *n* **24**
ostrich *n* **160, 165**
otter *n* **158**
Ottoman *n* **30**
oud *n* **129**
ounce *n* **174**
out *adj* **113**
out *adv* **180**
out field *n* **111**
out of bounds *adj* **112**
outboard motor *n* **105**
outbox *n* **83**
outdoor activities *n* **133**
outer core *n* **145**
outfield *adj* **113**
outfielders *n* **113**
outgoing *adj* **10**
outlay *n* **94**
outpatient *n* **21**
outside *adv, prep* **180**
outside center *n* **108**
outside hitter *n* **112**
outside lane *n* **96**
outside linebacker *n* **107**
outstanding *adj* **177**
oval *n* **74**
ovary *n* **04, 38**
oven *n* **27**
oven mitt *n* **29**
over par *adj* **115**
overhanging eaves *n* **44**
over-the-counter drugs *n* **49**
overalls *n* **37**
overcast *adj* **154**
overdraft *n* **45, 94**
overeat *v* **23**
overfishing *n* **155**
overhead compartment *n* **103**
overpass *n* **102**
overtime *n* **81**
own *v* **32**
Oxfords *n* **17**
oxygen *n* **78**
oxygen mask *n* **21, 50**
oyster *n* **54**
oyster mushroom *n* **56, 170**
oyster sauce *n* **60**
oystercatcher *n* **160**
ozone depletion *n* **155**
ozone layer *n* **155**

P

PA (personal assistant) *n* **81**
pacifier *n* **08**
pack *v* **11, 32**
pack your bags *v* **131**
pack your lunch *v* **09**
package *n* **45, 52**
paddle *n* **114, 119**
paddleboarding *n* **119**
paddock *n* **120**
paella *n* **72**
page *n* **138**
pail and shovel *n* **134**
pain au chocolat *n* **62**
pain *n* **19**
painkillers *n* **20, 49**
paint *n* **37**
paint *v* **37**
paint a wall *v* **35**
paint bucket *n* **37**
paint stripper *n* **37**
paint tray *n* **37**
paint tube *n* **141**
paintballing *n* **133**
paintbrush *n* **37**
painted lady butterfly *n* **162**
painter *n* **89**
painting *n* **26, 130, 141**
paisley *adj* **13**
pajamas *n* **14**
Pakistan *n* **150, 153**
Pakistani *adj* **153**
palace *n* **132**
palate *n* **04**
Palau *n* **150, 153**
Palauan *adj* **153**
Paleogene *adj* **157**
Paleogene *n* **157**
paleontologist *n* **77**
Paleozoic (old life) *adj* **157**
Paleozoic (old life) *n* **157**
palette *n* **141**
palette knife *n* **141**
palladium *n* **78**
pallet *n* **87**
palm *n* **02, 41**
palm hearts *n* **55**
palm oil *n* **60**
palm tree *n* **134**
palomar knot *n* **121**
pampas grass *n* **38, 167**
Pamukkale *n* **145**
pan *n* **174**
panama *n* **16**
Panama *n* **150, 152**
Panamanian *adj* **152**
pancake *n* **65, 71**
pancreas *n* **04**
panda *n* **159**
paneer *n* **64**
pangolin *n* **159**
panpipe *n* **129**
pansy *n* **38**
panther chameleon *n* **163**
panties *n* **14**
pantograph *n* **102**
pantry *n* **27**
pants *n* **15, 107**
panty liner *n* **49**
pantyhose *n* **14**
paparazzi *n* **127**
papaya *n* **58**
paper *adj* **176**
paper *n* **82, 155, 176**
paper clip, paper clips *n* **73, 82**
paper napkin *n* **70**
paperback *n* **138**
papier-mâché *n* **141**
paprika *n* **59**
Papua New Guinea *n* **150, 153**
Papua New Guinean *adj* **153**
papyrus sedge *n* **167**
par *n* **115**
para athlete *n* **125**
para ice hockey *n* **122**
parachute *n* **125**
parachuting *n* **125**
paragliding *n* **125**
Paraguay *n* **149, 152**
Paraguayan *adj* **152**
parallel *adj* **74**
parallel bars *n* **125**
parallelogram *n* **74**
paramedic *n* **21, 50, 90**
paramotor *n* **103**
parasailing *n* **119**
parasports *n* **125**
parchment *n* **175**
parents *n* **05**
park *n* **42, 133**
park *v* **98**
parking attendant *n* **96**
parking enforcement officer *n* **96**
parking lot *n* **42**
parking meter *n* **96**
parking space *n* **32**
parkour *n* **133**
Parmesan *n* **64**
parole *n* **85**
parry *v* **117**
parsley *n* **59**
parsnip *n* **56**
parson's chameleon *n* **163**
particle accelerator *n* **75**
particle board *n* **35**
particle *n* **75**
partner *n* **05, 07**
parts of the body *n* **01**
parts of the day *n* **171**
pass *n* **112**
pass *v* **73, 98, 107, 108, 110**
passenger airplane *n* **103**
passenger port *n* **106**
passenger seat *n* **100**
passengers *n* **102, 106**
passing lane *n* **96**
passion flower *n* **169**
passion fruit *n* **58**
passionate *adj* **10**

Passover *n* **07**
passport *n* **104**
passport control *n* **104**
password *n* **83**
pasta *n* **64, 72**
pasta shells *n* **64**
pastels *n* **141**
pasteurized *adj* **61**
pasting table *n* **37**
pastrami *n* **64**
pastry *n* **63**
pastry brush *n* **29**
pasture *n* **86**
patch *n* **101**
patchwork *n* **142**
pâté *n* **64, 71**
patella *n* **03**
path *n* **41**
pathology *n* **21**
patient *adj* **10, 93**
patient *n* **19, 20, 21**
patio *n* **25**
patio doors *n* **25**
patio garden *n* **41**
patio umbrella *n* **65**
patty pan *n* **56**
pause *v* **137**
paving *n* **41**
pavlova *n* **63**
pawn *n* **140**
pay *n* **81**
pay *v* **46**
pay by card *v* **94**
pay cut *n* **81**
pay-per-view channel *n* **137**
pay separately *v* **69**
pay slip *n* **81**
pay the bills *v* **09**
pay with cash *v* **94**
paying attention to detail *n* **93**
pea *n* **55**
peace lily *n* **38**
peach *n* **57**
peacock butterfly *n* **162**
peacock *n* **161**
peak *n* **147**
peanut *n* **58, 68**
peanut allergy *n* **23**
peanut butter *n* **60**
peanut oil *n* **60**
pear *n* **58, 169**
peasants *n* **79**
peat *n* **39**
peat bog *n* **79**
pecan *n* **58, 168**
pectoral *n* **03**
pedal *n* **101**
pedal *v* **101**
pedestrian crossing *n* **96**
pedestrian zone *n* **42**
pediatrics *n* **21**
pedicure *n* **18**
pediment *n* **44**
peel *v* **29**
peeled prawn *n* **54**
peeler *n* **28**
peep toes *n* **17**
pelican *n* **160**
pelvis *n* **03**
pen *n* **73, 82, 86**
penalty area *n* **109**
penalty bench *n* **110**
penalty kick *n* **109**
penalty spot *n* **109**
pencil *n* **73, 82, 141, 175**
pencil case *n* **73**
pencil sharpener *n* **73, 82**
pendant *n* **16**
pendulous nose *n* **159**
peninsula *n* **147**
penis *n* **04**
penne *n* **64**
penny candy *n* **67**
pen pal *n* **07**
penstock *n* **51**
pentagon *n* **74**
peony *n* **47, 168**
pepper *n* **26**
peppercorns *n* **59**
peppered moth *n* **162**
pepperoni *n* **64**
peppers *n* **56**
percent *n* **173**
percentage, percentages *n* **74, 173**
perch *n* **54**
percussion *n* **128**
peregrine falcon *n* **160**
perennial *n* **41**
performance *n* **126**
performer *n* **126**
performing arts *n* **91**
perfume *n* **18**
pergola *n* **41**
period *n* **175**
period drama *n* **137**
periodic table *n* **78**
periodical *n* **80**
permanent *adj* **81**
permanent exhibition *n* **130**
Permian *adj* **157**
Permian *n* **157**
perpendicular *n* **74**
Persian *n* **164**
persimmon *n* **58**
personal assistant (PA) *n* **90**
personal services *n* **91**
personal trainer *n* **124**
personality traits *n* **10**
perspire *v* **02**
Peru *n* **149, 152**
Peruvian *adj* **152**
pescatarian *adj* **23**
pescatarian *n* **23**
pesticide *n* **40, 55, 86**
pestle *n* **28, 76**
pet *n* **164**
pet food *n* **48**
pet services *n* **91**
pet store *n* **46**
pet supplies *n* **164**
pet therapy *n* **24**
petal *n* **38**
petri dish *n* **77**
pH level *n* **76**
pharmaceuticals *n* **91**
pharmacist *n* **49, 89**
pharmacy *n* **42, 49**
pharynx *n* **04**
pheasant *n* **53, 161**
Philippines *n* **151, 153**
Phillips screwdriver *n* **36**
philosopher *n* **79**
philosophy *n* **80**
phoenix *n* **139**
phone *n* **82**
phoropter *n* **22**
phosphorus *n* **78**
photo booth *v* **46**
photo finish *n* **116**
photocopier *n* **82**
photographer *n* **89**
photosynthesis *n* **77**
phrasal verbs *n* **178**
phrasebook *n* **131**
phyllo *n* **63**
physical education *n* **73**
physical therapist *n* **89**
physical therapy *n* **21**
physics *n* **73, 75, 80**
physiotherapist *n* **89**
piano *n* **128, 129**
piano overture *n* **128**
piccalilli *n* **60**
piccolo *n* **128**
pick *v* **57**
pick mushrooms *v* **170**
pick someone up *v* **98**
pick up *v* **11, 178**
pick-up *n* **129**
pickax *n* **87**
pickled *adj* **72**
pickled beetroot *n* **60**
pickled onions *n* **60**
pickles *n* **60, 72**
pickpocketing *n* **85**
picnic *n* **133**
picnic basket *n* **133, 134**
picnic bench *n* **135**
pie pan *n* **29**
pieces *n* **140**
pier *n* **106**
pig *n* **165**
pig farm *n* **86**
pigeon *n* **160**
pigeon pose *n* **24**
piglet *n* **165**
pigtails *n* **12**
pike perch *n* **54**
Pilates *n* **124**
pile up *v* **178**
pileated woodpecker *n* **160**
pillow *n* **26, 30**
pillowcase *n* **30**
pills *n* **20, 49**
pilot *n* **90, 103**
Pilsner *n* **68**
pin *n* **16, 33, 142**
PIN *n* **45**
pin *v* **117**
pinch *n* **29**
pincushion *n* **142**
pine nuts *n* **58**
pineapple *n* **58, 167**
pineapple juice *n* **65**
ping pong *n* **114**
pink *n* **141**
pinking shears *n* **142**
pint *n* **174**
pint glass *n* **27**
pipe cutter *n* **36**
pipe *n* **33, 87, 98**
pipe organ *n* **128**
pipefish *n* **166**
pipette *n* **76**
piping bag *n* **29**
pirouette *v* **126**
Pisces *n* **144**
pistachio *n* **58**
pistol *n* **88**
pit lane *n* **123**
pit stop *n* **123**
pita bread *n* **62, 72**
pitch *n* **107, 109, 111, 128**
pitch a tent *v* **135**
pitch *v* **113**
pitcher *n* **113**
pitcher plant *n* **168**
pitcher's mound *n* **113**
pixie *n* **139**
pizza *n* **70**
pizza cutter *n* **28**
pizza oven *n* **70**
pizzeria *n* **70**
place mat *n* **26**
place setting *n* **27**
place to live *n* **25**
placenta *n* **08**
placerias *n* **157**
plaice *n* **54**
plaid *adj* **13**
plain *n* **146**
plain *adj* **13**
plain flour *n* **62**
plaintiff *n* **85**
plait *n* **12**
plan your route *v* **148**
plane *n* **36**
plane *v* **35**
planets *n* **143**
plank pose *n* **24**
plankton *n* **77, 166**
planner *n* **82, 138**
plant cell *n* **77**
plant cutting *n* **39**
plant food *n* **39**
plant *n* **77, 167–169**
plant pot *n* **40**
plant *v* **39, 86**
plantains *n* **86**
plaque *n* **22**
plaster *n* **37, 49**
plaster *v* **37**
plastic *adj* **155, 176**
plastic *n* **155, 176**
plastic surgery *n* **21**
plastic waste *n* **155**
plate *n* **145**
plate tectonics *n* **145**
plateau *n* **146**
plateosaurus *n* **157**
platform *n* **84, 102, 118**
platforms *n* **17**
platform game *n* **136**
platform number *n* **102**
platinum *n* **78, 156**
platypus *n* **158**
play *n* **126**
play *v* **11, 113, 137, 140**
play a musical instrument *v* **09**
play suit *n* **13**
play (the trumpet) *v* **128**
play with your kids *v* **09**
player *n* **108, 113, 114, 140**
player's number *n* **107**
players' bench *n* **107, 109, 110**
players' dugout *n* **113**
players' entrance/ exit *n* **109**
playground *n* **43**
playing cards *n* **140**
playing surface *n* **108**
playpen *n* **08**
plead *v* **85**
pleasant *adj* **177**
pleased *adj* **06**
pleat *n* **14**
plié *v* **126**
Plimsoll line *n* **105**
plow *n* **86**
plug *n* **31, 33, 83**
plug in *v* **83**
plug-in hybrid *n* **97**
plum *n* **57, 169**
plum tomato *n* **56**
plumb line *n* **37**
plumber *n* **89**
plumbing *n* **33**

plunger *n* **31, 36**
plus sign *n* **74**
plush toy *n* **08**
Pluto *n* **143**
plutonium *n* **78**
plywood *n* **35**
poach *v* **29**
poached *adj* **72**
poached egg *n* **61, 71**
pocket *n* **15, 125, 142**
pod *n* **55**
podcast *n* **84**
podium *n* **116, 128**
poetry therapy *n* **24**
point *n* **111**
point *v* **11**
point guard *n* **112**
point out *v* **178**
points *n* **140**
poison dart frog *n* **163**
poisoning *n* **19**
Poland *n* **151, 153**
polar bear *n* **159**
polar region *n* **146**
Polaris *n* **144**
pole *n* **121**
pole position *n* **123**
Pole Star *n* **144**
pole stretcher *n* **50**
pole vault *n* **116**
police *n* **50**
police bike *n* **50**
police car *n* **50**
police cell *n* **50**
police dog *n* **50**
police hat *n* **50**
police officer *n* **50, 89**
police station *n* **42, 50**
Polish *adj* **153**
polish *n* **34**
polite *adj* **10**
politics *n* **80**
polka dot *adj* **13**
polka dot plant *n* **38**
pollock *n* **54**
pollution *n* **155**
polo *n* **120**
polo shirt *n* **14**
polonium *n* **78**
pom pom beanie *n* **16**
pomegranate *n* **58, 168**
pomelo *n* **57**
Pomeranian *n* **164**
pommel *n* **120**
pommel horse *n* **125**
poncho *n* **15**
pond *n* **41, 86**
ponytail *n* **12**
poodle *n* **164**
pool *n* **125**
pool ring *n* **134**
pop *n* **129**
Pop Art *n* **130**
pop concert *n* **129**
pop-up *n* **84**
pop-up tent *n* **135**
popcorn *n* **127**
poplar *n* **168**
popping crease *n* **111**
poppy *n* **38**
poppy seeds *n* **59**
popular music *n* **129**
porch *n* **25**
porch light *n* **25**
porcini *n* **170**
porcupine *n* **158**
porcupine fish *n* **166**
pores *n* **12**
pork *n* **53**
porpoise *n* **166**
port *n* **68, 106**
portable speakers *n* **95**
portcullis *n* **44**
porter *n* **131**
portfolio *n* **92, 94**
portion *n* **26**
Portugal *n* **151, 153**
Portuguese *adj* **153**
Portuguese man-of-war *n* **166**
position markers *n* **129**
positive *adj* **75**
positive electrode *n* **75**
post *v* **84**
post office *n* **42, 45**
Post-Impressionism *n* **130**
postal worker *n* **45**
postcard *n* **48, 132**
poster paint *n* **141**
postgraduate *n* **80**
postmark *n* **45**
pot *v* **39**
pot plant *n* **47**
potassium *n* **78**
potato *n* **56, 86**
potato cakes *n* **71**
potato fork *n* **40**
pothole *n* **101**
potion *n* **139**
potted plant *n* **41**
potter *n* **141**
potter's wheel *n* **141**
pottery *n* **141**
potting shed *n* **39**
potty *n* **08**
pouch *n* **158**
poultry *n* **48, 53, 165**
poultry farm *n* **86**
pounce *v* **159**
pound *n* **174**
pour *v* **29**
pour down *v* **178**
powder *n* **49**
powder puff *n* **18**
powdered milk *n* **61**
power *n* **33**
power cord *n* **83**
power forward *n* **112**
power lead *n* **83**
power outage *n* **33**
power station *n* **44**
power supply *n* **51**
practical *adj* **93**
practice swing *n* **115**
prairie *n* **146**
praseodymium *n* **78**
praying mantis *n* **162**
Precambrian *adj* **157**
Precambrian *n* **157**
prefab house *n* **32**
pregnancy *n* **08**
pregnancy test *n* **08**
pregnant *adj* **08**
premiere *n* **127**
preparation *n* **54**
prepositions *n* **148, 180**
prescription *n* **20, 49**
present *n* **07**
presentation *n* **82, 95**
presenter remote *n* **95**
presenting *n* **95**
preserved fruit *n* **60**
preserving jar *n* **60**
presser foot *n* **142**
pressure cooker *n* **28**
pressure gauge *n* **33**
pretty *adj* **177**
pretzel *n* **62**
preview *n* **137**
price *n* **69**
price list *n* **70**
price tag *n* **47**
prickly pear *n* **58, 168**
prima donna *n* **126**
primer *n* **37**
prince *n* **79**
princess *n* **79**
principal *n* **73**
print *v* **83**
printer *n* **82**
printing *n* **141, 175**
prism *n* **75**
prison *n* **85**
prison guards *n* **85**
prisoners *n* **85**
private bathroom *n* **131**
private investigator *n* **89**
private jet *n* **103**
private room *n* **21**
probe *n* **22**
problem-solving *n* **93**
proboscis monkey *n* **159**
proceed to checkout *v* **46**
processed food *n* **23**
producer *n* **126, 127**
production *n* **91**
professional *adj* **93**
professional attributes *n* **93**
professional expertise *n* **93**
program *n* **126, 137**
project management *n* **93**
projector *n* **82, 95**
promenade *n* **134**
promethium *n* **78**
propagate *v* **39**
propeller *n* **103, 105**
proposal *n* **82**
props *n* **126, 127**
prosciutto *n* **64**
prosecution *n* **85**
prosecutor *n* **85**
prostate gland *n* **04**
protactinium *n* **78**
protea *n* **38**
protective padding *n* **110**
protein *n* **23**
proton *n* **76**
protractor *n* **73, 74**
proud *adj* **06**
prow *n* **105**
prowl *v* **159**
prune *v* **39**
pruners *n* **40**
prunes *n* **58**
pruning knife *n* **40**
pruning saw *n* **40**
psychiatry *n* **21**
psychologist *n* **90**
psychotherapy *n* **24**
public address system *n* **102**
public footpath *n* **148**
public relations (PR) *n* **91**
public speaking *n* **93**
puck *n* **110**
puddle *n* **154**
puff pastry *n* **63**
pufferfish *n* **166**
pug *n* **164**
pull *v* **11**
pull-along toy *n* **08**
pulp *n* **03, 57**
pumice *n* **156**
pumice stone *n* **31**
pump *n* **101**
pumpkin *n* **56**
punch *v* **117**
punching bag *n* **117**
punctual *adj* **93**
puncture *n* **101**
puncture repair kit *n* **101**
punk *n* **129**
pupil *n* **01, 73**
puppet *n* **08**
puppy *n* **164**
purchasing *n* **91**
purple *n*, *adj* **141**
purple loosestrife *n* **168**
purr *v* **164**
purse *n* **16, 94**
push ups *n* **124**
push *v* **11**
put away *v* **178**
put on *v* **14, 178**
put on makeup *v* **09**
put the children to bed *v* **09**
put together *v* **178**
put up shelves *v* **35**
putt *v* **115**
putter *n* **115**
puzzle game *n* **136**
puzzles *n* **138**
pylon *n* **51**
pyramid *n* **74**
pyramids of Giza *n* **44**

Q

Qatar *n* **151, 153**
Qatari *adj* **153**
qibla prayer wall *n* **44**
quack *v* **165**
quad bike *n* **100**
quadriceps *n* **03**
quail *n* **53**
quail egg *n* **61**
qualifying *n* **123**
quart *n* **174**
quarter *num* **173**
quarter of an hour *n* **171**
quarter past one *n* **171**
quarter to two *n* **171**
quarterback *n* **107**
quarterdeck *n* **105**
quartz *n* **156**
quartzite *n* **156**
Quaternary *adj* **157**
Quaternary *n* **157**
quay *n* **106**
queen *n* **79, 140**
queen of the Andes *n* **167**
quest *n* **139**
question *v* **73**
question mark *n* **175**
quiet *adj* **176**
quilt *n* **30**
quilted jacket *n* **15**
quilting *n* **142**
quince *n* **58**
quiver *n* **125**
quiz show *n* **137**

R

rabbit *n* **53, 158, 164**
rabbit hutch *n* **164**
raccoon *n* **158**
race *n* **116**
race car *n* **97, 123**
race car driver *n* **123**
race number *n* **100**
race track *n* **123**
racecourse *n* **120**
racehorse *n* **120**
racing bike *n* **100, 101**
racing dive *n* **118**
racing events *n* **116**
racing overalls *n* **123**
rack *n* **100, 125**
racket *n* **114**
racket games *n* **114**
racquetball *n* **114**
radar *n* **105**
radar speed gun *n* **50**
radiated tortoise *n* **163**
radiator *n* **33, 98**
radicchio *n* **55**
radio antenna *n* **105**
radio *n* **50, 84, 88, 136**
radio DJ *n* **90**
radio station *n* **84**
radio telescope *n* **144**
radio waves *n* **75**
radioactivity *n* **75**
radiology *n* **21**
radish *n* **56**
radium *n* **78**
radius *n* **03, 74**
radon *n* **78**
raffia palm *n* **167**
rafter *n* **87**
rafting *n* **119**
Ragdoll *n* **164**
rail network *n* **102**
railing *n* **65**
railroad *n* **148**
railroad terminal *n* **106**
rain *n* **51, 154**
rain boots *n* **17**
rain forest *n* **146, 159**
rain gear *n* **135**
rainbow *n* **154**
rainbow trout *n* **54**
raincoat *n* **15**
raindrop *n* **154**
rainfly *n* **135**
rainy *adj* **154**
raise *n* **81**
raise *v* **11**
raised mudguard *n* **100**
raisin *n* **58**
rake *n* **40**
rake (leaves) *v* **39**
rake (soil) *v* **39**
rally *n* **114**
rally driving *n* **123**
ram *n* **165**
ramekin *n* **28**
ramen *n* **64, 72**
ramp *n* **96**
ranch house *n* **32**
rapeseed *n* **86**
rapeseed oil *n* **60**
rapids *n* **119, 146**
ras el hanout *n* **59**
rash *n* **19**
raspberry *n* **57**
raspberry jam *n* **60**
rat *n* **158**
rattle *n* **08**
rattlesnake *n* **163**
raven *n* **160**
raw *adj* **56**
raw meat *n* **53**
ray *n* **166**
razor blade *n* **31**
razor-shell *n* **54**
reach a consensus *v* **95**
reach an agreement *v* **95**
reaction *n* **76**
reaction direction *n* **76**
reactor *n* **51**
read *v* **73**
read a map *v* **148**
read a newspaper *v* **09**
reading *n* **138**
reading a map *n* **148**
reading glasses *n* **22, 49**
reading light *n* **103**
reading list *n* **80**
reading room *n* **80**
real estate *n* **32, 91**
real estate agent **89**
reality TV *n* **137**
realtor *n* **32**
reamer *n* **36**
rear light *n* **101**
rear suspension *n* **123**
rear wheel *n* **99**
rear wing *n* **97, 123**
reasonable *adj* **10**
rebound *n* **112**
receipt *n* **48, 69, 94**
receptacle *n* **38**
receptionist *n* **81, 90, 131**
reconnaissance aircraft *n* **88**
reconnaissance vehicle *n* **88**
record player *n* **136**
record store *n* **46**
record *v* **137**
recorder *n* **129**
recording studio *n* **84**
records *n* **136**
recover *v* **20**
recovery room *n* **21**
recruiter *n* **92**
rectangle *n* **74**
recycling *n* **91, 155**
recycling bin *n* **33, 34**
red *n* **141**
red blood cell *n* **77**
red cabbage *n* **55**
red card *n* **109**
red carpet *n* **127**
red currant *n* **57**
red deer *n* **158**
red fox *n* **159**
red giant *n* **144**
red hair *n* **12**
red line *n* **110**
red meat *n* **53**
red mullet *n* **54**
red panda *n* **159**
red salamander *n* **163**
red wine *n* **52, 68**
red-eyed tree frog *n* **163**
reed *n* **167**
reef *n* **147**
reel *n* **121**
reel in *v* **121**
referee *n* **107-109, 112**
referee crease *n* **110**
reflected radiation *n* **155**
reflection *n* **75**
reflector *n* **100, 101**
reflector strap *n* **100**
reflector telescope *n* **144**
reflexology *n* **24**
refraction *n* **75**
refractor telescope *n* **144**
refrigerator *n* **27**
refund *v* **46**
reggae *n* **129**
registered mail *n* **45**
registered trademark *n* **175**
regulator *n* **118**
reiki *n* **24**
reindeer *n* **159**
reins *n* **120**
relationships *n* **05, 07**
relaxation *n* **24**
relaxed *adj* **06**
relaxing *adj* **177**
relay race *n* **116**
release *v* **121**
reliable *adj* **10, 93**
remains *n* **79**
remarkable *adj* **177**
remember *v* **11**
remote *n* **137**
remote control *n* **26, 83, 136**
renew *v* **80**
renewable energy *n* **51**
renovating *n* **37**
rent *v* **32**
rent a cottage *v* **131**
rent out *v* **32**
renting a house *n* **32**
repair *v* **11, 33**
reply *v* **83**
reply to all *v* **83**
report *n* **82**
reporter *n* **137**
reproduction *n* **77**
reproductive *n* **04**
reproductive organs *n* **04**
reptiles *n* **163**
Republic of the Congo *n* **149, 152**
research *n* **91, 93**
research and development (R&D) *n* **91**
reserve *v* **80**
reservoir *n* **51**
residential area *n* **32**
residential buildings *n* **44**
residential district *n* **42**
resign *v* **81**
respectful *adj* **177**
respiratory *n* **04**
responsible *adj* **93**
rest *v* **20**
rest stop *n* **148**
restaurant *n* **42, 69, 131**
restaurant manager *n* **69**
restricted area *n* **112**
restroom *n* **47, 130, 131**
résumé *n* **92**
resurfacing *n* **87**
resuscitate *v* **20**
retail *n* **91**
retake *v* **73**
reticulated python *n* **163**
retina *n* **22**
retinal camera *n* **22**
retire *v* **07, 81**
retriever *n* **164**
return *n* **114**
return *v* **46, 80**
return crease *n* **111**
reusable cup *n* **70**
reverb *n* **129**
reverse *v* **96**
reversible direction *n* **76**
review *n* **138**
review *v* **73**
rewind *v* **137**
rewire the house *v* **35**
rhenium *n* **78**
rhinoceros *n* **158**
rhinoceros beetle *n* **162**
rhodium *n* **78**
rhododendron *n* **38**
rhombus *n* **74**
rhubarb *n* **58**
rib *n* **03, 53**
rib cage *n* **03**
ribs *n* **70**
ribbon *n* **63, 125, 142**
rice *n* **72, 86**
rice bowl *n* **27**
rice noodles *n* **64**
rice pudding *n* **63**
rich *adj* **52**
ride *v* **11**
ride passenger *v* **100**
rider *n* **100, 120**
ridge *n* **146**
ridge beam *n* **87**
riding boot *n* **17, 120**
riding crop *n* **120**
riding hat *n* **120**
rifle *n* **88**
rig *n* **129**
rigging *n* **119**
right angle *n* **74**
right bend *n* **96**
right cornerback *n* **107**
right defenseman *n* **110**
right defensive end *n* **107**
right defensive tackle *n* **107**
right guard *n* **107**
right of way *n* **96**
right safety *n* **107**
right side *n* **112**
right tackle *n* **107**
right wing *n* **108**
right winger *n* **110**
rim *n* **101**
rind *n* **61, 64**
ring *n* **16, 170**
ring binder *n* **82**
ring finger *n* **02**
ring ties *n* **40**
ring-tailed lemur *n* **159**
rings *n* **125, 143**
rinse *v* **22**
rip out *v* **178**
ripe *adj* **57**
rise *v* **62**
risotto *n* **72**
river *n* **147, 148**
river features *n* **147, 148**
road *n* **96**
road bike *n* **101**
road construction *n* **87, 96**
road markings *n* **96**
road signs *n* **96**
roadmap *n* **95**
roadmap *n* **148**
roar *v* **159**
roast *n* **29, 72**
robbers *n* **50**
robbery *n* **50, 85**
robe *n* **80**
rock *n* **129**

rock climbing n 125
rock garden n 41
rock star n 90
rocket n 143
rockhopper penguin n 161
rocks n 147, 156
rocking chair n 26
rocking horse n 08
rodeo n 120
roe deer n 158
roentgenium n 78
role-playing game n 136
roll n 62
roll v 29
roll bar n 97
roller n 37, 87
roller coaster n 133
roller extension pole n 37
roller shade n 26
rollerblading n 133
rollerskating n 125
rolling pin n 29
romaine lettuce n 55
romance n 138
Romania n 151, 153
Romanian adj 153
romantic adj 10, 177
romantic comedy n 127
romper n 13
roof n 25, 98
roof garden n 41
roof ladder n 50
roof rack n 97
roof tiles n 87
rook n 140, 160
room service n 131
room with a view n 131
roomer n 32
roommate n 32
rooster n 165
root n 03
rope n 117, 119, 125
rose n 38
rosé n 68, 52
rose of Sharon n 38
rose-ringed parakeet n 161
rosemary n 38, 59
rotor n 51
rotor blade n 103
rotten adj 57
rough n 115
round n 117
round neck n 14
round-trip n 131
roundabout n 96
route number n 99
router n 35, 83
rover n 143
row n 32
row n 103, 126
rowboat n 105
rower n 119
rowing n 119
rowing machine n 124
rubber adj 176
rubber n 176
rubber bands n 82
rubber boots n 40
rubber gloves n 34
rubber plant n 38
rubber tree n 169
rubidium n 78
ruby n 156
ruck n 108
rudder n 103, 119
rude adj 10
rug n 26
rugby n 108
rugby ball n 108
rugby jersey n 108
rugby pitch n 108
rugby positions n 108
rugby shirt n 108
ruler n 73, 74, 72, 174
rum n 68
rum and cola n 68
rump roast n 53
run away v 178
run out (of) v 178
run out of time v 95
run v 11, 111, 113
rung n 36
runner beans n 55
runners n 122
running n 124
running back n 107
running blades n 125
running machine n 124
running shoes n 17
running spikes n 17
runny nose n 19
runway n 104
rush hour n 42, 102
rushes n 41
Russian adj 153
Russian Federation n 150, 151, 153
rustic baguette n 62
rutabaga n 56
ruthenium n 78
rutherfordium n 78
Rwanda n 149, 152
Rwandan adj 152
rye bread n 62

S

saber n 117
saber-toothed cat n 157
sacred ibis n 160
sad adj 06
saddle n 101, 120
saddlebag n 120
safari park n 133
safe adj 113
safe n 131
safety area n 117
safety barrier n 122
safety glasses n 87
safety gloves n 87
safety goggles n 36, 76
safety notice board n 87
safety pin n 20
saffron n 59
sage n 59
Sagittarius n 144
sail n 119, 134
sail fish n 166
sailboat n 105
sailing n 119
sailor, sailors n 88, 99
sake cup n 27
salad n 55, 65
salad vegetables n 55
salami n 53, 64
salary n 81
sale n 47
sale sign n 47
sales n 91
sales assistant n 89
salmon fillet n 54
salt n 23, 26
salted adj 54, 61, 64
saltwater crocodile n 163
salty adj 52
Salvadoran adj 152
samara n 169
samarium n 78
Sammarinese adj 153
Samoa n 150, 153
Samoan adj 153
San Marino n 151, 153
sand n 35, 39, 134
sand v 37
sand dune n 146
sand martin n 160
sand rose n 156
sandals n 17
sandbox n 43
sandcastle n 134
sander n 35
sandpaper n 36–37
sandstone n 156
sandstorm n 154
sandwich n 65, 70, 72
sandwich pickle n 60
sanitary pad n 49
São Tomé and Príncipe n 149, 152
São Toméan adj 152
sapphire n 156
sardines n 54, 64
sari n 15
sarong n 15
sash window n 25
satellite n 143
satellite dish n 25, 136
satellite TV n 137
satire n 137
saturated fat n 23
Saturday n 172
Saturn n 143
sauce, sauces n 60, 64
saucepan n 28
Saudi adj 153
Saudi Arabia n 151, 153
sauerkraut n 60
sauna n 124
sausage, sausages n 53, 71
sausage patties n 71
sauté v 29
savannah n 146, 158
save up v 32
savings n 45
savings account n 45
savoy cabbage n 55
savory adj 52
saw v 35
sawfish n 166
saxophone n 128–129
scale n 20, 29, 54, 76, 104, 128, 148
scales n 45, 163, 174
scallop n 54
scalpel n 21, 77
scan n 21
scandium n 78
scanner n 48, 82, 104
scapula n 03
scarecrow n 86
scared adj 06
scarf n 16
scarlet n 141
scarlet ibis n 160
scarlet macaw n 161
scenic adj 132
schist n 156
scholarship n 80
school n 43, 73, 148
school bag n 73
school bus n 99
school equipment n 73
school shirt n 13
school students n 73
school tie n 13
school uniform n 13
school zone n 96
science, sciences n 73, 80
science fiction n 127, 138
scientist n 90
scimitar n 79
scissors n 20, 37, 82
sconce n 26
scoop n 28
scoop v 110
scootering n 133
score n 114, 128, 140
scoreboard n 107, 111
scorekeepers bench n 110
Scorpio n 144
scorpion n 162
Scotch and water n 68
scouring pad n 34
scrambled eggs n 61, 71
scrape n 19
scraper n 37
scratch v 164
screen n 45, 83, 111, 127, 136–137
screenplay n 127
screenwriter n 127
screw n 36
screw base n 33
scribe n 79
script n 126
scroll n 79
scrotum n 04
scrub the floor v 34
scrubbing brush n 34
scrubs n 13, 21
scrum n 108
scrum-half n 108
scuba diving n 118
sculpting n 141
sculptor n 89
sculpture n 130, 141
sea n 145
sea bass n 54
sea bed n 51
sea bream n 54
sea buckthorn n 169
sea cave n 147
sea krait n 163
sea lion n 166
sea serpent n 139
sea slug n 166
sea stack n 147
sea urchin n 166
sea vessels n 105
seaborgium n 78
seafood n 54
seafood allergy n 23
seafood platter n 54
seagull n 160
seahorse n 166
seal n 159, 166

sealant *n* **37**
seam *n* **111, 142**
seamount *n* **145**
seaplane *n* **103**
seashore *n* **147**
season *n* **137**
seasonal fruit *n* **57**
seasons *n* **172**
seat *n* **26, 33, 100, 102-103, 120**
seat back *n* **103**
seat belt, seat belts *n* **103, 123**
seat post *n* **101**
seated forward fold *n* **24**
seated twist *n* **24**
seating *n* **47, 126**
seaweed *n* **134, 166**
second *n* **171**
second *num* **173**
second base *n* **113**
second floor *n* **25, 47**
second hand *n* **171**
second row *n* **108**
secondary road *n* **148**
secretary *n* **90**
secretive *adj* **10**
sections *n* **48**
security *n* **104**
security *n* **109**
security bit *n* **36**
security guard *n* **89-90, 130**
sedan *n* **97**
sedative *n* **49**
sedimentary *adj* **156**
see *v* **11**
seed, seeds *n* **40, 58 168**
seed tray *n* **40**
seeded bread *n* **62**
seedless *adj* **57**
seesaw *n* **43**
segment *n* **57**
selenium *n* **78**
self checkout *n* **48**
self management *n* **93**
self tanner *n* **18**
self-help *n* **138**
self-inflating mattress *n* **135**
self-rising flour *n* **62**
selfish *adj* **10**
sell *v* **46**
semi-hard cheese *n* **61**
semi-soft cheese *n* **61**
semicolon *n* **175**
semiconductor *n* **75**
semimetals *n* **78**
seminal gland *n* **04**
send *v* **83**
send a package *v* **09**
Senegal *n* **149, 152**
Senegalese *adj* **152**
sensitive *adj* **10, 18**
sentence *n* **85**
sepal *n* **38**
September *n* **172**
Serbia *n* **151, 153**
Serbian *adj* **153**
serious *adj* **06, 10**
serve *v* **65, 114**
server *n* **65, 69, 89**
service charge *n* **69**
service focused *adj* **93**
service included *phr* **69**
service line *n* **114**
service not included *phr* **69**
service the car *v* **98**
service vehicle *n* **104**
services *n* **131**
serving spoon *n* **27**
sesame allergy *n* **23**
sesame oil *n* **60**
set *n* **114, 126**
set off *v* **98, 178**
set sail *v* **106**
set the alarm *v* **09**
set the table *v* **26, 34**
sets *n* **126**
setter *n* **112, 164**
seven *num* **173**
seventeen *num* **173**
seventh *num* **173**
seventy *num* **173**
sew *v* **142**
sewer drain pipe *n* **33**
sewing *n* **142**
sewing box *n* **142**
sewing machine *n* **142**
sewing needle *n* **142**
Seychelles *n* **149, 152**
Seychellois *adj* **152**
shade plants *n* **41**
shaft *n* **115**
shaggy bracket fungus *n* **170**
shaggy mane mushroom *n* **170**
shake *v* **11**
shake hands *v* **92**
shake your head *v* **02**
shale *n* **51**
shale gas *n* **51**
shallot *n* **56**
shallow *adj* **176**
shallow end *n* **118**
shaobing *n* **62**
shapes *n* **74**
share *v* **84**
share price *n* **94**
share your screen *v* **95**
shares *n* **94**
sharp *adj* **128**
sharpening stone *n* **36**
shave *v* **09, 12, 31**
shaved head *n* **12**
shaving cream *n* **31**
shears *n* **40**
shears *n* **142**
shed *n* **25, 39**
sheep *n* **165**
sheep farm *n* **86**
sheep's milk *n* **61**
sheep's milk cheese *n* **61**
sheer *v* **165**
sheer curtain *n* **26**
sheet *n* **30, 119**
shelf *n* **26-27**
shell *n* **58, 61, 163**
shelter *n* **44**
shelves *n* **27, 48**
sherry *n* **68**
shiatsu *n* **24**
shield *n* **40, 79**
shih tzu *n* **164**
shiitake mushroom *n* **56, 170**
shin *n* **01**
shin guard *n* **110**
shingles *n* **87**
shiny *adj* **176**
ship's captain *n* **89**
shipping *n* **91**
shipping container *n* **106**
ships *n* **105**
shipyard *n* **106**
shirt *n* **15**
shiver *v* **02**
shocked *adj* **06**
shocking *adj* **177**
shoe accessories *n* **17**
shoe brush *n* **17**
shoe polish *n* **17**
shoe store *n* **46**
shoe trees *n* **17**
shoelaces *n* **17**
shoes *n* **17**
shoe accessories *n* **17**
shoot *v* **112**
shooting guard *n* **112**
shoplifting *n* **85**
shopper *n* **47**
shopping *n* **46, 179**
shopping bag *n* **48**
shopping cart *n* **48**
shopping channel *n* **137**
shopping list *n* **46**
shopping mall *n* **42, 47**
shopping spree *n* **46**
short *adj* **12, 176**
short corner *n* **112**
short hair *n* **12**
short-sleeved shirt *n* **14**
shortbread *n* **63**
shorts *n* **14**
shot *n* **68**
shot put *n* **116**
shotgun *n* **88**
shoulder *n* **01**
shoulder bag *n* **16**
shoulder blade *n* **03**
shoulder pad *n* **15, 107, 110**
shoulder strap *n* **16**
shoulder-launched missile *n* **88**
shoulder-length hair *n* **12**
shout *v* **11**
shovel *n* **40, 87**
show *n* **137**
show of hands *n* **95**
show off *v* **178**
shower *n* **31**
shower block *n* **135**
shower curtain *n* **31**
shower door *n* **31**
shower gel *n* **31**
showjumping *n* **120**
shredder *n* **82**
shrinking glaciers *n* **155**
shrubs *n* **41**
shrug *v* **02**
shuffle *v* **140**
shutoff valve *n* **33**
shutter *n* **25**
shuttle bus *n* **99**
shuttlecock *n* **114**
shy *adj* **10**
Siamese *n* **164**
Siberian husky *n* **164**
siblings *n* **05**
side *n* **69, 74**
side car *n* **100**
side dishes *n* **72**
side effects *n* **49**
side order *n* **69**
side part *n* **12**
side plate *n* **27**
side shuffles *n* **124**
side street *n* **42**
side view *n* **97**
side-saddle *n* **120**
side-view mirror *n* **97**
sideboard *n* **26**
sideburns *n* **12**
sidedeck *n* **119**
sideline *n* **107, 112, 114**
sidestroke *n* **118**
sidewalk *n* **25, 43, 65**
sidewinder *n* **163**
Sierra Leone *n* **149, 152**
Sierra Leonean *adj* **152**
sieve *n* **28**
sieve *v* **39**
sift *v* **62**
sigh *v* **02**
sightseeing *n* **99, 132**
sign *n* **104**
sign a contract *v* **92**
signal *n* **102**
signal *v* **98**
signature *n* **45, 83**
signet ring *n* **16**
silicon *n* **78**
silk *n* **13**
silk tree *n* **168**
silly *adj* **10**
silo *n* **86**
silt *n* **39**
Silurian *adj* **157**
Silurian *n* **157**
silver *adj* **176**
silver *n* **78, 116, 156, 176**
silverware *n* **26, 27**
sim card *n* **48**
simmer *v* **29**
simulation game *n* **136**
sing *v* **11**
Singapore *n* **151, 153**
Singaporean *adj* **153**
singer *n* **89**
single *adj* **68**
single parent *n* **05**
single quotation mark *n* **175**
single room *n* **131**
single-burner camping stove *n* **135**
singles *n* **114**
sink *n* **27**
sinus *n* **04**
sip *v* **52**
sippy cup *n* **27**
sirloin steak *n* **53**
sister *n* **05**
sister-in-law *n* **05**
sit down *v* **11**
sit-up *n* **124**
sitar *n* **129**
sitcom *n* **137**
site *n* **135**
site manager *n* **89**
site manager's office *n* **135**
sites available *phr* **135**
six *num* **173**
sixteen *num* **173**
sixth *num* **173**
sixty *num* **173**
skate *n* **54, 122**
skate *v* **110**
skate wing *n* **54**
skateboard *n* **125**
skateboarding *n* **125, 133**
skein *n* **142**
skeleton *n* **03, 122**
sketch *n* **141**
sketch pad *n* **141**
skewer *n* **28**
ski *n* **119, 122**
ski boot *n* **17, 122**

ski instructor *n* **89**
ski jacket *n* **122**
ski jump *n* **122**
ski lodge *n* **122**
ski pole *n* **122**
ski resort *n* **122**
ski run *n* **122**
ski slope *n* **122**
skier *n* **122**
skiing *n* **122**
skillet *n* **28**
skim milk *n* **61**
skin *n* **01, 58**
skin care *n* **49**
skin type *n* **18**
skip *v* **124**
skipping rope *n* **133**
skirt *n* **14**
skull *n* **03**
skunk *n* **158**
skydiving *n* **125**
skyscraper *n* **42**
slalom *n* **122**
slate *n* **156**
sled *n* **122**
sledding *n* **122**
sledgehammer *n* **87**
sleep in *v* **178**
sleeping bag *n* **135**
sleeping compartment *n* **102**
sleeping mat *n* **135**
sleeping pills *n* **49**
sleepsuit *n* **13**
sleet *n* **154**
sleeve *n* **15**
sleeveless *adj* **15**
slice *n* **53, 114**
slice *v* **29, 62**
sliced bread *n* **62**
slicer *n* **62**
slide *n* **43, 77, 95**
slide *v* **113**
sliders *n* **17**
sling *n* **19-20**
slingback heels *n* **17**
slip *n* **14, 111**
slip-ons *n* **17**
slippers *n* **14, 17**
slit skirt *n* **15**
sloth *n* **159**
slotted spoon *n* **28**
Slovakia *n* **151, 153**
Slovakian *adj* **153**
Slovenia *n* **151, 153**
Slovenian *adj* **153**
slow *adj* **176**
slow down *v* **98**
slug *n* **162**
sluice gates *n* **51**
small *adj* **176**
small creatures *n* **162**
small forward *n* **112**
small intestine *n* **04**
smartpen *n* **95**
smartphone *n* **83**
smartwatch *n* **83**
smell *v* **11**
smile *v* **02**
smog *n* **154**
smoke *n* **50**
smoke alarm *n* **50**
smoked *adj* **54, 72**
smoked fish *n* **64**
smoked haddock *n* **64**
smoked mackerel *n* **64, 71**
smoked meat *n* **53**
smoked salmon *n* **64, 71**
smooth orange juice *n* **65**
smoothie *n* **52**
smuggling *n* **85**
snack bar *n* **48, 65**
snacks *n* **65**
snail *n* **162**
snake plant *n* **38**
snap *n* **13**
snap *n* **140**
snare drum *n* **128**
sneaker *n* **17**
sneeze *v* **02, 20**
snell knot *n* **121**
Snellen chart *n* **22**
sniff *v* **164**
snooker *n* **125**
snore *v* **02, 30**
snorkel *n* **118**
snorkel and mask *n* **15, 134**
snorkeling *n* **118**
snort *v* **165**
snow *n* **154**
snow goose *n* **160**
snow leopard *n* **159**
snow peas *n* **55**
snow tires *n* **97**
snowboarding *n* **122**
snowdrift *n* **154**
snowdrop *n* **167**
snowflake *n* **154**
snowmobile *n* **122**
snowstorm *n* **154**
snowsuit *n* **13**
snowy *adj* **154**
snowy owl *n* **161**
soap *n* **31**
soap dish *n* **31**
soap opera *n* **137**
soccer *n* **109**
soccer cleats *n* **17, 109**
soccer game *n* **109**
soccer jersey *n* **15, 109**
social media *n* **84**
social sciences *n* **80**
sociologist *n* **89**
sociology *n* **80**
sock, socks *n* **14, 107**
socket *n* **33**
socket wrench *n* **36**
soda *n* **70**
soda bread *n* **62**
sodium *n* **78**
sofa bed *n* **26**
soft *adj* **57, 176**
soft candy *n* **67**
soft cheese *n* **61**
soft down feathers *n* **161**
soft drink *n* **70**
softwood *n* **35**
soil *n* **39**
soil tiller *n* **40**
soil types *n* **39**
solar charger *n* **83**
solar energy *n* **51**
solar farm *n* **51**
solar panel *n* **51**
solar radiation *n* **155**
solar system *n* **143**
solar water heating *n* **51**
solder *n* **35-36**
solder *v* **35**
soldering iron *n* **35-36**
soldier *n* **88-89**
sole *n* **02, 17, 54, 115**
solid, solids *n* **74, 76**
solitaire *n* **140**
solo *n* **128**
Solomon Island *adj* **153**
Solomon Islands *n* **150, 153**
soluble *adj* **49**
solvent *n* **37**
Somalia *n* **149, 152**
Somalian *adj* **152**
sombrero *n* **16**
sometimes *adj* **172**
sommelier *n* **69**
son *n* **05**
son-in-law *n* **05**
song *n* **129**
soprano *n* **126**
sore throat *n* **19**
sorrel *n* **55, 59**
sort your trash *v* **155**
sorting unit *n* **33**
soufflé *n* **72**
soufflé dish *n* **28**
soul *n* **129**
sound bar *n* **136**
sound boom *n* **84**
sound engineer *n* **127**
sound hole *n* **129**
sound technician *n* **84**
soundtrack *n* **127**
soup *n* **69, 72**
soup bowl *n* **27**
soup spoon *n* **27**
sour *adj* **52, 57**
source *n* **147**
sources *n* **79**
sourdough bread *n* **62**
sourdough starter *n* **62**
south *n* **148**
South Africa *n* **149, 152**
South African *adj* **152**
South America *n* **149, 152**
South American *adj* **152**
South Korea *n* **150, 153**
South Korean *adj* **153**
South Pole *n* **75, 145**
South Sudan *n* **149, 152**
South Sudanese *adj* **152**
southeast *n* **148**
Southern Cross *n* **144**
Southern Hemisphere *n* **145**
southwest *n* **148**
souvenir *n* **132**
souvenir stall *n* **132**
sow *v* **39, 86**
soy allergy *n* **23**
soy milk *n* **61**
soy sauce *n* **60**
soy sauce dip *n* **72**
soybean oil *n* **60**
space *n* **143-144**
space exploration *n* **143**
space probe *n* **143**
space shuttle *n* **143**
space shuttle launch *n* **143**
space station *n* **143**
space suit *n* **143**
space telescope *n* **144**
spacecraft *n* **143**
spackle *n* **37**
spackle *v* **37**
spade *n* **40, 140**
spaghetti *n* **64, 72**
Spain *n* **151, 153**
spam *n* **83**
Spanish *adj* **153**
Spanish chestnut *n* **168**
spare tire *n* **98**
spark plug *n* **98**
sparkling *adj* **52**
sparkling wine *n* **68**
sparrow *n* **160**
spatula *n* **28, 76**
speak *v* **11**
speaker, speakers *n* **83, 129**
speaker stand *n* **136**
spear *n* **79**
spearfishing *n* **121**
special *adj* **177**
special effects *n* **127**
special offer *n* **48**
specials *n* **69**
species *n* **77**
species of birds *n* **160-161**
species of fungi *n* **170**
species of mammals *n* **158-159**
spectacled caiman *n* **163**
spectators *n* **110, 115-116**
speed boating *n* **119**
speed camera *n* **96**
speed limit *n* **96**
speed skating *n* **122**
speed up *v* **98**
speedboat *n* **105**
speeding *n* **85**
speedometer *n* **99-100**
speedway *n* **123**
spell *v* **11, 73**
spell book *n* **139**
sperm whale *n* **166**
sphere *n* **74**
sphinx *n* **139, 164**
spices *n* **59**
spicy *adj* **52, 56**
spicy sausage *n* **64**
spider monkey *n* **159**
spider plant *n* **38**
spikes *n* **115**
spin *n* **114**
spinach *n* **55**
spinal cord *n* **04**
spine *n* **03, 138**
spiral galaxy *n* **144**
spirit dispenser *n* **68**
spit *n* **147**
spleen *n* **04**
splinter *n* **19**
split the check *v* **69**
spoiler *n* **97**
spoke *n* **101**
sponge *n* **31, 34, 37**
sponge cake *n* **63**
spontaneous *adj* **10**
spores *n* **170**
sport fishing *n* **121**
sports bra *n* **15**
sports car *n* **97**
sports center *n* **43**
sports drink *n* **52**
sports field *n* **80**
sports game *n* **136**
sports jacket *n* **15**
sports shoes *n* **17**
sports show *n* **137**
sportsperson *n* **89**
sportswear *n* **15**
Spotted Lake *n* **145**
sprain *n* **19**
spray *n* **49**
spray *v* **39**
spray nozzle *n* **40**
sprayer *n* **40**
spring *n* **57, 172**
spring a leak *v* **33**
spring greens *n* **55**
spring onion *n* **55**
spring roll *n* **72**
springboard *n* **118, 125**
springbok *n* **158**
sprinkle *v* **29**
sprinkler *n* **40**

sprinter *n* **116**
sprocket *n* **101**
spruce *n* **167**
spy *n* **89**
square *n* **42, 74, 140**
square foot *n* **174**
square kilometer *n* **174**
square leg *n* **111**
square meter *n* **174**
square mile *n* **174**
squash *n* **114**
squat *n* **124**
squeak *v* **164**
squeegee *n* **34**
squid *n* **54**
squirrel *n* **158**
squirrel monkey *n* **159**
Sri Lanka *n* **150, 153**
Sri Lankan *adj* **153**
St. Basil's cathedral *n* **44**
St. Kitts and Nevis *n* **150, 152**
St. Lucia *n* **150, 152**
St. Lucian *adj* **152**
St. Vincent and The Grenadines *n* **150, 152**
stable *n* **86, 120**
staff *n* **81, 139**
stag beetle *n* **162**
stage *n* **126**
stage lights *n* **129**
stained glass window *n* **44**
stair gate *n* **08**
staircase *n* **25**
stairs *n* **25**
stake *v* **39**
stalactite *n* **146**
stalagmite *n* **146**
stalk *n* **55**
stall *n* **47**
stallion *n* **120, 165**
stamen *n* **38**
stamp, stamps *n* **45, 48**
stance *n* **115**
stand *n* **40, 109, 115, 121, 136**
stand up *v* **11**
standing ovation *n* **126**
stapler *n* **73, 82**
staples *n* **82**
star, stars *n* **144**
star anise *n* **59**
star chart *n* **144**
star cluster *n* **144**
Star of David *n* **44**
starfish *n* **134, 166**
starfruit *n* **58**
starling *n* **160**
start school *v* **07**
starting block *n* **116, 118**
starting grid *n* **123**
starting line *n* **116**
statement *n* **85**
station wagon *n* **97**
stationery *n* **82**
status *n* **104**
status update *n* **84**
stay in a hotel *v* **131**
steam *v* **29**
steam dome *n* **102**
steam train *n* **102**
steamed *adj* **72**
steel wool *n* **36**
steeplechase *n* **120**
steering wheel *n* **99**
stegosaurus *n* **157**
stem *n* **38, 170**
stemware *n* **27**
stencil *n* **37**
stepbrother *n* **05**
stepladder *n* **37**
stepmom *n* **05**
stepmother *n* **05**
steppe *n* **146**
steps *n* **25**
stepsister *n* **05**
stereo *adj* **136**
stern *n* **105, 119**
sternum *n* **03**
stethoscope *n* **20**
stew *n* **72**
stick *n* **110**
stick insect *n* **164**
sticky notes *n* **82**
sticky prong *n* **168**
stiff *adj* **176**
stifling *adj* **154**
stigma *n* **38**
stilettos *n* **17**
still *adj* **52**
stilt house *n* **32**
sting *n* **19, 162**
sting *v* **162**
stinkhorn *n* **170**
stir *v* **29**
stir-fry *n* **29, 72**
stir-fried *adj* **72**
stirrer *n* **68**
stirrup *n* **120**
stitch *n* **142**
stitches *n* **21, 113**
stitch length selector *n* **142**
stitch selector *n* **142**
stock exchange *n* **94**
stockbroker *n* **94**
stockings *n* **14**
stocks *n* **47, 94**
stomach *n* **04**
stomachache *n* **19**
stone *adj* **176**
stone *n* **16, 141, 176**
Stone age *n* **79**
stone fruit *n* **57**
stool *n* **65**
stop *v* **96, 137**
stop at (the hotel) *v* **148**
stop button *n* **99**
stop light *n* **43, 96**
stop light ahead *n* **96**
stoppage time *n* **109**
stopper *n* **76**
storage *n* **32**
store *n* **42**
store window *n* **25**
stories *n* **139**
stork *n* **160**
storm *n* **154**
storm drain *n* **43**
stormy *adj* **154**
stout *n* **68**
stove *n* **27**
straight *adj* **74**
straight hair *n* **12**
straightening iron *n* **12**
strainer *n* **28**
strait *n* **147**
strange *adj* **177**
strapless *adj* **15**
strategy game *n* **136**
stratosphere *n* **155**
straw *n* **70**
strawberry *n* **57**
strawberry jam *n* **60**
strawberry milkshake *n* **61, 65**
strawberry smoothie *n* **65**
stream *n* **137, 147**
street *n* **42**
street corner *n* **42**
street market *n* **46**
street sign *n* **43**
street stall *n* **70**
streetlight *n* **25, 43**
stress *n* **19**
stressed *adj* **06**
stretch *n* **124**
stretcher *n* **21**
strike *n* **113**
strike *v* **117**
strike out *v* **111**
string *n* **129**
string of pearls *n* **16**
strings *n* **114, 128**
strip *v* **37**
striped *n* **13**
stripes *n* **14**
stroke *n* **118**
stroller *n* **08**
strong *adj* **52**
strontium *n* **78**
stubble *n* **12**
studs *n* **16, 111**
study *n* **73**
studying the past *n* **79**
stuffed *adj* **72**
stuffed olives *n* **64**
stuffed vine leaves *n* **64**
stump *v* **111**
stumps *n* **111**
stunning *adj* **177**
stunt *n* **127**
style *n* **38**
style your hair *v* **12**
stylist *n* **89**
subject *n* **83**
submarine *n* **88, 105**
submersible *n* **166**
subscript *n* **76**
subsoil *n* **39**
substitutes *n* **109**
subterranean stream *n* **146**
subtitles *n* **137**
subtract *v* **11, 74**
suburb *n* **42**
subway map *n* **102**
subway train *n* **102**
subwoofer *n* **136**
succulents *n* **38, 41**
suck *v* **02**
suction hose *n* **34**
Sudan *n* **149, 152**
Sudanese *adj* **152**
sugar *n* **23**
sugar cane *n* **86, 167**
suit *n* **15**
suit (someone) *v* **14**
suitcase *n* **16, 104**
sulfite allergy *n* **23**
sulfur *n* **78, 156**
sum up *v* **95**
sumac *n* **59**
summer *n* **57, 172**
summer leaf *n* **169**
summer roll *n* **72**
summons *n* **85**
sumo wrestling *n* **117**
Sun *n* **143**
sun *n* **154**
sun hat *n* **14, 16, 134**
sunbathing *n* **133–134**
sunblock *n* **49, 134**
sunburn *n* **19, 134**
Sunday *n* **172**
sundew *n* **168**
sunflower, sunflowers *n* **38, 86**
sunflower oil *n* **60**
sunglasses *n* **22, 134**
sunlit zone *n* **166**
sunny *adj* **154**
sunrise *n* **171**
sunroof *n* **98**
sunscreen *n* **49, 134**
sunset *n* **171**
superb *adj* **177**
superfoods *n* **23**
supermarket *n* **48**
supernova *n* **144**
supervise *v* **92**
supervisor *n* **81, 92**
supplement *n* **23, 49**
support *n* **87**
support cane *n* **39**
supportive *adj* **10**
suppository *n* **49**
surf *n* **119**
surface *n* **39, 143**
surface cleaner *n* **34**
surface-to-air missile *n* **88**
surfboard *n* **119, 134**
surfcasting *n* **121**
surfer *n* **119**
surfing *n* **119, 134**
surgeon *n* **21, 90**
surgery *n* **21**
surgical mask *n* **21**
Suriname *n* **149, 152**
Surinamese *adj* **152**
surprised *adj* **06**
Surrealism *n* **130**
surround sound speaker *n* **136**
surveillance camera *n* **130**
surveyor *n* **90**
sushi *n* **54**
sushi set *n* **27**
suspect *n* **50, 85**
suspension *n* **98, 100**
suspension line *n* **125**
swallow *n* **160**
swallow *v* **52**
swallowtail butterfly *n* **162**
swamp *n* **146**
swarm *n* **162**
Swazi *adj* **152**
sweat *v* **02**
sweatpants *n* **15**
sweater *n* **14**
sweatshirt *n* **14**
Sweden *n* **151, 153**
sweep the floor *v* **34**
sweet *adj* **52, 56–57**
sweet chilli *n* **60**
sweet potato *n* **56**
sweet spreads *n* **60**
swift *n* **160**
swim trunks *n* **15, 134**
swimmer *n* **118**
swimming *n* **118**
swimming pool *n* **118, 131**
swimsuit *n* **15, 118, 134**
swing *n* **43, 115, 133**
swing *v* **115, 159**
Swiss *adj* **153**
Swiss chard *n* **55**
Swiss cheese plant *n* **38**
Switzerland *n* **151, 153**
swoop *v* **161**
sword *n* **79, 117**
swordfish *n* **54**
sycamore *n* **169**
Sydney Opera House *n* **44**
sympathetic *adj* **06**

symphony *n* **128**
symptoms *n* **19**
synagogue *n* **44**
synchronized swimming *n* **118**
synthetic *n* **13**
Syria *n* **150, 153**
Syrian *adj* **153**
syringe *n* **20, 49, 77**
syrup *n* **49**

T

T-shirt *n* **14**
T-strap heels *n* **17**
T11 (visual impairment) race *n* **116**
tabard *n* **13**
tabi boots *n* **17**
table *n* **26, 65**
table setting *n* **69**
table tennis *n* **114**
tablecloth *n* **26**
tablespoon *n* **27**
tablet *n* **83**
tablets *n* **20, 49**
tableware *n* **27**
tachometer *n* **99**
tack *v* **119, 142**
tackle *n* **108, 121**
tackle *v* **107**
tackle box *n* **121**
taco *n* **70**
tadpole *n* **77, 163**
taekwondo *n* **117**
tag *v* **113**
tagine *n* **28**
tai chi *n* **117, 133**
tail *n* **54, 103, 120, 143, 158–160**
tail feathers *n* **161**
tail light *n* **100**
tail plane *n* **103**
tailbone sacrum *n* **03**
tailgate *n* **97**
tailor *n* **46, 89**
tailor *v* **142**
tailor's chalk *n* **142**
tailored *adj* **15**
Taj Mahal *n* **44**
Tajikistan *n* **151, 153**
Tajikistani *adj* **153**
take *v* **11, 140**
take a bath *v* **09, 31**
take a break *v* **09**
take a nap *v* **09**
take a penalty *v* **109**
take a shower *v* **09, 31**
take a test *v* **73**
take in *v* **142**
take minutes *v* **95**
take notes *v* **73**
take off *v* **14, 98, 104, 178**
take on *v* **81**
take out the trash *v* **09, 34**
take questions *v* **95**
take the first left *v* **96, 148**
take the second right *v* **96, 148**
talented *adj* **10**
talk *v* **11**
talk show *n* **137**
talkative *adj* **10**
tall *adj* **12**
tamarillo *n* **58**
tambourine *n* **128**
tampon *n* **49**
tandem *n* **101**
tank *n* **88**
tank top *n* **14**
tanning bed *n* **18**
tanning goggles *n* **18**
tanning mitt *n* **18**
tantalum *n* **78**
Tanzania *n* **149, 152**
Tanzanian *adj* **152**
tap *n* **33**
tap water *n* **52**
tape *n* **20, 32, 82**
tape measure *n* **36, 142**
tapir *n* **159**
tarantula *n* **162**
target *n* **125**
target shooting *n* **125**
taro root *n* **56**
tarragon *n* **59**
Tasmanian devil *n* **158**
taste *v* **11, 29, 52**
tasty *adj* **52**
Taurus *n* **144**
tawny owl *n* **161**
taxi driver *n* **90**
taxi stand *n* **104**
tea *n* **52, 66, 71, 86**
tea infuser *n* **66**
tea strainer *n* **66**
tea with lemon *n* **66**
tea with milk *n* **66**
teacher *n* **73, 90**
teacup *n* **27**
team *n* **107**
team bench *n* **112**
team jersey *n* **107**
team leader *n* **92**
team player *n* **93**
teamwork *n* **92–93**
teapot *n* **27, 66**
tear *n* **22**
tear duct *n* **01**
tearful *adj* **06**
teaspoon *n* **27**
teat *n* **08**
technetium *n* **78**
technological revolution *n* **79**
technology *n* **83**
technology literate *adj* **93**
teddy bear *n* **30**
tee *n* **115**
tee off *v* **115**
teeing ground *n* **115**
teenagers *n* **05**
teepee *n* **32**
teeth *n* **01, 03**
telephone *n* **82**
telephone banking *n* **94**
telephone manner *n* **93**
telescope *n* **144**
television *n* **26, 136–137**
television studio *n* **84**
telling the time *n* **171**
tellurium *n* **78**
temperate forest *n* **146**
temperature *n* **154**
temperature display *n* **33**
temperature gauge *n* **99**
temple *n* **01, 44**
temporary *adj* **81**
temporary exhibition *n* **130**
ten *num* **173**
ten past one *n* **171**
ten to two *n* **171**
tenant *n* **32**
tend *v* **39**
tendon *n* **03**
tennessine *n* **78**
tennis *n* **114**
tennis court *n* **114**
tennis match *n* **114**
tennis shoes *n* **114**
tenon saw *n* **36**
tenor *n* **126**
tension control *n* **142**
tent peg *n* **135**
tent pole *n* **135**
tenth *num* **173**
terbium *n* **78**
terminal *n* **104**
termite *n* **162**
terrace *n* **25, 65**
terrible *adj* **177**
terrified *adj* **06**
terrifying *adj* **177**
test *n* **73**
test results *n* **20**
test tube *n* **76**
test tube rack *n* **76**
testicle *n* **04**
text *n* **138**
textbook *n* **73, 138**
textiles *n* **91**
Thai *adj* **153**
thallium *n* **78**
Thanksgiving *n* **07**
thatched cottage *n* **32**
thatched roof *n* **32**
thawb *n* **15**
theater *n* **42, 126**
theme park *n* **133**
therapy *n* **24**
thermal flask *n* **52, 135**
thermals *n* **135**
thermometer *n* **20, 76**
thermosphere *n* **155**
thesis *n* **80**
thick *adj* **176**
thigh *n* **01, 53**
thigh-high boot *n* **17**
thimble *n* **142**
thin *adj* **176**
think *v* **11**
third *num* **173**
third base *n* **113**
third man *n* **111**
thirteen *num* **173**
thirty *num* **173**
this way up *phr* **45**
thistle *n* **38, 169**
thoracic vertebrae *n* **03**
thorium *n* **78**
thorny devil *n* **163**
thoughtless *adj* **10**
thread *n* **84, 142**
thread *v* **142**
thread guide *n* **142**
thread reel *n* **142**
three *num* **173**
three times a week *adv* **172**
three-course meal *n* **69**
three-second area *n* **112**
three-wheeler *n* **100**
thrift shop *n* **46**
thrilled *adj* **06**
thriller *n* **127, 137**
thrilling *adj* **177**
throat *n* **04**
throat lozenge *n* **49**
throttle *n* **100**
throw *n* **26, 30**
throw *v* **11, 107–108, 113, 117**
throw away *v* **178**
throw-in *n* **109, 112**
throw-in line *n* **112**
thrush *n* **160**
thruster *n* **143**
thulium *n* **78**
thumb *n* **02**
thumbtack *n* **82**
thunder *n* **154**
thundery *adj* **154**
Thursday *n* **172**
thyme *n* **59**
thyroid gland *n* **04**
tiara *n* **16**
tibia *n* **03**
tic-tac-toe *n* **140**
ticket *n* **102, 104, 130**
ticket barrier *n* **102**
ticket office *n* **102, 102, 130**
tidal barrage *n* **51**
tidal energy *n* **51**
tide pool *n* **134**
tie *n* **15–16**
tie *v* **109**
tie bar *n* **16**
tie your hair back *v* **12**
tie-break *n* **114**
tiger *n* **157, 159**
tiger's eye *n* **156**
tight *adj* **13, 176**
tighthead prop *n* **108**
tilde *n* **175**
tile, tiles *n* **25, 35**
tile *v* **35, 37**
tiller *n* **119**
time *n* **104, 107, 171**
time management *n* **93**
time out *n* **107**
timer *n* **28, 76, 95**
timetable *n* **102, 132**
Timorese *adj* **153**
tin *n* **78, 156**
tip *n* **69, 122**
tiramisu *n* **63**
tire *n* **97, 100–101**
tire lever *n* **101**
tired *adj* **06**
tiring *adj* **177**
tissue *n* **49**
tissue box *n* **30**
titanium *n* **78**
title *n* **138**
toadstools *n* **170**
toast *n* **71**
toasted sandwich *n* **71**
toaster *n* **27**
tobacco *n* **86**
Tobagonian *adj* **152**
toco toucan *n* **160**
toddler *n* **05, 08**
toe *n* **02, 115**
toe box *n* **126**
toe clip *n* **101**
toe strap *n* **101**
toenail *n* **02**
toffee *n* **67**
Togo *n* **149, 152**
Togolese *adj* **152**
toilet *n* **31, 33**
toilet block *n* **135**
toilet brush *n* **31**
toilet cleaner *n* **34**
toilet float *n* **33**

toilet paper *n* **31**
toilet paper holder *n* **31**
toilet seat *n* **31**
toiletries *n* **18, 48**
tollbooth *n* **96**
tomato juice *n* **65**
tomato sauce *n* **70**
tomato *n* **56**
tomb *n* **79**
tombolo *n* **147**
ton *n* **174**
toner *n* **18**
Tonga *n* **150, 153**
Tongan *adj* **153**
Tonghi bottlebrush *n* **168**
tongs *n* **28, 68, 76**
tongue *n* **04, 17, 53**
tonne *n* **174**
tonsillitis *n* **19**
tool belt *n* **36, 87**
tool rack *n* **35**
toolbox *n* **36**
tools *n* **35-36, 40, 87**
toothache *n* **22**
toothbrush *n* **31**
toothpaste *n* **31**
top *n* **08**
top dress *v* **39**
top tier *n* **63**
topaz *n* **156**
topiary *n* **41**
topping *n* **70**
topsoil *n* **39**
torc *n* **16**
torch lily *n* **167**
tornado *n* **154**
tortellini *n* **64**
tortilla *n* **62**
tortoise *n* **164**
touch-in goal line *n* **108**
touchdown *n* **107**
tour bus *n* **132**
tour guide *n* **90, 130, 132**
tourer *n* **100**
touring bike *n* **101**
tourism *n* **91**
tourist *n* **132**
tourist attraction *n* **132**
tourist bus *n* **99**
tourist map *n* **48, 132**
tourist office *n* **42**
tourmaline *n* **156**
tournament *n* **115**
tow away *v* **96**
tow truck *n* **98**
towel bar *n* **31**
towels *n* **31**
tower *n* **44, 51**
tower crane *n* **87**
town *n* **43, 148**
town features *n* **42-43**
town house *n* **32, 43**
toy car *n* **08**
toy store *n* **46**
toybox *n* **08**
toys *n* **08, 164**
trachea *n* **04**
track *n* **102, 116**
track your order *v* **46**
tracksuit *n* **15**
tractor *n* **86**
traditional clothes *n* **15**
traffic *n* **96**
traffic barrier *n* **96**
traffic jam *n* **43, 96**
traffic light ahead *n* **96**
tragedy *n* **126**
trail map *n* **148**
trailer *n* **135**
train, trains *n* **15, 102**
train *v* **39, 124**
train driver *n* **90**
train set *n* **08**
train station *n* **42, 102, 148**
training cane *n* **39**
training wheels *n* **101**
tram *n* **99, 102**
trampoline *n* **08, 125**
transfer money *v* **45**
transformer *n* **33, 75**
transition metals *n* **78**
translator *n* **89**
transmission *n* **98**
transplant *v* **39**
transport helicopter *n* **88**
transportation *n* **91**
trap *n* **33**
trapezius *n* **03**
trapezoid *n* **74**
trapped insect *n* **168**
trapped radiation *n* **155**
trash *n* **83**
trash bag *n* **33-34**
trash can *n* **25, 27, 33, 82**
travel *n* **131**
travel agent *n* **46, 90**
travel card *n* **48**
travel writing *n* **138**
traveler's tree *n* **168**
trawler *n* **105**
tray *n* **69-70**
tray table *n* **103**
trays *n* **82**
tread *n* **101**
tread water *v* **118**
treadmill *n* **124**
treasure *n* **139**
treatment *n* **20-21**
treatments *n* **24**
treats *n* **164**
treble clef *n* **128**
treble fishhook *n* **121**
tree, trees *n* **41, 167-169**
tree climbing *n* **133**
tree house *n* **32, 133**
tree pose *n* **24**
tree pruner *n* **40**
trekking *n* **120**
trellis *n* **41**
trench *n* **145**
trench coat *n* **15**
trend *v* **84**
trial *n* **85**
triangle *n* **74, 128**
triangle *n* **74**
triangle pose *n* **24**
Triassic *adj n* **157**
Triassic *n* **157**
triathlon *n* **116**
tributary *n* **147**
triceratops *n* **157**
trilobite *n* **157**
trim *v* **39**
trimmer *n* **40**
Trinidad and Tobago *n* **150, 152**
Trinidadian *adj* **152**
trip over *v* **178**
triple bar vertical *n* **120**
triple jump *n* **116**
triplets *n* **05**
tripod *n* **76, 144**
trivia game *n* **136**
troll *n* **139**
troll *v* **84**
trolley *n* **102, 104, 131**
trolley bus *n* **99**
trolling *n* **84**
trombone *n* **128**
Tropic of Cancer *n* **145**
Tropic of Capricorn *n* **145**
tropics *n* **145**
troposphere *n* **155**
trot *v* **120, 165**
trout *n* **54**
trowel *n* **40, 87**
truck driver *n* **90**
truck-mounted crane *n* **87**
truffle, truffles *n* **56, 170**
trumpet *n* **128-129**
trumpetfish *n* **166**
trunk *n* **159**
trunk *n* **97**
try *n* **108**
try line *n* **108**
try on *v* **46**
try something on *v* **14**
tsunami *n* **145**
tuba *n* **128**
tubular bells *n* **128**
Tuesday *n* **172**
tuff *n* **156**
tugboat *n* **105**
tulip *n* **38**
tumble dryer *n* **34**
tumble turn *n* **118**
tumbler *n* **27**
turmeric *n* **59**
tuna *n* **54**
tundra *n* **146**
tune in *v* **136**
tuner *n* **129, 136**
tungsten *n* **78**
tuning buttons *n* **136**
tuning peg *n* **129**
Tunisia *n* **149, 152**
Tunisian *adj* **152**
turban *n* **16**
turbine *n* **51**
turbot *n* **54**
turkey *n* **53, 161, 165**
Turkish *adj* **153**
Turkish delight *n* **67**
Türkiye *n* **150, 151, 153**
Turkmen *adj* **153**
Turkmenistan *n* **151, 153**
turle knot *n* **121**
turn *v* **35, 118, 126**
turn down *v* **136, 178**
turn down the volume *v* **137**
turn left *v* **96, 148**
turn off *v* **83, 137, 178**
turn on *v* **83, 137, 178**
turn right *v* **96, 148**
turn signal *n* **97, 100**
turn up *v* **14, 136, 178**
turn up the volume *v* **137**
turner *n* **28**
turnip *n* **56**
turntable *n* **129**
turquoise *n* **141, 156**
turret *n* **44**
tutu *n* **126**
Tuvalu *n* **150, 153**
Tuvaluan *adj* **153**
tuxedo *n* **15**
TV *n* **26, 136**
TV channels *n* **137**
TV guide *n* **137-138**
TV schedule *n* **137**
TV set *n* **137**
TV shows *n* **137**
tweeter *n* **136**
tweezers *n* **18, 20, 77**
twelve *num* **173**
twentieth *num* **173**
twenty *num* **173**
twenty-five past one *n* **171**
twenty-five to two *n* **171**
twenty minutes *n* **171**
twenty past one *n* **171**
twenty thirty-three *n* **172**
twenty to two *n* **171**
twenty-first *num* **173**
twenty-one *num* **173**
twenty-two *num* **173**
twice a week *adv* **172**
twilight zone *n* **166**
twin bed *n* **30**
twin room *n* **131**
twine *n* **40**
twins *n* **05**
twist bar *n* **124**
twist ties *n* **40**
two *num* **173**
two hundred *num* **173**
two o'clock *n* **171**
two percent milk *n* **61**
two weeks *n* **172**
two-person tent *n* **135**
typeface *n* **175**
types of aircraft *n* **103**
types of buildings *n* **44**
types of buses *n* **99**
types of cars *n* **97**
types of fishing *n* **121**
types of houses *n* **32**
types of meat *n* **53**
types of motorcycles *n* **100**
types of motorsports *n* **123**
types of plants *n* **41**
types of soil *n* **39**
types of trains *n* **102**
tyrannosaurus rex *n* **157**

U

udon *n* **64**
Uganda *n* **149, 152**
Ugandan *adj* **152**
ugli fruit *n* **57**
ugly *adj* **177**
Ukraine *n* **151, 152**
Ukrainian *adj* **153**
ukulele *n* **129**
ulna *n* **03**
ultrasound *n* **08**
ultraviolet *n* **75**
ultraviolet rays *n* **155**
umbilical cord *n* **08**
umbrella *n* **16**
umbrella pine *n* **167**
umbrella plant *n* **38**
umlaut *n* **175**
umpire *n* **111, 113-114**
umpire's chair *n* **114**
unanimous vote *n* **95**
unapproachable *adj* **10**
uncle *n* **05**
unclog the sink *v* **35**

unclog the toilet *v* **35**
under *prep* **180**
under par *adj* **115**
undercoat *n* **37**
undergraduate *n* **80**
underpass *n* **96, 102**
underscore *n* **175**
undersea features *n* **145**
undershirt *n* **14**
understand *v* **11**
underwater camera *n* **118**
underwater diving *n* **118**
underwear *n* **14**
unemployment benefit *n* **81**
unenthusiastic *adj* **06**
uneven bars *n* **125**
unfasten *v* **14**
unfriendly *adj* **10**
unfurnished *adj* **32**
unhappy *adj* **06**
unicorn *n* **139**
unicycle *n* **101**
uniform, uniforms *n* **13, 50, 88**
unimpressed *adj* **06**
United Arab Emirates *n* **151, 153**
United Kingdom *n* **151, 153**
United States of America *n* **150, 152**
universe *n* **144**
university departments *n* **80**
university schools *n* **80**
unkind *adj* **10**
unleaded *n* **97**
unload the dishwasher *v* **34**
unpack *v* **11, 32**
unpasteurized *adj* **61**
unpeeled prawn *n* **54**
unpick *v* **142**
unpleasant *adj* **177**
unreasonable *adj* **10**
unreliable *adj* **10**
unsalted *adj* **61**
unsaturated fat *n* **23**
upload *v* **83**
upper deck *n* **99**
upper level *n* **47**
uppercase *n* **175**
upscale *adj* **47**
upset *adj* **06**
upstairs *adv, n* **25**
uranium *n* **78**
Uranus *n* **143**
urinary *n* **04**
urology *n* **21**
Uruguay *n* **149, 152**
Uruguayan *adj* **152**
USB drive *n* **83**
useful *adj* **177**
useful expressions *n* **179-180**
useless *adj* **177**
usher *n* **126**
uterus *n* **04, 08**
utility knife *n* **36-37**
utility power *n* **33**
UV tubes *n* **18**
Uzbek *adj* **153**
Uzbekistan *n* **151, 153**

V

V-neck *n* **14**
vacancies *n* **92, 131**
vacation *n* **81, 104**
vaccination *n* **08, 20**
vacuole *n* **77**
vacuum *n* **75**
vacuum cleaner *n* **34**
vacuum the carpet *v* **34**
vagina *n* **04**
Vaisakhi *n* **07**
valance *n* **30**
valley *n* **146**
valve *n* **101**
vampire *n* **139**
vanadium *n* **78**
vandalism *n* **85**
vanilla milkshake *n* **61**
vanity *n* **30**
Vanuatu *n* **150, 153**
Vanuatuan *adj* **153**
varnish *n* **37**
vase *n* **26**
Vatican City *n* **151**
vault *n* **125**
veal *n* **53**
vegan *adj* **23**
vegan *n* **23**
vegetable garden *n* **41, 86**
vegetables *n* **48, 55-56**
vegetarian *adj* **23**
vegetarian *n* **23**
veggie burger *n* **70**
veil *n* **15**
vein *n* **04**
Venetian blinds *n* **26**
Venezuela *n* **149, 152**
Venezuelan *adj* **152**
venison *n* **53**
vent *n* **145**
Venus *n* **143**
Venus fly-trap *n* **168**
verdict *n* **85**
vermilion flycatcher *n* **160**
vertebrate *n* **77**
verticals *n* **120**
vest *n* **14**
vest *n* **15**
vet *n* **89**
veteran *n* **88**
vial *n* **36**
vibraphone *n* **128**
Victoria Falls *n* **145**
vicuña *n* **158**
video chat *n* **83**
video conference *n* **83**
video games *n* **136**
video on demand *n* **137**
Vietnam *n* **150, 153**
Vietnamese *adj* **153**
view a house *v* **32**
viewing platform *n* **44**
viewpoint *n* **148**
villa *n* **32, 131**
village *n* **43**
villain *n* **127**
Vincentian *adj* **152**
vinegar *n* **60, 64**
vineyard *n* **86**
vintage *adj* **13**
vintage *n* **97**
vinyl records *n* **129**
viola *n* **128**
violet *n* **38**
violin *n* **128-29**
violin sonata *n* **128**
Virginia creeper *n* **168**
Virgo *n* **144**
virus *n* **19, 77**
visa *n* **104**
visible light *n* **75**
vision *n* **22**
visitor *n* **107**
visor *n* **100**
vitamins *n* **23, 49**
vivarium *n* **164**
vlog *n* **84**
vlogger *n* **84**
vocal cords *n* **04**
vodka *n* **68**
vodka and orange *n* **68**
voice recorder *n* **83**
volcano *n* **145**
volley *n* **114**
volleyball *n* **112**
volleyball positions *n* **112**
volt *n* **75**
voltage *n* **33**
volume *n* **74, 136, 174**
volunteer *v* **92**
vomit *v* **20**
vote *n* **85**
vulture *n* **160**

W

waders *n* **121**
wading pool *n* **25, 133**
waffle, waffles *n* **65, 70-71**
wages *n* **81**
waist *n* **01, 129**
waistband *n* **15, 142**
wait in line *v* **104**
wait on *v* **178**
wait up *v* **178**
waiter *n* **69, 89**
waiting room *n* **20, 102**
waitress *n* **69, 89**
wake up *v* **09, 178**
walk *v* **120**
walk the dog *v* **09**
walkie-talkie *n* **50**
walking boots *n* **135**
walking trail *n* **148**
wall *n* **25, 44, 87**
Wallace's flying frog *n* **163**
wallet *n* **94**
wallet *n* **16**
wallflower *n* **169**
wallpaper *n* **37**
wallpaper *v* **37**
wallpaper border *n* **37**
wallpaper brush *n* **37**
wallpaper hanger *n* **37**
wallpaper paste *n* **37**
wallpaper roll *n* **37**
wallpaper stripper *n* **37**
walnut *n* **58, 168**
walnut oil *n* **60**
walrus *n* **166**
wand *n* **139**
want *v* **46**
war *n* **79, 88**
war elephant *n* **79**
ward *n* **21**
wardrobe *n* **30**
warehouse *n* **44, 106**
warfare *n* **79**
warhorse *n* **79**
warm *adj* **154**
warm front *n* **155**
warning track *n* **113**
warp thread *n* **142**
warrant *n* **85**
warrior *n* **79**
warrior pose *n* **24**
warthog *n* **159**
wasabi *n* **60**
wash the car *v* **34**
wash your face *v* **09**
wash your hair *v* **09, 12**
washer *n* **36**
washer fluid *n* **97**
washer fluid reservoir *n* **98**
washing machine *n* **34**
wasp *n* **162**
wasp nest *n* **162**
waste *n* **33**
waste disposal *n* **135**
watch *n* **16**
watch TV *v* **09**
watching television *n* **137**
water *n* **48, 91, 118**
water *v* **39**
water bottle, water bottles *n* **101, 135**
water carrier *n* **135**
water chestnut *n* **56**
water cooler *n* **82**
water features *n* **145**
water garden *n* **41**
water hazard *n* **115**
water jet *n* **50**
water lilies *n* **167**
water phenomena *n* **145**
water plants *n* **41**
water polo *n* **119**
water rail *n* **161**
water shoes *n* **17**
water skier *n* **119**
water skiing *n* **119**
water sports *n* **119**
water the plants *v* **09, 34**
water vapor *n* **51**
watercolor *n* **130**
watercolor paints *n* **141**
watercress *n* **55**
waterfall *n* **146**
waterfront *n* **132**
watering *n* **40**
watering can *n* **40**
watermark *n* **94**
watermelon *n* **58**
waterproof fishing gear *n* **121**
wave *n* **75, 119, 134, 147**
wave *v* **02**
wavelength *n* **75**
wavy hair *n* **12**
wax *adj* **176**
wax *n* **18, 176**
waxcap *n* **170**
weapons *n* **79, 88**
wear *v* **14**
weasel *n* **158**
weather *n* **137, 154**

weather forecaster *n* **137**
weather map *n* **155**
weaver *n* **142**
weaverbird *n* **160**
weaving *n* **142**
webcam *n* **83**
wedding *n* **07**
wedding cake *n* **63**
wedding dress *n* **15**
wedge *n* **115**
wedge sandals *n* **17**
Wednesday *n* **172**
weedkiller *n* **39**
weeds *n* **41**
week *n* **172**
weekends *n* **172**
weekly *adj* **172**
weekly *adv* **172**
weevil *n* **162**
weft thread *n* **142**
weigh *v* **174, 178**
weight, weights *n* **121, 174**
weight belt *n* **118**
weight training *n* **124**
well-qualified *adj* **93**
werewolf *n* **139**
west *n* **148**
western *n* **127**
wet *adj* **154**
wet suit *n* **118, 134**
wet wipe, wet wipes *n* **08, 49**
wetlands *n* **146**
wharf *n* **106**
wheat allergy *n* **23**
wheat beer *n* **68**
wheel *n* **97, 101**
wheel pose *n* **24**
wheelbarrow *n* **40**
wheelchair *n* **21**
wheelchair access *n* **99**
wheelchair basketball *n* **125**
wheelchair curling *n* **122**
wheelchair race *n* **116**
wheelchair ramp *n* **130**
wheelchair rugby *n* **108, 125**
whiplash *n* **19**
whipped cream *n* **61**
whisk *n* **28**
whisk *v* **29**
whiskers *n* **158**
whiskey *n* **68**
whisper *v* **11**
white *adj* **140–141**
white *n* **140–141**
white blood cell *n* **77**
white bread *n* **62**
white chocolate *n* **67**
white coffee *n* **65**
white currant *n* **57**
white dwarf *n* **144**
white flour *n* **62**
White House *n* **44**
white meat *n* **53**
white mustard *n* **59**
white tea *n* **66**
white vinegar *n* **34**
white wine *n* **52, 68**
whiteboard *n* **73, 95**
whitening *n* **22**
whiting *n* **54**
whole milk *n* **61**
whole-grain bread *n* **62**
whole-grain mustard *n* **60**
whole-wheat flour *n* **62**
whooper swan *n* **161**
Wi-Fi *n* **83**
wicket *n* **111**
wicket-keeper *n* **111**
wide *adj* **176**
wide range *n* **48**
wide receiver *n* **107**
widow *n* **05**
width *n* **74**
wife *n* **05**
wig *n* **12**
wigwam *n* **32**
wildcat *n* **159**
wildebeest *n* **158**
wildlife photography *n* **133**
willow *n* **169**
win *v* **11, 109, 115, 140**
win a prize *v* **07**
wind *n* **51, 154**
wind energy *n* **51**
wind farm *n* **51**
wind turbine *n* **51**
windbreak *n* **134**
windlass *n* **105**
windmill *n* **44**
window cleaner *n* **90**
window shopping *n* **46**
windshield *n* **97, 100**
windsurfer *n* **119**
windsurfing *n* **119, 134**
windy *adj* **154**
wine *n* **68**
wine list *n* **69**
wine vinegar *n* **60**
wineglass *n* **27**
wing *n* **53, 103, 112, 161**
wings *n* **49, 126**
wink *v* **02**
winners' cup *n* **109**
winter *n* **172**
Winter Olympics *n* **122**
winter sports *n* **122**
wipe the surfaces *v* **34**
wiper *n* **97**
wire *n* **35, 83**
wire cutters *n* **36**
wire strippers *n* **36**
wireless *adj* **83**
wireless headphones *n* **136**
wires *n* **33**
wiring *n* **33**
wisteria *n* **38**
witch *n* **139**
witches' brew *n* **139**
with ice *adj* **68**
withdraw money *v* **45**
without ice *adj* **68**
witness *n* **85**
wizard *n* **139**
wok *n* **28**
wolf *n* **159**
woman *n* **05**
womb *n* **04, 08**
wombat *n* **158**
women's heptathlon *n* **116**
womenswear *n* **47**
wonderful *adj* **177**
wood *adj* **176**
wood *n* **35, 115, 141, 146, 176**
woods *n* **176**
wood duck *n* **161**
wood glue *n* **35**
wood preserver *n* **37**
wooden spoon *n* **28**
woodwind *n* **128**
woodworking *n* **141**
woofer *n* **136**
wool *adj* **176**
wool *n* **142, 176**
woolen *n* **13**
woolly mammoth *n* **157**
woolly rhinoceros *n* **157**
work *n* **81**
work *v* **11**
work bench *n* **35**
work boots *n* **17**
work from home *v* **81**
work full-time *v* **81**
work part-time *v* **81**
work shifts *v* **81**
workclothes *n* **13**
worker *n* **81**
working out *n* **124**
working well under pressure *n* **93**
workplace skills *n* **93**
workstation *n* **82**
worm *n* **162**
worried *adj* **06**
wound *n* **19**
wrap *n* **70**
wrap up the meeting *v* **95**
wren *n* **160**
wrench *n* **36, 98**
wrestling *n* **117**
wrinkles *n* **12**
wrist *n* **01–02**
wrist band *n* **107**
wrist weights *n* **124**
wristband *n* **114**
writ *n* **85**
write *v* **73**
write a will *v* **07**
writer *n* **90**
writing *n* **175**
writing equipment *n* **175**
written communication *n* **93**

X-ray, X-rays *n* **19, 21, 75**
X-ray machine *n* **104**
xenon *n* **78**
xylophone *n* **128**
yacht *n* **105, 119, 134**
yak *n* **159**
yam *n* **56, 86**
yard *n* **174**
yard line *n* **107**
yarmulke *n* **16**
yawn *v* **02**
year *n* **172**
yellow *n* **141**
yellow box fish *n* **166**
yellow card *n* **109**
yellow mustard *n* **60**
yellow surgeonfish *n* **166**
yellow tang *n* **166**
Yemen *n* **151, 153**
Yemeni *adj* **153**
yew *n* **167**
yield *v* **96**
yo-yo *n* **08**
yoga *n* **24**
yoga class *n* **24**
yoga pants *n* **24**
yoga teacher *n* **90**
yogurt n **61**
yolk *n* **61, 71**
young *adj* **12**
young frog *n* **77**
ytterbium *n* **78**
yttrium *n* **78**
yucca *n* **38**
yurt *n* **32**

Z

Zambia *n* **149, 152**
Zambian *adj* **152**
zebra *n* **158**
zero carbon *adj* **155**
zero point five *num* **173**
zest *n* **57**
ziggurat *n* **44**
Zimbabwe *n* **149, 152**
Zimbabwean *adj* **152**
zinc *n* **78, 156**
zip code *n* **45**
zipper *n* **17, 142**
zirconium *n* **78**
zodiac *n* **144**
zodiac constellations *n* **144**
zodiac symbols *n* **144**
zombie *n* **139**
zoo *n* **133**
zookeeper *n* **90**
zoologist *n* **77**
zoology *n* **77, 80**
zucchini *n* **56**

Italian word list

The numbers after each word or phrase refer to the units in which they can be found.

A

a destra **148**
a foglia **56**
a pois **13**
a quadri **13**
a righe **13**
a scacchi **13**
a sinistra **148**
abbaiare **164**
abbaino **25**
abbassare **136, 137, 178**
abbattere un muro **35**
abbigliamento **14, 100**
abbigliamento da donna **47**
abbigliamento da uomo **47**
abbigliamento formale **15**
abbigliamento informale **14**
abbigliamento sportivo **15**
abbigliamento termico **135**
abboccare **121**
abete **167**
abilità **11**
abilità di calcolo **93**
abissino **164**
abitacolo **123**
abiti da lavoro **13**
abiti tradizionali **15**
abito da flamenco **15**
abito da sera **15**
acacia **47**
acacia di Costantinopoli **168**
accanto **148**
accanto a **180**
accappatoio **31**
accedere **83**
accelerare **98**
acceleratore **99, 100**
acceleratore di particelle **75**
accendere **83, 135, 137, 178**
accendifuoco **135**
accensione **99**
accento acuto **175**
accento circonflesso **175**
accento grave **175**
accesso per disabili **99**
accessori **16, 17**
accessori di moda **16**
accettate **94**
acchiappamosche vermiglio **160**
acciughe **64**
accompagnare qualcuno **98**
acconciare i capelli **12**
accordatore **129**
accordo **128**
accordo commerciale **81**
accudire **178**
accusa **50, 85**
ace **114**
acero **169**
aceto **60, 64**
aceto balsamico **60**
aceto bianco **34**
aceto di malto **60**
aceto di sidro di mele **60**
aceto di vino **60**
acetosella **55, 59**
acido / acida **52, 76**
acqua **48, 91, 118**
acqua calda **31**
acqua del rubinetto **52**
acqua di cocco **58, 65**
acqua fredda **31**
acqua minerale **52, 68**
acqua ragia **37**
acqua santa **07**
acquamarina **156**
acquario **145, 164**
acquazzone **154**
acquerelli **141**
acquerello **130**
acquistare **32**
acquisti **91**
acquisto di una casa **32**
acro **174**
AD (amministratore delegato) **81**
addebito diretto **45**
addentare **52**
addetto alla reception / addetta alla reception **81, 90**
addetto alla sicurezza / addetta alla sicurezza **130**
addetto alle pulizie / addetta alle pulizie **89**
additivi **23**
addolorato / addolorata **06**
addome **01, 162**
addominali **03, 124**
addormentarsi **09**
aderente **13**
adesso **171**
adolescente **05**
adorabile **177**
adulti **05**
aerare **39**
aereo cargo **103**
aereo da ricognizione **88**
aereo da trasporto militare **88**
aereo leggero **103**
aereo passageri **103**
aerobica **124**
aeromobile **103**
aeronautica militare **88**
aeroporto **43, 104**
affamato / affamata **26**
affare **48**
affascinato / affascinata **06**
afferrare **11**
affettare **29, 62**
affettati **71**
affettatrice **62**
affidabile **10, 93**
affilacoltelli **28**
affittare un cottage **131**
affitto di una casa **32**
affittuario / affittuaria **32**
affluente **147**
affondare **117**
affondo **124**
affumicato / affumicata **54, 72**
afgano / afgana **153**
Afghanistan **151, 153**
afnio **78**
Africa **149, 152**
africano / africana **152**
agata **156**
agbada **15**
agenda **82, 138**
agente di borsa **94**
agente di polizia **50**
agente di polizia giudiziaria **85**
agente di polizia motociclista **50**
agente di viaggio **90**
agente immobiliare **32, 89**
agenzia di viaggi **46**
aggettivi **52, 176**
aggettivi del tempo **154**
aggiornamento dello stato **84**
aggirarsi furtivamente **159**
aggiungere **11, 29**
aggiungere al carrello **46**
aggiungere alla lista dei desideri **46**
aggiustare **11**
aggraziato / aggraziata **177**
aggrottare la fronte **02**
agitatore **68**
aglio **56**
agnello **53, 165**
ago **20**
ago da cucito **142**
ago da macchina **142**
agopressione **24**
agopuntura **24**
agosto **172**
agricoltura **86, 91**
agrumi **57**
aguglia **166**
aia **86**
aikido **117**
airbag **99**
airball **112**
airone **160**
aiuola **41**
aiutare **11**
aiuto cuoco **69**
al completo **131**
al settimo cielo **06**
al tegame **72**
al vapore **72**
ala **53, 103, 112, 161**
ala destra **108, 110**
ala grande **112**
ala interiore **162**
ala piccola **112**
ala posteriore **162**
ala sinistra **108, 110**
alano **164**
alba **171**
albanese **153**
Albania **151, 153**
albatro **160**
albergo **42, 131**
albero **41, 105, 119, 167, 168, 169**
albero del fuoco cileno **167**
albero del viaggiatore **168**
albero della gomma **169**
albero di avocado **167**
albero di fuoco **168**
albero di Giosuè **167**
albero di pecan **168**
albero motore **98**
albertonecte **157**
albicocca **57**
albicocche secche **58**
album **129**
albume **61, 71**
alcale **76**
alce **159**
alchechengi **57, 169**
alesatore **36**
alettone **103**
alettone anteriore **97, 123**
alettone posteriore **97, 123**
Aleuria aurantia **170**
alfabeto cirillico **175**
alfabeto devanagari **175**
alfabeto greco **175**
alfabeto latino **175**
alfiere **140**
alga **134, 166**
Algeria **149, 152**
algerino / algerina **152**
ali **49**
aliante **103**
alieno / aliena **139**
alimentazione **23**
alimentazione elettrica **51**
alimenti **52–72**
alimenti lavorati **23**
aliscafo **105**
allacciare **14**
allaccio della luce **135**
all'antica **177**
allargare **142**
allarme **25, 50**
allarme antincendio **50**
allegato **83**
allegro / allegra **06**
allenamento **124**
allenamento a circuito **124**
allenarsi **124**
allenatore / allenatrice **109, 112, 113**
allentato / allentata **176**
allergia **19**
allergia ai frutti di mare **23**
allergia ai solfiti **23**
allergia al grano **23**
allergia al sedano **23**
allergia al sesamo **23**
allergia alla frutta a guscio **23**
allergia alla senape **23**
allergia alla soia **23**
allergia alle arachidi **23**
allergia alle uova **23**
allergico / allergica **23**
allergie alimentari **23**

all'esterno **180**
allevamento ittico **86**
allevare **120**
allevato a terra / allevata a terra **53**
alligatore del Mississippi **163**
all'interno **180**
allocco **161**
alloggiare in albergo **131**
alloggio **131**
alloro **38**, **167**
alluce **02**
alluminio **78**, **156**
allungare **124**
alluvione **154**
aloe **167**
alogeni **78**
alpaca **165**
alpinismo **133**
alta definizione **137**
alta marea **147**
alta pressione **155**
altalena **43**, **133**
altalena a dondolo **43**
altezza **12**, **74**
altri animali domestici **164**
alto **45**
alto / alta **12**, **176**
altoparlante **102**, **136**
altoparlante anteriore **136**
altoparlante centrale **136**
altoparlante surround **136**
altoparlanti **83**
altopiano **146**
altura **146**
alunno / alunna **73**
alveare **86**, **162**
alzare **178**
alzare il volume **136**, **137**
alzarsi **09**, **11**, **178**
alzata di mano **95**
amaca **135**
amanita falloide **170**
amanita virosa **170**
amarillide **167**
amaro / amara **52**, **56**
ambiente **143–56**, **155**
ambizioso / ambiziosa **10**, **93**
ambulanza **21**, **50**
ambulanza militare **88**
America Centrale **150**, **152**
America del Nord **152**
American curl **164**
americio **78**
ametista **156**
amichevole **10**
amico / amica **07**
amico di penna / amica di penna **07**
ammasso stellare **144**
amministrazione **91**, **93**
ammiraglio **88**
ammissioni **80**
ammorbidente **34**
ammucchiare **178**
amo da pesca **121**
ampere **33**
ampiamente qualificato / ampiamente qualificata **93**
amplificatore **129**
amuleto **139**
anacardi **68**
anacardo **58**
analisi **93**
anamnesi dentale **22**
ananas **58**, **167**
anatra **53**, **165**
anatra mandarina **161**
anatra sposa **161**
anatroccolo **165**
ancora **105**, **119**
ancoretta **121**
andare a funghi **170**
andare a letto **09**
andare a prendere qualcuno **98**
andare a scuola **09**
andare al bar **09**
andare al galoppo **120**
andare al lavoro **09**
andare al passo **120**
andare al piccolo galoppo **120**
andare al trotto **120**
andare alla scuola materna **07**
andare all'asilo **07**
andare all'estero **104**, **131**
andare bene **14**, **46**, **73**
andare carponi **11**
andare dal medico **20**
andare dritto **96**, **148**
andare in **11**
andare in bicicletta **101**, **133**
andare in crociera **131**
andare in giro **96–106**
andare in kayak **119**
andare in maternità **81**
andare in moto d'acqua **119**
andare in motoscafo **119**
andare in mountain bike **133**
andare in pellegrinaggio alla Mecca **07**
andare in pensione **07**, **81**
andare in vacanza **131**
andare male **73**
andare sulla slitta **122**
andare sullo skateboard **125**
andare via **178**, **179**
andato a male / andata a male **52**
Andorra **151**, **153**
andorrano / andorrana **153**
anelli **125**, **143**
anello **16**, **112**, **170**
anello con sigillo **16**
anemone **134**, **166**
anestesista **90**
aneto **59**, **60**
anfibi **163**
angiosperme **157**
Angola **149**, **152**
angolano / angolana **152**
angolo **74**, **109**, **148**
angolo della strada **42**
angolo retto **74**
anguilla **54**
anguilla pellicano **166**
anguria **58**
anice **59**
anice stellato **59**
anidride carbonica **155**
animali da fattoria **165**
animali domestici **164**
annaffiare le piante **34**
annaffiatoio **40**
annaffiatura **40**
anniversario **07**
anno **172**
annoiato / annoiata **06**
annuale **41**
annuire **02**
annullare **178**
annusare **11**
ansioso / ansiosa **06**
antenna **25**, **97**, **162**
antenna parabolica **25**, **136**
antenna radio **105**
antera **38**
antibiotici **49**
antiche rovine **44**
anticipazione **137**
antico tempio greco **44**
antidolorifici **20**, **49**
antifurto **25**
antigelo **97**
Antigua e Barbuda **150**, **152**
antiguo o barbudano / antiguo o barbudana **152**
antimonio **78**
antinfiammatorio **49**
antipasto **69**
antisettico **20**
anulare **02**
anziano / anziana **05**, **12**
ape **162**, **165**
aperto / aperta **48**, **132**
apostrofo **175**
apparato cardiocircolatorio **04**
apparato digerente **04**
apparato respiratorio **04**
apparato riproduttivo **04**
apparato urinario **04**
apparecchi **83**
apparecchiare **34**
apparecchio **22**
appartamento **25**, **131**
appassionato / appassionata **10**
appendere **14**, **37**, **178**
appendere gli scaffali **35**
appendice **04**
appendicite **19**
appisolarsi **178**
applaudire **02**
applauso **126**
applique **26**
appoggio **40**
apprendista **92**
appuntamento **20**, **81**
appunti **95**
apribottiglie **28**, **68**
aprile **172**
apriscatole **28**
aquila arpia **160**
aquila calva **160**
aquila reale **160**
aquilegia **168**
aquilone **08**
ara scarlatta **161**
Arabia Saudita **151**, **153**
aracea americana **38**
arachide **58**
arachidi **68**
aragosta **54**
arance rosse **57**
arancia **57**
aranciata **52**
arancione **141**
arare **86**
araucaria **167**
arbitro **107**, **108**, **109**, **111**, **112**, **113**
arbusti **41**
arbusti da fiore **41**
archeologia **79**
archeologo / archeologa **79**
architetto **90**
architettura **44**
architrave **87**
archivio **79**
arciere **125**
arcipelago **147**
arco **41**, **44**, **74**, **79**, **125**
arco naturale **147**
arco plantare **02**
arcobaleno **154**
ardesia **156**
ardiglione **121**
area **74**, **174**
area bagni **135**
area campeggio **148**
area degli arbitri **110**
area dei tre secondi **112**
area del portiere **110**
area dell'allenatore **113**
area di campeggio **135**
area di meta **108**
area di rigore **109**
area di sosta **148**
area docce **135**
area giochi per bambini **133**
area pedonale **42**
area residenziale **32**
area ristorazione **47**
aree disponibili **135**
arena **120**
arenaria **156**
argano **105**
Argentina **149**, **152**
argentino / argentina **152**
argento **78**, **116**, **156**, **176**
argilla **39**, **141**
argon **78**
aria condizionata **33**, **99**
ariete **79**, **144**
aringa **54**
aringhe affumicate **71**
armadietti **118**, **124**
armadillo **159**
armadio **30**
armadio a muro **30**
armatura **79**
Armenia **150**, **153**
armeno / armena **153**
armi **79**, **88**
armonica **129**
arnia **165**
aromaterapia **24**
arpa **128**
arpione **121**
arrabbiato / arrabbiata **06**
arrampicata **125**
arrampicata su ghiaccio **122**
arrampicata sugli alberi **133**

arredamento **47**
arredato / arredata **32**
arresto **50**
arricciature **142**
arrivare **09**
arrivare a casa **09**
arrivare in anticipo **09**
arrivare in orario **09**
arrivare in ritardo **09**
arrivederci **179**
arrivo **43**
arrogante **10**
arrossire **02**
arrostire **29**
arsenico **78**
Art déco **130**
arte **73, 141**
arte concettuale **130**
arte topiaria **41**
arteria **04**
arteterapia **24**
arti **91, 141, 142**
arti dello spettacolo **91**
arti marziali **117**
articolazione **03**
articoli da toeletta **48**
articolo **138**
Artide **159**
artigiano / artigiana **79**
artiglio **161**
artista **90, 141**
ascella **01**
ascensore **25, 47, 131**
ascia **36, 50, 79**
asciugamani **31**
asciugamano da bagno **31**
asciugamano per capelli **18**
asciugamano per le mani **31**
asciugare i piatti **34**
asciugarsi **31**
asciugarsi i capelli **09**
asciugatrice **34**
ascoltare **11**
ascoltare la radio **09**
Asia **150, 151, 153**
asiatico / asiatica **153**
asino **165**
asma **19**
asola **15**
asparago **56**
aspettare alzato / aspettare alzata **178**
aspetto **12, 19–24**
aspetto generale **12**
aspidistra **167**
aspirafoglie **40**
aspirapolvere **34**
aspiratore **31**
aspirazione dell'aria del motore **123**
aspro / aspra **57**
assaggiare **11, 29, 52**
assale **100**
asse da stiro **34**
assegno **45, 94**
assemblea generale annuale **95**
assertivo / assertiva **10, 93**
assi del pavimento **26**
assistente all'infanzia **90**
assistente di volo **103, 104**
assistente personale **81, 90**
assistente socio-psicologico / assistente sociopsicologica **24**
asso **140**
assolo **128**
assorbente **49**
assorbente interno **49**
asta **115**
asta di estensione del rullo **37**
asta per microfono **84**
asta portaflebo **21**
astato **78**
asteoride **143**
asterisco **175**
astigmatismo **22**
astina di livello **98**
astronauta **144**
astronomia **144**
astuccio **22, 73**
atlante **73**
atleta **89, 116**
atletica **116, 125**
atletica leggera **116**
atmosfera **143, 155**
atollo **147**
atomo **76**
atrio **25, 102**
attaccante **109**
attacco **107**
attacco a baionetta **33**
attacco a vite **33**
atteggiamento pragmatico **93**
attento / attenta **10**
atterrare **104**
attinio **78**
attività **09**
attività all'aperto **133**
attività mineraria **91**
attività quotidiane **09**
attore / attrice **85, 89, 126**
attraccare **106**
attraversamento di animali selvatici **96**
attraversamento di bambini **96**
attrazione turistica **132**
attrazioni **132**
attrezzatura **129**
attrezzatura da cricket **111**
attrezzatura da golf **115**
attrezzatura da palestra **124**
attrezzatura dell'ufficio **82**
attrezzatura per il giardinaggio **40**
attrezzatura per le sale riunioni **82**
attrezzature per il campeggio **135**
attrezzi **36, 87**
attrezzi da giardinaggio **40**
attrezzi per il bricolage **35**
audioguida **130**
auditorium **80**
audizione **127**
aula **73**
aula di tribunale **85**
aumento **81**
auricolare **88**
auricolari **136**
aurora **144, 155**
Australia **150, 153**
australiano / australiana **153**
Austria **151, 153**
austriaco / austriaca **153**
autista **90, 99**
autista di autobus **90**
auto **97, 98, 99**
auto 4x4 **97**
auto da corsa **97, 123**
auto della polizia **50**
auto d'epoca **97**
auto elettrica **97**
auto ibrida **97**
auto ibrida plug-in **97**
auto sportiva **97**
autoabbronzante **18**
autobiografia **138**
autobus **43, 99**
autobus articolato **99**
autobus a due piani **99**
autobus turistico **99**
autogestione **93**
autogru **87**
autolavaggio **97**
autoradio **99**
autore / autrice **138**
autoribaltabile **87**
autostrada **96**
autovelox **96**
autunno **57, 172**
avambraccio **01**
avampiede **02**
avatar **84**
avere un bambino **07**
avere un giorno libero **81**
avere un incidente **98**
avere una perdita **33**
aviatore **88**
avocado **56**
avocado toast **71**
avvelenamento **19**
avventuroso / avventurosa **10**
avversario / avversaria **117**
avviare **95**
avvocato **85, 90**
avvolgitubo **40**
avvoltoio **160**
axolotl **163**
ayran **61**
ayurveda **24**
azalea **38**
Azerbaigian **150, 153**
azerbaigiano / azerbaigiana **153**
azienda **81**
azienda agricola **86**
azienda avicola **86**
azienda casearia **86**
azienda di ovinicoltura **86**
azienda ortofrutticola **86**
azienda suinicola **86**
azioni **11, 94, 117**
azoto **78**

B

babbuino **158**
baby monitor **08, 30**
bacca di goji **57**
bacca di sambuco **57**
bacche **57**
bacchetta di vetro **76**
bacchetta magica **139**
bacchette **27**
bacello **55**
bacheca **82**
bacheca degli avvisi di sicurezza **87**
bacino **03**
bacino di carenaggio **106**
backgammon **140**
backstop **113**
backswing **115**
badile **40, 87**
badminton **114**
baffi **12**
bagagli in eccedenza **104**
bagagliaio **97, 99**
bagaglio a mano **103, 104**
bagel **62, 71**
bagliore **144**
bagnino / bagnina **118, 134**
bagno **31**
bagno in camera **131**
bagnoschiuma **18, 31**
baguette **62**
Bahamas **150, 152**
bahamense **152**
Bahrein **151, 153**
bahreinita **153**
baia **147**
Baisakhi **07**
baita **32, 131**
baklava **63**
balaustra **25, 110**
balcone **25**
balenottera azzurra **166**
balestruccio **160**
ballare **11**
ballerine **17**
ballerino / ballerina **89, 126**
balletto **126**
balzare **159**
bambina **05**
bambini / bambine **05**
bambino **05**
bambino piccolo / bambina piccola **05, 08**
bambola **08**
bambù **41, 55, 167**
banana **58**
banane platano **86**
banca **45, 94**
bancale **87**
bancarella **70**
bancarella di souvenir **132**
banchina **106**
banco **73**
banco da lavoro **35**
banco del check-in **104**
banco della giuria **85**
banco di scogli **147**
bancomat **45**
bancone **68, 131**
banconote **45, 94**
band **129**
bandiera a scacchi **123**
bandierina **115**
bandierina per il calcio d'angolo **109**

bangladese **153**
Bangladesh **150, 153**
banjo **129**
baobab **169**
bar **42, 46, 65, 66, 68**
bar mitzvah / bat mitzvah **07**
barattolo **27, 52, 60**
barattolo in vetro **52**
barba **12**
barba corta **12**
barbabietola **56**
barbabietole sott'aceto **60**
barbadiano / barbadiana **152**
Barbados **150, 152**
barbagianni **161**
barbecue **41, 135**
barbiere **89**
barboncino **164**
barca a remi **105**
barca a vela **105**
barche **105**
barella **21, 50**
barella dell'ambulanza **50**
bario **78**
barista **65, 68, 69, 89**
baritono **126**
barra **119**
barra dei pesi **124**
barra portapacchi **97**
barracuda **166**
barre di combustibile **51**
barretta **48**
barretta di cioccolato **67**
barriera corallina **118, 145, 166**
barriera di sicurezza **96, 122**
barriera per le onde di marea **51**
basa **54**
basalto **156**
basco **16**
base **74, 76**
baseball **113**
basette **12**
basilico **59**
basilisco piumato **163**
basket **112**
bassa marea **147**
bassa pressione **155**
basset hound **164**
bassista **129**
basso **126**
basso / bassa **12, 176**
bassotto **164**
bastoncino di zucchero **67**
bastone **110, 139**
bastone da portiere **110**
bastone per torsioni **124**
bastoni **40**
batacchio **25**
battaglia **79, 88**
battere **111, 113**
batteri **157**
batteria **75, 83, 98**
batterio **77**
batterista **129**
battesimo **07**
batticarne **28**
battiscopa **30**
battistrada **101**
battito cardiaco **124**
battitore **111, 113**
batuffolo di cotone **18, 20**
Bauhaus **130**
bavaglino **13**
beagle **164**
bebè **05**
becchime **164**
becco **161**
becco Bunsen **76**
becher **76**
bed and breakfast **131**
begonia **38**
belare **165**
belga **153**
Belgio **151, 153**
Belize **150, 152**
beliziano / beliziana **152**
bella **12**
belladonna **169**
bellezza **18, 47**
bello / bella **12, 177**
beluga **166**
bemolle **128**
benda **20, 126**
benefit **81**
Benin **149, 152**
beninese **152**
benzina **97**
berberis **168**
bere **52**
bere acqua **20**
bere tè o caffè **09**
berillio **78**
berkelio **78**
berlina **97**
bermuda **14**
berrettino **16**
berretto **16**
berretto alla Sherlock Holmes **16**
berretto con pon pon **16**
bersaglio **125, 140**
bestiame **165**
bestseller **138**
betoniera **87**
betulla **168**
beuta **76**
bevanda **69**
bevanda energetica **52**
bevande **48, 52, 65**
bhangra **129**
Bhutan **150, 153**
biancheria da letto **30**
biancheria intima **14**
bianchetto **82**
bianco **140, 141**
biancospino **169**
biathlon **122**
biberon **08**
bibita **70**
bibita gassata **70**
bibita in lattina **70**
bibliografia **138**
biblioteca **43, 80, 148**
bibliotecario / bibliotecaria **80, 90**
bicchiere **27, 52**
bicchiere da birra **27**
bicchiere da cocktail **68**
bicchiere da sakè **27**
bicchiere da vino **27**
bicchieri **27, 68**
bici da strada **101**
bicicletta **101**
bicicletta da cicloturismo **101**
bicicletta da corsa **101**
bicicletta elettrica **101**
bicipiti **03**
bidet **31**
bidone della spazzatura **25**
bidone di compostaggio **40**
biella di accoppiamento **102**
Bielorussia **151, 153**
bielorusso / bielorussa **153**
biennale **41**
bietola **55**
Big Bang **144**
Big Ben **44**
biga **79**
biglietteria **102, 106, 130**
biglietto **102, 104, 130**
biglietto dell'autobus **99**
biglietto di andata e ritorno **131**
biglietto di buon compleanno **07**
biglietto di sola andata **131**
bikini **134**
bilancia **20, 29, 31, 45, 76, 104, 145, 174**
biliardo **125**
binario **102**
binocolo **22, 144**
biochimica **76**
biografia **138**
biologia **73, 77, 80**
biologico / biologica **23, 39, 53**
biologo / biologa **77**
biotecnologie **91**
biplano **103**
bird watcher **161**
bird watching **133**
birilli **08**
birillo **125**
birmano / birmana **153**
birra **52, 68**
birra ale **68**
birra analcolica **68**
birra di frumento **68**
birra lager **68**
birra stout **68**
bis **126**
bisaccia **120**
biscotti **63**
biscotti della fortuna **63**
biscotto con gocce di cioccolato **63**
biscotto fiorentino **63**
bismuto **78**
bistecchiera **28**
bistrot **69**
bisturi **21, 77**
bitta **105**
bloc-notes **82, 95**
bloccare **84, 112, 117**
blocco di calcestruzzo **87**
blocco di partenza **116, 118**
blog **84**
blogger **84**
blu **01, 141**
blu marino **141**
blues **129**
blusa **14**
boa **106, 119, 134**
boa arboricolo smeraldino **163**
bob **122**
bobbisti **122**
bobtail giapponese **164**
bocca **01**
boccaglio e la maschera **15, 134**
bocce **125**
body **15, 126**
bodyboard **134**
bodyboarding **119**
bohrio **78**
boletus dal cappello arancione **170**
Bolivia **149, 152**
boliviano / boliviana **152**
bolle di CO2 **62**
bollette **32**
bollire **29**
bollito / bollita **72**
bollitore elettrico **27**
boma **119**
bombardiere **88**
bomber **15**
bombo **162**
bombola **118**
bombola d'aria compressa **50**
bongo **128**
bonsai **38**
boogie-board **119**
border collie **164**
bordo della carta da parati **37**
bordo erbaceo **41**
bordocampo **107, 112, 114**
boro **78**
borraccia **101**
borragine **59**
borsa **16, 94**
borsa da spiaggia **134**
borsa della spesa **47, 48**
borsa dell'acqua calda **30**
borsa di studio **80**
borsa per il pronto soccorso **50**
borsa per pannolini **08**
borsa a tracolla **16**
borse **16**
borseggio **85**
borsone **16**
bosco **146**
Bosnia-Erzegovina **151, 153**
bosniaco o erzegovino / bosniaca o erzegovina **153**
botanica **77**
botanico / botanica **77**
Botswana **149, 152**
botswaniano / botswaniana **152**
botteghino **127**
bottiglia **52**
bottiglie d'acqua **135**
bottone **15**
bottone a pressione **13**
bottoni **142**
bougainville **168**
boundary **111, 113**
bouquet **15, 47**
boutique **46**
bowling **125**
box **08**
boxe **117**

boxer **14**, **164**
bozza **83**
bozzolo **162**
bracciale **21**
bracciale rigido **16**
bracciale / braccialetto **16**
bracciata **118**
braccio **01**, **50**, **87**, **126**
braccio per telecamera **84**
bracciolo **99**, **103**, **118**
brachiosauro **157**
bradipo **159**
Braille **175**
branda **135**
brandy **68**
Brasile **149**, **152**
brasiliano / brasiliana **152**
bravo / brava **177**
breakfast roll **71**
brezza **154**
bricolage **35**
bridge **125**, **140**
brie **64**
briglie **120**
brillante **177**
brioche **62**, **71**
britannico / britannica **153**
British shorthair **164**
brividi **19**
broccolo **55**, **56**
brodo **72**
bromo **78**
bronzo **116**, **176**
bruciare **29**
bruciatore **103**
bruciatura **19**
bruco **77**, **162**
brugole **36**
brunch **69**
Brunei **151**, **153**
bruneiano / bruneiana **153**
brutto / brutta **177**
bubolare **161**
buca **101**, **115**, **125**, **129**
buca delle lettere **25**, **45**
buca in un colpo **115**
bucaneve **167**
bucato e pulizie **34**
buccia **58**
bucket turn **118**
buco della serratura **25**
buco dell'ozono **155**
buco nero **144**
budget **94**
budino di riso **63**
bue muschiato **159**
bufalo **159**
buffet **69**
bulbo **41**
bulbo oculare **22**
Bulgaria **151**, **153**
bulgaro / bulgara **153**
bullone **36**
bulloni delle ruote **98**
bungalow **32**
bungee jumping **125**
bunker **115**
buon appetito **69**
buon ascoltatore / buona ascoltatrice **93**
buon pomeriggio **179**
buonanotte **179**
buonasera **179**
buongiorno **179**
buono sconto **48**
Burj Khalifa **44**
Burkina Faso **149**, **152**
burkinabé **152**
burmese **164**
burrasca **154**
burriera **28**
burrito **71**
burro **61**, **71**
burrocacao **18**
burro di arachidi **60**
burundese **152**
Burundi **149**, **152**
bus turistico **132**
bussola **119**, **135**, **148**
busta **45**, **82**
busta paga **81**
butanese **153**
buttare via **178**

C

cabina **50**, **103**, **105**, **134**
cabina di guida **102**
cabina di pilotaggio **103**
cabina per fototessere **46**
cablaggio **33**
cacao **65**, **169**
cacatua **161**, **164**
cacatua rosa **161**
caccia **88**
cacciapietre **102**
cacciare **159**
cacciatorpediniere **88**
cacciavite a stella **36**
cacciavite a testa piatta **36**
caco **58**
cactus **41**
cactus testa di vecchio **168**
caddie **115**
cadere **11**, **117**
caditoia **43**
cadmio **78**
caduco / caduca **41**
caduta delle foglie **172**
caffè **52**, **65**, **69**, **71**, **86**
caffè americano **65**
caffè freddo **65**
caffè nero **65**
caffettiera **27**
caffettiera a stantuffo **28**
caimano dagli occhiali **163**
calamari **54**
calamaro **54**
calamaro gigante **166**
calare l'ancora **106**
calcare **156**
calciare **11**, **107**, **108**, **118**
calcio **23**, **49**, **78**, **109**
calcio d'angolo **109**
calcio di rigore **109**
calcio di trasformazione **108**
calcio d'inizio **109**
calcio frontale **117**
calcio volante **117**
calcite **156**
calcolatrice **73**, **74**
calderone **139**
caldissimo / caldissima **154**
caldo / calda **154**, **176**
calendario **82**, **172**
calendula **38**
calici **27**
californio **78**
calla **167**
calligrafia **175**
callisia profumata **167**
calmarsi **178**
calmo / calma **06**, **10**, **93**
calorie **23**
calvo / calva **12**
calze **14**
calzini **14**
calzino **107**
camaleonte del Madagascar **163**
camaleonte di Jackson **163**
camaleonte di Parson **163**
cambiamento climatico **155**
cambiare **102**
cambiare canale **137**
cambiare i soldi **45**
cambiare le lenzuola **34**
cambiare marcia **101**
cambiare una lampadina **35**
cambiarsi **14**
cambiavalute **45**
cambio **104**
cambio automatico **99**
cambio manuale **99**
Cambogia **150**, **153**
cambogiano / cambogiana **153**
Cambriano **157**
cambusa **105**
camelia **38**
camembert **64**
camera con vista **131**
camera da letto **30**
camera d'aria **101**
camera doppia **131**
camera doppia con letti singoli **131**
camera magmatica **145**
camera singola **131**
cameraman **84**, **127**
cameriere / cameriera **65**, **69**, **89**
camerini **47**
Camerun **149**, **152**
camerunense **152**
camice da laboratorio **13**
camicetta **14**
camicetta folkloristica **15**
camicia **15**
camicia a maniche corte **14**
camicia da notte **14**
camicia della divisa scolastica **13**
caminetto **26**
camino **25**, **32**, **87**
camino vulcanico **145**
camion con pianale **87**
camion dei traslochi **32**
camion dei vigili del fuoco **50**
camion militare **88**
camionista **90**
cammello **158**
camomilla **66**
campagna **146**
campane tubolari **128**
campanello **25**, **99**
campanile **44**
campanula **167**, **169**
campeggio **135**
camper **135**
campionato **114**
campo **107**, **109**, **111**, **112**, **146**
campo da baseball **113**
campo da cricket **111**
campo da golf **115**
campo da rugby **108**
campo da tennis **114**
campo elettrico **75**
campo esterno **111**
campo magnetico **75**
campo sportivo **80**
campus universitario **80**
Canada **150**, **152**
canadese **152**
canale **137**, **147**
canale di scolo **43**
canale di televendite **137**
canale musicale **137**
canale pay per view **137**
canali televisivi **137**
canapa **169**
canarino **160**
cancellare **69**
cancelleria **82**
cancelletto **122**
cancelletto di sicurezza **08**
cancello **32**, **41**, **86**, **106**
Cancro **144**
candeggina **34**
candela **26**, **98**
candela magica **139**
candeline **63**
candidato / candidata **81**
candidature **92**
cane **122**
cane a testa in giù **24**
cane della polizia **50**
cane selvatico africano **158**
canestro **112**
canguro **158**
canini **03**
canna **101**, **121**, **167**
canna da giardino **40**
canna da pesca **121**
canna da zucchero **86**, **167**
cannella **59**
cannella macinata **59**
cannelloni **64**
cannolicchio **54**
cannone **79**, **88**
cannuccia **70**
Caño Cristales **145**
canoa **105**
canotta **14**
canottaggio **119**
canottiera **14**
canottiere **119**
canovaccio **28**
cantalupo **58**
cantante **89**
cantare **11**, **165**
cantiere **87**
cantiere navale **106**
cantieri stradali **87**
cantina **25**

canyon **146**
canzone **129**
capace di adattarsi **93**
capace di influenzare le persone **93**
capace di lavorare in gruppo **93**
capacità **174**
capacità decisionale **93**
capacità di guidare **93**
capacità oratorie **93**
capacità relazionali **93**
capanna **32**
capanno **25**, **39**
capasanta **54**
capelli **01**, **12**
capelli a spazzola **12**
capelli biondi **12**
capelli castani **12**
capelli corti **12**
capelli crespi **12**
capelli grassi **12**
capelli grigi **12**
capelli lisci **12**
capelli lunghi **12**
capelli lunghi fino alle spalle **12**
capelli mossi **12**
capelli neri **12**
capelli normali **12**
capelli ramati **12**
capelli ricci **12**
capelli rossi **12**
capelli secchi **12**
capezzolo **01**
capibara **159**
capire **11**
capitale netto **94**
capitano **105**
capitano della nave **89**
capitano di porto **106**
capitolo **138**
capo **147**
capo cantiere **89**
Capo Verde **149**, **152**
Capodanno **07**
capodoglio **166**
capoeira **117**
capolavoro **130**
capotasto **129**
capoufficio **81**
capoverdiano / capoverdiana **152**
capovolta in avanti **118**
cappa aspirante **27**
cappelliera **103**
cappello **170**
cappello da baseball **16**
cappello da cowboy **16**
cappello da cuoco **13**
cappello da golf **115**
cappello da poliziotto **50**
cappello da sole **14**, **16**, **134**
cappello di cera **170**
capperi **64**
cappotti **15**
cappuccino **65**
cappuccio **13**, **15**
capra **53**, **165**
capra delle nevi **159**
capretto / capretta **165**
Capricorno **145**
caprifoglio **38**
capriola all'indietro **118**
capriolo **158**
capsula **22**
capsula Petri **77**
capsule **49**
caraffa graduata **27**, **28**, **29**, **174**
Caraibi **150**, **152**
caraibico / caraibica **152**
carambola **58**
caramella gommosa **67**
caramella gommosa alla frutta **67**
caramelle **67**
caramelle assortite **67**
caramelle morbide **67**
carapace **163**
carattere **175**
caratteri arabi **175**
caratteri cinesi **175**
caratteri giapponesi **175**
caravan **135**
caravella portoghese **166**
carboidrati **23**
carboncino **141**
carbone **51**
carbonella **135**
Carbonifero **157**
carbonio **78**
carcerati / carcerate **85**
carcere **85**
carciofo **56**
cardamomo **59**
cardigan **14**
cardinale rosso **161**
cardio **54**
cardiologia **21**
cardo **38**, **169**
caribù **159**
carica **75**
caricabatterie solare **83**
caricare **83**, **165**
caricatore frontale **87**
carico **102**, **105**, **106**
carie **22**
carlinga **51**
carlino **164**
carne **53**
carne affumicata **53**
carne bianca **53**
carne cotta **53**, **64**
carne cruda **53**
carne e pollame **48**
carne macinata **53**
carne magra **53**
carne rossa **53**
carnevale **07**
carota **56**
carpa **54**
carpino **168**
carpo **03**
carrello **48**, **102**, **104**, **131**
carrello anteriore **103**
carrello dei dolci **63**, **69**
carrello di atterraggio **103**
carrello elevatore **87**, **106**
carrello per sacca da golf **115**
carriola **40**
carro armato **88**
carro attrezzi **98**
carrozzeria **98**, **123**
carrozzina **08**
carta **82**, **155**, **176**
carta celeste **144**
carta da filtro **76**
carta da parati **37**
carta dei vini **69**
carta di credito **45**, **94**
carta di debito **45**, **94**
carta di fondo **37**
carta d'imbarco **104**
carta fedeltà **47**
carta igienica **31**
carta meteorologica **155**
carta SIM **48**
carta stradale **148**
carta vetrata **36**, **37**
cartapesta **141**
cartella clinica **21**
cartelli stradali **96**
cartellino **130**
cartellino del prezzo **47**
cartellino giallo **109**
cartellino rosso **109**
cartello **104**
cartello dei saldi **47**
cartello stradale **43**
cartilagine **03**
cartina **132**, **148**
cartina della metropolitana **102**
cartina escursionistica **148**
cartina online **148**
cartina turistica **48**
cartine **148**
cartografo / cartografa **148**
cartolina **48**, **132**
cartone **52**, **141**
cartone animato **127**, **137**
cartone del latte **61**
casa **25–41**, **32**, **148**
casa a schiera **32**
casa base **113**
Casa Bianca **44**
casa bifamiliare **32**
casa delle bambole **08**
casa di città **32**
casa galleggiante **32**
casa indipendente **32**
casa prefabbricata **32**
casa sull'albero **32**, **133**
casa vacanze **131**
cascata **146**
Cascate Vittoria **145**
caschetto **12**
casco **50**, **100**, **107**, **110**, **111**, **113**, **117**, **120**, **123**, **143**, **146**
casco da bicicletta **101**
casco di protezione **87**
case **25**, **32**
case di città **43**
casella **140**
casello **96**
caserma dei vigili del fuoco **42**, **50**
casetta **39**
cassa **48**, **68**, **94**, **129**
cassa automatica **48**
cassa bluetooth **136**
cassa del pesce **54**
cassa toracica **03**
cassaforte **131**
cassapanca **30**
casse portatili **95**
cassero **105**
casseruola **28**
cassetta da pesca **121**
cassetta degli attrezzi **36**
cassetta delle lettere **25**, **45**
cassettiera **30**
cassetto **27**, **30**, **82**
cassetto per frutta e verdura **27**
cassiere / cassiera **45**, **48**
cassonetto **25**
cast **126**, **127**
castagna d'acqua **56**
castagne **58**
castagno **168**
castello **44**
castello di Himeji **44**
castello di sabbia **134**
casuario **160**
catamarano **105**
catapulta **79**
cataratta **22**
catarifrangente **100**, **101**
catch-up tv **137**
catena **101**
catena montuosa **146**
catenaccio **25**
catenina **16**
cattedrale di San Basilio **44**
cattivo / cattiva **127**
catturare **121**, **140**
catturare con la rete **121**
cauto / cauta **10**
cauzione **32**, **85**
cavalcata all'amazzone **120**
cavalcavia **96**
cavaliere **79**, **139**
cavallerizzo / cavallerizza **120**
cavalletta **162**
cavalletto **82**, **101**, **141**
cavallo **120**, **140**, **165**
cavallo a dondolo **08**
cavallo con maniglie **125**
cavallo da battaglia **79**
cavallo da corsa **120**
cavalluccio di legno **08**
cavalluccio marino **166**
cavatappi **28**, **68**
cavatorsoli **28**
cavezza **120**
cavi **33**
caviglia **01**, **02**
cavigliera **16**, **124**
cavità **22**
cavo **83**, **101**
cavo di alimentazione **83**
cavo di ricarica **83**
cavo HDMI **95**
cavolfiore **56**
cavolini di Bruxelles **55**
cavolo **55**
cavolo cinese **55**
cavolo nero **55**
cavolo rapa **55**
cavolo riccio **55**
cavolo rosso **55**
cazzuola **87**
CD **136**
ceco / ceca **153**
cediglia **175**
cedro del Libano **167**
celebrazioni **07**
celebrità **127**
celidonia **168**
cella **50**, **85**
cellula animale **77**
cellula vegetale **77**
cellulare **82**
Celsius **154**
cemento **35**, **176**

cena **26**, **72**
cenare **09**, **52**
cenere **145**
Cenozoico **158**
centauro **139**
centimetro **174**
cento **173**
centopiedi **162**
centrafricano / centrafricana **152**
centrale **112**
centrale elettrica **44**
centrale geotermica **51**
centrale idroelettrica **51**
centrale nucleare **51**
centro **74**, **107**, **110**, **112**
centro città **42**
centro commerciale **42**, **47**
centro del bersaglio **140**
centro per l'impiego **92**
centro sportivo **43**
centroamericano / centroamericana **152**
centrocampista **109**
centrotorta **63**
cera **176**
ceramica **176**
ceramiche **141**
Cerbero **139**
cercare **178**
cercatore **144**
cerchietto **16**
cerchio **74**, **125**
cerchio delle streghe **170**
cerchio di centrocampo **109**
cerchio di ingaggio **110**
cerchione **101**
cereali **71**
cereali per la colazione **48**
Cerere **143**
ceretta **18**
cerfoglio **59**
cerimonia di laurea **80**
cerio **78**
cerotto **20**, **49**
cerotto a nastro **20**
certificato di nascita **07**
cervello **04**
cervice uterina **04**
cervo **53**
cervo rosso **158**
cervo volante **162**
cesio **78**
cesoie **40**
cesoie tagliabordi **40**
cesta **164**
cestello per friggere **28**
cestino **48**, **82**, **83**, **101**
cestino da picnic **133**, **134**
cestino del pane **71**
cestino della spazzatura **27**, **33**
cestino per la raccolta differenziata **33**, **34**
cesto **110**
cesto da giardinaggio **40**
cesto della biancheria **31**, **34**
cesto di frutta **57**
cesto sospeso **41**
cetriolini sott'aceto **60**
cetriolino **60**
cetriolo **55**
chalet **32**, **131**
challah **62**
champagne **68**
chapati **62**
chat **83**
chattare online **09**
chavistello **25**
check-in online **104**
cheddar **64**
cheerleader **107**
cheeseburger **70**
cheesecake **63**
chef **69**, **90**
chest press **124**
chiacchierare con gli amici **09**
chiamare i familiari **09**
chiamare un amico / un'amica **09**
chiamare un idraulico **33**
chiaro **60**
chiaro / chiara **177**
chiave **25**, **129**
chiave a bussola **36**
chiave a rullino **36**
chiave di basso **128**
chiave di violino **128**
chiave inglese **36**, **98**
chiavetta USB **83**
chiavi **32**
chiazza di petrolio **155**
chicane **123**
chicchi **55**
chicco di grandine **154**
chiedere indicazioni **148**
chiesa **43**, **44**
chiesa ortodossa **44**
chiglia **105**, **119**
chignon **12**
chihuahua **164**
chilogrammo **174**
chilometro **174**
chilometro quadrato **174**
chimica **73**, **76**, **80**
chimico / chimica **76**
chiocciola **83**, **162**, **175**
chiodi di garofano **59**
chiodo **36**
chiosco **46**, **47**, **48**
chiosco dei fiori **47**
chiropratica **24**
chirurgia **21**
chirurgia plastica **21**
chirurgo / chirurga **21**, **90**
chitarra acustica **129**
chitarra elettrica **129**
chitarrista acustico / chitarrista acustica **129**
chitarrista elettrico / chitarrista elettrica **129**
chiurlo **161**
chiusa **106**
chiuso **48**
chiuso / chiusa **132**
chiusura **16**
choker **16**
chorizo **53**, **64**
chutney **60**, **72**
ciabatte slider **17**
Ciad **149**, **152**
ciadiano / ciadiana **152**
ciak **84**
ciambella **63**, **70**
ciambella al cioccolato **63**
ciambella alla marmellata **63**
ciao **179**
cibi **65**, **72**
cibi pronti **23**, **48**
cibo da asporto **70**
cibo in scatola **48**
cibo per animali **48**
cicala di mare **166**
ciclismo **101**
ciclo di vita **77**
ciclostoma **157**
cicogna **160**
cicoria **55**
cicuta **169**
cifre **175**
ciglia **01**
cigno nero **161**
cigno reale **161**
cigno selvatico **161**
Cile **149**
cileno / cilena **152**
ciliegia **57**
ciliegie **169**
ciliegio **169**
cilindro **74**
cima **55**
cimitero **43**
Cina **150**, **153**
cinema **42**, **127**
cinema multisala **127**
cinepresa **127**
cinese **153**
cinghia della ventola **98**
cinghia fermapiedi **119**
cinghiale **53**, **159**
cinquanta **173**
cinque **173**
cinque posizioni **112**
cinque spezie **59**
cinquecento **173**
cintura **15**, **16**, **103**, **117**, **142**
cintura degli attrezzi **87**
cintura nera **117**
cintura porta attrezzi **36**
cintura zavorrata **118**
cinture di sicurezza **123**
cinturino per pedali **101**
cinturone **50**
cioccolata calda **52**
cioccolato al latte **67**
cioccolato bianco **67**
cioccolato fondente **67**
ciotola **26**, **27**, **52**
ciotola dei cereali **71**
ciotola del riso **27**
ciotola della frutta **26**
cipolla **56**
cipolline sott'aceto **60**
cipollotto **55**
cipria **18**
Cipro **151**, **153**
cipriota **153**
circolo **115**
Circolo Polare Artico **145**
circonduzioni delle braccia **124**
circonferenza **74**
circuito **83**, **123**
cirripede **134**, **166**
cistifellea **04**
citazione **85**
citofono **25**
citoplasma **77**
citrino **156**
citronella **59**
città **42**, **42–51**, **43**, **148**
Città del Vaticano **151**
Città Proibita **44**
ciuccio **08**
civetta delle nevi **161**
clacson **99**, **100**
clamidosauro **163**
clarinetto **128**
classe **73**
classe business **103**
classe economy **103**
Classicismo **130**
clavicola **03**
clementina **57**
cliccare **83**
cliente **45**, **47**, **48**, **65**, **85**
clienti **69**, **81**
clima **155**
cloche **16**
cloro **78**
cloroplasto **77**
clown **89**
club sandwich **70**
cobalto **78**
cobra indiano **163**
coca cola **52**
coccige **03**
coccinella **162**
coccodrillo del Nilo **163**
coccodrillo marino **163**
cocktail **68**
cocktail analcolico **68**
coda **54**, **103**, **120**, **143**, **158**, **159**, **160**
coda di cavallo **12**
codice a barre **48**
codice postale **45**
codini **12**
coelophysis **157**
cofano **97**, **98**
cognata **05**
cognato **05**
coincidenza **104**
coinquilino / coinquilina **32**
colata di fango **146**
colazione **26**, **71**
colazione a buffet **71**
colazione all'inglese **71**
colesterolo **23**
colibrì **160**
colino **28**
colino da tè **66**
colla **82**, **101**, **141**
colla per carta da parati **37**
colla per il legno **35**
collaborare **92**
collage **141**
collana **16**
collant **14**
collare **19**
collega **07**, **81**, **92**
collegare **83**
colletto **15**, **142**
collezione **130**
collina pedemontana **147**
collirio **22**
collo **01**, **161**
collo del piede **02**
colloquio **81**
collutorio **31**
colmo **87**
Colombia **149**, **152**
colombiano / colombiana **152**

colonna sonora **128**
colonna vertebrale **03**
colori a olio **141**
colori acrilici **141**
Colosseo **44**
colpevole **06**, **85**
colpire **11**, **110**, **117**
colpire con un pugno **117**
colpo di frusta **19**
colpo di taglio **114**
coltellino svizzero **135**
coltello **27**
coltello da burro **27**
coltello da cucina **28**
coltello da pane **28**
coltivare **39**
colture **86**
comandi **99**, **100**, **136**
comandi dei fari **99**
comandi del riscaldamento **99**
combustibili fossili **51**, **155**
cometa **143**, **144**
comico / comica **89**
comignolo **25**
commedia **126**, **127**, **137**
commedia romantica **127**
commercialista **90**, **94**
commesso / commessa **89**
commissariato di polizia **42**, **50**
commissione **94**
commozione cerebrale **19**
comodino **30**
Comore **149**, **152**
comoriano / comoriana **152**
compagnia aerea **104**
comparse **127**
compasso **73**, **74**
compensato **35**
competenze informatiche **93**
competenze professionali **93**
competenze sul luogo di lavoro **93**
competenze tecnologiche **93**
competitivo / competitiva **93**
compilare **178**
compilare un modulo **92**
compitare **11**
compiti per casa **73**
compito in classe **73**
compleanno **07**
completo **15**
comporre **128**
compositore / compositrice **128**
compost **40**
compostiera **40**, **41**
composto **76**
comprare **46**
comprensivo / comprensiva **06**
comprensorio sciistico **122**
compresse **20**, **49**
compressioni toraciche **20**
computare **73**
computer **82**, **83**
computer fisso **83**
computer portatile **82**, **83**
comunicazione online **83**
comunicazione scritta **93**
con camere libere **131**
con ghiaccio **52**, **68**
con le spalle scoperte **15**
con motivo cachemire **13**
con motivo scozzese **13**
con piombo **97**
concerto pop **129**
conchiglie **64**
concimare **39**
concime **39**
concludere una riunione **95**
condannare **85**
condimenti **60**, **71**, **72**
condimento **70**, **72**
condito / condita **72**
condividere **84**
condividere lo schermo **95**
condominio **25**, **43**
condor delle Ande **160**
condotta forzata **51**
conduttore **75**
conduttore del notiziario / conduttrice del notiziario **137**
conduttore / conduttrice **89**
conferenza **95**
confettura **71**
confettura di fragole **60**
confettura di lamponi **60**
confezionare su misura **142**
confuso / confusa **06**
congelare **29**
conglomerato **156**
congolese **152**
conifere **41**, **157**, **167**
conigliera **164**
coniglio **53**, **158**, **164**
connettore a coccodrillo **75**
cono **74**, **87**
cono gelato **65**
Conocybe apala **170**
conoscente **07**
conoscere qualcuno **179**
consegna **45**
consegna a domicilio **48**, **70**
consegna online **91**
consiglio di amministrazione **95**
console **136**
console del dj **129**
costellazioni **144**
consulente finanziario / consulente finanziaria **94**
consulenza legale **85**
contachilometri **99**
contadino / contadina **79**, **86**, **89**
contagiri **99**
contagocce **76**
container **105**, **106**
contaminuti **28**
contare **11**, **74**
contatore elettrico **33**
contatto **83**
contenitore dei giocattoli **08**
contenitore ermetico **52**
contenitore per il compost **33**
contenitori **52**
contento / contenta **06**
continente **145**
conto corrente **45**
conto di risparmio **45**
contorni **72**, **148**
conto **69**
contrabbando **85**
contrabbasso **128**
contralto **126**
contrappeso **87**
contrarre i muscoli **124**
contrattare **46**
contratto **92**
contratto d'affitto **32**
controfigura **127**
controfiletto **53**
controllare gli pneumatici **98**
controllare le e-mail **09**
controllare l'olio **98**
controller **136**
controllo della tensione **142**
controllo immigrazione **104**
controllo passaporti **104**
controllore **102**
convenuto / convenuta **85**
convertire il loft **35**
cookie **84**
cooksonia **157**
coordinare **92**
coordinate **148**
coperchio **28**
copernicio **78**
coperta **26**, **30**
coperta elettrica **30**
copertina **138**
coperto **69**, **154**
copertura vegetale **41**
copiare **11**
copilota **103**
copione **126**
coppa del vincitore **109**
coppa di gelato **65**
coppia **07**
coppia di fidanzati **07**
coppia sposata **07**
coppola **16**
copricapi **16**
copriletto **30**
coprimozzo **98**
coprire con zolle erbose **39**
copyright **175**
coraggioso / coraggiosa **10**
corallo **166**
corda **125**
corda da saltare **124**
corda per saltare **08**
corde **114**, **117**, **129**
corde vocali **04**
cordolo **43**
cordone ombelicale **08**
Corea del Nord **150**, **153**
Corea del Sud **150**, **153**
coriandolo **59**
coristi / coriste **129**
cormorano **160**
corna **158**
cornamusa **129**
cornea **22**
cornerback destro **107**
cornerback sinistro **107**
cornice **26**, **130**
corniola **156**
corno francese **128**
corno inglese **128**
coro **128**
corpo **02**, **129**
corpo sano **24**
corpo umano **01**
corrente alternata **33**, **75**
corrente continua **33**, **75**
corrente elettrica **33**
correre **11**, **111**, **113**
correttore **18**
corridoio **103**, **126**
corridoio telescopico **104**
corriere **45**
corrimano **25**, **99**
corruzione **85**
corsa **124**
corsa a ostacoli **120**
corsa al trotto **120**
corsa dei carri **120**
corsa di cavalli **120**
corsa in carrozzina **116**
corsa motociclistica su pista **123**
corsa T11 (per atleti non vedenti) **116**
corsetto **14**
corsia **116**, **118**
corsia centrale **96**
corsia dei box **123**
corsia di destra **96**
corsia di emergenza **96**
corsia di sinistra **96**
corsia galleggiante **118**
corsie **48**
corsivo **175**
corso d'acqua sotterraneo **146**
cortado **65**
cortile **25**, **41**
corto / corta **13**, **176**
corvo **160**
corvo imperiale **160**
corvo nero **160**
coscia **01**, **53**
cose **176**, **177**
cospargere **29**
Costa d'Avorio **149**, **152**
Costa Rica **150**, **152**
costaricano / costaricana **152**
costellazione **144**
costellazioni zodiacali **144**
costola **03**
costoletta **53**
costolette **70**
costruire **11**, **87**
costruzioni **87**
costume **13**, **118**, **134**
costume da bagno **15**
costumi **127**
cotoletta **53**
cotonastro **169**
cotone **13**, **86**, **176**
cottage **32**
cottage con il tetto di paglia **32**
cotto / cotta **56**
cotto al forno / cotta al forno **72**
cover **111**
cozza **54**
crampo **19**, **118**
cranio **03**

cratere **143**, **145**
crauti **60**
cravatta **15**, **16**
cravatta della divisa scolastica **13**
creativo / creativa **93**
creature fantastiche **139**
credenza **26**
crema **49**
crema al limone **60**
crema idratante **18**
crema pasticcera **63**
crema per il viso **31**
crema per irritazioni da pannolino **08**
crema per le mani **18**
crema solare **49**, **134**
crema solare ad alta protezione **49**
crema spalmabile al cioccolato **60**
creme spalmabili dolci **60**
crêpe **70**
crepuscolo **171**
crescere **05**, **62**, **178**
crescione **55**
crescione d'acqua **55**
cresta **161**
Cretaceo **157**
cric **98**
criceto **158**, **164**
cricket **111**
criminale **85**
crimini **85**
crinale **146**
criniera **120**
cripton **78**
crisalide **77**
crisantemo **38**
cristallino **22**
cristallo **76**
cristalloterapia **24**
critico / critica **10**
croato / croata **153**
Croazia **151**, **154**
croccante **52**, **56**, **57**
crocchette di pollo **70**
Croce del Sud **144**
croco **38**, **167**
crogiolo **76**
croissant **62**, **71**
cromo **78**, **156**
cromosoma **77**
croquet **133**
crosta **61**, **62**, **64**, **145**
crostata di frutta **63**
crotalo ceraste **163**
crudités **72**
crudo / cruda **56**
cruna **142**
cruscotto **99**
Cuba **150**, **152**
cubano / cubana **152**
Cubismo **130**
cubo **74**
cucchiaino **27**
cucchiaio **27**
cucchiaio da minestra **27**
cucchiaio da portata **27**
cucchiaio di legno **28**
cucchiaio dosatore **28**
cuccia **164**
cucciolo / cucciola **159**, **164**
cucciolo di canguro **158**
cucina **27**, **28**, **29**, **69**
cucinare **29**
cucire **142**
cucito **142**
cucitrice **73**, **82**
cucitura **107**, **111**, **142**
cuciture **113**
cuffia **118**
cuffia bluetooth **83**
cuffie **82**, **84**, **95**, **136**
cuffie wireless **136**
cugino / cugina **05**
culla di vimini **08**, **30**
cumino **59**
cumino dei prati **59**
cumulo di neve **154**
cuocere a fuoco lento **29**
cuocere al vapore **29**
cuocere in forno **29**, **62**, **63**
cuocere in microonde **29**
cuociriso **27**
cuoio **13**
cuore **04**, **53**
cuore di carciofo **56**
cuori **140**
cuori di palma **55**
cupcake **63**
cupola **44**
cupola a cipolla **44**
curare **39**
curatore / curatrice **130**
curatore del museo / curatrice del museo **89**
curcuma **59**
cure **20**
curio **78**
curioso / curiosa **06**, **93**
curl dei bicipiti **124**
curling **122**
curling in carrozzina **122**
curriculum **92**
curry **59**, **72**
curva **74**
curva a destra **96**
cuscino **26**, **30**
custard **63**
custode dello zoo **90**
cuticola **02**
cycas **167**
cyclette **124**

D

dadi **140**
dado **36**
daino **158**
dalmata **164**
dama **140**
danese **153**
Danimarca **152**, **153**
dare da mangiare agli animali **34**
dare da mangiare al cane / al gatto **09**
dare il preavviso **32**
dare in affitto **32**
dare la precedenza **96**
darmstadio **78**
Dasypeltis scabra **163**
data di scadenza **49**
data prevista per il parto **08**
datore di lavoro / datrice di lavoro **81**
dattero **57**, **58**
davanti a **148**, **180**
decapottabile **97**
decathlon maschile **116**
decennio **172**
decidere **11**
decimali **173**
decimo / decima **173**
deciso / decisa **10**
decoder digitale **136**
decollare **104**, **178**
decorare **29**, **63**
decoratore / decoratrice **37**
decorazione **37**, **63**
defensive end destro **107**
defensive end sinistro **107**
defensive tackle destro **107**
defensive tackle sinistro **107**
defibrillatore **50**
deforestazione **155**
deglutire **52**
delfino **166**
delibera della giuria **85**
delizioso / deliziosa **52**, **177**
dello stabilimento **135**
delta **147**
deltaplano **125**
deltoide **03**
deludente **177**
deluso / delusa **06**
denaro **45**, **94**
denaro falso **94**
denim **13**
denominatore **74**
dente **03**
dente di leone **38**, **55**
dente vischioso **168**
denti **01**, **03**
denti da latte **22**
dentiera **22**
dentifricio **31**
dentista **22**, **89**
dentro **180**
denuncia **50**
deodorante **49**
deposito bagagli **102**
deposizione **85**
depresso / depressa **06**
depurazione **23**
deriva **119**
derivati del latte **61**
dermatologia **21**
derrick **51**
desertificazione **155**
deserto **146**
designer **89**
dessert **63**, **69**
destinazione **104**
detergente **18**
detergente per bagno **34**
detergente per il viso **18**
detergente per superfici **34**
determinato / determinata **93**
detersivo per il bucato **34**
detersivo per piatti **34**
deuce **114**
deviazione **96**
Devoniano **157**
di conforto **10**
di fronte **148**
di lana **13**
di lusso **47**
di media altezza **12**
di mezza età **12**
diabete **19**
diagonale **74**
diamante **113**, **156**
diametro **74**
diapositiva **95**
diarrea **19**
diaspro **156**
diavolo della Tasmania **158**
diavolo spinoso **163**
dicembre **172**
dichiararsi **85**
diciannove **173**
diciassette **173**
diciotto **173**
didgeridoo **129**
dieci **173**
dieresi **175**
diesel **97**
diesis **128**
dieta **23**
dieta equilibrata **23**
dieta ipocalorica **23**
dietro **148**
dietro a **180**
difensore **109**
difensore destro **110**
difensore sinistro **110**
difesa **85**, **107**
differenziare i rifiuti **155**
diffrazione **75**
diffusione **76**
diga **51**
digestivo **69**
digitale **38**, **84**
diluviare **178**
dimagrire **20**, **23**
dimensioni **74**
dimenticare **11**
dimetrodonte **157**
dimettere **21**
dimettersi **81**
dinamo **101**
dinastino **162**
diodo **75**
dipartimenti **80**
dipendente **81**
dipingere **37**
dipingere un muro **35**
dipinto **130**, **141**
dipinto a olio **130**
diploma di laurea **80**
dire l'ora **171**
direttore della filiale / direttrice della filiale **45**
direttore della fotografia / direttrice della fotografia **127**
direttore di sala / direttrice di sala **69**
direttore d'orchestra / direttrice d'orchestra **128**
direzione di rivoluzione **143**
direzione di una reazione **76**

direzione inversa **76**
direzione obbligatoria **96**
direzioni **148**, **180**
dirigere **128**
dirigibile **103**
disastroso / disastrosa **177**
discarica **155**
discesa **122**
discesa in corda doppia **125**
dischetto **109**
dischi in vinile **129**
disco **110**
disco da curling **122**
disco del freno **100**
disco fisso **83**
discutere **73**
disegnare **73**
disegno **141**
disegno tecnico **73**
diserbante **39**
disfare **142**
disgustoso / disgustosa **06**, **52**, **177**
Disir **139**
disonesto / disonesta **10**
dispensa **27**, **60**
dispensario **49**
dispenser di liquori **68**
dispersione **75**
display **136**
display della temperatura **33**
disponibile **10**
disprosio **78**
dissodatore **40**
dissuasori **43**
distanza **174**
distintivo **50**
distratto / distratta **06**
distribuire **140**, **178**
distributore d'acqua fresca **82**
distributore di benzina **42**, **97**
distribuzione **98**
ditale **142**
dito del piede **02**
divano **26**
divano letto **26**
diventare virale **84**
divertente **10**, **177**
divertito / divertita **06**
dividendi **94**
dividere **74**
dividere il conto **69**
divieto di accesso **96**
divieto di fotografare **130**
divieto di inversione a U **96**
divieto di sorpasso **96**
divieto di svolta a destra **96**
divieto di transito ai pedoni **96**
divieto di transito ai velocipedi **96**
divisa **50**, **88**
divisa chirurgica **13**, **21**
divisa da cuoco **13**
divisa scolastica **13**
divorziare **07**
divorziato / divorziata **05**
Diwali **07**
dizionario **73**, **138**
dj **84**
dj radiofonico / dj radiofonica **90**
DNA **77**
doberman **164**
doccia **31**
docente **89**
documentario **137**
documentario sulla natura **137**
documenti della presentazione **95**
documento **79**
dodici **173**
dogana **104**, **106**
dolce **52**, **56**, **57**
dolcetti **63**
dolciumi **48**, **67**
dolore **19**
domandare **73**
domenica **172**
domestico / domestica **89**
Dominica **150**, **152**
dominicano / dominicana **152**
dominicense **152**
domino **140**
donazione **130**
donna **05**
donna d'affari **81**, **90**
donnola **158**
dopo **171**
dopobarba **18**, **31**
doppio / doppia **68**
doppio **114**
doppio fallo **114**
dormire fino a tardi **178**
dormitorio **80**, **131**
dorsale oceanica **145**
dorso **118**, **138**
dorso del piede **02**
dosa **72**
dosaggio **49**
dosare **178**
dotto lacrimale **01**
dottorato **80**
dottore / dottoressa **19**, **20**, **21**, **89**
dove **179**
dracena **38**, **167**
drago **139**
dragoncello **59**
dramma in costume **137**
drenaggio **39**
drepanaspide **157**
dressage **120**
drink **68**
dritto **114**
dromedario **158**
drone armato **88**
drosera **168**
dubnio **78**
due **171**, **173**
due fuochi **135**
due punti **175**
due volte alla settimana **172**
due volumi **97**
duemila **172**
duna **146**, **147**
dune buggy **97**, **134**
duomo **102**
duro / dura **57**, **176**
DVD **136**

E

e commerciale **175**
e-mail **83**
eccellente **177**
eccentrico / eccentrica **10**
eccesso di velocità **85**
eccezionale **177**
echidna **158**
Echinocactus **168**
éclair **63**
eclissi di luna **143**
ecografia **08**, **21**
economia **80**
ecosistema **77**, **155**
ecoturismo **131**
Ecuador **149**, **152**
ecuadoregno / ecuadoregna **152**
eczema **19**
edam **64**
edera **169**
edicola **46**, **48**
edifici **42**, **43**, **44**
edifici famosi **44**
edifici residenziali **44**
edificio **148**
edificio abbandonato **44**
edificio governativo **43**
edificio moderno **44**
edificio storico **44**, **132**
editore / editrice **89**
educato / educata **10**
educazione fisica **73**
effetti collaterali **49**
effetti speciali **127**
effetto serra **155**
effettuare l'accesso **178**
efficiente **93**
Egitto **149**, **152**
egiziano / egiziana **152**
eglefino **54**
eglefino affumicato **64**
egoista **10**
Eid al-Fitr **07**
einsteinio **78**
El Salvador **150**, **152**
elastici **82**
elefante africano **158**
elefante asiatico **159**
elefante da battaglia **79**
elementi **76**
elementi morfologici sottomarini **145**
elettricista **89**
elettricità **33**, **51**, **75**
elettrizzante **177**
elettrizzato / elettrizzata **06**
elettrodo negativo **75**
elettrodo positivo **75**
elettrodomestici **47**
elettrodomestici da cucina **27**
elettrone **76**
elettronica **48**, **91**
elfo **139**
elfo dei cactus **161**
eliambulanza **50**
elica **103**, **105**
elicottero **103**
elicottero da trasporto **88**
elicottero d'attacco **88**
eliminare **83**, **113**
eliminare colpendo il wicket **111**
elio **78**
elisir **139**
elisuperficie **51**
ellittica **124**
elsa **117**
ematite **156**
ematoma **19**
embrione **08**
emicrania **19**
emigrare **07**
Emirati Arabi Uniti **151**, **153**
emiratino / emiratina **153**
emisfero australe **145**
emisfero boreale **145**
emissioni **51**, **155**
emissioni industriali **155**
emissioni zero **155**
emoji **84**, **175**
emorragia **19**
empanada **70**
Empire State Building **44**
emù **160**
emulsione **37**
enagra **38**
enciclopedia **73**, **138**
end zone **110**
endocrinologia **21**
endoscheletro **77**
energia **51**, **91**
energia da biomasse **51**
energia eolica **51**
energia geotermica **51**
energia idroelettrica **51**
energia mareomotrice **51**
energia nucleare **51**
energia pulita **51**
energia rinnovabile **51**
energia solare **51**
energico / energica **93**
enigmistica **138**
entrare **11**
entrata dei giocatori **109**
entusiasmante **177**
entusiasta **06**, **10**
epatica **167**
epiglottide **04**
episodio **137**
epistassi **19**
epoca d'oro islamica **79**
eptathlon femminile **116**
equatoguineano / equatoguineana **152**
equatore **145**
equazione **74**
equazione chimica **76**
equipaggiamento per la pesca **121**
equipaggio **119**
equiseti giganti **157**
equiseto **167**
equitazione **120**, **133**
era dell'informazione **79**
erba **25**, **41**, **167**
erba cipollina **59**
erba della pampa **167**
erba medica **86**
erbalismo **24**
erbe **59**

erbe **59**
erbe aromatiche **41**
erbe e spezie **59**
erbe infestanti **41**
erbicida **86**
erbio **78**
ere **158**
erica **38, 41**
Eritrea **149, 152**
eritreo / eritrea **152**
eroe / eroina **127, 139**
erogatore **118**
eruttare **145**
eruzione cutanea **19**
esagono **74**
esame del sangue **20, 21**
esaurire il tempo a disposizione **95**
esausto / esausta **06**
esca **121**
escavatore **87**
escursioni in quad **133**
escursionismo **133**
esercito **88, 91**
esercizi **124**
esibizione **126**
esilarante **177**
esofago **04**
esoscheletro **77**
esosfera **155**
espadrillas **17**
esperimento **76**
esplorazione dello spazio **143**
espressioni utili **179, 180**
espresso **65**
espresso doppio **65**
essere assente **95**
essere assolto / essere assolta **85**
essere di tendenza **84**
essere disoccupato / essere disoccupata **81**
essere eliminato **111**
essere espulso **109**
essere in pareggio **94**
essere in ritardo **09, 104, 171**
essere licenziato / essere licenziata **81**
essere promosso / essere promossa **81**
est **148**
est-timorese **153**
estate **57, 172**
estensore per torace **124**
estenuante **177**
esterni **113**
estintore **50**
estone **153**
Estonia **151, 153**
estradosso **103**
estratto conto **45**
estrazione **22**
estremo **108**
estroverso / estroversa **10**
estuario **147**
Eswatini **149, 152**
età **12**
età del bronzo **79**
età della pietra **79**
età del ferro **79**
etichette **40**
etilometro **50**
etiope **152**
Etiopia **149, 152**
ettaro **174**
Europa **151, 153**
europeo / europea **153**
europio **78**
eventi della vita **07**
evidenziatore **73, 82, 175**
evoluzione **77**
ex marito **05**
ex moglie **05**
Exotic Shorthair **164**
extra vergine **60**
eyeliner **18**

F

fabbrica **42**
fabbro **79, 90**
faccende domestiche **34**
facchino / facchina **131**
facciale **18**
facocero **159**
facoltà **80**
faesite **35**
faggio **168**
fagiano **53, 161**
fagioli secchi **55**
fagioli stufati **71**
fagiolini **55**
fagiolo **56**
fagotto **128**
Fahrenheit **154**
fai da te **47**
fairway **115**
falafel **70**
falangi **03**
falce di luna **143**
falco pellegrino **160**
falco pescatore **160**
falegname **89**
falegnameria **141**
falena dei vestiti **162**
falena di luna **162**
falena imperatrice **162**
falene **162**
fallire **94**
fallo **112, 114**
falò **135**
falso papiro **38**
famiglia **05**
fan **129**
fanalino posteriore **100**
fantasma **139**
fantastico / fantastica **177**
fantasy **127, 139**
fantino **120**
far arrampicare **39**
far bollire (le uova) **29**
far crescere **39**
far entrare **178**
far scattare **178**
faraglione **147**
farcito / farcita **72**
farcitura **63**
fard **18**
fare amicizia **07**
fare campeggio **135**
fare colazione **09**
fare corsa sul posto **124**
fare domanda per un lavoro **92**
fare esercizio fisico **09, 20**
fare gli straordinari **09**
fare i bagagli **131**
fare i compiti **09, 11**
fare i turni **81**
fare il back up **83**
fare il bagher **112**
fare il bagno **09, 31**
fare il bucato **34**
fare il check-in **131, 178**
fare il check-out **131, 178**
fare il giocoliere **11**
fare il letto **09, 34**
fare il pieno **178**
fare il plié **126**
fare il risvolto **14**
fare in camicia (le uova) **29**
fare la coda **104**
fare la doccia **09, 31**
fare la muta **164**
fare la pirouette **126**
fare la spesa **09, 34**
fare le fusa **164**
fare le pulizie **178**
fare l'occhiolino **02**
fare male **20**
fare pace **178**
fare qua qua **165**
fare retromarcia **96**
fare spallucce **02**
fare testamento **07**
fare trazioni alla sbarra **124**
fare un giro turistico **99, 132**
fare un gran sorriso **02**
fare un incantesimo **139**
fare un pupazzo di neve **11**
fare un riposino **09**
fare un tour **132**
fare una pausa **09**
fare una prenotazione **131**
fare una presentazione **95**
fare una verifica **73**
fare un'escursione **132**
fare uno swing **115**
fare volontariato **92**
faretra **125**
farfalla **77, 118, 162**
farfalla cavolaia **162**
farfalla cobra **162**
farfalla dalle ali di vetro **162**
farfalla monarca **162**
farfalla papilionide **162**
farfalla punteggiata delle betulle **162**
fari **50**
farina **62**
farina autolievitante **62**
farina bianca **62**
farina di grano duro **62**
farina di grano saraceno **62**
farina di ossa **39**
farina integrale **62**
farina marrone **62**
farina senza glutine **62**
faringe **04**
farmaci da banco **49**
farmacia **42, 49**
farmacista **49, 89**
farmaco **20, 49**
farmaco per la tosse **49**
faro **44, 97, 100, 106**
farsi crescere i capelli **12**
farsi tagliare i capelli **12**
fascia catarifrangente **100**
fasciatoi **47**
fasciatoio **30**
fasciatura **20, 49**
fast food **70**
fastidioso / fastidiosa **177**
fata **139**
fattoria **86, 165**
fattorino **48**
fattorino di cibo a domicilio **70**
fattura **94**
fauno **139**
fave **55**
favo **60**
favola **138, 139**
favoloso / favolosa **177**
fazzoletto **16, 49**
febbraio **172**
febbre **19**
febbre da fieno **19**
federa **30**
Federazione Russa **151, 153**
fedora **16**
fegato **04, 53**
feijoa **58**
felce **167**
felci **41, 157**
felice **06**
felicissimo / felicissima **06**
felpa **14**
femminile **04**
femore **03**
fenditure **51**
feng shui **24**
fenice **139**
fenicottero **160**
fennec **158**
fenomeni acquatici **145**
ferie annuali **81**
ferita **19**
ferita alla testa **19**
ferito **88**
feritoia **44**
fermablocco **82**
fermacravatta **16**
fermapiede **101**
fermare **137**
fermarsi **96**
fermarsi a **148**
fermata dell'autobus **25**
fermio **78**
ferramenta **46**
ferro **23, 49, 78, 115, 156**
ferro arricciacapelli **12**
ferro da maglia **142**
ferro da stiro **34**
ferro di cavallo **120**
fertilizzante **39**
fertilizzare **39**
feste **07**
feta **64**
feto **08**
fetta **53**
fetta di custard **63**
fez **16**
fiala **36**
fianco **01**
fibbia **16**
fibra di vetro **176**

fico **169**
fico del caucciù **38**
fico d'India **58**
fico secco **58**
fidanzata **07**
fidanzato **07**
fiducioso / fiduciosa **06**
fienile **86**
fieno **86**
Figi **150**, **153**
figiano / figiana **153**
figli **05**
figlio / figlia **05**
figlio unico / figlia unica **05**
fil di ferro **35**
fila **48**, **103**, **126**, **132**
filamento **38**
filetto **53**, **54**
filetto di razza **54**
filetto di salmone **54**
filiale **81**
filigrana **94**
Filippine **151**, **153**
filippino / filippina **153**
fillio **162**
film **127**
film d'azione **127**
film di arti marziali **127**
film di fantascienza **127**
film drammatico **127**
film storico **127**
film western **127**
filo **142**
filo a piombo **37**
filo di perle **16**
filo di trama **142**
filo d'ordito **142**
filo interdentale **22**, **31**
filo stendibiancheria **34**
filobus **99**
filone **62**
filosofia **80**
filosofo **79**
filtro dell'aria **98**, **100**
finanza **91**, **94**
fine della partita **109**
fine leg **111**
finestra **25**, **87**
finestra a ghigliottina **25**
finestra a golfo **25**
finestra ad arco **32**
finestra pop-up **84**
finestrino **99**, **102**, **103**
finferlo **56**, **170**
finire di lavorare **09**
finlandese **153**
Finlandia **151**, **153**
finocchio **55**, **59**
fiocchi di latte **61**
fiocco **119**
fiocco di neve **154**
fiordo **147**
fiore **38**, **169**
fiore della passione **169**
fioretto **117**
fiori **38**, **140**
fiorista **46**, **47**, **89**
firma **45**, **83**
firmare un contratto **92**
firme **47**
fisarmonica **129**
fischio finale **109**
fish and chips **70**
fisica **73**, **75**, **80**
fisioterapia **21**
fisioterapista **89**
fissione **75**
fit boxe **124**
fiume **147**
fiutare **164**
flan **64**
flat white **65**
flauto **128**, **129**
flauto di Pan **129**
flauto dolce **129**
flebo **21**
flerovio **78**
flessibile **93**, **176**
flessioni **124**
fluente nelle lingue **93**
fluoro **78**
fluviale **147**
FM **84**
foca **159**, **166**
focaccia **62**
foce **147**
focena **166**
fodera **15**
foglia **55**
foglia autunnale **169**
foglia d'alloro **59**
foglia estiva **169**
fogliame **47**
fogliame verde **172**
foglie di barbabietola **55**
foglie di fieno greco **59**
foglie di vite ripiene **64**
foglie nuove **172**
folaga **161**
folletto **139**
follower **84**
fondale marino **51**
fondotinta **18**
fontana **41**, **42**
fonti **79**
food truck **70**
football americano **107**
foratura **101**
forbici **20**, **37**, **82**, **142**
forbici a zigzag **142**
forbici da cucina **28**
forbici per capelli **12**
forbici per potatura **40**
forbicine per le unghie **18**
forca **40**
forcella **101**
forchetta **27**
forchetta da giardino **40**
forchettone **28**
forcone **40**
foresta **147**, **148**
foresta decidua **146**
foresta di conifere **146**
foresta di latifoglie **159**
foresta pluviale **146**, **159**
forfora **12**
forma per scarpe **17**
forma per stivali **17**
formaggi **64**
formaggio **61**, **71**
formaggio a pasta dura **61**
formaggio a pasta molle **61**
formaggio a pasta semidura **61**
formaggio a pasta semimolle **61**
formaggio di capra **61**
formaggio erborinato **61**
formaggio fresco **61**
formaggio grattugiato **61**
formaggio spalmabile **61**
formazioni acquatiche **145**
forme **74**
formica **162**
formichiere **159**
formidabile **177**
formula chimica **76**
fornello **27**
fornello da campeggio **135**
forno **27**
forno a microonde **27**
forno da pizza **70**
forottero **22**
forte **52**
fortunato / fortunata **06**
forza centrifuga **75**
forza centripeta **75**
forze armate **88**
fosforo **78**
fossa dell'orchestra **126**
fossa oceanica **145**
fossato **44**
fossette **12**
fossile **77**
fotocamera **83**
fotocopiatrice **82**
fotofinish **116**
fotografia naturalistica **133**
fotografo / fotografa **89**
fotosintesi **77**
fragile **45**
fragola **57**
frana **146**
francese **153**
Francia **151**, **153**
francio **78**
francobollo **45**, **48**
frangivento **134**
frappè **52**
frasario **131**
fratellastro **05**
fratelli **05**
fratello **05**
frattaglie **53**
frattura **19**
fratturazione idraulica **51**
frazione **74**
frazioni **173**
freccette **140**
freccia **79**, **97**, **100**, **125**
freddo / fredda **52**, **154**, **176**
fregata **88**, **160**
frenare **98**, **101**
french toast **71**
freno **99**, **100**, **101**
freno a mano **99**
frequenza **84**
fresa verticale **35**
fresco / fresca **52**, **54**, **56**, **154**
fresia **47**, **167**
friggere **29**
frigo **27**
frigo portatile **135**
frigorifero **27**
fringuello **160**
frisbee **133**
Frithia pulchra **168**
frittelle di patate **71**
fritto / fritta **72**
frizione **99**, **100**
frizzante **52**
frode **85**
frollino **63**
frontale **03**
frontalino **120**
fronte **01**, **88**
fronte caldo **155**
fronte freddo **155**
fronte occluso **155**
frontone **44**
frullato **52**
frullato di fragole **65**
frullatore **27**, **65**
frusta **28**
frustino **120**
frustrato / frustrata **06**
frutta **48**, **57**, **58**
frutta a guscio **58**
frutta con il nocciolo **57**
frutta conservata **60**
frutta fresca **71**
frutta secca **71**
frutta stagionale **57**
frutti **58**
frutti di mare **54**
fruttivendolo / fruttivendola **46**, **56**, **89**
frutto della passione **58**
frutto dell'albero del pane **56**
fucile **88**
fucile a canna liscia **88**
fucsia **168**
fullback **107**
fulmine **154**
fumaiolo **105**
fumetto **48**, **138**
fumo **50**
fune **119**
fune di sospensione **125**
funerale **07**
funghi **77**, **170**
funghi coltivati **170**
funghi fritti **71**
funghi velenosi **170**
fungo **56**
fungo dell'inchiostro **170**
fungo dell'olivo **170**
fungo enoki **56**, **170**
fungo Laetiporus **170**
fungo pleurotus **56**
fungo shiitake **56**, **170**
funivia **122**
fuoco **27**, **50**
fuori **180**
fuori campo **112**
fuori pista **122**
furetto **164**
furioso / furiosa **06**
furto d'auto **85**
fusello **142**
fusilli **64**
fusione **75**

G

gabbia **03**, **164**
gabbiano **134**, **160**
gabinetto **33**
Gabon **149**, **152**

gabonese **152**
gadolinio **78**
galassia a spirale **144**
galassia ellittica **144**
galateo telefonico **93**
galleggiante **33**, **121**
galleggiare **118**
galleria **126**, **130**
galleria d'arte **43**, **132**
gallerie **130**
galletta **62**, **71**
gallina **165**
gallio **78**
gallo **165**
galloccia **119**
gallone **174**
galoppare **165**
gamba **01**, **26**
gambero d'acqua dolce **54**
gambero non sgusciato **54**
gambero sgusciato **54**
Gambia **149**, **152**
gambiano / gambiana **152**
gambo **55**, **170**
gancio **87**
gancio da macellaio **53**
gancio e occhiello **142**
Gange **145**
gara **116**
gara automobilistica **123**
gara di accelerazione **123**
gara di Monster Truck **123**
gara di tuffi **118**
garage **25**
garanzia **47**
gardenia **38**
gare di corsa **116**
garofano **38**
garza **20**
gas **51**, **76**
gas di scisto **51**
gas flaring **51**
gas nobili **78**
gas serra **155**
gastornis **157**
gastroenterologia **21**
gastronomia **46**, **48**, **64**
gate d'imbarco **104**
gattino / gattina **164**
gatto Bombay **164**
gatto d'Angora **164**
gatto del Bengala **164**
gatto delle nevi **122**
gatto Himalayano **164**
gatto selvatico **159**
gaviale **163**
gazzella **158**
gel **49**
gel doccia **31**
gel per capelli **12**
gelata **154**
gelato **61**, **70**, **134**
gelido / gelida **154**
geloso / gelosa **06**
gemelli **144**
gemelli / gemelle **05**, **16**
gemme **156**
gene **77**
generale **88**
generatore **33**, **51**
generi **138**
genero **05**
generoso / generosa **10**
gengiva **03**
genio **139**
genitali **01**
genitore single **05**
genitori **05**
gennaio **172**
gentile **10**, **177**
geode **156**
geografia **73**, **146**, **147**
Georgia **150**, **153**
georgiano / georgiana **153**
geranio **38**
gerbera **47**
gerbillo **164**
Germania **151**, **153**
germanio **78**
germano reale **161**
germogli di soia **55**
geroglifici dell'Antico Egitto **175**
gesso **39**, **156**
gesso da sarto **142**
gestione dei progetti **93**
gestione del tempo **93**
gestire **92**
getto d'acqua **50**
geyser **146**
Ghana **149**, **152**
ghanese **152**
ghee **61**
ghepardo **158**
ghiacciaio **146**
ghiacciato / ghiacciata **154**
ghiaccio **68**, **154**
ghiacciolo **146**
ghiaia **35**, **40**
ghianda **169**
ghiandola prostatica **04**
ghiandola surrenale **04**
ghiera **115**
ghirlanda **47**
giaca **58**
giacca **15**
giacca a vento **15**
giacca ad alta visibilità **13**
giacca da cuoco **13**
giacca da sci **122**
giacca di jeans **15**
giacca sportiva **15**
giacimento petrolifero **51**
giada **156**
giaguaro **159**
giaietto **156**
giallo **141**
Giamaica **150**, **152**
giamaicano / giamaicana **152**
Giappone **150**, **153**
giapponese **153**
giardinaggio **39**, **133**
giardiniera **60**
giardiniere / giardiniera **89**
giardino **38–41**, **41**
giardino all'inglese **41**
giardino all'italiana **41**
giardino botanico **132**
giardino con patio **41**
giardino d'acqua **41**
giardino di erbe aromatiche **41**
giardino pensile **41**
giardino roccioso **41**
giarrettiera **14**
gibbone **159**
Gibuti **149**, **152**
gibutiano / gibutiana **152**
gigante / gigantessa **139**
gigante rossa **144**
giganti gassosi **143**
giglio **38**, **167**
gilbertese **153**
gilet **15**
gilet ad alta visibilità **87**
gilet da pesca **121**
gin tonic **68**
ginecologia **21**
ginecologo / ginecologa **08**
ginerio **38**
ginkgo **58**, **167**
ginnastica **125**
ginocchiera **100**, **107**
ginocchio **01**, **126**
giocare **11**, **113**, **140**
giocare a carte **140**
giocare con i bambini **09**
giocatore / giocatrice **108**, **114**, **140**
giocatore di basket / giocatrice di basket **112**
giocatrice di football **107**
giocatore di hockey su ghiaccio / giocatrice di hockey su ghiaccio **110**
giocatore di hockey su prato / giocatrice di hockey su prato **110**
giocatore di lacrosse / giocatrice di lacrosse **110**
giocatore intermedio **111**
giocatori / giocatrici **108**, **113**
giocattoli **08**, **164**
giocattoli per il bagnetto **31**
giocattolo da trainare **08**
giochi **08**, **140**
giochi con le racchette **114**
gioco a piattaforme **136**
gioco a premi **137**
gioco a quiz **136**
gioco da tavolo **08**, **140**
gioco d'avventura **136**
gioco d'azione **136**
gioco di logica **136**
gioco di ruolo **136**
gioco di simulazione **136**
gioco di sport **136**
gioco di strategia **136**
gioco multigiocatore **136**
giogaia **159**
gioielleria **46**, **141**
gioielli **16**
gioielliere / gioielliera **89**
Giordania **150**, **153**
giordano / giordana **153**
giornale **138**
giornalismo **91**
giornalista **90**
giorno **171**
giorno dei morti **07**
giostra dei cavalli **133**
giostrina **30**
giovane **12**
giovane rana **77**
Giove **143**
giovedì **172**
gipsofila **47**
giradischi **136**
giraffa **158**
girare a destra **96**, **148**
girare a sinistra **96**, **148**
girarsi **118**
girasole **38**, **86**
girino **77**, **163**
giro turistico **132**
girocollo **16**
girocottero **103**
giubbotto di salvataggio **105**, **119**
giubbotto imbottito **15**
giudice **85**, **90**, **114**
giugno **172**
giullare **79**
giumenta **120**, **165**
giunchi **41**
giunchiglia **38**
Giurassico **157**
giuria **85**
giusto / giusta **176**
gladiolo **47**
glassa **29**, **63**
glassare **62**, **63**
glicine **38**
globulo bianco **77**
globulo rosso **77**
gloria del Texas **168**
glossario **138**
gnatostoma **157**
gneis **156**
gnocchi **64**
gnomo **139**
gnu **158**
go **140**
go cart **123**
goalball **126**
gobba **159**
gobbo **84**
goblin **139**
gocce **49**
goccia di pioggia **154**
goccio **29**
goffo goffa **10**
gola **04**
golden retriever **164**
golena **147**
golf **115**
golf cart **115**
golfista **115**
golfo **147**
gomito **01**
gomma **101**, **176**
gomma a terra **98**
gomma da cancellare **73**, **82**
gomma da masticare **67**
gommone **105**, **134**
gommone di salvataggio **119**
gondola **103**
gong **128**
goniometro **73**, **74**
gonna **14**
gonna arricciata **142**
gonna con spacco **15**
gorilla **159**
gospel **129**
gradevole **177**
gradi **154**
gradinate **109**
graffetta **73**
graffette **82**
graffiti **85**
grafico a barre **95**
grafite **156**
grammo **174**

gran lavoratore / gran lavoratrice 93
granata 88
granato 156
grancassa 128
granchio 54, 134
granchio blu 166
granchio del cocco 166
granchio violinista 166
grande 176
grande dorsale 03
grande gluteo 03
grande gufo grigio 161
grande magazzino 47
Grande Moschea di Djenné 44
grande varietà 48
grandi numeri 173
grani di pepe 59
granito 156
grano 86
grassa 18
grassetto 175
grassi insaturi 23
grassi saturi 23
gratella 29
graticcio 41
grato / grata 06
grattacielo 42
grattarsi 164
grattugia 28
grattugiare 29
gravidanza 08
gravità 144
Great Blue Hole 145
Grecia 151, 153
greco / greca 153
green 115
gregge di pecore 165
grembiule 13, 29
gremlin 139
Grenada 150, 152
grenadino / grenadina 152
gridare 11
grifola frondosa 170
grifone 139
grigi 01
grigio 141
griglia di partenza 123
griglia pieghevole 135
grigliare 29
grigliato / grigliata 72
grillo 162
grondaia 25
gronde 32
gronde sporgenti 44
grotta marina 147
grotte 146
gru 106, 160
gru a ponte 106
gru a torre 87
gru galleggiante 106
gruccia appendiabiti 30
grugnire 165
guadagnare 81, 94
guadagnare yard 107
guancia 01
guanti 16, 107, 109
guanti da boxe 117
guanti da giardinaggio 40
guanti di gomma 34
guanti isolanti 143
guanti protettivi 87
guantino da battitore 113
guanto 100, 110, 115, 117, 122
guanto da forno 29
guanto da presa 110
guanto da ricevitore 113
guanto per autoabbronzante 18
guardalinee 109, 114
guardare la televisione 09, 137
guardare le vetrine 46
guardaroba 130
guardia costiera 106
guardia del corpo 90
guardia destra 107
guardia di sicurezza 89, 90
guardia sinistra 107
guardia tiratrice 112
guardie carcerarie 85
guarire 20
guarnire 29
guarnizione 36
Guatemala 150, 152
guatemalteco / guatemalteca 152
guava 58, 168
guerra 79, 88
guerriero 79
gufo crestato 161
gufo reale 161
guianese 152
guida 96, 98, 131, 132
guida turistica 90, 130, 132, 138
guida tv 137, 138
guidafilo 142
guidare 09, 96
guidone 119
Guinea 149, 152
Guinea Equatoriale 149, 152
Guinea-Bissau 149, 152
guineano / guineana 152
guineense 152
guinzaglio 164
gunnera 168
guscio 58, 61, 161
guscio della noce di cocco 57
gustoso / gustosa 52
Guyana 149, 152

hackeraggio 85
Haiti 150, 152
haitiano / haitiana 152
hakama 117
halal 72
halfback 107
halibut 54
hall dell'albergo 131
halloumi 64
Halloween 07
halva 67
hamburger 70
hamburger di pollo 70
hamburger vegetariano 70
handicap 115
Hang Son Doong 145
hangar 104
Hanukkah 07
harissa 60
hash brown 70, 71
hashmark 107
hashtag 83, 84, 175
hassio 78
heavy metal 129
henna 168
Hericium 170
Hibbertia scandens 168
hijab 16
hip hop 129
hockey 110
hockey su ghiaccio 110
hockey su prato 110
Holi 07
home cinema 136
home entertainment 136
Honduras 150, 152
honduregno / honduregna 152
horror 127
hosel 115
hostess 90
hot dog 70
hot pot cinese 72
hotel 42
hovercraft 105
Hugin e Munin 139
hula hoop 08
hummus 72
husky siberiano 164
Hydnum repandum 170
hypoestes phyllostachya 38

I

iarda 174
ibernazione 77
ibis sacro 160
ibis scarlatto 160
ibisco 38
ibisco cinese 169
iceberg 146
identikit 85
idolo moresco 166
idra 139
idrante 50
idraulico / idraulica 89
idrogeno 78
idroterapia 24
idrovolante 103
iena 158
igiene femminile 49
igienista dentale 22
igloo 32
igname 56
ignami 86
iguana marina 163
iguana verde 163
illuminazione 47
illuminismo 79
illustrazione 138
imballare 32
imbarazzato / imbarazzata 06
imbarcadero 106
imbarcarsi 104, 106
imbarcazioni 105
imbastire 142
imbianchino / imbianchina 89
imbottitura di protezione 110
imbracatura 122
imbuto 76
immaturo / immatura 10
immersione ad alte profondità 118
immersioni 118
immersioni subacquee 118
immobile 32
impacchettare 11
impala 158
imparare 73
imparare in fretta 93
impastare 62
impasto 62
impaurito / impaurita 06
impaziente 10
impennaggio 103
imperatore 79
imperatrice 79
impermeabile 15
impero 79
impianto elettrico 33
impianto idraulico 33
impianto di raffreddamento 98
impianto hi-fi 136
impianto idraulico 33
impiegato delle poste / impiegata delle poste 45
impiego 81
importante 177
importo 45
impostare la sveglia 09
impregnante 37
impresa 139
Impressionismo 130
impronta digitale 50
impugnatura 115
impulsivo / impulsiva 10
imputato / imputata 85
in attivo 45
in camicia 72
in campo 111
in passivo 45
in rosso 45
in salamoia 64
in salsa 72
in scatola 56
in senso antiorario 148
in senso orario 148
in tempo 171
inaffidabile 10
inalatore 20, 49
inavvicinabile 10
incapace 177
incendio 50
incentivo 81
inchinarsi 02
inchiostro 141, 175
inciampare 178
incidente 19
incinta 08
incisione 141
incisivi 03

incontrare **178**
incontrarsi **179**
incontro **114**
incontro di boxe **117**
incontro di tennis **114**
incredibile **177**
incrociatore **88**
incrocio **43**
incubatrice **08**
incubo **30**
indaco **141**
indagine **50**
indebitarsi **94**
India **150**, **153**
India Pale Ale (IPA) **68**
indiano / indiana **153**
indicare **11**, **178**
indicatore della temperatura **99**
indicazioni **132**
indice **02**, **138**
indifferente **06**
indio **78**
indipendente **93**
indirizzo **45**
indivia **55**
indivia riccia **55**
Indonesia **151**, **153**
indonesiano / indonesiana **153**
indossare **14**, **178**
indumenti **13**, **14**, **15**
indumenti da notte **14**
indumenti da pesca impermeabili **121**
indumenti dei bambini **13**
indumenti impermeabili **135**
industria aerospaziale **91**
industria chimica **91**
industria farmaceutica **91**
industria manifatturiera **91**
infanzia **08**
infastidito / infastidita **06**
infelice **06**
infermiere / infermiera **20**, **21**, **89**
infermieristica **80**
infezione **19**
infilare l'ago **142**
influencer **84**
influenza **19**
informatica **73**, **91**
infradito **17**, **134**
infrarosso **75**
infusore **66**
ingaggio **110**
ingegnere / ingegnera **90**
ingegneria **80**
ingegneria del petrolio **91**
ingegnoso / ingegnosa **93**
inghiottire **52**
inginocchiatoio **40**
inglese **73**
ingorgo **43**, **96**
ingrassare **20**
ingresso **25**, **130**
inguine **01**
iniziare la scuola **07**
iniziare una partita **115**
iniziativa **93**
injera **62**
innaffiare **39**
innaffiare le piante **09**
innamorarsi **07**
innestare **39**
inning **113**
innocente **85**
innocuo / innocua **177**
inoltrare **83**
Inonotus hispidus **170**
inquilino / inquilina **32**
inquinamento **155**
insaccati **64**
insalata **55**, **65**
insalata greca **72**
insalata iceberg **55**
insalata mista **72**
insalata tritata **72**
insegnante **73**, **90**
insegnante di musica **90**
insegnante di yoga **90**
insensibile **10**
inserviente **90**
insetti **162**
insetto intrappolato **168**
insetto stecco **164**
insonnia **19**, **30**
installare **33**
installatore di cucine / installatrice di cucine **90**
installazione **130**
insulina **49**
intagliare **35**
integratore **23**, **49**
intelligente **10**
intelligenza artificiale **83**
intercity **102**
intercostale **03**
interessante **177**
interessato / interessata **06**
interno **113**
interprete **89**
interrompere **95**
interruttore **33**
interruzione di corrente **33**
intervallo **109**, **126**
intervista **137**
intestino crasso **04**
intestino tenue **04**
intollerante **23**
intolleranza ai latticini **23**
intolleranza al glutine **23**
intolleranza al lattosio **23**
intonacare **37**
intonaco **37**
intossicazione alimentare **19**
intrattenimento **91**
intruglio della strega **139**
inutile **177**
inventivo / inventiva **93**
inverno **172**
invertebrati **162**
invertebrato / invertebrata **77**
investigatore / investigatrice **50**
investigatore privato / investigatrice privata **89**
investimento **94**
inviare **83**
inviare un messaggio diretto **84**
involtino estate **72**
involtino primavera **72**
involucro **103**
iodio **78**
ionosfera **155**
ipercalorico / ipercalorica **23**
ipertensione **19**
ipnoterapia **24**
ipocalorico / ipocalorica **23**
ipoteca **32**, **45**
ipotenusa **74**
ippocastano **169**
ippodromo **120**
ippopotamo **158**
ippovia **133**
iracheno / irachena **153**
Iran **151**, **153**
iraniano / iraniana **153**
Iraq **150**
iride **01**
iris **38**
Irish coffee **65**
Irlanda **151**, **153**
irlandese **153**
irragionevole **10**
irrigatore a pioggia **40**
irriguardoso / irriguardosa **10**
irritante **177**
irritato / irritata **06**
irruzione **50**
iscrizione **124**
Islanda **151**, **153**
islandese **153**
isobara **155**
isola **88**, **145**, **147**
isolamento **35**
Isole Marshall **150**, **153**
Isole Salomone **150**, **153**
ispettore / ispettrice **50**
Israele **150**, **153**
israeliano / istraeliana **153**
issopo **59**
istioforo **166**
istituto d'arte **80**
istmo **147**
istruttore di guida / istruttrice di guida **89**
istruttore di volo / istruttrice di volo **90**
istruzione **91**
Italia **151**, **153**
italiano / italiana **153**
itterbio **78**
ittiostega **157**
ittrio **78**
iurta **32**
ivoriano / ivoriana **152**

J

jack **129**, **140**
jalapeño **59**
jazz **129**
jeans **13**, **14**
jet privato **103**
jogging **133**
jolly **140**
judo **117**
jujitsu **117**
jumbo jet **103**
jumping jack **124**

K

K-pop **129**
Kalanchoe daigremontiana **168**
karaoke **136**
karate **117**
kayak **105**, **119**
Kazakistan **151**
kazako / kazaka **153**
kebab **70**, **72**
kefir **61**
kendo **117**
keniano / keniana **152**
Kenya **149**, **152**
ketchup **60**, **70**
kickboxing **117**
kickflip **125**
kilt **15**
kimchi **60**
kimono **15**
kippah **16**
kirghiso / kirghisa **153**
Kirghizistan **151**, **153**
Kiribati **150**, **153**
kit di pronto soccorso **20**, **49**
kit di riparazione delle forature **101**
kitesurf **119**
kittitiano o nevisiano / kittitiana o nevisiana **152**
kiwi **58**, **160**
K.O. **117**
koala **158**
kookaburra **160**
kosher **72**
kung fu **117**
Kuwait **151**, **153**
kuwaitiano / kuwaitiana **153**
Kwanzaa **07**

L

labbra **01**
labirinto di perline **08**
laboratorio **76**
labrador **164**
lacci delle scarpe **17**
laccio **17**
lacrima **22**
lacrosse **110**
laghetto **41**
lago **146**, **148**
lago Natron **145**
laguna **147**
lama **40**, **117**, **158**, **165**
lamelle **170**

lametta **31**
laminaria **166**
lampada **26**, **82**, **106**, **139**
lampada da comodino **30**
lampadina **101**
lampadina a incandescenza **33**
lampadina a LED **33**
lampadina fluorescente compatta (CFL) **33**
lampadine **33**
lampeggiante dei mezzi di soccorso **50**
lampione **25**, **43**
lampone **57**
lana **13**, **142**, **176**
lana d'acciaio **36**
lancetta dei minuti **171**
lancetta dei secondi **171**
lancetta delle ore **171**
lancia **79**
lanciagranate **88**
lanciare **11**, **107**, **108**, **111**, **113**, **117**
lanciare la lenza **121**
lanciatore **111**, **113**
lancio **143**
lancio del disco **116**
lancio del giavellotto **116**
lancio del martello **116**
lancio del peso **116**
lancio della navicella spaziale **143**
lantanio **78**
lanterna **135**
Laos **150**, **153**
laotiano / laotiana **153**
lapislazzulo **156**
larghezza **74**
largo / larga **13**, **176**
larice **167**
laringe **04**
lasagne **64**, **72**
lasciarsi **178**
laser **75**
laser-run **116**
lassativo **49**
lastricato **35**
latitudine **145**, **148**
lato **74**
latte **61**, **65**, **71**
latte condensato **61**
latte di capra **61**
latte di mandorla **61**
latte di mucca **61**
latte di pecora **61**
latte di soia **61**
latte in polvere **08**, **61**
latte intero **61**
latte macchiato **65**
latte parzialmente scremato **61**
latte scremato **61**
latticello **61**
latticini **23**, **48**
lattina **52**
lattuga **55**
lattuga Little Gem **55**
lattuga romana **55**
laurea **80**
laurea magistrale **80**
laurearsi **07**
laureato / laureata **80**
laurenzio **78**
lava **145**
lavabo **33**
lavagna **73**, **95**
lavagna a fogli mobili **82**, **95**
lavanda **38**
lavanderia a secco **46**
lavanderia self-service **46**
lavandino **22**
lavare i piatti **09**, **34**
lavare il pavimento **34**
lavare l'auto **09**, **34**
lavarsi i capelli **09**, **12**
lavarsi i denti **09**
lavarsi il viso **09**
lavastoviglie **27**, **34**
lavatrice **34**
lavavetri **34**, **90**
lavello **27**
lavorare **11**
lavorare a tempo pieno **81**
lavorare bene sotto pressione **93**
lavorare da casa **81**
lavorare part-time **81**
lavoratore / lavoratrice **81**
lavorazione del merletto **142**
lavori **89**, **90**
lavori di casa **34**
lavori di miglioria della casa **35**
lavori in corso **96**
lavori stradali **87**, **96**
lavoro **81**, **81–95**
lavoro a maglia **142**
lavoro a uncinetto **142**
lavoro di otto ore regolari **81**
lavoro di squadra **92**, **93**
lavoro d'ufficio **81**
lavoro fisso **81**
lavoro temporaneo **81**
leadership **93**
lecca lecca **67**
leccare **02**, **11**
lederhosen **15**
leg press **124**
lega **76**
lega per saldatura **35**, **36**
legacci **40**
legacci ad anello **40**
legamento **03**
legare i capelli **12**
legatura **175**
legge **80**, **85**
leggere **73**
leggere un giornale **09**
leggere una cartina **148**
leggero / leggera **176**
leggero piovasco **154**
leggings **14**
leggio **128**
legname **87**
legno **35**, **115**, **141**, **176**
legno massiccio **35**
legno tenero **35**
legumi **23**
lemure dalla coda ad anelli **159**
lente **22**, **75**
lente concava **75**
lente convessa **75**
lenti a contatto **22**, **49**
lentiggini **12**
lento / lenta **176**
lenza **121**
lenzuolo **30**
Leone **145**, **158**
leone marino **166**
leonessa **158**
leopardo **159**
leopardo delle nevi **159**
lepre **53**
lepre artica **159**
leprecauno **139**
lesioni **19**
lesosfera **155**
lesothiano / lesothiana **152**
Lesotho **149**, **152**
let **114**
lettera **45**, **82**
lettera di accompagnamento **92**
letteratura **73**, **80**
letteratura di viaggio **138**
lettere **175**
lettere maiuscole **175**
lettere minuscole **175**
lettiera **164**
lettino **30**
lettino abbronzante **18**
letto **30**
letto d'ospedale **21**
letto matrimoniale **30**
letto singolo **30**
lettone **153**
Lettonia **151**, **153**
lettore CD **136**
lettore di codice a barre **48**
lettore di e-book **83**, **138**
lettura **138**
leva del cambio **99**, **101**
leva del freno **101**
leva d'emergenza **102**
leva smontagomme **101**
levigatrice **35**
levistico **59**
lezione **73**
lezione di ginnastica **124**
lezione di yoga **24**
libanese **153**
Libano **150**, **153**
libbra **174**
libellula **162**
libera **112**
liberare **121**
Liberia **149**, **152**
liberiano / liberiana **152**
libertà condizionale **85**
Libia **149**, **152**
libico / libica **152**
libreria **26**, **46**
libretto **126**
libri **26**, **138**
libro **80**, **138**
libro con copertina rigida **138**
libro da colorare **138**
libro degli incantesimi **139**
libro di cucina **138**
libro di fantascienza **138**
libro di giardinaggio **138**
libro di testo **73**, **138**
libro fantasy **138**
libro per bambini **138**
libro sulla natura **138**
libro tascabile **138**
libro umoristico **138**
licantropo **139**
licenza di pesca **121**
Liechtenstein **151**, **153**
liechtensteinese **153**
lievitare **62**
lievito disidratato **62**
lievito fresco **62**
lievito madre **62**
lillà **38**
lima **36**
lime **57**
lime sott'aceto **60**
limetta per unghie **18**
limite di velocità **96**
limo **39**
limonata **52**
limone **57**, **68**
limousine **97**
limulo **166**
lince **159**
lince rossa **159**
linea blu **110**
linea dei **5** metri **108**
linea dei **10** metri **108**
linea dei **22** metri **108**
linea del lanciatore **111**
linea del pallone morto **108**
linea del servizio **114**
linea delle **50** yard **107**
linea di centrocampo **108**
linea di colpo **111**
linea di fondo **107**, **112**, **114**
linea di foul **113**
linea di gioco **115**
linea di goal **110**
linea di meta **107**, **108**
linea di metà campo **109**, **112**
linea di partenza **116**
linea di rimessa **112**
linea di tiro libero **112**
linea di touche **108**
linea ferroviaria **148**
linea ritornata **111**
linea rossa **110**
linebacker centrale **107**
linebacker esterno **107**
linee **74**
linee della griglia **148**
linee elettriche **102**
lineetta **175**
lingerie **47**
lingua **04**, **53**
lingua di terra **147**
lingue **73**, **80**
linguetta **17**
lino **86**
liquido **76**
liquido per tergicristalli **97**
liquirizia **67**
liquore **68**
lisciviazione **39**
lista dei libri da leggere **80**
lista della spesa **46**
listino prezzi **70**
litchi **57**
litio **78**
litorale **132**
litro **174**
Lituania **151**, **153**
lituano / lituana **153**
livella **35**, **36**, **87**
livellatrice **87**
livermorio **78**

loafer **17**
locale notturno **42**
locusta **162**
loganberry **57**
lokum **67**
longitudine **145**, **148**
lontano / lontana **176**
lontra **158**
lonza **53**
loquace **10**
lord / lady **79**
lorichetto **161**
loto **38**
love **114**
lozione per il corpo **31**
lucchetto **101**
luce **32**, **84**, **101**
luce da lettura **103**
luce del portico **25**
luce notturna **30**
luce posteriore **101**
luce ultravioletta **75**
luce visibile **75**
lucertola **163**
lucertola perlinata **164**
luci **50**, **143**
luci del palco **129**
lucidante **34**
lucido / lucida **37**, **176**
lucido da scarpe **17**
lucioperca **54**
ludo **140**
luglio **172**
lumaca **162**
lumaca di mare **166**
luminoso / luminosa **176**
Luna **143**
luna di miele **07**
luna nuova **143**
luna piena **143**
lunedì **172**
lunghezza **74**, **174**
lunghezza d'onda **75**
lungo / lunga **176**
lungo fino a terra / lunga fino a terra **15**
lungomare **134**
luogo in cui vivere **25**
lupino **38**
lupo **159**
lupo artico **159**
luppolo **169**
lussemburghese **153**
Lussemburgo **151**, **153**
lutezio **78**

M

macaco **159**
macadamia **168**
macaron **63**
maccheroni **64**
macchina a raggi X **104**
macchina da cucire **142**
macchina del caffè **65**, **68**
macchina per il ghiaccio **27**
macchina per rimuovere la carta da parati **37**
macchinari **87**
macchinari da palestra **124**
macchinina **08**
macchinista ferroviario / macchinista ferroviaria **90**
macedone **153**
Macedonia del Nord **151**, **153**
macellaio **46**, **53**
macellaio / macellaia **89**
macinare **29**
macis **59**
macramé **142**
Madagascar **149**, **152**
madre **05**
maestro di sci / maestra di sci **89**
magazzino **32**, **44**, **106**
maggio **172**
maggiorana **59**
maglia con scollo a V **14**
maglia da calcio **15**, **109**
maglia da rugby **108**
maglia della squadra **107**
maglia girocollo **14**
maglietta da rugby **108**
maglione **14**
magnesio **49**, **78**, **156**
magnete **75**
magnolia **167**
mago / maga **139**
mai **171**
maiale **53**, **165**
maialino **165**
Maine coon **164**
maionese **60**
mais **55**, **86**
mal di denti **22**
mal di gola **19**
mal di schiena **19**
mal di stomaco **19**
mal di testa **19**
malachite **156**
malattie **19**, **20**
Malawi **149**, **152**
malawiano / malawiana **152**
Maldive **150**, **153**
maldiviano / maldiviana **153**
maleducato / maleducata **10**
malese **153**
Malesia **151**, **153**
malgascio / malgascia **152**
Mali **149**, **152**
maliano / maliana **152**
malta **35**, **37**, **87**, **151**, **153**
maltese **153**
mamma **05**
mammiferi **158**, **159**
mammut lanoso **157**
manager **81**
manchego **64**
mancia **69**
manciata **29**
mandare avanti **137**
mandarino cinese **57**
mandarino satsuma **57**
mandato **85**
mandibola **01**, **03**
mandolina **28**
mandolino **129**
mandorle **58**, **68**
mandria **86**
mandria di mucche **165**
mandrillo **159**
mandrino **35**
maneggiare con cura **45**
manette **50**
manganello **50**
manganese **78**
mangiare **52**
mangiare fuori **69**, **178**
mangiare sul posto **70**
mangiare troppo **23**
mango **57**
mangostano **58**
mangrovia **169**
mangusta **159**
mani **02**
manica **15**
manica ad aletta **15**
manichetta antincendio **50**
manichino da sarto **142**
manico **16**, **28**, **40**, **87**, **110**, **113**, **114**, **129**
manicure **18**
maniglia **25**, **97**, **99**
maniglione **31**
manioca **56**
mannaia **28**
mano **01**
mano di fondo **37**
manometro **33**
manopola di messa a fuoco **77**, **144**
manopola di selezione dei punti **142**
manopola di selezione della lunghezza del punto **142**
manopola per regolare la tensione **142**
manopole **124**
manovre **119**
mantella **15**
mantello **145**
mantide religiosa **162**
mantovana **30**
manuale di auto-aiuto **138**
manubrio **101**, **124**
manutenzione delle aree verdi **89**
manzo **53**
manzo sotto sale **64**
mapo **57**
mappa turistica **132**
Mar Morto **145**
maracas **128**
maratona **116**
marca di bordo libero **105**
marcare **107**, **112**
marcatori **129**
marce **101**
marchio registrato **175**
marciapiede **25**, **43**, **65**
marcio / marcia **57**
mare **134**, **145**
margarina **61**
margherita **38**
margherita africana **38**
marina **106**
marina militare **88**
marinaio **88**
marinaio / marinaia **88**, **89**
marinato / marinata **64**, **72**
marionetta **08**
marito **05**
marketing **91**
marmellata di arance **60**, **71**
marmitta **98**, **100**
marmo **156**, **176**
marmosetta **159**
marocchino / marocchina **152**
Marocco **149**, **152**
marrella **157**
marrone **141**
marroni **01**
marshallese**153**
marshmallow **67**
marsupio **158**
Marte **143**
martedì **172**
martellare **35**
martello **36**
martello pneumatico **87**
martin pescatore **160**
Martini **68**
marzapane **63**
marzo **172**
mascara **18**
maschera **118**
maschera da baseball **113**
maschera d'ossigeno **21**, **50**
maschera facciale protettiva **107**, **110**, **111**
maschera per il viso **18**
maschera protettiva **117**
mascherina **20**
mascherina chirurgica **21**
mascherina per gli occhi **14**
maschile **04**
mascotte **109**
massaggio **24**
massiccio montuoso **146**
masticare **52**
mata mata **163**
matassa **142**
matematica **73**, **74**
materassino **135**
materassino autogonfiante **135**
materassino del fasciatoio **30**
materasso **30**
materasso ad aria **135**
materiale di scena **127**
materiale per scrivere **175**
materiali **35**, **73**, **176**
maternità **21**
matita **73**, **82**, **141**, **175**
matita per labbra **18**
matita per sopracciglia **18**
matite colorate **73**
matraccio **76**
matrigna **05**
matrimonio **07**
mattarello **29**
mattina **09**, **171**
mattoncini **08**
mattone **87**, **176**
mattoni **35**
maturo / matura **10**, **57**
matzo **62**
Mauritania **149**, **152**
mauritano / mauritana **152**
Mauritius **149**, **152**

mauriziano / mauriziana **152**
mazza **87**, **110**, **111**, **113**
mazza ferrata **79**
mazze da golf **115**
mazzetto aromatico **59**
mazzo **47**
mazzo di carte **140**
mazzuolo **36**, **141**
MDF **35**
meccanico / meccanica **89**, **98**
mèches **12**
medaglia **88**
medaglie **116**
media **84**, **91**
media online **84**
mediano d'apertura **108**
mediano di mischia **108**
medicina **80**
medicinale **49**
medico **19**, **20**, **21**
medio **02**
mediocre **177**
meditazione **24**
medusa **166**
megafono **50**
meganeura **157**
megaterio **157**
megattera **166**
meitnerio **78**
mela **58**
mela cotogna **58**
Melaleuca subulata **168**
melanzana **56**
mele selvatiche **58**
melissa **59**
melo selvatico **169**
melodia **129**
melograno **58**, **168**
melone charentais **58**
melone d'inverno **58**
melone galia **58**
melone verde **58**
meloni **58**
membrana cellulare **77**
mendelevio **78**
menestrello **79**
meno dieci **154**
mensa **80**
mensa militare **88**
mensola del caminetto **26**
menta **59**
mente sana **24**
mentina **67**
mento **01**
mentoniera **107**
menù **65**, **70**
menù alla carta **69**
menù del pranzo **69**
menù della cena **69**
menù fisso **69**
menù per bambini **69**
meraviglioso / meravigliosa **177**
mercante **79**
mercatino dell'artigianato **132**
mercato **46**
mercato agricolo **23**
mercoledì **172**
Mercurio **78**, **143**, **156**
meringa **63**
merlano **54**
merlatura **44**
merlo **160**
merluzzo **54**, **166**
merluzzo nero **54**
mesa **146**
meschino / meschina **10**
mescolare **29**, **62**
mese **172**
Mesozoico **158**
messa a terra **33**
messicano / messicana **152**
Messico **150**, **152**
mestichino **141**
mestieri **141**, **142**
mestolo **27**
meta **108**
metà **173**
metacarpo **03**
metal detecting **133**
metalli **78**, **156**
metalli alcalini **78**
metalli alcalino-terrosi **78**
metalli di transizione **78**
metallo **35**, **155**, **176**
metamorfosi **77**
metano **155**
metatarso **03**
meteo **137**
meteora **144**
meticoloso / meticolosa **10**
metro **174**
metro a nastro **36**
metro cubo **174**
metro da sarto **142**, **174**
metro quadrato **174**
metropolitana **102**
mettere **14**
mettere a letto i bambini **09**
mettere in pausa **137**
mettere in vaso **39**
mettere la freccia **98**
mettere l'esca **121**
mettere mi piace **84**
mettere via **178**
mettersi a dieta **23**
mezzanino **126**
mezzanotte **171**
mezzo litro **174**
mezzo soprano **126**
mezzogiorno **171**
mezz'ora **171**
miagolare **164**
mica **156**
micelio **170**
microbiologia **77**
microbiologo / microbiologa **77**
microfono **84**, **95**, **136**
Micronesia **150**, **153**
micronesiano / micronesiana **153**
microonde **75**
microscopio **77**
mid-off **111**
midollo spinale **04**
miele **60**, **71**
miele cristallizzato **60**
mietitrebbia **86**
miglio **86**, **174**
miglio quadrato **174**
migliore amico / migliore amica **07**
mignolo **02**
migrare **161**
miliardo **173**
milione **173**
milkshake **65**, **70**
milkshake al cioccolato **61**, **65**
milkshake alla fragola **61**, **65**
milkshake alla vaniglia **61**
mille **173**
millennio **172**
millepiedi **162**
milligrammo **174**
millimetro **174**
milza **04**
mimosa **168**
minareto **44**
minatore / minatrice **89**
minatori **51**
mindfulness **24**
minerali **23**, **156**
mini pannocchie di mais **55**
minibar **131**
miniera a cielo aperto **51**
miniera di carbone **51**
miniserra **39**
Minotauro **139**
minulo **02**
minuto **171**
miope **22**
mirtillo **57**
mirtillo rosso **57**
mirto **168**
mischia **108**
mischia spontanea **108**
mischiare **140**
missile balistico **88**
missile da crociera **88**
missile spalleggiabile **88**
missile terra-aria **88**
mista **18**
misura dei liquidi **174**
misurare **174**
misuratore di pressione **21**
misure **174**
misurini **28**
misurino **49**
mite **154**
mito **139**
mitocondrio **77**
mitologia greca **139**
mitra **88**
mixer **27**, **84**
mobile banking **94**
mobiletto **27**
mocassini **17**
mochi **63**
mocio **34**
moda **91**
modanatura **26**
modellistica **141**
modello dell'abito **142**
modulo di candidatura **92**
modulo di rientro **143**
modulo lunare **143**
mogano cinese **169**
moglie **05**
molari **03**
Moldavia **151**, **153**
moldavo / moldava **153**
molecola **76**
molibdeno **78**
molletta **34**
molo **106**
moltiplicare **74**
monastero **44**
mondo naturale **157–70**
monegasco / monegasca **153**
monete **45**, **94**
mongolfiera **103**
Mongolia **150**, **153**
mongolo / mongola **153**
monitor **21**
mono **136**
monociclo **101**
monocolo **22**
monopattino **133**
monopattino elettrico **100**
monoplano **103**
monorotaia **102**
monovolume **97**
montagna **147**
montagna sottomarina **145**
montagne russe **133**
montare **178**
montare la tenda **135**
monte di lancio **113**
montenegrino / montenegrina **153**
Montenegro **151**, **153**
montgomery **15**
montone **165**
monumenti **44**
monumento **42**, **132**
moquette **30**
mora **57**
mora di gelso **57**
morbido / morbida **57**, **176**
morbillo **19**
morchella **170**
morire **07**
morsetto **76**
morsetto a G **35**
morso **19**, **120**
mortaio **28**, **76**
mortaio e pestello **28**
mosca **121**, **162**, **168**
moschea **44**
moscovio **78**
mostarda integrale **60**
mostra **130**
mostra permanente **130**
mostra temporanea **130**
mostro **139**
motivato / motivata **93**
motivo Battenburg **50**
moto **100**
moto a tre ruote **100**
moto da corsa **100**
moto da turismo **100**
moto d'acqua **134**
moto della polizia **50**
moto elettrica **100**
moto fuoristrada **100**
motocicli **100**
motociclismo **123**
motociclista **100**
motocross **123**
motore **98**, **100**, **103**
motore a reazione **103**
motore fuoribordo **105**
motoscafo **105**
mountain bike **101**
mouse **83**
mozambicano / mozambicana **152**

Mozambico 149, 152
mozzafiato 177
mozzarella 64
mozzo 51, 101
mucca 165
muesli 71
muffa 170
muffin 63, 70
muffole 13
mughetto 38
mule 17
mulinello 121
mulino a vento 44
multa 85
multivitaminici 49
mungere 86
muovere 140
muoversi furtivamente 11
mura 44
muro 25, 87
muro della qibla 44
muschio 167
muscoli 03
muscoli ischiocrurali 03
musei 130
museo 43, 130, 132
museruola 120
musetto 123
musher 122
musica 73, 128, 129
musica classica 129
musica country 129
musica dance 129
musica folk 129
musica latina 129
musica pop 129
musical 126, 127
musicista 90
musicoterapia 24
muso 103
muta subacquea 118, 134
mutande 14
mutandine 14
mutuo 45
Myanmar 150, 153

N

nachos 70
Namibia 149, 152
namibiano / namibiana 152
nana bianca 144
nano 139
narici 01
narrativa 138
narrativa letteraria 138
narvalo 166
nascere 07
nascita 08
nascondersi 164
nascondino 133
nasica 159
naso 01
naso che cola 19
naso pendulo 159
nassa galleggiante 121
nastro 63, 125, 142
nastro adesivo 32
nastro adesivo di carta 37
nastro isolante 36
nastro medico 20
nastro trasportatore 48
nasturzio 169
Natale 07
naturale 52
naturopatia 24
naturoterapia 24
Nauru 150, 153
nauruano / nauruana 153
nausea 19
nautilo 166
nave 105
nave da carico 105
nave da crociera 105
nave da guerra 105
nave portacontainer 105, 106
navetta 99
navi 88
navicella spaziale 143
navigare 119
navigatore satellitare 99
nazionalità 152, 153
nebbia 154
nebbiolina 154
nebbioso / nebbiosa 154
nebulosa 144
negoziazione 93
negozio 42
negozio d'arte 46
negozio dell'usato 46
negozio di abbigliamento 47
negozio di alcolici 46
negozio di alimenti biologici 47
negozio di animali 46
negozio di antiquariato 46
negozio di articoli da regalo 46
negozio di borse 47
negozio di cibi biologici 23, 46
negozio di dolciumi 67
negozio di elettronica 46
negozio di giocattoli 46
negozio di musica 46
negozio di scarpe 46
negozio di souvenir 130
negozio duty-free 104
negozio specializzato in chiavi 46
neo 12
neodimio 78
Neogene 157
neon 78
neonato / neonata 08
neozelandese 153
Nepal 150, 153
nepalese 153
nero 140, 141
nervo 03, 22
nervoso / nervosa 06, 10
nespolo 169
netball 125
nettunio 78
Nettuno 143
neurologia 21
neutro 33
neutrone 76
neve 154
nevischio 154
nevoso / nevosa 154
Nicaragua 150, 152
nicaraguense 152
nichel 78, 156
nido 160
nido di vespe 162
Niger 149, 152
Nigeria 149, 152
nigeriano / nigeriana 152
nigerino / nigerina 152
nihonio 78
ninfea 167
niobio 78
nipote (di nonni) 05
nipote (di zii) 05
nipoti (di nonni) 05
nobelio 78
nobili 79
nocca 02
nocciola 01, 58
nocciolo 168
noce 58, 168
noce di cocco 58
noce moscata 59
noci 68
noci brasiliane 58
noci di cola 58
noci di Macadamia 58
noci pecan 58
nodi 121
nodo Arbor 121
nodo clinch 121
nodo di sangue 121
nodo Palomar 121
nodo Snell 121
nodo Turle 121
noioso noiosa 177
noleggio auto 104
non arredato / non arredata 32
non frizzante 52
non metalli 78
non pastorizzato 61
non piegare 45
non salato 61
nonni 05
nonno / nonna 05
nono / nona 173
noodle 64, 70, 72
noodle di riso 64
nord 148
Nord America 150
nordamericano / nordamericana 152
nordcoreano / nordcoreana 153
nordest 148
nordovest 148
normale 18
norvegese 153
Norvegia 152, 153
nota 128
notazione musicale 128
note 128
notevole 177
notiziario 137
notte 171
novanta 173
nove 173
novembre 172
nube di cenere 145
nucleo 76, 77
nucleo esterno 145
nucleo interno 145
numeratore 74
numeri 173
numeri cardinali 173
numeri ordinali 173
numero 112
numero del giocatore / numero della giocatrice 107
numero della linea 99
numero di binario 102
numero di conto 45
numero di gara 100
numero di gate 104
numero di volo 104
nuora 05
nuotatore / nuotatrice 118
nuoto 118
nuoto sincronizzato 118
Nuova Zelanda 150, 153
nuovo / nuova 176
nutrire 86
nuvola 154
nuvole 51
nuvoloso / nuvolosa 154

oasi 146
obiettivo 77, 127, 136
obliqui 03
oboe 128
oca 53, 165
oca canadese 160
oca delle nevi 160
oca egiziana 160
occhi 01
occhiali 22, 122
occhiali bifocali 22
occhiali da lettura 22, 49
occhiali da sole 22, 134
occhiali protettivi 36, 76, 87
occhiali protettivi per abbronzatura 18
occhialini 15, 118
occhiello 17, 121
occhio 01
occhio di tigre 156
occupazioni 89, 90
Oceania 150, 153
oceaniano / oceaniana 153
oceano 145, 147
ochetta 165
oculare 77, 136, 144
oculistica 21
odontoiatra 89
offensive tackle destro 107
offensive tackle sinistro 107
offerta del giorno 70
offerta speciale 48
offerte di lavoro 92
officina 98
oganessio 78
oggetto 83
ogni due giorni 172

ogni giorno **172**
ogni mese **172**
ogni ora **171**, **172**
ogni settimana **172**
ogre **139**
okra **55**
olandese **153**
oleandro **169**
oli essenziali **24**
oli in bottiglia **60**
Olimpiadi Invernali **122**
olio **60**, **64**, **97**
olio aromatizzato **60**
olio di arachide **60**
olio di cocco **60**
olio di colza **60**
olio di girasole **60**
olio di mais **60**
olio di mandorle **60**
olio di nocciola **60**
olio di noci **60**
olio di oliva **60**
olio di palma **60**
olio di sesamo **60**
olio di soia **60**
olio di vinaccioli **60**
olivastro **169**
olive **68**
olive nere **64**
olive ripiene **64**
olive verdi **64**
olivello spinoso **169**
olivo **169**
olmio **78**
olmo **169**
Olneya tesota **169**
oltrepassare **148**
Oman **151**, **153**
omanita **153**
ombelico **01**
ombrello **16**
ombrellone **65**, **134**
ombretto **18**
omelette **61**, **71**, **72**
omeopatia **24**
omero **03**
omino di pan di zenzero **63**
omogeneizzato **61**
oncia **174**
oncia liquida **175**
oncologia **21**
onda **75**, **119**, **134**, **147**
ondata di caldo **154**
onde radio **75**
onesto / onesta **10**, **93**
onice **156**
opaco / opaca **37**, **176**
opale **156**
open space **32**
opera **126**, **129**
opera esposta **130**
operaio edile / operaia edile **87**, **90**
operazione **21**
operazioni **74**
opinioni **177**
optometrista **22**
opuntia **168**
ora **171**
ora di punta **42**
orangotango **159**
orari **132**
orari di apertura **132**
orario **104**
orario di punta **102**
orario flessibile **81**
orata **54**
orbita **143**
orca **166**
orchestra **128**
orchidea **38**, **47**
orco **139**
ordinanza **85**
ordinare **46**, **69**
ordinare online **46**
ordine del giorno **95**
Ordoviciano **157**
orecchini **16**
orecchini a bottone **16**
orecchini a cerchio **16**
orecchio **01**
orecchio di lepre **170**
organi interni **04**
organi riproduttivi **04**
organizzare **92**
organizzato / organizzata **93**
organizzazione **93**
organo a canne **128**
orgoglioso / orgogliosa **06**
orice **159**
orientato al cliente / orientata al cliente **93**
orientato al servizio / orientata al servizio **93**
orienteering **133**, **148**
origami **141**
origano **59**
originale **93**
Orione **144**
oritteropo **158**
orlo **14**, **142**
ormeggiare **106**
ormeggio **106**
ornamenti **41**
ornitorinco **158**
oro **78**, **116**, **156**, **176**
orologio **16**, **44**, **171**
oroscopo **138**
orribile **177**
Orsa Maggiore **144**
orsacchiotto **30**
orso bruno **159**
orso polare **159**
ortensia **38**
ortica **169**
orto **41**, **86**
ortopedia **21**
orzo **86**
oscillare **159**
osmio **78**
ospedale **21**, **42**
ospedale da campo **88**
ospite **26**
ospiti **131**
osservare **178**
osservatorio **144**
ossidiana **156**
ossigeno **78**
osso **03**
osso rotto **19**
osso sacro **03**
ostacoli **116**, **120**
ostacolo a tre barre **120**
ostacolo d'acqua **115**
ostello **131**
osteopatia **24**
ostetrica **08**
ostrica **54**
ostrichiere **160**
otorinolaringoiatria **21**
ottagono **74**
ottanta **173**
ottavino **128**
ottavo **173**
ottavo / ottava **173**
ottenere il lavoro **92**
ottica **75**
ottico / ottica **22**, **46**, **89**
ottimista **10**
otto **173**
ottobre **172**
ottomana **30**
ottone **176**
ottoni **128**
ottotipo **22**
otturazione **22**
oud **129**
out **113**
ovaio / ovaia **04**
ovale **74**
ovario **38**
overture **128**
ovest **148**
ovolo malefico **170**

P

pacchetto **52**
pacciamare **39**
pacco **45**
pacco batterie **35**
paddle **114**
paddle-boarding **119**
padella **28**
padre / papà **05**
padrone di casa / padrona di casa **32**
paella **72**
paesaggio **132**, **146**
paese **43**
paesi **149**, **150**, **151**
Paesi Bassi **151**, **153**
paga **81**
pagaia **119**
pagare **46**
pagare con carta **94**
pagare in contanti **94**
pagare le bollette **09**
pagare separatamente **69**
pagina **138**
pagliaccetto **13**
paglietta **16**
pagnotta **62**
paguro **134**, **166**
pain au chocolat **62**
paintball **133**
Pakistan **150**, **153**
pakistano / pakistana **153**
pala **33**, **51**
pala del rotore **103**
palafitta **32**
palato **04**
Palau **150**, **153**
palauano / palauana **153**
palazzo **132**
palazzo di uffici **42**
palchetto **126**
palco **126**, **159**
Paleogene **157**
paleontologo / paleontologa **77**
Paleozoico **158**
palestra **124**, **131**
paletta **34**, **40**, **129**
paletta forata **28**
palettare **39**
paletti **111**
pali **108**
palla **08**, **109**, **110**, **112**
palla da bowling **125**
palla da cricket **111**
palla da football **107**
palla da rugby **108**
palla fitness **124**
palla foul **113**
pallacanestro in carrozzina **125**
palladio **78**
pallamano **125**
pallanuoto **119**
pallavolo **112**
palleggiare **112**
palleggiatore / palleggiatrice **112**
palleggio **114**
pallina **114**
pallina da golf **115**
pallino **125**
palloncino **08**
pallone da spiaggia **134**
pallonetto **114**
palma **134**
palma da cocco **167**
palma da datteri **167**
palma rafia **167**
palme **41**
palmo **02**
palo **107**, **109**
palo di foul **113**
palpebra **01**
palude **146**, **147**
Pamukkale **145**
pan di Spagna **63**
Panama **16**, **150**
panamense **152**
panca **124**
panca da picnic **135**
panca puniti **110**
panca segnapunti **110**
pancake **65**, **71**
pancetta **53**, **71**
panchina **107**, **109**, **110**
panchina dei giocatori **113**
panchina della squadra **112**
pancreas **04**
panda **159**
panda rosso **159**
pane **62**, **71**
pane alla frutta **62**
pane bianco **62**
pane con lievito madre **62**
pane con semi **62**
pane di farina integrale **62**
pane di mais **62**
pane di segale **62**
pane in cassetta **62**
pane nero **62**
pane tostato **71**
paneer **64**
panetteria **48**, **62**, **63**
panettiere / panettiera **62**

pangolino **159**
panificio **46**
panino **62**
panino glassato **63**
panna **61**, **71**
panna densa **61**
panna liquida **61**
panna montata **61**
pannello mobile **82**
pannello solare **51**
panni sporchi **34**
panno **34**
panno per la pulizia delle lenti **22**
panno per spolverare **34**
pannolino **08**
pannoloni per l'incontinenza **49**
panoramico / panoramica **132**
pantaloncini da mare **134**
pantaloni **15**, **107**
pantaloni alla cavallerizza **120**
pantaloni cargo da lavoro **13**
pantaloni da yoga **24**
pantaloni della tuta **15**
pantofolaio / pantofolaia **137**
pantofole **14**, **17**
pantografo **102**
papaia **58**
paparazzi **127**
papavero **38**
papavero comune **168**
papavero da oppio **168**
papillon **16**
papiro egiziano **167**
pappagallino **164**
pappagallo cenerino africano **161**
pappagallo ecletto **161**
paprika **59**
Papua Nuova Guinea **150**, **153**
papuano / papuana **153**
par **115**
para hockey sul ghiaccio **122**
parabraccia **110**
parabrezza **97**, **100**
paracadute **125**
paracadutismo **125**
paracollo **107**
paracosce **107**
paradenti **107**, **117**
parafango **100**
parafango rialzato **100**
parafianchi **107**
paragambe **110**, **111**
paragomiti **107**
paraguaiano / paraguaiana **152**
Paraguay **149**, **152**
parallela **74**
parallele **125**
parallele asimmetriche **125**
parallelogramma **74**
paralume **26**
paramedico **21**, **50**, **90**
paramotore **103**
paraorecchie **87**
parapendista **125**
parare **117**
parasailing **119**
paraschizzi **27**
paraspalle **107**, **110**
parasport **125**
parastinchi **110**
paratleta **125**
paratoie **51**
paraurti **97**
parcheggiare **98**
parcheggio **32**, **42**
parcheggio interrato **47**
parcheggio per biciclette **43**
parcheggio per disabili **96**
parchimetro **96**
parco **42**, **133**
parco divertimenti **133**
parco eolico **51**
parco fotovoltaico **51**
parco giochi **43**
parco nazionale **133**
pareggiare **109**
parentesi **175**
parenti non consanguinei **05**
parete **25**, **87**
parete cellulare **77**
parkour **133**
parlare **11**
parmigiano **64**
parotite **19**
parrocchetto dal collare **161**
parrocchetto ondulato **160**
parrucca **12**
parrucchiere **47**
parrucchiere / parrucchiera **89**
parte anteriore **03**
parte meno profonda **118**
parte più profonda **118**
parte posteriore **03**
partecipare a una riunione **95**
partenza **43**
partenze **104**
parti del corpo **01**
parti del giorno **171**
particella **75**
partire **98**, **178**
partita **114**
partita di baseball **113**
partita di calcio **109**
partner **05**, **07**
pascolo **86**
Pasqua **07**
Pasqua ebraica **07**
passaggio sopraelevato **102**
passaporto **104**
passaporto biometrico **104**
passare **107**, **108**, **110**, **112**
passare il filo interdentale **22**
passare il mocio **34**
passare l'aspirapolvere sul tappeto **34**
passavanti **119**
passeggeri **102**, **106**
passeggino **08**
passerella **105**
passero **160**
password **83**
pasta **64**, **72**
pasta dolce **63**
pasta fillo **63**
pasta per i bignè **63**
pasta sfoglia **63**
pastelli **141**
pasticceria **46**
pastiglia dei freni **101**
pastiglia per la gola **49**
pastiglie **20**, **49**
pastiglie per lavastoviglie **34**
pastinaca **56**
pasto di tre portate **69**
pastore tedesco **164**
pastorizzato **61**
pastrami **64**
patata **56**
patata dolce **56**
patata novella **56**
patate **86**
patatine **48**, **68**
patatine fritte **70**
patchwork **142**
pâté **64**, **71**
patella **134**, **166**
paterazzo **119**
patio **25**
patologia **21**
pattinaggio a rotelle **125**
pattinaggio artistico **122**
pattinaggio di velocità **122**
pattinaggio in linea **125**, **133**
pattinaggio sul ghiaccio **122**
pattinare **110**
pattino **122**
pattino da ghiaccio **110**
pavimentazione **41**
pavimento **25**, **30**
pavlova **63**
pavone **161**
paziente **10**, **93**
paziente ambulatoriale **21**
paziente **19**, **20**, **21**
peccio **167**
pecora **165**
pecorino **61**
pedalare **101**
pedale **101**
pedale del freno **100**
pedali **99**
pedana elastica **125**
pediatria **21**
pedice **76**
pedicure **18**
pediera **30**
pedine **140**
pedone **140**
pelapatate **28**
peli del viso **12**
pelle **01**, **13**, **18**, **107**, **176**
pellegrinaggio alla Mecca **07**
pellicano **160**
peluche **08**
pendente **16**
pendolari **102**
pene **04**
penisola **147**
penna **73**, **82**
penna a sfera **175**
penna stilografica **175**
pennarello **175**
penne **64**
pennello **37**, **141**
pennello per carta da parati **37**
pennello per dolci **29**
pennello per le labbra **18**
pennino **73**, **175**
pensare **11**
pensilina della fermata **99**
pensione **131**
pentagono **74**
pentathlon moderno **116**
pentola **28**
pentola a pressione **28**
peonia **47**, **168**
pepe **26**
peperoncini **64**
peperoncini freschi **59**
peperoncino **56**, **60**
peperoncino a scaglie **59**
peperoncino di Cayenna **59**
peperoncino dolce **60**
peperoncino in polvere **59**
peperoncino Thai **59**
peperone **56**
per nulla colpito / per nulla colpita **06**
pera **58**
percento **173**
percentuale **74**
percentuali **173**
percorso a piedi **148**
percorso del traghetto **148**
percussioni **128**
perdere **94**, **109**, **140**
perdere la palla **107**
perdere peso **23**
perdere un treno **102**
perdersi **148**
perdita di habitat **155**
perenne **41**
pergamena **79**, **175**
pergola **41**
pericolo **96**
periferia **42**
periodi geologici **157**
perito **90**
Permiano **157**
pero **169**
perone **03**
perorare **85**
perpendicolare **74**
persiano **164**
personaggio **138**
personal trainer **124**
personalità **10**, **11**
persone **01–11**
persone nella storia **79**
Perù **149**, **152**
peruviano / peruviana **152**
pesante **176**
pesare **174**, **178**
pesca **57**, **91**, **121**
pesca a mosca **121**
pesca d'altura **121**
pesca in acqua dolce **121**
pesca marittima **121**
pesca nettarina **57**
pesca sportiva **121**
pesca su ghiaccio **121**
pesca subacquea **121**
pescatore / pescatrice **89**, **121**
pesce **48**, **54**, **164**
pesce affumicato **64**

pesce chirurgo blu **166**
pesce chirurgo giallo **166**
pesce chirurgo pinna gialla **166**
pesce falco **166**
pesce gatto **54**
pesce istrice **166**
pesce marinato **64**
pesce pagliaccio **166**
pesce palla **166**
pesce persico **54**
pesce pipa **166**
pesce saltafango **166**
pesce scatola giallo **166**
pesce sega **166**
pesce spada **54**
pesce trombetta **166**
pesce volante **166**
pescetariano / pescetariana **23**
peschereccio **105**
pescheria **46**
pesci **145**
pesci della barriera corallina **118**
pescivendolo / pescivendola **54**, **89**
pesi **174**
pesi liberi **124**
peso **121**, **174**
pessimo / pessima **177**
pestello **28**, **76**
pesticida **40**, **86**
pesticidi **55**
pet therapy **24**
petalo **38**
petroliera **105**
petrolio **51**
pettinarsi **09**
pettinatura afro **12**
pettine **12**
pettinino per sopracciglia **18**
pettirosso europeo **160**
petto **01**, **53**
pettorale **03**
pettorina da lavoro **13**
pezzo di carne **53**
phon **12**
pialla **36**
piallare **35**
pianeta Terra **145**
pianeti **143**
pianeti nani **143**
piangere **02**
pianificare il percorso **148**
piano cottura **27**
piano cottura in vetroceramica **27**
piano d'azione **95**
piano di lavoro **27**
piano di sopra **25**
piano di sotto **25**
piano inferiore **99**
piano intermedio **47**
piano superiore **99**
piano terra **25**, **47**
pianoforte **128**, **129**
pianta **02**, **77**
pianta carnivora **168**
pianta delle monete cinesi **38**
pianta in vaso **41**, **47**
pianta ragno **38**
pianta rampicante **41**
piantare **39**, **86**
piante **41**, **167**, **168**, **169**
piante acquatiche **41**
piante alpine **41**
piante da appartamento **38**
piante da giardino **38**
piante erbacee **41**
piante grasse **38**, **41**
piante ombreggianti **41**
piante ornamentali **41**
piantina **130**, **132**
pianura **146**
piastra per capelli **12**
piastrellare **35**, **37**
piastrelle **35**
piattaforma **50**, **84**, **118**
piattaforma di osservazione **44**
piatti **72**, **128**
piattino **27**
piatto **174**
piatto del giradischi **129**
piatto di frutti di mare **54**
piatto fondo **27**
piatto piano **27**
piazza **42**
piazzale **97**
piazzola di partenza **115**
piccante **52**, **56**
picche **140**
picchetto **135**
picchio nero **160**
picchio pileato **160**
picchio rosso maggiore **160**
picchio verde **160**
piccione **160**
piccolo / piccola **176**
piccone **87**
pick-up **129**
picnic **133**
piede **01**, **174**
piede quadrato **174**
piedi **02**
piedino premi-stoffa **142**
piega **14**
piegamento in avanti da seduti **24**
piegare **14**
piegare i vestiti **34**
pieno / piena **26**, **135**, **176**
pietra **141**, **176**
pietra di luna **156**
pietra metamorfica **156**
pietra per affilare **36**
pietra pomice **31**, **156**
pietra preziosa **16**
pietre vive **168**
pigiama **14**
pigiama intero **13**
pignone **101**
pigro / pigra **10**
pila **75**
Pilates **124**
pillole per il mal di viaggio **49**
pilone **51**
pilone destro **108**
pilone sinistro **108**
pilota **90**, **103**, **123**
Pilsner **68**
piluccare **52**
pimento **59**
PIN **45**
pince **142**
pince del petto **142**
ping pong **114**
pinguino di Humboldt **161**
pinguino imperatore **161**
pinguino minore blu **161**
pinguino Papua **161**
pinguino saltarocce **161**
pinne **15**, **118**, **134**
pino domestico **167**
pinoli **58**
pinta **174**
pinza fermacarte **82**
pinzatrice **82**
pinze **28**, **68**, **76**
pinze a becchi lunghi **36**
pinze a becchi tondi **36**
pinze spelafili **36**
pinzette **18**, **20**, **77**
pioggerella **154**
pioggia **51**, **154**
pioggia acida **51**, **155**
piolo **36**, **135**
piombo **78**
pioppo **168**
piovoso / piovosa **154**
pipetta **76**
pipistrello **158**
piramide **74**
piramidi di Giza **44**
pirofila di vetro **28**
pirottino **28**
piscina **118**, **131**
piscina per bambini **133**
piscinetta **25**
piselli **55**
pisello **55**
pista **104**, **116**, **122**
pista ciclabile **43**, **101**
pista da hockey su ghiaccio **110**
pista di atletica **116**
pista senza ostacoli **120**
pistacchio **58**
pistola **88**
pistola per colla a caldo **35**
pita **62**, **72**
pitone reticolato **163**
pittura **37**, **141**
pittura paesaggistica **133**
piume della coda **161**
piumino **161**
piumino da cipria **18**
piumino per la polvere **34**
piumone **30**
pizza **70**
pizzeria **70**
pizzetto **12**
pizzico **29**
placca **22**, **145**
placca ago **142**
placca da forno **29**
placcare **107**, **108**
placenta **08**
placerias **157**
planare **161**
plancia **105**
plancton **77**, **166**
plastica **155**, **176**
platano **168**
platea **126**
plateosauro **157**
platessa **54**
platino **78**, **156**
playmaker **112**
Pleurotus ostreatus **170**
Plutone **143**
plutonio **78**
pneumatici invernali **97**
pneumatico **97**, **100**
pneumatico con battistrada profondo **100**
poco chiaro / poco chiara **177**
poco entusiasta **06**
poco profondo / poco profonda **176**
podcast **84**
podio **116**, **128**
poesiaterapia **24**
poggiapiedi **82**
poggiatesta **99**, **123**
point **111**
polacco / polacca **153**
polizia **50**
poliziesco **127**, **137**
poliziotto / poliziotta **89**
pollaio **86**
pollame **53**, **165**
pollice **02**, **174**
pollo **53**, **165**
pollo arrosto **72**
pollo fritto **70**
polmone **04**
polo **14**, **120**
polo negativo **75**
polo nord **75**, **145**
polo positivo **75**
polo sud **75**, **145**
Polonia **151**, **153**
polonio **78**
polpa **03**, **57**, **58**
polpaccio **01**, **03**
polpette di carne **72**
polpette di salsiccia **71**
polpo **54**, **166**
polsiera **124**
polsino **15**, **107**, **114**, **142**
polso **01**, **02**
poltrona **26**
poltrona del dentista **22**
polvere **49**
pomata **20**, **49**
pomello **25**
pomelo **57**
pomeriggio **09**, **171**
pomo d'Adamo **04**
pomodori ciliegini **55**
pomodoro **56**
pomodoro grigliato **71**
pomodoro in scatola **71**
pomodoro San Marzano **56**
pomolo **113**, **120**
pompa **101**
pompa ad aria **135**
pompa di benzina **97**
pompa elettrica **135**
pompa irroratrice a spalla **40**
pompelmo **57**
poncho **15**
ponte **43**, **105**, **129**
ponte levatoio **44**
ponte pedonale **104**
pontile **106**, **134**
pop **129**
Pop art **130**
popcorn **127**
popolani **79**

poppa **105**, **119**
porcellino d'India **164**
porciglione europeo **161**
porcino **170**
porcospino **158**
pori **12**
porridge **71**
porro **56**
porta **99**, **102**, **109**, **110**, **111**
porta della doccia **31**
porta d'ingresso **25**
portacandele **26**
portacanne **121**
portacoltelli **28**
portaerei **88**, **105**
portafoglio **16**, **94**
portafoglio digitale **94**
portagioie **16**
portalenti **22**
portamonete **94**
portantino **21**
portapacchi **100**
portaprovette **76**
portare **11**
portare a spasso il cane **09**
portare fuori la spazzatura **09**, **34**
portarotolo di carta igienica **31**
portasapone **31**
portasciugamano **31**
portatovagliolo **27**
portauovo **27**, **61**
portefinestre **25**
portello di accesso dell'equipaggio **143**
portellone posteriore **97**
portfolio **92**, **94**
portico **25**
portiera anteriore **97**
portiera posteriore **97**
portiere **109**, **110**, **111**
porto **68**, **106**
porto di pesca **106**
porto passeggeri **106**
Portogallo **151**, **153**
portoghese **153**
porzione **26**
POS **45**, **48**
posare i mattoni **35**
posare la moquette **35**
posate **26**, **27**
posizione dei piedi **115**
posizione del bambino **24**
posizione del cadavere **24**
posizione del cammello **24**
posizione del cobra **24**
posizione del corvo **24**
posizione del delfino **24**
posizione del guerriero **24**
posizione del piccione **24**
posizione del ponte **24**
posizione del triangolo **24**
posizione della mezza luna **24**
posizione della montagna **24**
posizione della panca **24**
posizione della ruota **24**
posizione della sedia **24**
posizione dell'albero **24**
posizione dell'angolo legato **24**
posizione dell'arco **24**
posizioni del football americano **107**
posizioni del rugby **108**
posizioni della pallavolo **112**
posizioni in campo **111**
posizioni nell'hockey su ghiaccio **110**
possedere **32**
post alto **112**
Post-impressionismo **130**
post-it **82**
posta aerea **45**
posta in arrivo **83**
posta in uscita **83**
postare **84**
postazione di lavoro **82**
posteggiatore / posteggiatrice **96**
posteggio dei taxi **104**
posti a sedere **47**, **126**
posti vacanti **92**
postino / postina **45**, **90**
posto a tavola **27**
posto di guida **99**
potare **39**
potassio **78**
potatore **40**
pothos Jade **38**
pothos regina di marmo **38**
pozione **139**
pozza tra le rocce **134**
pozzanghera **154**
pozzo del fuoco **135**
pozzo minerario **51**
pranzare **09**
pranzo **26**, **72**
pranzo di lavoro **81**
praseodimio **78**
prataiolo **170**
prateria **146**
pratico / pratica **93**
prato **41**
preavviso di semaforo **96**
Precambriano **157**
precedenti penali **85**
preciso / precisa **93**
prelevare denaro **45**
premi **164**
premolari **03**
premuroso / premurosa **10**
prendere **11**
prendere appunti **73**
prendere il sole **133**, **134**
prendere il treno **09**
prendere in affitto **32**
prendere in prestito **80**
prendere la palla **107**, **111**, **113**
prendere la prima a sinistra **96**, **148**
prendere la seconda a destra **96**, **148**
prendere l'autobus **09**
prendere un treno **102**
prendersi un giorno di malattia **81**
prenotare **69**, **80**
prenotare una vacanza **131**
preoccupato / preoccupata **06**
preparare il pranzo al sacco **09**
preparare la cena **09**
preparare la tavola **26**, **34**
preparazione **54**
preparazione del cibo **72**
preposizioni **180**
preposizioni di luogo **148**
presa elettrica **33**, **83**
presbite **22**
prese d'aria **123**
presentare **95**
presentare le dimissioni **81**
presentatore / presentatrice **84**, **137**
presentazione **82**, **95**
presentazioni **95**
preside **73**
presidente della giuria / presidentessa della giuria **85**
pressione sanguigna **20**
prestare attenzione ai dettagli **93**
presto **171**
pretzel **62**
previsioni del tempo **137**
prezzemolo **59**
prezzo **69**
prezzo del servizio **69**
prezzo delle azioni **94**
prima **126**, **127**
prima base **113**
prima posizione **123**
primadonna **126**
primavera **57**, **172**
primo / prima **173**
primo centro **108**
primo piano **25**, **47**
primo piatto **69**
primula **169**
Principato di Monaco **151**
principe / principessa **79**
prisma **75**
problemi ambientali **155**
proboscide **159**
procedere al pagamento **46**
processo **85**
procione **158**
prodotti agricoli locali **23**
prodotti caseari **61**
prodotti per animali domestici **164**
prodotti per bambini **48**
prodotti per la casa **48**
prodotti per la pelle **49**
prodotti per l'igiene orale **49**
produttore / produttrice **126**, **127**
produzione **91**
professionale **93**
professore / professoressa **80**
profondimetro **118**
profondità **74**
profondo / profonda **176**
profumeria **47**
profumo **18**
progettare l'architettura paesaggistica **39**
programma **126**, **137**
programma del mattino **137**
programma di attualità **137**
programma di cucina **137**
programma sportivo **137**
programmi **137**
proiettore **82**, **95**
prolunga **35**
promezio **78**
pronto soccorso **21**, **50**
proposta **82**
propulsore **143**
prosciutto **53**, **64**, **71**
prosciutto iberico **64**
protagonista **127**
protea **38**
proteine **23**
proteo **163**
protesi da corsa **125**
protezione **40**
protezione inguinale **117**
protezione per il torace **107**, **117**
protezione per pali **108**
protezione solare **134**
protoattinio **78**
protone **76**
prova **50**, **85**
provare **46**
provare qualcosa **14**
prove multiple **116**
provetta **76**
prua **105**, **119**
prugna **57**
prugne secche **58**
prugno **169**
psichiatria **21**
psicologo / psicologa **90**
psicoterapia **24**
pubblicità **91**, **137**
pubblico **126**, **127**
pubblico ministero **85**
pugno **02**
pulcinella di mare **160**
pulcino **161**, **165**
puledro / puledra **120**, **165**
pulire il bagno **34**
pulire il forno **34**
pulire la stalla **120**
pulire le finestre **34**
pulire le superfici **34**
pulito / pulita **54**, **176**
pullman **99**
pulmino **99**
pulsante per prenotare la fermata **99**
pungere **162**
pungiglione **162**
punk **129**
punta **115**, **122**, **126**
punta da legno **36**
punta da metallo **36**
punta da muro **36**
punta del trapano **35**
punta di asparago **56**
punta di sicurezza **36**
punta piatta da legno **36**
puntaspilli **142**
punte del trapano **36**
punteggio **114**, **140**
punti **21**, **140**
punti di azione **95**
puntina da disegno **82**
puntini di sospensione **175**
punto **142**, **175**
punto di congelamento **154**
punto di ebollizione **154**

punto e virgola **175**
punto esclamativo **175**
punto interrogativo **175**
punto panoramico **148**
puntuale **93**
puntura **19**
pupilla **01**
puttare **115**
putter **115**
puzzle **08**, **136**, **140**
puzzola **158**

Q

Qatar **151**, **153**
qatariota / qatariota **153**
quad **100**
quaderno **73**
quaderno per schizzi **141**
quadrato **74**
quadri **140**
quadricipiti **03**
quadro **26**
quadro elettrico **33**
quaglia **53**
qualificazioni **124**
qualità professionali **93**
quantità **68**
quaranta **173**
quaranta minuti **171**
quarterback **107**
quartiere storico **43**
quartieri **42**
quarto / quarta **173**
quarto (2 pinte) **174**
quarto d'ora **171**
quarzite **156**
quarzo **156**
Quaternario **157**
quattordici **173**
quattro **173**
quattro frecce **99**
quercia **169**
quindici **173**
quindicina **172**
quinte **126**
quinto / quinta **173**
quiz televisivo **137**
quota d'ingresso **132**
quote azionarie **94**
quotidiano **48**

R

rabarbaro **58**
raccattapalle **114**
racchetta **114**
racchetta da sci **122**
raccoglierba **40**
raccogliere **39**, **57**, **86**, **110**, **178**
raccoglitore ad anelli **82**
raccoglitori **82**
raccolta dei funghi **133**
raccomandata **45**
racquetball **114**
radar **105**
radersi **09**, **12**, **31**
radiatore **33**, **98**
radiatore a olio **33**
radiazione gamma **75**
radiazione intrappolata **155**
radiazione riflessa **155**
radiazione solare **155**
radicchio **55**
radice **03**
radio **03**, **50**, **78**, **84**, **136**
radioattività **75**
radiografia **19**, **21**
radiografia dentale **22**
radiologia **21**
radiosveglia **30**
radiotelescopio **144**
radiotrasmittente **88**
radon **78**
rafano **56**
raffreddamento dei freni **123**
raffreddarsi **124**
raffreddore **19**
rafting **119**
raganella dagli occhi rossi **163**
ragazzo / ragazza **05**
Ragdoll **164**
raggi ultravioletti **155**
raggi X **75**
raggio **74**, **101**
raggiungere **178**
raggiungere un accordo **95**
raggiungere un consenso **95**
ragionevole **10**
ragliare **165**
ragno saltatore **162**
ragno tessitore **162**
ragù alla bolognese **64**
rallentare **98**
rally **123**
rame **78**, **156**
ramen **64**, **72**
rami spogli **172**
rammendare **142**
ramo **169**
rampa di accesso **96**
rampa di atterraggio **122**
rampa di lancio **143**
rampa di salto **122**
rampa di uscita **96**
rampa per sedie a rotelle **130**
rana **77**, **118**
rana adulta **77**
rana di Darwin **163**
rana freccia **163**
rana pescatrice **54**, **166**
rana temporaria **163**
rana toro africana **163**
rana volante di Wallace **163**
ranuncolo **38**, **168**
rapa **56**
rapa svedese **56**
rapide **119**, **146**
rapina **50**, **85**
rapinatori **50**
rapporti **07**
ras el hanout **59**
raschietto **37**
rasoio elettrico **31**
rasoio usa e getta **31**
rastrellare (le foglie) **39**
rastrelliera **102**
rastrelliera per gli attrezzi **35**
rastrelliera portabici **101**
rastrello **40**
rastrello aeratore **40**
ratto **158**
ravanello **56**
ravioli **70**, **72**
razza **54**, **166**
razze di cani **164**
razze di gatti **164**
razzo ausiliario **143**
re **79**, **140**
reality **137**
realizzare le tende **35**
reattore **51**
reazione **76**
recensione **138**
reception **131**
reception dell'ufficio **81**
receptionist **131**
recessione economica **94**
recinto **86**, **120**
recinto dei maiali **86**
recinto di sabbia **43**
recinzione **41**
recipiente per l'acqua **135**
recitare **11**
reclamare **46**
recuperare il compito **73**
recupero **109**
red carpet **127**
reddito **94**
redigere il verbale **95**
redini **120**
refrazione **75**
regalare **178**
regalo **07**
reggae **129**
reggibraccio **19**, **20**
reggicalze **14**
reggisella **101**
reggiseno **14**
reggiseno sportivo **15**
regina **79**, **140**
regina delle Ande **167**
regione polare **146**
regista **84**, **126**, **127**
registrare **137**
registratore di cassa **48**
registratore vocale **83**
regno **79**
Regno Unito **151**, **153**
reiki **24**
relatore ospite / relatrice ospite **95**
relazione **82**
relazioni **05**
relazioni pubbliche **91**
remo **119**
rene **04**, **53**
reni **71**
renio **78**
renna **159**
reparti **21**, **48**, **91**
reparto **21**, **80**
reparto bambini **47**
reparto contabile **91**
reparto di terapia intensiva **21**
reparto maternità **21**
reparto pediatrico **21**
reparto ricerca e sviluppo **91**
repellente per gli insetti **49**
repellente per insetti **135**
reporter **137**
Repubblica Ceca **151**, **153**
Repubblica Centrafricana **149**, **152**
Repubblica del Congo **149**, **152**
Repubblica Democratica del Congo **149**, **152**
Repubblica Dominicana **150**, **152**
respingente **102**
respirare **02**
respiratore **118**
responsabile **81**
responsabile **93**
responsabile del colloquio **81**
responsabile del team **92**
responsabile IT **89**
restauro **130**
resti **79**
restituire **46**, **80**, **178**
restringimento dei ghiacciai **155**
rete **30**, **109**, **112**, **114**
rete elettrica **33**
rete ferroviaria **102**
retina **22**
retino **121**
retinografo **22**
retta **74**
rettangolo **74**
rettili **163**
rettili volanti **157**
rettilineo d'arrivo **123**
rever **15**
revisionare l'auto **98**
rianimare **20**
riassumere **95**
ribaltarsi **119**
ribes bianco **57**
ribes nero **57**
ribes rosso **57**
ricamo **142**
ricamo ad ago **142**
riccio **158**
riccio di mare **166**
ricerca **91**, **93**
ricercatore di mercato / ricercatrice di mercato **89**
ricetrasmittente **50**
ricetta **20**, **49**
ricettacolo **38**
ricevitore **107**, **113**
ricevuta **94**
riciclaggio **155**
riciclo **91**
ricino **169**
riconoscente **06**
ricordare **11**
ricorrere in appello **85**
ricoverare **21**
ridere **02**
ridio **78**
ridurre **23**
riduzione dello stipendio **81**

riempire la lavastoviglie **34**
rifacimento del manto stradale **87**
rifare l'impianto elettrico della casa **35**
riferimento **171–80**
rifiuti **33**, **155**
rifiuti alimentari **155**
rifiuti biodegradabili **33**
rifiuti edili **33**
rifiuti elettrici **33**
rifiuti pericolosi **33**
rifiuti plastici **155**
riflessione **75**
riflessologia **24**
rifornire **98**
rifugio **44**
rifugio sciistico **122**
riga centrale **12**
riga laterale **12**
righe **14**
righello **73**, **74**, **82**, **174**
rigido / rigida **176**
rilassamento **24**
rilassante **177**
rilassarsi **178**
rilassato / rilassata **06**, **10**
rilevatore di fumo **50**
rilevatore di velocità **50**
rimanere senza **178**
rimbalzo **112**
rimborsare **46**
rimedi erboristici **49**
rimessa **109**, **112**
rimorchiatore **105**
rimorchio per bagagli **104**
rimpallo **114**
rimuovere **96**
rimuovere i fiori morti **39**
ring **117**
ringhiera **65**
Ringraziamento **07**
rinnovare **80**
rinoceronte **158**
rinoceronte lanoso **157**
rinunciare **178**
rinunciare a **23**
Rio delle Amazzoni **145**
riordinare **34**
riparare **11**, **33**
riparare una foratura **101**
riparare una recinzione **35**
ripassare **73**
ripiano **27**
ripieno **70**
riposare **20**
riprendersi **20**
riprodurre **137**
riproduzione **77**
riscaldamento solare dell'acqua **51**
riscaldarsi **124**
riserva naturale **133**, **148**
riservato / riservata **10**
riserve **109**
riso **72**, **86**
risoluzione dei problemi **93**
risorse umane **91**
risotto **72**
risparmi **45**
risparmiare **32**
rispettare una scadenza **92**
rispettoso / rispettosa **177**
rispondere **73**, **83**
rispondere a tutti **83**
rispondere alle domande **95**
ristorante **42**, **69**, **131**
ristorante fast food **47**
ristorazione **91**
ristrutturare **178**
ristrutturazione della casa **37**
risultati dell'esame **20**
ritardo **102**
ritirare **11**
ritiro bagagli **104**
ritmo **129**
riunione **81**, **82**
riunirsi **95**
riva **147**
rivista **48**, **80**
rivista di gossip **138**
rivoluzione industriale **79**
rivoluzione tecnologica **79**
robot cattivo **139**
rocce **147**, **156**
rocchetto **142**
rocchetto di filo **142**
roccia ignea **156**
roccia sedimentaria **156**
rock **129**
rock star **90**
rodeo **120**
rodio **78**
rododendro **38**
roentgenio **78**
rollbar **97**
Romania **151**, **153**
romantico / romantica **10**, **177**
romanzo **138**
romanzo poliziesco **138**
rombo **54**, **74**
rompersi **98**, **178**
roncola **40**
rondine **160**
rondine riparia **160**
rondone **160**
ronzare **162**
rosa **38**, **141**
rosa canina **169**
rosa del deserto **156**
rosé **68**
rosmarino **38**, **59**
rospo comune **163**
rospo delle grandi pianure **163**
rossetta **158**
rossetto **18**
rosso **141**
rotaia **102**
rotaia sotto tensione **102**
rotazione **114**
rotella tagliapizza **28**
rotelle **101**
rotolo alla cannella **71**
rotolo di carta da parati **37**
rotonda **96**
rotore **51**
rotula **03**
rough **115**
roulotte **32**, **135**
round **117**
router **83**
rover **143**
rover lunare **143**
rovescio **114**
Ruanda **149**, **152**
ruandese **152**
rubidio **78**
rubinetto **27**, **31**, **33**
rubino **156**
rucola **55**
rugby **108**
rugby in carrozzina **108**, **125**
ruggire **159**
rughe **12**
rullo **37**, **87**
rum **68**
rum e cola **68**
rumeno / rumena **153**
rumoroso / rumorosa **176**
running back **107**
ruota **97**, **101**, **161**
ruota anteriore **99**
ruota del timone **119**
ruota di scorta **98**
ruota panoramica **133**
ruota per addominali **124**
ruota posteriore **99**
ruscello **147**
ruspa **87**
russare **02**, **30**
russo / russa **153**
rutenio **78**
rutherfordio **78**

S

sabato **172**
sabbia **35**, **39**, **134**
sabot **17**
sac-a-poche **29**
sacca da golf **115**
sacchetto **52**
sacchetto compostabile **155**
sacco a pelo **135**
sacco da boxe **117**
sacco dell'immondizia **33**, **34**
safety destro **107**
safety sinistro **107**
saggistica **138**
Sagittario **145**
Saint Kitts e Nevis **150**, **152**
Saint Vincent e Grenadine **150**, **152**
sala concerti **43**
sala da pranzo **26**
sala d'attesa **20**, **81**, **102**
sala di controllo **143**
sala di lettura **80**
sala di registrazione **84**
sala d'imbarco **104**
sala interrogatori **50**
sala macchine **105**
sala operatoria **21**
sala risveglio **21**
sala riunioni del consiglio di amministrazione **95**
salamandra pezzata **163**
salamandra rossa **163**
salame **53**, **64**
salame piccante **64**
salario **81**
salato **61**
salato / salata **52**, **54**, **64**
salcerella **168**
saldare **35**
saldatrice **35**, **36**
saldi **47**
sale **23**, **26**
salice **169**
salice grigio **169**
salire **100**, **178**
salire su una bicicletta **101**
salmone affumicato **64**, **71**
salmone dell'Atlantico **166**
salomonese **153**
salopette **13**
salotto **26**
salpare **106**
salsa **70**
salsa di ostriche **60**
salsa di pesce **60**
salsa di pomodoro **70**
salsa di soia **60**
salsa di soia da intingere **72**
salsa piccante **60**
salse **60**, **64**
salsicce **53**
salsiccia **71**
salsiccia piccante **64**
saltare **11**, **29**, **117**, **120**, **164**
saltare in padella **29**
saltare la corda **124**
saltato in padella / saltata in padella **72**
saltellare **11**
salti laterali **124**
salto a due **112**
salto a ostacoli **120**
Salto Ángel **145**
salto con gli sci **122**
salto con l'asta **116**
salto della corda **133**
salto in alto **116**
salto in lungo **116**
salto triplo **116**
salumi **53**, **64**
salutare con la mano **02**
salutare (formale) **179**
salutare (informale) **179**
salute **12–18**
saluti **179**
salvadoregno / salvadoregna **152**
salvagente **134**
salvagente a ciambella **105**, **119**, **134**
salvaslip **49**
salvavita **33**
Salve **179**
salvia **59**
salvietta umidificata **08**, **49**
salviette disinfettanti **20**
salvo **113**
samara **170**
samario **78**
sammarinese **153**
Samoa **150**, **153**
samoano / samoana **153**
San Marino **151**
sandali **17**
sandali alla schiava **17**
sandali con zeppa **17**
sandali in gomma **17**
sandwich **65**, **70**, **72**
sanguinaccio **71**
sanguinare **20**
sanità **91**
sansevieria **38**

Santa Lucia **150**, **152**
santaluciano / santaluciana **152**
sanvincentino / sanvincentina **152**
São Tomé e Príncipe **149**, **152**
saotomense **152**
sapone **31**
saporito / saporita **52**
saracinesca **44**
sardine **54**, **64**
sari **15**
sarong **15**
sarto / sarta **46**, **89**
sartoriale **15**
sassofono **128**, **129**
satellite **143**
satira **137**
satirione **170**
Saturno **143**
saudita **153**
sauna **124**
savana **146**, **158**
sbadigliare **02**
sbagliato / sbagliata **177**
sbalorditivo / sbalorditiva **177**
sbalordito / sbalordita **06**
sbarcare **106**
sbarra **116**, **124**, **125**
sbarre **30**
sbattere **161**
sbattere con la frusta **29**
sbattere le palpebre **02**
sbattere le uova **29**
sbiancante **22**
sbrinare il frigo **34**
sbucciare **29**
sbucciatura **19**
sbuffare **165**
scacchi **140**
scacchiera **140**
scaffale **26**, **80**
scaffali **27**, **48**
scafo **105**, **119**
scala **36**, **50**, **87**, **148**
scala a libretto **37**
scala antincendio **50**
scala da tetto **50**
scala mobile **47**, **104**
scala musicale **128**
scalare **11**
scaldabagno **33**
scale **25**
Scale e serpenti **140**
scalini **25**
scalogno **56**
scalpello **36**, **141**
scamone **53**
scanalatura **115**
scanalatura del paletto **111**
scandio **78**
scanner **82**, **104**
scapola **03**
scappare **178**
scarafaggio **162**
scaricare **83**
scarico **31**, **33**
scarlatto **141**
scarpa da ciclismo **17**
scarpa da ginnastica **17**
scarpa da golf **115**
scarpe **17**
scarpe basse **17**
scarpe brogue **17**
scarpe col tacco **17**
scarpe con cinturino a T **17**
scarpe con fibbia **17**
scarpe con plateau **17**
scarpe con tacco aperte sul tallone **17**
scarpe con tacco e cinturino alla caviglia **17**
scarpe con tacco a rocchetto **17**
scarpe con tacco a spillo **17**
scarpe da barca **17**
scarpe da baseball **17**
scarpe da calcio **17**, **109**
scarpe da corsa **17**
scarpe da corsa con tacchetti **17**
scarpe da cricket **111**
scarpe da football **107**
scarpe da ginnastica alte **17**
scarpe da golf **17**
scarpe da scoglio **17**
scarpe da tennis **114**
scarpe da trekking **135**
scarpe Derby **17**
scarpe Mary Jane **17**
scarpe Oxford **17**
scarpe per bambini **17**
scarpe senza lacci **17**
scarpe sportive **17**
scarpe spuntate **17**
scarpette **13**, **126**
scarponcini da trekking **17**
scarpone da sci **17**, **122**
scartavetrare **37**
scatola **52**
scatola da cucito **142**
scatola dei fusibili **98**
scatola del cambio **98**, **100**
scatola di fazzoletti **30**
scatole **32**
scavare **11**, **39**
scavare una galleria **159**
scavo **79**
scegliere **46**
scena del crimine **50**
scendere **100**, **178**
scendere da una bicicletta **101**
scendere in picchiata **161**
sceneggiatore / sceneggiatrice **127**
sceneggiatura **127**
scenografie **126**
scheda di lavoro **92**
scheda di memoria **83**
scheda elettronica **75**
scheda informativa **49**
schedario **82**
scheggia **19**
scheletro **03**
scherma **116**, **117**
schermata delle informazioni **104**
schermo **45**, **83**, **111**, **127**, **136**, **137**
schermo digitale **136**
schiacciapatate **28**
schiacciare **29**, **112**
schiacciato / schiacciata **72**
schiacciatore-ricevitore destro / schiacciatrice-ricevitrice destra **112**
schiacciatore-ricevitore esterno / schiacciatrice-ricevitrice esterna **112**
schiacciatore-ricevitore opposto / schiacciatrice-ricevitrice opposta **112**
schienale **26**
schienale del sedile **103**
schiudersi **161**
schiuma **65**, **119**
schiuma da barba **31**
schiumarola **28**
schizzo **141**
sci **119**, **122**
sci da discesa **122**
sci d'acqua **119**
sci di fondo **122**
sciabola **117**
sciacallo **158**
sciacquare **22**
scialuppa **105**
sciame **162**
sciame meteorico **144**
sciare **122**
sciarpa **16**
sciatore / sciatrice **122**
sciatore d'acqua / sciatrice d'acqua **119**
scienze **73**, **80**
scienze politiche **80**
scienze sociali **80**
scienziato / scienziata **90**
scimitarra **79**
scimmia cappuccina **159**
scimmia ragno **159**
scimmia scoiattolo **159**
scimmia urlatrice **159**
scimpanzé **159**
scinco dalla lingua blu **163**
scioccante **177**
scioccato / scioccata **06**
sciocco / sciocca **10**
sciogliere il burro **29**
scioglimento delle calotte polari **155**
scippo **85**
sciroppo **49**
sciroppo d'acero **60**
scisto **51**, **156**
scivolare **113**
scivolo **43**
Scleroderma citrinum **170**
scodella **27**
scogliera **147**
scoiattolo **158**
scoiattolo striato **159**
scoiattolo volante **158**
scolapasta **28**
scolapiatti **27**
scollatura **142**
scollo all'americana **15**
scompartimento **102**
scontento / scontenta **06**
scontrino **48**, **69**
scooter **100**
scopa **34**, **40**, **139**
scopa da curling **122**
scoperte **79**
scoperto **45**, **94**
scopetta **34**
scopino del water **31**
scoppio dello pneumatico **124**
scorie nucleari **51**
Scorpione **145**, **162**
scortese **10**
scorza **57**
scossa elettrica **19**
scossa sismica **145**
scotano **59**
scotch **82**
scotch con acqua **68**
scotta **119**
scottatura **19**, **134**
scovolino interdentale **22**
scricciolo **160**
scrittore / scrittrice **90**
scrittura **175**
scrittura a mano **175**
scrivania **82**
scrivania del computer **83**
scrivano **79**
scrivere **73**
scroto **04**
scuderia **86**, **120**
scudo **79**, **110**
scultore / scultrice **89**
scultura **130**, **141**
scuola **43**, **73**, **148**
scuola di danza **80**
scuola di musica **80**
scuolabus **99**
scuotere **11**
scuotere la testa **02**
scuro / scura **60**, **176**
seaborgio **78**
secca **18**
secchiello del ghiaccio **68**
secchiello e paletta **134**
secchio **34**, **37**, **40**
secchio per pittura **37**
secco **154**
secolo **172**
seconda base **113**
seconda linea **108**
secondo / seconda **173**
secondo **171**
secondo centro **108**
sedano **55**
sedano rapa **56**
sedativo **49**
sede principale **81**
sedersi **11**, **164**
sedia **26**, **82**
sedia a dondolo **26**
sedia a rotelle **21**
sedia a sdraio **134**
sedia con appoggio per ginocchia **82**
sedia da regista **84**
sedia del giudice **114**
sedici **173**
sedile **102**, **103**
sedile posteriore **99**
seduta **26**
sega **36**
sega circolare **35**
sega da potatura **40**
sega per tenoni **36**
segare **35**
seggiolino per bambini **101**
seggiolone **08**
seggiovia **122**
seghetto **36**
seghetto alternativo **35**
segnale **102**

segnaletica orizzontale **96**
segni zodiacali **144**
segno diviso **74**
segno meno **74**
segno per **74**
segno più **74**
segretario / segretaria **90**
seguire **84**
sei **173**
selce **156**
selenio **78**
sella **100**, **101**, **120**
sellino posteriore **100**
selvaggina **53**
semaforo **43**, **96**
seme **168**
semi **40**, **58**
semi di colza **86**
semi di coriandolo **59**
semi di finocchio **59**
semi di Nigella **59**
semi di papavero **59**
semi di senape **60**
semicerchio **112**
semiconduttore **75**
semimetalli **78**
seminare **39**, **86**
sempre **171**
sempreverde **41**
semprevivo maggiore **168**
senape **70**
senape bianca **59**
senape di Digione **60**
senape gialla **60**
senape inglese **60**
senape nera **59**
Senegal **149**, **152**
senegalese **152**
seno **01**, **04**
sensibile **10**, **18**
senso unico **42**
senso unico alternato **96**
sentenza **85**
sentiero pubblico **148**
sentimenti **06**
sentirsi meglio **20**
senza ghiaccio **68**
senza glutine **23**
senza grassi **61**
senza latticini **23**
senza lattosio **61**
senza maniche **15**
senza piombo **97**
senza semi **57**
senza spalline **15**
sepalo **38**
sequoia gigante **167**
sera **09**, **171**
serbatoio **51**
serbatoio d'acqua **33**
serbatoio del carburante **100**
serbatoio del liquido di raffreddamento **98**
serbatoio del liquido freni **98**
serbatoio del liquido per tergicristalli **98**
serbatoio dell'olio **100**
Serbia **151**, **153**
serbo / serba **153**
serie degli attinoidi **78**
serie dei lantanoidi **78**
serio / seria **06**, **10**
serpente a sonagli **163**
serpente corallo comune **163**
serpente di mare bocca gialla **166**
serpente di mare dagli anelli **163**
serpente di terra indiano **163**
serpente liana verde **163**
serpente marino **139**
serra **39**
serratura **99**
servire **65**, **114**, **178**
servizi **31**
servizi alla persona **91**
servizi bancari online **45**, **94**
servizi bancari telefonici **94**
servizi di pronto intervento **50**
servizi per animali domestici **91**
servizi per l'ufficio **91**
servizio clienti **47**, **93**
servizio di lavanderia **131**
servizio di pulizie **131**
servizio in camera **131**
servizio incluso **69**
servizio non incluso **69**
servizzi **131**
sessanta **173**
sesto / sesta **173**
set **114**, **126**
set cinematografico **127**
set da sushi **27**
seta **13**
setacciare **39**, **62**
setaccio **28**
settanta **173**
sette **173**
settembre **172**
setter **164**
settimana **172**
settimo / settima **173**
settore automobilistico **91**
settore bancario **91**
settore edile **91**
settore hospitality **91**
settore immobiliare **91**
settore tessile **91**
settori **91**
Seychelles **149**, **152**
seychellese **152**
sezione di alimenti biologici **23**
sezione notizie **84**
sfera **74**
sfera di cristallo **139**
sfiatatoio **166**
sfinge **139**
sfinge del galio **162**
sfingide **162**
sfogliare **138**
sfondo **126**
sfrondare **39**
sgabello **26**, **65**, **68**
sgarbato / sgarbata **10**, **177**
sgombro **54**
sgombro affumicato **64**, **71**
sgradevole **177**
shaker per cocktail **68**
sherry **68**
shiatsu **24**
shih-tzu **164**
shopping **46**, **47**, **48**, **49**, **179**
shopping online **48**
short corner **112**
shorts **14**
shottino **68**
siamese **164**
siccità **154**
sicomoro **169**
sicurezza **104**
sicuro / sicura **06**, **10**, **93**
sidecar **100**
sidro **68**
siepe **41**, **86**, **146**
Sierra Leone **149**, **152**
sierraleonese **152**
sifone **33**
sigillante per bagno **37**
silene dioica **168**
silenzioso / silenziosa **176**
silicio **78**
silo **86**
Siluriano **157**
simbolo chimico **76**
sinagoga **44**
sinfonia **128**
Singapore **151**, **153**
singaporiano / singaporiana **153**
singolo **114**
singolo / singola **68**
sintetico / sintetica **13**
sintomi **19**
sintonizzarsi **136**
sintonizzatore **136**
sipario **126**
sirena **139**
Siria **150**, **153**
siriano / siriana **153**
siringa **20**, **49**, **77**
sistema di gestione dei contenuti **84**
sistema di supporto vitale **143**
sistema di trasporto **115**
sistema endocrino **04**
sistema legale **85**
sistema linfatico **04**
sistema nervoso **04**
sistema solare **143**
sistemi audio **136**
sistemi e apparati **04**
sitar **129**
sitcom **137**
sito archeologico **132**
sito storico **79**
sito web della community **84**
sito web di notizie **84**
sito web di una rivista **84**
skateboard **125**, **133**
skeleton **122**
skydiving **125**
slacciare **14**
slalom **122**
slalom gigante **122**
slip **111**
slitta **122**
slitta trainata da cani **122**
slittino **122**
slogatura **19**
Slovacchia **151**, **153**
slovacco / slovacca **153**
Slovenia **151**, **153**
sloveno / slovena **153**
smaltimento dei rifiuti **135**
smalto **03**
smalto per le unghie **18**
smartpen **95**
smartphone **83**
smartwatch **83**
smeraldo **156**
smog **154**
smoking **15**
smorzata **114**
snack **65**, **68**
snack bar **65**
snap **140**
snooker **125**
snorkelling **118**
snowboard **122**
soccorso stradale **98**
social media **84**
sociologia **80**
sociologo / sociologa **89**
soda bread **62**
sodio **78**
soffiare **11**
soffitta **25**
soffitto **26**
soffocante **154**
sogliola **54**
sogno **30**
soldato / soldatessa **88**, **89**
Sole **143**, **154**
soleggiato / soleggiata **154**
solette **17**, **49**
solidi **74**
solido **76**
solitario **140**
sollevamento pesi **124**
sollevare **11**
solo / sola **06**
soltanto il weekend **172**
solubile **49**
soluzione per lenti a contatto **22**, **49**
solvente **37**
solvente per unghie **18**
Somalia **149**, **152**
somalo / somala **152**
sombrero **16**
sommare **74**
sommelier **69**
sommergibile **166**
sonaglio **08**
sonata per violino **128**
sonda **22**
sonda spaziale **143**
sonniferi **49**
sopra **180**
sopra il par **115**
sopracciglio **01**
soprano **126**
sorbo **169**
sorella **05**
sorellastra **05**
sorgente **147**
sorgere del sole **171**
sorpassare **98**
sorpreso / sorpresa **06**
sorridere **02**
sorseggiare **52**
sospensione **98**
sospensioni **100**
sospensioni anteriori **123**
sospensioni posteriori **123**
sospettato / sospettata **50**, **85**
sospirare **02**

sosta ai box **123**
sostegno per piante rampicanti **39**
sostenere un colloquio **92**
sostituire **46**
sottaceti **60**, **72**
sott'aceto **72**
sottaceto per sandwich **60**
sottile **176**
sotto **180**
sotto il par **115**
sotto tensione **33**
sottobicchiere **27**, **68**
sott'olio **64**
sottomarino **88**, **105**
sottopancia **120**
sottopassaggio **96**, **102**
sottosuolo **39**
sottotitoli **137**
sottoveste **14**
sottrarre **11**, **74**
soufflé **72**
soul **129**
sound bar **136**
souvenir **132**
sovrapesca **155**
sovratelo **135**
spaccare **117**
spacchettare **11**, **32**
spaccio di droga **85**
spada **79**, **117**
spaghetti **64**, **72**
Spagna **151**, **153**
spagnolo / spagnola **153**
spago **40**
spalla **01**
spallina imbottita **15**
spam **83**
sparecchiare **09**, **34**
spareggio **114**
spargimiele **60**
spari **88**
spartito **128**
spartitraffico **96**
spassoso / spassosa **177**
spatifillo **38**
spatola **28**, **76**
spaventapasseri **86**
spaventato / spaventata **06**
spaventoso / spaventosa **177**
spazio **143**, **144**
spazzare il pavimento **34**
spazzola **12**
spazzola da scarpe **17**
spazzola per lavare la schiena **31**
spazzolare **22**
spazzolino **31**
spazzolone **34**
specchietto **18**, **22**
specchietto retrovisore **97**
specchio **30**, **77**
speciale **177**
specialità **69**
specie **77**
specie a rischio **155**
specie marine **166**
spedire un pacco **09**
spedizioni **91**
spegnere **63**, **83**, **137**, **178**
speleologia **146**
speleologo / speleologa **146**
spese **94**
spese folli **46**
spesso / spessa **176**
spettacolo **126**
spettatori **110**, **115**, **116**
spettro elettromagnetico **75**
spezie **59**
Sphinx **164**
spia **89**
spiaggia **134**, **147**, **148**
spianare (il terreno) **39**
spicchio **57**
spiedo **28**
spigola **54**
spilla **16**
spilla da balia **20**
spillatrice per birra **68**
spillo **142**
spina **33**
spina dorsale **03**
spinaci **55**
spinato / spinata **54**
spingere **11**
spinotto **33**
spogliatoio **124**
spoiler **97**
spolverare **34**
spontaneo / spontanea **10**
sporco / sporca **176**
spore **170**
sport **107–25**, **125**
sport acquatici **119**
sport da combattimento **117**
sport d'acqua **119**
sport invernali **122**
sport motoristici **123**
sportello **45**
sportello prestiti **80**
sposa **07**
sposarsi **07**
sposato / sposata **05**
sposo **07**
spostare **11**
Spotted Lake **145**
spray **49**
spray nasale **20**
spray per capelli **12**
spremiaglio **28**
spremiagrumi **28**
spremuta di arancia **65**
springbok **158**
spruzzare **39**
spruzzino **40**
spugna **31**, **34**, **37**
spugnetta abrasiva **34**
spumante **68**
squadra **73**, **74**, **107**
squadra di casa **107**
squadra ospite **107**
squalo bianco **166**
squalo elefante **166**
squalo martello **166**
squama **54**
squamato / squamata **54**
squame **163**
square leg **111**
squash **114**
squat **124**
squittire **164**
Sri Lanka **150**, **153**
srilankese **153**
stabilizzatore **103**
staccare **37**
staff **81**
staffa **120**
staffetta **116**
staffetta mista **118**
stagionato / stagionata **72**
stagione **137**
stagioni **172**
stagista **81**
stagno **78**, **86**, **156**
stalagmite **146**
stalattite **146**
stallone **120**, **165**
stambecco **158**
stame **38**
stampa **141**, **175**
stampante **82**
stampare **83**
stampelle **19**
stampo per soufflé **28**
stancante **177**
stanco / stanca **06**
standing ovation **126**
stanza del bebè **30**
stanza privata **21**
star del cinema **127**
stare a galla **118**
stare bene a (qualcuno) **14**
starnutire **02**, **20**
stati d'animo **06**
Stati Uniti d'America **150**
station wagon **97**
stato **104**
statunitense **152**
stazione degli autobus **42**, **99**
stazione di ricarica per auto elettriche **97**
stazione ferroviaria **42**, **102**, **148**
stazione radio **84**
stazione spaziale **143**
stecca **125**
stecca di cannella **59**
stegosauro **157**
stella **144**
stella binaria **144**
stella di David **44**
stella di neutroni **144**
stella marina **134**, **166**
Stella Polare **144**
stelle **144**
stelo **38**
stencil **37**
stendere **29**
stendere il bucato **34**
stendersi **20**
stenografo / stenografa **85**
step **124**
steppa **146**
stereo **136**
sterna artica **160**
sterno **03**
stetoscopio **20**
steward **90**, **109**
stigma **38**
stile di nuoto sul fianco **118**
stile di vita sano **23**
stile libero **118**
stile Liberty **130**
stilista **90**
stilo **38**
stinco **01**
stipendio **81**
stirare **34**
stirare una camicia **09**
stivale **100**
stivale alto **17**
stivaletti **17**
stivaletti Chelsea **17**
stivaletti chukka **17**
stivaletti stringati **17**
stivaletto ortopedico **19**
stivali **17**
stivali al ginocchio **17**
stivali da cowboy **17**
stivali da equitazione **17**, **120**
stivali da lavoro **17**
stivali di gomma **17**, **40**
stivali Tabi **17**
stivaloni di gomma **121**
stomaco **04**
storia **73**, **79**, **80**
storia d'amore **138**
storia naturale **157**
storico / storica **79**
storie **139**
storno **160**
stoviglie **27**
strada **42**, **96**
strada a doppia carreggiata **96**
strada a senso unico **96**
strada d'accesso **106**
strada deformata **96**
strada laterale **42**
strada principale **148**
strada secondaria **148**
strade **96**
strallo **119**
strano / strana **177**
straordinari **81**
straordinario / straordinaria **177**
strappare **178**
strascico **15**
strato di lava **145**
strato di ozono **155**
strato superiore **63**
stratosfera **155**
strega **139**
strelizia **167**
stress **19**
stressato / stressata **06**
stretching **124**
stretto **147**
stretto / stretta **13**, **176**
strigliare **120**
strike **113**
stringere **142**
stringersi la mano **92**
stringinaso **118**
strisce pedonali **96**
striscione **109**
stronzio **78**
stropicciato / stropicciata **13**
strozzatura **129**
strumenti **129**
strumenti a corda **128**
strumenti a fiato **128**
strumenti dell'orchestra **128**
strumenti per la matematica **74**
struttura **135**

struttura **135**
struttura per arrampicarsi **43**
strutture per il campeggio **135**
struzzo **161**, **165**
stuccare **37**
stucco **37**
studente della laurea magistrale / studentessa della laurea magistrale **80**
studente della laurea triennale / studentessa della laurea triennale **80**
studenti / studentesse **73**
studi umanistici **80**
studio **26**, **73**, **73–80**
studio cinematografico **127**
studio del passato **79**
studio dentistico **22**
studio medico **20**
studio televisivo **84**
stufato **72**
stufetta **33**
stufetta a gas **33**
stupendo / stupenda **177**
sturalavandini **31**, **36**
sturare il lavandino **35**
sturare il water **35**
substrato roccioso **145**
subwoofer **136**
succhi **65**
succhiare **02**
succo **52**
succo d'ananas **65**
succo d'arancia **65**
succo di frutta **71**
succo di mango **65**
succo di mela **65**
succo di mirtillo rosso **65**
succo di pomodoro **65**
succoso / succosa **52**
sud **148**
Sud America **149**, **152**
Sudafrica **149**, **152**
sudafricano / sudafricana **152**
sudamericano / sudamericana **152**
Sudan **149**, **152**
Sudan del Sud **149**, **152**
sudanese **152**
sudare **02**
sudcoreano / sudcoreana **153**
sudest **148**
sudovest **148**
sudsudanese **152**
sula **160**
sumo **117**
sundae **63**
suocera **05**
suocero **05**
suola **17**, **115**
suona la sveglia **09**
suonare (la tromba) **128**
suonare uno strumento musicale **09**
supercibi **23**
superficie **39**, **143**
superficie di gioco **108**
supermercato **48**
supernova **144**
supervisionare **92**
supervisore **81**, **92**
supporto **87**, **115**, **136**
supporto per altoparlanti **136**
supporto per la telecamera **123**
supposta **49**
surf **119**, **134**
surfcasting **121**
surfista **119**
surgelati **48**
surgelato / surgelata **54**, **56**
surgelatore **27**
suricato **159**
Suriname **149**, **152**
surinamese **152**
Surrealismo **130**
sushi **54**
sussidio di disoccupazione **81**
sussurrare **11**
svagarsi **178**
svasso **161**
svedese **153**
sveglia **30**
svegliarsi **09**, **178**
svenire **20**
sverniciatore **37**
Svezia **151**, **153**
sviluppatore di app / sviluppatrice di app **89**
svincolo **96**
Svizzera **151**, **153**
svizzero / svizzera **153**
svuotare la lavastoviglie **34**
swazi **152**
swing **115**
swing di prova **115**

T

T-shirt **14**
tabacco **86**
tabellone **112**
tabellone delle partenze **102**
tabellone segnapunti **107**, **111**
tablet **83**
taccheggio **85**
tacchetti **111**, **115**
tacchino **53**, **161**, **165**
tacco **17**, **115**
taccola **55**
tachimetro **99**, **100**
taco **70**
taekwondo **117**
tagico / tagica **153**
Tagikistan **151**, **153**
tagli **53**
tagli di carne **53**
tagliabordi **40**
tagliaerba **40**
tagliare **29**, **35**, **39**, **142**
tagliare a dadini **29**
tagliare a fette **29**
tagliare a pezzetti **29**
tagliare l'erba **09**, **39**
tagliatubi **36**
tagliaunghie **18**, **49**
tagliauova **28**
tagliere **28**
tagliere di formaggi **69**
taglierino **36**, **37**
taglio **19**, **94**
taglio corto **12**
tai chi **117**, **133**
tailandese **153**
Tailandia **150**, **153**
Taj Mahal **44**
tajine **28**
talco **31**
talea **39**
talentuoso / talentuosa **10**
talk show **137**
tallio **78**
tallonatore **108**
tallone **01**, **02**
talpa **159**
tamarillo **58**
tamburello **128**
tamburo rullante **128**
tandem **101**
tantalio **78**
Tanzania **149**, **152**
tanzaniano / tanzaniana **152**
tapiro **159**
tapis roulant **124**
tapparella **25**
tappetino **24**, **124**, **125**
tappetino da bagno **31**
tappetino per il mouse **83**
tappeto **26**
tappetto volante **139**
tappezzare **37**
tappo **31**, **76**
tappo di sughero **60**
tarantola **162**
tardi **171**
targa **97**
tariffa **99**, **102**
tariffa d'ingresso **130**
tariffa oraria **81**
taro **56**
tarso **03**
tartaruga **164**
tartaruga dal collo di serpente **163**
tartaruga dal dorso di diamante **163**
tartaruga delle Galápagos **163**
tartaruga embricata **166**
tartaruga liuto **163**
tartaruga verde **163**
tartina **70**
tartufo **56**, **170**
tasca **15**, **142**
tassista **90**
tasso **167**
tasso del miele **158**
tasso di cambio **45**, **94**
tasso d'interesse **45**
tasso europeo **158**
tasti di sintonizzazione **136**
tastiera **45**, **83**, **129**
tasto **129**
tasto home **83**
tatami **117**
tavola **26**, **119**
tavola da surf **119**, **134**
tavola da volteggio **125**
tavola periodica **78**
tavolato **41**
tavoletta attiva **34**
tavoletta da nuoto **118**
tavoletta del water **31**, **33**
tavolino **26**, **103**
tavolo **65**
tavolo da lavoro **37**
tavolo operatorio **21**
tavolozza **141**
tazza **27**
tazza da tè **27**
tazza del gabinetto **33**
tazza del water **33**
tazza riutilizzabile **70**
tazzina da caffè **27**
tè **52**, **66**, **71**, **86**
tè alla menta **66**
tè bianco **66**
tè con il latte **66**
tè con il limone **66**
tè freddo **52**, **66**
tè nero **66**
tè verde **66**
teatro **42**, **73**, **126**
teatro dell'opera **126**
Teatro dell'Opera di Sydney **44**
tecnezio **78**
tecnico del suono **84**, **127**
tecnologia **73**, **83**
tedesco / tedesca **153**
tee **115**
teenager **05**
tegame **28**
tegame da forno **29**
teglia **28**, **29**
teglia da flan **29**
teglia da muffin **29**
tegola **25**
tegole **87**
teiera **27**, **66**
tela **141**
telaio **101**, **123**, **142**
telecamera **84**
telecamera di sorveglianza **130**
telecomando **26**, **83**, **136**, **137**
telecomando per presentazioni **95**
telefonare a **178**
telefono **82**
telefono di emergenza **96**
telenovela **137**
telescopio **144**
telescopio riflettore **144**
telescopio rifrattore **144**
telescopio spaziale **144**
televisione **136**, **137**
televisione / TV **26**
televisore **137**
tellurio **78**
telo di protezione **37**
telo impermeabile **135**
tema **73**
tempera **141**
temperatura **154**
temperino **73**, **82**
tempesta di neve **154**
tempesta di sabbia **154**

tempestoso /
tempestosa **154**
tempia **01**
tempio **44**
tempo **107**, **171**
tempo atmosferico **154**
tempo libero **126-42**
temporale **154**
temporalesco /
temporalesca **154**
tenda automatica **135**
tenda da sole **65**
tenda della doccia **31**
tenda familiare **135**
tenda per due
persone **135**
tende **26**
tende avvolgibili **26**
tende di tulle **26**
tendine **03**
tendine d'Achille **03**
tenere **11**, **117**
tenere una
teleconferenza **95**
tennessinio **78**
tennis **114**
tenore **126**
tepee **32**
terapia **21**
terapia di gruppo **24**
terbio **78**
tergicristallo **97**
terminal **104**
terminal ferroviario **106**
terminal petrolifero **106**
terminal traghetti **106**
termite **162**
termometro **20**, **76**
termometro auricolare **20**
termometro da carne **28**
termosfera **155**
Terra **143**, **145**
terra grassa **39**
terraferma **145**
terrario **164**
terrazza **25**, **65**
terremoto **145**
terreno **39**
terreno coltivato **86**, **146**
terreno erboso **146**
terribile **177**
terriccio **39**
terrificante **177**
terrina **28**
terrorizzato /
terrorizzata **06**
terza base **113**
terza linea ala aperta **108**
terza linea ala chiusa **108**
terza linea centro **108**
terzo / terza **173**
terzo uomo **111**
tesi **80**
tesoro **139**
tessera della biblioteca **80**
tessera per i trasporti **48**
tessitore **160**
tessitore / tessitrice **142**
tessitura **142**
tessuto **142**
test di gravidanza **08**
testa **01**, **04**, **162**
testa rasata **12**
testata **98**
testicolo **04**
testiera **30**
testimone **116**
testimone **85**
testo **138**
testuggine raggiata **163**
tettarella **08**
tetto **25**, **98**
tetto di paglia **32**
tettonica delle placche **145**
tettuccio apribile **98**
thawb **15**
thermos **52**, **135**
thread **84**
thriller **127**, **137**
tiara **16**
tibia **03**
tifa **167**
tifosi **107**, **109**
tiglio **169**
tigre **157**, **159**
tigre dai denti a
sciabola **157**
tilde **175**
timbro postale **45**
time out **107**
timer **76**, **95**
timer da cucina **28**
timido / timida **10**
timo **59**
timone **103**, **119**
Timor Est **151**, **153**
timpano **128**
tinta per capelli **18**
tinta unita **13**
tiramisù **63**
tirante **135**
tirare **11**, **112**
tirare il drive **115**
tirare su **121**
tirare un calcio
di rigore **109**
tirare un chip **115**
tiro al bersaglio **125**
tiro con l'arco **125**
tirocinante **81**
tiroide **04**
tisana **52**, **66**
titanio **78**
titolo **138**
toast **71**
tocco **80**
toeletta **30**
toffee **67**
toga **80**
togliere **14**
togliere le erbacce **39**
Togo **149**, **152**
togolese **152**
toilette **47**, **130**, **131**
tomba **79**
tombino **43**
tombolo **147**
tonchio **162**
Tonga **150**, **153**
tongano / tongana **153**
tonico **18**
tonnellata **174**
tonno **54**
tono **128**
tono più alto **128**
tono più basso **128**
tonsillite **19**
topazio **156**
topinambur **56**
topo **158**, **164**
toppa **101**
torba **39**
torbiera **79**
torcia **135**
torcia frontale **135**, **146**
tordo **160**
torio **78**
tormalina **156**
tormenta **154**
tornado **154**
tornante **123**
tornare indietro **137**, **148**
tornello **102**
torneo **115**
tornio **141**
tornire **35**
Toro **144**, **165**
torque **16**
torre **44**, **51**, **140**
torre del bagnino **134**
torre di controllo **104**
torre di controllo del
traffico aereo **43**
torre di perforazione **51**
torre di raffreddamento **51**
Torre Eiffel **44**
torre pendente di Pisa **44**
torretta **44**
torretta di comando **105**
torrido / torrida **154**
torrione **44**
torrone **67**
torsione da seduti **24**
torsolo **57**
torta **63**
torta a strati **63**
torta al cioccolato **63**
torta alla frutta **63**
torta di compleanno **63**
torta nuziale **63**
torte **63**
tortellini **64**
tortilla **62**
tortini **64**
tortino **72**
tosare **165**
tosse **19**
tossire **20**
tostapane **27**
touchdown **107**
tovaglia **26**
tovaglietta
all'americana **26**
tovagliolo **27**, **72**
tovagliolo di carta **70**
tra **148**, **180**
tracciare l'ordine **46**
trachea **04**
tracolla **16**
traffico **96**
tragedia **126**
traghetto **105**, **106**
traguardo **116**, **123**
tram **99**, **102**
tramonto **171**
trampolino **08**, **118**
trampolino elastico **125**
trapanare **35**
trapano **22**
trapano a batteria **35**
trapano elettrico **35**
trapano manuale **35**, **36**
trapezio **03**, **74**
trapiantare **39**
trapunta **30**
trapuntatura **142**
trasferimento in
navetta **104**
trasferire denaro **45**
trasferirsi **32**
trasformatore **33**, **75**
traslocare **32**
trasmettere **84**
trasmettere in
streaming **137**
trasmissione **98**
trasporto **91**
trasporto merci per via
aerea **104**
trattamenti di bellezza **18**
trattamenti e terapie **24**
trattare **92**
trattenere il respiro **02**
tratti della personalità **10**
trattino **175**
trattino basso **175**
trattore **86**
trave **87**, **125**
trave metallica **87**
traversa **42**, **108**, **109**
tre **173**
tre gemelli **05**
tre volte alla settimana **172**
treccia **12**
treccia alla francese **12**
treccine **12**
treccine aderenti
alla testa **12**
tredici **173**
trekking a cavallo **120**
tremare **02**
tremendo / tremenda **177**
tremolo **129**
trench **15**
treni **102**
trenino elettrico **08**
treno **102**
treno a levitazione
magnetica **102**
treno a vapore **102**
treno ad alta velocità **102**
treno diesel **102**
treno elettrico **102**
treno merci **102**
treno proiettile **102**
trenta **173**
treppiede **76**, **144**
triangolo **74**, **128**
triangolo da biliardo **125**
Triassico **157**
triathlon **116**
tribunale **43**, **85**
triceratopo **157**
tricheco **166**
tricipiti **03**
triglia di scoglio **54**
trilobite **157**
Trinidad e Tobago
150, **152**
trinidadiano o
tobagoniano /
trinidadiana o
tobagoniana **152**
tris **140**
triste **06**
tritadocumenti **82**
tritoma **167**
tritone **139**
tritone crestato **163**
troll **139**

trolling **84**
tromba **128, 129**
trombetta dei morti **170**
trombone **128**
troncarami **40**
tronchese **36**
tropici **145**
Tropico del Cancro **145**
Tropico del Capricorno **145**
troposfera **155**
trota **54**
trota corallina **166**
trota iridea **54**
trottare **165**
trottola **08**
trousse **18**
trovare un lavoro **07**
truccarsi **09**
trucco **18**
truciolato **35**
tsunami **145**
tuba **128**
tuba di Falloppio **04**
tubatura **33, 87**
tubetto di colore **141**
tubi UV **18**
tubo di aspirazione **34**
tubo di scarico **98, 100**
tucanetto smeraldino **160**
tucano toco **160**
tuffarsi **112, 118**
tuffatore / tuffatrice **118**
tuffi **118**
tuffo da grandi altezze **118**
tuffo di piedi **118**
tuffo di testa **118**
tufo vulcanico **156**
tulio **78**
tulipano **38**
tumbler **27**
tundra **146**
tungsteno **78**
Tunisia **149, 152**
tunisino / tunisina **152**
tuono **154**
tuorlo **61, 71**
turbante **16**
turbato / turbata **06**
turbina **51**
turbina eolica **51**
turchese **141, 156**
Turchia **151, 153**
turco / turca **153**
turismo **91**
turista **132**
Turkmenistan **151, 153**
turkmeno / turkmena **153**
tuta **13**
tuta da corsa **123**
tuta da ginnastica **15**
tuta da lavoro **13, 37**
tuta da motociclista **100**
tuta da sci **13**
tuta intera **13**
tuta mimetica **88**
tuta spaziale **143**
tutina **13**
tutù **126**
Tuvalu **150, 153**
tuvaluano / tuvaluana **153**
tv per bambini **137**
tv satellitare **137**
tv via cavo **137**
tweeter **136**
tyrannosaurus rex **157**

U

uccelli **160, 161**
uccellino **161**
uccello del paradiso **160**
Ucraina **151, 153**
ucraino / ucraina **153**
udienza **85**
udon **64**
ufficiale giudiziario / ufficiale giudiziaria **85**
ufficiali di gara **112**
ufficio **82**
ufficio bagagli smarriti **104**
ufficio del responsabile dello stabilimento / ufficio della responsabile dello stabilimento **135**
ufficio del turismo **42, 132**
ufficio dell'amministratore delegato **81**
ufficio dell'avvocato **85**
ufficio legale **91**
ufficio oggetti smarriti **102**
ufficio postale **42, 45**
Uganda **149, 152**
ugandese **152**
ugello **40**
ugello spruzzatore **40**
uguale **74**
ukulele **129**
ulna **03**
ultimo piano **47**
ultraleggero **103**
ululone dal ventre di fuoco **163**
umidità **154**
umido **154**
una **171**
una e cinque **171**
una e dieci **171**
una e mezza **171**
una e trentacinque **171**
una e un quarto **171**
una e venti **171**
una e venticinque **171**
una volta alla settimana **172**
uncinetto **142**
undici **173**
ungere **29**
ungherese **153**
Ungheria **151, 153**
unghia **02**
unghia del piede **02**
unicorno **139**
uniforme da pompiere **13**
uniforme militare **13**
uniformi **13**
unità per la raccolta differenziata **33**
università **43, 80**
universo **144**
uno **173**
uno virgola sette **173**
uomo **05**
uomo d'affari **81, 90**
uomo primitivo **157**
uova **61**
uova di rana **77, 163**
uova strapazzate **61, 71**
uovo **77**
uovo al tegamino **61, 71**
uovo d'anatra **61**
uovo di gallina **61**
uovo di quaglia **61**
uovo d'oca **61**
uovo in camicia **61, 71**
uovo sodo **61, 71**
uragano **154**
uranio **78**
Urano **143**
uria **160**
urologia **21**
uruguaiano / uruguaiana **152**
Uruguay **149, 152**
usciere / usciera **126**
uscire **11, 83, 178**
uscire con gli amici **09**
uscire dal lavoro **09**
uscire di casa **09**
uscita **48**
uscita dei giocatori **109**
uscita di emergenza **103, 131**
usignolo **160**
utensile di modellazione **141**
utensili da cucina **28**
utensili di selce **79**
utensili per il bricolage **35**
utero **04, 08**
utile **177**
utilizzo del computer **93**
uva **57**
uva passa **58**
uva spina **57**
uvetta **58**
uvetta sultanina **58**
Uzbekistan **151, 153**
uzbeko / uzbeka **153**

V

vacanza **104**
vaccinazione **08, 20**
vacuolo **77**
vagina **04**
vagone **102**
vagone letto **102**
vagone ristorante **102**
Vaisakhi **07**
valanga **122**
valigetta **16**
valigia **16, 104**
valigie **104, 131**
valle **146**
valore di pH **76**
valuta **45, 94**
valuta digitale **94**
valvola **101**
valvola di intercettazione **33**
vampiro **139**
vanadio **78**
vandalismo **85**
vanessa del cardo **162**
vanessa io **162**
vanga **40**
vaniglia **59**
vantaggio **114**
vantarsi **178**
vanuatiano / vanuatiana **153**
Vanuatu **150, 153**
vapore acqueo **51**
varano di Komodo **163**
varicella **19**
varie ed eventuali **95**
vasaio / vasaia **141**
vasca da bagno **31**
vasca idromassaggio **25, 124**
vaschetta per i semi **40**
vaschetta per il bagnetto **08**
vaschetta per pittura **37**
vasetto **60**
vasino **08**
vaso **26, 40**
vassoi **82**
vassoio **69, 70**
vassoio della colazione **131**
vecchio / vecchia **176**
vedere **11**
vedere una casa **32**
vedersi **178**
vedovo / vedova **05**
vedova nera **162**
vegano / vegana **23**
vegetariano / vegetariana **23**
veicoli militari **88**
veicolo anfibio **88**
veicolo corazzato **88**
veicolo da ricognizione **88**
veicolo di servizio **104**
veicolo spaziale **143**
vela **119, 125, 134**
vela maestra **119**
velivolo da combattimento **88**
velo **15**
veloce **176**
velocista **116**
vena **04**
vendere **46**
vendita al dettaglio **91**
vendita al dettaglio online **91**
vendite **91**
venerdì **172**
Venere **143**
venere acchiappamosche **168**
veneziane **26**
Venezuela **149, 152**
venezuelano / venezuelana **152**
ventesimo / ventesima **173**
venti **173**
venti minuti **171**
ventidue **173**
ventilato / ventilata **154**
ventilatore **33**
ventilatore da soffitto **33**
vento **51, 154**

ventola dell'aria 103
ventoso / ventosa 154
ventunesimo / ventunesima 173
ventuno 173
verbale 82
verbi 106, 120, 162, 178
verbi comuni 178
verde 141
verdi 01
verdura 48, 55, 56
verdure biologiche 55
verdure cotte 72
verdure da insalata 55
verdure primaverili 55
Vergine 145
verifica 73
verme 162
vernice 37
vernice di base 37
versare 29, 45
vertebra cervicale 03
vertebra lombare 03
vertebrato / vertebrata 77
verticale 24
vertice 74
vertigini 19
vertebra toracica 03
verza 55
vescia 170
vescia gigante 170
vescica 19
vescicola seminale 04
vespa 162
vestaglia 14
vestirsi 09
vestirsi elegante 178
vestito 14
vestito da damigella 15
vestito da sposa 15
veterano di guerra 88
veterinario / veterinaria 89
vetrata colorata 44
vetrina 25
vetrino 77
vetro 35, 155, 176
vetta 147
Via Lattea 144
via principale 46
viaggiare con lo zaino in spalla 131
viaggiare dietro 100
viaggio 131
viaggio di lavoro 81
viale 43
vialetto 41
vibrafono 128
vibrisse 158
vicino / vicina 07, 176
vicolo 42
video on demand 137
videocamera 83, 136
videocamera subacquea 118
videochiamata 83
videoconferenza 83
videogiochi 91, 136
videoproiettore 73
Vietnam 150, 153
vietnamita 153
vigile del fuoco / vigilessa del fuoco 89
vigile urbano / vigilessa urbana 96
vigili del fuoco 50
vigneto 86
vigogna 158
villa 32
vincere 11, 109, 115, 140
vincere un premio 07
vinili 136
vino 68
vino bianco 52, 68
vino rosé 52
vino rosso 52, 68
vintage 13
viola 38, 128, 141
viola del pensiero 38
violacciocca 47, 169
violenza dei tifosi 85
violino 128, 129
violoncello 128
virare 119
virata 118
virata aperta 118
virgola 175
virgoletta doppia 175
virgoletta singola 175
virus 19, 77
vischio 168
visiera 100
visiera placcata in oro 143
visita di controllo 22
visita guidata 132
visita medica 20
viso 01
vista 22
vista frontale 97
vista laterale 97
visto 104
vita 01
vita in città 42–51
vita negli oceani 166
vita quotidiana 178
vitamine 23, 49
vite 36, 168
vite americana 168
vitello 53
vitello / vitella 165
vivaio 46
vlog 84
vlogger 84
voce principale 129
vodka 68
vodka con succo d'arancia 68
vogatore 124
volano 114
volante 99
volare 11, 162
volare con il deltaplano 125
volare con il parapendio 125
volée 114
volere 46
volo diretto 104
volo internazionale 104
volo interno 104
volpe artica 159
volpe rossa 159
volpino della Pomerania 164
volt 75
voltaggio 33
volume 74, 136, 175
volume dei liquidi 174
vomitare 20
vongola 54
voto 73, 85
voto unanime 95
vulcano 145
vuoto 75
vuoto / vuota 176

waffle 65, 70, 71
warning track 113
wasabi 60
water 31
webcam 83
wedge 115
weekend 172
whisky 68
Wi-Fi 83
wicket mediano 111
wigwam 32
windsurf 119, 134
wireless 83
wok 28
wombat 158
woofer 136
wrap 70
wrestling 117

xanthorrhoea 167
xenon 78
xilofono 128
yacht 105, 119, 134
yak 159
yard line 107
Yemen 151, 153
yemenita 153
yo-yo 08
yoga 24
yogurt 61
yogurt alla frutta 71
yogurt gelato 61
yucca 38

Z

zafferano 59
zaffiro 156
zaino 16, 73, 135
Zambia 149, 152
zambiano / zambiana 152
zampa 53
zampe lunghe 159
zanzara 162
zanzariera 135
zappa 40
zebra 158
zenzero 59
zerbino 25
zero 173
zia 05
ziggurat 44
Zimbabwe 149, 152
zimbabweano / zimbabweana 152
zinco 78, 156
zio 05
zip 17, 142
zirconio 78
zoccoli 17
zoccolo 120, 158
zodiaco 144
zolfo 78, 156
zombie 139
zona adeopelagica 166
zona batipelagica 166
zona commerciale 42
zona di attacco 110
zona di difesa 110
zona di meta 107
zona di pericolo 117
zona di sicurezza 117
zona fuori dal diamante 113
zona industriale 42
zona mesopelagica 166
zona neutrale 107, 110
zona pelagica 166
zona residenziale 42
zone umide 146
zoo 133
zoologia 77, 80
zoologo / zoologa 77
zoosafari 133
zucca 56
zucca acorn 56
zucca bianca 56
zucca di Halloween 139
zucca invernale 56
zucca violina 56
zucchero 23
zucchero filato 67
zucchina 56
zucchino 56
zuppa 69, 72
zuppa con noodle 72

Acknowledgments

The publisher would like to thank:
Dr. Steven Snape for his assistance with hieroglyphs. Elizabeth Blakemore for editorial assistance; Mark Lloyd, Charlotte Johnson, and Anna Scully for design assistance; Simon Mumford for national flags; Sunita Gahir and Ali Jayne Scrivens for additional illustration; Adam Brackenbury for art colour correction; Claire Ashby and Romaine Werblow for images; William Collins for fonts; Lori Hand, Kayla Dugger, and Jane Perlmutter for Americanization; Justine Willis for proofreading; Elizabeth Blakemore for indexing; Helen Peters for the wordlists; Christine Stroyan for audio recording management and ID Audio for audio recording and production.

DK India
Senior Art Editors Vikas Sachdeva, Ira Sharma; **Art Editor** Anukriti Arora;
Assistant Art Editors Ankita Das, Adhithi Priya; **Editors** Hina Jain, Saumya Agarwal;
DTP Designer Manish Upreti

DK WHAT WILL YOU LEARN NEXT?

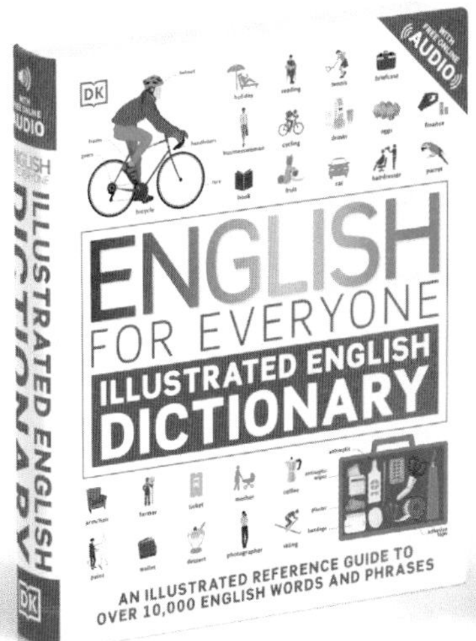
WITH FREE ONLINE AUDIO
ENGLISH FOR EVERYONE
ILLUSTRATED ENGLISH DICTIONARY
AN ILLUSTRATED REFERENCE GUIDE TO OVER 10,000 ENGLISH WORDS AND PHRASES

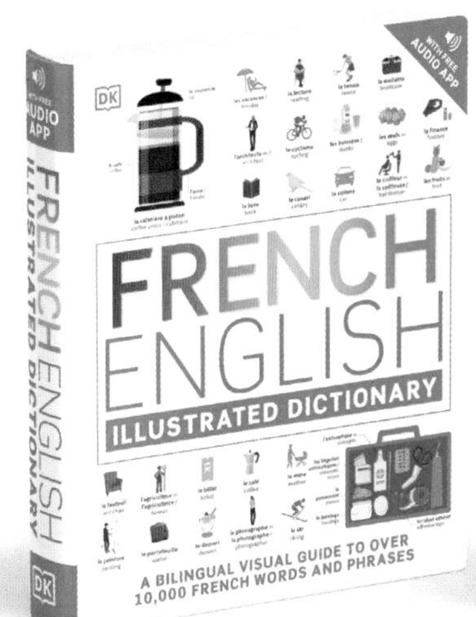
WITH FREE AUDIO APP
FRENCH ENGLISH
ILLUSTRATED DICTIONARY
A BILINGUAL VISUAL GUIDE TO OVER 10,000 FRENCH WORDS AND PHRASES

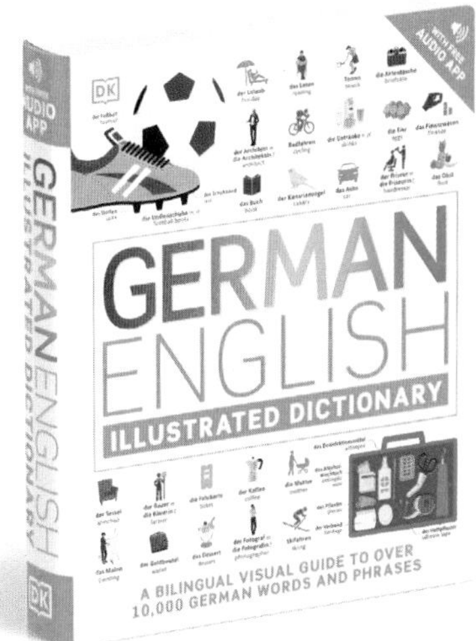
WITH FREE AUDIO APP
GERMAN ENGLISH
ILLUSTRATED DICTIONARY
A BILINGUAL VISUAL GUIDE TO OVER 10,000 GERMAN WORDS AND PHRASES

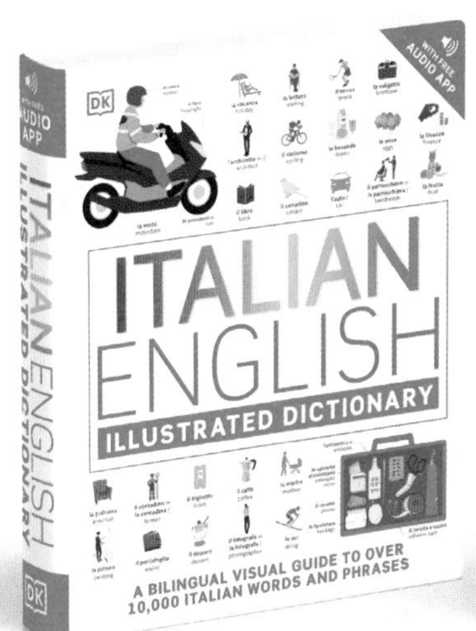
WITH FREE AUDIO APP
ITALIAN ENGLISH
ILLUSTRATED DICTIONARY
A BILINGUAL VISUAL GUIDE TO OVER 10,000 ITALIAN WORDS AND PHRASES

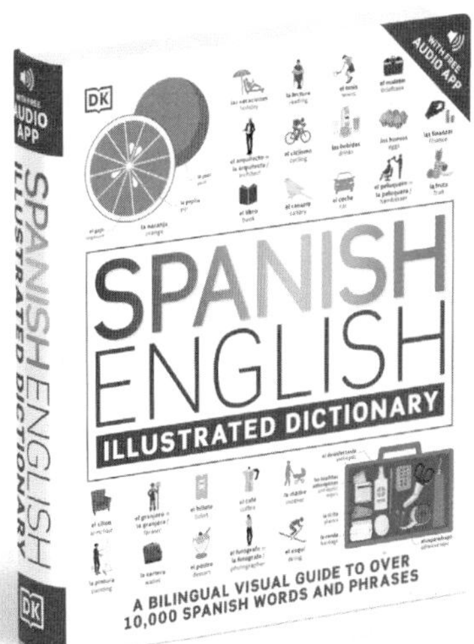
WITH FREE AUDIO APP
SPANISH ENGLISH
ILLUSTRATED DICTIONARY
A BILINGUAL VISUAL GUIDE TO OVER 10,000 SPANISH WORDS AND PHRASES